# The Earth and Its Peoples

## A Global History

BRIEF EDITION    SIXTH EDITION

# The Earth and Its Peoples

## A Global History

**Richard W. Bulliet**
*Columbia University*

**Pamela Kyle Crossley**
*Dartmouth College*

**Daniel R. Headrick**
*Roosevelt University*

**Steven W. Hirsch**
*Tufts University*

**Lyman L. Johnson**
*University of North Carolina–Charlotte*

**David Northrup**
*Boston College*

CENGAGE
Learning·

Australia • Brazil • Mexico • Singapore • United Kingdom • United States

**The Earth and Its Peoples: A Global History,
Brief Edition Sixth Edition**
Richard W. Bulliet, Pamela Kyle Crossley,
Daniel R. Headrick, Steven W. Hirsch,
Lyman L. Johnson, David Northrup

Product Director: Suzanne Jeans

Product Manager: Brooke Barbier

Senior Content Developer: Tonya Lobato

Content Coordinator: Cara Swan

Product Assistant: Katie Coaster

Media Developer: Kate MacLean

Marketing Brand Manager: Kyle Zimmerman

Senior Content Project Manager: Carol Newman

Senior Art Director: Cate Barr

Manufacturing Planner: Sandee Milewski

Senior Rights Acquisition Specialist: Jennifer
Meyer Dare

Production Service/Compositor: Lachina
Publishing Services

Text and Cover Designer: Dick Hannus, Hannus
Design Associates

Cover Image: A man seated near a river with a
boat. From an album with scenes of scholarly
lives. China, Qing dynasty. Ink, and watercolor
painting on silk, 28.3 x 27.3 cm. Inv. MG22755.
RMN-Grand Palais/Art Resource, NY

For product information and technology assistance, contact us at
**Cengage Learning Customer & Sales Support, 1-800-354-9706**

For permission to use material from this text or product,
submit all requests online at **www.cengage.com/permissions**.
Further permissions questions can be emailed to
**permissionrequest@cengage.com.**

Library of Congress Control Number: 2013946152

ISBN-13: 978-1-285-44551-9
ISBN-10: 1-285-44551-1

**Cengage Learning**
200 First Stamford Place, 4th Floor
Stamford, CT 06902
USA

Cengage Learning is a leading provider of customized learning solutions with office locations around the globe, including Singapore, the United Kingdom, Australia, Mexico, Brazil and Japan. Locate your local office at **international.cengage.com/region**.

Cengage Learning products are represented in Canada by Nelson Education, Ltd.

For your course and learning solutions, visit **www.cengage.com**.

Purchase any of our products at your local college store or at our preferred online store **www.cengagebrain.com**.

**Instructors:** Please visit **login.cengage.com** and log in to access instructor-specific resources.

Printed in Canada
1 2 3 4 5 6 7 17 16 15 14 13

# BRIEF CONTENTS

# CONTENTS

## PART TWO
## The Formation of New Cultural Communities, from 1500 B.C.E.   80

## Greece and Iran, 1000–30 B.C.E.   82

## An Age of Empires: Rome and Han China, 753 B.C.E.–330 C.E.   106

## India and Southeast Asia, 1500 B.C.E.–1025 C.E.   132

## 7

## Peoples and Civilizations of the Americas, from 1200 B.C.E.   156

## 8

## Networks of Communication and Exchange, 300 B.C.E.–1100 C.E.   186

## 9

## The Sasanid Empire and the Rise of Islam, 200–1200   206

**PART EIGHT**

## Perils and Promises of a Global Community, 1945 to the Present    654

### The Cold War and Decolonization, 1945–1999    656

### New Challenges in a New Millennium    684

# MAPS

# FEATURES

## ENVIRONMENT & TECHNOLOGY

## ISSUES IN WORLD HISTORY

## DIVERSITY & DOMINANCE

## MATERIAL CULTURE

In preparing the sixth edition of this book, we examined the flow of topics from chapter to chapter and decided that certain rearrangements within chapters and in the order of chapters would accommodate the needs of instructors and students better than the template they had followed since the first edition. The first change was reversing the order of the third and fourth chapters to have early Mediterranean and Middle Eastern history directly follow the discussion of the origins of civilization in the Nile Valley and Mesopotamia.

The second change addressed the problem of when and how to discuss the history of pre-Columbian America. The time span to be covered, ranging from roughly 1500 B.C.E. to 1500 C.E., was too long to fit easily into the book's division into eight parts. The new structure we have adopted relocates the long pre-Aztec and pre-Inka narrative from Part Three, Growth and Interaction of Cultural Communities, to the end of Part Two, The Formation of New Cultural Communities. This change puts the status of the earliest civilizations in the Western Hemisphere on the same footing as the early civilizations of Greece, China, and South and Southeast Asia. It has the added benefit of making the history of East Asia in the Tang and Song periods directly precede the history of the Mongol empire, which allows instructors to have an uninterrupted focus on East Asia. The histories of the Aztecs and Inkas have been shifted to the chapter on tropical history located in Part Four, Interregional Patterns of Culture and Contact. This allows for a discussion of the overall influence of tropical environments and places them in close proximity to our treatment of the coming of Europeans to the New World.

A third structural change has shortened the length of the book by one chapter. To lessen the impression that Europe's domination of the world should always be the primary focus of student attention between the eighteenth and mid-twentieth centuries we have combined the two separate chapters on European imperialism, Chapters 22 and 24 in previous editions, into one. We feel that this change provides a better balance between the saga of European imperialism, accounts of resistance to imperialism, and the rise of independence movements in different parts of the world.

In a related change, we have relocated the chapter dealing with the histories of India, Latin America, and Africa in the first half of the twentieth century from after World War II, the former Chapter 27, to a position between the world wars. The aim of this largely new chapter, titled "Revolutions in Living," is to portray that period not only as a time of political change in parts of the world subjected to European imperialism, but also as one of transformation of daily lives of people in both the industrialized and nonindustrialized worlds. The added focus of the chapter fills a gap between discussion of the Industrial Revolution in the eighteenth and nineteenth centuries and the advent of major technological changes in the post-World War II era.

Finally in this new edition, contributor and East Asian specialist Michael Wert of Marquette University brought a fresh perspective to many of our chapters dealing with East Asia, helping ensure that our coverage is at the forefront of emerging scholarship.

The authors believe that these changes, along with myriad smaller changes detailed below, significantly enhance the overall goal of *The Earth and Its Peoples*, namely, to be a textbook that speaks not only for the past but also to today's student and teacher. Students and instructors alike should take away from this text a broad, and due to the changes, more flowing impression of human societies beginning as sparse and disconnected communities reacting creatively to local circumstances; experiencing ever more intensive stages of contact, interpenetration, and cultural expansion and amalgamation; and arriving at a twenty-first-century world in which people increasingly visualize a single global community.

Process, not progress, is the keynote of this book: a steady process of change over time, at first differently experienced in various regions, but eventually connecting peoples and traditions from all parts of the globe. Students should come away from this book with a sense that the problems and promises of their world are rooted in a past in which people of every sort, in every part of the world, confronted problems of a similar character and coped with them as best they could. We believe that our efforts will help students see where their world has come from and learn thereby something useful for their own lives.

## Central Themes and Goals of the Text

We have subtitled *The Earth and Its Peoples* "A Global History" because the book explores the common challenges and experiences that unite the human past. Although the dispersal of early humans around the world resulted in many different economic, social, political, and cultural systems, all societies displayed analogous patterns in meeting their needs and exploiting their environments. Our challenge was to select the particular data and episodes that would best illuminate these global patterns of human experience.

To meet this challenge, we adopted two themes to serve as the spinal cord of our history: "technology and environment" and "diversity and dominance." The first theme represents the commonplace material bases of all human societies at all times. It grants no special favor to any cultural group even as it embraces subjects of the broadest topical, chronological, and geographical range. The second theme expresses the reality that every human society has constructed or inherited structures of domination. We examine practices and institutions of many sorts: military, economic, social, political, religious, and cultural, as well as those based on kinship, gender, and literacy. Simultaneously we recognize that alternative ways of life and visions of societal organization continually manifest themselves both within and in dialogue with every structure of domination.

With respect to the first theme, it is vital for students to understand that technology, in the broad sense of experience-based knowledge of the physical world, underlies all human activity. Writing is a technology, but so is oral transmission from generation to generation of lore about medicinal or poisonous plants. The magnetic compass is a navigational technology, but so is a Polynesian mariner's hard-won knowledge of winds, currents, and tides that made possible the settlement of the Pacific islands.

All technological development has come about in interaction with environments, both physical and human, and has, in turn, affected those environments. The story of how humanity has changed the face of the globe is an integral part of this central theme. Yet technology and the environment do not explain or underlie all important episodes of human experience. The theme of "Diversity and Dominance" informs all our discussions of politics, culture, and society. Thus, when narrating the histories of empires, we describe a range of human experiences within and beyond the imperial frontiers without assuming that the imperial institutions are a more suitable topic for discussion than the economic and social organization of pastoral nomads or the lives of peasant women. When religion and culture occupy our narrative, we focus not only on the dominant tradition but also on the diversity of alternative beliefs and practices.

## Organization

The brief edition of *The Earth and Its Peoples*, sixth edition, retains the eight broad chronological divisions of previous editions to define its conceptual scheme of global historical development.

In **Part One: The Emergence of Human Communities, to 1500 B.C.E.**, we examine important patterns of human communal organization primarily in the Eastern Hemisphere. Small, dispersed human communities living by foraging spread to most parts of the world over tens of thousands of years. They responded to enormously diverse environmental conditions, at different times and in different ways discovering how to cultivate plants and utilize the products of domestic animals. On the basis of these new modes of sustenance, populations grew, permanent towns appeared, and political and religious authority, based on collection and control of agricultural surpluses, spread over extensive areas.

**Part Two: The Formation of New Cultural Communities, from 1500 B.C.E.** introduces the concept of a "cultural community," in the sense of a coherent pattern of activities and symbols pertaining to a specific human community. While all human communities develop distinctive cultures, including those discussed in Part One, historical development in this stage of global history prolonged and magnified the impact of some cultures more than others. In the geographically contiguous African-Eurasian landmass, as well as the Western Hemisphere, the cultures that proved to have the most enduring influence traced their roots to the second and first millennia B.C.E.

**Part Three: Growth and Interaction of Cultural Communities, 300 B.C.E.–1200 C.E.** deals with early episodes of technological, social, and cultural exchange and interaction on a continental scale both within and beyond the framework of imperial expansion. These are so different from earlier interactions arising from more limited conquests or extensions of political boundaries that they constitute a distinct era in world history, an era that set the world on the path of increasing global interaction and interdependence that it has been following ever since.

In **Part Four: Interregional Patterns of Culture and Contact, 1200–1550**, we take a look at the world during three centuries that saw both intensified cultural and commercial contact and increasingly confident self-definition of cultural communities in Europe, Asia, Africa, and the Americas. The Mongol conquest of a vast empire extending from the Pacific Ocean to eastern Europe greatly stimulated trade and interaction. In the West, strengthened European kingdoms began maritime expansion in the Atlantic, forging direct ties with sub-Saharan Africa and entering into conflict with the civilizations of the Western Hemisphere.

**Part Five: The Globe Encompassed, 1500–1750** treats a period dominated by the global effects of European expansion and continued economic growth. European ships took over, expanded, and extended the maritime trade of the Indian Ocean, coastal Africa, and the Asian rim of the Pacific Ocean. This maritime commercial enterprise had its counterpart in European colonial empires in the Americas and a new Atlantic trading system. The contrasting capacities and fortunes of traditional land empires and new maritime empires, along with the exchange of domestic plants and animals between the hemispheres, underline the technological and environmental dimensions of this first era of complete global interaction.

In **Part Six: Revolutions Reshape the World, 1750–1870**, the word *revolution* is used in several senses: in the political sense of governmental overthrow, as in France and the Americas; in the metaphorical sense of radical transformative change, as in the Industrial Revolution; and in the broadest sense of a perception of a profound change in circumstances and worldview. Technology and environment lie at the core of these developments. With the rapid ascendancy of the Western belief that science and technology could overcome all challenges, technology became not only an instrument of transformation but also an instrument of domination, to the point of threatening the integrity and autonomy of cultural traditions in nonindustrial lands and provoking strong movements of resistance.

**Part Seven: Global Diversity and Dominance, 1850–1945**, examines the development of a world arena in which people conceived of events on a global scale. Imperialism, international economic connections, and world-encompassing ideological tendencies, such as nationalism and socialism, present the picture of a globe becoming increasingly involved with European political and ideological concerns. Two world wars arising from European rivalries provide a climax to these developments, and European exhaustion affords other parts of the world new opportunities for independence and self-expression.

**Part Eight: Perils and Promises of a Global Community, 1945 to the Present**, divides at the turn of the millennium not because 2000 is a round number but because the terrorist attacks of 9/11 triggered, and now symbolize, so many changes in the world's political, economic, social, and ideological attitudes. Where the challenges of the Cold War and postcolonial nation building dominated the second half of the twentieth century, the promises and perils of globalization have been the hallmark of the twenty-first. Technology is a key topic in Part Eight because the threat of nuclear weapons and the urgency of supplying the growing world demand for oil overshadowed the late twentieth century, and the transformation of information technology has shaped the twenty-first, with worries about the impact of new technologies on the environment forming a constant and growing concern throughout the period.

The brief edition is produced in two formats: A complete edition covers the entire chronology from prehistory to the present, and a two-volume edition can be used for the two-semester survey. Volume I covers the period from prehistory to 1550, and Volume II covers 1500 to the present. There is a brief introduction to Volume II that orients students to the general political and social climate of the world before and up to 1500.

## Changes in the Brief Sixth Edition

Several changes have been made to the organization of the text to make the narrative more logical and accessible. In Part One, Chapters 2 and 3 have been swapped for better continuity with Part Two. Chapter 3 now contains a substantial new section on pastoral nomadism in the Eurasian steppe. Additionally, descriptions of early civilizations in the Western Hemisphere have been shifted to Chapter 7 in order to facilitate a more unified discussion of Pre-Columbian America. The placement of Chapter 8 has been corrected in this edition, moving from Part Two to Part Three where it fits logically with the part focus on the growth and interaction of cultural communities.

Part Four features a new organization and contains heavily revised chapter material. Chapter 13 (formerly Chapter 14) has expanded coverage of eastern Europe and the Ottoman empire. A largely new Chapter 14 bears a new title, "Southern Empires, Southern Seas," and includes treatment of the Aztec and Inka empires that were previously covered much earlier in the book. Chapter 15 reflects new research on South Asian and Polynesian maritime cultures.

In Part Five, Chapter 18 has expanded to include the history of Russia, hence a new opening featuring a Russian popular hero and the change of title to "Territorial Empires Between Europe and China." Chapter 19 has a new discussion of Korean history and the Imjin War.

The organization of Part Six has been modified as well. Chapters 20 and 21 have been reversed in sequence to provide better continuity to discussions of revolutions in Europe and parallel changes in the Americas. Chapter 20 includes a new discussion of proto-industrialization as well as augmented discussions of the spread of industrialization to continental Europe and North America and the early career of Karl Marx. The section "Protest and Reform" has been broadly revised to include machine breaking in the textile sector and rural resistance to mechanization in the Captain Swing riots.

Part Seven has been the focus of our revision efforts and features a new organization highlighting global issues, much streamlined content, and one brand new chapter on culture and technology. The opening chapter of Part Seven now combines accounts of European imperialism that were previously contained in Chapters 22 and 24. Chapter 24 features a revised discussion of early Japanese industrialization as well as an expanded treatment of Marx and Marxism and a new discussion of Mikhail Bakunin and anarchism. Chapter 26 combines in a new chapter a discussion of technology and lifestyle changes that occurred between 1900 and 1945 with accounts of political movements in India, Latin America, and Africa that were previously located in Chapter 27.

The final Part Eight includes an updated discussion about the Cold War confrontation between West and East plus a revised discussion of apartheid and South Africa's struggle for independence. The final chapter updates world affairs through the first half of 2013.

## Features and Pedagogical Aids

As with previous editions, the sixth edition offers a number of valuable features and pedagogical aids designed to pique student interest in specific world history topics and help them process and retain key information.

Our **Material Culture** feature calls particular attention to the many ways in which objects and processes of everyday life can help us understand human history on a broad scale. Thus essays like "Wine and Beer in the Ancient World" and "Cotton Clothing" are not only interesting in and of themselves but also suggestive of how today's world historians find meaning in the ordinary dimensions of human life.

The **Environment and Technology** feature, which has been a valuable resource in all prior editions of *The Earth and Its Peoples*, serves to illuminate the major theme of the text by demonstrating the shared material bases of all human societies across time.

Historical essays for each of the eight parts called ***Issues in World History*** were specifically designed to alert students to broad and recurring conceptual issues that are of great interest to contemporary historians; this feature has proved to be an instructor and student favorite.

Finally, **Diversity and Dominance**, also core to the theme of the text, is the primary source feature that brings a myriad of real historical voices to life in a common struggle for power and autonomy.

Pedagogical aids include the following:

**Chapter Opening Focus Questions**  These questions are keyed to every major subdivision of the chapter through a system of color-coding and serve to help students focus on the core chapter concepts. The unique color-coded system helps students keep track of where they are in the text and easily identify which focus question corresponds to each section of the chapter. The color-coding carries through to the end of each chapter, where the focus questions for each section are answered and summarized.

**Section Reviews**  Short bullet-point reviews appear at the end of each major section in every chapter and remind students of key information.

**Chapter Conclusions**  Every chapter ends with a comparative conclusion that will help students synthesize chapter material and understand how it fits into the larger picture.

**Key Terms with Definitions**  Students can handily find definitions for bolded key terms right on the page of the text where the term first appears.

**Chapter Reviews**  Keyed to the chapter opening focus questions through a system of color-coding, the chapter reviews summarize the most important concepts addressed in the chapter, making studying more efficient and effective.

**Pronunciation Guide**  Phonetic spellings for unfamiliar names and terms have been integrated into the text.

## Supplements

A wide array of supplements accompany this text to assist students with different learning needs and to help instructors master today's various classroom challenges.

### Instructor Resources

**MindTap™ [ISBN: 9781285843056]** The Personal Learning Experience. MindTap for *The Earth and Its Peoples* is a personalized, online digital learning platform providing students with *The Earth and Its Peoples* content and related interactive assignments and app services—while giving you a choice in the configuration of coursework and curriculum enhancement. Through a carefully designed chapter-based learning path, students can access the ebook (MindTap Reader, see description below); Aplia™ assignments developed for the most important concepts in each chapter (see Aplia description below); brief quizzes; and a set of web applications known as MindApps to help you create the most engaging course for your students. The MindApps range from ReadSpeaker (which reads the text out-loud to students) to Kaltura (allowing you to insert inline video and audio into your curriculum) to ConnectYard (allowing you to create digital "yards" through social media—all without "friending" your students). MindTap for *The Earth and Its Peoples* goes well beyond an eBook, a homework solution/ digital supplement, a resource center website, or a Learning Management System. It is truly a Personal Learning Experience that allows you to synchronize the text reading and engaging assignments and quizzes. To learn more, ask your Cengage Learning sales representative to demo it for you—or go to www.cengage.com/MindTap.

**Aplia™ [ISBN: 9781285780382]** is an online interactive learning solution that improves comprehension and outcomes by increasing student effort and engagement. Founded by a professor to enhance his own courses, Aplia provides automatically graded assignments with detailed, immediate explanations on every question. The interactive assignments have been developed to address the major concepts covered in *The Earth and Its Peoples* and are designed to promote critical thinking and engage students more fully in learning. Question types include questions built around animated maps, primary sources such as newspaper extracts, or imagined scenarios, like engaging in a conversation with a an historical figure or finding a diary and being asked to fill in some blanks; more in-depth primary source question sets address a major topic with a number of related primary sources and questions that promote deeper analysis of historical evidence. Many of the questions incorporate images, video clips, or audio clips. Students get immediate feedback on their work (not only what they got right or wrong, but why), and they can choose to see another set of related questions if they want more practice. A searchable eBook is available inside the course as well so that students can easily reference it as they work. Map-reading and writing tutorials are also available to get students off to a good start.

Aplia's simple-to-use course management interface allows instructors to post announcements, upload course materials, host student discussions, e-mail students, and manage the gradebook; a knowledgeable and friendly support team offers assistance and personalized support in customizing assignments to the instructor's course schedule. To learn more and view a demo for this book, visit www.aplia.com.

**MindTap Reader** for *The Earth and Its Peoples* is an eBook specifically designed to address the ways students assimilate content and media assets. MindTap Reader combines thoughtful navigation ergonomics, advanced student annotation, note-taking, and search tools, and embedded media assets such as video and MP3 chapter summaries, primary source documents with critical thinking questions, and interactive (zoomable) maps. Students can use the eBook as their primary text or as a multimedia companion to their printed book. The MindTap Reader eBook is available within the MindTap and Aplia online offerings found at www.cengagebrain.com.

**Online PowerLecture with Cognero®** [ISBN: 9781285455075]  This PowerLecture is an all-in-one online multimedia resource for class preparation, presentation, and testing. Accessible through cengage.com/login with your faculty account, you will find available for download: book-specific Microsoft® PowerPoint® presentations; a Test Bank in both Microsoft® Word® and Cognero® formats; an Instructor Manual; Microsoft® PowerPoint® Image Slides; and a JPEG Image Library. The Test Bank, offered in Microsoft® Word® and Cognero® formats, contains multiple-choice and essay questions for each chapter. Cognero® is a flexible, online system that allows you to author, edit, and manage test bank content for The Earth and Its People, 6e. Create multiple test versions instantly and deliver through your LMS from your classroom, or wherever you may be, with no special installs or downloads required.

The **Instructor's Manual** contains for each chapter: an outline and summary; critical thinking questions; in-class activities; lecture launching suggestions; a list of key terms with definitions; and suggested readings and Web resources. The Microsoft® PowerPoint® presentations are ready-to-use, visual outlines of each chapter. These presentations are easily customized for your lectures and offered along with chapter-specific Microsoft® PowerPoint® Image Slides and JPEG Image Libraries. Access your Online PowerLecture at www.cengage.com/login.

**CourseReader**  CourseReader is an online collection of primary and secondary sources that lets you create a customized electronic reader in minutes. With an easy-to-use interface and assessment tool, you can choose exactly what your students will be assigned—simply search or browse Cengage Learning's extensive document database to preview and select your customized collection of readings. In addition to print sources of all types (letters, diary entries, speeches, newspaper accounts, etc.), their collection includes a growing number of images and video and audio clips.

Each primary source document includes a descriptive headnote that puts the reading into context and is further supported by both critical thinking and multiple-choice questions designed to reinforce key points. For more information visit www.cengage.com/coursereader.

**Cengagebrain.com**  Save your students time and money. Direct them to www.cengagebrain.com for choice in formats and savings and a better chance to succeed in your class. Cengagebrain.com, Cengage Learning's online store, is a single destination for more than 10,000 new textbooks, eTextbooks, eChapters, study tools, and audio supplements. Students have the freedom to purchase a-la-carte exactly what they need when they need it. Students can save 50% on the electronic textbook, and can pay as little as $1.99 for an individual eChapter.

**Reader Program** Cengage Learning publishes a number of readers, some containing exclusively primary sources, others a combination of primary and secondary sources, and some designed to guide students through the process of historical inquiry. Visit Cengage.com/history for a complete list of readers.

**Custom Options** Nobody knows your students like you, so why not give them a text that is tailor-fit to their needs? Cengage Learning offers custom solutions for your course—whether it's making a small modification to *The Earth and Its Peoples* to match your syllabus or combining multiple sources to create something truly unique. You can pick and choose chapters, include your own material, and add additional map exercises along with the Rand McNally Atlas to create a text that fits the way you teach. Ensure that your students get the most out of their textbook dollar by giving them exactly what they need. Contact your Cengage Learning representative to explore custom solutions for your course.

## Student Resources

*Writing for College History*, **First Edition [ISBN: 9780618306039]** Prepared by Robert M. Frakes, Clarion University. This brief handbook for survey courses in American history, Western Civilization/European history, and world civilization guides students through the various types of writing assignments they encounter in a history class. Providing examples of student writing and candid assessments of student work, this text focuses on the rules and conventions of writing for the college history course.

*The History Handbook*, **Second Edition [ISBN: 9780495906766]** Prepared by Carol Berkin of Baruch College, City University of New York and Betty Anderson of Boston University. This book teaches students both basic and history-specific study skills such as how to read primary sources, research historical topics, and correctly cite sources. Substantially less expensive than comparable skill-building texts, The History Handbook also offers tips for Internet research and evaluating online sources.

*Doing History: Research and Writing in the Digital Age*, **Second Edition [ISBN: 9781133587880]** Prepared by Michael J. Galgano, J. Chris Arndt, and Raymond M. Hyser of James Madison University. Whether you're starting down the path as a history major, or simply looking for a straightforward and systematic guide to writing a successful paper, you'll find this text to be an indispensible handbook to historical research. This text's "soup to nuts" approach to researching and writing about history addresses every step of the process, from locating your sources and gathering information, to writing clearly and making proper use of various citation styles to avoid plagiarism. You'll also learn how to make the most of every tool available to you—especially the technology that helps you conduct the process efficiently and effectively.

*The Modern Researcher*, **Sixth Edition [ISBN: 9780495318705]** Prepared by Jacques Barzun and Henry F. Graff of Columbia University. This classic introduction to the techniques of research and the art of expression is used widely in history courses, but is also appropriate for writing and research methods courses in other departments. Barzun and Graff thoroughly cover every aspect of research, from the selection of a topic through the gathering, analysis, writing, revision, and publication of findings, presenting the process not as a set of rules but through actual cases that put the subtleties of research in a useful context. Part One covers the principles and methods of research; Part Two covers writing, speaking, and getting one's work published.

***Rand McNally Historical Atlas of the World*, Second Edition [ISBN: 9780618841912]** This valuable resource features over 70 maps that portray the rich panoply of the world's history from preliterate times to the present. They show how cultures and civilization were linked and how they interacted. The maps make it clear that history is not static. Rather, it is about change and movement across time. The maps show change by presenting the dynamics of expansion, cooperation, and conflict. This atlas includes maps that display the world from the beginning of civilization; the political development of all major areas of the world; expanded coverage of Africa, Latin America, and the Middle East; the current Islamic World; and the world population change in 1900 and 2000.

## Acknowledgments

In preparing the sixth edition, we benefited from the critical readings of many colleagues. Our sincere thanks go in particular to contributor Michael Wert of Marquette University who lent his fresh perspective to our coverage of East Asia. We thank Beatrice Manz of the History Department at Tufts University who provided guidance on the new Pastoral Nomads section in Part One. We are also indebted to the following instructors who lent their insight over various editions: Hedrick Alixopuilos, Santa Rosa Junior College; Hayden Bellenoit, U.S. Naval Academy; Dusty Bender, Central Baptist College; Cory Crawford, Ohio University; Adrian De Gifis, Loyola University New Orleans; Peter de Rosa, Bridgewater State University; Aaron Gulyas, Mott Community College; Darlene Hall, Lake Erie College; Vic Jagos, Scottsdale Community College; Adrien Ivan, Vernon College; Andrew Muldoon, Metropolitan State College of Denver; Percy Murray, Shaw University; Dave Price, Santa Fe College; Anthony Steinhoff, University of Tennessee-Chattanooga; Anara Tabyshalieva, Marshal University; Susan Autry, Central Piedmont Community College; Anna Collins, Arkansas Tech University; William Connell, Christopher Newport University; Gregory Crider, Winthrop University; Shawn Dry, Oakland Community College; Nancy Fitch, California State University, Fullerton; Christine Haynes, University of North Carolina at Charlotte; Mark Herman, Edison College; Ellen J. Jenkins, Arkansas Tech University; Frank Karpiel, The Citadel; Ken Koons, Virginia Military Institute; David Longfellow, Baylor University; Heather Lucas, Georgia Perimeter College; Jeff Pardue, Gainesville State College; Craig Patton, Alabama A & M University; Linda Scherr, Mercer County Community College; Robert Sherwood, Georgia Military College; Brett Shufelt, Copiah-Lincoln Community College; Kristen Walton, Salisbury University; Christopher Ward, Clayton State University; William Wood, Point Loma Nazarene University.

When textbook authors set out on a project, they are inclined to believe that 90 percent of the effort will be theirs and 10 percent that of various editors and production specialists employed by their publisher. How very naïve. This book would never have seen the light of day had it not been for the unstinting labors of the great team of professionals who turned the authors' words into beautifully presented print. Our debt to the staff of Cengage Learning remains undiminished in the sixth edition. Brooke Barbier, product manager, has offered us firm but sympathetic guidance throughout the revision process. Tonya Lobato, senior product developer, offered astute and sympathetic assistance as the authors worked to incorporate many new ideas and subjects into the text. Carol Newman, senior content project manager, moved the work through the production stages to meet a challenging schedule. Abbey Stebing did an outstanding job of photo research.

We thank also the many students whose questions and concerns, expressed directly or through their instructors, shaped much of this revision. We continue to welcome all readers' suggestions, queries, and criticisms. Please contact us at our respective institutions.

# ABOUT THE AUTHORS

**RICHARD W. BULLIET**    Professor of Middle Eastern History at Columbia University, Richard W. Bulliet received his Ph.D. from Harvard University. He has written scholarly works on a number of topics: the social and economic history of medieval Iran (The Patricians of Nishapur and Cotton, Climate, and Camels in Early Islamic Iran), the history of human-animal relations (The Camel and the Wheel and Hunters, Herders, and Hamburgers), the process of conversion to Islam (Conversion to Islam in the Medieval Period), and the overall course of Islamic social history (Islam: The View from the Edge and The Case for Islamo-Christian Civilization). He is the editor of the Columbia History of the Twentieth Century. He has published four novels, coedited The Encyclopedia of the Modern Middle East, and hosted an educational television series on the Middle East. He was awarded a fellowship by the John Simon Guggenheim Memorial Foundation and was named a Carnegie Corporation Scholar.

**PAMELA KYLE CROSSLEY**    Pamela Kyle Crossley received her Ph.D. in Modern Chinese History from Yale University. She is currently the Robert and Barbara Black Professor of History at Dartmouth College. Her books include The Wobbling Pivot: An Interpretive History of China Since 1800; What Is Global History?; A Translucent Mirror: History and Identity in Qing Imperial Ideology; The Manchus; Orphan Warriors: Three Manchu Generations and the End of the Qing World; and (with Lynn Hollen Lees and John W. Servos) Global Society: The World Since 1900.

**DANIEL R. HEADRICK**    Daniel R. Headrick received his Ph.D. in History from Princeton University. Professor of History and Social Science, Emeritus, at Roosevelt University in Chicago, he is the author of several books on the history of technology, imperialism, and international relations, including The Tools of Empire: Technology and European Imperialism in the Nineteenth Century; The Tentacles of Progress: Technology Transfer in the Age of Imperialism; The Invisible Weapon: Telecommunications and International Politics; Technology: A World History; Power Over Peoples: Technology, Environments and Western Imperialism, 1400 to the Present;

and When Information Came of Age: Technologies of Knowledge in the Age of Reason and Revolution, 1700–1850. His articles have appeared in the Journal of World History and the Journal of Modern History, and he has been awarded fellowships by the National Endowment for the Humanities, the John Simon Guggenheim Memorial Foundation, and the Alfred P. Sloan Foundation.

**STEVEN W. HIRSCH**   Steven W. Hirsch holds a Ph.D. in Classics from Stanford University and is currently Associate Professor of Classics and History at Tufts University. He has received grants from the National Endowment for the Humanities and the Massachusetts Foundation for Humanities and Public Policy. His research and publications include The Friendship of the Barbarians: Xenophon and the Persian Empire, as well as articles and reviews in the Classical Journal, the American Journal of Philology, and the Journal of Interdisciplinary History. He is currently completing a comparative study of ancient Greco-Roman and Chinese civilizations.

**LYMAN L. JOHNSON**   Professor Emeritus of History at the University of North Carolina at Charlotte, Lyman L. Johnson earned his Ph.D. in Latin American History from the University of Connecticut. A two-time Senior Fulbright-Hays Lecturer, he also has received fellowships from the Tinker Foundation, the Social Science Research Council, the National Endowment for the Humanities, and the American Philosophical Society. His recent books include Workshop of Revolution: Plebeian Buenos Aires and the Atlantic World, 1776-1810; Death, Dismemberment, and Memory; The Faces of Honor (with Sonya Lipsett-Rivera); Aftershocks: Earthquakes and Popular Politics in Latin America (with Jürgen Buchenau); Essays on the Price History of Eighteenth-Century Latin America (with Enrique Tandeter); and Colonial Latin America (with Mark A. Burkholder). He also has published in journals, including the Hispanic American Historical Review, the Journal of Latin American Studies, the International Review of Social History, Social History, and Desarrollo Económico. He has served as president of the Conference on Latin American History.

**DAVID NORTHRUP**   David Northrup earned his Ph.D. in African and European History from the University of California, Los Angeles. He has published scholarly works on African, Atlantic, and world history. His most recent books are How English Became the Global Language, the third edition of Africa's Discovery of Europe, 1450–1850, and the Diary of Antera Duke, an Eighteenth-Century African Slave Trader. He taught at a rural secondary school on Nigeria, Tuskegee Institute in Alabama, Boston College, and Venice International University and is a past president of the World History Association.

# NOTE ON SPELLING AND USAGE

Where necessary for clarity, dates are followed by the letters C.E. or B.C.E. The abbreviation C.E. stands for "Common Era" and is equivalent to A.D. (anno Domini, Latin for "in the year of the Lord"). The abbreviation B.C.E. stands for "before the Common Era" and means the same as B.C. ("before Christ"). In keeping with our goal of approaching world history without special concentration on one culture or another, we chose these neutral abbreviations as appropriate to our enterprise. Because many readers will be more familiar with English than with metric measurements, however, units of measure are generally given in the English system, with metric equivalents following in parentheses.

In general, Chinese has been Romanized according to the pinyin method. Exceptions include proper names well established in English (e.g., Canton, Chiang Kaishek) and a few English words borrowed from Chinese (e.g., kowtow). Spellings of Arabic, Ottoman Turkish, Persian, Mongolian, Manchu, Japanese, and Korean names and terms avoid special diacritical marks for letters that are pronounced only slightly differently in English. An apostrophe is used to indicate when two Chinese syllables are pronounced separately (e.g., Chang'an).

For words transliterated from languages that use the Arabic script—Arabic, Ottoman Turkish, Persian, Urdu—the apostrophe indicating separately pronounced syllables may represent either of two special consonants, the hamza or the ain. Because most English-speakers do not hear the distinction between these two, they have not been distinguished in transliteration and are not indicated when they occur at the beginning or end of a word. As with Chinese, some words and commonly used place-names from these languages are given familiar English spellings (e.g., Quran instead of Qur'an, Cairo instead of al-Qahira). Arabic romanization has normally been used for terms relating to Islam, even where the context justifies slightly different Turkish or Persian forms, again for ease of comprehension.

Before 1492 the inhabitants of the Western Hemisphere had no single name for themselves. They had neither a racial consciousness nor a racial identity. Identity was derived from kin groups, language, cultural practices, and political structures. There was no sense that physical similarities created a shared identity. America's original inhabitants had racial consciousness and racial identity imposed on them by conquest and the occupation of their lands by Europeans after 1492. All of the collective terms for these first American peoples are tainted by this history. Indians, Native Americans, Amerindians, First Peoples, and Indigenous Peoples are among the terms in common usage. In this book the names of individual cultures and states are used wherever possible. Amerindian and other terms that suggest transcultural identity and experience are used most commonly for the period after 1492.

There is an ongoing debate about how best to render Amerindian words in English. It has been common for authors writing in English to follow Mexican usage for Nahuatl and Yucatec Maya words and place-names. In this style, for example, the capital of the Aztec state is spelled Tenochtitlán, and the important late Maya city-state is spelled Chichén Itzá. Although these forms are still common even in the specialist literature, we have chosen to follow the scholarship that sees these accents as unnecessary. The exceptions are modern place-names, such as Mérida and Yucatán, which are accented. A similar problem exists for the spelling of Quechua and Aymara words from the Andean region of South America. Although there is significant disagreement among scholars, we follow the emerging consensus and use the spellings khipu (not quipu), Tiwanaku (not Tiahuanaco), and Wari (not Huari). In this edition we have introduced the now common spelling Inka (not Inca) but keep Cuzco for the capital city (not Cusco), since this spelling facilitates locating this still-important city on maps.

# The Earth and Its Peoples

A Global History

# Part One

# The Emergence of Human Communities, to 1500 B.C.E.

© Cengage Learning

| | 8000 B.C.E. | 7000 B.C.E. | 6000 B.C.E. | 5000 B.C.E. |
|---|---|---|---|---|
| **AMERICAS** | | • **7000** Incipient plant domestication in Peru | | • **5000** Maize, beans, and squash domestication in Mesoamerica |
| **EUROPE** | Spread of Indo-European languages | | • **6000** Farming in southern Europe | |
| **AFRICA** | • **8000** Farming in eastern Sahara | | | • **5500** Farming in Egypt |
| **MIDDLE EAST** | • **8000** Domestication of plants and animals in Fertile Crescent | | | • **5000** Irrigation in Mesopotamia |
| **ASIA AND OCEANIA** | | • **6500** Rice cultivation in China | | • **5000** Farming in India |

Human beings evolved over several million years from primates in Africa. Able to walk upright and possessing large brains, hands with opposable thumbs, and the capacity for speech, early humans used teamwork and created tools to survive in diverse environments. They spread relatively quickly to almost every habitable area of the world, hunting and gathering wild plant products. Around 10,000 years ago some groups began to cultivate plants, domesticate animals, and make pottery vessels for storage. This led to permanent settlements—at first small villages but eventually larger towns as well.

The earliest complex societies arose in the great river valleys of Iraq, Egypt, Pakistan, and northern China. In these arid regions agriculture depended on river water, and centers of political power arose to organize the labor required to dig and maintain irrigation channels. Kings and priests dominated these early societies from the urban centers, helped by administrators, scribes, soldiers, merchants, craftsmen, and others with specialized skills. Surplus food grown in the countryside by a dependent peasantry sustained the activities of these groups.

Certain centers came to dominate broader expanses of territory, seeking access to raw materials, especially metals. This development also stimulated long-distance trade and diplomatic relations between major powers. Artisans made weapons, tools, and ritual objects from bronze. Culture and technology spread to neighboring regions, such as southern China, Nubia, Syria-Palestine, Anatolia, and the Aegean.

| 4000 B.C.E. | 3000 B.C.E. | 2000 B.C.E. | 1000 B.C.E. |
|---|---|---|---|
| • **4000** Quinoa and potato domestication in Peru | • **3000** Farming in central Mexico | • **2000** Farming in Peru | • **1200** Rise of Olmec civilization in Mesoamerica<br>• **900** Rise of Chavín civilization in Peru |
| • **4000** Megaliths | **3000–1100** Aegean civilization | | • **1000** Iron metallurgy |
| | • **3100** Unification of Egypt   **2575–2134** Old Kingdom Egypt | **2040–1640** Middle Kingdom Egypt<br>• **2000** Rise of Kush in Nubia   **1532–1070** New Kingdom Egypt | • **800** Rise of Nubian Kingdom at Napata |
| | • **3100** Mesopotamian civilization   Advent of horses in western Asia **2000** •<br>• **2350** Akkadian kingdom | • **1750** Hammurabi's law code<br>**1700–1200** Hittites dominant in Anatolia | • **911** Rise of Neo-Assyrian Empire |
| | Bronze metallurgy in China **2000** •<br>**2600–1900** Indus Valley civilization | **1600–1027** Shang kingdom in China | **1027–221** Zhou kingdom in China |

# Nature, Humanity, and the First River-Valley Societies

© Cengage Learning

Were the people who lived tens of thousands of years ago different from people today? Did their eyes see beauty, their ears hear music, and their minds wonder at the meaning of the world around them and the celestial bodies above them? Biologically, members of *Homo sapiens* have not changed much over time, but very little evidence exists to tell us what our ancestors were like inside—in their thoughts, imaginations, and emotions.

We might find clues in the splendid creative abilities of early humans that first came to light in 1940 near Lascaux in southwestern France, where youths stumbled upon a vast underground cavern whose walls were covered with paintings of animals, including many that had been extinct for thousands of years. Such art immediately suggested that those who made it were as sophisticated as the people who live today. Even though the original significance of these paintings is a mystery, we have a sense of these cave artists' common humanity with ourselves.

Paintings and engravings on stone created tens of thousands of years ago by early humans have been found on every continent. The oldest recognizable human art, a carefully crosshatched bone from Blombos Cave east of Cape Town, South Africa, dates from over 70,000 years ago. The oldest cave paintings discovered in southwestern France date from 32,000 years ago. To even the most skeptical person, these artistic troves reveal rich imaginations and sophisticated skills, qualities also apparent in the stone tools and in the evidence of complex social relations uncovered from prehistoric sites. Just as the skeletal remains of *Homo sapiens* of tens of thousands of years ago show they had modern bodies, the art they made suggests they had modern minds.

The production of such artworks and tools over wide areas and long periods of time demonstrates that skills and ideas were not simply individual expressions but were deliberately passed along within societies. These learned patterns of action and expression constitute **culture**. Culture includes material objects, such as dwellings, clothing, tools, and crafts, along with nonmaterial values, beliefs,

and languages. Although it is true that some animals also learn new ways, their activities are determined primarily by inherited instincts. Only human communities trace profound cultural developments over time. The development, transmission, and transformation of cultural practices and events are the subject of **history**.

## EARLY HUMANS

■ *In light of scientific advances in our understanding of human origins, what have we learned about our relationship to the earth and other living species?*

Since Charles Darwin argued in *The Descent of Man* (1871) that human beings had come into existence through the process of natural selection called **evolution**, it has been popular (and controversial) to say that we are descended from apes. In fact, apes and humans share a common ancestor. Over 99 percent of human DNA, the basic genetic blueprint, is identical to that of the great apes. But three traits distinguish humans from apes and other primates. The first of these traits to appear was walking upright on two legs. This frees the forelimbs from any role in locomotion and enhances the development of a thumb that can manipulate objects skillfully. Modern humans' second distinctive trait was a very large brain. Besides enabling humans to think abstractly, experience profound emotions, and construct complex social relationships, this larger brain controls the fine motor movements of the hand and of the tongue, increasing humans' tool-using capacity and facilitating the development of speech. The physical possibility of language, however, depends on a third distinctive human trait: the location of the larynx (voice box). In humans it lies much lower in the neck

**culture** Socially transmitted patterns of action and expression. *Material culture* refers to physical objects such as dwellings, clothing, tools, and crafts. Culture also includes arts, beliefs, knowledge, and technology.

**history** The study of past events and changes in the development, transmission, and transformation of cultural practices.

**evolution** The biological theory that, over time, changes occurring in plants and animals, mainly as a result of natural selection and genetic mutation, result in new species.

than in any other primate, making it possible to create a wide range of sounds.

About 65 million years ago, primates—members of a class of four-limbed, social animals known as mammals—came to prominence. Biologists classify humans as members of a family of primates known as **hominids** (HOM-uh-nids). The first hominids are now dated to about 7 million years ago. Beginning approximately 4.5 million years ago, several species of hominids known as **australopithecines** (aw-strah-loh-PITH-uh-seens) evolved in southern and eastern Africa.

In northern Ethiopia in 1974, Donald Johanson unearthed a well-preserved skeleton of a twenty-five-year-old female whom he nicknamed "Lucy," supporting the 1924 finding by Raymond Dart that a transitional "human" he named *Australopithecus africanus* (aw-strah-loh-PITH-uh-kuhs ah-frih-KAH-nuhs) (African southern ape) walked upright like a human but had a brain the size of an ape's. A wealth of fossil evidence had been mounting that the tropical habitat of the African apes was the cradle of humanity. The discovery of fossilized footprints in Tanzania in 1977 provided spectacular visual evidence that australopithecines walked on two legs.

**Bipedalism** evolved because it provided australopithecines an advantage for survival. Some studies suggest that walking and running on two legs is very energy efficient. Another theory is that bipeds survived better because they could carry armfuls of food back to their mates and children.

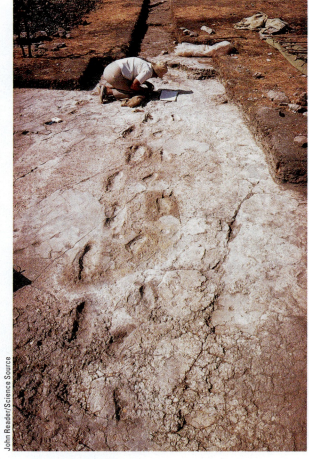

John Reader/Science Source

**Fossilized Footprints** Archaeologist Mary Leakey (shown at top) found these remarkable footprints of a hominid adult and child at Laetoli, Tanzania. The pair had walked through fresh volcanic ash that solidified after being buried by a new volcanic eruption. Dated to 3.5 million years ago, the footprints are the oldest evidence of bipedalism yet found.

## Climate Change, Food, and Stone Tools

Climate changes between 2 and 3 million years ago led to the evolution of a new species. Falling temperatures culminated in the **Great Ice Age**, or Pleistocene (PLY-stuh-seen) epoch, extending from about 2 million to 11,000 years ago, when it was followed by our era, the Holocene (HOH-loh-seen). These temperature changes and altered rainfall and vegetation imposed great strains on plant and animal species. What most distinguished **Homo habilis** (HOH-moh HAB-uh-luhs) (handy human) from the australopithecines was a brain nearly 50 percent larger. Greater intelligence may have enabled Homo habilis to locate things to eat throughout the seasons of the year. Seeds and other fossilized remains

**hominid** The biological family that includes humans and humanlike primates.

**australopithecines** The several extinct species of humanlike primates that existed from about 4.5 million years ago to 1.4 million years ago (genus *Australopithecus*).

**bipedalism** The ability to walk upright on two legs, characteristic of hominids.

**Great Ice Age** Geological era that occurred between ca. 2 million and 11,000 years ago.

*Homo habilis* The first human species (now extinct). It evolved in Africa about 2.3 million years ago.

# Chronology

| | Geological Epochs | Species and Migrations | Technological Advances |
|---|---|---|---|
| 7,000,000 B.C.E. | | 7,000,000 B.C.E. Earliest hominids | |
| 4,000,000 B.C.E. | | 4,500,000 B.C.E. Australopithecines | |
| | | 2,300,000 B.C.E. Early *Homo habilis* | 2,600,000 B.C.E. Earliest stone tools; hunting and gathering (foraging) societies |
| 2,000,000 B.C.E. | 2,000,000–9000 B.C.E. Pleistocene (Great Ice Age) | 1,800,000–350,000 B.C.E. *Homo erectus* | 2,000,000–8000 B.C.E. Paleolithic (Old Stone Age) |
| 1,000,000 B.C.E. | | 400,000–100,000 B.C.E. Archaic *Homo sapiens* | 500,000 B.C.E. Use of fire |
| 100,000 B.C.E. | | 100,000 B.C.E. Anatomically modern *Homo sapiens* in Africa | |
| | | 50,000 B.C.E. Behaviorally modern *Homo sapiens* possessing language | |
| | | Migrations to Eurasia | |
| | | 46,000 B.C.E. Modern humans in Australia | 30,000 B.C.E. First cave paintings |
| | | 18,000 B.C.E. Modern humans in Americas | |
| 10,000 B.C.E. | 9000 B.C.E.–present Holocene | | 8000–2000 B.C.E. Neolithic (New Stone Age); earliest agriculture |

found in ancient Homo habilis camps indicate that the new species ate a greater variety of more nutritious foods than did australopithecines.

Moreover, unlike australopithecines, *Homo habilis* made tools. Abundant evidence of stone tools first appeared at ancient human sites around 2.6 million years ago, causing this period to be called the **Stone Age**. The **Paleolithic** (or Old Stone Age) period lasted until 10,000 years ago. Specimens of crude early tools found in the Great Rift Valley of eastern Africa reveal that *Homo habilis* made tools by chipping flakes off the edges of volcanic stones. Lacking the skill to hunt and kill large animals, *Homo habilis* probably obtained animal protein by scavenging meat. The razor-sharp edges of the volcanic flakes would have been highly effective for skinning and butchering

wild animals. These two changes—increased meat eating and toolmaking—appear to be closely linked.

By 1 million years ago *Homo habilis* and all the australopithecines had become extinct. In their habitat lived a new hominid, **Homo erectus** (HOH-moh ee-REK-tuhs) (upright human), which first appeared in eastern Africa about 1.8 million years ago. (It is uncertain whether *Homo erectus* evolved from *Homo*

**Stone Age** The historical period characterized by the production of tools from stone and other nonmetallic substances.

**Paleolithic** The period of the Stone Age associated with the evolution of humans.

**Homo erectus** An extinct human species. It evolved in Africa about 1.8 million years ago.

*habilis* or both species descended from *Australopithecus*.) A nearly complete skeleton of a twelve-year-old male of the species discovered in 1984 in Kenya shows that *Homo erectus* closely resembled modern people from the neck down. These creatures possessed brains a third larger than those of *Homo habilis*. Members of *Homo erectus* were also scavengers, but they were more clever. They created the multipurpose hand ax, for example, that could be used for scraping skins, digging up edible roots, or hurling at animals. *Homo erectus* even hunted elephants by driving them into swamps, where they became trapped and died. These early humans may have also used fire; evidence suggests that fires were deliberately set as early as 1.4 million years ago, and hearths were being kept as early as 500,000 years ago. Very successful in dealing with different environments, *Homo erectus* underwent hardly any biological changes for over a million years.

DNA and fossil evidence indicates that **Homo sapiens** (HOH-moh SAY-pee-enz) (wise human) first evolved in Africa sometime between 400,000 and 100,000 years ago. The brains of *Homo sapiens* were a third larger than those of *Homo erectus*, whom they gradually superseded. Members of *Homo sapiens* were far more skillful hunters. Using their superior intelligence, they could track animals and make a spear. Despite these abilities, anthropologists believe early humans would have reserved meat for feasts.

Archaeological and genetic evidence suggest that a further development, probably connected to the emergence of language, produced the first behaviorally modern humans, with the intellectual and social capabilities that we have. There is no scholarly consensus on when, why, or how humans developed the capacity to speak. Assuming that the shape of the throat and low position of the larynx are essential, it ought to be relevant that these features were still evolving in *Homo habilis* and *Homo erectus*. Some scholars link the development of language in the fullest sense to the period around 50,000 years ago when *Homo sapiens* began to migrate out of Africa.

Early humans first expanded their range in eastern and southern Africa. Then they ventured out of Africa, perhaps following migrating herds of animals or searching for more abundant food supplies in a time of drought. Early migrations from Africa into southern Eurasia were followed by treks across land bridges during ice ages, when giant ice sheets lowered ocean levels. About 46,000 years ago, modern humans also traveled by boat to New Guinea and Australia. The reasons for these migrations are uncertain, but the end results are vividly clear: an ancestral group from which all humans are descended (which may have comprised as few as 5,000 individuals) successfully colonized every habitable environment across the globe, including deserts and arctic lands.

## Life in Paleolithic Communities

Archaeological evidence from Ice Age campsites suggests that early humans lived in highly mobile bands of **foragers** (hunting and food-gathering peoples)—big enough to defend their members from predators and divide responsibilities and small enough not to deplete the food supply in the vicinity. The band would move regularly to follow migrating animals and take advantage of seasonally ripening plants. Where the climate was severe or where natural shelters like caves did not exist, people erected huts of branches, stones, bones, skins, and leaves.

Although the oldest evidence of fibers woven into cloth dates from about 26,000 years ago, the appearance of the body louse around 70,000 years ago has been linked to people beginning to wear close-fitting garments. Early peoples would have likely worn animal skins. An "Iceman" from 5,300 years ago, whose frozen remains were found in the European Alps in 1991, was wearing many different garments made of animal skins sewn with cord fashioned from vegetable fibers and rawhide.

Ice Age women would have done most of the gathering and cooking, which they could do while caring for small children. Researchers studying present-day foragers infer that day-to-day nourishment would have come mostly from wild plant foods that women collected in skins or baskets woven from leaves. They would have dug edible roots out of the ground. Men,

**Homo sapiens** The current human species. It evolved in Africa sometime between 400,000 and 100,000 years ago.

**foragers** People who support themselves by hunting wild animals and gathering wild edible plants and insects.

© Smetek/STERN/Picture Press

**The Iceman** This is an artist's rendition of what the Iceman might have looked like. Notice his tools, remarkable evidence of the technology of his day.

with stronger arms and shoulders, would have been better suited for hunting animals, particularly large animals, and some early cave art suggests male hunting activities. Since male hunters only occasionally succeeded in bringing down their prey, women gatherers provided the bulk of the band's daily diet, and it is likely that women held a respected position for this reason. Women past childbearing age would have

been the most knowledgeable and productive food gatherers.

Even before *Homo sapiens*, the two-parent family would have been common. While other large mammals are mature at two or three years of age, humans are not able to care for themselves until much later, making the nurturing of children a biological imperative. The human reproductive cycle was also unique. In many other species sexual contact only occurs during a special mating season or when the female is fertile. In contrast, an enduring bond between human parents made it much easier for vulnerable offspring to receive the care they needed during the long period of their childhood.

Early music and dance have left no traces, but there is abundant evidence of painting and drawing. Because many cave paintings feature wild animals that were hunted for food, some believe they were meant to record hunting scenes or formed part of magical and religious rites to ensure successful hunting. However, a newly discovered cave in southern France features rhinoceroses, panthers, bears, and other animals that probably were not hunted. Other drawings include people dressed in animal skins and smeared with paint. In many caves there are stencils of human hands. Are these the signatures of the artists or the world's oldest graffiti? Some scholars suspect that other marks in cave paintings and on bones from this period may represent efforts at counting or writing. Other theories suggest that cave and rock art represent concerns with fertility, efforts to educate the young, or elaborate mechanisms for time reckoning.

Without written texts it is difficult to know about the religious beliefs of early humans. Sites of deliberate human burials from about 100,000 years ago give some hints. The fact that an adult was often buried with stone implements, food, clothing, and red-ochre powder suggests that early people revered their leaders, relatives, and companions enough to honor them after death and implies a belief in an afterlife.

Today we recognize that the Old Stone Age, whose existence was scarcely dreamed of two centuries ago, was a formative period. Although accidents, erratic weather, and disease might take a heavy toll on a foraging band, day-to-day existence was probably not particularly hard or unpleasant. Studies suggest that, in plant- and game-rich areas, obtaining necessary food, clothing, and shelter would have occupied only from three to five hours a day. This would have left a great deal of time for artistic endeavors, toolmaking, and social life. Important in its own right, this period also laid the foundation for major changes ahead as human communities passed from being food gatherers to food producers.

## THE AGRICULTURAL REVOLUTIONS

■ *How did plant and animal domestication set the scene for the emergence of complex societies?*

Around 10,000 years ago global climate changes seem to have induced some societies to enhance their food supplies with domesticated plants and animals. More and more people became food producers over the following millennia. Although hunting and gathering did not disappear, this transition from foraging to food production was one of the great turning points in history because it fostered a rapid increase in population and greatly altered humans' relationship to nature.

## Plant Cultivation and Domesticated Animals

Because agriculture arose in combination with new kinds of stone tools, archaeologists called this period the **Neolithic**, or New Stone Age, and the rise of agriculture the *Neolithic Revolution*. While archeologists were first alerted to the beginning of a food production revolution by the presence of new, specialized tools for agriculture, such as polished stone heads to work the soil and stone mortars to pulverize grain, the name *Neolithic Revolution* can be misleading: first, stone tools were not its essential component, and second, it was not a single event but occurred in a series of transformations in different parts of the world that likely began when forager bands, returning year after year to the same seasonal camps, deliberately scattered the seeds of desirable plants in locations where they would thrive and discouraged the growth of competing plants by clearing them away. By 8000 B.C.E. wheat and barley had been domesticated in the Middle East; sorghum in Africa; and rice in China (possibly as early as 10,000 B.C.E.). By about 5000 B.C.E. the inhabitants of the American continents, who first arrived around 18,000 B.C.E. were domesticating maize (mayz) (corn) in Mexico, manioc in Brazil and Panama, and beans and squash in Mesoamerica. Thus a better term is **Agricultural Revolutions**, which emphasizes that the central change was in food production and that agriculture arose independently in many places.

In most cases agriculture included the domestication of animals—dogs at first to help hunters track game, and later sheep, goats, cattle, donkeys, humped-back Zebu (ZEE-boo), and water buffalo from the Middle East and northern Africa to India and China. In the Americas, domesticated llamas provided transportation and wool, while guinea pigs, dogs, and turkeys furnished meat. Varieties of domesticated animals spread from one region to another. Once cattle became tame enough to be yoked to plows, they became essential to grain production.

**Neolithic** The period of the Stone Age associated with the ancient Agricultural Revolution(s).

**Agricultural Revolutions** The change from food gathering to food production that occurred between ca. 8000 and 2000 B.C.E. Also known as the Neolithic Revolution.

In addition, animal droppings provided valuable fertilizer.

In the more arid parts of Africa and western and Central Asia, **pastoralism**, a way of life dependent on large herds of small and large stock, predominated. As the Sahara approached its maximum dryness around 2500 B.C.E., pastoralists replaced farmers, who migrated southward (see Chapter 8). Moving their herds to new pastures and watering places throughout the year made pastoralists almost as mobile as foragers and discouraged accumulation of bulky possessions and construction of substantial dwellings. Early herders probably relied more heavily on milk than on meat, since killing animals reduced their herds. During wet seasons, they may also have done some hasty crop cultivation or bartered meat and skins for plant foods with nearby farming communities.

Why did the Agricultural Revolutions occur? Some theories assume that growing crops had obvious advantages, such as the promise of a secure food supply. However, most experts believe that climate change drove people to abandon hunting and gathering in favor of agriculture or pastoralism. With the end of the Great Ice Age between 6000 and 2000 B.C.E., the temperate lands became exceptionally warm. This is the same time when people in many parts of the world adopted agriculture. The precise nature of the crisis probably varied. In the Middle East, shortages of wild food caused by dryness or overhunting may have stimulated food production. Elsewhere, a warmer, wetter climate could turn grasslands into forests, reducing supplies of game and wild grains.

In many drier parts of the world, where wild food remained abundant, people did not take up agriculture. The inhabitants of Australia relied exclusively on foraging until recent centuries, as did some peoples on other continents. Amerindians in the arid grasslands from Alaska to the Gulf of Mexico hunted bison, and salmon-fishing sustained groups in the Pacific Northwest. Abundant supplies of fish, shellfish, and aquatic animals permitted food gatherers east of the Mississippi River to thrive. In the equatorial rain forest and in the southern part of Africa, conditions favored retention of the older ways.

Whatever the causes, the gradual adoption of food production transformed most parts of the world.

A hundred thousand years ago, world population, mostly living in the temperate and tropical regions of Africa and Eurasia, did not exceed 2 million. The population may have fallen even lower during the last glacial epoch, between 32,000 and 13,000 years ago. Agriculture supported a gradual population increase, perhaps to 10 million by 5000 B.C.E., and then mushroomed to between 50 and 100 million by 1000 B.C.E.[1]

## Life in Neolithic Communities

Evidence that an ecological crisis may have triggered the transition to food production has prompted a reexamination of the assumption that farmers enjoyed better lives than foragers. Early farmers probably had to work much harder and for much longer periods than food gatherers. Long days spent clearing and cultivating land yielded meager harvests. Guarding herds from predators, guiding them to fresh pastures, and tending to their needs imposed similar burdens.

There were other problems as well. Although early farmers were less likely to starve, their diet was less varied and nutritious than that of foragers. Skeletal remains show that Neolithic farmers were shorter on average than earlier foragers. Death from contagious diseases ravaged farming settlements, which were contaminated by human waste, infested by disease-bearing vermin and insects, and inhabited by domestic animals—especially pigs and cattle—whose diseases could infect people.

However, a dependable supply of food that could be stored between harvests to see people through the nonproductive seasons, droughts, and other calamites proved decisive in the long run. Over several millennia, farmers came to outnumber nonfarmers, and in most cases, farmers seem to have displaced foragers by gradual infiltration rather than by conquest. The families who chose farming settled permanently near their fields. As they did in forager bands,

[1] Colin McEvedy and Richard Jones, *Atlas of World Population History* (New York: Penguin Books, 1978), 13–15.

**pastoralism** A way of life dependent on moving large herds of small and large stock to new pastures and watering places throughout the year.

kinship and marriage bound farming communities together.

The religions of foragers tended to center on sacred groves, springs, and wild animals. In contrast, the rituals of farmers often centered on the Earth Mother. Pastoralists tended to worship the all-powerful (and usually male) sky-god. Assemblages of **megaliths** ("big stones") seem to relate to religious beliefs. Stonehenge, a famous megalithic site in England constructed about 2000 B.C.E., marked the position of the sun and other celestial bodies at key points in the year.

Most early farmers lived in small villages, but in some parts of the world a few villages grew into towns, which served as centers of trade and specialized crafts. One early town in the Middle East that has been extensively excavated is Çatal Hüyük (cha-TAHL hoo-YOOK) in central Turkey. The ruins of Çatal Hüyük date to between 7000 and 5000 B.C.E. and cover 32 acres (13 hectares). Its residents lived in mud-brick rooms with elaborate decorations. Çatal Hüyük had no defensive wall. Instead, the outer walls of its houses formed a continuous barrier without doors or large windows. Residents entered their house by means of ladders through holes in the roof.

Long-distance trade at Çatal Hüyük featured obsidian, a hard volcanic rock that craftspeople made into tools, weapons, mirrors, and ornaments. Other residents made fine pottery, wove baskets and woolen cloth, made stone and shell beads, and worked leather and wood. House sizes varied, but there is no evidence of a dominant class or centralized political structure. Wall paintings, remarkably similar to earlier cave paintings, reveal the continuing importance of hunting. Scenes depict men and women adorned with leopard skins. Men were buried with weapons rather than farming tools, and wild foods—acorns, wild grains, and game animals—still featured prominently in the residents' diet. But fields around the town produced crops of barley and wheat and vegetables. Domesticated pigs were kept along with goats and sheep.

Çatal Hüyük had one religious shrine for every two houses. Many rooms contain depictions of horned wild bulls, female breasts, goddesses, leopards, and handprints. Rituals involved burning grains, legumes (LEG-yooms), and meat but not sacrificing live animals. Statues of plump female deities

far outnumber statues of male deities, suggesting that the inhabitants primarily venerated a goddess of fertility. According to the site's principal excavator, "it seems extremely likely that the cult of the goddess was administered mainly by women."[2]

Metalworking became an important specialized occupation in the late Neolithic period. At Çatal Hüyük objects of copper and lead—metals that occur naturally in fairly pure form—date to about 6400 B.C.E. Silver and gold also appear at early dates in various parts of the world. Because of their rarity and softness, those metals did not replace stone tools and weapons. The discovery of decorative and ceremonial objects of metal in graves suggests they were symbols of status and power.

Towns, specialized crafts, and religious shrines forced farmers to produce extra food for nonfarmers like priests and artisans. The building of permanent houses, walls, and towers, not to mention megalithic monuments, also called for added labor. Stonehenge, for example, took 30,000 person-hours to build. Whether these tasks were performed freely or coerced is unknown.

---

[2] James Mellaart, *Çatal Hüyük: A Neolithic Town in Anatolia* (New York: McGraw-Hill, 1967), 202.

**SECTION REVIEW**

- Around 10,000 years ago humans began to cultivate plants, selecting for those with the highest nutritional yield, and to domesticate animals. These Agricultural Revolutions arose in various parts of the world.
- Climate change at the end of the last Ice Age is probably the major reason for the switch from food gathering to food production.
- The lives of farmers are, in many respects, harder and more hazardous than those of hunter-gatherers, but the more secure food supply made possible by agriculture led to a great increase in human population.
- In some places small agricultural villages developed into towns that were centers of trade and home to sophisticated craftspeople and people in other specialized professions. Farmers had to produce surpluses to feed nonfarming specialists.

**megaliths** Structures and complexes of very large stones constructed for ceremonial and religious purposes in Neolithic times.

rivers deposited. The Syrian and Arabian deserts lie to the west and southwest, the Persian Gulf to the southeast.

Floods in this plain, caused by snow melting in the northern mountains, could be sudden and violent. They could ruin crops and change the course of rivers, cutting off fields and towns from water and communication. In this environment, the people of ancient Mesopotamia saw themselves at the mercy of gods who embodied the forces of nature. Because of the unpredictable floods and a hot, dry climate where evaporation of flood drainage leeched toxic salt into the soil, Mesopotamia came late to farming, approximately in 5000 B.C.E. But shortly after 3000 B.C.E. the Mesopotamians had constructed an irrigation system to control the supply of water from the Tigris and Euphrates. This struggle against nature is reflected in the Babylonian myths (**Babylon** was the most important city in southern Mesopotamia). The myths say that human beings were created by Marduk, the chief god of Babylon, from the bloody defeat of Tiamat (TIE-ah-mut), a female figure who personified the salt sea.

**"Civilization"**  The Mesopotamians, like other peoples throughout history, equated civilization with their own way of life, but *civilization* is an ambiguous concept, and the charge that a particular group is "uncivilized" has been used throughout human history to justify many distressing acts. Thus it is important to explain the rise of complex societies in Mesopotamia and Egypt from approximately 3500 to 1500 B.C.E. (see Map 1.1). (China, developing slightly later, is discussed in Chapter 3.)

Our starting point roughly coincides with the origins of writing, allowing us to observe aspects of human experience not revealed by archaeological evidence alone. The people living in Mesopotamia at the start of the "historical period"—the period for which we

**Neolithic Goddess**  Many versions of a well-nourished and pregnant female figure were found at Çatal Hüyük. Here she is supported by twin leopards whose tails curve over her shoulders. To those who inhabited the city some 8,000 years ago, the figure likely represented fertility and power over nature. The Art Archive/Museum of Anatolian Civilisations Ankara/Gianni Dagli Orti

## MESOPOTAMIA

■ *How did Mesopotamian civilization emerge, and what technologies promoted its advancement?*

*Mesopotamia* means "land between the rivers" in Greek. The name reflects the centrality of the Tigris (TIE-gris) and Euphrates (you-FRAY-teez) Rivers to the way of life in this region. Mesopotamia lies mostly within modern Iraq. To the north and east, an arc of mountains extends from northern Syria and southeastern Anatolia to the Zagros (ZAG-rohs) Mountains, which separate the plain from the Iranian Plateau. This is an alluvial plain—a flat, fertile expanse built up over many millennia by silt that the

**Babylon**  The largest and most important city in Mesopotamia. It achieved particular eminence as the capital of the Amorite king Hammurabi in the eighteenth century B.C.E.

**Map 1.1  River-Valley Civilizations, 3500–1500 B.C.E.**  The earliest complex societies arose in the floodplains of large rivers: in the fourth millennium B.C.E. in the valley of the Tigris and Euphrates Rivers in Mesopotamia and the Nile River in Egypt, in the third millennium B.C.E. in the valley of the Indus River in Pakistan, and in the second millennium B.C.E. in the valley of the Yellow River in China. © Cengage Learning

# Chronology

| | Mesopotamia | | Egypt |
|---|---|---|---|
| **3500 B.C.E.** | | | 3100–2575 B.C.E.  Early Dynastic |
| **3000 B.C.E.** | 3000–2350 B.C.E.  Early Dynastic (Sumerian) | | |
| **2500 B.C.E.** | | | 2575–2134 B.C.E.  Old Kingdom |
| | 2350–2230 B.C.E.  Akkadian (Semitic) | | 2134–2040 B.C.E.  First Intermediate Period |
| **2000 B.C.E.** | 2112–2004 B.C.E.  Third Dynasty of Ur (Sumerian) | | 2040–1640 B.C.E.  Middle Kingdom |
| | 1900–1600 B.C.E.  Old Babylonian (Semitic) | | 1640–1532 B.C.E.  Second Intermediate Period |
| **1500 B.C.E.** | | | 1532–1070 B.C.E.  New Kingdom |

have written evidence—were the **Sumerians**. Archaeological evidence places them in southern Mesopotamia by 5000 B.C.E. and perhaps even earlier. Writing first appeared in Mesopotamia before 3300 B.C.E. According to one plausible theory, it may have originated to keep track of property, and it used a system known as **cuneiform**, which is Latin for "wedge-shaped" because of the wedge-shaped impressions created from pressing the point of a reed into a moist clay tablet.

The *Epic of Gilgamesh*, whose roots date to before 2000 B.C.E., defines *civilization* as the people of ancient Mesopotamia understood it. Gilgamesh, an early king (who may be depicted on the sculpture shown here), sends a temple prostitute to tame Enkidu (EN-kee-doo), a wild man who lives like an animal in the grasslands. Using her sexual charms to win Enkidu's trust, the temple prostitute tells him:

> Come with me to the city, to Uruk (OO-rook), to the temple of Anu and the goddess Ishtar . . . to Uruk, where the processions are and music, let us go together through the dancing to the palace hall where Gilgamesh presides.[3]

She clothes Enkidu and teaches him to eat cooked food, drink beer, and bathe and oil his body. Her words and actions signal the principal traits of civilized life in ancient Mesopotamia.

Scholars define **civilization** as having certain political, social, economic, and technological traits: (1) cities as administrative centers, (2) a political system based on control of a defined territory rather than kinship connections, (3) many people engaged in specialized, non-food-producing activities, (4) status distinctions based largely on accumulation of substantial wealth by some groups, (5) monumental building, (6) a system for keeping permanent records, (7) long-distance trade, and (8) major advances in science and the arts.

### Cities, Kings, and Religion

The *Epic of Gilgamesh* shows both the ambition of kings and their value to the community. Gilgamesh, who is probably based on a historical king of Uruk, stirs resentment by demanding sexual favors

The Art Archive/Alamy

**Gilgamesh Strangling a Lion**   This eighth-century B.C.E. sculpture of a king, possibly Gilgamesh, from the palace of the Assyrian king Sargon II, represents the magical power and omnipotence of kingship. The Gilgamesh story was still popular in Mesopotamia twenty centuries after the king of Uruk's lifetime.

from new brides, but the community relies on his immense strength, wisdom, and courage. In his quest of everlasting glory, Gilgamesh walls the city magnificently, stamping his name on every brick. His journey

**Sumerians**   The people who dominated southern Mesopotamia through the end of the third millennium B.C.E.

**cuneiform**   A system of writing in which wedge-shaped symbols represented words or syllables. It originated in Mesopotamia and was used initially for Sumerian and Akkadian but later was adapted to represent other languages of western Asia. Literacy was confined to a relatively small group of administrators and scribes.

**civilization**   An ambiguous term often used to denote more complex societies but sometimes used by anthropologists to describe any group of people sharing a set of cultural traits.

---

[3] David Ferry, *Gilgamesh: A New Rendering in English Verse* (New York: Noonday Press, 1992).

to the faraway Cedar Mountains reflects the king's role in accessing valuable resources.

Mesopotamians opened new land to agriculture by building and maintaining their irrigation networks. Successful construction and maintenance of these irrigation systems required leaders who were able to organize large numbers of people to work together. Other projects called for similar coordination: harvesting, sheep shearing, building fortification walls and large public buildings, and warfare. Scholars have long believed that the earliest cities and complex societies arose in southern Mesopotamia as a result of the need to organize labor, especially for the creation and maintenance of irrigation channels. However, recent archaeological discoveries in northern Mesopotamia, where agriculture first developed in this part of the world and was sustained by rainfall, are suggesting a more complicated picture, as a number of sites in northeast Syria appear to have developed urban centers, bureaucracy, and other elements of social complexity at roughly the same time.

Most cities evolved from villages. When a successful village grew, small satellite villages developed nearby and eventually merged with the main village to form an urban center. Mesopotamian cities controlled the agricultural land and collected crop surpluses from villages in their vicinity. In return, the city provided rural districts with military protection against raiders and a market where villagers could acquire manufactured goods. Many early Mesopotamian city dwellers went out each day to labor in nearby fields. Others specialized in pottery, artwork, weapons, tools, and other crafts forged out of metal. The term **city-state** refers to a self-governing urban center and the agricultural territories it controls.

Little is known about the political systems of early Mesopotamian city-states. The two centers of power seen in written records are the temple and the palace of the king. The temples owned extensive agricultural lands, and head priests managed their wealth and played prominent political and economic roles in early communities. Temples contained the shrine of the chief deity, chapels for lesser deities, and offices and housing for priests and temple staff. The compound focused on the **ziggurat** (ZIG-uh-rat), a multistory, mud-brick, pyramid-shaped tower. Scholars are still debating the ziggurat's function and

meaning. Gods were anthropomorphic (an-thru-po-MORE-fik)—like humans in forms and conduct—and the temple would have been considered the god's residence. Priests tried to anticipate the gods' needs and appease them, with the high priest performing the central acts in the rituals. Certain priests entertained the gods with music, others exorcised evil spirits, and still others interpreted dreams and divined the future by examining the organs of sacrificed animals, reading patterns in rising incense smoke, or casting dice. Priests passed their office to their sons.

It is unknown whether common people had much access to temple buildings and how religious practices and belief affected their everyday lives, but the survival of many **amulets** (small charms meant to protect the bearer from evil) suggests a widespread belief in magic. Elite and common folk would have come together for the great festivals, such as the twelve-day New Year's festival held at harvest each spring where the Babylonian Creation Epic would have been read.

In the third millennium B.C.E., Sumerian documents show the emergence of the *lugal* (LOO-gahl), or "big man"—we would call him a king. The location of the temple in the heart of the city and the less prominent siting of the king's palace symbolize the later emergence of royalty. A plausible theory maintains that certain men chosen by the community to lead the armies in time of war extended their authority in peacetime. Some Mesopotamian kings claimed divinity, but this concept did not take root. Normally, the king portrayed himself as the deity's earthly representative and saw to the upkeep and building of temples and the proper performance of ritual. The king's power grew at the expense of the priests, and priests and temples gradually became dependent on the pal-

**city-state**  A small independent state consisting of an urban center and the surrounding agricultural territory. A characteristic political form in early Mesopotamia, Archaic and Classical Greece, Phoenicia, and early Italy.

**ziggurat**  A massive pyramidal stepped tower made of mud bricks. It is associated with religious complexes in ancient Mesopotamian cities, but its function is unknown.

**amulet**  Small charm meant to protect the bearer from evil. Found frequently in archaeological excavations in Mesopotamia and Egypt, amulets reflect the religious practices of the common people.

ace. Other royal responsibilities included maintaining city walls and defenses, extending and repairing irrigation channels, guarding property rights, warding off outside attackers, and establishing justice. Although the lugal's position was not hereditary, it often passed from a father to a capable son.

Sargon (SAHR-gone), ruler of the city of Akkad (AH-kahd) around 2350 B.C.E., was the first to unite many cities under one king and capital. By razing the walls of conquered cities and installing governors backed by garrisons of Akkadian troops, Sargon, and the four family members who succeeded him, established a reign that lasted over 120 years. They gave land to soldiers to ensure their loyalty. For reasons that remain obscure, the Akkadian state fell around 2230 B.C.E.

The Sumerian language and culture became dominant again in the cities of the southern plain under the Third Dynasty of Ur (2112–2004 B.C.E.). Through campaigns of conquest and marriage alliances, this dynasty of five kings flourished for a century, maintaining tight control through a rapidly expanding bureaucracy of administrators and obsessive record keeping. Messengers and well-maintained road stations enabled rapid communication, and an official calendar, standardized weights and measures, and uniform writing practices increased the efficiency of the central administration.

The Third Dynasty of Ur built a great wall 125 miles (201 kilometers) long to protect against nomadic Amorites (AM-uh-rite), but the Amorites toppled the dynasty and founded a new city at Babylon, not far from Akkad. Toward the end of a long reign, **Hammurabi** (HAM-uh-rah-bee) (r. 1792–1750 B.C.E.) launched a series of aggressive military campaigns, and Babylon became the capital of what historians call the "Old Babylonian" state, which stretched beyond Sumer and Akkad into the north and northwest from 1900 to 1600 B.C.E. Hammurabi's Law Code, inscribed on a polished black stone pillar, reflects social divisions that may also have been valid at other times. Society was divided into three classes: (1) the free, landowning class, largely living in the cities, which included royalty, high-ranking officials, warriors, priests, merchants, and some artisans and shopkeepers; (2) the class of dependent farmers and artisans, whose legal attachment to royal, temple, or private estates made them the primary rural workforce; and (3) the class of slaves, primarily employed in domestic service. Penalties for crimes prescribed in the Law Code depended on the class of the offender, with the most severe punishments reserved for the lower orders.

## Trade and Mesopotamian Society

Conquest gave some Mesopotamian city-states access to vital resources. Trade offered an alternative, and long-distance commerce flourished in most periods. Evidence of seagoing vessels appears as early as the fifth millennium B.C.E. Wood, metals, and stone came from foreign lands in exchange for wool, cloth, barley, and vegetable oil. Cedar forests in Lebanon and Syria yielded wood, Anatolia yielded silver, Egypt gold, and the eastern Mediterranean and Oman (on the Arabian peninsula) copper. Tin, which in alloy with copper made bronze, came from Afghanistan (in southern Central Asia), and chlorite, a greenish, easily carved stone, from the Iranian plateau. Jewelers and stonecarvers used black diorite from the Persian Gulf, blue lapis lazuli (LAP-is LAZ-uh-lee) from Afghanistan, and reddish carnelian (kahr-NEEL-yuhn) from Pakistan. In the third millennium B.C.E., merchants worked for the palace or temple and exchanged surpluses from the royal or temple farmlands for raw materials and luxury goods. Coined money played no role, but fixed weights of precious metal, primarily silver, or measures of grain could be exchanged for the calculated value. In the second millennium B.C.E., merchants became more independent and merchant guilds gained influence.

In the Old Babylonian period, as the class of people who were not dependent on the temple or palace grew in numbers and importance, the amount of land and other property in private hands increased, and the hiring of free laborers became more common. But we know little about the daily lives of ordinary Mesopotamians, especially those in villages or on

**Hammurabi** Amorite ruler of Babylon (r. 1792–1750 B.C.E.). He conquered many city-states in southern and northern Mesopotamia and is best known for a code of laws, inscribed on a black stone pillar, illustrating the principles to be used in legal cases.

large estates in the countryside, because they left few archaeological or written remains. Slaves, dependent workers, and hired laborers were all compensated with commodities such as food and oil in quantities proportional to their age, gender, and tasks. Slavery was not as fundamental to the economy as it would be in the later societies of Greece and Rome (see Chapters 4 and 5). Many slaves came from mountain tribes, either captured in war or sold by slave traders. Others were people unable to pay their debts. Normally slaves were not chained, but they were identified by a distinctive hairstyle; if given their freedom, a barber shaved off the telltale mark.

It is likewise difficult to discover much about the experiences of women. The written sources were produced by male **scribes**—trained professionals who applied their reading and writing skills to tasks of administration—and for the most part reflect elite male activities. Anthropologists theorize that women lost social standing and freedoms in societies where agriculture superseded hunting and gathering because women no longer provided most of the community's food. Food production in Mesopotamia depended on the heavy physical labor that fell to men of plowing, harvesting, and digging irrigation channels. Since food surpluses permitted families to have more children, bearing and rearing children became the primary occupation of many women, preventing them from acquiring the specialized skills of the scribe or artisan. Women could own property, maintain control of their dowry (a sum of money given by the woman's father to support her in her husband's household), and even engage in trade. Some worked outside the household in textile factories and breweries or as prostitutes, tavern keepers, bakers, or fortunetellers. Non-elite women who stayed at home helped with farming, planted vegetable gardens, cooked, cleaned, fetched water, tended the household fire, and wove baskets and textiles.

The standing of women seems to have declined further in the second millennium B.C.E., perhaps because of the rise of an urbanized middle class and an increase in private wealth. The laws favored the rights of husbands. Although Mesopotamian society was generally monogamous, a man could take a second wife if the first gave him no children, and in later Mesopotamian history kings and wealthy men had

several wives. Marriage alliances arranged between families made women into instruments for preserving and increasing family wealth. Alternatively, a family might decide to avoid a daughter's marriage—and the resulting loss of a dowry—by dedicating her to the temple service of a deity as a "god's bride." Later constraints on women's lives in the region, such as largely confining themselves to the home and wearing veils in public (see Chapter 9), may have originated in the second millennium B.C.E.

## Technology and Science

The term *technology*, from the Greek word *techne*, meaning "skill" or "specialized knowledge," normally refers to the tools and machines that humans use to manipulate the physical world. Many scholars now use the term more broadly for any specialized knowledge used to transform the natural environment and human society. Writing was one such form of early technology.

Careful observation of the skies and advances in mathematics that used a number-system expressed as fractions or multiples of 60 (in contrast to our base-10 system; this is the origin of the seconds and minutes we use in calculating time today) made the Mesopotamians sophisticated practitioners of astronomy. Priests compiled lists of omens or unusual sightings on earth and in the heavens, together with a record of the events that coincided with them. They consulted these texts at critical times, for they believed that the recurrence of such phenomena could provide clues to future developments. The underlying premise was that the elements of the material universe, from the microscopic to the macrocosmic, were interconnected in mysterious but undeniable ways.

Clay, Mesopotamia's most abundant resource, went into the making of mud bricks. Whether dried in the sun or baked in an oven for greater durability, these constituted the main building material. Reed mats, laid between the mud-brick layers of ziggurats, served the same engineering purpose as girders in

**scribe** In the governments of many ancient societies, a professional position reserved for men who had undergone the lengthy training required to be able to read and write using cuneiform, hieroglyphics, or other early, cumbersome writing systems.

modern high-rise construction. The abundance of good clay also made pottery the most common material for dishes, storage vessels, and oil lamps (see Material Culture: Lamps and Candles). By 4000 B.C.E. the potter's wheel, spun by hands and feet, made possible rapid manufacture in precise and complex shapes.

Other technologies that enabled the Mesopotamians to meet the challenges of their physical environment included wheeled carts and sled-like platforms dragged by cattle to transport goods. In northern Mesopotamia, donkeys were the chief pack animals for overland caravans before the advent of the camel around 1200 B.C.E. (see Chapter 8). Evidence of boats used in river and sea trade appears as early as the fifth millennium B.C.E.

The Mesopotamians had to import metals, but they also became skilled in metallurgy, refining ores containing copper and alloying them with arsenic or tin to make **bronze**. Craftsmen poured molten bronze into molds to produce tools and weapons. The cooled and hardened bronze took a sharper edge than stone, was less likely to break, and was more easily repaired. Stone implements remained in use among poor people, who could not afford bronze.

Early military forces were nonprofessional militias of able-bodied men called up for short periods when needed. The powerful states of the later third and second millennia B.C.E. built up armies of well-trained and well-paid full-time soldiers. In the early

second millennium B.C.E. horses appeared in western Asia, and the horse-drawn chariot came into vogue. Infantry found themselves at the mercy of swift chariots carrying a driver and an archer who could easily run them down. Using increasingly effective siege machinery, Mesopotamian soldiers could climb over, undermine, or knock down the walls protecting the cities of their enemies.

# EGYPT

■ *What role did the environment and religion play in the evolution of Egyptian civilization?*

No place exhibits the impact of the natural environment on the history and culture of a society better than ancient Egypt. Though located at the intersection of Asia and Africa, Egypt was less a crossroads than an isolated land protected by surrounding barriers of desert and a harborless, marshy seacoast. Whereas Mesopotamia was open to migration or invasion and was dependent on imported resources, Egypt's natural isolation and material self-sufficiency fostered a unique culture that for long periods had relatively little to do with other civilizations.

## The Land of Egypt: "Gift of the Nile"

The world's longest river, the Nile flows northward from Lake Victoria and several large tributaries in the highlands of tropical Africa, carving a narrow valley between a chain of hills on either side until it reaches the Mediterranean Sea (see Map 1.2). Though bordered mostly by desert, the banks of the river support lush vegetation. About 100 miles (160 kilometers) from the Mediterranean, the river divides into channels to form a triangular delta. Most of Egypt's population lives on the twisting, green ribbon of land along the river or in the Nile Delta. Bleak deserts of mountains, rocks, and dunes occupy the rest of the country. The ancient Egyptians distinguished between the low-lying, life-sustaining "Black

## SECTION REVIEW

- Mesopotamia developed in the plain of the unpredictable Tigris and Euphrates Rivers, and Mesopotamian gods embodied the often-violent forces of nature.

- The first people to develop a complex society that produced written records were the Sumerians.

- Mesopotamia was home to a coalition of city-states that grew out of villages and controlled rural territory.

- At the expense of the priesthood, kings assumed responsibility for administrative, legal, and military activities.

- The urban civilization of Mesopotamia developed a high degree of social division, a hierarchy in which women steadily lost standing.

- The Mesopotamians developed a wide range of technologies, the most important of which was writing.

**bronze**  An alloy of copper with a small amount of tin (or sometimes arsenic), which is harder and more durable than copper alone. The term *Bronze Age* is applied to the era—the dates of which vary in different parts of the world—when bronze was the primary metal for tools and weapons.

# Material Culture

## Lamps and Candles

It is hard to imagine today how dark the world was after the sun went down throughout most of human history. The glow of a fire did not extend far. Nor were torches easy to make or long-lasting. A stick wrapped with oil-soaked cloth at one end does make an effective torch, but humans were in need of light long before they figured out how to make cloth. As for flammable oil, vegetable oils extracted from the seeds of olive or palm trees, or from plants like flax, lettuce, and corn, became abundant only with the spread of plant domestication in the Neolithic period. Prior to that, animal fat or tallow could be used, though it had the disadvantage of smelling like meat.

The Agricultural Revolutions made available not only vegetable oils but also pottery, and later metal, vessels that could be used as lamps. A fireproof vessel would be filled with oil, and a wick would be placed so that one end was immersed in the oil and the other open to the air. The oil would saturate the wick, and a flame touched to the wick would vaporize a small amount of oil and ignite the resultant gas. A poor wick might sputter, smoke, or go out. The pith, or inner porous core of plants of the rush family, could be used as wicks in rush lamps, or the oil-soaked pith stiffened by part of the outer skin of the rush could be stood upright and lit like slender candles in rush lights.

Aside from the pith of rushes, wicks were usually made of string or a sliver of wood. Since a wick of greater diameter produces a larger flame, braiding was used to make a thicker string. Of all natural fibers, cotton makes the best wicks because of its absorbency. Different varieties of cotton were native to India and pre-Columbian America, but cotton became a major crop in the Middle East only in the early Islamic period of the eighth century C.E. Christian Europe knew cotton only as an expensive import until the twelfth century, when a cotton industry was founded in northern Italy. Access to superior wicks contributed to an increase in European candle use.

Waxes differ from oils in being solid at room temperature. Molding wax around a wick produces a candle. Beeswax provided an ideal material for odorless candles and was in use for lighting as early as ancient Egyptian times. However, beeswax was scarce and expensive. Some premodern trade routes, such as those going south to the

**Ancient Lamp Vessel** *This 2,500-year-old oil lamp from Megiddo in Israel has grooves for two wicks. It is made of bronze, a valuable metal. Pottery lamps were much cheaper and show up abundantly in ancient archaeological sites.*

Erich Lessing/Art Resource, NY

Middle East along the rivers of Russia, featured beeswax as a major product. Beeswax candles came to play a prominent and often symbolic role in Christian, Jewish, and Buddhist religious rituals. Mosques, on the other hand, were traditionally lit by oil lamps.

Though whaling was practiced in certain coastal regions in prehistoric times, the extraction of whale oil on an industrial scale began in the sixteenth century and grew rapidly over the next three hundred years. Oil extracted from the whale's fat, or blubber, was widely used for lamps. Of even greater value was a wax called spermaceti that was made from an oily substance in the heads of sperm whales. A large whale might yield three tons of spermaceti. It burned without odor in candles and became the standard for candle making until the discovery of paraffin, a wax made from petroleum, in 1830. Paraffin generally replaced spermaceti as the preferred wax for candles.

The small flames of oil lamps and candles did not produce much illumination. *Candela* is the name of the unit of light intensity that became increasingly precise over the course of the nineteenth and twentieth centuries. It is intended to represent the light produced by a single candle, though many technical specifications, such as the color of the light, make it only an approximation. An even rougher approximation equates 120 candelas with the illumination provided by a 100-watt light bulb. This last approximation suggests how little light a single lamp or candle could provide in premodern times for reading, sewing, or doing any kind of fine work after sundown.

### QUESTIONS FOR ANALYSIS

1. How would the provision of artificial light affect patterns of life with the change of seasons?
2. What human activities, such as storytelling, might have been enhanced by a lack of light?
3. How did gradual adoption of gaslights (1792) and the electric light bulb (1879) change people's lives?

Land" of dark soil and the elevated, deadly "Red Land" of the desert. The fifth-century B.C.E. Greek traveler Herodotus (he-RAH-duh-tuhs) called Egypt the "gift of the Nile."

The river was the main means of travel and communication, with the most important cities located upstream away from the Mediterranean. Because the river flows from south to north, the Egyptians called the southern part of the country "Upper Egypt" and the northern delta "Lower Egypt." The First Cataract of the Nile, the northernmost of a series of impassable rocks and rapids below Aswan (AS-wahn) (about 500 miles [800 kilometers] south of the Mediterranean), formed Egypt's southern boundary in most periods, but Egyptian control sometimes extended farther south into what was called "Kush" (later Nubia, today part of southern Egypt and northern Sudan). The Egyptians also settled a chain of large oases west of the river, green and habitable "islands" in the midst of the desert.

While the hot, sunny climate favored agriculture, rain rarely fell south of the delta, and irrigation channels carried water into the valley to increase the area suitable for planting. Unlike the Tigris and Euphrates, the Nile flooded at exactly the right time for grain agriculture. When the waters receded, they left behind a moist, fertile layer of mineral-rich silt in which farmers could easily plant their crops. An Egyptian creation myth featured the emergence of a life-supporting mound of earth from a primeval swamp.

The level of the flood's crest determined the abundance of the next harvest. Too little water left fertile land unirrigated and hence uncultivable, plunging the country into famine. The ebb and flow of successful and failed regimes seems to have been linked to the cycle of floods. Nevertheless, remarkable stability characterized most eras, and Egyptians viewed the universe as an orderly and beneficent place.

Egypt had other resources besides the Nile. Papyrus reeds growing in marshes yielded fibers that made good sails, ropes, and a kind of paper. The wild animals and birds and the abundant river fish attracted hunters and fishermen. Building stone was quarried and floated downstream from southern Egypt. And the state organized armed expeditions and forced labor to exploit copper and turquoise

**Map 1.2 Ancient Egypt** The Nile River, flowing south to north, carved out of the surrounding desert a narrow green valley that became heavily settled in antiquity.

© Cengage Learning

deposits in the Sinai Desert to the east and gold from Nubia to the south.

The farming villages that appeared in Egypt as early as 5500 B.C.E. relied on domesticated plant and animal species that had originated several millennia earlier in western Asia. Egypt's emergence as a focal point of civilization, however, stemmed at least partially from a gradual change in climate from the fifth to the third millennium B.C.E. Before that time, the Sahara, today the world's largest desert, had a relatively mild and wet climate. Its lakes and grasslands supported a variety of plant and animal species as well as populations of hunter-gatherers (see Chapter 8). As the Sahara became a desert, displaced groups migrated into the Nile Valley, where they developed a sedentary way of life.

## Divine Kingship

The increasing population called for greater complexity in political organization, including a form of local kingship. Later generations of Egyptians saw the unification of smaller units into a single state by Menes (MEH-neez), a ruler from the south, as a pivotal event. Kings of Egypt bore the title "Ruler of the Two Lands"—Upper and Lower Egypt—and wore two crowns symbolizing the unification of the country. Unlike Mesopotamia, therefore, Egypt was unified early in its history.

Following the practice of Manetho, an Egyptian priest from the third century B.C.E., historians divide Egyptian history into thirty dynasties (sequences of kings from the same family). The rise and fall of dynasties often reflect the dominance of different parts of the country. More generally, scholars refer to the "Old," "Middle," and "New Kingdoms," each a period of centralized political power and brilliant cultural achievement, punctuated by "Intermediate Periods" of political fragmentation and cultural decline. Although experts debate the specific dates for these periods, the chronology reflects current opinion.

The Egyptian state centered on the king, often known by the New Kingdom term **pharaoh**, from an Egyptian phrase meaning "palace." From the Old Kingdom on, if not earlier, Egyptians considered the king to be a god sent to earth to maintain **ma'at** (muh-AHT), the divinely authorized order of the uni-

verse. He was the indispensable link between his people and the gods, and his benevolent rule ensured the welfare and prosperity of the country.

So much depended on the kings that their deaths evoked elaborate efforts to ensure the well-being of their spirits on their journey to rejoin the gods. Carrying out funerary rites, constructing royal tombs, and sustaining the kings' spirits in the afterlife by perpetual offerings in adjoining funerary chapels demanded massive resources. Flat-topped, rectangular tombs made of mud brick sufficed for the earlier rulers, but around 2630 B.C.E. Djoser (JO-sur), a Third Dynasty king, constructed a stepped **pyramid**—a series of stone platforms laid one on top of the other—at Saqqara (suh-KAHR-uh), near Memphis. Rulers of the Fourth Dynasty filled in the steps to create the smooth-sided, limestone pyramids that most often symbolize ancient Egypt. Between 2550 and 2490 B.C.E. the pharaohs Khufu (KOO-foo) and Khafre (KAF-ray) erected huge pyramids at Giza, several miles north of Saqqara.

Egyptians accomplished this construction with stone tools (bronze was still expensive and rare) and no machinery other than simple levers, pulleys, and rollers. Calculations of the human muscle power needed to build a pyramid within a ruler's lifetime suggest that large numbers of people must have been pressed into service for part of each year, probably during the flood season, when no agricultural work could be done. The Egyptian masses probably considered this demand for labor a kind of religious service that would help ensure prosperity. The age of the great pyramids lasted only about a century, although construction of pyramids on a smaller scale continued.

**pharaoh**  The central figure in the ancient Egyptian state. Believed to be an earthly manifestation of the gods, he used his absolute power to maintain the safety and prosperity of Egypt.

**ma'at**  Egyptian term for the concept of divinely created and maintained order in the universe. The divine ruler was the earthly guarantor of this order.

**pyramid**  A large, triangular stone monument, used in Egypt and Nubia as a burial place for the king. The largest pyramids, erected during the Old Kingdom near Memphis, reflect the Egyptian belief that the proper and spectacular burial of the divine ruler would guarantee the continued prosperity of the land.

**Pyramids of Menkaure, Khafre, and Khufu at Giza, ca. 2500 B.C.E.** With a width of 755 feet (230 meters) and a height of 480 feet (146 meters), the Great Pyramid of Khufu is the largest stone structure ever built. The construction of these massive edifices depended on relatively simple techniques of stonecutting, transport (the stones were floated downriver on boats and rolled to the site on sledges), and lifting (the stones were dragged up the face of the pyramid on mud-brick ramps). However, the surveying and engineering skills required to level the platform, lay out the measurements, and securely position the blocks were very sophisticated and have withstood the test of time.

## Administration and Communication

Ruling dynasties usually placed their capitals in the area of their original power base. **Memphis**, near today's Cairo at the apex of the Nile Delta, held this central position during the Old Kingdom. **Thebes**, far to the south, supplanted it during the Middle and New Kingdom periods (see Map 1.2). A complex bureaucracy kept detailed records of the country's resources. At the village, district, and central government levels, bureaucrats kept track of land, products, and people, extracting as taxes as much as 50 percent of the annual revenues of the country. This income supported the palace, bureaucracy, and army, paid for building and maintaining temples, and made possible great monuments celebrating the king's grandeur. The government maintained a monopoly over key sectors of the economy and controlled long-distance trade. The urban middle-class traders who increasingly managed the commerce of Mesopotamia had no parallel in Egypt.

A writing system had been developed before the beginning of the Early Dynastic period. **Hieroglyphics** (high-ruh-GLIF-iks), the earliest form of this system, featured picture symbols standing for words, syllables, or individual sounds. Hieroglyphic writing long continued to be used on monuments and ornamental inscriptions, but by 2500 B.C.E., administrators and copyists had developed a cursive script, in which the original pictorial nature of the symbol was less apparent, for their everyday needs. The Egyptians used writing for many purposes other than administrative record keeping. Their written literature included tales of adventure and magic, love poetry, religious hymns, and instruction manuals on technical subjects. Scribes in workshops attached to the temples made copies of traditional texts.

Egyptians wrote with ink on a writing material called **papyrus** (puh-PIE-ruhs), made from the stems of the papyrus reed that grew in the Nile marshes. Papyrus makers laid out the stems in a vertical and horizontal grid pattern, moistened them, and then

**Memphis** The capital of Old Kingdom Egypt, near the head of the Nile Delta. Early rulers were interred in the nearby pyramids.

**Thebes** Capital city of Egypt and home of the ruling dynasties during the Middle and New Kingdoms. Monarchs were buried across the river in the Valley of the Kings.

**hieroglyphics** A system of writing in which pictorial symbols represented sounds, syllables, or concepts. It was used for official and monumental inscriptions in ancient Egypt. Because of the long period of study required to master this system, literacy in hieroglyphics was confined to a relatively small group of scribes and administrators.

**papyrus** A reed that grows along the banks of the Nile River in Egypt. From it was produced a coarse, paperlike writing medium used by the Egyptians and many other peoples in the ancient Mediterranean and Middle East.

pounded them with a soft mallet until they adhered into a sheet of writing material. The plant grew only in Egypt, and papyrus was exported in large quantities throughout the ancient world. The word *paper* comes from Greek and Roman words for papyrus.

Strong monarchs appointed and promoted officials on the basis of ability and accomplishment, giving them grants of land cultivated by dependent peasants. Low-level officials worked in villages and district capitals; high-ranking officials served in the royal capital. During the Old Kingdom, the tombs of officials lay near the monumental tomb of the king so that they could serve him in death as they had in life.

Egyptian history exhibits a recurring tension between the centralizing power of the monarchy and the decentralizing tendencies of the bureaucracy. The shift of officials' tombs from the vicinity of the royal tomb to the home districts where they spent much of their time and exercised power more or less independently signaled the breakdown of centralized power in the late Old Kingdom and First Intermediate Period. Another sign was the tendency of administrative posts to become hereditary. The early monarchs of the Middle Kingdom restored centralized control by reducing the power and prerogatives of the old elite and creating a new class of administrators.

The common observation that Egypt was a land of villages without real cities stems from its capitals being primarily extensions of the palace and central administration. Compared to Mesopotamia, a far larger percentage of Egyptians lived in farming villages, and Egypt's wealth derived to a higher degree from cultivating the land. The towns and cities that did exist unfortunately lie buried beneath modern urban sites, since Egypt has too little land in its cultivable regions to afford abandonment of a large area.

Egypt largely stuck to itself during the Old and Middle Kingdoms, all foreigners being technically regarded as enemies. When necessary, local militia units backed up a small standing army of professional soldiers. Nomadic groups in the eastern and western deserts and Libyans to the northwest posed a nuisance more than a real danger. The king maintained limited contact with other advanced civilizations in the region, and Egypt's interests abroad focused on maintaining access to valuable resources rather than on acquiring territory. Trade with the coastal towns of the Levant (luh-VANT) (modern Israel, the Palestinian territories, Lebanon, and Syria) brought in cedar wood in return for grain, papyrus, and gold.

Egypt's strongest interest involved goods from the south. Nubia had rich sources of gold (Chapter 3 examines the rise in Nubia of a civilization influenced by Egypt but also vital, original, and long-lasting), and the southern course of the Nile offered the easiest passage to sub-Saharan Africa. In the Old Kingdom, Egyptian noblemen led donkey caravans south to trade for gold, incense, and products of tropical Africa such as ivory, ebony, and exotic animals. Forts along the border protected Egypt from attack. In the early second millennium B.C.E. Egyptian forces invaded Nubia, extending the border to the Third Cataract of the Nile and taking possession of the gold fields.

## The People of Egypt

The estimated million to a million and a half inhabitants of Egypt included various physical types, ranging from dark-skinned people related to the populations of sub-Saharan Africa to lighter-skinned people akin to the populations of North Africa and western Asia. Though Egypt experienced no migrations or invasions on a scale common in Mesopotamian history, settlers periodically trickled into the Nile Valley and mixed with the local people.

Egypt had less pronounced social divisions than Mesopotamia, where a formal class structure emerged. The king and high-ranking officials enjoyed status, wealth, and power. Below them came lower-level officials, local leaders, priests and other professionals, artisans, and well-to-do farmers. Peasants, at the bottom, constituted the vast majority of the population.

Peasants lived in rural villages and devoted themselves to the seasonally changing tasks of agriculture: plowing, sowing, tending emerging shoots, reaping, threshing, and storing. They maintained irrigation channels, basins, and dikes. Fish and meat from domesticated animals—cattle, sheep, goats, and poultry—supplemented a diet based on wheat or barley, beer, and vegetables. Villagers shared implements, work animals, and storage facilities and helped one another at peak times in the agricultural cycle and in building projects. They prayed and feasted together at festivals to the local gods. Periodically they had to contribute labor to state projects. If taxation or compulsory service was too great a burden, flight into the desert was the only escape.

This account of village life depends on bits and pieces of archaeological and literary evidence. Tomb paintings of the elite sometimes depict the lives of common folk. The artists employed conventions to indicate status: obesity for the wealthy and comfortable, baldness and deformity for the working classes. Egyptian poets frequently employed metaphors of farming and hunting, and papyrus documents preserved in the hot, dry sands tell of property transactions and legal disputes among ordinary people. Slavery existed on a limited scale but was of limited economic significance and was softened by humane treatment and the possibility of being freed.

Some information is available about the lives of women of the upper classes, but it is filtered through the brushes and pens of male artists and scribes. Tomb paintings show women of the royal family and elite classes accompanying their husbands and engaging in typical domestic activities. They are depicted with dignity and affection, though they are clearly subordinate to the men. The artistic convention of depicting men with a dark red and women with a yellow flesh tone implies that the elite woman's proper sphere was indoors, away from the searing sun. In the beautiful love poetry of the New Kingdom, lovers address each other in terms of apparent equality and express emotions of romantic love.

Legal documents show that Egyptian women could own property, inherit property from their parents, and will their property to whomever they wished. Marriage, usually monogamous, was not confirmed by any legal or religious ceremony and essentially constituted a decision by a man and woman to establish a household together. Either party could dissolve the relationship, and the divorced woman retained rights over her dowry. At certain times queens and queen-mothers played significant behind-the-scenes roles in the politics of the court, and priestesses sometimes supervised the cults of female deities. In general, the limited evidence suggests that women in ancient Egypt enjoyed greater respect and more legal rights and social freedom than women in Mesopotamia and other ancient societies.

## Belief and Knowledge

Egyptian religion was rooted in the landscape of the Nile Valley and the vision of cosmic order that it evoked. The sun rose every day in a clear and cloudless sky, and the river flooded on schedule every year, ensuring a bounteous harvest. Recurrent cycles and periodic renewal seemed a part of the natural world. Egyptians imagined the sky to be a great ocean surrounding the inhabited world. The sun-god Re (ray) traversed its waterway in a boat by day, then returned through the Underworld at night, fighting off the attacks of demonic serpents so that he could be born anew in the morning. In one especially popular story Osiris (oh-SIGH-ris), a god who once ruled Egypt, is slain by his jealous brother Set, who scatters his dismembered remains. Isis, Osiris's sister and wife, finds and reassembles the pieces, while Horus, his son, takes revenge on Set. Restored to life and installed as king of the Underworld, Osiris represents hope for a new life in a world beyond this one.

The king, represented as Horus and as the son of Re, fit into the pattern of the dead returning to life and the sun-god renewing life. As Egypt's chief priest, he intervened with the gods on behalf of his land and people. Egyptian rulers zealously built new temples, refurbished old ones, and made lavish gifts to the gods, at the same time overseeing construction of their own tombs. Thus much of the country's wealth went for religious purposes in a ceaseless effort to win the gods' favor, maintain the continuity of divine kingship, and ensure the renewal of the life-giving forces.

Some deities normally appeared with animal heads; others always took human form. Few myths about the origins and adventures of the gods have survived, but there must have been a rich oral tradition. Many towns had temples for locally prominent deities. When a town became the capital of a ruling dynasty, the chief god of that town became prominent across the land. Thus did Ptah (puh-TAH) of Memphis, Re of Heliopolis (he-lee-OP-uh-lis), and Amon (AH-muhn) of Thebes become gods of all Egypt, serving to unify the country and strengthen the monarchy.

During great festivals, the priests paraded a boat-shaped litter carrying the shrouded statue and cult items of the deity around the town. This brought large numbers of people into contact with the deity in an outpouring of devotion and celebration. Little is known about the day-to-day beliefs and practices of the common people, however. At home, family members made small offerings to Bes, the god of marriage and domestic happiness, to local deities, and to the family's ancestors. They relied on amulets and depictions of demonic figures to protect the bearer and ward off evil forces. In later times Greeks and Romans commented on the Egyptian devotion to magic.

Egyptians believed in the afterlife and prepared extensively for a safe passage and a comfortable existence once they arrived. A common belief was that death was a journey beset with hazards. The Egyptian Book of the Dead, present in many excavated tombs, contained rituals and spells to protect the journeying spirit. The weighing of the deceased's heart in the presence of the judges of the Underworld presented the ultimate challenge—the one that determined whether the person had led a good life and deserved to reach the blessed destination.

Obsession with the afterlife led to great concern about the physical condition of the dead body and led Egyptians to perfect techniques of mummification for preserving it. The idea probably derived from the slow decomposition of bodies buried in hot, dry sand on the edge of the desert, an early practice. The elite classes spent the most on mummification. Vital organs were removed, preserved, and stored in stone jars laid out around the corpse. Body cavities were filled with various packing materials. After immersing the cadaver for long periods in dehydrating and preserving chemicals, Egyptians wrapped it in linen. The **mummy** was then placed in one or more decorated wooden caskets within a tomb.

Building tombs at the edge of the desert left the lowlands free for farming. Pictures and samples of food and objects from everyday life accompanied the mummy to provide whatever he or she might need in the next life. Much of what is now known about ancient Egyptian life comes from examining utilitarian and luxury household objects found in tombs. Small figurines called shawabtis (shuh-WAB-tees) represented the servants whom the deceased might need

## SECTION REVIEW

- In the benign environment of the Nile Valley, a unified Egypt emerged from a collection of small kingdoms.
- The ruler was the divine pharaoh responsible for maintaining the cosmic order.
- The state was administered from royal capitals and through a bureaucracy in which scribes kept detailed records in hieroglyphic script.
- Less urban than Mesopotamia, Egypt primarily concerned itself with maintaining the flow of important resources.
- Social divisions in Egypt were less pronounced than in Mesopotamia, slavery was limited, and women enjoyed greater freedom than elsewhere in the ancient world.
- Egyptian religion reflected the predictability of the environment and centered on the afterlife, the inspiration for many of Egypt's important technologies.

or the laborers he might send as substitutes if asked to provide compulsory labor. The elite classes attached chapels to their tombs and left endowments to subsidize the daily attendance of a priest and offerings of foodstuffs to sustain their spirits for all eternity.

The forms of the tomb also reflected wealth and status. Simple pit graves or small mud-brick chambers sufficed for the common people. The privileged classes built larger tombs. Kings erected pyramids and other grand edifices, employing subterfuge to hide the sealed chamber containing the body and treasures, as well as curses and other magical precautions to foil tomb robbers. Rarely did they succeed, however. Archaeologists have seldom discovered an undisturbed royal tomb.

The ancient Egyptians explored many areas of knowledge and developed advantageous technologies. They learned about chemistry through the mummification process, which also provided opportunities to learn about human anatomy, and Egyptian doctors were in demand in courts throughout western Asia. They developed mathematics to measure the dimensions of fields and to calculate the quantity of agricultural produce owed to the state. Through careful observation of the stars they constructed the most

**mummy**  A body preserved by chemical processes or special natural circumstances, often in the belief that the deceased will need it again in the afterlife.

accurate calendar in the world, and they knew that when the star Sirius appeared on the horizon shortly before sunrise, the Nile flood surge was imminent. Pyramids, temple complexes, and other monumental building projects called for great skill in engineering. Long underground passageways were excavated to connect mortuary temples by the river with tombs near the desert's edge. On several occasions Egyptian kings dredged out a canal more than 50 miles (80 kilometers) long in order to join the Nile Valley to the Red Sea and expedite the transport of goods.

## CONCLUSION

The first modern humans emerged in Africa and migrated to every corner of the earth. Research suggests that climate change drove these foragers to abandon hunting and gathering and adopt the practices of agriculture and pastoralism. In the warmer era following the Great Ice Age around 9000 B.C.E., populations on every inhabited continent except Australia underwent this great transformation, selecting high-yield strains of plants for cultivation and breeding livestock.

It is no accident that the first civilizations to develop high levels of political centralization, urbanization, and technology were situated in river valleys where rainfall was insufficient for reliable agriculture. Dependent on river water to irrigate the cultivated land that fed their populations, Mesopotamian and Egyptian rulers channeled considerable human resources into the construction and maintenance of canals, dams, and dikes. This effort required the formation of political centers that could organize the necessary labor force.

In both Egypt and Mesopotamia, kingship emerged as the dominant political form. The Egyptian king's divine origins and symbolic association with the forces of renewal made him central to the welfare of the entire country and gave him religious authority superseding the temples and priests. Egyptian monarchs lavished much of the country's wealth on their tombs, believing that a proper burial would ensure the continuity of kingship and the attendant blessings that it brought to the land and people. Mesopotamian rulers, who were not normally regarded as divine but still dominated the religious institutions, built new cities, towering walls, splendid palaces, and religious edifices as lasting testaments to their power.

The unpredictable and violent floods in the Tigris-Euphrates Basin were a constant source of alarm for the people of Mesopotamia. In contrast, the predictable, opportune, and gradual Nile floods were eagerly anticipated events in Egypt. The relationship with nature stamped the worldview of both peoples. Mesopotamians tried to appease their harsh deities so as to survive in a dangerous world. Gilgamesh, the hero of the Mesopotamian epic, is tormented by terrifying visions of the afterlife: disembodied spirits of the dead stumbling around in the darkness of the Underworld for all eternity, eating dust and clay and slaving for the heartless gods of that realm. Egyptians, on the other hand, largely trusted in and nurtured the supernatural powers that, they believed, guaranteed orderliness and prosperity.

Although the populations of Egypt and Mesopotamia were ethnically diverse, both regions experienced a remarkable degree of cultural continuity. New immigrants readily assimilated to the dominant language, belief system, and lifestyles of the civilization. Mesopotamian women's apparent loss of freedom and legal privilege in the second millennium B.C.E. also may have been related to the higher degree of urbanization and class stratification in this society. In contrast, Egyptian pictorial documents, love poems, and legal records indicate respect and greater equality for women in the valley of the Nile.

## CHAPTER REVIEW

### EARLY HUMANS

■ *In light of scientific advances in our understanding of human origins, what have we learned about our relationship to the earth and other living species?* (page 5)

The theory of evolution, supported by an enormous body of evidence, leads to far-reaching conclusions. Every living species evolved from a common ancestor. Humans are descended from earlier hominid species that evolved in Africa beginning about 7 million years ago. Every modern human descended from communities that evolved in Africa 50,000 years ago, with some groups migrating to the other habitable continents. All human communities are directly related to each other, to all other living species, and to the earth.

## THE AGRICULTURAL REVOLUTIONS

■ *How did plant and animal domestication set the scene for the emergence of complex societies?* (page 10)

Domestic plants and animals made it possible for sizable populations to live even in regions that offered little support for foraging groups. As farming became the main source of food, settlement in villages became a normal way of life. In time, this led to complex political structures and the division of labor characteristic of civilized life.

## MESOPOTAMIA

■ *How did Mesopotamian civilization emerge, and what technologies promoted its advancement?* (page 13)

The first Mesopotamian people to keep written records were the Sumerians. Some Sumerian towns grew into city-states composed of an urban center that ruled surrounding agricultural land. Priests originally dominated these states, but they gave way to kings who assumed religious, administrative, legal, and military responsibilities. Sharp social divisions were reflected in the class-based penalties of the Law Code of Hammurabi. Mesopotamian gods embodied the uncertain forces of the environment. The people strove to appease them through rites focused on temples maintained by priests. Mesopotamian culture pioneered cuneiform writing, canal irrigation, bronze casting, and monumental architecture.

## EGYPT

■ *What role did the environment and religion play in the evolution of Egyptian civilization?* (page 19)

Protected by deserts and coastal marshes and nurtured by the predictable flooding of the Nile River, Egyptian civilization was relatively self-sufficient and secure. As the Sahara Desert dried and the population in the Nile Valley increased, political organization became more complex, eventually unifying into a single kingdom under a divine king, the pharaoh. Less urban and socially stratified than Mesopotamian society, Egypt relied on peasant farmers with few slaves and a comparatively free female population. Egyptian religion embodied the orderly and benign qualities of the Nile and involved a complex vision of the afterlife. Much wealth went for religious purposes preparing for the afterlife and glorifying the pharaoh. To this end, Egyptians constructed monuments, tombs, and temples and applied their knowledge of chemistry and anatomy to mummification.

## Key Terms

| | |
|---|---|
| culture (p. 5) | Babylon (p. 13) |
| history (p. 5) | Sumerians (p. 15) |
| evolution (p. 5) | cuneiform (p. 15) |
| hominid (p. 6) | civilization (p. 15) |
| australopithecines (p. 6) | city-state (p. 16) |
| bipedalism (p. 6) | ziggurat (p. 16) |
| Great Ice Age (p. 6) | amulet (p. 16) |
| *Homo habilis* (p. 6) | Hammurabi (p. 17) |
| Stone Age (p. 7) | scribe (p. 18) |
| Paleolithic (p. 7) | bronze (p. 19) |
| *Homo erectus* (p. 7) | pharaoh (p. 22) |
| *Homo sapiens* (p. 8) | ma'at (p. 22) |
| foragers (p. 8) | pyramid (p. 22) |
| Neolithic (p. 10) | Memphis (p. 23) |
| Agricultural Revolutions (p. 10) | Thebes (p. 23) |
| | hieroglyphics (p. 23) |
| pastoralism (p. 11) | papyrus (p. 23) |
| megaliths (p. 12) | mummy (p. 26) |

# CHAPTER 2

## from 2000 B.C.E.

# The Middle East and the Mediterranean

© Cengage Learning

## CHAPTER PREVIEW

### THE COSMOPOLITAN MIDDLE EAST, 1700–1100 B.C.E.

■ *How did a cosmopolitan civilization develop in the Middle East during the Late Bronze Age, and what forms did it take?*

### THE AEGEAN WORLD, 2000–1100 B.C.E.

■ *What civilizations emerged in the Aegean world, and what relationship did they have to the older civilizations to the east?*

### THE ASSYRIAN EMPIRE, 911–612 B.C.E.

■ *How did the Assyrian Empire rise to power and eventually dominate most of the ancient Middle East?*

### ISRAEL, 2000–500 B.C.E.

■ *How did the civilization of Israel develop, following both familiar cultural patterns and a unique course of its own?*

### PHOENICIA AND THE MEDITERRANEAN, 1200–500 B.C.E.

■ *How did the Phoenicians rise to commercial dominance over much of the Mediterranean world?*

### FAILURE AND TRANSFORMATION, 750–550 B.C.E.

■ *What factors prompted the transformation of the ancient Middle East between 750 and 550 B.C.E.?*

### Conclusion

**ENVIRONMENT & TECHNOLOGY:** Ancient Textiles and Dyes

29

Ancient stories—even when not historically accurate—provide valuable insights into how people thought about their origins and identity. One story concerned the founding of the city of Carthage (KAHR-thuhj) in present-day Tunisia, which for centuries dominated the waters and water-borne commerce of the western Mediterranean. Tradition held that Dido, a member of the royal family of the Phoenician city-state of Tyre (tire) in southern Lebanon, fled with her supporters to the western Mediterranean after her husband was murdered by her brother, the king. On the North African coast the refugees made friendly contact with local people, who offered them as much land as a cow's hide could cover. By cleverly cutting the hide into narrow strips, they marked out a substantial territory for Kart Khadasht, the "New City" (called *Carthago* by their Roman enemies).

This story highlights the spread of cultural patterns from older centers to new regions in the Mediterranean lands and western Asia. Trade, diplomatic contacts, military conquests, and the relocation of large numbers of people spread knowledge, beliefs, practices, and technologies.

By the early first millennium B.C.E. many societies of the region were entering the **Iron Age**. Iron offered advantages over bronze. It was a single metal rather than an alloy, and there were many sources of iron ore. Once the technology had been mastered—iron has to be heated to a higher temperature than bronze, and its hardness depends on the amount of carbon added during the forging process—iron tools were found to have harder, sharper edges than bronze tools.

The first part of this chapter resumes the story of Mesopotamia and Egypt in the second millennium B.C.E.: their relations with neighboring peoples, the development of a prosperous, "cosmopolitan" network of states in the Middle East, and the destruction and decline that set in around 1200 B.C.E. We also look at how the Minoan and Mycenaean civilizations of the Aegean Sea adopted the technologies and cultural patterns of the older Middle Eastern centers and prospered from participation in long-distance trade.

The remainder of the chapter examines three societies from 1000 to 500 B.C.E.: the Assyrians of

northern Mesopotamia; the Israelites; and the Phoenicians of Lebanon and their colonies in the western Mediterranean, mainly Carthage.

## THE COSMOPOLITAN MIDDLE EAST, 1700–1100 B.C.E.

■ *How did a cosmopolitan civilization develop in the Middle East during the Late Bronze Age, and what forms did it take?*

Both Mesopotamia and Egypt succumbed to outside invaders in the seventeenth century B.C.E. Eventually the outsiders were either ejected or assimilated, and conditions of stability and prosperity were restored. Between 1500 and 1200 B.C.E. large states dominated the Middle East (see Map 2.1), controlling the smaller states and kinship groups as they competed with, and sometimes fought against, one another for control of commodities and trade routes.

Historians have called the Late Bronze Age a "cosmopolitan" era, meaning a time of widely shared cultures and lifestyles. Diplomatic relations and commercial contacts between states fostered the flow of goods and ideas, and elite groups shared similar values and high standards of living. The peasants in the countryside, who constituted the majority of the population, saw some improvement in their standard of living but reaped fewer benefits from the increasing contacts and trade.

**Western Asia**   By 1500 B.C.E. Mesopotamia was divided into two distinct political zones: Babylonia in the south and Assyria in the north (see Map 2.1). The city of Babylon had gained ascendancy under the dynasty of Hammurabi in the eighteenth and seventeenth centuries B.C.E., but Kassite (KAS-ite) people from the Zagros (ZAH-grohs) Mountains to the east had seized power by 1460 B.C.E. Though Kassite names derive from their native language, the Kassites otherwise embraced Babylonian

> **Iron Age**  Historians' term for the period during which iron was the primary metal for tools and weapons. The advent of iron technology began at different times in different parts of the world.

# Chronology

| | Western Asia | Egypt | Syria–Palestine | Mediterranean |
|---|---|---|---|---|
| **2000 B.C.E.** | **2000 B.C.E.** Horses in use<br><br>**1700–1200 B.C.E.** Hittites dominant in Anatolia | **2040–1640 B.C.E.** Middle Kingdom<br><br>**1640–1532 B.C.E.** Hyksos dominate northern Egypt<br><br>**1532 B.C.E.** Beginning of New Kingdom | **1800 B.C.E.** Abraham migrates to Canaan | **2000 B.C.E.** Rise of Minoan civilization on Crete; early Greeks arrive in Greece<br><br>**1600 B.C.E.** Rise of Mycenaean civilization in Greece |
| **1500 B.C.E.** | **1500 B.C.E.** Hittites develop iron metallurgy<br><br>**1460 B.C.E.** Kassites assume control of southern Mesopotamia<br><br>**1200 B.C.E.** Destruction of Hittite kingdom | **1470 B.C.E.** Queen Hatshepsut dispatches expedition to Punt<br><br>**1353 B.C.E.** Akhenaten launches reforms<br><br>**1290–1224 B.C.E.** Reign of Ramesses the Great<br><br>**1200–1150 B.C.E.** Sea Peoples attack Egypt<br><br>**1070 B.C.E.** End of New Kingdom | **1500 B.C.E.** Early "alphabetic" script developed at Ugarit<br><br>**1250–1200 B.C.E.** Israelite occupation of Canaan<br><br>**1150 B.C.E.** Philistines settle southern coast of Israel | **1450 B.C.E.** Destruction of Minoan palaces in Crete<br><br>**1200–1150 B.C.E.** Destruction of Mycenaean centers in Greece |
| **1000 B.C.E.** | **1000 B.C.E.** Iron metallurgy begins<br><br>**911 B.C.E.** Rise of Neo-Assyrian Empire<br><br>**744–727 B.C.E.** Reforms of Tiglathpileser<br><br>**668–627 B.C.E.** Reign of Ashurbanipal<br><br>**626–539 B.C.E.** Neo-Babylonian kingdom | **750 B.C.E.** Kings of Kush control Egypt<br><br>**671 B.C.E.** Assyrian conquest of Egypt | **1000 B.C.E.** Jerusalem made Israelite capital<br><br>**969 B.C.E.** Hiram of Tyre comes to power<br><br>**960 B.C.E.** Solomon builds First Temple<br><br>**920 B.C.E.** Division into two kingdoms of Israel and Judah<br><br>**721 B.C.E.** Assyrian conquest of northern kingdom<br><br>**701 B.C.E.** Assyrian humiliation of Tyre | **1000 B.C.E.** Iron metallurgy<br><br>**814 B.C.E.** Foundation of Carthage |
| **600 B.C.E.** | **612 B.C.E.** Fall of Assyria | | **587 B.C.E.** Capture of Jerusalem<br><br>**515 B.C.E.** Deportees from Babylon return to Jerusalem<br><br>**450 B.C.E.** Completion of Hebrew Bible; Hanno the Phoenician explores West Africa | **500–200 B.C.E.** Rivalry of Carthaginians, Greeks, and Romans in western Mediterranean |

**Map 2.1    The Middle East in the Second Millennium B.C.E.**  Although warfare was not uncommon, treaties, diplomatic missions, and correspondence in Akkadian cuneiform fostered cooperative relationships
between states. All were tied together by extensive networks of exchange centering on the trade in metals. Peripheral regions, such as Nubia and the Aegean Sea, were drawn into the web of commerce.
© Cengage Learning

language and culture and intermarried with the
native population. During their 250 years in power,
the Kassite rulers of Babylonia defended their core
area and traded for raw materials, but they did not
pursue territorial conquest.

The Assyrians of the north proved more ambitious. As early as the twentieth century B.C.E. the city
of Ashur (AH-shoor) on the northern Tigris anchored
a busy trade route stretching across the northern
plain to the Anatolian Plateau (modern Turkey).
Assyrian merchants settled outside the walls of Anatolian cities and exchanged textiles and tin (a component of bronze) for Anatolian silver. In the eighteenth
century B.C.E., an Assyrian dynasty briefly controlled
the upper Euphrates River near the present-day Syria-
Iraq border. The trade routes connecting Mesopota-

mia to Anatolia and the Syria-Palestine coast were
key to the power of this "Old Assyrian" kingdom.
After 1400 B.C.E. a resurgent "Middle Assyrian" kingdom engaged in campaigns of conquest and economic expansion.

Other ambitious states developed around the
Mesopotamian heartland, including Elam (EE-
luhm) in southwest Iran and Mitanni (mih-TAH-nee)
between the upper Euphrates and Tigris Rivers. Most
formidable were the **Hittites** (HIT-ites), who became

**Hittites**  A people from central Anatolia who established an
empire in Anatolia and Syria in the Late Bronze Age. With
wealth from the trade in metals and military power based
on chariot forces, the Hittites vied with New Kingdom Egypt
for control of Syria-Palestine before falling to unidentified
attackers around 1200 B.C.E.

the foremost power in Anatolia from around 1700 to 1200 B.C.E. From their capital at Hattusha (haht-tush-SHAH), near present-day Ankara (ANG-kuh-ruh) in central Turkey, they deployed the fearsome new technology of horse-drawn war chariots. They exploited Anatolia's rich deposits of copper, silver, and iron to play a key role in international commerce and were the first to develop a technique for making tools and weapons of iron, a process they kept secret because it provided military and economic advantages.

During the second millennium B.C.E. Mesopotamian political and cultural concepts spread across western Asia. Akkadian (uh-KAY-dee-uhn) became the language of diplomacy and correspondence between governments. The Elamites (EE-luh-mites) and Hittites, among others, adapted the cuneiform system to write their own languages. In the Syrian coastal city-state of Ugarit (OO-guh-reet), thirty cuneiform symbols were used to write consonant sounds, an early use of the alphabetic principle and a considerable advance over the hundreds of signs required in conventional writing.

## New Kingdom Egypt

After flourishing for nearly four hundred years (see Chapter 1), the Egyptian Middle Kingdom collapsed in the seventeenth century B.C.E. Egypt entered a period of political fragmentation and economic decline. Around 1640 B.C.E. northern Egypt came under foreign rule for the first time at the hands of the Hyksos (HICK-soes), or "Princes of Foreign Lands."

Historians are uncertain who the Hyksos were. Semitic peoples had been migrating from the Levant (present-day Syria, Jordan, Lebanon, Israel, and the Palestinian territories) into the eastern Nile Delta for centuries. In the chaotic conditions of this time, other people may have joined them, establishing control first in the delta and then in the middle of the country. The Hyksos possessed war chariots and composite bows made of wood and horn for greater range, which gave them an advantage over the Egyptians. They intermarried with Egyptians and assimilated to native ways, speaking the Egyptian language and maintaining Egyptian institutions and culture. Nevertheless, unlike in Mesopotamia, the Egyptians continued to regard the Hyksos as "foreigners."

As with the formation of the Middle Kingdom five hundred years earlier, the reunification of Egypt under a native dynasty was accomplished by princes from Thebes. After three decades of warfare, Kamose (KAH-mose) and Ahmose (AH-mose) expelled the Hyksos from Egypt and inaugurated the New Kingdom, which lasted from about 1532 to 1070 B.C.E.

New Kingdom Egypt saw a shift from traditional Egyptian isolationism to aggressive expansion northward into Syria-Palestine and southward into Nubia. Timber, gold, and copper in taxes and tribute (payments from conquered peoples) were the prizes of this expansion. The occupied lands also provided a buffer against foreign attack. In Nubia, Egypt imposed direct control and pressed the native population to adopt Egyptian language and culture. In the Syria-Palestine region, the Egyptians stationed garrisons at strategically placed forts and supported local rulers willing to collaborate.

The New Kingdom was a period of innovation. Egyptian soldiers, administrators, diplomats, and merchants traveled widely, bringing back new fruits and vegetables, new musical instruments, and new technologies, such as an improved potter's wheel and weaver's loom.

At least one woman held the throne of New Kingdom Egypt. When her husband died, Queen **Hatshepsut** (hat-SHEP-soot) claimed the royal title for herself (r. 1473–1458 B.C.E.). In inscriptions she often used the male pronoun for herself, and drawings and sculptures show her wearing the long beard of the ruler of Egypt.

Around 1470 B.C.E. Hatshepsut sent a naval expedition down the Red Sea to the fabled land of Punt (poont), an exotic land that historians believe may have been near the coast of eastern Sudan or Eritrea. Hatshepsut was seeking the source of myrrh (murr), a reddish-brown resin that the Egyptians burned in religious rites and used in medicines and cosmet-

**Hatshepsut** Queen of Egypt (r. 1473–1458 B.C.E.). She dispatched a naval expedition to Punt (possibly northeast Sudan or Eritrea), the faraway source of myrrh. There is evidence of opposition to a woman as ruler, and after her death her name and image were frequently defaced.

**The Mortuary Temple of Queen Hatshepsut at Deir el-Bahri, Egypt, ca. 1460** B.C.E. This beautiful complex of terraces, ramps, and colonnades featured relief sculptures and texts commemorating the famous expedition to Punt. Hatshepsut, facing resistance from traditionalists opposed to a woman ruling Egypt, sought to prove her worth by publicizing the opening of direct contact with the source of highly prized myrrh. EugenZ/Shutterstock.com

ics. When the expedition returned with myrrh and sub-Saharan luxury goods—ebony, ivory, cosmetics, live monkeys, panther skins—Hatshepsut celebrated the achievement in a great public display and in words and pictures on the walls of her mortuary temple at Deir el-Bahri (DARE uhl–BAH-ree). After her death, her image was defaced and her name blotted out wherever it appeared, presumably by officials opposed to a woman ruler.

A century later another untraditional ruler ascended the throne as Amenhotep (ah-muhn-HOE-tep) IV. He soon began to refer to himself as **Akhenaten** (ah-ken-AHT-n) (r. 1353–1335 B.C.E.), meaning "beneficial to the Aten" (AHT-n) (the disk of the sun), and spread his belief in Aten as the supreme deity. He closed the temples of other gods, challenging the age-old supremacy of the chief god Amon (AH-muhn) and the power and influence of his priests.

Some scholars have credited Akhenaten with the invention of monotheism—the belief in one exclusive god. It is likely, however, that Akhenaten was attempting to reassert the superiority of the king over the priests and to renew belief in the king's divinity. Worship of Aten was confined to the royal family: the people of Egypt were pressed to revere the divine ruler.

Akhenaten built a new capital at modern-day Amarna (uh-MAHR-nuh), halfway between Memphis and Thebes (see Map 2.1). He relocated thousands of Egyptians to construct the site and serve the ruling elite. His artists created a new style that broke with the conventions of earlier art: the king, his wife Nefertiti (nef-uhr-TEE-tee), and their daughters were depicted in fluid, natural poses with strangely elongated heads and limbs and swelling abdomens.

Akhenaten's reforms were strongly resented by government officials and priests whose privileges and wealth were linked to the traditional system. After his death the temples were reopened; Amon was reinstated as chief god; the capital was returned to Thebes; and the priests regained their influence. The boy-king Tutankhamun (tuht-uhnk-AH-muhn) (r. 1333–1323 B.C.E.), famous solely because his was the only royal tomb found by archaeologists that had not been pillaged by robbers, reveals both in his name (meaning "beautiful in life is Amon") and in his insignificant reign the ultimate failure of Akhenaten's revolution.

The rulers of a new dynasty, the Ramessides (RAM-ih-sides), returned to the policy of conquest and

> **Akhenaten** Egyptian pharaoh (r. 1353–1335 B.C.E.). He built a new capital at Amarna, fostered a new style of naturalistic art, and created a religious revolution by imposing worship of the sun-disk.

**Ramesses II in a War Chariot Attacks Nubian Enemies** This is a restoration of a thirteenth century B.C.E. painting on the wall of a temple at Beit el Wali. Other paintings depict the pharaoh attacking Asiatic enemies and making offerings to the high god Amon. www.BibleLandPictures.com/Alamy

expansion that Akhenaten had neglected. **Ramesses II** (RAM-ih-seez)—sometimes called Ramesses the Great—ruled for sixty-six years (r. 1290–1224 B.C.E.) and dominated his age. Living into his nineties, he may have fathered more than a hundred children. Since 1990 archaeologists have been excavating a network of corridors and chambers carved deep into a hillside near Thebes, where many sons of Ramesses were buried.

## Commerce and Communication

Early in his reign Ramesses II fought a major battle against the Hittites at Kadesh in northern Syria (1285 B.C.E.). Although Egyptian propaganda boasted of a great victory, the lack of territorial gains suggests that it was essentially a draw. In subsequent years Egyptian and Hittite diplomats negotiated a treaty, which was strengthened by Ramesses' marriage to a Hittite princess. At issue was control of Syria-Palestine, strategically located between the great powers of the Middle East and at the end of the east-west trade route across Asia. The inland cities—such as Mari (MAH-ree) on the upper Euphrates and Alalakh (UH-luh-luhk) in western Syria—were hubs of international trade. The coastal towns—particularly Ugarit and the Phoenician towns of the Lebanese seaboard—extended commerce to the lands ringing the Mediterranean Sea.

Commerce in metals energized long-distance trade. Assyrian trafficked in silver from Anatolia (above) and Egyptians gratified their passion for Nubian gold (see Chapter 3). Copper came from Anatolia and Cyprus, tin from Afghanistan and possibly the British Isles. Both ores traveled long distances and passed through many hands before reaching their final destinations.

New modes of transportation expedited communications and commerce across great distances and inhospitable landscapes. Horses, domesticated by nomadic peoples in Central Asia, were brought into

**Ramesses II** A long-lived ruler of New Kingdom Egypt (r. 1290–1224 B.C.E.). He reached an accommodation with the Hittites of Anatolia after a standoff in battle at Kadesh in Syria. He built on a grand scale throughout Egypt.

- The Late Bronze Age saw the rise of a cosmopolitan culture in the ancient Middle East.

- Mesopotamia was divided between Babylonia and the increasingly powerful Assyrians.

- In Anatolia, the technologically advanced Hittites became the major political force, and both they and other outlying peoples absorbed Mesopotamian cultural and political concepts.

- After a century of foreign domination, the New Kingdom in Egypt ushered in a period of expansion abroad and innovation at a home.

- During the Late Bronze Age, long-distance trade in metals expanded, and the arrival of the horse made possible larger states and empires.

Mesopotamia through the Zagros Mountains around 2000 B.C.E. and reached Egypt before 1600 B.C.E. The speed of the horse contributed to the creation of large states and empires, enabling soldiers and government agents to cover great distances quickly. Swift, maneuverable horse-drawn chariots became the premier instrument of war.

Sometime after 1500 B.C.E. in western Asia, but not for another thousand years in Egypt, people began to make common use of camels, though the animal was domesticated much earlier in southern Arabia. Their strength made them ideal pack animals, and their ability to go without water made possible travel across barren terrain.

# THE AEGEAN WORLD, 2000–1100 B.C.E.

■ *What civilizations emerged in the Aegean world, and what relationship did they have to the older civilizations to the east?*

In this era of far-flung trade and communication, the emergence of the Minoan (mih-NO-uhn) civilization on the island of Crete and the Mycenaean (my-suh-NEE-uhn) civilization of Greece demonstrates the fertilizing influence of older centers on outlying lands and peoples. The landscape of southern Greece and the Aegean islands is rocky and arid, with small plains lying between ranges of hills. The limited arable land was suitable for grains, grapevines, and olive

trees. Flocks of sheep and goats grazed the slopes. Sharply indented coastlines, natural harbors, and small islands within sight of one another made the sea the fastest and least costly mode of travel. Lacking metals and timber, Aegean peoples had to import these commodities from abroad. As a result, the rise, success, and eventual fall of the Minoan and Mycenaean societies were closely tied to their commercial and political relations with other peoples in the region.

## Minoan Crete

The **Minoan** civilization that had come into being on the island of Crete by 2000 B.C.E. (see Map 2.1) featured centralized government, monumental building, bronze metallurgy, writing, and record keeping. Archaeologists named this civilization after King Minos, who, in Greek legend, ruled a naval empire in the Aegean and kept the monstrous Minotaur (MIN-uh-tor) (half-man, half-bull) in a mazelike labyrinth built by the ingenious inventor Daedalus (DED-ih-luhs).

The ethnicity of the Minoans is uncertain, and their writing has not been deciphered. But their sprawling palace complexes at Cnossos (NOS-suhs), Phaistos (FIE-stuhs), and Malie (mahl-YAH) and the distribution of Cretan pottery and other artifacts around the Mediterranean and Middle East testify to widespread trading connections. Egyptian, Syrian, and Mesopotamian influences can be seen in the design of the Minoan palaces, but the absence of identifiable representations of Cretan rulers contrasts sharply with the grandiose depictions of kings in the Middle East and suggests a different conception of authority. Also noteworthy are the absence of fortifications at the palace sites and the presence of high-quality indoor plumbing.

Statuettes of women with elaborate headdresses and serpents coiling around their limbs may represent fertility goddesses. Colorful frescoes (paintings done on the moist plaster surfaces of walls) in the palaces portray groups of women in frilly skirts conversing

**Minoan** Prosperous civilization on the Aegean island of Crete in the second millennium B.C.E. The Minoans engaged in far-flung commerce around the Mediterranean and exerted powerful cultural influences on the early Greeks.

or watching performances as well as young acrobats vaulting over the horns of an onrushing bull, either for sport or as a religious activity. Servants carrying jars and fishermen throwing nets and hooks from their boats suggest a joyful attitude toward work, but this may say more about elite ideals than about the reality of daily toil. Stylized vase paintings depicting plants with swaying leaves and playful octopuses winding their tentacles around the surface of the vase communicate a delight in nature's beauty.

All the Cretan palaces except at Cnossus, along with the houses of the elite and peasants in the countryside, were deliberately destroyed around 1450 B.C.E. Because Mycenaean Greeks took over at Cnossus, most historians regard them as the culprits.

## Mycenaean Greece

Most historians believe that speakers of an Indo-European language ancestral to Greek migrated into the Greek peninsula around 2000 B.C.E. Through intermarriage, blending of languages, and melding of cultural practices, the indigenous population and the newcomers created the first Greek culture. For centuries this society remained simple and static. Farmers and shepherds lived in Stone Age conditions, wringing a bare living from the land. But in 1876 a German businessman, Heinrich Schliemann (SHLEE-muhn), intent on proving true the ancient Greek *Iliad* and *Odyssey* epics that spoke of Agamemnon (ag-uh-MEM-non), the king of **Mycenae** (my-SEE-nee), discovered proof of an advanced civilization that lasted from around 1600 to 1150 B.C.E. Schliemann found deep, rectangular **shaft graves** with not only the bodies of men, women, and children but also gold jewelry, ornaments, weapons, and utensils. Clearly, some people had acquired wealth, authority, and the capacity to mobilize human labor. Subsequent excavation uncovered a large palace complex, massive walls, and more shaft graves.

The sudden appearance of Mycenaean culture in mainland Greece is puzzling. There is no evidence of Cretan political control of the mainland, but these early Greeks were clearly influenced by the Minoan palaces, centralized economy, and administrative bureaucracy, as well as the writing system. They adopted Minoan styles of architecture, pottery, and fresco and vase painting. Historians speculate that trade, piracy, and the booty brought back by mercenaries (soldiers who served for pay in foreign lands) might be responsible.

Excavations revealed other settlements with the same features discovered at Mycenae: a citadel built on a hilltop and surrounded by high, thick walls. The fortified enclosure—made of stones so large that later Greeks believed the one-eyed giant Cyclopes (SIGH-kloe-pees) had lifted them into place—provided refuge for the entire community in time of danger and contained the palace and administrative complex. The large central hall with an open hearth and columned porch was surrounded by courtyards, living quarters for the royal family and their retainers, offices, storerooms, and workshops. Brightly painted scenes of war, the hunt, and daily life, as well as decorative motifs from nature, covered the palace walls.

Additional information is provided by over four thousand baked clay tablets written in a script called **Linear B**. Like its predecessor, the undecipherable Minoan script called Linear A, Linear B uses pictorial signs to represent syllables, but the language is an early form of Greek. Palace administrators kept track of people, animals, and objects in exhaustive detail, listing the number of chariot wheels in storerooms, the rations paid to workers, and the gifts dedicated to various gods. However, individual people—even kings—receive no mention, leaving us largely in the dark about the political and legal system, social structure, gender relations, religious beliefs, or even historical events.

---

**Mycenae**  Site of a fortified palace complex in southern Greece that controlled a Late Bronze Age kingdom. In ancient epic poems, Mycenae was the base of King Agamemnon, who commanded the Greeks besieging Troy. Contemporary archaeologists call the complex Greek society of the second millennium B.C.E. "Mycenaean."

**shaft graves**  A term used for the burial sites of elite members of Mycenaean Greek society in the mid-second millennium B.C.E. At the bottom of deep shafts lined with stone slabs, the bodies were laid out along with gold and bronze jewelry, implements, weapons, and masks.

**Linear B**  A set of syllabic symbols, derived from the writing system of Minoan Crete, used in the Mycenaean palaces of the Late Bronze Age to write an early form of Greek. It was used primarily for palace records, and the surviving Linear B tablets provide substantial information about the economic organization of Mycenaean society and tantalizing clues about political, social, and religious institutions.

Dea/G Nimatallah/De Agostini Editore/Age Fotostock

**Fresco from the Aegean Island of Thera, ca. 1650 B.C.E.** This picture shows the arrival of a fleet in a harbor as people watch from the walls of the town. The Minoan civilization of Crete was famous in legend for its naval power. The fresco reveals the appearance and design of ships in the Bronze Age Aegean. In the seventeenth century B.C.E., the island of Thera was devastated by a massive volcanic explosion, thought by many to be the origin of the myth of Atlantis sinking beneath the sea.

The seafaring skill of Minoans and Mycenaeans encouraged long-distance trade. Commercial vessels depended primarily on sails, and their crews navigated during daylight hours to keep the land in sight and then went ashore at night to eat and sleep. The ships' shallow keels enabled the crews to pull them up onto the beach.

Cretan and Greek pottery and crafted goods are found not only in the Aegean but also in other parts of the Mediterranean and Middle East, sometimes in enough quantity and variety to suggest settlements of Aegean peoples. The oldest artifacts are Minoan; then Minoan and Mycenaean objects are found side by side; and eventually Greek wares replace Cretan goods altogether. This indicates that Cretan mer-

chants pioneered trade routes and were later joined by Mycenaean traders, who supplanted them in the fifteenth century B.C.E.

The many Aegean pots found throughout the region must have once contained such products as wine and olive oil. Other possible exports include textiles, weapons, and other crafted goods, as well as slaves and mercenary soldiers. As for imports, amber (from northern Europe) and ivory carved in Syria have been discovered at Aegean sites, and the large population of southern Greece may have relied on imports of grain. Above all, the Aegean lands needed metals, both gold and the copper and tin needed to make bronze. Sunken ships carrying copper ingots have been found on the floor of the Mediterranean.

Only the elite classes owned metal goods, which may have been symbols of their superior status.

Mycenaeans were tough, warlike, and acquisitive. They traded with those who were strong and took from those who were weak. This way of life led to conflict with the Hittite kings of Anatolia in the fourteenth and thirteenth centuries B.C.E. Documents in the archives at the Hittite capital refer to the king and land of Ahhijawa (uh-key-YAW-wuh), most likely a Hittite rendering of *Achaea* (uh-KEY-uh), a term used for the Greeks. They indicate that relations were sometimes friendly, sometimes strained, and that the people of Ahhijawa took advantage of Hittite preoccupation or weakness. The *Iliad*, which Schliemann had tried to prove true over a century ago, can be seen against this backdrop of Mycenaean belligerence and opportunism, telling a tale of the Achaeans' ten-year siege and eventual destruction of Troy, a city on the fringes of Hittite territory controlling the sea route between the Mediterranean and Black Seas. Archaeology has confirmed a destruction at Troy around 1200 B.C.E.

## The Fall of Late Bronze Age Civilizations

Hittite difficulties with Ahhijawa and the Greek attack on Troy foreshadowed the troubles that culminated in the destruction of many of the old centers of the Middle East and Mediterranean around 1200 B.C.E. In this period, for reasons not well understood, large numbers of people were on the move. As migrants swarmed into one region, they displaced other peoples, who then joined the tide of refugees. Around 1200 B.C.E. unidentified invaders destroyed the Hittite capital, Hattusha, and the Hittite kingdom. The tide of destruction moved south into Syria, and the great coastal city of Ugarit was swept away. Egypt managed to beat back two attacks: an assault on the Nile Delta around 1220 B.C.E. by "Libyans and Northerners coming from all lands," and a major invasion by the "Sea Peoples" about thirty years later. Although the Egyptian ruler claimed a great victory, the Philistines (FIH-luh-steen) occupied the coast of Palestine (this is the origin of the name subsequently used for this region), and Egypt soon withdrew. The Egyptians also lost their foothold in Nubia, opening the way for the emergence of the native kingdom centered on Napata (see Chapter 3).

Among the invaders listed in the Egyptian inscriptions are the Ekwesh (ECK-wesh), who could be Achaeans—that is, Greeks. Whether or not the Mycenaeans participated in these or other invasions, their own centers also experienced collapse. The rulers apparently saw trouble coming; at some sites they began to build more extensive fortifications and took steps to guarantee water supplies. But their efforts were in vain. Nearly all the palaces were destroyed in the first half of the twelfth century B.C.E.

Curiously, archaeological records contain no trace of foreign invaders. However, the demise of Mycenaean civilization at roughly the same time as the fall of other regional civilizations suggests that external factors played a role. The position of the Mycenaean ruling class may have depended on the import of vital commodities and the profits from trade, and they may have suffered from the destruction of trading partners and disruption of routes. Competition for limited resources may have led to internal unrest and, ultimately, political collapse.

The end of Mycenaean civilization illustrates the interdependence of the major centers of the Late Bronze Age. The destruction of the palaces ended the domination of the ruling class. The administrative apparatus revealed in the Linear B tablets disappeared, and writing passed out of use along with the

## SECTION REVIEW

- Influenced by contact with older cultures, Minoan Crete was the first European civilization to develop complex government and advanced technologies.

- The Minoans participated in extensive long-distance trade, which prompted a blending of foreign and indigenous cultural forms and practices.

- Minoan civilization was deliberately destroyed, perhaps by Mycenaean Greeks.

- In Greece, Mycenaean civilization rose suddenly and developed common patterns of settlement, organization, and technology.

- The Mycenaeans participated in long-distance trade and piracy activities, which likely became the basis of later heroic legends.

- Large migrations precipitated the collapse of many Late Bronze Age civilizations, including the Mycenaean, after which Greece entered a Dark Age.

palace officials who had utilized it. Archaeological studies indicate the depopulation of some regions of Greece and a flow of people to other regions that escaped destruction. The Greek language persisted, and a thousand years later people were still worshiping gods mentioned in the Linear B tablets. People also continued to make the vessels and implements that they were familiar with, although with a marked decline in artistic and technical skill. Mycenaean cultural uniformity gave way to regional variations in shapes, styles, and techniques, reflecting the increased isolation of different Greek areas. The peoples of the region entered a centuries-long "Dark Age" of poverty, isolation, and loss of knowledge.

## THE ASSYRIAN EMPIRE, 911–612 B.C.E.

■ *How did the Assyrian Empire rise to power and eventually dominate most of the ancient Middle East?*

New centers emerged in the centuries after 1000 B.C.E. The chief force for change was the powerful and aggressive **Neo-Assyrian Empire** (911–612 B.C.E.). Compared to the flat expanse of Babylonia to the south, the Assyrian homeland in northern Mesopotamia is hillier and has a more temperate climate and greater rainfall. Peasant farmers, accustomed to defending themselves against marauders, provided the foot-soldiers for the ceaseless Neo-Assyrian campaigns: westward across the plain and desert as far as the Mediterranean, north into mountainous Urartu (ur-RAHR-too) (modern Armenia), east across the Zagros range onto the Iranian Plateau, and south along the Tigris River to Babylonia.

These campaigns followed important trade routes and provided immediate booty and the prospect of tribute and taxes. They also secured access to iron and silver and brought the Assyrians control of international commerce. Driven by pride, greed, and religious conviction, the Assyrians defeated the other great kingdoms of the day. At its peak their empire stretched from Anatolia, Syria-Palestine, and Egypt in the west, across Armenia and Mesopotamia, and as far as western Iran. Although historians sometimes apply the term *empire* to earlier regional powers, the Assyrians created a new kind of empire, larger in extent than anything seen before and dedi-

cated to the enrichment of the imperial center at the expense of the subjugated periphery.

The king was literally and symbolically the center of the Assyrian universe. All the land belonged to him, and all the people, even the highest-ranking officials, were his servants. Assyrians believed that the gods chose the king as their earthly representative. Normally the king chose a son as successor, and his choice was confirmed by divine oracles and the Assyrian elite. In the revered ancient city of Ashur the high priest anointed the new king's head with oil and gave him the insignia of kingship: a crown and scepter. The kings also were buried in Ashur.

Messengers and spies brought the king information from every corner of the empire. The king appointed officials, heard complaints, dictated correspondence to an army of scribes, and received foreign envoys. He was the military leader, responsible for planning campaigns, and was often away from the capital commanding operations in the field.

Among other responsibilities, the king supervised the state religion, devoting much time to elaborate public and private rituals and to upkeep of the temples. He consulted the gods through rituals of divination. All actions were carried out in the name of Ashur, the chief god. Military victories were cited as proof of Ashur's superiority over the gods of the conquered peoples.

Relentless government propaganda secured popular support for military campaigns that mostly benefited the king and the nobility. Royal inscriptions posted throughout the empire catalogued recent victories, extolled the unshakeable determination of the king, and promised ruthless punishments to anyone who resisted. Relief sculptures depicting hunts, battles, sieges, executions, and deportations covered the walls of the royal palaces. Looming over most scenes was the king, larger than anyone else, muscular and fierce. Few visitors to the Assyrian court could fail to be awed and intimidated.

**Neo-Assyrian Empire**  An empire extending from western Iran to Syria-Palestine, conquered by the Assyrians of northern Mesopotamia between the tenth and seventh centuries B.C.E. They used force and terror and exploited the wealth and labor of their subjects. They also preserved and continued the cultural and scientific developments of Mesopotamian civilization.

Hulton Archive/Stringer/Getty Images

**Wall Relief from the Palace of Sennacherib at Nineveh** Against a backdrop of wooded hills representing the landscape of Assyria, workers are hauling a huge stone sculpture from the riverbank to the palace under the watchful eyes of officials and soldiers. They accomplish this task with simple equipment—a lever, a sledge, and thick ropes—and a lot of human muscle power.

## Conquest and Control

Superior military organization and technology lay behind Assyria's unprecedented conquests. Early armies consisted of men who served in return for grants of land and peasants and slaves contributed by large landowners. Later, King Tiglathpileser (TIG-lath-pih-LEE-zuhr) (r. 744–727 B.C.E.) created a core army of professional soldiers made up of Assyrians and the most formidable subject peoples. At its peak the Assyrian state could mobilize a half-million troops, including lightly armed bowmen and slingers, armored spearmen, cavalry equipped with bows or spears, and four-man chariots.

Iron weapons and cavalry gave Assyrian soldiers an advantage. However, Assyrian engineers also developed machinery and tactics for besieging fortified towns. They tunneled under the walls, built mobile towers for archers, and applied battering rams to weak points. Couriers and signal fires provided long-distance communication, while a network of spies gathered intelligence.

Terror tactics discouraged resistance and rebellion. Civilians were thrown into fires, prisoners were skinned alive, and the severed heads of defeated rulers hung on city walls, all of which was well publicized. **Mass deportation**—the forced uprooting of entire communities and resettlement elsewhere—broke the spirit of rebellious peoples. Although this tactic had a long history in the ancient Middle East, the Neo-Assyrian monarchs used it on an unprecedented scale, and up to 4 million people may have been relocated. Deportation also shifted human resources from the periphery to the center, where the deportees worked on royal and noble estates, opened new lands for agriculture, and built palaces and cities.

**mass deportation** The forcible removal and relocation of large numbers of people or entire populations. The mass deportations practiced by the Assyrian and Persian Empires were meant as a terrifying warning of the consequences of rebellion. They also brought skilled and unskilled labor to the imperial center.

The Assyrians never discovered an effective method of governing an empire of such vast distances, varied landscapes, and diverse peoples. Control tended to be tight at the center and in lands closest to the core area, and less so farther away. The Assyrian kings waged many campaigns to reinstate control over territories subdued in previous wars.

Assyrian officials oversaw the collection of tribute and taxes, maintained law and order, raised troops, undertook public works, and provisioned armies and administrators passing through their territory. The expectation of land or shares of booty and taxes, fear of punishment, and oaths of allegiance bound the elite and skilled professionals—priests, diviners, scribes, doctors, and artisans—to the monarch. Provincial governors were subject to frequent inspections by royal overseers.

The Assyrians ruthlessly exploited the wealth and resources of their subjects to fund their military campaigns and administration. Wealth from the periphery was funneled to the center, where the king and nobility grew rich. Triumphant kings expanded the ancestral capital and religious center at Ashur and built magnificent new royal cities encircled by high walls and containing ornate palaces and temples. Dur Sharrukin (DOOR SHAH-roo-keen), the "Fortress of Sargon," was completed in a mere ten years by a massive labor force composed of prisoners of war and Assyrian citizens who owed periodic service to the state.

Nevertheless, the Assyrian Empire was not simply parasitic. There is some evidence of royal investment in provincial infrastructure. The cities and merchant classes thrived on expanded long-distance commerce, and some subject populations were surprisingly loyal to their Assyrian rulers.

## Assyrian Society and Culture

Surviving sources primarily shed light on the deeds of kings and elites. Only a little is known about the lives and activities of the millions of Assyrian subjects. The government did not distinguish between native Assyrians and the increasingly large number of immigrants and deportees in the Assyrian homeland. All were referred to as "human beings," entitled to the same legal protections and liable for the same labor and military service.

### SECTION REVIEW

- One of the most important civilizations to emerge after the upheavals of the Late Bronze Age was the Neo-Assyrian Empire.
- Led by all-powerful kings, the Assyrians waged campaigns of aggressive expansion.
- The Assyrians' military success rested on superior organization and technology, such as iron weapons, cavalry, and the ability to attack fortifications.
- The Assyrians controlled subject peoples through terror tactics and mass deportations.
- The Assyrian state exploited subject territories, transporting wealth from the periphery to the center of the empire.
- Assyrian scholars preserved and added to the long intellectual and scientific legacy of Mesopotamian civilization.

Over time the inflow of outsiders changed the ethnic makeup of the core area.

The vast majority of subjects worked on the land. The agricultural surpluses they produced allowed substantial numbers of people—the standing army, government officials, religious experts, merchants and artisans—to engage in specialized activities.

Most trade took place at the local level, with individual artisans and small workshops producing pottery, tools, and clothing. The state fostered long-distance trade, since imported luxury goods—metals, fine textiles, dyes, gems, and ivory—brought in substantial customs revenues and pleased the elite. Silver was the basic medium of exchange, weighed out for each transaction in a time before the invention of coins.

Assyrian scholars preserved and built on the achievements of their Mesopotamian predecessors. When archaeologists excavated the palace of Ashurbanipal (ah-shur-BAH-nee-pahl) (r. 668–627 B.C.E.), one of the last Assyrian kings, at Nineveh (NIN-uh-vuh), they discovered more than twenty-five thousand tablets or fragments. The **Library of Ashurbanipal** contained official documents as well as literary and

**Library of Ashurbanipal** A large collection of writings drawn from the ancient literary, religious, and scientific traditions of Mesopotamia. It was assembled by the seventh-century B.C.E. Assyrian ruler Ashurbanipal. The many tablets unearthed by archaeologists constitute one of the most important sources of present-day knowledge of the long literary tradition of Mesopotamia.

scientific texts. Some were originals that had been brought to the capital; others were copies made at the king's request. The "House of Knowledge" referred to in some documents may have been an academy that attracted learned men to the imperial center. Much of what we know about Mesopotamian art, literature, science, and earlier history comes from discoveries at Assyrian sites.

## ISRAEL, 2000–500 B.C.E.

■ *How did the civilization of Israel develop, following both familiar cultural patterns and a unique course of its own?*

The small land of Israel probably appeared insignificant to the Assyrian masters of western Asia, but it would play an important role in world history. Two interconnected dramas played out here between around 2000 and 500 B.C.E. First, a loose collection of nomadic groups engaged in herding and caravan traffic became a sedentary, agricultural people, developed complex political and social institutions, and became integrated into the commercial and diplomatic networks of the Middle East. Second, these people transformed the austere cult of a desert god into the concept of a single, all-powerful, and all-knowing deity, in the process creating ethical and intellectual traditions that underlie the beliefs and values of Judaism, Christianity, and Islam.

The land and people at the heart of this story have gone by various names: Canaan, Israel, Palestine; Hebrews, Israelites, Jews. For the sake of consistency, the people are referred to here as *Israelites*, the land they occupied in antiquity as **Israel**.

Israel is a crossroads linking Anatolia, Egypt, Arabia, and Mesopotamia. Its natural resources are few. The Negev Desert and the vast wasteland of the Sinai (SIE-nie) lie to the south. The Mediterranean coastal plain was in the hands of others, particularly the Philistines, throughout much of this period. Galilee to the north, with its sea of the same name, was a relatively fertile land of grassy hills and small plains. The narrow ribbon of the Jordan River runs down the eastern side of the region into the Dead Sea, so named because its high salt content is toxic to life.

## Origins, Exodus, and Settlement

The fundamental source of information about ancient Israel is the collection of writings preserved in the **Hebrew Bible** (called the Old Testament by Christians). The Hebrew Bible brings together several collections of materials that originated with different groups and advocated particular interpretations of past events. Traditions about the Israelites' early history were long transmitted orally. Not until the tenth century B.C.E. were they written down in a script borrowed from the Phoenicians. The text that we have today dates from the fifth century B.C.E., with a few later additions, and reflects the point of view of the priests who controlled the Temple in Jerusalem. The Hebrew language of the Bible reflects the speech of the Israelites until about 500 B.C.E., when it was supplanted by Aramaic. Historians disagree about how accurately this document represents Israelite history. However, it provides a foundation to be used critically and tested against archaeological discoveries.

The history of ancient Israel follows a familiar pattern in the ancient Middle East. Nomadic pastoralists, occupying marginal land between the inhospitable desert and settled agricultural areas, sometimes engaged in trade and sometimes raided the farms and villages of settled peoples, but eventually they settled down to an agricultural way of life and later developed a unified state.

The Hebrew Bible tells the story of Abraham and his descendants. Born in the city of Ur in southern Mesopotamia, Abraham rejected the idol worship of his homeland and migrated with his family and livestock across the Syrian desert. Eventually he arrived in the land of Israel, which had been promised to him and his descendants by the Israelite god, Yahweh.

**Israel** In antiquity, the land between the eastern shore of the Mediterranean and the Jordan River, occupied by the Israelites from the early second millennium B.C.E. The modern state of Israel was founded in 1948.

**Hebrew Bible** A collection of sacred books containing diverse materials concerning the origins, experiences, beliefs, and practices of the Israelites. Most of the extant text was compiled by members of the priestly class in the fifth century B.C.E. and reflects the concerns and views of this group.

These "recollections" of the journey of Abraham (who, if he was a real person, probably lived around 1800 B.C.E.) may compress the experiences of generations of pastoralists who migrated from the grazing lands between the upper reaches of the Tigris and Euphrates Rivers to the Mediterranean coastal plain. They camped by a permanent water source in the dry season and drove herds of sheep, cattle, and donkeys to a well-established sequence of grazing areas during the rest of the year. The animals provided them with milk, cheese, meat, and cloth.

The nomadic Israelites and the settled peoples were suspicious of one another. This friction between herders and farmers permeates the story of the innocent shepherd Abel, who was killed by his farmer brother Cain.

Abraham's son Isaac and then his grandson Jacob became the leaders of this migratory group of herders. In the next generation the squabbling sons of Jacob's several wives sold their brother Joseph as a slave to passing merchants heading for Egypt. Through luck and ability Joseph became a high official at the pharaoh's court. Thus he was in a position to help his people when drought struck and forced the Israelites to migrate to Egypt. The sophisticated Egyptians looked down on these rough herders and eventually enslaved them and put them to work on royal building projects.

Several points need to be made about this biblical account. First, the Israelite migration to Egypt and later enslavement may have been connected to the rise and fall of the Hyksos. Second, although surviving Egyptian sources do not refer to Israelite slaves, they do complain about Apiru (uh-PEE-roo), a derogatory term applied to caravan drivers, outcasts, bandits, and other marginal groups. Some scholars believe there may be a connection between the similar-sounding terms *Apiru* and *Hebrew*. Third, the period of alleged Israelite slavery coincided with the ambitious building programs launched by several New Kingdom pharaohs. However, there is little archaeological evidence of an Israelite presence in Egypt.

The Bible further relates that Moses, an Israelite with connections to the Egyptian royal family, led the Israelites out of captivity. The narrative of their departure, the Exodus, is overlaid with folktale motifs, including the ten plagues that Yahweh

inflicted on Egypt to persuade the pharaoh to release the Israelites, and the miraculous parting of the waters of the Red Sea that enabled the refugees to escape. Oral tradition may have embellished memories of a real emigration from Egypt followed by years of wandering in the wilderness of Sinai.

During their reported forty years in the desert, the Israelites entered into a "covenant" or pact with their god, Yahweh: they would be his "Chosen People" if they promised to worship him exclusively. This pact was confirmed by tablets that Moses brought down from the top of Mount Sinai, inscribed with the Ten Commandments that set out the basic tenets of Jewish belief and practice. The Commandments prohibited murder, adultery, theft, lying, and envy and demanded respect for parents and rest from work on the Sabbath, the seventh day of the week.

Joshua, Moses's successor, led the Israelites from the east side of the Jordan River into the land of Canaan (KAY-nuhn) (modern Israel and the Palestinian territories), where they attacked and destroyed Canaanite (KAY-nuh-nite) cities. Archaeological evidence confirms the destruction of some Canaanite towns between 1250 and 1200 B.C.E., though not precisely the towns mentioned in the biblical account. Shortly thereafter, lowland sites were resettled and new sites were established in the hills. The material culture of the new settlers was cruder but continued Canaanite patterns.

Most scholars doubt that Canaan was conquered by a unified Israelite army. In a time of widespread disruption, movements of peoples, and decline and destruction of cities throughout this region, it is more likely that Israelite migrants took advantage of the disorder and were joined by other groups and even refugees from the Canaanite cities.

In a pattern common throughout history, the new coalition of peoples invented a common ancestry. The "Children of Israel," as they called themselves, were divided into twelve tribes supposedly descended from the sons of Jacob and Joseph. Each tribe was installed in a different part of the country. Its chief was primarily responsible for mediating disputes and safeguarding the group. Charismatic figures, famed for their daring in war or genius in arbitration, were called "Judges" and enjoyed a special standing that transcended tribal boundaries. The tribes also shared access to a shrine

**The Western Wall in Jerusalem** The sole remaining remnant of King Herod's magnificent Second Temple, the religious center of ancient Judaism. It replaced Solomon's Temple, destroyed in the Babylonian conquest of 586 B.C.E., but was destroyed by the Romans in 70 C.E. in the course of suppressing a revolt in Judaea. The site is also sacred to Islam, with the golden Dome of the Rock in the background.

Protasov AN/Shutterstock.com

in the hill country at Shiloh (SHIE-loe), which housed the Ark of the Covenant, a sacred chest containing the tablets that Yahweh had given Moses.

### Rise of the Monarchy

The troubles afflicting the eastern Mediterranean around 1200 B.C.E. also brought the Philistines to the coastal plain of Israel, where they came into frequent conflict with the Israelites. The long-haired strongman Samson, who toppled a Philistine temple, and the shepherd boy David, whose sling felled the towering warrior Goliath, became biblical heroes. A religious leader named Samuel recognized the need for a strong central authority and anointed Saul as the first king of Israel around 1020 B.C.E. When Saul perished in battle, the throne passed to David (r. ca. 1000–960 B.C.E.), who oversaw Israel's transition from tribal confederacy to unified monarchy. He strengthened royal authority by making the captured hill city of Jerusalem his capital. Soon after, David brought the Ark to Jerusalem, making the city the religious as well as political center of the kingdom.

The reign of David's son Solomon (r. ca. 960–920 B.C.E.) marked the high point of the Israelite monarchy. Alliances and trade linked Israel with near and distant lands. Solomon and Hiram, the king of Phoenician Tyre, dispatched a fleet into the Red Sea to bring back gold, ivory, jewels, sandalwood, and exotic animals. The story of the visit to Solomon by the queen of Sheba may be mythical, but it reflects the reality of trade with Saba (SUH-buh) in south Arabia (present-day Yemen) or the Horn of Africa (present-day Somalia). Such wealth supported a lavish court life, a sizable bureaucracy, and an intimidating chariot army that made Israel a regional power. Solomon undertook an ambitious building program employing slaves and the compulsory labor of citizens. To strengthen the link between religious and secular authority, he built the **First Temple** in Jerusalem.

The Temple priests became a powerful and wealthy class, receiving a share of the annual harvest in return for making animal sacrifices to Yahweh. The expansion of Jerusalem, new commercial opportunities, and the increasing prestige of the Temple hierarchy contributed to a growing gap between urban and rural, rich and poor. Fiery prophets, claiming revelation from Yahweh, accused the monarchs and aristocracy of corruption, impiety, and neglect of the poor.

**First Temple** A monumental sanctuary built in Jerusalem by King Solomon in the tenth century B.C.E. to be the religious center for the Israelite god Yahweh. The Temple priesthood conducted sacrifices, received a tithe or percentage of agricultural revenues, and became economically and politically powerful.

The Israelites lived in extended families, several generations residing together under the authority of the eldest male. Male heirs were of paramount importance, and first-born sons received a double share of the inheritance. If a couple had no son, they could adopt one, or the husband could have a child by the wife's slave attendant. If a man died childless, his brother was expected to marry his widow and sire an heir.

Women provided the family with vital goods and services, but they could not inherit property or initiate divorce. An unfaithful wife could be put to death. Peasant women labored with other family members in agriculture or herding in addition to caring for the house and children. As the society became urbanized, some women worked outside the home as cooks, perfumers, wet nurses (a recent mother hired to suckle another person's child), prostitutes, and singers of laments at funerals. A few women reached positions of power, such as Deborah the Judge, who led troops in battle against the Canaanites. "Wise women" composed sacred texts in poetry and prose. This reality has been obscured, in part by the male bias of the Hebrew Bible, in part because the status of women declined as Israelite society became more urbanized.

## Fragmentation and Dispersal

After Solomon's death around 920 B.C.E., resentment over royal demands and the neglect of tribal rights split the monarchy into two kingdoms: Israel in the north, with its capital at Samaria (suh-MAH-ree-yuh); and Judah (JOO-duh) in the southern territory around Jerusalem. The two were sometimes at war, sometimes allied.

This period saw the final formulation of **monotheism**, the belief in Yahweh as the one and only god. Nevertheless, many Israelites were attracted to the ecstatic rituals of the Canaanite storm-god Baal (BAHL) and the fertility goddess Asherah (uh-SHARE-uh). Prophets condemned the adoption of foreign ritual and threatened that Yahweh would punish Israel severely.

The two Israelite kingdoms and other small states in the region laid aside their rivalries to mount a joint resistance to the Neo-Assyrian Empire, but to no avail. In 721 B.C.E. the Assyrians destroyed the northern kingdom of Israel and deported much of its

### SECTION REVIEW

- As the Hebrew Bible suggests, the Israelites began as nomadic pastoralists who, after a period of enslavement, settled permanently in Canaan.
- Pressure from hostile Philistines forced the Israelites to adopt a more complex government.
- The resulting monarchy unified the Israelites into the kingdom of Israel, which reached its height under Solomon.
- During the monarchy, the temple priests became a powerful class, and Israelite society became more urban and economically divided.
- Patrilineal extended families became the basic social unit, and the status of women declined.
- After the breakup of Israel, Jewish monotheism reached its final form, successive conquests created the Diaspora, and a distinctive Jewish identity emerged.

population to the east. New settlers were brought in from Syria, Babylon, and Iran, changing the area's ethnic, cultural, and religious character. The kingdom of Judah survived more than a century, sometimes rebelling, sometimes paying tribute to the Assyrians or the Neo-Babylonian kingdom (626–539 B.C.E.) that succeeded them.

When the Neo-Babylonian monarch Nebuchadnezzar (NAB-oo-kuhd-nez-uhr) captured Jerusalem in 587 B.C.E., he destroyed the Temple and deported to Babylon the royal family, the aristocracy, and many skilled workers such as blacksmiths and scribes. The deportees prospered so well in their new home "by the waters of Babylon" that half a century later most of their descendants refused the offer of the Persian monarch Cyrus (see Chapter 3) to return to their homeland. This was the origin of the **Diaspora** (die-ASS-peh-rah)—a Greek word meaning "dispersion" or "scattering." This dispersion outside the homeland of

**monotheism** Belief in the existence of a single divine entity. Some scholars cite the devotion of the Egyptian pharaoh Akhenaten to Aten (sun-disk) and his suppression of traditional gods as the earliest instance. The Israelite worship of Yahweh developed into an exclusive belief in one god, and this concept passed into Christianity and Islam.

**Diaspora** Greek word meaning "dispersal," used to describe the communities of a given ethnic group living outside their homeland. Jews, for example, spread from Israel to western Asia and Mediterranean lands in antiquity and today can be found throughout the world.

many Jews—as we may now call these people, since an independent Israel no longer existed—continues to this day. To maintain their religion and culture, the Diaspora communities developed institutions like the synagogue (Greek for "bringing together"), a communal meeting place that served religious, educational, and social functions.

The Babylonian Jews who did make the long trek back to Judah met with a cold reception from the local population. Persevering, they rebuilt the Temple in modest form and edited the Hebrew Bible into roughly its present form.

Exile and loss of political autonomy sharpened Jewish identity. Jews lived by a rigid set of rules. Dietary restrictions forbade the eating of pork and shellfish and mandated that meat and dairy products not be consumed together. Ritual baths were used to achieve spiritual purity. The Jews venerated the Sabbath (Saturday, the seventh day of the week) by refraining from work and from fighting, following the example of Yahweh, who, according to the Bible, rested on the seventh day after creating the world. These strictures and others, including a ban on marrying non-Jews, tended to isolate the Jews from other peoples, but they also fostered a powerful sense of community.

# PHOENICIA AND THE MEDITERRANEAN, 1200–500 B.C.E.

■ *How did the Phoenicians rise to commercial dominance over much of the Mediterranean world?*

While the Israelites were forging a united kingdom, the people who occupied the Mediterranean coast to the north were developing their own distinctive **Phoenician** (fi-NEE-shun) civilization. Historians generally used this Greek word instead of *Can'ani*—Canaanites—the word they used for themselves.

### The Phoenician City-States

Many Canaanite settlements were destroyed during the violent upheavals and mass migrations around 1200 B.C.E. discussed earlier. Aramaeans (ah-ruh-MAY-uhn)—nomadic pastoralists like the early Israelites—migrated into the interior portions of Syria while Israelites and Philistines gained domination farther south.

By 1100 B.C.E. Canaanite territory had shrunk to a narrow strip of Lebanon between the mountains and the sea. New political forms and seaborne commerce provided the key to Canaanite survival. Sometime after 1000 B.C.E. the Canaanites encountered the Greeks, who referred to them as *Phoinikes*, or Phoenicians. The term may mean "red men" and refer to the color of their skin, or it may refer to the precious purple dye they extracted from the murex snail (see Environment and Technology: Ancient Textiles and Dyes).

Rivers and rocky spurs sliced the Lebanese coastal plain into a series of small city-states, chief among them Byblos (BIB-loss), Sidon (SIE-duhn), and Tyre. Trading raw materials (cedar and pine, metals, incense, papyrus), foodstuffs (wine, spices, salted fish), and crafted luxury goods (textiles, carved ivory, glass) brought wealth and influence to the Phoenician city-states.

### Expansion into the Mediterranean

Before 1000 B.C.E. Byblos was the most important Phoenician city-state. The English word *bible* comes from the Greek *biblion*, meaning "book written on papyrus from Byblos." The Greeks recognized the Phoenicians as the inventors of the alphabet, which used about two dozen symbols, each representing a sound. (The Greeks later added symbols for vowel sounds—see Chapter 4.) Little Phoenician writing survives, however, probably because scribes used perishable papyrus. As a result, little is known about the internal affairs of the Phoenician cities beyond the names of some kings.

After 1000 B.C.E. Tyre surpassed Byblos. Located on an offshore island, Tyre was practically impregnable. It had two harbors—one facing north, the other south—that were connected by a canal. The city boasted a large marketplace, a magnificent palace complex with treasury and archives, and temples to the gods Melqart (MEL-kahrt) and Astarte (uh-STAHR-tee). Some of its

> **Phoenicians** Canaanites living on the coast of modern Lebanon and Syria in the first millennium B.C.E. From major cities such as Tyre and Sidon, Phoenician merchants and sailors explored the Mediterranean, engaged in widespread commerce, and founded Carthage and other colonies in the western Mediterranean.

# environment & technology

## Ancient Textiles and Dyes

Throughout human history the production of textiles—cloth for clothing, blankets, carpets, and coverings of various sorts—required an expenditure of human labor second only to the work necessary to provide food. Nevertheless, textile production in antiquity has left few archaeological traces. The plant fibers and animal hair used for cloth quickly decompose except in rare circumstances. Some textile remains have been found in the hot, dry conditions of Egypt, the cool, arid Andes of South America, and the peat bogs of northern Europe. But most of our knowledge of ancient textiles depends on the discovery of equipment used in textile production—such as spindles, loom weights, and dyeing vats—and on pictorial representations and descriptions in texts.

Cloth production usually has been the work of women for a simple but important reason: responsibility for child rearing limits women's ability to participate in other activities but does not consume all their time and energy. In many societies textile production has been complementary to child-rearing activities, for it can be done in the home, is relatively safe, does not require great concentration, and can be interrupted without consequence. The growing and harvesting of plants such as cotton or flax (from which linen is made) and the shearing of wool from sheep and, in the Andes, llamas are outdoor activities, but the subsequent stages of production can be carried out inside the home. The basic methods of textile production did not change much from early antiquity until the late eighteenth century C.E., when the fabrication of textiles was transferred to mills and mass production began.

When textile production has been considered "women's work," most of the output has been for household consumption. However, women weavers in Peru developed new raw materials, new techniques, and new decorative motifs around three thousand years ago. They began to use the wool of llamas and alpacas in addition to cotton. Three women worked side by side and passed the weft from hand to hand in order to produce a fabric of greater width. Women weavers also introduced embroidery and decorated garments with new religious motifs, such as the jaguar-god. Their high-quality textiles were given as tribute to the elite and were used to trade for luxury goods.

More typically, men dominated commercial production. In ancient Phoenicia, fine textiles with bright, permanent colors became a major export product. Most prized was the red-purple known as Tyrian purple because Tyre was the major source. Persian and Hellenistic kings wore robes dyed this color, and a white toga with a purple border was the sign of a Roman senator.

The production of Tyrian purple was an exceedingly laborious process. The spiny dye-murex snail lives on the sandy Mediterranean bottom at depths ranging from 30 to 500 feet (10 to 150 meters). Nine thousand snails were needed to produce 1 gram (0.035 ounce) of dye. The dye was made from a colorless liquid in the snail's hypobranchial gland. The gland sacs were removed, crushed, soaked with salt, and exposed to sunlight and air for some days; then they were subject to controlled boiling and heating.

Huge mounds of broken shells on the Phoenician coast are testimony to the ancient industry. The snail may have been rendered nearly extinct at many locations, and some scholars speculate that Phoenician colonization in the Mediterranean was motivated in part by the search for new sources of snails.

**Scythian Felt Cloth from Pazyryk, ca. 500 B.C.E.** *Found in a subterranean tomb in Siberia, the textile was preserved by the permafrost. It depicts a winged figure with a human upper body and antlers.*

Felt decoration depicting a fenix/Hermitage, St. Petersburg, Russia/De Agostini Picture Library/A. Dagli Orti/The Bridgeman Art Library

**Map 2.2 Colonization of the Mediterranean** In the ninth century B.C.E., the Phoenicians of Lebanon began to explore and colonize parts of the western Mediterranean, including the coast of North Africa, southern and eastern Spain, and the islands of Sicily and Sardinia. The Phoenicians were primarily interested in access to valuable raw materials and trading opportunities. © Cengage Learning

thirty thousand inhabitants lived in suburbs on the mainland. Its one weakness was its dependence on the mainland for food and fresh water.

After 900 B.C.E. Tyre turned its attention westward, establishing colonies on Cyprus, a copper-rich island 100 miles (161 kilometers) from the Syrian coast (see Map 2.2). By 700 B.C.E. a string of settlements in the western Mediterranean formed a "Phoenician triangle" composed of the North African coast from western Libya to Morocco; the south and southeast coast of Spain, including Gades (GAH-days) (modern Cadiz [kuh-DEEZ]) on the Strait of Gibraltar, controlling passage between the Mediterranean and the Atlantic Ocean; and the islands of Sardinia, Sicily, and Malta off the coast of Italy (see Map 2.2). Many settlements were situated on promontories or offshore islands in imitation of Tyre. The Phoenician trading network spanned the entire Mediterranean.

Frequent and destructive Assyrian invasions of Syria-Palestine and the lack of arable land to feed a swelling population probably motivated Tyrian expansion. Overseas settlement provided an outlet for excess population, new sources of trade goods, and new trading partners. Tyre maintained its autonomy until 701 B.C.E. by paying tribute to the Assyrian kings. In that year it finally fell to an Assyrian army that stripped it of much of its territory and population, allowing Sidon to become the leading city in Phoenicia.

## Carthage's Commercial Empire

Thanks to Greek and Roman reports about their wars, historians know more about **Carthage** and the other Phoenician

**Carthage** City located in present-day Tunisia, founded by Phoenicians around 800 B.C.E. It became a major commercial center and naval power in the western Mediterranean until defeated by Rome in the third century B.C.E.

colonies than they do about the Phoenician home-land. For example, the account of the origins of Carthage that begins this chapter comes from Roman sources but probably is based on a Carthaginian original. Archaeological excavation has roughly confirmed the city's traditional foundation date of 814 B.C.E. The new settlement grew rapidly and soon dominated other Phoenician colonies in the west.

Located just outside the present-day city of Tunis in Tunisia, on a promontory jutting into the Mediterranean, Carthage stretched between the original hilltop citadel and a double harbor. The inner harbor could accommodate 220 warships. A watchtower allowed surveillance of the surrounding area, and high walls made it impossible to see in from the outside. The outer commercial harbor was filled with docks for merchant ships and shipyards. In case of attack, the harbor could be closed off by a huge iron chain.

Government offices ringed a large central square where magistrates heard legal cases outdoors. The inner city was a maze of narrow, winding streets, multistory apartment buildings, and sacred enclosures. Farther out lay a sprawling suburban district where the wealthy built spacious villas amid fields and vegetable gardens. This entire urban complex was enclosed by a wall 22 miles (35 kilometers) in length. At the most critical point—the 2–1/2-mile-wide (4-kilometer) isthmus connecting the promontory to the mainland—the wall was over 40 feet (13 meters) high and 30 feet (10 meters) thick and had high watchtowers.

With a population of roughly 400,000, Carthage was one of the largest cities in the world by 500 B.C.E. The population was ethnically diverse, including people of Phoenician stock, indigenous peoples ancestral to modern-day Berbers, and immigrants from other Mediterranean lands and sub-Saharan Africa. The Phoenicians readily intermarried with other peoples.

Each year two "judges" were elected from upper-class families to serve as heads of state and carry out administrative and judicial functions. The real seat of power was the Senate, where members of the leading merchant families, who sat for life, directed the affairs of the state. An inner circle of thirty or so senators made the crucial decisions. The leadership occasionally convened an Assembly of the citizens to elect public officials or vote on important issues, particularly when they were divided or wanted to stir up popular enthusiasm for some venture.

There is little evidence at Carthage of the kind of social and political unrest that plagued Greece and Rome. A merchant aristocracy (unlike an aristocracy of birth) was not a closed group, and a climate of economic and social mobility allowed newly successful families and individuals to push their way into the circle of influential citizens. The ruling class also made sure that everyone benefited from the riches of empire.

Carthaginian power rested on its navy, which dominated the western Mediterranean for centuries. Phoenician towns provided a network of friendly ports. The Carthaginian fleet consisted of fast, maneuverable galleys (oared warships). Each bore a sturdy, pointed ram in front that could pierce the hull of an enemy vessel below the water line, while marines (soldiers aboard a ship) fired weapons. Innovations in the placement of benches and oars eventually made room for as many as 170 rowers.

Carthaginian foreign policy, reflecting the economic interests of the dominant merchant class, focused on protecting the sea lanes, gaining access to raw materials, and fostering trade. Foreign merchants were free to sail to Carthage to market their goods, but if they tried to operate elsewhere on their own, they risked having their ships sunk by the Carthaginian navy. Treaties between Carthage and other states included formal recognition of this maritime commercial monopoly.

The archaeological record provides few clues about the commodities traded by the Carthaginians. These may have included perishable goods—foodstuffs, textiles, animal skins, slaves—and raw metals whose Carthaginian origin would not be evident. Carthaginian ships carried goods manufactured elsewhere, and products brought to Carthage by foreign traders were re-exported.

There is also evidence for trade with sub-Saharan Africa. Hanno (HA-noe), a Carthaginian captain of the fifth century B.C.E., claimed to have sailed through the Strait of Gibraltar into the Atlantic Ocean

**The Tophet of Carthage** Here, from the seventh to second centuries B.C.E., the cremated bodies of sacrificed children were buried. Archaeological excavation has confirmed the claim in ancient sources that the Carthaginians sacrificed children to their gods at times of crisis. Stone markers, decorated with magical signs and symbols of divinities as well as family names, were placed over ceramic urns containing the ashes and charred bones of one or more infants or, occasionally, older children.

Werner Forman Archive/Glow Images

and to have explored the West African coast (see Map 2.2). Other Carthaginians explored the Atlantic coast of Spain and France and secured control of an important source of tin in the "Tin Islands," probably Cornwall in southwestern England.

### War and Religion

Carthage did not directly rule a large territory. A belt of fertile land in northeastern Tunisia, owned by Carthaginians but worked by native peasants and imported slaves, provided a secure food supply. Beyond this core area the Carthaginians ruled most of their "empire" indirectly and allowed other Phoenician communities in the western Mediterranean to remain independent. These communities looked to Carthage for military protection and followed its lead in foreign policy. Only Sardinia and southern Spain came under the control of a Carthaginian governor and garrison, presumably to safeguard their resources.

Trade may explain the unusual fact that citizens were not required to serve in the army: they were of more value as traders and sailors. Another sign that war was not the primary business of the state was the separation of military command from civilian government. Generals were chosen by the Senate and kept in office for as long as they were needed. Since the indigenous North African population was not politically or militarily well organized, Carthage had little to fear close to home. When Carthage was drawn into a series of wars with the Greeks and Romans from the fifth through third centuries B.C.E., it relied on mercenaries from the most warlike peoples in its dominions or from neighboring areas. These well-paid mercenaries were under the command of Carthaginian officers.

Like the deities of Mesopotamia (see Chapter 1), the Carthaginian gods—chief among them Baal Hammon (BAHL ha-MOHN), a male storm-god, and Tanit (TAH-nit), a female fertility figure—were powerful and capricious entities. Roman sources report that members of the Carthaginian elite would sacrifice their own male children in times of crisis. Excavations at Carthage and other western Phoenician towns have turned up *tophets* (TOE-fet)—walled enclosures with thousands of small, sealed urns containing the burned bones of children. Originally practiced by the upper classes, child sacrifice became more common and involved broader elements of the population after 400 B.C.E.

Plutarch (PLOO-tawrk), a Greek who lived around 100 C.E., long after the demise of Carthage, wrote the following on the basis of earlier sources:

> The Carthaginians are a hard and gloomy people, submissive to their rulers and harsh to their subjects, running to extremes of cowardice in times of fear and of cruelty in times of anger; they keep obstinately to their decisions, are austere, and care little for amusement or the graces of life.[1]

We should not take the hostile opinions of Greek and Roman sources at face value. Still, it is clear that the Carthaginians were perceived as different and that cultural barriers, leading to misunderstanding and prejudice, played a significant role in ongoing conflicts. The struggle between Carthage and Rome for control of the western Mediterranean was especially protracted and bloody (see Chapter 5).

# FAILURE AND TRANSFORMATION, 750–550 B.C.E.

■ *What factors prompted the transformation of the ancient Middle East between 750 and 550 B.C.E.?*

The extension of Assyrian power over the entire Middle East had enormous consequences for all the

peoples of the region and caused the stories of Mesopotamia, Israel, and Phoenicia to converge. In 721 B.C.E. the Assyrians destroyed the northern kingdom of Israel, and for over a century the southern kingdom of Judah faced relentless pressure. Assyrian threats spurred the Phoenicians to colonize and exploit the western Mediterranean. Even Egypt, for so long impregnable behind its desert barriers, fell to Assyrian invaders in the mid-seventh century B.C.E.

Closer to the Assyrian homeland, the southern plains of Sumer and Akkad, the birthplace of Mesopotamian civilization, were reduced to a protectorate, while Babylon was alternately razed and rebuilt by Assyrian kings. Urartu and Elam, Assyria's great power rivals, were destroyed. By 650 B.C.E. Assyria stood supreme in western Asia. But the arms race with Urartu, the frequent expensive campaigns, and the protection of lengthy borders sapped Assyrian resources. Brutality and exploitation aroused the hatred of conquered peoples. At the same time, changes in the ethnic composition of the army and the population of the homeland had reduced popular support for the Assyrian state.

Two new political entities spearheaded resistance to Assyria. First, Babylonia had been revived by the Neo-Babylonian, or Chaldaean (chal-DEE-uhn), dynasty (the Chaldaeans had infiltrated southern Mesopotamia around 1000 B.C.E.). Second, the Medes (MEED), an Iranian people, were extending their kingdom on the Iranian Plateau in the seventh century B.C.E. The two powers launched a series of attacks on the Assyrian homeland that destroyed the chief cities by 612 B.C.E.

The rapidity of the Assyrian fall was stunning, and the destruction systematically carried out by the vic-

---

[1] Plutarch, *Moralia*, 799 D, trans. B. H. Warmington, *Carthage* (Harmondsworth, England: Penguin, 1960), 163.

tors led to the depopulation of northern Mesopotamia. The Medes took over the Assyrian homeland and the northern plain as far as eastern Anatolia, but most of the territory of the old empire fell to the **Neo-Babylonian kingdom** (626–539 B.C.E.), thanks to the energetic campaigns of kings Nabopolassar (NAB-oh-poe-lass-uhr) (r. 625–605 B.C.E.) and Nebuchadnezzar (NEB-uh-kuh-nez-uhr) (r. 604–562 B.C.E.). Babylonia underwent a cultural renaissance, pursuing mathematics, astronomy, and astrology, resurrecting old cults and festivals, rebuilding temples, and ultimately becoming the greatest metropolis of the sixth-century B.C.E. world.

## CONCLUSION

The Late Bronze Age in the Middle East was a "cosmopolitan" era of shared lifestyles and technologies. Besides the already ancient river-valley kingdoms, the period from 2000 to 500 B.C.E. saw two kinds of societies emerge in the Middle East and the Mediterranean world. One was small kingdoms like Israel and Minoan Crete or even city-states like those of Phoenicia and Carthage that lived from trade rather than tribute. These small states and societies were vulnerable to attack by larger, more powerful neighbors, and sometimes they succumbed. Yet just as often, they survived or reappeared. The other kind of kingdom was the great and powerful Assyrian Empire, which used advanced military tactics and weapons, and sheer brutality, to conquer and exploit an area of unprecedented size and diversity. The far-reaching expansion and the subsequent rapid fall of the Assyrian Empire were the most important factors in the transformation of the ancient Middle East.

> **Neo-Babylonian kingdom**   Under the Chaldaeans (nomadic kinship groups that settled in southern Mesopotamia in the early first millennium B.C.E.), Babylon again became a major political and cultural center in the seventh and sixth centuries B.C.E. After participating in the destruction of Assyrian power, the monarchs Nabopolassar and Nebuchadnezzar took over the southern portion of the Assyrian domains.

## CHAPTER REVIEW

### THE COSMOPOLITAN MIDDLE EAST, 1700–1100 B.C.E.

■ *How did a cosmopolitan civilization develop in the Middle East during the Late Bronze Age, and what forms did it take?* (page 30)

Historians have called the Late Bronze Age a "cosmopolitan" era, meaning a time of widely shared cultures and lifestyles. The cultural patterns that originated in the river-valley civilizations of Egypt and Mesopotamia persisted into this era. Peoples such as the Amorites, Kassites, and Chaldaeans, who migrated into the Tigris-Euphrates plain, adopted its language, religious beliefs, political and social institutions, and forms of artistic expression. Similarly, the Hyksos, who migrated into the Nile Delta and controlled much of Egypt for a time, adopted the ancient ways of Egypt. When the founders of the New Kingdom finally ended Hyksos domination, they reinstituted the united monarchy and the religious and cultural traditions of earlier eras.

### THE AEGEAN WORLD, 2000–1100 B.C.E.

■ *What civilizations emerged in the Aegean world, and what relationship did they have to the older civilizations to the east?* (page 36)

The Late Bronze Age expansion of commerce and communication stimulated the emergence of new civilizations, including those of the Minoans and Mycenaean

Greeks in the Aegean Sea. These civilizations borrowed heavily from the technologies and cultural practices of Mesopotamia and Egypt, creating dynamic syntheses of imported and indigenous elements. Cretan art and architecture display the wide range of cultural influences from the Minoans' extensive trading contacts, as well as the unique forms of Minoan civilization. The Mycenaean Greeks built their own civilization under the influence of Minoan Crete, and their palaces served as centers for crafts, trade, and administrative record keeping. Trade brought the Mycenaeans, like the Minoans, into steady contact with older eastern civilizations.

## THE ASSYRIAN EMPIRE, 911–612 B.C.E.

■ *How did the Assyrian Empire rise to power and eventually dominate most of the ancient Middle East?* (page 40)

Ultimately, the very interdependence of the societies of the Middle East and eastern Mediterranean made them vulnerable to the destructions and disorder of the decades around 1200 B.C.E. The entire region slipped into a "Dark Age" of isolation, stagnation, and decline that lasted several centuries. The early centuries after 1000 B.C.E. saw a resurgence of political organization and international commerce, as well as the spread of technologies and ideas. The Neo-Assyrian Empire, the great power of the time, represented a continuation of the Mesopotamian tradition, though the center of empire moved to the north. The king wielded supreme authority in all areas, and state propaganda presented him as all-powerful and victorious. The Assyrians won control of their empire through superior organization and military technology and maintained it through terror and mass deportation of subject peoples. Assyrian social structure mirrored that of earlier Mesopotamian cultures, with most people working the land. Assyrian scholarship built on earlier traditions, and Ashurbanipal's library collected the literary and scientific heritage of Mesopotamia.

## ISRAEL, 2000–500 B.C.E.

■ *How did the civilization of Israel develop, following both familiar cultural patterns and a unique course of its own?* (page 43)

Our main textual source of information about the Israelites, the Hebrew Bible, must be reconciled with archaeological findings. It recounts that the Israelites began as nomadic pastoralists who wandered from Mesopotamia to the Mediterranean coastal plain and then to Egypt, where they suffered enslavement. During the Exodus, Yahweh and the Israelites entered into a covenant. The Israelites then settled permanently in Canaan, where they coalesced into a political federation, the "Children of Israel." Conflict with the Philistines forced them to adopt a more complex political structure. The resulting monarchy reached its height under Solomon, during whose reign the Temple priests rose to prominence and Israelite society grew more urban and economically stratified. After Solomon's death the kingdom divided into Israel and Judah, and the monotheism that Judaism would bequeath to the world reached its final form. While the long, slow evolution of the Israelites from wandering groups of herders to an agriculturally based monarchy followed a pattern common in ancient western Asia, the religious and ethical concepts that they formulated were unique and have had a powerful impact on world history.

## PHOENICIA AND THE MEDITERRANEAN, 1200–500 B.C.E.

■ *How did the Phoenicians rise to commercial dominance over much of the Mediterranean world?* (page 47)

After the upheavals of the Late Bronze Age, the Phoenician city-states along the coast of Lebanon flourished. Under pressure from the Neo-Assyrian Empire, the Phoenicians, with Tyre in the lead, began spreading westward into the Mediterranean. Carthage became the most important city outside the Phoenician homeland.

Ruled by leading merchant families, it extended its commercial empire throughout the western Mediterranean, maintaining power through naval superiority.

## FAILURE AND TRANSFORMATION, 750–550 B.C.E.

■ *What factors prompted the transformation of the ancient Middle East between 750 and 550 B.C.E.?* (page 52)

In their drive for empire, the Assyrians destroyed many older states and, directly or indirectly, displaced large numbers of people. Their brutality, as well as the population shifts that resulted from their deportations, undercut support for their state. The Chaldaeans and Medes led resistance to Assyrian rule, and the empire swiftly collapsed. This conquest led to the depopulation of northern Mesopotamia.

## Key Terms

Iron Age (p. 30)
Hittites (p. 32)
Hatshepsut (p. 33)
Akhenaten (p. 34)
Ramesses II (p. 35)
Minoan (p. 36)
Mycenae (p. 37)
shaft graves (p. 37)
Linear B (p. 37)
Neo-Assyrian Empire (p. 40)
mass deportation (p. 41)

Library of Ashurbanipal (p. 42)
Israel (p. 43)
Hebrew Bible (p. 43)
First Temple (p. 45)
monotheism (p. 46)
Diaspora (p. 46)
Phoenicians (p. 47)
Carthage (p. 49)
Neo-Babylonian kingdom (p. 53)

# New Civilizations in East Asia, Africa, and Europe

© Cengage Learning

Around 2200 B.C.E. an Egyptian official named Harkhuf (HAHR-koof), who lived at Aswan (AS-wahn) on the southern boundary of Egypt, set out on his fourth trek to a place called Yam, far to the south in the land that later came to be called Nubia. He brought gifts from the Egyptian pharaoh for the ruler of Yam, and he returned home with three hundred donkeyloads of incense, ebony, ivory, and other exotic products. Despite the diplomatic fiction of exchanging gifts, we should probably consider Harkhuf a trader; and the prize of his trip was so special that the eight-year-old boy pharaoh, Pepi II, could not contain his excitement. He wrote:

> Come north to the residence at once! Hurry and bring with you this pygmy whom you brought from the land of the horizon-dwellers live, hale, and healthy, for the dances of the god, to gladden the heart, to delight the heart of king Neferkare [Pepi] who lives forever! When he goes down with you into the ship, get worthy men to be around him on deck, lest he fall into the water! When he lies down at night, get worthy men to lie around him in his tent. Inspect ten times at night! My majesty desires to see this pygmy more than the gifts of the mine-land and of Punt![1]

Scholars identify Yam with Kerma, later the capital of the kingdom of Nubia, on the upper Nile in modern Sudan. For Egyptians, Nubia was a wild and dangerous place. But it was developing a more complex political organization that fostered trade with Egypt and tropical regions farther south (where pygmies would have lived).

In this chapter we bring into the picture parts of the world outside the largely self-sufficient older river-valley civilizations of Mesopotamia and Egypt and the newer Mediterranean civilizations that were shaped by networks of long-distance trade. The societies examined in this chapter emerged later in East Asia, sub-Saharan Africa, the Eurasian steppes, and continental Europe.

In the second millennium B.C.E. a civilization based on irrigation agriculture arose in the valley of the Yellow River and its tributaries in northern China. In the same epoch, in Nubia (southern Egypt and northern Sudan), the first complex society in tropical Africa continued to develop from the roots observed earlier by Harkhuf. The first millennium B.C.E. witnessed the rise of a new kind of nomadism on the Eurasian steppes and the spread of Celtic peoples across much of continental Europe. These societies had no contact with one another and represent a variety of responses to environmental and historical circumstances. However, they have certain features in common and collectively point to a distinct stage in the development of human societies.

## EARLY CHINA, 2000–221 B.C.E.

■ *How did early Chinese rulers use religion to justify and strengthen their power?*

On the eastern edge of the vast Eurasian landmass, Neolithic cultures developed as early as 8000 B.C.E., and a more complex civilization evolved in the second and first millennia B.C.E. Under the Shang and Zhou dynasties, many of the institutions and values of classical Chinese civilization emerged and spread south and west. As elsewhere, the rise of cities, specialization of labor, bureaucratic government, writing, and other advanced technologies depended on intensive agriculture along a great river system—the Yellow River (Huang He [hwahng-HUH]) and its tributaries.

**Geography and Resources** With mountains and deserts to the west and north making overland travel difficult and slow (see Map 3.1), the great river systems of eastern China—the Yellow and the Yangzi (yang-zuh) Rivers and their tributaries—provide the main axes of east-west movement. In the eastern river valleys dense populations practiced intensive agriculture; on the steppe lands of Mongolia, the deserts and oases of Xinjiang (shin-jyahng), and the high plateau of Tibet, sparser populations lived largely by herding. Within the eastern agricultural zone, the north and the south have strikingly different environments. Monsoons drench southern China with heavy rainfall in the summer,

[1] Quoted in Miriam Lichtheim, ed., *Ancient Egyptian Literature: A Book of Readings* (Berkeley: University of California Press, 1978).

**Map 3.1  China in the Shang and Zhou Periods, 1750–221 B.C.E.**  The Shang dynasty arose in the second millennium B.C.E. in the floodplain of the Yellow River. While southern China benefits from the monsoon rains, northern China depends on irrigation. As population increased, the Han Chinese migrated from their eastern homeland to other parts of China, carrying with them their technologies and cultural practices. Other ethnic groups predominated in more outlying regions, and the nomadic peoples of the northwest constantly challenged Chinese authority. © Cengage Learning

the most beneficial time for agriculture. Rainfall is more erratic in northern China. As in Mesopotamia, where civilization developed in relatively unfriendly environments, China's early history unfolded in the demanding environment of the northern plains. By the third century C.E., however, the gradual flow of population toward the warmer southern lands caused the political and intellectual center to move south.

Since prehistoric times, winds blowing from Central Asia had deposited a yellowish-brown dust called **loess** (less) on the North China Plain, creating an

abundance of potentially productive land (this dust suspended in the water gives the Yellow River its distinctive hue and name). The thick soil was extremely fertile and soft enough to be worked with wooden digging sticks. However, in some areas, forests had to be cleared; more importantly, recurrent floods on the Yellow River necessitated earthen dikes and overflow

> **loess**  A fine, light silt deposited by wind and water. It constitutes the fertile soil of the Yellow River Valley in northern China.

# Chronology

| | China | Eurasian Steppes | Celtic Europe | Nubia |
|---|---|---|---|---|
| **8000 B.C.E.** | **8000–2000 B.C.E.** Neolithic cultures | | | **4500 B.C.E.** Early agriculture in Nubia |
| **2500 B.C.E.** | | | | **2200 B.C.E.** Harkhuf's expeditions to Yam |
| **2000 B.C.E.** | **2000 B.C.E.** Bronze metallurgy <br><br> **1750–1045 B.C.E.** Shang dynasty | | | **1750 B.C.E.** Rise of kingdom of Kush based on Kerma |
| **1500 B.C.E.** | | | | **1500 B.C.E.** Egyptian conquest of Nubia |
| **1000 B.C.E.** | **1045–221 B.C.E.** Zhou dynasty <br><br><br><br><br><br> **600 B.C.E.** Iron metallurgy | **1000 B.C.E.** Initial development of pastoral nomadism <br><br><br><br><br><br> **700 B.C.E.** Scythians drive out Cimmerians and settle area north of Black Sea | **1000 B.C.E.** Origin of Celtic culture in central Europe <br> **1000 B.C.E.** Celtic elites trade for Mediterranean goods | **1000 B.C.E.** Decline of Egyptian control in Nubia <br><br><br> **750 B.C.E.** Rise of kingdom based on Napata <br> **712–660 B.C.E.** Nubian kings rule Egypt |
| **500 B.C.E.** | **551–479 B.C.E.** Life of Confucius <br><br><br><br><br><br><br><br><br> **221–206 B.C.E.** Legalism becomes philosophy of Qin Empire | **440 B.C.E.** Greek historian Herodotus reports on nomadic Scythians <br><br> **ca. 300 B.C.E.** Ruler of Chinese state of Zhao equips troops like nomad horsemen <br> **100 B.C.E.** Chinese historian Sima Qian describes Xiongnu nomads | **500–300 B.C.E.** Migrations across Europe <br><br><br> **390 B.C.E.** Celts sack Rome | **300 B.C.E.–350 C.E.** Kingdom of Meroë |

channels. In this landscape, agriculture demanded the coordinated efforts of large groups of people. To cope with the periodic droughts, catch basins (reser- voirs) were dug to store river water and rainfall. As the population grew, people built retaining walls to partition the hillsides into flat arable terraces.

**Shang Period Bronze Vessel** Vessels such as this large wine jar were used in rituals by the Shang ruling class to make contact with their ancestors. As both the source and the proof of the elite's authority, these vessels were often buried in Shang tombs. The complex shapes and elaborate decorations testify to the artisans' skill. Covered ritual 'Fang-yi' wine vessel with 'Tao-tie' motif, Shang Dynasty (cast bronze with grey patina), Chinese School, (12th century B.C.)/Arthur M. Sackler Museum, Harvard University Art Museums, USA/Bequest of Grenville L. Winthrop/The Bridgeman Art Library

The staple crops in the northern region were millet, a grain indigenous to China, and wheat, originally from the Middle East. Rice required a warmer climate and prospered in the south. The cultivation of rice in the Yangzi River Valley and the south required a great outlay of labor. Rice paddies—the fields where rice is grown—must be flat and surrounded by irrigation channels to bring or drain water according to

precise schedules. Seedlings sprout in a nursery and are transplanted one by one to the paddy, which is then flooded. Flooding eliminates weeds and rival plants and supports microscopic organisms that keep the soil fertile. When the crop is ripe, the paddy is drained; the rice stalks are harvested with a sickle; and the edible kernels are separated out. The reward for this effort is a harvest that can feed more people per cultivated acre than any other grain, which explains why the south eventually became more populous than the north.

Archaeological evidence shows that the Neolithic population of China grew millet, raised pigs and chickens, and used stone tools. They made pottery on a wheel and fired it in high-temperature kilns. They also pioneered silk production, first raising silkworms on mulberry trees, then unraveling their cocoon filaments to spin into thread. Lacking stone, they built walls by hammering soil inside temporary wooden frames until it became hard as cement. By 2000 B.C.E. they had begun casting bronze (roughly a thousand years after the Middle East Bronze Age).

Legends say that the ancient dynasty of the Xia (shah) ruled the core region of the Yellow River Valley. Some archeologists identify the Xia with the Neolithic Longshan cultural complex in the centuries before and after 2000 B.C.E. However, history proper begins with the rise of the **Shang** (shahng) clans, which coincides with the earliest written records.

### The Shang Period, 1750– 1045 B.C.E.

The Shang originated in the part of the Yellow River Valley that lies in the present-day province of Henan (heh-nahn). After 1750 B.C.E., they extended their control north into Mongolia, west as far as Gansu (gahn-soo), and south to the Yangzi River Valley. The warrior aristocracy that dominated Shang society reveled in warfare, hunting (for recreation and to fine-tune battle skills), exchanging gifts, and feasting.

**Shang** The dominant people in the earliest Chinese dynasty for which we have written records (ca. 1750–1045 B.C.E.).

The king ruled the core area of the Shang state directly, while aristocrats served as generals, ambassadors, and supervisors of public projects. Other members of the royal family and high-ranking nobility governed outlying provinces. The most distant regions were governed by native rulers who swore allegiance to the Shang king. The king was often on the road, traveling to the courts of his subordinates to reinforce their loyalty.

Frequent military campaigns, often against the nomadic people who occupied the steppe and desert regions to the north and west, occupied the warrior class and yielded considerable plunder. Prisoners of war taken in these campaigns served as slaves in the Shang capital.

The Shang kingdom had several capitals, the last and most important near modern Anyang (ahn-yahng) (see Map 3.1). Shang cities were centers of political control and religion. Surrounded by massive walls of pounded earth, they contained palaces, administrative buildings, storehouses, royal tombs, shrines of gods and ancestors, and housing for aristocrats. Commoners lived in agricultural villages outside these centers. Urban street grids aligned with the north star and gates opening to the cardinal directions demonstrate an ongoing Chinese concern with feng shui (fung shway), the spatial orientation of buildings according to a sense of cosmic order.

Writing was the key to effective administration. Pictograms (pictures representing objects and concepts) and phonetic symbols representing the sounds of syllables were combined to form a complex system of hundreds of signs. Only a small educated elite had the time to master this system. Despite substantial changes through the ages, the fundamental principles of the Chinese system still endure. As a result, people speaking languages that sound quite different, such as Mandarin and Cantonese, can read and understand the same text.

Shang ideology glorified the king as the intermediary between the people and Heaven. Shang religion also revered and made sacrifices to male ancestors, who were believed to be intensely interested in the fortunes of their descendants. Burials of kings entailed sacrifices, not only of animals but also of humans, including noble officials of the court, women, servants, soldiers, and prisoners of war.

Before taking any action, the Shang rulers used divination to determine the will of Heaven.

Bronze weapons and ritual vessels symbolized authority and nobility, and Shang tombs contain many such objects. The relatively modest tomb of one queen yielded 450 bronze articles (ritual vessels, bells, weapons, and mirrors)—remarkable because copper and tin, the principal ingredients of bronze, were not plentiful in northern China. (Also found in the same tomb were numerous objects of jade, bone, ivory, and stone, seven thousand cowrie shells, sixteen sacrificed men, women, and children, and six dogs!)

Finding and mining deposits of copper and tin, transporting the refined metal to the capital, and crafting these beautifully wrought weapons and vessels constituted a major Shang enterprise. Bronzesmiths working in foundries outside the main cities also made chariot fittings and musical instruments. Stylized depictions of real and imaginary animals were a favorite decorative theme.

Far-reaching networks of trade brought to the Shang jade, ivory, and mother of pearl (a hard, shiny substance from the interior of mollusk shells) used for jewelry, carved figurines, and decorative inlays. Some evidence suggests that Shang China may have exchanged goods and ideas with distant Mesopotamia. The horse-drawn chariot, which the Shang adopted from nomads of the northwest, became a formidable instrument of war.

## The Zhou Period, 1045–221 B.C.E.

Shang domination of central and northern China lasted more than six centuries. In the eleventh century B.C.E. the last Shang king was defeated by Wu, the ruler of **Zhou** (joe), a dependent state in the Wei (way) River Valley. The Zhou line of kings (ca. 1027–221 B.C.E.) was the longest lasting and most revered of all dynasties in Chinese history. The Zhou preserved the essentials of Shang culture and added new elements of ideology and technology.

**Zhou**  The people and dynasty that took over the dominant position in north China from the Shang and created the concept of the Mandate of Heaven to justify their rule. The Zhou era, particularly the vigorous early period (1045–771 B.C.E.), was remembered in Chinese tradition as a time of prosperity and benevolent rule.

To justify their seizure of power to the restive remnants of Shang clans, the early Zhou monarchs styled themselves "Sons of Heaven," and their rule was called the **Mandate of Heaven**. According to the new theory advanced by their propagandists, the supreme deity, known as Heaven, would support the king as long as he served as a wise, principled, and energetic guardian of the people. Prosperity and stability proved divine favor, but royal misbehavior, a fault attributed to the last Shang ruler, could forfeit Heaven's mandate. Corruption, violence, and insurrection were signs of divine displeasure.

The Zhou kings continued some of the Shang rituals, but there was a marked decline in the practice of divination and in extravagant sacrifices and burials. The priestly power of the ruling class, the only ones who had been able to make contact with the spirits of ancestors during the Shang period, faded away. The resulting separation of religion and government made way for the development of important philosophical and mystical systems. The bronze vessels that had been sacred implements in the Shang period now became family treasures.

The early period of Zhou rule, the eleventh through ninth centuries B.C.E., is sometimes called the Western Zhou era because of the location of the capitals in the western part of the kingdom. These centuries saw the development of a sophisticated administrative apparatus. The Zhou built a series of capital cities with pounded-earth foundations and walls. The major buildings all faced south, in keeping with the feng shui principles of harmonious relationship with the terrain, the forces of wind, water, and sunlight, and the invisible energy perceived to be flowing through the natural world. All government officials, including the king, were supposed to be models of morality, fairness, and concern for the welfare of the people.

Like the Shang, the Zhou regime was decentralized. Members and allies of the royal family ruled more than a hundred largely autonomous territories. Elaborate court ceremonials, embellished by music and dance, impressed on observers the glory of Zhou rule and reinforced the bonds of obligation between rulers and ruled.

Around 800 B.C.E. Zhou power began to wane. Ambitious local rulers operated ever more independently and waged war on one another, while nomadic peoples attacked the northwest frontiers (see Map 3.1). In 771 B.C.E. members of the Zhou lineage relocated to a new, more secure, eastern capital near Luoyang (LWOE-yahng), initiating the five-hundred-year Eastern Zhou era. There they continued to hold the royal title and receive at least nominal homage from the local rulers, the real power brokers of the age. Historians conventionally divide this period of political fragmentation, shifting centers of power, and fierce competition among numerous small states into the Spring and Autumn Period (771–481 B.C.E.), after a collection of chronicles that give annual entries for those two seasons, and the Warring States Period (from 480 to the unification of China in 221 B.C.E.).

Numerous competing kingdoms meant numerous capital cities, some of which became quite large. To the north, long walls of pounded earth were constructed, the ancestors of the Great Wall of China, to protect the kingdoms from each other and from nomads. Chinese armies adopted the nomad practice of putting fighters on horseback. The northwest nomads were probably also the source of the ironworking skills that led to iron replacing bronze as the primary metal for tools and weapons around 600 B.C.E. Bureaucracies in many states expanded their functions, composing law codes, collecting taxes directly, imposing monetary standards, and managing large-scale public works projects.

Eventually this activity led to a philosophy called **Legalism**, which argued that maintaining the

**Mandate of Heaven** Chinese religious and political ideology developed by the Zhou, according to which it was the prerogative of Heaven, the chief deity, to grant power to the ruler of China and to take away that power if the ruler failed to conduct himself justly and in the best interests of his subjects.

**Legalism** In China, a political philosophy that emphasized the unruliness of human nature and justified state coercion and control. The ruling class invoked it to validate the authoritarian nature of the regime and its profligate expenditure of subjects' lives and labor. It was later superseded by a more benevolent Confucian doctrine of governmental moderation.

wealth and power of the state justified an authoritarian political control. Legalists maintained that human nature is essentially wicked and that people behave properly only if compelled by strict laws and harsh punishments. They believed that every aspect of human society ought to be controlled and personal freedom sacrificed for the good of the state.

## Confucianism, Daoism, and Chinese Society

Bureaucratic government superseded aristocratic rule in some of the major Zhou states. To maintain their influence, aristocrats sought a new role as advisers to the rulers. Kongzi (kohng-zuh) (551–479 B.C.E.)—known in the West by the Latin form of his name, **Confucius**—lived through the political flux and social change of this anxious time. Coming from one of the smaller states, he had not been particularly successful in obtaining administrative posts. However, his doctrine of duty and public service, initially aimed at fellow aristocrats, was to become a central influence in Chinese thought.

Many elements in Confucius's teaching had roots in earlier Chinese belief, including folk religion and the rites of the Zhou royal family, such as the veneration of ancestors and elders and worship of the deity Heaven. Confucius drew a parallel between the family and the state. Just as the family is a hierarchy, with the father at its top, sons next, then wives and daughters in order of age, so too the state is a hierarchy, with the ruler at the top, the public officials as the sons, and the common people as the women.

Confucius took a traditional term for the feelings between family members, *ren (ruhn)* and expanded it into a universal ideal of benevolence toward all humanity, which he believed was the foundation of moral government. Government exists, he said, to serve the people, and the administrator or ruler gains respect and authority by displaying fairness and integrity. Confucian teachings emphasized benevolence, avoidance of violence, justice, rationalism, loyalty, and dignity.

Though Confucius had little influence in his own time, his later follower Mencius (Mengzi, 371–289 B.C.E.), who opposed despotism and argued against the authoritarian ideology of the Legalists, made the master's teachings much better known (see Diversity and Dominance: Human Nature and Good Government in the *Analects* of Confucius and the Legalist Writings of Han Fei). Confucianism eventually became the dominant political philosophy and the core of the educational system for government officials.

The Warring States Period also saw the rise of the school of thought known as Daoism. If Confucianism emphasized social engagement, its great rival, **Daoism (DOW-ism)**, urged withdrawal from the empty formalities, rigid hierarchy, and distractions of Chinese society. According to tradition, Laozi (low-zuh), the originator of Daoism (believed to have lived in the sixth century B.C.E., though some scholars doubt his existence), sought to stop the warfare of the age by urging humanity to follow the *Dao*, or "path." Daoists accepted the world as they found it, adhering to the "path" of nature and avoiding useless struggles. They avoided violence if at all possible and took the minimal action necessary for a task; rather than fight the current of a stream, a wise man allows the onrushing waters to pass around him. This passivity arose from the Daoist's sense that the world was always changing and lacked any absolute morality or meaning. In the end, Daoists believed, all that matters is the individual's fundamental understanding of the "path."

The original Daoist philosophy was greatly expanded in subsequent centuries to incorporate popular beliefs, magic, and mysticism. Daoism represented an important stream of thought throughout Chinese history. By idealizing individuals who find their own "path" to right conduct, it offered an alternative to the Confucian emphasis on hierarchy and duty and to the Legalists' approval of force.

**Confucius**  Western name for the Chinese philosopher Kongzi (551–479 B.C.E.). His doctrine of duty and public service had a great influence on subsequent Chinese thought and served as a code of conduct for government officials.

**Daoism**  Chinese school of thought, originating in the Warring States Period with Laozi. Daoism offered an alternative to the Confucian emphasis on hierarchy and duty, emphasizing instead understanding the "path" of nature.

# Diversity & Dominance

## Human Nature and Good Government in the *Analects* of Confucius and the Legalist Writings of Han Fei

**A**lthough monarchy (the rule of one man) was the standard form of government in ancient China and was rarely challenged, political theorists and philosophers thought a great deal about the qualities of the ideal ruler, his relationship to his subjects, and the means by which he controlled them. These considerations about how to govern people were inevitably molded by fundamental assumptions about the nature of human beings. In the Warring States Period, as the major states struggled desperately with one another for survival and expansion, such discussions took on a special urgency, and the Confucians and Legalists came to represent two powerful, and largely contradictory, points of view.

The Analects *are a collection of sayings of Confucius, probably compiled and written down several generations after he lived, though some elements may have been added even later. They cover a wide range of matters, including ethics, government, education, music, and rituals. Taken as a whole, they are a guide to living an honorable, virtuous, useful, and satisfying life. While subject to reinterpretation according to the circumstances of the times, Confucian principles have had a great influence on Chinese values and behavior ever since.*

*Han Fei (280–233 b.c.e.), who was, ironically, at one time the student of a Confucian teacher, became a Legalist writer and political adviser to the ruler of the ambitious state of Qin* (chin), *who emerged from the same Wei River Valley as the Zhou and succeeded the Zhou as China's ruling class (see Chapter 5). The Qin dynasty was the first to put into practice Legalist political methods. Eventually Han Fei lost out in a power struggle at court and was forced to kill himself.*

*The following selections illuminate the profound disagreements between Confucians and Legalists over the essential nature of human beings and how the ruler should conduct himself in order to most effectively govern his subjects and protect his kingdom.*

### Confucius

**4:5** Confucius said: "Riches and honors are what all men desire. But if they cannot be attained in accordance with the *dao* [the path] they should not be kept. Poverty and low status are what all men hate. But if they cannot be avoided while staying in accordance with the *dao*, you should not avoid them. If a Superior Man departs from *ren* [humaneness], how can he be worthy of that name? A Superior Man never leaves *ren* for even the time of a single meal. In moments of haste he acts according to it. In times of difficulty or confusion he acts according to it."

**16:8** Confucius said: "The Superior Man stands in awe of three things: (1) He is in awe of the decree of Heaven. (2) He is in awe of great men. (3) He is in awe of the words of the sages. The inferior man does not know the decree of Heaven; takes great men lightly and laughs at the words of the sages."

**4:14** Confucius said: "I don't worry about not having a good position; I worry about the means I use to gain position. I don't worry about being unknown; I seek to be known in the right way."

**7:15** Confucius said: "I can live with coarse rice to eat, water for drink and my arm as a pillow and still be happy. Wealth and honors that one possesses in the midst of injustice are like floating clouds."

**13:6** Confucius said: "When you have gotten your own life straightened out, things will go well without your giving orders. But if your own life isn't straightened out, even if you give orders, no one will follow them."

**12:2** Zhonggong asked about the meaning of *ren*. The Master said: "Go out of your home as if you were receiving an important guest. Employ the people as if you were assisting at a great ceremony. What you don't want done to yourself, don't do to others. Live in your town without stirring up resentments, and live in your household without stirring up resentments."

**1:5** Confucius said: "If you would govern a state of a thousand chariots (a small-to-middle-size state), you must pay strict attention to business, be true to your word, be economical in expenditure and love the people. You should use them according to the seasons."

**2:3** Confucius said: "If you govern the people legalistically and control them by punishment, they will avoid crime, but have no personal sense of shame. If you govern them by means of virtue and control them with propriety, they will gain their own sense of shame, and thus correct themselves."

**12:7** Zigong asked about government. The Master said, "Enough food, enough weapons and the confidence of the people." Zigong said, "Suppose you had no alternative but to give up one of these three, which one would ➤

be let go of first?" The Master said, "Weapons." Zigong said, "What if you had to give up one of the remaining two, which one would it be?" The Master said, "Food. From ancient times, death has come to all men, but a people without confidence in its rulers will not stand."

**12:19** Ji Kang Zi asked Confucius about government saying: "Suppose I were to kill the unjust, in order to advance the just. Would that be all right?" Confucius replied: "In doing government, what is the need of killing? If you desire good, the people will be good. The nature of the Superior Man is like the wind, the nature of the inferior man is like the grass. When the wind blows over the grass, it always bends."

**2:19** The Duke of Ai asked: "How can I make the people follow me?" Confucius replied: "Advance the upright and set aside the crooked, and the people will follow you. Advance the crooked and set aside the upright, and the people will not follow you."

**2:20** Ji Kang Zi asked: "How can I make the people reverent and loyal, so they will work positively for me?" Confucius said, "Approach them with dignity, and they will be reverent. Be filial and compassionate and they will be loyal. Promote the able and teach the incompetent, and they will work positively for you."

## Han Fei

Past and present have different customs; new and old adopt different measures. To try to use the ways of a generous and lenient government to rule the people of a critical age is like trying to drive a runaway horse without using reins or whips. This is the misfortune that ignorance invites. . . .

Humaneness [*ren*] may make one shed tears and be reluctant to apply penalties, but law makes it clear that such penalties must be applied. The ancient kings allowed law to be supreme and did not give in to their tearful longings. Hence it is obvious that humaneness cannot be used to achieve order in the state. . . .

The best rewards are those that are generous and predictable, so that the people may profit by them. The best penalties are those that are severe and inescapable, so that the people will fear them. The best laws are those that are uniform and inflexible, so that the people can understand them. . . .

Hardly ten men of true integrity and good faith can be found today, and yet the offices of the state number in the hundreds. . . . Therefore the way of the enlightened ruler is to unify the laws instead of seeking for wise men, to lay down firm policies instead of longing for men of good faith. . . .

When a sage rules the state, he does not depend on people's doing good of themselves; he sees to it that they are not allowed to do what is bad. If he depends on people's doing good of themselves, then within his borders he can count fewer than ten instances of success. But if he sees to it that they are not allowed to do what is bad, then the whole state can be brought to a uniform level of order. Those who rule must employ measures that will be effective with the majority and discard those that will be effective with only a few. Therefore they devote themselves not to virtue but to law. . . .

When the Confucians of the present time counsel rulers, they do not praise those measures that will bring order today, but talk only of the achievements of the men who brought order in the past. . . . No ruler with proper standards will tolerate them. Therefore the enlightened ruler works with facts and discards useless theories. He does not talk about deeds of humaneness and rightness, and he does not listen to the words of scholars. . . .

Nowadays, those who do not understand how to govern invariably say, "You must win the hearts of the people!" . . . The reason you cannot rely on the wisdom of the people is that they have the minds of little children. If the child's head is not shaved, its sores will spread; and if its boil is not lanced, it will become sicker than ever . . . for it does not understand that the little pain it suffers now will bring great benefit later. . . .

Now, the ruler presses the people to till the land and open up new pastures so as to increase their means of livelihood, and yet they consider him harsh; he draws up a penal code and makes the punishments more severe in order to put a stop to evil, and yet the people consider him stern. . . . He makes certain that everyone within his borders understands warfare and sees to it that there are no private exemptions from military service; he unites the strength of the state and fights fiercely in order to take its enemies captive, and yet the people consider him violent. . . . [These] types of undertaking all ensure order and safety to the state, and yet the people do not have sense enough to rejoice in them.

### QUESTIONS FOR ANALYSIS

1. What do Confucius and Han Fei believe about the nature of human beings? Are they intrinsically good and well-behaved, or bad and prone to misbehave?

2. What are the qualities of an ideal ruler for Confucius and Han Fei?

3. By what means can the ruler influence his subjects in Confucian thought? How should the ruler compel obedience in the people in Legalist thought?

4. What do Confucians and Legalists think about the value of the past as a model for the present?

5. Why might Confucius's passionate concern for ethical behavior on the part of officials and rulers arise at a time when the size and power of governments were growing?

*Sources:* Confucius selections from "The Analects of Confucius," translated by A. Charles Muller, from http://www.acmuller.net/con-dao/analects.html. Reprinted by permission of Charles Muller. Passages from "The Five Vermin" from Han Fei Tzu, translated by Burton Watson. Copyright © 1964 Columbia University Press. Reprinted with permission of the publisher.

**Chinese Bronze Bells** This set of 65 bells was discovered in the tomb of Marquis Yi, the ruler of one of the warring states in the 5th century B.C.E. Bells in different sizes were central components of ancient Chinese "orchestras." In the Eastern Zhou era, each state had its own distinctive set of instruments, an assertion of independence and local pride. Asian Art & Archaeology, Inc./Corbis

Social organization also changed in this period. The kinship structures of the Shang and early Zhou periods, based on the clan (a relatively large group of related families), gave way to the three-generation family of grandparents, parents, and children as the fundamental social unit. Only men could conduct rituals and make offerings to the ancestors, though women could help maintain the household's ancestral shrines. Fathers held authority over women and children, arranged marriages for their offspring, and could sell the labor of family members. A man was limited to one wife but was permitted additional sexual partners, who had the lower status of concubines. The elite classes used marriage to create political alliances, and it was common for the groom's family to offer a substantial "bride-gift," a proof of the wealth and standing of his family, to the family of the prospective bride. A man whose wife died had a duty to remarry in order to produce male heirs to keep alive the cult of the ancestors, whereas women were discouraged from remarrying.

These differences in male and female activities were explained by the concept of **yin** and **yang**, the complementary nature of male and female roles in the natural order. The male principle (yang) was equated with the sun: active, bright, and shining; the female principle (yin) corresponded to the moon: passive, shaded, and reflective. Female gentleness balanced male toughness, female endurance and need for completion balanced male action and initiative, and female supportiveness balanced male leadership. In its earliest form, the theory considered yin and yang as equal and alternately dominant, like day and night, creating balance in the world. However, as a result of the changing role of women in the Zhou period and the pervasive influence of Confucian ideology, the male principle came to be seen as superior to the female.

**yin/yang** In Chinese belief, complementary factors that help to maintain the equilibrium of the world. Yang is associated with masculine, light, and active qualities; yin with feminine, dark, and passive qualities.

- Neolithic farming communities grew in the Yellow and Yangzi River Valleys and adapted to the very different environments in each.

- The Shang dynasty emerged in the Yellow River Valley and grew to encompass parts of the Yangzi River Valley.

- Shang technologies included pictographic writing, bronze work, and artifacts related to royal divination, male ancestor worship, and the power of the warrior aristocracy.

- The first king of the Zhou dynasty defeated the Shang, claiming the Mandate of Heaven as justification for this victory.

- Like the Shang, the Zhou state was decentralized, and it devolved into a collection of independent and hostile states.

- Legalism became the major political philosophy, but Confucianism and Daoism also emerged and established most of the basic principles of Chinese culture.

# NUBIA, 2300 B.C.E.–350 C.E.

■ *How did the technological and cultural influences of Egypt affect the formation of Nubia?*

Since the first century B.C.E. the name *Nubia* has been applied to a 1,000-mile (1,600-kilometer) stretch of the Nile Valley lying between Aswan and Khartoum (kahr-TOOM) and straddling the southern part of the modern nation of Egypt and the northern part of Sudan. The ancient Egyptians called it *Tasety*, meaning "Land of the Bow," after the favorite weapon of the warriors. Nubia is the only trade corridor and continuously inhabited stretch of territory connecting sub-Saharan Africa (the lands south of the Sahara Desert) with North Africa. It was richly endowed with natural resources such as gold, copper, and semiprecious stones.

Egypt's quest for Nubian gold helps explain the early rise of a civilization with a complex political organization, social stratification, metallurgy, monumental building, and writing. However, most scholars today have moved away from the traditional view that Nubian civilization derived from Egypt and emphasize the mutually beneficial interactions between the two lands and the growing evidence that Nubian culture drew on influences from sub-Saharan Africa.

## Early Cultures and Egyptian Domination, 2300–1100 B.C.E.

The central geographical feature of Nubia, as of Egypt, is the Nile River. The Nubian segment of the Nile flows through a landscape of rocky desert, grassland, and fertile plain. In a torrid climate with minimal rainfall, agriculture depended on river irrigation. Six cataracts, barriers formed by large boulders and rapids, obstructed boat traffic. Boats operating between the cataracts and caravans skirting the river made travel possible.

In the fifth millennium B.C.E., bands of people in northern Nubia made the transition from seminomadic hunting and gathering to a settled life based on grain agriculture and cattle herding. The majority of the population came to live in agricultural villages alongside the river. Even before 3000 B.C.E. Egyptian craftsmen worked in ivory and in ebony wood that must have come from tropical Africa by way of Nubia.

As we saw with the journey of Harkhuf at the beginning of this chapter, Nubia enters the Egyptian historical record around 2300 B.C.E. in accounts of trade missions. At that time Aswan, just north of the First Cataract, was the southern limit of Egyptian control. Egyptian noblemen stationed there led donkey caravans south in search of gold, incense, ebony, ivory, slaves, and exotic animals from tropical Africa. This was dangerous work, requiring delicate negotiations with local Nubian chiefs to secure protection, but it brought substantial rewards to those who succeeded.

During the Middle Kingdom (ca. 2040–1640 B.C.E.), Egypt adopted a more aggressive stance toward Nubia. Egyptian rulers sought to control the gold mines in the desert east of the Nile and to cut out the Nubian middlemen who drove up the cost of luxury goods from the tropics. A string of mud-brick forts on islands and riverbanks south of the Second Cataract was built to protect Egypt's southern frontier and regulate the flow of commerce. These Egyptian garrisons were sufficiently intimidating that relations with the indigenous population of northern Nubia, while intermittent, were generally peaceful.

Farther south, where the Nile makes a great U-shaped turn in a fertile plain, a more complex political entity was evolving from the chiefdoms of the third millennium B.C.E. The Egyptians gave the name **Kush** to the kingdom whose capital was located at Kerma, one of the earliest urbanized centers in tropical Africa. Beginning around 1750 B.C.E. the kings of Kush marshaled a labor force to build monumental walls and structures of mud brick. Royal burials containing dozens and even hundreds of sacrificed servants and wives, along with sumptuous objects, testify to the wealth and power of the rulers of Kush and suggest a belief in some sort of afterlife. Kushite craftsmen showed skill in metalworking, whether for weapons or jewelry, and their pottery surpassed anything produced in Egypt.

During the expansionist New Kingdom (ca. 1532–1070 B.C.E.) the Egyptians penetrated more deeply into Nubia (see Chapter 2). They destroyed Kush and its capital and extended their frontier to the Fourth Cataract. A high-ranking Egyptian official called "Overseer of Southern Lands" or "King's Son of Kush" ruled Nubia from a new administrative center at Napata (nah-PAH-tuh), near Gebel Barkal (JEB-uhl BAHR-kahl), the "Holy Mountain," believed to be the home of a local god. Egypt exploited the gold mines of Nubia to help buttress its commerce with other lands. Fatalities were high among native workers in the brutal desert climate, and the army had to ward off attacks from desert nomads.

Five hundred years of Egyptian domination in Nubia left many marks. The Egyptian government imposed Egyptian culture on the native population. To guarantee the good behavior of their relatives in Nubia, children from elite families were brought to the Egyptian royal court; to absorb Egyptian language, culture, and religion, which they later carried home with them. Other Nubians served Egyptians as archers; the manufactured goods that they brought back to Nubia have been found in their graves. The Nubians built Egyptian-style towns and erected stone temples to Egyptian gods, particularly Amon. The frequent depiction of Amon with the head of a ram may reflect a blending of the chief Egyptian god with a Nubian ram deity.

## The Kingdom of Meroë, 800 B.C.E.–350 C.E.

Egypt's weakness after 1200 B.C.E. led to the collapse of its authority in Nubia, and in the eighth century B.C.E. a powerful new native kingdom emerged in southern Nubia. Its history can be divided into two parts. During the early period, between the eighth and fourth centuries B.C.E., Napata, the former Egyptian headquarters, was the primary center. During the later period, from the fourth century B.C.E. to the fourth century C.E., the center was farther south, at **Meroë** (MER-oh-ee), near the Sixth Cataract.

For half a century, from around 712 to 660 B.C.E., the kings of Nubia ruled all of Egypt as the Twenty-fifth Dynasty. They conducted themselves in the age-old manner of Egyptian rulers, using Egyptian titles, costumes, and burial customs. However, they kept their Nubian names and were depicted with physical features suggesting peoples of sub-Saharan Africa. Building on a monumental scale for the first time in centuries and reinvigorating Egyptian art, architecture, and religion, they inaugurated an artistic and cultural renaissance. The Nubian kings resided at Memphis, the Old Kingdom capital, while Thebes, the New Kingdom capital, was the residence of a celibate female member of the king's family who was titled "God's Wife of Amon."

The Nubian dynasty made a disastrous mistake in 701 B.C.E. when it offered help to local rulers in Syria-Palestine who were struggling against the Assyrian Empire. The Assyrians retaliated by invading Egypt and driving the Nubian monarchs back to their southern domain by 660 B.C.E. Napata again became the chief royal residence and religious center of the kingdom. However, Egyptian cultural influences remained strong. Court documents continued to be written in Egyptian hieroglyphs, and the mummified remains of the rulers were buried in modestly sized sandstone pyramids along with hundreds of shawabti (shuh-WAB-tee) figurines.

**Kush**  An Egyptian name for Nubia, the region alongside the Nile River south of Egypt, where an indigenous kingdom with its own distinctive institutions and cultural traditions arose beginning in the early second millennium B.C.E.

**Meroë**  Capital of a flourishing kingdom in southern Nubia from the fourth century B.C.E. to the fourth century C.E. In this period Nubian culture shows more independence from Egypt and the influence of sub-Saharan Africa.

**Gebel Barkal** The "Holy Mountain" of Nubia, located in northern Sudan at a great bend in the Nile near the Fourth Cataract. At its base sat the ancient city of Napata, first the capital of the New Kingdom Egyptian occupying forces, then of the independent state of Kush from the eighth to fourth centuries B.C.E. Several pillars survive from the temple of Amon, as well as a number of small burial pyramids. KENNETH GARRETT/National Geographic Stock

By the end of the fourth century B.C.E. the center of gravity had shifted south to Meroë, perhaps because Meroë was better situated for agriculture and trade, the economic mainstays of the Nubian kingdom. As a result, sub-Saharan cultural patterns gradually replaced Egyptian ones. Egyptian hieroglyphs gave way to a new set of symbols, still essentially undeciphered, for writing the Meroitic language. People continued to worship Amon as well as Isis, an Egyptian goddess connected to fertility and sexuality, but those deities had to share the stage with Nubian deities like the lion-god Apedemak. Meroitic art combined Egyptian, Greco-Roman, and indigenous traditions.

Women of the royal family played an important role in Meroitic politics, another reflection of the influence of sub-Saharan Africa. The Nubians employed a matrilineal system in which the king was succeeded by the son of his sister. Nubian queens sometimes ruled by themselves and sometimes in partnership with their husbands. Greek, Roman, and biblical sources refer to a queen of Nubia named Candace. Since these sources relate to different times,

*Candace* was probably a title rather than a proper name. At least seven queens ruled between 284 B.C.E. to 115 C.E. They are depicted in scenes reserved for male rulers in Egyptian imagery, smiting enemies in battle and being suckled by the mother-goddess Isis. Roman sources marvel at the fierce resistance put up by a one-eyed warrior-queen.

Meroë was a huge city for its time, more than a square mile in area, and it overlooked fertile grasslands and dominated converging trade routes. Great reservoirs were dug to catch precious rainfall. The city was a major center for iron smelting (after 1000 B.C.E. iron had replaced bronze as the primary metal for tools and weapons). The Temple of Amon was approached by an avenue of stone rams, and the enclosed "Royal City" was filled with palaces, temples, and administrative buildings. In 2002 archaeologists using a magnetometer to detect structures buried in the sand discovered a large palace, which they plan to excavate.

Meroë collapsed in the early fourth century C.E., overrun by nomads from the western desert who had become more mobile because of the arrival of the

- Fertile and rich in natural resources, Nubia became an important source of raw materials in Egypt.

- Egyptian cultural influence moved deeper into Nubia as the Middle and New Kingdoms extended Egyptian authority farther south.

- The rich Nubian kingdom of Kush fell to the New Kingdom, but after five hundred years a Nubian dynasty rose and took control of Egypt itself for a short time.

- After the fall of this dynasty, Meroë assumed control of southern Nubia, which was dominated by sub-Saharan cultural practices.

- Meroë was a large and powerful city in its prime, but it was already weak by the time it fell to nomadic invaders.

camel in North Africa. However, Meroë had already been weakened when profitable commerce with the Roman Empire was diverted to the Red Sea and to the rising kingdom of Aksum (AHK-soom) in present-day Ethiopia (see Chapter 8).

# PASTORAL NOMADS OF THE EURASIAN STEPPES, 1000–100 B.C.E.

■ *How was the rise of steppe nomadism dependent on interactions with settled agricultural peoples, and what new challenges did the nomads pose to farming societies?*

For most of human history people were foraging **nomads** ("wanderers" in Greek) who moved from one temporary encampment to another, mostly as a strategy for feeding themselves. But with the Agricultural Revolutions humans began to settle in one place, build permanent homes, acquire more possessions, and create more complex societies (see Chapter 1).

The domestication of herd animals, such as sheep, goats, and cattle, made a new kind of nomadism possible. People lived off the products of their animals, consuming the meat, milk and other dairy products, clothing themselves with hair and hides, and utilizing animal manure to fuel fires. We have already seen several examples of nomadic peoples: the Amorites who migrated into southern Mesopotamia and assimilated with the peoples there to eventually found Baby-

lon (see Chapter 1); the Aramaeans, whose language, Aramaic, became widespread in Syria-Palestine; and the early Israelites, whose migratory lifestyle was recorded in the Hebrew Bible (see Chapter 2). Many scholars believe that the proto-Indo-Europeans, speakers of the language or languages ancestral to the large family of Indo-European languages found across much of Europe and Asia, were nomadic herders who migrated from an original homeland north of the Black and Caspian Seas. They are believed to have first domesticated horses, which enhanced their ability to herd other animals (see Chapter 2).

## Steppe Nomads

Our concern here is with a new kind of pastoral nomadism that arose across the vast Eurasian **Steppes** (a word of Russian origin)—a treeless ecological zone of grass-and-shrub-covered plains that extend from Hungary in eastern Europe across Ukraine and southern Russia, Central Asia, Mongolia, and southern Siberia. In the first millennium B.C.E. the peoples who occupied these relatively arid lands did not wander randomly but rather drove their herds to familiar encampments appropriate to their needs in different seasons, being careful not to overexploit pastures and water sources so that they could be used when they returned. There were, no doubt, significant ethnic and linguistic differences among these peoples, who operated within certain territorial bounds worked out with other groups. They became horse-riding warriors who under normal circumstances were as prone to fight each other as to raid the lands and possessions of the farmers in neighboring areas. In fact, the success of their way of life depended on a symbiotic interaction with settled agricultural peoples, often by trading animal products (live animals, meat, hides, wool, cheese) for agricultural products and manufactured goods (metalwork and textiles), and sometimes by raiding and stealing. These various tribes shared many features of technology, culture,

**nomads** People without permanent, fixed places of residence, whose way of life and means of subsistence require them to periodically migrate, often with their herds of domesticated animals, to a familiar series of temporary seasonal encampments.

**steppe** An ecological region of grass- and shrub-covered plains that is treeless and too arid for agriculture.

**Scythian Gold Pectoral** This gold pectoral (decorative item worn over the breast), found in Ukraine and dating to the fourth century B.C.E., displays the beauty and quality of craftsmanship of Scythian art. The lower register shows griffins attacking a horse, while two men with quivers examine a fleece shirt in the upper register.

Ria Novosti/Alamy

and political and social organization, due, in large part, to their mobility and the speed with which objects and ideas could move across this open landscape. Indeed, the steppe was the conduit by which products, such as wheat, and technologies, including bronze and iron metalworking, chariots, and cavalry warfare, traveled from western and Central Asia to East Asia.

## The Scythians

While the origins of pastoral nomadism on the steppes are shrouded in the mists of prehistory, archaeological information and the accounts of literate ancient peoples tell us something about them. The first Greek historian, Herodotus, writing in 440 B.C.E., claims that the nomadic Cimmerians, driven out of their northern homelands by another nomadic people, the **Scythians**, invaded Anatolia (modern Turkey) in the seventh century B.C.E. These Cimmerians are also mentioned in Assyrian records. The Greeks used the term *Scythian* broadly, lumping together various peoples who spoke similar languages and lived north and east of their Aegean homeland (in present-day Ukraine and southern Russia). These peoples,

however, would not have regarded themselves as belonging to the same ethnic group.

Herodotus traveled in the region where Greeks had established colonies around the coasts of the Black Sea and derived information from Greek traders who traveled far inland and Scythian natives who interacted with the Greeks. He depicts the fundamental quality of the Scythians as people without cities or permanent homes, who migrate together with their herds of sheep, goats, and cattle and their prized horses. Scythians belonged to kinship groups ruled by kings. They and their families lived in carts that were also used to transport their few possessions. Herodotus also makes clear that there were different groups of Scythians practicing somewhat different ways of life. Besides the purely nomadic groups, there were others that engaged in a mixed pastoral and agricultural economy, and some groups (perhaps influenced by the nearby Greek settlers) were settled agriculturalists, evidence of the important interdependency of nomadic pastoralists with agricultural peoples.

Herodotus also describes the Scythians as exceedingly warlike and savage—their chief god equated with the Greek god of war, Ares—who are said to drink the blood of their enemies, cut off their heads as trophies, and make goblets out of their skulls, napkins and coats from their skins. In religious practices the Scythians had no images of the gods, no shrines and no altars, and employed a sacrificial ritual quite different from that of the Greeks that sometimes included human sacrifice. When their kings died, they were accompanied in the grave by murdered servants, guards, and horses. Herodotus's comparatively lengthy account of the Scythian barbarians suggests he may have wanted to emphasize how different they were as a way of "reflecting" what was characteristically Greek.

While likely taking pleasure in relating his story at the expense of the powerful Persians, Herodotus shows how these exceedingly mobile nomads drew the Persian king Darius ever further into unknown Scythian territory, their lack of permanent settlements and cultivated fields presenting no obvious targets for the

**Scythians** Term used by the ancient Greeks for the nomadic peoples living on the steppe north of the Black and Caspian Seas.

Persians to attack and hold hostage. They practiced a "scorched earth" policy of burning the grass and destroying the wells, and they clearly felt no shame in retreat. The Persian king realized that the Scythians were toying with him when, as the armies were finally drawn up for battle, a hare darted across an open space and all the Scythians took off in pursuit of it. As Herodotus tells the story, it was all Darius could do to make a successful escape home with part of his army. Herodotus may have misunderstood Darius's real purpose—to drive the Scythians far from Persian-controlled lands—but he nevertheless illustrated brilliantly the unique difficulties that nomads presented to even powerful ancient states and empires, many of whom found it cheaper to just buy off the nomads by giving them "gifts" in return for not attacking.

## China and the Nomads

Chinese accounts of the peoples of the eastern side of the Eurasian Steppes, also known as Inner Asia, usually match those of the Greeks and Romans. As the Chinese states of the Spring and Autumn and Warring States Periods came under increasing pressure from swift-moving, horse-borne warriors, they began to build walls along their northern frontiers to keep the raiders out, and in the late fourth century B.C.E. the forward-thinking ruler of the state of Zhao took the unprecedented step of outfitting some of his troops with trousers and mounting them on horseback.

Our fullest Chinese account of the northern nomads comes from Sima Qian (ca. 100 B.C.E.), who in many ways corresponds to Herodotus as "the father of history" in East Asia. Like Herodotus, he may have been using his description of the lifestyle of the Xiongnu (SHONG-noo) nomads to highlight characteristic aspects of Chinese civilization. Sima Qian served at the court and had access to archival records and earlier historical texts. He also traveled on official business among the barbarians. He reports that the Xiongnu had no cities, no fixed dwellings, no agriculture, and no writing. They migrated with their herds to pastures and sources of water. They were trained as warriors from an early age, and for this reason the young and fit were given preference over the old and useless. Although tough and warlike by nature, they felt no shame in retreating. Their armies lacked disci-

pline and order, and they largely fought for their own personal gain. They swooped in like birds and vanished just as quickly, cutting off the heads of their vanquished enemies. Human sacrifice was part of their royal funerals. In Sima Qian's account, a former Chinese official who has defected to the nomads points out that, unlike the Chinese, their lives were simple and unencumbered by excessive rules, rituals, or bureaucracy. Here, again, we should note that because the Xiongnu either controlled or were allied to groups that practiced agriculture, they had access to items they could not produce themselves. Many scholars believe that the Xiongnu and several other nomadic peoples on the East Asian steppe spoke Turkish languages, while the Yuezhi, (YOUAY-jee) located further west, spoke an Indo-European language.

In addition to information we can cull from ancient texts like those of Herodotus and Sima Qian, we also have information from archaeological excavation of the large burial mounds of the elite, and in a number of cases the permafrost of Siberia, which has preserved materials, such as textiles, that normally do not survive in the archaeological record. The art of the nomads—mainly golden jewelry and horse fittings and colorful carpets and other textiles—is beautiful to the modern eye, with its emphasis on animals, real and fantastic, often shown in combat, in twisting, interlocked poses that conform gracefully to the surface on which they are displayed.

As we will see in subsequent chapters, the relatively small, fractious tribes of steppe nomads were, at the least, a constant nuisance to the sedentary agricultural peoples living to the south of them. However, from time to time they united in great confederacies under charismatic leaders, and then they presented a serious military threat. The Han Chinese emperors would be at war for centuries with the Xiongnu; the Parthians would take over Iran and much of Mesopotamia and become Rome's only great-power rival (see Chapter 5); the Late Roman Empire would be hard-pressed by Avars and Huns; and in the medieval period the Mongols and several Turkish peoples would overrun most of Asia (see Chapter 12).

While nomadism has become increasingly rare, it has been estimated that 30 to 40 million people still practice this ancient way of life, primarily in Central Asia and the West African Sahel region.

# CELTIC EUROPE, 1000–50 B.C.E.

■ *What were the causes behind the spread of Celtic peoples across much of continental Europe and the later retreat of Celtic cultures to the western edge of the continent?*

The southern peninsulas of Europe—present-day Spain, Italy, and Greece—share in the mild climate of all the Mediterranean lands and are separated from "continental" Europe to the north by high mountains (the Pyrenees and Alps). Consequently, the history of southern Europe in antiquity is primarily connected to that of the Middle East, at least until the Roman conquests north of the Alps (see Chapters 4 and 5).

Continental Europe (including the modern nations of France, Germany, Switzerland, Austria, the Czech Republic, Slovakia, Hungary, Poland, and Romania) was more forested but was well suited to agriculture and herding. It contained broad plains with good soil and had a temperate climate with cold winters, warm summers, and ample rainfall. Large, navigable rivers (the Rhone, Rhine, and Danube) facilitated travel and the exploitation of natural resources like timber and metals.

Humans had lived in this part of Europe for many thousands of years, but their lack of a writing system limits our knowledge of the earliest inhabitants. Around 500 B.C.E., Celtic peoples spread across a substantial portion of Europe, and by coming into contact with the literate societies of the Mediterranean, entered the historical record. Information about the early **Celts** (kelts) comes from the archaeological

record, Greek and Roman authors, and the Celtic oral traditions of Wales and Ireland that were written down during the European Middle Ages.

## The Spread of the Celts

The term *Celtic* refers to a branch of the Indo-European family of languages found throughout Europe and in western and southern Asia. Scholars link the Celtic language group to archaeological remains first appearing in parts of present-day Germany, Austria, and the Czech Republic after 1000 B.C.E. Celtic elites were trading with Mediterranean societies for craft goods and wine. This contact may have stimulated the new styles of Celtic manufacture and art that appeared at this time.

These new cultural features coincided with Celtic migrations to many parts of Europe. The motives behind these population movements, their precise timing, and the manner in which they were carried out are not well understood, but probably included pressure from Germanic peoples still farther east who would eventually displace them. Celts occupied nearly all of France and much of Britain and Ireland, and they merged with indigenous peoples to create the Celtiberian culture of northern Spain. Other Celtic groups overran northern Italy in the fifth century B.C.E., sacking Rome in 390; raided central Greece; and settled in central Anatolia (modern Turkey). By 300 B.C.E. Celtic peoples were spread across Europe north of the Alps, from present-day Hungary to Spain and Ireland.

Although these widely diffused Celtic groups shared elements of language and culture, there was no Celtic "nation." Instead they were divided into hundreds of small, loosely organized kinship groups. Traditional depictions of Celtic society come largely from the observations of Greek and Roman writers. However, current scholarship focuses on the differences as much as the similarities among Celtic peoples. It is unlikely that the ancient Celts ever identified themselves as belonging to anything akin to our modern conception of "Celtic civilization."

The Greeks and Romans remarked particularly on the appearance of male Celts—their burly

**Celts** Peoples sharing common linguistic and cultural features that originated in Central Europe in the first half of the first millennium B.C.E.

size, long red hair (which they often made stiff and upright by applying a cement-like solution of lime), shaggy mustaches, and loud, deep voices. Trousers (usually an indication of horse-riding peoples) and twisted gold neck collars were similarly distinctive, but not as unusual as the terrifying warriors who fought naked and collected the skulls of defeated enemies. The surviving accounts describe the Celts as wildly fond of war, courageous, childishly impulsive and emotional, and fond of boasting and exaggeration, yet quick-witted and eager to learn.

## Celtic Society

The Roman general Gaius Julius Caesar, who conquered Gaul (present-day France) between 58 and 51 B.C.E. (see Chapter 5) penned the greatest source of information about Celtic society. Many Celtic groups in Gaul had once been ruled by kings, but by 60 B.C.E they periodically chose public officials, perhaps under Greek and Roman influence. Their society was divided into an elite class of warriors, professional groups of priests and bards (singers of poems about glorious deeds of the past), and commoners. The warriors owned land and flocks of cattle and sheep and monopolized both wealth and power, while the common people labored on their land. The Celts built houses (usually round in Britain, rectangular in France) out of wattle and daub—a wooden framework filled in with clay and straw—with thatched straw roofs. Several such houses belonging to related families might be surrounded by a wooden fence for protection.

The warriors of Welsh and Irish legend reflect a stage of political and social development less complex than that of the Celts in Gaul. They raided one another's flocks, reveled in drunken feasts, and engaged in contests of strength and wit. At banquets warriors would fight to the death just to claim the choicest cut of the meat, the "hero's portion."

**Druids**, the Celtic priests in Gaul and Britain, formed a well-organized fraternity that performed religious, judicial, and educational functions. Trainees spent years memorizing prayers, secret rituals, legal precedents, and other traditions. The priesthood was the one Celtic institution that crossed tribal lines. The Druids sometimes headed off warfare between feuding groups and served as judges in cases involving Celts from different groups. In the first cen-

**The Gundestrup Cauldron**  This silver vessel was found in a peat bog in Denmark, but it must have come from elsewhere. It is usually dated to the second or first century B.C.E. On the inside right are Celtic warriors on horse and on foot, with lozenge-shaped shields and long battle-horns. On the inside left is a horned deity, possibly Cernunnos. Universal History Archive/Getty Images

tury C.E. the Roman government attempted to stamp out the Druids, probably because of concern that they might serve as a rallying point for Celtic opposition to Roman rule and also because of their involvement in human sacrifices.

The Celts supported large populations by tilling the heavy but fertile soils of continental Europe, and their metallurgical skills probably surpassed those of the Mediterranean peoples. Celts living on the Atlantic shore of France built sturdy oceangoing boats, and they developed extensive trade networks along Europe's large, navigable rivers. One lucrative commodity was tin, which Celtic traders from southwest England brought to Greek buyers in southern France. By the first century B.C.E. some hill-forts were evolving into urban centers.

Women's lives were focused on child rearing, food production, and some crafts. Their situation was superior to that of women in the Middle East

**Druids**  The class of religious experts who conducted rituals and preserved sacred lore among some ancient Celtic peoples.

and in the Greek and Roman Mediterranean. Greek and Roman sources depict Celtic women as strong and proud. Welsh and Irish tales portray self-assured women who sit at banquets with their husbands, engage in witty conversation, and provide ingenious solutions to vexing problems. Marriage was a partnership to which both parties contributed property, and each had the right to inherit the estate if the other died. Celtic women also had greater freedom in their sexual relations than did their southern counterparts.

Tombs of elite women have yielded rich collections of clothing, jewelry, and furniture for use in the next world. Daughters of the elite were married to leading members of other tribes to create alliances. When the Romans invaded Celtic Britain in the first century C.E., they sometimes were opposed by Celtic tribes headed by queens, although some experts see this as an abnormal circumstance created by the Roman invasion itself.

## Belief and Knowledge

Historians know the names of more than four hundred Celtic gods and goddesses, mostly associated with particular localities or kinship groups. More widely revered deities included Lug (loog), the god of light, crafts, and inventions; the horse-goddess Epona (eh-POH-nuh); and the horned god Cernunnos (KURN-you-nuhs). "The Mothers," three goddesses depicted together holding symbols of abundance, probably played a part in a fertility cult. Halloween and May Day preserve the ancient Celtic holidays of Samhain (SAH-win) and Beltaine (BEHL-tayn), respectively, which took place at key moments in the agricultural cycle.

The early Celts did not build temples, but instead worshiped wherever they felt the presence of divinity—at springs, groves, and hilltops. At the sources of the Seine and Marne Rivers in France, archaeologists have found huge caches of Celtic wooden statues thrown into the water by worshipers.

Wagons filled with extensive grave goods show up in elite burials, suggesting a belief in some sort of afterlife. In Irish and Welsh legends, heroes and gods pass back and forth between the natural and supernatural worlds much more readily than in the mythology of other cultures, and magical occurrences are

**SECTION REVIEW**

- From central and eastern Europe, Celtic peoples spread across the continent.
- These peoples shared language and culture but no single state.
- Although Celtic societies varied in complexity, they all shared the institutions of the Druid priesthood, practiced agriculture, and developed sophisticated technologies.
- Celtic women enjoyed relatively high status, and some even led warriors against Roman invaders.
- Celtic religion involved a vast array of deities and some sort of afterlife.
- Celtic culture declined under Roman rule, and the Germanic migrations pushed it to the western margin of Europe.

commonplace. Celtic priests set forth a doctrine of reincarnation—the rebirth of the soul in a new body.

The evolution of Celtic society in Spain, southern Britain, France, and parts of central Europe slowed after the Roman conquests from the second century B.C.E. to the first century C.E. The peoples in these lands largely assimilated Roman ways (see Chapter 5). From the third century C.E. on, Germanic invaders from the east diminished the Celts still further. Only on the western fringes of the European continent—in Brittany (northwest France), Wales, Scotland, and Ireland—did Celtic peoples maintain their language, art, and culture into modern times.

## CONCLUSION

The civilizations of early China, Nubia, the Eurasian Steppes, and the Celts emerged in very different ecological contexts in widely separated parts of the Eastern Hemisphere, and the patterns of organization, technology, behavior, and belief that they developed were, in large part, responses to the challenges and opportunities of those environments.

In the North China Plain, as in the river-valley civilizations of Mesopotamia and Egypt, the presence of great, flood-prone rivers and the lack of dependable rainfall led to the formation of powerful institutions capable of organizing large numbers of people to dig and maintain irrigation channels and build dikes. An authoritarian central government has been a recurring feature of Chinese history, beginning with the Shang monarchy and the warrior elite.

In Nubia, the initial impetus for the formation of a strong state was the need for protection from desert nomads and from the Egyptian rulers who coveted Nubian gold and other resources. Control of these resources and of the trade route between sub-Saharan Africa and the north, as well as the agricultural surplus to feed administrators and specialists in the urban centers, made the rulers and elites of Kerma, Napata, and Meroë wealthy and formidable.

Pastoral nomads found ways to exploit the challenging environment of the Eurasian Steppes. The very nature of their lifestyle, based on migrating with their herds of domesticated animals to seasonal camping grounds, meant that they had no permanent settlements and maintained small, kinship-based groups. Thus, under normal circumstances, their political organization was relatively simple. However, in moments of crisis, or when a charismatic military leader came to the fore, they could unite in formidable confederacies.

The Celtic peoples of continental Europe never developed a strong state. They occupied fertile lands with adequate rainfall for agriculture, grazing territory for flocks, and timber for fuel and construction. Kinship groups dominated by warrior elites and controlling compact territories were the usual form of organization.

# CHAPTER REVIEW

## EARLY CHINA, 2000–221 B.C.E.
*How did early Chinese rulers use religion to justify and strengthen their power?* (page 57)

Throughout history, elites have used religion to bolster their position. The Shang rulers of China were indispensable intermediaries between their kingdom and powerful and protective ancestors and gods. Bronze vessels were used to make offerings to ancestral spirits, and royal and elite families were buried in elaborate tombs that were intended to serve the occupant in the afterlife. Their Zhou successors developed the concept of the ruler as divine Son of Heaven who ruled in accord with the Mandate of Heaven.

## NUBIA, 2300 B.C.E.–350 C.E.
*How did the technological and cultural influences of Egypt affect the formation of Nubia?* (page 67)

The civilization that developed in Nubia was powerfully influenced by its interactions with the more complex and technologically advanced neighboring society in Egypt. Nubia was engaged in trade with Egypt for most of its history, and Egyptians often sought to connect and dominate the gold trade. In the New Kingdom period, the Egyptian government imposed Egyptian culture, language, and religion on the native population, and Nubian architecture came to be based on Egyptian models. In the eighth century B.C.E. the kingdom of Meroë emerged and Nubia controlled all of Egypt for half a century. While they kept their Nubian names, the rulers imitated the style of Egyptian rulers and retained many Egyptian traditions. By the fourth century, power shifted south to Meroë and sub-Saharan African cultural influences replaced Egyptian ones.

## PASTORAL NOMADS OF THE EURASIAN STEPPES, 1000–100 B.C.E.
*How was the rise of steppe nomadism dependent on interactions with settled agricultural peoples, and what new challenges did the nomads pose to farming societies?* (page 70)

The economy of the steppe nomads depended on the agricultural products and manufactured goods (metalwork and textiles) they could trade for animal products (live animals, meat, hides, wool, cheese). These horse-riding warriors were described as exceedingly brutal and warlike and were also known to raid agricultural settlements for the products they wanted. In this regard they were at the very least a nuisance to farming communities. However, their mobility and speed brought objects, ideas, and technologies—such as wheat, bronze and iron metalworking, chariots, and cavalry warfare—all the way from western and Central Asia to East Asia.

## CELTIC EUROPE, 1000–50 B.C.E.

*What were the causes behind the spread of Celtic peoples across much of continental Europe and the later retreat of Celtic cultures to the western edge of the continent?* (page 73)

The Celtic peoples migrated into Europe from the east, probably because of pressure from Germanic peoples who would eventually displace them. The Celtic elites of central Europe initially traded for luxury goods with the Mediterranean, and when they began to expand into lands to the west and south after 500 B.C.E. they came into even closer contact with the Mediterranean peoples. Eventually, many Celtic groups were incorporated into the Roman Empire. Druids, the Celtic priests in Gaul and Britain, performed religious and other functions. Rather than constructing temples, the Celts worshiped hundreds of gods and goddesses in natural surroundings, where they felt the presence of divinity. By the first century C.E. the Romans had conquered parts of Europe and assimilated many Celts to their ways.

## Key Terms

loess (p. 58)

Shang (p. 60)

Zhou (p. 61)

Mandate of Heaven (p. 62)

Legalism (p. 62)

Confucius (p. 63)

Daoism (p. 63)

yin/yang (p. 66)

Kush (p. 68)

Meroë (p. 68)

nomads (p. 70)

steppe (p. 70)

Scythians (p. 71)

Celts (p. 73)

Druids (p. 74)

# Animal Domestication

Because the earliest domestication of plants and animals took place long before the existence of written records, we cannot be sure how and when humans first learned to plant crops and make use of tamed animals. Historians usually link the two processes as part of an Agricultural Revolution, but they were not necessarily connected.

The domestication of plants is much better understood than the domestication of animals. Foraging bands of humans primarily lived on wild seeds, fruits, and tubers. Eventually some humans tried planting seeds and tubers, favoring varieties that they particularly liked, and a variety that may have been rare in the wild became more common. When such a variety suited human needs, usually by having more food value or being easier to grow or process, people stopped collecting the wild types and relied on farming and further developing their new domestic type.

In the case of animals, the basis of selection to suit human needs is less apparent. Experts looking at ancient bones and images interpret changes in hair color, horn shape, and other visible features as indicators of domestication. But these visible changes did not generally serve human purposes. It is usually assumed that animals were domesticated for their meat, but even this is questionable. Dogs, which may have become domestic tens of thousands of years before any other species, were not eaten in most cultures, and cats, which became domestic much later, were eaten even less often. As for the uses most commonly associated with domestic animals, some of the most important, such as milking cows, shearing sheep, and harnessing oxen and horses to pull plows and vehicles, first appeared thousands of years after domestication.

Cattle, sheep, and goats became domestic around ten thousand years ago in the Middle East and North Africa. Coincidentally, wheat and barley were being domesticated at roughly the same time in the same general area. This is the main reason historians generally conclude that plant and animal domestication are closely related. Yet other major meat animals, such as chickens, which originated as jungle fowl in Southeast Asia, and pigs, which probably became domestic separately in several parts of North Africa, Europe, and Asia, have no agreed-upon association with early plant domestication. Nor is plant domestication connected with the horses and camels that became domestic in western Asia and the donkeys that became domestic in the Sahara region around six thousand years ago. Moreover, though the wild forebears of these species were probably eaten, the domestic forms were usually not used for meat.

In the Middle East humans may have originally kept wild sheep, goats, and cattle for food, though wild cattle were large and dangerous and must have been hard to control. It is questionable whether, in the earliest stages, keeping these animals captive for food would have been more productive than hunting. It is even more questionable whether the humans who kept animals for this purpose had any reason to anticipate that life in captivity would cause them to become domestic.

Human motivations for domesticating animals can be better assessed after a consideration of the physical changes involved in going from wild to domestic. Genetically transmitted tameness, defined as the ability to live with and accept handling by humans, lies at the core of the domestication process. In separate experiments with wild rats and foxes in the twentieth century, scientists found that wild individuals with strong fight-or-flight tendencies reproduce poorly in captivity, whereas individuals with the lowest adrenaline levels have the most offspring in captivity. In the wild, the same low level of excitability would have made these individuals vulnerable to predators and kept their reproduction rate down. However, early humans probably preferred the animals that seemed the tamest and destroyed those that were most wild. In the rat and fox experiments, after twenty generations or so, the surviving animals were born with much smaller adrenal glands and greatly reduced fight-or-flight reactions. Since adrenaline production normally increases in the transition to adulthood, many of the low-adrenaline animals also retained juvenile characteristics, such as floppy ears and pushed-in snouts, both indicators of domestication.

Historians disagree about whether animal domestication was a deliberate process or the unanticipated outcome of keeping animals for other purposes. Some assume that domestication was an understood and reproducible process. Others argue that, since a twenty-generation time span for wild cattle and other large quadrupeds would have amounted to several human lifetimes, it is unlikely that the people who ended up with domestic cattle had any recollection of how the process started. This would also rule out the possibility that people who had unwittingly domesticated one species would have attempted to repeat the process with other species, since they did not know what they and their ancestors had done to produce genetically transmitted tameness.

Historians who assume that domestication was an understood and reproducible process tend to conclude that humans domesticated every species that could be domesticated. This is unlikely. Twentieth-century efforts to domesticate bison, eland, and elk have not fully succeeded, but they have generally not been maintained for as long as twenty generations. Rats and foxes have more rapid reproduction rates, and the experiments with them succeeded.

Animal domestication is probably best studied on a case-by-case basis as an unintended result of other processes. In some instances, sacrifice probably played a key role. Religious traditions of animal sacrifice rarely utilize, and sometimes prohibit, the ritual killing of wild animals. It is reasonable to suppose that the practice of capturing wild animals and holding them for sacrifice eventually led to the appearance of genetically transmitted tameness as an unplanned result.

Horses and camels were domesticated relatively late, and most likely not for meat consumption. The societies within which these animals first appeared as domestic species already had domestic sheep, goats, and cattle for meat, and they used oxen to carry loads and pull plows and carts. Horses, camels, and later reindeer may represent successful experiments with substituting one draft animal for another, with genetically transmitted tameness an unexpected consequence of separating animals trained for riding or pulling carts from their wilder kin.

Once human societies had developed the full range of uses of domestic animals—meat, eggs, milk, fiber, labor, transport—the likelihood of domesticating more species diminished. In the absence of concrete knowledge of how domestication had occurred, it was usually easier for people to move domestic livestock to new locations than to attempt to develop new domestic species. Domestic animals accompanied human groups wherever they ventured, and this practice triggered enormous environmental changes as domestic animals, and their human keepers, competed with wild species for food and living space.

# Part Two

# The Formation of New Cultural Communities, from 1500 B.C.E.

ARCTIC OCEAN

NORTH AMERICA

EUROPE

ASIA

Rome Macedonia
Greece Anatolia
Carthage Assyria
Israel
Egypt MIDDLE
Nubia EAST
Persia Indus
Valley Ganges
Plain
India
China
Indochine

NORTH ATLANTIC OCEAN

Mesoamerica

PACIFIC OCEAN

AFRICA

Malay Peninsula
Sumatra
Java

PACIFIC OCEAN

Peru

SOUTH AMERICA

SOUTH ATLANTIC OCEAN

INDIAN OCEAN

AUSTRALIA

0   1000 2000 3000 Km.
0    1000    2000    3000 Mi.

© Cengage Learning

| | 1000 B.C.E. | 800 B.C.E. | 600 B.C.E. |
|---|---|---|---|
| **AMERICAS** | 1200–400 Olmec civilization in Mesoamerica | | |
| | | 900–250 Chavín civilization in Peru | Gold metallurgy in Chavín **500** • |
| **EUROPE** | • **1000** Iron metallurgy | 800–500 Archaic period in Greece | Celts spread across Europe **500** • / Roman Republic **507** • | **477–404** Athenian Empire and democracy |
| **AFRICA** | Rise of Nubian kingdom at Napata **800** • | • **814** Carthage founded / **712–660** Nubian domination of Egypt | Hanno of Carthage explores West African coast **465** • |
| **MIDDLE EAST** | **1000** David establishes Jerusalem as capital of Israel / **911–612** Neo-Assyrian Empire | Babylonian conquest of Jerusalem **587** • | **522–486** Darius I rules Persian Empire |
| **ASIA AND OCEANIA** | • **1000** Aryans settle Ganges Plain / **1027–221** Zhou kingdom in China | Iron metallurgy in China **600** • | **563–483** Life of the Buddha / **551–479** Life of Confucius |

From 1000 B.C.E. to 400 C.E., important changes occurred in the ways of life established in the river-valley civilizations in the two previous millennia, and the scale of human institutions and activities increased. On the shores of the Mediterranean and in Iran, India, and Southeast Asia, new centers arose in lands watered by rainfall and worked by a free peasantry. These societies developed new patterns of political and social organization and economic activity, and they moved in new intellectual, artistic, and spiritual directions.

The rulers of the empires of this era constructed extensive networks of roads and promoted urbanization. These measures brought more rapid communication, trade over greater distances, and the broad diffusion of religious ideas, artistic styles, and technologies. Large cultural zones unified by common traditions emerged—Iranian, Hellenistic, Roman, Hindu, and Chinese—and exercised substantial influence on subsequent ages.

The expansion of agriculture and trade and improvements in technology led to population increases, the spread of cities, and the growth of a comfortable middle class. In many places iron replaced bronze as the preferred metal for weapons, tools, and utensils, and metals were available to more people than in the preceding age. People using iron tools cleared extensive forests around the Mediterranean, in India, and in eastern China. Iron weapons gave an advantage to the armies of Greece, Rome, and imperial China.

New systems of writing, more easily and rapidly learned, moved the preservation and transmission of knowledge out of the control of specialists and gave birth to new ways of thinking, new genres of literature, and new types of scientific endeavor.

In the Western Hemisphere, the development of urban, agricultural civilizations in the Andes, the Yucatán lowlands, and the central plateau of Mexico, first noted among the Olmec of Mesoamerica and the Chavín culture of Peru, climaxed in the Maya and Andean cultures. These cultural exchanges and interactions were counterparts to changes in Eurasia and Africa during the same era.

| 400 B.C.E. | 200 B.C.E. | B.C.E. C.E. | 200 C.E. |
|---|---|---|---|
| | • **300** Migrants from Mesoamerica bring irrigation farming to Arizona | | **250–900** Classic period of Maya civilization |
| | | • **100** Teotihuacan founded | **200–700** Moche culture in coastal Peru |
| • **399** Trial and death of Socrates | **264–201** Rome defeats Carthage | **31 B.C.E.–14 C.E.** Augustus establishes Principate | • **212** Caracalla grants Roman citizenship to all free males |
| | • **290** Rome takes control of Italy   **200–30** Rome absorbs Hellenistic eastern Mediterranean | **45–58** Paul spreads Christianity | • **324** Constantinople founded |
| **400** B.C.E.–300 C.E. Kingdom of Meroë in Nubia | | | |
| | **323–30** Ptolemies rule Hellenistic kingdom in Egypt | • **30** Rome conquers Egypt | |
| | **334–323** Alexander of Macedonia conquers western Asia | • **30** Crucifixion of Jesus | |
| | **301–64** Seleucid kingdom in western Asia | **66–73** Jewish Revolt crushed by Rome | |
| | **324–184** Maurya Empire in India | • **ca. 50** Funan establishes first empire in Southeast Asia | **320–550** Gupta Empire in India |
| | • **221** Qin emperor unites eastern China | | |
| | **206 B.C.E.–220 C.E.** Han Empire in China | | |

# CHAPTER 4

## 1000–30 B.C.E.

# Greece and Iran

© Cengage Learning

The Greek historian Herodotus (heh-ROD-uh-tuhs) (ca. 485–425 B.C.E.) relates that the Persian king Darius (duh-RIE-us) I, whose empire stretched from eastern Europe to northwest India, questioned some Greek and Indian sages. Under what circumstances, he asked the Greeks, would they eat their deceased fathers' bodies? The Greeks, who practiced cremation, recoiled in revulsion. Darius then asked the Indians whether they would ever burn the bodies of their dead parents. This similarly repelled them because they practiced ritual eating of the bodies of the dead. Herodotus argues from this that every group of people regards its own practices as "natural" and superior. This story reminds us that ancient sources such as Herodotus's writings are sometimes accurate, as Herodotus is about Greek funerary customs, and sometimes wildly inaccurate, as are his views on Indian rituals.

The story also reminds us that the Persian Empire and the Hellenistic Greek kingdoms that succeeded it brought together peoples and cultural systems from Europe, Africa, and Asia that previously had little direct contact with one another. This cross-cultural interaction both alarmed and stimulated the peoples involved, in some instances giving rise to new cultural synthesis.

This chapter recounts the experience of the Persians and Greeks in the first millennium B.C.E. Historians traditionally consider the rivalry of Greeks and Persians the first act of an age-long drama: the clash of East and West, of fundamentally different ways of life destined to collide. Ironically, Greeks and Persians had more in common than they realized. They spoke related languages belonging to the Indo-European family, and they inherited similar cultural traits, forms of social organization, and religious outlooks from their shared past.

## ANCIENT IRAN, 1000–500 B.C.E.

■ *How did the Persian Empire rise from its Iranian homeland and succeed in controlling vast territories and diverse cultures?*

Iran, the "land of the Aryans," links western Asia with southern and Central Asia. In the sixth century B.C.E.

the Persians of southwest Iran created the largest empire the world had yet seen. Heirs to the Assyrian and Babylonian imperial tradition, they introduced distinctly Iranian elements and developed new forms of political and economic organization.

Scant written evidence from within the Persian Empire forces us to rely on works by Greeks—ignorant outsiders at best, usually hostile, and interested primarily in events that affected themselves. This leaves us largely uninformed about developments in the central and eastern portions of the Persian Empire, though archaeology and close analysis of the few writings from within the empire can supplement and help correct the Greek perspective.

### Geography and Resources

Iran is bounded by the Zagros (ZUHG-roes) Mountains on the west, the Caucasus (KAW-kuh-suhs) Mountains and Caspian Sea to the northwest and north, and the mountains of Afghanistan (ancient Arachosia) and the desert of Baluchistan (buh-loo-chi-STAN) (ancient Gedrosia) on the east and southeast. The southern limit is a barren seacoast on the Persian Gulf and Indian Ocean. The northeast lies open to attacks or population movements from Central Asia.

Winter precipitation in the mountains feeds streams that either flow away from the central plateau into rivers that drain into seas or flow into the plateau and terminate in salt lakes and deserts. Husbanding water is the key to survival in Iran's arid interior. Lacking a great river like the Nile, Indus, or Tigris-Euphrates, ancient Iran had a sparse population, most numerous in the moister north and west and decreasing toward the arid south and east. The Great Salt Desert, covering much of eastern Iran and Baluchistan, did not support life. Mountain barriers separated scattered settlements on the southern coastal plains from the interior plateau.

Wheat and barley grown during the comparatively wet winter season were the most common crops. However, by 800 B.C.E. Iranian farmers had worked out techniques for digging underground irrigation channels that prevented evaporation and used gravity to deliver water from the subsurface water table in the foothills of the mountains to fields in otherwise uncultivable desert. Constructing these channels and the vertical shafts that gave access to them demanded cooperative labor, but since each village had its own channel, the large-scale, government-sponsored irrigation projects typical of Mesopotamia were probably not required. This factor favored the rise of local aristocracies capable of defending their lands.

The mountains yielded copper, tin, iron, gold, and silver, all exploited on a limited scale in antiquity, as well as wood for fuel, construction, and crafts, the hillsides being more heavily wooded than they are now. Export goods consisted largely of metals and products from further east carried across Iran by traders.

## The Rise of the Persian Empire

The term *Iranians* as used for premodern history describes a group of peoples speaking related languages and sharing certain cultural characteristics that lived in a broad swath of territory between the Zagros Mountains and Central Asia, with some groups as far east as northwest China. One group, the Medes (*Mada* in Iranian),* gained political dominance in northwestern Iran in the late second millenium B.C.E, influenced in part by the ancient centers in Mesopotamia and Urartu (modern Armenia and northeast Turkey). The Medes played a major role in destroying the Assyrian Empire in the late seventh century B.C.E. and extended their control westward across Assyria into Anatolia (modern Turkey). They also projected power southeastward into the land of the Elamites, which was increasingly identified with an immigrant Iranian people known as the Persians (*Parsa*).

The Persian rulers, called Achaemenids (a-KEY-muh-nid) because they traced their lineage back to an ancestor named Achaemenes, cemented relations with the Median court through marriage. **Cyrus** (*Kurush*), the son of a Persian chieftain and a Median princess, united the Persian tribes and overthrew the Median monarch around 550 B.C.E. The differences between these two peoples being slight—notably in dialect and costume—Cyrus placed both Medes and Persians in positions of responsibility and retained the framework of Median rule. The Greeks could not readily tell them apart and may not have recorded their history accurately.

Patriarchal family organization among the Medes and Persians, like that of the Greeks, Romans, and most other Indo-European peoples, gave the male head of the household authority over family members. The warrior class dominated the other two social and occupational classes, the priests and peasants. Noble warriors, the most illustrious being the king, owned land and took pleasure in hunting, fighting, and feasting. The priests, or magi (*magush*), supervised sacrifices and other rituals. Village-based farmers and shepherds made up the third class.

Over the course of two decades the energetic Cyrus (r. 550–530 B.C.E.) redrew the map of western Asia. In 546 B.C.E. he won a cavalry battle outside Sardis, the capital of Lydia in western Anatolia, reportedly because the smell of his camels caused a panic among his opponents' horses. All Anatolia, including the Greek city-states on the western coast, came under Persian control. In 539 B.C.E. he swept into southern Mesopotamia, where the Neo-Babylonian dynasty had ruled since the collapse of Assyrian power (see Chapter 2). Disaffected elements within Babylon surrendered the city to Cyrus. Cyrus respected the Babylonian priesthood and had his son crowned king in accordance with local traditions.

Cyrus died in 530 B.C.E. while campaigning against nomadic Iranians in the northeast. His son Cambyses (kam-BIE-sees) (*Kambujiya*, r. 530–522 B.C.E.) set his sights on Egypt. Defeating the Egyptians in bloody battle, the Persians sent exploratory expeditions south to Nubia and west to Libya. Greek sources depict Cambyses as a cruel and impious madman, but contemporary Egyptian documents reflect a practical outlook. Like his father, he cultivated local priests and notables and respected their traditions.

---

* Familiar Greek names of Iranian groups and individuals are followed by the original Iranian names in parentheses.

**Cyrus** Founder of the Achaemenid Persian Empire. Between 550 and 530 B.C.E. he conquered Media, Lydia, and Babylon. Revered in the traditions of both Iran and the subject peoples, he employed Persians and Medes in his administration and respected the institutions and beliefs of subject peoples.

# Chronology

| | Greece and the Hellenistic World | Persian Empire |
|---|---|---|
| 1500 B.C.E. | 1150–800 B.C.E.  Greece's "Dark Age" | |
| 1000 B.C.E. | | ca. 1000 B.C.E.  Persians settle in southwest Iran |
| 800 B.C.E. | ca. 800 B.C.E.  Greek seafaring resumes | |
| 500 B.C.E. | | 550–530 B.C.E.  Reign of Cyrus |
| | | 480–479 B.C.E.  Xerxes invades Greece |
| 400 B.C.E. | 431–404 B.C.E.  Peloponnesian War | |
| 300 B.C.E. | | 334–323 B.C.E.  Alexander the Great defeats Persia |
| 100 B.C.E. | 30 B.C.E.  Rome annexes Egypt | |

When Cambyses died in 522 B.C.E., **Darius I** (duh-RIE-uhs) (*Darayavaush*), seized the throne, crushing challengers with skill, energy, and ruthlessness. The Medes now played lesser roles; most important posts went to leading Persian nobles. Darius (r. 522–486 B.C.E.) extended Persian control eastward to the Indus Valley and westward into Europe, bridging the Danube River and chasing the nomadic Scythian (SITH-ee-uhn) peoples north of the Black Sea. In maritime matters, Darius dispatched a fleet to explore the route from the Indus Delta to the Red Sea and completed a canal linking the Red Sea with the Nile.

## Imperial Organization and Ideology

Each of the empire's twenty provinces, stretching from eastern Europe to Pakistan, was placed under a Persian **satrap** (SAY-trap), or governor, usually a relative or connection by marriage. The satrap's court mirrored the royal court on a smaller scale. Governorships frequently became hereditary, so that satraps' families lived in the province governed by their head, acquired knowledge about local conditions, and formed connections with the local elite. The farther a province was from the empire's center, the more autonomy the satrap had, since slow communications made contact with the royal center difficult.

Darius prescribed how much precious metal each province owed annually, and the satrap collected and sent it. Some went for necessary expenditures, but most was hoarded. This practice increasingly took precious metal out of circulation, forcing up the price of gold and silver and making it hard for provinces to meet their quotas. Evidence from Babylonia shows increasing taxes and official corruption and a corresponding economic decline by the fourth century B.C.E.

Royal roads, well maintained and patrolled, connected outlying provinces to the imperial center. Way stations sheltered important travelers and couriers, and garrisons controlled movement at strategic points: mountain passes, river crossings, and important urban centers. The ancient Elamite capital of Susa, in southwest Iran, served as the imperial administrative center, the destination for Greeks and others with requests and messages for the king.

**Darius I**  Third ruler of the Persian Empire (r. 521–486 B.C.E.). He crushed the widespread initial resistance to his rule and gave major government posts to Persians rather than to Medes. He established a system of provinces and tribute, began construction of Persepolis, and expanded Persian control in the east (Pakistan) and west (northern Greece).

**satrap**  The governor of a province in the Achaemenid Persian Empire, often a relative of the king. He was responsible for protection of the province and for forwarding tribute to the central administration. Satraps in outlying provinces enjoyed considerable autonomy.

It took at least three months to make the journey to Susa. For Greek ambassadors, the time spent travelling, waiting for an audience, and returning home could take a year or more.

The king lived and traveled with numerous wives and children. Information about the royal women comes from foreign sources and is thus suspect. The Book of Esther in the Hebrew Bible tells how King Ahasuerus (uh-HAZZ-yoo-ear-uhs) (Xerxes [ZERK-sees] to the Greeks) picked the Jewish woman Esther as a wife, putting her in a position to save the Jewish people from a plot to massacre them. Greek sources depict royal women as pawns in power struggles and as intriguers, poisoning rival wives and plotting their sons' paths to the throne.

The king's entourage also included (1) the sons of Persian aristocrats, who were educated at court and also served as hostages for their parents' loyalty; (2) noblemen who attended the king when not on other assignments; (3) administrative officers; (4) the royal bodyguard; and (5) courtiers and slaves. Long gone were the simple days when the king hunted and caroused with his warrior companions. Inspired by Mesopotamian conceptions of monarchy, the Persian king became an aloof figure of majesty and splendor: "The Great King, King of Kings, King in Persia, King of Countries." He referred to everyone, even the Persian nobility, as "my slaves," and anyone who approached him had to bow down before him.

The king owned vast tracts of land throughout the empire, some of which he gave to his supporters. Donations called "bow land," "horse land," and "chariot land" in Babylonian documents obliged the recipient to provide military service. The *paradayadam* (meaning "walled enclosure"—the term has come into English as *paradise*), consisting of gardens or orchards belonging to the king or high nobility, symbolized the prosperity of the king and his servants.

Traditions remembered Darius as issuing the "laws of the King," appointing royal judges throughout the empire, and encouraging the codification of the laws of subject peoples. As master of a decentralized empire, he allowed each people their own traditions and ordinances.

Sometimes the kings returned to **Persepolis** (per-SEH-poe-lis) (*Parsa*), a ceremonial capital in the Persian homeland in southwest Iran that had been founded by Darius and completed by his son Xerxes (Ahasueras to the Hebrews). The palaces, audience halls, treasury buildings, and barracks built on an artificial platform extending from a mountainside took inspiration from Mesopotamia, where the Assyrian kings had created fortress-cities to advertise their power.

Texts found in Persepolis and inscribed in Elamite cuneiform on baked clay tablets show government officials distributing food and other goods to workers of various nationalities, some of them prisoners of war working on construction projects, irrigation networks, or royal estates. Women received less than men of equivalent status, but pregnant women and new mothers received more. Skilled workers of either sex received more than the unskilled.

The relief sculptures on the foundations, walls, and stairwells at Persepolis feature representatives of the peoples of the empire—recognizable by distinctive hairstyles, beards, dress, hats, and footwear—bringing gifts to the king. These images do not depict a real ceremony but rather advertise the vast extent, abundant resources, and cooperative spirit of the empire. One scene shows erect subjects effortlessly shouldering a giant platform bearing Darius's throne. Similar scenes from the Assyrian Empire show the subjects staggering under the weight. Persepolis probably served as a setting of New Year's festivals, coronations, marriages, and funerals. Tombs cut into the cliffs at nearby Naqsh-i Rustam (NUHK-shee ROOS-tuhm) sheltered the remains of Darius and his successors.

Several dozen inscriptions cut into cliff faces provide perspectives on the imperial ideology. At Naqsh-i Rustam, for example, Darius claims:

> Ahuramazda (ah-HOOR-uh-MAZZ-duh) [the chief deity], when he saw this earth in commotion, thereafter bestowed it upon me, made me king. . . . By the favor of Ahuramazda I put it down in its place. . . . I am of such a sort that I am a friend to right, I am not a friend to wrong. It is not my desire that the weak

**Persepolis**  A complex of palaces, reception halls, and treasury buildings erected by the Persian kings Darius I and Xerxes in the Persian homeland. It is believed that the New Year's festival was celebrated here, as well as the coronations, weddings, and funerals of the Persian kings, who were buried in cliff-tombs nearby.

**Sculpted Images on a Stairwell at Persepolis, ca. 500 B.C.E.** Persepolis, in the Persian homeland, was built by Darius I and his son Xerxes, and it was used for ceremonies of special importance to the Persian king and people–coronations, royal weddings, funerals, and the New Year's Festival. Relief images like these on the stone foundations, walls, and stairways, representing members of the court and embassies bringing gifts, broadcast a vision of the grandeur and harmony of the Persian Empire.

arazu/Shutterstock.com

man should have wrong done to him by the mighty; nor is that my desire, that the mighty man should have wrong done to him by the weak.[1]

Darius's inscriptions also show that the Persians honored promises and telling the truth. Several inscriptions castigate evildoers as followers of "The Lie."

Since the religion of **Zoroastrianism** (zo-ro-ASS-tree-uh-niz-um) recognized Ahuramazda as god, it seems certain that Darius and his successors were Zoroastrians. Questions surround the origins of this religion. Worshipers believe that Zarathustra (Zoroaster in Greek) wrote hymns called *Gathas*, the dialect and physical setting of which indicate an origin in northern Afghanistan. Scholarly guesses place Zarathustra's life sometime between 1700 and 500 B.C.E. According to Zarathustra, Ahuramazda, "the wise lord," created the world. Angra Mainyu (ANG-ruh MINE-yoo), "the hostile spirit," and a host of demons threaten it. In this dualist universe, the struggle between good and evil plays out for 12,000

years. At the end of time, good will prevail, and the world will return to the pure state of creation. In the meantime, humanity participates in this cosmic struggle, and individuals reap rewards or torments in the afterlife according to their actions.

The Persians also drew on pre-Zoroastrian moral and metaphysical concepts. Alive to the beauties of nature, they venerated water, which they kept pure, and fire, which burned continuously at altars. Bodily purity, a matter of intense concern, ceased with death. Zoroastrians exposed corpses to carrion-eating birds and the elements to avoid sullying the earth through burial or fire through cremation. Some earlier gods, such as Mithra, a sun-deity and defender of oaths and compacts, retained divine status despite Zarathustra's focus on one god.

Zoroastrianism preached belief in one supreme deity, maintained high ethical standards, and

---

[1] Quoted in Roland G. Kent, *Old Persian: Grammar, Texts, Lexicon*, 2nd ed. (New Haven, CT: American Oriental Society, 1953), 138, 140.

**Zoroastrianism** A religion originating in ancient Iran that became the official religion of the Achaemenids. It centered on a single benevolent deity, Ahuramazda, who engaged in a struggle with demonic forces before prevailing and restoring a pristine world. It emphasized truth-telling, purity, and reverence for nature.

**SECTION REVIEW**

- Early Iranians developed complex societies that enabled them to carry settled agriculture from mountain valleys to the less hospitable plains.

- The Medes instituted a complex political order and, after helping to destroy the Assyrian Empire, subdued the Persians.

- Under Cyrus, the Persians overthrew the Medes, and the two cultures merged.

- Cyrus and his successors expanded the empire, respecting the local traditions of conquered peoples.

- The empire reached its fullest extent under Darius I, who created its basic administrative structure and imperial ideology.

- The religion of the empire was Zoroastrianism, which may have influenced Judaism and Christianity.

promised salvation. Expanding with the advance of the Persian Empire, it may have exerted influence on Judaism and thus, indirectly, on Christianity. God and the Devil, Heaven and Hell, reward and punishment, the Messiah and the End of Time: all appear in this belief system. Yet the Islamic conquest of Iran in the seventh century C.E. (see Chapter 9) triggered the faith's decline, and only tiny communities still survive in Iran. Some larger communities, called Parsees, live in South Asia.

# THE RISE OF THE GREEKS, 1000–500 B.C.E.

■ *What were the most distinctive elements of Greek civilization, and how and why did they evolve in the Archaic and Classical periods?*

The cultural features that emerged in resource-poor Greece in the first millennium B.C.E. depended on access to foreign markets and sources of raw materials. Greek merchants and mercenaries brought home not only raw materials and crafted goods but also ideas. Population pressure, poverty, war, and political crisis prompted Greeks to venture throughout the Mediterranean and western Asia, carrying with them their language and culture and exerting influence on other societies. Greek identity and interest in geography, ethnography, and history grew from experience with non-Greek practices and beliefs, as well as from a two-century-long rivalry with the Persian Empire.

**Geography and Resources**   Bounded by the Atlantic, the Alps, the Syrian Desert, and the Sahara, the lands of the Mediterranean climatic zone share seasonal weather patterns and many plants and animals. In summer a stalled weather front near the entrance of the Mediterranean holds up storms from the Atlantic and allows winds from the Sahara to flow over the region. In winter, the front dissolves and ocean storms roll in, bringing waves, wind, and cold. Such similarities facilitated migration within the zone, since people did not have to change familiar practices and occupations.

Greek civilization arose on the Greek mainland, the Aegean islands, and the western coast of Anatolia. As we saw in Chapter 2, small plains between low mountain ranges characterize southern Greece, a land with no navigable rivers. The islands dotting the Aegean, inhabited from early times, made sailing from Greece to Ionia (western Anatolia) comparatively easy. From about 1000 B.C.E. Greeks began to settle Ionia, where rivers with broad, fertile plains made for a comfortable life. These coastal Greeks maintained closer contact with Greeks across the Aegean than with the peoples of Anatolia's rugged interior. The sea served as a connector, not a barrier.

Mainland farmers depended on rainfall to water their crops. In the south, limited land, thin topsoil, and sparse rainfall supported only small populations. Farmers planted the plains with barley, which is hardier than wheat, and the edge of the plain with olive trees. Grapevines grew on the terraced lower slopes of the foothills. Sheep and goats grazed the hillsides. Northern Greece, with more rainfall and broader plains, supported herds of cattle and horses. Resources included abundant building stone and fine marble but few metal deposits or forests.

The difficulty and expense of overland transport, the availability of good anchorages, and the need to import metals, timber, and grain drew the Greeks to the sea. They obtained timber from the northern Aegean, gold and iron from Anatolia, copper from Cyprus, tin from the western Mediterranean, and grain from the Black Sea, Egypt, and Sicily. Though never comfortable with "the wine-dark sea," as Homer called it, the Greeks relied on it, their small, frail ships hugging the coastline or island-hopping where possible.

## The Emergence of the Polis

After the destruction of the Mycenaean palace-states (see Chapter 2), Greece lapsed into a "Dark Age" (ca. 1150–800 B.C.E.), a time of depopulation, poverty, and backwardness that left few traces in the archaeological record. Decline of trade and lack of access to resources lay behind the poverty of the Dark Age. Within Greece, regional distinctiveness in pottery and crafts indicates declining interconnections.

By reestablishing contact between the Aegean and the Middle East, Phoenician traders (see Chapter 2) gave Greek civilization a push that inaugurated the Archaic period of Greek history (ca. 800–480 B.C.E.). Greek seafarers reappeared in the Mediterranean waters looking for raw materials, trade opportunities, and fertile farmland.

Lifelike human and animal figures and imaginative mythical beasts on painted Greek pottery signal new ideas from the east, as does the adoption of an alphabetical writing system of Phoenician inspiration. Cuneiform or hieroglyphics, systems in which several hundred symbols stood for syllables rather than letters, took years of training and remained the preserve of an elite scribal class. By contrast, the alphabetic symbols made literacy easy to acquire.

First used for economic purposes or for preserving oral poetry, the Greek alphabet facilitated new forms of literature, law codes, religious dedications, and epitaphs. Yet Greek culture continued to center on storytelling, rituals, and performances. Theatrical drama, philosophical dialogues, and political and courtroom oratory demonstrate the dynamic interaction of speaking and writing.

Population grew rapidly during the Archaic period, as we know from a five- to sevenfold increase in cemeteries around Athens during the eighth century B.C.E. On the previously uncultivated margins of the plains, herding gave way to intensive farming. This increasing population and prosperity stimulated the importation of food and raw materials, a merging of villages into urban centers, and specialization of labor. Freed from farming and rising surpluses, some people developed skills in crafts, commerce, and religion.

The Greek **polis** (POE-lis), or city-state, ranging in size from a few thousand souls to several hundred thousand in the case of Athens, consisted of an urban center and the surrounding countryside. Typically, a fortified hilltop, the *acropolis* (uh-KRAW-poe-lis) ("top of the city"), offered refuge in emergencies, with the town spread around its base. In the open area around government buildings and markets, called an *agora* (ah-go-RAH) ("gathering place"), citizens debated the decisions of leaders and organized for war. Walls surrounded the urban center; but population growth prompted construction beyond them. Food came from surrounding farms, though many who lived within the walls worked nearby fields. Unlike the dependent rural workers of Mesopotamia, Greek farmers enjoyed full citizenship.

By the early seventh century B.C.E., frequent city-state conflicts had led to a new kind of warfare based on **hoplites** (HAWP-lite)—heavily armored infantrymen who fought in close formation. Protected by helmet, breastplate, and leg guards, each hoplite brandished a thrusting spear while guarding his left side and the right side of the hoplite beside him with a round shield, keeping a sword in reserve. Victory depended on maintaining one's battle line while breaking open the enemy's. The losers suffered most of their casualties while fleeing.

Private citizens, mostly farmers called up for brief periods rather than professional soldiers, served as hoplites. Courage to stand one's ground counted for more than strength for bearing weapons and armor. When an army approached, the farmers of the polis under attack mustered to defend their land and buildings. The clash of hoplite lines resulted in quick decision. Battles rarely lasted more than a few hours, with the survivors promptly returning home to their farms.

**polis** The Greek term for a city-state, an urban center and the agricultural territory under its control. It was the characteristic form of political organization in southern and central Greece in the Archaic and Classical periods. Of the hundreds of city-states in the Mediterranean and Black Sea regions settled by Greeks, some were oligarchic, others democratic, depending on the powers delegated to the Council and the Assembly.

**hoplite** A heavily armored Greek infantryman of the Archaic and Classical periods who fought in the close-packed phalanx formation. Hoplite armies—militias composed of middle- and upper-class citizens supplying their own equipment—were for centuries superior to all other military forces.

As population growth strained the agricultural resources of the small plains, many city-states sent excess population abroad to establish independent colonies. Sometimes people were chosen by lot to be colonists and forbidden to return on pain of death. At other times people in search of adventure or an escape from poverty volunteered. Colonists sought the approval of the god Apollo at his sanctuary at Delphi and then departed by sea carrying a fire from the communal hearth of the mother-city, a symbol of the kinship and religious ties that would connect the two communities. The "founder," a prominent member of the mother-city, chose a hill or other natural refuge, assigned parcels of land, and drafted laws. Sometimes colonists intermarried with local inhabitants; alternatively, they drove them away or reduced them to semiservility.

From the mid-eighth through mid-sixth centuries B.C.E., colonists spread Greek culture to the northern Aegean area, the Libyan coast of North Africa, and around the Black Sea, with southern Italy and Sicily becoming heavily Greek. Establishing new homes, farms, and communities posed many challenges, but the similarity in climate and ecology helped the Greek settlers transplant their way of life.

Greeks called themselves *Hellenes* (HELL-leans) (*Graeci* is what the Romans later called them) to distinguish themselves from *barbaroi* (literally "non-Greek speakers," whence the English word *barbarian*). Interaction with new peoples and exposure to their cultures made the Greeks aware of their unity of language, religion, and lifestyle. It also introduced them to new ideas and technologies. Developments in the colonial world traveled back to the Greek homeland: urban planning, forms of political organization, and new intellectual currents.

Coinage, invented in the early sixth century B.C.E. in Lydia (western Anatolia), spread throughout the Greek world and beyond. Scarcity, durability, divisibility, and ease of use made silver, gold, bronze, and copper appropriate for minting into metal pieces of state-guaranteed weight and purity. (Societies in other parts of the world used items with similar qualities, including beads, hard-shelled beans, and cowrie shells.) Coinage made weighing quantities of metal obsolete and fostered quicker trading transactions, better record keeping, and easier wealth storage.

Trade grew, as did the total wealth of communities, but different weight standards used by different states often confused exchanges of currencies.

Colonization relieved pressures within Archaic Greek communities but did not eliminate political instability. At some point, the Dark Age kings depicted in Homer's *Iliad* and *Odyssey* were superseded by councils representing noble families that derived their wealth and power from landownership. The peasants who farmed these lands kept only a portion of their harvest. Debt-slaves, people who lost their freedom when they could not repay money or seed borrowed from the lord, also worked the land. Free peasants owned small farms and joined urban-based craftsmen and merchants as part of a "middle class."

In the mid-seventh and sixth centuries B.C.E., **tyrants**—individuals who seized power in violation of normal political institutions—gained control of many city-states. Often disgruntled aristocrats with middle-class backing, they appealed to hoplite soldiers, whose numbers increased with growing prosperity and lower prices for weaponry, and granted these supporters political rights.

Some tyrants passed their positions on to sons, but communities eventually expelled the tyrant families and opted for oligarchy (OLL-ih-gahr-key), in which a group of the wealthiest men held power, or **democracy**, in which all free adult males shared power. This broadening of the political system was made possible by the absence of a professional military class.

Even before they invaded the Greek peninsula at the end of the third millennium B.C.E., the Greeks worshiped several sky-gods, such as Zeus, who sent storms and lightning, and Poseidon, who was master

**tyrant**  The term the Greeks used to describe someone who seized and held power in violation of the normal procedures and traditions of the community. Tyrants appeared in many Greek city-states in the seventh and sixth centuries B.C.E., often taking advantage of the disaffection of the emerging middle class and, by weakening the old elite, unwittingly contributing to the evolution of democracy.

**democracy**  System of government in which all "citizens" (however defined) have equal political and legal rights, privileges, and protections, as in the Greek city-state of Athens in the fifth and fourth centuries B.C.E.

**Vase Painting Depicting a Sacrifice to the God Apollo, ca. 440 B.C.E.** For the Greeks, who believed in a multitude of gods who looked and behaved like humans, the central act of worship was the sacrifice, the ritualized offering of a gift. Sacrifice created a relationship between the human worshiper and the deity and raised expectations that the god would bestow favors in return. Here we see a number of male devotees, wearing their finest clothing and garlands in their hair, near a sacred outdoor altar and statue of Apollo. The god is shown at the far right, standing on a pedestal and holding his characteristic bow and laurel branch. The first worshiper offers the god bones wrapped in fat. All of the worshipers will feast on the meat carried by the boy. Bildarchiv Preussischer Kulturbesitz/Art Resource, NY

of the sea and earthquakes. These deities were given personalities by Homer's *Iliad* and *Odyssey*, heroic epics that were memorized by schoolboys and recited by performers. The gods are portrayed as anthropo-morphic (an-throh-poh-MORE-fik), or humanlike in appearance (though taller, more beautiful, and more powerful, with a supernatural radiance), with humanlike emotions of love, anger, and jealousy. But unlike humans, they are immortal.

State religious ceremonies conferred civic identity. **Sacrifice**, the central ritual, took place at altars in front of the temples where the gods were thought to reside. Gifts as humble as a small cake or a cup of wine poured on the ground accompanied prayers for favor and protection. In grander sacrifices, people would kill one or more animals, smear the altar with its blood, and burn parts of its body so that the aroma would ascend to the gods.

Oracles situated at sacred sites responded to human pleas for information, advice, or prediction. At Delphi in central Greece, the most honored site, the god Apollo spoke through his priestesses, the Pythia (PITH-ee-uh), whose obscure utterances were interpreted by the male priests who administered

the sanctuary. There were also fertility cults that were usually based on female deities and appealed to the agricultural majority of the population, but our dependence on literary texts that express the values of an educated urban elite limits our knowledge of them.

## New Intellectual Currents

Prosperity, new technologies, and social and political development led to innovations in intellectual outlook and artistic outlook, including a growing emphasis on the individual. In early Greek communities, the family enveloped the individual, and land belonged collectively to the family, including ancestors and descendants. Ripped from this communal network and forced to resettle elsewhere, colonists became models of individualism, as did the tyrant who seized power for himself alone.

**sacrifice** A gift given to a deity, often with the aim of creating a relationship, gaining favor, and obligating the god to provide some benefit to the sacrificer, sometimes in order to sustain the deity and thereby guarantee the continuing vitality of the natural world.

This valuing of the uniqueness, talents, and rights of the individual was a form of humanism, which remains a central tenet of Western civilization.

In the new lyric poetry, short verses deal with personal subjects drawn from the poet's experience. Archilochus (ahr-KIL-uh-kuhs), a soldier and poet living in the first half of the seventh century B.C.E., wrote:

> Some barbarian is waving my shield, since I was obliged to leave that perfectly good piece of equipment behind under a bush. But I got away, so what does it matter? Let the shield go; I can buy another one equally good.[2]

Here Archilochus pokes fun at the heroic ideal that scorned soldiers who ran from the enemy. In challenging traditional values and expressing personal feelings, lyric poets pointed toward the modern Western conception of poetry.

In religion, thinkers now known as pre-Socratic philosophers called into question Homer's representations of the gods. Xenophanes (zeh-NOFF-eh-nees), living in the sixth century B.C.E., protested:

> But if cattle and horses or lions had hands, or were able to draw with their hands and do the works that men can do, horses would draw the forms of the gods like horses, and cattle like cattle, and they would make their bodies such as they each had themselves.[3]

The term *pre-Socratic* refers to philosophers before Plato, a student of Socrates, who in the later fifth century B.C.E. shifted the focus of philosophy to ethical questions. They rejected traditional explanations of the origins and nature of the world and sought more rational answers. How was the world created? What is it made of? Why does it change? Some postulated that earth, air, fire, and water, the primal elements, combine or dissolve to form the substances found in nature. One taught that microscopic atoms (from a Greek word meaning "indivisible") move through the void of space, colliding randomly and combining in various ways to form the natural world—an intuition that resembles modern atomic theory. Most pre-Socratics came from Ionia and southern Italy, where Greeks lived close to non-Greeks. Encountering peoples with different ideas may have stimulated some of their thoughts.

Also in Ionia in the sixth century B.C.E., men later referred to as logographers (loe-GOG-ruff-er) ("writers of prose accounts") gathered information on ethnography (the physical characteristics and cultural practices of a people), Mediterranean geography, the foundation of cities, and the origins of famous families. They called their accumulation of information *historia*, "investigation/research." The most famous of these works, the *Historia* by **Herodotus** (ca. 485–425 B.C.E.) from Halicarnassus in southwest Anatolia, contains geographic and ethnographic reports, legends, and marvels in its early parts and later focuses on the Persian-Greek wars of the previous generation. Herodotus opens his work as follows:

> I, Herodotus of Halicarnassus, am here setting forth my history, that time may not draw the color from what man has brought into being, nor those great and wonderful deeds, manifested by both Greeks and barbarians, fail of their report, and, together with all this, the reason why they fought one another.[4]

His search for causes reveals the thinking of a true historian. Thus did *historia* begin to narrow and acquire the modern meaning of *history*, with Herodotus gaining the nickname *Father of History*.

## Athens and Sparta

Athens and Sparta, the preeminent city-states of the late Archaic and Classical periods, differed in character despite environmental and cultural similarities. The Spartans' ancestors migrated into the

---

[2] Richmond Lattimore, *Greek Lyrics*, 2d ed. (Chicago: University of Chicago Press, 1960), 2.

[3] G. S. Kirk and J. E. Raven, *The Presocratic Philosophers: A Critical History with a Selection of Texts* (Cambridge, England: Cambridge University Press, 1957), 169.

---

[4] Herodotus, *The History*, trans. David Grene (Chicago: University of Chicago Press, 1988), 33. (Herodotus 1.1)

**Herodotus** Heir to the technique of *historia* ("investigation/research") developed by Greeks in the late Archaic period. He came from a Greek community in Anatolia and traveled extensively, collecting information in western Asia and the Mediterranean lands. He traced the antecedents and chronicled the wars between the Greek city-states and the Persian Empire, thus originating the Western tradition of historical writing.

Peloponnese (PELL-uh-puh-neze), the southernmost part of Greece, around 1000 B.C.E. Their community resembled others until the seventh century B.C.E., when the population increases and shortage of farmland that affected all communities prompted them to react differently. Instead of sending out colonies, the Spartans invaded the fertile plain of Messenia to the west. The resulting takeover, aided perhaps by hoplite tactics, saw the Messenians reduced to the status of helots (HELL-ut), the most abused and exploited population on the Greek mainland.

The Spartan state quickly turned into a military camp, always prepared for a helot uprising. The state divided Messenia and Laconia, the Spartan homeland, into several thousand lots, each assigned to a Spartan citizen. Helots worked the land and turned over a part of their harvest to their Spartan masters. Freed from farming, the Spartans devoted their lives to military affairs.

The Spartan army outclassed all others because it did not rely on militias summoned only during crises. The Spartans paid a price, however. Taken from their families and put into barracks at age seven, boys underwent a severe regime of discipline, beatings, and deprivation. The demands of the state consumed a Spartan male's whole life.

The economic, political, and cultural revival of the Archaic Greek world passed Sparta by: no poets or artists, no precious metals or coinage, no commerce or other activities that could introduce inequality. The fifth-century B.C.E. Athenian historian Thucydides (thoo-SID-ih-dees) remarked that in his day Sparta looked like a large village and that no future observer of the site would be able to guess its power.

Other Greeks admired the Spartans' courage, commitment, and martial skills but abhorred their arrogance, ignorance, and cruelty. The Spartan Council of Elders and two kings, who commanded in battle, practiced a cautious and isolationist foreign policy. Reluctant to venture far for fear of a helot uprising, they worked for peace through the Peloponnesian League, a system of alliances with their neighbors.

Athens, by comparison, possessed an unusually large and populous territory: the fertile plains of Attica with their groves of olive trees. By the fifth century B.C.E., Athens numbered approximately 300,000 people. Villages and a few larger towns dotted the peninsula where the urban center stood beside the sheer-sided Acropolis some 5 miles (8 kilometers) from the sea.

In 594 B.C.E., to avoid civil war, the Athenians conferred lawgiving powers on Solon, an aristocrat with ties to the merchant community. Solon divided the citizens into four classes based on the annual yield of their farms. The top three classes could hold state offices. The lowest class, with little or no property, held no offices but could participate in meetings of the Assembly. Although a far cry from democracy, this linkage between rights, privileges, and wealth broke the power of a dominant cluster of aristocratic families and favored social and political mobility. By abolishing debt slavery, Solon also guaranteed the freedom of Athenian citizens.

Despite Solon's efforts, in 546 B.C.E., an aristocrat named Pisistratus (pie-SIS-truh-tuhs) seized power. Because most Athenians still lived in villages, identified primarily with a district, and accepted the leadership of landlords who lived in sturdy manor houses, Pisistratus turned to the urban population for support. He undertook building projects, including a Temple of Athena on the Acropolis, and instituted or expanded popular urban festivals: the City Dionysia (die-ul-NIZ-eeuh), later famous for dramatic performances, and the Panathenaea (pan-ath-un-NEE-uh), a religious procession combined with athletic and poetic competitions.

With Spartan assistance, the Athenians expelled Pisistratus's sons, who had inherited his position. In the 460s and 450s B.C.E. **Pericles** (PER-eh-kleez) led a democratic movement to transfer all power to popular organs of government: the Assembly, the Council of 500, and the People's Courts. Henceforward, Athenians of moderate or slender means could hold office and participate in politics. Selected by lot for even the highest positions, officials now received pay for their

**Pericles**  Aristocratic leader who guided the Athenian state through the transformation to full participatory democracy for all male citizens, supervised construction of the Acropolis, and pursued a policy of imperial expansion that led to the Peloponnesian War. He formulated a strategy of attrition but died from the plague early in the war.

services and so could afford to leave their other occupations. Some key offices—managing public money, commanding military forces—were filled by elections that took into account the candidates' abilities.

The Assembly of all citizens held open debates several times a month in which anyone could speak to the issues of the day. Members of the Council of 500 took turns presiding and representing the Athenian state. Through effective political organizing, Pericles dominated Athenian politics from 461 B.C.E. until his death in 429 B.C.E.

Athens's economic position paralleled its political evolution. From the time of Pisistratus, Athenian pottery became increasingly prominent throughout the Mediterranean. These pots often contained olive oil, Athens's chief export, but elegant painted vases were also luxury commodities in themselves. Trade-related increases in the size and prosperity of the middle class help explain the growth of Athenian democracy.

## THE STRUGGLE OF PERSIA AND GREECE, 546–323 B.C.E.

■ *How did the Persian Wars and their aftermath affect the politics and culture of ancient Greece and Iran?*

In the fifth and fourth centuries B.C.E., Greek life was dominated by the Persian-Greek wars. Although the Persians probably considered developments farther east more important, in the end, the encounters of Greeks and Persians profoundly affected the history of the eastern Mediterranean and western Asia.

### Early Encounters

Cyrus's conquest of Lydia in 546 B.C.E. led to the subjugation of the Ionian Greek cities. Some groups and individuals collaborated with the Persian government, but in 499 B.C.E. Greeks and other subject peoples on the western frontier staged the Ionian Revolt. The Persians needed five years and a massive infusion of troops and resources to stamp out the insurrection.

The failed revolt led to the **Persian Wars**: two Persian attacks on Greece in the early fifth century B.C.E. In 490 B.C.E. Darius dispatched a naval fleet to punish Eretria (er-EH-tree-uh) and Athens, two mainland Greek states allied with the Ionian rebels. Disloyal citizens betrayed Eretria to the Persians, who marched the survivors off to exile. In this, as in many other things, Persians copied their Assyrian predecessors, although they did not boast of mass deportations. Athens would probably have suffered a similar fate if its hoplites had not defeated the lighter-armed Persian troops in a sharp engagement at Marathon, 26 miles (42 kilometers) from Athens.

After Xerxes (*Khshayarsha*, r. 486–465 B.C.E.) succeeded his father in 486 B.C.E., he gathered a huge invasion force, including contingents from all over the Persian Empire and a large fleet. Crossing the Hellespont (the narrow strait separating Europe and Asia) and traversing Thrace, the Persian throng descended into central and southern Greece. Xerxes sent messengers ahead demanding of the city-states "earth and water"—tokens of submission.

Many city-states complied. But in southern Greece the Spartans formed an alliance that historians call the Hellenic League. At the pass of Thermopylae (thuhr-MOP-uh-lee) in central Greece, three hundred Spartans and their king fought to the last man to buy time for their fellows to escape. The Persians sacked Athens, but the outnumbered Athenians

**Persian Wars** Conflicts between Greek city-states and the Persian Empire, ranging from the Ionian Revolt (499–494 B.C.E.) through Darius's punitive expedition that failed at Marathon (490 B.C.E.) and the defeat of Xerxes's massive invasion of Greece by the Spartan-led Hellenic League (480–479 B.C.E.). This first major setback for Persian arms launched the Greeks into their period of greatest cultural productivity. Herodotus chronicled these events in the first "history" in the Western tradition.

lured the Persian navy into narrow waters at Salamis (SAH-lah-miss), where, despite their numbers, they could not maneuver. The Persians lost their advantage, and the Athenians administered a devastating defeat. A rout of the Persian army at Plataea (pluh-TEE-uh) the following spring relieved the immediate threat.

Athens's stubborn refusal to submit and the effectiveness of the Athenian navy earned the city great respect. Naval strategies dominated the next phase of the war, which was designed to liberate Greek states still under Persian control. This focus gave Athens priority over land-based, isolationist Sparta. The Delian (DEE-lih-yuhn) League, formed in 477 B.C.E., brought the Greek states together. In less than twenty years, League forces led by Athenian generals swept the Persians from the waters of the eastern Mediterranean and freed all Greek communities except those in distant Cyprus.

## The Height of Athenian Power

Scholars date the Classical period of Greek history (480–323 B.C.E.) to this defense of the Greek homeland. Ironically, Athens exploited its crucial role in these events to become an imperial power. Some Greek allies contributed money instead of troops, and the Athenians used the money to strengthen their navy. They treated other members of the Delian League as subjects and demanded annual contributions. States attempting to leave the League were brought back by force, stripped of their defenses, and subordinated to Athens.

Athenian naval technology transformed Greek warfare and brought power and wealth to Athens itself. Unlike commercial sailing ships, which over time had developed a stabler and more capacious round-bodied design, slender military vessels relied on large numbers of rowers. Having little deck room or storage space, these ships hugged the coastline and put ashore nightly to replenish food supplies and let the crew sleep. Fifty-oared ships had dominated naval warfare until the late sixth century B.C.E. when sleek, fast **triremes** (TRY-reems), powered by 170 rowers, brought an end to crude engagements in which warriors cleared the enemy's decks with spears and arrows before boarding and fighting hand to hand. Approximately 115 by 18 feet (35 by 6 meters) in size,

**Replica of Ancient Greek Trireme** Greek warships had a metal-tipped ram in front to pierce the hulls of enemy vessels and a pair of steering rudders in the rear. Though equipped with masts and sails, in battle these warships were propelled by 170 rowers. This modern, full-size replica, manned by international volunteer crews, is helping scholars to determine attainable speeds and maneuvering techniques. Replica of the trireme 'Olympia' at sea (photo)/Private Collection/Ancient Art and Architecture Collection Ltd./Mike Andrews/The Bridgeman Art Library

the trireme positioned rowers on three levels with oars of different lengths to avoid interference. The fragile vessels could achieve up to 7 knots in short bursts. Athenian crews, by constant practice, became the best in the eastern Mediterranean. They disabled enemy vessels by sheering off their oars, smashing their hulls below the water line with an iron-tipped prow, or forcing collisions by running around them in ever-tightening circles.

The primacy of the fleet contributed to a democratic system in which each male citizen had, at least in principle, an equal voice. The middle or upper class produced hoplites, who bought their own armor and weapons. Rowers came from the lower classes, but they insisted on full rights as protectors of the community.

Athenian maritime power reached farther than any citizen militia. Victors in Greek wars seldom occupied enemy lands permanently (the exception being Sparta's takeover of Messenia). Booty with

**trireme** Greek and Phoenician warship of the fifth and fourth centuries B.C.E. It was sleek and light, powered by 170 oars arranged in three vertical tiers. Manned by skilled sailors, it was capable of short bursts of speed and complex maneuvers.

minor adjustments to boundary lines sufficed. But Athens could exert continual domination and readily did so to promote commerce. Athens's port, Piraeus (pih-RAY-uhs), became the most important commercial center in the eastern Mediterranean.

Annual dues from subject states subsidized the increasingly expensive Athenian democracy and paid the construction costs of the Parthenon, a majestic temple to Athena on the Acropolis. The Athenian leader Pericles gained extraordinary popularity by hiring many Athenians to construct and decorate this and other monuments. When political enemies protested Pericles's use of Delian League funds for construction, he replied: "They [Athens's subjects] do not give us a single horse, nor a soldier, nor a ship. All they supply is money. It is no more than fair that after Athens has been equipped with all she needs to carry on the war, she should apply the surplus to public works, which, once completed, will bring her glory for all time."[5]

The proceeds of empire indirectly subsidized the festivals at which the dramatic tragedies of Aeschylus (ESS-kuh-luss), Sophocles, and Euripedes (yer-RIP-uh-deez) and the comedies of Aristophanes (ar-uh-STOFF-uh-neez) were performed. The brightest and most creative artists and thinkers flocked to Athens. Traveling teachers called Sophists ("wise men") provided instruction in logic and public speaking to fee-paying pupils. The new discipline of rhetoric—the crafting of attractive and persuasive arguments—gave those with training and quick wits a great advantage in politics and the courts. Greeks became connoisseurs of oratory, eagerly listening for each innovation yet so aware of the power of words that *sophist* came to mean one who uses cleverness to manipulate reality.

These new intellectual currents came together in 399 B.C.E. when the philosopher **Socrates** (ca. 470–399 B.C.E.) went on trial charged with corrupting the youth of Athens and not believing in the city's gods. A sculptor by trade, Socrates spent his time conversing with young men who enjoyed hearing him deflate the

pretensions of those who thought themselves wise. He wryly commented that he knew one more thing than everyone else: that he knew nothing.

At his trial, Socrates easily disposed of the actual charges: he was a deeply religious man, and the families of the young men he associated with supported him. He argued that the real basis of the prosecution was twofold: (1) blame for attempts by several of his aristocratic students to overthrow the Athenian democracy, and (2) blame for the controversial teachings of the Sophists, which many believed undermined morality and religious tradition. In Athenian trials, juries of hundreds of citizens decided guilt and punishment, often spurred by emotion more than legal principles. Convicted by a close vote, Socrates maintained his innocence and said he should be rewarded for his services instead. This statement led the jury to condemn him to death by drinking hemlock. Socrates's disciples considered him a martyr, and smart young men like Plato withdrew from public life and dedicated themselves to philosophical pursuits.

Socrates himself wrote nothing, preferring to converse with people he met in the street. His student Plato (ca. 428–347 B.C.E.), who learned from books and habitually wrote down his thoughts, may represent the first truly literate generation. On the outskirts of Athens, Plato founded the Academy, a school where young men could pursue higher education. Yet even Plato reflected the oral nature of his upbringing by writing dialogues—an oral form—in which his protagonist, Socrates, uses the "Socratic method" of question and answer to reach a deeper understanding of values such as justice, excellence, and wisdom. Plato refused to write down the most advanced teachings of the Academy. Higher reality, he believed, appeared only in pale reflection in the sensible world and could be grasped only by "initiates" who had completed the earlier stages.

---

[5] Plutarch, *Pericles* 12, trans. Ian Scott-Kilvert, *The Rise and Fall of Athens: Nine Greek Lives by Plutarch* (Harmondsworth: Penguin Books, 1960), 178.

**Socrates**  Athenian philosopher (ca. 470–399 B.C.E.) who shifted the emphasis of philosophical investigation from questions of natural science to ethics and human behavior. He attracted young disciples from elite families but made enemies by revealing the ignorance and pretensions of others, culminating in his trial and execution by the Athenian state.

## Inequality in Classical Greece

The Athenian democracy that historically underlies modern traditions of democracy included only a small percentage of Attica's population: true citizens—free adult males of pure Athenian ancestry. Excluding women, children, slaves, and foreigners, this group amounted to 30,000 or 40,000 people out approximately 300,000. Equally exclusive practices probably existed in less well-known Greek democracies.

Slaves, mostly foreigners, constituted perhaps one-third of the population of Attica in the fifth and fourth centuries B.C.E. The average Athenian family owned at least one slave. Slaves ran the shop or worked the farm while the master attended meetings of the Assembly or served on one of the boards overseeing the day-to-day activities of the state. As "living pieces of property," slaves did any work, submitted to any sexual acts, and suffered any punishments their owners ordained, though some communities prohibited arbitrarily killing slaves. Overall, Greece saw few of the extremes of cruelty and abuse inflicted on slaves in other places and times.

Farms being small, most slaves performed domestic service rather than field labor, often working with the master or mistress on the same tasks. Daily contact fostered relationships between owners and slaves that made it hard for owners to act inhumanely. Still, Greek thinkers justified slavery by arguing that *barbaroi* (non-Greeks) lacked the capacity to reason and thus were better off under Greek owners. The stigma attached to slavery was so great that most Athenians refused to work as wage laborers because following an employer's orders resembled being his slave.

The position of women varied. Spartan women, who were expected to bear and raise strong children, exercised regularly and enjoyed a level of public visibility and outspokenness that shocked other Greeks. At the opposite extreme, Athenians confined and oppressed women. Ironically, the exploitation of women in Athens reflects the high degree of freedom that Athenian men enjoyed in the democratic state.

Inequality marked Athenian marriages. A man of thirty—reasonably educated, a war veteran, and experienced in business and politics—commonly married, after negotiating with her parents, a teenage girl

**Vase Painting Depicting Women at an Athenian Fountain House, ca. 520 B.C.E.** Paintings on Greek vases provide the most vivid pictorial record of ancient Greek life. The subject matter usually reflects the interests of the aristocratic males who purchased the vases—warfare, athletics, mythology, drinking parties—but sometimes we are given glimpses into the lives of women and the working classes. These women are presumably domestic servants sent to fetch water for the household from the public fountain. The large water jars they are filling are like the one on which this scene is depicted. Scala/Art Resource, NY

with no formal education and minimal training in weaving, cooking, and household management. Coming into the home of a husband she hardly knew, the wife had no political rights and limited legal protection. Given the differences in age, social experience, and authority, the relationship between husband and wife resembled that of father and daughter. The function of marriage was to produce children, preferably male. The ancients were sufficiently ashamed of infanticide—the killing through exposure of

# Material Culture

## Wine and Beer in the Ancient World

The most prized beverages of ancient peoples were wine and beer. Sediments found in jars excavated at a site in northwest Iran prove that techniques for the manufacture of wine were known as early as the sixth millennium B.C.E. Beer dates back at least as far as the fourth millennium B.C.E. Archaeological excavations have brought to light the equipment used in preparing, transporting, serving, and imbibing these beverages.

In Egypt and Mesopotamia, beer, which was made from wheat or barley by a rather elaborate process, was the staple drink of both the elite and the common people. Women prepared beer for the family in their homes, and breweries produced large quantities for sale. Because the production process left chaff floating on the surface of the liquid, various means were employed to filter out this unwelcome byproduct. Sculptures on Mesopotamian stone reliefs and seals show several drinkers drawing on straws immersed in a large bowl. Archaeologists have found examples of the perforated metal cones that fit over the submerged ends of the straws and filtered the liquid beer drawn through them. It is likely that the sharing of beer from a common vessel by several people had social implications, creating a bond of friendship among the participants. Archaeologists have also found individual beer "mugs" resembling a modern watering can: closed bowls with a perforated spout to filter the chaff and a semicircular channel carrying the liquid into the drinker's mouth.

In Greece, Rome, and other Mediterranean lands, where the climate was suitable for cultivating grape vines, wine was the preferred beverage. Vines were prepared in February and periodically pruned and their unwanted tendrils pinched off. The full-grown grapes were picked in September, then crushed (with a winepress or by people trampling on them) to produce a liquid that was sealed in casks for fermentation. The new vintage was sampled the following February. Exuberant religious festivals marked key moments in the cycle. Initially expensive and therefore confined to the wealthy and for religious ceremonies, in later antiquity wine became available to a wider spectrum of people. Unlike beer, which requires refrigeration, wine can be stored for a long time in sealed containers and thus could be transported and traded across the Mediterranean lands, continental Europe, and western Asia. The usual containers for wine were long, conical pottery jars, which the Greeks called *amphoras*.

The Greeks normally mixed wine with water, and they developed an elaborate array of vessels, made of pottery, metal, and glass, to facilitate mixing, serving, and drinking the precious liquid (see the photo of the silver and bronze wine set). *Kraters* were large mixing bowls into which the wine and water were poured. The *hydria* was used to carry water, and a heater could be used to warm the water when that was desired. Another special vessel could be used to chill the wine by immersion in cold water. Ladles (long-handled spoons) and elegantly narrow vessels with spouts were used to pour the concoction into the drinkers' cups. The most popular shapes for individual drinking vessels were a shallow bowl with two handles, called a *kylix*, and the *kantharos*, a large, deep, two-handled cup. Another popular implement in Greece and western Asia was the *rhyton*, a horn-shaped vessel that tapered into the head and forepaws of an animal with a small hole at the base. The drinker would fill the horn, holding his thumb over the hole until he was ready to drink or pour, then move his thumb and release a thin stream of wine that appeared to be coming out of the animal's mouth.

The drinking equipment belonging to wealthy Greeks was often decorated with representations of the god of wine, Dionysus, holding a kantharos and surrounded by

unwanted children—to say little about it. But it is likely that more girls than boys were abandoned.

The husband spent the day outdoors attending to work or political responsibilities; he dined with male friends at night (see Material Culture: Wine and Beer in the Ancient World). The wife stayed home to cook, clean, raise the children, and supervise the servants. The closest relationship in the family was likely to be between the wife and her slave attendant, a woman of roughly the same age. The servant could be sent on errands. The wife stayed home, except to attend funerals and certain festivals or to make discreet visits to female relatives. Greek men claimed that confinement to the home stifled female promiscuity and prevented illegitimate births that could threaten family property and erode regulation of citizenship

**Dionysus in the Vineyard** *This Greek vase of the late sixth century B.C.E. depicts Dionysus, the god of wine. Carrying a large kantharos or drinking vessel, he is enveloped by vines carrying bunches of ripe grapes, and accompanied by several Satyrs (mythical creatures combining human features with those of goats or horses) and his human bride Ariadne. Greek drinking paraphernalia often depicted Dionysus and elements of his mythology and cult.* Photo By DEA/G. DAGLI ORTI/ De Agostini/Getty Images

a dense tangle of vines and grape clusters. His entourage included the half-human, half-horse Centaurs and the Maenads, literally "crazy women." These were female worshipers who drank wine and engaged in frenzied dancing until they achieved an ecstatic state and sensed the presence of the god.

Greeks, Romans, and other Mediterranean peoples used wine for more conventional religious ceremonies, pouring libations on the ground or on the altar as an offering to the gods. It was also used on occasion for medical purposes, as a disinfectant and painkiller, or as an ingredient in various medicines. Above all, wine was featured at the banquets and drinking parties that forged and deepened social bonds. In the Greek world, the *symposion* (meaning "drinking together") was held after the meal. The host presided over the affair, making the crucial decision about the proportion of water to wine, suggesting topics of conversation, and trying to keep some semblance of order. There might also be entertainment in the form of musicians, dancers, and acrobats.

In Shang China, magnificent bronze vessels whose surfaces were covered with abstract designs and representations of otherworldly animals were fashioned for use in elaborate ceremonies at ancestral shrines (see photo on page 60). The vessels contained offerings of wine and food for the spirits of the family's ancestors, who were imagined to still need sustenance in the afterlife. The treasured bronze vessels were often buried with their owners so that they could continue to employ them after death. In later periods, as the ancestral sacrifices became less important, beautiful bronze vessels, as well as their ceramic counterparts, became part of the equipment at the banquets of the well-to-do.

## QUESTIONS FOR ANALYSIS

1. What social benefits arise from drinking together?
2. How does wine serve religious purposes?
3. What evidence is there that collective drinking was practiced by the privileged social classes?

rights. Athenian law allowed a husband to kill an adulterer caught in the act with his wife.

Without documents written by women, we cannot tell how Athenian women felt about their situation. Women's festivals, such as the Thesmophoria (thes-moe-FOE-ree-uh), provided a rate opportunity for women to get out. During this three-day festival, the women of Athens lived together and managed

their own affairs in a great encampment, carrying out mysterious rituals to enhance the fertility of the land. Bold and self-assertive women appeared on the Athenian stage: the defiant Antigone (an-TIG-uh-nee) of Sophocles's play, who buried her brother despite the king's prohibition; and the wives in Aristophanes's comedy *Lysistrata* (lis-us-STRAH-tuh), who withheld sex from their husbands until the men ended a war.

Although imagined by men and probably reflecting a fear of strong women, these characters must partly reflect the playwrights' mothers, sisters, and wives.

To find his intellectual and emotional "equal," men often looked to other men. Bisexuality arose as much from the social structure as from biological inclinations. An older man commonly admired, pursued, and mentored a youth, thus making bisexuality part of the youth's education and initiation into the adult male community. Though commonplace among intellectual groups that loom large in the written sources, the frequency of bisexuality and the confinement of women among the Athenians remains uncertain.

## Failure of the City-State and Triumph of the Macedonians

Athens's rise to empire led in 431 B.C.E. to the outbreak of the **Peloponnesian War**, a struggle for survival between Athenian and Spartan alliances that encompassed most of the Greek world. To insulate themselves from attack by land, in midcentury the Athenians had built three long walls connecting the city with the port of Piraeus and the adjacent shoreline. As long as Athens controlled the sea-lanes and could provision itself, a land-based siege could not starve it into submission.

At the start of the war, Pericles broke precedent by refusing to engage the Spartan-led armies that invaded Attica each year, knowing that the enemy hoplites must soon return to their farms. Thus, instead of culminating in a short, decisive battle, the Peloponnesian War dragged on for nearly three decades with great loss of life and resources. It sapped the morale of all Greece and ended only with the defeat of Athens in a naval battle in 404 B.C.E. Because the Persian Empire had bankrolled the construction of ships by the Spartan alliance, Sparta finally was able to take the conflict into Athens's own element, the sea.

The victorious Spartans, who had entered the war championing "the freedom of the Greeks," took over Athens's overseas empire until their increasingly highhanded behavior aroused the opposition of other city-states. Indeed, the fourth century B.C.E. was a time of nearly continuous skirmishing among Greek states. The independent polis that lent glory to Greek culture also fostered rivalries and fears among neighbors.

This lack of unity allowed the Persians to recoup old losses. By the King's Peace of 387 B.C.E., encompassing most of the war-weary Greek states, all of western Asia, including the Ionian Greek communities, went to Persia. The Persian king guaranteed a status quo that kept the Greeks divided and weak until rebellions in Egypt, Cyprus, and Phoenicia, combined with troubles from some western satraps, diverted his attention from thoughts of another Greek invasion.

Meanwhile, in northern Greece Philip II (r. 359–336 B.C.E.) was transforming his previously backward kingdom of Macedonia into the premier military power. (Although southern Greeks had long doubted the "Greekness" of the rough and rowdy Macedonians, modern scholarship considers their language and culture as Greek at base, though influenced by non-Greek neighbors.) Philip improved the traditional hoplite formation and increased its striking power and mobility by equipping soldiers with longer thrusting spears and less armor. Using horses bred in Macedonia's broad grassy plains, he also experimented with coordinating infantry and cavalry. Finally, his engineers developed new siege weapons, including the first catapults—machines using the power of twisted cords that, when relaxed, hurled arrows or stones great distances.

In 338 B.C.E. Philip defeated a southern coalition and established the Confederacy of Corinth to control the Greek city-states. Appointed military commander of all the Greeks, he planned a campaign against Persia and established a bridgehead on the Asiatic side of the Hellespont. These plans may have reflected the advice of Greek thinkers who urged an anti-Persian crusade to unify their quarrelsome countrymen.

An assassin cut short Philip's ambitions in 336 B.C.E. **Alexander** (356–323 B.C.E.), his son and heir, crossed into Asia in 334 B.C.E., vowing revenge for

**Peloponnesian War** A protracted (431–404 B.C.E.) and costly conflict between the Athenian and Spartan alliance systems that convulsed most of the Greek world. The war was largely a consequence of Athenian imperialism. Possession of a naval empire allowed Athens to fight a war of attrition. Ultimately, Sparta prevailed because of Athenian errors and Persian financial support.

**Alexander** King of Macedonia in northern Greece. Between 334 and 323 B.C.E. he conquered the Persian Empire, reached the Indus Valley, founded many Greek-style cities, and spread Greek culture across the Middle East. Later known as Alexander the Great.

Xerxes's invasion a century and half earlier. In 331 B.C.E. he defeated the Persians in three pitched battles against the western satraps at the village of Gaugamela (GAW-guh-mee-luh), north of Babylon.

Alexander the Great, as he came to be called, maintained the Persian administration system but replaced Persian officials with Macedonians and Greeks. To control strategic points, he settled wounded and aged ex-soldiers in a series of Greek-style cities, beginning with Alexandria in Egypt. After his victory at Gaugamela, he experimented with leaving cooperative Persian officials in place, also admitting some Persians and other Iranians into his army and court circle. Adopting elements of Persian dress and court ceremonials, he married several Iranian women who had useful royal or aristocratic connections, and he pressed his leading comrades to do the same.

In opting for these unexpected policies, which the Macedonian nobility fiercely resented, Alexander probably acted from both pragmatic and idealistic motives. His Asian campaign began with visions of glory, booty, and revenge. But the farther east he traveled, the more he saw himself as the legitimate successor of the Persian king (a claim facilitated by the death of Darius III). Alexander may have recognized that he had responsibilities to all the peoples who fell under his control and that administering so vast an empire would require the cooperation of local leaders. In this, he was following the example of the Achaemenids.

## SECTION REVIEW

- Greek rebellion against Persian domination provoked the Persian Wars.

- During successive Persian invasions, Athens and Sparta led Greek resistance.

- Victory left Athens a naval power with imperial aspirations, and its wealth nourished the great cultural achievements of the Classical period.

- Athenian democracy rested upon several forms of inequality, including the subjugation of women and slaves.

- Rivalry between Sparta and Athens sparked the Peloponnesian War, which destroyed Athens and weakened all the city-states.

- Macedonia then became the dominant power in Greece, conquering city-states and, under Alexander the Great, the Persian Empire.

# THE HELLENISTIC SYNTHESIS, 323–30 B.C.E.

■ *How did Greeks and non-Greeks interact and develop new cultural syntheses during the Hellenistic Age?*

Historians call the epoch following Alexander's conquests the **Hellenistic Age** (323–30 B.C.E.) because the lands in northeastern Africa and western Asia that came under Greek rule became "Hellenized"—that is, powerfully influenced by Greek culture. Greeks migrated in large numbers from their overcrowded homeland to serve as a privileged class of soldiers and administrators on the new frontiers, where they replicated the lifestyle of the city-state. This era of large kingdoms, containing ethnically mixed populations, great cities, powerful rulers, pervasive bureaucracies, and vast disparities in wealth, differed profoundly from the Archaic and Classical ages with their small, homogeneous, independent city-states. The Hellenistic world more closely resembled our own in its long-distance trade and communications, new institutions like libraries and universities, new kinds of scholarship and science, and sophisticated tastes in art and literature.

When he died suddenly in 323 B.C.E. at the age of thirty-two, Alexander had no plans for the succession. A half century of chaos followed as the most ambitious and ruthless of his generals struggled to succeed him. When the dust cleared, they had broken the empire into three major kingdoms, each ruled by a Macedonian dynasty: the Seleucid (sih-LOO-sid), Ptolemaic (tawl-uh-MAY-ik), and Antigonid (an-TIG-uh-nid) kingdoms (see Map 4.1). The Antigonids ruled the Macedonian homeland and tried with varying success to extend their control over southern Greece; the Ptolemies ruled Egypt; and the Seleucids inherited the majority of Alexander's conquests in Asia. A rough balance of power prevented any of the three from gaining the upper hand and enabled smaller states to survive by playing off the great powers.

**Hellenistic Age** Historians' term for the era, usually dated 323–30 B.C.E., in which Greek culture spread across western Asia and northeastern Africa after the conquests of Alexander the Great. The period ended with the fall of the last major Hellenistic kingdom to Rome, but Greek cultural influence persisted until the spread of Islam in the seventh century C.E.

The Seleucids, who ruled the bulk of Alexander's empire, faced the greatest challenges. The Indus Valley and Afghanistan soon split off, and over the course of the third and second centuries B.C.E. Iran fell to the Parthians (see Chapter 8). Thereafter Mesopotamia, Syria, and parts of Anatolia constituted the Seleucid core, with the kings ruling from Antioch (AN-tee-awk) in Syria. Like the Persians before them, they governed many different ethnic groups organized under various political and social forms. In the farming villages, where most of the population resided, the Seleucids maintained an administration modeled on the Persian system. They also continued Alexander's policy of founding Greek-style cities to serve as administrative centers and attract colonists from Greece. The Seleucids desperately needed Greek soldiers, engineers, and administrators.

In Europe, the Antigonid dynasty ruled the Macedonian homeland and parts of northern Greece. Compact and ethnically homogeneous, the Antigonid kingdom experienced little of the hostility that the Seleucid and Ptolemaic rulers faced. Macedonian garrisons gave the Antigonids a toehold in central and southern Greece, and the shadow of Macedonian intervention always threatened the south. The southern states responded by joining confederations, such as the Achaean (uh-KEY-uhn) League in the Peloponnese, in which the member-states maintained local autonomy but pooled resources and military power.

Athens and Sparta stood apart from these confederations. Never abandoning their myth of invincibility, the Spartans made a number of heroic but futile stands against Macedonian armies. Athens, now cherished for the artistic and literary accomplishments of the fifth century B.C.E., pursued a policy of neutrality. The city became a large museum filled with the relics and memories of a glorious past, as well as a university town that attracted the children of the well-to-do from all over the Mediterranean and western Asia.

## Egypt Under the Ptolemies

The dynasty of the **Ptolemies** (TAWL-uh-meze) ruled Egypt and sometimes laid claim to Palestine. Since most Egyptians belonged to one ethnic group and lived in villages alongside the Nile, the Ptolemies ruled from **Alexandria**, which was situated near the mouth of the westernmost branch of the Nile and linked Egypt with the Mediterranean world. Memphis and Thebes, the capitals of ancient Egypt, had been located upriver. In the language of the Ptolemaic bureaucracy, Alexandria was technically "beside Egypt" rather than in it, as if to emphasize the gulf between rulers and subjects and the fact that it was not on the Nile River.

Like the Seleucids, the Ptolemies encouraged Greek immigration. In return for collaboration in the military or civil administration, the immigrants received land and a privileged position in the new society. But the Ptolemies did not plant Greek-style cities throughout the Egyptian countryside and made no effort to force the Greek language or customs on the Egyptian population. So separate was the ruling class from the subject population that only the last Ptolemy, Queen Cleopatra (r. 51–30 B.C.E.), who lost her kingdom to Rome, bothered to learn the Egyptian language.

The advent of new masters brought few changes to the Egyptian peasants. Vast revenues poured into the royal treasury from rents (the king owned most of the land), taxes, and royal monopolies on olive oil, salt, papyrus, and other key commodities. Nevertheless, from the early second century B.C.E., native insurrections in the countryside, though quickly stamped out by government forces and Greek and Hellenized settlers, indicate growing resentment of the Greeks' exploitation and arrogance.

Alexandria, the greatest Hellenistic city with a population of nearly half a million, had at its heart the royal compound, containing the palace and administrative buildings. The magnificent Mausoleum of Alexander enshrined Alexander's body, which the first Ptolemy had stolen during its return to Macedonia for burial. He had hoped that the luster of the

**Ptolemies**  The Macedonian dynasty, descended from one of Alexander the Great's officers, that ruled Egypt for three centuries (323–30 B.C.E.). From their magnificent capital at Alexandria on the Mediterranean coast, the Ptolemies largely took over the system created by Egyptian pharaohs to extract the wealth of the land, rewarding Greeks and Hellenized non-Greeks serving in the military and administration.

**Alexandria**  City on the Mediterranean coast of Egypt founded by Alexander. It became the capital of the Hellenistic kingdom of the Ptolemies. It contained the famous Library and the Museum, a center for leading scientific and literary figures. Its merchants engaged in trade with areas bordering the Mediterranean and the Indian Ocean.

**Map 4.1  Hellenistic Civilization**  After the death of Alexander the Great in 323 B.C.E., his vast empire soon split apart into a number of large and small political entities. A Macedonian dynasty was established on each continent: the Antigonids ruled the Macedonian homeland and tried with varying success to extend their control over southern Greece; the Ptolemies ruled Egypt; and the Seleucids inherited the majority of Alexander's conquests in Asia, though they lost control of the eastern portions because of the rise of the Parthians of Iran in the second century B.C.E. This period saw Greeks migrating in large numbers from their overcrowded homeland to serve as a privileged class of soldiers and administrators on the new frontiers, where they replicated the lifestyle of the city-state. © Cengage Learning

great conqueror, who was declared to be a god, would give him legitimacy as a ruler.

The famed Library of Alexandria had several hundred thousand volumes. The Museum, or "House of the Muses" (divinities who presided over the arts and sciences), supported the work of the great poets, philosophers, doctors, and scientists. A great lighthouse—a multistory tower with a fiery beacon visible at a distance of 30 miles (48 kilometers)—guided seafarers to two harbors serving the commerce of the Mediterranean, the Red Sea, and the Indian Ocean.

Alexandrian Greeks enjoyed citizenship in a polis, complete with Assembly, Council, and officials overseeing local affairs. They took advantage of Greek-style amenities and institutions: public baths and shaded arcades, theaters featuring revivals of ancient plays, and concert halls for musical performances and demonstrations of oratory. Young men of the privileged elite took classes at gymnasiums where athletics and fitness combined with music and literature in the curriculum. Jews had their own civic corporation, government, officials, and courts and

SECTION REVIEW

- The death of Alexander the Great and the breakup of his empire inaugurated the Hellenistic Age.
- Large kingdoms were ruled by Macedonian dynasties in which Greek culture was fused with local traditions.
- More Greek city-states retained autonomy through alliances, but Sparta and Athens stood apart and lost power.
- Egypt under the Ptolemies was the most successful Hellenistic state, and its capital Alexandria became the greatest Hellenistic city.

predominated in two of the five main residential districts. The sights, sounds, and smells of Syria, Anatolia, and the Egyptian countryside lent distinctiveness to other quarters.

## Hellenistic Societies

In all the Hellenistic states, ambitious members of the indigenous populations learned the Greek language and adopted elements of the Greek lifestyle, because doing so helped them become part of the privileged and wealthy ruling class. Language and customs more than physical traits made a person a Greek. The Hellenistic Age saw a spontaneous synthesis of Greek and indigenous ways. Egyptians migrated to Alexandria, and Greeks and Egyptians intermarried in the villages of the countryside. Greeks living amid the monuments and descendants of the ancient civilizations of Egypt and western Asia learned the mathematical and astronomical wisdom of Mesopotamia, the mortuary rituals of Egypt, and the attractions of foreign religions. With little official planning or blessing and stemming for the most part from the day-to-day experiences of ordinary people, a great multicultural experiment unfolded as Greek and Middle Eastern cultural traits clashed and merged.

## CONCLUSION

Greece and Iran represent two ways in which societies with shared Indo-European linguistic and religious roots adapted to different geographical environments and indigenous cultures. Although scholars can easily trace resemblances among gods, customs, and philosophical outlooks in these areas, the people themselves had no sense of kinship with one another. Only briefly, under Alexander the Great, did they come into direct contact in meaningful ways, and the resulting Hellenistic culture touched all three regions.

While some technologies, such as coinage, took hold in all areas and trade flourished, both overland and across the Mediterranean Sea, local circumstances dictated political and social formations. The ancient cultural centers of Egypt and Mesopotamia influenced the Greeks and the Persians.

It is intriguing to compare Greek civilization to ancient China in the Zhou era (see Chapter 3). Too far apart to have had any influence on each other, both reveal striking similarities. Their most innovative developments took place during periods of political fragmentation, rivalry, and warfare—the Archaic and Classical periods of Greek history and the Spring and Autumn and Warring States Periods in China—rather than in the more stable centuries under the Roman and Han emperors (Chapter 5 will compare Rome and early imperial China). Their differences are equally revealing and underlie the ways in which Western and East Asian civilizations have diverged, with implications for our own times.

## CHAPTER REVIEW

### ANCIENT IRAN, 1000–500 B.C.E.

■ *How did the Persian Empire rise from its Iranian homeland and succeed in controlling vast territories and diverse cultures?* (page 83)

The Medes, who were the first Iranians to build a complex political order, helped destroy the Assyrian Empire. Cyrus then united the Persians and overthrew the Medes, prompting the two similar cultures to blend. Expansion into Mesopotamia, Syria, and Anatolia connected the Persian Empire with older cultural and commercial networks. Under Darius I, the empire reached its fullest extent and basic governmental structure: provinces governed by satraps, tribute money funneled to the center, and a decentralized legal system. An extensive road and post system connected the imperial center with the periphery.

## THE RISE OF THE GREEKS, 1000–500 B.C.E.
■ *What were the most distinctive elements of Greek civilization, and how and why did they evolve in the Archaic and Classical periods?* (page 88)

A rugged geography inhibiting overland travel turned the Greeks to the sea. The focus of this Greek civilization was the polis, whose citizens participated in government and defended it as hoplites. Population pressures spurred overseas colonization, which spread Greek culture throughout the Mediterranean world. The late Archaic period saw the emergence of new forms of literary and intellectual endeavor, such as history and philosophical inquiry, that matured in the Classical period.

## THE STRUGGLE OF PERSIA AND GREECE, 546–323 B.C.E.
■ *How did the Persian Wars and their aftermath affect the politics and culture of ancient Greece and Iran?* (page 94)

Athens, Sparta, and their allies repulsed Persian invasions on land and at sea. Victory left Athens a naval power with an overseas empire and sufficient wealth from tribute and trade to finance temples on the Acropolis and other cultural achievement in drama and philosophy. Warlike Sparta and artistic, cosmopolitan Athens represented opposite extremes of Greek culture, but rivalry between then exploded into the Peloponnesian War, which shattered Athens and weakened the other city-states. Exploring this weakness, Persia recovered old losses but encountered Macedonian expansion and ultimate defeat by Alexander the Great.

## THE HELLENISTIC SYNTHESIS, 323–30 B.C.E.
■ *How did Greeks and non-Greeks interact and develop new cultural syntheses during the Hellenistic Age?* (page 101)

The death of Alexander the Great ushered in the Hellenistic Age. From his empire his generals carved kingdoms for themselves, founding Macedonian dynasties that presided over an international Greek culture. The Seleucids ruled the largest kingdom, founding Greek-style cities but ruling in the Persian manner. Both they and the Ptolemies encouraged Greek immigration, but in Egypt Greeks remained a class apart and had little to do with native Egyptians. The Antigonids ruled Macedonia, but the southern and central Greek cities resisted them through alliances. Sparta and Athens remained apart, both losing power in the region. Alexandria became the major Hellenistic city, a showcase of the cultural synthesis that marked the age.

## Key Terms

| | |
|---|---|
| Cyrus (p. 84) | Herodotus (p. 92) |
| Darius I (p. 85) | Pericles (p. 93) |
| satrap (p. 85) | Persian Wars (p. 94) |
| Persepolis (p. 86) | trireme (p. 95) |
| Zoroastrianism (p. 87) | Socrates (p. 96) |
| polis (p. 89) | Peloponnesian War (p. 100) |
| hoplite (p. 89) | Alexander (p. 100) |
| tyrant (p. 90) | Hellenistic Age (p. 101) |
| democracy (p. 90) | Ptolemies (p. 102) |
| sacrifice (p. 91) | Alexandria (p. 102) |

# An Age of Empires: Rome and Han China

© Cengage Learning

According to Chinese sources, in the year 166 C.E. a group of travelers identifying themselves as envoys from Andun, the king of distant Da Qin, arrived at the court of the Chinese emperor Huan, one of the Han dynasty rulers. Andun was Marcus Aurelius Antoninus, the emperor of Rome.

These first known "Romans" to reach China probably hailed from one of Rome's eastern provinces, perhaps Egypt or Syria, and may have stretched the truth in claiming to be official representatives of the Roman emperor. The Chinese officials had had no direct contact with the Roman Empire, however, and so the travelers, probably merchants hoping to trade for highly prized Chinese silk, easily got away with the imposture.

Direct or regular contact between the empires never developed, but the episode reveals that in the early centuries C.E. Rome and China dimly recognized each other's existence across the far-flung trading networks that spanned the Eastern Hemisphere. Both states, moreover, emerged from the last centuries B.C.E. and the first centuries C.E. as a new kind of empire, both qualitatively and quantitatively.

Since neither empire influenced the other, what caused them to arise and flourish at the same time? Some stress supposedly common factors, such as climate change or challenges from Central Asian nomads, but no theory has won the general support of scholars. The Roman Empire encompassed the lands surrounding the Mediterranean Sea and substantial portions of inland Europe and the Middle East. The Han Empire, named for China's ruling family, stretched from the Pacific Ocean to the oases of Central Asia. The largest empires the world had yet seen, they nevertheless managed to centralize control, achieve unprecedented stability and longevity, and assert dominance over the many cultures and peoples within their borders.

# ROME'S CREATION OF A MEDITERRANEAN EMPIRE, 753 B.C.E.–330 C.E.

■ *How did Rome create and maintain its vast Mediterranean empire?*

The boot-shaped Italian peninsula, with the large island of Sicily, constitutes a bridge almost linking Europe and North Africa (see Map 5.1). Rome too lay at a crossroads, being situated at the midpoint of the peninsula, about 15 miles (24 kilometers) from its western coast, where a north-south road intersected an east-west river route. The Tiber River on one side and a double ring of seven hills on the other afforded natural protection to the site.

The Apennine Mountains form Italy's spine, separating the eastern and western coastal plains, and the arc of the Alps shields it on the north. Navigable rivers and passes through the Apennines, and even through the snowcapped Alps, eased travel by merchants and armies. The Mediterranean climate afforded a long growing season and favorable conditions for a wide variety of crops. Hillside forests, today largely gone, provided timber for construction and fuel. Iron and other metals came from the region of Etruria in the northwest.

Although hills account for 75 percent of the Italy's land area, the coastal plains and river valleys provide arable land, with fertile volcanic soil capable of supporting a much larger population than Greece. As it expanded within Italy, the Roman state tapped these human resources.

## A Republic of Farmers

According to legend, Romulus, cast adrift on the Tiber River as a baby and nursed by a she-wolf, founded Rome in 753 B.C.E. Archaeological research, however, has revealed occupation on the Palestine Hill, one of the city's seven hills, dating to 1000 B.C.E. Several hilltop communities merged shortly before 600 B.C.E., forming an urban nucleus made possible by the draining of a swamp on the site of the future Roman Forum (civic center).

The Latin speech and cultural patterns of the inhabitants of the site resembled those of most of the other peoples of the peninsula. However, tradition remembered Etruscan immigrants (who were linguistically and culturally different from the technologically advanced Romans) arriving in the seventh century B.C.E., and Rome came to pride itself on offering refuge to exiles and outcasts.

Agriculture anchored the economy of early Rome, and land constituted wealth. Landowners brought

**Map 5.1  The Roman Empire**  The Roman Empire came to encompass all the lands surrounding the Mediterranean Sea, as well as parts of continental Europe. When Augustus died in 14 C.E., he left instructions to his successors not to expand beyond the limits he had set, but Claudius invaded southern Britain in the mid-first century and the soldier-emperor Trajan added Romania early in the second century. Deserts and seas provided solid natural boundaries, but the long and vulnerable river borders in central and eastern Europe would eventually prove expensive to defend and vulnerable to invasion by Germanic and Central Asian peoples. © Cengage Learning

**Legend:**
- Roman Empire by death of Augustus, 14 C.E.
- Territory added by death of Hadrian, 138 C.E.
- Territory gained and lost, with dates held
- Parthian Empire, ca. 200 C.E.
- ★ Major battle

CALEDONIA (85–105 C.E.)

Hadrian's Wall 122 C.E.

Eburacum (York)

BRITAIN

Camulodunum (Colchester)
Londinium (London)

GERMANIA (4–9 C.E.)

LOWER GERMANY

Colonia Claudia Agrippinensis (Cologne)

Moguntiacum (Mainz)

UPPER GERMANY

BELGICA

Alesia 52 B.C.E.

LUGDUNENSIS

GAUL

Lutetia Parisiorum (Paris)

Lugdunum (Lyons)

AQUITANIA

Burdigala (Bordeaux)

Nemausus (Nîmes)

NARBONENSIS

Massilia (Marseilles)

Narbo

Tarraco

Saguntum

TARRACONENSIS

SPAIN

LUSITANIA

Emerita Augusta (Mérida)

Corduba (Córdoba)

BAETICA

Balearic Is.

Corsica

Sardinia

ALPS

CISALPINE GAUL

Mediolanum (Milan)

RAETIA

NORICUM

PANNONIA

Vindobona (Vienna)

Aquincum (Budapest)

DACIA (107–272 C.E.)

Singidunum (Belgrade)

DALMATIA

MOESIA

Arretium

ETRURIA

ITALY

Rome

Ostia

Pompeii

Mt. Vesuvius

Brundisium

Adriatic Sea

THRACE

Byzantium

MACEDONIA

Thessalonica

EPIRUS

Actium 31 B.C.E. ★

ACHAEA

Corinth

Athens

Syracuse

Sicily

Malta

Crete

Rhodes

Carthage

NUMIDIA

AFRICA PROCONSULARIS

Leptis Magna

Cyrene

CYRENAICA

MAURETANIA

NORTH AFRICA

SAHARA

Mediterranean Sea

BITHYNIA AND PONTUS

Pergamum

ASIA

Ephesus

ANATOLIA

GALATIA

CAPPADOCIA

PAMPHYLIA

LYCIA

CILICIA

Tarsus

Cyprus

Antioch

SYRIA

Damascus

Palmyra

Jerusalem

Petra

JUDAEA

ARABIA

Red Sea

EGYPT

Alexandria

Bahriya Oasis

Nile R.

ARABIAN DESERT

ARMENIA (114–117 C.E.)

ASSYRIA (116–117 C.E.)

MESOPOTAMIA (115–117 C.E.)

Tigris R.

Euphrates R.

Ctesiphon

Seleucia

Babylon

Susa

Ecbatana

PARTHIA

Nisa

Persepolis

Persian Gulf

CAUCASUS MTS.

Black Sea

Caspian Sea

Aral Sea

Volga R.

Don R.

Dnieper R.

BOSPORAN KINGDOM

Vistula R.

Elbe R.

Rhine R.

Rhône R.

Ebro R.

Po R.

Danube R.

Baltic Sea

North Sea

ATLANTIC OCEAN

0   200   400 Km.
0   200   400 Mi.

# Chronology

| | Rome | China |
|---|---|---|
| 1000 B.C.E. | 1000 B.C.E. First settlement on site of Rome | |
| 500 B.C.E. | 507 B.C.E. Establishment of the Republic | 480–221 B.C.E. Warring States Period |
| 300 B.C.E. | 264–202 B.C.E. Wars against Carthage guarantee Roman control of western Mediterranean | 221 B.C.E. Qin emperor unites eastern China |
| 200 B.C.E. | 200–146 B.C.E. Wars against Hellenistic kingdoms lead to control of eastern Mediterranean | 206 B.C.E. Han dynasty succeeds Qin<br>140–87 B.C.E. Emperor Wu expands the Han Empire |
| 100 B.C.E. | 88–31 B.C.E. Civil wars and failure of the Republic<br>31 B.C.E.–14 C.E. Augustus establishes the Principate | 25 C.E. Han capital transferred from Chang'an to Luoyang |
| 30 C.E. | Between 30 and 36 C.E. Crucifixion of Jesus | |
| 200 C.E. | 235–284 C.E. Third-Century Crisis | 220 C.E. Fall of Han dynasty |
| 300 C.E. | 324 C.E. Constantine moves capital to Constantinople | |

social status and political privilege while buttressing fundamental values. Most early Romans cultivated their own small plots of land, but a few families managed to acquire large tracts of land. The heads of these wealthy families served in the Senate, a "Council of Elders" that dominated the politics of the Roman state. Their families constituted the senatorial class. Tradition maintains that seven kings ruled Rome between 753 and 507 B.C.E., Romulus being the first and the tyrannical Tarquinius Superbus the last. In 507 B.C.E. members of the senatorial class, led by Brutus "the Liberator," deposed Tarquinius Superbus and instituted a *res publica*, a "public possession," or republic.

Far from being a democracy, the **Roman Republic**, which lasted from 507 to 31 B.C.E., vested power in several assemblies. Male citizens could attend their sessions, but the votes of the wealthy counted for more than the votes of the poor. The hierarchy of state officials, elected for one year, culminated in two consuls, who presided over the Senate and other assemblies and commanded the army on campaigns.

Technically an advisory council, first to the kings and later to the annually changing Republican officials, the **Roman Senate** increasingly made policy and governed. Senators nominated their sons for public offices and filled senatorial vacancies with former officials. This self-perpetuating body, whose members served for life, brought together the

state's wealth, influence, and political and military experience.

Roman families consisted of several generations as well as domestic slaves. The oldest living male, the *paterfamilias*, exercised absolute authority over every family member. This *auctoritas*, enjoyed by important male members of the society as a whole, enabled a man to inspire and demand obedience from his inferiors.

Complex ties of obligation, such as the **patron/ client relationship**, bound together individuals and families. *Clients* sought the help and protection of *patrons*, men of wealth and influence. A senator might have dozens or even hundreds of clients to whom he provided legal advice and representation,

**Roman Republic** The period from 507 to 31 B.C.E., during which Rome was largely governed by the aristocratic Roman Senate.

**Roman Senate** A council whose members were the heads of wealthy, landowning families. Originally an advisory body to the early kings, in the era of the Roman Republic the Senate effectively governed the Roman state and the growing empire. Under Senate leadership, Rome conquered an empire of unprecedented extent in the lands surrounding the Mediterranean Sea.

**patron/client relationship** In ancient Rome, a fundamental social relationship in which the patron—a wealthy and powerful individual—provided legal and economic protection and assistance to clients, men of lesser status and means, and in return the clients supported the political careers and economic interests of their patron.

**Statue of a Roman Carrying Busts of His Ancestors, First Century B.C.E.**
Roman society was extremely conscious of status, and the status of an elite Roman family was determined in large part by the public achievements of ancestors and living members. A visitor to a Roman home found portraits of distinguished ancestors in the entry hall, along with labels listing the offices they held. Portrait heads were carried in funeral processions.
Alinari/Art Resource, NY

under the jurisdiction of the paterfamilias of her husband's family. Unable to own property or represent herself in legal proceedings, she had to depend on a male guardian to advocate her interests.

Despite these limitations, Roman women were less constrained than their Greek counterparts (see Chapter 4). Over time they gained greater personal protection and economic freedom. Some took advantage of a form of marriage that left a woman under the jurisdiction of her father and independent after his death. Many stories involve strong women who greatly influenced their husbands or sons and thereby helped shape Roman history. Roman poets expressed love for women who appeared educated and outspoken, and the careers of the early emperors abound with tales of self-assured and assertive queen-mothers and consorts.

Like other Italian peoples, Romans believed in invisible forces known as *numina*. Vesta, the living, pulsating energy of fire, dwelled in the hearth; Janus guarded the door; and the Penates watched over food stored in the cupboard. Other deities resided in hills, caves, grottoes, and springs. Small offerings of cakes and liquids supplicated the favor of these spirits. Certain gods operated in larger spheres—for example, Jupiter, the god of the sky, and Mars, initially a god of agriculture as well as war.

The Romans strove to maintain the *pax deorum* ("peace of the gods"), a covenant between the gods and the Roman state. Boards of priests drawn from the aristocracy performed sacrifices and other rituals to win the gods' favor. In return, the Roman state counted on the gods for success in its undertakings. When the Romans encountered the Greeks of southern Italy, they equated their major deities with gods from the Greek pantheon, such as Zeus (Jupiter) and Ares (Mars), and took over the myths attached to them.

physical protection, and monetary loans in tough times. In turn, the client followed his patron out to battle, supported him in the political arena, worked on his land, and even contributed to his daughter's dowry. Throngs of clients awaited their patrons in the morning and accompanied them to the Forum for the day's business. Especially large retinues brought great prestige. Middle-class clients of the aristocracy might be patrons of poorer men. Rome thus accepted and institutionalized inequality and made of it a system of mutual benefits and obligations.

Roman women played no public role and hence appear infrequently in sources. Nearly all information pertains to those in the upper classes. In early Rome, a woman never ceased to be a child in the eyes of the law. She started out under the absolute authority of her paterfamilias. When she married, she came

## Expansion in Italy and the Mediterranean

The fledgling Roman Republic of 500 B.C.E. did not stand out among the city-states of Latium, a region of central Italy. Three and a half centuries later, Rome commanded a huge empire encompassing virtually all the Mediterranean lands. Expansion began slowly but picked up momentum, peaking in the third and second centuries B.C.E.

Some scholars ascribe Rome's success to the greed and aggressiveness of a people fond of war. Others observe that the structure of the Roman state encouraged recourse to war, because the two consuls had only one year in office in which to gain military glory. The Romans invariably claimed that they were only defending themselves. It is possible that fear drove the Romans to expand their territory, as the vulnerability of new conquests necessitated ever more buffers against attack.

Ongoing friction between the pastoral hill peoples of the Apennines, who depended on herding, and the farmers of the coastal plains sparked Rome's conquest of Italy. In the fifth century B.C.E., Rome achieved leadership within a league of central Italian cities organized for defense against the hill peoples. In the fourth century B.C.E., the Romans occasionally defended the wealthy and sophisticated cities of Campania, the region on the Bay of Naples possessing the richest farmland in the peninsula. By 290 B.C.E., after three wars with the peoples of Samnium in central Italy, the Romans had extended their "protection" over nearly the entire peninsula.

The Romans consolidated their hold over Italy by granting the political, legal, and economic privileges of citizenship to conquered populations. In this, they contrasted with the Greeks, who did not share citizenship with outsiders (see Chapter 4). The Romans co-opted the most influential elements within the conquered communities and made Rome's interests their interests. Rome also demanded that its Italian subjects provide soldiers, thus creating a seemingly inexhaustible reservoir of manpower that bolstered military success. Rome could endure higher casualties than the enemy and prevail by sheer numbers.

Between 264 and 202 B.C.E. Rome fought two protracted wars against the Carthaginians, those energetic descendants of the Phoenicians who had settled in Tunisia and dominated the commerce of the western Mediterranean (see Chapter 2). The Roman state emerged as the master of the western Mediterranean and acquired its first overseas provinces in Sicily, Sardinia, and Spain (see Map 5.1). Between 200 and 146 B.C.E. a series of wars pitted the Roman state against the major Hellenistic kingdoms in the eastern Mediterranean. Reluctant to occupy such distant territories, the Romans withdrew their troops. But when the settlements they imposed failed to take root, a frustrated Roman government took over direct administration of these turbulent lands. The conquest of the Celtic peoples of Gaul (modern France; see Chapter 3) by Rome's most brilliant general, Gaius Julius Caesar, between 59 and 51 B.C.E. led to the first territorial acquisitions in Europe's heartland.

The Romans resisted extending to distant provinces the governing system and privileges of citizenship they employed in Italy. Indigenous elite groups willing to collaborate with Rome enjoyed considerable autonomy, including responsibility for local administration and tax collection. Every year a senator, usually someone who had held high office, served as governor in each province. Accompanied by a surprisingly small retinue of friends and relations who served as advisers and deputies, the governor defended the province against outside attack and internal disruption, oversaw the collection of taxes, and judged legal cases.

Over time, this system proved inadequate. Officials chosen through political connections often lacked competence, and the one-year period of service gave them little time to gain experience. A few governors extorted huge sums of money from the provincial populace. Rome still depended on the institutions and attitudes of a city-state to govern an ever-growing empire.

## The Failure of the Republic

The frequent wars and territorial expansion of the third and second centuries B.C.E. set off changes in the Italian landscape. Peasant farmers spent long periods of time away from home on military service, while most of the wealth generated by conquest and empire ended up helping the upper classes purchase Italian land. Investors easily acquired the property of absent soldier-farmers by purchase, deception, or intimidation. The small self-sufficient farms of the Italian countryside, whose peasant owners provided the backbone of the Roman legions (units of 6,000 soldiers), gave way to *latifundia*, literally "broad estates," or ranches.

The new owners had ample space to graze herds of cattle or grow grapes for wine in the place of less profitable wheat. Thus, much of Italy, especially in the cities, became dependent on expensive imported grain. Meanwhile, cheap slave labor provided by war prisoners made it hard for peasants who had lost their farms to find work in the countryside (see Diversity and Dominance: Socioeconomic Mobility, Winners and Losers in Imperial Rome and Han China). They moved to Rome and other cities, but they found no work there either and ended up living in poverty. The growing urban masses, idle and prone to riot, would play a major role in the political struggles of the late Republic.

The decline of peasant farmers in Italy produced a shortage of men who owned the minimum amount of property required for military service. During a war that the Romans fought in North Africa at the end of the second century B.C.E., Gaius Marius—a "new man," as the Romans labeled politically active individuals from outside the traditional ruling class—achieved political prominence by accepting poor, propertyless men into his legions, to whom he promised farms upon retirement from military service. These grateful troops helped Marius get elected to an unprecedented (and illegal) six consulships.

Between 88 and 31 B.C.E., several ambitious individuals—Sulla, Pompey, Julius Caesar, Mark Antony, and Octavian—commanded armies that were more loyal to them than to the state. Their use of Roman troops to increase their personal power led to civil wars between military factions. The generals who seized Rome on several occasions executed their political opponents and exercised dictatorial control.

By 31 B.C.E., however, Julius Caesar's grandnephew and heir, Octavian (63 B.C.E.–14 C.E.), had eliminated all rivals and set about refashioning the Roman system of government while retaining the offices, honors, and social prerogatives of the senatorial class. A dictator in fact, he never called himself king or emperor, claiming merely to be *princeps*, "first among equals"—hence the term **Roman Principate** for the period following the Roman Republic. **Augustus**, a title Octavian received from the Senate, implied prosperity and piety and became the name by which he is known to posterity. Augustus's ruthlessness, patience, and intuitive grasp of psychology enabled him to manipulate each group

in society. When he died in 14 C.E., after forty-five years of carefully veiled rule, scarcely anyone could remember the Republic. During his reign, the empire expanded into Egypt and parts of the Middle East and central Europe, leaving only the southern half of Britain and modern Romania to be added later.

So popular was Augustus that four members of his family succeeded to the position of "emperor" (as we call it) despite serious personal and political shortcomings. After the mid-first century C.E., other families obtained the post. In theory, the Senate affirmed the early emperors; in reality, the armies chose them. By the second century C.E., the so-called Good Emperors instituted a new mechanism of succession: each designated as his successor a mature man of proven ability whom he adopted as his son and with whom he shared offices and privileges.

Augustus had allied himself with the **equites (EH-kwee-tays)**, the class of well-to-do Italian merchants and landowners second in wealth and social status only to the senatorial class. These competent and self-assured individuals became the core of a new civil service. At last Rome had an administrative bureaucracy capable of managing a large empire with considerable honesty, consistency, and efficiency.

## An Urban Empire

Calling the Roman Empire of the first three centuries C.E. an "urban" empire does not mean that most people lived in cities and towns. Perhaps 80 percent of the 50 to 60 million people lived in agricultural villages or isolated farms. The network of towns and

---

**Roman Principate**  A term used to characterize Roman government in the first three centuries C.E., based on the ambiguous title *princeps* ("first citizen") adopted by Augustus to conceal his military dictatorship.

**Augustus**  Honorific name of Octavian, founder of the Roman Principate, the military dictatorship that replaced the failing rule of the Roman Senate. After defeating all rivals, between 31 B.C.E. and 14 C.E. he laid the groundwork for several centuries of stability and prosperity in the Roman Empire.

*equites*  In ancient Italy, prosperous landowners second in wealth and status to the senatorial aristocracy. The Roman emperors allied with this group to counterbalance the influence of the old aristocracy and used the equites to staff the imperial civil service.

Cast of Trajan's Column, Detail of soldiers building fortifications in Dacia/De Agostini Picture Library/G. Dagli Orti/The Bridgeman Art Library

**Scene from Trajan's Column, Rome, ca. 113 C.E.** The Roman emperor Trajan erected a marble column 125 feet (38 meters) in height to commemorate his triumphant campaign in Dacia (modern Romania). The relief carving, which snakes around the column for 656 feet (200 meters), illustrates numerous episodes of the conquest and provides a detailed pictorial record of the equipment and practices of the Roman army in the field. This panel depicts soldiers building a fort.

cities served as administrative centers, however, with corresponding benefits for the urban populace.

Numerous towns had several thousand inhabitants. A handful of major cities—Alexandria in Egypt, Antioch in Syria, and Carthage—had populations of several hundred thousand. Rome itself had approximately a million residents. The largest cities put huge strains on the government's technical ability to provide food and remove sewage.

In Rome, the upper classes lived in elegant hillside townhouses. The house centered around an *atrium*, a rectangular courtyard with an open skylight that let in light and rainwater for drinking and washing. A dining

room for dinner and drinking parties, an interior garden, a kitchen, and perhaps a private bath surrounded the atrium, with bedrooms on the upper level. Pebble mosaics on the floors and frescoes of mythological scenes or outdoor vistas on the wall and ceilings gave a sense of openness in the absence of windows. Many aristocrats owned a number of villas in the countryside as retreats from the pressures of city life.

The poor inhabited crowded slums in the lowlying parts of the city. Damp, dark, and smelly, with few furnishings, these wooden tenements suffered from frequent fires. Fortunately, Romans could spend the day outdoors for most of the year.

## Socioeconomic Mobility, Winners and Losers in Imperial Rome and Han China

Throughout human history, most people have been born into societies in which there was little opportunity or likelihood that they could significantly improve their social or economic circumstances. However, in complex and urbanized civilizations like imperial Rome or Han China, economic advancement—which is, then, generally linked to a higher social status—is more achievable for various reasons, including conditions of peace and stability favorable to commerce brought by the imperial power, the construction of roads over which goods can be conveyed, increased wealth and higher standards of living for many, the presence of large numbers of potential customers in urban centers, and innovative technologies for producing high-quality products. However, two further points need to be made. First, in situations of open economic competition, there are losers as well as winners. And, second, the existence of new forms of wealth and its acquisition by new groups of people tends to destabilize and threaten traditional institutions and values. We are fortunate in having texts from early imperial Rome and Han China that illustrate these processes from the vantage point of "the losers."

Juvenal wrote poetic satires of Roman society in the late first and early second centuries C.E. Of course satire, by its very nature, exaggerates, but to be effective and funny it has to be based on something real. The main speaker in Juvenal's *Third Satire* is a friend of the poet named Umbricius, who has decided to abandon the ever more dangerous and frustrating city of Rome for a quieter town on the Bay of Naples.

. . .'There is no room in the city
for respectable skills,' he said, 'and no reward for one's efforts.

Today my means are less than yesterday; come tomorrow,
the little left will be further reduced. . .
What can I do in Rome? I can't tell lies; if a book
is bad I cannot praise it and beg for a copy; the stars
in their courses mean nothing to me; I'm neither willing nor
    able
to promise a father's death; I've never studied the innards
of frogs; I leave it to others to carry instructions and presents
to a young bride from her lover; none will get help from me
in a theft; that's why I never appear on a governor's staff;. . .
Who, these days, inspires affection except an accomplice –
one whose conscience boils and seethes with unspeakable
    secrets?. . .
I shan't mince words. My fellow Romans, I cannot put up with
    a city of Greeks. . .
They make for the Esquiline, or the willow's Hill, intent on
    becoming
the vital organs and eventual masters of our leading houses.
Nimble wits, a reckless nerve, and a ready tongue. . .
What of the fact that the nation excels in flattery, praising
the talk of an ignorant patron, the looks of one who is ugly. . .
the whole country's a play. You chuckle, he shakes with a
    louder
guffaw; he weeps if he spots a tear in the eye of his patron,
yet he feels no grief; on a winter's day if you ask for a brazier,
he dons a wrap; if you say 'I'm warm,' he starts to perspire.
So we aren't on equal terms; he always has the advantage
who night and day alike is able to take his expression
from another's face, to throw up his hands and cheer if his
    patron
produces an echoing belch or pees in a good straight line. . .
There's no room here for any Roman. . .
That same man, moreover, provides a cause and occasion
for universal amusement if his cloak is ripped and muddy,
if his toga is a little stained, and one of his shoes gapes open. . .
Of all that luckless poverty involves, nothing is harsher
than the fact that it makes people funny.'

Umbricius complains about the difficulty that educated, middle-class Romans like Juvenal and himself have in finding gainful employment and making a decent living. They cannot compete with the swarms of "Greeks"—by which he means people from the Greek-speaking Eastern Mediterranean, which would include Greeks proper, Syrians, and Egyptians—who are such accomplished actors, flatterers, and liars that they ingratiate themselves with the rich and powerful and get all the good jobs and contracts. The real Romans, who have too much dignity to stoop to this level, are left on the outside looking in. As they descend into poverty in a city in which the cost of lodging, food, and everything else is exorbitantly high, they are scorned and humiliated.

We see in this poem a resurgence of long-standing Roman prejudice toward the Greeks. Ironically, the presence of so many Easterners at Rome was a product of the empire, both because large numbers of prisoners of war initially serving as slaves in Italy gained their freedom and Roman citizenship, and because the capital city was a magnet attracting the most able and ambitious people in the empire to come to Rome to make their fortune.

A striking Han Chinese parallel to Juvenal's *Third Satire* can be found in an essay on friendship written by Wang Fu. He lived in the first half of the second century C.E. and never obtained an official post, leading him to complain that the system was not operating with fairness.

*People compete to flatter and to get close to those who are wealthy and prominent. . . People are also quick to snub those who are poor and humble. . . If a person makes friends with the rich and prominent, he will gain the benefits of influential recommendations for advancement in office and the advantages of generous presents and other emoluments. But if he makes friends with the poor and humble, he will lose money either from giving them handouts or from unrepaid loans. . . This is the reason that crafty, calculating individuals can worm their way up the official ladder while ordinary scholars slip ever more into obscurity. Unless the realm has a brilliant ruler, there may be no one to discern this. . . Alas! The gentlemen of today speak nobly but act basely. Their words are upright, but their hearts are false. Their actions do not reflect their words, and their words are out of harmony with*

*their thoughts. . . In their lofty speeches they refer to virtuous and righteous persons as being worthy. But when they actually recommend people for office, they consider only such requirements as influence and prominence. If a man is just an obscure scholar, even if he possesses the virtue of Yan Hui and Min Ziqian, even if he is modest and diligent, even if he has the ability of Yi Yin and Lu Shang, even if he is filled with the most devoted compassion for the people, he is clearly not going to be employed in this world.*

As Wang Fu sees it, men of ambition focused all their attention on cultivating the rich and powerful in order to get the recommendations that led to official appointments, and in the process they ignored their real friends, whereas men of talent who could not or would not play this game were overlooked and scorned for their poverty. While appointment to public office was supposed to be meritocratic, based, first, on knowledge of the classic Confucian texts as determined by an exam and then by performance in office, Wang Fu's essay makes clear that what mattered most was connections to powerful people and the recommendations those people made to their peers in the government.

## QUESTIONS FOR ANALYSIS

1. What kinds of abilities lead to success in imperial Rome and China?
2. Are the authors of these two texts just whining because they have had little success, or are they justified in claiming that the situation is unfair?
3. How are the new circumstances of increased socioeconomic mobility damaging traditional institutions and values?

*Sources:* First selection [translated by Niall Rudd, *Juvenal, The Satires* (Oxford 1992)]. Second selection [translated by Lily Hwa, in Patricia Buckley Ebrey (ed.), *Chinese Civilization, A Sourcebook*, 2nd ed. (The Free Press, 1993)]

**Roman Shop Selling Food and Drink** The bustling town of Pompeii on the Bay of Naples was buried in ash by the eruption of Mt. Vesuvius in 79 C.E. Archaeologists have unearthed the streets, stores, and houses of this typical Roman town. Shops such as this sold hot food and drink served from clay vessels set into the counter. Shelves and niches behind the counter contained other items. In the background can be seen a well-paved street and a public fountain where the inhabitants could fetch water.

Other cities and towns, including the ramshackle settlements that sprang up beside frontier forts, mirrored the capital city in political organization, physical layout, and appearance. A town council and two annually elected officials drawn from prosperous members of the community maintained law and order and collected both urban and rural taxes. In return for the privilege of running local affairs and in appreciation for the state's protection of their wealth and position, this "municipal aristocracy" served Rome loyally. In striving to imitate Roman senators, they lavishly endowed their communities with attractive elements of Roman urban life: a forum, government buildings, temples, gardens, baths, theaters, amphitheaters, and games and public entertainments of all sorts. These amenities made the situation of the urban poor superior to that of the rural poor. Poor

people in a city could pass time at the baths, seek refuge from the elements under the colonnades, and attend the games.

Hard work and drudgery marked life in the countryside, relieved only by occasional festival days and the everyday pleasures of sex, family, and conversation. Rural people had to fend for themselves in dealing with bandits, wild animals, and other hazards. People outside urban centers had little direct contact with the government beyond occasional run-ins with bullying soldiers and the dreaded arrival of the tax collector.

The concentration of ownership reversed temporarily during the civil wars that ended the Republic; it resumed under the emperors. But the end of new conquests reduced the number of slaves and forced landowners to find new labor. Landlords turned to tenant farmers, whom they allowed to live on and cultivate plots of land in return for a portion of their crops. The landowners themselves still lived in the cities and hired foremen to manage their estates. Thus wealth based on rural productivity became concentrated in the cities.

In the *pax Romana* ("Roman peace"), the safety and stability guaranteed by Roman might, commerce flourished, allowing some urban dwellers to become rich from manufacture and trade. Meat and vegetables were usually exchanged locally because transportation was costly and many products spoiled quickly. The city of Rome, however, depended on grain shipments from Sicily, North Africa, and Egypt to feed its huge population. Special naval squadrons performed this task.

Some exporters dealt in glass, metalwork, delicate pottery, and other fine manufactured products. The centers of production, first located in Italy, moved into the provinces as knowledge of the necessary skills spread. Roman armies on the frontiers provided a large market, and their presence promoted the prosperity of border provinces. Other merchants traded in luxury items from beyond the empire's boundaries, especially Chinese silks, Indian spices, and Arabian incense. The tax revenues of rich provinces like Gaul (France) and Egypt flowed to Rome to support the emperor and the central government, and to the frontier provinces to subsidize the armies.

While Hellenism dominated the eastern Mediterranean (see Chapter 4), **Romanization**, the spread of the Latin language and Roman way of life, proved an enduring consequence of empire among the diverse peoples in the western provinces. As the language of the conquerors spread among the common people as well as the elite, it became the basis for Portuguese, Spanish, French, Italian, and Romanian. However, in frontier areas along the Rhine and Danube Rivers, where Roman control was tenuous and migration by Germanic peoples was changing the ethnic balance by the third century C.E., Latin made only limited headway.

The Roman government did not force Romanization. The inhabitants of the provinces themselves chose Latin and adopted cultural practices like wearing a *toga* (the traditional cloak worn by Roman male citizens). Making this choice brought advantages, as learning English and wearing Western clothing do today. Latin facilitated dealings with the Roman administration and helped merchants get contracts to supply the military. Many also must have been drawn by the aura of success surrounding the language and culture of a people who had created so vast an empire.

As towns sprang up and acquired the Roman urban amenities, they attracted ambitious members of the indigenous populations. The empire gradually and reluctantly extended Roman citizenship, with its attendant privileges, legal protections, and certain tax exemptions, to people living outside Italy. Completing a twenty-six-year term of service in the native military units that backed up the Roman legions earned soldiers citizenship that could pass to their descendants. Emperors granted citizenship to individuals or entire communities as a reward for service. Then in 212 C.E. the emperor Caracalla granted citizenship to all free, adult, male inhabitants of the empire.

The gradual extension of citizenship mirrored the empire's transformation from an Italian dominion over the Mediterranean lands into a commonwealth of peoples. As early as the first century C.E., some of the leading literary and intellectual figures came from the provinces. By the second century even the emperors hailed from Spain, Gaul, and North Africa.

## The Rise of Christianity

The Jewish homeland of Judaea (see Chapter 2), roughly equivalent to present-day Israel, came under direct Roman rule in 6 C.E. Over the next half century, the insensitivity of the Roman governors to the Jewish belief in one god increased tension with the inhabitants. Various kinds of opposition to Roman rule

---

*pax Romana*  Literally, "Roman peace," it connoted the stability and prosperity that Roman rule brought to the lands of the Roman Empire in the first two centuries C.E. The movement of people and trade goods along Roman roads and safe seas allowed for the spread of cultural practices, technologies, and religious ideas.

**Romanization**  The process by which the Latin language and Roman culture became dominant in the western provinces. Indigenous peoples in the provinces often chose to Romanize because of the political and economic advantages that it brought, as well as the allure of Roman success.

sprang up. Many Jews anticipated the arrival of the Messiah, the "Anointed One," presumed to be a military leader who would liberate the Jewish people and drive the Romans out.

It is in this context that we must see the career of **Jesus**, a young carpenter from the Galilee region in northern Israel. In place of what he considered excessive concern with money and power among Jewish leaders and perfunctory religious observance by mainstream Jews, Jesus prescribed a return to the personal faith and spirituality of an earlier age. He eventually attracted the attention of the Jewish authorities in Jerusalem, who regarded popular reformers as potential troublemakers. Sometime between 30 and 36 C.E. they turned him over to the Roman governor, Pontius Pilate. Jesus was imprisoned, condemned, and executed by crucifixion, a punishment usually reserved for common criminals. His followers, the Apostles, subsequently sought to spread his teachings and their belief that he had been resurrected (returned from death to life) among their fellow Jews.

**Paul**, a Jew from the Greek city of Tarsus in southeast Anatolia, converted to the new creed and between 45 and 58 C.E. devoted himself to spreading the word. Traveling throughout Syria-Palestine, Anatolia, and Greece, he found most Jews unwilling to accept his claim that Jesus was the Messiah and had ushered in a new age. Frustrated, Paul redirected his efforts to non-Jews (sometimes called *gentiles*) who were also experiencing a spiritual hunger. He set up a string of Christian (from the Greek name *christos*, meaning "anointed one," given to Jesus by his followers) communities in the eastern Mediterranean.

Paul's career exemplifies the cosmopolitan nature of the Roman Empire in this era. Speaking both Greek and Aramaic, he moved comfortably between the Greco-Roman and Jewish worlds. He used Roman roads, depended on the peace guaranteed by Roman arms, called on his Roman citizenship to protect him from local authorities, and moved from city to city in his quest for converts.

In 66 C.E., tensions in Roman Judaea erupted in a revolt that lasted until 73. The Jerusalem-based Christian community, which focused on converting Jews, fell victim to the Roman reconquest. This cleared the field for Paul's non-Jewish converts, and Christian-

ity began to diverge more and more from its Jewish roots. The sect grew slowly but steadily. Many early converts came from disenfranchised groups: women, slaves, and the urban poor. They hoped to receive the respect not accorded them in the larger society and to obtain positions of responsibility when the early Christian communities elected them leaders. However, as the religious movement grew and prospered, it developed a hierarchy of priests and bishops and engaged in bitter disputes over theological doctrine (see Chapter 10).

As monotheists forbidden to worship other gods, early Christians met persecution from Roman officials, who often took their refusal to worship the emperor as a sign of disloyalty. Nevertheless, occasional government attempts at suppression and mob attacks did not keep converts from joining the Christian movement. By the late third century C.E. adherents to Christianity were a sizable minority within the empire and included many educated and prosperous people holding local and imperial posts.

During the Greek Classical period, a number of "mystery" cults had gained popularity by claiming to provide secret information about the nature of life and death and promising a blessed afterlife to their adherents. In the Hellenistic and Roman periods, belief systems making similar promises arose in the eastern Mediterranean and spread throughout the Greco-Roman lands, responding to a spiritual and intellectual hunger not satisfied by paganism. These included the cults of the mother-goddess Cybele in Anatolia, the Egyptian goddess Isis, and the Iranian sun-god Mithra. As we shall see, the ultimate victory

**Jesus** A Jew from Galilee in northern Israel who sought to reform Jewish beliefs and practices. He was executed as a revolutionary by the Romans. Hailed as the Messiah and son of God by his followers, he became the central figure in Christianity, a belief system that developed in the centuries after his death.

**Paul** A Jew from the Greek city of Tarsus in Anatolia, he initially persecuted the followers of Jesus but, after receiving a revelation on the road to Syrian Damascus, became a Christian. Taking advantage of his Hellenized background and Roman citizenship, he traveled throughout Syria-Palestine, Anatolia, and Greece, preaching the new religion and establishing churches. Finding his greatest success among pagans ("gentiles"), he began the process by which Christianity separated from Judaism.

**Roman Aqueduct near Tarragona, Spain** The growth of towns and cities challenged Roman officials to provide an adequate supply of water. Aqueducts channeled water from a source, sometimes many miles away, to an urban complex, using only the force of gravity. To bring an aqueduct from high ground into the city, Roman engineers designed long, continuous rows of arches that maintained a steady downhill slope. Scholars sometimes can roughly estimate the population of an ancient city by calculating the amount of water that was available to it. Lenar Musin/Shutterstock.com

of Christianity over these rivals arose from historical circumstances as much as from spiritual appeal.

## Technology and Transformation

The relative safety of travel brought by Roman arms and engineering helped the early Christians to spread their faith. Surviving remnants of roads, fortification walls, aqueducts, and buildings testify to the Romans' engineering expertise. In peacetime, army engineers built bridges, siege works, and ballistic weapons. Romans also pioneered the use of arches for the even distribution of weight without the use of thick supporting walls. **Aqueducts**—long elevated or underground conduits—used gravity to bring water from its source to urban centers. Another invention was concrete—a mixture of lime powder, sand, and water—that could be poured into molds to create vast vaulted and domed interior spaces, unlike the rectilinear pillar-and-post construction of the Greeks and Egyptians.

Defending borders that stretched for thousands of miles posed a great administrative challenge. In a document released after his death, Augustus advised against expanding the empire because of the costs of administration and defensive strategy. Mountains,

> **aqueduct** A conduit, either elevated or underground, that used gravity to carry water from a source to a location—usually a city—that needed it. The Romans built many aqueducts in a period of substantial urbanization.

deserts, and seas protected the empire at most points. But the lengthy Rhine/Danube frontier in Germany and central Europe was vulnerable and thus had to be guarded by forts whose relatively small garrisons were not always up to the task of repelling raiders. On more desolate frontiers in Britain and North Africa, the Romans built long walls to keep out the peoples who lived beyond.

Most of Rome's neighbors lacked sufficient technology and military organization to pose a serious threat. The one exception lay on the eastern frontier, where the Parthian kingdom controlled the lands that are today Iran and Iraq (see Chapter 4). Rome and Parthia fought exhaustingly for centuries, with neither side gaining significant territory.

The Roman state prospered for two and a half centuries after Augustus stabilized the political situation and instituted a program of reforms. But in the third century C.E. cracks in the edifice became visible. Historians call the period from 235 to 284 C.E. the **third-century crisis**, a time when political, military, and economic problems nearly destroyed the empire. Rulers changed frequently, as twenty or more men claimed the office of emperor during this period. Most reigned for only a few months or years before being overthrown by a rival or killed by their own troops. Germanic peoples on the Rhine/Danube frontier took advantage of the disorders to raid deep into the empire. For the first time in centuries, Roman cities built protective walls. Some regions, feeling a lack of imperial protection, turned to anyone who promised to put their interests first.

Political and military emergencies devastated the empire's economy. Buying the loyalty of the army and paying to defend the increasingly permeable frontiers drained the treasury. The resultant demands for more tax revenues from the provinces, as well as the interruption of commerce by fighting, eroded urban prosperity. Shortsighted emperors, desperate for cash, secretly reduced the amount of precious metal in Roman coins and pocketed the excess. But the public quickly caught on, and the devalued coinage became less and less acceptable in the marketplace. Indeed, the empire reverted to a barter economy, which curtailed large-scale and long-distance commerce even more.

The municipal aristocracy, once the empire's most vital and public-spirited class, suffered heav-

ily. As town councilors, its members had to make up shortfalls in taxes owed to the state. As the decline in trade eroded their wealth, many evaded their civic duties and even went into hiding. At the same time, population shifted out of the cities and into the countryside, as my people sought employment and protection from both raiders and government officials on the estates of wealthy and powerful country landowners.

Just when things looked bleakest, one man pulled the empire back from the brink. Diocletian, like several other emperors, hailed from one of the eastern European provinces most vulnerable to invasion. Of humble origins, he rose through the ranks of the army and gained power in 284. He was so successful that he ruled for more than twenty years and died in bed.

To halt inflation (the process by which prices rise as money loses value), Diocletian issued an edict specifying the maximum prices for various commodities and services. To ensure an adequate labor supply in vital services, he froze people in their professions and made them train their sons to succeed them. This unprecedented regulation of prices and vocations had unforeseen consequences. A "black market" arose among buyers and sellers who chose to ignore the price controls. More broadly, many imperial citizens began to see the government as an oppressive entity that no longer deserved their loyalty.

When Diocletian resigned in 305, the old divisiveness reemerged as various claimants battled for the throne. The eventual winner was a general named **Constantine** (r. 306–337), who reunited the empire under his sole rule. In 312, Constantine won a key battle at the Milvian Bridge over the Tiber River near Rome. He later claimed that before the battle, he had seen in the sky a cross (the sign of the Christian God) superimposed on the sun. Believing that the Christian God had helped him achieve the victory, Con-

**third-century crisis**  Historians' term for the political, military, and economic turmoil that beset the Roman Empire during much of the third century C.E.: frequent changes of ruler, civil wars, barbarian invasions, decline of urban centers, and near-destruction of long-distance commerce and the monetary economy. After 284 C.E. Diocletian restored order by making fundamental changes.

**Constantine**  Roman emperor (r. 312–337). After reuniting the Roman Empire, he moved the capital to Constantinople and made Christianity a favored religion.

stantine converted to Christianity. Throughout his reign, he supported the Christian church, although he tolerated other beliefs as well. Historians disagree about whether Constantine's conversion resulted from spiritual motives or from a pragmatic desire to unify the empire under a single religion. Regardless of the reason, large numbers of people now converted because they saw that Christians had advantages over non-Christians in seeking offices and favors.

Constantine also transferred the capital in 324 from Rome to Byzantium, an ancient Greek city on the Bosporus (BAHS-puhr-uhs) strait connecting the Mediterranean and the Black Sea. Renamed Constantinople (cahn-stan-tih-NO-pul) ("City of Constantine"), it represented a concentration of attention on the threatened imperial borders in eastern Europe (see Map 5.1). The cities and middle class of the eastern provinces had withstood the third-century crisis better than those in the west. In addition, more educated people and more Christians were living in the east (see Chapter 10).

Some see the conversion of Constantine and the transfer of the imperial capital as events marking the end of Roman history. But many of the important changes that culminated during Constantine's reign had their roots in the previous two centuries, and the Roman Empire as a whole survived for at least another century. Moreover, the eastern, or Byzantine, portion of it (discussed in Chapter 10) survived Constantine by more than a thousand years. Neverthe-

less, the Roman Empire of the fourth century differed fundamentally from what had existed before, a fact that justifies seeing Constantine's reign as the beginning of a new epoch in the West.

## THE ORIGINS OF IMPERIAL CHINA, 221 B.C.E.–220 C.E.

■ *How did imperial China evolve under the Qin and Han dynasties?*

A fragmentation seemingly dictated by geography characterized the early history of China (see Chapter 3). The Shang (ca. 1750–1045 B.C.E.) and Western Zhou (1045–771 B.C.E.) wielded authority over a relatively compact zone in northeastern China. The last few centuries of nominal Zhou rule—the Warring States Period—saw rivalry among a group of small states, a situation reminiscent of the contemporary Greek city-states (see Chapter 4). As in Greece, competition and conflict fostered many elements of a national culture.

In the second half of the third century B.C.E. the Qin (chin) state of the Wei (way) River Valley conquered its rivals and created China's first empire (221–206 B.C.E.). But it barely survived the death of its founder, Shi Huangdi (shih wahng-dee). Power passed to a new dynasty, the Han, which ruled China from 206 B.C.E. to 220 C.E. (see Map 5.2). The imperial tradition of political and cultural unity thus begun lasted into the twentieth century and still has meaning for China today.

### Resources and People

China, an imperial state controlling lands of great diversity in topography, climate, plant and animal life, and human population, faced greater obstacles to long-distance communication and a uniform way of life than did the Roman Empire. Rome's territories were roughly similar in climate and agriculture, but Rome benefited from an internal sea—the Mediterranean—that facilitated rapid and inexpensive transport. Different resources, technologies, institutions, and values made the Chinese empire possible.

Agriculture produced the wealth and taxes that supported the institutions of imperial China. The main tax, a percentage of the annual harvest,

### SECTION REVIEW

- From a collection of farming communities, Rome evolved into a republic dominated by wealthy land-owning families who controlled the Senate.
- Through a series of wars, the Republic grew into an overseas empire.
- Political crises destroyed the Republic, and under Augustus and his successors, Rome expanded as a prosperous urban empire.
- Christianity emerged from tensions between Jewish and Roman culture and spread through the preaching of Paul of Tarsus.
- The third-century crisis nearly destroyed the empire until Diocletian's reforms stabilized the state briefly.
- Constantine reunited the empire, granted tolerance to Christianity, and moved the capital to Byzantium.

**Map 5.2  Han China**  The Qin and Han rulers of northeast China extended their control over all of eastern China and extensive territories to the west. A series of walls in the north and northwest, built to check the incursions of nomadic peoples from the steppes, were joined together to form the ancestor of the present-day Great Wall of China. An extensive network of roads connecting towns, cities, and frontier forts promoted rapid communication and facilitated trade. The Silk Road carried China's most treasured products to Central, South, and West Asia and the Mediterranean lands.

© Cengage Learning

funded government activities ranging from the luxurious lifestyle of the royal court to the military garrisons on the frontiers. The imperial capitals, first Chang'an (chang-ahn) (modern Xi'an [shee-ahn]), and later Luoyang (LWOE-yang), housed large populations that had to be fed. As intensive agriculture

spread in the Yangzi River Valley, the need to transport southern crops to the north spurred the construction of canals to connect the Yangzi with the Yellow River. The government also stored surplus grain during prosperous times for sale at reasonable prices during shortages.

To assess its labor resources, the government periodically conducted a census. Results survive for the years 2 C.E. and 140 C.E. The earlier survey indicates approximately 12 million households and 60 million people; the later, not quite 10 million households and 49 million people. Then as now, the vast majority of the population lived in the eastern river-valley regions that supported intensive agriculture. By early Han times, the demographic center in the Yellow River Valley and North China Plain had begun to shift south to the Yangzi River Valley.

In the intervals between seasonal agricultural tasks, able-bodied men donated one month of labor to public building projects—palaces, temples, fortifications, and roads—or to transporting goods, excavating and maintaining canals, cultivating imperial estates, or mining. The state also required two years of military service. On the frontiers, conscripted young Chinese men built walls and forts, kept an eye on barbarian neighbors, fought when necessary, and grew crops to support themselves. Registers of land and households enabled imperial officials to keep track of money and services due. Like the Romans, the Chinese governments depended on a large population of free peasants to contribute taxes and services to the state.

Throughout the Han dynasty, the Han Chinese gradually expanded into the territory of other ethnic groups. Population growth in the core regions and a shortage of good lands spurred the pioneers onward. Sometimes the government organized new settlements at strategic sites and on the frontiers. Neighboring kingdoms also invited Chinese settlers so they could exploit their skills and learn their technologies.

Han people preferred regions suitable to the agriculture they had practiced in the eastern river valleys. On the northern frontier, they pushed back nomadic populations. They also expanded into the tropical forests of southern China and settled in the western oases. Places not suitable for their preferred kind of agriculture, particularly the steppe and deserts, did not attract them.

## Hierarchy, Obedience, and Belief

The Han Chinese brought with them their social organization, values, language, and other cultural practices. The Chinese family, the basic social unit, included not only the living generation but also the ancestors. The Chinese believed their ancestors maintained an ongoing interest in the fortunes of the family and therefore consulted, appeased, and venerated them to maintain their favor. Viewed as a living, self-renewing organism, the family required sons to perpetuate itself and ensure the immortality offered by the ancestor cult.

The doctrine of Confucius (Kongzi), which had its origins in the sixth century B.C.E. (see Chapter 3), became a fundamental source of values in the imperial period. Confucianism considered hierarchy a natural social phenomenon and assigned tasks and rules of conduct to each person. Absolute authority rested with the father, who presided over the rituals that linked living family members to the ancestors. Each person had a place and responsibilities based on gender, age, and relationship to other family members, and people saw themselves as part of an interdependent unit rather than as individual agents. The same concepts operated in society as a whole. Peasants, soldiers, administrators, and rulers all made distinctive contributions to the welfare of society. Confucianism optimistically maintained that education, imitation of role models, and self-improvement could guide people to the right path. Because the state mirrored the family, the basic family values of loyalty, obedience to authority, respect for elders and ancestors, and concern for honor and appropriate conduct carried over into the relationships between individuals and the state.

Contemporary written sources say little about the experience of women. Confucian ethics stressed the impropriety of women participating in public life. Traditional wisdom about appropriate female conduct appears in a story of the mother of the Confucian philosopher Mencius (Mengzi):

> A woman's duties are to cook the five grains, heat the wine, look after her parents-in-law, make clothes, and that is all! . . . [She] has no ambition to manage affairs outside the house. . . . She must follow the "three submissions." When she is young, she must submit to her parents. After her marriage, she must submit to her husband. When she is widowed, she must submit to her son.[1]

---

[1] Patricia Buckley Ebrey, ed., *Chinese Civilization and Society: A Sourcebook* (New York: Free Press, 1981), 33–34.

This ideal, perpetuated by males of the upper classes who composed most of the surviving texts, placed women under considerable pressure to conform. Women of the lower classes, less affected by Confucian ways of thinking, may have been less constrained than their more "privileged" counterparts.

After her parents arranged her marriage, a young bride went to live with her husband's family, who saw her as a stranger until she proved herself. Ability and force of personality (as well as the capacity to produce sons) could make a difference, but dissension between the wife and her mother-in-law and sisters-in-law grew out of their competition for influence with husbands, sons, and brothers and for a larger share of the economic resources held in common by the family.

Like the early Romans, the Chinese believed that divinity resided within nature rather than outside or above it. They worshiped and tried to appease the forces of nature. The state maintained shrines to the lords of rain, winds, and soil, as well as to certain great rivers and high mountains. Gathering at mounds or altars dedicated to local earth spirits, people sacrificed sheep and pigs and beat drums to promote fertility. Unusual natural phenomena like eclipses or heavy rains prompted them to tie a red cord around the sacred spot, symbolically restraining the deity. A belief that supernatural forces, bringing good and evil fortune, flowed through the landscape led experts in *feng shui*, "earth divination," to determine the most favorable location and orientation for buildings and graves. The faithful adapted their lives to the complex rhythms of nature.

Most people believed in ghosts and spirits. Some sought potions that would impart immortality. The desire to cheat death included taking life-enhancing drugs or building ostentatious tombs, flanked by towers or covered by mounds of earth, and filling them with what they believed they would need for a blessed afterlife. The objects in these tombs provide a wealth of knowledge about Han society.

**Silk Burial Banner from Mawangdui**   This banner was placed on the coffin containing the mummified body of Lady Dai, wife of the ruler of a dependent kingdom in southern China, in the mid-second century B.C.E. The lower and upper portions depict the Underworld and Heaven, while the middle register shows the deceased and her family offering sacrifices to help her soul ascend to Heaven.

## The First Chinese Empire

From the mid-third century B.C.E., the state of **Qin** began to methodically conquer the other "warring states" of China, and by 221 B.C.E. it had united the northern plain and the Yangzi River Valley under one rule. After defeating the last of his rivals in 221 B.C.E., the ruthless and energetic young king gave himself a title that symbolized the creation of the first Chinese empire—**Shi Huangdi**, or "First Emperor." The name *China* is probably derived from *Qin* (pronounced "chin").

The new regime sought to eliminate rival centers of authority. Its first target was the landowning aristocracy of the conquered states, already weakened by centuries of interstate rivalry. It abolished primogeniture—the right of the eldest son to inherit all the landed property—requiring estates to be broken up and passed on to several heirs. It also weakened the system that created aristocratic wealth by abolishing slavery and establishing a free peasantry. Slaves and peasant serfs, who previously worked the lands for the aristocracy and owed landlords a substantial portion of their harvest, now owed taxes and labor, as well as military service, to the state.

In place of the aristocracy, Shi Huangdi created a centrally controlled administrative structure with district officials who owed their appointments to the king and who were watched over by his agents. The Qin government's commitment to standardization helped create a unified Chinese civilization. A code of law, in force throughout the empire, applied punishments evenhandedly to all members of society. The Qin also imposed standardized weights and measures, a single coinage, a common system of writing, and even a specified axle-length for carts so that they would create a single set of ruts in the road.

Thousands of miles of roads, comparable in scale to the roads of the Roman Empire, connected the parts of the empire and helped move Qin armies quickly. The Qin also built canals to connect the northern and southern river systems, at first for military purposes but eventually for transporting commercial goods as well. The 20-mile-long (32.2-kilometer-long) Magic Canal, which ingeniously linked two rivers that flowed in opposite directions with strong currents, is still in use. The frontier walls of the old states were gradually combined into a continuous barricade, the precursor of the Great Wall, which protected cultivated lands from raids by northern steppe nomads (see Chapter 3), although a recent study suggests that its primary function was to take in newly captured territory where large numbers of Chinese peasants could be dispatched and ordered to begin cultivation.[2]

Mobilizing manpower for irrigation and flood control, military service, road and wall construction, and the building of a monumental tomb for the ruler taught the king's administrators organizational skills and strengthened their hand against the nobles. But such projects also required that the Qin government relocate large numbers of people and institute an oppressive program of forced labor and military service.

Li Si (luh suh), the prime minister, persuaded Shi Huangdi that Confucian scholars were subverting the goals of the regime with appeals to the past that demanded benevolent and nonviolent conduct from rulers. A crackdown ensued in which Confucian books were burned and scholars brutally executed. The Qin ruler favored instead a philosophy known as Legalism (see Chapter 3), a system of discipline and obedience maintained through the rigid application of rewards and punishments. Its major proponent, Li Si himself, considered the will of the ruler supreme.

The recent discovery of a manual of Qin laws used by an administrator, with prescriptions less extreme than expected, suggests that the sins of the Qin may have been exaggerated by later sources. Nevertheless, rebellions ended the dynasty after the death of Shi Huangdi and attest to both the resentment of the aristocracy and the anger of the commoners. The regime

[2] Nicola Di Cosmo, *Ancient China and Its Enemies: The Rise of Nomadic Power in East Asian History* (Cambridge: Cambridge University Press, 2002), 155–158.

**Qin** A people and state in the Wei River Valley of eastern China that conquered rival states and created the first Chinese empire (221–206 B.C.E.). The Qin ruler, Shi Huangdi, standardized many features of Chinese society and ruthlessly marshaled subjects for military and construction projects, engendering hostility that led to the fall of his dynasty shortly after his death. The Qin framework was largely taken over by the succeeding Han dynasty.

**Shi Huangdi** Founder of the short-lived Qin dynasty and creator of the Chinese Empire (r. 221–210 B.C.E.). He is remembered for his ruthless conquests of rival states, standardization of practices, and forcible organization of labor for military and engineering tasks. His tomb, with its army of life-size terracotta soldiers, has been partially excavated.

**Terracotta Soldiers from the Tomb of Shi Huangdi, "First Emperor" of China, Late Third Century** B.C.E. Near the monumental tomb that he built for himself, the First Emperor filled a huge underground chamber with more than seven thousand life-size baked-clay statues of soldiers. The terra-cotta army was unearthed in the 1970s.

had lasted only fifteen years, but the achievements of the Qin—the unification of China and the creation of a Chinese style of civilization—would endure.

### The Long Reign of the Han

When the dust cleared, Liu Bang (le-oo bahng), possibly a peasant by background, established a new dynasty, the **Han** (206 B.C.E.–220 C.E.). Rejecting the excesses and mistakes of the Qin, he restored the institutions of a venerable past. Though he retained much of the administrative structure and Legalist ideology put in place by the Qin, he also revised Confucianism to address the circumstances of a large, centralized political entity and to temper the Qin Legalist methods. This Confucianism emphasized the benevolence of government and the appropriateness of particular rituals and behaviors in a manifestly hierarchical society. The Han administration became the standard for later ages, and the Chinese people today refer to themselves ethnically as Han.

As in the Zhou monarchy (see Chapter 3), people thought that the emperor, the "Son of Heaven," enjoyed the Mandate of Heaven, wielding authority like a father in a family and linking the living generations with the ancestors. The emperor brought the support of the powerful imperial ancestors and guaranteed the harmonious interactions of Heaven and earth. More than his Roman counterpart, he was regarded as a divinity on earth. His word was law. Failure to govern well, however, could lose him the backing of Heaven. Given the belief that events in Heaven, the natural world, and human society corresponded, floods, droughts, and earthquakes could be seen as both the consequences and symptoms of an ethical failure and mismanagement. Natural disasters, and

**Han** A term used to designate (1) the ethnic Chinese people who originated in the Yellow River Valley and spread throughout regions of China suitable for agriculture and (2) the dynasty of emperors who ruled from 206 B.C.E. to 220 C.E.

the misery that ensued, could spawn revolution. If the revolution was successful, Heaven was seen to have withdrawn its support from an unworthy ruler.

After eighty years of imperial consolidation, Emperor Wu (r. 140–87 B.C.E.) launched a period of military expansion south into Fujian, Guangdong, and present-day North Vietnam, north into Manchuria and present-day North Korea, and west into Inner Mongolia and Xinjiang (SHIN-jyahng). Extending his control into the northwest, Emperor Wu laid the foundations for the so-called Silk Road (see Chapter 8), the series of trade routes that connected China, via Inner and Central Asia, to India, the Middle East, and the Mediterranean. As the name suggests, silk was the most important trade commodity linking the peoples of the Eastern Hemisphere. A Chinese text claims that Emperor Wu sent agents to the "Southern Sea," which may refer to India or Southeast Asia, to acquire prized Roman glass, indicating the reach of China in maritime trade routes as well as the overland Silk Road. However, controlling the routes and territories proved expensive, so Wu's successors curtailed further expansion.

The Han Empire endured, with a brief interruption, for more than four hundred years. People lived in various milieus—cities, rural villages and farms, or military camps on the frontiers. **Chang'an**, in the Wei River Valley, the strategic region from which the Zhou and Qin dynasties had emerged, served as the capital from 200 B.C.E. to 25 C.E.—the period of the Early, or Western, Han. From 25 to 220 C.E., the Later, or Eastern, Han established its base in the more centrally located Luoyang.

Protected by a ring of hills but with ready access to the fertile plain, Chang'an was surrounded by a wall of pounded earth and brick 15 miles (24 kilometers) in circumference. In 2 C.E. its population was 246,000. Contemporaries described it as a bustling place, filled with courtiers, officials, soldiers, merchants, craftsmen, and foreign visitors. Broad thoroughfares running north and south intersected with others running east and west. High walls protected and restricted access to the imperial palaces, administrative offices, barracks, and storehouses. Temples and marketplaces were scattered about the civic center. Chang'an became a model of urban planning, its main features imitated in cities and towns through-

out China (it is estimated that between 10 and 30 percent of the population lived in urban centers).

Han literature describes the appearance of the capitals and the activities taking place in the palace complexes, public areas, and residential streets. Moralizing writers criticized the excesses of the elite. Living in multistory houses, wearing fine silks, traveling in ornate horse-drawn carriages, well-to-do officials and merchants devoted their leisure time to art and literature, occult religious practices, elegant banquets, and various entertainments—music and dance, juggling and acrobatics, dog and horse races, and cock and tiger fights. In stark contrast, the common people inhabited a sprawling warren of alleys, living in dwellings packed "as closely as the teeth of a comb."

Secluded within the palace compound, surrounded by his many wives and children, servants, courtiers, and officials, the emperor presided over an unceasing round of pomp and ritual emphasizing the worship of Heaven and imperial ancestors, as well as the practical business of government. When the emperor died, his chief widow chose his heir from the male members of the ruling clan, thus making the royal compound a hive of intrigue.

A prime minister, a civil service director, and nine ministers charged with military, economic, legal, and religious responsibilities ran the central government. As in imperial Rome, Han officials depended on local officials for the day-to-day administration of the vast empire, allying themselves with the **gentry**, a class just below the aristocracy of moderately prosperous landowners. They were usually men with education and expertise, resembling the Roman *equites* favored by Augustus. Wealthy merchant families, however, were viewed with suspicion and accused of greedily driving up prices and living off the work of others. During hard times, advisers to the emperors

**Chang'an**  City in the Wei River Valley in eastern China. It became the capital of the early Han Empire. Its main features were imitated in the cities and towns that sprang up throughout the Han Empire.

**gentry**  In China, the class of prosperous families, next in wealth below the rural aristocrats, from which the emperors drew their administrative personnel. Respected for their education and expertise, these officials became a privileged group and made the government more efficient and responsive than in the past.

blamed merchants for China's economic ills and proposed banning them and their children from holding government posts.

The new gentry class, with imperial support, adopted a version of Confucianism that provided a system for training officials to be intellectually capable and morally worthy of their roles and set forth a code of conduct for measuring their performance. Chinese tradition speaks of an imperial university located outside Chang'an and said to have thirty thousand students, as well as provincial centers of learning. From these centers, students entered government service. Exempt from taxes and compulsory military or labor services, they led comfortable lives by the standards of the time. While the granting of government jobs on the basis of performance on the exams theoretically should have given everyone an equal chance, in reality the sons of the gentry had distinct advantages because they received better training in Confucian classics. The Han period was rich in intellectual developments, thanks to the relative prosperity of the era, the growth of urban centers, and state support of scholars. Gradually, the gentry became a new aristocracy of sorts, and scholar-officials became a self-perpetuating, privileged class.

Daoism, which originated in the Warring States Period (see Chapter 3), took deeper root among the common people in the Han period. With its emphasis on the *Dao*, or "path," of nature, its valuing of harmony with the cycles and patterns of the natural world, and its search for enlightenment through solitary contemplation and physical and mental discipline rather than education, Daoism called into question age-old beliefs and values and rejected the hierarchy and rules of Confucianism. It urged passive acceptance of the disorder of the world, denial of ambition, contentment with simple pleasures, and trust in one's own instincts.

## Technology and Trade

Chinese tradition, which seems to recognize the importance of technology for the success and spread of Chinese civilization, credits the legendary first five emperors with the introduction of major new technologies.

The advent of bronze tools around 1500 B.C.E. helped open land for agriculture on the North China Plain. A millennium later, iron arrived, and the Chinese took full advantage of this technology. Chinese metalworkers used more advanced techniques than metalworkers elsewhere in the world. Whereas Roman blacksmiths produced wrought-iron tools and weapons by hammering heated iron, the Chinese mastered the technique of liquefying iron and pouring it into molds. The resulting cast-iron and steel tools and weapons had higher carbon content and were harder and more durable.

In the succeeding centuries, improvements in crossbows and cavalry helped the Chinese military to beat off the attacks of nomads (see Chapter 3). The watermill, which harnessed the power of running water to turn a grindstone, appeared in China long before it did in Europe. The horse collar and breast strap harnessing, which did not constrict the horse's breathing, also allowed horses in China to pull heavier loads than European horses could.

The Han rulers continued the Qin road-building program. Besides using the roads to move troops and supplies, the government created a network of official couriers—a postal service—using horses, boats, and even footpaths, with food and shelter provided at relay stations. Canal construction also continued, and river navigation improved.

Silk dominated China's export trade. Silk cocoons are secreted into the leaves of mulberry trees by silkworms. The Chinese understood this and kept it a closely guarded secret, which gave them a monopoly on the manufacture of silk. Carried through the Central Asian oases to the Middle East, India, and the Mediterranean, and passing through the hands of middlemen who added their own fees to the price, this beautiful textile may have increased in value a hundred-fold by the end of its journey. Controlling the Silk Road and its profits justified periodic military campaigns into Inner Asia and the installation there of garrisons and Chinese colonies (see Chapter 8).

## The Decline of the Han Empire

For the Han, as for the Romans, maintaining frontier security, particularly in the north and northwest, posed a serious challenge. In the end, non-Chinese people raiding across the frontier or moving into imperial territory proved a major factor in bringing the empire down.

**Gold Belt Buckle, Xiongnu, Second Century B.C.E.** The Xiongnu, herders in the lands north of China, shared the artistic conventions of nomadic peoples across the steppes of Asia and eastern Europe, such as this fluid, twisting representation of the animals on which they depended for their livelihood. Shi Huangdi's military incursion into their pasturelands in the late third century B.C.E. catalyzed the formation of the Xiongnu Confederacy, whose horse-riding warriors challenged the Chinese for centuries. The Metropolitan Museum of Art. Image source/Art Resource, NY

Pastoralists and farmers had always exchanged goods on the frontier, but the different ways of life of farmers, who usually accepted Han rule, and herders who preferred their own kings, gave rise to conflict (see Chapter 3). Sometimes herders resorted to raiding agricultural communities, and for centuries the Chinese kingdoms struggled with these tough, horse-riding warriors, building long walls along the frontier to keep them away from vulnerable farmlands. Shortly before the Qin unification of China, several states had begun to train soldiers on horseback to contend with the mobile nomads.

Shi Huangdi sent a large force to drive the nomads far north. His generals succeeded momentarily, extending Chinese territory beyond the great northern loop of the Yellow River. But Shi Huangdi's attack on the nomads had an unanticipated consequence. The threat to their way of life created by the Chinese invasion drove the normally fragmented and quarreling nomad groups to unite in a great confederacy. In the Han period, this **Xiongnu** (SHE-OONG-noo) Confederacy of Turkic peoples threatened the empire. Frequent wars cost lives and resources and gave rise to insulting stereotypes on both sides. The settled Chinese thought of nomads as "barbarians"—rough and uncivilized—much as the Romans viewed the Germanic peoples on their own frontiers.

Access to good horses and pastureland became a state priority in the war against the Xiongnu. Other strategies included maintaining garrisons and colonies of soldier-farmers on the frontier, settling compliant nomads within the borders to serve as a buffer, bribing nomad chiefs to promote disunity, and paying protection money. The "tributary system," in which nomad rulers accepted Chinese supremacy and exchanged tribute payments for marriages to Chinese princesses, receptions at court, and imperial gifts worth more than the tribute, often worked well.

Yet military vigilance burdened Han finances and made the economic troubles of later Han times worse. Despite attempts at major reforms to address economic problems, including giving surplus land to landless peasants, some members of the Han family and other elements of the elite resisted their loss of status and property, and the imperial court was weakened. By the end of the first century B.C.E. nobles and successful merchants again acquired control of huge estates, and many peasants sought their protection against the exactions of the imperial government. The Han government was forced to give up conscription, and instead had to pay foreign soldiers and officers—who were not always loyal—to defend its borders. This trend spread over the next two centuries. Poems in the first century C.E. complain of corrupt officials, unchecked attacks by barbarians, uprisings of desperate and hungry peasants, the spread of banditry, widespread poverty, and despair. The dynasty survived till 220 C.E., when the Han king was forced to abdicate, and China entered a period of political fragmentation and economic and cultural regression that lasted until the rise of the Sui (sway) and Tang (thang) dynasties in the late sixth and seventh centuries C.E., a story that we take up in Chapter 11.

**Xiongnu** A confederation of nomadic peoples living beyond the northwest frontier of ancient China. Chinese rulers tried a variety of defenses and stratagems to ward off these "barbarians," as they called them, and finally succeeded in dispersing the Xiongnu in the first century C.E.

- Imperial China rested on a foundation of agriculture, and periodic censuses ensured a ready supply of labor for public works.

- The extended family was the basic social unit, and Confucianism provided the value system.

- The Qin established the first empire and a unified Chinese civilization, subordinating the individual to the state to standardize everything from laws to writing—a standardization that contributed to the accomplishment of massive public works.

- Under the Han dynasty, the empire grew, the Confucian scholar-official rose to prominence, and Daoism gained more popularity with common people.

- The Qin and Han periods saw technological advancement, steady urbanization, and expansion of the silk trade.

- The burden of defense against nomadic invaders weakened the empire, which collapsed because of several factors, ushering in a period of fragmentation.

## CONCLUSION

Agriculture was the fundamental economic activity and source of government revenues in both Roman and Chinese civilization. Both empires depended initially on a free peasantry—sturdy farmers who could be pressed into military service or other forms of compulsory labor. Conflicts over who owned the land and how it was used caused political and social turmoil in both places. Roman and Chinese autocratic rulers secured their positions by breaking the power of old aristocratic families, seizing their excess land, and giving it to small farmers and to themselves. Later, when wealthy noblemen again gained control of vast estates worked by dependent tenant farmers, the authority of the state eroded.

From ethnically homogeneous cores, both empires spread into territories with diverse ecosystems, populations, and ways of life. The cultural unity that resulted has persisted, at least in part, to the present day. Military conquest paved the way, but Italian and Han settlers, outstripping the resources of their core areas, moved into new regions, bringing their languages, beliefs, customs, and technologies. Conquered peoples were also attracted to the culture and success of the ruler nation. To administer far-flung territories and large populations, both empires delegated considerable autonomy to local officials based in the cities and towns. Administrators were drawn from educated and capable members of a prosperous middle class.

Roads built to expedite the movement of troops became the highways of commerce and culture. Urban networks provided local administrative bases, furthering commerce and radiating imperial culture to the countryside. While a large majority of the population lived in the country, city dwellers enjoyed the advantages of empire. Rome and Chang'an provided models for outlying cities. Travelers could find in outlying regions the same types and styles of buildings and public spaces that they knew from the capital.

Similar problems of defense—long borders located far from the capital and aggressive neighbors—prompted both empires to build walls and chains of forts to protect against incursions. Frontier defense was so costly that it eventually eroded both empires' prosperity. As governments demanded more taxes and services from the civilian population, they lost the loyalty of the people, many of whom sought protection on the estates of powerful landowners. The Roman and Han governments eventually came to rely on soldiers hired from the same "barbarian" peoples confronting them on the frontiers. As the empires became weaker, the borders were overrun and the central governments collapsed. Ironically, the triumphant immigrant groups respected the imperial culture so deeply that they strove to maintain it once they were in power.

Though the empires failed in similar fashion, the long-term consequences differed. In China the imperial model revived in subsequent eras, but the lands of the Roman Empire never reunified. One reason is that the two cultures had different attitudes toward the individual and the state. In China individuals were deeply embedded in families with precisely defined hierarchies, unquestioning obedience, and solemn rituals of deference to elders and ancestors. Respect for authority was deep-seated. Confucianism, which sanctified family hierarchy and provided a code of conduct for public officials, preceded the imperial system. The cultural base could adapt with little change to diverse political circumstances. The Roman family also respected hierarchy and obedience, but it was not the organizational model of the Roman state. Confucianism had no Roman equivalent to orient society when the state collapsed.

Moreover, opportunities for economic and social mobility were greater in the Roman Empire than in ancient China. Whereas the merchant class in China was frequently disparaged and constrained by the government, the absence of government interference in the Roman Empire resulted in greater economic mobility and a thriving and influential middle class in the towns and cities. The Roman army also differed from the Chinese, the former being composed of professional soldiers who increasingly gained privileges and took part in political conflict, and the latter relying on draftees who served for two years and remained on the margins of power struggles.

Although Roman emperors tried to create an ideology to bolster their position, Republican traditions and Christianity's insistence on monotheism negated the

Roman emperor's pretensions to divinity. The dynastic principle never took root, and the cult of the emperor had little spiritual content. Thus, in the lands that had once constituted the western part of the Roman Empire, there was no compelling basis for reviving the position of emperor and the territorial claims of empire in later ages. In contrast, the Chinese believed that the emperor was the divine Son of Heaven and drew authority from the power of the royal ancestors.

# CHAPTER REVIEW

## ROME'S CREATION OF A MEDITERRANEAN EMPIRE, 753 B.C.E.–330 C.E.

■ *How did Rome create and maintain its vast Mediterranean empire?* (page 107)

The Romans were successful empire builders because of their superior military organization and training and a series of very capable generals. They co-opted the ruling elites and brought peace and prosperity to the peoples of the lands they annexed. Yet Rome's military success led to social and economic disruption and acute political struggles. Out of this crisis emerged the Principate, which persevered for several centuries. The emperors developed more effective administrative techniques, and local elites embraced Roman culture.

## THE ORIGINS OF IMPERIAL CHINA, 221 B.C.E.–220 C.E.

■ *How did imperial China evolve under the Qin and Han dynasties?* (page 121)

In China, the "First Emperor" established the Qin Empire and put key elements of a unified Chinese civilization in place. The preceding Shang and Zhou states, though not empires, had controlled the North China Plain and

developed the concept of the Mandate of Heaven, a claim to divine backing for the ruler as the Son of Heaven. Furthermore, the Legalist political philosophy justified authoritarian measures. But the harshness of the new order generated resistance that soon brought down the Qin, and its Han successors built a durable imperial regime on a moderated version of Qin structures that incorporated Confucian principles.

## Key Terms

Roman Republic (p. 109)
Roman Senate (p. 109)
patron/client relationship (p. 109)
Roman Principate (p. 112)
Augustus (p. 112)
*equites* (p. 112)
*pax Romana* (p. 117)
Romanization (p. 117)
Jesus (p. 118)
Paul (p. 118)
aqueduct (p. 119)
third-century crisis (p. 120)
Constantine (p. 120)
Qin (p. 125)
Shi Huangdi (p. 125)
Han (p. 126)
Chang'an (p. 127)
gentry (p. 127)
Xiongnu (p. 129)

# India and Southeast Asia

© Cengage Learning

In the Bhagavad-Gita (BUH-guh-vahd GEE-tuh), the most renowned Indian sacred text, the legendary warrior Arjuna (AHR-joo-nuh) rides out in his chariot to the open space between two armies preparing for battle. Torn between his social duty to fight for his family's claim to the throne and his conscience, which balks at the prospect of killing relatives, friends, and former teachers in the enemy camp, Arjuna slumps down in his chariot and refuses to fight. But his driver, the god Krishna (KRISH-nuh) in disguise, persuades him, in a carefully structured dialogue, both of the necessity to fulfill his duty as a warrior and of the proper frame of mind for performing these acts. In the climactic moment of the dialogue Krishna endows Arjuna with a "divine eye" and permits him to see the true appearance of God:

> It was a multiform, wondrous vision,
> with countless mouths and eyes
> and celestial ornaments,
> Everywhere was boundless divinity
> containing all astonishing things,
> wearing divine garlands and garments,
> anointed with divine perfume.
> If the light of a thousand suns
> were to rise in the sky at once,
> it would be like the light
> of that great spirit.
> Arjuna saw all the universe
> in its many ways and parts,
> standing as one in the body
> of the god of gods.[1]

In all of world literature, this is one of the most compelling attempts to depict the nature of deity. Graphic images emphasize the vastness, diversity, and multiplicity of the god, but in the end we learn that Krishna is the organizing principle behind all creation, that behind diversity and multiplicity lies a higher unity.

This is an apt metaphor for Indian civilization. The enormous variety of the Indian landscape is mirrored in the patchwork of ethnic and linguistic groups that occupy it, the political fragmentation that has marked most of Indian history, the elaborate hierarchy of social groups into which the Indian population is divided, and the thousands of deities who are worshiped at innumerable holy places that dot the subcontinent. Yet, in the end, one can speak of an Indian civilization united by shared views and values.

This chapter surveys the history of South and Southeast Asia from approximately 1500 B.C.E. to 1025 C.E., highlighting the evolution of features that define Indian civilization. Considerable attention is given to Indian religious conceptions, due both to religion's profound role in shaping Indian society and the sources of information available to historians. For reasons that will be explained below, writing came late to India, and ancient Indians did not develop the same kind of historical consciousness as other peoples of antiquity and took little interest in recording specific historical events.

## THE INDUS VALLEY CIVILIZATION

■ *What does material evidence tell us about the Indus Valley civilization and the most likely reason for its collapse?*

Civilization developed almost as early in South Asia as in Mesopotamia and Egypt (see Chapter 2). Just as each Middle Eastern civilization centered on a great river valley, so civilization in the Indian subcontinent originated on the fertile floodplain of the Indus River, where farming created the food surplus essential to urbanized society.

**Natural Environment** A plain of more than 1 million acres (400,000 hectares) stretches between the mountains of western Pakistan and the Thar (tahr) Desert to the east in Sind (sinned), the central portion of the Indus Valley (see Map 6.1). Silt carried downstream and deposited on the land by the Indus River over many centuries has elevated the riverbed and its banks above the level of the plain. Twice a year, the river overflows and inundates surrounding land as far as 10 miles (16 kilometers) distant. Snowmelt from the Pamir (pah-MEER) and Himalaya (him-uh-LAY-uh) Mountains

[1] Barbara Stoler Miller, *The Bhagavad-Gita: Krishna's Counsel in Time of War* (New York: Bantam, 1986), 98–99.

feeds the floods in March and April. In August, the monsoons bring rains from the southwest that cause a second flood. Though extremely dry for the rest of the year, Sind's floods make two crops a year possible. In ancient times, the Hakra (HAK-ruh) River (sometimes referred to as the Saraswati), which has since dried up, ran parallel to the Indus about 25 miles (40 kilometers) to the east and supplied water to a second cultivable area.

Adjacent regions shared distinctive cultural traits with this core area. In Punjab (literally "five waters"), to the northeast, five rivers converge to form the main course of the Indus. Closer to the northern mountains, the Punjab receives more rainfall but less floodwater than Sind. Culturally similar settlements extend from the Punjab as far east as Delhi (DEL-ee) in northwest India. Settlement also extended south through the Indus delta in southern Sind down into India's hook-shaped Kathiawar (kah-tee-uh-WAHR) Peninsula, an area of alluvial plains and coastal marshes. The Indus Valley civilization, as scholars labeled this area of cultural homogeneity when they first discovered it ninety years ago, covered an area roughly equivalent to modern France.

**Material Culture**    Although archaeologists have located several hundred communities that flourished from approximately 2600 to 1900 B.C.E., the remains of two urban sites known by the modern names **Harappa** and **Mohenjo-Daro** (moe-hen-joe–DAHR-oh) best typify the Indus Valley civilization. Unfortunately, the high water table at these sites makes excavation of the earliest levels of settlement nearly impossible.

Scholars once believed that the people who created this civilization spoke Dravidian (dru-VID-ee-uhn) languages related to those spoken today in southern India. Invaders from the northwest speaking Indo-European languages, they thought, conquered these people around 1500 B.C.E., causing some of them to migrate to the southeast. Skeletal evidence, however, indicates that the population of the Indus Valley has remained stable from ancient ties to the present. Settled agriculture in this region seems to date back to at least 5000 B.C.E.

The writing system of the Indus Valley people contained more than four hundred signs to represent syllables and words. Archeologists have recovered thousands of inscribed seal stones and copper tablets. The inscriptions are so brief, however, that no one has yet deciphered them, though some scholars believe they represent an early Dravidian language.

Harappa, 3.5 miles (5.6 kilometers) in circumference, may have housed a population of 35,000, and Mohenjo-Daro several times that. These cities show marked similarities in planning and construction: high, thick, encircling walls of brick; streets laid out in a rectangular grid; and covered drainpipes that carried away waste. The consistent width of streets and length of city blocks, and the uniformity of the mud bricks used in construction, suggest a strong central authority, located possibly in the citadel—an elevated, enclosed compound containing large buildings. Scholars think the well-ventilated structures near the citadel stored grain for use and for export. The presence of barracks may point to some regimentation of skilled artisans.

Though it is presumed that these urban centers controlled the surrounding farmlands, different centers may have served different functions, which might account for their locations. Mohenjo-Daro seems to dominate the great floodplain of the Indus. Harappa, which is nearly 500 miles (800 kilometers) to the north, sits in the zone where farmlands give way to pasturelands. No settlements have been found west of Harappa, which may have served as a gateway for copper, tin, precious stones, and other resources from the northwest. Coastal towns in the south engaged in seaborne trade with the Persian Gulf, as well as in fishing and gathering highly prized seashells. Although published accounts of the Indus Valley civilizations tend to treat Mohenjo-Daro and Harappa, the most extensively excavated sites, as the norm, most people surely lived in smaller settlements, which exhibit the same artifacts and the same standardization of styles and shapes as the large cities.

**Harappa**  Site of one of the great cities of the Indus Valley civilization of the third millennium B.C.E. It was located on the northwest frontier of the zone of cultivation (in modern Pakistan).

**Mohenjo-Daro**  Largest of the cities of the Indus Valley civilization, centrally located in the extensive floodplain of the Indus River in contemporary Pakistan.

# Chronology

| | India | Southeast Asia |
|---|---|---|
| 3000 B.C.E. | 2600 B.C.E. Beginning of Indus Valley civilization<br>1900 B.C.E. End of Indus Valley civilization | 3000 B.C.E. Malay peoples begin migrating from southern China into mainland Southeast Asia |
| 1500 B.C.E. | ca. 1500 B.C.E. Migration of Indo-European peoples into northwest India | Before 1000 B.C.E. Beginning of migrations from mainland Southeast Asia to islands in Pacific and Indian Oceans |
| 1000 B.C.E. | ca. 1000 B.C.E. Indo-Europeans settle the Ganges Plain | |
| 500 B.C.E. | ca. 500 B.C.E. Beginnings of Buddhism and Jainism<br>300 B.C.E. Tamil kingdoms<br>324 B.C.E. Mauryan Empire founded | |
| 1 C.E. | 320 C.E. Gupta Empire founded | ca. 50–560 C.E. Funan dominates southern Indochina and the Isthmus of Kra |
| 500 C.E. | 606–647 C.E. Reign of Harsha Vardhana | ca. 500 C.E. Trade route develops through Strait of Malacca<br>683 C.E. Rise of Srivijaya in Sumatra<br>770–825 C.E. Construction of Borobodur in Java |
| 1000 C.E. | | 1025 C.E. Decline of Srivijaya |

Metal appears more frequently in Indus Valley sites than in Mesopotamia and Egypt. Tools and other useful objects outweigh in importance the decorative objects—jewelry and the like—so often found in those other regions. Whereas metal goods were largely the possessions of elite in the Middle East, in the Indus Valley they belonged to a broad cross-section of the population.

Technologically, the Indus Valley people showed skill in irrigation, used the potter's wheel, and fired bricks in kilns for use in the foundations of large public buildings (sun-dried bricks exposed to floodwaters would have dissolved quickly). Smiths worked with various metals—gold, silver, copper, and tin. The varying ratios of tin to copper in their bronze objects suggest awareness of the hardness of different mixtures. They used less tin, a relatively scarce metal, in objects that did not require maximum hardness, like knives, and more tin in things like axes that had to be harder.

Archaeological finds point to widespread trading contacts. Mountain passes through the northwest granted access to the valuable resources of eastern Iran and Afghanistan, as well as to ore deposits in western India. These resources included metals (such as copper and tin), precious stones (lapis lazuli, jade, and turquoise), building stone, and timber. Rivers provided thoroughfares for transporting goods within the zone of Indus Valley culture.

Inhabitants of the Indus Valley and of Mesopotamia obtained raw materials from some of the same sources. The discovery of Indus Valley seal stones in the Tigris-Euphrates Valley indicates that merchants from the former region may have acted as middlemen in long-distance trade, obtaining raw materials from the northwest and shipping them to the Persian Gulf.

We know little about the political, social, economic, and religious structures of Indus Valley society. Efforts to link artifacts and images to cultural features characteristic of later periods of Indian history, including a sociopolitical institution (a system of hereditary occupational groups, the predominant role of priests), architectural forms (bathing tanks like those later found in Hindu temples, private interior courtyards in houses), and religious beliefs and practices (depictions of gods and sacred animals on seal stones, a cult of the mother-goddess), remain speculative. Further knowledge on these matters awaits additional archaeological finds and the deciphering of the Indus Valley script.

## Transformation of the Indus Valley Civilization

The Indus Valley cities were abandoned sometime after 1900 B.C.E. Archaeologists once thought that invaders destroyed them, but they now believe this civilization suffered "systems failure"—a breakdown of the fragile interrelationship of political, social, and economic systems that sustained order and prosperity. The precipitating cause may have been one or more natural disasters, such as an earthquake or massive flooding. Gradual ecological changes may also have played a role as the Hakra river system dried up and salinization (an increase in the amount of salt in the soil, inhibiting plant growth) and erosion increased.

Towns left dry by a change of riverbed, seaports removed from the coast by silt deposited in deltas, and regions suffering loss of fertile soil would have necessitated the relocation of populations and a change in the livelihood of those who remained. The causes, patterns, and pace of change probably varied, with urbanization persisting longer in some areas. The urban centers eventually succumbed, however, and village-based farming and herding took their place. As the interaction between regions lessened, regional variation replaced the standardization of technology and style of the previous era.

Historians can do little more than speculate about the causes behind the changes and the experiences of the people who lived in the Indus Valley around 1900 B.C.E. Two tendencies bear remembering, however. In most cases like this, the majority of the population adjusts to the new circumstances. But members of the political and social elite, who depend on the urban centers and complex political and economic structures, lose the source of their authority and merge with the population as a whole.

# FOUNDATIONS OF INDIAN CIVILIZATION

■ *What historical forces led to the development of complex social groupings in ancient India?*

India is called a *subcontinent* because it is a large—roughly 2,000 miles (3,200 kilometers) in both length and breadth—and physically isolated landmass within the continent of Asia. The Himalayas (him-AH-lay-uhs), the world's highest mountains, form a barrier to the north; the Indian Ocean bounds it on the east, south, and west (see Map 6.1). The one frontier easily accessible to invaders and migrating peoples lies to the northwest. But people using this corridor must cross over the mountain barrier of the Hindu Kush (HIHN-doo KOOSH) in Afghanistan and the Thar (tahr) Desert east of the Indus River.

## The Indian Subcontinent

This region divides into three topographical zones. The mountainous northern zone takes in the heavily forested foothills and high meadows on the edge of the Hindu Kush and Himalaya ranges. Next come the great basins of the Indus and Ganges (GAHN-jeez) Rivers. Originating in the Himalayas, these rivers flood annually, leaving layers of silt that over time have created large fertile plains. The Vindhya range and the Deccan (de-KAN), an arid, rocky plateau reminiscent of the American Southwest, separate northern India from the third zone, the peninsula proper. The Malabar Coast in the west, the Coromandel Coast in the east with its web of rivers descending from the Deccan, the flatlands of Tamil Nadu on the southern tip of the peninsula, and the island of Sri Lanka often have followed paths of political and cultural development separate from those of northern India.

## SECTION REVIEW

- As in Mesopotamia and Egypt, and roughly in the same time period, the wide, fertile Indus Valley supported a large urban civilization.

- Cities like Harappa and Mohenjo-Daro and their artifacts display uniformity of planning and construction and standardization of styles and shapes.

- The Indus Valley people developed sophisticated technologies, including a still-undecipherable writing system.

- Cities exchanged goods with each other and maintained extensive trade contacts with other ancient civilizations.

- The Indus Valley civilization collapsed when the cities were abandoned, probably as a result of natural disasters or environmental changes.

**Map 6.1 Ancient India** Mountains and ocean largely separate the Indian subcontinent from the rest of Asia. Migrations and invasions usually came through the Khyber Pass in the northwest. Seaborne commerce with western Asia, Southeast Asia, and East Asia often flourished. Peoples speaking Indo-European languages migrated into the broad valleys of the Indus and Ganges Rivers in the north. Dravidian-speaking peoples remained the dominant population in the south. The diversity of the Indian landscape, the multiplicity of ethnic groups, and the primary identification of people with their class and caste lie behind the division into many small states that has characterized much of Indian political history.

© Cengage Learning

The mountainous northern rim shelters the subcontinent from cold Siberian winds and gives it a subtropical climate. The **monsoon** (seasonal wind) comes annually when the Indian Ocean lags behind the Asian landmass in heating and cooling with the changing seasons. The temperature difference between water and land acts like a bellows, producing a great wind over the ocean. The southwest monsoon begins in June off the coast of East Africa, picks up moisture from the Indian Ocean, and delivers heavy precipitation to the Ganges Basin and the rainforest belt on India's western coast. The moist, flat Ganges Delta (modern Bengal) favors rice production. Elsewhere, wheat, barley, and millet predominate. Indus Valley farmers, in contrast, see little precipitation and therefore rely on extensive irrigation.

Indian Ocean mariners learned to ride the monsoon winds across open waters from northeast to southwest in January and to make the return voyage in July. Ships ventured across the Arabian Sea to the Persian Gulf, the southern coast of Arabia, and East Africa, and east across the Bay of Bengal to Indochina and Indonesia (see Chapter 8).

**monsoon** Seasonal winds in the Indian Ocean caused by the differences in temperature between the rapidly heating and cooling landmasses of Africa and Asia and the slowly changing ocean waters. These strong and predictable winds have long been ridden across the open sea by sailors, and the large amounts of rainfall that they deposit on parts of India, Southeast Asia, and China allow for the cultivation of several crops a year.

## The Vedic Age, 1500–500 B.C.E.

Many features of later Indian civilization surely date back to the Indus Valley civilization of the third and early second millennia B.C.E. Since the writing from that period remains undeciphered, the earliest textual knowledge about Indian roots comes from the period of 1500–500 B.C.E., called the Vedic Age after the religious texts known as the **Vedas**. While most historians believe that Indo-European-speaking nomads migrated into northwest India at the beginning of the period, others argue for a much earlier Indo-European presence deriving from the spread of agriculture (see Chapter 3).

After the collapse of the Indus Valley civilization, the central authority presumed to have organized large-scale irrigation disappeared and the region became home to bands of Vedic-speaking cattle herders who also engaged in farming. As with other Indo-European peoples—Celts, Greeks, Iranians, Romans—patriarchal traditions made the father dominant in the family just as the king ruled the group as a whole. Warriors boasted of their martial skill and courage, relished combat, feasted on beef, and filled their leisure time with chariot racing and gambling.

After 1000 B.C.E., some groups pushed eastward into the Ganges Plain. Iron tools—harder than bronze and able to hold a sharper edge—allowed settlers to fell trees and work the newly cleared land with ox-drawn plows. The fertile plain, watered by the annual monsoon, sustained two or three crops a year. As in Greece at roughly the same time, the use of iron tools must have led to a population increase.

Stories about this era, not written down until much later but preserved by an oral tradition, speak of rivalry and warfare between two groups: the Aryas, speakers of Vedic Sanskrit and practitioners of the sacrificial religion prescribed in the Vedas; and the Dasas, indigenous speakers of Dravidian languages, whose religion, it is pointedly noted in the Vedas, did not involve sacrifice to or worship of the Vedic gods. Some scholars argue that the real process by which Arya groups became dominant in the north involved the absorption of some Dasas into Arya populations and a merging of elites from both groups. For the most part, however, Aryas pushed the Dasas south into central and southern India, where their descen-

dants still live. Indo-European languages descended from those of the Aryas predominate in northern India today, while Dravidian languages prevail in the south.

The cultural and religious differences between the Aryas and the indigenous peoples contributed to sharp social divisions. A system of **varnas**, literally "colors" but usually translated as "castes," indicated something akin to classes. Individuals belonged by birth to one of four varnas: *Brahmins*, the group comprising priests and scholars; *Kshatriyas* (kshuh-TREE-yuhs), warriors and the king; *Vaishyas* (VIESH-yuhs), all other Aryas; and *Shudras* (SHOOD-ras), non-Aryans who were servants and slaves of the other three varnas. The designation *Shudra* originally may have been reserved for Dasas. Indeed, the term *dasa* came to mean "slave." Eventually a fifth group emerged: the Untouchables. Excluded from the caste system and shunned by the other castes, they worked in demeaning or polluting trades such as tanning, which involved touching dead animals, and sweeping away ashes after cremations.

According to one creation myth, a primordial man named Purusha allowed himself to be sacrificed. From his mouth sprang the varna of Brahmin priests. From his arms came the Kshatriya warriors; from his thighs the Vaishya merchants, artisans, and peasants; and from his feet the Shudra workers.

Within the broad varna divisions, the population further divided into numerous smaller groups, called **jatis**, or *castes*. Each jati had its proper occupation, duties, and rituals. Members of a given jati lived and married within the group and ate only with members

---

**Vedas** Early Indian sacred "knowledge"—the literal meaning of the term—long preserved and communicated orally by Brahmin priests and eventually written down. These religious texts, including the thousand poetic hymns to various deities contained in the *Rig Veda*, are our main source of information about the Vedic period (ca. 1500–500 B.C.E.).

**varna/jati** Two categories of social identity of great importance in Indian history. Varnas are the four major social divisions: the Brahmin priest class, the Kshatriya warrior/administrator class, the Vaishya merchant/farmer class, and the Shudra laborer class. Within the system of varnas are many jatis, regional groups of people who have a common occupational sphere and who marry, eat, and generally interact with other members of their group.

of the group. Elaborate rules governed interactions between groups. Members of higher-status groups feared pollution from contacting lower-caste individuals and had to undergo rituals of purification to remove any taint.

The caste system became connected to a belief in reincarnation. Brahmin priests taught that every living creature had an immortal essence: the *atman*, or "self." Separated from the body at death, the atman returned in the body of an insect, an animal, or a human depending on the **karma**, or deeds, of the atman in its previous incarnations. People of exemplary goodness returned in a higher caste. Those who misbehaved fell to a lower caste or even a lower life form. The underlying message ran: You are where you deserve to be, and the only way to improve your lot in the next incarnation is to accept your current station and its attendant duties.

Many of the Vedic deities, mostly male, were associated with the heavens. Indra, like Zeus a god of war and master of the thunderbolt, commanded the greatest devotion and represented the chieftains who led the warriors into battle. Agni, the fire-god, consumed the sacrifice and bridged the spheres of gods and humans. Vedic religion centered on sacrifice, the dedication to a god of a valued possession, often a living creature. The offerings invigorated the gods and thereby sustained their creative powers and promoted stability in the world.

Brahmin priests alone knew the rituals and prayers. The *Rig Veda*, a collection of more than a thousand poetic hymns to various deities, and the *Brahmanas*, detailed prose descriptions and explanations of ritual procedures, all in the Sanskrit language of the Arya upper classes, passed orally from one generation of priests to the next. Writing did not spread in India until the Gupta period (320–550 C.E.), possibly because the Brahmins opposed its introduction. The priests' "knowledge" (the term *veda* means just that) earned them rewards for officiating at sacrifices and gave them social and political power as the intermediaries between gods and humans.

As elsewhere in the ancient world, the lives of Indian women left few traces. Limited evidence indicates that in the Vedic period women studied sacred lore, composed religious hymns, and participated in sacrifices. They could own property and usually did

not marry until their middle or late teens. A number of strong and resourceful women appear in the *Mahabharata* epic (discussed later in this chapter). In the *Ramayana* epic, on the other hand, we see the familiar motif of the hero Rama rescuing his wife Sita after she has been abducted.

The internal divisions of Indian society, the complex hierarchy of groups, and the claims of some to superior virtue and purity provided each individual with a clear identity and role and offered the benefits of group solidarity and support. Sometimes groups even upgraded their status within the system, which was not entirely static and provided a mechanism for releasing social tensions. Many of these features have persisted into modern times.

## Challenges to the Old Order: Jainism and Buddhism

After 700 B.C.E. reactions against Brahmin power and privilege emerged. People who objected to the rigid social hierarchy could always retreat to the forest that covered much of ancient India. Never far away, these wild places symbolized freedom from societal constraints. Individuals who wandered in the forest sometimes attracted followers. Questioning priestly power and the necessity of sacrifices, they offered alternate paths to salvation: individual pursuit of insight into the nature of the self and the universe through physical and mental discipline (*yoga*), which included dietary restrictions and meditation. They taught that by distancing oneself from desire for the things of this world, one could achieve **moksha**, or liberation, a "deep, dreamless sleep" that released one from the endless reincarnations through union with the divine force of the universe. The

**karma**   In Indian tradition, the residue of deeds performed in past and present lives that adheres to a "spirit" and determines what form it will assume in its next life cycle. The doctrines of karma and reincarnation were used by the elite in ancient India to encourage people to accept their social position and do their duty.

**moksha**   The Hindu concept of the spirit's "liberation" from the endless cycle of rebirths. There are various avenues—such as physical discipline, meditation, and acts of devotion to the gods—by which the spirit can distance itself from desire for the things of this world and be merged with the divine force that animates the universe.

**Carved Stone Gateway Leading to the Great Stupa at Sanchi**  Pilgrims traveled long distances to visit stupas, mounds containing relics of the Buddha. The complex at Sanchi, in central India, was begun by Ashoka in the third century B.C.E., though the gates probably date to the first century C.E. This relief shows a royal procession bringing the remains of the Buddha to the city of Kushinagara.

*Upanishads* (ooh-PAH-nee-shad), which continue the explanations of ritual begun in the *Brahmanas*, also reflect this questioning of Vedic religion.

Jainism (JINE-iz-uhm) and Buddhism challenged not only Vedic ritualism but also the authority of the Vedic priests. Jainism took its name from the teacher Mahavira (540–468 B.C.E.), known to his followers as Jina, "the Conqueror." Mahavira respected the life force so much that he commanded strict nonviolence. Jains wore masks to avoid inadvertently inhaling small insects and brushed off the seat before sitting down. Some practiced extreme asceticism by embracing nudity and eventually starving themselves to death. Less zealous Jains engaged in com-

merce in cities, since agricultural work inevitably involved killing.

Buddhism, a far more successful movement, stemmed from the life of Siddhartha Gautama (563–483 B.C.E.), known as the **Buddha**, "the Enlightened One," about whom myriad legends have arisen. From a Kshatriya family in what is now Nepal, he enjoyed the princely lifestyle to which he had been born until

**Buddha**  An Indian prince named Siddhartha Gautama, who renounced his wealth and social position. After becoming "enlightened" (the meaning of *Buddha*), he enunciated the principles of Buddhism. This doctrine evolved and spread throughout India and to Southeast, East, and Central Asia.

he experienced a change of heart and gave up family and privilege to become a wandering ascetic. After six years, he decided that asceticism was no more likely to produce spiritual insight than his earlier luxurious life, so he opened a "Middle Path." Sitting under a tree in a deer park near Benares on the Ganges River, he gained a sudden and profound insight, which he set forth as "Four Noble Truths": (1) life is suffering; (2) suffering arises from desire; (3) the solution to suffering lies in curbing desire; and (4) desire can be curbed if a person follows the "Eightfold Path" of right views, aspirations, speech, conduct, livelihood, effort, mindfulness, and meditation. Rising up, the Buddha preached his First Sermon, a central text of Buddhism, and set into motion the "Wheel of the Law." He soon attracted followers, some of whom took vows of celibacy, nonviolence, and poverty.

At first, Buddhism centered on the individual, denying the usefulness of the gods to a person seeking enlightenment. What mattered was living moderately to minimize desire and suffering and searching for spiritual truth through self-discipline and meditation. One should seek *nirvana*, literally "snuffing out the flame," a release from the cycle of reincarnations and enjoyment of perpetual tranquility. Whereas the *Upanishad* tradition emphasized the eternal survival of the atman, the "self" or nonmaterial essence of the individual, Buddhism regarded the individual as a composite of features such as breath and wind, but without a soul.

At his death, Buddha left no final instructions, urging his disciples to "be their own lamp." As his followers spread his philosophy throughout India and into Central, Southeast, and East Asia, its wide appeal subverted its individualistic and atheistic underpinnings, and Buddhist monasteries with hierarchies of monks and nuns came into being. Worshipers erected *stupas* (STOO-puh) (large earthen mounds symbolizing the universe) over relics of the cremated founder and other holy men and walked around them in a clockwise direction. Believers began to worship the Buddha himself as a god. Many Buddhists also revered *bodhisattvas* (boe-dih-SUT-vuhs), men and women who had achieved enlightenment and were on the threshold of nirvana but chose rebirth into mortal bodies to help others along the path to salvation.

Early representations show the Buddha only indirectly, through symbols such as his footprints, begging bowl, or the tree under which he achieved enlightenment, as if to emphasize his achievement of a state of nonexistence. From the second century C.E., however, statues of the Buddha and bodhisattvas proliferated, sculpted in styles that showed the influence of the Greek settlements established in Bactria (modern Afghanistan) by Alexander the Great.

A schism emerged within Buddhism. Devotees of **Mahayana** (mah-huh-YAH-nuh) ("Great Vehicle") **Buddhism** embraced the popular new features. Practitioners of **Theravada** (there-uh-VAH-duh) ("Teachings of the Elders") **Buddhism** followed most of the original teachings of the founder.

## The Rise of Hinduism

Challenged by the new religious movements, Vedic religion evolved by the fourth century C.E. into **Hinduism**, the dominant religion in South Asia today. (The term *Hinduism* originated with Islamic invaders in the eleventh century C.E. as a label for the diverse practices they encountered: "what the Indians do.") Though based on the Vedic religion of northern India, Hinduism incorporated Dravidian cultural elements from the south, such as intense devotion to a deity and the prominence of goddesses.

Brahmin priests survived the transition with their social status and influence intact, but sacrifice lost its central place. Opportunities for individual worshipers to have direct contact with deities increased. Hinduism emphasized the worshiper's personal devotion to a particular deity, usually Vishnu

**Mahayana Buddhism** "Great Vehicle" branch of Buddhism followed in China, Japan, and Central Asia. The focus is on reverence for Buddha and for bodhisattvas, enlightened persons who have postponed nirvana to help others attain enlightenment.

**Theravada Buddhism** "Way of the Elders" branch of Buddhism followed in Sri Lanka and much of Southeast Asia. Theravada remains close to the original principles set forth by the Buddha; it downplays the importance of gods and emphasizes austerity and the individual's search for enlightenment.

**Hinduism** A general term for a wide variety of beliefs and ritual practices that have developed in the Indian subcontinent since antiquity. Hinduism has roots in ancient Vedic, Buddhist, and south Indian religious concepts and practices. It spread along the trade routes to Southeast Asia.

**Hindu Temple at Khajuraho**   This sandstone temple of the Hindu deity Shiva, representing the celestial mountain of the gods, was erected at Khajuraho, in central India, around 1000 C.E., but it reflects the architectural symbolism of Hindu temples developed in the Gupta period. Worshipers made their way through several rooms to the image of the deity, located in the innermost "womb-chamber" directly beneath the tallest tower.

(VIHSH-noo) or Shiva (SHEE-vuh), or Devi (DEH-vee) ("the Goddess"). The goddess is of Dravidian origin, and her incorporation into the cult shows how Arya and indigenous cultures fused to form Hindu civilization. Vishnu, who has a clear Arya pedigree, remains more popular in northern India, and Shiva is dominant in the south. These deities appear in many guises, bear various cult names, and give rise to a complex symbolism of stories, companion animals, birds, and objects.

Vishnu, the preserver, benevolently helps his devotees in time of need. Hindus believe that whenever demonic forces threaten the cosmic order, an *avatara*, or incarnation of Vishnu, appears on the earth. His avatars include the legendary hero Rama, the cowherd-god Krishna, and the Buddha (a clear attempt to co-opt the rival religion's founder). Shiva, who lives in ascetic isolation on Mount Kailasa in the

Himalayas, represents a cyclical process of creation and destruction that is symbolized in statues showing him dancing. Devi can manifest herself as a full-bodied mother-goddess representing fertility and procreation, as Shiva's loving wife Parvati, or as the frightening deity who, under the name Kali or Durga, lets loose violence and destruction.

The multiplicity of gods (330 million according to one tradition), sects, and local practices within Hinduism reflects the ethnic, linguistic, and cultural diversity of India. Yet within this variety, there is unity. A worshiper's devotion to one god or goddess does not entail denial of the other main deities or the host of lesser divinities and spirits. Ultimately, all are manifestations of a single divine force pervading the universe. The underlying unity appears in the way various manifestations of Devi represent different female potentials, as well as in composite statues—

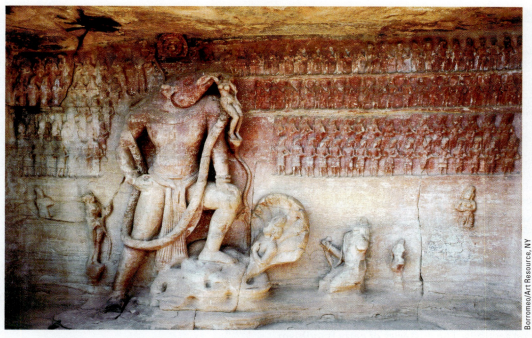

**Vishnu Rescuing the Earth Goddess, Fifth Century C.E.** This sculpture, carved into the rock wall of a cave at Udayagiri in eastern India, depicts Vishnu in his incarnation as a boar rescuing the Earth Goddess from the vast ocean. As the god treads triumphantly on a subdued snake demon and the joyful goddess clings to his snout, a chorus of gods and sages applaud the miracle.

half Shiva, half Vishnu—signifying complementary aspects of one cosmic principle.

Hindus may approach god and obtain divine favor through special knowledge of sacred truths, mental and physical discipline, or extraordinary devotion to the deity. Worship centers on the temples, which range from humble shrines to richly decorated stone edifices built under royal patronage. Statues beckon the deity to take up temporary residence within the image and be available to eager worshipers. *Puja*, or service to the deity, can include bathing, clothing, or feeding the statue. Glimpsing the divine image conveys blessings.

Sacred places where a worshiper can directly sense and benefit from the divine power dot the Indian subcontinent. Mystery and sanctity surround certain mountains, caves, trees, plants, and rocks. *Tirthayatra*, the term for pilgrimage site, means "journey to a river crossing," illustrating the association of Hindu places with flowing water. The Ganges River is especially sacred. Millions of worshipers travel each year to bathe and receive the restorative and purifying power of its waters. Pilgrimages to shrines foster contact and the exchange of ideas among people from different parts of India, helping to create a broad Hindu identity and the concept of India as a single civilization.

Religious duties depend on social standing and gender as well as stage of life. Young men from the three highest classes (Brahmin, Kshatriya, and Vaishya) undergo ritual rebirth through the ceremony of the sacred thread, marking attainment of manhood and readiness to receive religious knowledge. The life cycle then passes through four stages: (1) student of the sacred texts, (2) married householder with children and material goods, (3) forest dweller meditating on the meaning of existence after the birth of his grandchildren, and (4) wandering ascetic awaiting death. The person living such a life fulfills first his duties to society and then his duties to himself, leaving him disconnected from the world and prepared for moksha (liberation).

- The Indian subcontinent is divided by a variety of natural barriers and as a whole is isolated from the rest of Asia except for the northwest.
- Indian seafarers used the monsoons to travel to the Middle East, East Africa, and Southeast Asia.
- During the Vedic Age, the Aryas migrated into northern India, and their conquest of the Dasas introduced the caste system.
- Brahmin priests presided over the Vedic religion and led ritual sacrifices.
- Jainism and Buddhism, which stressed more individual approaches, rose to challenge Brahmin power.
- In response, Vedic religion transformed into Hinduism.

Hinduism responded to the needs of people for personal deities with whom they could establish direct connections. The austerity of early Buddhism, its denial of the importance of gods, and its demand that individuals find their own path to enlightenment may have required too much of ordinary people. What eventually made Mahayana Buddhism popular—gods, saints, and myths—also made it more easily absorbed into the vast social and cultural fabric of Hinduism.

# INDIAN IMPERIAL EXPANSION AND COLLAPSE

■ *In the face of powerful forces that tended to keep India fragmented, how did the Mauryan Empire of the fourth to second centuries B.C.E. and the Gupta Empire of the fourth to sixth centuries C.E. succeed in unifying much of India?*

Political unity has rarely lasted in India. The varied terrain—mountains, foothills, plains, forests, steppes, deserts—favors different forms of organization and economic activity. Peoples occupying topographically diverse zones may also differ in language and cultural practices. Caste and family have generated the strongest feelings of personal identity, allegiance to a higher political authority being a secondary concern. Nevertheless, two empires arose in the Ganges Plain: the Mauryan (MORE-yuhn) Empire of the fourth

to second centuries B.C.E. and the Gupta (GOOP-tuh) Empire of the fourth to sixth centuries C.E.

## The Mauryan Empire, 324–184 B.C.E.

Among the many kinship groups and independent states that dotted the north Indian landscape, the kingdom of Magadha, in the modern state of Bihar, began to play an influential role around 600 B.C.E. thanks to wealth based on agriculture, iron mines, and strategic location astride the trade routes of the eastern Ganges Basin. In the late fourth century B.C.E. Chandragupta Maurya (MORE-yuh), a man of Vaishya or Shudra origins, took control of Magadha and founded the **Mauryan Empire**. Greek tradition claimed that Alexander the Great met an Indian native named "Sandracotus," an apparent corruption of "Chandragupta," when his armies reached the Punjab (northern Pakistan) in 326 B.C.E., implying that he might have served as a role model for the new ruler.

Greek rule in the Punjab collapsed after Alexander's death, allowing Chandragupta (r. 324–301 B.C.E.) and his successors Bindusara (r. 301–273 B.C.E.) and Ashoka (r. 273–232 B.C.E.) to extend Mauryan control over the entire subcontinent except its southern tip.

Tradition holds that Kautilya, a crafty elderly Brahmin, guided Chandragupta and wrote a treatise on government, the *Arthashastra* (ahr-thuh-SHAHS-truh). Although recent studies have shown that the existing form of the *Arthashastra* dates only to the third century C.E., its core text may well go back to Kautilya. This pragmatic guide to political success advocates the so-called *mandala* (man-DAH-luh) (circle) theory of foreign policy: "My enemy's enemy is my friend." It also presents schemes for enforcing and increasing the collection of tax revenues and prescribes the use of spies to keep watch on one's subjects.

A quarter of all agricultural output went in taxes to support the Mauryan government. Relatives and associates of the king governed districts based on

**Mauryan Empire** The first state to unify most of the Indian subcontinent. It was founded by Chandragupta Maurya in 324 B.C.E. and survived until 184 B.C.E. From its capital at Pataliputra in the Ganges Valley it grew wealthy from taxes on agriculture, iron mining, and control of trade routes.

ethnic boundaries. The imperial army—with infantry, cavalry, and elephant divisions—secured central authority, which also controlled mining, shipbuilding, and arms making. Standard coinage fostered support for the government and promoted trade.

The Mauryan kings ruled Pataliputra (modern Patna), where five tributaries join the Ganges. Descriptions by foreign visitors testify to the international connections of the Indian monarchs. Surrounded by a timber wall and moat, the city extended along the river for 8 miles (13 kilometers). Six governing committees oversaw manufacturing, trade, sales, taxes, the welfare of foreigners, and the registration of births and deaths.

**Ashoka**, Chandragupta's grandson, began his reign by extending the boundaries of the empire. After killing, wounding, or deporting thousands of people during his conquest of Kalinga (modern Orissa, a coastal region southeast of Magadha), remorse overcame him and he converted to Buddhism, thereafter preaching nonviolence, morality, moderation, and religious tolerance in both government and private life.

Ashoka publicized this program through edicts inscribed on great rocks and polished sandstone, the earliest decipherable Indian texts:

> For . . . many hundreds of years the sacrificial slaughter of animals, violence toward creatures, unfilial conduct toward kinsmen, and improper conduct toward Brahmins and ascetics have increased. Now with the practice of morality by King [Ashoka], the sound of war drums has become the call to morality. . . . You [government officials] are appointed to rule over thousands of human beings in the expectation that you will win the affection of all men. All men are my children. Just as I desire that my children will fare well and be happy in this world and the next, I desire the same for all men. . . . King [Ashoka] . . . desires that there should be the growth of the essential spirit of morality or holiness among all sects. . . . There should not be glorification of one's own sect and denunciation of the sect of others for little or no reason. For all the sects are worthy of reverence for one reason or another.[2]

Despite his commitment to employ peaceful means whenever possible, Ashoka reminded potential transgressors that "the king, remorseful as he is, has the strength to punish the wrongdoers who do not repent."

## Commerce and Culture in an Era of Political Fragmentation

The Mauryan Empire prospered for a time after Ashoka's death in 232 B.C.E. Then, weakened by dynastic disputes, it collapsed under attacks in the northwest in 184 B.C.E. Five hundred years passed before another state succeeded in extending control over northern India. In the meantime, settlers descended from troops left in northern Afghanistan by Alexander the Great established the Greco-Bactrian kingdom (180–50 B.C.E.), and two nomadic groups from Central Asia followed them, set off by the pressure of Han Chinese forces on the Xiongnu (see Chapter 5). The Shakas, an Iranian people, were dominant from 50 B.C.E. to 50 C.E., followed by the Kushans (KOO-shahn) (50 to 240 C.E.), originally from Xinjiang in northwest China. At its height the Kushan kingdom controlled much of present-day Uzbekistan, Afghanistan, Pakistan, and northwest India, fostering trade through both the overland Silk Road and Indian Ocean seaports (see Chapter 8). The eastern Ganges region reverted to the patchwork of small principalities that had characterized the Mauryan era.

Despite the political fragmentation, however, economic, cultural, and intellectual development continued. The roads and towns of the Mauryas fostered commerce within the subcontinent, while land and sea routes linked India to China, Southeast Asia, Central Asia, the Middle East, East Africa, and the lands of the Mediterranean. Guilds of merchants and artisans regulated the lives of their members and had an important voice in local affairs. They supported culture and endowed the religious sects, particularly Buddhism and Jainism, with temples and monuments.

---

[2] B. G. Gokhale, *Asoka Maurya* (New York: Twayne, 1966), 152–153, 156–157, 160.

**Ashoka** Third ruler of the Mauryan Empire in India (r. 273–232 B.C.E.). He converted to Buddhism and broadcast his precepts on inscribed stones and pillars, the earliest surviving Indian writing.

During the last centuries B.C.E. and first centuries C.E. the two greatest Indian epics, the *Ramayana* (ruh-MAH-yuh-nuh) and the *Mahabharata* (muh-huh-BAH-ruh-tuh), based on centuries-old oral predecessors, achieved their final form. They place the events they describe in the distant past, but their proud kings, beautiful queens, family wars, heroic conduct, and chivalric values seem to reflect the late Vedic period, when Aryan warrior societies moved onto the Ganges Plain.

The *Ramayana* relates the exploits of Rama, a heroic prince who came to be considered an incarnation of Vishnu. When the chief of the demons kidnaps his wife, Sita, he destroys the demons with the help of his brother and a troop of monkeys. The vast *Mahabharata*—eight times the length of the Greek *Iliad* and *Odyssey* combined—tells how two sets of cousins, the Pandavas and Kauravas, quarreled over succession to the throne and fought a cataclysmic battle at Kurukshetra. The battle is so destructive on both sides that Yudhishthira, the eldest of the Pandava brothers and their leader, accepts the fruits of victory only reluctantly.

The **Bhagavad-Gita** is a self-contained (and perhaps originally separate) episode set in the battle. The hero Arjuna shrinks from fighting his kinsmen until his charioteer, the god Krishna, tutors him on the necessity of fulfilling his duty as a warrior. Death means nothing in a universe of endless reincarnation. The Bhagavad-Gita resolves the tension in Indian civilization between duty to society and duty to one's own soul. Dutiful action taken without regard for personal benefits serves society and may earn release from the cycle of rebirths.

Science and technology flourished in this era as well. Indian doctors applied herbal remedies and served in the courts of western and southern Asia. Panini (late fourth century B.C.E.) undertook a detailed analysis of Sanskrit, which arrested its natural development and turned it into a formal, literary language. Prakrits—popular dialects—emerged to become the ancestors of the modern languages of northern and central India.

Historians of southern India consider the period from the third century B.C.E. to the third century C.E. dominated by three often feuding **Tamil kingdoms**—of Cholas, Pandyas, and Cheras—a "classical" period

for Tamil art and literature. Under the patronage of the Pandya kings and guided by an academy of five hundred authors, Tamil writers composed grammatical treatises, collections of ethical proverbs, epics, and short poems about love, war, wealth, and the beauty of nature while performers excelled in music, dance, and drama.

## The Gupta Empire, 320–550 C.E.

Like its Mauryan predecessor, the **Gupta Empire** grew from the kingdom of Magadha and had its capital at Pataliputra. Its founder called himself Chandra Gupta (r. 320–335), borrowing the name of the Mauryan founder. Though they never controlled as much land as the Mauryans, the Gupta monarchs took the title "Great King of Kings."

Trade, agriculture, and iron mining brought prosperity to the Guptas as they had to the Mauryans, and the kings followed similar methods of taxation and administration. In addition to a 25 percent tax on agriculture, users of the irrigation network paid fees, and some commodities were subject to special taxes. The state maintained monopolies over mining and production, exploited state-owned farmlands, and required subjects to work a specified number of days on maintaining roads, wells, and irrigation works.

The Gupta administration and intelligence network were smaller and less pervasive than those of the Mauryans. A powerful army maintained tight control of the empire's core, but provincial governors had a free hand, which they sometimes used to exploit the populace. Governorships often passed from father to

**Mahabharata** A vast epic chronicling the events leading up to a cataclysmic battle between related kinship groups in early India. It includes the Bhagavad-Gita.

**Bhagavad-Gita** The most important work of Indian sacred literature, a dialogue between the great warrior Arjuna and the god Krishna on duty and the fate of the spirit.

**Tamil kingdoms** The kingdoms of southern India, inhabited primarily by speakers of Dravidian languages, which developed in partial isolation, and somewhat differently, from the Arya north. They produced epics, poetry, and performance arts. Elements of Tamil religious beliefs were merged into the Hindu synthesis.

**Gupta Empire** A powerful Indian state based, like its Mauryan predecessor, on a capital at Pataliputra in the Ganges Valley. It controlled most of the Indian subcontinent through a combination of military force and its prestige as a center of sophisticated culture.

son within high-ranking military or administrative families. The most distant areas, controlled by kinship groups or subordinate kings, made annual donations of tribute. Garrisons stationed at frontier points kept trade routes open and ensured the collection of customs duties.

A constant round of solemn rituals, dramatic ceremonies, and cultural events in Pataliputra demonstrated to visitors from remote areas the benefits of belonging to the empire. Modern historians call such a regime a **theater-state**. Rulers and subjects in the Gupta theater-state had an economic relationship. The former accumulated luxury goods and profits from trade and redistributed them to dependents through gifts and other means. Subordinate princes gained prestige by emulating the center and maintained close ties through visits, gifts, and marriages with all the Gupta family. Gupta patronage also supported the Indian mathematicians, who invented the concept of zero and developed the Arabic numerals and place-value notations (see Environment and Technology: Indian Mathematics).

The moist climate of the Ganges Plain does not favor the preservation of buildings and artifacts, so archaeology has little to say about the Gupta era. However, a Chinese Buddhist monk named Faxian (fah-shee-en), who made a pilgrimage to the homeland of his faith around 400 C.E., penned a description of the Gupta kingdom:

> The cities and towns of this country are the greatest of all in the Middle Kingdom. The inhabitants are rich and prosperous, and vie with one another in the practice of benevolence and righteousness. . . . The heads of the Vaishya families in them establish in the cities houses for dispensing charity and medicines. All the poor and destitute in the country, orphans, widowers, and childless men, maimed people, and cripples, and all who are diseased, go to those houses, and are provided with every kind of help.[3]

At this time, the civil disabilities of women, which had always existed as custom, hardened into law with the emergence of books like *The Law of Manu*. Indian women lost the right to own or inherit

property, and girls married at an increasingly early age, sometimes at six or seven. The husband could thus ensure his wife's virginity and, by bringing her up in his own household, could train her to suit his purposes. As in Confucian China, a woman owed obedience to her father, then her husband, and finally her sons (see Chapter 3). In certain parts of India, a practice called *sati* (suh-TEE) required a widow to cremate herself on her husband's funeral pyre. Widows who refused to follow this custom could not remarry and suffered social rejection.

Entering a Jainist or Buddhist religious community offered some women an escape from male control. Women from powerful families and courtesans trained in poetry and music, as well as sexual technique, sometimes enjoyed high social standing and gave money for Buddhist stupas and other shrines.

The Gupta monarchs sought sanctity through reviving Vedic practices, and Brahmin priests regained influence. Yet the kings also patronized Buddhist and Jain endeavors. Buddhist monasteries with hundreds or even thousands of monks and nuns in residence flourished in the cities. Northern India drew Buddhist pilgrims from Southeast and East Asia to the birthplace of their faith.

The classic form of the Hindu temple, which evolved during the Gupta era, symbolizes the sacred mountain or palace where the gods of mythology reside. Sitting atop a raised platform surmounted by high towers, it mirrors the order of the universe. From an exterior courtyard, worshipers approached the central shrine containing the statue of the deity. In rich temples, painted or sculpted gods and mythical events covered the walls. Frescoes and statues also adorned cave temples carved into cliffs.

The vibrant commerce of the period of fragmentation continued under the Guptas. Coins served as a medium of exchange, and artisan guilds influenced the economic, political, and religious life of towns. The Guptas sought control of the ports on

---

[3] James Legge, *The Travels of Fa-hien: Fa-hien's Record of Buddhistic Kingdoms* (Delhi: Oriental Publishers, 1971), 77–79.

**theater-state** Historians' term for a state that acquires prestige and power by developing attractive cultural forms and staging elaborate public ceremonies (as well as redistributing valuable resources) to attract and bind subjects to the center. Examples include the Gupta Empire in India and Srivijaya in Southeast Asia.

# environment & technology

## Indian Mathematics

**T**he so-called Arabic numerals used in most parts of the world today were developed in India. The Indian system of place-value notation was far more efficient than the unwieldy numerical systems of Egyptians, Greeks, and Romans, and the invention of zero was a profound intellectual achievement. This system is used even more widely than the alphabet derived from the Phoenicians (see Chapter 2) and is, in one sense, the only truly global language.

In its fully developed form the Indian method of arithmetic notation employed a base-ten system. It had separate columns for ones, tens, hundreds, and so forth, as well as a zero sign to indicate the absence of units in a given column. This system makes possible the economical expression of even very large numbers. It also allows for the performance of calculations not possible in a system like the numerals of the Romans, where any real calculation had to be done mentally or on a counting board.

A series of early Indian inscriptions using the numerals from 1 to 9 are deeds of property given to religious institutions by kings or other wealthy individuals. They were incised in the Sanskrit language on copper plates. The earliest known example has a date equivalent to 595 C.E. A sign for zero is attested by the eighth century, but textual evidence leads to the inference that a place-value system and the zero concept were already known in the fifth century.

This Indian system spread to the Middle East, Southeast Asia, and East Asia by the seventh century. Other peoples quickly recognized its capabilities and adopted it, sometimes using indigenous symbols. Europe received the new technology somewhat later. Gerbert of Aurillac, a French Christian monk, spent time in Spain between 967 and 970, where he was exposed to the mathematics of the Arabs. A great scholar and teacher who eventually became Pope Sylvester II (r. 999–1003), he spread word of the "Arabic" system in the Christian West.

Knowledge of the Indian system of mathematical notation eventually spread throughout Europe, partly through the use of a mechanical calculating device—an improved version of the Roman counting board, with counters inscribed with variants of the Indian numeral forms. Because the counters could be turned sideways or upside down, at first there was considerable variation in the forms.

**Copper Plate with Indian Numerals** *This property deed from western India shows an early form of the symbol system for numbers that spread to the Middle East and Europe and today is used all over the world.* Facsimile by Georges Ifrah. Reproduced by permission of Georges Ifrah.

But by the twelfth century they had become standardized into forms close to those in use today. As the capabilities of the place-value system for calculations became clear, the counting board fell into disuse. This led to the adoption of the zero sign—not necessary on the counting board, where a column could be left empty—by the twelfth century. Leonardo Fibonacci, a thirteenth-century C.E. Italian who learned algebra in Muslim North Africa and employed the Arabic numeral system in his mathematical treatise, gave additional impetus to the movement to discard the traditional system of Roman numerals.

Why was this marvelous system of mathematical notation invented in ancient India? The answer may lie in the way its range and versatility correspond to elements of Indian cosmology. The Indians conceived of immense spans of time—trillions of years (far exceeding current scientific estimates of the age of the universe as approximately 14 billion years)—during which innumerable universes like our own were created, existed for a finite time, then were destroyed. In one popular creation myth, Vishnu is slumbering on the coils of a giant serpent at the bottom of the ocean, and worlds are being created and destroyed as he exhales and inhales. In Indian thought our world, like others, has existed for a series of epochs lasting more than 4 million years, yet the period of its existence is but a brief and insignificant moment in the vast sweep of time. The Indians developed a number system that allowed them to express concepts of this magnitude.

## SECTION REVIEW

- Chandragupta Maurya took control of the kingdom of Magadha and established the Mauryan Empire.

- The collapse of Greek rule in the Punjab enabled Chandragupta and his successors to expand the empire.

- The empire reached its fullest extent under Ashoka, after whose death it disintegrated.

- Economic and cultural activity continued during an era of fragmentation; to the south, Tamil culture entered its classical period.

- Also centered in Magadha, the Gupta Empire was less centralized than the Mauryan, but it thrived on the same economic bases.

- The Guptas revived Vedic practices and presided over both the legal hardening of gender discrimination and the expansion of overseas trade.

the Arabian Sea but lost trade as the Roman Empire weakened. However, trade with Southeast and East Asia increased. Merchants from eastern and southern India voyaged to the Malay (muh-LAY) Peninsula and the islands of Indonesia to exchange cotton cloth, ivory, metalwork, and animals for Chinese silk or Indonesian spices. The overland Silk Road from China brought further trade but was vulnerable to disruption by Central Asian nomads (see Chapter 8).

The Gupta Empire collapsed around 550 C.E. under pressure from nomadic invaders from the steppes of Central Asia (see Chapter 3). In the early seventh century, Harsha Vardhana (r. 606–647 C.E.), the ruler of the region around Delhi, briefly restored imperial power. An account of his region by a courtier named Bana shows him to be a fervent Buddhist, poet, patron of artists, and dynamic warrior. After Harsha's death, northern India reverted to its political fragmentation and remained divided until the Islamic invasions of the eleventh and twelfth centuries (see Chapter 14).

## SOUTHEAST ASIA, 50–1025 C.E.

■ *How did the geography of Southeast Asia contribute to its commerce and to the influence of Hinduism and Buddhism?*

Southeast Asia consists of three geographical zones: the Indochina mainland, the Malay Peninsula, and thousands of islands extending on an east-west axis far out into the Pacific Ocean (see Map 6.2). Encompassing a vast area of land and water, this region is now occupied by the countries of Myanmar (myahn-MAH) (Burma), Thailand, Laos, Cambodia, Vietnam, Malaysia, Singapore, Indonesia, Brunei (broo-NIE), and the Philippines. Poised between the ancient centers of China and India, Southeast Asia has been influenced by the cultures of both civilizations. The region first rose to prominence and prosperity because of its intermediate role in the trade exchanges between southern and eastern Asia.

The strategic importance of Southeast Asia is enhanced by the region's natural resources. This is a geologically active zone; the islands are the tops of a chain of volcanoes. Lying along the equator, Southeast Asia has a tropical climate. The temperature hovers around 80 degrees Fahrenheit (30 degrees Celsius), and the monsoon winds provide dependable rainfall throughout the year. Thanks to several growing cycles each year, the region is capable of supporting a large human population. The most fertile agricultural lands lie along the floodplains of the largest silt-bearing rivers or contain rich volcanic soil deposited by ancient eruptions.

## Early Civilization

Rain forest covers much of Southeast Asia. As early as 2000 B.C.E. people in this region were clearing land for farming by cutting and burning the vegetation. The cleared land was farmed for several growing seasons. When the soil was exhausted, the farmers abandoned the patch, allowing the forest to reclaim it, while they cleared and cultivated other nearby fields in similar fashion. Rice was the staple food—labor-intensive, but able to support a large population. A number of domesticated plant and animal species spread from Southeast Asia to other regions, including rice, soybeans, sugar cane, yams, bananas, coconuts, chickens, and pigs.

The Malay peoples who became the dominant population in this region were the product of several waves of migration from southern China beginning around 3000 B.C.E. Some indigenous peoples merged with the Malay newcomers; others retreated to remote mountain and forest zones. Subsequently, rising population and disputes within communities

**Map 6.2 Southeast Asia** Southeast Asia's position between the ancient centers of civilization in India and China had a major impact on its history. In the first millennium C.E. a series of powerful and wealthy states arose in the region by gaining control of major trade routes: first Funan, based in southern Vietnam, Cambodia, and the Malay Peninsula, then Srivijaya on the island of Sumatra, then smaller states on the island of Java. Shifting trade routes led to the rise and fall of the various centers. © Cengage Learning

prompted streams of people to leave the Southeast Asian mainland for the islands. By the first millennium B.C.E. Southeast Asians had developed impressive navigational skills. They knew how to ride the monsoon winds and interpret the patterns of swells, winds, clouds, and bird and sea life. Over a period of several thousand years groups of Malay peoples in large, double outrigger sailing canoes spread out across the Pacific and Indian Oceans—half the circumference of the earth—to settle thousands of islands.

The inhabitants of Southeast Asia clustered along riverbanks or in fertile volcanic plains. Their fields and villages were never far from the rain forest, with its wild animals and numerous plant species. Forest trees provided fruit, wood, and spices, and the shallow waters surrounding the islands teemed with fish. This region was also an early center of metallurgy. Metal-smiths heated copper and tin ore to the right temperature for producing and shaping bronze

implements by using hollow bamboo tubes to funnel oxygen to the furnace.

Northern Indochina, by its geographic proximity, was vulnerable to Chinese pressure and cultural influences, and it was under Chinese political control for a thousand years (111 B.C.E.–939 C.E.). Farther south, larger states emerged in the early centuries C.E. in response to two powerful forces: commerce and Hindu-Buddhist culture. Southeast Asia was situated along the trade routes that merchants used to carry Chinese silk westward to India and the Mediterranean. The movements of nomadic peoples had disrupted the old land route across Central Asia, but in India demand for silk was increasing—both for domestic use and for transshipment to satisfy the fast-growing luxury market in the Roman Empire. Gradually merchants extended this exchange network to include goods from Southeast Asia, such as aromatic woods, resins, and cinnamon, pepper, cloves, nutmeg, and other spices. Southeast Asian centers rose to prominence by serving this trade network and controlling key points.

The other force leading to the rise of larger political entities was the influence of Hindu-Buddhist culture imported from India. Commerce brought Indian merchants and sailors into the ports of Southeast Asia. As Buddhism spread, Southeast Asia became a way station for Indian missionaries and East Asian pilgrims going to and coming from the birthplace of their faith. Shrewd Malay rulers looked to Indian traditions as a rich source of ideas and prestige. They borrowed Sanskrit terms such as *maharaja* (mah-huh-RAH-juh) ("great king"), utilized Indian models of bureaucracy, ceremonial practices, and forms of artistic representation, and employed priests, administrators, and scribes skilled in Sanskrit writing to expedite government business. Their special connection to powerful gods and higher knowledge raised them above their rivals.

The Southeast Asian kingdoms, however, were not just passive recipients of Indian culture. They took what was useful to them and synthesized it with indigenous beliefs, values, and institutions—for example, local concepts of chieftainship, ancestor worship, and forms of oaths. Moreover, they trained their own people in the new ways, so that the bureaucracy contained both foreign experts and native disciples. The whole process amounted to a cultural dialogue between India and Southeast Asia, in which both were active participants.

The first major Southeast Asian center, called **Funan** (FOO-nahn) by Chinese visitors, flourished between the first and sixth centuries C.E. (see Map 6.2). Its capital was at the modern site of Oc-Eo in southern Vietnam. Funan occupied the delta of the Mekong (MAY-kawng) River, a "rice bowl" capable of supporting a large population. The rulers mobilized large numbers of laborers to dig irrigation channels and prevent destructive floods. By extending its control over most of southern Indochina and the Malay Peninsula, Funan was able to dominate the trade route from India to China. The route began in the ports of northeast India, crossed the Bay of Bengal, continued by land over the Isthmus of Kra on the Malay Peninsula, and then crossed the South China Sea (see Map 6.2). Indian merchants found that offloading their goods from ships and carrying them

across the narrow strip of land was safer than making the 1,000-mile (1,600-kilometer) voyage around the Malay Peninsula—a dangerous trip marked by treacherous currents, rocky shoals, and pirates. Once the portage across the isthmus was finished, the merchants needed food and lodging while waiting for the monsoon winds to shift so they could make the last leg of the voyage to China by sea. Funan stockpiled food and provided security for those engaged in this trade—in return for customs duties and other fees.

Chinese observers have left reports of the prosperity and sophistication of Funan, emphasizing the presence of walled cities, palaces, archives, systems of taxation, and state-organized agriculture. Nevertheless, Funan declined in the sixth century. The most likely explanation is that international trade routes changed and Funan no longer held a strategic position.

### The Srivijayan Kingdom

By the sixth century a new, all-sea route had developed. Merchants and travelers from south India and Sri Lanka sailed through the Strait of Malacca (between the west side of the Malay Peninsula and the northeast coast of the island of Sumatra) and into the South China Sea. This route presented both human and navigational hazards, but it significantly shortened the traveling time.

A new center of power, **Srivijaya** (shree-vuh-JAH-yuh)—Sanskrit for "Great Conquest"—dominated the new southerly route by 683 C.E. The capital of the Srivijayan kingdom was at modern-day Palembang in southeastern Sumatra, 50 miles (80 kilometers) up the broad and navigable Musi River, with a good natural harbor. The kingdom was well situated to control the southern part of the Malay Peninsula, Sumatra, parts

**Funan**  An early complex society in Southeast Asia between the first and sixth centuries C.E. It was centered in the rich rice-growing region of southern Vietnam, and it controlled the passage of trade across the Malaysian isthmus.

**Srivijaya**  A state based on the Indonesian island of Sumatra between the seventh and eleventh centuries C.E. It amassed wealth and power by a combination of selective adaptation of Indian technologies and concepts, control of the lucrative trade routes between India and China, and skillful showmanship and diplomacy in holding together a disparate realm of inland and coastal territories.

of Java and Borneo, and the Malacca (muh-LAH-kuh) and Sunda straits—vital passageways for shipping (see Map 6.2).

The Srivijayan kingdom gained ascendancy over its rivals and assumed control of the international trade route by fusing four distinct ecological zones into an interdependent network. The core area was the productive agricultural plain along the Musi River. The king and his clerks, judges, and tax collectors controlled this zone directly. Control was less direct over the second zone, the upland regions of Sumatra's interior, with its commercially valuable forest products. Local rulers there were bound to the center by oaths of loyalty, elaborate court ceremonies, and the sharing of profits from trade. The third zone consisted of river ports that had been Srivijaya's main rivals. They were conquered and controlled thanks to an alliance between Srivijaya and neighboring sea nomads, pirates who served as a Srivijayan navy in return for a steady income.

The fourth zone was a fertile "rice bowl" on the central plain of the nearby island of Java—a region so productive, because of its volcanic soil, that it houses and feeds the majority of the population of present-day Indonesia. Srivijayan monarchs maintained alliances, cemented by intermarriage, with several ruling dynasties in this region, and the Srivijayan kings claimed descent from the main Javanese dynasty. These arrangements gave Srivijaya access to large quantities of foodstuffs that people living in the capital and merchants and sailors visiting the various ports needed.

The kings of Srivijaya who constructed and maintained this complex network of social, political, and economic relationships were men of energy and skill. Although their authority depended in part on force, it owed more to diplomatic and even theatrical talents. Like the Gupta monarchy, Srivijaya was a theater-state, securing its preeminence and binding dependents by its sheer splendor and its ability to attract labor, talent, and luxury products. The court was the scene of ceremonies designed to dazzle observers and reinforce an image of wealth, power, and sanctity. Subordinate rulers took oaths of loyalty carrying dire threats of punishment for violations, and in their home locales they imitated the splendid ceremonials of the capital.

The Srivijayan king, drawing upon Buddhist conceptions, presented himself as a bodhisattva, one who has achieved enlightenment and utilizes his precious insights for the betterment of his subjects. The king was believed to have magical powers, controlling powerful forces of fertility associated with the rivers in flood and mediating between the spiritually potent realms of the mountains and the sea. He was also said to be so wealthy that he deposited bricks of gold in the river estuary to appease the local gods, and a hillside near town was covered with silver and gold images of the Buddha. The gold originated in East or West Africa and came to Southeast Asia through trade with the Muslim world (see Chapter 9).

The kings built and patronized Buddhist monasteries and schools. In central Java, local dynasties allied with Srivijaya built magnificent temple complexes to advertise their glory. The most famous of these, **Borobodur** (booh-roe-boe-DOOR), built between 770 and 825 C.E., was the largest human construction in the Southern Hemisphere.

The kings of Srivijaya carried out this marvelous balancing act for centuries. But the system was vulnerable to shifts in the pattern of international trade. Some such change must have contributed to the decline of Srivijaya in the eleventh century, even though the immediate cause was a destructive raid on the capital by forces of the Chola kingdom of southeast India in 1025 C.E.

After the decline of Srivijaya, leadership passed to new, vigorous kingdoms on the eastern end of Java, and the maritime realm of Southeast Asia remained prosperous and connected to international trade networks. Through the ages Europeans remained dimly aware of this region as a source of spices and other luxury items. Some four centuries after the decline of Srivijaya, an Italian navigator serving under the flag of Spain—Christopher Columbus—sailed westward across the Atlantic Ocean, seeking to establish a direct route to the fabled "Indies" from which the spices came.

**Borobodur** A massive stone monument on the Indonesian island of Java, erected by the Sailendra kings around 800 C.E. The winding ascent through ten levels, decorated with rich relief carving, is a Buddhist allegory for the progressive stages of enlightenment.

**Aerial View of the Buddhist Monument at Borobodur, Java** The great monument of volcanic stone was more than 300 feet (90 meters) in length and over 100 feet (30 meters) high. Pilgrims made a 3-mile-long (nearly 5-kilometer-long) winding ascent through ten levels intended to represent the ideal Buddhist journey from ignorance to enlightenment. Numerous sculptured reliefs depicting Buddhist legends provide glimpses of daily life in early Java.

Robert Harding Picture Library Ltd/Alamy

## CONCLUSION

This chapter traces the emergence of complex societies in India and Southeast Asia between the second millennium B.C.E. and the first millennium C.E. Because of migrations, trade, and the spread of belief systems, an Indian style of civilization spread throughout the subcontinent and adjoining regions and eventually made its way to the mainland and island chains of Southeast Asia. In this period were laid cultural foundations that in large measure still endure.

The development and spread of belief systems—Vedism, Buddhism, Jainism, and Hinduism—have a central place in this chapter because nearly all the surviving sources are religious. Ancient Indians held a strikingly different view of time than did their Israelite, Greek, and Chinese contemporaries, and they did not generate historiographic texts. The distinctive Indian conception—of vast epochs in which universes are created and destroyed again and again and the essential spirit of living creatures is reincarnated repeatedly—made the particulars of any brief moment seem relatively insignificant.

Political and social division has been the norm throughout much of the history of India, a consequence of the diversity of the subcontinent and the complex mix of ethnic and linguistic groups inhabiting it. The elaborate structure of classes and castes was a response to this diversity. Strong central governments, such as those of the Mauryan and Gupta kings, rose to dominance by gaining control of resources and important trade routes and developing effective military and administrative institutions. However, the periods of fragmentation and multiple small centers of power seemed as economically and intellectually dynamic as the periods of unity.

Many distinctive social and intellectual features of Indian civilization—the class and caste system, models of kingship and statecraft, and Vedic, Jain, and Buddhist belief systems—originated in the great river valleys of the north, where descendants of Indo-European immigrants predominated. Hinduism embraced elements drawn from the Dravidian cultures of the south as well as from Buddhism. The capacity of the Hindu tradition to assimilate a wide range of popular beliefs facilitated the spread of a common Indian civilization across the subcontinent, although there was considerable variation from one region to another.

Southeast Asia, as a crossroads of trade, was influenced by both China and India. Commerce brought migrants and merchants from both regions to Southeast Asia. As Buddhism spread, Southeast Asia became a way station for Indian missionaries and Chinese pilgrims. Malay rulers looked to Indian traditions as a rich source of ideas and prestige, and they used Indian models of bureaucracy, ceremonial practices, and forms of artistic representation. Thus the Southeast Asian kingdoms synthesized foreign cultural influences with indigenous beliefs, values, and institutions.

# CHAPTER REVIEW

## THE INDUS VALLEY CIVILIZATION

■ *What does material evidence tell us about the Indus Valley civilization and the most likely reason for its collapse?* (page 133)

The cities of Harappa and Mohenjo-Daro provide evidence of early civilization in the fertile Indus Valley. Both display a striking uniformity of planning and construction, including high brick walls and a rectangular grid of streets. Excavated artifacts exhibit standard shapes and styles, with some evidence indicating trade with resource-rich regions to the north and Mesopotamia in the west. Unfortunately, the writing system of this civilization remains undeciphered. The abandonment of the cities signaled the end of this civilization. The probable cause was "systems failure" resulting from ecological changes in the river valley and along the coast.

## FOUNDATIONS OF INDIAN CIVILIZATION

■ *What historical forces led to the development of complex social groupings in ancient India?* (page 136)

Arya kinship groups moving into northwest India after 1500 B.C.E. established a religiously sanctioned class (varna) system of priests, warriors, landowners and merchants, and peasants and laborers. With further subdivisions into castes (jati), this system ordered the

relations among ethnically, linguistically, and culturally diverse populations. Various forms of resistance to the secular and religious domination of the Brahmins arose, including the more egalitarian Buddhist and Jain belief systems. Traditionalists responded to this through Hinduism, which provided people with a number of ways to make a personal connection with the gods.

## INDIAN IMPERIAL EXPANSION AND COLLAPSE

■ *In the face of powerful forces that tended to keep India fragmented, how did the Mauryan Empire of the fourth to second centuries B.C.E. and the Gupta Empire of the fourth to sixth centuries C.E. succeed in unifying much of India?* (page 144)

Despite geographical obstacles, religious diversity, and social orientation toward the caste system, the Mauryan (fourth to second centuries B.C.E.) and Gupta (fourth to sixth centuries C.E.) rulers brought most of the subcontinent under their control. Both dynasties exploited the agricultural productivity of the Ganges Plain, monopolized mining and weapons production, built standing armies, and developed complex bureaucracies and networks of spies. These centralizing factors encouraged urban growth, long-distance trade, and new forms of art and literature.

## SOUTHEAST ASIA, 50–1025 C.E.

■ *How did the geography of Southeast Asia contribute to its commerce and to the influence of Hinduism and Buddhism?* (page 149)

Southeast Asia, a region rich in resources with a tropical climate favorable for agriculture, generated a lively trade, both locally and with South and East Asia. Geographically situated between the Indian Ocean and the South China Sea, the Malay Peninsula had either to be crossed at its narrowest point or sailed around to connect markets with consumers. South Asian sailors, merchants, and pilgrims brought Hinduism and Buddhism to the region. Kingdoms in southern Indochina, the Malay Peninsula, and Java found their ideas appealing. Malay rulers blended Indian religions with local traditions to produce a distinctive civilization.

## Key Terms

Harappa (p. 134)

Mohenjo-Daro (p. 134)

monsoon (p. 137)

Vedas (p. 138)

*varna/jati* (p. 138)

karma (p. 139)

*moksha* (p. 139)

Buddha (p. 140)

Mahayana Buddhism (p. 141)

Theravada Buddhism (p. 141)

Hinduism (p. 141)

Mauryan Empire (p. 144)

Ashoka (p. 145)

*Mahabharata* (p. 146)

Bhagavad-Gita (p. 146)

Tamil kingdoms (p. 146)

Gupta Empire (p. 146)

theater-state (p. 147)

Funan (p. 151)

Srivijaya (p. 151)

Borobodur (p. 152)

# Peoples and Civilizations of the Americas

© Cengage Learning

Humans reached the Western Hemisphere through a series of migrations from Asia. Some scholars believe that the first migrations occurred as early as 35,000 to 25,000 B.C.E., but most accept a later date of 20,000 to 13,000 B.C.E. Although some limited contacts with other cultures—for example, with Polynesians—may have occurred later, the peoples in the Western Hemisphere were virtually isolated from the rest of the world for at least 15,000 years. Thus, while technological innovations passed back and forth among the civilizations of Asia, Africa, and Europe, the peoples of the Americas faced the challenges of the natural environment on their own.

As people spread throughout the hemisphere, they encountered environments that ranged from polar extremes to tropical rain forests to towering mountain ranges. In two areas, Mesoamerica (Mexico and northern Central America) and the mountainous Andean region of South America, conditions proved conducive to the emergence of complex societies. Domestication of maize, beans, squash, and sweet potatoes occurred there well before 3000 B.C.E. In the following millennia, technological innovations like metallurgy and a limited trade led to greater social stratification and the beginnings of urbanization in both regions. Cultural elites used their increasing political and religious authority to organize great numbers of laborers for projects such as large-scale irrigation and drainage works, cleared forests, and hillside terracing, thus providing the economic platform for the construction of urban centers.

The Amerindian[1] hereditary elites organized their societies to meet these challenges, even as

---

[1] Before 1492, the inhabitants of the Western Hemisphere had no single name for themselves, no sense that physical similarities created a shared identity. Identity derived from kin groups, language, cultural practices, and political structures. Conquest and the occupation by Europeans after 1492 imposed on America's original inhabitants a racial consciousness and racial identity. All collective terms for these first American peoples reflect this history. *Indians, Native Americans, Amerindians, First Peoples,* and *Indigenous Peoples* find common usage. This book uses the names of individual cultures and states wherever possible. It tries to reserve *Amerindian* and other terms that suggest transcultural identity and experience for the period after 1492.

their ambitions ignited new conflicts. No single set of political institutions or technologies worked in every environment, and American cultures varied widely. Productive and diversified agriculture and cities that rivaled the Chinese and Roman capitals in size and beauty developed in Mesoamerica and the Andean region of South America. In the rest of the hemisphere, indigenous peoples maintained a wide variety of settlement patterns, political forms, and cultural traditions based on combinations of hunting and agriculture.

# FORMATIVE OLMEC AND CHAVÍN CIVILIZATIONS, 1200–200 B.C.E.

■ How did the Olmec and Chavín civilizations influence later Mesoamerican and Andean civilizations?

By 1000 B.C.E. the major urban centers of Mesoamerica and the Andes, dominated by monumental structures devoted to religion and the elite, had become civilizations and begun to project their political and cultural power over broad territories. These civilizations, the Olmec of Mesoamerica and the Chavín of the Andes, would persist for more than a thousand years.

## The Mesoamerican Olmec, 1200–400 B.C.E.

Mesoamerica is a region of great geographic and climatic diversity. It is extremely active geologically, experiencing both earthquakes and volcanic eruptions. Mountain ranges break the region into microenvironments, including the temperate climates of the Valley of Mexico and the Guatemalan highlands, the tropical forests of the Petén and Gulf of Mexico coast, the rain forest of the southern Yucatán and Belize, and the drier scrub forest of the northern Yucatán (see Map 7.1).

Within each of these ecological niches, Amerindian peoples made use of a wide variety of indigenous plants, including maize, beans, and squash, as well as minerals like obsidian, quartz, and jade. But no animals were domesticated. Eventually, contacts across environmental boundaries led to trade and cultural exchange with emerging centers in the region and ultimately with Central and South America.

**Map 7.1  Olmec and Chavín Civilizations**  The regions of Mesoamerica (most of modern Mexico and Central America) and the Andean highlands of South America have hosted impressive civilizations since early times. The civilizations of the Olmec and Chavín were the originating civilizations of these two regions, providing the foundations of architecture, city planning, and religion. © Cengage Learning

Enhanced trade, increasing agricultural productivity, and rising population led, in turn, to urbanization and the appearance of powerful political and religious elites. Yet even though all Mesoamerican civilizations shared fundamental elements of material culture, technology, religious belief and ritual, political organization, art, architecture, and sports, the region was never unified politically.

The most influential early Mesoamerican civilization was the **Olmec**, flourishing between 1200 and 400 B.C.E. (see Map 7.1). The center of Olmec

civilization was located near the tropical Atlantic coast of what are now the Mexican states of Veracruz and Tabasco. The earliest settlements in the region depended on rich plant diversity and fishing,

**Olmec**  The first Mesoamerican civilization. Between about 1200 and 400 B.C.E., the Olmec people of central Mexico created a vibrant civilization that included intensive agriculture, wide-ranging trade, ceremonial centers, and monumental construction. The Olmec had great cultural influence on later Mesoamerican societies.

# Chronology

| | Mesoamerica | Northern Peoples | Andean Region |
|---|---|---|---|
| 3000 B.C.E. | **Before 3000 B.C.E.** Domestication of maize, beans, and squash | | **Before 3000 B.C.E.** Domestication of potato, quinoa, sweet potato, and llama |
| | **Before 2000 B.C.E.** Early urbanization | **Before 2000 B.C.E.** Domestication of squash and seed crops like sunflower | **Before 2000 B.C.E.** Early urbanization |
| 2000 B.C.E. | **1200 B.C.E.** Beginning of Olmec civilization | | |
| 1000 B.C.E. | | | **900 B.C.E.** Beginning of Chavín civilization |
| 500 B.C.E. | **400 B.C.E.** End of Olmec civilization **100 B.C.E.** First stage of Teotihuacan temple complex | | **200 B.C.E.** End of Chavín civilization |
| 100 C.E. | **250** Maya early classic period begins | **100–400** Hopewell culture in Ohio River Valley | **200** Moche begin to dominate Peruvian coast |
| 500 C.E. | **750** Teotihuacan destroyed **800–900** Maya classic-era cities abandoned **968** Toltec capital of Tula founded | **700** Beginning of Anasazi culture in Four Corners region **800** Beginning of Mississippian culture | **500–1000** Tiwanaku and Wari control Andean highlands **700** End of Moche domination **900** Chimú begins to dominate Peruvian coast |
| 1000 C.E. | **1175** Tula destroyed **Until 1500** Culhuacán and Cholula continue Toltec tradition | **1050–1250** Cahokia reaches peak population **1150** Anasazi center of Pueblo Bonito abandoned; other Anasazi centers enter crisis after 1200 | **1470s** End of Chimú domination |
| 1500 C.E. | | **1500** End of Mississippian culture | |

but by 3000 B.C.E. the staples of the Mesoamerican diet—maize, beans, and squash—had been domesticated. Manioc, a calorie-rich root crop originating in Brazil, was also grown in the floodplains. The first stage of urbanization was tied to the trade and

use of products like salt, cacao (chocolate beans), potters' clay, and limestone. It is unclear whether Olmec urban centers were rival city-states or were subject to a centralized political authority, but scholars agree that San Lorenzo (1200–900 B.C.E.), with a

**Olmec Head**  Giant heads sculpted from basalt are a widely recognized legacy of Olmec culture. Sixteen heads have been found, the largest approximately 11 feet (3.4 meters) tall. Experts in Olmec archaeology believe the heads are portraits of individual rulers, warriors, or ballplayers. Some were depicted wearing the padded helmet used as protection in the sacred ballgame.

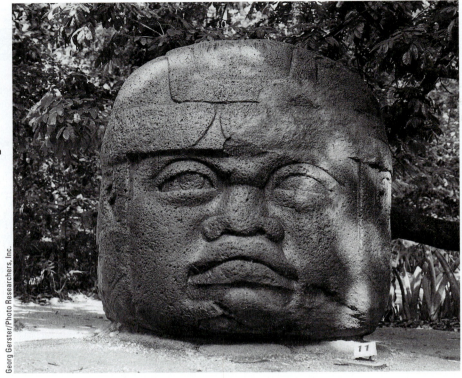

Georg Gerster/Photo Researchers, Inc.

population between 10,000 to 18,000, was the largest and most important Olmec center. San Lorenzo's cultural influence ultimately extended south and west to the Pacific coast of Central America and north to central Mexico. Also founded around 1200 B.C.E., La Venta (LA BEN-tah) became the preeminent Olmec center when San Lorenzo was abandoned or destroyed around 900 B.C.E. After La Venta's collapse around 600 B.C.E., Tres Zapotes (TRACE zah-POE-tace) became the largest Olmec center, although it was much smaller than either of its predecessors.

Little is known about Olmec political structure, but it seems likely that the rise of major urban centers coincided with the appearance of a form of kingship that combined religious and secular roles. San Lorenzo and other Olmec cities served primarily as religious centers, laid out in alignment with the religious observation of the stars (a practice that led to a calendar used to predict seasonal rains and guide planting and harvesting and that likely influenced later innovations of the Maya). The deities of the polytheistic Olmec had both male and female natures.

Human and animal characteristics were blended in the motifs found on ceramics, sculptures, and buildings. Rulers and their close kin came to be associated with the gods through bloodletting ceremonies and human sacrifice and through the staging of elaborate rituals that brought together urban and rural populations. Rulers were especially associated with the jaguar. Priests and shamans who foretold the future and acted as healers claimed the ability to make direct contact with supernatural powers by transforming themselves into powerful animals, such as crocodiles, snakes, and sharks. These transformative powers were also associated with a ballgame played with a solid rubber ball in banked courts located near the center of temple precincts. Versions of this game survived until the arrival of Europeans in the sixteenth century.

The urban elite's power grew with the development of persuasive religious ideologies and compelling religious rituals that helped organize and subordinate neighboring rural populations. As a result, urban centers were dominated by religious architecture, including pyramids, monumental mounds, and raised platforms. Large artificial platforms and mounds of packed earth framed the collective rituals and political activities that brought the rural population to the cities at special times in the year. This massive urban architecture required thousands of laborers recruited from surrounding rural areas. Skilled artisans who lived in or near the urban core decorated the buildings with carvings and sculptures. Olmec artisans also produced exquisite carved jade figurines, necklaces, and ceremonial knives and axes. The diffusion of these Olmec products among distant locations suggests a specialized merchant class that traded for obsidian, jade, and pottery.

The mounting wealth and power of the elite and the growing populations of Olmec cities depended on a bargain struck with the much larger populations of the surrounding countryside. The rural masses provided the labor that constructed the pyramids, platforms, and ball courts of the urban centers as well as the food that sustained urban populations. In exchange, they participated in the awe-inspiring ceremonies that explained human origins or unforeseen natural events and helped guide collective life.

Each major Olmec center was eventually abandoned, its monuments defaced and buried and its buildings destroyed. Archaeologists interpret these events differently; some see them as evidence of internal upheavals or military defeat by neighboring peoples, and others suggest that they were associated with the death of a ruler. Regardless of the causes for Olmec decline, the influence of this civilization endured for centuries. Every subsequent Mesoamerican civilization utilized the rich legacy of Olmec material culture, technology, religious belief and ritual, political organization, art, architecture, and sports.

## Early South American Civilization: Chavín, 900–200 B.C.E.

Geography played an important role in the development of human society in the Andes. The region's diverse environments—a mountainous core, arid coastal plain, and dense interior jungles—challenged human populations, encouraging the development of specialized regional production as well as complex social institutions and

cultural values that facilitated interregional exchanges and shared labor responsibilities. These adaptations to environmental challenge became enduring features of Andean civilization.

The earliest urban centers in this region were villages of a few hundred people built along the coastal plain or in the foothills near the coast. The abundance of fish and mollusks along the coast of Peru provided a dependable supply of food that helped make the development of early cities possible. The coastal populations traded these products along with decorative shells for maize, other foods, and textiles produced in the foothills. The two regions also exchanged ceremonial practices, religious motifs, and aesthetic ideas. Recent discoveries demonstrate that as early as 2600 B.C.E. the vast site called Caral had developed many of the characteristics now viewed as the hallmarks of later Andean civilization, including ceremonial plazas, pyramids, elevated platforms and mounds, and extensive irrigation works. The scale of public works in Caral suggests a population of thousands and a political structure capable of organizing the production and distribution of maritime and agricultural products over a broad area.

**Chavín**, one of the most impressive of South America's early urban civilizations (see Map 7.1), inherited many of the cultural and economic characteristics of Caral. The capital city, Chavín de Huantar (cha-BEAN day WAHN-tar), was located at 10,300 feet (3,139 meters) in the eastern range of the Andes north of the modern city of Lima. Between 900 and 200 B.C.E., a period roughly coinciding with Olmec civilization in Mesoamerica, Chavín dominated a densely populated region that included large areas of the Peruvian coastal plains and Andean foothills. Chavín de Huantar's location at the intersection of trade routes connecting the coast with populous mountain valleys and tropical lowlands on the eastern flank of the Andes allowed the city's rulers to control trade

**Chavín** The first major urban civilization in South America (900–200 B.C.E.). Its capital, Chavín de Huántar, was located high in the Andes Mountains of Peru. Chavín became politically and economically dominant in a densely populated region that included two distinct ecological zones, the Peruvian coastal plain and the Andean foothills.

among these distinct ecological zones and gain an important economic advantage over regional rivals.

Chavín's dominance as a ceremonial and commercial center depended on earlier developments in agriculture and trade, including the introduction of maize cultivation from Mesoamerica. Maize increased the food production of the coast and interior foothills, allowing greater levels of urbanization. As Chavín grew, its trade linked the coast to inland producers of quinoa (a local grain), potatoes, and llamas in the high mountain valleys and, to a lesser extent, the Amazonian production of coca and fruits.

Reciprocal labor obligations that permitted the construction and maintenance of roads, bridges, temples, palaces, and large irrigation and drainage projects, as well as textile production, developed as well. In later times, groups of related families who held land communally and claimed descent from a common ancestor organized these labor obligations. Group members thought of each other as brothers and sisters and were obliged to aid one another, providing a model for the organization of labor and distribution of goods at every level of Andean society.

**Llamas**, the only domesticated beasts of burden in the Americas, played an important role in the integration of the Andean region. They were first domesticated in the mountainous interior of Peru and were crucial to Chavín's development. Llamas provided meat and wool and helped transport goods. A single driver could control ten to thirty animals, each carrying up to 70 pounds (32 kilograms); a human porter could carry only about 50 pounds (22.5 kilograms). The increased use of llamas to move goods from one ecological zone to another promoted specialization of production and increased trade.

The enormous scale of the capital and the dispersal of Chavín's pottery styles, religious motifs, and architectural forms over a wide area suggest that Chavín imposed some form of political integration and trade dependency on its neighbors that may have relied in part on military force. However, most modern scholars believe that, as in the case of the Olmec civilization, Chavín's influence depended more on the development of an attractive and convincing religious belief system and related rituals. Chavín's most potent religious symbol, a jaguar deity, was dispersed over a broad area, and archaeological

evidence suggests that Chavín de Huantar served as a pilgrimage site.

The architectural signature of Chavín was a large complex of multilevel platforms made of packed earth or rubble and faced with cut stone or adobe (sun-dried brick made of clay and straw). Small buildings used for ritual purposes or as elite residences were built on these platforms. Nearly all the buildings were decorated with relief carvings of serpents, condors, jaguars, or humans. The largest building at Chavín de Huantar measured 250 feet (76 meters) on each side and rose to a height of 50 feet (15 meters). About one-third of its interior was hollow, containing narrow galleries and small rooms that may have housed the remains of royal ancestors.

American metallurgy was first developed in the Andean region. The later introduction of metallurgy in Mesoamerica, like the appearance of maize agriculture in the Andes, suggests sustained contact between the two regions. Archaeological investigations of Chavín de Huantar and smaller centers have revealed remarkable three-dimensional silver, gold, and gold alloy ornaments that represent a clear advance over earlier technologies. Bronze and iron, however, were unknown.

Improvements in both the manufacture and decoration of textiles are also associated with the rise of Chavín. The quality of these products, which were probably used by the elite or in religious rituals, added to the reputation and prestige of the culture and aided in the projection of its power and influence. The most common decorative motif in sculpture, pottery, and textiles was a jaguar-man similar in conception to the Olmec symbol. In both civilizations and in many other cultures in the Americas, this powerful predator provided an enduring image of religious authority and a vehicle through which the gods could act in the world.

Class distinctions also appear to have increased in Chavín. Priests directed religious life, and there is

**llama**  A hoofed animal indigenous to the Andes Mountains. It was the only domesticated beast of burden in the Americas before the arrival of Europeans. The use of llamas to transport goods made possible specialized production and trade among people living in different ecological zones and fostered the integration of these zones by Chavín and later Andean states.

evidence that both local chiefs and a more powerful chief or king dominated Chavín's politics. Excavations of graves reveal that superior-quality textiles as well as gold crowns, breastplates, and jewelry distinguished rulers from commoners.

There is no convincing evidence, like defaced buildings or broken images, that the eclipse of Chavín (unlike the Olmec centers) was associated with conquest or rebellion. However, recent investigations have suggested that increased warfare throughout the region around 200 B.C.E. disrupted Chavín's trade and undermined the authority of the governing elite. Regardless of what caused the collapse of this powerful culture, the technologies, material culture, statecraft, architecture, and urban planning associated with Chavín influenced the Andean region for centuries.

# CLASSIC-ERA CULTURE AND SOCIETY IN MESOAMERICA, 200–900

■ *What were the most important shared characteristics of Mesoamerican cultures in the classic period?*

Between 200 and 900 C.E., the peoples of Mesoamerica entered a period of remarkable cultural creativity. Despite differences in language and the absence

of regional political integration, Mesoamericans were unified by similarities in material culture, religious beliefs, and social structures forged in the Olmec era. Building on this legacy, the peoples of what is now Central America and south and central Mexico developed new political institutions, made great strides in astronomy and mathematics, and improved agricultural productivity.

Archaeologists call the mix of achievements after 300 C.E. the classic period. Population grew, a greater variety of products were traded over longer distances, social hierarchies became more complex, and great cities served as governing and religious centers. Impressive platforms and pyramids were devoted to religious functions. Large urban populations, divided into classes, served hereditary political and religious elites who also controlled the nearby towns and countryside.

The agricultural foundation of Mesoamerican civilization had been developed centuries earlier. The major agricultural technologies—irrigation, wetland drainage, and hillside terracing—preceded the cities built after 200 C.E. by more than a thousand years. What made the achievements of the classic era possible was the extended reach and power of religious and political leaders. The impressive architecture and great size of Teotihuacan (teh-o-tee-WAH-kahn) and the great Maya cities such as Tikal illustrate both Mesoamerican aesthetic achievements and the development of powerful political institutions.

**Teotihuacan**    At the height of its power, from 450 to 600 C.E., **Teotihuacan** (100 B.C.E.–750 C.E.), located about 30 miles (48 kilometers) northeast of modern Mexico City, housed between 125,000 and 150,000 inhabitants. The largest city in the Americas, it outshone all but a few contemporary European and Asian cities.

The religious architecture of Teotihuacan included enormous pyramids dedicated to the sun and moon and more than twenty smaller temples devoted to other gods, all of which flanked a central avenue. The god Quetzalcoatl (kate-zahl-CO-ah-tal),

**Teotihuacan** A powerful city-state in central Mexico (100 B.C.E.–750 C.E.). Its population was about 150,000 at its peak in 600.

**The Temple of the Sun**  The temple of the sun in the background is the largest pyramid in Tenochtitlan. The smaller temple of Quetzalcoatl in foreground displays the serpent images associated with this culture god common to most Mesoamerican civilizations.

G. Dagli Orti/The Art Archive

the feathered serpent, was considered the originator of agriculture and the arts. Like the Olmec, Teotihuacan's population practiced human sacrifice as a sacred duty toward the gods and as a necessity for the well-being of human society. The excavation of the temple of Quetzalcoatl uncovered scores of sacrificial victims.

Teotihuacan's urban population had grown rapidly from the forced relocation of villagers following volcanic eruptions. Nevertheless, more than two-thirds of the city's residents continued to farm, walking from their city homes to their fields. The elite used the city's growing labor resources to expand agriculture by draining swamps, building irrigation works, and cutting terraces into hillsides. They also expanded **chinampas** (chee-NAM-pahs), misleadingly called "floating gardens." These narrow artificial islands, anchored by trees and created by heaping lake muck and waste material on beds of reeds, were crucial in sustaining the growing population because the subsurface irrigation resisted frost and thus permitted year-round agriculture.

The housing of commoners changed as the population grew. Apartment-like stone buildings housed, among other people, the craftspeople who produced

goods for export. Teotihuacan pottery has turned up throughout central Mexico and even in the Maya region of Guatemala. More than 2 percent of the urban population crafted similarly widespread obsidian tools and weapons.

The city's role as a religious center signified divine approval of the increasingly prosperous elite. Members of the elite controlled the state bureaucracy, tax collection, and commerce. Their diet and style of dress reflected their prestige, and they lived in separate aristocratic compounds. Temple and palace murals confirm the central position and great prestige of the priestly class. Pilgrims came to Teotihuacan from far away, and some became permanent residents.

Unlike other classic-period societies, the people of Teotihuacan did not have a single ruler. The deeds of the rulers do not feature in public art, nor were rulers represented by statues as in other Mesoamerican civilizations. Thus historians debate the role of the military at Teotihuacan. Unlike later postclassic

**chinampas**  Raised fields constructed along lakeshores in central Mexico to increase agricultural yields.

civilizations, Teotihuacan was not an imperial state controlled by a military elite, and the absence of walls or other defensive structures before 500 suggests relative peace. However, archaeology points to a powerful military protecting long-distance trade and compelling peasants to hand over their surplus production. Representations of soldiers in typical Teotihuacan dress in the Maya region of Guatemala may indicate that the military were used to expand trade.

The forces that brought about the end of Teotihuacan about 750 remain a mystery, but evidence of weaknesses appears as early as 500, when the urban population declined to about 40,000 and the city began to build defensive walls. Fortifications and pictorial evidence from murals suggest that the city's final decades were violent. Indications of conflict within the ruling elite and of mismanagement of resources have challenged earlier theories of conquest by a nearby rival city or by nomadic peoples from the north. Class conflict and the breakdown of public order may explain the destruction of the most important temples in the city center, the defacing of religious images, and the burning of elite palaces. The eclipse of Teotihuacan reverberated throughout Mexico and into Central America.

## The Maya

Contemporary with Teotihuacan, the **Maya** developed a civilization in the region that today includes Guatemala, Honduras, Belize, and southern Mexico. The difficulties of a tropical climate and fragile soils make the cultural and architectural achievements of the Maya all the more remarkable. Although they shared a single culture, they never unified politically. Instead, rival kingdoms led by hereditary rulers competed for dominance (see Map 7.2).

Today, Maya farmers cut down small trees and brush and burn the dead vegetation to fertilize the land. This swidden agriculture produces high yields for a few years, but it exhausts the soil's nutrients, eventually forcing a move to more fertile land. The high population levels of the Maya classic period (250–900 C.E.) required more intensive forms of agriculture. Maya living near the major urban centers achieved high yields by draining swamps and building elevated fields. They used irrigation in areas with long dry seasons and built terraced hillsides in the cooler

**Map 7.2 Maya Civilization, 250–1400 C.E.** The Maya never created an integrated and unified state. Instead Maya civilization developed as a complex network of independent city-states. © Cengage Learning

highlands. Nearly every household planted a garden to provide condiments and fruits. The Maya also practiced forest management, favoring the growth of useful trees and shrubs and promoting the conservation of deer and other animals hunted for food.

During the classic period, city-states proliferated, the most powerful controlling groups of smaller dependent cities. Religious temples and rituals linked the power of kings to the gods. Unlike earlier sites, these cities had dense central precincts dominated by buildings that were commonly aligned with the movements of the sun and Venus. High pyramids and elaborately decorated palaces, often built on high ground or on constructed mounds, surrounded open plazas, an awesome prospect for the masses drawn in for religious and political rituals.

**Maya** Mesoamerican civilization concentrated in Mexico's Yucatán Peninsula and in Guatemala and Honduras but never unified into a single empire. Major contributions were in mathematics, astronomy, and development of the calendar.

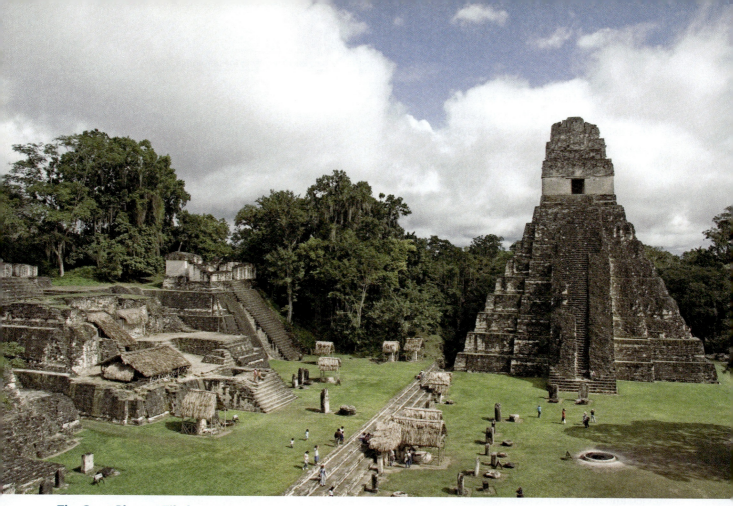

**The Great Plaza at Tikal** The impressive architectural and artistic achievements of the classic-era Maya are still visible in the ruins of Tikal, in modern Guatemala. Maya centers provided a dramatic setting for the rituals that dominated public life. Construction of Tikal began before 150 B.C.E.; the city was abandoned about 900 C.E. A ball court and residences for the elite were part of the Great Plaza. Daniel Loncarevic/Shutterstock.com

Bas-reliefs and bright paint covered nearly all public buildings. Common motifs included religious allegories, the genealogies of rulers, and important historical events. Carved altars and stone monoliths arose near major temples. As was true throughout the hemisphere, this rich legacy of monumental architecture was constructed without the aid of wheels—no pulleys, wheelbarrows, or carts—or metal tools. Masses of men and women aided only by levers and stone tools cut and carried construction materials and lifted them into place.

The Maya cosmos consisted of three layers connected along a vertical axis that traced the course of the sun. The earthly arena of human existence came between the heavens, conceptualized as a sky-monster, and a dark underworld. A sacred tree rose through the three layers, its roots in the underworld and its branches in the heavens. The temple precincts of Maya cities physically represented this cosmology: the pyramids as sacred mountains reaching to the heavens and their doorways as portals to the underworld.

Rulers and other members of the elite decorated their bodies with paint and tattoos and wore elaborate costumes of textiles, animal skins, and feathers to project both secular power and divine sanction. Kings communicated directly with the supernatural residents of the other worlds and with deified royal ancestors through bloodletting rituals and hallucinogenic trances. Scenes of rulers drawing blood from lips, ears, and penises are common in frescoes and on painted pottery.

Warfare in particular was infused with religious meaning and elaborate rituals. Scenes of battle and the torture and sacrifice of captives appear frequently. The king, his kinsmen, and other ranking nobles fought personally, with the goal of securing captives rather than territory. Elite captives were nearly always sacrificed; commoners usually became slaves.

Few women directly ruled Maya kingdoms, though women from ruling lineages did play important political and religious roles. The consorts of male rulers participated in bloodletting rituals and in other public ceremonies. Their noble blood helped legitimate their husbands' rule. Though generally patrilineal (tracing descent in the male line), some male rulers traced their lineages from both the male and female lines. Some rulers emphasized the female line if it held higher status. Women were also healers and shamans. In addition, scholars believe that women played a central role in religious rituals of the home. Among the lower classes, women were essential to the management of family life and the household economy, maintaining garden plots and weaving.

Building on Olmec contributions, the Maya developed the calendar, mathematics, and writing. The complexity of their calendric system, with each day marked by three separate dating systems, reflects their interest in time and the cosmos. Like other Mesoamerican peoples, the Maya calendar tracked a ritual cycle (260 days divided into thirteen months of 20 days) as well as a solar calendar (365 days divided into eighteen months of 20 days, plus 5 "unfavorable days" at the end of the year). The concurrence of these two calendars every 52 years was considered especially ominous. Alone among Mesoamerican peoples, the Maya also maintained a continuous "long count" calendar, which began at a fixed date in the past that scholars have identified as 3114 B.C.E., a date probably associated with creation.

The Maya systems of mathematics, which underlay the calendar, incorporated the concept of the zero and place value but had limited notational signs. Maya writing used hieroglyphs that signified whole words or concepts as well as phonetic cues or syllables. Aspects of public life, religious belief, and the biographies of rulers and their ancestors were

## SECTION REVIEW

- Between 200 and 900 C.E., Mesoamerican peoples built civilizations with characteristics derived from Olmec culture.
- Their achievements were made possible by the increased power of political and religious leaders.
- Both Teotihuacan and the Maya city-states were supported by intensive agriculture and contained monumental religious architecture.
- Teotihuacan grew into a powerful economic and religious center without a single ruler or powerful military elite.
- The Maya city-states were ruled by kings and elites that practiced ritualized warfare.
- Maya women appear to have enjoyed high status, and both civilizations adopted practices and technologies from their Olmec predecessors.

recorded in bark-paper books, on pottery, and on the stone columns and monumental buildings of the urban centers.

Abandonment or destruction befell many of the major urban centers between 800 and 900, although a small number survived for centuries. In many areas, decades of urban population decline and increased warfare preceded the collapse. Some experts maintain that the destruction of Teotihuacan after 650 disrupted trade, thus undermining the legitimacy of Maya rulers who used trade goods in rituals. Others suggest that the population pressure led to environmental degradation and declining agricultural productivity. This, in turn, might have caused social conflict and warfare as desperate elites sought additional agricultural land through conquest.

# THE POSTCLASSIC PERIOD IN MESOAMERICA, 900–1300

■ *What role did warfare play in the postclassic period of Mesoamerica?*

The collapse of Teotihuacan and many of the major Maya centers occurred over more than a century and a half, making the division between classic and postclassic periods somewhat arbitrary. In fact, some important classic-period civilizations survived unscathed, and essential cultural characteristics in religious belief and practice, architecture, urban planning, and social organization carried over to the postclassic period.

Nevertheless, important differences exist. The population of Mesoamerica apparently expanded in the postclassic period, causing an intensification of agricultural practices and increased warfare. Governing elites increased the size of their armies and developed political institutions that facilitated their control of large and culturally diverse territories acquired through conquest.

### The Toltecs

Scholars speculate that the **Toltecs** (TOLL-teks) originated as a satellite population protecting the northern frontier of Teotihuacan from nomad raids. After migrating south, they created an important postclassic civilization based on the cultural legacy of Teotihuacan, including the preservation of Teotihuacan religious architecture and rituals and the use of irrigation and terraced hillsides.

The Aztecs and their fifteenth-century contemporaries erroneously believed that the Toltecs were the source of nearly all of Mesoamerica's cultural achievements (see Chapter 15). As one Aztec source declared:

> In truth [the Toltecs] invented all the precious and marvelous things.... All that now exists was their discovery.... And these Toltecs were very wise; they were thinkers, for they originated the year count, the day count. All their discoveries formed the book for interpreting dreams.... And so wise were they [that] they understood the stars which were in the heavens.[2]

Actually, the most important Toltec innovations came from politics and war. Their civilization was dependent on military power, and they created the first conquest state. Their political influence extended from their political capital at Tula (TOO-la), founded in 968 C.E. north of modern Mexico City, to Central America. The violent imagery of their military achievements and religious rituals dominated the Mesoamerican imagination in the late postclassic period. Nearly all the public buildings and temples in

Tula carried scenes of human sacrifice, including the decoration of a prominent ceremonial platform with images of impaled skulls, the **tzompantli** (zohm-PAHNT-lee). The massive architecture of the city center also featured impressive statues of warriors and serpents, colonnaded patios, and numerous temples. At its peak Tula had a population of approximately 60,000.

Like the earlier Teotihuacan, Tula and its subject dependencies had a multiethnic character, hosting distinct culture and language communities. At the height of their power, the Toltecs forged a military alliance with another multiethnic state with historic ties to Teotihuacan, **Culhuacán** (kool-whah-KHAN), located to the south. Together they established networks of tribute and trade throughout the central Mexican region.

Accounts dictated to Catholic priests by native informants during the Spanish conquest do not agree on the demise of the Toltecs. Most sources seem to indicate that two rulers shared power at Tula and that this division of power eventually weakened the Toltec state. Sometime around 1150 C.E. a struggle between elite groups identified with rival religious cults undermined Toltec society. According to Aztec legends, Topiltzin (tow-PEELT-zeen)—one of the two rulers and a priest of the cult of Quetzalcoatl—and his followers bitterly accepted exile in the east. One text relates the following:

> Thereupon he [Topiltzin] looked toward Tula, and then wept.... And when he had done these things ... he went to reach the seacoast. Then he fashioned a raft of serpents. When he had arranged the raft, he placed himself as if it were his boat. Then he set off across the sea.[3]

[3] Quoted in Nigel Davies, The Toltec Heritage: *From the Fall of Tula to the Rise of Tenochtitlán* (Norman: University of Oklahoma Press, 1980), 3.

**Toltecs** Powerful postclassic empire in central Mexico (900–1175 C.E.). It influenced much of Mesoamerica. Aztecs claimed ties to this earlier civilization.

**tzompantli** Images of impaled skulls in scenes of human sacrifice included in the decoration of a prominent public buildings and temples in Tula.

**Culhuacán** Multiethnic Mesoamerican state south of and historically connected with Teotihuacan.

[2] From the Florentine Codex, quoted in Inga Clendinnen, *Aztecs* (New York: Cambridge University Press, 1991), 213.

**Tula** The capital of the Toltecs was dominated by massive public architecture like these carved stone figures. DEA/G.DAGLI ORTI/Getty Images

Toltec decline set in after 1150. By 1175 internal conflict and northern invaders had wreaked destruction upon the once-dominant city of Tula, triggering a centuries-long process of cultural and political assimilation to produce a new Aztec political order based on the Toltec heritage (see Chapter 15).

### Cholula

Located near the Mexican city of Puebla, Cholula developed at about the same time as Teotihuacan. It is situated to serve as an exchange point linking the Maya southeast with the Valley of Mexico and with the Mixtec peoples of the southwest. Like Teotihuacan, it was a major religious center and included one of the largest pyramids of Mesoamerica. As a key trade and religious pilgrimage destination, it had a large culturally and linguistically diverse population, including a large Toltec community. Cholula's original ties to the Toltecs are unclear, but sometime after 1000 C.E. its resident Toltec population appealed for help to Culhuacán. Just as Topiltzin would later try to save Tula, his father, Mixcoatl, went to the aid Cholula. While the fate of this vulnerable Toltec community is not known, Cholula survived as an

## SECTION REVIEW

- Postclassic civilizations carried on the basic forms of religious belief and ritual, architecture, city planning, and social organization of their predecessors.

- Mesoamerican populations increased, causing intensified agriculture and warfare.

- The Toltecs built upon Teotihucan's legacy, creating a powerful empire through military conquest and alliances. Their influence spread across central Mexico.

- The architecture of the Toltec capital Tula was decorated with militaristic themes and images of human sacrifice, indicating the increased violence of the postclassic period.

- After the collapse of Tula in the twelfth century, elements of Toltec culture and political culture survived in Culhuacán and Cholula.

important regional power until the Spanish conquest, thus connecting the legacies of both Teotihuacan and the Toltecs to the rise of the powerful Aztec Empire (see Chapter 15).

# NORTHERN PEOPLES

■ *In what ways did Mesoamerica influence the cultural centers in North America?*

Mesoamerica's classic period ended around 900 C.E. By then, settled life and complex social and political structures based on improved agriculture and population growth had appeared in the southwestern desert region of today's United States and in eastern river alleys. Along the Ohio River, Amerindian peoples living in large villages created monumental earthworks, practiced hunting and gathering, and harvested locally domesticated seed crops, such as sunflowers. In both areas, cultivating maize introduced from Mesoamerica required large-scale irrigation projects. However, the two regions evolved different political traditions. The Anasazi (ah-nah-SAH-zee) and their neighbors in the Southwest maintained a relatively egalitarian social structure and a political organization based on kinship and age. The mound builders of the East had hereditary chiefs who wielded both secular and religious authority over the political center and subordinate small towns.

## Southwestern Desert Cultures

Immigrants from Mexico brought irrigation agriculture to Arizona around 300 B.C.E. With two harvests per year, population grew and villages appeared. The Hohokam of the Salt and Gila River Valleys show strong Mexican influence, with platform mounds and ball courts similar to those of Mesoamerica. Hohokam pottery, clay figurines, cast copper bells, and turquoise mosaics also reflect this influence. By 1000 C.E. the Hohokam had constructed an elaborate irrigation system that included one canal more than 18 miles (30 kilometers) in length. Hohokam agricultural and ceramic technology gradually spread, but it was the Anasazi to the north who left the most vivid legacy.

Archaeologists use **Anasazi**, a Navajo word meaning "ancient ones," to identify a number of dispersed desert cultures located in the Four Corners region of Arizona, New Mexico, Colorado, and Utah. Between 450 and 750 C.E. the early Anasazi lived in large villages and grew maize, beans, and squash. Their cultural life centered in underground buildings called kivas, which they may have used for weaving cotton and making pottery with geometric patterns. After 900, they began to construct large multistory residential and ritual centers.

Chaco Canyon sheltered one of the largest communities: eight large towns in the canyon itself and more on surrounding mesas, suggesting a regional population of 15,000. Each town contained hundreds of rooms arranged in tiers around a central plaza. At Pueblo Bonito, the largest town, a four-story block of residences and storage spaces contained more than 650 rooms. This town, abandoned in 1150, had thirty-eight kivas, including a great kiva more than 65 feet (19 meters) in diameter.

Social life and craft activities took place in small, open plazas or common rooms. While men were often away from the village hunting, trading, and doing irrigation work, women prepared food and cared for children, as well as shared in agricultural tasks and

**Anasazi** Important culture of what is now the southwest United States (700–1300 C.E.). Centered on Chaco Canyon in New Mexico and Mesa Verde in Colorado, the Anasazi culture built multistory residences and worshiped in subterranean buildings called kivas.

**Mesa Verde Cliff Dwelling** Located in southern Colorado, the Anasazi cliff dwellings of the Mesa Verde region hosted a population of about 7,000 in 1250 C.E. The construction of housing complexes and religious buildings in the area's large caves was prompted by increased warfare in the region. Kenneth Murray/Photo Researchers, Inc.

many crafts. Among modern Pueblos, the cultural descendants of the Anasazi, houses and furnishings belong to women's extended families that include their mothers and sisters.

Late in Chaco's development, traders provided turquoise to Toltec-period peoples in northern Mexico to exchange for shell jewelry, copper bells, macaws, and trumpets. More important signs of Mesoamerican influence, such as pyramid-shaped mounds, ball courts, and class distinctions signaled by burials or residences, do not appear at Chaco. It seems more likely that the Chaco Canyon culture developed from earlier societies in the region.

Drought probably forced the abandonment of Chaco Canyon in the twelfth century. Nevertheless, the Anasazi continued in the Four Corners region for more than a century. Anasazi settlements on the Colorado Plateau and in Arizona used large natural caves high above valley floors. Such hard-to-reach locations suggest increased warfare, probably provoked by population pressure on limited arable land. The Pueblo peoples of the Rio Grand Valley and Arizona still live in multistory villages and worship in kivas.

## Mound Builders: The Hopewell and Mississippian Cultures

From around 100 C.E. the Hopewell culture spread through the Ohio River Valley. Hopewell people constructed large villages and monumental earthworks. Once established, their influence spread west to Illinois, Michigan, and Wisconsin, east to New York and Ontario, and south to Alabama, Louisiana, Mississippi, and even Florida. For sustenance the

Hopewell people depended on hunting and gathering and a limited agriculture based on domesticated seed crops. Hopewell is an early example of a North American **chiefdom**—a territory with a population as large as 10,000 and rule by a hereditary leader with both religious and secular responsibilities. Chiefs organized periodic rituals of feasting and gift giving that established bonds among diverse kinship groups and guaranteed access to specialized crops and craft goods. They also managed long-distance trade for luxury goods and additional food supplies.

The largest Hopewell towns in the Ohio River Valley served as ceremonial and political centers and had several thousand inhabitants. Large mounds housing elite burials and serving as platforms for temples and the chief's residence dominated these centers. Elite burial vaults contain valuable goods like river pearls and copper jewelry and sometimes include the bodies of women and retainers apparently sacrificed to accompany a dead chief into the afterlife. The abandonment of major Hopewell sites around 400 C.E. has no clear environmental or political explanation.

Hopewell technology and mound building were linked to the development of the Mississippian culture (800–1500 C.E.). Although the dependence on maize, beans, and squash suggests an indirect link to Mesoamerica, the urbanized Mississippian chiefdoms resulted instead from the accumulated effects of small increases in agricultural productivity, the adoption of the bow and arrow, and the expansion of trade networks. The largest towns shared a common urban plan based on a central plaza surrounded by large platform mounds. There, people bartered essential commodities, such as flint used for weapons and tools.

The Mississippian culture culminated in the urban site of Cahokia, located near East St. Louis, Illinois. North America's largest mound, a terraced structure 100 feet (30 meters) high and 1,037 by 790 feet (316 by 241 meters) at the base, stands at its center, an area of elite housing and temples ringed by areas where commoners lived. At its height in about 1200 C.E., Cahokia had a population of about 20,000—as large as the great Maya city of Tikal.

Cahokia controlled surrounding agricultural lands and a large number of secondary towns ruled by subchiefs. One tomb containing more than fifty

**SECTION REVIEW**

- In parts of North America, agricultural improvements and population growth stimulated the development of complex societies.

- In Chaco Canyon, the Anasazi practiced irrigated agriculture and produced architecture that suggests an egalitarian society.

- Some Chaco Canyon settlements exerted broad territorial influences until changing conditions forced relocation to less accessible sites.

- The Hopewell peoples built large villages with monumental earthworks and organized themselves into hierarchical chiefdoms.

- The Mississippian culture built on these patterns, with great sites such as Cahokia revealing stratified societies.

young women and retainers sacrificed to accompany a ruler after death suggests the exalted position of Cahokia's chiefs. Nothing links the decline and eventual abandonment of Cahokia (1250) to military defeat or civil war, although climate changes and population pressures may have undermined its vitality. Smaller Mississippian centers flourished in the southeastern United States until the arrival of Europeans.

# ANDEAN CIVILIZATIONS, 200–1400

■ *How did the Amerindian peoples of the Andean area adapt to their environment and produce socially complex and politically advanced societies?*

Much of the Andean region's mountainous zone seems too high for agriculture and human habitation, and the arid plain of its Pacific coastland poses a difficult challenge to cultivation. To the east of the Andes Mountains, the hot, humid tropical environment of the Amazon headwaters also discouraged the organization of complex societies. Yet the Amerindian peoples of the Andean area developed some of the most socially complex and politically advanced societies of the Western Hemisphere (see Map 7.3).

**chiefdom** Form of political organization with rule by a hereditary leader who held power over a collection of villages and towns. Less powerful than kingdoms and empires, chiefdoms were based on gift giving and commercial links.

record keeping followed in Mesoamerica, this system enabled the inhabitants to construct large-scale drainage and irrigation works and to terrace hillsides to control erosion and provide additional farmland, all of which increased agricultural production. People worked collectively on road building, urban construction, and even textile production.

The clan, or **ayllu** (aye-YOU), provided the foundation for Andean achievement. Members of an ayllu held land communally and claimed descent from a common ancestor, though they were not always related in fact. Ayllu members thought of themselves as brothers and sisters with obligations to help one another in tasks beyond the ability of a single household.

When territorial states became ruled by hereditary aristocracies and kings after 1000 B.C.E., these obligations were organized on a larger scale. The **mita** (MEET-ah) system required ayllu members to work the fields and care for the llama and alpaca herds owned by religious establishments, the royal court, and the aristocracy. Each ayllu met a yearly quota of workers for specific tasks. Mita laborers built and maintained roads, bridges, temples, palaces, and large irrigation and drainage projects. They also produced textiles and goods essential to ritual life, such as beer made from maize and coca (dried leaves chewed as a stimulant and now also the source of cocaine).

Jobs divided along gender lines, but the work of men and women was interdependent. Men hunted and served as soldiers and administrators, while women had responsibilities in textile production, agriculture, and the home. One early Spanish commentator remarked:

> [Women] did not just perform domestic tasks, but also [labored] in the fields, in the cultivation of their lands, in building houses, and carrying burdens.... And more than once I heard that while women were carrying those burdens, they would feel labor pains,

**Map 7.3** Andean Civilizations, 200 B.C.E.–1532 C.E. In response to environmental challenges posed by an arid coastal plain and high interior mountain ranges, Andean peoples made complex social and technological adaptations. Irrigation systems, the domestication of the llama, metallurgy, and shared labor obligations helped provide a firm economic foundation for powerful, centralized states.
© Cengage Learning

## Cultural Response to Environmental Challenge

People living in the high mountain valleys and on the dry coastal plains overcame significant environmental challenges through effective organization of labor. The record-keeping system used—a device of knotted colored cords called **khipus** (KEY-pooz)—helped administrations record population counts and tribute obligations. Though more limited than the

**khipus** System of knotted colored cords used by preliterate Andean peoples to record information.

**ayllu** Andean lineage group or kin-based community.

**mita** Andean labor system based on shared obligations to help kinsmen and work on behalf of the ruler and religious organizations.

**Moche Warrior** The Moche of ancient Peru were among the most accomplished ceramic artists of the Americas. Moche potters produced representations of gods and spirits, scenes of daily life, and portrait vases of important people. This warrior is armed with a mace, shield, and protective helmet. The Trustees of the British Museum/Art Resource, NY

and giving birth, they would go to a place where there was water and wash the baby and themselves. Putting the baby on top of the load they were carrying, they would then continue walking as before they gave birth.[4]

The unique environmental challenges of the Andean region led to distinctive highland and coastal cultures. Here, more than in Mesoamerica, geography influenced regional cultural integration and state formation. Because the region's mountain ranges created a multitude of small ecological areas with specialized resources, each community sought to control a variety of environments to gain access to essential goods. Coastal regions produced maize, fish, and cotton; mountain valleys contributed quinoa, potatoes, and tubers; higher elevations contributed the wool and meat of llamas and alpacas; and the Amazonian region provided coca and fruits. Colonists sent to exploit these ecological niches remained linked to their original region and ayllu by marriage and ritual. Historians commonly refer to this system of controlled exchange across ecological boundaries as vertical integration, or verticality.

## Moche

Around 200 C.E., some four centuries after the collapse of Chavín, the **Moche** (MO-che) achieved dominance among the Andean civilizations in the north coastal region of Peru. While they did not establish a centralized state, they did deploy military force, and major urban centers like Cerro Blanco (see Map 7.3) established hegemony over smaller towns and villages. In the major Moche cities, elaborate religious rituals tied hereditary rulers to the gods, creating a potent ideology that was key to Moche expansion.

The Moche cultivated maize, quinoa, beans, manioc, and sweet potatoes with the aid of massive irrigation works. At higher elevations, they produced coca, which was used ritually. Complex network of canals and aqueducts connecting fields with water sources as far away as 75 miles (121 kilometers) depended on mita labor. Large herds of alpacas and llamas transported goods across the region's difficult terrain. Their wool, along with cotton, provided the raw material for textile production, and their meat was an important part of the Moche diet.

Murals and decorated ceramics show Moche society to be stratified and theocratic. Labor organi-

---

[4] Quoted in Irene Silverblatt, *Moon, Sun, and Witches: Gender Ideologies and Class in Inca and Colonial Peru* (Princeton, NJ: Princeton University Press, 1987), 10.

**Moche** Civilization of north coast of Peru (200–700 C.E.). An important Andean civilization that built extensive irrigation networks as well as impressive urban centers dominated by brick temples.

zations helped to promote class divisions. Wealth and power, along with political control, lay in the hands of priests and military leaders, a situation reinforced by military conquest. The elite lived above the commoners atop large platforms at Moche ceremonial centers. The power of the elite was highly individualized and associated with divine sanction, and they literally looked down on the commoners whose labor supported them. Their rich attire, including tall headdresses and elaborate gold jewelry that covered the lower portion of the face with a gold plate suspended from the nose and gold plugs for ears, confirmed their connections to the gods.

One tomb of a warrior-priest buried in the Lambeyeque Valley contained a treasure that included gold, silver, and copper jewelry, textiles, feather ornaments, and shells (see Diversity and Dominance: Burials as Historical Texts). Two women and three men were executed and then buried with this powerful man in order to serve him in the afterlife.

Commoners lived by subsistence farming and labored for their ayllu and the elite. Agriculture, the care of llama herds, and the household economy involved both men and women. Commoners lived in one-room buildings clustered in the outlying areas of cities and in surrounding agricultural zones.

Moche textiles, ceramics, and metallurgy give evidence of numerous skilled artisans. As in Chavín, women played a major role in textile production, and even elite women devoted time to weaving. Moche craftspeople produced highly individualized portrait vases, ceramics decorated with line drawings representing myths and rituals, and vessels depicting explicit sexual acts. Their metalwork included gold and silver objects devoted to religious and decorative functions or to elite adornment, as well as heavy copper and copper alloy tools for agricultural and military purposes.

The archaeological record makes clear that the rapid decline of major centers coincided with a succession of natural disasters in the sixth century and the rise of a new military power in the Andean highlands. When an earthquake altered the course of the Moche River, major flooding caused serious damage, and a thirty-year drought expanded the area of coastal sand dunes, which then blew sand onto fragile agricultural lands, overwhelming the irrigation sys-

tem. As the land dried, periodic heavy rains caused erosion, which further damaged fields and weakened the economy. Despite massive efforts to keep the irrigation canals open and despite the construction of new urban centers in less vulnerable valleys to the north, Moche civilization never fully recovered. In the eighth century, a new military power, the **Wari (WAH-ree)**, put pressure on trade routes linking the coastal region with the highlands and thus contributed to the disappearance of the Moche.

## Tiwanaku and Wari

After 500 C.E., Wari and Tiwanaku were the two powerful civilizations that dominated the Andean highlands. The ruins of **Tiwanaku (tee-wah-NA-coo)** (see Map 7.3), stand at nearly 13,000 feet (3,962 meters) near Lake Titicaca in modern Bolivia. Tiwanaku's expansion depended on the adoption of technologies that increased agricultural productivity. Modern excavations provide the outline of vast drainage projects that reclaimed nearly 200,000 acres (80,000 hectares) of rich lakeside marshes for agriculture. This system of raised fields and ditches permitted intensive cultivation similar to that achieved by the use of chinampas in Mesoamerica. Fish and llamas added protein to a diet largely dependent on potatoes and grains. Llamas were also crucial for long-distance trade that brought in maize, coca, tropical fruits, and medicinal plants. The resulting abundance permitted a dense cycle of feasting and religious observance that fueled the rise of a powerful elite.

Tiwanaku's construction featured high-quality stone masonry. Thousands of laborers were mobilized to cut and move the large stones many miles for large terraced pyramids, sunken plazas, walled enclosures, and a reservoir. With copper alloy tools their only metallic resource, Tiwanaku's artisans cut stone so precisely that little mortar was needed to fit the blocks. They also produced gigantic human statuary. Together, these sacred structures, oriented to reflect celestial cycles and distant Andean peaks, provided an awe-inspiring setting for the religious rituals that

**Wari** Andean civilization culturally linked to Tiwanaku, perhaps beginning as a colony of Tiwanaku.

**Tiwanaku** Name of capital city and empire centered on the region near Lake Titicaca in modern Bolivia (375–1000 C.E.).

# Diversity & Dominance

## Burials as Historical Texts

Efforts to reveal the history of the Americas before the arrival of Europeans depend on the work of archaeologists. The burials of rulers and other members of elites can be viewed as historical texts that describe how textiles, precious metals, beautifully decorated ceramics, and other commodities were used to reinforce the political and cultural power of ruling lineages. In public, members of the elite were always surrounded by the most desirable goods and rarest products as well as by elaborate rituals and ceremonies. The effect was to create an aura of godlike power. The material elements of political and cultural power were also integrated into the experience of death and burial as members of the elite were sent into the afterlife.

The first photograph is of an excavated Moche tomb in Sipán, Peru. The Moche (200–ca. 700 C.E.) were one of the most important of the civilizations of the Andean region and masters of metallurgy, ceramics, and textiles. The excavations at Sipán revealed a "warrior-priest" buried with an amazing array of gold ornaments, jewels, textiles, and ceramics. Also buried with him were five human sacrifices: two women, perhaps wives or concubines, two male servants, and a warrior. Three of these victims—the warrior, one woman, and a male servant—are each missing a foot, perhaps cut off to guarantee their continued faithfulness to the deceased ruler in the afterlife.

The second photograph shows the excavation of a classic-era (250–ca. 800 C.E.) Maya burial at Río Azul in Guatemala. After death this elite male was laid out on a carved wooden platform and cotton mattress and his body was painted with decorations. Mourners covered his body in rich textiles and surrounded him with valuable goods. These included a necklace of individual stones carved ➤

© Heinze Plenge/NGS Image Collection

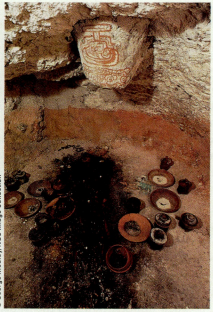

© George Mobley/NGS Image Collection

**Burials Reveal Ancient Civilizations** *(Left) Around 300 C.E., this Moche warrior-priest was buried amid rich tribute at Sipán in Peru. Also buried were the bodies of retainers or kinsmen probably sacrificed to accompany this powerful man. The body lies with the head on the right and the feet on the left. (Right) Similarly, the burial of a member of the Maya elite at Río Azul in northern Guatemala indicates the care taken to surround the powerful with fine ceramics, jewelry, and other valuable goods.*

➤ in the shape of heads, perhaps a symbol of his prowess in battle, and high-quality ceramics, some filled with foods consumed by the elite like cacao. The careful preparation of the burial chamber had required the work of numerous artisans and laborers, as was the case in the burial of the Moche warrior-priest. In death, as in life, these early American civilizations acknowledged the high status, political power, and religious authority of their elites.

legitimized the elite's domination of society and the city's control of distant territories.

At its height around 800 C.E., Tiwanaku had a population of around 60,000. Its highly stratified society was ruled by a hereditary elite. Most men and women devoted themselves to agriculture and the care of llamas; however, the elite controlled the ayllus of the surrounding region, and as their military power grew, they also drafted labor from conquered and incorporated populations. Thousands of skilled artisans expanded and embellished the ceremonial architecture and produced metal goods, textiles, and pottery. Tiwanaku ceramics found in distant places suggest a specialized merchant class. Military

Paulo Afonso/Shutterstock.com

**The Ritual Center of Tiwanaku** During the Middle Horizon period Tiwanaku was one of the most impressive cities in the Andean region. The ritual center was characterized by beautiful stone construction, sunken plazas, and by large carved stone representations of the gods.

conquests and the establishment of distant colonial populations also brought to Tiwanaku more exotic products, like colorful shells, gold and copper, and fine textiles.

Sometime after 1000 C.E. urban Tiwanaku was abandoned. There is evidence that severe drought led to precipitous population loss and to the breakdown of the long-distance trade. The destruction of monumental effigies and other religious symbols suggests that worsening material conditions undermined the legitimacy of the elite.

The contemporary site of Wari, about 450 miles (751 kilometers) to the northwest, had cultural and technological links to Tiwanaku, but most scholars argue that Wari was a politically centralized state with its own distinct culture and powerful military, rather than a dependency of Tiwanaku. Recent research indicates an aggressive Wari expansion lubricated by captive-taking and human sacrifice. Wari exceeded Tiwanaku in size, measuring nearly 4 square miles (10 square kilometers). A massive wall surrounded the city center, which included a large temple and multifamily housing. Housing for commoners sprawled across a suburban zone. Unlike most other urban centers in the Andes, Wari had no central planning.

The relatively small scale of Wari's monumental architecture and the near absence of cut stone masonry in public and private buildings distinguish Wari from Tiwanaku. Wari ceramic style also differs, allowing experts to trace Wari's expansion to the coastal area previously controlled by the Moche and to the northern highlands. This expansion occurred at a time of climate change and increasing warfare throughout the Andes that led ultimately to the eclipse of both Tiwanaku and Wari after 1000 C.E.

## Chimú

On the north coast of Peru, the **Chimú** Empire, or Chimor, appeared after 900 C.E. Chimú control extended from Ecuador's Pacific coast in the north to central Peru and depended on the labor provided by conquered dependencies. Distinct regions provided laborers, who made their own adobe bricks, to build palaces and religious monuments in Chan Chan, the massive Chimú capital. Tribute labor also expanded the scale

of Moche irrigation works in the difficult arid environment of the Peruvian coast. Dependent peoples were compensated for their loss of autonomy by larger and more predictable harvests.

While the grandeur of Wari and Tiwanaku can still be seen in surviving monumental stone architecture, the once-great Chan Chan, built from adobe, has been much diminished by a thousand years of erosion. Nevertheless, its imperial character is clear. Nine large residential compounds provided the urban nucleus. Each one housed a ruler and became his mausoleum upon his death. With each succession, the new ruler would construct a new palace compound. Chan Chan primarily served as the residential precinct of the elite and those who provided them with luxury goods like gold jewelry and high-quality textiles and pottery, rather than as a commercial or religious center, and there was little urban planning. High walls separated the elite from the dispersed humble habitations of commoners. Both the urban architecture and the organization of labor expressed the profound social and economic distance that separated royalty and populace.

**Chimú** Powerful Peruvian civilization based on conquest. Located in the region earlier dominated by Moche. Conquered by Inka in 1465.

### SECTION REVIEW

- Andean societies overcame the challenges of their environment through superior political organization based on the ayllu and mita.
- The Moche developed a powerful state based on irrigated agriculture, exchange between ecological regions, and a powerful religious elite.
- The construction of canals and the development of raised-field agriculture made possible the rise of the religious and political center of Tiwanaku.
- Both Tiwanaku and Wari used powerful militaries to extend their dominion over large regions and create long-distance networks of trade.
- The Chimú created a powerful new empire in the region previously dominated by the Moche.

This system depended on a series of conquests and a potent military. Unlike earlier Andean civilizations, the Chimú Empire did not collapse because of environmental catastrophe or social unrest. Instead, it survived into the fifteenth century, when it fell victim to a more powerful rival, the Inka (see Chapter 15), who maintained many of Chimú's technologies and political institutions.

## CONCLUSION

The Toltecs of Mesoamerica and the Chimú of the Andean region were potent representatives of cultures that had developed over nearly two thousand years. Each was created militarily, its survival depending as much on the power of its armies as on the productivity of its economy or the wisdom of its rulers. Each also depended on political institutions, economic forms, technologies, and religious practices that were first put in place by the Olmec and Chavín.

Mesoamerica and the Andean region were environmentally challenging territories where a succession of native states found ways to produce and distribute products from distinct ecological zones as well as ways to organize ethnically diverse populations into coherent polities. From the beginning, rulers in both regions legitimized their authority religiously, serving as priestly intermediaries with the gods or claiming direct descent from the gods. The major cities of every important civilization from the time of the Olmec and Chavín to 1300 C.E. operated as religious as well as political centers. Their urban centers were dominated by monumental religious architecture decorated with symbols connecting elites to the gods and legitimizing the power of elites over the rural laborers that made these early civilizations possible.

With the important exception of metallurgy developed in the Andes and transferred to Mesoamerica after 500 C.E., ancient technologies from the Olmec and Chavín were the basis for Toltec and Chimú construction of irrigation canals, raised fields, terraced hillsides, and, in the case of Mesoamerica, chinampas. The growing size of cities, the mounting power of government, and the expanding scale of empire all depended more on the mobilization of ever-larger workforces than on new technologies.

There were important differences between Mesoamerica and the Andean region. In Mesoamerica the Toltecs imposed tribute obligations on defeated peoples but left local hereditary elites in place. In the Andes reciprocal labor obligations were used to produce and distribute goods.

We can find similar patterns in North America. The transfer of agricultural technology from Mesoamerica, with its dependence on corn, beans, and squash, influenced the mound-building cultures of the Ohio and Mississippi River Valleys and the desert cultures of the Southwest. The Anasazi in what is now the southwest United States utilized irrigation, a technology crucial to both Mesoamerican and Andean cultures. Both the desert and mound-building cultures of North America experienced cycles when powerful new political centers expanded the territories they controlled and consolidated their power until overwhelmed by environmental challenges or displaced by military rivals.

Great civilizations in both Mesoamerica and the Andean region had risen and been overwhelmed in earlier epochs, as had the major powers of the Four Corners desert region and the Ohio and Mississippi River Valleys. In all these cases, a long period of cultural and political adjustment led eventually to the creation of new indigenous institutions, the adoption of new technologies, and the appearance of new centers of power in new locations. With the appearance of the Aztec and Inka Empires in the fourteenth century (see Chapter 15), America would experience its final cycle of autonomous indigenous crisis and adjustment. At the end of the fifteenth century the future of Amerindian peoples would become linked to the cultures of the Old World.

## CHAPTER REVIEW

### FORMATIVE OLMEC AND CHAVÍN CIVILIZATIONS, 1200–200 B.C.E.
■ *How did the Olmec and Chavín civilizations influence later Mesoamerican and Andean civilizations?* (page 157)

The people of the Americas lived in virtual isolation from the rest of the world for at least 15,000 years. During this period, they learned to adapt to their natural environment on their own. The Olmec organized their population to dig irrigation and drainage canals and to cultivate the land. Chavín agriculture depended on the introduction of maize cultivation as well as trade with other regions. Llamas were used to transport goods along newly constructed roads and bridges. Artificial platforms and mounds of packed earth dominated both civilizations' urban centers. Olmec urban centers were planned to be aligned with the stars through religious observation of the heavens. Though both civilizations passed away, their successors chose to retain their technologies and cultural features like mound-centered urban sites.

### CLASSIC-ERA CULTURE AND SOCIETY IN MESOAMERICA, 200–900
■ *What were the most important shared characteristics of Mesoamerican cultures in the classic period?* (page 163)

Mesoamerican civilization was based largely on a relationship with the gods and the environment. At Teotihuacan, people worshiped many gods and constructed pyramids devoted to the sun, the moon, and Quetzalcoatl. Human sacrifice was deemed essential to the well-being of society. Maya city-states also featured impressive temples, often built on high ground and reflecting the Maya cosmos. As both political leaders and priests, rulers participated in bloodletting rituals and hallucinogenic trances. The people of Teotihuacan brought marginal lands into production and expanded the use of chinampas. The Maya contended with a tropical climate and fragile soils. People living near cities manipulated

their environment by draining swamps and building elevated fields.

### THE POSTCLASSIC PERIOD IN MESOAMERICA, 900–1300
■ *What role did warfare play in the postclassic period of Mesoamerica?* (page 167)

The Toltecs were known for their military achievements. The governing elites increased the size of their armies and developed political institutions that facilitated their control of large and culturally diverse territories acquired through conquest. Images of war, violence, and human sacrifice appear on nearly all the Toltec public buildings and temples and dominated the Mesoamerican imagination in the late postclassic period. Warriors were featured in impressive statues. Labor from conquered peoples constructed massive religious buildings and agricultural works, and military alliances secured trade routes throughout the central Mexican region.

### NORTHERN PEOPLES
■ *In what ways did Mesoamerica influence the cultural centers in North America?* (page 170)

Cultural centers in the southwest United States exhibit strong Mexican influence. Hohokam sites have platform mounds and ball courts, as well as pottery, clay figurines, and turquoise mosaics. To the north lived the Anasazi, who left the most vivid legacy of desert culture. One of the largest communities of the Anasazi was located in Chaco Canyon. Though Chaco trade goods show up in Toltec-period sites in northern Mexico, the Chaco culture seems to have developed independently. Beginning around 100 C.E., the Hopewell culture spread through the Ohio River Valley. Hopewell earthen mounds housed elite burials and served as platforms for temples and homes for chiefs. Similar mound building occurred in the Mississippian culture. Apart from food crops, evidence of a Mesoamerican influence on either culture is rare.

## ANDEAN CIVILIZATIONS, 200–1400

■ *How did the Amerindian peoples of the Andean area adapt to their environment and produce socially complex and politically advanced societies?* (page 172)

Both the Andes Mountains and the bordering coastal plain posed great environmental challenges. The Amerindian response was effective organization of human labor for digging irrigation works, terracing hillsides, and building roads. Andean societies functioned through clans called ayllus that provided labor and goods to their hereditary chiefs. They also exchanged goods across ecological boundaries. Each community's production suited its ecological niche: coastal regions produced maize, fish, and cotton; mountain valleys contributed quinoa and potatoes; higher elevations contributed the wool and meat of animals; and the Amazonian region provided coca and fruits. The institutions of the ayllu and the state managed exchanges that fostered integration and growth.

### Key Terms

Olmec (p. 158)
Chavín (p. 161)
llama (p. 162)
Teotihuacan (p. 163)
chinampas (p. 164)
Maya (p. 165)
Toltecs (p. 168)
tzompantli (p. 168)
Culhuacán (p. 168)

Anasazi (p. 170)
chiefdom (p. 172)
khipus (p. 173)
ayllu (p. 173)
mita (p. 173)
Moche (p. 174)
Wari (p. 175)
Tiwanaku (p. 175)
Chimú (p. 178)

# Oral Societies and the Consequences of Literacy

The availability of written documents is a key factor used by historians to divide human prehistory from history. When we can read what people of the past thought and said about their lives, we begin to understand their cultures, institutions, values, and beliefs in ways that are not possible based only on the material remains unearthed by archaeologists.

Literacy and nonliteracy are not absolute alternatives. Personal literacy ranges from illiteracy through many shades of partial literacy (the ability to write one's name or to read simple texts with difficulty) to the fluent ability to read that is possessed by anyone reading this textbook. And there are degrees of societal literacy, ranging from nonliteracy through so-called craft literacy—in which a small specialized elite uses writing for limited purposes, such as administrative record keeping—up to the near-universal literacy and the use of writing for innumerable purposes that is the norm in the developed world in our times.

The vast majority of human beings of the last five to six thousand years, even those living in societies that possessed the technology of writing, were not themselves literate. If most people in a society rely on the spoken word and memory, that culture is essentially "oral" even if some members know how to write. The differences between oral and literate cultures are immense, affecting not only the kinds of knowledge that are valued and the forms in which information is preserved, but also the very use of language, the categories for conceptualizing the world, and ultimately the hard-wiring of the individual human brain (now recognized by neuroscientists to be strongly influenced by individual experience and mental activity).

Ancient Greece of the Archaic and Classical periods (ca. 800–323 B.C.E.) offers a particularly instructive case study because we can observe the process by which writing was introduced into an oral society as well as the far-reaching consequences. The Greeks of the Dark Age and early Archaic period lived in a purely oral society; all knowledge was preserved in human memory and passed on by telling it to others. The *Iliad* and the *Odyssey* (ca. 700 B.C.E.), Homer's epic poems, reflect this state of affairs. Scholars recognize that the creator of these poems was an oral poet, almost certainly not literate, who had heard and memorized the poems of predecessors and retold them his own way. The poems are treasuries of information that this society regarded as useful—events of the past; the conduct expected of warriors, kings, noblewomen, and servants; how to perform a sacrifice, build a raft, put on armor, and entertain guests; and much more.

Embedding this information in a story and using the colorful language, fixed phrases, and predictable rhythm of poetry made it easier for poet and audience to remember vast amounts of material. The early Greek poets, drawing on their strong memories, skill with words, and talent for dramatic performance, developed highly specialized techniques to assist them in memorizing and presenting their tales. They played a vital role in the preservation and transmission of information and thus enjoyed a relatively high social standing and comfortable standard of living. Analogous groups can be found in many other oral cultures of the past, including the bards of medieval Celtic lands, Norse skalds, West African griots, and the tribal historians of Native American peoples.

Nevertheless, human memory, however cleverly trained and well practiced, can only do so much. Oral societies must be extremely selective about what information to preserve in the limited storage medium of human memory, and they are slow to give up old information to make way for new.

Sometime in the eighth century B.C.E. the Greeks borrowed the system of writing used by the Phoenicians of Lebanon and, in adapting it to their language, created the first purely alphabetic writing, employing several dozen symbols to express the sounds of speech. The Greek alphabet, although relatively simple to learn as compared to the large and cumbersome sets of symbols in such craft literacy systems as cuneiform, hieroglyphics, or Linear B, was probably known at first only to a small number of people and used for restricted purposes. Scholars believe that it may have taken three or four centuries for knowledge of reading and writing to spread to large numbers of Greeks and for the written word to become the primary storage medium for the accumulated knowledge of Greek civilization. Throughout that time Greece was still primarily an oral society, even though some Greeks, mostly highly educated members of the upper classes, were beginning to write down poems, scientific speculations, stories about the past, philosophic musings, and the laws of their communities.

It is no accident that some of the most important intellectual and artistic achievements of the Greeks, including early science, history, drama, and rhetoric, developed in the period when oral and literate ways existed side by side. Scholars have persuasively argued that writing, by opening up a virtually limitless capacity to store information, released the human mind from the hard discipline of memorization and ended the need to be so painfully selective about what was preserved. This made previously unimaginable innovation and experimentation possible. The Greeks began to organize and categorize information in linear ways, perhaps inspired by the linear sequence of the alphabet; and they began to engage in abstract thinking now that it was no longer necessary to put everything in a story format. We can observe changes in the Greek language as it developed a vocabulary full of abstract nouns, accompanied by increasingly complex sentence structure now that the reader had time to go back over the text.

Nevertheless, all the developments associated with literacy were shaped by the deeply rooted oral habits of Greek culture. It is often said that Plato (ca. 429–347 B.C.E.) and his contemporaries of the later Classical period may have been the first generation of Greeks who learned much of what they knew from books. Even so, Plato was a disciple of the philosopher Socrates, who wrote nothing, and Plato employed the oral form of the dialogue, a dramatized sequence of questions and answers, to convey his ideas in written form.

The transition from orality to literacy met stiff resistance in some quarters. Groups whose position in the oral culture was based on the special knowledge only they possessed—members of the elite who judged disputes, priests who knew the time-honored formulas and rituals for appeasing the gods, oral poets who preserved and performed the stories of a heroic past—resented the consequences of literacy. They did what they could to inflame the common people's suspicions of the impiety of literate men who sought scientific explanations for phenomena, such as lightning and eclipses, that had traditionally been attributed to the will and action of the gods. The elite attacked the so-called Sophists, or "wise men," who charged fees to teach what they claimed were the skills necessary for success, accusing them of subverting traditional morals and corrupting the young.

Other societies, ancient and modern, offer parallel examples of these processes. Oral "specialists" in antiquity, including the Brahmin priests of India and the Celtic Druids, preserved in memory valuable religious information about how to win the favor of the gods. These groups jealously guarded their knowledge because it was the basis of their livelihood and social standing. In their determination to select and to maintain control over those who received this knowledge, they resisted committing it to writing, even after that technology was available. The ways in which oral authorities feel threatened by writing and resist it can be seen in the following quotation from a twentieth-century C.E. "griot," an oral rememberer and teller of the past in Mali in West Africa:

We griots are depositories of the knowledge of the past. . . . Other peoples use writing to record the past, but this invention has killed the faculty of memory among them. They do not feel the past anymore, for writing lacks the warmth of the human voice. With them everybody thinks he knows, whereas learning should be a secret. . . . What paltry learning is that which is congealed in dumb books! . . . For generations we have passed on the history of kings from father to son. The narrative was passed on to me without alteration, for I received it free from all untruth.[1]

This point of view is hard for us to grasp, living as we do in an intensely literate society in which the written word is often felt to be more authoritative and objective than the spoken word. It is important, in striving to understand societies of the past, not to superimpose our assumptions on them and to appreciate the complex interplay of oral and literate patterns in many of them.

---

[1] D. T. Niane, *Sundiata: An Epic of Old Mali* (Harlow, UK: Longman, 1986), 41.

# Part Three

# Growth and Interaction of Cultural Communities, 300 B.C.E.–1200 C.E.

© Cengage Learning

| | 300 B.C.E. | B.C.E. C.E. | | 300 C.E. | |
|---|---|---|---|---|---|
| **EUROPE** | | • **146** Rome destroys Carthage, begins direct control of territories ouside Europe | | Council of Nicaea **325** • <br> Reign of Roman emperor Diocletian **284–305** | Fall of Roman Empire in West **476** • |
| **AFRICA** | **500 B.C.E.–1000 C.E.** Bantu migrations | | • **ca. 100** Bananas and yams reach Africa from Southeast Asia | • **ca. 330** First Christian bishop in Ethiopia | |
| **MIDDLE EAST** | • **300** Petra flourishes as caravan city in Jordan | **248 B.C.E.–226 C.E.** Kingdom of Parthia in Iran | | • **276** Prophet Mani martyred <br> **226–650** Sasanid Empire in Iraq and Iran | |
| **ASIA AND OCEANIA** | • **128** Chinese general Zhang Jian explores Silk Road <br> **206 B.C.E.–220 C.E.** Han Empire in China | | • **ca. 100** Stirrup developed in Afghanistan | • **200–400** Rice introduced to Japan from Korea | |

184

In 300 B.C.E., societies had only limited contacts beyond their frontiers. By 1200 C.E., this situation had changed. Traders, migrating peoples, and missionaries brought peoples together. Products and technologies moved along long-distance trade networks: the Silk Road across Asia, Saharan caravan routes, and sea-lanes connecting the Indian Ocean coastlands.

Migrating Bantu peoples from West Africa spread iron and new farming techniques through much of sub-Saharan Africa and helped foster a distinctive African culture. Conquering Arabs from the Arabian peninsula, inspired by the Prophet Muhammad, established Muslim rule from Spain to India, laying the foundation of a new culture.

In Asia, missionaries and pilgrims helped Buddhism spread from India to Sri Lanka, Tibet, Southeast Asia, and East Asia. The new faith interacted with older philosophies and religions to produce distinctive cultural patterns. Simultaneously, the Tang Empire in China disseminated Chinese culture and technologies throughout Inner and East Asia.

In Europe, monks and missionaries spread Christian beliefs that became enmeshed with new political and social structures: a struggle between royal and church authority in western Europe; a union of religious and imperial authority in the Byzantine east; and a similar but distinctive society in Kievan Russia. The Crusades reconnected western Europe with the lands of the east.

| 600 C.E. | 900 C.E. | 1200 C.E. |
|---|---|---|
| ca. **400–800** Decline of cities and monetary economy in West | • **800** Charlemagne crowned emperor | • **988** Christianity established in Kievan Russia<br>• **1095** First Crusade<br>• **962** Holy Roman Empire founded |
| | • **750** Trans-Saharan trade routes become active | • **1076** Fall of kingdom of Ghana |
| **570–632** Life of Muhammad<br>**634–711** Islamic conquests of western Asia, North Africa<br>**661–750** Umayyad Caliphate | **750–850** Abbasid Caliphate at its height | • **1071** Turks defeat Byzantines at Manzikert<br>• **1187** Saladin recaptures Jerusalem |
| **589–618** Sui Empire reunites China<br>**618–907** Tang Empire in China and Central Asia | • **840** Buddhism suppressed in China<br>**960–1127** Song Empire reunites China | • **1127** Southern Song Empire founded<br>• **1185** Kamakura Shogunate founded in Japan |

185

# CHAPTER 8

## 300 B.C.E.–1100 C.E.

# Networks of Communication and Exchange

© Cengage Learning

## CHAPTER PREVIEW

### THE SILK ROAD
- *What factors contributed to the growth of trade along the Silk Road?*

### THE INDIAN OCEAN MARITIME SYSTEM
- *How did geography affect Indian Ocean trade routes?*

### ROUTES ACROSS THE SAHARA
- *Why did trade begin across the Sahara Desert?*

### SUB-SAHARAN AFRICA
- *What accounts for the substantial degree of cultural unity in Africa south of the Sahara?*

### THE SPREAD OF IDEAS
- *Why do some goods and ideas travel more easily than others?*

### Conclusion

**DIVERSITY & DOMINANCE:** Travel Accounts of Africa and India

186

nspired by the tradition of the Silk Road, a Chinese poet named Po Zhuyi (boh joo-yee) nostalgically wrote:

> Iranian whirling girl, Iranian whirling girl—
> Her heart answers to the strings,
> Her hands answer to the drums.
> At the sound of the strings and drums, she raises her arms,
> Like whirling snowflakes tossed about, she turns in her twirling dance.
> Iranian whirling girl,
> You came from Sogdiana (sog-dee-AH-nuh).
> In vain did you labor to come east more than ten thousand tricents.
> For in the central plains there were already some who could do the Iranian whirl,
> And in a contest of wonderful abilities, you would not be their equal.[1]

The western part of Central Asia, the region around Samarkand (SAM-mar-kand) and Bukhara (boh-CAR-ruh) known in the eighth century C.E. as Sogdiana, was 2,500 miles (4,000 kilometers) from the Chinese capital of Chang'an (chahng-ahn). The route between these points was called in later times the **Silk Road**, after one of the major products that were traded. Caravans took more than four months to trek across the mostly unsettled deserts, mountains, and grasslands, carrying with them agricultural goods, manufactured products, and ideas. Musicians and dancing girls traveled, too—as did camel pullers, merchants, monks, and pilgrims. The Silk Road was a means of connecting peoples and parts of the world as well as a social system.

With every expansion of territory, the growing wealth of temples, kings, and emperors enticed traders to venture ever farther afield for precious goods. For the most part, the customers were wealthy elites. But the new products, agricultural and industrial processes, and foreign ideas and customs these long-distance traders brought with them sometimes affected an entire society.

[1] Victor H. Mair, ed., *The Columbia Anthology of Traditional Chinese Literature* (New York: Columbia University Press, 1994), 485; translated by Victor H. Mair.

Travelers and traders seldom owned much land or wielded political power. Socially isolated (sometimes by law) and secretive because any talk about markets, products, routes, and travel conditions could help their competitors, they nevertheless contributed more to drawing the world together than did all but a few kings and emperors.

This chapter examines the social systems and historical impact of exchange networks that developed between 300 B.C.E. and 1100 C.E. in Europe, Asia, and Africa. The Silk Road and the Indian Ocean Maritime System illustrate long-distance trade in this era. At the same time, shorter trade routes developed across the Sahara, and the Bantu-speaking peoples within sub-Saharan Africa began folk migration throughout Africa, carrying with them technologies, language, and ideas. A third pattern of cultural contact and exchange is illustrated by the spread of religion. Chapter 5 discussed the growth of Christianity in the Roman Empire; this chapter discusses the spread of Christianity in Africa and Asia and that of Buddhism in Asia.

## THE SILK ROAD

■ *What factors contributed to the growth of trade along the Silk Road?*

Archaeology and linguistic studies show that the peoples of Central Asia engaged in long-distance movement and exchange from at least 1500 B.C.E. In Roman times Europeans became captivated by the idea of a trade route linking the lands of the Mediterranean with China by way of Mesopotamia, Iran, and Central Asia. The Silk Road, as it came to be called in the modern era, experienced several periods of heavy use (see Map 8.1). The first began around 100 B.C.E.

### Origins and Operations

While the Seleucid kings who succeeded to the eastern parts of Alexander the Great's empire in the third century B.C.E. focused their energies on Mesopotamia and Syria, an Iranian nomadic leader

**Silk Road**  Caravan routes connecting China and the Middle East across Central Asia and Iran.

**Map 8.1  Asian Trade and Communication Routes**  The overland Silk Road was vulnerable to political disruption, but it was much shorter than the maritime route from the South China Sea to the Red Sea, and ships were more expensive than pack animals. Moreover, China's political centers were in the north. © Cengage Learning

**Expansion of Buddhism**

- Area of origin
- 5th to 2d century B.C.E.
- 2d century B.C.E. to 3d century C.E.
- 3d to 8th century C.E.

→ Spread of Buddhism
━ Silk Road
━ Indian Ocean trade routes

# Chronology

| | Silk Road | Indian Ocean Trade | Saharan Trade |
|---|---|---|---|
| **500 B.C.E.** | **247 B.C.E.** Parthian rule begins in Iran<br><br>**128 B.C.E.** General Zhang Jian reaches Ferghana<br><br>**100 B.C.E.–300 C.E.** Kushans rule northern Afghanistan and Sogdiana | | **500 B.C.E.–ca. 1000 C.E.** Bantu migrations<br><br>**ca. 200 B.C.E.** Camel nomads in southern Sahara<br><br>**46 B.C.E.** First mention of camels in northern Sahara |
| **1 C.E.** | | **1st century C.E.** Indonesian migration to Madagascar | |
| **300 C.E.** | **ca. 400** Buddhist pilgrim Faxian travels Silk Road | **ca. 900** Arab and Persian merchants in Canton | **ca. 300** Beginning of camel nomadism in northern Sahara |

established an independent kingdom in northeastern Iran. By 247 B.C.E. these **Parthians**, a people originally from east of the Caspian Sea, had become a major force. They left few written sources, and recurring wars with Greeks and Romans to the west prevented travelers from the Mediterranean region from gaining firm knowledge of their kingdom. It seems likely, however, that they helped foster the Silk Road by being located on the threshold of Central Asia and sharing customs with steppe nomads in Inner Asia farther to the east.

In 128 B.C.E. a Chinese general named Zhang Jian (jahng jee-en) made his first exploratory journey across the deserts and mountains of Inner Asia on behalf of Emperor Wu of the Han dynasty (see Chapter 5). After crossing the broad and desolate Tarim Basin north of Tibet, he reached the fertile valley of Ferghana (fer-GAH-nuh) and for the first time encountered westward-flowing rivers. There he found horse breeders whose animals far outclassed any horses he had seen. Later Chinese historians looked on General Zhang, who ultimately led eighteen expeditions, as the originator of overland trade with the western lands, and they credited him with personally introducing a whole garden of new plants and trees to China.

Long-distance travel suited the people of the steppes more than the Chinese. The populations of Ferghana and neighboring regions included many nomads who followed their herds. Their migrations had little to do with trade, but they provided pack animals and controlled transit across their lands. The trading demands that brought the Silk Road into being were Chinese eagerness for western products, especially horses, and on the western end, the organized Parthian state, which had captured the flourishing markets of Mesopotamia from the Seleucids and maintained relations with other markets in India.

By 100 B.C.E., Greeks, and later Romans, could buy Chinese silk from Parthian traders in Mesopotamian border entrepôts. Yet caravans also bought and sold goods along the way in prosperous Central Asian cities like Samarkand and Bukhara. These cities grew and flourished, often under the rule of local princes.

General Zhang definitely seems to have brought two plants to China: alfalfa and wine grapes. The former provided the best fodder for horses. In addition, Chinese farmers adopted pistachios, walnuts, pomegranates, sesame, coriander, spinach, and other new

**Parthians** Iranian ruling dynasty between ca. 250 B.C.E. and 226 C.E.

Lee Boltin/The Bridgeman Art Library

**Scythian Breastplate** This superbly crafted gold ornament from the fourth century B.C.E. features animal combat in the lower tier, flower motifs in the center, and scenes from Scythian pastoral life in the upper. Two men prepare a fleece garment in the middle of the upper tier while on either side young animals are suckling and a ewe is being milked. Note the contrast between the simplicity of nomadic life and the luxury represented by the gold ornament itself.

## SECTION REVIEW

- The rise of the Parthian kingdom helped foster the Silk Road to meet European demand for Chinese silk and Chinese demand for horses.
- General Zhang led expeditions that established the route from China through Central Asia.
- Central Asian nomads facilitated the movement of goods through their lands.
- Central Asian cities grew as a result of Silk Road trade.
- In addition to silk, agricultural products traveled both ways along the Silk Road.

crops. Chinese artisans and physicians made good use of other trade products, such as jasmine oil, oak galls (used in tanning animal hides, dyeing, and making ink), sal ammoniac (for medicines), copper oxides, zinc, and precious stones.

In addition, traders going west from China carried new fruits such as peaches and apricots, which the Romans mistakenly attributed to other eastern lands, calling them Persian plums and Armenian plums, respectively. They also carried cinnamon, ginger, and other spices that could not be grown in the West.

## Nomadism in Central and Inner Asia

The Silk Road could not have functioned without pastoral nomads to provide animals, animal handlers, and protection. In Chapter 3, a portrayal of steppe nomads appears in the history of the Greek writer Herodotus. He describes them as fearsome horse archers, herdsmen, and hunters living in the Central Asian lands to the north of the Black and Caspian Seas and moving their enormous herds regularly to prevent overgrazing. Their lightweight homes, made of felt spread over a portable framework, were transported on two- or four-wheeled wagons drawn by oxen. This custom continued for another two thousand years in the grasslands and deserts extending eastward to the borders of China.

Nomads used the products grown by farmers, but their wanderings required self-sufficiency, so they subsisted on meat and milk and looked to settled regions primarily for the bronze or iron used in bridles, stirrups, cart fittings, and weapons. They acquired metal implements in trade and reworked them to suit their purposes. Scythians (as steppe nomads were called by the Greeks) in the Ukraine worked extensively with iron as early as the fourth century B.C.E., and Turkish-speaking peoples had large ironworking stations south of the Altai Mountains in western Mongolia in the 600s C.E. Steppe nomads situated near settled areas also traded wool, leather, and horses for wood, silk, vegetables, and grain.

## THE INDIAN OCEAN MARITIME SYSTEM

■ *How did geography affect Indian Ocean trade routes?*

While a land route was established in Central Asia, a multilingual, multiethnic society of seafarers established the **Indian Ocean Maritime System**, a trade network across the Indian Ocean and the South China Sea. These people left few records and seldom played a visible part in the rise and fall of kingdoms and empires, but they forged increasingly strong economic and social ties between the coastal lands of East Africa, southern Arabia, the Persian Gulf, India, Southeast Asia, and southern China.

This trade took place in three distinct regions: (1) In the South China Sea, Chinese and Malays (including Indonesians) dominated trade. (2) From the east coast of India to the islands of Southeast Asia, Indians and Malays were the main traders. (3) From the west coast of India to the Persian Gulf and the east coast of Africa, merchants and sailors were predominantly Persians and Arabs. However, Chinese and Malay sailors could and did voyage to East Africa, and Arab and Persian traders reached southern China before 900 C.E.

From the time of Herodotus in the fifth century B.C.E., Greek writers regaled their readers with stories of marvelous voyages down the Red Sea into the Indian Ocean or around Africa from the west. Most often, they attributed such trips to the Phoenicians, the most fearless of Mediterranean seafarers. Occasionally a Greek appears. One such was Hippalus, a Greek ship's pilot who was said to have discovered the seasonal monsoon winds that facilitate sailing across the Indian Ocean (see Diversity and Dominance: Travel Accounts of Africa and India).

Of course, the regular, seasonal alternation of steady winds could not have remained unnoticed for thousands of years, waiting for an alert Greek to happen along. The great voyages and discoveries made before written records became common should surely be attributed to the peoples who lived around the Indian Ocean rather than to interlopers from the Mediterranean Sea. The story of Hippalus resembles the Chinese story of General Zhang Jian, whose role in opening trade with Central Asia overshadows the anonymous contributions made by the indigenous peoples. The Chinese may indeed have learned from General Zhang and the Greeks from Hippalus, but other people played important roles anonymously.

Indian Ocean voyages differed in several ways from Mediterranean voyages. Mediterranean sailors of the time of Alexander used square sails and long banks of oars to maneuver among the sea's many islands and small harbors. In contrast, Indian Ocean vessels relied on roughly triangular lateen sails and normally did without oars in running before the wind on long ocean stretches. Whereas Mediterranean shipbuilders nailed their vessels together, the planks of Indian Ocean ships were pierced, tied together with palm fiber, and caulked with bitumen. Mediterranean sailors rarely ventured out of sight of land. Indian Ocean sailors, thanks to the monsoon winds, could cover long reaches entirely at sea.

These technological differences prove that the world of the Indian Ocean developed differently from the world of the Mediterranean Sea, where the Phoenicians and Greeks established colonies that maintained contact with their home cities (see Chapters 2 and 4). The traders of the Indian Ocean, where distances were greater and contacts less frequent, seldom retained political ties with their homelands. The colonies they established were sometimes socially distinctive but rarely independent of the local political powers.

**Iranian Rider on Silk Road Camel**
Glazed ceramic figurines of camels and horses are found in many Inner Asian burials of the Tang period. Most of the camel riders, like this one, have beards and big noses stereotyping people from Central Asia far to the west. Soft pointed caps first appear in images of Scythians living north of Iran. The absence of a saddle and the rider's diminutive size suggest a humorous caricature.
Werner Forman/Universal Images Group/Getty Images

**Indian Ocean Maritime System** In premodern times, a network of seaports, trade routes, and maritime culture linking countries on the rim of the Indian Ocean from Africa to Indonesia.

# Diversity & Dominance

## Travel Accounts of Africa and India

The most revealing description of ancient trade in the Indian Ocean and the economic forces shaping the Indian Ocean trading system is found in The Periplus of the Erythraean Sea, *a sailing itinerary (periplus in Greek). Composed in the first century C.E. by an unknown Greco-Egyptian merchant, it highlights the diversity of peoples and products from the Red Sea to the Bay of Bengal. Historians believe that the descriptions of market towns were based on firsthand experience. The following passages deal with East Africa and the coastal lands of the Indian subcontinent (see Map 8.1).*

Of the designated ports on the Erythraean Sea [Indian Ocean], and the market-towns around it, the first is the Egyptian port of Mussel Harbor. To those sailing down from that place, on the right hand . . . there is Berenice. The harbors of both are at the boundary of Egypt. . . .

On the right-hand coast next below Berenice is the country of the Berbers. Along the shore are the Fish-Eaters, living in scattered caves in the narrow valleys. Further inland are the Berbers, and beyond them the Wild-flesh-Eaters and Calf-Eaters, each tribe governed by its chief . . . .

Below the Calf-Eaters there is a little market-town on the shore . . . called Ptolemais of the Hunts, from which the hunters started for the interior under the dynasty of the Ptolemies. . . . But the place has no harbor and is reached only by small boats. . . .

Beyond this place, the coast trending toward the south, there is the Market and Cape of Spices [and] an abrupt promontory at the very end of the Berber coast toward the east. . . . A sign of an approaching storm . . . is that the deep water becomes more turbid and changes its color. When this happens they all run to a large promontory called Tabae, which offers safe shelter. . . .

Beyond Tabae [lies] . . . another market-town called Opone. . . . [I]n it the greatest quantity of cinnamon is produced . . . and slaves of the better sort, which are brought to Egypt in increasing numbers. . . .

[Ships also come] from the places across this sea, . . . bringing to these . . . market-towns the products of their own places; wheat, rice, clarified butter, sesame oil, cotton cloth . . . and honey from the reed called sacchari [sugar cane]. Some make the voyage especially to these market-towns, and others exchange their cargoes while sailing along the coast. This country is not subject to a King, but each market-town is ruled by its separate chief.

Beyond Opone, the shore trending more toward the south . . . this coast [the Somali region of Azania, or East Africa] is destitute of harbors . . . until the Pyralax islands [Zanzibar]. . . . [A] little to the south of south-west . . . is the island Menuthias [Madagascar], . . . low and wooded, in which there are rivers and many kinds of birds and the mountain-tortoise. There are no wild beasts except the crocodiles; but there they do not attack men. In this place there are sewed boats, and canoes hollowed from single logs. . . .

Two days' sail beyond, there lies the very last market-town of the continent of Azania, which is called Rhapta [Dar es-Salaam]. . . name[d] from the sewed boats (rhapton ploiarion) . . . in which there is ivory in great quantity, and tortoise-shell. Along this coast live men of piratical habits, very great in stature, and under separate chiefs for each place. . . . And these markets of Azania are the very last of the continent. . . .

Now the whole country of India has very many rivers, and very great ebb and flow of the tides. . . . Parts of the dry land are sea, and [parts are]. . . dry where ships were sailing just before; and the rivers, under the inrush of the flood tide, when the whole force of the sea is directed against them, are driven upwards more strongly against their natural current. . . .

The country inland . . . is inhabited by numerous tribes. . . . Above these is the very warlike nation of the Bactrians, who are under their own king. And Alexander, setting out from these parts, penetrated to the Ganges. . . . [T]o the present day ancient drachmae are current in Barygaza, coming from this country, bearing inscriptions in Greek letters, and the devices of those who reigned after Alexander. . . .

Inland from this place and to the east, is the city called Ozene [Ujjain]. . . . [F]rom this place are brought down all things needed for the welfare of the country. . . and many things for our trade: agate and carnelian, Indian muslins. . . .

There are imported into this market-town wine, Italian preferred, also Laodicean and Arabian; copper, tin, and lead; coral and topaz; thin clothing and inferior sorts of all kinds . . . gold and silver coin, on which there is a profit when exchanged for the money of the country. . . . And for the King there are brought into those places very costly vessels of silver, singing boys, beautiful maidens for the harem, fine wines, thin clothing of the finest weaves, and the choicest ointments. There are exported from these places [spices], ivory, agate and carnelian . . . cotton cloth of all kinds, silk cloth. . . .

[T]he adjoining coast extends in a straight line from north to south. . . . The inland country back from the coast toward the east comprises many desert regions and great mountains; and all kinds of wild beasts—leopards, tigers, elephants, enormous serpents, hyenas, and baboons of many sorts; and many populous nations, as far as the Ganges. . . .

Beyond this, the course trending toward the north, there are many barbarous tribes, among whom are the Cirrhadae, a race of men with flattened noses, very savage; another tribe, the Bargysi; and the Horse-faces and the Long-faces, who are said to be cannibals.

After these, the course turns toward the east again, and . . . [the] Ganges comes into view. . . . [J]ust opposite . . . there is an island in the ocean, the last part of the inhabited world toward the east, under the rising sun itself[,] . . . and it has the best tortoise-shell of all the places on the Erythraean Sea.

After this region under the very north, the sea outside ending in a land called This, there is a very great inland city called Thinae, from which raw silk and silk yarn and silk cloth are brought on foot. . . . But the land of This is not easy of access; few men come from there, and seldom.

*The Chinese traveler Xuanzang (600–664) journeyed across Inner Asia to India, making pilgrimage to Buddhist holy places and searching for Sanskrit scriptures to take back to China with him. His descriptions of the places he visited reflect his interests. The following passages come from his description of India.*

## Towns and Buildings

The towns and villages have inner gates; the walls are wide and high; the streets and lanes are tortuous, and the roads winding. The thoroughfares are dirty and the stalls arranged on both sides of the road with appropriate signs. Butchers, fishers, dancers, executioners, and scavengers, and so on, have their abodes without the city. In coming and going these persons are bound to keep on the left side of the road till they arrive at their homes. Their houses are surrounded by low walls, and form the suburbs. The earth being soft and muddy, the walls of the town are mostly built of brick or tiles. The towers on the walls are constructed of wood or bamboo; the houses have balconies and belvederes, which are made of wood, with a coating of lime or mortar, and covered with tiles. The different buildings have the same form as those in China: rushes, or dry branches, or tiles, or boards are used for covering them. The walls are covered with lime and mud, mixed with cow's dung for purity. At different seasons they scatter flowers about. Such are some of their different customs.

## Dress and Appearance

Their clothing is not cut or fashioned; they mostly affect fresh-white garments; they esteem little those of mixed color or ornamented. The men wind their garments round their middle, then gather them under the armpits, and let them fall down across the body, hanging to the right. The robes of the women fall down to the ground; they completely cover their shoulders. They wear a little knot of hair on their crowns, and let the rest of their hair fall loose. Some of the men cut off their moustaches, and have other odd customs. . . . In North India, where the air is cold, they wear short and close-fitting garments. . . . The dress and ornaments worn by the nonbelievers are varied and mixed. Some wear peacocks' feathers; some wear as ornaments necklaces made of skull bones; some have no clothing, but go naked; some wear leaf or bark garments; some pull out their hair and cut off their moustaches; others have bushy whiskers and their hair braided on the top of their heads. The costume is not uniform, and the color, whether red or white, not constant.

## QUESTIONS FOR ANALYSIS

1. How do the differing interests of a trader and a religious pilgrim show up in what they report?
2. How do these narratives show the influence of the countries the authors are coming from?
3. Given the different viewpoints of travelers, what is the value of travel accounts as sources for history?

*Source*: Samuel Beal, *Buddhist Records of the Western World, Translated from the Chinese of Hiuen Tsiang* (A.D. *629*) (London: Trubner and Company, 1884; reprint Delhi: Oriental Books Reprint Corporation, 1969), 73–76.

**Indian Ocean Sailing Vessel** Ships like this one, in a rock carving on the Buddhist temple of Borobodur in Java, probably carried colonists from Indonesia to Madagascar.

## Origins of Contact

By 2000 B.C.E. Sumerian records indicate regular trade between Mesopotamia, the islands of the Persian Gulf, Oman, and the Indus Valley. However, this early trading contact broke off, and later Mesopotamian trade references mention East Africa more often than India.

A similarly early chapter in Indian Ocean history concerns migrations from Southeast Asia to Madagascar, the world's fourth largest island, situated off the southeastern coast of Africa. About two thousand years ago, people from one of the many Indonesian islands of Southeast Asia established themselves in that forested, mountainous land 6,000 miles (9,500 kilometers) from home. They could not possibly have carried enough supplies for a direct voyage across the Indian Ocean, so their route must have touched the coasts of India and southern Arabia. No physical remains of their journeys have been discovered, however.

Apparently, the sailing canoes of these people plied the seas along the increasingly familiar route for several hundred years. Settlers farmed the new land and entered into relations with Africans who found their way across the 250-mile-wide (400-kilometer-wide) Mozambique (moe-zam-BEEK) Channel around the fifth century C.E. Descendants of the seafarers preserved the language of their homeland and some of its culture, such as the cultivation of bananas, yams, and other native Southeast Asian plants. These food crops spread to mainland Africa. But the memory of their distant origins gradually faded, not to be recovered until modern times, when scholars unraveled the linguistic link between the two lands.

## The Impact of Indian Ocean Trade

The demand for products from the coastal lands inspired mariners to persist in their long ocean voyages. Africa produced exotic animals, wood, and ivory. Since ivory also came from India, Mesopotamia, and North Africa, the extent of African ivory exports cannot be determined. The highlands of northern Somalia and southern Arabia grew the scrubby trees whose aromatic resins were valued as frankincense and myrrh. Pearls abounded in the Persian Gulf, and evidence of ancient copper mines has been found in Oman in southeastern Arabia. India shipped spices and manufactured goods, and more spices came from Southeast Asia, along with manufactured items, particularly pottery, obtained in trade with China. In sum, the Indian Ocean trading region had a great variety of highly valued products. Given the long distances and the comparative lack of islands, however, the volume of trade there was undoubtedly much lower than in the Mediterranean Sea.

The culture of the Indian Ocean ports was often isolated from the hinterlands, particularly in the west. The coasts of the Arabian peninsula, the African side of the Red Sea, southern Iran, and northern India (today's Pakistan) were mostly barren desert. Ports in all these areas tended to be small, and many suffered from meager supplies of fresh water. Farther south in India, the monsoon provided ample water, but steep mountains cut off the coastal plain from the interior of the country. Thus few ports between Zanzibar and Sri Lanka had substantial inland populations within easy reach. The head of the Persian Gulf was one exception: ship-borne trade was possible from the port of Apologus (the precursor of modern Basra) as far north as Babylon.

By contrast, eastern India, the Malay Peninsula, and Indonesia afforded more hospitable and densely populated shores with easier access to inland populations. Though the fishers, sailors, and traders of the western Indian Ocean system supplied a long series of kingdoms and empires, none of these consumer societies became primarily maritime in orientation, as the Greeks and Phoenicians did in the Mediterranean. In contrast, seaborne trade and influence seem to have been important even to the earliest states of Southeast Asia (see Chapter 6).

In coastal areas throughout the Indian Ocean system, small groups of seafarers sometimes had a significant social impact despite their usual lack of political power. Women seldom accompanied the men on long sea voyages, so sailors and merchants often married local women in port cities. The families thus established were bilingual and bicultural. As in many other situations in world history, women played a crucial though not well-documented role as media-

- The Indian Ocean Maritime System grew from the voyages of diverse seafaring traders.
- Unlike the Mediterranean, the Indian Ocean developed no network of colonies with home ties.
- The system originated in early Mesopotamian trade routes and the migration of Southeast Asian peoples to Madagascar.
- Trade in a broad range of goods flourished in ports where distinct cultures evolved.

tors between cultures. Not only did they raise their children to be more cosmopolitan than children from inland regions, but they also introduced the men to customs and attitudes that they carried with them when they returned to sea. As a consequence, the designation of specific seafarers as Persian, Arab, Indian, or Malay often conceals mixed heritages and a rich cultural diversity.

# ROUTES ACROSS THE SAHARA

■ *Why did trade begin across the Sahara Desert?*

The windswept Sahara, a desert stretching from the Red Sea to the Atlantic Ocean and broken only by the Nile River, isolates **sub-Saharan Africa** from the Mediterranean world (see Map 8.2). The current dryness of the Sahara dates only to about 2500 B.C.E. The period of drying out that preceded that date lasted twenty-five centuries and encompassed several cultural changes. During much of that time, travel between a slowly shrinking number of grassy areas was comparatively easy. However, by 300 B.C.E., scarcity of water was restricting travel to a few difficult routes initially known only to desert nomads. Trade over **trans-Saharan caravan routes**, at first only a trickle, eventually expanded into a significant stream.

**sub-Saharan Africa** Portion of the African continent lying south of the Sahara.

**trans-Saharan caravan routes** Trading network linking North Africa with sub-Saharan Africa across the Sahara.

**Map 8.2 Africa and the Trans-Saharan Trade Routes** The Sahara and the surrounding oceans isolated most of Africa from foreign contact before 1000 C.E. The Nile Valley, a few trading points on the east coast, and limited transdesert trade provided exceptions to this rule; but the dominant forms of sub-Saharan African culture originated far to the west, north of the Gulf of Guinea. © Cengage Learning

## Early Saharan Cultures

Sprawling sand dunes, sandy plains, and vast expanses of exposed rock make up most of the great desert. Stark and rugged mountain and highland areas separate its northern and southern portions. The cliffs and caves of these highlands, the last spots where water and grassland could be found as the climate changed, preserve rock paintings and engravings that constitute the primary evidence for early Saharan history.

Though dating is difficult, what appear to be the earliest images, left by hunters in much wetter times, depict elephants, giraffes, rhinoceroses, crocodiles, and other animals that have long been extinct in the region. Overlaps in the artwork indicate that the hunting societies were gradually joined by new cultures based on cattle breeding and well adapted to the sparse grazing that remained. Domestic cattle probably originated separately in northern Africa, western Asia, and southern Pakistan. They certainly reached the Sahara before it became completely dry. The beautiful paintings of cattle and scenes of daily life seen in the Saharan rock art depict pastoral societies that bear little similarity to any in western Asia. The people seem physically akin to today's West Africans, and the customs depicted, such as dancing and wearing masks, as well as the breeds of cattle, particularly those with piebald coloring (splotches of black and white), strongly suggest later societies to the south of the Sahara. These factors support the hypothesis that some southern cultural patterns originated in the Sahara.

Overlaps in artwork also show that horse herders succeeded the cattle herders. The rock art changes dramatically in style, from the superb realism of the cattle pictures to sketchier images that are often strongly geometric. Moreover, the horses are frequently shown drawing light chariots. According to the most common theory, intrepid charioteers from the Mediterranean shore drove their flimsy vehicles

Henri Lhote

**Cattle Herders in Saharan Rock Art** These paintings represent the most artistically accomplished type of Saharan art. Herding societies of modern times living in the Sahel region south of the Sahara strongly resemble the society depicted here.

across the desert and established societies in the few remaining grassy areas of the central Saharan highlands. Some scholars suggest possible chariot routes that refugees from the collapse of the Mycenaean and Minoan civilizations of Greece and Crete (see Chapter 2) might have followed deep into the desert in search of a new homeland somewhere to the south. Nevertheless, as with the cattle herders, the identity of the Saharan horse breeders and the source of their passion for drawing chariots remain a mystery. Only with the coming of the camel is it possible to make firm connections with the Saharan nomads of today through the depiction of objects and geometric patterns still used by the veiled, blue-robed Tuareg (TWAH-reg) people of the highlands in southern Algeria, Niger, and Mali.

Some historians maintain that the Romans inaugurated an important trans-Saharan trade, but they lack firm archaeological evidence. More plausibly, Saharan trade relates to the spread of camel domestication. Supporting evidence comes from rock art, where overlaps of images imply that camel riders in desert costume constitute the latest Saharan population. The camel-oriented images are decidedly the crudest to be found in the region.

The first mention of camels in North Africa comes in a Latin text of 46 B.C.E. Since the native camels of Africa probably died out before the era of domestication, the domestic animals most likely reached the Sahara from Arabia, probably by way of Egypt around 200 B.C.E. They could have been adopted by pastoral peoples farther to the west, from one central Saharan highland to the next, only much later spreading northward and coming to the attention of the Romans. Camel herding, which began in the northern Sahara around 300 C.E., made it easier for people to move away from the Saharan highlands and roam the deep desert.

### Trade Across the Sahara

Linkage between two different trading systems, one in the south, the other in the north, developed slowly. Southern traders concentrated on supplying salt from large deposits in the southern desert to the peoples of sub-Saharan Africa. Traders from the equatorial forest zone brought forest products, such as kola nuts (a condiment and source of

**SECTION REVIEW**

- Early Saharan cultures included hunting societies and, in isolated areas, groups of cattle breeders.
- Later, horse and camel herders joined these groups.
- Camel-riding nomads most likely pioneered the trans-Saharan trade routes, linking North African and sub-Saharan trade networks.

caffeine) and edible palm oil, to trading centers near the desert's southern fringe. Each group received the products they needed in their homelands from the other, or from the farming peoples of the **Sahel** (SAH-hel)—literally "the coast" in Arabic, the southern borderlands of the Sahara (see Map 8.2). Middlemen who were native to the Sahel played an important role in this trade, but precise historical details are lacking.

In the north, Roman colonists supplied Italy with agricultural products, primarily wheat and olives. Surviving mosaic pavements depicting scenes from daily life show that people living on the farms and in the towns of the interior consumed Roman manufactured goods and shared Roman styles. This northern pattern began to change only in the third century C.E. with the decline of the Roman Empire, the abandonment of many Roman farms, the growth of nomadism, and a lessening of trade across the Mediterranean.

## SUB-SAHARAN AFRICA

■ *What accounts for the substantial degree of cultural unity in Africa south of the Sahara?*

The Indian Ocean network and later trade across the Sahara provided sub-Saharan Africa, the portion of Africa south of the Sahara, with a few external contacts. The most important African network of cultural exchange from 300 B.C.E. to 1100 C.E., however, arose within the region and took the form of folk migration. These migrations and exchanges put in place enduring characteristics of African culture.

**Sahel** Belt south of the Sahara; literally "coastland" in Arabic.

## A Challenging Geography

Many geographic obstacles impede access to and movement within sub-Saharan Africa (see Map 8.2). The Sahara, the Atlantic and Indian Oceans, and the Red Sea form the boundaries of the region. With the exception of the Nile, a ribbon of green traversing the Sahara from south to north, the major river systems empty into oceans: the Senegal, Niger, and Zaire (zah-EER) Rivers empty into the Atlantic, and the Zambezi River empties into the Mozambique Channel of the Indian Ocean. Rapids limit the use of these rivers for navigation.

Stretching over 50 degrees of latitude, sub-Saharan Africa encompasses dramatically different environments. A 4,000-mile (6,500-kilometer) trek from the southern edge of the Sahara to the Cape of Good Hope would take a traveler from the flat, semi-arid **steppes** of the Sahel region to tropical **savanna** covered by long grasses and scattered forest, and then to **tropical rain forest** on the lower Niger and in the Zaire Basin. The rain forest gives way to another broad expanse of savanna, followed by more steppe and desert, and finally by a region of temperate highlands at the southern extremity, located as far south of the equator as Greece and Sicily are to its north. East-west travel is comparatively easy in the steppe and savanna regions—a caravan from Senegal to the Red Sea would have traversed a distance comparable to that of the Silk Road—but difficult in the equatorial rain-forest belt and across the mountains and deep rift valleys that abut the rain forest to the east and separate East from West Africa.

## The Development of Cultural Unity

Cultural heritages shared by the educated elites within each region of the world—heritages that some anthropologists call **"great traditions"**—typically include a written language, common legal and belief systems, ethical codes, and other intellectual attitudes. They loom large in written records as traditions that rise above the diversity of local customs and beliefs commonly distinguished as **"small traditions."**

By the year 1 C.E. sub-Saharan Africa had become a distinct cultural region, though one not shaped by imperial conquest or characterized by a shared elite culture, a "great tradition." The cultural unity of sub-Saharan Africa rested on similar characteristics shared to varying degrees by many popular cultures, or "small traditions." These had developed during the region's long period of isolation from the rest of the world after the drying up of the Sahara and had been refined, renewed, and interwoven by repeated episodes of migration and social interaction. Historians know little about this complex prehistory beyond the beginnings of ironworking and the spread of domesticated grains, such as pearl millet (from Mali) and teff (from Ethiopia), around the third millennium B.C.E. Thus, to a greater degree than in other regions, they call on anthropological descriptions, oral history, and comparatively late records of various "small traditions" to reconstruct the broad outlines of cultural formation.

Sub-Saharan Africa's cultural unity is less immediately apparent than its diversity. By one estimate, Africa is home to two thousand distinct languages, many corresponding to social and belief systems endowed with distinctive rituals and cosmologies. There are likewise numerous food production systems, ranging from hunting and gathering—very differently carried out by the Mbuti (m-BOO-tee) Pygmies of the equatorial rain forest and the Khoisan (KOI-sahn) peoples of the southwestern deserts—to the cultivation of bananas, yams, and other root crops in forest clearings and of sorghum, originally from Egypt, and millet in the savanna lands. Pastoral societies, particularly those depending on cattle, display somewhat less diversity across the Sahel and savanna belt from Senegal to Kenya. Equatorial regions have distinctive breeds of dwarf goats that are resistant to tsetse fly infection.

**steppe** An ecological region of grass- and shrub-covered plains that is treeless and too arid for agriculture.

**savanna** Tropical or subtropical grassland, either treeless or with occasional clumps of trees. Most extensive in sub-Saharan Africa but also present in South America.

**tropical rain forest** High-precipitation forest zones of the Americas, Africa, and Asia lying between the Tropic of Cancer and the Tropic of Capricorn.

**"great traditions"** Historians' term for a literate, well-institutionalized complex of religious and social beliefs and practices adhered to by diverse societies over a broad geographical area.

**"small traditions"** Historians' term for a localized, usually nonliterate, set of customs and beliefs adhered to by a single society, often in conjunction with a "great tradition."

Sub-Saharan Africa covered a larger and more diverse area than any other cultural region in the first millennium C.E. and had a lower overall population density. Thus societies and polities had ample room to form and reform, and a substantial amount of space separated different groups. The contacts that did occur did not last long enough to produce rigid cultural uniformity.

In addition, for centuries external conquerors could not penetrate the region's natural barriers and impose a uniform culture. The Egyptians occupied Nubia (see Chapter 3), and some traces of Egyptian influence appear in Saharan rock art farther west, but the Nile cataracts and the vast swampland in the Nile's upper reaches blocked movement farther south. The Romans sent expeditions against pastoral peoples living in the Libyan Sahara but could not incorporate them into the Roman world.

## African Cultural Characteristics

European travelers who got to know the sub-Saharan region well in the nineteenth and twentieth centuries observed broad commonalities underlying African life and culture. In agriculture, the common technique was cultivation by hoe and digging stick. Plows were never used despite an abundance of cattle in the Sahel. Musically, different groups of Africans played many instruments, especially types of drums, but common features, particularly in rhythm, gave African music as a whole a distinctive character. Music played an important role in social rituals, as did dancing and wearing masks, which often showed great artistry in their design.

African kingdoms varied, but kingship displayed common features, most notably the ritual isolation of the king himself. Fixed social categories—age groupings, kinship divisions, distinct gender roles and relations, and occupational groupings—also show resemblances from one region to another, even in societies too small to organize themselves into kingdoms. Though not hierarchical, these categories played a role similar to the divisions between noble, commoner, and slave prevalent where kings ruled. Such indications of cultural unity have led modern observers to identify a common African quality throughout most of the region, even though most sub-Saharan Africans themselves did not perceive it.

An eminent Belgian anthropologist, Jacques Maquet, has called this quality "Africanicity."

Some historians hypothesize that these common cultural features emanated from the peoples who once occupied the southern Sahara. In Paleolithic times, periods of dryness alternated with periods of wetness as the Ice Ages that locked up much of the world's fresh water in glaciers and icecaps came and went. When European glaciers receded with the waning of the last Ice Age, a storm belt brought increased wetness to the Saharan region. Rushing rivers scoured deep canyons. Now filled with fine sand, those canyons are easily visible on flights over the southern parts of the desert. As the glaciers receded farther, the storm belt moved northward to Europe, and dryness set in gradually after 5000 B.C.E. As a consequence, runs the hypothesis, the region's population migrated southward, becoming increasingly concentrated in the Sahel, which may have been the initial incubation center for Pan-African cultural patterns.

Increasing dryness and the resulting difficulty in supporting the population would have driven some people out of this core into more sparsely settled lands to the east, west, and south. In a parallel development farther to the east, migration away from the growing aridity of the desert seems to have contributed to the settling of the Nile Valley and the emergence of the Old Kingdom of Egypt (see Chapter 1). Local populations that were originally cattle herders around one lake in what is now waterless desert had, by the seventh millennium, developed large villages with deep wells and sorghum and millet cultivation. The fifth millennium witnessed the construction there of an astronomically oriented ring of stones two thousand years older than Stonehenge (see Chapter 1), along with a cattle cult featuring animals buried in stone-built chambers, which is a likely precursor to the cult of cattle worship in dynastic Egypt.

## The Advent of Iron and the Bantu Migrations

Archaeology confirms that agriculture had become common between the equator and the Sahara by the early second millennium B.C.E. It then spread southward, displacing hunting and gathering as a way of life. Moreover, botanical evidence indicates that banana trees, probably introduced to southeastern

Africa from Southeast Asia, made their way north and west, retracing in the opposite direction the presumed migration routes of early agriculturists.

Archaeologists also uncovered traces of copper mining in the Sahara from the early first millennium B.C.E. Copper appears in the Niger Valley somewhat later and in the Central African copper belt after 400 C.E. Most important of all, iron smelting began in northern sub-Saharan Africa in the early first millennium C.E. and spread southward from there.

Many historians believe that the secret of smelting iron, which requires very high temperatures, was discovered only once, by the Hittites of Anatolia (modern Turkey) around 1500 B.C.E. (see Chapter 2). If that is the case, it is hard to explain how iron smelting reached sub-Saharan Africa. The earliest evidence of ironworking from the kingdom of Meroë, situated on the upper Nile and in cultural contact with Egypt, is no earlier than the evidence from West Africa (northern Nigeria). Even less plausible than the Nile Valley as a route of technological diffusion is the idea of a spread southward from Phoenician settlements in North Africa, since archaeological evidence has failed to substantiate the vague Greek and Latin accounts of Phoenician excursions to the south. A more plausible scenario focuses on Africans' discovering for themselves how to smelt iron. Some historians suggest that they might have done so while firing pottery in kilns. No firm evidence exists to prove or disprove this theory.

Linguistic analysis provides the strongest evidence of extensive contacts among sub-Saharan Africans in the first millennium C.E.—and offers suggestions about the spread of iron. More than three hundred languages spoken south of the equator belong to the branch of the Niger-Congo family known as **Bantu**, after the word meaning "people" in most of the languages.

The distribution of the Bantu languages both north and south of the equator is consistent with a divergence beginning in the first millennium B.C.E. By comparing core words common to most of the languages, linguists have drawn some conclusions about the original Bantu-speakers, whom they call "proto-Bantu." These people engaged in fishing, using canoes, nets, lines, and hooks. They lived in permanent villages on the edge of the rain forest, where they

## SECTION REVIEW

- An environmentally diverse region, sub-Saharan Africa includes many barriers to travel and communication.
- Sub-Saharan Africa achieved a cultural unity of similar "small traditions."
- Shared characteristics include agricultural methods, approaches to music, forms of kingship, and fixed social categories.
- The likely mechanism of this unity was the Bantu migrations, which were also responsible for the spread of iron smelting throughout sub-Saharan Africa.

grew yams and grains and harvested wild palm nuts from which they pressed oil. They possessed domesticated goats, dogs, and perhaps other animals. They made pottery and cloth. Linguists surmise that the proto-Bantu homeland was near the modern boundary of Nigeria and Cameroon.

Because the presumed home of the proto-Bantu lies near the known sites of early iron smelting, migration by Bantu-speakers seems a likely mechanism for the southward spread of iron. The migrants probably used iron axes and hoes to hack out forest clearings and plant crops. According to this scenario, their actions would have established an economic basis for new societies capable of sustaining much denser populations than could earlier societies dependent on hunting and gathering alone. Thus the period from 500 B.C.E. to 1000 C.E. saw a substantial transfer of Bantu traditions and practices southward, eastward, and westward and their transformation, through intermingling with preexisting societies, into Pan-African traditions and practices.

## THE SPREAD OF IDEAS

■ *Why do some goods and ideas travel more easily than others?*

Ideas, like social customs, religious attitudes, and artistic styles, can spread along trade routes and through folk migrations. In both cases, documenting

**Bantu** Collective name of a large group of sub-Saharan African languages and of the peoples speaking these languages.

the dissemination of ideas, particularly in preliterate societies, poses a difficult historical problem.

## Ideas and Material Evidence

Historians know about some ideas only through the survival of written sources. Other ideas do not depend on writing but are inherent in material objects studied by archaeologists and anthropologists. Customs surrounding the eating of pork are a case in point. Scholars disagree about whether pigs became domestic in only one place, from which the practice of pig keeping spread elsewhere, or whether several peoples hit on the same idea at different times and in different places.

Southeast Asia was an important early center of pig domestication. Anthropological studies tell us that the eating of pork became highly ritualized in this area and that it was sometimes allowed only on ceremonial occasions. On the other side of the Indian Ocean, wild swine were common in the Nile swamps of ancient Egypt. There, too, pigs took on a sacred role, being associated with the evil god Set, and eating them was prohibited. The biblical prohibition on the Israelites' eating pork, echoed later by the Muslims, probably came from Egypt in the second millennium B.C.E.

In a third locale in eastern Iran, an archaeological site dating from the third millennium B.C.E. provides evidence of another religious taboo relating to pork. Although the area around the site was swampy and home to many wild pigs, not a single pig bone has been found. Yet small pig figurines seem to have been used as symbolic religious offerings, and the later Iranian religion associates the boar with an important god.

What accounts for the apparent connection between domestic pigs and religion in these far-flung areas? There is no way of knowing. It has been hypothesized that pigs were first domesticated in Southeast Asia by people who had no herd animals—sheep, goats, cattle, or horses—and who relied on fish for most of their animal protein. The pig therefore became a special animal to them. The practice of pig raising, along with religious beliefs and rituals associated with the consumption of pork, could conceivably have spread from Southeast Asia along the maritime routes of the Indian Ocean, eventually reaching Iran and Egypt. But no evidence survives to support this hypothesis. In this case, therefore, material evidence

**Gandharan Sculpture**   The art of Gandhara in northwest Pakistan featured Hellenistic styles and techniques borrowed from the cities founded by Alexander the Great in Afghanistan. Though much Gandharan art is Buddhist in spirit, this fourth-century C.E. image of a flower-bearer is strongly Greek in the naturalistic treatment of the head and left arm.   Erich Lessing/Art Resource, NY

can only hint at the spread of religious ideas, leaving the door open for other explanations.

A more certain example of objects indicating the spread of an idea is the practice of hammering a carved die onto a piece of precious metal and using the resulting coin as a medium of exchange. From its origin in the Lydian kingdom in Anatolia in the first millennium B.C.E. (see Chapter 4), the idea of trading by means of struck coinage spread rapidly to Europe, North Africa, and India. Was the low-value copper coinage of China, made by pouring molten metal into a mold, also inspired by this practice from far away? It may have been, but it might also derive from indigenous Chinese metalworking.

## The Spread of Buddhism

While material objects associated with religious beliefs and rituals are important indicators of

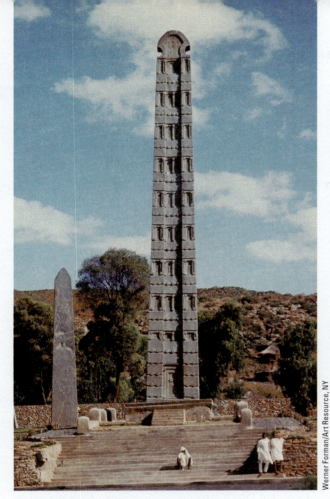

One such traveler was the Chinese pilgrim Faxian (fah-shee-en) (died between 418 and 423 C.E.), who left a written account of his travels. Faxian began his trip in the company of a Chinese envoy to an unspecified ruler or people in Central Asia. After traveling from one Buddhist site to another across Afghanistan and India, he reached Sri Lanka, a Buddhist land, where he lived for two years. He then embarked for China on a merchant ship with two hundred men aboard. A storm drove the ship to Java, which he chose not to describe since it was Hindu rather than Buddhist. After five months ashore, Faxian finally reached China on another ship.

Less reliable accounts make reference to missionaries traveling to Syria, Egypt, and Macedonia, as well as to Southeast Asia. One of Ashoka's sons allegedly led a band of missionaries to Sri Lanka. Later, his sister brought a company of nuns there, along with a branch of the sacred Bo tree under which the Buddha had received enlightenment. At the same time, there are reports of other monks traveling to Burma, Thailand, and Sumatra. Ashoka's missionaries may also have reached Tibet by way of trade routes across the Himalayas.

The different lands that received the story and teachings of the Buddha preserved or adapted them in different ways. Theravada Buddhism, "Teachings of the Elder," was centered in Sri Lanka. Holding closely to the Buddha's earliest teachings, it maintained that the goal of religion, available only to monks, is nirvana, the total absence of suffering and the end of the cycle of rebirth (see Chapter 6). This teaching contrasted with Mahayana, or "Great Vehicle" Buddhism, which stressed the goal of becoming a bodhisattva, a person who attains nirvana but chooses to remain in human company to help and guide others.

**The Spread of Christianity**   The post-Roman development of Christianity in Europe is discussed in Chapter 10. The Christian faith enjoyed an earlier spread in Asia and Africa before its confrontation with Islam (described in Chapter 9). Jerusalem in Palestine, Antioch in Syria, and Alexandria in Egypt became centers of Christian authority soon after the crucifixion, but the spread of Christianity to Armenia and Ethiopia illustrates the connections between religion, trade, and imperial politics.

**Stele of Aksum** This 70-foot (21-meter) stone is the tallest remnant of a field of steles, or standing stones, marking the tombs of Aksumite kings. The carvings of doors, windows, and beam ends imitate common features of Aksumite architecture, suggesting that each stele symbolized a multistory royal palace. The largest steles date from the fourth century C.E.

the spread of spiritual ideas, written sources deal with the spread of today's major religions. Buddhism grew to become, with Christianity and Islam (see Chapter 9), one of the most popular and widespread religions in the world. In all three cases, the religious ideas spread without dependency on a single ethnic or kinship group.

King Ashoka, the Mauryan ruler of India (see Chapter 6), and Kanishka, the greatest king of the Kushans who ruled northern Afghanistan between 100 B.C.E. and 300 C.E., strongly promoted Buddhism; but the monks, missionaries, and pilgrims of various ethnicities who crisscrossed India, followed the Silk Road, or took ships on the Indian Ocean played a greater role in bringing the Buddha's teachings to Southeast Asia, China, Korea, and ultimately Japan (see Map 8.1).

Situated in eastern Anatolia (modern Turkey), **Armenia** served recurrently as a battleground between Iranian states to the south and east and Mediterranean states to the west. Each imperial power wanted to control this region so close to the frontier where Silk Road traders met their Mediterranean counterparts. In Parthian times, Armenia's kings favored Zoroastrianism (see Chapter 4). The invention of an Armenian alphabet in the early fifth century opened the way to a wider spread of Christianity. The Iranians did not give up domination easily, but within a century the Armenian Apostolic Church had become the center of cultural life.

Far to the south Christians similarly sought to outflank Iran. The Christian emperors in Constantinople (see Chapter 5) sent missionaries along the Red Sea trade route to seek converts in Yemen and **Ethiopia**. In the fourth century C.E. a Syrian philosopher traveling with two young relatives sailed to India. On the way back the ship docked at a Red Sea port occupied by Ethiopians from the prosperous kingdom of Aksum. Being then at odds with the Romans, the Ethiopians killed everyone on board except the two boys, Aedisius—who later narrated this story—and Frumentius. Impressed by their learning, the king made the former his cupbearer and the latter his treasurer and secretary.

When the king died, his wife urged Frumentius to govern Aksum on her behalf and that of her infant son, Ezana. As regent, Frumentius sought out Roman Christians among the merchants who visited the country and helped them establish Christian communities. When he became king, Ezana, who may have become a Christian, permitted Aedisius and Frumentius to return to Syria. The patriarch of Alexandria, on learning about the progress of Christianity in Aksum, elevated Frumentius to the rank of bishop, though he had not previously been a clergyman, and sent him back to Ethiopia as the first leader of its church.

The spread of Christianity into Nubia, the land south of Egypt along the Nile River, proceeded from Ethiopia rather than Egypt. Politically and economically, Ethiopia became a power at the western end of the Indian Ocean trading system, occasionally even extending its influence across the Red Sea and asserting itself in Yemen (see Map 8.2).

## SECTION REVIEW

- Material evidence can only offer hints about the spread of some ideas.
- Material and documentary evidence show the spread of Buddhism from India along the land and sea trade routes to elsewhere in Asia.
- Lands in which Buddhism took hold adapted its teachings in different ways, a process that resulted in the split between Mahayana and Theravada.
- Christianity spread through a combination of trade and imperial politics, with significant Christian societies emerging in Armenia and Ethiopia.

## CONCLUSION

The growing networks of transportation and trade that developed in the third century B.C.E. linked societies and cultures throughout the Eastern Hemisphere. Merchants and pilgrims were the first to pioneer connections across long distances and often forbidding terrains, such as across Central Asia, the Himalayas, or the Sahara Desert. Due to the cost of travel, merchants could only carry items of great value and small bulk, such as silk and precious metals. But they also brought animals, such as camels, that could withstand the trip. Seeds of useful plants, agricultural products, and new technologies were spread by traders. The Bantu, for example, spread metallurgy, as well other cultural forms such as the Bantu languages, far and wide in sub-Saharan Africa and, unlike other traders, also brought a degree of cultural dominance that strongly affected later African history.

Christianity and Buddhism also spread along trade routes, at least to some degree, and gave rise to new forms of cultural diversity even as overall doctrinal unity made these religions dominant. As "great traditions," the new faiths based on conversion linked priests, monks, nuns, and religious scholars across vast distances. However, these same religions merged with myriad "small traditions" to provide for the social and spiritual needs of peoples living in many lands under widely varying circumstances.

In short, in the last centuries before the Common Era, travel and commerce increasingly brought together the various parts of Eurasia and Africa and their once-separate cultures and civilizations.

**Armenia** One of the earliest Christian kingdoms, situated in eastern Anatolia and the western Caucasus and occupied by speakers of the Armenian language.

**Ethiopia** East African highland nation lying east of the Nile River.

# CHAPTER REVIEW

## THE SILK ROAD
- *What factors contributed to the growth of trade along the Silk Road?* (page 187)

Occasional contacts across the heart of Asia undoubtedly occurred for many centuries before the Silk Road regularized communication. Cooperative relations between caravan traders and pastoral nomads in the Central Asian grasslands were the key to this regularization. The fact that the Parthian rulers of Iran were themselves of nomadic origin and shared customs with steppe nomads played an important role. Chinese eagerness for western products, especially horses, and Greek, and later Roman, desire for Chinese silk, plus the interest east and west in agricultural and metal products, such as bridles, stirrups, and weapons for military use, made for a prosperous trade for Central Asian nomads and pastoralists, as well as all those who bought and sold goods in market towns along the Silk Road.

## THE INDIAN OCEAN MARITIME SYSTEM
- *How did geography affect Indian Ocean trade routes?* (page 190)

Maritime trade in general is strongly affected by such things as wind patterns, the presence of islands, and good seaports. The monsoon system in particular determined the seasons of trade across the Indian Ocean. In addition, coastal areas that had ample water supplies and easy communications with inland markets and population centers developed different relations with sea traders than did regions where coastal deserts were cut off from the interior by mountains.

## ROUTES ACROSS THE SAHARA
- *Why did trade begin across the Sahara Desert?* (page 195)

The beginnings of trade across the barren wastes of the Sahara bear comparison with the Silk Road and Indian Ocean trade. Political and economic contacts between pastoral nomads who supplied caravan animals played an important role, but trade was also influenced by the location of markets on both northern and southern sides, as well as the connections those markets had with suppliers and consumers farther away from the desert.

## SUB-SAHARAN AFRICA
- *What accounts for the substantial degree of cultural unity in Africa south of the Sahara?* (page 198)

The Sahara changed over time from a verdant state to one of exceptional dryness. This change forced cattle-herding peoples who lived in the areas that were drying up to move southward. This movement, in turn, contributed to the widespread migrations of Bantu-speaking peoples. Their shared linguistic and cultural characteristics led to a high degree of cultural similarity despite the fact that the various migrating groups settled in places that were not so close together as to encourage complex political developments stretching over large parts of the continent.

## THE SPREAD OF IDEAS
- *Why do some goods and ideas travel more easily than others?* (page 201)

The Bantu migrations contrast with contacts made along trade routes in terms of the sorts of cultural characteristics that enjoy wide geographic spread. Migrating in groups, the Bantu were able to maintain their social structures and rituals along with their techniques of agriculture and metal using. Along overland and seaborne trade routes where the number of travelers was comparatively small, on the other hand, the social practices of the merchants had less influence than the good they carried, which were often highly prized. To be sure, religious missionaries often traveled by caravan or ship, but the doctrines they preached seldom fully replaced earlier religions.

## Key Terms

Silk Road (p. 187)

Parthians (p. 189)

Indian Ocean Maritime System (p. 191)

sub-Saharan Africa (p. 195)

trans-Saharan caravan routes (p. 195)

Sahel (p. 198)

steppes (p. 199)

savanna (p. 199)

tropical rain forest (p. 199)

"great traditions" (p. 199)

"small traditions" (p. 199)

Bantu (p. 201)

Armenia (p. 204)

Ethiopia (p. 204)

# The Sasanid Empire and the Rise of Islam

© Cengage Learning

A technology we take for granted, paper-making, was originally invented in China. After Arab conquests in the seventh century C.E. established an Islamic caliphate stretching from Spain to Central Asia, knowledge of papermaking spread from China to the Middle East. Paper provided a medium that was superior to papyrus and parchment and well suited to a variety of purposes. Maps, miniature paintings, and, of course, books became increasingly common and inexpensive. With cheaper books came bookstores, and one of the most informative manuscripts of the period of the Islamic caliphate is a *Fihrist*, or descriptive catalogue, of the books sold at one bookstore in Baghdad.

Abu al-Faraj Muhammad al-Nadim, a man with good connections at the caliph's court, compiled the catalogue, though his father probably founded the bookstore. Its latest entry dates to ca. 990, al-Nadim's death date. Superbly educated, al-Nadim wrote such well-informed comments on books and authors that his catalogue presents a detailed survey of the intellectual world of Baghdad.

The first of the *Fihrist*'s ten books deals with Arabic language and sacred scriptures: the Quran, the Torah, and the Gospel. The second covers Arabic grammar, and the third writings from people connected with the caliph's court: historians, government officials, singers, jesters, and the ruler's boon companions. *Al-Nadim* means "boon companion," so it is assumed that the author knew this milieu well. After dealing with Arabic poetry, Muslim sects, and Islamic law in Books 3 through 6, he comes to Greek philosophy, science, and medicine in Book 7.

Most things we would find today in a bookstore are relegated to the final three chapters. Book 8 divides into three sections, the first being "Story Tellers and Stories." Here he lists a Persian book called *A Thousand Stories*, which in translation became *The Arabian Nights*. Al-Nadim's version no

longer survives; the collection we have today comes from a manuscript written five hundred years later.

Then come books about "Exorcists, Jugglers, and Magicians," followed by "Miscellaneous Subjects and Fables." These include books on "Freckles, Twitching, Moles, and Shoulders," "Horsemanship, Bearing of Arms, the Implements of War," "Veterinary Surgery," "Birds of Prey, Sport with Them and Medical Care of Them," "Interpretation of Dreams," "Perfume," "Cooked Food," "Poisons," and "Amulets and Charms."

Non-Muslim sects and foreign lands—India, Indochina, and China—fill Book 9, leaving Book 10 for a few final notes on philosophers not mentioned previously.

All together, the thousands of titles and authors commented on by al-Nadim provide both a panorama of what interested book buyers in tenth-century Baghdad and a saddening picture of how profound the loss of knowledge has been since that glorious era.

**Baghdad Bookstore**  With the advent of papermaking, manufacturing books became increasingly common and inexpensive. As a result, bookstores also became more common. Notice how books are shelved on their sides in wall cubicles.

# THE SASANID EMPIRE, 224–651

■ *How did the Sasanid Empire evolve under the influence of east-west trade?*

The rise in the third century of a new Iranian state, the **Sasanid** (SAH-suh-nid) **Empire**, continued the old rivalry between Rome and the Parthians along the Euphrates frontier. However, behind this façade of continuity, a social and economic transformation took place that set the stage for a new and powerful religiopolitical movement: Islam.

## Politics and Society

Ardashir, a descendant of an ancestor named Sasan, defeated the Parthians around 224 and established the Sasanid kingdom. The new rulers confronted the Romans, whom later historians frequently refer to as the Byzantines after about 330. The rival empires launched numerous attacks on each other between the 340s and 628, but in times of peace, the empires flourished, allowing goods transported over the Silk Road to enter the Mediterranean.

The Sasanid and Byzantine Empires were alike in maintaining central control of imperial finances and military power. The political hinterlands of the mountains and plateaus of Iran proper were often ruled by the cousins of the shah (king) or by powerful families descending from the pre-Sasanid Parthian nobility. Each empire also found effective ways of integrating frontier peoples as mercenaries or caravaneers. There were differences, however. Despite the dominance of aristocratic families, long-lasting political fragmentation of the medieval European variety (see Chapter 10) did not develop in the Sasanid Empire. Also, although many nomads lived in the mountain and desert regions, no folk migrations took place comparable to that of the Germanic peoples who defeated Roman armies and established kingdoms in formerly Roman territory from about the third century C.E. on.

Cities were small walled communities that served more as military strong-points than as centers of population and production. Sasanid silver work and silk fabrics testify to the sumptuous lifestyle of the warrior elite. Society revolved around a local aristocracy that lived on rural estates and cultivated the arts of hunting, feasting, and war just like the warriors described in the sagas of ancient kings and heroes sung at their banquets.

The Silk Road brought many new crops to Mesopotamia. Sasanid farmers pioneered in planting cot-

> **Sasanid Empire** Iranian empire, established around 224, with a capital in Ctesiphon, Mesopotamia. The Sasanid emperors established Zoroastrianism as the state religion. Islamic Arab armies overthrew the empire around 651.

**Sasanid Silver Plate with Gold Decoration** The Sasanid aristocracy, based in the countryside, invested part of its wealth in silver plates and vessels. This image of a Sasanid king hunting on horseback also reflects a favorite aristocratic pastime. Erich Lessing/Art Resource, NY

# Chronology

| | The Arab Lands | Iran and Central Asia |
|---|---|---|
| 200 | 570–632 Life of the Prophet Muhammad | 224–651 Sasanid Empire |
| 600 | 634 Conquests of Iraq and Syria commence<br>639–642 Conquest of Egypt by Arabs<br>656–661 Ali caliph; first civil war<br>661–750 Umayyad Caliphate rules from Damascus | Before 1000 B.C.E. Beginning of migrations from mainland Southeast Asia to islands in Pacific and Indian Oceans |
| 700 | 711 Berbers and Arabs invade Spain from North Africa<br>750 Beginning of Abbasid Caliphate<br>755 Umayyad state established in Spain<br>776–809 Caliphate of Harun al-Rashid | 711 Arabs capture Sind in India<br>747 Abbasid revolt begins in Khurasan |
| 800 | 835–892 Abbasid capital moved from Baghdad to Samarra | 875 Independent Samanid state founded in Bukhara |
| 900 | 909 Fatimids seize North Africa, found Shi'ite Caliphate<br>929 Abd al-Rahman III declares himself caliph in Cordoba<br>945 Shi'ite Buyids take control in Baghdad<br>969 Fatimids conquer Egypt | 945 Buyids from northern Iran take control of Abbasid Caliphate |
| 1000 | 1055 Seljuk Turks take control in Baghdad<br>1099 First Crusade captures Jerusalem<br>1171 Fall of Fatimid Egypt<br>1187 Saladin recaptures Jerusalem<br>1250 Mamluks control Egypt<br>1258 Mongols sack Baghdad and end Abbasid Caliphate<br>1260 Mamluks defeat Mongols at Ain Jalut | 1036 Beginning of Turkish Seljuk rule in Khurasan |

ton, sugar cane, rice, citrus trees, eggplants, and other crops adopted from India and China. Although the acreage devoted to new crops increased slowly, these products became important consumption and trade items during the succeeding Islamic period.

## Religion and Empire

Religion permeated all aspects of community life. Most subjects of the Byzantine emperors and Sasanid shahs identified themselves first and foremost as members of a religious community. Their schools and law courts were religious, they looked on religious leaders as moral guides in daily life, and most books discussed religious subjects. In some areas, priests represented their flocks even in such secular matters as tax collection. The establishment of the Zoroastrian

faith (see Chapter 4) as a state religion similar to Christianity in the Byzantine Empire (see Chapter 10) marked the fresh emergence of religion as an instrument of politics both within and between the empires.

Both Zoroastrianism and Christianity practiced intolerance. A late-third-century inscription in Iran boasts of the persecutions of Christians, Jews, and Buddhists carried out by the Zoroastrian high priest. Yet sizable Christian and Jewish communities remained, especially in Mesopotamia. Similarly, from the fourth century onward, councils of Christian bishops declared many theological beliefs heretical—so unacceptable that they were un-Christian.

Christians became pawns in the political rivalry with the Byzantines and were sometimes persecuted, sometimes patronized, by the Sasanid kings. In 431 a council of bishops called by the Byzantine emperor declared the Nestorian Christians heretics for over-emphasizing the humanness of Christ. The Nestori-ans believed that human characteristics and divinity coexisted in Jesus and that Mary was not the mother of God, as many other Christians maintained, but the mother of the human Jesus. After the bishops' ruling, the Nestorians sought refuge under the Sasanid shah and eventually extended their missionary activities along the Central Asian trade routes.

A parallel episode within Zoroastrianism trans-pired in the third century when Mani, preaching a faith theologically derived from Zoroastrianism—a dualistic struggle between Good and Evil—founded a new religion in Mesopotamia: Manichaeism. Although at first Mani enjoyed the favor of the shah, he and many of his followers were martyred in 276. His religion survived and spread widely, particularly along the Silk Road but also into North Africa and Europe. Nestorian missionaries competed with Man-ichaean missionaries for converts in Central Asia.

The Arabs became enmeshed in this web of reli-gious conflict. Along their Euphrates frontier, the Sasanids subsidized nomadic Arab chieftains to pro-tect their empire from invasion. The Byzantines did the same with Arabs on their Jordanian frontier. The border protectors for the Byzantines adopted a Mono-physite theology, which emphasized Christ's divine nature; the allies of the Sasanids, the Nestorian faith. Even in the interior deserts, Semitic polytheism, with its worship of natural forces and celestial bodies, began to encounter the religiopolitical ideas of the Sasanid and Byzantine Empires. These ideas would contribute to the subsequent rise of Islam and a new political empire based on religion.

## SECTION REVIEW

- The Sasanids overthrew the Parthians and continued their predecessors' rivalry with Rome.
- Sasanid farmers pioneered the cultivation of Silk Road crops. Sasanid kings made Zoroastrianism the state religion, and other religions, particularly Christianity, experienced both toleration and persecution.
- Diverse religious ideas spread and competed, especially along the Silk Road and in the Arab border areas.

# THE ORIGINS OF ISLAM

■ *How did the traditions and religious views of pre-Islamic peoples become integrated into the culture shaped by Islam?*

The Arabs of 600 C.E. lived exclusively in the Arabian peninsula and on the desert fringes of Syria, Jordan, and Iraq. Outside the Euphrates and Jordanian fron-tiers where Arabs protected the Sasanid and Byzan-tine Empires, respectively, Arab pastoralists remained isolated and independent, seldom engaging the attention of the shahs and emperors. It was far-ther to the south in these interior Arabian lands that the religion of Islam took form.

## The Arabian Peninsula Before Muhammad

Throughout history more people living on the Arabian peninsula have subsisted as farmers than as pastoral nomads. Farming villages supported the compara-tively dense population of Yemen, where abundant rainfall waters the highlands during the spring monsoon, and small inlets along the southern coast favored fishing and trading communities. But the enormous sea of sand known as the "Empty Quarter" isolated many southern regions from the Arabian interior. In the seventh century, most people in south-ern Arabia knew more about Africa, India, and the Persian Gulf than about the forbidding interior and the scattered camel- and sheep-herding nomads who lived there.

Caravan trading provided a rare link among peoples. Nomads derived income from providing camels, guides, and safe passage to merchants bring-ing the primary product of the south, the aromatic resins frankincense and myrrh, to northern custom-ers. Return caravans brought manufactured products from Mesopotamia and Syria.

Nomad dominance of the caravan trade received a boost from the invention of militarily efficient camel saddles. This invention contributed to the rise of Arab-dominated caravan cities and to Arab pastoral-ists becoming the primary suppliers of animal power throughout the region. By 600 C.E., wheeled vehicles—mostly ox carts and horse-drawn chariots—had all but disappeared from the Middle East, replaced by camels and donkeys.

**Mecca**, a late-blooming caravan city, occupies a barren mountain valley halfway between Yemen and Syria and somewhat inland from the Red Sea coast. A nomadic kin group known as the Quraysh (koo-RAYSH) settled in Mecca in the fifth century and assumed control of trade. Mecca rapidly achieved a measure of prosperity, partly because it was too far from Byzantine Syria, Sasanid Iraq, and Ethiopian-controlled Yemen for them to attack it.

A cubical shrine with idols inside called the Ka'ba (KAH-buh), a holy well called Zamzam, and a sacred precinct surrounding the two wherein killing was prohibited contributed to the emergence of Mecca as a pilgrimage site. Some Meccans associated the shrine with stories known to Jews and Christians. They regarded Abraham (Ibrahim in Arabic) as the builder of the Ka'ba, and they identified a site outside Mecca as the location where God asked Abraham to sacrifice his son. The son was not Isaac (Ishaq in Arabic), the son of Sarah, but Ishmael (Isma'il in Arabic), the son of Hagar, cited in the Bible as the forefather of the Arabs.

## Muhammad in Mecca

Born in Mecca in 570, **Muhammad** grew up an orphan in the house of his uncle. He engaged in trade and married a Quraysh widow named Khadija (kah-DEE-juh), whose caravan interests he superintended. Their son died in childhood, but several daughters survived. Around 610 Muhammad began meditating at night in the mountainous terrain around Mecca. During one night vigil, known to later tradition as the "Night of Power and Excellence," a being whom Muhammad later understood to be the angel Gabriel (Jibra'il in Arabic) spoke to him:

> Proclaim! In the name of your Lord who created. Created man from a clot of congealed blood. Proclaim! And your Lord is the Most Bountiful. He who has taught by the pen. Taught man that which he knew not.[1]

For three years Muhammad shared this and subsequent revelations only with close friends and family. This period culminated in his conviction that he was hearing the words of God (Allah [AH-luh] in Arabic). Khadija, his uncle's son Ali, his friend Abu Bakr (ah-boo BAK-uhr), and others close to him shared this conviction. The revelations continued until Muhammad's death in 632.

Like most people of the time, including Christians and Jews, the Arabs believed in unseen spirits: gods, demonic *shaitans*, and desert spirits called *jinns* who were thought to possess seers and poets. Therefore, when Muhammad recited his rhymed revelations in public, many people believed he was inspired by an unseen spirit, even if it was not, as Muhammad asserted, the one true god.

Muhammad's earliest revelations called on people to witness that one god had created the universe and everything in it, including themselves. At the end of time, their souls would be judged, their sins balanced against their good deeds. The blameless would go to paradise; the sinful would taste hellfire:

> By the night as it conceals the light;
> By the day as it appears in glory;
> By the mystery of the creation of male and female;
> Verily, the ends ye strive for are diverse.
> So he who gives in charity and fears God,
> And in all sincerity testifies to the best,
> We will indeed make smooth for him the path to Bliss.
> But he who is a greedy miser and thinks himself self-sufficient,
> And gives the lie to the best,
> We will indeed make smooth for him the path to misery.[2]

The revelation called all people to submit to God and accept Muhammad as the last of his messengers. Doing so made one a **Muslim**, meaning one who makes "submission," **Islam**, to the will of God.

[2]Quran. Sura 92, verses 1–10.

**Mecca**  City in western Arabia; birthplace of the Prophet Muhammad and ritual center of the Islamic religion.

**Muhammad**  Arab prophet (570–632 C.E.); founder of religion of Islam.

**Muslim**  An adherent of the Islamic religion; a person who "submits" (in Arabic, *Islam* means "submission") to the will of God.

**Islam**  Religion expounded by the Prophet Muhammad on the basis of his reception of divine revelations, which were collected after his death into the Quran. In the tradition of Judaism and Christianity, and sharing much of their lore, Islam calls on all people to recognize one creator god—Allah—who rewards or punishes believers after death according to how they led their lives.

[1]Quran. Sura 96, verses 1–5.

Because earlier messengers mentioned in the revelations included Noah, Moses, and Jesus, Muhammad's hearers connected his message with Judaism and Christianity, religions they were already familiar with. Yet his revelations charged the Jews and Christians with being negligent in preserving God's revealed word. Thus, even though they identified Abraham/Ibrahim, whom Muslims consider the first Muslim, as the builder of the Ka'ba (which superseded Jerusalem as the focus of Muslim prayer in 624), Muhammad's followers considered his revelation more perfect than the Bible because it had not gone through an editing process.

Some scholars maintain that Muhammad appealed especially to people distressed over wealth replacing kinship as the most important aspect of social relations and over neglect of orphans and other powerless people. Most Muslims, however, put less emphasis on a social message than on the power and beauty of Muhammad's recitations.

### Formation of the Umma

Fearing that accepting Muhammad as the sole agent of the one true God would threaten their power and prosperity, Mecca's leaders pressured his kin to disavow him and persecuted the weakest of his followers. Stymied by this hostility, Muhammad and his followers fled Mecca in 622 to take up residence in the agricultural community of **Medina** 215 miles (346 kilometers) to the north. This hijra (HIJ-ruh)—Mohammad's journey from Mecca to Medina—marks the beginning of the Muslim calendar.

Prior to the hijra, Medinan representatives had met with Muhammad and agreed to accept and protect him and his followers because they saw him as an inspired leader who could calm their perpetual feuding. Together, the Meccan migrants and major groups in Medina bound themselves into a single **umma** (UM-muh), a community defined by acceptance of Islam and of Muhammad as the "Messenger of God," his most common title. Partly because three Jewish kin groups chose to retain their own faith, the direction of prayer was changed from Jerusalem toward the Ka'ba in Mecca, now thought of as the "House of God."

Having left their Meccan kin groups, the immigrants in Medina felt vulnerable. During the last decade of his life, Muhammad took active responsibility for

his umma. Fresh revelations provided a framework for regulating social and legal affairs and stirred the Muslims to fight against the still-unbelieving city of Mecca. At various points during the war, Muhammad charged the Jewish kin groups, whom he had initially hoped would recognize him as God's messenger, with disloyalty, and he finally expelled or eliminated them. The sporadic war, largely conducted by raiding and negotiating with desert nomads, sapped Mecca's strength and convinced many Meccans that God favored Muhammad. In 630 Mecca surrendered, and Muhammad and his followers made the pilgrimage to the Ka'ba unhindered.

Muhammad stayed in Medina, which had grown into a bustling city-state. Delegations came to him from all over Arabia and returned home with believers who could teach about Islam and collect alms, or charity for the poor. Muhammad's mission to bring God's message to humanity had brought him unchallenged control of a state that was coming to dominate the Arabian peninsula.

In 632, after a brief illness, Muhammad died. Within twenty-four hours a group of Medinan leaders, along with three of Muhammad's close friends, determined that Abu Bakr, one of the earliest believers and the father of Muhammad's favorite wife A'isha (AH-ee-shah), should succeed him. They called him the *khalifa* (kah-LEE-fuh), or "successor," the English version of which is *caliph*. But calling Abu Bakr a successor did not clarify his powers. Everyone knew that neither Abu Bakr nor anyone else could receive revelations, and they likewise knew that Muhammad's revelations made no provision for succession or for any government purpose beyond maintaining the umma.

Abu Bakr continued and confirmed Muhammad's religious practices, notably the so-called Five Pillars of Islam: (1) avowal that there is only one god and Muhammad is his messenger, (2) prayer five times a day, (3) fasting during the lunar month of Ramadan, (4) paying alms, and (5) making the pilgrimage

**Medina**  City in western Arabia to which the Prophet Muhammad and his followers emigrated in 622 to escape persecution in Mecca.

**umma**  The community of all Muslims. A major innovation against the background of seventh-century Arabia, where traditionally kinship rather than faith had determined membership in a community.

to Mecca at least once during one's lifetime. He also reestablished and expanded Muslim authority over Arabia's communities, some of which had abandoned their allegiance to Medina or followed various would-be prophets. Muslim armies fought hard to confirm the authority of the newborn **caliphate**. In the process, some fighting spilled over into non-Arab areas in Iraq.

Reportedly, Abu Bakr ordered the men who had written down Muhammad's revelations to collect them in a book. Hitherto written haphazardly on pieces of leather or bone, these now became a single document gathered into chapters. Muslims believe the **Quran** (kuh-RAHN), or the Recitation, acquired its final form around the year 650. They see it not as the words of Muhammad but as the unalterable word of God. Theologically, it compares not so much to the Bible, a book written by many hands over many centuries, as to the person of Jesus Christ, whom Christians consider an earthly manifestation of God.

Though united in accepting God's will, the umma soon disagreed over the succession to the caliphate. When rebels assassinated the third caliph, Uthman (ooth-MAHN), in 656 and the assassins nominated Ali, Muhammad's first cousin and the husband of his daughter Fatima, to succeed him, civil war broke out. Ali had been passed over three times previously, even though many people considered him to be the Prophet's natural heir. Those who believed Ali was the Prophet's heir came to be known as **Shi'ites**, after the Arabic term *Shi'at Ali* ("Party of Ali").

When Ali accepted the nomination to be caliph, two of Muhammad's close companions and his favorite wife A'isha challenged him. Ali defeated them in the Battle of the Camel (656), so called because the fighting raged around the camel on which A'isha was seated in an enclosed woman's saddle.

After the battle, the governor of Syria, Mu'awiya (moo-AH-we-yuh), a kinsman of the slain Uthman from the Umayya clan of the Quraysh, renewed the challenge. Inconclusive battle gave way to arbitration. The arbitrators decided that Uthman, whom his assassins considered corrupt, had not deserved death and that Ali had erred in accepting the caliphate. Ali rejected these findings, but before fighting could resume, one of his own supporters killed him for agreeing to the arbitration. Mu'awiya offered Ali's

## SECTION REVIEW

- Islam emerged among the nomadic pastoralists and caravan traders of the Arabian peninsula.
- Mecca grew as a caravan city and pilgrimage site identified with Jewish and Christian stories.
- Muhammad experienced revelations that called people to submit to God's will.
- Facing hostility in Mecca, Muhammad and his followers fled to Medina, where they formed the umma.
- As caliph succeeding Muhammad, Abu Bakr confirmed the Five Pillars of Islam and ordered the composition of the Quran.
- Civil war within the umma resulted in the Sunni/Shi'ite division and the foundation of the Umayyad Caliphate.

son Hasan a dignified retirement and thus emerged as caliph in 661.

Mu'awiya chose his own son, Yazid, to succeed him, thereby instituting the **Umayyad** (oo-MY-ad) **Caliphate**. When Hasan's brother Husayn revolted in 680 to reestablish the right of Ali's family to rule, Yazid ordered Husayn and his family killed. Sympathy for Husayn's martyrdom helped transform Shi'ism from a political movement into a religious sect.

Several variations in Shi'ite belief developed, but Shi'ites all agree that Ali was the rightful successor to Muhammad and that God's choice as Imam, leader of the Muslim community, has always been one or another of Ali's descendants. They see the caliphal office as more secular than religious. Because the Shi'ites seldom held power, their religious feelings came to focus on outpourings of sympathy for Husayn and other martyrs and on messianic dreams that one of their Imams would someday triumph.

**caliphate** Office established in succession to the Prophet Muhammad, to rule the Islamic empire; also the name of that empire.

**Quran** Book composed of divine revelations made to the Prophet Muhammad between roughly 610 and his death in 632; the sacred text of the religion of Islam.

**Shi'ites** Muslims belonging to the branch of Islam believing that God vests leadership of the community in a descendant of Muhammad's son-in-law Ali. Shi'ism is the state religion of Iran.

**Umayyad Caliphate** First hereditary dynasty of Muslim caliphs (661 to 750). From their capital at Damascus, the Umayyads ruled an empire that extended from Spain to India. Overthrown by the Abbasid Caliphate.

Those Muslims who supported the first three caliphs gradually came to be called "People of Tradition and Community"—in Arabic, *Ahl al-Sunna wa'l-Jama'a*, **Sunnis** for short. Sunnis consider the caliphs to be Imams. As for Ali's followers who had abhorred his acceptance of arbitration, they evolved into small and rebellious Kharijite sects (from *kharaja*, meaning "to secede or rebel") claiming righteousness for themselves alone. These three divisions of Islam, the last now quite minor, still survive.

## THE RISE AND FALL OF THE CALIPHATE, 632–1258

■ *Was the Baghdad caliphate really the high point of Muslim civilization?*

The Islamic caliphate built on the conquests the Arabs carried out after Muhammad's death gave birth to a dynamic and creative religious society. By the late 800s, however, one piece after another of this huge realm broke away. Yet the idea of a caliphate, however unrealistic, remains today a touchstone of Sunni belief in the unity of the umma.

Sunni Islam never gave a single person the power to define true belief, expel heretics, and discipline clergy. Thus, unlike Christian popes and patriarchs, the caliphs had little basis for reestablishing their universal authority once they lost political and military power.

### The Islamic Conquests, 634–711

Arab conquests outside Arabia began under the second caliph, Umar (r. 634–644). Arab armies wrenched Syria (636) and Egypt (639–642) away from the Byzantine Empire and defeated the last Sasanid shah, Yazdigird III (r. 632–651). After a decade-long lull, expansion began again. Tunisia fell and became the governing center from which was organized, in 711, the conquest of Spain by an Arab-led army mostly composed of Berbers from North Africa. In the same year, Sind—the southern Indus Valley in today's Pakistan—succumbed to invaders from Iraq. The Muslim dominion remained roughly stable in size for three centuries until conquest began anew in the eleventh century. India and Anatolia experienced invasions; sub-Saharan Africa and other regions saw Islam expand peacefully by trade and conversion.

Muhammad's close companions, men of political and economic sophistication inspired by his charisma, guided the conquests. The social structure and hardy nature of Arab society lent itself to flexible military operations; and the authority of Medina, reconfirmed during the caliphate of Abu Bakr, ensured obedience.

The decision made during Umar's caliphate to prohibit Arabs from assuming ownership of conquered territory proved important. Umar tied army service, with its regular pay and windfalls of booty, to residence in military camps—two in Iraq (Kufa and Basra), one in Egypt (Fustat), and one in Tunisia (Qairawan). East of Iraq, Arabs settled around small garrison towns at strategic locations and in one large garrison at Marv in present-day Turkmenistan. This policy kept the armies together and ready for action and preserved normal life in the countryside, where some three-fourths of the population lived. Only a tiny proportion of the Syrian, Egyptian, Iranian, and Iraqi populations understood the Arabic language.

The million or so Arabs who participated in the conquests over several generations constituted a small, self-isolated ruling minority living on the taxes paid by a vastly larger non-Arab, non-Muslim subject population. The Arabs had little material incentive to encourage conversion, and there is no evidence of coherent missionary efforts to spread Islam during the conquest period.

### The Umayyad and Early Abbasid Caliphates, 661–850

The Umayyad caliphs presided over an Arab realm rather than a religious empire. Ruling from Damascus, their armies consisted almost entirely of Muslim Arabs. Sasanid and Byzantine administrative practices continued in force. Only gradually did the caliphs replace non-Muslim secretaries and tax officials with Muslims and introduce Arabic as the language of government. Distinctively Muslim silver and gold coins introduced at the end

**Sunnis**  Muslims belonging to branch of Islam believing that the community should select its own leadership. The majority religion in most Islamic countries.

of the seventh century symbolized the new order. Henceforward, silver dirhams and gold dinars bearing Arabic religious phrases circulated in monetary exchanges from Morocco to the frontiers of China.

The Umayyad dynasty fell in 750 after a decade of growing unrest. Converts to Islam numbered no more than 10 percent of the indigenous population, but they were still important because of the comparatively small number of Arab warriors. These converts resented Arab social domination. In addition, non-Syrian Arabs envied the Syrian domination of caliphal affairs, and pious Muslims looked askance at the secular and even irreligious behavior of the caliphs. Finally, Shi'ites and Kharijites attacked the Umayyad family's legitimacy as rulers, launching a number of rebellions.

In 747 a rebellion began in Khurasan (kor-uh-SAHN), in what is today northeastern Iran, and overthrew the last Umayyad caliph three years later, though one family member escaped to Spain to found an Umayyad principality there in 755. Many Shi'ites supported the rebellion, thinking they were fighting for the family of Ali. As it turned out, the family of Abbas, one of Muhammad's uncles, controlled the secret organization that coordinated the revolt. Upon victory they established the **Abbasid** (ah-BASS-id) **Caliphate**. Some of the Abbasid caliphs who ruled after 750 befriended their relatives in Ali's family, and one even flirted with transferring the caliphate to them. The Abbasid family, however, held on to the caliphate until 1258, when Mongol invaders killed the last of them in Baghdad (see Chapter 12).

Initially, the Abbasid dynasty made a fine show of leadership and piety. Theology and religious law became preoccupations at court and among a growing community of scholars devoted to interpreting the Quran, collecting the sayings of the Prophet, and compiling Arabic grammar. (In recent years, some Western scholars have maintained that the Quran, the sayings of the Prophet, and the biography of the Prophet were all composed around this time to provide a foundation myth for the regime. This reinterpretation of Islamic origins has not been generally accepted either in the scholarly community or among Muslims.) Some caliphs sponsored ambitious projects to translate great works of Greek, Persian, and Indian thought into Arabic.

With its roots among the semi-Persianized Arabs of Khurasan, the new dynasty gradually adopted the ceremonies and customs of the Sasanid shahs. Government grew increasingly complex in Baghdad, the newly built capital city on the Tigris River. As more non-Arabs converted to Islam, the ruling elite became more cosmopolitan. Greek, Iranian, Central Asian, and African cultural currents met in the capital and gave rise to an abundance of literary works, a process facilitated by the introduction of papermaking from China. Arab poets neglected the traditional odes extolling life in the desert and wrote instead wine songs (despite Islam's prohibition of alcohol) or poems in praise of their patrons.

The translation of Aristotle into Arabic, the founding of the main currents of theology and law, and the splendor of the Abbasid court—reflected in stories of *The Arabian Nights* set in the time of the caliph Harun al-Rashid (hah-ROON al–rah-SHEED) (r. 776–809)—in some respects warrant calling the early Abbasid period a "golden age." Yet the refinement of Baghdad culture only slowly made its way into the provinces. Egypt remained predominantly Christian and Coptic-speaking in the early Abbasid period. Iran never adopted Arabic as a spoken tongue. Most of Berber-speaking North Africa rebelled and freed itself of direct caliphal rule after 740.

Gradual conversion to Islam among the conquered population accelerated in the second quarter of the ninth century. Social discrimination against non-Arab converts gradually faded, and the Arabs themselves—at least those living in cosmopolitan urban settings—lost their previously strong attachment to kinship and ethnic identity.

## Political Fragmentation, 850–1050

Abbasid decline became evident in the second half of the ninth century as conversion to Islam accelerated (see Map 9.1). No government ruling so vast an empire could hold power easily. Caravans traveled only 20 miles (32 kilometers) a day, and the couriers of

**Abbasid Caliphate** Descendants of the Prophet Muhammad's uncle, al-Abbas, the Abbasids overthrew the Umayyad Caliphate and ruled an Islamic empire from their capital in Baghdad (founded 762) from 750 to 1258.

the caliphal post system usually did not exceed 100 miles (160 kilometers) a day. News of frontier revolts took weeks to reach Baghdad. Military responses might take months.

During the first two Islamic centuries, revolts against Muslim rule had been a concern. The Muslim umma had therefore clung together, despite the long distances. But with the growing conversion of the population to Islam, fears that Islamic dominion might be overthrown faded. Once they became the overwhelming majority, Muslims realized that a highly centralized empire did not necessarily serve the interests of all the people.

By the middle of the ninth century, revolts targeting Arab or Muslim domination gave way to movements within the Islamic community concentrating on seizure of territory and formation of principalities. None of the states carved out of the Abbasid Caliphate after that time repudiated or even threatened Islam. They did, however, cut the flow of tax revenues to Baghdad, thereby increasing local prosperity. Increasingly starved for funds by breakaway provinces and by an unexplained fall in revenues from Iraq itself, the caliphate experienced a crisis in the late ninth century. Distrusting generals and troops from outlying areas, the caliphs purchased Turkish slaves, **mamluks** (MAM-luke), from Central Asia and established them as a standing army. Well trained and hardy, the Turks proved an effective but expensive military force. When the government could not pay them, the mamluks took it on themselves to seat and unseat caliphs, a process made easier by the construction of a new capital at Samarra, north of Baghdad on the Tigris River.

The Turks dominated Samarra without interference from an unruly Baghdad populace that regarded them as rude and highhanded. However, the money and effort that went into the huge city, which was occupied only from 835 to 892, further sapped the caliphs' financial strength and deflected labor from more productive pursuits.

In 945, after several attempts to find a strongman to save it, the Abbasid Caliphate fell under the control of rude mountain warriors from Daylam in northern Iran. Led by the Shi'ite Buyid (BOO-yid) family, they conquered western Iran as well as Iraq. Each Buyid commander ruled his own principality. After two centuries of glory, the sun began to set on Baghdad.

The Abbasid caliph remained, but the Buyid princes controlled him. Being Shi'ites, the Buyids had no special reverence for the Sunni caliph. The Shi'ite teachings they followed held that the twelfth and last Imam had disappeared around 873 and would return as a messiah only at the end of time. Thus they had no Shi'ite Imam to defer to and retained the caliph only to help control their predominantly Sunni subjects.

Dynamic growth in outlying provinces paralleled the caliphate's gradual loss of temporal power. In the east in 875, the dynasty of the Samanids (sah-MAN-id), one of several Iranian families to achieve independence, established a glittering court in Bukhara, a major city on the Silk Road (see Map 9.1). Samanid princes patronized literature and learning, but the language they favored was Persian written in Arabic letters. For the first time, a non-Arabic literature rose to challenge the eminence of Arabic within the Islamic world.

In the west, the Berber revolts against Arab rule led to the appearance after 740 of the city-states of Sijilmasa (sih-jil-MAS-suh) and Tahert (TAH-hert) on the northern fringe of the Sahara. The Kharijite beliefs of these states' rulers interfered with their east-west overland trade and led them to develop the first regular trade across the Sahara Desert. Once traders looked to the desert, they discovered that Berber speakers in the southern Sahara were already carrying salt from the desert into the Sahel region. The northern traders discovered that they could trade salt for gold by providing the southern nomads, who controlled the salt sources but had little use for gold, with more useful products, such as copper and manufactured goods. Sijilmasa and Tahert became wealthy cities, the former minting gold coins that circulated as far away as Egypt and Syria.

The earliest known sub-Saharan beneficiary of the new exchange system was the kingdom of **Ghana** (GAH-nuh). It first appears in an Arabic text of the late eighth century as the "land of gold." Few details

> **mamluks** Under the Islamic system of military slavery, Turkish military slaves formed an important part of the armed forces of the Abbasid Caliphate of the ninth and tenth centuries. Mamluks eventually founded their own state, ruling Egypt and Syria (1250–1517).
>
> **Ghana** First known kingdom in sub-Saharan West Africa between the sixth and thirteenth centuries C.E. Also the modern West African country once known as the Gold Coast.

**Map 9.1 Rise and Fall of the Abbasid Caliphate** Though Abbasid rulers occupied the caliphal seat in Iraq from 750 to 1258, when Mongol armies destroyed Baghdad, real political power waned sharply and steadily after 850. The rival caliphates of the Fatimids (909–1171) and Spanish Umayyads (929–976) were comparatively short-lived. © Cengage Learning

survive about the early years of this realm, which was established by the Soninke (soh-NIN-kay) people and covered parts of Mali, Mauritania, and Senegal, but it prospered until 1076, when it was conquered by nomads from the desert. It was one of the first lands outside the orbit of the caliphate to experience a gradual and peaceful conversion to Islam.

The North African city-states lost their independence after the Fatimid (FAH-tuh-mid) dynasty, whose members claimed (perhaps falsely) to be Shi'ite Imams descended from Ali, established itself in Tunisia in 909. After consolidating their hold on northwest Africa, the Fatimids culminated their rise to power by conquering Egypt in 969. Claiming the title of caliph in a direct challenge to the Abbasids, the Fatimid rulers governed from a palace complex outside the old conquest-era garrison city of Fustat (fuss-TAHT). They named the complex Cairo. For the first time Egypt became a major cultural, intellectual, and political center of Islam. The abundance of Fatimid gold coinage, now channeled to Egypt from West Africa, made the Fatimids an economic power in the Mediterranean.

Cut off from the rest of the Islamic world by the Strait of Gibraltar and, from 740 onward, by independent city-states in Morocco and Algeria, Umayyad Spain developed a distinctive Islamic culture blending Roman, Germanic, and Jewish traditions with those of the Arabs and Berbers. Historians disagree on how rapidly and completely the Spanish population converted to Islam. If we assume a process similar to that in the eastern regions, it seems likely that the most rapid surge in Islamization occurred in the middle of the tenth century.

As in the east, governing cities symbolized the Islamic presence in al-Andalus, as the Muslims called their Iberian territories. Cordoba, Seville, Toledo, and other cities grew substantially, becoming much larger

217

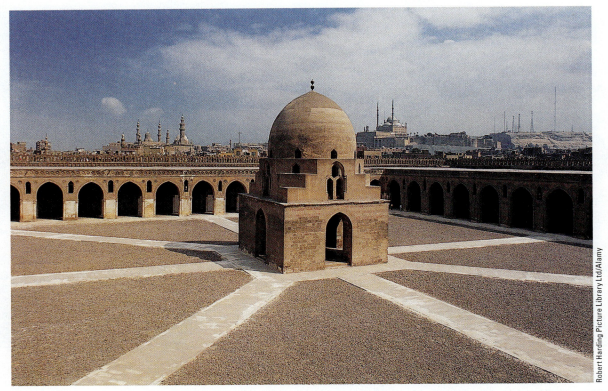

**Mosque of Ibn Tulun in Fustat** Completed in 877, this mosque symbolized Egypt becoming for the first time a quasi-independent province under its governor. The kiosk in the center of the courtyard contains fountains for washing before prayer. Before its restoration in the thirteenth century, the mosque had a spiral minaret and a door to an adjoining governor's palace.

and richer than contemporary cities in neighboring France. Converts to Islam and their descendants, unconverted Arabic-speaking Christians, and Jews joined with the comparatively few descendants of Arab settlers to create new architectural and literary styles. In the countryside, where the Berbers preferred to settle, a fusion of preexisting agricultural technologies with new crops, notably citrus fruits, and irrigation techniques from the east gave Spain the most diverse and sophisticated agricultural economy in Europe.

The rulers of al-Andalus took the title *caliph* only in 929, when Abd al-Rahman (AHB-d al–ruh-MAHN) III (r. 912–961) did so in response to a similar declaration by the newly established (909) Fatimid ruler in Tunisia. By the century's end, however, this caliphate encountered challenges from breakaway movements that eventually splintered al-Andalus into a number of small states. Political decay did not impede cultural growth. Some of the greatest writers and

thinkers in Jewish history worked in Muslim Spain in the eleventh and twelfth centuries, sometimes writing in Arabic, sometimes in Hebrew. Judah Halevi (1075–1141) composed exquisite poetry and explored questions of religious philosophy. Maimonides (1135–1204) made a major compilation of Judaic law and expounded on Aristotelian philosophy. At the same time, Islamic thought in Spain attained its loftiest peaks in Ibn Hazm's (994–1064) treatises on love and other subjects, the Aristotelian philosophical writings of Ibn Rushd (IB-uhn RUSHED) (1126–1198, known in Latin as Averroës [uh-VERR-oh-eez]) and Ibn Tufayl (IB-uhn too-FILE) (d. 1185), and the mystic speculations of Ibn al-Arabi (IB-uhn ahl–AH-rah-bee) (1165–1240). Christians, too, shared in the intellectual and cultural dynamism of al-Andalus. Translations from Arabic to Latin made during this period had a profound effect on the later intellectual development of western Europe (see Chapter 10).

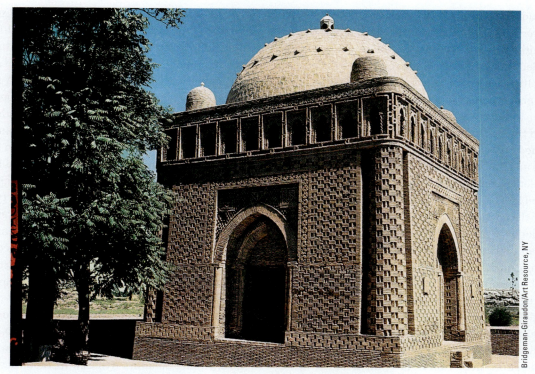

**Tomb of the Samanids in Bukhara** This early-tenth-century structure has the basic layout of a Zoroastrian fire temple: a dome on top of a cube. However, geometric ornamentation in baked brick marks it as an early masterpiece of Islamic architecture. The Samanid family achieved independence as rulers of northeastern Iran and western Central Asia in the tenth century.

The Samanids, Fatimids, and Spanish Umayyads, three of many regional principalities, represent the political diversity and awakening of local awareness that coincided with Abbasid decline. Yet drawing and redrawing political boundaries did not result in the rigid division of the Islamic world into kingdoms. Religious and cultural developments, particularly the rise in cities of a social group of religious scholars known as the **ulama** (oo-leh-MAH)—Arabic for "people with (religious) knowledge"—worked against any permanent division of the Islamic umma.

### Assault from Within and Without, 1050–1258

The role played by Turkish mamluks in the decline of Abbasid power established an enduring stereotype of the Turk as a ferocious, unsophisticated warrior. This image gained strength in the 1030s when the Seljuk (sel-JOOK) family established a Turkish Muslim state based on nomadic power. Taking the Arabic title *Sultan*, meaning "power," and the revived Persian title *Shahan-shah*, or King of Kings, the Seljuk ruler Tughril (TUUG-ruhl) Beg created a kingdom that stretched from northern Afghanistan to Baghdad, which he occupied in 1055. After a century under the thumb of the Shi'ite Buyids, the Abbasid caliph breathed easier under the slightly lighter thumb of the Sunni Turks. The Seljuks pressed on into Syria and Anatolia, administering a lethal blow to Byzantine power at the Battle of Manzikert (MANZ-ih-kuhrt) in 1071. The Byzantine army fell back on Constantinople, leaving Anatolia open to Turkish occupation.

Under Turkish rule, which coincided with a severe climatic cooling that reduced harvests in Iran,

**ulama** Muslim religious scholars. From the ninth century onward, the primary interpreters of Islamic law and the social core of Muslim urban societies.

Iraq, and eastern Anatolia, cities shrank as pastoralists overran their agricultural hinterlands. Irrigation works suffered from lack of maintenance in the unsettled countryside, and tax revenues fell. Quarreling twelfth-century princes fought over cities, but few Turks participated in urban cultural and religious life. The gulf between a religiously based urban society and the culture and personnel of the government deepened. When factional riots broke out between Sunnis and Shi'ites, or between rival schools of Sunni law, rulers generally remained aloof, even as destruction and loss of life mounted.

By the early twelfth century, unrepaired damage from floods, fires, and civil disorder had reduced old Baghdad on the west side of the Tigris to ruins. The withering of Baghdad reflected a broader environmental problem: the collapse of the canal system on which agriculture in the Tigris and Euphrates Valley depended. For millennia a center of world civilization, Mesopotamia underwent substantial population loss and never again regained its geographical importance.

The Turks alone cannot be blamed for the demographic and economic misfortunes of Iran and Iraq. Too-robust urbanization, spurred largely by a boom in Iranian cotton production, resulted in strained food resources when the climate deteriorated after 1000. Baghdad, a city with a torrid climate today, experienced heavy winter snowfalls that killed date trees. The growing practice of paying soldiers and courtiers with land grants led to absentee landlords using agents to collect taxes. These agents gouged villagers to meet their quotas and took little interest in improving production, thus intensifying the agricultural crisis.

Internecine feuding was preoccupying the Seljuk family when the first Christian Crusaders reached the Holy Land and captured Jerusalem in 1099 (see Chapter 10). Though charged with the stuff of romance, the Crusades had little lasting impact on the Islamic lands. The four Crusader principalities of Edessa, Antioch, Tripoli, and Jerusalem simply became pawns in the shifting pattern of politics already in place. Newly arrived knights eagerly attacked the Muslim enemy, whom they called "Saracens" (SAR-uh-suhn); but veteran Crusaders recognized that practicing diplomacy and seeking partners of convenience among rival Muslim princes offered a sounder strategy.

The Muslims finally unified to face the European enemy in the mid-twelfth century. Nur al-Din ibn Zangi (NOOR uhd–DEEN ib-uhn ZAN-gee) established a strong state based in Damascus and sent an army to terminate the Fatimid Caliphate in Egypt. A nephew of the Kurdish commander of that expedition, Salah-al-Din, known in the West as Saladin, took advantage of Nur al-Din's timely death to seize power and unify Egypt and Syria. The Fatimid dynasty fell in 1171. In 1187 Saladin recaptured Jerusalem from the Europeans. He then took the title Khadim al-Haramain (KAH-dim al-ha-ra-MAYN), literally "Servant of the Two Holy Places," meaning Mecca and Medina, in a challenge to the caliph's claim to be the paramount Sunni potentate. Revitalizing the pilgrimage became a core concern for later rulers in Egypt and Syria, particularly after the termination of the Baghdad caliphate in 1258.

Saladin's descendants fought off subsequent Crusades. After one such battle, however, in 1250, Turkish mamluk troops seized control of the government in Cairo, ending Saladin's dynasty. In 1260 these mamluks rode east to confront a new invader. At the Battle of Ain Jalut (ine jah-LOOT) (Spring of Goliath) in Syria, they met and defeated an army of Mongols from Central Asia (see Chapter 12), thus stemming an invasion that had begun several decades before and legitimizing their claim to dominion over Egypt and Syria.

During the ensuing Mamluk period a succession of slave-soldier sultans ruled Egypt and Syria until 1517. Fear of new Mongol attacks receded after 1300, but by then the new ruling system had become fixed. Young Turkish or Circassian slaves, the latter from the eastern end of the Black Sea, were imported from non-Muslim lands, raised in training barracks, and converted to Islam. Owing loyalty to the Mamluk officers who purchased them, they formed a military class that was socially disconnected from the Arabic-speaking native population.

The Mongol invasions, especially their destruction of the Abbasid Caliphate in Baghdad in 1258, shocked the world of Islam. The Mamluk sultan enthroned a relative of the last Baghdad caliph in Cairo, but the Egyptian Abbasids were mere puppets serving Mamluk interests. From Iraq eastward, non-Muslim rule lasted for much of the thirteenth century. Although the Mongols left few ethnic or

## SECTION REVIEW

- By 711, Arab armies had conquered an empire stretching from Sind in the east to Spain in the west.
- The Umayyad caliphs ruled an ethnic empire; they governed from Damascus using Sasanid and Byzantine administrative methods.
- The Umayyads fell to rebels who established the Abbasid Caliphate at Baghdad, while surviving Umayyads fled to Spain.
- Influenced by Persian culture, the Abbasids presided over significant spiritual, intellectual, and artistic activity.
- Abbasid decline led to fragmentation of the caliphate into independent states, but the Islamic umma remained intact.
- Political divisions continued as successor states to the former caliphate fell, replaced by Seljuk Turk, Crusader, Mamluk, and Mongol states.

linguistic traces in these lands, their initial destruction of cities and slaughter of civilian populations, their diversion of Silk Road trade from Baghdad to more northerly routes ending at Black Sea ports, and their casual disregard, even after conversion to Islam, for Muslim religious life and urban culture hastened currents of change already under way.

# ISLAMIC CIVILIZATION

■ *How did regional diversity affect the development of Islamic civilization?*

Though increasingly unsettled in its political dimension and subject to economic disruptions caused by war, the ever-expanding Islamic world underwent a fruitful evolution in law, social structure, and religious expression. Religious conversion and urbanization reinforced each other to create a distinct Islamic civilization. The immense geographical and human diversity of the Muslim lands allowed many "small traditions" to coexist with the developing "great tradition" of Islam.

## Law and Dogma

The Shari'a, the law of Islam, provided the foundation of Islamic civilization. Yet aside from certain Quranic verses conveying specific divine ordinances—most pertaining to personal and family matters—Islam had no legal system in the time of Muhammad. Arab custom and the Prophet's own authority offered the only guidance. After Muhammad died, the umma tried to follow his example. This became harder and harder to do, however, as those who knew Muhammad best passed away and many Arabs found themselves living in far-off lands. Non-Arab converts to Islam, who at first tried to follow Arab customs they had little familiarity with, had an even harder time.

Islam slowly developed laws to govern social and religious life. The full sense of Islamic civilization, however, goes well beyond the basic Five Pillars mentioned earlier. Some Muslim thinkers felt that the reasoned consideration of a mature man offered the best resolution of issues not covered by Quranic revelation. Others argued for the sunna, or tradition, of the Prophet as the best guide. To understand that sunna they collected and studied thousands of reports, called **hadith** (hah-DEETH), purporting to convey the precise words or deeds of Muhammad. It became customary to precede each hadith with a chain of oral authorities leading back to the person who had direct acquaintance with the Prophet.

Many hadith dealt with ritual matters, such as how to wash before prayer. Others provided answers to legal questions not covered by Quranic revelation or suggested principles for deciding such matters. By the eleventh century most legal thinkers had accepted the idea that Muhammad's personal behavior provided the best role model and that the hadith constituted the most authoritative basis for law after the Quran itself.

Yet the hadith posed a problem because the tens of thousands of anecdotes included both genuine and invented reports, the latter sometimes politically motivated, as well as stories derived from non-Muslim religious traditions. Only a specialist could hope to separate a sound from a weak tradition. As the hadith grew in importance, so did the branch of learning devoted to their analysis. Scholars discarded thousands for having faulty chains of authority. The most reliable they collected into books that gradually

**hadith** A tradition relating the words or deeds of the Prophet Muhammad; next to the Quran, the most important basis for Islamic law.

achieved authoritative status. Sunnis placed six books in this category; Shi'ites, four.

As it gradually evolved, the Shari'a embodied a vision of an umma in which all subscribed to the same moral values and political and ethnic distinctions lost importance. Every Muslim ruler was expected to abide by and enforce the religious law. In practice, this expectation often lost out in the hurly-burly of political life. But the Shari'a proved an important basis for an urban lifestyle that varied surprisingly little from Morocco to India.

## Converts and Cities

Conversion to Islam, more the outcome of people's learning about the new rulers' religion than an escape from the tax on non-Muslims, as some scholars have suggested, helped spur urbanization. Conversion did not require extensive knowledge of the faith. To become a Muslim, a person simply stated, in the presence of a Muslim: "There is no God but God, and Muhammad is the Messenger of God."

Few converts spoke Arabic, and fewer could read the Quran. Many converts knew no more of the Quran than the verses they memorized for daily prayers. Muhammad had established no priesthood to define and spread the faith. Thus new converts, whether Arab or non-Arab, faced the problem of finding out for themselves what Islam was about and how they should act as Muslims. This meant spending time with Muslims, learning their language, and imitating their practices.

In many areas, conversion involved migrating to an Arab governing center. The alternative, converting to Islam but remaining in one's home community, was difficult because religion had become the main component of social identity in Byzantine and Sasanid times. Converts to Islam thus encountered discrimination if they stayed in their Christian, Jewish, or Zoroastrian communities. Migration both averted discrimination and took advantage of the economic opportunities opened up by tax revenues flowing into the Arab governing centers.

The Arab military settlements of Kufa and Basra in Iraq blossomed into cities and became important centers for Muslim cultural activities. As conversion rapidly spread in the mid-ninth century, urbanization accelerated in other regions, most visibly in

Iran, where most cities previously had been quite small. Nishapur in the northeast grew from fewer than 10,000 pre-Islamic inhabitants to between 100,000 and 200,000 by the year 1000. Other Iranian cities experienced similar growth. In Iraq, Baghdad and Mosul joined Kufa and Basra as major cities. In Syria, Aleppo and Damascus flourished under Muslim rule. Fustat in Egypt developed into Cairo, one of the largest and greatest Islamic cities. The primarily Christian patriarchal cities of Jerusalem, Antioch, and Alexandria, not being Muslim governing centers, shrank and stagnated.

Conversion-related migration meant that cities became heavily Muslim before the countryside did. This reinforced the urban orientation deriving from the fact that Muhammad and his first followers came from the commercial city of Mecca. Mosques in large cities served both as ritual centers and as places for learning and social activities.

Islam colored all aspects of urban social life. Initially the new Muslims imitated Arab dress and customs, particularly favoring plain linen or cotton over the silk brocade of the non-Muslim Iranian elite. In the absence of a central religious authority, local variations developed in the way people practiced Islam and in the hadith they attributed to the Prophet. This gave the rapidly growing religion the flexibility to accommodate many different social situations.

By the tenth century, urban growth was affecting the countryside by expanding the consumer market. Citrus fruits, rice, and sugar cane, introduced by the Sasanids, increased in acreage and spread to new areas. Cotton became a major crop in Iran and elsewhere and stimulated textile production. Irrigation works expanded. Abundant coinage facilitated a flourishing intercity and long-distance trade that provided regular links between isolated districts and integrated the pastoral nomads, who provided pack animals, into the region's economy. Trade encouraged the manufacture of cloth, metal goods, and pottery.

Science and technology also flourished. Building on Hellenistic traditions and their own observations and experience, Muslim doctors and astronomers developed skills and theories far in advance of their European counterparts. Working in Egypt in the eleventh century, the mathematician and physicist Ibn al-Haytham (IB-uhn al–HY-tham) wrote more than a

**Women Playing Chess in Muslim Spain**   As shown in this thirteenth-century miniature, women in their own quarters, without men present, wore whatever clothes and jewels they liked. Notice the henna decorating the hands of the woman in the middle. The woman on the left, probably a slave, plays an oud.   Album/Art Resource, NY

hundred works. Among other things, he determined that the Milky Way lies far beyond earth's atmosphere, proved that light travels from a seen object to the eye and not the reverse, and explained why the sun and moon appear larger on the horizon than overhead.

## Women and Islam

Seclusion of women and veiling in public already existed in Byzantine and Sasanid times. Women seldom traveled. Those living in rural areas worked in the fields and tended animals, while urban and elite women did not leave their homes without covering themselves (see Material Culture: Head Coverings). Through interpretation of specific verses from the Quran, these practices now became fixtures of Muslim social life. Public roles for women were generally barred, and women who sometimes became literate and studied with relatives did so away from the gaze of unrelated men. Only slave women could perform before unrelated men as musicians and dancers. A misogynistic tone is also sometimes found in Islamic writings. One saying attributed to the Prophet observed: "I was raised up to heaven and saw that most of its denizens were poor people; I was raised into the hellfire and saw that most of its denizens were women."[3]

Nevertheless, Muslim women fared better legally under Islamic law than did Christian and Jewish women under their respective religious codes. While a man could have sexual relations with as many slave concubines as he pleased, and marry as many as four wives, Muslim law put the financial burden of supporting a family exclusively on the husband, who could not legally compel his wife to help out. Women could also remarry if their husbands divorced them, and they received a cash payment upon divorce. Although a man could divorce his wife without stating a cause, a woman could initiate divorce under specified conditions. Women could also practice birth control. They could testify in court, although their testimony counted as half that of a man. They

[3]Richard W. Bulliet, *Islam: The View from the Edge* (New York: Columbia University Press, 1994), 87.

# Material Culture

## Head Coverings

Covering the head is one of the most universal of human cultural characteristics. It is also one of the most common ways of signaling social status. Examples can be drawn from every part of the world, from earliest times down to the modern era. In premodern Chinese society, the color and design of a man's cap indicated his rank as clearly as the insignia on military head coverings does today. In most European societies in the seventeenth and eighteenth centuries, men and frequently women of the higher social orders wore wigs, a practice that still survives in the costume of British judges. Head coverings were particularly important for royalty. From ancient Egypt, where the earliest pharaonic crowns symbolized the union of the northern and southern parts of the Nile Valley, down to the twentieth century and the jewel-studded crown of the shah of Iran, each land developed its own distinctive royal headdress. This also held true for Native American societies in pre-Columbian times and for African and Polynesian societies. In some societies, such as Sasanid Iran and the Ottoman Empire in what is today Turkey, each ruler's crown or turban had a distinctive design that symbolized his rule.

Head coverings have also played significant roles in religion. In orthodox Judaism, for example, men wear hats or skullcaps, and married women wear wigs, as signs of acceptance of God's laws. In Islam, head coverings for women, borrowed from pre-Islamic practice in the Middle East, have become politically controversial in recent years; but prior to the twentieth century it was considered equally improper for a Muslim man to go bareheaded.

Wearing no hat at all was usually a characteristic of slaves or of the poorest elements in society. But it could also signify a deliberate desire to be regarded as humble. Sumerian priests, Buddhist monks and nuns, and certain Sufis in the Muslim world shaved their heads clean. In Europe, early Christian monks and priests shaved the crown of their heads in the Roman Catholic tradition. This form of tonsure competed with and eventually superseded an Irish Catholic practice of shaving the front of the head. Yet head shaving did not always signify humility. Japanese samurai, or warriors, also shaved the front of their heads.

Head coverings for women, as well as wigs and hair-dressing styles, sometimes show greater diversity than those for men. This has been particularly true in societies where women of high status mix with men on public occasions. A magnificent wig, hat, or coiffure under these

**Muslim Head Coverings** *The man standing before a governor in this thirteenth-century miniature painting wears a simple skullcap indicating his low social status. The two attendants wear turbans, but the governor's turban is built into a high, conical shape. The folds and tails of turbans signified not only rank, but also place of origin. To this day, men from western Afghanistan wear tightly wound white turbans with long tails while men from eastern Afghanistan wear loose colorful turbans.* Abu Zayd standing before the governor of Ramba in Baghdad, Arabic miniature, 1237./De Agostini Picture Library/J.E. Bulloz/The Bridgeman Art Library

circumstances might speak as much for the social rank of the woman's husband as for her own.

Given this long history of distinctive head coverings, the abandonment of both men's and women's hats in the second half of the twentieth century marked a major turning point in the history of symbolism. Around the world, the hat-making industry has greatly contracted. Whether one visits China, Egypt, India, France, or Brazil, one finds it difficult to determine the rank or status of most people by looking at what they have on their heads. Heads of government typically pose for group photographs with no hats on at all. Aside from conservative religious groups, the head coverings that remain most often indicate occupations: military, police, construction, athletics, and so on.

The reasons for this change are unclear. The spread of democracy and decline of aristocracy may have contributed to it, but hats have become equally uncommon in dictatorships. A more likely cause is the worldwide role of news photographs, movies, and other pictorial media. The media developed in Europe and the United States tend to take Western customs as normal and exoticize non-Western styles as "native costumes." People everywhere have thus felt pressure to switch to Western styles, including bareheadedness, to fit into the image of the modern world.

### QUESTIONS FOR ANALYSIS

1. What might covering the head, or removing a head cover, signify in America today?
2. How desirable is it to be able to distinguish a person's job or social position by looking at his or her head covering?
3. What does wearing a baseball cap convey?

could also go on pilgrimage. In addition, Islamic law guaranteed daughters a share in inheritance equal to half that of a son; the majority of women inherited some amount of money or real estate, and this remained their private property to keep or sell.

In the absence of writings by women about women from this period, the status of women must be deduced from the writings of men. Two episodes involving the Prophet's wife A'isha, the daughter of Abu Bakr, provide examples of how Muslim men appraised women in society. Only eighteen when Muhammad died, A'isha lived for another fifty years. Early reports stress her status as Muhammad's favorite, the only virgin he married and the only wife to see the angel Gabriel. These reports emanate from A'isha herself, who was an abundant source of hadith. As a fourteen-year-old she had become separated from a caravan and rejoined it only after traveling through the night with a man who found her alone in the desert. Gossips accused her of being untrue to the Prophet, but a revelation from God proved her innocence. The second event was her participation in the Battle of the Camel, fought to derail Ali's caliphate. These two episodes came to epitomize what Muslim men feared most about women: sexual infidelity and meddling in politics. Even though the earliest literature dealing with A'isha stresses her position as Muhammad's favorite, his first wife, Khadija, and his daughter, Ali's wife Fatima, eventually surpassed A'isha as ideal women. Both appear as model wives and mothers with no suspicion of sexual irregularity or political manipulation.

As the seclusion of women became commonplace in urban Muslim society, some writers extolled homosexual relationships, partly because a male lover could appear in public or go on a journey. Although Islam deplored homosexuality, one ruler wrote a book advising his son to follow moderation in all things and thus share his affections equally between men and women. Another ruler and his slave-boy became models of perfect love in the verses of mystic poets.

Islam allowed slavery but forbade Muslims from enslaving other Muslims or so-called People of the Book—Jews, Christians, and Zoroastrians, who revered holy books respected by the Muslims. Being enslaved as a prisoner of war constituted an exception. Later centuries saw a constant flow of slaves into Islamic territory from Africa and Central Asia. A hereditary slave society, however, did not develop. Usually slaves converted to Islam, and many masters then freed them as an act of piety. The offspring of slave women and Muslim men were born free.

## The Recentering of Islam

Early Islam centered on the caliphate, the political expression of the unity of the umma. No formal organization or hierarchy, however, directed the process of conversion. Thus there emerged a multitude of local Islamic communities so disconnected from each other that numerous competing interpretations of the developing religion arose. Inevitably, the centrality of the caliphate diminished (see Map 9.1). The appearance of rival caliphates in Tunisia and Cordoba accentuated the problem of decentralization. The rise of the ulama as community leaders did not prevent growing fragmentation because the ulama themselves divided into contentious factions. During the twelfth century factionalism began to abate, and new socioreligious institutions, including a revitalized pilgrimage to Mecca, emerged to provide the umma with a different sort of religious center. These new developments stemmed in part from an exodus of religious scholars from Iran in response to economic and political disintegration during the late eleventh and twelfth centuries. The flow of Iranians to the Arab lands and to newly conquered territories in India and Anatolia increased after the Mongol invasion. Immigrant scholars were warmly received. Fully versed in Arabic as well as their native Persian, they brought with them a view of religion developed in Iran's urban centers. A type of religious college, the *madrasa* (MAH-dras-uh), gained sudden popularity outside Iran, where madrasas had been known since the tenth century. Scores of madrasas, many founded by local rulers, appeared throughout the Islamic world. In the fourteenth century, Mecca became a major educational center for the first time since Muhammad's generation.

Iranians also contributed to the growth of mystic groups known as *Sufi* brotherhoods in the twelfth and thirteenth centuries. The doctrines and rituals of certain Sufis spread from city to city, giving rise to the first geographically extensive Islamic religious organizations. Sufi doctrines varied, but a quest for a sense of union with God through rituals and training was a common denominator. Sufism had begun in early Islamic times and had doubtless benefited from the ideas and beliefs of people from religions with mystic traditions who converted to Islam.

The early Sufis had been saintly individuals given to ecstatic and poetic utterances and wonder-working. They attracted disciples but did not try to organize them. The growth of brotherhoods, a less ecstatic form of Sufism, set a tone for society in general. It soon became common for most Muslim men, particularly in the cities, to belong to at least one brotherhood.

A sense of the social climate the Sufi brotherhoods fostered can be gained from a twelfth-century manual:

> Every limb has its own special ethics. . . . The ethics of the tongue. The tongue should always be busy in reciting God's names (dhikr) and in saying good things of the brethren, praying for them, and giving them counsel. . . . The ethics of hearing. One should not listen to indecencies and slander. . . . The ethics of sight. One should lower one's eyes in order not to see forbidden things.[4]

Special dispensations allowed people who merely wanted to emulate the Sufis and enjoy their company to follow less demanding rules:

> It is allowed by way of dispensation to possess an estate or to rely on a regular income. The Sufis' rule in this matter is that one should not use all of it for himself, but should dedicate this to public charities and should take from it only enough for one year for himself and his family. . . .
>
> There is a dispensation allowing one to watch all kinds of amusement. This is, however, limited by the rule: What you are forbidden from doing, you are also forbidden from watching.[5]

As some Sufi brotherhoods spread in the countryside, local shrines and pilgrimages to the tombs of Muhammad's descendants and saintly Sufis became popular.

---

[4]Abu Najib al-Suhrawardi, *A Sufi Rule for Novices*, trans. Menahem Milson (Cambridge, MA: Harvard University Press, 1975), 45–58.

[5]Ibid., 73–82.

## SECTION REVIEW

- The foundation of Islamic civilization is the Shari'a, which is derived from the Quran and the hadith.
- Urbanization and religious conversion reinforced each other and prompted the expansion of agriculture, trade, science, and technology.
- Women in general enjoyed relatively high status under Islamic law, though urban women tended to live in seclusion.
- Islamic attitudes toward homosexuality were ambivalent, and slavery was an accepted and continuous practice.
- Migrations of Iranian scholars centered Islam on the madrasa and contributed to the rise of Sufism.

## CONCLUSION

The Sasanid Empire that held sway in Iran and Iraq from the third to the seventh century resembled the contemporary realm of the Byzantine Roman emperors. Both states forged strong relations between the ruler and the dominant religion, Zoroastrianism in the former empire, Christianity in the latter. Priestly hierarchies paralleled state administrative structures, and the citizenry came to think of themselves more as members of a faith community than as subjects of a ruler. This gave rise to conflict among religious sects and also raised the possibility of the founder of a new religion commanding both political and religious loyalty on an unprecedented scale. This possibility was realized in the career of the prophet Muhammad in the seventh century.

Islam culminated the trend toward identity based on religion. The concept of the umma united all Muslims in a universal community embracing enormous diversity of language, appearance, and social custom. Though Muslim communities adapted to local "small traditions," by the twelfth century a religious scholar could travel anywhere in the Islamic world and blend easily into the local Muslim community.

By the ninth century, the forces of conversion and urbanization fostered social and religious experimentation in urban settings. From the eleventh century onward, political disruption, the spread of pastoral nomadism, and climatic deterioration slowed this early economic and technological dynamism. Muslim communities then turned to new religious institutions, such as the madrasas and Sufi brotherhoods, to create the flexible and durable community structures that carried Islam into new regions and protected ordinary believers from capricious political rule.

# CHAPTER REVIEW

## THE SASANID EMPIRE, 224–651

■ *How did the Sasanid Empire evolve under the influence of east-west trade?* (page 208)

Originating in southwest Iran, the Sasanids inherited the Parthian's involvement in trade along the Silk Road, but were more active than their predecessors in introducing new crops. Despite repeated wars with the Byzantine Empire, trade and cultural influences passed between the adversaries. Sasanid kings supported Zoroastrianism as the state religion, continuing a larger trend toward the politicization of religion. Other religions often suffered persecution, but the Sasanid king welcomed Nestorian Christians fleeing persecution in Byzantium. Nestorians traveled the Silk Road as missionaries while Manichaeans, persecuted by the Sasanids found opportunities for growth in Byzantine territory as well as along the Silk Road.

## THE ORIGINS OF ISLAM

■ *How did the traditions and religious views of pre-Islamic peoples become integrated into the culture shaped by Islam?* (page 210)

During Mohammed's lifetime, virtually all Muslims were Arabs from central or southern Arabia. Their cultural traditions underlie many verses of the Quran. But the conquests brought many other peoples under the rule of the caliphate. Non-Arabs who converted to Islam, as well as Arabs from previously Christian and Jewish groups in Syria and Iraq, brought with them some of the traditions and religious views of their former faith communities. Bits of this cultural heritage sometimes became incorporated into the body of lore accepted as the sayings of Muhammad. Other materials, notably in science and philosophy, were translated in book form into Arabic, and still more seeped into the rich store of legend and customary knowledge in different parts of the caliphate.

## THE RISE AND FALL OF THE CALIPHATE, 632–1258

■ *Was the Baghdad caliphate really the high point of Muslim civilization?* (page 214)

A division of the caliphate into smaller political units accompanied this growth in ethnic diversity. The glittering cosmopolitan Baghdad of the early Abbasid Caliphate lost its luster as the conversion of non-Arabs to Islam increased and other cities from Spain to Central Asia evolved into regional Muslim centers. Despite Baghdad's reputation, these later centers, looked at collectively, contributed more to the distinctiveness of medieval Islamic culture than did Baghdad.

## ISLAMIC CIVILIZATION

■ *How did regional diversity affect the development of Islamic civilization?* (page 221)

Spain, Egypt, and Iran were three regions that flourished as Baghdad declined. Each developed a particular intellectual, religious, and artistic character within the overall unity of Islam. Politically as well, regional variation was important. The coming of the Turks and Mongols left North Africa and Spain mostly untouched, the Crusades were of negligible importance for Iran, and the confrontations of Spanish Muslims with Christians to their north meant little to the Egyptians. Yet all of those events contributed to the shaping of medieval Islamic civilization as a whole.

## Key Terms

Sasanid Empire (p. 208)
Mecca (p. 211)
Muhammad (p. 211)
Muslim (p. 211)
Islam (p. 211)
Medina (p. 212)
umma (p. 212)
caliphate (p. 213)
Quran (p. 213)
Shi'ites (p. 213)
Umayyad Caliphate (p. 213)
Sunnis (p. 214)
Abbasid Caliphate (p. 215)
mamluks (p. 216)
Ghana (p. 216)
ulama (p. 219)
hadith (p. 221)

# Christian Societies Emerge in Europe

© Cengage Learning

In 800, **Charlemagne** (SHAHR-leh-mane) (from Latin *Carolus magnus*, "Charles the Great") was the first in western Europe to bear the title *emperor* in over three hundred years. Rome's decline and Charlemagne's rise marked a shift of focus for Europe—away from the Mediterranean and toward the north and west. As German custom and Christian piety transformed the Roman heritage to create a new civilization, Irish monks preaching in Latin became important intellectual leaders in Germanic lands. The memory of Greek and Roman philosophy faded, and the urban life that had begun in the later days of the Roman Empire declined. Historians originally called this era **medieval**, literally "middle age," because it comes between the era of Greco-Roman civilization and the intellectual, artistic, and economic changes of the Renaissance in the fourteenth century. In fact, many aspects of medieval culture were as rich and creative as those that came earlier and later.

Charlemagne was not the only ruler in Europe to claim the title *emperor*. Another emperor held sway in the Greek-speaking east, where Rome's political and legal heritage continued in the Eastern Roman or **Byzantine Empire**. While western Europeans lived amid the ruins of empire, the Byzantines maintained and reinterpreted Roman traditions. The authority of the Byzantine emperors also blended with the influence of the Christian church in a cultural synthesis that helped shape the emerging kingdom of **Kievan Russia**. Byzantium's centuries-long conflict with Islam helped spur the crusading passion that overtook western Europe in the eleventh century.

The comparison between western and eastern Europe appears paradoxical. Byzantium inherited a robust and self-confident late Roman society and economy, while western Europe could not achieve political unity and suffered severe economic decline. Yet by 1200 western Europe was showing renewed vitality and flexing its military muscles, while Byzantium was showing signs of decline and military weakness. As we explore these different historical paths, we must remember that the emergence of Christian Europe included both developments.

# THE BYZANTINE EMPIRE, 600–1200

■ *How did the Byzantine Empire maintain Roman imperial traditions in the east?*

The Byzantine emperors established Christianity as their official religion (see Chapter 5). They also represented a continuation of Roman imperial rule and tradition. Whereas only provincial forms of Roman law survived in the west, Byzantium inherited imperial law intact. Combining the imperial role with political oversight over the Christian church, the emperors made a comfortable transition into the role of all-powerful Christian monarchs. The Byzantine drama, however, played on a steadily shrinking stage. Territorial losses and almost constant military pressure from north and south deprived the empire of long periods of peace.

**Church and State**   In 324, in the nineteenth year of his reign, the emperor Constantine (r. 306–337) led a procession marking the expanded limits of his new capital: the millennium-old Greek city of Byzantium, located on a long narrow inlet at the entrance of the Bosphorus strait. In the forum of the new Constantinople (cahn-stan-tih-NO-pul), he erected a 120-foot-tall (36-meter-tall) column topped with a statue of Apollo, and he retained the old Roman title *pontifex maximus* (PAHN-tih-fex MAX-ih-mus) (chief priest). Nevertheless, he leaned toward Christianity—historians disagree on when he embraced it fully—and he and his mother studded both his capital and the Christian centers of Jerusalem and Rome with important churches.

**Charlemagne**   King of the Franks (r. 768–814); emperor (r. 800–814). Through a series of military conquests he established the Carolingian Empire, which encompassed all of Gaul and parts of Germany and Italy. Though illiterate himself, he sponsored a brief intellectual revival.

**medieval**   Literally "middle age," a term that historians of Europe use for the period from roughly 500 to 1300, signifying its intermediate point between Greco-Roman antiquity and the Renaissance.

**Byzantine Empire**   Historians' name for the eastern portion of the Roman Empire from the fourth century onward, taken from *Byzantion*, an early name for Constantinople, the Byzantine capital city. The empire fell to the Ottomans in 1453.

**Kievan Russia**   State established at Kiev in Ukraine around 880 by Scandinavian adventurers asserting authority over a mostly Slavic farming population.

Constantine appointed the patriarch of Constantinople and involved himself in doctrinal disputes over which beliefs constituted heresy. In 325 he called hundreds of bishops to a council at Nicaea (nye-SEE-uh) (modern Iznik in northwestern Turkey) to resolve disputes over religious doctrine. The bishops rejected the views of a priest from Alexandria named Arius, who maintained that Jesus was of lesser importance than God the Father. The Arian doctrine enjoyed greatest popularity among the Germanic peoples then migrating along the Danube frontier and into the western Roman lands. An Arian bishop named Ulfilas (ca. 311–383), himself belonging to the Germanic peoples known as Goths,

translated the Bible into Gothic, reportedly using an alphabet of his own devising. This set the Arians apart from Christians, who relied on scriptures written in Latin or Greek.

Following the Arian controversy, disputes over theology and quarrels among the patriarchs of Constantinople, Alexandria, and Antioch continued to tear at the Byzantine Empire. As discussed in Chapter 9, religion permeated society, and the literature of the period shows the widespread concern for religious affairs. A fourth-century bishop reported: "Everything is full of those who are speaking of unintelligible things. . . . I wish to know the price of bread; one answers, "The Father is greater than the Son." I

**Map 10.1 The Spread of Christianity** By the early eighth century, Christian areas around the southern Mediterranean from northern Syria to northern Spain, accounting for most of the Christian population, had fallen under Muslim rule; the slow process of conversion to Islam had begun. This accentuated the importance of the patriarchs of Constantinople, the popes in Rome, and the later converting regions of northern and eastern Europe. © Cengage Learning

# Chronology

| | Western Europe | Eastern Europe |
|---|---|---|
| **600** | **711** Muslim conquest of Spain<br>**732** Battle of Tours | **634–650** Muslims conquer Byzantine provinces of Syria, Egypt, and Tunisia |
| **800** | **800** Coronation of Charlemagne<br>**843** Treaty of Verdun divides Carolingian Empire among Charlemagne's grandsons<br>**910** Monastery of Cluny founded<br>**962** Beginning of Holy Roman Empire | **ca. 880** Varangians take control of Kiev<br>**980** Vladimir becomes grand prince of Kievan Russia |
| **1000** | **1054** Formal schism between Latin and Orthodox Churches<br>**1066** Normans under William the Conqueror invade England<br>**1076–1078** Climax of investiture controversy<br>**1095** Pope Urban II preaches First Crusade | **1081–1118** Alexius Comnenus rules Byzantine Empire, calls for western military aid against Muslims |
| **1200** | | **1204** Western knights sack Constantinople in Fourth Crusade |

inquire whether my bath is ready; one says, 'The son has been made out of nothing.'"[1]

Early Christians had established communities in many cities (see Map 10.1). The bishops in the four most prominent cities—Jerusalem, Antioch, Alexandria, and Rome—became recognized as patriarchs or paramount leaders, and Constantine made Constantinople a fifth patriarchate (PAY-tree-ar-kayt). Although recognized as important, theologians like St. Augustine (354–430), the bishop of Hippo in North Africa, were not patriarchs.

The patriarchs appointed bishops throughout their regions, and each bishop consecrated priests within his area of jurisdiction, called a *diocese* or *see*. Church rules set by the patriarch or by councils of bishops guided priests in serving ordinary believers. Priests commemorated Christ's sacrifice on the cross in the consumption of wine and a wafer or bread in the Mass, or church service. Church leaders differed on the precise form of other rituals and on which should be considered sacred mysteries, or

sacraments. Before baptism became standardized as a ritual for newborns, for example, it was sometimes postponed until late in life so that the person could benefit from the forgiveness of sin that it conveyed.

One area of disagreement within the church hierarchy centered on Jesus' relationship to God the Father and to the Holy Spirit. The bishops gathered for the Council of Nicaea agreed that, contrary to the Arian view, the three formed a divine Trinity in which three manifestations of god somehow came together. But they did not all understand the Trinity in the same way. They also disagreed on whether Mary was the mother of God or the mother of a human named Jesus. Some Christians thought that images of God or Jesus or Mary, called *icons*, were proper objects to pray before because they stimulated pious thoughts; others, known as *iconoclasts*, or image-breakers, condemned the practice as too much like praying to pagan statues.

In another dispute, Monophysite (muh-NAH-fi-site) (Greek for "one nature") doctrine emphasized the divinity of Jesus Christ and minimized his human characteristics. Finding abhorrent the idea that Christ suffered like an ordinary human on the cross, some Monophysites maintained that another man

---

[1] A.A. Vasiliev, *History of the Byzantine Empire, 324–1435*, vol. 1 (Madison: University of Wisconsin Press, 1978), 79–80.

**Byzantine Church from a Twelfth-Century Manuscript**
The upper portion shows the church façade and domes. The lower portion shows the interior with a mosaic of Christ enthroned at the altar end. Image Asset Management Ltd./SuperStock

had been substituted for him. Versions of Monophysitism persist to this day in Egyptian, Ethiopian, and Armenian churches.

For some four centuries after 300, disagreements like these led to charges and countercharges of heresy. A heresy was a belief or practice so unacceptable as to be un-Christian. The most severe disagreements resulted in a **schism** (SKIZ-uhm) or formal theological break.

Christianity progressed most rapidly in urban centers. Though the country folk (Latin *pagani*, whence the word *pagan* used as a negative label for polytheists) long retained worship of the old gods, the emperor Julian (r. 361–363) tried in vain to restore the old polytheism as the state cult. When a blind Christian addressed Julian by the pejorative term *apostate*

(renegade from Christianity), the emperor said, "You are blind, and your God will not cure you." To this the Christian replied, "I thank God for my blindness, since it prevents me from beholding your impiety."[2] In 392 the emperor Theodosius banned all pagan ceremonies. The following year he terminated the eleven-hundred-year-old tradition of the Olympic Games, which had originated as religious rites but had become increasingly professionalized in Roman times.

Having a single ruler endowed with supreme legal and religious authority prevented the breakup of the Eastern Empire into petty principalities, despite near-constant border wars. A strong emperor might temporarily recover lost ground, as Justinian (r. 527–565) did in seizing Tunisia from Germanic Vandals and reasserting Byzantine control along the east coast of Italy. To the the north and east, however, various enemies, including the Germanic Goths, the nomadic Huns of Central Asia, and the Sasanids of the Iranian Empire, posed severe threats at different times. Bribes, diplomacy, and occasional military victories usually persuaded the Goths and Huns to settle peacefully or move on and attack western Europe. War with the Sasanids, however, flared up repeatedly for almost three hundred years. Finally, a new enemy appeared from the Arabian peninsula: followers of the Arab prophet Muhammad (see Chapter 9). Between 634 and 650, Arab armies destroyed the Sasanid Empire and captured Byzantine Egypt, Syria, and Tunisia. By the end of the twelfth century at least two-thirds of the Christians in these former Byzantine territories had adopted the Muslim faith.

The loss of such populous and prosperous provinces shook the empire and reduced its power. Although the empire had largely recovered and reorganized militarily by the tenth century, it never regained the lost lands and eventually succumbed to Muslim conquest in 1453. The later Byzantine emperors faced new enemies in the north and south. Following the wave of Germanic migrations, Slavic and Turkish peoples appeared on the northern frontiers

---

[2] Ibid., 71.

**schism**  A formal split within a religious community.

as part of centuries-long population migrations in Eurasian steppelands. Other Turks led by the Seljuk family became the primary foe in the south.

At the same time, relations with the popes and provinces of western Europe steadily worsened. In the mid-ninth century the patriarchs of Constantinople had challenged the territorial jurisdiction of the peoples of Rome and some of the practices of the Latin Church. These arguments culminated in 1054 in a formal schism between the Latin Church and the Orthodox Church—a break that has been only partially mended.

## Society and Urban Life

Imperial authority and urban prosperity in the eastern provinces of the old Roman Empire initially sheltered Byzantium from the economic reverses and population losses suffered from the third century on. However, the territorial losses to Arab invaders coming on the heels of a devastating sixth-century epidemic of bubonic plague, known as "the plague of Justinian," gave Byzantium a taste of decline. Popular narratives of saints' lives show a transition from stories about educated saints hailing from cities to stories about saints who originated as peasants. In many areas, barter replaced money transactions; some cities declined in population and wealth; and the traditional class of local urban notables nearly disappeared.

As the urban elite class shrank, the importance of high-ranking aristocrats at the imperial court and of rural landowners gained importance. Power organized by family began to rival power from class-based officeholding. By the end of the eleventh century, a family-based military aristocracy had emerged. Of Byzantine emperor Alexius Comnenus (uh-LEX-see-uhs kom-NAY-nuhs) (r. 1081–1118) it was said: "He considered himself not a ruler, but a lord, conceiving and calling the empire his own house."[3]

The situation of women changed, too. After the seventh century women increasingly found themselves confined to the home. Some sources indicate that when they went out, they concealed their faces behind veils. Paradoxically, however, from 1028 to 1056 women ruled the Byzantine Empire alongside their husbands. The increase in the seclusion of women resembles simultaneous developments in neighboring Islamic countries, but a firm linkage between them has yet to be found.

Economically, the Byzantine emperors continued the Late Roman practice of setting prices, organizing grain shipments to the capital, and monopolizing luxury goods like Tyrian purple cloth. Such government intervention may have slowed technological development and economic innovation. In the countryside, Byzantine farmers continued to use slow oxcarts and light scratch plows, which were efficient for many, but not all, soil types, long after farmers in western Europe had begun to adopt more efficient techniques.

Because Byzantium's Roman inheritance remained so much more intact than western Europe's, few people recognized the slow deterioration. Gradually, however, pilgrims and visitors from the west saw the reality beyond the awe-inspiring, incense-filled domes of cathedrals and beneath the glitter and silken garments of the royal court. An eleventh-century French visitor wrote:

> The city itself [Constantinople] is squalid and fetid and in many places harmed by permanent darkness, for the wealthy overshadow the streets with buildings and leave these dirty, dark places to the poor and to travelers; there murders and robberies and other crimes which love the darkness are committed. Moreover, since people live lawlessly in this city, which has . . . almost as many thieves as poor men, a criminal knows neither fear nor shame, because crime is not punished by law and never entirely comes to light. In every respect she exceeds moderation; for, just as she surpasses other cities in wealth, so too, does she surpass them in vice.[4]

A Byzantine contemporary, Anna Comnena, the brilliant daughter of Emperor Alexius Comnenus, expressed the view from the other side. She scornfully described a prominent churchman and philosopher who happened to be from Italy: "Italos . . . was unable with his barbaric, stupid temperament to grasp the profound truths of philosophy; even in the act of learning he utterly rejected the teacher's guiding

[3] A. P. Kazhdan and Ann Wharton Epstein, *Change in Byzantine Culture in the Eleventh and Twelfth Centuries* (Berkeley: University of California Press, 1985), 71.

[4] Ibid., 248.

hand, and full of temerity and barbaric folly, [believed] even before study that he excelled all others."[5]

## Cultural Achievements

Justinian's collection of Roman laws endured far longer than his restoration of Byzantine rule in Italy and North Africa. At his command a team of seventeen legal scholars made a systematic compilation, in Latin, of a thousand years of Roman legal tradition. The *Corpus Juris Civilis*, or Body of Civil Law, as it has been called since the sixteenth century, consisted of four sections: the laws themselves, a digest for lawyers and judges containing quotations from well-known commentaries, and a student textbook. A collection of recent Justinian decrees not previously collected made up the fourth section added later. In the eleventh century a legal scholar named Irnerius (ca. 1055–ca. 1130) revived the study of this code (see Chapter 13) at the University of Bologna (boe-LOAN-yuh) in Italy, and it subsequently became the basis of most modern European legal systems.

Constantinople's cathedral, the Hagia Sophia (Ah-yah SOH-fee-uh) ("Sacred Wisdom"), also dates in its present form to the reign of Justinian and his influential wife, the empress Theodora. Its great dome became a hallmark of Byzantine architecture. Artistic creativity appeared in the design and ornamentation of other churches and monasteries as well. Byzantine religious art, featuring stiff but arresting images of holy figures against gold backgrounds, strongly influenced painting in western Europe down to the thirteenth century, and Byzantine musical traditions strongly affected the chanting employed in medieval Latin churches.

Other important Byzantine achievements date to the empire's long period of political decline. In the ninth century, two brothers named Cyril and Methodius embarked on a highly successful mission to the Slavs of Moravia (part of the modern Czech Republic). Like the Gothic bishop Ulfilas in the fourth century, they preached in the local language, and their followers perfected a writing system, called Cyrillic (sih-RIL-ik), that came to be used by Slavic Christians adhering to the Orthodox—that is, Byzantine—rite. Their careers also mark the beginning of a competition between

**SECTION REVIEW**

- With Christianity as a state religion, the Eastern Roman Empire retained its unity and became the Byzantine Empire, continuing the Roman imperial and legal traditions in the east.

- Doctrinal and territorial disputes led to a formal schism that split the Orthodox Church from the Catholic Church in the west.

- Plagues and invasions caused significant cultural and political shifts and decline in the Byzantine Empire.

- The culture of the Byzantine Empire made many important aesthetic contributions to the art of Europe.

- Byzantine missionaries spread their faith and the Cyrillic alphabet into eastern Europe.

the Greek and Latin forms of Christianity for the allegiance of the Slavs. The use today of the Cyrillic alphabet among the Russians and other Slavic peoples of Orthodox Christian faith, and of the Roman alphabet among the Slavic Poles, Czechs, and Croatians, testifies to this competition.

# EARLY MEDIEVAL EUROPE, 600–1000

■ *How did the culture of early medieval Europe develop in the absence of imperial rule?*

The disappearance of the imperial legal framework that had persisted to the final days of the Western Roman Empire (see Chapter 5) and the rise of various kings, nobles, and chieftains changed the legal and political landscape of western Europe. In region after region, the family-based traditions of the Germanic peoples, which often fit local conditions better than previous practices, supplanted the edicts of the Roman emperors (see Map 10.2).

Fear and physical insecurity led communities to seek the protection of local strongmen. In places where looters and pillagers might appear at any moment, a local lord with a castle at which peasants could take refuge counted for more than a distant king. Dependency of weak people on strong people became a hallmark of the post-Roman period in western Europe.

## The Time of Insecurity

By 530 the Western Roman Empire had fragmented into a handful of dissimilar kingdoms

---

[5] Ibid., 255.

**Viking Runestone** Pre-Christian symbols and myths from northern Europe appear on stones like this one from Sweden. An inscription containing names written in the runic alphabet had elaborately intertwined ornaments at the ends, a feature that reappears in the Christian Book of Kells. The scene at the top is thought to depict Odin, the chief god of the Vikings.
Werner Forman/Art Resource, NY

under Germanic rulers. The Franks held much of Gaul, the Visigoths ruled Spain, and the Ostrogoths ruled in Italy and present-day Austria and Hungary. By 600 the Lombards had replaced the Ostrogoths in northern Italy, and the Byzantine Empire had regained footholds in the south and around Ravenna along the east coast. The city of Rome lost most of its population and its political importance but retained prominence as the seat of the bishop of Rome. Local noble families competed for control of this position, which over several centuries acquired the title *pope* (supreme cleric) in the Latin-speaking church.

The educated few, most of them Christian priests and monks, spoke and wrote a simplified form of Latin, but the uneducated masses who had lived under Roman rule spoke Romance dialects that eventually became modern Portuguese, Spanish, French, Italian, and Romanian. In the north and east of the Rhine River, where Roman culture had scarcely penetrated, people spoke Germanic and related Scandinavian languages. East of the Elbe River, Slavic speakers formed a third major group. Whatever sense of unity Europe may have experienced under Roman rule gave way to strongly localized identities.

In 711 a frontier raiding party of Muslim Arabs and Berbers crossed the Strait of Gibraltar and defeated the Visigoths in Spain (see Chapter 9). After pushing the remaining Christian chieftains into the northern mountains, the Muslims moved on to France. They occupied much of the southern coast and penetrated as far north as Tours, less than 150 miles (240 kilometers) from the English Channel, before the Frankish leader Charles Martel, Charlemagne's grandfather, stopped their most advanced raiding party in 732 at the Battle of Tours.

Military effectiveness was the key element in the rise of the Carolingian (kah-roe-LIN-gee-uhn) family (from Latin *Carolus*, "Charles"), first as protectors of the Frankish (French) kings, then as kings themselves under Charlemagne's father Pepin (r. 751–768), and finally with Charlemagne as emperor. Charlemagne's Carolingian Empire encompassed all of Gaul and parts of Germany and Italy. When Charlemagne's son Louis the Pious died, the Germanic tradition of splitting property among sons led to the Treaty of Verdun (843), which divided the empire into three parts. French-speaking in the west (France) and middle (Burgundy), and German-speaking in the east (Germany), the three

**Map 10.2 Germanic Kingdoms** Though German kings asserted authority over most of western Europe, German-speaking peoples were most numerous east of the Rhine River. In most other areas, Celtic languages such as Irish or languages derived from Latin predominated. Though the absolute number of Germanic settlers seems to have been fairly limited, the Germanic Anglo-Saxon tongue increasingly supplanted the Celtic Welsh and Scottish in Britain.

© Cengage Learning

regions never reunited (see Map 10.2). Nevertheless, the Carolingian economic system based on landed wealth and a brief intellectual revival sponsored personally by Charlemagne—himself illiterate—provided a common heritage.

In 793, Viking sea raiders from Scandinavia attacked and plundered an English coastal monastery, the first of hundreds of similar raids. Local sources from France, the British Isles, and Muslim Spain reflect widespread dread of Viking warriors descending from multi-oared, dragon-prowed boats to pillage monasteries, villages, and towns. Versatile Viking vessels could both brave the stormy North Atlantic and maneuver up rivers. By the ninth century raiders from Denmark and Norway were harrying the British and French coasts while Varangians (va-RAN-gee-anz) (Swedes) pursued raiding and trading interests along the rivers of eastern Europe and Russia. In the 800s and 900s Viking captains organized the settlement of Iceland and Greenland, and, around the year 1000, they reached the northern tip

of Newfoundland, which they called *Vinland* ("the land of grapevines").

Vikings long settled on lands they had seized in Normandy (in northwestern France) organized the most important and ambitious expeditions in terms of numbers of men and horses and long-lasting impact. William the Conqueror, the duke of Normandy, invaded England in 1066 and brought Anglo-Saxon domination of the island to an end. Other Normans (from "north men") attacked Muslim Sicily in the 1060s and, after thirty years of fighting, permanently severed it from the Muslim world.

## A Self-Sufficient Economy

Archaeology and monastic records reveal a profound economic transformation that accompanied the new Germanic political order. The new rulers cared little for the Romans' urban-based culture, which accordingly shrank in importance. Change was more rapid in some regions than others, but most cities lost population, or even became

**Boatbuilding Scene from the Bayeux Tapestry** Eleventh-century shipwrights prepare vessels for William of Normandy's invasion of England. Building ships under the orders of Duke William, detail from the Bayeux Tapestry, before 1082 (wool embroidery on linen), French School, (11th century)/ Musee de la Tapisserie, Bayeux, France/With special authorisation of the city of Bayeux/The Bridgeman Art Library

villages. Roman roads fell into disuse and disrepair. Small thatched houses sprang up beside abandoned villas, and marble public buildings became dilapidated. Paying for purchases in coin largely gave way to bartering goods and services. Although trade across the Mediterranean did not entirely stop after the Muslim conquests, archaeological investigations of sunken ships show contact more with North African ports than with Egypt and Syria, and western Europe came to rely on meager local resources.

Roman centralization had channeled the wealth and production of the empire to the capital, which in turn radiated Roman culture to the provinces. As literacy and other aspects of Roman life declined and as Germanic territorial lords replaced Roman governors, Germanic and Celtic cultural traditions became more dominant, and self-sufficient farming estates known as **manors** became centers of agricultural production. The lack of a central government, poor communication, and warfare made unprotected country houses vulnerable to pillaging, so farmers in isolated regions gave their land to large landowners in return for protection. Many became warriors, maintained a force of armed men, or swore allegiance to landowners who had armed forces to protect them.

Depending on local custom, protection ranged from a ditch and wooden stockade to a stone wall surrounding a fortified keep (a stone building). Fortification tended to increase until the twelfth century, when stronger monarchies made it less necessary.

Manor life reflected personal status. A well-appointed manor possessed fields, gardens, grazing lands, fishponds, a mill, a church, workshops for making farm and household implements, and a village where the farmers dependent on the lord of the manor lived. Nobles and their families exercised almost unlimited power over the **serfs**—agricultural workers who belonged to the manor, tilled its fields, and owed other dues and obligations. Serfs could not leave the manor where they were born and attach themselves to another lord. Most peasants in England, France, and western Germany were unfree serfs in the tenth and eleventh centuries. In Bordeaux (bore-DOE), Saxony,

**manor** In medieval Europe, a large, self-sufficient landholding consisting of the lord's residence (manor house), outbuildings, peasant village, and surrounding land.

**serf** In medieval Europe, an agricultural laborer legally bound to a lord's property and obligated to perform set services for the lord. In Russia, later, some serfs worked as artisans and in factories; serfdom was not abolished there until 1861.

237

and a few other regions, free peasantry survived based on the egalitarian social structure of the Germanic peoples during their period of migration. Outright slavery, the mainstay of the Roman economy (see Chapter 5), diminished as more and more peasants became serfs in return for a lord's protection. At the same time, taking prisoners to serve as slaves became less important as an object of warfare.

The average western European of the ninth century was probably better nourished than his or her descendants three hundred years later, when population was increasing and the nobility monopolized the resources of the forests. While nobles ate better than peasants, even the peasant diet of the north was reasonably balanced, featuring beer, lard or butter, and bread made of barley, rye, or wheat, and supplemented by pork from herds of swine fed on forest acorns and beechnuts, and by game from the same forests. The Roman diet based on wheat, wine, and olive oil persisted in the south.

## Early Medieval Society in the West

Reversion to a self-sufficient economy limited the freedom and potential for personal achievement of most people, but an emerging class of nobles reaped great benefits. During the Germanic migrations and later among the Vikings of Scandinavia, men regularly answered the call to arms issued by war chiefs, to whom they swore allegiance. All warriors shared in the booty gained from raiding. As settlement enhanced the importance of agricultural tasks, laying down the plow and picking up the sword at the chieftain's call became harder.

Those who continued to join the war parties included a growing number of horsemen. Mounted warriors became the central force of the Carolingian army. At first, fighting from horseback did not make a person either a nobleman or a landowner. By the tenth century, however, nearly constant warfare to protect land rights or support the claims of a lord brought about a gradual transformation in the status of the mounted warrior. At different rates in different areas, landholding became almost inseparable from military service.

The German foes of the Roman legions had equipped themselves with helmets, shields, and swords, spears, or throwing axes. Most fought on foot.

Horsemen, using stirrups first invented by Central Asian pastoralists around the first century C.E., were able to stand in the saddle, lean forward, and absorb the impact when their lances struck the enemy at full gallop. This type of warfare required grain-fed horses that were larger and heavier than the small, grass-fed animals of the Central Asian nomads. Thus agricultural Europe rather than the European steppelands produced the charges of armored knights that by the eleventh century came to dominate the battlefield.

Knights wore an open-faced helmet and a long linen shirt, or hauberk (HAW-berk), studded with small metal disks. A century later, knightly equipment commonly included a visored helmet that covered the head and neck and a hauberk of chain mail. More armor for knight and horse meant a greater financial outlay. Since land was the basis of wealth, a knight needed financial support from land revenues. Accordingly, kings began to reward armed service with grants of land from their own property. Lesser nobles with extensive properties built their own military retinues the same way.

A grant of land in return for a pledge to provide military service was often called a **fief**. At first, kings granted fiefs to their noble followers, known as **vassals**, on a temporary basis. By the tenth century, most fiefs could be inherited as long as the specified military service continued to be provided. Starting in the sixteenth century, it became common to refer to medieval Europe as a "feudal society" (from the Latin *feodum*, meaning land awarded for military service) in which kings and lords gave land to vassals in return for sworn military support.

By analyzing original records, more recent historians have discovered this to be an oversimplification. Relations between landholders and serfs and between lords and vassals differed too much from one place to another to fit together in anything resembling a regular system. The lord of a manor rather than the king provided local governance and justice, and members of the clergy, along with the extensive agricultural lands owned by monasteries and convents, fell under

**fief** In medieval Europe, land granted in return for a sworn oath to provide specified military service.

**vassal** In medieval Europe, a sworn supporter of a king or lord committed to rendering specified military service to that king or lord.

**Noblewoman Directing Construction of a Church** This picture of Berthe, wife of Girat de Roussillon, acting as mistress of the works comes from a tenth-century manuscript that shows a scene from the ninth century. Wheelbarrows rarely appear in medieval building scenes. Copyright Brussels, Royal Library of Belgium

the jurisdiction of the church, further limiting the reach and authority of the monarch.

While practices varied between and within realms, the "typical" medieval realm consisted of lands directly owned by a king or a count and administered by royal officers, with the king's or count's major vassals holding and administering other lands in return for military service. These vassals, in turn, granted land to their own vassals. Kings and lords commanded the service of their vassals for only part of the year. Vassals could hold land from several different lords and owe loyalty to each one. Moreover, the allegiance that a vassal owed to one lord could entail military service to that lord's master in time of need.

Noblewomen became enmeshed in this tangle of obligations as heiresses and as candidates for marriage. A man who married the widow or daughter of a lord with no sons could gain control of that lord's property. Marriage alliances affected entire kingdoms. Noble daughters and sons had little say in marriage matters; issues of land, power, and military service took precedence.

Nevertheless, a noblewomen could own land or administer her husband's estates when he was away at war. Nonnoble women usually worked alongside their menfolk, performing agricultural tasks such as raking and stacking hay, shearing sheep, and picking vegetables. As artisans, women spun, wove, and sewed clothing. The Bayeux (bay-YUH) Tapestry, a piece of embroidery 230 feet (70 meters) long and 20 inches (51 centimeters) wide depicting William the Conqueror's invasion of England in 1066 (see page 237), was designed and executed entirely by women, though historians do not agree on who those women were.

## SECTION REVIEW

- Post-Roman European society was marked by the prevalence of Germanic traditions and the dependency of the weak on the strong.

- The eighth century through the mid-eleventh was a period of great insecurity, with Charlemagne's empire providing short-lived stability.

- After the fall of the empire, technological sophistication and urban life declined, and self-sufficient manors dominated agriculture.

- The mounted warrior elite came to dominate a society shaped by the exchange of rights and obligations.

- Noblewomen were part of the exchange system, while nonnoble women worked alongside men.

# THE WESTERN CHURCH

■ *What role did the Western Church play in the politics and culture of Europe?*

Just as eastern European Christians followed the religious guidance of the patriarch of Constantinople, so did the pope wield authority over church affairs in western Europe. And while Orthodox missionaries spread Christianity among the Slavs, Catholic missionaries added territory to Christendom with forays into the British Isles and the lands of the Germans.

In the west Roman nobles lost control of the **papacy**—the office of the pope—after the tenth century, and it became a more powerful international office. Councils of bishops—which normally set rules called canons to regulate the priests and laypeople under their jurisdiction—became increasingly responsive to papal direction.

Nevertheless, regional disagreements over church regulations, shortages of educated and trained clergy, difficult communications, and political disorder posed formidable obstacles to unifying church standards and practices. Clerics in some parts of western Europe were still issuing prohibitions against the worship of rivers, trees, and mountains as late as the eleventh century. Church problems included lingering polytheism, lax enforcement of prohibitions against priests marrying, nepotism (giving preferment to close kin), and simony (selling ecclesiastical appointments, often to laymen). The persistence of the papacy in asserting its legal jurisdiction over clergy, combating polytheism and heretical beliefs, and calling on secular rulers to recognize the pope's authority constituted a rare force for unity and order in a time of disunity and chaos (see Diversity and Dominance: The Struggle for Christian Morality).

## Politics and the Church

The pope needed allies. Although Charlemagne's father Pepin was a strong supporter of the papacy, the relationship between kings and popes was tense, since both thought of themselves as ultimate authorities. In 962 the pope crowned the first "Holy Roman Emperor" (Charlemagne never held this full title). This designation of a secular political authority as the guardian of collective Christian interests proved more apparent then real. Essentially a loose confederation of German princes who named one of their own as emperor, the **Holy Roman Empire** had little influence west of the Rhine River.

Although the pope crowned the early Holy Roman Emperors, this did not signify political superiority. The law of the church (known as *canon law* because each law was called a *canon*) gave the pope exclusive legal jurisdiction over clergy and church property wherever located. But bishops who held land as vassals owed military support or other services and dues to kings and princes. The secular rulers demanded the power to appoint those bishops because that was the only way to guarantee fulfillment of their duties as vassals. The popes disagreed.

In the eleventh century, this conflict over the control of ecclesiastical appointments came to a head. Hildebrand (HILL-de-brand), an Italian monk, capped a career of reorganizing church finances when the cardinals (a group of senior bishops) meeting in Rome selected him to be Pope Gregory VII in 1073. His personal notion of the papacy (preserved among his letters) represented an extreme position:

§ The pope can be judged by no one;
§ The Roman church has never erred and never will err till the end of time;
§ The pope alone can depose and restore bishops;
§ He alone can call general councils and authorize canon law;
§ He can depose emperors;
§ He can absolve subjects from their allegiance;
§ All princes should kiss his feet.[6]

Such claims antagonized lords and monarchs, who had become accustomed to *investing*—that is, conferring a ring and a staff as symbols of authority on bishops and abbots in their domains. Historians

---

[6] R. W. Southern, *Western Society and the Church in the Middle Ages* (Harmondsworth, England: Penguin, 1970), 102.

**papacy** The central administration of the Roman Catholic Church, of which the pope is the head.

**Holy Roman Empire** Loose federation of mostly German states and principalities, headed by an emperor elected by the princes. It lasted from 962 to 1806.

apply the term **investiture controversy** to the medieval struggle between the church and the lay lords to control ecclesiastical appointments; the term also refers to the broader conflict of popes versus monarchs. When Holy Roman Emperor Henry IV defied Gregory's reforms, Gregory excommunicated him in 1076, thereby cutting him off from church rituals. Stung by the resulting decline in his influence, Henry stood barefoot in the snow for three days outside a castle in northern Italy waiting for Gregory, a guest there, to receive him. Henry's formal act of penance induced Gregory to forgive him and restore him to the church; but the reconciliation, an apparent victory for the pope, proved hollow. In 1078 Gregory deposed Henry but then had to flee from Rome to Salerno, where he died two years later.

A compromise was reached in 1122 at Worms, a town in Germany. In the Concordat of Worms, Emperor Henry V renounced his right to choose bishops and abbots or bestow spiritual symbols upon them. In return, Pope Calixtus II permitted the emperor to invest papally appointed bishops and abbots with any lay rights or obligations before their spiritual consecration. Such compromises did not fully solve the problem, but they reduced tensions between the two sides.

Assertions of royal authority triggered other conflicts as well. Though barely twenty when he became king of England in 1154, Henry II, a great-grandson of William the Conqueror, acted to strengthen the power of the Crown and weaken the nobility. He appointed traveling justices to enforce his laws and made juries, a holdover from traditional Germanic law, into powerful legal instruments. He also established the principle that criminal acts violated the "king's peace" and should be tried and punished in accordance with charges brought by the Crown instead of in response to charges brought by victims.

Henry had a harder time controlling the church. His closest friend and chancellor, or chief administrator, Thomas à Becket (ca. 1118–1170), lived the grand and luxurious life of a courtier. In 1162 Henry persuaded Becket to become a priest and assume the position of archbishop of Canterbury, the highest church office in England. Becket agreed but cautioned that from then on he would act solely in the interest of the church. When Henry sought to try clerics accused of crimes in royal instead of ecclesiastical courts, Archbishop Thomas, now leading an austere and pious life, resisted. In 1170 four of Henry's knights, knowing that the king desired Becket's death, murdered the archbishop in Canterbury Cathedral. Their crime backfired, and an outpouring of sympathy caused Canterbury to become a major pilgrimage center. In 1173 the pope declared the martyred Becket a saint. His authority badly damaged, Henry allowed himself to be publicly whipped twice in penance for the crime.

Henry II's conflict with Thomas à Becket, like the Concordat of Worms, yielded no clear victor. The problem of competing legal traditions made political life in western Europe more complicated than in Byzantium. So-called feudal law, rooted in Germanic custom, gave supreme power to the king. Canon law, based on Roman precedent, visualized a single church with jurisdiction over all of Western Christendom. In the eleventh century Roman imperial law, contained in the *Corpus Juris Civilis*, added a third tradition.

## Monasticism

**Monasticism** featured prominently in the religious life of almost all medieval Christian lands. The origins of group monasticism lay in the eastern lands of the Roman Empire. Pre-Christian practices such as celibacy, continual devotion to prayer, and living apart from society (alone or in small groups) came together in Christian form in Egypt. A hermit named Anthony (ca. 251–356), sometimes called the Father of All Monks, attracted many followers to his life of extreme privation in the Egyptian desert.

Monasticism in western Europe, however, involved groups of monks or nuns living together in organized communities. The person most responsible for introducing this practice in the Latin west was

**investiture controversy** Dispute between the popes and the Holy Roman Emperors over who held ultimate authority over bishops in imperial lands.

**monasticism** Living in a religious community apart from secular society and adhering to a rule stipulating chastity, obedience, and poverty. It was a prominent element of medieval Christianity and Buddhism. Monasteries were the primary centers of learning and literacy in medieval Europe.

# Diversity & Dominance

## The Struggle for Christian Morality

### Ireland

The medieval church believed that Christians could be absolved of their sins by performing public or private penalties, or acts of humiliation. Priests listened to the believers confess their sins and then set the nature and duration of the penance. Books called penitentials guided the priests by stipulating the appropriate penance for specific sins. These books varied over time and tended to reflect local conditions. One of the earliest is attributed to Saint Patrick, who began his missionary work in Ireland in 432. The selections below deal not just with penalties for sin but also with efforts to impose church discipline on priests.

§ There shall be no wandering cleric in a parish.

§ If any cleric, from sexton [church caretaker] to priest, is seen without a tunic, and does not cover the shame and nakedness of his body; and if his hair is not shaven according to the Roman custom, and if his wife goes about with her head unveiled, he shall be alike despised by laymen and separated from the Church.

§ A monk and a virgin, the one from one place, the other from another, shall not dwell together in the same inn, nor travel in the same carriage from village to village, nor continually hold conversation with each other.

§ It is not permitted to the Church to accept alms from pagans.

§ A Christian who believes that there is a vampire in the world, that is to say, a witch, is to be anathematized [condemned by the Church]; whoever lays that reputation upon a living being, shall not be received into the Church until he revokes with his own voice the crime that he has committed and accordingly does penance with all diligence.

§ A Christian who defrauds anyone with respect to a debt in the manner of the pagans, shall be excommunicated [barred from Christian society] until he pays the debt.

### England and Southern Germany

Boniface (ca. 675–754), a widely esteemed bishop of the southern German city of Mainz, began life with the name Winfrid in Anglo-Saxon Britain. After working as a missionary in Frisia in the Netherlands, he devoted the bulk of his life to establishing Christianity and respect for Christian law and morality in southern Germany. His letters reflect his passion for reforming personal behavior along Christian lines.

#### Boniface to Pope Zacharias, 742

We must confess, our father and lord, that after we learned from messengers that your predecessor in the apostolate [i.e., papacy], Gregory of reverend memory . . . had been set free from the prison of the body and had passed on to God, nothing gave us greater joy or happiness than the knowledge that the Supreme Arbiter had appointed your fatherly clemency to administer the canon law and to govern the Apostolic See. . . .

Some of the ignorant common people, Alemanians, Bavarians, and Franks, hearing that many of the offenses prohibited by us are practiced in the city of Rome imagine that they are allowed by the priests there and reproach us for causing them to incur blame in their own lives. They say that on the first day of January year after year, in the city of Rome and in the neighborhood of St. Peter's church by day or night, they have seen bands of singers parading the streets in pagan fashion, shouting and chanting sacrilegious songs and loading tables with food day and night, while no one in his own house is willing to lend his neighbor fire or tools or any other convenience. They say also that they have seen there women with amulets and bracelets of heathen fashion on their arms and legs, offering them for sale to willing buyers. . . .

#### Boniface and Other Bishops to King Ethelbald of Mercia (a Saxon Kingdom in England), 746–747

We have heard that you are very liberal in almsgiving, and congratulate you thereon. . . . We have heard also that you repress robbery and wrongdoing, perjury, and rapine with a strong hand, and that you have established peace within your kingdom. . . .

But amidst all this, one evil report as to the manner of life of Your Grace has come to our hearing, which has greatly grieved us and which we would wish were not true. We have learned from many sources that you have never taken to yourself a lawful wife.... If you had willed to do this for the sake of chastity and abstinence ... we should rejoice, for that is not worthy of blame but rather of praise. But if, as many say—but which God forbid!—you have neither taken a lawful spouse nor observed chastity for God's sake but, moved by desire, have defiled your good name before God and man by the crime of adulterous lust, then we are greatly grieved because this is a sin in the sight of God and is the ruin of your fair fame among men.

And now, what is worse, our informants say that these atrocious crimes are committed in convents with holy nuns and virgins consecrated to God, and this, beyond all doubt, doubles the offense....

## Northern Germany and Scandinavia

*A*dam of Bremen's *History of the Archbishops of Hamburg-Bremen consists of four sections. The third is devoted to the Archbishop Adalbert, whose death in 1072 stirred Adam to write. References to classical poets, the lives of saints, and royal documents show that Adam, a churchman, had a solid education and access to many sources, including conversations with kings and nobles.*

This remarkable man [i.e., Archbishop Adalbert] may ... be extolled with praise of every kind in that he was noble, handsome, wise, eloquent, chaste, temperate. All these qualities he comprised in himself and others besides, such as one is wont to attach to the outer man: that he was rich, that he was successful, that he was glorious, that he was influential. All these things were his in abundance. Moreover, in respect of the mission to the heathen, which is the first duty of the Church at Hamburg, no one so vigorous could ever be found....

As soon as the metropolitan [i.e., Archbishop Adalbert] had entered upon his episcopate, he sent legates to the kings of the north in the interest of friendship. There were also dispersed throughout all Denmark and Norway and Sweden and to the ends of the earth admonitory letters in which he exhorted the bishops and priests living in those parts ... fearlessly to forward the conversion of the pagans.... [One Danish king] forgot the heavenly King as things prospered with him and married a blood relative from Sweden. This mightily displeased the lord archbishop,

who sent legates to the rash king, rebuking him severely for his sin, and who stated finally that if he did not come to his senses, he would have to be cut off with the sword of excommunication. Beside himself with rage, the king then threatened to ravage and destroy the whole diocese of Hamburg. Unperturbed by these threats, our archbishop, reproving and entreating, remained firm, until at length the Danish tyrant was prevailed upon by letters from the pope to give his cousin a bill of divorce....

In Norway ... King Harold surpassed all the madness of tyrants in his savage wildness. Many churches were destroyed by that man; many Christians were tortured to death by him. But he was a mighty man and renowned for the victories he had previously won in many wars with barbarians in Greece and in the Scythian regions [while assisting the Byzantine empress Zoë fight the Seljuk Turks]. After he came into his fatherland, however, he never ceased from warfare; he was the thunderbolt of the north.... And so, as he ruled over many nations, he was odious to all on account of his greed and cruelty. He also gave himself up to the magic arts and, wretched man that he was, did not heed the fact that his most saintly brother [Saint Olaf, one of Harold's predecessors] had eradicated such illusions from the realm and striven even unto death for the adoption of the precepts of Christianity....

Across the Elbe [east of the river Hamburg is on] and in Slavia our affairs were still meeting with great success. For Gottschalk ... married a daughter of the Danish king and so thoroughly subdued the Slavs that they feared him like a king, offered to pay tribute, and asked for peace with subjection. Under these circumstances our Church at Hamburg enjoyed peace, and Slavia abounded in priests and churches....

## QUESTIONS FOR ANALYSIS

1. How are the practices of non-Christians used as good and bad examples for Christians?
2. What limits, if any, do church officials recognize in their role as moral judges?
3. How does the church confront royal authority?

*Sources*: Excerpts from John T. McNeill and Helena M. Gamer, *Medieval Handbooks of Penance* (New York: Columbia University Press, 1938), 77–78; *The Letters of Saint Boniface*, tr. Ephraim Emerton (New York: Columbia University Press, 2000), 56, 59–60, 103–105; and *History of the Archbishops of Hamburg-Bremen*, tr. Francis J. Tschan (New York: Columbia University Press, 1959 [new ed. 2002]), 114–133.

Benedict of Nursia (ca. 480–547) in Italy. Benedict began his pious career as a hermit in a cave but eventually organized several monasteries, each headed by an abbot. In the seventh century monasteries based on his model spread far beyond Italy. *The Rule of Saint Benedict*, written to govern the monks' behavior, envisions a balanced life of devotion and work, along with obligations of celibacy, poverty, and obedience to the abbot. Those who lived by this or other monastic rules became *regular clergy*, in contrast to *secular clergy*, priests who lived in society instead of in seclusion. The *Rule* of Benedict was the starting point for most forms of western European monastic life and remains in force today in Benedictine monasteries.

Though monks and nuns made up a small percentage of the total population, their secluded way of life reinforced the separation of religious affairs from ordinary politics and economics. Monasteries followed Jesus' axiom to "render unto Caesar what is Caesar's and unto God what is God's" better than the many town-based bishops who behaved like lords.

Monasteries preserved literacy and learning in the early medieval period, although some rulers, like Charlemagne, encouraged scholarship at court. Regular clergy saw copying manuscripts and even writing books as a religious calling, thereby preserving many Roman works that would otherwise have disappeared. The survival of Greek works depended more on Byzantine and Muslim scribes in the east.

Monasteries could plant Christianity in new lands, as Irish monks did in parts of Germany, service the needs of travelers, organize agricultural production on their lands, and raise abandoned infants. Convents provided refuge for widows and other women who lacked male protection or desired a spiritual life. Yet oversight was a problem. A bishop might have authority over an abbot or abbess (head of a convent), but he could not exercise constant vigilance over what went on behind monastery walls.

A reform movement focused on monastic discipline took shape in the Benedictine abbey of Cluny (KLOO-nee) in eastern France. William the Pious, the first duke of Aquitaine, founded Cluny in 910 and freed it of lay authority. A century later the local bishop conferred similar freedom. Cluny's abbots pursued a vigorous campaign, eventually allying with reforming popes like Gregory VII to improve monastic

## SECTION REVIEW

- In western Europe, the papacy became the most powerful international institution and thus a source of cultural unity.
- Popes sought secular allies by engaging the support of kings and conferring the title *Holy Roman Emperor*.
- Pope Gregory VII asserted papal primacy and touched off the investiture controversy with the Holy Roman Empire.
- Although the Concordat of Worms partially resolved the controversy, conflicts between secular and papal authority continued.
- Western monasticism originated with Benedict of Nursia, and monasteries and convents became important cultural centers.
- Failing monastic discipline led to the Cluniac and Cistercian reform movements.

discipline and administration. A magnificent new abbey church—with later additions, the largest in the world—symbolized Cluny's preeminence.

At the peak of Cluny's influence, nearly a thousand Benedictine abbeys and priories (lower-level monastic houses) in various countries accepted the authority of its abbot. The Benedictine *Rule* made each monastery independent; but the Cluniac reformers stipulated that every abbot and prior (head of a priory) be appointed by the abbot of Cluny. Monastic reform gained new impetus in the second half of the twelfth century with the rapid rise of the Cistercian order, which emphasized a life of asceticism and poverty.

# KIEVAN RUSSIA, 900–1200

■ *What was the significance of the adoption of Orthodox Christianity by Kievan Russia?*

Though Latin and Orthodox Christendom followed different paths in later centuries, which of them would flourish more was not apparent in 900. Many Slavs living in the north eventually accepted the Catholicism of Rome as taught by German missionaries. The Serbs and other southern Slavs took their faith from Constantinople. The conversion of Kievan Russia, farther to the east, shows how economics, politics, and religious life were closely intertwined. The choice of Orthodoxy over Catholicism had important consequences for later European history.

## The Rise of the Kievan Empire

The territory between the Black and Caspian Seas in the south and the Baltic and White Seas in the north divides into a series of east-west zones. Frozen tundra in the far north gives way to a cold forest zone, then to a more temperate forest, then to a mix of forest and steppe grasslands, and finally to grassland only. Several navigable rivers, including the Volga, the Dnieper (d-NYEP-er), and the Don, run from north to south across these zones.

Early historical sources reflect repeated linguistic and territorial changes, seemingly under pressure from population migrations. Most of the Germanic peoples, along with some Iranian and west Slavic peoples, migrated into eastern Europe from Ukraine and Russia in Roman times. The peoples who remained behind spoke eastern Slavic languages, except in the far north and south: Finns and related peoples lived in the former region, Turkish-speakers in the latter.

Forest dwellers, farmers, and steppe nomads complemented each other economically. Nomads traded animals for the farmers' grain; and honey, wax, and furs from the forests became important exchange items. Traders could travel east and west by steppe caravan (see Chapter 8), or they could use boats on the rivers to move north and south.

Hoards containing thousands of Byzantine and Islamic coins buried in Poland and on islands in the Baltic Sea where fairs were held attest to the trading activity of Varangians (Swedish Vikings) who sailed across the Baltic and down Russia's rivers. They exchanged forest products and slaves for manufactured goods and coins, which they may have used as jewelry rather than as money, at markets controlled by the Khazar Turks, whose powerful kingdom centered around the mouth of the Volga River.

Historians debate the early meaning of the word *Rus* (from which *Russia* is derived), but at some point it came to refer to Slavic-speaking peoples ruled by Varangians. Unlike western European lords, the Varangian princes and their *druzhina* (military retainers) lived in cities, while the Slavs farmed. The princes occupied themselves with trade and fending off enemies. The Rus of the city of Kiev (KEE-yev),

which was taken over by Varangians around 880, controlled trade on the Dnieper River and dealt more with Byzantium than with the Muslim world because the Dnieper flows into the Black Sea. The Rus of Novgorod (NOHV-goh-rod) played the same role on the Volga. The semilegendary account of the Kievan Rus conversion to Christianity must be seen against this background.

In 980 Vladimir (VLAD-ih-mir) I, a ruler of Novgorod who had fallen from power, returned from exile to Kiev with a band of Varangians and made himself the grand prince of Kievan Russia (see Map 10.3). Though his grandmother Olga had been a Christian, Vladimir built a temple on Kiev's heights and placed there the statues of the six gods his Slavic subjects worshiped. The earliest Russian chronicle reports that Vladimir and his advisers decided against Islam as the official religion because of its ban on alcohol, rejected Judaism (the religion to which the Khazars had converted) because they thought that a truly powerful god would not have let the ancient Jewish kingdom be destroyed, and even spoke with German emissaries advocating Latin Christianity. Why Vladimir chose Orthodox Christianity over the Latin version is not precisely known. The magnificence of Constantinople seems to have been a consideration. After visiting Byzantine churches, his agents reported: "We knew not whether we were in heaven or on earth, for on earth there is no such splendor of [sic] such beauty, and we are at a loss how to describe it. We know only that God dwells there among men, and their service is finer than the ceremonies of other nations."[7]

After choosing a reluctant bride from the Byzantine imperial family, Vladimir converted to Orthodox Christianity, probably in 988, and opened his lands to Orthodox clerics and missionaries. The patriarch of Constantinople appointed a metropolitan (chief bishop) at Kiev to govern ecclesiastical affairs. Churches arose in Kiev, one of them on the ruins of Vladimir's earlier hilltop temple, and writing was introduced, using the Cyrillic alphabet devised earlier for the western Slavs. This extension of Orthodox Christendom northward provided a barrier against the eastward expansion of Latin Christianity. Kiev

---

[7] S. A. Zenkovsky, ed., *Medieval Russia's Epics, Chronicles, and Tales* (New York: New American Library, 1974), 67.

**Map 10.3 Kievan Russia and the Byzantine Empire in the Eleventh Century** By the mid-eleventh century, the princes of Kievan Russia had brought all the eastern Slavs under their rule. The loss of Egypt, Syria, and Tunisia to Arab invaders in the seventh to eighth centuries had turned Byzantium from a far-flung empire into a fairly compact state. From then on the Byzantine rulers looked to the Balkans and Kievan Russia as the primary arena for extending their political and religious influence. © Cengage Learning

became firmly oriented toward trade with Byzantium and turned its back on the Muslim world, though the Volga trade continued through Novgorod.

Struggles within the ruling family and with other enemies, most notably the steppe peoples of the south, marked the later political history of Kievan Russia. But down to the time of the Mongols in the thirteenth century (see Chapter 12), the state remained and served as an instrument for the Christianization of the eastern Slavs.

## Society and Culture

In Kievan Russia political power derived from trade rather than from landholding, so the manorial agricultural system of western Europe never developed. Farmers practiced shifting cultivation of their own lands. They would burn a section of forest, then lightly scratch the ash-strewn surface with a plow. When fertility waned, they would move to another section of forest. Poor land and a short growing season in the most northerly latitudes made food scarce. Living on their own estates, the druzhina evolved from infantry into cavalry and focused their efforts more on horse breeding than on agriculture.

Large cities like Kiev and Novgorod may have reached thirty thousand or fifty thousand people—roughly the size of contemporary London or Paris, but far smaller than Constantinople or major Muslim

**SECTION REVIEW**

- The Kievan state rose from Varangian-ruled cities that controlled river trade in Russia.

- Vladimir of Novgorod took over Kiev and converted to Orthodox Christianity.

- Trade was the basis of political power, farmers practiced shifting agriculture, and warrior retainers evolved into a mounted elite.

- Cities were large by western European standards and served as craft centers.

- Christianity took hold slowly, but the church assumed increasingly active roles in political and economic life.

- Kievan Russia experienced its peak in the twelfth and early thirteenth centuries.

akg-images/RIA Nowosti

**Cathedral of Saint Dmitry in Vladimir** Built between 1193 and 1197, this Russian Orthodox cathedral shows Byzantine influence. The three-arch façade, small dome, and symmetrical Greek Cross floor plan strongly resemble features of the Byzantine church shown on page 232.

metropolises like Baghdad and Nishapur. Many cities amounted to little more than fortified trading posts. Yet they served as centers for the development of crafts, some, such as glassmaking, based on skills imported from Byzantium. Artisans enjoyed higher status in society than peasant farmers. Construction relied on wood from the forests, although Christianity brought the building of stone cathedrals and churches on the Byzantine model.

Christianity penetrated the general population slowly. Several polytheist uprisings occurred in the eleventh century, particularly in times of famine and passive resistance led some groups to reject Christian burial and persist in cremating the dead and keeping the bones of the deceased in urns. Women continued to use polytheist designs on their clothing and bracelets, and as late as the twelfth century they were still turning to polytheist priests for charms to cure sick children. Traditional Slavic marriage practices involving casual and polygamous relations particularly scandalized the clergy.

Christianity eventually triumphed, and its success led to increasing church engagement in political and economic affairs. In the twelfth century, Christian clergy became involved in government administration, some of them collecting fees and taxes related to trade. Direct and indirect revenue from trade provided the rulers with the money they needed to pay their soldiers. The rule of law also spread as Kievan Russia experienced its peak of culture and prosperity in the century before the Mongol invasion of 1237.

# WESTERN EUROPE REVIVES, 1000–1200

■ *How did Mediterranean trade help revive western Europe?*

Between 1000 and 1200 western Europe slowly emerged from nearly seven centuries of subsistence economy. Population and agricultural production climbed, and a growing food surplus found its way to town markets, speeding the return of a money-based economy and providing support for larger numbers of craftspeople, construction workers, and traders.

Historians have attributed western Europe's revival to population growth spurred by new technologies and to the appearance in Italy and Flanders, on the coast of the North Sea, of self-governing cities devoted primarily to seaborne trade. For monarchs, the changes facilitated improvements in central administration, greater control over vassals, and consolidation of realms on the way to becoming stronger kingdoms.

### The Role of Technology

A lack of concrete evidence confirming the spread of technological innovations frustrates efforts to relate revival to technological change. Nevertheless, most historians agree that technology played a significant role in the near doubling of the population of western Europe between 1000 and 1200. The population of England seems to have risen from 1.1 million in 1086 to 1.9 million in 1200, and the population of the territory of modern France seems to have risen from 5.2 million to 9.2 million over the same period.

The history of plows and draft harnesses illustrates the difficulty of drawing historical conclusions from scattered evidence. Farmers in southern Europe and Byzantium continued to use the Roman plow, which scratched shallow grooves, as was appropriate for loose, dry Mediterranean soils. But a new plow cut deep into the soil with a knifelike blade, while a curved board mounted behind the blade lifted the cut layer and turned it over, making it possible to farm the heavy, wet clays of the northern river valleys. This required more energy, which meant harnessing several teams of oxen or horses. Horses plowed faster than oxen but were more delicate. Iron horseshoes, which were widely adopted in this period, helped protect their hooves, but like the plow itself, they added to the farmer's expenses.

Another issue was harnesses. Roman horse harnesses put such pressure on the animal's throat that a horse pulling a heavy load risked strangulation. A mystery surrounds the adoption of more efficient designs. The **horse collar**, which moves the point of traction from the animal's throat to its shoulders,

first appeared around 800 in a miniature painting, and it is shown clearly as a harness for plow horses in the Bayeux Tapestry, embroidered after 1066. The simpler breast-strap harness, appearing around 500, was not as suitable for the heaviest work but was preferred in southern Europe. In both cases, linguists have tried to trace key technical terms to Chinese or Turko-Mongol words and have argued for an eastern origin. Yet third-century Roman farmers in Tunisia and Libya used both types of harness to hitch horses and camels to plows and carts. This technology, which is still employed in Tunisia, appears clearly on Roman bas-reliefs and lamps; but there is no more concrete evidence of its movement northward into Europe than there is of similar harnessing moving across Asia. Thus the question of where efficient harnessing came from and whether it began in 500 or in 800, or was known even earlier but not extensively used, cannot be easily resolved.

Hinging on this problem is the question of when and why landowners in northern Europe began to use teams of horses to pull plows through soils that were too heavy for teams of oxen. Horses moved faster but cost more, particularly after the population increase raised the prices of the grain needed to feed them. Thus, it is difficult to say that one technology was always better. Agricultural surpluses did grow and better plowing did play a role in this growth, but areas that continued to use oxen and even old-style plows seem to have also shared in the general population growth of the period.

### Cities and the Rebirth of the Trade

Independent cities governed and defended by communes appeared first in Italy and Flanders and then elsewhere. Communes were groups of leading citizens who banded together to defend their cities and demand the privilege of self-government from their lay or ecclesiastical lord. Lords who granted such privileges benefited from the commune's economic dynamism. Lacking extensive farmlands, these

> **horse collar** Harnessing method that increased the efficiency of horses by shifting the point of traction from the animal's throat to the shoulders; its adoption favors the spread of horse-drawn plows and vehicles.

**Vertical Two-Beam Loom** These women weavers set up their loom out-of-doors. The vertical strands are the warp threads around which the weft is interwoven. The pole across the bottom of the loom holds the warp threads taut. The kneeling weaver holds a beater to compact the weft at the loom's bottom. In Europe, horizontal looms were more common and paved the way for the mechanization of weaving.

cities enacted laws to encourage manufacturing and trade. Cities in Italy that had shrunk within walls built by the Romans now pressed against those walls, forcing the construction of new ones. Pisa, for example, built a new wall in 1000 and expanded it in 1156.

Islands at the northern end of the Adriatic Sea had been largely uninhabited in Roman times. Now settlers organized themselves into the city of Venice. In the eleventh century it became the dominant sea power in the Adriatic, competing with Pisa and Genoa, on the western side of Italy, for leadership in the trade with Muslim ports. One merchant's list mentions trade in some three thousand "spices" (including dyestuffs, textile fibers, and raw materials), some of them products of Muslim lands and some coming

via the Silk Road or the Indian Ocean trading system (see Chapter 8). Among them were eleven types of alum (for dyeing), eleven types of wax, eight types of cotton, four types of indigo, five types of ginger, four types of paper, and fifteen types of sugar. Trade from the Indian Ocean and Asia increasingly flowed through Egypt and Syria as climatic cooling caused agricultural decline in Iraq and Iran.

Ghent, Bruges (broozh), and Ypres (EEP-r) in Flanders rivaled the Italian cities in prosperity and trade. Granted privileges by the counts of Flanders, these cities centralized the fishing and wool trades of the North Sea region. Around 1200 raw wool from England began to be woven into woolen cloth for a very large market.

Coinage also signaled the upturn in economic activity. In the ninth and tenth centuries most gold coins had come from Muslim lands and the Byzantine Empire. Worth too much for most trading purposes, they seldom reached Germany, France, and England; the widely imitated Carolingian silver penny sufficed. With the economic revival of the twelfth century came the minting of silver coins in Scandinavia, Poland, and other outlying regions. In the following century, Italian cities followed with a new and abundant gold coinage.

## THE CRUSADES, 1095–1204

■ *What were the origins and impact of the Crusades?*

Revival coincided with and contributed to the **Crusades**, a series of religiously inspired Christian military campaigns against Muslims in the eastern Mediterranean. Four great expeditions between 1095 and 1204, the last redirected against Constantinople, which the Catholic knights looted, constituted the region's largest military undertakings since the fall of Rome. As a result of the Crusades, noble courts and burgeoning cities in western Europe consumed more goods from the east and later adopted ideas, artistic styles, and industrial processes from the lands of Islam.

### The Roots of the Crusades

Several social and economic currents of the eleventh century contributed to the Crusades. First, church reformers seeking to soften warlike habits popularized the Truce of God, a movement to limit fighting between Christian lords by specifying times of truce, such as during Lent (the forty days before Easter) and on Sundays. Many knights welcomed a religiously approved alternative to fighting other Christians. Second, ambitious rulers, like the Norman chieftains who invaded England and Sicily, were looking for new lands to conquer. Nobles, particularly younger sons in areas where the oldest son inherited everything, were hungry for land and titles. Third, Italian merchants wanted trading posts in Muslim territory. However, without the rivalry between popes and kings already discussed, and without the desire of the church to demonstrate political authority, the Crusades might never have occurred.

Several factors focused attention on the Holy Land, which had been under Muslim rule for four centuries. **Pilgrimages** played an important role in European religious life. In western Europe, pilgrims traveled under royal protection. Some were actually thieves, beggars, and peddlers, but genuinely pious pilgrims thronged to old churches and sacred relics. Rome and Constantinople were favored destinations, but the most intrepid went to Jerusalem and Antioch to fulfill a vow or to atone for a sin.

Pilgrims who crossed northern Spain to pray at the shrine of Santiago de Compostela learned of Christian kings fighting to dislodge the Muslims to the south. The Umayyad Caliphate in al-Andalus had broken up in the eleventh century, leaving its smaller successor states prey to Christian attacks from the north (see Chapter 9). The word *crusade*, taken from Latin *crux* for "cross," was first used in Spain. Pilgrims returning from Palestine urged both churchmen and nobles to consider the Muslim a proper target for Christian arms. Muslims generally

**Crusades** (1095–1204) Armed pilgrimages to the Holy Land by Christians determined to recover Jerusalem from Muslim rule. The Crusades brought an end to western Europe's centuries of intellectual and cultural isolation.

**pilgrimage** Journey to a sacred shrine by Christians seeking to show their piety, fulfill vows, or gain absolution for sins. Other religions also have pilgrimage traditions, such as the Muslim pilgrimage to Mecca and the pilgrimages made by early Chinese Buddhists to India in search of sacred Buddhist writings.

tolerated Christian pilgrims, but after 1071, when the Seljuks defeated the Byzantines at Manzikert (see Chapter 9), security along the pilgrimage route through Anatolia, already none too good, deteriorated further.

Despite the theological differences between the Orthodox and Roman Churches, the Byzantine emperor Alexius Comnenus asked the pope and western European rulers for help against the Muslims. Pope Urban II responded at the Council of Clermont in 1095. He addressed a huge crowd of people gathered in a field and called on them, as Christians, to stop fighting one another and go to the Holy Land to fight Muslims. "God wills it!" exclaimed voices in the crowd. People cut cloth into crosses and sewed them on their shirts to symbolize their willingness to march on Jerusalem. Thus began the First Crusade, though people at the time more often used the word *peregrinatio*, "pilgrimage." Urban promised to free Crusaders who had committed sins from their normal penance, or acts of atonement, the usual reward for peaceful pilgrims to Jerusalem.

The First Crusade captured Jerusalem in 1099 and established four Crusader principalities, the most important being the Latin Kingdom of Jerusalem. The next two expeditions strove with diminishing success to protect these gains. Muslim forces retook Jerusalem in 1187. By the time of the Fourth Crusade in 1204, the original religious ardor had so diminished that the commanders agreed, at the urging of the Venetians, to sack Constantinople first to defray the cost of transporting the army by ship.

## The Impact of the Crusades

Exposure to Muslim culture in Spain, Sicily, Mediterranean seaports, and the Crusader principalities awakened Europeans to things lacking in their own lives. Borrowings from Muslim society occurred gradually and are not always easy to date, but Europeans began to produce pasta, paper, sugar, cotton cloth, colored glass, and many other formerly exotic items.

Europeans also learned of Greek philosophical, scientific, and medical writings—and equally important Arab and Iranian works—which were translated into Latin. Some manuscripts came from conquered territory: Sicily, Spain, the Holy Land,

and Constantinople. For others, translators worked in parts of Spain still under Muslim rule. Generations passed before all these works were studied and understood, but they eventually transformed the intellectual world of Europe.

Changes in noble lifestyle took place more quickly. Eleanor of Aquitaine (1122?–1204), the most influential woman of the crusading era, accompanied her husband, King Louis VII of France, on the Second Crusade (1147–1149). The Arab influenced court life of her uncle Raymond, who ruled the Crusader principality of Antioch, particularly appealed to her. Once back in France, a lack of male offspring led to an annulment of her royal marriage, and she married Henry of Anjou in 1151. Three years later he inherited the throne of England as Henry II. Eleanor's sons, John and Richard Lion-Heart, famed in romance as the chivalrous foe of Saladin during the Third Crusade (1189–1192), rebelled against their father but eventually succeeded him as kings of England. In Aquitaine, a powerful duchy in southern France, Eleanor maintained her own court for a time. Poet-singers called troubadours enjoyed her favor and made her court a center for music based on the idea of "courtly love," an idealization of feminine beauty and grace that influenced later European ideas of romance. Surviving troubadour melodies show the influence of poetry styles then current in Muslim Spain. The favorite troubadour instrument, moreover, was the lute, a guitarlike instrument with a bulging belly whose design and name (Arabic *al-ud*) came from Muslim Spain.

## SECTION REVIEW

- The Crusades coincided with and fueled the western European revival.
- Several religious, political, and economic factors prompted the Crusades, the most immediate of which was the decline of Byzantine power under Seljuk pressure.
- Responding to Byzantine calls for aid, Pope Urban II proclaimed the First Crusade in 1095.
- As a result of the Crusaders, western Europeans gradually absorbed Muslim technological and intellectual achievements.
- Contact with Muslim culture affected the elite most immediately by shaping court life and the troubadour tradition of courtly love.

## CONCLUSION

The division of the Roman Empire by Constantine into an eastern and western branch marked Europe from that time on. When the Western Roman Empire collapsed, the Germanic tribes that settled on its territory formed numerous competing kingdoms and principalities. For several centuries, the only unifying factor was the Catholic Church, which provided intellectual and some administrative continuity with the vanished Roman Empire. Secular authorities, however, arose to contest the political authority of the church. Thus, western Europe remained divided among competing states and power centers. After the Viking invasions tapered off in the late tenth century, the economy, culture, and population of western Europe showed a dynamism that spread to areas of northern Europe never reached by the Romans. It also carried over into expansionism against the Muslims of the Holy Land and against Constantinople itself.

Eastern Europe evolved very differently, under the influence of Constantinople. Though it lost many provinces, the Eastern Roman Empire was not overrun by barbarians as the west had been, but retained its imperial structure for another thousand years. Though Christianity replaced all earlier religions as it did in the west, it was in the form of the Orthodox Church, a subordinate branch of the imperial Byzantine government, rather than an independent and competing organization like the Catholic Church in the west. As northeastern Europe (Russia, Ukraine, Belarus) filled in after the viking raiders settled down to trade and build cities, its peoples adopted the Orthodox form of Christianity and with it the subordination of church to state that prevailed in the Byzantine Empire.

## CHAPTER REVIEW

### THE BYZANTINE EMPIRE, 600–1200
■ *How did the Byzantine Empire maintain Roman imperial traditions in the east?* (page 229)

Divergent ecclesiastical practices paralleled a political separation that dated from the fourth-century division of the roman empire into an eastern portion, the Byzantine Empire ruled from Constantinople, and a western portion that became increasingly fragmented as warlike Germanic peoples assumed more and more control. For the east, the collection and analysis of imperial laws symbolized continuing imperial rule. The emperor also assumed control over the Christian church.

### EARLY MEDIEVAL EUROPE, 600–1000
■ *How did the culture of early medieval Europe develop in the absence of imperial rule?* (page 234)

In the west, the heritage of Rome consisted more in the elite use of Latin and the popular rise of Romance languages. The Roman Empire became more and more a shared memory as great buildings decayed into ruins. This memory, however, could be used as a basis of political power, as the rule of Charlemagne demonstrates. After Charlemagne's death, Viking invasions continued to disrupt European life, but their migrations laid the foundations of powerful states in Russia and Normandy. Although some long-distance trade continued, poor infrastructure and the absence of centralized authority led to the rise of a self-sufficient economy based on the manor. The lords and warriors who protected serfs became a mounted military elite that dominated the system of rights and obligations loosely termed "feudalism."

### THE WESTERN CHURCH
■ *What role did the Western Church play in the politics and culture of Europe?* (page 240)

Unlike the Eastern Church, where the emperor played a dominating role, the bishops and abbots who spoke for western Christendom sought complete control of both the political and the social realm. They ultimately came into conflict with kings and dukes who resented these claims to power, but the lower ranks of society became increasingly immersed in a Christian culture based on respect for the clergy.

## KIEVAN RUSSIA, 900–1200

■ *What was the significance of the adoption of Orthodox Christianity by Kievan Russia?* (page 244)

The Eastern and Western Churches competed in converting the Slavic peoples. The Poles became Roman Catholics, while the Russians established their own Orthodox Church on the Byzantine pattern. Since the rulers of Kiev were of Scandinavian origin like the Norman rulers of northern France, England, and Sicily, there was potentially a basis for continuing interconnections across northern Europe. The decision to follow the Byzantine form of Christianity eliminated that possibility and raised a barrier between Russia and western Europe that lasted for centuries.

## WESTERN EUROPE REVIVES, 1000–1200

■ *How did Mediterranean trade help revive western Europe?* (page 247)

Prosperous communes established in major Italian cities, based to some extent on rapid population growth, stimulated an expansion in Mediterranean trade. "Spices" imported from the East were resold in other European markets while Italian merchants opened new trading connections in the Middle East, some of them with Crusader states.

## THE CRUSADES, 1095–1204

■ *What were the origins and impact of the Crusades?* (page 250)

A combination of factors including population growth, contests for authority between monarchs and the Catholic church, and a loss of Byzantine territory to Muslims led to a series of military expeditions bent on seizing the Holy Land, and Jerusalem in particular, from the Muslims. The Crusading era led to many changes in European intellectual and cultural life ranging from the stimulus of scientific and philosophical ideas translated from Arabic into Latin; to the adoption of Muslim manufacturing practices, such as glassmaking and papermaking; to the popularization of troubadour poetry and lute playing from Muslim Spain.

## Key Terms

Charlemagne (p. 229)

medieval (p. 229)

Byzantine Empire (p. 229)

Kievan Russia (p. 229)

schism (p. 232)

manor (p. 237)

serf (p. 237)

fief (p. 238)

vassal (p. 238)

papacy (p. 240)

Holy Roman Empire (p. 240)

investiture controversy (p. 241)

monasticism (p. 241)

horse collar (p. 248)

Crusades (p. 250)

pilgrimage (p. 250)

# Inner and East Asia

© Cengage Learning

The origins of East Asia, characterized by a shared writing system, political ideology, and culture, can be traced to the Sui (sway) and Tang (tahng) Empires. The powerful and expansive Tang Empire (618–907) ended four centuries of rule by short-lived and competing states (see Chapter 5) and became a model for emerging regimes on the Korean Peninsula, in northeast Asia, on the Japanese islands, and, to a certain extent, in continental Southeast Asia. But the formation of East Asia did not occur in isolation. Missionaries from India, along with Chinese pilgrims returning with sacred Sanskrit texts, encouraged the spread of Buddhism. Travelers from India and Persia also brought with them their native religions, artistic aesthetic, popular entertainments, technology, and even cuisine. Nestorian Christian churches and Jewish places of worship existed alongside Buddhist temples and monasteries. A legend credits an uncle of Mohammad with erecting the Red Mosque at Canton in the mid-seventh century. Foreigners worked in the Tang bureaucracy, served in the military, and maintained close ties to the royal family. Many historians characterize the Tang Empire as "cosmopolitan" because of its breadth and diversity, and it left an indelible mark on the Chinese imagination long after it fell. It was succeeded by the Song (soong) Empire. Extraordinarily productive and advanced in terms of technology, economy, and government, the Song Empire was not as globally connected and never approached the Tang's dominance over East Asia.

Other East Asian societies in Japan, Korea, and Vietnam found Confucian values and Chinese culture appealing, but they developed separate social and political institutions and economic systems.

## THE SUI AND TANG EMPIRES, 581–755

■ *What was the importance of Inner and Central Asia as a region of interchange during the Tang period?*

The reunification of China took place under the Sui dynasty, father and son rulers who held power from 581 until Turks from Inner Asia (the part of the Eurasian steppe east of the Pamir Mountains) defeated the son in 615. He was assassinated three years later, and the Tang filled the political vacuum.

The small kingdoms of northern China and Inner Asia that had come and gone during the centuries following the fall of the Han Empire had structured themselves around a variety of political ideas and institutions. Some favored the Chinese tradition, with an emperor, a bureaucracy using the Chinese language exclusively, and a Confucian state philosophy (see Chapter 5). Others reflected Tibetan, Turkish, or other regional cultures and depended on Buddhism to legitimate their rule. Throughout the period the relationship between northern China and the deserts and steppe of Inner Asia remained a central focus of political life, a key commercial linkage, and a source of new ideas and practices.

The Sui rulers called their new capital Chang'an in honor of the old Han capital nearby in the Wei (way) River Valley (modern Shaanxi province). Though northern China constituted the Sui heartland, population centers along the Yangzi (yahng-zeh) River in the south grew steadily and pointed to what would be the future direction of Chinese expansion. To facilitate communication and trade with the south, the Sui built the 1,100-mile (1,771-kilometer) **Grand Canal** linking the Yellow River with the Yangzi, and they also constructed irrigation systems in the Yangzi Valley. On their northern frontier, the Sui also improved the Great Wall, the barrier against nomadic incursions that had been gradually constructed by several earlier states.

Sui military ambition, which extended to Korea and Vietnam as well as Inner Asia, required high levels of organization, manpower, and such resources as livestock, wood, iron, and food supplies. The same was true of their massive public works projects. These burdens proved more than the Sui could sustain. Overextension compounded the political dilemma stemming from the military defeat and subsequent assassination of the second Sui emperor. These circumstances opened the way for another strong leader to establish a new state.

**Grand Canal** The 1,100-mile (1,771-kilometer) waterway linking the Yellow and the Yangzi Rivers. It was begun in the Han period and completed during the Sui Empire.

Horse figures, relief from Emperor T'ai Tsung's tomb in Hsi-An (Shensi), Chinese civilization, 7th century/De Agostini Picture Library/The Bridgeman Art Library

**Iron Stirrups**   This bas-relief from the tomb of Li Shimin depicts the type of horse on which the Tang armies conquered China and Inner Asia. Saddles with high supports in front and back, breastplates, and cruppers (straps beneath the tail that help keep the saddle in place) point to the importance of high speeds and quick maneuvering. Central and Inner Asian horsemen had iron stirrups available from the time of the Huns (fifth century). Earlier stirrups were of leather or wood. Stirrups could support the weight of shielded and well-armed soldiers rising in the saddle to shoot arrows or use lances.

In 618 the powerful Li family took advantage of Sui disorder to carve out an empire of similar scale and ambition. They adopted the dynastic name Tang (Map 11.1). The brilliant emperor **Li Shimin** (lee shir-meen) (r. 626–649) extended his power primarily westward into Inner Asia. Though he and succeeding rulers of the **Tang Empire** retained many Sui governing practices, they avoided overcentralization by allowing local nobles, gentry, officials, and religious establishments to exercise significant power.

The Tang emperors and nobility descended from the Turkish elites that built small states in northern China after the Han, as well as from Chinese officials and settlers who had moved there. They appreciated the pastoral nomadic culture of Inner Asia (see Chapter 8) as well as Chinese traditions. Some of the most impressive works of Tang art, for example, are

large pottery figurines of the horses and two-humped camels used along the Silk Road, brilliantly colored with glazes devised by Chinese potters. Reflecting a similar influence, clothing styles changed in north China, as working people switched from robes to the pants favored by the Turks from Central Asia. Cotton replaced hemp in clothes worn by commoners, and textiles sported Persian and Central Asian designs. In warfare, the Tang combined Chinese weapons—the crossbow and armored infantrymen—with Inner

**Li Shimin**   One of the founders of the Tang Empire and its second emperor (r. 626–649). He led the expansion of the empire into Inner Asia.

**Tang Empire**   Empire unifying China and part of Inner Asia (618–907). The Tang emperors presided over a magnificent court at their capital, Chang'an.

# Chronology

| | Inner Asia | China | Northeast Asia | Japan |
|---|---|---|---|---|
| **200** | | **220–589** China disunited<br><br>**581–618** Sui unification | **313–668** Three Korean kingdoms: Koguryō, Paekche, Silla | |
| **600** | **751** Battle of Talas River | **618** Tang Empire founded<br>**626–649** Li Shimin reign<br>**690–705** Wu Zhao reign<br>**755–763** An Lushan rebellion | **668** Silla victory in Korea | **645–655** Taika era<br>**710–784** Nara as capital<br><br>**752** "Eye-Opening" ceremony<br>**794** Heian era |
| **800** | | **840** Suppression of Buddhism<br>**879–881** Huang Chao rebellion<br>**907** End of Tang Empire<br><br>**960** Song Empire founded | **916** Liao Empire founded<br>**918** Koryo founded: Korean Peninsula unified | **866–1180** Fujiwara influence |
| **1000** | | | **1115** Jin Empire founded | **ca. 1000** *The Tale of Genji* |
| **1200** | | **1127–1279** Southern Song period | | **1185** Kamakura Shogunate founded |

Asian expertise in horsemanship and the use of iron stirrups. At their peak, from about 650 to 751, when they were defeated in Central Asia (present-day Kyrgyzstan) by an Arab Muslim army at the Battle of Talas River, the Tang armies were a formidable force.

During the Tang dynasty China also consolidated Chinese trade in the southern coastal region, increasing access to the Indian Ocean. Shipbuilders excelled at compass design and the construction of very large oceangoing vessels. Commercial ships, built to sail from south China to the Philippines and southern Asia, carried twice as much as contemporary vessels in the Mediterranean Sea or the western parts of the Indian Ocean trading system (see Chapter 8). As travel along the Silk Road and to the various ports of the Indian Ocean trading system increased, the economies of the seaports and entrepôts involved in trade became increasingly commercialized, leading to networks of private traders devising new instruments of credit and finance. By about the year 1000 the magnitude of exports from Tang territories, facilitated by China's excellent transportation systems, dwarfed Chinese imports from Europe, West Asia, and South Asia.

## Chang'an: Metropolis at the Center of East Asia

Much of the global exchange in China during the Sui and Tang dynasties occurred in the capital Chang'an. Well-maintained roads and water transport connected Chang'an to the coastal towns of south China, most importantly Guangzhou (gwahng-jo) (Canton). As the center of the **tributary system**, which began in

**tributary system** A system in which, from the time of the Han Empire, countries in East and Southeast Asia not under the direct control of empires based in China nevertheless enrolled as tributary states, acknowledging the superiority of the emperors in China in exchange for trading rights or strategic alliances.

Han times, Chang'an received regular embassies from independent countries who came to acknowledge the Chinese emperor's supremacy by paying tribute (see Chapter 5). Central Asians, Tibetans, Vietnamese, Japanese, and Koreans regularly visited the capital. In the main parts of the city, restaurants, inns, temples, mosques, and street stalls lined the thoroughfares, creating a vigorous commercial world in which material goods and cultural influences mixed. The Tang court promoted polo, a pastime from the steppes, and followed the Inner Asian tradition of allowing noblewomen to compete. Various stringed instruments reached China from the Silk Road, along with Turkish folk melodies. Grape wine from West Asia and tea, sugar, and spices from India and Southeast Asia transformed the Chinese diet. Such changes reflected new economic and trade relationships (see Material Culture: Salt).

More than simply a political and trade center, Chang'an became the premier study-abroad destination in Asia; rulers sent intellectuals to learn statecraft, the techniques of running a government, to bring back to their home governments. Monks from Korea and Japan went to study with Chinese Buddhists and with Indian masters. Visitors brought the most recent ideas home, and Chang'an became the center of a continent-wide system of communication.

During the Tang period, Chang'an and its surrounding suburbs, with a population of nearly 2 million, was the largest metropolitan area in the world at the time. Its sophisticated gridlike layout, with its palace located in the north Pole Star position to reflect the celestial order, was imitated by Korean and Japanese capitals. Most people lived in suburbs that extended beyond the main gates. Many also dwelt in outlying

**Map 11.1  The Tang Empire in Inner and Eastern Asia, 750**  For over a century the Tang Empire controlled China and a very large part of Inner Asia. The defeat of Tang armies in 751 by a force of Arabs, Turks, and Tibetans at the Talas River in present-day Kyrgyzstan ended Tang westward expansion. To the south the Tang dominated Annam, and Japan and the Silla kingdom in Korea were leading tributary states of the Tang. © Cengage Learning towns that had special responsibilities like maintaining nearby imperial tombs. The diverse population included Asian, Arab, and Persian merchants, who became long-time residents of the city. In Chang'an and other trading centers, foreigners, whether merchants, students, or ambassadors, resided in special compounds enclosed by brick walls and wooden gates that guards locked from curfew (between eight and ten o'clock) till dawn to control crime. By the end of the Tang period, West Asians in Chang'an probably numbered over 100,000. There were so many Iranians living in the city that the government had to set up a special department to handle Iranian-Tang affairs.

## Buddhism and the Tang Empire

As the Tang Empire expanded westward, intensified contact with Central Asia and India strengthened Buddhist influence throughout China. Mahayana (mah-HAH-YAH-nah), or "Great Vehicle," Buddhism predominated. Mahayana fostered faith in enlightened beings—bodhisattvas—who postpone nirvana (see Chapter 5) to help others achieve enlightenment. This permitted the absorption of local gods and goddesses into Mahayana sainthood and thereby made conversion more attractive to the common people. Mahayana also encouraged translating Buddhist scripture into local languages, and it accepted religious practices not based on written texts. The adaptability of Mahayana views to different societies and classes of people invigorated travel, language learning, and cultural exchange.

Though Buddhism and Confucianism proved attractive to many different peoples, regional cultures and identities remained strong. At the height of the Tang Empire (between 600 and 751), **Uighur (WEE-ger)** merchants and scribes along the trading routes from Persia to China showed enthusiasm for Buddhist teachings, and Chinese Buddhists on pilgrimage to India advanced contacts between India and **Tibet**. Regular contact and Buddhist influences consolidated the Tang-Tibet relationship. Regional commitments to Tibetan, Uighur, and other languages and writing systems coexisted with the widespread use of written Chinese.

The Tang rulers followed Inner Asian precedents in their political use of Buddhism. State cults based

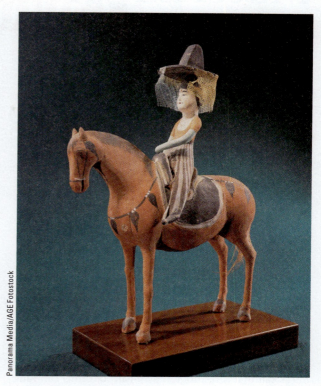

Panorama Media/AGE Fotostock

**Tang Horsewoman**   This ceramic tomb figurine from the far northwest, a region populated largely by Turkic speaking peoples, is unusual in being painted rather than glazed. The woman's costume suggests that she is of high rank, but not Chinese. Note the difference between the rider's light, toe-only stirrup and the full iron military stirrup shown on page 256.

on Buddhism had flourished in Inner Asia and north China since the fall of the Han. Some interpretations of Buddhist doctrine accorded kings and emperors the spiritual function of welding humankind into a harmonious Buddhist society. Protecting spirits were to help the ruler govern and prevent harm from coming to his people. Early Tang princes competing for political influence enlisted monastic leaders to pray for them, preach on their behalf, counsel aristocrats to support them, and—perhaps most important—

**Uighurs**   A group of Turkish-speakers who controlled their own centralized empire from 744 to 840 in Mongolia and Central Asia.

**Tibet**   Country centered on the high, mountain-bounded plateau north of India. Tibetan political power occasionally extended farther to the north and west between the seventh and thirteenth centuries.

# Material Culture

## Salt

Though sodium chloride, or table salt, is one of the world's most abundant chemicals, it's abundance in some areas and scarcity in others has frequently given it an important role in economic history. Here are some examples.

Outcroppings of rock salt known as salt licks play a nutritional role in the lives of many wild mammals. Prehistoric human hunters sought game at these natural animal gathering places, and some scholars believe that human provision of salt played an important role in domesticating some species.

Trade in salt from the southern regions of the Sahara Desert is described as early as the ninth century C.E., but it is probably much older because the Saharan deposits formed an important nutritional source for salt-poor sub-Saharan Africa. The legendary exchange of salt for equivalent quantities of gold symbolizes this commercial importance. Bilma, an oasis town in eastern Niger, still produces salt that is distributed by means of camel caravans trekking across the sand dunes of the Ténére Desert.

In ancient Rome, a strong-smelling sauce known as *garum* became a cooking staple and an important export item. *Garum* was made by crushing cut-up fish, with their entrails, in a small amount of brine. The salt prevented the sauce from spoiling. For common people, using *garum* was a way of avoiding the tax on salt.

Early in the fourteenth century C.E. a Flemish fisherman devised a method of preserving herring, a small fish. After the head and certain internal organs were removed, enzymes from the pancreas began to digest the flesh and make it tender. Then the fish were packed with salt in casks. Salted herring and its raw materials, salt and herring, became mainstays of the commerce of Scotland, northern Germany, and, in particular, the Netherlands. A Dutch proverb maintains that the city of Amsterdam was built on herring casks.

In France, a salt tax known as the *gabelle* became a permanent part of royal revenues in the late fourteenth century C.E. Everyone over the age of eight was forced to buy a minimum amount of salt every week at a price fixed by the government. Most of the salt was produced by evaporating seawater, but inland provinces in the east exploited salt marshes. Popular resentment against the tax contributed to the French Revolution in 1789. A year later the *gabelle* was canceled.

In nineteenth-century China, where the salt tax had been a mainstay of government revenues since the Tang dynasty, brine (saltwater) wells around the western city of Zigong became the basis for one of the country's most prosperous industries. The family-based trusts that contribute monastic wealth to their war chests. In return, the monasteries received tax exemptions, land privileges, and gifts.

## Upheavals and Repression, 750–879

Under the Uighurs, caravan cities like Kashgar and Khotan (see Map 11.1) enjoyed commercial ties with both the Islamic world and China. The location of Tibet also made it a crossroads for trade with China, Southeast Asia, South Asia, and Central Asia. The later years of the Tang Empire saw increasing turmoil as a result of conflict with Tibetans and Turkish Uighurs. One result was a backlash against "foreigners," which to Confucians included Buddhists. The Tang elites came to see Buddhism as undermining the Confucian idea of the family as the model for the state. The Confucian scholar Han Yu (768–824) spoke powerfully for a return to traditional Confucian practices. In "Memorial on the Bone of Buddha" written to the emperor in 819 on the occasion of ceremonies to receive a bone of the Buddha in the imperial palace, he scornfully disparages the Buddha and his followers:

> Now Buddha was a man of the barbarians who did not speak the language of China and wore clothes of a different fashion. His sayings did not concern the ways of our ancient kings, nor did his manner of dress conform to their laws. He understood neither the duties that bind sovereign and subject nor the affections of father and son. If he were still alive today and came to our court by order of his ruler, Your Majesty might condescend to receive him,

extracted the salt from as deep as 3,000 feet were comparable in capital accumulation, management skill, and technological innovation to contemporary European corporations.

In 1930 the British monopoly on salt production in India became the center of a peaceful protest led by Mahatma Gandhi. With seventy-eight followers he marched 240 miles to the seacoast, where the protestors picked up small lumps of salt, thereby breaking the law against private harvesting of salt. Though many were imprisoned, the Salt March became an important model of civil disobedience.

Though salt naturally brings a certain taste to mind, its historic roles relate more to the chemical properties of the salty moisture on the outside of preserved foods. Pieces of pork transform into ham, cucumbers and other vegetables become pickles, and sturgeon eggs become caviar. Since a high concentration of salt kills bacteria, salted foods can be transported and stored for long periods without spoiling or becoming dangerous to eat.

Producing salt from seawater and other sources of brine requires evaporation or boiling. But salt is also available in solid form and can be mined. Cities like Salzburg (literally "Salt Town") in Austria may grow up around salt mines. Underground layers of salt, sometimes hundreds of feet thick, are the residue of dried-up prehistoric seas or oceans. In addition to being processed for consumption, rock salt is used on icy roads. Since saltwater freezes at a lower temperature than fresh water, salt deposited on snow or ice causes melting.

VOLKMAR K. WENTZEL/National Geographic Stock

**Camel Caravan Carrying Salt in West Africa** *Natural salt deposits, such as those at Bilma in the southern Sahara Desert in Niger, have time and again become the bases for extensive regional and international trade. Transporting the salt can be a challenge, however. Camel transport made salt trading an integral part of the trade between the Saharan region and the agricultural countries of West Africa. In northern Europe the salt springs at Lüneburg near Hamburg, Germany, fed into a maritime trading network throughout the Baltic and North Sea region. Coastal lands could extract salt from seawater by evaporation, though in colder climates, such as Japan, boiling was needed to supplement the power of natural sunlight and heat.*

### QUESTIONS FOR ANALYSIS

1. Why did salt become such an important trade product?
2. Why would a tax on salt be easy to administer?
3. How many uses of salt can you think of?

but . . . he would then be escorted to the borders of the state, dismissed, and not allowed to delude the masses. How then, when he has long been dead, could his rotten bones, the foul and unlucky remains of his body, be rightly admitted to the palace? Confucius said, "Respect spiritual beings, while keeping at a distance from them."[1]

Buddhism was also attacked for encouraging women in politics. Wu Zhao (woo jow), a woman who had married into the imperial family, seized control of the government in 690 and declared herself emperor. She based her legitimacy on claiming to be a bodhisattva, an enlightened soul who had chosen to

remain on earth to lead others to salvation. She also favored Buddhists and Daoists over Confucians in her court and government.

Later Confucian writers expressed contempt for Wu Zhao and other powerful women and lamented the influence of women at the Tang court, which had caused "the hearts of fathers and mothers everywhere not to value the birth of boys, but the birth of girls."[2] Confucian elites heaped every possible charge on prominent women who offended them, accusing Emperor Wu of grotesque tortures and murders, including tossing the dismembered but still living bodies of enemies into wine vats and cauldrons.

[1] Theodore de Bary, ed., *Sources of Chinese Tradition*, vol. 1, 2d ed. (New York: Columbia University Press, 1999), 584.

[2] Quoted in David Lattimore, "Allusion in T'ang Poetry," in *Perspectives on the T'ang*, ed. Arthur F. Wright and David Twitchett (New Haven, CT: Yale University Press, 1973), 436.

**Buddhist Cave Painting at Dunhuang** Hundreds of caves dating to the period when Buddhism enjoyed popularity and government favor in China survive in Gansu province, which was beyond the reach of the Tang rulers when they turned against Buddhism. This cave, dated to the period 565–576, depicts the historical Buddha flanked by bodhisattvas. Scenes of the Buddha preaching appear on the wall to the left.

*Pierre Colombel/Corbis* (rotated, left margin)

Serious historians dismiss the stories about Wu Zhao as stereotypical characterizations of "evil" rulers. Eunuchs (castrated palace servants) charged by historians with controlling Chang'an and the Tang court and publicly executing rival bureaucrats represent a similar stereotype. In fact Wu seems to have ruled effectively and was not deposed until 705, when extreme old age (eighty-plus) incapacitated her. Nevertheless, traditional Chinese historians commonly describe unorthodox rulers and all-powerful women as evil, and the truth about Wu will never be known.

Even Chinese gentry living in safe and prosperous localities associated Buddhism with social ills. People who worried about "barbarians" ruining their society pointed to Buddhism as evidence of the foreign evil, since it had such strong roots in Inner Asia and Tibet. Because Buddhism shunned earthly ties, monks and nuns severed relations with the secular world in search of enlightenment. They paid no taxes, served in no army. They deprived their families of advantageous marriage alliances and denied

descendants to their ancestors. The Confucian elites saw all this as threatening to the family and to the family estates that underlay the Tang economic and political structure.

By the ninth century, hundreds of thousands of people had entered tax-exempt Buddhist institutions. In 840 the government moved to crush the monasteries, whose tax exemption had allowed them to accumulate land, serfs, and precious objects, often as gifts. Within five years 4,600 temples had been destroyed. Now an enormous amount of land and 150,000 workers were returned to the tax rolls.

Buddhist centers like the cave monasteries at Dunhuang were protected by local warlords loyal to Buddhist rulers in Inner Asia. Nevertheless, China's cultural heritage suffered a great loss in the dissolution of the monasteries. Some sculptures and grottoes survived only in defaced form. Wooden temples and façades sheltering great stone carvings burned to the ground. Monasteries became legal again in later times, but Buddhism never recovered the influence of early Tang times.

## The End of the Tang Empire, 879–907

The campaigns of expansion in the seventh century had left the empire dependent on local military commanders and a complex tax collection system. Reverses like the Battle of the Talas River in 751, where Arabs halted Chinese expansion into Central Asia, led to military demoralization and underfunding. In 755 An Lushan, a Tang general on the northeast frontier, led about 200,000 soldiers in rebellion. The emperor fled Chang'an and executed his favorite concubine, Yang Guifei (yahng gway-fay), who was rumored to be An Lushan's lover. (Another woman reviled by Confucians for her influence in government, she was blamed for the outbreak of the An Lushan rebellion.) The rebellion lasted for eight years and resulted in new powers for the provincial military governors who helped suppress it. Even so, Chang'an never recovered, symbolizing Tang's waning influence over satellite states in Korea and Japan.

A disgruntled member of the gentry, Huang Chao (wang show), led the most devastating uprising between 879 and 881. Despite his ruthless treatment of the villages he controlled, his rebellion attracted poor farmers and tenants who could not protect themselves from local bosses and oppressive landlords, or who simply did not know where else to turn in the deepening chaos. The new hatred of "barbarians" spurred the rebels to murder thousands of foreign residents in Canton and Beijing (bay-jeeng).

Local warlords finally wiped out the rebels, but Tang society did not find peace. Refugees, migrant workers, and homeless people became common sights. Residents of northern China fled to the southern frontiers as groups from Inner Asia moved into localities in the north. Though Tang emperors continued in Chang'an until a warlord terminated their line in 907, they never regained power after Huang Chao's rebellion.

# CHINA AND ITS RIVALS

■ *What were the effects of the fracturing of power in Inner Asia and China?*

In the aftermath of the Tang, three new states emerged and competed to inherit its legacy (see Map 11.2). The Liao (lee-OW) Empire of the Khitan (kee-THAN) people, pastoral nomads related to the Mongols living on the northeastern frontier, established their rule in the north. They centered their government on several cities, but the emperors preferred life in nomad encampments. In western China, the Minyak people (cousins of the Tibetans) established a state they called "Tanggut" (1038–1227) (TAHNG-gut) to show their connection with the fallen empire. The third state, the Chinese-speaking **Song Empire**, came into being in 960 in central China.

These states embodied the political ambitions of peoples with different religious and philosophical systems—Mahayana Buddhism among the Liao, Tibetan Buddhism among the Tangguts, and Confucianism among the Song. Cut off from Inner Asia, the Song used advanced seafaring and sailing technologies to forge maritime connections with other states in East, West, and Southeast Asia. The Song elite shared the late Tang dislike of "barbaric" or "foreign" influences as they tried to cope with multiple enemies that heavily taxed their military capacities. Meanwhile, Korea, Japan, and some Southeast Asian states strengthened political and cultural ties with China.

---

### SECTION REVIEW

- After the period of disunity following the fall of the Han, China was united under the Sui, followed by the Tang with its founder Li Shimin.

- Tang culture was based on both Chinese tradition and Inner Asian nomadic culture and war expertise.

- Trade led to the spread of Buddhism, prosperity, and a cosmopolitan legacy in the arts and lifestyle of the Tang Empire.

- Uighur and Tibetan turmoil created political problems for the Tang Empire that steadily weakened it.

- In China, this turmoil resulted in a backlash against foreign and female cultural influences and especially Buddhism, as Tang elites led a neo-Confucian reaction.

- The Tang fell due to a combination of destabilizing forces.

---

**Song Empire** Empire in central and southern China (960–1126) while the Liao people controlled the north. Empire in southern China (1127–1279; the "Southern Song") while the Jin people controlled the north. Distinguished for its advances in technology, medicine, astronomy, and mathematics.

## The Liao and Jin Challenge

The Liao Empire of the Khitan people extended from Siberia to Inner Asia. Variations on the Khitan name became the name for China in these distant regions: "Kitai" for the Mongols, "Khitai" for the Russians, and "Cathay" for Italian merchants like Marco Polo who reported on China in Europe.

The Liao rulers prided themselves on their pastoral traditions as horse and cattle breeders, the continuing source of their military might, and they made no attempt to create a single elite culture. They encouraged Chinese elites to use their own language, study their own classics, and see the emperor through Confucian eyes; and they encouraged other peoples to use their own languages and see the emperor as a champion of Buddhism or as a nomadic chieftain. On balance, Buddhism far outweighed Confucianism in this and other northern states, where rulers depended on their roles as bodhisattvas or as Buddhist kings to legitimate power. Liao rule lasted from 916 to 1125.

The Liao was the most powerful empire at the time, with the largest army in East Asia. Superb horsemen and archers, the Khitans also challenged the Song with siege machines from China and Central Asia. A truce concluded in 1005 required the Song emperor to pay the Liao great quantities of cash and silk annually. A century later, the Song tired of paying tribute and secretly allied with the Jurchens of northeastern Asia, who also resented Liao rule. In 1115 the Jurchens first destroyed the Liao capital in Mongolia and proclaimed their own empire, the Jin (see Map 11.2), and then turned on the Song.

The Jurchens grew rice, millet, and wheat, but they also spent a good deal of time hunting, fishing, and tending livestock. Using Khitan military arts and political organization, they became formidable enemies in an all-out campaign against the Song in 1127. They laid siege to the Song capital, Kaifeng (kie-fuhng), and captured the Song emperor. Within a few years the Song withdrew south of the Yellow River and established a new capital at Hangzhou (hahng-jo), leaving central as well as northern China in Jurchen control. Annual payments to the Jin Empire staved off further warfare. Historians generally refer to this period as the "Southern Song" (1127–1279).

## Song Industries

The Southern Song came closer to initiating an industrial revolution than any other premodern state. Many Song advances in technology, medicine, astronomy, and mathematics had come to China in Tang times, sometimes from very distant places. Song officials, scholars, and businessmen had the motivation and resources to adapt this Tang lore to meet their military, agricultural, and administrative needs.

Song mathematicians introduced the use of fractions, first employing them to describe the phases of the moon. From lunar observations, Song astronomers constructed a very precise calendar and, alone among the world's astronomers, noted the explosion of the Crab Nebula in 1054. Song inventors drew on their knowledge of celestial coordinates, particularly the Pole Star, to refine compass design. The magnetic compass, an earlier Chinese invention, shrank in size and gained a fixed pivot point for the needle. With a protective glass cover, the compass now became suitable for seafaring, a use first recorded in 1090.

Development of the seaworthy compass coincided with new techniques in building China's main oceangoing ship, the **junk**. A stern-mounted rudder improved the steering of the large ship in rough seas, and watertight bulkheads helped keep it afloat in emergencies. The shipwrights of the Persian Gulf soon copied these features in their ship designs.

Because they needed iron and steel to make weapons for their army of 1.25 million men, the Song rulers fought their northern rivals for control of mines in north China. Production of coal and iron soared. By the end of the eleventh century cast iron production reached about 125,000 tons (113,700 metric tons) annually, putting it on a par with the output of eighteenth-century Britain. Engineers became skilled at high-temperature metallurgy using enormous bellows, often driven by water wheels, to superheat the molten ore. Military engineers used iron to buttress defensive works because it was impervious to fire or concussion, and armorers mass-produced body

**junk** A very large flatbottom sailing ship produced in the Tang, Song, and Ming Empires, specially designed for long-distance commercial travel.

armor. Iron construction also appeared in bridges and small buildings. Mass-production techniques for bronze and ceramics in use in China for nearly two thousand years were adapted to iron casting and assembly.

To counter cavalry assaults, the Song experimented with **gunpowder**, which they initially used to propel clusters of flaming arrows. During the wars against the Jurchens in the 1100s the Song introduced a new and terrifying weapon. Shells launched from Song fortifications exploded in the midst of the enemy, blowing out iron shrapnel and dismembering men and horses. However, the short range of these shells limited them to defensive uses.

## Economy and Society in Song China

In a warlike era, Song elite culture idealized civil pursuits, and civilians outranked military men socially. Private academies, designed to train young men for the official examinations, became influential in culture and politics. New interpretations of Confucian teachings became so important and influential that the term **neo-Confucianism** is used for Song and later versions of Confucian thought.

Zhu Xi (jew she) (1130–1200), the most important early neo-Confucian thinker, reacted to the many centuries during which Buddhism and Daoism had overshadowed the precepts of Confucius. He and others worked out a systematic approach to cosmology that focused on the central conception that human nature is moral, rational, and essentially good. To combat the Buddhist dismissal of worldly affairs as a transitory distraction, they reemphasized individual moral and social responsibility. Their human ideal was the sage, a person who could preserve mental stability and serenity while dealing conscientiously with troubling social problems. Whereas earlier Confucian thinkers had written about sage kings and political leaders, the neo-Confucians espoused the spiritual idea of universal sagehood, a state that could be achieved through proper study of the new Confucian principles and cosmology.

Popular Buddhist sects also persisted during the Song, demonstrating that anti-Buddhist feelings were

**Map 11.2   Liao and Song Empires, ca. 1100**  The states of Liao in the north and Song in the south generally ceased open hostilities after a treaty in 1005 stabilized the border and imposed an annual payment on Song China. © Cengage Learning

not as ferocious as Confucian polemics against Buddhism might suggest. Some Buddhists elaborated on Tang-era folk practices derived from India and Tibet. The best known, Chan Buddhism (known as **Zen** in Japan and as Son in Korea), asserted that mental discipline alone could win salvation.

**gunpowder**  A mixture of saltpeter, sulfur, and charcoal, in various proportions. The formula, brought to China in the 400s or 500s, was first used to make fumigators to keep away insect pests and evil spirits. In later centuries it was used to make explosives and grenades and to propel cannonballs, shot, and bullets.

**neo-Confucianism**  Term used to describe new approaches to understanding classic Confucian texts that became the basic ruling philosophy of China from the Song period to the twentieth century.

**Zen**  The Japanese word for a branch of Mahayana Buddhism based on highly disciplined meditation. It is known in Sanskrit as *dhyana*, in Chinese as *chan*, and in Korean as *son*.

**Su Song's Astronomical Clock** This gigantic clock built at Kaifeng between 1088 and 1092 combined mathematics, astronomy, and calendar-making with skillful engineering. The team overseen by Su Song placed an armillary sphere on the observation platform and linked it with chains to the water-driven central mechanism shown in the cutaway view. The water wheel also rotated the Buddha statues in the multistory pagoda the spectators are looking at. Other devices displayed the time of the day, the month, and the year.

From Joseph Needham's *Science and Civilization in China*, Vol 4. After the original diagram in Su Song's treatise Xinyi Xiangfayao, 1092.

Meditation, a key Chan practice, was employed by Confucians as well as Buddhists. It afforded prospective officials relief from studying for civil service examinations, which continued into the Song from the Tang period. Unlike the ancient Han policy of hiring and promoting on the basis of recommendations, Song-style examinations involved a large bureaucracy. Test questions, which changed each time the examinations were given, often related to economic management or foreign policy even though they were always based on Confucian classics.

Hereditary class distinctions meant less than they had in Tang times, when noble lineages played a greater role in the structure of power. The new system recruited the most talented men, whatever their origin. Yet men from wealthy families enjoyed an advantage, for preparation for the tests consumed so much time that peasant boys could rarely compete. Success in the examinations brought good marriage prospects, the chance for a high salary, and enormous prestige. Failure could bankrupt a family and ruin

a man both socially and psychologically. This put great pressure on candidates, who spent days writing essays in tiny, dim, airless examination cells.

For some, preparation became easier thanks to a technical change from woodblock to an early form of **movable type**, which made printing cheaper. To promote its ideological goals, the Song government authorized the mass production of test preparation books in the years before 1000. Although a man had to be literate to read the preparation books and basic education was still rare, a growing number of candidates without noble, gentry, or elite backgrounds entered the Song bureaucracy.

**movable type** Type in which each individual character is cast on a separate piece of metal. It replaced woodblock printing, allowing for the arrangement of individual letters and other characters on a page, rather than requiring the carving of entire pages at a time. It may have been invented in Korea in the thirteenth century.

**Song River Transport**
This seventeenth-century painting shows the emperor Huizong (r. 1100–1126), in red, supervising the ceremonial transfer of pierced stones and a tree. The purpose of their transfer is unknown. Note the differences between the workshop at lower left and the residence at lower right where women, children, and even a pet dog are enjoying life outside the enclosed courtyard.

The availability of printed books changed country life as well, since landlords gained access to expert advice on planting and irrigation techniques, harvesting, tree cultivation, threshing, and weaving. Landlords frequently gathered their tenants and workers to show them illustrated texts on the crafts of farming and explain their meaning. New agricultural land was developed south of the Yangtze River, and iron implements such as plows and rakes, first used in the Tang era, were adapted to southern wet-rice cultivation. The growing profitability of agriculture interested ambitious members of the gentry. Still a frontier for Chinese settlers under the Tang, the south saw increasing concentration of land in the hands of a few wealthy families. In the process, the indigenous inhabitants of the region retreated into the mountains or southward toward Vietnam.

During the 1100s the total population of the Chinese territories, spurred by prosperity, rose above 100 million. The leading Song cities were still among the largest cities in the world. Health and crowding posed problems in the Song capitals. Multistory wooden apartment houses fronted on narrow streets— sometimes only 4 or 5 feet (1.2 to 1.5 meters) wide— that were clogged by peddlers or families spending time outdoors. The crush of people called for new

**Female Musicians** A group of entertainers from a Song period copy of a lost Tang painting titled "Night Revels of Han Xizai." The emperor ordered the painter to document the lifestyle of a man who preferred music, dance, and poetry to accepting appointment as Prime Minister. The mood of genteel indulgence appealed to Song era elites. Chinese women were not veiled, but foot-binding became common under the Song. The Night Revelry of Han Xizai, by Gu Hongzhong the court painter sent by his suspicious monarch to spy on Han and to make a record of Han's licentious behaviour/Werner Forman Archive/The Bridgeman Art Library

techniques in waste management, water supply, and firefighting. In Hangzhou engineers diverted the nearby river to flow through the city, flushing away waste and disease. Arab and European travelers who had firsthand experience with the Song capital, and who were sensitive to urban conditions in their own societies, expressed amazement at Hangzhou's amenities: restaurants, parks, bookstores, wine shops, tea houses, theaters, and other entertainments.

The idea of credit, originating in the robust long-distance trade of the Tang period, spread widely under the Song. Intercity or interregional credit—what the Song called "flying money"—depended on the acceptance of guarantees that the paper could be redeemed for coinage at another location. The public accepted the practice because credit networks tended to be managed by families, so that brothers and cousins were usually honoring each other's certificates.

"Flying money" certificates differed from government-issued paper money, which the Song pioneered. In some years, military expenditures consumed 80 percent of the government budget. The state responded to this financial pressure by distributing paper money. But this made inflation so severe that by the beginning of the 1100s paper money was trading for only 1 percent of its face value. Eventually the government withdrew paper money and instead imposed new taxes, sold monopolies, and offered financial incentives to merchants.

Hard-pressed for the revenue needed to maintain the army, canals, roads, waterworks, and other state functions, the government finally resorted to tax farming, selling the rights to tax collection to private individuals. Tax farmers made their profit by collecting the maximum amount and sending an agreed-upon smaller sum to the government. This meant exorbitant rates for taxable services, such as tolls, and much heavier tax burdens on the common people.

Rapid economic growth undermined the remaining government monopolies and the traditional strict regulation of business. Now merchants and artisans as well as gentry and officials could make fortunes. With land no longer the only source of wealth, the traditional social hierarchy common to an agricultural economy weakened, while cities, commerce, consumption, and the use of money and credit boomed. Urban life reflected the elite's growing taste for fine fabrics, porcelain, exotic foods, large houses, and exquisite paintings and books.

Along with the revival of Confucianism that began under the Tang and intensified under the Song, women experienced subordination, legal disenfranchisement, and social restriction. Merchants spent long periods away from home, and many maintained several wives in different locations. They often depended on wives to manage their homes and even their businesses in their absence. Although women took on responsibility for the management of their husbands' property, their own property rights suffered legal erosion. Under Song law, a woman's property automatically passed to her husband, and women could not remarry if their husbands divorced them or died.

As the subordination of women proved compatible with Confucianism, it became fashionable to educate girls just enough to read simplified versions of Confucian philosophy that emphasized the lowly role of women. Literacy made these young women more desirable as companions for the sons of gentry or noble families and as mothers in lower-ranking families aspiring to improve their status. The poet Li Qingzhao (lee CHING-jow) (1083–1141) acknowledged and made fun of her unusual status as a highly celebrated female writer:

Although I've studied poetry for thirty years
I try to keep my mouth shut and avoid reputation.
Now who is this nosy gentleman talking about my
    poetry

Like Yang Ching-chih (yahng SHING-she)
Who spoke of Hsiang Ssu (sang sue) everywhere he
    went.[3]

(Her reference is to a hermit poet of the ninth century who was continually and extravagantly praised by a court official.)

Female footbinding first appeared among slave dancers at the Tang court, but it did not become widespread until the Song period. The bindings forced the toes under and toward the heel, so that the bones eventually broke and the woman could not walk on her own. In noble and gentry families, footbinding began between ages five and seven. In less wealthy families, girls worked until they were older, so footbinding began only in a girl's teens.

Many literate men condemned the maiming of innocent girls and the general uselessness of footbinding. Nevertheless, bound feet became a status symbol. By 1200 a woman with unbound feet had become undesirable in elite circles, and mothers of elite status, or aspiring to such status, almost without exception bound their daughters' feet. They knew that girls with unbound feet faced rejection. Working women and the indigenous peoples of the south, where northern practices took a longer time to penetrate, did not practice footbinding. Consequently they enjoyed considerably more mobility and economic independence than did elite Chinese women.

[3] Quoted at "Women's Early Music, Art, Poetry," *http://music.acu.edu/www/iawm/pages/reference/tzusongs.html.*

## SECTION REVIEW

- Several rival states replaced the fallen Tang Empire, and the close relations between Central Asia and East Asia ended.
- The Liao and Jin Empires encouraged culturally diverse societies and confronted Song China with formidable military threats.
- The Song Empire of central and southern China built upon Tang achievements in technology and science and promoted civil ideals.
- Under the Song, print culture developed, urban populations rose, commercial activity grew through innovation, and women were subordinated to men.

# NEW KINGDOMS IN EAST ASIA

■ *To what extent do shared practices justify thinking of East Asia as a unified cultural region in the post-Tang era?*

The best possibilities for expanding the Confucian worldview of the Song lay with newly emerging kingdoms to the east and south. Korea, Japan, and Vietnam, like Song China, devoted great effort to the cultivation of rice, a practice that fit well with Confucian social ideas. Tending the young rice plants, irrigating the rice paddies, and managing the harvest required coordination among many village and kin groups and rewarded hierarchy, obedience, and self-discipline. Confucianism also justified using agricultural profits to support the education, safety, and comfort of the literate elite. In each of these new kingdoms Song civilization melded with indigenous cultural and historical traditions to create a distinctive synthesis.

## Chinese Influences

Korea, Japan, and Vietnam had first centralized power under ruling houses in the early Tang period, and their state ideologies continued to resemble that of the early Tang, when Buddhism and Confucianism seemed compatible. Government offices went to noble families and did not depend on passing examinations on Confucian texts. Landowning and agriculture remained the major sources of income, and landowners faced no challenges from a merchant class or urban elite.

Nevertheless, learned men prized literacy in classical Chinese and a good knowledge of Confucian texts. Though formal education was available to only a small number of people, the ruling and landholding elites sought to instill Confucian ideals of hierarchy and harmony among the general population.

## Korea

Our first knowledge of Korea, Japan, and Vietnam comes from early Chinese officials and travelers. When the Qin Empire established its first colony in the Korean peninsula in the third century B.C.E., Chinese bureaucrats began documenting Korean history and customs. Han writers noted the horse breeding, strong hereditary elites, and **shamanism** (belief in the ability of certain individuals to contact ancestors and the invisible spirit world) of Korea's small kingdoms. But Korea quickly absorbed Confucianism and Buddhism.

Mountainous in the east and north, Korea was heavily forested until modern times. The land that can be cultivated (less than 20 percent) lies mostly in the south, where a warm climate and monsoon rains support two crops per year. Population movements from Manchuria, Mongolia, and Siberia in the north and toward Japan in the east spread languages that were very different from Chinese but distantly related to the Turkish tongues of Inner Asia .

In the early 500s the dominant landholding families made inherited status—the "bone ranks"—permanent in Silla (SILL-ah or SHILL-ah), a kingdom in the southeast of the peninsula. In the early 660s Silla defeated the southwestern kingdom of Paekche, which had played a major role as a maritime power in transmitting Chinese culture to Japan. Then in 668 the northern Koguryŏ kingdom came to an end after prolonged conflict with the Sui and Tang. Koguryŏ was so influential in Northeast Asia that the Liao and Jin Empires, and subsequent Korean kingdoms, claimed to inherit its legacy.

Supported by the Tang, Silla took control of much of the Korean peninsula. The Silla rulers imitated Tang government and examined officials on the Confucian classics. They also sent Buddhist monks to China. But the intellectual exchange was not one-directional: writings by the monk Wonhyo known as the "Korean Commentary" greatly influenced Buddhism in China. The fall of the Tang in the early 900s coincided with Silla's collapse and enabled the ruling house of **Koryo** (KAW-ree-oh), from which the modern name *Korea* derives, to rule a united peninsula for the next three centuries. Threatened constantly by the Liao and then the Jin in northern China, Koryo maintained amicable relations with Song China in the south. The Koryo

---

**shamanism** The practice of identifying special individuals (shamans) who will interact with spirits for the benefit of the community. Characteristic of the Korean kingdoms of the early medieval period and of early societies of Central Asia.

**Koryo** Korean kingdom founded in 918 and destroyed by a Mongol invasion in 1259.

DeA Picture Library/Art Resource, NY

**Silla Warrior** This ewer—the projection in front is the pour spout—reflects Korea's early use of cavalry. Horses were probably introduced to Japan by way of Korea.

kings supported Buddhism and made superb printed editions of Buddhist texts.

The oldest surviving woodblock print in Chinese characters comes from Korea in the middle 700s. Commonly used during the Tang period, woodblock printing required great technical skill. A calligrapher would write the text on thin paper, which would then be pasted upside down on a block of wood. Once wetted, the characters showed through from the back, and an artisan would carve away the wooden surface surrounding each character. A fresh block had to be carved for each printed page. Korean artisans developed their own advances in printing. By Song times, Korean experiments with movable type had reached China, where further improvements led to metal or porcelain type from which texts could be cheaply printed.

## Japan

Japan consists of four main islands and many smaller ones stretching in an arc from as far south as Georgia to as far north as Maine. The nearest point of contact with

the Asian mainland lies 100 miles away in southern Korea. In early times Japan was even more heavily forested than Korea, with only 11 percent of its land area suitable for cultivation. Mild winters and monsoon rains supported the earliest population centers on the coastlands of the Inland Sea between Honshu and Shikoku Islands. The first rulers to extend their power broadly in the fourth and fifth centuries C.E. were based in the Yamato River Basin on the Kinai Plain at the eastern end of the sea.

The first Chinese description of Japan, dating from the fourth century, tells of an island at the eastern edge of the world that is divided into hundreds of small communities, with the largest one, called Yamatai, ruled over by a shamaness named Himiko or Pimiko. The location of the early Yamatai kingdom remains a source of debate, but archaeological finds point to frequent interaction with China and Korea. In the mid-600s these rulers, acting on knowledge gained from Korean contacts and embassies to Chang'an sent by five different kings, implemented the Taika (TIE-kah) and other reforms, giving the Yamato regime the key features of Tang government. A legal code, an official variety of Confucianism, and an official reverence for Buddhism blended with the local recognition of indigenous and immigrant chieftains as territorial administrators. Within a century, a centralized government with a complex system of law had emerged, as attested by a massive history in the Confucian style.

Women from the aristocracy became royal consorts and thereby linked their kinsmen with the royal court. At the death of her husband in 592, Suiko, a woman from the immigrant aristocratic family of Soga, became empress. She occupied the throne until 628, enjoying a longer reign than any other ruler down to the nineteenth century. Asuka, her capital, saw a flowering of Buddhist art, and her nephew Shotoku opened relations with Sui China and is credited with promulgating a "Constitution" in 604 that had lasting influence on Japan's governing philosophy.

The Japanese mastered and improved on several Chinese skills. They copied Chinese building techniques so well that Nara (NAH-rah) and Kyoto, Japan's early capitals, provide invaluable evidence of the wooden architecture long since vanished from China. During the eighth century Japan in some ways surpassed China in Buddhist studies. In 752 dignitaries from all over Mahayana Buddhist Asia gathered at the enormous Todaiji temple, near Nara, to celebrate the "eye-opening" of the "Great Buddha" statue.

Though the Japanese adopted Chinese building styles and some street plans, Japanese cities were built without walls. One reason was that central Japan was not plagued by constant warfare. Also, the Confucian Mandate of Heaven, which justified dynastic changes, played no role in legitimating Japanese government. The *tenno*, or "heavenly sovereign"—often called "emperor" in English—belonged to a family believed to have ruled Japan since the beginning of history. The dynasty never changed. A prime minister and the leaders of the native religion, in later times called Shinto, the "way of the gods," exercised real control.

By 750 the government in the capital city Nara had reached its zenith. Roads reached out to provincial capitals, and the rulers pushed their rice-growing culture into the territory of the related Hayato people

of southern Kyushu and into northeastern Honshu, where the Emishi, a non-Japanese indigenous population, practiced slash-and-burn agriculture.

In 794 the central government moved to Kyoto, usually called by its ancient name, Heian (hay-ahn). Though power became decentralized toward the end, legally centralized government lasted there until 1185. During this time members of the **Fujiwara** (foo-jee-WAH-rah) clan—a family of priests, bureaucrats, and warriors who had succeeded the Soga clan in influence from 866 to 1180—controlled power and protected the emperor. Fujiwara dominance favored men of Confucian learning over the generally illiterate warriors. Noblemen of the Fujiwara period read the Chinese classics and appreciated painting and poetry.

Gradually the Fujiwara nobles began to entrust responsibility for local government, policing, and tax collection to their warriors, known as *samurai*, literally "one who serves." Though often of humble origins, a small number of warriors had achieved wealth and power by the late 1000s. By the middle 1100s the nobility had lost control, and civil war between rival warrior clans engulfed the capital.

Like other East Asian states influenced by Confucianism, the elite families of Fujiwara Japan did not encourage education for women. The hero of the celebrated Japanese novel about Fujiwara court culture, *The Tale of Genji*, written around the year 1000 and often regarded as the world's first novel, remarks: "Women should have a general knowledge of several subjects, but it gives a bad impression if they show themselves to be attached to a particular branch of learning."[4] However, within the marriage politics of the day, having interesting and talented women helped the Fujiwara monopolize the monarch's attention on their own women rather than those of other families.

Fujiwara noblewomen lived in near-total isolation, generally spending their time on cultural pursuits and the study of Buddhism. To communi-

---

[4] Quoted in Ivan Morris, *The World of the Shining Prince: Court Life in Ancient Japan* (New York: Penguin Books, 1979), 221–222.

> **Fujiwara** Aristocratic family that dominated the Japanese imperial court between the ninth and twelfth centuries.

cate with their families or among themselves, they depended on writing. The simplified syllabic script that they used represented the Japanese language in its fully inflected form (the Chinese classical script used by Fujiwara men could not do so). Sei Shonagon (SAY SHOH-nah-gohn), a lady attending one of the royal consorts, composed her *Pillow Book* between 996 and 1021. Most likely named for being kept by the author's pillow so she could jot down occasional thoughts, this famous work begins:

> Spring is best at dawn as gradually the hilltops lighten, while the light grows brighter until there are purple-tinged clouds trailing through the sky.

> Summer is best at night. That goes without saying when there is a full moon. But when fireflies flit here and there in a dark sky, that too is wonderful. It is even wonderful when it is raining.[5]

Military clans acquired increasing importance during the period 1156–1185, and warfare between rival families culminated in the establishment of the **Kamakura** (kah-mah-KOO-rah) **Shogunate** in eastern Honshu, far from the old religious and political center at Kyoto. The standing of the Fujiwara family fell as nobles and the emperor hurried to accommodate the new warlords. *The Tale of the Heike*, an anonymously composed thirteenth-century epic account of the clan war, reflects a Buddhist appreciation of the impermanence of worldly things, a view that became common among the new warrior class. This class eventually absorbed some of the Fujiwara aristocratic values, but the monopoly of power by a nonmilitary civil elite had come to an end.

### Vietnam

Not until Tang times did the relationship between Vietnam and China become close enough for economic and cultural interchange to play an important role. Occupying the coastal regions east of the mountainous spine of mainland Southeast Asia, Vietnam's economic and political life centered on two fertile river valleys, the Red River in the north and the Mekong (may-KONG) in the south. The rice-based agriculture of Vietnam

[5] Quoted in Ivan Morris, trans., *The Pillow Book of Sei Shonagon* (New York: Columbia University Press, 1991), section 1.

**SECTION REVIEW**

- Korea, Japan, and Vietnam adapted Chinese cultural and political models, including the Tang blend of Confucianism and Buddhism.

- In all three cultures, landowning and agriculture remained the principal source of wealth.

made the region well suited for integration with southern China. In both regions the wet climate and hilly terrain demanded expertise in irrigation.

Early Vietnamese peoples may have preceded the Chinese in using draft animals in farming and working with metal. But in Tang and Song times the elites of "Annam" (ahn-nahm)—as the Chinese called early Vietnam—adopted Confucian bureaucratic training, Mahayana Buddhism, and other aspects of Chinese culture. Annamese elites continued to rule in the Tang style after that dynasty's fall. Annam assumed the name *Dai Viet* (die vee-yet) in 936 and maintained good relations with Song China as an independent country.

Champa, located in what is now southern Vietnam, rivaled the Dai Viet state. The cultures of India and the Malay Peninsula strongly influenced Champa through maritime networks of trade and communication. During the Tang period, Champa fought with Dai Viet, but both kingdoms cooperated with the less threatening Song. Among the tribute gifts brought to the Song court by Champa emissaries was **Champa rice** (originally from India). Chinese farmers soon made use of this fast-maturing variety to improve their yields of the essential crop.

Vietnam shared the general Confucian interest in hierarchy, but attitudes toward women, like those in Korea and Japan, differed from the Chinese model. None of the societies adopted footbinding. In Korea strong family alliances that functioned like political and economic organizations allowed women a role in

**Kamakura Shogunate**  The first of Japan's decentralized military governments (1185–1333).

**Champa rice**  Quick-maturing rice that can allow two harvests in one growing season. Originally introduced into Champa from India, it was later sent to China as a tribute gift by the Champa state.

negotiating and disposing of property. Before the adoption of Confucianism, Annamese women had enjoyed higher status than women in China, perhaps because both women and men participated in wet-rice cultivation. The Trung sisters of Vietnam, who lived in the second century C.E. and led local farmers in resistance against the Han Empire, still serve as national symbols in Vietnam and as local heroes in southern China.

## CONCLUSION

The Tang Empire put into place a solid system of travel, trade, and communications that allowed cultural and economic influences to move quickly from Central Asia to Japan. Diversity within the empire produced great wealth and new ideas. In northern and Central Asia, these refinements included state ideologies based on Buddhism, bureaucratic practices based on Chinese traditions, and military techniques combining nomadic horsemanship and strategies with Chinese armaments and weapons. As a result of China's great size, ancient culture, and advanced technology, smaller states of East Asia such as Vietnam, Korea, and Japan modeled their political and cultural life on China. But tensions among rival groups weakened the

political structure and led to great violence and misery.

Though smaller than its predecessor, the Song Empire showed great productivity, circulating goods and money throughout East Asia and stimulating the economies of neighbors. In Song China, the spread of Tang technological knowledge resulted in major advances in technology and industry, increased productivity in agriculture, and deeper exploration of ideas relating to time, cosmology, and mathematics. Song China dominated military technology and engineering, privatized commerce, and used movable type to promote its ideological goals. The brilliant achievements of the Song period came from mutually reinforcing developments in economy and technology.

Korea, Japan, and Vietnam developed distinct social, economic, and political systems. Buddhism became the preferred religion in all three regions, but Chinese influences, largely deriving from a universal esteem for Confucian thought and writings, put down deep roots. In the absence of a land border with China, Japan retained greater political independence than Korea and Vietnam. All of these societies made advances in agricultural technology and productivity and raised their literacy rates as printing spread. The culture of Japan's imperial center reached a high level of perfection, but the political system was ultimately based on a warrior aristocracy.

## CHAPTER REVIEW

### THE SUI AND TANG EMPIRES, 581–755
■ *What was the importance of Inner and Central Asia as a region of interchange during the Tang period?* (page 255)

Though the Tang emperors presided over one of the most celebrated periods in Chinese history, they were of Turkish descent and made extensive use of the military and cultural practices of Inner Asian nomads. Silk Road trade flourished under the Tang, and the new popularity of Buddhism entering China from the northwest gateway greatly affected Chinese culture. Nevertheless, most Tang officials came from long-established aristocratic Chinese families.

### CHINA AND ITS RIVALS
■ *What were the effects of the fracturing of power in Inner Asia and China?* (page 263)

After the Tang fell, warlords of different ethnic identities fought for control of northern China. The southward flight of people across the Yangzi River led to the formation of power centers well removed from the northwest frontier. The Song dynasty brought political and economic prominence to southern China. But in Korea and Vietnam, the collapse of the Tang encouraged local independence. Chinese culture continued to be admired and imitated, but the new ruling families rejected the Chinese bureaucratic structure even while recognizing that China provided the greatest market for their trade, particularly under the robust economic conditions of the Southern Song.

## NEW KINGDOMS IN EAST ASIA

■ *To what extent do shared practices justify thinking of East Asia as a unified cultural region in the post-Tang era?* (page 269)

A reverence for Confucian classics spread from China to all neighboring lands and formed the core of elite education. Buddhism also spread at both the elite and popular levels. However, neither played as strong a political role as Islam did in the Middle East or Christianity in Europe. As a consequence, East Asia emerged during this period as a region with strong cultural links but without a common philosophical or religious tradition of rulership.

## Key Terms

Grand Canal (p. 255)
Li Shimin (p. 256)
Tang Empire (p. 256)
tributary system (p. 257)
Uighurs (p. 259)
Tibet (p. 259)
Song Empire (p. 263)
junk (p. 264)
gunpowder (p. 265)
neo-Confucianism (p. 265)
Zen (p. 265)
movable type (p. 266)
shamanism (p. 270)
Koryo (p. 270)
Fujiwara (p. 272)
Kamakura Shogunate (p. 273)
Champa rice (p. 273)

# Religious Conversion

*Religious conversion* has two meanings that often get confused. The term can refer to the inner transformation an individual may feel on joining a new religious community or becoming revitalized in his or her religious belief. Conversions of this sort are often sudden and deeply emotional. In historical terms, they may be important when they transform the lives of prominent individuals.

In its other meaning, religious conversion refers to a change in the religious identity of an entire population, or a large portion of a population. This generally occurs slowly and is hard to trace in historical documents. As a result, historians have sometimes used superficial indicators to trace the spread of a religion. Doing so can result in misleading conclusions, such as considering the spread of the Islamic faith to be the result of forced conversion by Arab conquerors, or taking the routes traveled by Christian or Buddhist missionaries as evidence that the people they encountered adopted their spiritual message, or assuming that a king or chieftain's adherence to a new religion immediately resulted in a religious change among subjects or followers.

In addition to being difficult to document, religious conversion in the broad societal sense has followed different patterns according to changing circumstances of time and place. Historians have devised several models to explain the different conversion patterns. According to one model, while religious labels in a society change quickly, such as through mass baptism, devotional practices remain largely the same. Evidence for this model can be found in the continuation of old religious customs among people who identify themselves as belonging to a new religion. Another model sees religious change as primarily a function of economic benefit or escape from persecution. Taking this approach makes it difficult to explain the endurance of certain religious communities in the face of hardship and discrimination. Nevertheless, most historians pay attention to economic advantage in their assessments of mass conversion. A third model associates a society's religious conversion with its desire to adopt a more sophisticated way of life, by shifting, for example, from a religion that does not use written texts to one that does.

One final conceptual approach to explaining the process of mass religious change draws on the quantitative models of innovation diffusion that were originally developed to analyze the spread of new technologies in the twentieth century. According to this approach, new ideas, whether in the material or religious realm, depend on the spread of information. A few early adopters—missionaries, pilgrims, or conquerors, perhaps—spread word of the new faith to the people they come in contact with, some of whom follow their example and convert. Those converts in turn spread the word to others, and a chain reaction picks up speed in what might be called a bandwagon effect. The period of bandwagon conversion tapers off when the number of people who have not yet been offered an opportunity to convert diminishes. The entire process can be graphed as a logistic or S-shaped curve. Figure 1, the graph of conversion to Islam in Iran based on changes from Persian (non-Islamic) to Arabic (Islamic) names in family genealogies, shows such a curve over a period of almost four centuries.

In societies that were largely illiterate, like those in which Buddhism, Christianity, and Islam slowly achieved spiritual dominance, information spread primarily by word of mouth. The proponents of the new religious views did not always speak the same language as the people they hoped to bring into the faith. Under these circumstances, significant conversion—that is, conversion that involved some understanding of the new religion, as opposed to forced baptism or imposed mouthing of a profession of faith—must surely have started with fairly small numbers.

Language was crucial. Chinese pilgrims undertook lengthy travels to visit early Buddhist sites in India. There they acquired Sanskrit texts, which they translated into Chinese. These translations became the core texts of Chinese Buddhism. In early Christendom, the presence of bilingual (Greek-Aramaic) Jewish communities in the eastern parts of the Roman Empire facilitated the early spread of the religion beyond its Aramaic-speaking homeland. By contrast, Arabic, the language of Islam, was spoken only in the Arabian peninsula and the desert borderlands that extended northwards from Arabia between Syria, Jordan, and Iraq. This initial impediment to the spread of knowledge about Islam dissolved only when intermarriage with non-Muslim, non-Arab women, many of them taken captive and distributed as booty during the conquests, produced bilingual offspring. Bilingual preachers of the Christian faith were similarly needed in the Celtic, Germanic, and Slavic language areas of western and eastern Europe.

This slow process of information diffusion, which varied from region to region, made changing demands on religious leaders and institutions. When a faith was professed primarily by a ruler, his army, and his dependants, religious leaders gave the highest priority to servicing the needs of the ruling minority and perhaps discrediting, denigrating, or exterminating the practices of the majority. Once a few centuries had passed and the new faith had become the religion of the great majority of the population, religious leaders turned to establishing popular institutions and reaching out to the common people. Historical interpretation can benefit from knowing where a society is in a long-term process of conversion.

These various models reinforce the importance of distinguishing between emotional individual conversion experiences and broad changes in a society's religious identity. New converts are commonly thought of as especially zealous in their faith, and that description is often apt in instances of individual conversion experiences. It is less appropriate, however, to broader episodes of conversion. In a conversion wave that starts slowly, builds momentum in the bandwagon phase, and then tapers off, the first individuals to convert are likely to be more spiritually motivated than those who join the movement toward its end. Religious growth depends on making the faith as attractive to late converts as to ecstatic early converts.

**Figure 1** Conversion to Islam in Iran

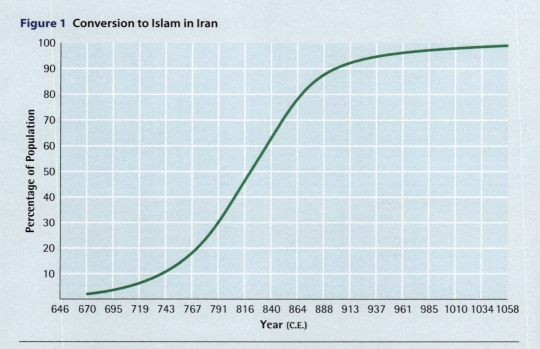

*Source*: Richard W. Bulliet, *Conversion to Islam in the Medieval Period*, Cambridge, MA: Harvard University Press, 1979, 23. Copyright © 1979 by the President and Fellows of Harvard College.

# Part Four

# Interregional Patterns of Culture and Contact, 1200–1550

© Cengage Learning

| | 1200 | 1250 | 1300 | 1350 |
|---|---|---|---|---|
| **AMERICAS** | • **1200** Population of Cahokia reaches 30,000<br>**1200–1300** Collapse of Anasazi centers | | | • **1325** Aztecs found Tenochtitlan |
| **EUROPE** | • **1215** Magna Carta | • **1240** Mongol conquest of Russia | • **1300** First clocks<br>• **1286** Champagne fairs begin to promote regional trade | **1337–1453** Hundred Years War<br>• **1347** Black Death |
| **AFRICA** | Kingdom of Benin founded **ca. 1250** • | **1240–1500** Mali Empire | • **1270** Solomonic dynasty founded in Ethiopia | • **1324–1325** Mansa Musa's pilgrimage to Mecca brings Islamic learning to Mali |
| **MIDDLE EAST** | • **1221** Mongols attack Iran | • **1260** Mamluks defeat Mongols at Ain Jalut<br>• **1258** Mongols take Baghdad, end Abbasid Caliphate | • **1300** Emergence of Ottomans in Anatolia<br>**1295–1304** Rule of Muslim Il-khan Ghazan | |
| **ASIA AND OCEANIA** | • **1200** Polynesians settle New Zealand<br>• **1206** Delhi Sultanate founded in India<br>**1206–1227** Reign of Genghis Khan | Polynesians settle Hawaii **1300** •<br>• **1274, 1281** Mongol attacks on Japan<br>**1265–1294** Reign of Khubilai Khan | • **1336** Ashikaga Shogunate founded<br>Yuan Empire in China **1279–1368**<br>Ming Empire founded in China **1368** • | |

## CHAPTER 12
Mongol Eurasia and Its Aftermath, 1200–1500

## CHAPTER 13
Europe East and West, 1200–1500

## CHAPTER 14
Southern Empires, Southern Seas, 1200–1500

## CHAPTER 15
The Maritime Revolution, to 1550

Part IV begins with the Mongol conquests under Chinggis Khan, whose empire made Mongolia the center of an administrative and trading system linking Europe, the Middle East, Russia, and East Asia. Overland trade along the Silk Road peaked under the Mongols. Some lands flourished; others groaned under tax burdens and physical devastation.

Societies that escaped conquest also felt the Mongol impact. Around the eastern Mediterranean coast and in eastern Europe, Southeast Asia, and Japan, fear of Mongol attack stimulated defense planning and accelerated processes of urbanization, technological development, and political centralization.

By 1500, Mongol dominance had waned. Eurasia's overland trade faded, and merchants, soldiers, and explorers took to the seas. From China, the admiral Zheng He made state-sponsored long-distance voyages under a new Ming Empire that were spectacular but without long-term results. Meanwhile, Africans explored the Atlantic, and Polynesians colonized the central and eastern Pacific in the 1300s and 1400s. By 1500 Christopher Columbus had reached the Americas; within twenty-five years a Portuguese ship would sail around the world.

The overland routes of Eurasia had generated massive wealth in East Asia and a growing hunger for commerce in Europe. These factors similarly spurred the development of maritime trade. The Ming expanded Chinese influence in Southeast Asia. The Ottomans overthrew the Byzantine Empire and became a major factor in Mediterranean and Black Sea trade, and Christian monarchs in Spain and Portugal, victorious over Muslim enemies, also lay the foundations for new overseas empires. Exposure to the achievements, wealth, and resources of the Americas, sub-Saharan Africa, and Asia guaranteed the further expansion of European exploration and maritime power. Meanwhile in the Western Hemisphere the Aztecs and Inkas were establishing the large Amerindian empires that were destined to clash with invading Europeans.

| 1400 | 1450 | 1500 | 1550 |
|---|---|---|---|

- 1438–1533 Inca Empire
- 1533 Pizarro conquers Inca Empire
- 1492 Columbus reaches Caribbean
- 1520 Cortés conquers Aztec Empire

- 1418–1460 Voyages of Henry the Navigator
- 1462–1505 Ivan III unites Russia
- Portugal establishes trading empire in Indian Ocean 1499–1572
- 1400–1550 Italian Renaissance
- 1454 Gutenberg Bible printed
- 1492 Christian reconquest of Spain

- 1400–1450 Great Zimbabwe at its peak
- 1471 Portuguese establish Elmina
- 1526 Christian king of Kongo urges end of slave trade
- 1499 Vasco da Gama rounds Africa
- 1539 Portuguese aid Ethiopia

- 1370–1405 Reign of Timur
- 1415 Portuguese seize Morocco
- 1453 Ottomans take Constantinople
- 1517 Ottomans conquer Egypt

- 1405–1433 Voyages of Zheng He
- ca. 1449 Ulugh Beg builds observatory in Samarkand
- 1500 Annam conquers Champa
- 1510, 1511 Portuguese seize Goa, Malacca
- 1392 Yi kingdom founded in Korea
- 1482 Japanese invasion of Korea

# CHAPTER 12

## 1200–1500

# Mongol Eurasia and Its Aftermath

© Cengage Learning

**CHAPTER PREVIEW**

### THE RISE OF THE MONGOLS, 1200–1260

- *What accounts for the magnitude and speed of the Mongol conquests?*

### THE MONGOLS AND ISLAM, 1260–1500

- *How did Mongol expansion and Islam affect each other?*

### REGIONAL RESPONSES IN WESTERN EURASIA

- *What benefits resulted from the integration of Eurasia into the Mongol Empire?*

### MONGOL DOMINATION IN CHINA, 1271–1368

- *How did Mongol rule in China foster cultural and scientific exchange?*

### THE EARLY MING EMPIRE, 1368–1500

- *In what ways did the Ming Empire continue or discontinue Mongol practices?*

### CENTRALIZATION AND MILITARISM IN EAST ASIA, 1200–1500

- *What are some of the similarities and differences in how Korea and Japan responded to the Mongol threat?*

### Conclusion

**DIVERSITY + DOMINANCE:** Observations of Mongol Life

When Temüjin (TEM-uh-jin) was a boy, a rival group murdered his father. Temüjin's mother tried to shelter him, but she could not find a safe haven, so at fifteen Temüjin sought refuge with the leader of the Keraits (keh-rates), a warring confederation whose people spoke Turkish and respected both Christianity and Buddhism. Temüjin learned the importance of religious tolerance, the necessity of dealing harshly with enemies, and the variety of Inner Asia's cultural and economic traditions.

In 1206 the **Mongols** and their allies acknowledged Temüjin as **Chinggis Khan** (CHING-iz KAHN) (sometimes known as Genghis), or supreme leader. His advisers spoke many languages and belonged to different religions. His deathbed speech, which cannot be literally true even though a contemporary recorded it, captures the strategy behind Mongol success: "If you want to retain your possessions and conquer your enemies, you must make your subjects submit willingly and unite your diverse energies to a single end."[1] By implementing this strategy, Chinggis Khan became the most famous conqueror in history, initiating an expansion of Mongol dominion that by 1250 stretched from Poland to northern China.

European and Asian sources of the time vilified the Mongols as agents of death, suffering, and conflagration, a still-common viewpoint based on reliable accounts of horrible massacres. However, scholars today stress the positive developments that transpired under Mongol rule. The tremendous extent of the Mongol Empire promoted the movement of people and ideas from one end of Eurasia to the other. Trade routes improved, markets expanded, and the demand for products grew. Trade on the Silk Road, which had declined with the fall of the Tang Empire (see Chapter 11), revived.

Between 1218 and about 1350 in western Eurasia and down to 1368 in China, the Mongols focused on specific economic and strategic interests, usually permitting local cultures to survive and develop. In some regions, local reactions to Mongol domination sowed seeds of regional and ethnic identity that blossomed in the period of Mongol decline. Regions as widely separated as Russia, Iran, China, Korea, and Japan benefited from the Mongol stimulation of economic and cultural exchange and also found in their opposition to the Mongols new bases for political consolidation and affirmation of cultural difference.

## THE RISE OF THE MONGOLS, 1200–1260

■ *What accounts for the magnitude and speed of the Mongol conquests?*

The Mongol Empire owed much of its success to the cultural institutions and political traditions of the Eurasian steppes and deserts. The pastoral way of life known as nomadism (see Chapter 3) gives rise to imperial expansion only occasionally, and historians disagree about what triggers these episodes. In the case of the Mongols, the personal contributions of Chinggis Khan and his successors remains uncertain.

**Mongol Nomadism** The pastoral nomads of the Eurasian Steppes played an on-again, off-again role in European, Middle Eastern, and Chinese history for hundreds of years before the rise of the Mongols (see Chapter 8). The Mongol way of life probably did not differ materially from that of those earlier peoples (see Diversity and Dominance: Observations of Mongol Life). Traditional accounts maintain that the Mongols put their infants on goats to accustom them to riding in preparation for their migratory lifestyle. Like earlier pastoral nomads of the steppes, Mongols moved with their flocks and herds. Powerful families ratified the decisions of the leader, the *khan*, in a public decision-making process

[1]Quotation adapted from Desmond Martin, *Chingis Khan and His Conquest of North China* (Baltimore: The John Hopkins Press, 1950), 303.

**Mongols** A people of this name is mentioned as early as the records of the Tang Empire, living as nomads in northern Eurasia. After 1206 they established an enormous empire under Chinggis Khan, linking western and eastern Eurasia.

**Chinggis Khan** The title of Temüjin when he ruled the Mongols (1206–1227). It means the "oceanic" or "universal leader." Chinggis Khan was the founder of the Mongol Empire.

that brought together the many voices of independent individual Mongols and their families. Yet people who disagreed with a decision could strike out on their own. Even during military campaigns, warriors moved with their families and possessions.

Menial work in camps fell to slaves—either prisoners of war or people who sought refuge in slavery to escape starvation. Weak groups secured land rights and protection from strong groups by providing them with slaves, livestock, weapons, silk, or cash. More powerful groups, such as Chinggis Khan's extended family and descendants, lived almost entirely off tribute, so they spent less time and fewer resources on herding and more on warfare designed to secure greater tribute.

Leading families combined resources and solidified intergroup alliances through arranged marriages and acts of allegiance, a process that helped generate political federations. Marriages were arranged in childhood—in Temüjin's case, at the age of eight—and children thus became pawns of diplomacy. Women from prestigious families could wield power in negotiation and management, though they ran the risk of assassination or execution just like men.

The wives and mothers of Mongol rulers traditionally managed state affairs during the interregnum between a ruler's death and the selection of a successor. Princes and heads of ministries treated such regents with great deference and obeyed their commands without question. Since a female regent could not herself succeed to the position of khan, her political machinations usually focused on gaining the succession for a son or other male relative. Families often included believers in two or more religions, most commonly Buddhism, Christianity, or Islam. Virtually all Mongols observed the practices of traditional shamanism, rituals in which special individuals visited and influenced the supernatural world. Whatever their faith, the Mongols believed in world rulership by a khan who, with the aid of his shamans, could speak to and for an ultimate god, represented as Sky or Heaven. This universal ruler transcended particular cultures and dominated them all.

## The Mongol Conquests, 1215–1283

Shortly after his acclamation in 1206, Chinggis initiated two decades of Mongol aggression. By 1209 he had cowed the Tanggut (TAHNG-gut) rulers of northwest China, and in 1215 he captured the Jin capital of Yanjing, today known as Beijing (bay-jeeng). He turned westward in 1219 with an invasion of Khwarezm (kaw-REZM), a state east of the Caspian Sea that included much of Iran. After 1221, when most of Iran had fallen, Chinggis left the command of most campaigns to subordinate generals.

Ögödei (ERG-uh-day), Chinggis's son, became the Great Khan in 1227 after his father's death. He completed the destruction of the Tanggut and the Jin and put their territories under Mongol governors. By 1234 he controlled most of northern China and was threatening the Southern Song (see Chapter 11). Two years later Chinggis's grandson Batu (BAH-too) (d. 1255) attacked Russian territories, took control of the towns along the Volga (VOHL-gah) River, and conquered Kievan Russia, Moscow, Poland, and Hungary in a five-year campaign. Only the death of Ögödei in 1241, which caused a suspension of campaigning, saved Europe from invasion. With Chinggis's grandson Güyük (gi-yik) installed as the new Great Khan, the conquests resumed. In the Middle East a Mongol army sacked Baghdad in 1258 and executed the last Abbasid caliph (see Chapter 9).

Chinggis Khan's original objective had probably been collecting tribute, but the success of the Mongol conquests created a new situation. Ögödei unquestionably sought to rule a united empire based at his capital, Karakorum (kah-rah-KOR-um), but after his death family unity began to unravel. The Golden Horde in Russia, the Chagatai (JAH-guh-die) lands in Central Asia, and the Il-khans in Iran were subordinate domains (see Map 12.1); but when Khubilai (KOO-bih-lie) declared himself Great Khan in 1265, the descendants of Chinggis's son Chagatai (d. 1242) and other branches of the family refused to accept him. As Karakorum was destroyed in the ensuing fighting, Khubilai transferred his court to the old Jin capital now renamed Beijing. In 1271 he declared himself founder of the **Yuan Empire**.

Chagatai's descendants continued to dominate Central Asia and enjoyed close relations with the region's Turkish-speaking nomads. This, plus a continuing hatred of Khubilai, contributed to Central

**Yuan Empire** Empire created in China and Siberia by Khubilai Khan.

# Chronology

| | Mongolia and China | Central Asia and Middle East | Russia | Korea, Japan, and Southeast Asia |
|---|---|---|---|---|
| **1200** | **1206** Temüjin chosen Chinggis Khan of the Mongols | **1219–1223** Invasion of Iran | | |
| | **1234** North China seized | | **1236** Russia invaded | |
| | | **1258** Mongols sack Baghdad | | **1258** Mongols conquer Koryo |
| | **1271** Founding of Yuan Empire | | | |
| | **1279** Southern Song attacked | | | **1274, 1281** Mongols attack Japan |
| **1300** | | | | **1333–1338** End of shogunate |
| | | | **1346** Plague in Kaffa | |
| | | **ca. 1350** Plague in Egypt | | |
| | **1368** Ming Empire founded | | | **1392** Korean Choson kingdom |
| **1400** | | **1453** Ottomans capture Constantinople | | |
| | | | **1462–1505** Ivan III tsar | |

Asia becoming an independent Mongol center and to the spread of Islam there.

After the Yuan destroyed the Southern Song (see Chapter 11) in 1279, Mongol troops attacked Annam—now northern Vietnam—and in 1283 invaded the kingdom of Champa in southern Vietnam. When the initially successful Mongols suffered a defeat, Khubilai was so infuriated that he postponed an invasion of Japan to focus on the Vietnamese kingdoms. In 1287, the Vietnamese troops, under the command of Tran Hung Dao, Vietnam's most famous military hero, defeated the Mongol forces in a final battle. A plan to invade Java by sea also failed, as did two invasions of Japan in 1274 and 1281.

The Mongols seldom outnumbered their enemies, but they were extraordinary riders and utilized superior bows. The Central Asian bow, made by laminating layers of wood, leather, and bone, could shoot one-third farther (and was correspondingly more difficult to pull) than the bows used by sedentary enemies. Rarely did an archer expend all of the five dozen arrows in his quiver. As the battle opened, arrows shot from a distance decimated enemy marksmen. Then the Mongols charged the enemy's infantry to fight with sword, lance, javelin, and mace. The Mongol cavalry met its match only at the Battle of Ain Jalut (ine jah-LOOT), where an under-strength force confronted Turkish-speaking mamluks whose war techniques matched their own (see Chapter 9).

The Mongols also fired flaming arrows and hurled enormous projectiles—sometimes flaming—from catapults. The original catapults, built on portable Chinese models, had short range and poor accuracy. But during western campaigns in Central Asia, the Mongols encountered a design that was half again as powerful and used it to hammer the cities of Iran and Iraq. Cities that resisted faced slaughter. The terror of certain death was spread by the annihilation of Balkh (bahlk) (in present-day northern Afghanistan) and other cities. Surrender was the only option. Each conquered area contributed men to the "Mongol" armies; in the Middle East, a few Mongol officers commanded armies of recently recruited Turks and Iranians.

**Map 12.1  The Mongol Domains in Eurasia in 1300**  After the death of Chinggis Khan in 1227, his empire was divided among his sons and grandsons. Son Ögödei succeeded Chinggis as Great Khan. Grandson Khubilai expanded the domain of the Great Khan into southern China by 1279. Grandson Hülegü was the first Il-khan in the Middle East. Grandson Batu founded the Khanate of the Golden Horde in southern Russia. Son Chagatai ruled the Chagatai Khanate in Central Asia.  © Cengage Learning

EUROPE

RUSSIA

• Moscow

• Kiev

Black Sea

Danube R.

Mediterranean Sea

AFRICA

Jerusalem •

ARABIA

Red Sea

Nile R.

Tigris R.  Baghdad •

Euphrates R.

Caspian Sea

Volga R.

• Bolgar

Aral Sea

Syr Darya R.

Amu Darya R.

Bukhara •  • Samarkand

IL-KHAN EMPIRE

KHANATE OF THE GOLDEN HORDE

ASIA

KHANATE OF CENTRAL ASIA

• Khotan

HIMALAYA MTS.

Indus R.

Ganges R.

Delhi •

SULTANATE OF DELHI

INDIA

Brahmaputra R.

Arabian Sea

Bay of Bengal

INDIAN OCEAN

MONGOLIA

Karakorum •

GOBI

EMPIRE OF THE GREAT KHAN

Shangdu •

Beijing •

MANCHURIA

Amur R.

KOREA

JAPAN

Sea of Japan (East Sea)

East China Sea

Tropic of Cancer

• Kaifeng

Huang He (Yellow R.)

Yangzi R.

SOUTHERN SONG (Fell 1279)

Hangzhou •

Guangzhou •

South China Sea

NANZHAO

ANNAM

Mekong R.

KHMER

BURMA

Irrawaddy R.

Salween R.

Pagan •

VIJAYANAGAR EMPIRE

1,000 Mi.

1,000 Km.

500

500

Mongol campaigns before 1240

Mongol campaigns after 1240

Route of Marco Polo

N

**Overland Trade and Disease**

Commercial integration under Mongol rule affected all parts of the empire. Like earlier nomad elites, Mongol nobles had the exclusive right to wear silk, almost all of which came from China. New styles and huge quantities of silk flowed westward to feed the luxury trade in the Middle East and Europe, and artistic motifs from Japan and Tibet reached as far as England and Morocco. Porcelain, another eastern luxury, became important in trade and strongly influenced later tastes in the Islamic world.

Merchants encountered ambassadors, scholars, and missionaries over the long routes to the Mongol courts. Some of the resulting travel literature, like the account of the Venetian Marco Polo (mar-koe POE-loe) (1254–1324), freely mixed the fantastic with the factual. Stories of immense wealth stimulated a European ambition to find easier routes to Asia.

Exchange also spread disease. In the mid-thirteenth century, flea-infested marmots and other rodents became infected and passed their disease to dogs and people. Though other diseases contributed to the mortality of the resulting pandemic, **bubonic plague**, which probably originated in Central Asia, was certainly involved. An earlier theory that southern China was the point of origin seems unlikely as unusually cold Chinese winters from 1344 to 1353 would have impeded the reproduction of fleas. Plague incapacitated the Mongol army during its assault on the city of Kaffa (KAH-fah) in Crimea (cry-MEE-ah) in 1346. They withdrew, but the plague remained. From Kaffa diseased rats carried the fleas to Europe and Egypt by ship (see Chapter 13).

Typhus, influenza, and smallpox traveled the same route. Thus peaceful trade created the "great pandemic" of 1347–1352 and caused deaths far in excess of what the Mongol armies inflicted. Epidemics were exacerbated, however, by the Mongol destruction of dams, irrigation channels, farmland, and crops. By cutting down the trees that helped keep the desert at bay, the Mongols turned large portions of China into the prairie plateaus of the steppe.

> **bubonic plague**  A bacterial disease of fleas that can be transmitted by flea bites to rodents and humans; humans in late stages of the illness can spread the bacteria by coughing. Because of its very high mortality rate and the difficulty of preventing its spread, major outbreaks have created crises in many parts of the world.

**Passport**  The Mongol Empire facilitated the movement of products, merchants, and diplomats over long distances. Travelers frequently encountered new languages, laws, and customs. The *paisa* (from a Chinese word for "card" or "sign"), with its inscription in Mongolian, proclaimed that the traveler had the ruler's permission to travel through the region. Europeans later adopted the practice, thus making the *paisa* the ancestor of modern passports.  The Metropolitan Museum of Art/Image source/Art Resource, NY

## SECTION REVIEW

- The society of the nomadic Mongols functioned through kinship and tribute ties, in which women often played important roles.

- Chinggis Khan began the Mongol conquest to win tribute from Eurasian kingdoms.

- His successors turned to territorial rule, yet internal politics split the empire into smaller states in China and Central Asia.

- The Mongols won territory through superior battle tactics and integrated it into a vast overland commercial network.

- That network allowed the bubonic plague and other diseases to spread across Asia into Europe.

## Observations of Mongol Life

The Mongols, despite the power, geographical extent, and durability of their empire, are known mainly from the observations made by non-Mongols who either traveled in their territory or worked for them. The following passages come from three such authors.

William of Rubruck, a Franciscan friar, journeyed to the court of the Great Khan Mönke in 1253–1255 after living for some period of time in Crusader territory in the Middle East. He carried a letter from the French king, Louis IX (ruled 1226–1270), asking that the friar and a companion be allowed to stay with the Mongols, preach Christianity, and comfort German prisoners. William never made contact with the Germans, but his highly personal observations on Mongol life fascinated European readers.

The dwelling in which they sleep is based on a hoop of interlaced branches, and its supports are made of branches, converging at the top around a smaller hoop, from which projects a neck like a chimney. They cover it with white felt: quite often they also smear the felt with chalk or white clay and ground bones to make it gleam whiter, or sometimes they blacken it. . . . These dwellings are constructed to such a size as to be on occasion thirty feet across: I myself once measured a breadth of twenty feet between the wheeltracks of a wagon, and when the dwelling was on the wagon it protruded beyond the wheels by at least five feet on either side. . . .

The married women make themselves very fine wagons. . . . One rich Mo'al [i.e., Mongol] or Tartar has easily a hundred or two hundred such wagons with chests. Baatu has twenty-six wives, each of whom has a large dwelling, not counting the other, smaller ones placed behind the large one, which are chambers, as it were, where the maids live: to each of these dwellings belong a good two hundred wagons. When they unload the dwellings, the chief wife pitches her residence at the westernmost end, and the others follow according to rank. . . . Hence the court of one wealthy Mo'al will have the appearance of a large town, though there will be very few males in it. . . .

The History of the World-Conqueror by the Iranian historian 'Ata-Malik Juvaini, who worked for the Mongols in Iran, was written in elegant Persian during the 1250s. It combines a glorification of the Mongol rulers with an unflinching picture of the cruelties and devastation inflicted by their conquests.

He [i.e., Chinggis Khan] paid great attention to the chase and used to say that the hunting of wild beasts was a proper occupation for the commanders of armies; and that instruction and training therein was incumbent on warriors and men-at-arms. . . . Whenever the Khan sets out on the great hunt (which takes place at the beginning of the winter season), he issues orders that the troops stationed around his headquarters and in the neighborhood . . . shall make preparation for the chase. . . .

The right wing, left wing and center of the army are drawn up and entrusted to the great emirs; and they set out together with the Royal Ladies and the concubines, as well as provisions of food and drink. For a month, or two, or three they form a hunting ring and drive the game slowly and gradually before them, taking care lest any escape from the ring. . . . Finally . . . the troops come to a halt all around the ring, standing shoulder to shoulder. The ring is now filled with the cries and commotion of every manner of game and the roaring and tumult of every kind of ferocious beast. . . .

When the ring has been so much contracted that the wild beasts are unable to stir, first the Khan rides in together with some of his retinue; then after he has wearied of the sport, they dismount upon high ground in the center . . . to watch the princes likewise entering the ring, and after them, in due order, the noyans [chiefs], the commanders and the troops. Several days pass in this manner; then, when nothing is left of the game but a few wounded and emaciated stragglers, old men and greybeards humbly approach the Khan, offer up prayers for his well-being and intercede for the lives of the remaining animals asking that they be suffered to depart to someplace nearer to grass and water. . . .

➤ Now war—with its killing, counting of the slain and sparing of the survivors—is after the same fashion, and indeed analogous in every detail, because all that is left in the neighborhood of the battlefield are a few broken-down wretches.

In 1330 Hu Szu-hui, a physician of Chinese-Turkish family background, presented the Yuan emperor with a manual entitled *Proper and Essential Things for the Emperor's Food and Drink*. His work reflects both the meat-heavy diet of the steppes and traditional Chinese concern with good nutrition.

## Foods That Cure Various Illnesses [60 entries]

### Donkey's Head Gruel

It cures apoplexy-vertigo, debility of hand and foot, annoying pain of extremities, and trouble in speaking:

*Black donkey's head (one; remove hair and wash clean), black pepper (two measures), tsaoko cardamom (two measures). Cook ingredients until overcooked. Add the five spices in fermented black bean juice. Flavor with the spices. Flavor evenly. Eat on an empty stomach.*

### Fox Meat Gruel

It cures infantile convulsion, epilepsy, spiritual confusion, indistinct speech, and inappropriate singing and laughing:

*Fox meat. (The quantity does not matter. Include organ meat.) [To] ingredient add the five spices according to the regular method. Cook until overcooked. When done eat on an empty stomach.*

### Bear Meat Gruel

It cures the various winds, foot numbness-insensitivity, and five flaccidities, tendon and muscle spasms:

*Bear meat (one measure). [To] ingredient add the five spices in fermented black beans. [Add] onions and sauce. Cook. When done eat on an empty stomach.*

### Sheep's Stomach Gruel

It cures the various apoplexies:

*Sheep's stomach (one; wash clean), non-glutinous rice (two measures), green onions (several), salted fruits, Chinese flower pepper (remove the closed up corns, roast to bring out the juice; 30 corns), sprouting ginger (two measures and a half cut up finely). Combine the six ingredients evenly and*

*put inside the sheep's stomach. Cook until overcooked. When done, flavor with the five spices. Eat on an empty stomach.*

## Foodstuffs That Mutually Conflict [55 entries]

Horse meat cannot be eaten together with granary rice.

Sheep's liver cannot be eaten together with pepper. It wounds the heart.

Hare meat cannot be eaten together with ginger.

Beef cannot be eaten together with chestnuts.

Mare's milk cannot be eaten together with fish hash. It produces obstruction of the bowels.

Venison cannot be eaten together with catfish.

Beef stomach cannot be eaten together with dog meat.

Quail meat cannot be eaten together with pork. The face will turn black.

Pheasant eggs cannot be eaten together with onions. It produces vermin.

Lettuce cannot be eaten together with cream.

Ground mustard cannot be eaten together with hare meat. It produces sores.

## QUESTIONS FOR ANALYSIS

1. How does the subject matter of these passages reveal the different viewpoints of a European, an Iranian, and a Chinese?

2. What in these passages might indicate whether the Mongols were Muslims, Christians, Buddhists, or Confucians?

3. Why would you expect the observations of a traveler to be more or less valuable as historical sources than those of someone who served a Mongol ruler?

*Sources:* From *The Mission of Friar William of Rubruck. His Journey to the Court of the Great Khan Mönke 1253–1255*, translated by Peter Jackson, pp. 73–74. Copyright ©1990. From Ata-Malik Juvani's *The History of the World Conqueror*, translated by Andrew Boyle, pp. 27–29, Cambridge, Mass.: Harvard University Press, Copyright © 1958 by Manchester University Press. Paul D. Buell and Eugene N. Anderson, *A Soup for the Qan*, 2000, pp. 428–429, 438–440.

# THE MONGOLS AND ISLAM, 1260–1500

■ *How did Mongol expansion and Islam affect each other?*

From the perspective of Mongol imperial history, political rivalries determined which branches of the family adopted Islam and which did not. From the standpoint of Islamic history, however, recovery from the devastation that culminated in the destruction of the Abbasid Caliphate in Baghdad in 1258 attests to the vitality of the faith and the ability of Muslims to overcome adversity. Within fifty years of its darkest hour, Islam reemerged as a potent ideological and political force.

**Mongol Rivalry**    By 1260 the **Il-khan** (IL-con) state, established by Chinggis's grandson Hülegü, controlled Iran, Azerbaijan, Mesopotamia, and parts of Armenia. North of the Caspian Sea the Mongols who had conquered southern Russia established the capital of their Khanate of the **Golden Horde** (also called the Kipchak [KIP-chahk] Khanate) at Sarai (sah-RYE) on the Volga River. Like the Il-khans, they ruled an indigenous Muslim population, mostly Turkish-speaking.

Some members of the Mongol imperial family professed Islam before the Mongol assault on the Middle East, and Turkish Muslims served the family in various capacities. Hülegü himself, though a Buddhist, had a trusted Shi'ite adviser and granted privileges to the Shi'ites. However, the Mongols under Hülegü's command came only slowly to Islam.

Islamic doctrines clashed with Mongol ways. Muslims abhorred the Mongols' worship of Buddhist and shamanist idols. Furthermore, Mongol law specified slaughtering animals without spilling blood, which involved opening the chest and stopping the heart. This horrified Muslims, who were forbidden to consume blood and slaughtered animals by slitting their throats and draining the blood.

Islam became a point of inter-Mongol tension when Batu's successor as leader of the Golden Horde declared himself a Muslim. He swore to avenge the murder of the Abbasid caliph and laid claim to the Caucasus—the mountains between the Black and Caspian Seas—which the Il-khans also claimed.

Some European leaders believed that if they helped the non-Muslim Il-khans repel the Golden Horde from the Caucasus, the Il-khans would help them relieve Muslim pressure on the Crusader principalities in Syria, Lebanon, and Palestine (see Chapter 9). This resulted in a brief correspondence between the Il-khan court and Pope Nicholas IV (r. 1288–1292) and a diplomatic mission that sent two Christian Turks to western Europe as Il-khan ambassadors in the late 1200s. The Golden Horde responded by seeking an alliance with the Muslim mamluks in Egypt (see Chapter 9) against both the Crusaders and the Il-khans. Before the Europeans' diplomatic efforts could bear fruit, a new Il-khan ruler, Ghazan (haz-ZAHN) (1271–1304), declared himself a Muslim in 1295. Conflicting indications of Sunni and Shi'ite affiliation, such as divergent coin inscriptions, indicate that Ghazan had a casual attitude toward theological matters. It is similarly unclear whether the Muslim Turkish nomads who served in his army were Shi'ite or Sunni.

**Islam and the State**    The Il-khans gradually came to appreciate the traditional urban culture of the Muslim territories they ruled. Nevertheless, they used tax farming to extract maximum wealth from their subjects. The government sold tax-collecting contracts to small partnerships, mostly consisting of merchants who might also finance caravans, small industries, or military expeditions. Whoever offered to collect the most revenue for the government won the contracts. They could use whatever methods they chose and keep anything over the contracted amount.

Tax farming initially lowered administrative costs; but over the long term, the extortions of the tax farmers drove many landowners into debt and servitude. Agricultural productivity declined, making it hard to supply the army. So the government resorted

**Il-khan** A "secondary" or "peripheral" khan based in Persia. The Il-khans' khanate was founded by Hülegü, a grandson of Chinggis Khan, and was based at Tabriz in the Iranian province of Azerbaijan. It controlled much of Iran and Iraq.

**Golden Horde** Mongol khanate founded by Chinggis Khan's grandson Batu. It was based in southern Russia and quickly adopted both the Turkish language and Islam. Also known as the Kipchak Horde.

**Tomb of Timur in Samarkand** The turquoise tiles that cover the dome are typical of Timurid architectural decoration. Timur's family ornamented his capital with an enormous mosque, three large religious colleges facing one another on three sides of an open plaza, and a lane of brilliantly tiled Timurid family tombs in the midst of a cemetery. Timur brought craftsmen to Samarkand from the lands he conquered to build these magnificent structures.

Robert Harding Picture Library Ltd/Alamy

**Timur** (TEE-moor), known to Europeans as Tamer-lane, maneuvered himself into command of the Chagatai forces and launched campaigns into western Eurasia, apparently seeing himself as a new Chinggis Khan. By ethnic background he was a Turk with only an in-law relationship to the family of the Mongol conqueror. This prevented him from assuming the title *khan*, but not from sacking the Muslim sultanate of Delhi in northern India in 1398 or defeating the sultan of the rising Ottoman Empire in Anatolia in 1402. He was reportedly preparing to march on China when he died in 1405. However, Timur's descendants could not hold the empire together.

## Culture and Science in Islamic Eurasia

The Il-khans and Timurids (descendants of Timur) presided over a brilliant cultural flowering in Iran, Afghanistan, and Central Asia based on blending Iranian and Chinese artistic trends and cultural practices. The dominant cultural tendencies were Muslim, however. Timur died before he could reunite Iran and China, but by transplanting Middle Eastern scholars, artists, and craftsmen to his capital, Samarkand, he fostered the cultural achievements of his descendants.

The historian Juvaini (joo-VINE-nee) (d. 1283), who recorded Chinggis Khan's deathbed speech, came from the city of Balkh, which the Mongols had devastated in 1221. His family switched their allegiance to the Mongols, and both Juvaini and his older brother assumed high government posts. The Il-khan Hülegü, seeking to immortalize and justify his conquests, enthusiastically supported Juvaini's writing of the first comprehensive narrative of Chinggis Khan's empire.

Juvaini combined a florid style with historical objectivity, often criticizing the Mongols. This approach served as an inspiration to **Rashid al-Din** (ra-SHEED ad-DEEN), Ghazan's prime minister, when he attempted the first history of the world. Rashid

to taking land to grow its own grain. Like property held by religious trusts, this land paid no taxes. Thus the tax base shrank even as the demands of the army and the Mongol nobility continued to grow.

Ghazan faced many economic problems. Citing Islam's humane values, he promised to reduce taxes, but the need for revenue kept the decrease from becoming permanent. The Chinese practice of printing paper money had been tried unsuccessfully by a predecessor. Now it was tried again. This time the experiment pushed the economy into a depression that lasted beyond the end of the Il-khan state in 1349. Mongol nobles competed among themselves for the decreasing revenues, and fighting among Mongol factions destabilized the government.

While the Golden Horde and the Il-khan Empire quarreled, a new power was emerging in the Central Asian Khanate of Chagatai (see Map 12.1). The leader

**Timur** Member of a prominent family of the Mongols' Chagatai Khanate, Timur through conquest gained control over much of Central Asia and Iran. He consolidated the status of Sunni Islam as orthodox, and his descendants, the Timurids, maintained his empire for nearly a century and founded the Mughal Empire in India.

**Rashid al-Din** Adviser to the Il-khan ruler Ghazan, who converted to Islam on Rashid's advice.

al-Din's work included the earliest known general history of Europe, derived from conversations with European monks, and a detailed description of China based on information from an important Chinese Muslim official stationed in Iran. The miniature paintings that accompanied some copies of Rashid al-Din's work included depictions of European and Chinese people and events and reflected the artistic traditions of both cultures. The Chinese compositional techniques helped inaugurate the greatest period of Islamic miniature painting under the Timurids. Rashid al-Din traveled widely and collaborated with administrators from other parts of the far-flung Mongol dominions. His idea that government should be in accord with the moral principles of the majority of the population buttressed Ghazan's adherence to Islam.

Under the Timurids, the tradition of the Il-khan historians continued. After conquering Damascus, Timur himself met there with the greatest historian of the age, Ibn Khaldun (ee-bin hal-DOON) (1332–1406), a Tunisian. In a scene reminiscent of Ghazan's answering Rashid al-Din's questions on the history of the Mongols, Timur and Ibn Khaldun exchanged historical, philosophical, and geographical viewpoints. Like Chinggis, Timur saw himself as a world conqueror. At their capitals of Samarkand and Herat (in western Afghanistan), later Timurid rulers sponsored historical writing in both Persian and Chagatai Turkish.

A Shi'ite scholar named **Nasir al-Din Tusi** (nah-SEER ad-DEEN TOO-si) represents the beginning of Mongol interest in the scientific traditions of the Muslim lands. Nasir al-Din may have joined the entourage of Hülegü during a campaign in 1256 against the Assassins, a Shi'ite religious sect derived from the Fatimid dynasty in Egypt and at odds with his more mainstream Shi'ite views (see Chapter 9). Nasir al-Din wrote on history, poetry, ethics, and religion, but he made his most outstanding contributions in mathematics and cosmology. Following Omar Khayyam (oh-mar kie-YAM) (1038?–1131), a poet and mathematician of the Seljuk (SEL-jook) period, he laid new foundations for algebra and trigonometry. Some followers working at an observatory built for Nasir al-Din at Maragheh (mah-RAH-gah), near the Il-khan capital of Tabriz, used the new mathematical techniques to reach a better understanding of celestial orbits.

Observational astronomy and calendar making had engaged the interest of earlier Central Asian rulers, particularly the Uighurs (WEE-ger) and the Seljuks. Under the Il-khans, the astronomers of Maragheh excelled in predicting eclipses, and astrolabes, armillary spheres, three-dimensional quadrants, and other instruments acquired new precision.

These techniques spread worldwide. The remarkably accurate eclipse predictions and tables prepared by Il-khan and Timurid astronomers reached the hostile Mamluk lands in Arabic translation. Byzantine monks took them to Constantinople and translated them into Greek, Christian scholars working in Muslim Spain rendered them into Latin, and in India the sultan of Delhi ordered Sanskrit versions of them. Following one of these routes, the mathematical tables and geometric models of lunar motion devised by one of Nasir al-Din's students somehow became known to Nicholas Copernicus (1473–1543), a Polish monk and astronomer (see Chapter 13). Copernicus adopted this lunar model as his own, virtually without revision, and then proposed it as the proper model for planetary movement as well—but with the planets circling the sun.

The interest in astronomy led to the building of observatories. The Great Khan Khubilai (discussed later in this chapter) summoned a team of Iranians to Beijing to build an observatory for him. Timur's grandson Ulugh Beg (oo-loog bek) (1394–1449), whose avocation was astronomy, constructed a great observatory in Samarkand and actively participated in compiling observational tables that were later translated into Latin and used by European astronomers.

A further advance made under Ulugh Beg came from the mathematician Ghiyas al-Din Jamshid al-Kashi (gee-YASS ad-DIN jam-SHEED al-KAH-shee), who noted that Chinese astronomers had long used one ten-thousandth of a day as a unit in calculating the occurrence of a new moon. This seems to have inspired him to employ decimal notation, by which quantities less than one could be represented by a

**Nasir al-Din Tusi**  Persian mathematician and cosmologist whose academy near Tabriz provided a model for heavenly motions that helped to inspire the Copernican model of the solar system.

## SECTION REVIEW

- For the Mongols of the Il-khan and Golden Horde states, Islam became a matter of political rivalry.

- In the Il-khan state Islamic values struggled with economic needs, and the resulting unrest left it open to invasions by Golden Horde Mongols.

- At the same time, Timur took control of the Chagatai territory and began his own imperial conquests.

- Under the Il-khans and Timurids, Iran and Central Asia experienced a flowering of Islamic culture.

- These rulers fostered great achievements in historical writing, literature, art, mathematics, and astronomy.

marker to show place. Al-Kashi's proposed value for *pi* ($\pi$) was far more precise than any previously calculated. This innovation arrived in Europe by way of Constantinople, where a Greek translation of al-Kashi's work appeared in the fifteenth century.

# REGIONAL RESPONSES IN WESTERN EURASIA

■ *What benefits resulted from the integration of Eurasia into the Mongol Empire?*

Safe, reliable overland trade benefited Mongol ruling centers and commercial cities along the Silk Road. But the countryside, ravaged by conquest, sporadic violence, and heavy taxes, suffered terribly. As Mongol control weakened, regional forces in Russia, eastern Europe, and Anatolia reasserted themselves. Sometimes this meant collaborating with the Mongols; at other times it meant using local ethnic or religious traditions to resist or roll back Mongol influence.

### Russia and Rule from Afar

The Golden Horde, a later term for the state established by Chinggis's grandson Batu before 1236, started as a unified state but gradually lost unity as some districts crystallized into smaller khanates. The White Horde, for instance, ruled much of southeastern Russia in the fifteenth century, and the Crimean khanate on the northern shore of the Black Sea succumbed to Russian power only in 1783.

East-west routes across the steppe and north-south routes along the rivers of Russia and Ukraine (you-CRANE) conferred importance on certain trading entrepôts, as they had under Kievan Russia (see Chapter 10). The Golden Horde capital was (Old) Sarai, just north of where the Volga flows into the Caspian Sea (see Map 12.1). The Mongols ruled their Russian domains to the north and east from afar. To facilitate control, they granted privileges to the Orthodox Church, which then helped reconcile the Russian people to their distant masters.

The politics of language played a role in subsequent history. Old Church Slavonic, an ecclesiastical language, revived; but Russian steadily acquired greater importance and eventually became the dominant written language. Russian scholars shunned Byzantine Greek, previously the main written tongue, even after the Golden Horde permitted renewed contacts with Constantinople. The Golden Horde enlisted Russian princes to act as their agents, primarily as tax collectors and census takers.

The flow of silver and gold into Mongol hands starved the local economy of precious metal. Like the Il-khans, the Golden Horde attempted to introduce paper money as a response to the currency shortage. The unsuccessful experiment left such a vivid memory that the Russian word for money (*denga* [DENG-ah]) comes from the Mongolian word for the stamp (*tamga* [TAHM-gah]) used to create paper currency. In reality, commerce depended more on direct exchange of goods than on currency transactions.

**Alexander Nevskii** (nih-EFF-skee) (ca. 1220–1263), the prince of Novgorod, persuaded some fellow princes to submit to the Mongols. In return, the Mongols favored both Novgorod and the emerging town of Moscow, ruled by Alexander's son Daniel. As these towns eclipsed devastated Kiev as political, cultural, and economic centers, they drew people northward to open new agricultural land far from the Mongol steppes. Decentralization continued in the 1300s, with Moscow only very gradually becoming Russia's dominant political center.

In appraising the Mongol era, some historians stress Mongol destructiveness and brutality in tax collecting. Ukraine, a fertile and well-populated region in

**Alexander Nevskii** Prince of Novgorod (r. 1236–1263). He submitted to the invading Mongols in 1240 and received recognition as the leader of the Russian princes under the Golden Horde.

the late Kievan period (1000–1230), suffered severe population loss from these sources. Isolated from developments to the west, Russia and parts of eastern Europe are portrayed as suffering under the "Mongol yoke."

Other historians point out that even before the Mongols struck, Kiev had declined economically and ceased to mint coins. Yet the Russian territories regularly paid the heavy Mongol taxes in silver, indicating both economic surpluses and an ability to convert goods into cash. The burdensome taxes stemmed less from the Mongols than from their tax collectors, Russian princes who often exempted their own lands and shifted the load to the peasants.

As for Russia's cultural isolation, skeptics observe that before the Mongol invasion, the powerful and constructive role played by the Orthodox Church oriented Russia primarily toward Byzantium (see Chapter 10). Although this situation did not eliminate contacts with western Europe, repeated wars with the expanding Catholic principality of Lithuania on Russia's western border discouraged extensive relations.

The traditional structure of local government survived Mongol rule, as did the Russian princely families, who continued to battle among themselves for dominance. The Mongols merely added a new player to those struggles. Ivan (ee-VAHN) III, the prince of Moscow (r. 1462–1505), established himself as an autocratic ruler in the late 1400s. Before Ivan, the title **tsar** (from *caesar*), of Byzantine origin, applied only to foreign rulers, whether the emperors of Byzantium or the Turkish khans of the steppe. Ivan's use of the title probably represents an effort to establish a basis for legitimate rule with the decline of the Golden Horde and the disappearance of the Byzantine Empire.

## New States in Eastern Europe and Anatolia

Anatolia and parts of Europe responded dynamically to the Mongol challenges. Raised in Sicily, the Holy Roman Emperor Frederick II (r. 1212–1250) appreciated Muslim culture and did not recoil from negotiating with Muslims. When the pope threatened to excommunicate him unless he waged a crusade, Frederick nominally regained Jerusalem through a flimsy treaty with the Mamluk sultan in Egypt. Dissatisfied, the pope continued to quarrel with the emperor, leaving Hungary, Poland, and Lithuania to deal with the Mongol

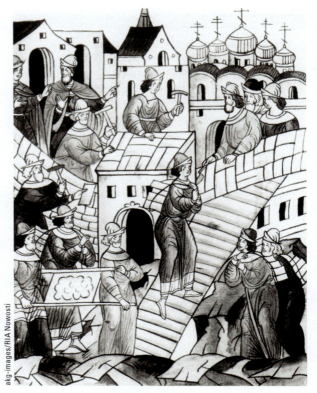

akg-images/RIA Nowosti

**Transformation of the Kremlin** Like other northern Europeans, the Russians preferred to build in wood, which was easy to handle and comfortable to live in. But they fortified important political centers with stone ramparts. In the 1300s, the city of Moscow emerged as a new capital, and its old wooden palace, the Kremlin, was gradually transformed into a stone structure.

onslaught on their own. Many princes capitulated and went to (Old) Sarai to offer their submission to Batu.

However, the Teutonic (two-TOHN-ik) Knights resisted. These German-speaking warriors sought to Christianize the pagan populations of northern Europe and colonize their territories with German settlers. They also fought against other Christians. To protect Slav territory, Alexander Nevskii joined the Mongols in fighting the Teutonic Knights and their Finnish allies. The latter suffered a catastrophe in 1242, when many broke through an icy northern lake and drowned. This event destroyed the power of the Knights, and the northern Crusades virtually ceased.

**tsar (czar)**  From Latin *caesar*, this Russian title for a monarch was first used in reference to a Russian ruler by Ivan III (r. 1462–1505).

The "Mongol" armies encountered by the Europeans consisted mostly of Turks, Chinese, Iranians, a few Europeans, and at least one Englishman, who went to crusade in the Middle East but joined the Mongols and served in Hungary. But most commanders were Mongol.

Initial wild theories describing the Mongols as coming from Hell or from caves where Alexander the Great confined monsters gradually yielded to a more sophisticated understanding as European embassies to Mongol courts returned with reliable intelligence. In some quarters terror gave way to appreciation. Europeans learned about diplomatic passports, coal mining, movable type, high-temperature metallurgy, higher mathematics, gunpowder, and, in the fourteenth century, the casting and use of bronze cannon. Yet with the outbreak of bubonic plague in the late 1340s, the memory of Mongol terror helped ignite religious speculation that God might again be punishing the Christians (see Chapter 13).

In the fourteenth century several regions, most notably Lithuania (lith-oo-WAY-nee-ah), escaped the Mongol grip. When Russia fell to the Mongols, Lithuania had experienced an unprecedented centralization and military strengthening. Like Alexander Nevskii, the Lithuanian leaders maintained their independence by cooperating with the Mongols. In the late 1300s Lithuania capitalized on its privileged position to dominate Poland and ended the Teutonic Knights' hope of regaining power.

In the Balkans independent kingdoms separated themselves from the chaos of the Byzantine Empire and thrived amidst the political uncertainties of the Mongol period. The Serbian king Stephen Dushan (ca. 1308–1355) proved the most effective leader. Seizing power from his father in 1331, he took advantage of Byzantine weakness to turn the archbishop of Serbia into an independent patriarch. In 1346 the patriarch crowned him "tsar and autocrat of the Serbs, Greeks, Bulgarians, and Albanians," a title that fairly represents the wide extent of his rule. As in the case of Timur, however, his kingdom declined after his death in 1355 and disappeared entirely after a defeat by the Ottomans at the battle of Kosovo in 1389.

The Turkish nomads whose descendants established the **Ottoman Empire** came to Anatolia in the same wave of Turkish migrations as the Seljuks (see

Chapter 9). Though Il-khan influence was strong in eastern Anatolia, a number of small Turkish principalities emerged in the west. The Ottoman principality was situated in the northwest, close to the Sea of Marmara. This location not only put the Ottomans in a position to cross into Europe and take part in the dynastic struggles of the declining Byzantine state, but it also attracted Muslim religious warriors who wished to do battle with Christians on the frontiers. The defeat of the Ottoman sultan by Timur in 1402 was only a temporary setback. In 1453 Sultan Mehmet II captured Constantinople and brought the Byzantine Empire to an end.

The Ottoman sultans, like the rulers of Russia, Lithuania, and Serbia, seized opportunities that arose with the decay of Mongol power. The powerful states they created put strong emphasis on religious and linguistic identity, factors that the Mongols themselves did not stress. As we shall see, Mongol rule stimulated similar reactions in the lands of East and Southeast Asia.

## MONGOL DOMINATION IN CHINA, 1271–1368

■ *How did Mongol rule in China foster cultural and scientific exchange?*

After conquering northern China in the 1230s, Great Khan Ögödei told a Confucian adviser that he

**Ottoman Empire**  Islamic state founded by Osman in northwestern Anatolia around 1300. After the fall of the Byzantine Empire, the Ottoman Empire was based at Istanbul (formerly Constantinople) from 1453 to 1922. It encompassed lands in the Middle East, North Africa, the Caucasus, and eastern Europe.

planned to turn the heavily populated North China Plain into a pasture for livestock. The adviser reacted calmly but argued that taxing the cities and villages would bring greater wealth. The Great Khan agreed, but he imposed an oppressive tax-farming system instead of the fixed-rate method traditional to China.

The Chinese suffered under this system during the early years, but the Yuan Empire, established by Chinggis Khan's grandson Khubilai in 1271, also brought benefits: secure trade routes, exchange of experts between eastern and western Eurasia, and transmission of information, ideas, and skills.

## The Yuan Empire, 1271–1368

The Yuan sought a fruitful synthesis of the Mongol and Chinese traditions. **Khubilai Khan** gave his oldest son a Chinese name and had Confucians participate in the boy's education. In public announcements and the crafting of laws, he took Confucian conventions into consideration, while Buddhist and Daoist leaders who visited the Great Khan came away believing that they had all but convinced him of their beliefs.

Buddhist priests from Tibet called **lamas** (LAH-mah) became popular with some Mongol rulers. Their idea of a militant universal ruler bringing the whole world under control of the Buddha and thus pushing it nearer to salvation mirrored an ancient Inner Asian idea of universal rulership.

**Beijing**, the Yuan capital, became the center of cultural and economic life. Karakorum had been geographically remote, but Beijing served as the eastern terminus of caravan routes that began near Tabriz, the Il-khan capital, and (Old) Sarai, the Golden Horde capital. A horseback courier system utilizing hundreds of stations maintained communications along routes that were generally safe for travelers. Ambassadors and merchants arriving in Beijing found a city that was much more Chinese in character than Karakorum had been.

Called Great Capital (Dadu) or City of the Khan (khan-balikh [kahn-BAL-ik], Marco Polo's "Cambaluc"), Khubilai's capital included the Forbidden City, a closed imperial complex with wide streets and a network of linked lakes and artificial islands. In summer, Khubilai practiced riding and shooting at a palace and park in Inner Mongolia. This was Shangdu (shahng-DOO), the "Xanadu" (ZAH-nah-doo) with its "stately pleasure dome" celebrated by the English poet Samuel Taylor Coleridge.

Before the Mongols reunited the country, three separate states with different languages, writing systems, forms of government, and elite cultures competed in China (see Chapter 11). The Tanggut and Jin Empires controlled the north, and the Southern Song controlled most of the area south of the Yellow River. The Great Khans destroyed all three, encouraging the restoration or preservation of many features of Chinese government and society and organizing China into provinces where the appointment of provincial governors systematized control in all parts of the country.

The Mongol-ruled Yuan state was cosmopolitan, attracting many non-Chinese who helped the Mongols govern China. By law, Mongols ranked highest. Below them came Central Asians and Middle Easterners, then northern Chinese, and finally southern Chinese. This ranking reflected a hierarchy of functions. The Mongols were the empire's warriors, the Central Asians and Middle Easterners its census takers and tax collectors. The northern Chinese outranked the southern Chinese because they came under Mongol control almost two generations earlier.

Confucian culture was still promoted in the Yuan Empire. Chinese "Confucians" (under the Yuan, a formal and hereditary status) were reactionary: they fared poorly in securing government appointments, and they also disparaged the merchants in China, many of whom were from the Middle East or Central Asia, as well as physicians, who took Muslim and Hellenistic approaches to medicine. Nevertheless, Confucian education, dress, and rituals were adopted all the way to the newly acquired Yunnan (YOON-nahn), where Sayyid Ajall Shams al-Din (SAY-id a-JELL Shams ad-DEEN), a Muslim governor from Central Asia, was creating a vibrant trade between Tibet, Burma, the Vietnamese kingdoms, and China.

**Khubilai Khan** Last of the Mongol Great Khans (r. 1260–1294) and founder of the Yuan Empire.

**lama** In Tibetan Buddhism, a teacher.

**Beijing** China's northern capital, first used as an imperial capital in 906 and now the capital of the People's Republic of China.

The reintegration of East Asia (though not Japan) with the overland Eurasian trade, which had lapsed with the fall of the Tang (see Chapter 11), stimulated the urban economies. Many cities prospered: in north China by being on the caravan routes; in the interior by being on the Grand Canal; and along the coast by participation in maritime grain shipments from south China. With merchants a privileged group and so few government posts open to the old Chinese elite, many families that had previously spent fortunes on educating sons for government service now went into commerce. Corporations—investor groups that behaved as single commercial and legal units and shared the risk of doing business—handled most economic activities, starting with financing caravans and expanding into tax farming and lending money to the Mongol aristocracy. Central Asians and Middle Easterners headed most corporations in the early Yuan period; but as Chinese bought shares, many acquired mixed membership, or even complete Chinese ownership.

Many gentry families moved from their traditional homes in the country into the city. City life increasingly catered to the tastes of merchants instead of scholars. Specialized shops selling clothing, grape wine, furniture, and religiously butchered meats became common. Teahouses offered sing-song girls, drum singers, operas, and other entertainments previously considered coarse. Writers published works in the style of everyday speech. And the increasing influence of the northern, Mongolian-influenced Chinese language, often called Mandarin in the West, resulted in lasting linguistic change.

Cottage industries linked to the urban economies dotted the countryside, where 90 percent of the people lived. Some villages cultivated mulberry trees and cotton using dams, water wheels, and irrigation systems patterned in part on Middle Eastern models. Treatises on planting, harvesting, threshing, and butchering were published. One technological innovator, Huang Dao Po (hwahng DOW poh), brought knowledge of cotton growing, spinning, and weaving from her native Hainan Island to the fertile Yangzi Delta.

But the agricultural base had been damaged by war, overtaxation, and the passage of armies and could not satisfy the financial needs of the Mongol aristocracy. The countryside did poorly during the Yuan period. Initially, the Mongol princes evicted many farmers and subjected the rest to brutal tax collection. By the time the Yuan shifted to lighter taxes and encouragement of farming at the end of the 1200s, it was too late. Servitude or homelessness had overtaken many farmers, and neglect of dams and dikes caused disastrous flooding, particularly on the Yellow River.

Following earlier precedent, the imperial government made up the financial shortfall with paper money. But people doubted the value of the notes, which were unsecured. Copper coinage partially offset the failure of the paper currency. During the Song, exports of copper to Japan, where the metal was scarce, had caused a severe shortage in China, leading to a rise in the value of copper in relation to silver. By cutting off trade with Japan, the Mongols stabilized the value of copper coins.

According to Song records from before the Mongol conquest and the Ming census taken after their overthrow—each, of course, subject to inaccuracy or exaggeration—China's population may have shrunk by 40 percent during eighty years of Mongol rule, with many localities in northern China losing up to five-sixths of their inhabitants. Scholars have suggested several causes: prolonged warfare, rural distress causing people to resort to female infanticide, epidemics, a southward flight of refugees, and flooding on the Yellow River. The last helps explain why losses in the north exceeded those in the south and why the population along the Yangzi River markedly increased.

## The Fall of the Yuan Empire

In the 1340s strife broke out among the Mongol princes. Within twenty years farmer rebellions and inter-Mongol feuds engulfed the land. Amidst the chaos, a charismatic Chinese leader, Zhu Yuanzhang (JOO yuwen-JAHNG), mounted a campaign that destroyed the Yuan Empire and brought China under control of his new empire, the Ming, in 1368. Many Mongols—as well as the Muslims, Jews, and Christians who had come with them—remained in China. Most of their descendants took Chinese names and became part of the diverse cultural world of China.

Many other Mongols, however, who had never moved out of their home territories in Mongolia, now

- The Great Khans reunified China, expanded its borders, and fostered a synthesis of ideas and cultural traditions.
- Khubilai Khan made Beijing the capital of the Yuan Empire and presided over a social hierarchy with Mongols at the top and southern Chinese at the bottom.
- Mongol rule systematized government, but cities benefited more from Mongol policies than did the countryside.
- Mongol-protected trade routes encouraged a steady exchange of scientific and cultural ideas.
- China's population shrank as a result of Mongol conquest and rule.
- Internal strife weakened the Yuan Empire, which fell to the Ming in 1368, but many Mongols remained in China.

welcomed back refugees from the Yuan collapse. Though Turkish peoples were becoming predominant in the steppe regions in the west, including territories still ruled by descendants of Chinggis Khan, Mongols continued to predominate in Inner Asia, the steppe regions bordering on Mongolia. Some Mongol groups adopted Islam; others favored Tibetan Buddhism. But religious affiliation proved less important than Mongol identity in fostering a renewed sense of unity.

The Ming thus fell short of dominating all the Mongols. The Mongols of Inner Asia paid tribute to the extent that doing so facilitated their trade. Other Mongols, however, remained a continuing threat on the northern Ming frontier.

# THE EARLY MING EMPIRE, 1368–1500

■ *In what ways did the Ming Empire continue or discontinue Mongol practices?*

Historians of China, like historians of Russia and Iran, divide over the overall impact of the Mongol era. Since the **Ming Empire** reestablished many practices that are seen as purely Chinese, it receives praise from people who ascribe central importance to Chinese traditions. On the other hand, historians who look upon the Mongol era as a pivotal historical moment when communication across the vast interior of Eurasia served to bring east and west together

sometimes see the inward-looking Ming as less productive than the Yuan.

**Ming China on a Mongol Foundation**

Zhu Yuanzhang, a former monk, soldier, and bandit, had watched his parents and other family members die of famine and disease, conditions he blamed on Mongol misrule. During the Yuan Empire's chaotic last decades, he vanquished rival rebels and assumed imperial power under the name Hongwu (r. 1368–1398).

Hongwu moved the capital to Nanjing (nahn-JING) ("southern capital") on the Yangzi River, turning away from the Mongols' Beijing ("northern capital"; see Map 12.2). Though Zhu Yuanzhang the rebel had espoused a radical Buddhist belief in a coming age of salvation, once in power he used Confucianism to depict the emperor as the champion of civilization and virtue.

Hongwu choked off relations with Central Asia and the Middle East and imposed strict limits on imports and foreign visitors. Silver replaced paper money for tax payments and commerce. These practices, illustrative of an anti-Mongol ideology, proved as economically unwise as some of the Yuan economic policies and did not last. Eventually, the Ming government came to resemble the Yuan. Ming rulers retained the provincial structure and continued to observe the hereditary professional categories of the Yuan period. Muslims made calendars and astronomical calculations at a new observatory at Nanjing, a replica of Khubilai's at Beijing. The Mongol calendar continued in use.

Continuities with the Yuan became more evident after an imperial prince seized power through a coup d'état to rule as the emperor **Yongle** (yoong-LAW) (r. 1403–1424). He returned the capital to Beijing,

**Ming Empire** Empire based in China that Zhu Yuanzhang established after the overthrow of the Yuan Empire. The Ming emperor Yongle sponsored the building of the Forbidden City and the voyages of Zheng He. The later years of the Ming saw a slowdown in technological development and economic decline.

**Yongle** The third emperor of the Ming Empire (r. 1403–1424). He sponsored the building of the Forbidden City, a huge encyclopedia project, the expeditions of Zheng He, and the reopening of China's borders to trade and travel.

**Map 12.2 The Ming Empire and Its Allies, 1368–1500** The Ming Empire controlled China but had a hostile relationship with peoples in Mongolia and Inner Asia who had been under the rule of the Mongol Yuan emperors. Mongol attempts at conquest by sea were continued by the Ming mariner Zheng He. Between 1405 and 1433 he sailed to Southeast Asia and then beyond, to India, the Persian Gulf, and East Africa. © Cengage Learning

enlarging and improving Khubilai's Forbidden City, which now acquired its present features: moats, orange-red outer walls, golden roofs, and marble bridges. Yongle intended this combination fortress, religious site, bureaucratic center, and imperial residential park to overshadow Nanjing, and it survives today as China's most imposing traditional architectural complex.

Yongle also restored commercial links with the Middle East. Because hostile Mongols still controlled much of the caravan route, Yongle explored maritime connections. In Southeast Asia, Annam became a Ming province as the early emperors continued

the Mongol program of aggression. This focus on the southern frontier helped inspire the naval expeditions of the trusted imperial eunuch **Zheng He** (JEHNG HUH) from 1405 to 1433.

A Muslim eunuch whose father and grandfather had made the pilgrimage to Mecca, Zheng He had a good knowledge of the Middle East; and his religion

**Zheng He** An imperial eunuch and Muslim, entrusted by the Ming emperor Yongle with a series of state voyages that took his gigantic ships through the Indian Ocean, from Southeast Asia to Africa.

eased relations with the states of the Indian subcontinent, where he directed his first three voyages. Subsequent expeditions reached Hormuz on the Persian Gulf, sailed the southern coast of Arabia and the Horn of Africa (modern Somalia), and possibly reached as far south as the Strait of Madagascar.

On early voyages Zheng He visited long-established Chinese merchant communities in Southeast Asia to cement their allegiance to the Ming Empire and collect taxes. When a community on the island of Sumatra resisted, he slaughtered the men to set an example. The expeditions added some fifty new tributary states to the Ming imperial universe, but trade did not increase as dramatically. Sporadic embassies reached Beijing from rulers in India, the Middle East, Africa, and Southeast Asia. During one visit the ruler of Brunei (broo-NYE) died and received a grand burial at the Chinese capital. The expeditions stopped in the 1430s after the deaths of Yongle and Zheng He.

Why did the Chinese not develop seafaring for commercial and military gain? Contemporaries considered the voyages a personal project of Yongle, an upstart ruler who had always sought to prove his worthiness. Building the Forbidden City in Beijing and sponsoring gigantic encyclopedia projects might be taken to reflect a similar character. Yongle may also have been emulating Khubilai Khan's sea expeditions against Japan and Southeast Asia. This would fit with the rumor spread by Yongle's political enemies that he was actually a Mongol.

A less speculative approach starts with the fact that the new commercial opportunities fell short of expectations, despite bringing foreign nations into the Ming orbit. In the meantime, Japanese coastal piracy intensified, and Mongol threats in the north and west grew. The human and financial demands of fortifying the north, redesigning and strengthening Beijing, and outfitting campaigns against the Mongols ultimately took priority over the quest for maritime empire.

## Technology and Population

The Ming government limited mining, partly to maintain the value of metal coins and partly to tax the industry. As a consequence, metal implements became more expensive for farmers. Techniques for making the high-quality bronze and steel used for weapons also declined, and Japan quickly surpassed China in the production of extremely high-quality swords.

After the death of Emperor Yongle in 1424, shipbuilding skills deteriorated, and few advances occurred in printing, timekeeping, and agricultural technology. Agricultural production peaked around the mid-1400s and remained level for more than a century. New weaving techniques did appear, but technological development in this field had peaked by 1500.

Reactivation of the examination system for recruiting government officials (see Chapter 11) drew large numbers of ambitious men into a renewed study of the Confucian classics. This change reduced the vitality of commerce, where they had previously been employed, just as population growth was creating a labor surplus. Records indicating a growth from 60 million at the end of the Yuan period in 1368 to nearly 100 million by 1400 may not be entirely reliable, but rapid population growth encouraged the production of staples—wheat, millet, and barley in the north and rice in the south—at the expense of commercial crops such as cotton that had stimulated many technological innovations under the Song. Staple crops yielded lower profits, which further discouraged capital improvements. New foods, such as sweet potatoes from the Western Hemisphere, became available but were little adopted. Population growth in southern and central China caused deforestation and raised the price of wood.

Against the Mongol horsemen in the north the Ming used scattershot mortars, explosive canisters, and a few cannon from contacts with the Middle East and later with Europeans. But shipyards and ports shut down to avoid Japanese pirates and prevent Chinese from migrating to Southeast Asia. Fearing a loss of technological secrets, the government also censored the chapters on gunpowder and guns in early Ming encyclopedias. Korea and Japan moved ahead of China—Japan in steel and Korea in the design and production of firearms and ships, in printing techniques, and in the sciences of weather prediction and calendar making. The desire to tap the wealthy Ming market spurred some of these advances.

## The Ming Achievement

In the late 1300s and the 1400s the wealth and consumerism of the early Ming stimulated high achievement in literature, the decorative arts, and painting. The plain writing of the Yuan period had produced some of the world's earliest novels. This genre flourished under the Ming: in *Water Margin*, which originated in the raucous drum-song performances loosely related to Chinese opera, and in *Romance of the Three Kingdoms*, which describes the attempts of an upright but doomed war leader and his followers to restore the Han Empire of ancient times and resist the power of the cynical but brilliant villain. *Romance of the Three Kingdoms* and *Water Margin* express the militant but joyous pro-China sentiment of the early Ming era and remain among the most appreciated Chinese fictional works.

Probably the best-known product of Ming technological advance was porcelain. The imperial ceramic works at Jingdezhen (JING-deh-JUHN) experimented with new production techniques and new ways of organizing workers and dividing up jobs. "Ming ware," a blue-on-white style developed in the 1400s from Indian, Central Asian, and Middle Eastern motifs, became especially prized. Other Ming goods in high demand included furniture, lacquered screens, and silk, all of which found ready markets in Southeast Asia and the Pacific, India, the Middle East, and East Africa.

# CENTRALIZATION AND MILITARISM IN EAST ASIA, 1200–1500

■ *What are some of the similarities and differences in how Korea and Japan responded to the Mongol threat?*

Korea, Japan, and Annam, the other major states of East Asia, were all affected by confrontation with the Mongols, but with differing results. Japan and Annam escaped Mongol conquest, becoming more effective and expansive regimes with enhanced commitments to independence. Korea revitalized interest in its own language and history. Though the Mongols conquered Korea after a difficult war that resulted in much Korean suffering, members of the Korean elite associated closely with the Yuan Empire. After the fall of the Yuan, merchants continued the international connections established in the Mongol period, while Korean armies consolidated a new kingdom and fended off pirates.

## Korea from the Mongols to the Choson Dynasty, 1231–1500

Korea had been the answer to the Mongols' search for coastal areas from which to launch naval expeditions and choke off the sea trade of their adversaries. When the Mongols attacked in 1231, the Choe family assumed the role of military commander and protector of the Koryo (KAW-ree-oh) king (not unlike the shoguns of Japan). The Choe's refusal to sue for peace, or emerge from their capital on Kanghwa Island to drive the Mongols from the Korean peninsula, led to widespread misery among the populace and frustration among military men and nobles alike. The last of the Choe commanders was killed by his underlings in 1258. Soon afterward the king surrendered to the Mongols and became a subject monarch by linking his family to the Great Khan by marriage.

By the mid-1300s the Koryo kings were of mostly Mongol descent and favored Mongol dress, customs, and language. The kings, their families, and their entourages often traveled between China and Korea, thus exposing Korea to the philosophical and artistic styles of Yuan China: neo-Confucianism, Chan Buddhism (called Son in Korea), and celadon (light green) pottery.

Mongol control broke down centuries of comparative isolation. Cotton was introduced in southern Korea; gunpowder came into use; and the art of calendar making stimulated astronomical observation and mathematics. Avenues of advancement opened for Korean scholars willing to learn Mongolian, landowners willing to open their lands to falconry and grazing, and merchants servicing the new royal exchanges with Beijing. These developments contributed to the rise of a new landed and educated class.

When the Yuan Empire fell in 1368, the Koryo ruling family remained loyal to the Mongols until a rebellious general, Yi Songgye (YEE SONG-gye), forced it to recognize the new Ming Empire. In 1392, Yi Songgye established a new kingdom called **Choson** (Cho-sun) with a capital in Seoul and sought to reestablish a distinctive Korean identity. Like Russia and Ming China, the Choson regime publicly rejected the period of Mongol domination. Yet the Choson government continued to employ Mongol-style land surveys, taxation in kind, and military garrison techniques.

Like the Ming emperors, the Choson kings revived the study of the Confucian classics, an activity that required knowledge of Chinese and showed the dedication of the state to learning. This revival may have led to a key technological breakthrough in printing technology. Koreans had begun using Chinese woodblock printing in the 700s. This technology worked well in China, where a large number of buyers wanted copies of a comparatively small number of texts. But in Korea, the comparatively few literate men had interests in a wide range of texts. Movable wooden or ceramic type appeared in Korea in the early thirteenth century and may have been invented there. But the texts were frequently inaccurate and difficult to read. In the 1400s Choson printers, working directly with the king, developed a reliable device to anchor the pieces of type to the printing plate: they replaced the old beeswax adhesive with solid copper frames. This innovation improved the legibility of the printed page, and high-volume, accurate production became possible. Combined with the phonetic *han'gul* (HAHN-goor) writing system, this printing technology laid the foundation for a high literacy rate in Korea.

Choson publications told readers how to produce and use fertilizer, transplant rice seedlings, and engineer reservoirs. Building on Eurasian knowledge imported by the Mongols and introduced under the Koryo, Choson scholars developed a meteorological science of their own. They invented or redesigned instruments to measure wind speed and rainfall and perfected a calendar based on minute comparisons of the Chinese and Islamic systems.

In agriculture, farmers expanded the cultivation of cash crops, the reverse of what was happening in Ming China. Cotton, the primary crop, enjoyed such high value that the state accepted it for tax payments.

SSPL/The Image Works

**Movable Type**   The improvement of cast bronze tiles, each showing a single character, eliminated the need to cast or carve whole pages. Individual tiles—the ones shown are Korean—could be moved from page frame to page frame and gave an even and pleasing appearance. All parts of East Asia eventually adopted this form of printing for cheap, popular books. In the mid-1400s Korea also experimented with a fully phonetic form of writing, which in combination with movable type allowed Koreans unprecedented levels of literacy and access to printed works.

The Choson army used cotton uniforms, and cotton became the favored fabric of the Korean elite. With cotton gins and spinning wheels powered by water, Korea advanced more rapidly than China in mechanization and began to export considerable amounts of cotton to China and Japan.

Although both the Yuan and the Ming withheld the formula for gunpowder from the Korean government, Korean officials acquired the information by subterfuge. By the later 1300s they had mounted

**Choson**   The Choson dynasty ruled Korea from the fall of the Koryo kingdom to the colonization of Korea by Japan.

**Defending Japan** Japanese warriors board Mongol warships with swords to prevent the landing of the invasion force in 1281.

cannon on ships that patrolled against pirates and used gunpowder-driven arrow launchers against enemy personnel and the rigging of enemy ships. Combined with skills in armoring ships, these techniques made the small Choson navy a formidable defense force.

## Political Transformation in Japan, 1274–1500

Having secured Korea, the Mongols looked toward Japan, a target they could easily reach from Korea. Their first 30,000-man invasion force in 1274 included Mongol cavalry and archers and sailors from Korea and northeastern Asia. Its weaponry included light catapults and incendiary and explosive projectiles of Chinese manufacture. The Mongol forces landed successfully and decimated the Japanese cavalry, but a great storm on Hakata (HAH-kah-tah) Bay on the north side of Kyushu (KYOO-shoo) Island prevented the establishment of a beachhead and forced the Mongols to sail back to Korea.

The invasion hastened social and political changes that were already under way. Under the Kamakura (kah-mah-KOO-rah) Shogunate established in 1185—a different powerful family actually exercised control—the shogun, or military leader, distributed land and privileges to his followers. In return they paid him tribute and supplied him with soldiers. This stable, but decentralized, system depended on balancing the power of regional warlords. Lords in

the north and east of Japan's main island were remote from those in the south and west. Beyond devotion to the emperor and the shogun, little united them until the terrifying Mongol threat materialized.

After the return of his fleet, Khubilai sent envoys to Japan demanding submission. Japanese leaders executed them and prepared for war. The shogun took steps to centralize his military government, effectively increasing the influence of warlords from the south and west of Honshu (Japan's main island) and from the island of Kyushu, where invasion seemed most likely.

Military planners studied Mongol tactics and retrained and outfitted Japanese warriors for defense against advanced weaponry. Farm laborers drafted from all over the country constructed defensive fortifications. This effort demanded, for the first time, a national system to move resources toward western points rather than toward the imperial or shogunal centers to the east.

The Mongols attacked again in 1281. They brought 140,000 warriors, including many non-Mongols, as well as thousands of horses, in hundreds of ships. However, the wall the Japanese had built to cut off Hakata Bay from the mainland deprived the Mongol forces of a reliable landing point. Japanese swordsmen rowed out and boarded the Mongol ships lingering offshore. Their superb steel swords shocked the invaders. After a prolonged standoff, a typhoon struck and sank perhaps half of the Mongol ships. An epidemic decimated the remaining Mongol troops. What was left of them sailed away, never again to harass Japan. Religious institutions later claimed that their prayers for help brought a "divine wind"—*kamikaze* (kah-me-kah-zay)—that drove away the Mongols.

Nevertheless, the Mongol threat continued to influence Japanese development. Prior to his death in 1294, Khubilai had in mind a third invasion. His successors did not carry through with it, but the shoguns did not know that the Mongols had given up. They rebuilt coastal defenses well into the fourteenth century, helping to consolidate the social position of Japan's warrior elite and stimulating the development of a national infrastructure for trade and communication. But the Kamakura Shogunate, based on regionally collected and regionally dispersed revenues, suffered financial strain in trying to pay for centralized road and defense systems.

Between 1333 and 1338 the emperor Go-Daigo broke the centuries-old tradition of imperial seclusion and aloofness from government and tried to reclaim power from the shoguns. This ignited a civil war that destroyed the Kamakura system. In 1338, with the Mongol threat waning, the **Ashikaga** (ah-shee-KAH-gah) **Shogunate** took control at the imperial center of Kyoto.

Provincial warlords enjoyed renewed independence. Around their imposing castles, they sponsored the development of market towns, religious institutions, and schools. The application of technologies imported in earlier periods, including water wheels, improved plows, and Champa rice, increased agricultural productivity. Growing wealth and relative peace stimulated artistic creativity, mostly reflecting Zen Buddhist beliefs held by the warrior elite. In the simple elegance of architecture and gardens, in the ritual of the tea ceremony, and in the eerie, stylized performances of the Noh theater and the contemplative landscapes of artists, the aesthetic code of Zen became established in the Ashikaga era.

Despite the technological advancement, artistic productivity, and rapid urbanization of this period, competition among warlords and their followers led to regional wars. By the later 1400s these conflicts resulted in the near destruction of the warlords. The great Onin War in 1477 left Kyoto devastated and the Ashikaga Shogunate a central government in name only. Ambitious but low-ranking warriors, some with links to trade with the continent, began to scramble for control of the provinces.

After the fall of the Yuan in 1368, Japan resumed overseas trade, exporting raw materials and swords, as well as folding fans, invented in Japan during the period of isolation. Japan's primary imports from China were books and porcelain. The volatile political environment in Japan gave rise to partnerships between warlords and local merchants. All worked to strengthen their own towns and treasuries through overseas commerce or, sometimes, through piracy.

## The Emergence of Vietnam, 1200–1500

Before the first Mongol attack in 1257, the states of Annam (the Chinese name for northern Vietnam) and Champa (southern Vietnam) had clashed frequently. Annam (called Dai Viet in Vietnamese in this period) looked toward China and had once been subject to the Tang. Chinese political ideas, social philosophies, dress, religion, and language heavily influenced its official culture. Champa related more closely to the trading networks of the Indian Ocean; its official culture was strongly influenced by Indian religion, language, architecture, and dress.

Champa's relationship with China depended in part on how close its enemy, Annam, was to China at any particular time. During the Song period Annam was neither formally subject to China nor particularly threatening to Champa militarily, so Champa inaugurated a trade and tribute relationship with China that spread fast-ripening Champa rice throughout East Asia.

The Mongols exacted tribute from both Annam and Champa until the fall of the Yuan Empire in 1368. However, because Mongol political and military ambitions were mostly focused elsewhere, they had

*kamikaze* The "divine wind," which the Japanese credited with blowing Mongol invaders away from their shores in 1281.

**Ashikaga Shogunate** The second of Japan's military governments headed by a shogun (a military ruler). Sometimes called the Muromachi Shogunate.

**Noh Drama Performance**
This slow, rhythmic, chanted form of drama appealed to the military elite with its stories of warriors, women, gods, and demons. The minimal stage is normally bare except for a painting at the rear of a pine tree, symbolizing the means by which deities descend to earth. The actors wear masks and lavish costumes. Four instrumentalists playing flutes and three types of drums punctuate the chanting.

Scenes of urban life under the 'Bakufu' government from a performance of Noh Drama, Tosa School, 1800, Japanese, (detail from six-fold screen, see 67712), (colour woodblock print). Private Collection/Photo © Bonhams, London, UK/The Bridgeman Art Library

minimal impact on Vietnam's politics and culture. The two Vietnamese kingdoms soon resumed their warfare. When Annam moved its army to reinforce its southern border, Ming troops occupied the capital, Hanoi, and installed a puppet government. Almost thirty years elapsed before Annam regained independence and resumed a tributary status. By then the Ming were turning to meet Mongol challenges to their north. In a series of ruthless campaigns, Annam terminated Champa's independence, and by 1500 the ancestor of the modern state of Vietnam, still called Annam, had been born.

The new state still relied on Confucian bureaucratic government and an examination system, but some practices differed from those in China. The Vietnamese legal code, for example, preserved group landowning and decision making within the villages, as well as women's property rights. Both developments probably had roots in an early rural culture based on the growing of rice in wet paddies; by this time the Annamese considered them distinctive features of their own culture.

## CONCLUSION

The Mongols were the most successful warriors the world had ever seen. In less than a hundred years, they had conquered an empire that covered half of Eurasia and reached from Poland to Vietnam. And yet half a century later, their empire had broken apart and they had lost most of what they had gained. Why were their conquests so short-lived compared with those of the Romans or the Arabs?

### SECTION REVIEW

- Mongol conquest devastated Korea, but Mongol rule opened it to new ideas and technologies.
- The Choson dynasty succeeded the Koryo dynasty and fostered local identity while encouraging economic expansion and technological innovation.
- In Japan, the Mongol threat forced military and organizational innovations, but the expense of these defenses weakened the Kamakura Shogunate.
- Go-Daigo's failed attempt to reassert imperial power resulted in the rise of the Ashikaga Shogunate.
- The warring states of Vietnam avoided Mongol conquest but paid tribute to the Yuan Empire.
- After the Ming withdrawal, Annam conquered Champa, establishing a unified state on both Confucian and local practices.

The Mongols, though ferocious warriors, were too few in number to manage a huge empire, and so they turned to the peoples they had conquered—Chinese, Persians, Turks, and Arabs—to carry out the tasks of administration. They were famous for tolerating many religions and cultures among the people who accepted their rule, but they had no common religion or ideology upon which to build a lasting political culture. Some Mongols converted to Islam, others converted to Buddhism, and still others became Chinese in language and culture. As the Mongol armies were widely scattered, subject peoples whose cultures had never been erased by the Mongols reasserted themselves politically and militarily.

Once Mongol rule was in place, travel across the breadth of Eurasia became safer and easier than it had ever been before or was to be for centuries. Trade flourished, and ideas and technologies spread widely. Yet with trade came the plague, which decimated all the regions that the Mongols occupied. Instead of a Roman or Arab legacy of culture, administration, and religion, subject peoples remembered the Mongols for the violence and brutality of their conquest. However, the reality or threat of Mongol attack and domination encouraged centralization of government, improvement of military techniques, and renewed stress on local cultural identity. Thus, in retrospect, despite its traditional association with death and destruction, the Mongol period appears as a watershed, establishing new connections between widespread parts of Eurasia and leading to the development of strong, assertive, and culturally creative regional states.

# CHAPTER REVIEW

## THE RISE OF THE MONGOLS, 1200–1260
■ *What accounts for the magnitude and speed of the Mongol conquests?* (page 281)

Nomadic mobility and endurance, expertise in military technology, and systematic army organization made the armies of Chinggis Khan all but invincible. While the Mongols did not usually outnumber their enemies, they were experts on horseback and used superior bows. Turkish pastoral peoples who suffered defeat often enrolled in the Mongol ranks, thus magnifying the power of the Mongols themselves.

## THE MONGOLS AND ISLAM, 1260–1500
■ *How did Mongol expansion and Islam affect each other?* (page 288)

As rivalries mounted between the Il-khan and the Golden Horde states, Islam became a point of contention. Rulers who converted to Islam were initially lax in their observance and affiliations. The Il-khans came to value urban Muslim culture, but their merciless taxation policies contributed to a weakness that allowed the Golden Horde to make inroads on Il-khan territory. Meanwhile, Timur rose to power in Chagatai territory and undertook wide-ranging conquests. The Il-khans, Timur, and his successors presided over a flowering of Islamic culture that drew upon Iranian and Chinese cultural elements to contribute notable achievements in historical writing, art, mathematics, and astronomy.

## REGIONAL RESPONSES IN WESTERN EURASIA
■ *What benefits resulted from the integration of Eurasia into the Mongol Empire?* (page 291)

The Great Khans attracted emissaries and traders from all over Eurasia to their court, revitalizing the Silk Road. Cultural contact between east and west had greater long-term impact than the Mongols' political power. Muslim astronomers and calendar makers found a welcome reception in China, and Chinese artistic styles became popular in Iran. Mongol occupation, or the threat of Mongol conquest, also helped non-Mongol political leaders galvanize popular support for local state building.

## MONGOL DOMINATION IN CHINA, 1271–1368

■ *How did Mongol rule in China foster cultural and scientific exchange?* (page 293)

In China, Yuan rule reestablished connections with Inner Asia that had earlier benefited Tang rule (see Chapter 11). The empire rewarded administrative and military skills more than ethnic or linguistic identity. Muslims from Central Asia brought astronomical expertise to China just as Chinese administrators brought their techniques to Iran. Beijing, the Yuan capital, developed a dynamic cultural scene that produced some of the first Chinese novels. Yet the period also produced war casualties, spread of disease, and migration to southern China.

## THE EARLY MING EMPIRE, 1368–1500

■ *In what ways did the Ming Empire continue or discontinue Mongol practices?* (page 296)

The Ming overthrew the Yuan and reaffirmed Chinese ethnicity as a basis for rule. Leaving Beijing, they located their capital in the south and relied on study of the Confucian classics and the examination system for choosing imperial officials. Nevertheless, Mongols still served in the army, and after a time Beijing again became the capital. Though some Yuan administrative practices continued, contact and trade with Inner Asia dwindled because of political disunity in the old Mongol core area.

## CENTRALIZATION AND MILITARISM IN EAST ASIA, 1200–1500

■ *What are some of the similarities and differences in how Korea and Japan responded to the Mongol threat?* (page 299)

The conquered Korean rulers remained loyal to the Yuan and benefited from new technologies and administrative techniques. When the Yuan fell, however, a Korean dynasty emerged that stressed non-Mongol ethnicity and reviled the earlier Mongol domination, even while retaining many of the innovations of that period.

After twice repelling Mongol invasions, Japan remained highly militarized. Paradoxically, regional warlords embraced cultural innovations, many of Chinese inspiration, that subsequently became central to Japanese identity. Zen Buddhism, Noh drama, and the ritual of the tea ceremony united the Japanese elite even as the warlords, with their samurai armies, seized control from the ineffective imperial government.

## Key Terms

Mongols (p. 281)

Chinggis Khan (p. 281)

Yuan Empire (p. 282)

bubonic plague (p. 285)

Il-khan (p. 288)

Golden Horde (p. 288)

Timur (p. 289)

Rashid al-Din (p. 289)

Nasir al-Din Tusi (p. 290)

Alexander Nevskii (p. 291)

tsar (p. 292)

Ottoman Empire (p. 293)

Khubilai Khan (p. 294)

lama (p. 294)

Beijing (p. 294)

Ming Empire (p. 296)

Yongle (p. 296)

Zheng He (p. 297)

Choson (p. 300)

*kamikaze* (p. 302)

Ashikaga Shogunate (p. 302)

# Europe East and West

© Cengage Learning

# RURAL GROWTH AND CRISIS

■ *How well did inhabitants of western Europe, rich and poor, urban and rural, deal with their natural environment?*

In the summer of 1454, a year after the Ottoman Sultan captured the Greek Christian city of Constantinople, Aeneas Sylvius Piccolomini (uh-NEE-uhs SIL-vee-uhs pee-kuh-lo-MEE-nee), destined in four years to become pope, expressed doubts as to whether anyone could persuade the rulers of Christian Europe to take up a new crusade against the Muslims: "Christendom has no head whom all will obey—neither the pope nor the emperor receives his due."

The Christian states thought more of fighting each other. French and English armies had been battling for over a century. The German emperor presided over dozens of states but did not really control them, and the numerous kingdoms and principalities of Spain and Italy could not unite. The Catholic rulers of Hungary, Poland, and Lithuania, on the front line against the Muslim Ottomans, seemed very far away from the western monarchs. With only slight exaggeration, Aeneas Sylvius moaned, "Every city has its own king, and there are as many princes as there are households." He attributed this lack of unity to European preoccupation with personal welfare and material gain, which had increased during the previous century after a devastating plague had carried off a third of Europe's population.

Yet despite all these divisions, disasters, and wars, historians now see the period from 1200 to 1500 (Europe's late Middle Ages) as a time of unusual progress. Prosperous cities adorned with splendid architecture, institutions of higher learning, and cultural achievements counterbalanced the avarice and greed that Aeneas Sylvius lamented. Frequent wars caused havoc and destruction, but they also promoted the development of military technology and more unified monarchies.

Although their Muslim and Byzantine neighbors commonly called Catholic Europeans "Franks," they ordinarily referred to themselves as "Latins," underscoring their allegiance to the Roman church and the Latin language used in its rituals.

Between 1200 and 1500, the European mainland brought more land under cultivation using new farming techniques and made greater use of machinery and mechanical forms of energy. Yet for the nine out of ten people who lived in the countryside, hard labor brought meager returns, and famine, epidemics, and war struck often. After the devastation of the Black Death between 1347 and 1351, social changes speeded up by peasant revolts released many persons from serfdom and brought some improvements to rural life. By contrast, eastern Europe, a region of vast open spaces and sparse population, saw serfdom increase, as nobles, faced with a labor shortage, forced farm workers to till their lands.

## Peasants, Population, and Plague

In 1200, most western Europeans lived as serfs tilling the soil on large estates owned by the nobility and the church (see Chapter 10). They owed their lord both a share of their harvests and numerous labor services. These obligations combined with inefficient farming practices meant that peasants received meager returns for their hard work. Even with numerous religious holidays, peasants labored some fifty-four hours a week, more than half the time in support of the local nobility. Each noble family, housed in its stone castle, required the labor of fifteen to thirty peasant families living in one-room thatched cottages containing little furniture and no luxuries.

Scenes of rural life show both men and women at work in the fields, but equality of labor did not mean equality at home. In the peasant's hut as elsewhere in medieval Europe, women were subordinate to men. The influential theologian Thomas Aquinas (uh-KWY-nuhs) (1225–1274) spoke for his age when he argued that although both men and women were theoretically created in God's image, "the image of God is found in man, and not in woman: for man is the beginning and end of woman; as God is the beginning and end of every creature."[1]

Rural poverty resulted partly from rapid population growth. In 1200, China's population may have exceeded Europe's by two to one; by 1300, the population of each was about 80 million. China's population fell because of the Mongol conquest (see Chapter 12), while Europe's doubled between 1100 and 1340. Some historians believe the reviving economy stimulated the increase. Others argue that severe epidemics were few, and warmer-than-usual European temperatures after 950, referred to as the Medieval Warm Period by climate historians, reduced mortality from starvation and exposure.

More people required more productive farming and new agricultural settlements. One widespread new technique, the **three-field system**, replaced the custom of leaving half the land fallow (uncultivated) every year to regain its fertility. Farmers grew crops on two-thirds of their land each year, alternating wheat and rye with oats, barley, or legumes. The third field was left fallow. The oats restored nitrogen to the depleted soil and produced feed for plow horses. In much of Europe, however, farmers continued to let half of their land lie fallow and use oxen (less efficient but cheaper than horses) to pull their plows.

Population growth also encouraged new agricultural settlements. In the twelfth and thirteenth centuries, large numbers of Germans migrated into the fertile lands east of the Elbe River from the Baltic Sea in the north to Transylvania (part of modern Romania) in the south. The Order of Teutonic Knights, founded in the Holy Land but given a (temporary) European base of operations by the king of Hungary in 1211, slaughtered or drove away native inhabitants who had not yet adopted Christianity (see Chapter 12). During the thirteenth century, they conquered, resettled, and administered a vast area along the Baltic that later became Prussia (see Map 13.1).

> **three-field system**   A rotational system for agriculture in which two fields grow food crops and one lies fallow. It gradually replaced the two-field system in medieval Europe.

Kharbine-Tapabor/The Art Archive at Art Resource, NY

**Rural French Peasants**   Many scenes of peasant life in winter are visible in this small painting by the Flemish Limbourg brothers from the 1410s. Above the snow-covered beehives one man chops firewood, while another drives a donkey loaded with firewood to a little village. At the lower right a woman, blowing on her frozen fingers, heads past the huddled sheep and hungry birds to join other women warming themselves in the cottage (whose outer wall the artists have cut away).

Draining swamps and clearing forests also brought new land under cultivation. But as population rose, even lands with poor soil or those vulnerable to flooding, frost, or drought were farmed. Average crop yields fell accordingly after 1250, and more people lived at the edge of starvation. According to one historian, "By 1300, almost every child born in western Europe faced the probability of extreme hunger at least once or twice during his expected 30 to 35 years of life."[2] One unusually cold spell at the end of the Medieval Warm Period produced the Great

---

[1] Quoted in Marina Warner, *Alone of All Her Sex: The Myth and Cult of the Virgin Mary* (New York: Random House, 1983), 179.

[2] Harry Miskimin, *The Economy of the Early Renaissance, 1300–1460* (Englewood Cliffs, NJ: Prentice Hall, 1969), 26–27.

# Chronology

| | Technology and Environment | Culture | Politics and Society |
|---|---|---|---|
| **1200** | **1200s** Widespread use of crossbows and windmills<br><br>**1250** Growing deforestation | **1209** Franciscan Friars<br><br>**1216** Dominican Friars<br>**1225–1274** Philosopher-monk Thomas Aquinas | **1200s** Champagne fairs flourish<br>**1204** Fourth Crusade<br><br>**1211** Teutonic Knights in Hungary<br>**1215** Magna Carta issued |
| **1300** | **1315–1317** Great Famine<br><br>**1347–1351** Black Death | **1300–1500** Rise of universities<br>**1313–1375** Giovanni Boccaccio, humanist writer<br><br>**ca. 1390–1441** Jan van Eyck, painter | **1337** Start of Hundred Years' War<br><br>**1381** Wat Tyler's Rebellion |
| **1400** | **1400s** Cannon and hand-held firearms in use<br><br>**1454** Gutenberg Bible | **1452–1519** Leonardo da Vinci, artist<br><br>**1492** Expulsion of Jews from Spain | **1415** Portuguese take Ceuta<br>**1431** Joan of Arc burned<br>**1453** End of Hundred Years' War; Ottomans take Constantinople<br><br>**1492** Fall of Muslim state of Granada |

Famine of 1315–1317, which affected much of Europe north of the Alps.

The **Black Death** reversed the population growth. Victims developed boils the size of eggs in their groins and armpits, black blotches on their skin, foul body odors, and severe pain. In most cases, death came within a few days. This terrible plague—bubonic plague was the primary form of the Black Death—had been carried from Inner Asia by fleas infesting the fur of certain rats and had moved westward with the Mongol armies (see Chapter 12). In 1346, the Mongols attacked the city of Kaffa (KAH-fah) on the Black Sea; a year later, Genoese (JEN-oh-eez) traders in Kaffa carried the disease to Italy and southern France. For two years, the Black Death spread across Europe, in some places carrying off two-thirds of the population. Town officials closed their gates to people from infected areas and burned the victims' possessions but could not halt the advance of the disease. Even if medieval doctors had understood its source, eliminating the rats that thrived on urban refuse would have been difficult. Average losses in western Europe amounted to one in three.

The plague brought home to people how sudden and unexpected death could be. Some people became more religious, giving money to the church or lashing themselves with iron-tipped whips to atone for their sins. Others chose reckless enjoyment, spending their money on fancy clothes, feasts, and drinking.

Periodic returns of plague made recovery from population losses slow and uneven. Europe's population in 1400 equaled that in 1200. Not until after 1500 did it rise above its preplague level.

**Black Death** An outbreak of bubonic plague that spread across Asia, North Africa, and Europe in the mid-fourteenth century, carrying off vast numbers of persons.

**Map 13.1 Europe in 1453** This year marked the end of the Hundred Years' War between France and England and the fall of the Byzantine capital city of Constantinople to the Ottoman Empire. Muslim advances into southeastern Europe were offset by the Latin Christian reconquests of Islamic holdings in southern Italy and the Iberian Peninsula and by the conversion of Lithuania. © Cengage Learning

**Spread of Latin Christendom**

- In 1000 C.E.
- Added 1000–1200
- Lost 1000–1200 (Regained 1200–1500)
- Added 1200–1500
- Lost 1200–1500
- English holdings, 1360
- Boundary of the Holy Roman Empire

**Burying Victims of the Black Death**  This scene from Tournai, Flanders, captures the magnitude of the plague.

## Social Rebellion

In addition to its demographic and psychological effects, the Black Death triggered social changes in western Europe. Workers who survived demanded higher pay for their services. When authorities tried to freeze wages at the old levels, peasants rose up against wealthy nobles and churchmen. During a widespread revolt in France in 1358, known as the *Jacquerie*, peasants looted castles and killed dozens of persons. In a large revolt in England in 1381 led by Wat Tyler, an estimated 50,000 peasants and craftsmen invaded London, calling for an end to serfdom and obligations to landowners and murdering the archbishop of Canterbury and other officials. Authorities put down these rebellions with great bloodshed and cruelty, but they could not stave off the higher wages and other social changes the rebels demanded.

Serfdom practically disappeared in western Europe as peasants bought their freedom or ran away. Some English landowners who could no longer hire enough fieldworkers began pasturing sheep for their wool. Others grew crops that required less care or made greater use of draft animals and labor-saving tools. Because the plague had not killed livestock and game, survivors had abundant meat and leather. Thus, the welfare of the rural masses generally improved after the Black Death, though the gap between rich and poor remained wide.

In urban areas, employers raised wages to attract workers. Guilds (discussed later in this chapter) shortened the period of apprenticeship. Competition within crafts also became more common. Although the overall economy shrank with the decline in population, per capita production actually rose.

## Mills and Mines

Mining, primarily in Germany and east-central Europe, and metalworking and craft mechanization everywhere expanded so greatly in the centuries before 1500 that some historians speak of an "industrial revolution" in medieval Europe. This is too strong a term, but the landscape fairly bristled with mechanical devices. Mills powered by water or wind ground grain, sawed logs, crushed olives, operated bellows, and pounded linen rags for making paper.

Watermills multiplied at a faster rate than the population. In 1086, 5,600 watermills flanked England's many rivers. After 1200, mills spread rapidly across the European mainland. By the early fourteenth century, entrepreneurs had crammed 68 watermills into a 1-mile (1.61-kilometer) section of the Seine (sen) River in Paris. Undershot wheels that depended on the river flowing beneath them were less efficient than overshot wheels where water channeled to fall over the top of the wheel combined the force of gravity with the water's current. Windmills multiplied in comparatively dry lands like Spain and in northern Europe, where water wheels froze in winter.

Designs for watermills dated back to Roman times, and the Islamic world, which inherited Hellenistic technologies, knew of, but failed to develop, both water wheels and windmills. European-style heavy investment in water or wind power made no sense in Muslim lands, where single animals typically operated mills and irrigation devices, because grazing on arid and semiarid wastes made animal power from oxen and camels virtually free. In Europe, by contrast, where grain crops fed both humans and animals, population growth increased the cost of animal energy, particularly of horsepower. One result was that the family name *Miller* became very important in European languages but was rarely used in Arabic, Persian, Turkish.

Owners invested heavily in building mills, but since nature furnished the energy to run them for free, they returned great profits. While individuals or monasteries constructed some mills, most were built by groups of investors. Rich millers often aroused the jealousy of their neighbors. In his *Canterbury Tales*, the English poet Geoffrey Chaucer (ca. 1340–1400) captured their unsavory reputation by portraying a miller as "a master-hand at stealing grain" by pushing down on the balance scale with his thumb.[3]

Waterpower aided the great expansion of iron making. Water powered the stamping mills that pulverized iron ore, the lifting devices that drained water from deep mines, and the bellows (first documented in the West in 1323) that raised temperatures to the point where liquid iron could be poured into molds. Blast furnaces producing high-quality iron are documented from 1380.

In addition to iron mines in many countries, new silver, lead, and copper mines in Austria and Hungary supplied metal for coins, church bells, cannon, and statues. Techniques of deep mining developed in central Europe spread west in the latter part of the fifteenth century. A building boom stimulated stone quarrying in France during the eleventh, twelfth, and thirteenth centuries.

---

[3]Quotations here and later in the chapter are from Geoffrey Chaucer, *The Canterbury Tales*, trans. Nevill Coghill (New York: Penguin Books, 1952), 25, 29, 32.

## SECTION REVIEW

- Population growth stimulated improved farming methods and agricultural expansion, but peasant life did not significantly improve.
- Famine and the Black Death reversed the population growth and resulted in social change throughout Europe.
- Improved mill designs and other technology stimulated further industrial growth, which, in turn, changed the landscape.

Industrial growth and urban sprawl changed the landscape. Quarries and mines scarred the hillsides, and dams and canals altered the flow of rivers. Increasingly from 1250 onward forests were cleared for farmland, as well as for ship and building timber and for use in leather tanning, iron smelting, and glassmaking. A single iron furnace could consume all the trees within five-eighths of a mile (1 kilometer) in just forty days. Although some powerful landowners established hunting preserves and those forests were protected, many of Europe's once-dense forests were lost. Urban tanneries, slaughterhouse runoff, and human waste polluted streams. England's Parliament enacted the first recorded antipollution law in 1388, but enforcement proved difficult. More lightly populated, central and eastern Europe experienced less environmental degradation.

## URBAN REVIVAL

■ *What social and economic factors led to the growth of cities in late medieval Europe?*

In the tenth century, no town on the European mainland could compete in size, wealth, or comfort with the cities of Byzantium and Islam. Yet by the later Middle Ages, the Mediterranean, Baltic, and Atlantic coasts boasted wealthy port cities, as did some major rivers draining into these seas. Some Byzantine and Muslim cities still exceeded those of the West in size, but not in commercial, cultural, and administrative dynamism, as marked by impressive new churches, guild halls, and residences.

## Trading Cities

Most urban growth after 1200 resulted from manufacturing and trade, both between cities and their hinterlands and over long distances. Northern Italy particularly benefited from maritime trade with the port cities of the eastern Mediterranean and, through them, the markets of the Indian Ocean and East Asia. In northern Europe, commercial cities in the county of Flanders (roughly today's Belgium) and around the Baltic Sea profited from regional networks and from overland and sea routes to the Mediterranean.

A Venetian-inspired assault in 1204 against the city of Constantinople, misleadingly named the "Fourth Crusade," temporarily eliminated Byzantine control of the waterway between the Mediterranean and the Black Sea and thereby allowed Venice to seize Crete and expand its trading colonies around the Black Sea. Another boon to Italian trade came from the westward expansion of the Mongol Empire, which opened trade routes from the Mediterranean to China (see Chapter 12).

When Mongol decline interrupted the caravan trade in the fourteenth century, Venetian merchants purchased eastern silks and spices brought by other middlemen to Constantinople, Damascus, and Cairo. Three times a year, Venice dispatched convoys of two or three galleys, with sixty oarsmen each, capable of bringing back 2,000 tons of goods.

The sea trade of Genoa on northern Italy's west coast probably equaled that of Venice. Genoese merchants established colonies in the western and eastern Mediterranean and around the Black Sea. In northern Europe, an association of trading cities known as the **Hanseatic** (han-see-AT-ik) **League** traded extensively in the Baltic, including the coasts of Prussia, newly conquered by German knights. Their merchants ranged eastward to Novgorod in Russia and westward across the North Sea to London.

In the late thirteenth century, Genoese galleys from the Mediterranean and Hanseatic ships from the Baltic were converging on the trading and manufacturing cities in Flanders. Artisans in the Flemish towns of Bruges (broozh), Ghent (gent [hard *g* as in *get*]), and Ypres (EE-pruh) transformed raw wool from England into a fine cloth that was softer and smoother than the coarse "homespuns" from simple

Flemish Weaver (engraving), English School, (19th century)/Private Collection/© Look and Learn/The Bridgeman Art Library

506.—Flemish Weaver.   (From a Print of 1568.)

**Flemish Weavers, Ypres** The spread of textile weaving gave employment to many people in the Netherlands. The city of Ypres in Flanders (now northern Belgium) was an important textile center in the thirteenth century. This drawing from a fourteenth-century manuscript shows a man and a woman weaving cloth on a horizontal loom.

village looms. Dyed in vivid hues, these Flemish textiles appealed to wealthy Europeans, who also appreciated fine textiles from Asia.

Along the overland route connecting Flanders and northern Italy, important trading fairs developed in the Champagne (sham-PAIN) region of Burgundy. The Champagne fairs began as regional markets, exchanging manufactured goods, livestock, and farm produce once or twice a year. When the king of France gained control of Champagne at the end of the twelfth century, royal guarantees of safe conduct to merchants

> **Hanseatic League** An economic and defensive alliance of the free towns in northern Germany, founded about 1241 and most powerful in the fourteenth century.

turned these markets into international fairs that were important for currency exchange and other financial transactions. A century later, fifteen Italian cities had permanent consulates in Champagne to represent the interests of their citizens. During the fourteenth century, the large volume of trade made it cheaper to ship Flemish woolens to Italy by sea than to pack them overland on animal backs. Champagne's fairs consequently lost some international trade, but they remained important as regional markets.

In the late thirteenth century, the English monarchy raised taxes on exports of raw wool, making cloth manufacture in England more profitable than in Flanders. Flemish specialists crossed the English Channel and introduced the spinning wheel, perhaps invented in India, and other devices to England. Annual raw wool exports fell from 35,000 sacks of wool at the beginning of the fourteenth century to 8,000 in the mid-fifteenth century, while English wool cloth production rose from 4,000 pieces just before 1350 to 54,000 a century later.

Florence also replaced Flemish imports with its own woolens industry financed by local banking families. In 1338, Florence manufactured 80,000 pieces of cloth, while importing only 10,000. Elsewhere in northern Italy a new industry appeared to manufacture cotton cloth, which had previously been imported across the Mediterranean. These changes in the textile industry show how competition promoted the spread of manufacturing and encouraged new specialties. Other Italian industries that grew on the basis of techniques borrowed from the Muslim world were papermaking, glassblowing, ceramics, and sugar refining.

In the fifteenth century, Venice surpassed its European rivals in the volume of its trade in the Mediterranean as well as across the Alps into central Europe. Its craftspeople manufactured luxury goods once obtainable only from eastern sources, including cotton and sugar grown with slave labor on the islands of Crete, Cyprus, and Sicily. This industry later became the model for the slave-based sugar economy of the New World (see Chapter 15). Exports of Italian and northern European woolens to the eastern Mediterranean also rose. In the space of a few centuries, western European cities had used the eastern trade to increase their prosperity and then reduce their dependence on eastern goods.

## Civic Life

Most northern Italian and German cities were independent states, much like the port cities of the Indian Ocean Basin (see Chapter 14). Other European cities held royal charters exempting them from the authority of local nobles. Their autonomy enabled them to adapt to changing market conditions more quickly than cities controlled by imperial authorities, as in China and the Islamic world. Since anyone who lived in a chartered city for over a year could claim freedom, urban life promoted social mobility.

Europe's Jews mostly lived in cities. Spain had the largest communities because of the tolerance of earlier Muslim rulers, but there were also sizable populations as far east as Magdeburg in Prussia. Commercial cities generally welcomed Jews with manufacturing and business skills. Despite official protection by certain Christian princes and kings, however, Jews endured violent religious persecutions or expulsions in times of crisis, such as during the Black Death (see Diversity and Dominance: Persecution and Protection of Jews, 1272–1349). In 1492, the Spanish monarchs expelled all Jews in the name of religious and ethnic purity. Only the papal city of Rome left its Jews undisturbed throughout the centuries before 1500.

Within most towns and cities, powerful associations known as guilds dominated civic life. **Guilds** brought together craft specialists, such as silversmiths or merchants working in a particular trade, to regulate business practices and set prices. Guilds also trained apprentices and promoted members' interests with the city government. By denying membership to outsiders and Jews, guilds protected the interests of families that already belonged to them. They also perpetuated male dominance of most skilled jobs.

Nevertheless, in a few places, women could join guilds either on their own or as the wives, widows, or daughters of male guild members. Large numbers of poor women also toiled in nonguild jobs in urban textile industries and in the food and beverage trades, generally receiving lower wages than men.

**guild**  In medieval Europe, an association of men (rarely women), such as merchants, artisans, or professors, who worked in a particular trade and banded together to promote their economic and political interests. Guilds were also important in other societies, such as the Ottoman and Safavid Empires.

Some women advanced socially through marriage to wealthy men. One of Chaucer's *Canterbury Tales* concerns a woman from Bath, a city in southern England, who became wealthy by marrying a succession of old men for their money (and then two other husbands for love), "aside from other company in youth." She was also a skilled weaver, Chaucer says: "In making cloth she showed so great a bent, / She bettered those of Ypres and of Ghent."

By the fifteenth century, a new class of wealthy merchant-bankers was operating on a vast scale and specializing in money changing and loans and making investments on behalf of other parties. Merchants great and small used their services. They also handled the financial transactions of ecclesiastical and secular officials and arranged for the transmission to the pope of funds known as Peter's pence, a collection taken up annually in every church in western Europe. Princes and kings supported their wars and lavish courts with credit. Some merchant-bankers even developed their own news services, gathering information on any topic that could affect business.

Florentine financiers offered checking accounts, organized private shareholding companies (the forerunners of modern corporations), and improved bookkeeping techniques. In the fifteenth century, the Medici (MED-ih-chee) family of Florence operated banks in Italy, Flanders, and London. Medicis also controlled the government of Florence and commissioned art works. The Fuggers (FOOG-uhrz) of Augsburg, who had ten times the Medici bank's lending capital, topped Europe's banking fraternity by 1500. Beginning as cloth merchants under Jacob "the Rich" (1459–1525), the family's many activities included trade in Hungarian copper, essential for casting cannon.

Since Latin Christians generally considered charging interest (usury) sinful, Jews predominated in moneylending. Christian bankers devised ways to get around the condemnation of usury. Some borrowers repaid loans in a different currency at a rate of exchange favorable to the lender. Others added to their repayment a "gift" for the lender. For example, in 1501, church officials agreed to repay a Fugger loan of 6,000 gold ducats in five months along with a "gift" of 400 ducats, which would have amounted to an effective interest rate of 16 percent except that the church failed to repay the loan on time.

Yet most residents of European cities suffered in poverty, ill-health, and squalor. European cities generally lacked such amenities as the public baths and water supply systems that had existed in Roman times and still survived in Islamic lands.

## Gothic Cathedrals

Master builders and stone masons counted among the skilled people in greatest demand. Though cities competed with one another in the magnificence of their guild halls and town halls, **Gothic cathedrals**, first appearing about 1140 in France, cost the most and brought the greatest prestige. The pointed, or Gothic, arch, replacing the older round, or Romanesque, arch, signaled the new design. External (flying) buttresses stabilizing the high, thin, stone columns below the arches constituted another distinctive feature. This design enabled master builders to push the Gothic cathedrals to great heights and fill the outside walls between the arches with giant windows depicting religious scenes in brilliantly colored stained glass. During the next four centuries, interior heights soared ever higher and walls became dazzling curtains of stained glass.

The men who designed and built the cathedrals had little or no formal education and limited understanding of the mathematical principles of civil engineering. Masons could miscalculate, causing parts

**Gothic cathedrals** Large churches originating in twelfth-century France; built in an architectural style featuring pointed arches, tall vaults and spires, flying buttresses, and large stained-glass windows.

# Diversity & Dominance

## Persecution and Protection of Jews, 1272–1349

*Because they did not belong to the dominant Latin Christian faith, Jews suffered from periodic discrimination and persecution. For the most part, religious and secular authorities tried to curb such anti-Semitism. Jews, after all, were useful citizens who worshiped the same God as their Christian neighbors. Still, it was hard to know where to draw the line between justifiable and unjustifiable discrimination. The famous reviser of Catholic theology, St. Thomas Aquinas, made one such distinction in his Summa Theologica with regard to attempts at forced conversion.*

Now, the practice of the Church never held that the children of Jews should be baptized against the will of their parents. . . .

There are two reasons for this position. One stems from danger to faith. For, if children without the use of reason were to receive baptism, then after reaching maturity they could easily be persuaded by their parents to relinquish what they had received in ignorance. This would tend to do harm to the faith.

The second reason is that it is opposed to natural justice . . . it [is] a matter of natural right that a son, before he has the use of reason, is under the care of his father. Hence, it would be against natural justice . . . for anything to be arranged for him against the will of his parents.

*The hostility toward the Jews that Aquinas opposed was much in the air, for in 1272 Pope Gregory X issued several decrees of protection for the legal rights of Jews.*

Since it occasionally happens that some Christians lose their Christian children, the Jews are accused by their enemies of secretly carrying off and killing these same Christian children, and of making sacrifices of the heart and blood of these very children. It happens, too, that the parents of these children, or some other Christian enemies of these Jews, secretly hide these very children in order that they may be able to injure these Jews, and in order that they may be able to extort from them a certain amount of money by redeeming them from their straits.

And most falsely do these Christians claim that the Jews have secretly and furtively carried away these children and killed them, and that the Jews offer sacrifice from the heart and the blood of these children, since their law in this matter precisely and expressly forbids Jews to sacrifice, eat, or drink the blood, or eat the flesh of animals having claws. This has been demonstrated many times at our court by Jews converted to the Christian faith: nevertheless very many Jews are often seized and detained unjustly because of this.

We decree, therefore, that Christians need not be obeyed against Jews in such a case or situation of this type, and we order that Jews seized under such a silly pretext be freed from imprisonment, and that they shall not be arrested henceforth on such a miserable pretext, unless—which we do not believe—they be caught in the commission of the crime. We decree that no Christian shall stir up anything against them, but that they should be maintained in that status and position in which they were from the time of our predecessors, from antiquity till now.

We decree, in order to stop the wickedness and avarice of bad men, that no one shall dare to devastate or to destroy a cemetery of the Jews or to dig up human bodies for the sake of getting money [by holding them for ransom]. Moreover, if anyone, after having known the content of this decree, should—which we hope will not happen—attempt audaciously to act contrary to it, then let him suffer punishment in his rank and position, or let him be ➤

punished by the penalty of excommunication, unless he makes amends for his boldness by proper recompense. Moreover, we wish that only those Jews who have not attempted to contrive anything toward the destruction of the Christian faith be fortified by the support of such protection. . . .

*Despite such decrees, violence against Jews might burst out when fears and emotions were running high. This selection is from the official chronicles of the upper-Rhineland towns.*

In the year 1349 there occurred the greatest epidemic that ever happened. . . . [S]o many people perished that it would be horrible to describe. The pope at Avignon stopped all sessions of court, locked himself in a room, allowed no one to approach him and had a fire burning before him all the time. And from what this epidemic came, all wise teachers and physicians could only say that it was God's will. . . . [I]t is estimated about sixteen thousand people died.

In the matter of this plague the Jews throughout the world were reviled and accused in all lands of having caused it through the poison which they are said to have put into the water and the wells—that is what they were accused of—and for this reason the Jews were burnt all the way from the Mediterranean into Germany, but not in Avignon, for the pope protected them there.

Nevertheless they tortured a number of Jews in Berne and Zofingen who admitted they had put poison into many wells, and they found the poison in the wells. Thereupon they burnt the Jews in many towns and wrote of this affair to Strasbourg, Freibourg, and Basel in order that they too should burn their Jews. . . . The deputies of the city of Strasbourg . . . said that they knew no evil of [the Jews]. . . . [But] a great indignation and clamor against the deputies from Strasbourg [caused] the Bishop and the lords and

the Imperial Cities . . . to do away with the Jews. The result was that they were burnt in many cities, and wherever they were expelled they were caught by the peasants and stabbed to death or drowned. . . .

On Saturday—that was St. Valentine's Day—they burnt the Jews on a wooden platform in their cemetery. . . . And everything that was owed to the Jews was cancelled, and the Jews had to surrender all pledges and notes that they had taken for debts. The council, however, took the cash that the Jews possessed and divided it among the working-men proportionately. The money was indeed the thing that killed the Jews. If they had been poor and if the feudal lords had not been in debt to them, they would not have been burnt.

## QUESTIONS FOR ANALYSIS

1. Why do Aquinas and Pope Gregory oppose prejudicial actions against Jews?
2. Why did prejudice increase at the time of the Black Death?
3. What factors account for the differences between the views of Christian leaders and the Christian masses?

*Sources*: First selection source is Pocket Books, a division of Simon & Schuster, Inc., and the Vernon & Janet Bourke Living Trust from *The Pocket Aquinas*, edited with translations by Vernon G. Bourke. Copyright © 1960 by Washington Square Press. Copyright renewed © 1988 by Simon & Schuster, Inc. Second and third selections from Jacob R. Marcus, ed., *The Jew in the Medieval World: A Source Book, 315–1791* (Cincinnati: Union of American Hebrew Congregations, 1938), 152–154, 45–47. Reprinted with permission of the Hebrew Union College Press, Cincinnati.

of the cathedrals to collapse. The record-high choir vault of Beauvais Cathedral, for instance—154 feet (47 meters) in height—came tumbling down in 1284. But with experience, success rose from the rubble of their mistakes. The cathedral spire in Strasbourg reached 466 feet (142 meters)—as high as a forty-story building. Such heights were unsurpassed until the nineteenth century.

# LEARNING, LITERATURE, AND THE RENAISSANCE

■ *What factors were responsible for the promotion of learning and the arts in Europe?*

Throughout the Middle Ages, people in western Europe lived amid reminders of the achievements of the Romans. They wrote and worshiped in a version of their language, traveled their roads, and obeyed some of their laws. The vestments and robes of popes, kings, and emperors followed the designs of Roman officials. Yet the learning of Greco-Roman antiquity virtually disappeared outside of Byzantium and the Muslim world.

A small revival of learning at the court of Charlemagne in the ninth century was followed by a larger renaissance (rebirth) in the twelfth century in which cities became centers of intellectual and artistic life. The universities established across the Latin countries of Europe after 1200 contributed to this cultural revival. Then in the mid-fourteenth century, the pace of intellectual and artistic life quickened in what is often called the **Renaissance**, which began in northern Italy and later spread to northern and eastern Europe. Some Italian authors saw the Italian Renaissance as a sharp break with an age of darkness.

## Universities and Scholarship

Before 1100, Byzantine and Islamic scholarship generally surpassed scholarship in western Europe. When Latin Christians wrested southern Italy from the Byzantines and Sicily and Toledo from the Muslims in the eleventh century, they acquired many manuscripts of Greek and Arabic works. These included works by Plato and Aristotle (AR-ih-stah-tahl) and Greek treatises on medicine, mathematics, and geography, as well as scientific

and philosophical writings by Muslim writers. Latin translations of the Iranian philosopher Ibn Sina (IB-uhn SEE-nah) (980–1037), known in the West as Avicenna (av-uh-SEN-uh), had great influence because of their sophisticated blend of Aristotelian and Islamic philosophy. Jewish scholars contributed significantly to the translation and explication of Arabic and other manuscripts.

The thirteenth century saw the foundation of two new religious orders, the Dominicans (1216) and the Franciscans (1209). Living according to a rule but not confined to monasteries, these friars (brothers) brought preaching to the common people and carried the Christian message abroad as missionaries. Some of their most talented members taught in the independent colleges that arose after 1200. Though some aspects of these institutions may derive from institutions of higher Islamic learning called *madrasas* that proliferated after 1100 (see Chapter 10), the Latin countries of Europe innovated the idea of **universities** as degree-granting corporations imparting both religious and nonreligious learning.

Between 1300 and 1500, sixty universities, from St. Andrews in Scotland to Krakow and Prague in eastern Europe, joined the twenty established before that time. Students banded together to start some of them; guilds of professors founded others. Teaching guilds, like craft guilds, set standards for the profession, trained apprentices and masters, and defended their professional interests.

Universities set curricula and instituted final examinations for degrees. Students who passed the exams that ended their apprenticeship received a "license" to teach, while those who completed longer training and defended a masterwork of scholarship became "masters" and "doctors." The University of Paris gradually absorbed the city's various colleges,

**Renaissance (European)**  A period of intense artistic and intellectual activity, said to be a "rebirth" of Greco-Roman culture. Usually divided into an Italian Renaissance, from roughly the mid-fourteenth to mid-fifteenth century, and a Northern (trans-Alpine) Renaissance, from roughly the early fifteenth to early seventeenth century.

**universities**  Degree-granting institutions of higher learning. Those that appeared in the countries of western Europe from about 1200 onward became the model of all modern universities.

but the colleges of Oxford and Cambridge remained independent, self-governing organizations.

Since all universities used Latin, students and masters moved freely across political and linguistic borders, seeking the courses and professors they wanted. Some universities offered specialized training. Legal training centered on Bologna in Italy (buh-LOHN-yuh); Montpellier in southern France and Salerno in Sicily focused on medicine; Paris and Oxford excelled in theology.

Some topics, such as astronomy, were studied outside the university. Both Greek and Arabic traditions presumed that the planets traced circular orbits around the earth, the circle being a perfect geometrical figure. Celestial observations did not always fit this presumption, however. Fifteenth-century astronomers in both Europe and the lands of Islam theorized explanations for the observational deviations. At the very end of the fifteenth century, the Polish-German astronomer Nicolaus Copernicus (co-PER-ni-cus), basing his ideas mainly on the Greek Ptolemy but also aware of more recent writings in Arabic, hit on the idea of planets orbiting the sun instead of the earth. His work, finally published as he lay dying of a stroke in 1543, would pose a challenge to the church's assumption that the earth was the center of God's universe.

Though the new learning sometimes raised inconvenient questions, students aspiring to ecclesiastical careers, and their professors, conferred special prominence on theology, seen as the "queen of the sciences" encompassing all true knowledge. Hence, thirteenth-century theologians sought to reconcile the rediscovered philosophical works of Aristotle and the commentaries of Avicenna with the Bible's revealed truth. These efforts to synthesize reason and faith were known as **scholasticism** (skoh-LAS-tih-sizm).

Thomas Aquinas wrote the most notable scholastic work, the *Summa Theologica* (SOOM-uh thee-uh-LOH-jih-kuh), between 1267 and 1273. Although his exposition of Christian belief organized on Aristotelian principles came to be accepted as a masterly demonstration of the reasonableness of Christianity, scholasticism upset many traditional thinkers. Some church authorities tried to ban Aristotle from the curriculum. However, the considerable freedom of medieval universities from both secular and religious authorities enabled the new ideas to prevail over the fears of church administrators.

## Humanists and Printers

This period also saw important literary contributions. The Italian Dante Alighieri (DAHN-tay ah-lee-GYEH-ree) (1265–1321) completed a long, elegant poem, the *Divine Comedy*, shortly before his death. This supreme expression of medieval preoccupations tells the allegorical story of Dante's journey through the nine circles of Hell and the seven terraces of Purgatory, followed by his entry into Paradise. The Roman poet Virgil guides him through Hell and Purgatory; Beatrice, a woman he had loved from afar since childhood and whose death inspired the poem, guides him to Paradise.

The *Divine Comedy* foreshadows the literary fashions of the later Italian Renaissance. Like Dante, later Italian writers made use of Greco-Roman classical themes and mythology and sometimes courted a broader audience by writing not in Latin but in their local language (Dante used the vernacular spoken in Tuscany [TUS-kuh-nee]).

The poet Geoffrey Chaucer, many of whose works show the influence of Dante, wrote in vernacular English. The *Canterbury Tales*, a lengthy poem written in the last dozen years of his life, contains often humorous and earthy tales told by fictional pilgrims on their way to the shrine of Thomas à Becket in Canterbury (see Chapter 10). They present a vivid cross-section of medieval people and attitudes.

Dante influenced a literary movement of the **humanists** that began in his native Florence in the mid-fourteenth century. The term refers to their interest in grammar, rhetoric, poetry, history, and moral philosophy (ethics)—subjects known collectively as the humanities, an ancient discipline. With the brash exaggeration characteristic of new intellectual fashions, humanist writers like the poet Francesco Petrarch

**scholasticism** A philosophical and theological system, associated with Thomas Aquinas, devised to reconcile Aristotelian philosophy and Roman Catholic theology in the thirteenth century.

**humanists (Renaissance)** European scholars, writers, and teachers associated with the study of the humanities (grammar, rhetoric, poetry, history, languages, and moral philosophy), influential in the fifteenth century and later.

**Dante's *Divine Comedy*** This fifteenth-century painting by Domenico di Michelino shows Dante holding a copy of the *Divine Comedy*. Hell is depicted to the poet's right and the terraces of Purgatory behind him, surmounted by the earthly and heavenly Paradise. The city of Florence, with its recently completed cathedral, appears to Dante's left.

(fran-CHES-koh PAY-trahrk) (1304–1374) and the poet and storyteller Giovanni Boccaccio (jo-VAH-nee boh-KAH-chee-oh) (1313–1375) proclaimed a revival of a Greco-Roman tradition they felt had for centuries lain buried under the rubble of post-Roman decay.

This idea of a rebirth of learning dismisses too readily the monastic and university scholars who for centuries had been recovering all sorts of Greco-Roman learning, as well as writers like Dante (whom the humanists revered), who anticipated humanist interests by a generation. Yet the humanists had a great impact as educators, advisers, and reformers. Their greatest influence came in reforming secondary education. They introduced a curriculum centered on the languages and literature of Greco-Roman antiquity, which they felt provided intellectual discipline, moral lessons, and refined tastes. This curriculum dominated European secondary schools well into the twentieth century.

Many humanists tried to duplicate the elegance of classical Latin and (to a lesser extent) Greek, which they revered as the pinnacle of learning, beauty, and wisdom. Boccaccio gained fame with his vernacular writings, which resemble Dante's, and especially for the *Decameron*, an earthy work that has much in common with Chaucer's boisterous tales. Under Petrarch's influence, however, Boccaccio turned to writing in classical Latin.

As humanist scholars mastered Latin and Greek, they turned their language skills to restoring the original texts of Greco-Roman writers and of the Bible. By comparing different manuscripts, they eliminated errors introduced by generations of copyists. To aid in this task, Pope Nicholas V (r. 1447–1455) created the Vatican Library, buying scrolls of Greco-Roman writings and paying to have accurate copies and translations made. Working independently, the Dutch scholar Erasmus (uh-RAZ-muhs) of Rotterdam

**A French Printshop, 1537** A workman operates the "press," quite literally a screw device that presses the paper to the inked type. Other employees examine the printed sheets, each of which holds four pages. When folded and sewn together, the sheets make a book. The man on the right is selecting pieces of type from a compartmented box and placing them in a frame for printing.

The Art Archive

(ca. 1466–1536) produced a critical edition of the New Testament in Greek. Erasmus corrected many errors and mistranslations in the Latin text that had been in general use throughout the Middle Ages.

The influence of the humanists grew as the new technology of printing made their critical editions of ancient texts, literary works, and moral guides more available. The Chinese and the Arabs used carved woodblocks for printing, and block-printed playing cards circulated in Europe before 1450, but after that date three European improvements revolutionized printing: (1) movable pieces of type consisting of individual letters, independently invented in Korea (see Chapter 12), (2) walnut oil-based ink suitable for printing on paper without smearing, and (3) the

**printing press**, a mechanical device that pressed sheets of paper onto inked type.

Johann Gutenberg (yoh-HAHN GOO-ten-burg) (ca. 1394–1468) of Mainz led the way. The Gutenberg Bible of 1454, the first book in the West printed from movable type, exhibited a beauty and craftsmanship testifying to the printer's years of experimentation. Humanists worked closely with the printers, who spread the new techniques to Italy and France. Erasmus did editing and proofreading for the Venetian

**printing press** A mechanical device for transferring text or graphics from a woodblock or type to paper using ink. Presses using movable type first appeared in Europe in about 1450.

scholar-printer Aldo Manuzio (1449–1515), whose press published many critical editions of classical Latin and Greek texts.

By 1500, at least 10 million printed volumes flowed from presses in 238 European towns, launching a revolution that affected students, scholars, and a growing literate population. These readers consumed unorthodox political and religious tracts along with ancient texts.

### Renaissance Artists

Although the artists of the fourteenth and fifteenth centuries continued to depict biblical subjects, the Greco-Roman revival led some, especially in Italy, to portray ancient deities and myths. Another popular trend involved scenes of daily life.

Neither theme was entirely new, however. Renaissance art, like Renaissance scholarship, owed a debt to earlier generations. Italian painters of the fifteenth century credited the Florentine painter Giotto (JAW-toh) (ca. 1267–1337) with single-handedly reviving the "lost art of painting." In religious scenes, Giotto replaced the stiff, staring figures of the Byzantine style, which were intended to overawe viewers, with more natural and human portraits with whose depictions of grief and love viewers could identify. Rather than floating on backgrounds of gold leaf, his saints inhabit earthly landscapes. North of the Alps, the Flemish painter Jan van Eyck (yahn vahn IKE) (ca. 1390–1441) mixed his pigments with linseed oil in place of the usual egg yolk. Oil paints dried more slowly and gave pictures a superior luster. Italian painters quickly copied van Eyck's technique, though his own masterfully realistic paintings on religious and domestic themes remained distinctive.

Leonardo da Vinci (lay-own-AHR-doh dah-VIN-chee) (1452–1519) used oil paints for his *Mona Lisa*. Renaissance artists like Leonardo worked in many media, including bronze sculptures and frescos (painting on wet plaster) like *The Last Supper*. Leonardo's notebooks also contain imaginative designs for airplanes, submarines, and tanks. His younger contemporary Michelangelo (my-kuhl-AN-juh-low) (1472–1564) painted frescoes of biblical scenes on the ceiling of the Sistine Chapel in the Vatican, sculpted

**SECTION REVIEW**

- Greco-Roman learning returned to the Latin countries of Europe through a series of revivals that culminated with the Renaissance.

- An infusion of Greek and Islamic scholarship during the eleventh century helped to prompt the revival of the twelfth and thirteenth centuries.

- Colleges and universities grew, with theology as the preeminent discipline.

- Foreshadowed by Dante, humanism, with its focus on classical languages, literature, ethics, and education, emerged in Italy.

- The influence of the humanists spread through the new print technology.

- Renaissance artists enlarged the thematic and technical resources of painting, sculpture, and architecture.

statues of David and Moses, and designed the dome for a new Saint Peter's Basilica in Rome.

The patronage of wealthy and educated merchants and prelates underlay the artistic blossoming in the cities of northern Italy and Flanders. The Florentine banker Cosimo de' Medici (1389–1464) and his grandson Lorenzo (1449–1492), known as "the Magnificent," spent immense sums on paintings, sculpture, and public buildings. In Rome, the papacy (PAY-puh-see) launched a building program that culminated in the construction of the new Saint Peter's Basilica and a residence for the pope.

These scholarly and artistic achievements exemplify the innovation and striving for excellence of the late Middle Ages. The new literary themes and artistic styles of this period had lasting influence on Western culture. But the innovations in the organization of universities, in printing, and in scientific thought had wider implications, for they were later adopted by cultures all over the world.

## POLITICAL AND MILITARY TRANSFORMATIONS

■ *What social, political, and military developments contributed to the rise of European nations in this period?*

Stronger and more unified states and armies developed in Europe in parallel with the economic and cultural revivals. Crusades against Muslim states brought consolidation to Spain and Portugal. In Italy and Germany, however, political power remained in the hands of small states and loose alliances. Farther to the east, Lithuania, dynastically linked to Poland, became one of Europe's largest states while Hungary confronted the Ottoman Empire.

## Monarchs, Nobles, and the Church

Thirteenth-century states continued early medieval state structures (see Chapter 10). Hereditary monarchs topped the political pyramid, but modest treasuries and the rights of nobles and the church limited their powers. Powerful noblemen who controlled vast estates had an important voice in matters of state. The church guarded closely its traditional rights and independence. Towns, too, had acquired rights and privileges. Towns in Flanders, the Hanseatic League, and Italy approached independence from royal interference. In theory the ruler's noble vassals owed military service in time of war. In practice, vassals sought to limit the monarch's power.

In the year 1200, knights still formed the backbone of European armies, but improved crossbows could shoot metal-tipped arrows with enough force to pierce helmets and light body armor. Professional crossbowmen, hired for wages, became increasingly common and much feared. Indeed, a church council in 1139 outlawed the crossbow—ineffectively—as being too deadly for use against Christians. The arrival in Europe of firearms based on the Chinese invention of gunpowder (see Chapter 12) further transformed the medieval army, first on the Ottoman frontier and then further west.

The church also resisted royal control. In 1302, the outraged Pope Boniface VIII (r. 1294–1303) asserted that divine law made the papacy superior to "every human creature," including monarchs. King Philip "the Fair" of France (r. 1285–1314) responded by sending an army to arrest the pope, a chastisement that hastened Pope Boniface's death. Philip then engineered the election of a French pope, who established a new papal residence at Avignon (ah-vee-NYON) in southern France in 1309.

A succession of French-dominated popes residing in Avignon improved church discipline but at the price of compromising papal neutrality. The **Great Western Schism** between 1378 and 1415 saw rival papal claimants at Avignon and Rome vying for Christian loyalties. The papacy eventually regained its independence and returned to Rome, but the long crisis broke the pope's ability to challenge the rising power of monarchs like Philip.

The English monarchy wielded more centralized power as a result of consolidation that took place after the Norman conquest of 1066. Between 1200 and 1400, the Anglo-Norman kings incorporated Wales and reasserted control over most of Ireland. Nevertheless, under King John (r. 1199–1216), royal power suffered a severe setback. Forced to acknowledge the pope as his overlord in 1213, he lost his bid to reassert claims to Aquitaine in southern France the following year and then yielded to his nobles by signing the Magna Carta in 1215. This "Great Charter" affirmed that monarchs were subject to established law, confirmed the independence of the church and the city of London, and guaranteed the nobles' hereditary rights.

## The Hundred Years' War

The conflict between the king of France and his vassals known as the **Hundred Years' War** (1337–1453) grew out of a marriage alliance between Princess Isabella of France and King Edward II of England (r. 1307–1327). Because Edward was a vassal who had inherited French lands from his Norman ancestors, the marriage should have ensured his loyalty. However, when the French royal line produced no other sons, Isabella's son, King Edward III of England (r. 1327–1377), laid claim to the French throne in 1337.

Early in the war, hired Italian crossbowmen reinforced the French cavalry, but the English longbow proved superior. Adopted from the Welsh, the 6-foot (1.8-meter) longbow could shoot farther and more rapidly than the crossbow. Its arrows could not pierce armor, but concentrated volleys found gaps in

> **Great Western Schism**  A division in the Latin (Western) Christian Church between 1378 and 1415, when rival claimants to the papacy existed in Rome and Avignon.
>
> **Hundred Years' War (1337–1453)**  Series of campaigns over control of the throne of France, involving English and French royal families and French noble families.

the knights' defenses or struck their less-protected horses. Heavier and more encompassing armor provided a defense but limited a knight's movements. Once pulled off his steed by a foot soldier armed with a pike (hooked pole), he could not get up.

Later in the Hundred Years' War, firearms gained prominence. The first cannon scared the horses with smoke and noise but did little damage. As they grew larger, however, they proved effective in battering the walls of castles and towns. The first artillery use against the French, at the Battle of Agincourt (1415), gave the English an important victory.

Faced with a young French peasant woman called Joan of Arc, subsequent English gains stalled. Acting, she believed, on God's instructions, she put on armor and rallied the French troops to defeat the English in 1429. Shortly afterward, she fell into English hands; she was tried by English churchmen and burned at the stake as a witch in 1431.

In the final battles, French cannon demolished the walls of once-secure castles held by the English and their allies. Armies now depended less on knights and more on bowmen, pikemen, musketeers, and artillerymen.

The war proved a watershed in the rise of **new monarchies** in France and England, centralized states with fixed "national" boundaries and stronger representative institutions. English monarchs after 1453 consolidated control over territory within the British Isles, though the Scots defended their independence. The French monarchs also turned to consolidating control over powerful noble families in Burgundy and Brittany.

The new monarchies needed a way to finance their full-time armies. Some nobles agreed to money payments in place of military service and to additional taxes in time of war. For example, in 1439 and 1445, Charles VII of France (r. 1422–1461) successfully levied a new tax on his vassals' land. This not only paid the costs of the war with England but also gave the monarchy a financial base for the next 350 years.

Merchants' taxes also provided revenues. Taxes on the English wool trade, begun by King Edward III, paid most of the costs of the Hundred Years' War. Some rulers taxed Jewish merchants or extorted large

contributions from wealthy towns. Individual merchants sometimes curried royal favor with loans. The fifteenth-century French merchant Jacques Coeur (cur) gained many social and financial benefits for himself and his family by lending money to French courtiers, but his debtors accused him of murder and had his fortune confiscated.

In the west, the church provided a third source of revenue through voluntary contributions to support a war. English and French monarchs won the right to appoint important church officials in their realms in the fifteenth century. In the east, religion became increasingly a political issue as Catholic Lithuania fought a series of wars with Orthodox Russia with little regard for which faith the common people adhered to.

The shift in power to the monarchs and away from the nobility and the church did not deprive nobles of their social position and roles as government officials and military officers. Moreover, the kings of England and France in 1500 had to deal with representative institutions that had not existed in 1200. The English Parliament proved a permanent check on royal power: the House of Lords contained the great nobles and church officials; the House of Commons represented the towns and the leading citizens of the counties. In France, the Estates General, a similar but less effective representative body, represented the church, the nobles, and the towns.

## Iberian Unification

Spain and Portugal's **reconquest of Iberia** from Muslim rule expanded the boundaries of Latin Christianity. The knights who pushed the borders of their kingdoms southward furthered both Christianity and their own interests. The spoils of victory included irrigated farmland, rich cities, and ports on

**new monarchies** Historians' term for the monarchies in France, England, and Spain from 1450 to 1600. The centralization of royal power was increasing within more or less fixed territorial limits.

**reconquest of Iberia** Beginning in the eleventh century, military campaigns by various Iberian Christian states to recapture territory taken by Muslims. In 1492 the last Muslim ruler was defeated, and Spain and Portugal emerged as united kingdoms.

the Mediterranean Sea and Atlantic Ocean. Serving God, growing rich, and living off the labor of others became a way of life for the Iberian nobility.

The reconquest took several centuries. Toledo fell and became a Christian outpost in 1085. In 1147 English Crusaders bound for the Holy Land helped take Lisbon, which then displaced the older city of Oporto (meaning "the port"), from which Portugal took its name, as both capital and the kingdom's leading city. After a Christian victory in 1212 broke the back of Muslim power, the reconquest accelerated. Within decades, Portuguese and Castilian forces captured the prosperous cities of Cordova (1236) and Seville (1248) and drove the Muslims from the southwestern region known as Algarve (ahl-GAHRV) ("the west" in Arabic). Only the small kingdom of Granada hugging the Mediterranean coast remained in Muslim hands.

By incorporating Algarve in 1249, Portugal attained its modern territorial limits. After a pause to colonize, forcibly Christianize, and consolidate this land, Portugal took the crusade to North Africa. In 1415, Portuguese knights seized the port of Ceuta (say-OO-tuh) in Morocco, where they learned more about the Saharan caravan trade in gold and slaves. During the next few decades, Portuguese mariners sailed down the Atlantic coast of Africa seeking rumored African Christian allies and access to this trade (see Chapter 15).

Elsewhere in Iberia, the reconquest continued. Princess Isabella of Castile married Prince Ferdinand of Aragon in 1469. A decade later, when they inherited their respective thrones, the two kingdoms united to become Spain. Their conquest of Granada in 1492 secured the final piece of Muslim territory for the new kingdom.

Ferdinand and Isabella sponsored the first voyage of Christopher Columbus in 1492 (see Chapter 15). In a third momentous event of that year, the monarchs expelled the Jews from their kingdoms. Attempts to convert or expel the remaining Muslims led to a revolt at the end of 1499 that lasted until 1501. The Spanish rulers expelled the last Muslims in 1502. Portugal expelled the Jews in 1496, including 100,000 refugees from Spain. For some time afterward the Spanish Inquisition, a tribunal established by the two monarchs, exerted itself in identifying and punishing

**SECTION REVIEW**

- Between 1200 and 1500, monarchs, nobles, and the church struggled over political power.
- Tensions between the French monarchy and the papacy resulted in the Great Western Schism.
- In England, royal power was checked by the papacy and nobility, the latter imposing the Magna Carta on King John.
- The Hundred Years' War between the French monarchy and its vassals introduced new military technologies.
- The war also stimulated the rise of the new centralized monarchies of England and France.
- Spain and Portugal continued the reconquest of Muslim Iberia, a process completed by Ferdinand and Isabella even as the Muslim Ottomans expanded their rule in the east.

Jews, called *Marranos*, and Muslims, called *Moriscos*, who had nominally converted to Christianity but secretly retained their old, forbidden faiths.

## The Ottoman Frontier

As Islam receded in the west, it advanced in the east as the Ottoman Empire (see Chapter 12) inflicted defeat after defeat on the Christian Balkan kingdoms. The Ottoman military was balanced between cavalry archers, primarily Turks, and slave infantrymen armed with hand-held firearms.

Slave soldiery had a long history in Islamic lands (see Chapter 9), but the conquest of the Balkans in the late fourteenth century gave the Ottomans access to a new military resource: Christian prisoners of war enslaved and converted to Islam. These "new troops," called *yeni cheri* in Turkish and *Janissaries* (JAN-i-say-ree) in English, gave the Ottomans unusual military flexibility. Not coming from a nomadic background like the Turks, they readily accepted the idea of fighting on foot and learning to use guns, which at that time were still too heavy and awkward for a horseman to load and fire. The Janissaries lived in barracks and trained all year round.

The process of selection for Janissary training changed early in the fifteenth century. The new system, called the *devshirme*, imposed a regular levy of male children on Christian villages in the Balkans. Selected children were placed with Turkish families to learn their language and then sent to Istanbul for instruction in Islam, military training, and, for the most talented, opportunities to become senior military commanders and heads of government departments. The Christian European contest between nobles, monarchs, and church authorities scarcely existed in the Ottoman realm.

## CONCLUSION

For seven hundred years after the fall of Rome, western Europe was impoverished economically and culturally compared to the Roman Empire at its height, but also and more importantly, compared to the Byzantine Empire, to the Muslim empires, and to China and India during the same period. At the same time that the Ottomans were expanding their borders in the East, division, disasters, and wars characterized the "Latins" of Europe. Farming techniques were inefficient and farming communities near starvation. But from this unlikely place emerged a new more powerful and prosperous Europe,

with kingdoms and their borders forerunners of modern nation-states.

Technological innovation and learning transformed Europe. Crossbows, then gunpowder technology from China, changed the nature of warfare. New wind and water mills substituted inanimate energy for human and animal labor. Farmers increased their yields by planting more of their land and using horses in place of oxen. Commercial expansion, mines, and deforestation took a toll on the land, but the growth of cities, guilds, and banking changed the economy of Europe. Europe became an amalgam of trading cities where now even the textile trade, once an Eastern specialty, surpassed that of the East.

The universities of the later Middle Ages multiplied across Europe, spreading Muslim and classical Greco-Roman knowledge through the common Latin language and invigorating an interest in humanism. The printing press brought learning and literature to more people, and the courts and the church patronized artists, writers, and musicians and built beautiful new buildings. Though the Black Death had decimated the population and set the economy back many decades, by 1500 Europe had rebounded and was preparing to expand beyond the oceans.

## CHAPTER REVIEW

### RURAL GROWTH AND CRISIS

■ *How well did inhabitants of western Europe, rich and poor, urban and rural, deal with their natural environment?* (page 307)

Ecologically, the peoples of western Europe harnessed the power of wind and water and mined and refined their mineral wealth at the cost of localized pollution and deforestation. However, the inability to improve food production and distribution in response to population growth created a demographic crisis that climaxed with the Black Death, which devastated Europe in the mid-fourteenth century.

### URBAN REVIVAL

■ *What social and economic factors led to the growth of cities in late medieval Europe?* (page 312)

Politically, basic features of the modern European state began to emerge. Frequent wars caused kingdoms of moderate size to develop exceptional military strength. The ruling class saw economic strength as the twin of political power and promoted commercial activities such as trade, manufacturing, and finance in the cities, the profits of which they taxed.

## LEARNING, LITERATURE, AND THE RENAISSANCE

■ *What factors were responsible for the promotion of learning and the arts in Europe?* (page 318)

Culturally, autonomous universities and printing supported the advance of knowledge though merchant cities also produced a class of literate and leisured individuals. Art and architecture reached unsurpassed peaks in the Renaissance with major innovations in visual styles and building techniques. Late medieval society also displayed a fundamental fascination with luxury goods and manufacturing techniques, many of them acquired from the Muslim world and adapted to a more prosperous and sophisticated consumer society.

## POLITICAL AND MILITARY TRANSFORMATIONS

■ *What social, political, and military developments contributed to the rise of European nations in this period?* (page 322)

Many of the tools that western Europe would use to challenge Eastern supremacy—printing, firearms, and navigational devices—originally came from the East. However, western European success depended as much on strong motives for expansion. From the eleventh century onward, population pressure, religious zeal, economic enterprise, and intellectual curiosity drove an expansion of territory and resources that took the Crusaders to the Holy Land, merchants to the eastern Mediterranean and Black Seas, the English into Wales and Ireland, German settlers across the Elbe River, and Iberian Christians into the Muslim south. The early voyages into the Atlantic, discussed in Chapter 15, extended these activities.

## Key Terms

three-field system (p. 308)

Black Death (p. 309)

Hanseatic League (p. 313)

guild (p. 314)

Gothic cathedrals (p. 315)

Renaissance (European) (p. 318)

universities (p. 318)

scholasticism (p. 319)

humanists (Renaissance) (p. 319)

printing press (p. 321)

Great Western Schism (p. 323)

Hundred Years' War (p. 323)

new monarchies (p. 324)

reconquest of Iberia (p. 324)

# Southern Empires, Southern Seas

© Cengage Learning

**S**ultan Abu Bakr (a-BOO BAK-uhr) customarily offered hospitality to distinguished visitors to his city of Mogadishu, an Indian Ocean port on the northeast coast of Africa. In 1331, he provided food and lodging for Muhammad ibn Abdullah **Ibn Battuta** (IB-uhn ba-TOO-tuh) (1304–1369), a young Muslim scholar from Morocco who had set out to explore the Islamic world. With a pilgrimage to Mecca and travel throughout the Middle East behind him, Ibn Battuta was touring the trading cities of the Red Sea and East Africa. Subsequent travels took him to Central Asia and India, China and Southeast Asia, Muslim Spain, and sub-Saharan West Africa. Recounting some 75,000 miles (120,000 kilometers) of travel over twenty-nine years, Ibn Battuta's journal provides invaluable information on these lands.

Hospitality being considered a noble virtue among Muslims, regardless of physical and cultural differences, the reception at Mogadishu mirrored that at other cities. Ibn Battuta noted that Sultan Abu Bakr had skin darker than his own and spoke a different native language (Somali), but as brothers in faith, they prayed together at Friday services, where the sultan greeted his foreign guest in Arabic, the common language of the Islamic world: "You are heartily welcome, and you have honored our land and given us pleasure." When Sultan Abu Bakr and his jurists heard and decided cases after the mosque service, they used the religious law familiar in all Muslim lands.

Islam aside, the most basic links among the diverse peoples of Africa and southern Asia derived from the tropical environment itself. A network of overland and maritime routes joined their territories, providing avenues for the spread of beliefs, technologies, and goods. Ibn Battuta sailed with merchants down the coast of East Africa and joined trading caravans across the Sahara from Morocco to West Africa. His path to India followed overland trade routes, and a merchant ship carried him on to China.

Maritime routes would also prove critical in connecting the Old World to the Western Hemisphere and its unique agricultural products from diverse high-altitude tropical microclimates. Working with simple stone tools, the Aztecs and Inka cre-

ated remarkable monuments and urban centers and a vast trading network—without the use of horses or camels. Virtually isolated from the rest of the world, these empires were the culmination of long historical developments in Mesoamerica and the Andes.

## TROPICAL AFRICA AND ASIA

■ *How did environmental differences shape cultural differences in tropical Africa and Asia?*

The tropical regions of Africa and Asia shared environmental similarities but differed markedly in their interactions with other parts of the world (see Chapter 8). The western regions of Africa were semi-isolated by the Atlantic Ocean and Sahara Desert, while Africa's east coast was in maritime contact with the lands bordering the Indian Ocean. Overland routes through Afghanistan to the Middle East and Central Asia affected India and in turn influenced developments in both mainland and island Southeast Asia.

### The Tropical Environment in Africa and Asia

Because of the angle of the earth's axis, the sun's rays warm the **tropics** year-round. The equator marks the center of the tropical zone, and the Tropic of Cancer and Tropic of Capricorn its outer limits. Africa lies almost entirely within the tropics, as do southern Arabia, most of India, and both mainland and island Southeast Asia. In the Western Hemisphere (discussed later in this chapter) the regions that produced the earliest civilizations, Mesoamerica and the Andes and Pacific coast of South America, also lay in the tropics.

Lacking the hot and cold seasons of temperate lands, the rainy and dry seasons of the Afro-Asian tropics derive from atmospheric patterns across the surrounding oceans. Winds flow away from areas

---

**Ibn Battuta** Moroccan Muslim scholar, the most widely traveled individual of his time. He wrote a detailed account of his visits to Islamic lands from China to Spain and the western Sudan.

**tropics** Equatorial region between the Tropic of Cancer and the Tropic of Capricorn. It is characterized by generally warm or hot temperatures year-round, though much variation exists due to altitude and other factors. Temperate zones north and south of the tropics generally have a winter season.

of high atmospheric pressure toward areas of low pressure. The earth's rotation causes these winds to move in a clockwise direction (anticyclone) north of the equator and a counterclockwise direction south of the equator. Thus a permanent high-pressure air mass over the South Atlantic delivers heavy rainfall to the western coast of Africa during much of the year. However, in December and January, large high-pressure zones over northern Africa and Arabia produce a southward movement of dry air that limits the inland penetration of the moist ocean winds.

In the lands around the Indian Ocean, the rainy and dry seasons reflect the influence of alternating winds known as **monsoons**. A gigantic high-pressure zone over the Himalaya (him-AH-la-yuh) Mountains peaks from December to March, producing southern Asia's dry season by forcing strong southward and westward air movements (the northeast monsoon) in the western Indian Ocean. Between April and August, a low-pressure zone over India reverses the process by drawing moist oceanic air from the south and west (the southwest monsoon) and brings southern Asia the heavy rains of its wet season, called the monsoon season.

Areas with the heaviest rainfall—the broad belt along the equator in coastal West Africa and West-Central Africa, parts of coastal India, and Southeast Asia—have dense rain forests. Lighter rains produce other forest patterns. The English word *jungle* comes from an Indian word for the tangled undergrowth in the forests that once covered most of tropical India.

Some other parts of the tropics rarely see rain at all. The world's largest desert, the Sahara, stretches across northern Africa and continues eastward across Arabia, southern Iran, Pakistan, and northwest India. Another desert occupies southwestern Africa. Tropical India and Africa fall mostly between the deserts and rain forests and experience moderate rainy seasons. These lands range from fairly wet woodlands to the much drier grasslands characteristic of much of East Africa.

Altitude produces other climatic variations. Thin atmospheres at high altitudes hold less heat than atmospheres at lower elevations. Snow covers some of the volcanic peaks of eastern Africa all or part of the year. The snowcapped Himalayas that form India's northern frontier rise so high that they block cold air

from moving south, giving northern India a more tropical climate than its latitude would suggest. The plateaus of inland Africa and the Deccan (DEK-uhn) Plateau of central India also enjoy cooler temperatures than the coastal plains.

## Human Ecosystems

A careful observer touring the tropics in 1200 would have noticed how different societies used the plants, animals, and other resources of their physical environments. Some peoples continued to rely primarily on hunting, fishing, and gathering and lived in small, mobile groups. For Pygmy (PIG-mee) hunters in the dense forests of Central Africa, small size permitted pursuit of prey through dense undergrowth. Hunting also prevailed among some inland groups in Borneo, New Guinea, and the Philippines.

A Portuguese expedition led by Vasco da Gama visited the arid coast of southwestern Africa in 1497 and saw there a healthy group of people feeding themselves on "the flesh of seals, whales, and gazelles, and the roots of wild plants." Fishing, which was common along all the major lakes and rivers as well as in the oceans, could be combined with farming or with ocean trade, particularly in Southeast Asia.

Depending on what a particular ecosystem can support, the density of population can also vary greatly. Herding provided sustenance in areas too arid for agriculture. Pastoralists consumed milk and sometimes blood from their herds but did not eat a lot of meat since their animals were of greater value to them alive than dead. The deserts of northern Africa and Arabia had small populations that ranged widely with their camels, goats, and donkeys. Some, like the Tuareg (TWAH-reg) of the western Sahara, proved invaluable as caravan guides because of their intimate knowledge of the desert. Along the Sahara's southern edge the cattle-herding Fulani (foo-LAH-nee) gradually extended their range until by 1500

**monsoon** Seasonal winds in the Indian Ocean caused by the differences in temperature between the rapidly heating and cooling landmasses of Africa and Asia and the slowly changing ocean waters. These strong and predictable winds have long been ridden across the open sea by sailors, and the large amounts of rainfall that they deposit on parts of India, Southeast Asia, and China allow for the cultivation of several crops a year.

# Chronology

| | Tropical Africa | Tropical Asia | Western Hemisphere |
|---|---|---|---|
| 1200 | **1230s** Mali Empire founded<br>**1270** Solomonic dynasty in Ethiopia founded | **1206** Delhi Sultanate founded in India<br>**1298** Delhi Sultanate annexes Gujarat | |
| 1300 | **1324–1325** Mansa Musa's pilgrimage to Mecca | **1398** Timur sacks Delhi; Delhi Sultanate declines | **1300** Aztec capital Tenochtitlan founded |
| 1400 | **1400s** Great Zimbabwe at its peak<br><br>**1433** Tuareg retake Timbuktu; Mali declines | **1430s** Inka expansion begins | |
| 1500 | | **1500** Port of Malacca at its peak | **1500–1525** Inka conquer Ecuador<br>**1502** Moctezuma II crowned Aztec ruler |

they had spread throughout the western and central Sudan. Other cattle herders lived on either side of the Nile in Sudan and in Somalia.

Pastoral groups in India were fewer and located mostly in the Himalayas or the deserts of the northwest. In contrast, South and Southeast Asia's wet climate favored intensive cultivation, and high yields supported dense populations. In 1200, over 100 million people lived in South and Southeast Asia, more than four-fifths of them on the fertile Indian mainland— a little less than the population of China, nearly double the population of Europe, and triple the population in all of Africa.

Rice cultivation dominated in the fertile Ganges Plain of northeast India, mainland Southeast Asia, and southern China. In drier areas, farmers grew grains—wheat, sorghum, and millet—and legumes such as peas and beans whose ripening cycles matched the pattern of the rainy and dry seasons. Tree crops, such as kola nuts in West Africa, coconuts in Southeast Asia, and bananas everywhere, made major contributions to the diet, as did the root crops characteristic of rain forest clearings.

The spread of farming, including the movement to Africa of Indo-Malayan bananas and root crops like yams and cocoyams, also known as taro, did not necessarily change the natural environment. In most of sub-Saharan Africa and much of Southeast Asia, extensive rather than intensive cultivation prevailed. Instead of enriching fields with manure and vegetable compost so they could be cultivated year after year, farmers abandoned fields when the natural fertility of the soil fell and cleared new fields. Ashes from the brush, grasses, and tree limbs they cut down and burned boosted the new fields' fertility. Shifting to new land every few years made efficient use of labor in areas with comparatively poor soils and abundant space.

## Water Systems and Irrigation

In the inland delta of the Niger River in West Africa, naturally fertilizing annual floods enabled farmers to grow rice for sale to the trading cities along the Niger bend. However, in India and Southeast Asia, many tropical farmers had to bring water to their crops. Conserving some of the monsoon rainfall for use during the dry season helped in Vietnam, Java, Malaya, and Burma (now Myanmar), which had terraced hillsides with special water-control systems for growing rice. Villagers in southeast India built stone and earthen dams across rivers to store water for gradual release through elaborate irrigation canals. Similar dam and canal systems supplied water farther north.

As had been true since the first river-valley civilizations (see Chapter 1), governments built and controlled the largest irrigation systems. The **Delhi** (DEL-ee) **Sultanate** (1206–1526) in northern India developed extensive new water-control systems. One large reservoir had fields of sugar cane, cucumbers, and melons planted along its rim as the water level fell during the dry season. Irrigation canals built in the Ganges Plain in the fourteenth century remained unsurpassed for five hundred years. Such systems made it possible to grow crops throughout the year.

Since the tenth century, the island of Ceylon (ancient Serandip; modern Sri Lanka [sree LAHNG-kuh]) off India's southern tip possessed the world's greatest concentration of irrigation reservoirs and canals.

**East African Pastoralists**  Herding large and small livestock has long been a way of life in drier parts of the tropics.

These facilities supported a large Sinhalese-speaking (sin-huh-LEEZ) kingdom in arid northern Ceylon. In Southeast Asia, another impressive system of reservoirs and canals served Cambodia's capital city, Angkor (ANG-kor).

Eventually both these systems deteriorated. Between 1250 and 1400, the irrigation complex in Ceylon fell into ruin when invaders from south India disrupted the Sinhalese government. As a result, malaria spread by mosquitoes breeding in the irrigation canals ravaged the population. In the fifteenth century, the great Cambodian system fell into ruin when the government that maintained it collapsed. Neither system was ever rebuilt. The vulnerability of complex irrigation systems built by powerful governments contrasts with village-based irrigation systems. Invasion and natural calamity might damage the latter, but they usually bounced back because they depended on local initiative and simpler technologies.

## Mineral Resources

Between 1200 and 1500, as the rain forests of coastal West Africa and Southeast Asia opened up for farming, ironworking provided the hoes, axes, and knives farmers used to clear and cultivate their fields. Iron also supplied spear and arrow points, needles, and nails. Indian armorers became known for forging strong and beautiful swords. In Africa, many people attributed magical powers to iron smelters and blacksmiths.

The Copperbelt of southeastern Africa came into prominence during the fourteenth and fifteenth centuries. Smelters cast the metal into large X-shaped ingots (metal castings) that local coppersmiths worked into wire and decorative objects. A mining town in the western Sudan visited by Ibn Battuta produced two sizes of copper bars that served as currency in place of coins. Coppersmiths in the West African city of Ife (now in southern Nigeria) cast highly realistic copper and brass (an alloy of copper and zinc) statues and heads that now rank as masterpieces of world art. They utilized the "lost-wax" method, in which molten metal melts a thin layer of wax sandwiched between clay forms, replacing the "lost" wax with hard metal.

African gold moved in quantity across the Sahara and into the Indian Ocean and Red Sea trades. Some came from streambeds along the upper Niger River and in modern Ghana (GAH-nuh). Far to the south, beyond the Zambezi (zam-BEE-zee) River (in modern Zimbabwe [zim-BAHB-way]), archaeologists have discovered thousands of mineshafts, dating from 1200, that were sunk up to 100 feet (30 meters) into the ground to get at gold ores. In northern India, panning

**Delhi Sultanate**  Centralized Indian empire of varying extent, created by Muslim invaders.

- The environment of tropical Africa and Asia is governed by wind patterns across oceans and the resulting rainfall.

- Deserts and rain forests mark the extreme climate variations in these regions, while mountain ranges produce further variations.

- Depending on the regional environment, people fed themselves mainly through hunting and gathering, herding, or farming.

- In West Africa, India, and Southeast Asia, human societies depended on river and irrigation systems of varying complexity.

- Iron, copper, and gold were central to the local economies and long-distance trade systems of tropical Africa and Asia.

for gold remained important in the streams descending from the mountains, but India's gold and silver mines seem to have been exhausted by this period. Thus, Indians imported considerable quantities of gold for jewelry and temple decoration from Iran and the Ottoman Empire, as well as from Southeast Asia and Africa.

# NEW ISLAMIC EMPIRES

■ *Under what circumstances did the first Islamic empires arise in Africa and India?*

Despite the Mongol destruction of the Baghdad caliphate in 1258 (see Chapter 12), Islam continued to spread. In fact, the territorial expansion of Islam between 1200 and 1500 exceeded the Arab conquests of the seventh century. The Ottoman conquests in Europe extended Muslim domains in the Mediterranean heartland, but most of the expansion took place in the Muslim south in Africa, South Asia, and Southeast Asia.

The empires of Mali in West Africa and Delhi in northern India formed the largest and richest tropical states during Islam's second period of expansion. Both utilized administrative and military systems introduced from the Islamic heartland. **Mali**, an indigenous African dynasty that rose in the 1230s, grew out of the peaceful influence of Muslim merchants and scholars, while the Delhi Sultanate was founded and ruled by invading Turkish and Afghan Muslims.

## Mali in the Western Sudan

Muslim rule in North Africa beginning in the seventh century (see Chapter 9) greatly stimulated trade across the Sahara. In the centuries that followed, the faith of Muhammad spread slowly to the lands south of the desert, which the Arabs called the *bilad al-sudan* (bih-LAD uhs-soo-DAN), "land of the blacks."

Muslim Berbers invading out of the desert in 1076 caused the collapse of Ghana, the empire that preceded Mali in the western Sudan (see Chapter 9). Takrur (TAHK-roor), a kingdom on the Atlantic coast whose king had become the first sub-Saharan ruler to adopt Islam in the 1030s, allied with the invaders but remained a small state when the Berbers' interests in Morocco and Spain drew their attention away from the sub-Saharan region. Farther east, a truce that had endured since 652 between Christian Nubia along the Nile and Muslim Egypt fell apart in the thirteenth century as the Mamluks of Cairo made repeated attacks (see Chapter 9). The small Christian kingdoms weakened and fell over the next two centuries, but Christian Ethiopia successfully withstood Muslim advances. In general, however, Islam's spread south of the Sahara followed a pattern of gradual and peaceful conversion. The expansion of commercial contacts in the western Sudan and on the East African coast greatly promoted the conversion process.

Shortly after 1200, Takrur expanded under King Sumanguru (soo-muhn-GOO-roo), only to suffer a major defeat some thirty years later at the hands of Sundiata (soon-JAH-tuh), the upstart leader of the Malinke (muh-LING-kay) people. Though both leaders professed Islam, Malinke legends recall their battles as clashes between powerful magicians, suggesting how much old and new beliefs mingled. Sumanguru could reportedly appear and disappear at will, assume dozens of shapes, and catch arrows in midflight. Sundiata defeated Sumanguru's much larger forces through superior military maneuvers and by wounding his adversary with a special arrow that robbed him of his magical powers. Other victories followed, and the Mali Empire was born (see Map 14.1).

**Mali** Empire created by indigenous Muslims in western Sudan of West Africa from the thirteenth to fifteenth century. It was famous for its role in the trans-Saharan gold trade.

**Map 14.1 Africa, 1200–1500** Many African states had beneficial links to the trade that crossed the Sahara and the Indian Ocean. Before 1500, sub-Saharan Africa's external ties were primarily with the Islamic world. © Cengage Learning

Legend:
- Benin
- Bornu
- Ethiopia
- Ghana
- Hausa States
- Kongo
- Mali
- Oyo
- Songhai
- Swahili Coast
- Yoruba
- Zimbabwe
- → Trans-Saharan trade routes
- → Coastal trade routes

Sundiata's empire depended on a well-developed agricultural base and control of the regional and trans-Saharan trade routes, as had Ghana before it. Mali, however, controlled a greater area than Ghana, including not only the core trading area of the upper Niger but also the gold fields of the Niger headwaters to the southwest. Moreover, its rulers fostered the spread of Islam among the empire's political and

334

**Djinguere Ber Mosque in Timbuktu** Built almost entirely of earth and organic materials, this fourteenth-century mosque can accommodate 2,000 worshipers. Mansa Kankan Musa, the most famous ruler of the Empire of Mali, is said to have paid Abu Ishaq al-Sahili, a native of Granada in Muslim Spain, 200 kilograms of gold for designing this masterful combination of Islamic and African traditions. Nik Wheeler/Corbis

trading elites. Control of the gold and copper trades and contacts with North African Muslim traders gave Mali unprecedented prosperity.

Under the ruler **Mansa Kankan Musa** (MAHN-suh KAHN-kahn MOO-suh) (r. 1312–1337), the empire's reputation for wealth spread far and wide. Mansa Musa's pilgrimage to Mecca in 1324–1325 fulfilled his personal duty as a Muslim and at the same time put on display his exceptional wealth. He traveled with a large entourage. Besides his senior wife and five hundred of her ladies in waiting and their slaves, one account says there were also sixty thousand porters and a vast caravan of camels carrying supplies and provisions. For purchases and gifts, he brought along eighty packages of gold, each weighing 122 ounces (3.8 kilograms). In addition, five hundred slaves each carried a golden staff. Mansa Musa dispersed so many gifts when he passed through Cairo that the value of gold was depressed for years.

Two centuries after its founding, Mali began to disintegrate. Mansa Musa was succeeded by Mansa Suleiman (r. 1341–1360), but his successors could not prevent rebellions breaking out among the diverse peoples subjected to Malinke rule, while other groups attacked from without. The desert Tuareg retook their city of Timbuktu (tim-buk-TOO) in 1433. By 1500, the rulers of Mali had dominion over little more than the Malinke heartland.

The cities of the upper Niger survived Mali's collapse, but some trade and intellectual life moved east to the central Sudan. Shortly after 1450, several Hausa city-states officially adopted Islam, becoming famous for cotton textiles and leatherworking. The central Sudanic state of Kanem-Bornu (KAH-nuhm–BOR-noo)

**Mansa Kankan Musa** Ruler of Mali (r. 1312–1337). His pilgrimage through Egypt to Mecca in 1324–1325 established the empire's reputation for wealth in the Mediterranean world.

also expanded in the late fifteenth century from the ancient kingdom of Kanem, whose rulers had accepted Islam in about 1085. At its peak around 1250, Kanem had absorbed the state of Bornu south and west of Lake Chad and gained control of routes crossing the central Sahara. As Kanem-Bornu's armies conquered new territories, they also spread the rule of Islam.

## The Delhi Sultanate in India

Beginning in the early eleventh century, the divided states of northwest India, having long ago lost the defensive unity of the Gupta Empire (see Chapter 6), fell prey to raids by the powerful sultan Mahmud (mah-MOOD) based in Ghazna, Afghanistan. From 1206 to 1526, repeated campaigns by successive rulers led to a series of Afghan and Turkish dynasties ruling from the city of Delhi. One partisan Muslim chronicler wrote: "The city [Delhi] and its vicinity was freed from idols and idol-worship, and in the sanctuaries of the images of the [Hindu] Gods, mosques were raised by the worshippers of one God."[1] Turkish adventurers from Central Asia flocked to join the invading armies and overwhelmed the small Indian states, which were often at war with one another.

Between 1206 and 1236, the Muslim invaders extended their rule over the Hindu princes and chiefs in much of northern India. Sultan Iltutmish (il-TOOT-mish) (r. 1211–1236) consolidated the conquest in a series of military expeditions that made his realm the largest in India (see Map 14.2). The caliph in Baghdad, soon to be killed by the Mongols, officially recognized the Delhi Sultanate as a Muslim realm. Incorporating north India into the Islamic world marked the beginning of the invaders' transformation from brutal conquerors to somewhat more benign rulers. Though doctrinally opposed to idol worship, Muslim commanders granted the Hindus freedom from persecution in return for paying the *jizya*, a tax required of Jews and Christians.

Iltutmish astonished his ministers by passing over his weak and pleasure-seeking sons and designating as his heir his beloved and talented daughter Raziya (RAH-zee-uh). He reportedly said, "My sons

are devoted to the pleasures of youth: no one of them is qualified to be king. . . . There is no one more competent to guide the State than my daughter." Her brother, who was given to riding his elephant through the bazaar and showering the crowds with coins, ruled ineptly for seven months before the ministers relented and put Raziya on the throne. A chronicler who knew her explained why this able ruler lasted less than four years (r. 1236–1240):

> Sultan Raziya was a great monarch. She was wise, just, and generous, a benefactor to her kingdom, a dispenser of justice, the protector of her subjects, and the leader of her armies. She was endowed with all the qualities befitting a king, but she was not born of the right sex, and so in the estimation of men all these virtues were worthless. May God have mercy upon her![2]

Doing her best to prove herself a proper king, Raziya dressed like a man and led her troops atop an elephant. In the end, however, the Turkish chiefs imprisoned her; she escaped but was killed by a robber soon afterward.

After a half century of stagnation and rebellion, the ruthless but efficient policies of Sultan Ala-ud-din Khalji (uh-LAH–uh–DEEN KAL-jee) (r. 1296–1316) increased control over the empire's outlying provinces. Successful frontier raids and high taxes filled his treasury, wage and price controls in Delhi kept down the cost of maintaining a large army, and a network of spies stifled intrigue. When a Mongol threat from Central Asia eased, Ala-ud-din's forces marched southward, capturing the rich trading state of **Gujarat** (goo-juh-RAHT) in 1298 and then briefly seizing the southern tip of the Indian peninsula.

Sultan Muhammad ibn Tughluq (TOOG-look) (r. 1325–1351) enlarged the sultanate to its greatest extent at the expense of the independent Indian states but balanced his aggression with religious toleration. He even attended Hindu religious festivals. However, his successor, Firuz Shah (fuh-ROOZ shah) (r. 1351–1388), alienated powerful Hindus by taxing

[2]Minhaju-s Siraj, Tabakat-i Nasiri, in ibid., 2:332–333.

[1]Hasan Nizami, Taju-l Ma-asir, in Henry M. Elliot, *The History of India as Told by Its Own Historians*, ed. John Dowson (London: Trübner and Co., 1869–1871), 2:219.

**Gujarat** Region of western India famous for trade and manufacturing; the inhabitants are called Gujaratis.

**Map 14.2 South and Southeast Asia, 1200–1500** The rise of new empires and the expansion of maritime trade reshaped the lives of many tropical Asians. © Cengage Learning

the Brahmin elite. Muslim chroniclers praised him for constructing forty mosques, thirty colleges, and a hundred hospitals.

A small minority in a giant land, the Delhi sultans relied on force to keep their subjects submissive, on military reprisals to put down rebellion, and on pillage and high taxes to sustain the ruling elite in luxury and power. The sultanate never escaped the disadvantage of foreign origins and alien religious identity, but some sultans did incorporate a few Hindus into their administrations, and some members of the Muslim elite married women from prominent Hindu families, though the brides had to convert to Islam.

Personal and religious rivalries within the Muslim elite, along with Hindu discontent, threatened the Delhi Sultanate whenever it showed weakness and finally hastened its end. In the mid-fourteenth century, Muslim nobles challenged the sultan's dominion and established the independent Bahmani (bah-MAHN-ee) kingdom (1347–1482) on the

Deccan Plateau. Defending against the southward push of Bahmani armies, the Hindu states of south India united to form the Vijayanagar (vee-JAY-yah-nah-GAR) Empire (1336–1565), which at its height controlled rich trading ports on both coasts of south India and held Ceylon as a tributary state.

Hindu Vijayanagar and the Muslim Bahmani state turned a blind eye to religious differences when doing so favored their interests. Bahmani rulers sought to balance Muslim domination by incorporating Hindu leaders into the government, marrying Hindu wives, and appointing Brahmins to high offices. Vijayanagar rulers hired Muslim horsemen and archers to strengthen their military forces and formed an alliance with the Muslim-ruled state of Gujarat.

By 1351, when all of south India had cast off Delhi's rule, much of north India rose in rebellion. In the east, Bengal broke away from the sultanate in 1338. In the west, Gujarat regained its independence by 1390.

**SECTION REVIEW**

- Islam spread into western sub-Saharan Africa usually by peaceful conversion through trading contacts.

- Founded by Sundiata, Mali depended on agriculture and control of trade routes, and Islam spread among its elites.

- Mali reached its height under Mansa Kankan Musa but declined after the death of his successor, and power shifted eastward.

- Muslim invaders from Afghanistan conquered much of Hindu northern India to establish the Delhi Sultanate.

- The sultanate grew to encompass most of India; the sultans ruled through force, pillage, and heavy taxation.

- Though efficient, the sultanate suffered from internal struggles and fell under pressure from rival states and invaders.

The weakening of Delhi's central authority tempted fresh Mongol interest in the area. In 1398, the Turko-Mongol leader Timur (see Chapter 12) captured the city of Delhi. When his armies withdrew the next year with vast quantities of loot and tens of thousands of captives, the largest city in southern Asia lay empty and in ruins. The Delhi Sultanate never recovered.

For all its shortcomings, the Delhi Sultanate triggered the development of centralized political authority in India. Prime ministers and provincial governors serving under the sultans established a bureaucracy, improved food production, promoted trade, and put in circulation a common coinage. Despite the many conflicts that Muslim conquest and rule provoked, Islam gradually acquired a permanent place in South Asia.

# INDIAN OCEAN TRADE

■ *How did cultural and ecological differences promote trade, and in turn how did trade and other contacts promote state growth and the spread of Islam?*

When the collapse of the Mongol Empire in the fourteenth century disrupted overland routes across Central Asia, the Indian Ocean assumed greater strategic importance in tying together the peoples of Eurasia and Africa. Between 1200 and 1500, the volume of trade in the Indian Ocean increased. The Indian Ocean routes also facilitated the spread of Islam.

## Monsoon Mariners

The prosperity of Islamic and Mongol empires in Asia, cities in Europe, and new kingdoms in Africa and Southeast Asia stimulated and contributed to the vitality of the Indian Ocean network. The demand for luxuries—precious metals and jewels, rare spices, fine textiles, and other manufactures—rose. Larger ships made shipments of bulk cargoes of ordinary cotton textiles, pepper, food grains (rice, wheat, barley), timber, horses, and other goods profitable.

Some goods were transported from one end of this trading network to the other, but few ships or crews made a complete circuit. Instead, the Indian Ocean trade divided into two legs: from the Middle East across the Arabian Sea to India and from India across the Bay of Bengal to Southeast Asia.

Shipyards in ports on the Malabar Coast (southwestern India) and in the Persian Gulf built large numbers of **dhows** (dow), the characteristic cargo and passenger ships of the Arabian Sea. They grew from an average capacity of 100 tons in 1200 to 400 tons in 1500. On a typical expedition, a dhow might sail west from India to Arabia and Africa on the northeast monsoon winds (December to March) and return on the southwest monsoons (April to August). Small dhows kept the coast in sight. Relying on the stars to guide them, skilled pilots steered large vessels by the quicker route straight across the water. A large dhow could sail from the Red Sea to mainland Southeast Asia in two to four months, but few did so. Eastbound cargoes and passengers from dhows reaching India were likely to be transferred to junks, which dominated the eastern half of the Indian Ocean and the South China Sea (see Environment and Technology: The Indian Ocean Dhow).

Junks, the largest, most technologically advanced, and most seaworthy vessels of the time, appeared first in China and spread with Chinese influence overseas. Enormous nails held together hulls of heavy spruce or fir planks, in contrast with dhows, whose planks were sewn together with palm fiber. Below the deck, watertight compartments minimized flooding in case of damage to the ship's hull. The largest junks reportedly had twelve sails made of bamboo strips woven into

**dhows**  Characteristic cargo and passenger ships of the Arabian Sea.

## The Indian Ocean Dhow

The sailing vessels that crossed the Indian Ocean shared the diversity of that trading area. The name by which we know them, *dhow*, comes from the Swahili language of the East African coast. The planks of teak from which their hulls were constructed were hewn from the tropical forests of south India and Southeast Asia. Their pilots, who navigated by stars at night, employed techniques that Arabs had used to find their way across the desert. Some pilots used a magnetic compass, which originated in China.

Dhows came in various sizes and designs, but all had two distinctive features in common. The first was hull construction. The hulls of dhows consisted of planks that were sewn together, not nailed. Cord made of fiber from the husk of coconuts or other materials was passed through rows of holes drilled in the planks. Because cord is weaker than nails, outsiders considered this shipbuilding technique strange. Marco Polo fancifully suggested that it indicated sailors' fear that large ocean magnets would pull any nails out of their ships. Better explanations observe that pliant sewn hulls were cheaper to build than rigid nailed hulls and were less likely to be damaged if the ships ran aground on coral reefs.

The second distinctive feature of dhows was their sails made of palm leaves or cloth. Sails that were either triangular (lateen) or had a very short leading edge were suspended from tall masts and could be turned to catch the wind.

**Dhow** *This modern model shows the vessel's main features.*

SSPL/Getty Images

Sewn hulls and lateen sails had appeared centuries earlier, but two innovations appeared between 1200 and 1500. First, a rudder positioned at the stern (rear end) of the ship replaced the large side oar that formerly had controlled steering. Second, shipbuilders increased the size of dhows to accommodate bulkier cargoes.

mats and carried a crew of a thousand men, including four hundred soldiers. A large junk might accommodate a hundred passenger cabins and a cargo of over 1,000 tons. Junks dominated China's foreign shipping to Southeast Asia and India, but the Chinese did not control all of the junks that plied these waters. During the fifteenth century, similar vessels came out of Bengal and Southeast Asia.

Decentralized and cooperative commercial interests, rather than political authorities, connected the several regions that participated in the Indian Ocean trade. The **Swahili** (swah-HEE-lee) **Coast**

supplied ivory, wood, and gold from inland areas of Africa. Ports around the Arabian peninsula supplied horses, incense, and manufactured goods from the Mediterranean region. Merchants in the cities of coastal India received goods from east and west, sold some locally, passed others along, and added Indian goods to the trade. The Strait of Malacca (meh-LAK-eh), between the eastern end of the Indian Ocean and

**Swahili Coast** East African shores of the Indian Ocean between the Horn of Africa and the Zambezi River; from the Arabic *sawahil*, meaning "shores."

the South China Sea, provided a meeting point for trade from Southeast Asia, China, and the Indian Ocean. In each region, certain ports functioned as giant emporia, consolidating goods from smaller ports and inland areas for transport across the seas.

## Africa: The Swahili Coast and Zimbabwe

Trade expanded steadily along the East African coast from about 1250, giving rise to between thirty and forty separate city-states by 1500.

After 1200, masonry buildings as much as four stories high replaced mud and thatch dwellings, and archaeological finds include Chinese porcelain, imported glass beads, and other exotic goods. Coastal and island peoples shared a common culture and a language built on African grammar and vocabulary but incorporating many Arabic and Persian terms and written in Arabic script. In time, these people became known as "Swahili," from the Arabic word *sawahil* (suh-WAH-hil), meaning "shores."

What attracted the Arab and Iranian merchants whom oral traditions associate with the Swahili Coast's commercial expansion? By the late fifteenth century, the major port of Kilwa, described by Ibn Battuta as "one of the most beautiful and well-constructed towns in the world," was annually exporting a ton of gold mined by inland Africans much farther south. Much of it came from or passed through a powerful state on the plateau south of the Zambezi River. At its peak in about 1400, its capital city, now known as **Great Zimbabwe**, occupied 193 acres (78 hectares) and had some eighteen thousand inhabitants.

Between about 1250 and 1450, local African craftsmen built stone structures for Great Zimbabwe's rulers, priests, and wealthy citizens. The largest structure, an enclosure the size and shape of a large football stadium with walls of unmortared stone 17 feet (5 meters) thick and 32 feet (10 meters) high, served as the king's court. A large conical stone tower was among the many buildings inside the walls.

As in Mali, mixed farming and cattle herding provided the economic basis of the Great Zimbabwe state, but long-distance trade brought added wealth. Trade began regionally with copper ingots from the upper Zambezi Valley, salt, and local manufactures. Gold exports to the coast expanded in the fourteenth

and fifteenth centuries and brought Zimbabwe to its peak. However, historians suspect that the city's residents depleted nearby forests for firewood while their cattle overgrazed surrounding grasslands. The resulting ecological crisis hastened the empire's decline in the fifteenth century.

The city of **Aden** (A[as in hat]-den) near the southwestern tip of the Arabian peninsula had a double advantage in the Indian Ocean trade. Monsoon winds brought enough rainfall to supply drinking water to a large population and grow grain for export, and its location made it a convenient stopover for trade with India, the Persian Gulf, East Africa, and Egypt. Aden's merchants dealt in cotton cloth and beads from India; spices from Southeast Asia; horses from Arabia and Ethiopia; pearls from the Red Sea; manufactured luxuries from Cairo; slaves, gold, and ivory from Ethiopia; and grain, opium, and dyes from Aden's own hinterland.

Common commercial interests generally promoted good relations among the different religions and cultures of this region. For example, in the mid-thirteenth century, a wealthy Jew from Aden named Yosef settled in Christian Ethiopia, where he acted as an adviser. South Arabia had been trading with neighboring parts of Africa since before the time of King Solomon of Israel. The dynasty that ruled Ethiopia after 1270 boasted (legendary) descent from Solomon and the Queen of Sheba from across the Red Sea. Ethiopia's Solomonic dynasty greatly increased trade through the Red Sea port of Zeila (ZAY-luh), including trade in slaves, amber, and animal pelts, which went to Aden and on to other destinations.

Friction sometimes arose, however. In the late fifteenth century, Ethiopia's territorial expansion and efforts to increase control over the trade provoked conflicts with Muslims who ruled the coastal states of the Red Sea.

**Great Zimbabwe** City, now in ruins (in the modern African country of Zimbabwe), whose many stone structures were built between about 1250 and 1450, when it was a trading center and the capital of a large state.

**Aden** Port city in the modern south Arabian country of Yemen. It has been a major trading center in the Indian Ocean since ancient times.

Embassy Photo/Visual Connection Archive

**Royal Enclosure, Great Zimbabwe**  Inside these oval stone walls the rulers of the trading state of Great Zimbabwe lived. Forced to enter the enclosure through a narrow corridor between two high walls, visitors were meant to be awestruck.

## India: Gujarat and the Malabar Coast

The state of Gujarat in western India prospered from the expanding trade of the Arabian Sea and the rise of the Delhi Sultanate. Blessed with a rich agricultural hinterland and a long coastline, Gujarat attracted new trade after the Mongol destruction of Baghdad in 1258 disrupted the northern land routes. Despite the violence of its forced incorporation into the Delhi Sultanate in 1298, Gujarat prospered from increased commercial interaction with Delhi's ruling class. Independent again after 1390, the Muslim rulers of Gujarat extended their control over neighboring Hindu states and regained their preeminent position in the Indian Ocean trade.

Gujaratis exported cotton textiles and indigo to the Middle East and Europe in return for gold and silver. They also shipped cotton cloth, carnelian beads, and foodstuffs to the Swahili Coast in exchange for ebony, slaves, ivory, and gold. During the fifteenth century, Gujarat's trade zone expanded eastward to the Strait of Malacca. There Gujarati merchants helped spread the Islamic faith among East Indian traders, some of whom even imported specially carved gravestones from Gujarat.

Unlike Kilwa and Aden, Gujarat manufactured goods for trade. According to the thirteenth-century Venetian traveler Marco Polo, Gujarat's leatherworkers dressed enough skins in a year to fill several ships to Arabia and other places. They made sleeping mats for export to the Middle East "in red and blue leather, exquisitely inlaid with figures of birds and beasts, and skillfully embroidered with gold and silver wire," as well as leather cushions embroidered in gold.

Later observers compared the Gujarati city of Cambay (modern name Khambhat) with cities in Flanders and northern Italy (see Chapter 13) in the scale, craftsmanship, and diversity of its textile industries. Cotton, linen, and silk cloth, along with carpets and quilts, found a large market in Europe, Africa, the Middle East, and Southeast Asia. Cambay also produced polished gemstones, gold jewelry, carved ivory, stone beads, and both pearls and mother of pearl. At the height of its prosperity in the fifteenth century, its well-laid-out streets and open places boasted fine stone houses with tiled roofs. Although Muslim residents controlled most of Gujarat's overseas trade, its Hindu merchant caste profited so much from related commercial activities that their wealth and luxurious lives became the envy of other Indians.

More southerly cities on the well-watered Malabar Coast of India imitated Gujarat's success. Calicut (KAL-ih-cut) (modern name Kozhikode) and other coastal cities prospered from local cotton, grains, and spices. They also served as clearing-houses for the long-distance trade of the Indian Ocean. The zamorin (ZAH-much-ruhn) (ruler) of Calicut presided over a loose federation of its Hindu rulers that united the coastal region, but steep mountains known as the Western Ghats cut the coast off from the inland areas on the Deccan Plateau. As in eastern Africa and Arabia, rulers tolerated religious and ethnic groups who contributed to commercial profits. Most trading activity lay in the hands of Muslims, many originally from Iran and Arabia, who intermarried with local Indian Muslims. Jewish merchants also operated from Malabar's trading cities.

## Southeast Asia

At the eastern end of the Indian Ocean, the Strait of Malacca between the Malay Peninsula and the island of Sumatra provided the principal passage into the South China Sea (see Map 14.2). As trade increased in the fourteenth and fifteenth centuries, this commercial choke point became the site of political rivalry. The mainland kingdom of Siam controlled most of the upper Malay Peninsula, while the Java-based kingdom of Majapahit (mah-jah-PAH-heet) extended its dominion over the lower Malay Peninsula and much of Sumatra. Majapahit, however, could not suppress Chinese pirates based at the Sumatran city of Palembang (pah-lem-BONG) who preyed on ships sailing through the strait. In 1407, a fleet from China commanded by the admiral Zheng He (see Chapter 12) smashed the pirates' power and took their chief back home for trial.

Majapahit, weakened by internal struggles, could not take advantage of China's intervention, making the chief beneficiary the newer port of **Malacca** (or Melaka), which dominated the narrowest part of the strait. Under a prince from Palembang, Malacca

### SECTION REVIEW

- Traversed by dhows and junks, the maritime trade network of the Indian Ocean tied together peoples of Asia, Africa, and Europe.
- Decentralized commercial interests rose throughout the network, including the Swahili city-states that exported African gold from Great Zimbabwe.
- Aden dealt in a variety of goods from Africa, Arabia, and Southeast Asia and traded with Zeila on the Red Sea.
- Despite political turmoil, the cities of Gujarat and the Malabar Coast prospered through agriculture, manufacture, and trade.
- Through astute alliances, Malacca grew into the predominant emporium of Southeast Asia.

had grown from an obscure fishing village into an important port through a series of astute alliances. Nominally subject to the king of Siam, Malacca also secured an alliance with China that was sealed by the visit of the imperial fleet in 1407. The conversion of an early ruler from Hinduism to Islam helped promote trade with Muslim merchants from Gujarat and elsewhere. Merchants also appreciated Malacca's security and low taxes.

Malacca served not just as a meeting point but also as an emporium for Southeast Asian products: rubies and musk from Burma, tin from Malaya, gold from Sumatra, cloves and nutmeg from the Moluccas (or Spice Islands, as Europeans later dubbed them). Shortly after 1500, when Malacca was at its height, one resident counted eighty-four languages spoken among the merchants gathered there, who came from as far away as Turkey, Ethiopia, and the Swahili Coast. Four officials administered the foreign merchant communities: one for the Gujaratis, one for other Indians and Burmese, one for Southeast Asians, and one for the Chinese and Japanese. Malacca's wealth and its cosmopolitan residents set the standard for luxury in Malaya for centuries to come.

**Malacca**  Port city in the modern Southeast Asian country of Malaysia, founded about 1400 as a trading center on the Strait of Malacca.

# SOCIAL AND CULTURAL CHANGE

■ *What social and cultural changes are reflected in the history of peoples living in tropical Africa and Asia during this period?*

As a result of state growth, commercial expansion, and the spread of Islam between 1200 and 1500, Muslim political and commercial elites grew in numbers and power. Religious agents sought converts both within and beyond the boundaries of Muslim states. Africa and India's local art, rituals, and even theological doctrines combined with those of Islam to form syncretic religious formations, often in the guise of Sufi brotherhoods, reminiscent of the syncretism of the Hellenistic period (see Chapter 4).

## Architecture, Learning, and Religion

Social and cultural changes typically affected cities more than rural areas. As travelers often observed, wealthy merchants and ruling elites spent lavishly on mansions, palaces, and places of worship while the lives of common people were less affected. Most mosques, local pilgrimage sites, and Sufi shrines surviving from this period blend older traditions and new influences. For example, African Muslims produced Middle Eastern mosque designs in local building materials: sun-baked clay reinforced by wooden crossbeams in the western Sudan, masonry using blocks of coral on the Swahili Coast. Once their homelands came under Muslim rule, south Asian artisans were free to travel to newly Islamized regions like Gujarat and older Muslim lands like Afghanistan and Iran, bringing with them Hindu temple architectural ideas and sometimes material for Muslim places of worship. The congregational mosque at Cambay, built in 1325, utilized pillars, porches, and arches taken from sacked Hindu and Jain (jine) temples. The congregational mosque erected at the Gujarati capital of Ahmedabad (AH-muhd-ah-bahd) in 1423 had the open courtyard typical of mosques everywhere, but the surrounding verandas incorporated many Gujarati details and architectural conventions.

Mosques, churches, and temples were centers of education as well as prayer and ritual. Muslims promoted literacy among their sons (and sometimes their daughters) so that they could read sacred texts. In some lands south of the Sahara, Ethiopia excepted, Islam provided the first exposure to literate culture. In much of South Asia, literacy in Indo-European languages like Sanskrit and Dravidian languages like Tamil had been established many centuries before. Even there, however, a migration of Arabic and Persian vocabulary into local languages produced significant changes. Scholars adapted the Arabic alphabet to write local languages like Hausa in Mali and numerous tongues in the Malay Peninsula and island Southeast Asia.

Persian became the court language of the Delhi Sultanate, but **Urdu** (ER-doo), a Persian-influenced form of the local Hindustani tongue of northern India, eventually became an important literary language written in Arabic characters. Muslims also introduced paper into their new lands. This was an improvement over palm leaves and other fragile materials, but tropical humidity and insect life made preservation of written knowledge difficult nevertheless.

Muslim scholars everywhere studied the Quran along with Islamic law and theology. A few demonstrated a high level of interest in mathematics, medicine, science, and philosophy, partly derived from ancient Greek writings translated into Arabic (see Chapter 9). In sixteenth-century **Timbuktu** (see Map 14.1), over 150 schools taught the Quran while leading clerics taught advanced classes in mosques or homes. Books imported from North Africa brought high prices. Al-Hajj Ahmed, a scholar who died in Timbuktu in 1536, possessed some seven hundred volumes, an unusually large library for that time. In Southeast Asia, Malacca became a center of Islamic learning from which scholars spread Islam throughout the region. Other important centers of learning developed in Muslim India, particularly in Delhi, the capital.

**Urdu** A Persian-influenced literary form of Hindi written in Arabic characters and used as a literary language since the 1300s.

**Timbuktu** City on the Niger River in the modern country of Mali. It was founded by the Tuareg as a seasonal camp sometime after 1000. As part of the Mali Empire, Timbuktu became a major terminus of the trans-Saharan trade and a center of Islamic learning.

Even in conquered lands, Muslim rulers seldom required conversion. Example and persuasion by merchants and Sufis proved more effective in winning new believers. Muslim domination of long-distance trade assisted the adoption of Islam. Commercial transactions could take place across religious boundaries, but the common code of morality and law that Islam provided encouraged trust and drew many local merchants to Islam. From the major trading centers along the Swahili Coast, in the Sudan, in coastal India, and in Southeast Asia, Islam's influence spread along regional trade routes.

Islam also spread among rural peoples, such as the pastoral Fulani of West Africa and Somali. In Bengal, Muslim religious figures working for state officials oversaw the conversion of jungle into rice paddies and thereby gained converts among the people who came to work the land and inhabit the new villages. At first the new converts melded Islamic beliefs with Hindu traditions, seeing Muhammad, for example, as a manifestation of the god Vishnu. Over time, however, more standard versions of Islam gained headway.

Marriage also played a role. Single Muslim men traveling to and settling in tropical Africa and Asia often married local women. Their children grew up in the paternal faith because Islamic doctrine specified the transmission of religious identity in the male line. Some wealthy men had dozens of children from up to four wives and additional slave concubines. Servants and slaves in such households normally professed Islam.

In India, Muslim invasions eliminated the last strongholds of long-declining Buddhism, including, in 1196, the great Buddhist center of study at Nalanda (nuh-LAN-duh) in Bihar (bee-HAHR). Its manuscripts were burned, and thousands of monks were killed or driven into exile in Nepal and Tibet. With Buddhism reduced to a minor faith in the land of its birth, Islam emerged as India's second most important religion, displacing Hinduism as the elite religion in most of maritime Southeast Asia and slowly supplanting a variety of local cults. In mainland Southeast Asia, Buddhism and Islam vied for supremacy, with Islam prevailing in the south and Buddhism farther north in Thailand, Cambodia, and Burma (Myanmar).

## Social and Gender Distinctions

A growth in slavery accompanied the rising prosperity of the elites. Military campaigns in India, according to Islamic sources, reduced hundreds of thousands of Hindu "infidels" to slavery. Delhi overflowed with slaves. Sultan Ala ud-Din owned 50,000 and Firuz Shah 180,000, including 12,000 skilled artisans. Sultan Tughluq sent 100 male slaves and 100 female slaves as a gift to the emperor of China in return for a similar gift.

When gold cut into the profitability of trans-Saharan trade, Mali and Bornu sent slaves across the Sahara to North Africa. The expanding Ethiopian Empire regularly sent captives to Aden traders at Zeila. Many eunuchs (castrated males) were included. According to modern estimates, Saharan and Red Sea traders sold about 2.5 million enslaved Africans between 1200 and 1500. African slaves from the Swahili Coast played conspicuous roles in the navies, armies, and administrations of some Indian states, especially in the fifteenth century. A few African slaves even reached China, where a source from about 1225 says rich families preferred gatekeepers with bodies "black as lacquer." Later Chinese paintings show Portuguese ships manned almost entirely by African seamen.

With "free" labor abundant and cheap, few slaves worked as farmers. In some places, hereditary castes of slaves dominated certain trades and military units. Indeed, the rulers of the Delhi Sultanate included a number of the powerful military caste of Turkish mamluk slaves (see Chapter 9). A slave general in the western Sudan named Askia Muhammad seized control of the Songhai Empire (Mali's successor) in 1493. Less fortunate slaves, like the men and women who mined copper in Mali, did hard menial work.

Wealthy households used many slave servants. Eunuchs guarded the harems of wealthy Muslims, but women predominated as household slaves, serving also as entertainers and concubines. Some rich men aspired to having a concubine from every part of the world. One of Firuz Shah's nobles reportedly had two thousand harem slaves, including women from Turkey and China.

Hindu commentaries suggest that the position of Hindu women may have improved somewhat. The ancient practice of sati (suh-TEE)—that is, of an upper-caste widow throwing herself on her husband's funeral pyre—remained a meritorious act strongly approved by social custom. But Ibn Battuta makes it clear that sati was strictly optional. Since the Hindu commentaries devote considerable attention to the rights of widows without sons to inherit their husbands' estates, one may even conclude that sati was rare.

A woman's male master—father, husband, or owner—determined her status, and Indian parents still gave their daughters in marriage before the age of puberty. But consummation of the marriage took place only when the young woman was ready. Wives faced far stricter rules of fidelity and chastity than their husbands and could be abandoned for any serious breach, but other offenses against law and custom usually brought lighter penalties than for men. Women seldom played active roles in commerce, administration, or religion.

Women involved themselves with child rearing, food preparation, and, when not prohibited by religious restrictions, brewing. In many parts of Africa, women commonly made beer from grains or bananas. These mildly alcoholic beverages played an important part in male rituals of hospitality and relaxation. Throughout tropical Africa and Asia, women toted heavy loads of food, firewood, and water balanced on their heads and did much of the farm work, as well as making clothing and clay pots. In India, women typically spun at home, leaving weaving to men now that the spinning wheel, possibly a local invention, reduced the cost of weaving by making the process faster. In West Africa, women often sold agricultural products, pottery, and other craftwork in the markets.

Differences between Muslims and Hindus on matters relating to gender were not as great as the formal religious texts of the two religious traditions would suggest. South Asian tradition tended to outweigh Muslim practices imported from Arabia and Persia, and African Islam showed similar inclinations in the area of gender. In Mali's capital, Ibn Battuta was appalled that Muslim women both free and slave did not completely cover their bodies and veil their faces when appearing in public. He considered their nakedness an offense to women's (and men's) modesty. Elsewhere in Mali, he berated a Muslim merchant from Morocco for permitting his wife to sit on a couch and chat with her male friend. The husband replied, "The association of women with men is agreeable to us and part of good manners, to which no suspicion attaches." Ibn Battuta refused to visit the merchant again.

## THE WESTERN HEMISPHERE

■ *What were the key differences between the societies of Africa and Asia and the empires of the Aztecs and Inkas?*

Though isolated from the Eastern Hemisphere by oceans that were not crossed until the end of the fifteenth century, the tropical regions of the Western Hemisphere shared many of the climatic characteristics of the Old World tropics (see Chapter 7). However, the region's two most powerful urbanized empires, the Aztecs of Mexico and the Inka of Peru, developed at altitudes above 7,000 feet (11,265 meters), thus experiencing lower average rainfall and temperature than is common across the tropics. They also differed in being themselves centers of civilization rather than subsidiary to dominating political and economic powers located in temperate lands to the north or south.

Mesoamerica had witnessed a series of urbanized societies—Olmec, Maya, Toltec—from the

---

### SECTION REVIEW

- Social and cultural life changed as a result of state formation, commercial expansion, and the spread of Islam.

- These changes mostly affected cities, where elites financed building programs, fostering hybrid styles of religious architecture.

- Islam spread mainly through peaceful adaptation and promoted education and scholarship.

- With rising prosperity came the expansion of slavery, which was endorsed by Islam.

- The position of Indian women seems to have improved, and the spread of Islam did not mean adoption of Arab gender customs.

second millennium B.C.E. onward, and the mountains and coastal deserts of the Andean region had an equally long sequence, including Moche, Tiwanaku, Wari, and Chimū (see Chapter 7). Apart from these advanced regions, which saw the rise of powerful empires between 1300 and 1500 C.E., most Western Hemisphere societies of the period subsisted at more basic levels as hunters and gatherers or village agriculturalists.

## Mesoamerica: The Aztecs

The Mexica (meh-SHE-ca) pushed into central Mexico from the north during the collapse of the Toltecs (see Chapter 7). When they arrived, the Mexica were organized as an **altepetl** (al-TEH-peh-tel)—an ethnic state led by a tlatoani (tlah-toh-AHN-ee) or ruler and the common political unit of the region. A group of **calpolli** (cal-POH-yee), each with up to a hundred families, served as the foundation of the altepetl, controlling land allocation, tax collection, and local religious life. Adapting to the political and social practices that they found among the urbanized agriculturalists of the valley, the Mexica first served their more powerful neighbors as serfs and mercenaries. As their strength grew, they relocated to small islands near the shore of Lake Texcoco.

Military successes allowed the Mexica to seize control of additional agricultural land along the lakeshore and to forge military alliances with neighboring altepetl. Once these more complex political and economic arrangements were in place, the Mexica-dominated alliance became the Aztec Empire. With increased economic independence, greater political security, and territorial expansion, the **Aztecs** transformed their political organization by introducing a monarchical system similar to that found in more powerful neighboring states. A council of powerful aristocrats selected new rulers from among male members of the ruling lineage. Once selected, the ruler had to renegotiate the submission of dependencies and then demonstrate his divine mandate by undertaking new military conquests. War acquired religious meaning, providing the ruler with legitimacy and increasing the prestige of successful warriors.

Around 1325 C.E. the Aztecs began the construction of their twin capitals, **Tenochtitlan** (teh-noch-TIT-lan) and Tlatelolco (tla-teh-LOHL-coh) (together the foundation for modern Mexico City). The population of Tenochtitlan and Tlatelolco combined with that of the cities and towns of the surrounding lakeshore was approximately 500,000 by 1500 C.E. Three causeways connected this island capital to the lakeshore. Planners laid out the urban center as a grid where canals and streets intersected at right angles to facilitate the movement of people and goods.

Although warfare gave increased power and privilege to males, women held substantial power and exercised broad influence in Aztec society. The roles of women and men were clearly distinguished, but women were held in high esteem. Scholars call this "gender complementarity." Following the birth of a boy, his umbilical cord was buried on the battlefield and he was given implements to signal his occupation or his role as a warrior. In the case of a girl, her umbilical cord was buried near the hearth and she was given weaving implements and female clothing. Women dominated the household and the markets, and sometimes served as teachers and priestesses. They were also seen as the founders of lineages, including the royal line.

Aztec military successes and territorial expansion allowed the warrior elite to seize land and peasant labor as spoils of war. In time, the royal family and highest-ranking members of the aristocracy possessed extensive estates that were cultivated by slaves and landless commoners. The lower classes received some material rewards from imperial expansion but lost their influence over decisions. Some commoners

> **altepetl** An ethnic state in ancient Mesoamerica, the common political building block of that region.
>
> **calpolli** A group of up to a hundred families that served as a social building block of an altepetl in ancient Mesoamerica.
>
> **Aztec** The Mexica-dominated alliance that created a powerful empire in central Mexico (1325–1521).
>
> **Tenochtitlan** Capital of the Aztec Empire, located on an island in Lake Texcoco. Its population was above 150,000 on the eve of the Spanish conquest. Mexico City was constructed on its ruins.

were able to achieve some social mobility through success on the battlefield.

However, by 1500 C.E. great inequalities in wealth and privilege characterized Aztec society. One of the Spaniards who participated in the conquest of the Aztec Empire remembered his first meeting with the Aztec ruler Moctezuma (mock-teh-ZU-ma) II (r. 1502–1520): "Many great lords walked before the great Montezuma [Moctezuma II], sweeping the ground on which he was to tread and laying down cloaks so that his feet should not touch the earth. Not one of these chieftains dared look him in the face."[3] While commoners lived in small dwellings and ate a limited diet of staples, members of the nobility lived in large, well-constructed, two-story houses and consumed a diet rich in animal protein.

A specialized class of merchants controlled long-distance trade. Given the absence of draft animals and wheeled vehicles in Mesoamerica, lightweight and valuable products like gold, jewels, feathered garments, cacao, and animal skins dominated this commerce. Merchants also provided political and military intelligence. Commerce took place without money or credit. Cacao beans, quills filled with gold, and cotton cloth were the standard units of value used to barter for goods. Aztec expansion integrated producers and consumers in the central Mexican economy. Hernán Cortés (1485–1547), the Spanish adventurer who eventually conquered the Aztecs, expressed his admiration for the abundance of the Aztec marketplace:

> One square in particular is twice as big as that of Salamanca and completely surrounded by arcades where there are daily more than sixty thousand folk buying and selling. Every kind of merchandise such as may be met with in every land is for sale. . . . There is nothing to be found in all the land which is not sold in these markets, for over and above what I have mentioned there are so many and such various things that on account of their very number . . . I cannot detail them.[4]

[3]Bernal Diaz del Castillo, *The Conquest of the New Spain*, trans. J.M. Cohen (London: Penguin Books, 1963), 217.

Although powerful and wealthy, merchants were never accepted into the ranks of the high nobility.

The Aztec state met the challenge of feeding an urban population of approximately 150,000 by efficiently organizing the labor of calpolli and of additional laborers sent by defeated peoples to expand agricultural land. Land reclamation centered on dikes more than 5 miles (9 kilometers) long by 23 feet (7 meters) wide that separated the fresh and salt water parts of Lake Texcoco. The dikes, whose construction consumed 4 million person-days, supported greater irrigation. Aztec **chinampas**—raised fields along lakeshores—contributed maize, fruits, and vegetables to the Tenochtitlan markets. The imposition of a **tribute system** on conquered peoples also helped relieve the capital's population pressure. Unlike the tribute system of Tang China, where tribute had a more symbolic character (see Chapter 11), one-quarter of the Aztec capital's food came from tribute payments of maize, beans, and other foods.

Religious rituals dominated public life in Tenochtitlan. As in other cultures of the Mesoamerican world, human sacrifice was common. Some scholars note that sacrifices took place before large crowds that included leaders from enemy and subject states, as well as the Aztec masses. The Aztecs worshiped numerous gods, most of which had a dual nature—both male and female. The chief god of the Mexica was Huitzilopochtli (wheat-zeel-oh-POSHT-lee) or southern hummingbird. Originally associated with war, it was later identified with the sun. Tenochtitlan was architecturally dominated by a great twin temple devoted to Huitzilopochtli and Tlaloc, the storm-god, symbolizing the two bases of the Aztec economy: war and agriculture.

[4]Hernando Cortéz, *Five Letters, 1519–1926*, trans. J. Bayard Morris (New York: Norton, 1991), 87.

**chinampas** Raised fields constructed along lakeshores in central Mexico to increase agricultural yields.

**tribute system** A system in which defeated peoples were forced to pay a tax in the form of goods and labor. The forced transfer of food, cloth, and other goods subsidized the development of large cities. An important component of the Aztec and Inka economies.

Werner Forman/Universal Images Group/Getty Images

**Inka Tunic**  Andean weavers produced beautiful textiles from cotton and from the wool of llamas and alpacas. The Inka inherited this rich craft tradition and produced some of the world's most remarkable textiles. The quality and design of each garment indicated the weaver's rank and power in this society. This tunic was an outer garment for a powerful male.

**The Andes: The Inka**

In little more than a hundred years, the **Inka** developed a vast imperial state, which they called "Land of Four Corners." By 1525 the empire had a population of more than 6 million and stretched from the Maule River in Chile to northern Ecuador and from the Pacific coast across the Andes to the upper Amazon and, in the south, into Argentina. In the early fifteenth century, the Inka were one of many competing military powers in the southern highlands, an area of limited political significance after the collapse of Wari (see Chapter 7).

The Inka were traditional highland pastoralists whose prosperity and military strength depended on vast herds of llamas and alpacas. Centered in the valley of Cuzco, they were initially organized as a chiefdom based on reciprocal gift giving and the redistribution of food and textiles. Strong and resourceful leaders consolidated political authority in the 1430s and undertook ambitious military expansion.

The Inka state utilized Andean social customs and economic practices. Tiwanaku had used colonists to provide supplies of resources from distant, ecologically distinct zones. The Inka built on this legacy by

**Inka**  Largest and most powerful Andean empire. Controlled the Pacific coast of South America from Ecuador to Chile from its capital of Cuzco.

conquering additional territories and increasing the scale of forced exchanges. Crucial to this process was the development of a large military. Unlike the peoples of Mesoamerica, who distributed specialized goods through markets and tribute relationships, Andean peoples used state power to broaden and expand the vertical exchange system that had permitted self-governing extended family groups called *ayllus* to exploit a range of ecological niches.

Collective efforts by mita labor, a system of forced service to the ruler (see Chapter 7), made the Inka Empire possible. Cuzco, the imperial capital, and the provincial cities, the royal court, the imperial armies, and the state's religious cults all rested on this foundation. The mita system also created the material surplus that provided the bare necessities for the old, weak, and ill of Inka society. Each ayllu contributed approximately one-seventh of its adult male population to meet these collective obligations. These draft laborers served as soldiers, construction workers, craftsmen, and runners to carry messages along post roads. They also drained swamps, terraced mountainsides, filled in valley floors, built and maintained irrigation works, and built storage facilities and roads. Inka laborers constructed 13,000 miles (20,930 kilometers) of road, facilitating military troop movements, administration, and trade.

The hereditary chiefs of ayllus, a group that included women, carried out local administrative and judicial functions. As the Inka expanded, they generally left local rulers in place. By doing so they risked rebellion, but they controlled these risks by a thinly veiled system of hostage taking and the use of military garrisons. Rulers of defeated regions sent their heirs to live at the Inka court in Cuzco, and representations of important local gods were brought to Cuzco to join the imperial pantheon. These measures promoted imperial integration while providing hostages to ensure the good behavior of subject peoples.

Conquests magnified the authority of the Inka ruler and led to the creation of an imperial bureaucracy drawn from his kinsmen. The royal family claimed descent from the sun, the primary Inka god. Members of the royal family lived in palaces maintained by armies of servants. Political and religious rituals dominated the lives of the ruler and his family and helped legitimize their authority. Because extending imperial boundaries by warfare was a king's duty, each new ruler began his reign with conquest.

Tenochtitlan, the Aztec capital, had a population of about 150,000 in 1520. At the height of Inka power in 1530, Cuzco had a population of less than 30,000. Nevertheless, Cuzco contained impressive buildings of carefully cut stones fitted together without mortar. The city was laid out in the shape of a giant puma (a mountain lion), and its center contained the palaces of rulers as well as the major temples. The richest was the Temple of the Sun, its interior lined with sheets of gold and its patio decorated with golden representations of llamas and corn. The ruler made every effort to awe and intimidate visitors and residents alike with a nearly continuous series of rituals, feasts, and sacrifices. Sacrifices of textiles, animals, and other goods sent as tribute dominated the city's calendar. The destruction of these valuable commodities, and a small number of human sacrifices, conveyed an impression of splendor and sumptuous abundance to validate the ruler's claimed descent from the sun.

Inka cultural achievement rested on the strong foundation of earlier Andean civilizations. We know that astronomical observation was a central concern of the priestly class, as in Mesoamerica. The collective achievements of Andean peoples were accomplished with a limited record-keeping system adapted from earlier Andean civilizations. Administrators used knotted colored cords, called **khipus** (KEY-pooz), for public administration, population counts, and tribute obligations. Inka weaving and metallurgy, also based on earlier regional development, was more advanced than in Mesoamerica. Inka craftsmen produced utilitarian tools and weapons of copper and bronze as well as decorative objects of gold and silver, while women produced textiles of extraordinary beauty from cotton and llama and alpaca wool.

**khipus** System of knotted colored cords used by preliterate Andean peoples to record information.

Although the Inka did not introduce new technologies, they increased economic output and added to the region's prosperity. Ruling large populations in environmentally distinct regions allowed the Inka to multiply exchanges between ecological niches. But imperial economic and political expansion reduced equality and diminished local autonomy. The imperial elite, living in richly decorated palaces in Cuzco and other urban centers, were increasingly isolated from the masses. Even provincial nobility were held at arm's length. Commoners faced execution if they look directly at the ruler's face.

After only a century of regional dominance, the Inka Empire faced a crisis in 1525. The death of the ruler Huayna Capac at the conclusion of the conquest of Ecuador initiated a bloody struggle for the throne. The rivalry of two sons compelled both the professional military and the hereditary Inka elite to choose sides. The resulting civil war weakened the imperial state and ignited the resentments of regionalism and ethnic diversity on the eve of the arrival of Europeans.

## CONCLUSION

Tropical Africa and Asia contained 40 percent of the world's population and over a quarter of its habitable land. Between 1200 and 1500, commercial, political, and cultural currents drew the region's peoples closer together. The Indian Ocean became the world's most important and richest trading area. The Delhi Sultanate brought the greatest political unity to India since the decline of the Guptas, and Mali extended the political and trading role pioneered by Ghana in the western Sudan. Trade and empire followed closely the enlargement of Islam's presence and the accompanying diversification of Islamic customs.

Yet many social and cultural practices remained stable. Most tropical Africans and Asians never ventured far outside the rural communities where their families had lived for generations. Their lives followed the patterns of agricultural or pastoral life, the cycle of religious observances, traditional occupational and kinship divisions, and the individual's passage through the stages of life from childhood to elder status. Village communities proved remarkably hardy. They might be ravaged by natural disaster or pillaged by advancing armies, but over time most recovered. Empires and kingdoms rose and fell, but village life endured.

In the Western Hemisphere, the powerful empires of the Aztecs and Inka rose in Mesoamerica and the Andean region, respectively. Each was heir to a series of preceding cultures, but they had in common an unprecedented territorial size. The Aztecs excelled at irrigation and trade, the Inka at labor organization and road building. Both empires were warlike and religious, and their success depended on the economic subordination of conquered peoples as well as specialized production in a variety of environmentally distinct regions.

# CHAPTER REVIEW

## TROPICAL AFRICA AND ASIA

■ *How did environmental differences shape cultural differences in tropical Africa and Asia?* (page 329)

By 1500 tropical Africa and Asia contained nearly 40 percent of the world's population but just over a quarter of its habitable land. Living in every type of ecosystem, from lush rain forests to arid deserts, tropical peoples had become intimately familiar with their environments, learning not merely to survive but also to prosper in them. African pastoralists tended herds of domestic animals in dry regions, while in Asia the more favorable soil and rainfall enabled farmers to cultivate rice, as well as grains and legumes.

## NEW ISLAMIC EMPIRES

■ *Under what circumstances did the first Islamic empires arise in Africa and India?* (page 333)

The period from 1200 to 1500 saw the rise of the first powerful Islamic states outside the Middle East. Chief among these were the Delhi Sultanate, which brought South Asia its greatest political unity since the decline of the Guptas, and the Mali Empire in the western Sudan, which extended the political and trading role pioneered by Ghana. Mali was founded by an indigenous African dynasty that had earlier adopted Islam, while invading Turkish and Afghan Muslims founded the Delhi Sultanate.

## INDIAN OCEAN TRADE

■ *How did cultural and ecological differences promote trade, and in turn how did trade and other contacts promote state growth and the spread of Islam?* (page 338)

Of greatest importance to the spread of Islam throughout tropical Africa and Asia was the Indian Ocean, which directly connected lands as distant as North and East Africa, Arabia, India, and Southeast Asia. Having mastered the seasonal monsoons, merchant sailors made the Indian Ocean the world's most important and richest trading area. A host of Muslim city-states arose: Kilwa along the Swahili Coast, Aden at the entrance to the Red Sea, Gujarat in India, and Malacca at the entrance to the South China Sea.

## SOCIAL AND CULTURAL CHANGE

■ *What social and cultural changes are reflected in the history of peoples living in tropical Africa and Asia during this period?* (page 343)

With the enlargement of Islam's presence in the tropical world came changes that could be brutal as well as beneficial. Slavery, common in many parts of the world at this time, was an integral part of commerce and social life. A woman's status was largely determined by her father, husband, or owner, and women were generally precluded from holding important positions in religious or political life. Muslim culture in this period also brought great benefits, however. The centrality of the Quran in social life contributed to a rise in literacy, first in Arabic but later in native languages as well. Centers of higher education arose in which subjects such as mathematics, medicine, and science were significantly advanced.

## THE WESTERN HEMISPHERE

■ *What were the key differences between the societies of Africa and Asia and the empires of the Aztecs and Inkas?* (page 345)

As the Western Hemisphere's long isolation drew to a close, the Aztecs and Inka used military conquest and political alliance to establish empires in Mesoamerica and the Andes. Divine monarchies that included human sacrifice, their societies were highly stratified and depended on the tribute system of defeated peoples, particularly labor obligations, food tribute, and exchange relationships, rather than their own technological innovation. Unlike in the Eastern Hemisphere, these societies lived in diverse microclimates at high altitudes, a situation that contributed to specialized agricultural niches of such Western Hemisphere crops as cacao, corn, and squash—which were farmed using the methods and technologies of their predecessors. Large territories included roads for long-distance trade, though the absence of large domestic animals meant that transport and trade focused more on lightweight, high value goods than on the bulky cargos shipped on the Indian Ocean. While writing existed for the Aztecs, the Inka utilized khipus—knots on strings—to keep records and a barter system for trading.

## Key Terms

Ibn Battuta (p. 329)

tropics (p. 329)

monsoon (p. 330)

Delhi Sultanate (p. 332)

Mali (p. 333)

Mansa Kankan Musa (p. 335)

Gujarat (p. 336)

dhows (p. 338)

Swahili Coast (p. 339)

Great Zimbabwe (p. 340)

Aden (p. 340)

Malacca (p. 342)

Urdu (p. 343)

Timbuktu (p. 343)

altepetl (p. 346)

calpolli (p. 346)

Aztec (p. 346)

Tenochtitlan (p. 346)

chinampas (p. 347)

tribute system (p. 347)

Inka (p. 348)

khipus (p. 349)

# The Maritime Revolution

© Cengage Learning

In 1511 young Ferdinand Magellan sailed from Europe around the southern tip of Africa and eastward across the Indian Ocean as a member of the first Portuguese expedition to explore the East Indies (maritime Southeast Asia). Eight years later, this time in the service of Spain, he led an expedition that sought to reach the East Indies by sailing westward. By the middle of 1521 Magellan's expedition had achieved its goal by sailing across the Atlantic, rounding the southern tip of South America, and crossing the Pacific Ocean—but at a high price.

Of the five ships that had set out from Spain in 1519, only three made the long passage across the vast Pacific. Dozens of sailors died from starvation and disease during the voyage. In the Philippines, Magellan, having survived numerous mutinies during the voyage, died in battle on April 27, 1521, while aiding a local ruler who had promised to become a Christian.

To consolidate their dwindling resources, the expedition's survivors burned the least seaworthy of their remaining three ships and consolidated men and supplies. In the end only the *Victoria* made it home across the Indian Ocean and back to Europe. Nevertheless, the *Victoria*'s return to Spain on September 8, 1522, was a crowning example of Europeans' determination to make themselves masters of the oceans. A century of daring and dangerous voyages backed by the Portuguese crown had opened new routes through the South Atlantic to Africa, Brazil, and the rich trade of the Indian Ocean. Rival voyages sponsored by Spain since 1492 opened new contacts with the American continents. A maritime revolution was under way that would change the course of history.

This new maritime era marked the end of a long period when Asia had been the source of the most useful technologies and the most influential systems of belief. It was also home to the most powerful states and the richest overland and maritime trading networks. The success of European voyages of exploration in the following century would redirect the world's center of power, wealth, and innovation to the West.

This maritime revolution broadened and deepened contacts, alliances, and conflicts across ancient cultural boundaries. Some of these contacts ended tragically for individuals like Magellan. Some proved disastrous for entire populations: Amerindians, for instance, suffered conquest, colonization, and a rapid decline in numbers. And sometimes the results were mixed: Asians and Africans found both risks and opportunities in their new relations with Europe.

## GLOBAL MARITIME EXPANSION BEFORE 1450

■ What were the objectives and major accomplishments of the voyages of exploration undertaken by Chinese, Polynesians, and other non-Western peoples?

By 1450 daring mariners had discovered and settled most of the islands of the Pacific, the Atlantic, and the Indian Ocean, and a great trading system united the peoples around the Indian Ocean. But no one had yet crossed the Pacific in either direction. Even the smaller Atlantic remained a barrier to contact between the Americas, Europe, and Africa. The inhabitants of Australia were also nearly cut off from contact with the rest of humanity. All this was about to change.

**The Indian Ocean** Connected through trade, the archipelagos and coastal regions of Southeast Asia were divided politically, culturally, and religiously, but their languages all originated from a common Austronesian root. Scholars often use the term *Malayo Indonesians* or *Malay* to describe the early peoples of this maritime realm.

The region's sailors were highly skilled navigators, ship builders, and sail makers who influenced Chinese and Arab maritime advances. They discovered two direct sea routes between Sri Lanka and the South China Sea through the Straits of Malacca and Sunda, thus opening a profitable link to China's silk markets, and they also used the seasonal monsoon winds of the Indian Ocean to extend their voyages for thousands of miles, ultimately reaching East Africa and settling in Madagascar (see Chapter 8).

By the first century C.E. India and Southeast Asia were trading across the region for spices, gold, and aromatic woods, even sending spices as far west as Rome through Mediterranean intermediaries (see

Chapter 5). Their success attracted African, Arab, and Chinese merchants, creating a large, integrated, and highly profitable market in the centuries that followed. By 1000 the dhows (dow) of Arabs and Africans as well as Malay *jongs* and Chinese junks came together in the region's harbors for commerce.

The rise of Islam (see Chapter 9) gave Indian Ocean trade an important boost. The great Muslim cities of the Middle East provided a demand for valuable commodities, and networks of Muslim traders who shared a common language, ethic, and law actively spread their religion to distant trading cities. By 1400 there were Muslim trading communities all around the Indian Ocean. Chinese merchant communities were present as well.

Indian Ocean traders operated independently of the empires and states they served, but when Ming rulers overthrew Mongol rule in China, they became interested in these wealthy ports and reestablishing China's predominance and prestige abroad. The Ming moved to establish direct contacts with the peoples around the Indian Ocean, sending out seven imperial fleets between 1405 and 1433. Admiral Zheng He (jung huh) (1371–1435) commanded the expeditions. A Chinese Muslim with ancestral connections to the Persian Gulf, Zheng was a fitting emissary to the increasingly Muslim-dominated Indian Ocean Basin (see Chapter 14).

The enormous size of these expeditions, far larger than needed for exploration or promoting trade, indicates that the Ming sought to inspire awe. The first consisted of sixty-two specially built "treasure ships," large Chinese junks each about 300 feet long by 150 feet wide (90 by 45 meters). There were also at least a hundred smaller vessels. Each treasure ship had nine masts, twelve sails, many decks, and a carrying capacity of 3,000 tons (six times the capacity of Columbus's entire fleet). One expedition carried over 27,000 individuals, including infantry and cavalry troops. The ships were armed with small cannon, but highly accurate crossbows dominated most Chinese sea battles.

One Chinese-Arabic interpreter kept a journal recording local customs and beliefs. He observed new flora and fauna, noting exotic animals such as the black panther of Malaya and the tapir of Sumatra. In India he described the division of the coastal population into five classes, which correspond to the four Hindu varna and a separate Muslim class, and the fact that traders in the Indian port of Calicut (KAL-ih-kut) could perform error-free calculations by

**Chinese Junk** This modern drawing shows how much larger the Chinese ships were compared to one of Vasco da Gama's vessels. Watertight interior bulkheads made junks the most seaworthy large ships of the fifteenth century. Sails made of pleated bamboo matting hung from the junk's masts, and a stern rudder provided steering. European ships of exploration, though smaller, were faster and more maneuverable.

Dugald Stermer

# Chronology

| | Pacific Ocean | Atlantic Ocean | Indian Ocean |
|---|---|---|---|
| **Pre-1400** | **300 B.C.E.–1200 C.E.** Polynesian settlement of Pacific islands<br>**By 1000** Sporadic Polynesian contacts with American mainland<br>**1200–1300** Polynesian societies in Hawaii, Tonga, and elsewhere develop clear class structures with hereditary chiefs | **770–1200** Viking voyages<br><br>**1300s** Settlement of Madeira, Azores, Canaries<br>**Early 1300s** Mali voyages | |
| **1400** | | **1418–1460** Voyages of Henry the Navigator<br>**1440s** Slaves from West Africa<br>**1482** Portuguese at Gold Coast and Kongo<br>**1486** Portuguese at Benin<br>**1488** Bartolomeu Dias reaches Indian Ocean<br>**1492** Columbus reaches Caribbean<br>**1492–1500** Spanish conquer Hispaniola<br>**1493** Columbus returns to Caribbean (second voyage)<br>**1498** Columbus reaches mainland of South America (third voyage) | **1405–1433** Voyages of Zheng He<br><br><br><br><br><br><br>**1497–1498** Vasco da Gama reaches India |
| **1500** | **1518** Smallpox arrives in Caribbean<br><br>**1519–1522** Magellan expedition | **1500** Cabral reaches Brazil<br><br><br>**1519–1521** Cortés conquers Aztec Empire<br>**1531–1533** Pizarro conquers Inka Empire<br>**1536** Rebellion of Inka in Peru | **1505** Portuguese bombard Swahili Coast cities<br>**1510** Portuguese take Goa<br>**1511** Portuguese take Malacca<br>**1515** Portuguese take Hormuz<br><br>**1535** Portuguese take Diu<br><br>**1538** Portuguese defeat Ottoman fleet<br>**1539** Portuguese aid Ethiopia |

counting on their fingers and toes rather than using the Chinese abacus. After his return, the interpreter went on tour in China, telling of these exotic places and "how far the majestic virtue of [China's] imperial dynasty extended."[1]

---

[1]Ma Huan, *Ying-yai Sheng-lan: "The Overall Survey of the Ocean's Shores,"* ed. Feng Ch'eng-Chün, trans. J. V. G. Mills (Cambridge, England: Cambridge University Press, 1970), 180.

While curiosity about the region was likely one motive, the fact that the fleets visited major commercial ports suggests that expanding China's trade was an objective as well, and it appears that China's lavish gifts to local rulers stimulated the Swahili market for silk and porcelain. But interest in new contacts was not limited to the Chinese. At least three trading cities on the Swahili (swah-HEE-lee) Coast of East Africa sent delegations to China between 1415 and 1416.

Delegates from Malindi presented the Chinese emperor with a giraffe, creating quite a stir among normally reserved imperial officials. These African delegations may have encouraged more contacts because the next three of Zheng's voyages reached the African coast. Unfortunately, no documents record how Africans and Chinese reacted to each other.

Later Ming emperors would focus their attention on internal matters, facing opposition to the expeditions from some Chinese officials who opposed increased contact with peoples they regarded as barbarians incapable of making contributions to China. Such opposition caused a suspension in the voyages from 1424 to 1431. The final Chinese expedition sailed between 1432 and 1433. But long-established Chinese merchant communities continued as major participants in Indian Ocean trade. As the sultan of Malacca, one of the most prosperous trade centers (see Chapter 14), described the era in 1468, "We have learned that to master the blue oceans people must engage in commerce and trade. All the lands within the seas are united in one body. Life has never been so affluent in preceding generations as it is today."[2]

## The Pacific Ocean

Around 3000 B.C.E. Austronesian-speaking seafarers from Southeast Asia reached the island of New Guinea. Contact with the island's original population eventually forged a new cultural identity between these peoples, called *Lapita* by archaeologists. Lapita settlers colonized the island chains of Melanesia (mel-uh-NEE-zhuh), reaching Tonga, Fiji, and Samoa around 1000 B.C.E. By 500 B.C.E. a linguistically and culturally distinct Polynesian culture had emerged from this Lapita origin.

While European sailors were still staying close to shore, Polynesians had mastered long-distance maritime exploration. Pushing east from Tonga, Samoa, and Fiji, they colonized the Marquesas (mar-KAY-suhs) and the Cook and Society archipelagos by approximately 300 B.C.E. Before 500 C.E. Polynesian colonies were established on the Hawaiian Islands 2,200 miles (3,541 kilometers) away. Colonists also

settled Easter Island, 2,300 miles (3,702 kilometers) to the southeast, by 800 C.E., and finally, New Zealand by 1200 C.E. Polynesian voyagers even made periodic contact with the mainland of South America after 1000 C.E., passing on the domesticated Asian chicken and returning with the sweet potato.

Both DNA and linguistic evidence make clear that the Polynesian settlement of the islands of the eastern Pacific was no accident, but rather part of a systematic cultural drive to discover new lands. Following voyages of reconnaissance, Polynesian mariners carried out colonizing expeditions in fleets of large double-hulled canoes that relied on scores of paddlers as well as sails. Their largest canoes reached 120 feet (37 meters) in length and carried crews of fifty. A wide platform connected the two hulls and permitted the transportation of animals and plants crucial to the success of distant and isolated settlements. Long-range expeditions took pigs, dogs, and chickens with them as well as domesticated plants such as taro, bananas, yams, and breadfruit. Their success depended upon reliably navigating thousands of miles of ocean using careful observation of the currents and stars as the crews searched for evidence of land (see Map 15.1).

While all Polynesian societies descended from the same culture and most depended on farming and fishing, differences in geography and climate led to varying colonization experiences. In Hawaii low-lying native forests were converted to farmland using controlled burns, and fishponds were built to increase fish yields. As a result, the Polynesian communities of Hawaii thrived into the era of European expansion. However, in Easter Island, among the most isolated of the Polynesian colonies, population growth led to total deforestation, soil erosion, intense resource competition, and, ultimately, a brutal cycle of warfare that drastically reduced the population. The hierarchical social and political structures that are in evidence throughout the Polynesian archipelagos and New Zealand around 1200–1300 led to chronic warfare elsewhere as well, as hereditary chiefs competed for resources.

## The Atlantic Ocean

From the early Middle Ages, Viking raiders used their small, open ships to attack northern Europe's coastal settlements. Like the Polynesians, the Vikings

[2]Quotation in Craig A. Lockard, "'The Sea Common to All': Maritime Frontiers, Port Cities, and Chinese Traders in the Southeast Asian Age of Commerce, ca. 1400–1750," *Journal of World History* 21, no. 2 (2010): 228.

navigated by their knowledge of the heavens and the seas rather than by maps and other navigational devices. They first settled Iceland in 770, established a colony on Greenland in 982, and sighted North America in 986. Fifteen years later Leif Ericsson established a short-lived Viking settlement on the island of Newfoundland, which he called *Vinland*. When the climate turned colder after 1200, the settlements in Greenland declined and Vinland was abandoned.

Some southern Europeans applied their Mediterranean experience to Atlantic exploration. In the fourteenth century, Genoese and Portuguese expeditions settled the islands of Madeira (muh-DEER-uh), the Azores (A-zorz), and the Canaries.

There is some evidence that Africans also explored the Atlantic in this period. The Syrian geographer al-Umari (1301–1349) relates that when Mansa Kankan Musa (MAHN-suh KAHN-kahn MOO-suh), the ruler of the West African empire of Mali, passed through Egypt on his lavish pilgrimage to Mecca in 1324 (see Chapter 14), he told of Atlantic voyages undertaken by his predecessor, Mansa Muhammad. Muhammad had sent out four hundred vessels with men and supplies, telling them, "Do not return until you have reached the other side of the ocean or if you have exhausted your food or water." After a long time one canoe returned, reporting that the others were lost in a "violent current in the middle of the sea." Muhammad himself then set out at the head of a second, even larger, expedition, from which no one returned.

On the other side of the Atlantic, Amerindian voyagers from the Caribbean coast of South America colonized the West Indies. By the year 1000 the **Arawak** (AR-uh-wahk) (also called *Taino*) had followed the small islands of the Lesser Antilles (Barbados, Martinique, and Guadeloupe) to the Greater Antilles (Cuba, Hispaniola, Jamaica, and Puerto Rico) as well as to the Bahamas. The Carib followed the same route in later centuries, and by the late fifteenth century they had overrun most Arawak settlements in the Lesser Antilles and were raiding parts of the Greater Antilles. Both Arawak and Carib peoples also made contact with the North American mainland.

The transfer of maize cultivation to South America after its domestication in Mesoamerica suggests contact among Amerindian peoples, including the use of boats along the Pacific coast. After 100, mari-

**SECTION REVIEW**

- Polynesians explored and settled the eastern Pacific from the Marquesas to Hawaii and Easter Island.
- The Indian Ocean became a center of commerce and cultural exchange. Between 1405 and 1433 Chinese admiral Zheng He's seven expeditions established contacts with South Asian and African peoples.
- Vikings, Amerindians, and Africans also pursued long-distance explorations and settlement.

ners in two-masted balsa rafts as long as 36 feet (11 meters) were sailing north from the coast of Ecuador bringing pottery, jewelry made of copper as well as gold and silver, and textiles. The rafts could carry over 20 metric tons and ten or more crew members. Favorable winds and Pacific currents facilitated travel north, but these crafts were also capable of returning south, often with cargos of spondylus shells (a spiny bivalve considered sacred by ancient peoples). Through such contact metallurgy was introduced to Mesoamerica around 650.

# EUROPEAN EXPANSION, 1400–1550

■ *In this era of long-distance exploration, did Europeans have any special advantages over other cultural regions?*

While the pace and intensity of maritime contacts increased in many parts of the world before 1450, it was the epic sea voyages sponsored by the European kingdoms of Portugal and Spain that launched the maritime revolution that would profoundly alter world history, ending the isolation of the Americas and increasing global interaction.

Overseas expansion arose from two related phenomena. First, Portuguese and Spanish rulers had strong economic, religious, and political motives to expand their influence. And second, improvements in maritime and military technologies gave them the means to master treacherous and unfamiliar ocean environments, seize control of existing maritime trade routes, and conquer new lands.

**Arawak** Amerindian peoples who inhabited the Greater Antilles of the Caribbean at the time of Columbus.

**Map 15.1  Exploration and Settlement in the Indian and Pacific Oceans Before 1500**  Over many centuries, mariners originating in Southeast Asia gradually colonized the islands of the Pacific and Indian Oceans. The Chinese voyages led by Zheng He in the fifteenth century were lavish official expeditions. © Cengage Learning

## Motives for Exploration

The immediate cause of the voyages in the fifteenth century was the ambitions and adventurous personalities of the rulers of Portugal and Spain, but the underlying causes were four trends evident in the countries of western Europe since about the year 1000: (1) the revival of urban life and trade, (2) the unique alliance between merchants and rulers, (3) a struggle with Islamic powers for dominance of the Mediterranean that mixed religious motives with the desire for trade, and (4) growing intellectual curiosity about the outside world.

By 1450 the city-states of northern Italy had well-established trade links to northern Europe, the Indian Ocean, and the Black Sea, and their merchant princes had also sponsored an intellectual and artistic Renaissance. The Italian trading states of Venice and Genoa maintained commercial ties in the Mediterranean that depended on lucrative alliances with Muslims from the East. Even after the expansion of the Ottoman Empire disrupted this trade, these cities did not take the lead in exploring the Atlantic. However, many individual Italians played leading roles in the Atlantic explorations.

In contrast, the Iberian kingdoms had been engaging in anti-Muslim warfare since the eighth century. By 1250 the Iberian kingdoms of Portugal, Castile, and Aragon had reconquered all the Muslim lands except the kingdom of Granada (see Chapter 13). The dynastic marriage of Isabella of Castile and Ferdinand of Aragon in 1469 facilitated the conquest of Granada in 1492 and the formation of Spain, sixteenth-century Europe's most powerful state.

Christian militancy continued to drive Portugal and Spain in their overseas ventures. But the Iberian rulers and their adventurous subjects also sought material returns. Their modest share of the Mediterranean trade made them more willing than the Italians to seek new routes to Africa and Asia via the Atlantic. Both kingdoms participated in the shipbuilding and the gunpowder revolutions that were under way in Atlantic Europe, and both were especially open to new geographical knowledge.

## Portuguese Voyages

When the Muslim government of Morocco in northwestern Africa weakened in the fifteenth century, the Portuguese attacked, conquering the city of Ceuta (say-OO-tuh) in 1415. Despite the capture of several more ports along Morocco's Atlantic coast, they could not push inland and gain direct access to the gold trade. So they sought contact with the gold producers by sailing down the African coast.

Prince Henry (1394–1460), third son of the king of Portugal, had led the attack on Ceuta. Because from 1418 on he devoted the rest of his life to promoting exploration, he is known as **Henry the Navigator**. His official biographer emphasized Henry's desire to convert Africans to Christianity, make contact with Christian rulers in Africa, and launch joint crusades with them against the Ottomans. Profit also figured in his dreams. His initial explorations focused on Africa, but reaching India became the eventual goal of Portuguese explorers. While called "the Navigator," Henry himself never ventured far from home. Instead, he founded a research center at Sagres (SAH-gresh) to study navigation built on the pioneering efforts of Italian merchants and fourteenth-century Jewish cartographers, and to improve navigational instruments, including the magnetic compass, first developed in China, and the astrolabe, an instrument of Arab or Greek invention that enabled mariners to determine their latitude at sea by measuring the position of the sun or the stars. This center collected geographical information from sailors and travelers and sponsored new expeditions to explore the Atlantic. Henry's ships established permanent contact with the islands of Madeira in 1418 and with the Azores in 1439.

The Portuguese also developed a new type of long-distance sailing vessel. Large crews of oarsmen prevented Mediterranean galleys from carrying enough supplies for long voyages, and the square-rigged vessels of northern Europe could not sail into the wind. The Portuguese **caravel** (KAR-uh-vel) solved both problems. Much smaller than either the largest European ships or the Chinese junks, it could enter shallow coastal waters and explore upriver and yet also had the strength to weather ocean storms. When equipped with triangular lateen sails, caravels had great maneuverability and could sail at greater speeds into the wind. The addition of small cannon made them good fighting ships as well. The caravels' economy, speed, agility, and power justified a con-

temporary's claim that they were "the best ships that sailed the seas."[3]

Pioneering captains had to overcome the common fear that South Atlantic waters were boiling hot or contained ocean currents that would prevent any ship entering them from ever returning home. It took Prince Henry from 1420 to 1434 to coax an expedition to venture beyond southern Morocco (see Map 15.2). It would ultimately take the Portuguese four decades to cover the 1,500 miles (2,400 kilometers) from Lisbon to Sierra Leone (see-ER-uh lee-OWN); it then took only three additional decades to explore the remaining 4,000 miles (6,400 kilometers) to the southern tip of the African continent. With experience, navigators learned to return home speedily by sailing northwest into the Atlantic to the latitude of the Azores, where they picked up prevailing westerly winds. The knowledge that ocean winds tend to form large circular patterns helped later explorers discover many other ocean routes.

During the 1440s Portuguese raiders on the northwest coast of Africa and the Canary Islands began to return with slaves, finding a profitable market in an Iberia still recovering from the population losses of the Black Death. The total number of Africans captured or purchased on voyages exceeded eighty thousand by the end of the century and rose steadily thereafter. However, gold quickly became more important once the Portuguese contacted the trading networks that flourished in West Africa and reached across the Sahara. By 1457 enough African gold was coming back to Portugal for the kingdom to issue a new gold coin bearing a large cross and called the *cruzado*, another reminder of how deeply the Portuguese entwined religious and secular motives.

---

[3]Alvise da Cadamosto in *The Voyages of Cadamosto and Other Documents*, ed. and trans. G. R. Crone (London: Hakluyt Society, 1937), 2.

**Henry the Navigator** Portuguese prince who promoted the study of navigation and directed voyages of exploration down the western coast of Africa in the fifteenth century.

**caravel** A small, highly maneuverable three-masted ship used by the Portuguese and Spanish in the exploration of the Atlantic.

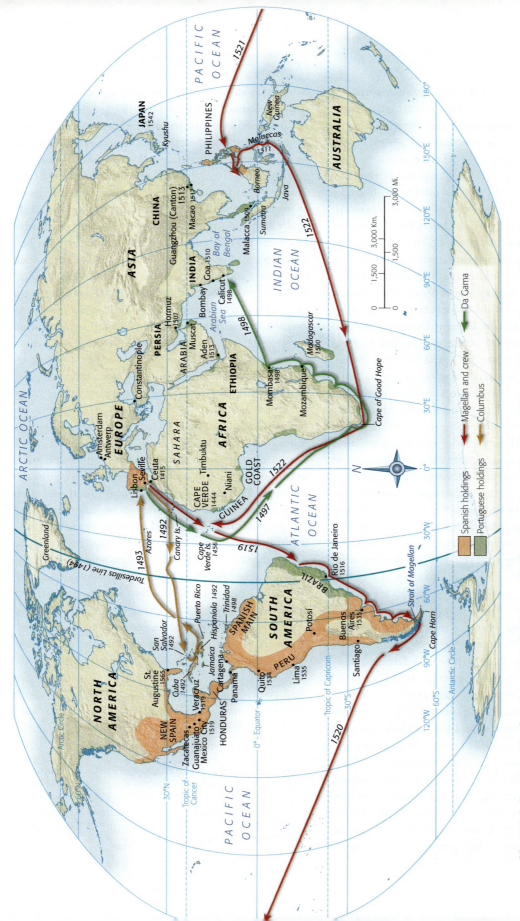

**Map 15.2 European Exploration, 1420–1542** Portuguese and Spanish explorers showed the possibility and practicality of inter-continental maritime trade. Before 1540 European trade with Africa and Asia was much more important than that with the Americas, but after the Spanish conquest of the Aztec and Inka Empires, transatlantic trade began to increase. Notice the Tordesillas line, which in theory separated the Spanish and Portuguese spheres of activity. © Cengage Learning

Royal sponsorship continued, but private commercial interests accelerated the pace of exploration. In 1469 a Lisbon merchant named Fernão Gomes purchased from the Crown the privilege of exploring 350 miles (550 kilometers) of African coast in return for a trade monopoly. He discovered the uninhabited island of São Tomé (sow toh-MAY) on the equator and following the example of the Venetians in the eastern Mediterranean converted it into a major producer of sugar dependent on slave labor. In the next century the island would serve as a model for the sugar plantations of Brazil and the Caribbean. Gomes also explored the **Gold Coast**, which became the headquarters of Portugal's West African trade.

The desire to find a passage around Africa to the rich spice trade of the Indian Ocean spurred the final thrust down the African coast. In 1488 **Bartolomeu Dias** rounded the southern tip of Africa and entered the Indian Ocean, and in 1497–1498 **Vasco da Gama** sailed around Africa and reached India. Then, in 1500, ships under the command of Pedro Alvares Cabral (kah-BRAHL) sailed too far west and accidentally reached the South American mainland, establishing Portugal's claim to Brazil. The gamble that Prince Henry had begun eight decades earlier was about to pay off handsomely.

### Spanish Voyages

Spain's early discoveries owed more to haste and blind luck than to careful planning. Only in the last decade of the fifteenth century did the Spanish monarchs turn their attention from the conquest and organization of previously Muslim territories to overseas exploration. By that time, the Portuguese had already found their route to the India.

The leader of the overseas mission was **Christopher Columbus** (1451–1506), a Genoese mariner. His four voyages between 1492 and 1504 established the existence of a vast new world across the Atlantic. But Columbus refused to accept this momentous discovery, insisting he had found a shorter route to the Indian Ocean.

As a young man Columbus participated in Portuguese explorations along the African coast, but he dreamed of a shorter way to the riches of the East. By his reckoning (based on a serious misreading of a ninth-century Arab authority), the Canaries were a mere 2,400 nautical miles (4,450 kilometers) from Japan. The actual distance was five times greater.

It was not easy for Columbus to find a sponsor to underwrite his theory that Asia could be reached by sailing west. The Portuguese twice rejected his plan, and a Castilian commission questioned his geographical assumptions. Though more sympathetic, Queen Isabella rejected it, too. But his persistence paid off, and in 1492, the queen and her husband, King Ferdinand of Aragon, agreed to fund a modest expedition.

Columbus recorded in his log that he and his crew of ninety men "departed Friday the third day of August of the year 1492" toward "the regions of India." Their mission, the royal contract stated, was "to discover and acquire certain islands and mainland in the Ocean Sea." He carried letters of introduction from the Spanish sovereigns to Eastern rulers, including one to the "Grand Khan" (meaning the Chinese emperor), and brought along an Arabic interpreter. The expedition traveled in three small ships, the *Santa María*, the *Niña*, and the *Pinta*. The *Niña* and the *Pinta* were caravels.

Unfavorable headwinds had impeded other attempts to explore the Atlantic west of the Azores, but Columbus chose a southern route because he had learned in his earlier voyages along the African coast that there were west-blowing winds at the latitude of the Canaries. In October 1492 the expedition reached the islands of the Caribbean. Columbus called the inhabitants Indians because he believed he had reached the East Indies. His second voyage to the Caribbean in 1493 did nothing to change his mind. Even when, two months after Vasco da Gama reached India in 1498, Columbus first sighted the mainland of

**Gold Coast** Region of the Atlantic coast of West Africa occupied by modern Ghana; named for its gold exports to Europe from the 1470s onward.

**Bartolomeu Dias** Portuguese explorer who in 1488 led the first expedition to sail around the southern tip of Africa from the Atlantic and sight the Indian Ocean.

**Vasco da Gama** Portuguese explorer. In 1497–1498 he led the first naval expedition from Europe to sail to India, opening an important commercial sea route.

**Christopher Columbus** Genoese mariner who in the service of Spain led expeditions across the Atlantic, reestablishing contact between the peoples of the Americas and the Old World and opening the way to Spanish conquest and colonization.

**Os montes claros em affrica**

**Serra lioa**    **Castello damina**

**Portuguese Map of Western Africa, 1502** This map shows in great detail a section of African coastline that Portuguese explorers charted and named in the fifteenth century. The cartographer illustrated the African interior, which was almost completely unknown to Europeans, with drawings of birds and views of coastal sights: Sierra Leone (Serra lioa), named for a mountain shaped like a lion, and the Portuguese Castle of the Mine (Castello damina) on the Gold Coast.

akg-images

South America on his third voyage, he insisted it was part of Asia. But by then other Europeans were convinced that he had discovered islands and continents previously unknown to the Old World. Amerigo Vespucci's explorations, first on behalf of Spain and then for Portugal, led mapmakers to name the new continents "America," after him.

To prevent disputes about exploiting these lands and spreading Christianity among their peoples, Spain and Portugal agreed to split the world between them. The Treaty of Tordesillas (tor-duh-SEE-yuhs), negotiated by the pope in 1494, drew an imaginary line down the middle of the Atlantic Ocean. Lands east of the line in Africa and southern Asia were Portugal's to exploit; lands to the west in the Americas were reserved for Spain. Cabral's discovery of Brazil, however, gave Portugal a valid claim to the part of South America located east of the line.

Where would Spain's and Portugal's spheres of influence divide in the East? Given Europeans' ignorance of the earth's true size in 1494, it was not clear whether the Moluccas (muh-LOO-kuhz), the source of valuable spices in the East Indies, were on Portugal's or Spain's side of the Tordesillas line extended around the globe. The size of the Pacific Ocean would determine the boundary. In the end, the Moluccas turned out to lie well within Portugal's sphere, as Spain formally acknowledged in 1529.

In 1519 **Ferdinand Magellan** (ca. 1480–1521) sought to complete Columbus's interrupted westward voyage by sailing around the Americas and across the Pacific. Despite his death during this voyage on behalf of the king of Spain, Magellan was considered the first person to encircle the globe because a decade earlier he had sailed from Europe to the East Indies on an expedition sponsored by his native Portugal. His two voyages took him across the Tordesillas line and through the separate spheres claimed by Portugal and Spain; they also established the basis for Spanish colonization of the Philippines after 1564.

Columbus and those who followed in his wake laid the foundation for the colonial empires of Spain and other European nations. In turn, these empires promoted a major new trading network whose importance rivaled and eventually surpassed that of the Indian Ocean. Portugal's entry into the Indian Ocean led quickly to a major European presence and profit. Both the eastward and the westward voyages of exploration marked a tremendous expansion of Europe's role in world history.

**Ferdinand Magellan** Portuguese navigator who led the Spanish expedition of 1519–1522 that was the first to sail around the world.

# ENCOUNTERS WITH EUROPE, 1450–1550

■ *What were the different outcomes of European interactions with Africa, India, and the Americas?*

European actions alone did not determine the global consequences of these new contacts. The ways in which Africans, Asians, and Amerindians perceived these visitors and interacted with them influenced developments as well. Everywhere indigenous peoples evaluated the Europeans as potential allies or enemies. In general, Africans and Asians recognized the benefits and dangers of European contact. However, the long isolation of the Amerindians from the rest of the world made them vulnerable to European diseases, limiting their ability to resist European settlement.

## Western Africa

Many Africans welcomed trade with the Portuguese, since it offered new markets for exports and access to imports cheaper than those transported overland from the Mediterranean. Miners in the hinterland, which the Portuguese had first visited in 1471, had long sold their gold to merchants from trading cities along the southern edge of the Sahara for transshipment to North Africa. Recognizing the possibility of more favorable terms, coastal Africans negotiated with the royal representative of Portugal, who arrived in 1482 seeking permission to erect a trading fort.

This Portuguese noble and his officers (likely including the young Christopher Columbus) were eager to make a proper impression. They dressed in their best clothes, erected a reception platform, celebrated a Catholic Mass, and signaled the start of negotiations with trumpets, tambourines, and drums. The African king, Caramansa, staged his entrance with equal ceremony, arriving with a large retinue of attendants and musicians. Through an African interpreter, the two leaders exchanged flowery speeches pledging goodwill and mutual benefit.

Caramansa then gave permission for a small trading fort, assured, he said, by the appearance of the royal delegate that they were honorable persons, unlike the "few, foul, and vile" Portuguese visitors of the previous decade.

Neither side made a show of force, but Caramansa warned that if the Portuguese acted aggressively, he and his people would move away, depriving their fort of food and trade. Trade at the post of Saint George of Elmina (the Arabic word for "seaport") enriched both sides. The Portuguese crown had soon purchased gold equal to one-tenth of the world's production at the time. In return, Africans received shiploads of

**Bronze Figure of Benin Ruler** Both this prince and his horse are protected by chain mail introduced in the fifteenth century to Benin by Portuguese merchants. Antenna Gallery Dakar Senegal/ G.Dagli Orti/The Art Archive

goods brought by the Portuguese from Asia, Europe, and other parts of Africa.

After a century of aggressive expansion, the kingdom of Benin in the Niger Delta was near the peak of its power when it first encountered the Portuguese. Its oba (king) presided over an elaborate bureaucracy from a spacious palace in his large capital city, also known as Benin. In response to a Portuguese visit in 1486, the oba sent an ambassador to Portugal to learn more about these strangers. He then established a royal monopoly on Portuguese trade, selling pepper and ivory tusks (for export to Portugal) as well as stone beads, textiles, and prisoners of war (for resale at Elmina). In return, Portuguese merchants provided Benin with copper and brass, fine textiles, glass beads, and a horse for the king's royal procession. In the early sixteenth century, as the demand for slaves for the Portuguese sugar plantations on the nearby island of São Tomé grew, the oba first raised the price of slaves and then imposed restrictions that limited their sale.

Early contacts generally involved a mix of commercial, military, and religious exchanges. Some African rulers appreciated the advantage of European firearms. Because African religions were generally not exclusive, coastal rulers were also willing to test the value of the Christian practices promoted by the Portuguese. The rulers of Benin and Kongo, the two largest coastal kingdoms, accepted Portuguese missionaries and soldiers as allies in battle to determine the efficacy of the religion and the weaponry.

However, Portuguese efforts to persuade the king and nobles of Benin to accept the Catholic faith ultimately failed. Early kings showed some interest, but after 1538 rulers declined to receive more missionaries. They also closed the market in male slaves for the rest of the sixteenth century. We do not know why Benin chose to limit its contacts with the Portuguese, but the result makes clear that these rulers had the power to control their contacts with Europeans.

Farther south, on the lower Congo River, the manikongo (mah-NEE-KONG-goh) (king of Kongo) also sent delegates to Portugal, established a royal monopoly on trade, and expressed interest in missionary teachings. But here the royal family made Catholicism the kingdom's official faith. Lacking ivory and pepper, Kongo sold more slaves to acquire the goods brought by the Portuguese and to pay missionary expenses. Soon the royal trade monopoly broke down. In 1526 the Christian manikongo, Afonso I (r. 1506–ca. 1540), wrote to his royal "brother," the king of Portugal, begging for his help in stopping the trade because unauthorized Kongolese were kidnapping and selling people, even members of good families (see Diversity and Dominance: Kongo's Christian King). Alfonso received no reply from Portugal, whose interests were now concentrated in the Indian Ocean. Soon rebellion and the relocation of the slave trade from his kingdom to the south weakened the manikongo's authority.

**Eastern Africa**

Different still were the reactions of the Muslim rulers of the coastal trading states of eastern Africa. As Vasco da Gama's fleet sailed up the coast in 1498, most rulers gave the Portuguese a cool reception, suspicious of the painted crusaders' crosses on their sails. The ruler of Malindi, however, saw the Portuguese as an ally who could help him expand Malindi's trade, and he provided da Gama with a pilot to guide him to India. The suspicions of the other rulers were proven correct seven years later when a Portuguese war fleet bombarded and looted most of the coastal cities of eastern Africa in the name of Christ and commerce, while sparing Malindi.

Christian Ethiopia also saw the benefit of an alliance with the Portuguese. In the fourteenth and fifteenth centuries, Ethiopian conflicts with Muslim states along the Red Sea Increased. After the Ottoman Turks conquered Egypt and launched a fleet in the Indian Ocean to counter the Portuguese in 1517, the warlord of the Muslim state of Adal (now Djibouti) attacked Ethiopia. A decisive victory in 1529 put the Christian kingdom in jeopardy, making Portuguese support crucial.

For decades, delegations from Portugal and Ethiopia had explored a Christian alliance. Queen Helena of Ethiopia, who acted as regent for her young sons after her husband's death in 1478, sent a letter in 1509 to "our very dear and well-beloved brother," the king of Portugal, along with a gift of two tiny crucifixes said to be made of wood from the cross on which Christ was crucified. She proposed joining forces—her army and Portugal's fleet—to fight the Ottomans;

however, Helena's death in 1522 occurred before the alliance could be arranged. Ethiopia's situation then grew more desperate.

Finally, a small Portuguese force commanded by Vasco da Gama's son Christopher arrived to aid Ethiopia in 1539. With Portuguese help, another queen rallied the Ethiopians. Muslim forces captured and tortured to death Christopher da Gama, but they retreated when their own leader fell in battle. Portuguese aid helped save the Ethiopian kingdom from extinction, but a permanent alliance faltered because Ethiopian rulers refused to transfer their Christian affiliation from the patriarch of Alexandria to the Latin patriarch of Rome (the pope).

As these examples illustrate, African encounters with the Portuguese before 1550 varied considerably. Africans and Portuguese might become royal brothers, bitter opponents, or partners in a mutually profitable trade, but Europeans remained a minor presence in most of Africa in 1550. By then the Portuguese had become far more interested in the Indian Ocean trade.

### Indian Ocean States

Vasco da Gama's arrival on the Malabar Coast of India in May 1498 did not impress the citizens of Calicut. The Chinese fleets of gigantic junks that had called at Calicut sixty-five years earlier dwarfed his four small ships, which were no larger than many of the dhows already filling the harbor. The samorin (ruler) of Calicut and his Muslim officials showed mild interest, but the gifts da Gama brought provoked derisive laughter: twelve pieces of fairly ordinary striped cloth, four scarlet hoods, six hats, and six wash basins. When da Gama tried to defend his gifts as those of an explorer, not a merchant, the samorin cut him short, asking whether he had come to discover men or stones: "If he had come to discover men, as he said, why had he brought nothing?"

Coastal rulers soon discovered that the Portuguese had no intention of remaining poor competitors in the Indian Ocean trade. Upon da Gama's return to Portugal in 1499, the jubilant King Manuel styled himself "Lord of the Conquest, Navigation, and Commerce of Ethiopia, Arabia, Persia, and India." Previously the Indian Ocean had been an open sea, used by merchants (and pirates) of all the surrounding coasts. Now the Portuguese crown intended to make it Portugal's sea, to be used on Portuguese terms alone.

Portugal's hope of controlling the Indian Ocean stemmed from the superiority of its ships and weapons, especially over the lightly armed merchant dhows. In 1505 a Portuguese fleet of eighty-one ships and some seven thousand men bombarded Swahili Coast cities. Indian ports were the next targets. Goa, on the west coast of India, fell to a well-armed fleet in 1510, becoming the base from which the Portuguese menaced the trading cities of Gujarat (goo-juh-RAHT) to the north and Calicut and other Malabar Coast cities to the south. The port of Hormuz, controlling entry to the Persian Gulf, fell in 1515. Aden, at the entrance to the Red Sea, successfully resisted, but the capture of the Gujarati port of Diu in 1535 consolidated Portuguese dominance of the western Indian Ocean.

Meanwhile, Portuguese explorers had reconnoitered the Bay of Bengal and the waters farther east. The city of Malacca (muh-LAH-kuh) on the strait between the Malay Peninsula and Sumatra became the focus of their attention. During the fifteenth century, Malacca had become the main entrepôt for the trade from China, Japan, India, the Southeast Asian mainland, and the Moluccas. The city's more than 100,000 residents spoke eighty-four different languages, including those of merchants from Cairo, Ethiopia, and the Swahili Coast. Many non-Muslim residents supported letting the Portuguese join its cosmopolitan trading community, perhaps hoping to offset the growing solidarity of Muslim traders. In 1511, however, the Portuguese seized Malacca with a force of a thousand fighting men, including three hundred recruited in southern India.

Force was not always necessary. On the China coast, local officials and merchants persuaded the imperial government to allow the Portuguese to establish a trading post at Macao (muh-COW) in 1557. Subsequently, Portuguese ships nearly monopolized trade between China and Japan.

Control of major port cities enabled the Portuguese to enforce their demands that all spices be carried in Portuguese ships, as well as goods on the major ocean routes such as between Goa and Macao. The Portuguese also tried to control and tax other Indian Ocean trade. Merchant ships entering and leaving their ports had to carry a Portuguese passport and

## Kongo's Christian King

The new overseas voyages brought conquest to some and opportunities for fruitful borrowings and exchanges to others. The decision of the ruler of the kingdom of Kongo to adopt Christianity in 1491 added cultural diversity to Kongolese society and in some ways strengthened the hand of the king. From then on Kongolese rulers sought to introduce Christian beliefs and rituals while at the same time Africanizing Christianity to make it more intelligible to their subjects. In addition, the kings of Kongo sought a variety of more secular aid from Portugal, including schools and medicine. Trade with the Portuguese introduced new social and political tensions, especially in the case of the export trade in slaves for the Portuguese sugar plantations on the island of São Tomé to the north.

Two letters sent to King João (zhwao) III of Portugal in 1526 illustrate how King Afonso of Kongo saw his kingdom's new relationship with Portugal and the problems that resulted from it. (Afonso adopted that name when baptized as a young prince.) After the death of his father in 1506, Afonso successfully claimed the throne and ruled until 1542. His son Henrique became the first Catholic bishop of the Kongo in 1521.

These letters were written in Portuguese and penned by the king's secretary João Teixera (tay-SHER-uh), a Kongo Christian, who, like Afonso, had been educated by Portuguese missionaries.

6 July 1526

To the very powerful and excellent prince Dom João, our brother:

On the 20th of June just past, we received word that a trading ship from your highness had just come to our port of Sonyo. We were greatly pleased by that arrival for it had been many days since a ship had come to our kingdom, for by it we would get news of your highness, which many times we had desired to know, . . . and likewise as there was a great and dire need for wine and flour for the holy sacrament; and of this we had had no great hope for we have the same need frequently. And that, sir, arises from the great negligence of your highness's officials toward us and toward shipping us those things. . . .

Sir, your highness should know how our kingdom is being lost in so many ways that we will need to provide the needed cure, since this is caused by the excessive license given by your agents and officials to the men and merchants who come to this kingdom to set up shops with goods and many things which have been prohibited by us, and which they spread throughout our kingdoms and domains in such abundance that many of our vassals, whose submission we could once rely on, now act independently so as to get the things in greater abundance than we ourselves; whom we had formerly held content and submissive and under our vassalage and jurisdiction, so it is doing a great harm not only to the service of God, but also to the security and peace of our kingdoms and state.

And we cannot reckon how great the damage is, since every day the mentioned merchants are taking our people, sons of the land and the sons of our noblemen and vassals and our relatives, because the thieves and men of bad conscience grab them so as to have the things and wares of this kingdom that they crave; they grab them and bring them to be sold. In such a manner, sir, has been the corruption and deprivation that our land is becoming completely depopulated, and your highness should not deem this good nor in your service. And to avoid this we need from these kingdoms [of yours] no more than priests and a few people to teach in schools, and no other goods except wine and flour for the holy sacrament, which is why we beg of your highness to help and assist us in this matter. Order your agents to send here neither merchants nor wares, because it is our will that in these kingdoms there should not be any dealing in slaves nor outlet for them, for the reasons stated above. Again we beg your highness's agreement, since otherwise we cannot cure such manifest harm. May Our Lord in His mercy have your highness always under His protection and may you always do the things of His holy service. I kiss your hands many times.

From our city of Kongo. . . .

The King, Dom Afonso ➤

18 October 1526

Very high and very powerful prince King of Portugal, our brother,

Sir, your highness has been so good as to promise us that anything we need we should ask for in our letters, and that everything will be provided. And so that there may be peace and health of our kingdoms, by God's will, in our lifetime. And as there are among us old folks and people who have lived for many days, many and different diseases happen so often that we are pushed to the ultimate extremes. And the same happens to our children, relatives, and people, because this country lacks physicians and surgeons who might know the proper cures for such diseases, as well as pharmacies and drugs to make them better. And for this reason many of those who had been already confirmed and instructed in the things of the holy faith of Our Lord Jesus Christ perish and die. And the rest of the people for the most part cure themselves with herbs and sticks and other ancient methods, so that they live putting all their faith in these herbs and ceremonies, and die believing that they are saved; and this serves God poorly.

And to avoid such a great error, I think, and inconvenience, since it is from God and from your highness that all the good and the drugs and medicines have come to us for our salvation, we ask your merciful highness to send us two physicians and two pharmacists and one surgeon, so that they may come with their pharmacies and necessary things to be in our kingdoms, for we have extreme need of each and every one of them. We will be very good and merciful to them, since sent by your highness, their work and coming should be for good. We ask your highness as a great favor to do this for us, because besides being good in itself it is in the service of God as we have said above.

Moreover, sir, in our kingdoms there is another great inconvenience which is of little service to God, and this is that many of our people, out of great desire for the wares and things of your kingdoms, which are brought here by your people, and in order to satisfy their disordered appetite, seize many of our people, freed and exempt men. And many times noblemen and the sons of noblemen, and our relatives are stolen, and they take them to be sold to the white men who are in our kingdoms and take them hidden or by night, so that they are not recognized. And as soon as they are taken by the white men, they are immediately ironed and branded with fire. And when they are carried off to be embarked, if they are caught by our guards, the whites allege that they have bought them and cannot say from whom, so that it is our duty to do justice and to restore to the free their freedom. And so they went away offended.

And to avoid such a great evil we passed a law so that every white man living in our kingdoms and wanting to purchase slaves by whatever means should first inform three of our noblemen and officials of our court on whom we rely in this matter, namely Dom Pedro Manipunzo and Dom Manuel Manissaba, our head bailiff, and Gonçalo Pires, our chief supplier, who should investigate if the said slaves are captives or free men, and, if cleared with them, there will be no further doubt nor embargo and they can be taken and embarked. And if they reach the opposite conclusion, they will lose the aforementioned slaves. Whatever favor and license we give them [the white men] for the sake of your highness in this case is because we know that it is in your service too that these slaves are taken from our kingdom; otherwise we should not consent to this for the reasons stated above that we make known completely to your highness so that no one could say the contrary, as they said in many other cases to your highness, so that the care and remembrance that we and this kingdom have should not be withdrawn. . . .

We kiss your hands of your highness many times.

From our city of Kongo, the 18th day of October,

The King, Dom Afonso

## QUESTIONS FOR ANALYSIS

1. What sorts of things does King Afonso desire from the Portuguese?
2. What is he willing and unwilling to do in return?
3. What problem with his own people has the slave trade created, and what has King Afonso done about it?
4. Does King Afonso see himself as an equal to King João or his subordinate? Do you agree with that analysis?

Source: From António Brásio, ed., *Monumenta Missionaria Africana: Africa Ocidental (1471–1531)* (Lisbon: Agência Geral do Ultramar, 1952), I: 468, 470–471, 488–491. Translated by David Northrup.

**Portuguese in India**   In the sixteenth century Portuguese men moved to the Indian Ocean Basin to work as administrators and traders. This Indo-Portuguese drawing from about 1540 shows a Portuguese man speaking to an Indian woman, perhaps making a proposal of marriage.

Album/Art Resource, NY

pay customs duties. Portuguese patrols seized vessels that did not comply, confiscated their cargoes, and either killed the captain and crew or sentenced them to forced labor.

Reactions to this power grab varied. Like the emperors of China, the Mughal (MOO-gahl) emperors of India largely ignored Portugal's maritime intrusions. The Ottomans confronted the Christian intruders more aggressively. They supported Egypt's defensive efforts in 1501 and 1509 and then sent their own fleet into the Indian Ocean in 1538. However, Ottoman galleys proved no match for the faster, better-armed Portuguese vessels in the open ocean. They retained their advantage only in the Red Sea and Persian Gulf, where they controlled many ports.

Smaller trading states also could not challenge the Portuguese because their mutual rivalry kept them from forming a common front. Some cooperated with the Portuguese to safeguard their prosperity and security, while others engaged in evasion and resistance. When the merchants of Calicut put up sustained resistance, the Portuguese embargoed all trade with Aden, Calicut's principal trading partner, and centered their trade on the port of Cochin, which had once been a dependency of Calicut. Some Calicut merchants evaded their patrols, but Calicut's impor-

tance shrank as Cochin gradually became the major pepper-exporting port on the Malabar Coast.

Farther north, Gujarat initially resisted Portuguese attempts at monopoly and in 1509 joined Egypt's futile effort to sweep the Portuguese from the Arabian Sea. But in 1535, finding his state weakened by Mughal attacks, the ruler allowed the Portuguese to build a fort at Diu in return for their support. Once established, the Portuguese gradually extended their control, and by midcentury they were licensing and taxing all Gujarati ships. Even after the Mughals took control of Gujarat in 1572, the Mughal emperor Akbar permitted the Portuguese to continue their maritime monopoly in return for allowing one pilgrim ship a year to travel to Mecca without paying a fee.

The Portuguese never gained complete control of the Indian Ocean trade, but their domination of key ports and trade routes brought them considerable profits from spices and other luxury goods. The Portuguese broke the trading monopoly of Venice and Genoa by selling pepper at much lower prices.

The consequences flowing from these events were dramatic. The Portuguese were able to fund an aggressive colonization of Brazil, while Asian and East African traders were at the mercy of their warships. But because the Portuguese concentrated on maritime trade routes in Asia and Africa, Portugal had little impact on the Asian and African mainlands, in sharp contrast to what was occurring in the Americas.

## The Americas

The Spanish and Portuguese monarchies had similar motives for expansion and used identical ships and weapons, but the Spanish established a territorial rather than a trading empire in the Americas. The outcomes had little to do with differences between the two kingdoms. Rather, the isolation of the Amerindian peoples was key, making their responses to outside contacts different from those of African and Indian Ocean peoples. Isolation had slowed the development of metallurgy and other militarily useful technologies in the Americas and also made these large populations more susceptible to new diseases. It was the spread of deadly new diseases, especially smallpox, among Amerindians after 1518 that weakened their ability to resist and facilitated Spanish and Portuguese occupation.

The first Amerindians to encounter Columbus were the Arawak of Hispaniola (modern Haiti and the Dominican Republic) in the Greater Antilles and the Bahamas to the north (see Map 15.2). They cultivated maize (corn), cassava (yuca), sweet potatoes, and hot peppers, as well as cotton and tobacco. Although the islands did not have large gold deposits and, unlike West Africans, the Arawak had not previously traded gold over long distances, the natives were skilled at working gold. They extended a cautious welcome, but they soon learned to tell exaggerated stories about gold in other places to persuade the Spanish to move on.

Columbus brought several hundred settlers, as well as missionaries, on his second trip to Hispaniola in 1493. The settlers provoked the Arawak by demanding indigenous labor to look for gold, stealing gold ornaments and food, and sexually assaulting native women. The Arawak rebelled in 1495 but were slaughtered by the tens of thousands, no match for Spanish horses, body armor, and steel swords. Thousands more were forced to labor for the Spanish. Meanwhile, cattle, pigs, and goats introduced by the settlers devoured the Arawaks' food crops, causing deaths from famine and disease, particularly smallpox. A governor appointed by the Spanish crown in 1502 institutionalized these demands by forcing the surviving Arawak to become laborers under the control of Spanish settlers.

The actions of the Spanish in the Antilles were similar to those used by the Spanish against the Muslims in previous centuries: they sought to serve God by defeating, controlling, and converting nonbelievers and to become rich in the process. Individual **conquistadors** (kon-KEY-stuh-dor) (conquerors) extended that pattern around the Caribbean. Some raided the Bahamas for gold and labor as both became scarce on Hispaniola. New expeditions searched for gold and Amerindian laborers across the Caribbean region, capturing thousands of Amerindians and relocating them to Hispaniola as slaves. The island of Borinquen (Puerto Rico) was conquered in 1508 and Cuba between 1510 and 1511.

An ambitious and ruthless nobleman, **Hernán Cortés** (kor-TEZ) (1485–1547) undertook a new expedition to the mainland. Cortés left Cuba in 1519 with six hundred fighting men to assault the Mexican mainland in search of slaves and trade. After learning of the rich Aztec Empire in central Mexico, he expanded the exploitation and conquest carried out in the Greater Antilles.

Many subject peoples resented the tribute payments, forced labor, and large-scale human sacrifices demanded by the Aztecs. Consequently, some embraced the Spanish as allies. The Aztecs also had powerful native enemies, including the Tlaxcalans (thlash-KAH-lans), who became crucial allies of Cortés. Individual Amerindians also calculated the potential benefit or threat represented by these strange visitors. Malintzin (mah-LEENT-zeen) (also called Malinche), a native woman given to Cortés shortly after his arrival in the Maya region, became his translator, key source of intelligence, and mistress. As peoples and as individuals, native allies were crucial to the Spanish campaign.

While the emperor **Moctezuma II** (mock-teh-ZOO-ma) (r. 1502–1520) hesitated to use force and

---

**conquistadors** Early-sixteenth-century Spanish adventurers who conquered Mexico, Central America, and Peru.

**Hernán Cortés** Spanish explorer and conquistador who led the conquest of Aztec Mexico in 1519–1521 for Spain.

**Moctezuma II** Aztec emperor who died while in custody of the Spanish conquistador Hernán Cortés.

Montezuma wearing on his back the royal standard of green Quetzal bird feathers, copied from a native artist (colour litho)/Private Collection/Peter Newark American Pictures/The Bridgeman Art Library

**Coronation of Emperor Moctezuma**  This painting by an unnamed Aztec artist depicts the Aztec ruler's coronation. Moctezuma, his nose pierced by a bone, receives the crown from a prince in the palace at Tenochtitlan.

attempted diplomacy instead, Cortés pushed toward the Aztec capital of Tenochtitlan (teh-noch-TIT-lan). Spanish forces overcame opposition with firearms, cavalry tactics, and steel swords. As the Spanish approached his island capital, the emperor went out in a great procession, dressed in his finery, to welcome Cortés.

Despite Cortés's initial pledge of friendship, Moctezuma was quickly imprisoned. The Spanish looted his treasury, interfered with the city's religious rituals, and eventually massacred hundreds during a festival. The Aztecs rebelled, killing half the Spanish force and four thousand of Cortés's native allies. In the confusion Moctezuma also lost his life, either killed by the Spanish or in the Aztec attack.

The survivors, strengthened by Spanish reinforcements and aided by the Tlaxcalans, renewed their attack and captured Tenochtitlan in 1521. Their victory was aided by a smallpox epidemic that killed more of the city's defenders than did the fighting. One source remembered that the disease "spread over the people as a great destruction." Many Amerindians as well as Europeans blamed the devastating spread of

this disease on supernatural forces. Cortés and other Spanish leaders then led expeditions to the north and south accompanied by the Tlaxcalans and other indigenous allies. Everywhere epidemic disease, especially smallpox, helped crush indigenous resistance.

Meanwhile, Spanish settlers in Panama began hearing of another empire to the south. The Inka Empire stretched nearly 3,000 miles (5,000 kilometers) south of the equator along the Pacific coast (see Chapter 14). During its expansion, it had enforced labor demands and taxes on conquered peoples and exiled rebellious populations. When the Inka ruler Huayna Capac (WHY-nah KAH-pak) died in 1525, a civil war ensued as his sons fought for the throne. **Atahuallpa** (ah-tuh-WAHL-puh) (r. 1531–1533), the candidate of the northern army, defeated Huascar, the candidate of the royal court at Cuzco, but political leadership was weakened and the military

**Atahuallpa**  Last ruling Inka emperor of Peru. He was executed by the Spanish.

**Francisco Pizarro**  Spanish explorer who led the conquest of the Inka Empire of Peru in 1531–1533.

decimated. At this critical time **Francisco Pizarro** (pih-ZAHR-oh) (ca. 1478–1541) and his force of 180 men, thirty-seven horses, and two cannon entered the region.

Pizarro had come to the Americas in 1502 at the age of twenty-five to seek his fortune. He had participated in the conquest of Hispaniola and in Balboa's expedition across the Isthmus of Panama to the Pacific. In the 1520s he gambled his fortune on exploring the Pacific coast south of the equator, where he learned of the riches of the Inka. With a license from the king of Spain, he set out from Panama in 1531 to conquer them.

Having seen signs of the civil war after landing, Pizarro arranged to meet the Inka emperor, Atahuallpa, near the Andean city of Cajamarca (kah-hah-MAHR-kah) in November 1532. With supreme boldness and brutality, Pizarro's small band of armed men attacked Atahuallpa and his followers as they entered an enclosed courtyard. Though surrounded by an Inka army of at least forty thousand, the Spaniards were able to use their cannon to create confusion while their swords brought down thousands of the emperor's lightly armed retainers and servants.

Atahuallpa attempted to purchase his freedom. Noting the glee with which the Spaniards seized gold and silver, Atahuallpa offered what he thought would satisfy even the greediest among them: rooms filled to shoulder height with gold and silver. But after receiving 13,400 pounds (6,000 kilograms) of gold and 26,000 pounds (12,000 kilograms) of silver, the Spaniards still executed Atahuallpa. His death broke the unity of an empire already battered by civil war.

### The Execution of Inka Ruler Atahuallpa

Felipe Guaman Poma de Ayala, a native Andean from the area of Huamanga in Peru, drew this representation of the execution. While Pizarro sentenced Atahuallpa to death by strangulation, not beheading, Guaman Poma's illustration forcefully made the point that Spain had imposed an arbitrary and violent government on the Andean people.

**SECTION REVIEW**

- African kingdoms reacted in various ways to the opportunities and threats created by the arrival of the Portuguese, but only Kongo embraced Christianity and accepted a large Portuguese military presence in the sixteenth century.

- The Portuguese used military force to consolidate a trade empire in the Indian Ocean.

- After the Spanish occupied the Caribbean, Cortés led an expedition that conquered the Aztecs, who were weakened by disease.

- The Spanish under Pizarro conquered the Inka Empire, already suffering from civil war, and then fell on each other; but surviving conquistadors continued to explore the Americas.

In 1533, the Spanish had taken Cuzco, but in 1536 Pizarro had to put down another massive native rebellion. The remaining Inka now retreated, creating a small kingdom in the mountains that lasted until 1572. In 1541, Pizarro himself met a violent death at the hands of Spanish rivals, but the conquest of the mainland continued. Incited by the fabulous wealth of the Aztecs and Inka, conquistadors extended Spanish conquest and exploration in South and North America, dreaming of new treasures.

## CONCLUSION

The rapid expansion of European empires and the projection of European military power around the world, one of the most important events in world history, would have seemed unlikely in 1492. No European power matched the military and economic strength of China, and few could rival the Ottomans. Spain lacked strong national institutions and Portugal had a small population; both had limited resources. Because of these limitations, the monarchs of Spain and Portugal allowed their subjects greater initiative. While royal sponsorship was often crucial in the Portuguese contacts with Africa and the first voyages to Asia, many of the commercial and military expeditions were effectively organized and financed as private companies. Very often the kings of Spain and Portugal struggled to catch up with their restless and ambitious subjects, sometimes taking decades to establish royal control in new colonies.

The pace and character of European expansion in Africa and Asia were different than in the Americas. In Africa local rulers were generally able to limit European military power to coastal outposts and to control European trade. Only in the Kongo were the Portuguese able to project their power inland. When the Europeans arrived in the Indian Ocean, mature markets and specialized production for distant consumers already existed. Here Portuguese (and later Dutch and British) naval power allowed Europeans to harvest large profits and influence regional commercial patterns, but most indigenous populations continued to enjoy effective autonomy for centuries.

In the Americas, however, the terrible effects of epidemic disease and the destructiveness of the Spanish conquests led to the rapid creation of European settlements and the subordination of the surviving indigenous population. As we shall see in Chapter 16, American gold, silver, and sugar eventually produced great wealth but only through the introduction of new technologies, the imposition of oppressive forms of labor, most notably slavery, and the development of new roads and ports.

What gave the European maritime revolution unprecedented importance had more to do with what happened after 1550 than what happened prior. The overseas empires of the Europeans would endure longer than the Mongols' and would continue to expand for three centuries after 1600. Unlike the Chinese, the Europeans did not turn their backs on the world after an initial burst of exploration. Not content with dominance in the Indian Ocean trade, Europeans opened an Atlantic maritime network that grew to rival the Indian Ocean network in the wealth of its trade; they also pioneered trade across the Pacific. The maritime expansion, begun in the period from 1450 to 1550, marked the beginning of a new age of global interaction.

# CHAPTER REVIEW

## GLOBAL MARITIME EXPANSION BEFORE 1450

■ *What were the objectives and major accomplishments of the voyages of exploration undertaken by Chinese, Polynesians, and other non-Western peoples?* (page 355)

The voyages of exploration undertaken by the Malays, Chinese, and Polynesians pursued diverse objectives. Malay voyagers were crucial participants in the development of the rich and varied commerce of Southeast Asia and initiated connections between these markets and Arabia and Africa. The great voyages of the Chinese in the early fifteenth century were motivated by an interest in trade, curiosity, and the desire to project imperial power. For the Polynesians, the discovery and settlement of new lands was a recurring objective because most of the islands that were settled were too small to support large populations. The Vikings, Africans, and Amerindians all undertook long-distance explorations as well, although with fewer lasting consequences.

## EUROPEAN EXPANSION, 1400–1550

■ *In this era of long-distance exploration, did Europeans have any special advantages over other cultural regions?* (page 359)

This projection of European influence between 1450 and 1550 was in some ways similar to that of other cultural regions in that it expanded commercial linkages, increased cross-cultural contacts, and served the ambitions of political leaders. But in the aftermath of several centuries of Spanish and Portuguese combat against Muslim kingdoms in Iberia, it was driven by unusually powerful urges to fight Muslims, acquire their riches, and spread Christianity. During those years European explorers opened new long-distance trade routes across the world's three major oceans, for the first time establishing regular contact among all the continents.

## ENCOUNTERS WITH EUROPE, 1450–1550

■ *What were the different outcomes of European interactions with Africa, India, and the Americas?* (page 365)

Europeans created colonial empires in the Americas quite rapidly, while their progress in Africa and Asia was much slower. Many Amerindians welcomed the Spanish settlers at first, only to have the Spanish tax their labors, steal their food, introduce disease and warfare, and eventually subjugate them. In contrast, Portuguese visitors to Africa remained a minor presence in 1550. In some regions, the Portuguese were welcomed as trading partners; in others they were regarded as potential political and military allies. The real focus of the Portuguese was to capture the rich trade of the Indian Ocean. While they never gained complete control, they used their superior military strength to dominate key ports and major trade routes.

## Key Terms

Arawak (p. 359)

Henry the Navigator (p. 361)

caravel (p. 361)

Gold Coast (p. 363)

Bartolomeu Dias (p. 363)

Vasco da Gama (p. 363)

Christopher Columbus (p. 363)

Ferdinand Magellan (p. 364)

conquistadors (p. 371)

Hernán Cortés (p. 371)

Moctezuma II (p. 371)

Atahuallpa (p. 372)

Francisco Pizarro (p. 372)

# Climate and Population to 1500

**D**uring the millennia before 1500, human populations expanded in three momentous surges. The first occurred after 50,000 B.C.E. when humans emigrated from their African homeland to all of the inhabitable continents. After that, the global population remained steady for many millennia. During the second expansion, between about 5000 and 500 B.C.E., population rose from about 5 million to 100 million as agricultural societies spread around the world (see Figure 1). Population growth then slowed for several centuries before a third surge took world population to over 350 million by 1200 C.E. (Figure 2 shows population in China and Europe.)

For a long time historians tended to attribute these population surges to cultural and technological advances. Indeed, a great many changes in culture and technology are associated with adaptation to different climates and food supplies in the first surge and with the domestication of plants and animals in the second. However, historians have not found a cultural or technological change to explain the third surge, nor can they explain why creativity would have stagnated for long periods between the surges. Something else must have been at work.

Recently historians have begun to pay more attention to the impact of long-term variations in

© Cengage Learning

**Figure 1** World Population, 5000–1 B.C.E.

global climate. By examining ice cores drilled out of glaciers, scientists have been able to compile records of thousands of years of climate change. The comparative width of tree rings from ancient forests has provided additional data on periods of favorable and unfavorable growth. Such evidence shows that cycles of population growth and stagnation followed changes in global climate.

Historians now believe that global temperatures were above normal for extended periods from the late 1100s to the late 1200s C.E. In the temperate lands where most of the world's people lived, above-normal temperatures meant a longer growing season, more bountiful harvests, and thus a more adequate and reliable food supply. The ways in which societies responded to the Medieval Warm Period (see Chapter 13) and the simultaneous cooling of the Middle East are as important as the climate change, but it is unlikely that human agency alone would have produced Europe's medieval surge. One notable response was that of the Vikings, who increased the size and range of their settlements in the North Atlantic, although their raids also caused death and destruction.

Some of the complexities involved in the interaction of human agency, climate, and other natural factors are also evident in the demographic changes that followed the Medieval Warm Period. During the 1200s the Mongol invasions caused death and disruption of agriculture across Eurasia. China's population, which had been over 100 million in 1200, declined by a third or more by 1300. The Mongol invasions did not cause harm west of Russia, but climate changes in the 1300s resulted in population losses in Europe. Unusually heavy rains caused crop failures and a prolonged famine in northern Europe from 1315 to 1319.

The freer movement of merchants within the Mongol Empire also facilitated the spread of disease across Eurasia, culminating in the great pandemic known as the Black Death in Europe. The demographic recovery under way in China was reversed. The even larger population losses in Europe may have been affected by the decrease in global temperatures to their lowest point in many millennia between 1350 and 1375. After 1400 improving economic conditions enabled population to recover more rapidly in Europe than in China, where the conditions of rural life remained harsh.

Because many other historical circumstances interact with changing weather patterns, historians have a long way to go in deciphering the role of climate in history. Nevertheless, it is a factor that can no longer be ignored.

**Figure 2** Population in China and Europe, 1–1500 C.E.

# Part Five

# The Globe Encompassed, 1500–1750

© Cengage Learning

| | 1500 | 1550 | 1600 | 1650 |
|---|---|---|---|---|
| **AMERICAS** | • **1500** Portuguese discover Brazil | • **1540** Viceroyalty of Peru<br>• **1535** Viceroyalty of Mexico<br>• **1545** Silver discovered at Potosí, Bolivia | Brazil is world's main source of sugar **1600** • | Dutch bring sugar and slavery to West Indies **1640s** •<br>**1607–1640** England and France found colonies |
| **EUROPE** | **1500–1600** Spain's golden century<br>• **1519** Protestant Reformation begins | • **1545** Catholic Reformation begins<br>• **1550** Scientific Revolution begins | • **1588** English defeat Spanish Armada<br>**1600–1700** Netherlands' golden century | **1618–1648** Thirty Years War |
| **AFRICA** | • **1505** Portuguese begin assault on Swahili cities | | • **1591** Morocco conquers Songhai Empire<br>Expansion of transatlantic slave trade **1640's** • | |
| **MIDDLE EAST** | | **1520–1566** Reign of Ottoman sultan Suleiman the Magnificent | • **1571** Ottoman defeat at Lepanto<br>**1588–1629** Reign of Safavid shah Abbas the Great | • **1622** Iranians expel Portuguese from Hormuz |
| **ASIA AND OCEANIA** | | • **1526** Mughal Empire founded in India<br>**1556–1605** Reign of Mughal emperor Akbar | • **1582** Russia conquers Sibir Khanate | • **1603** Tokugawa Shogunate founded in Japan<br>"Closing" of Japan **1639** •<br>Qing Empire begins in China **1644** • |

The decades between 1500 and 1800 witnessed a tremendous expansion of commercial, cultural, and biological exchanges around the world. New long-distance sea routes linked Europe with sub-Saharan Africa and the already established maritime networks of the Indian Ocean and East Asia. Spanish and Portuguese voyages ended the isolation of the Americas and created new webs of exchange in the Atlantic and Pacific. Overland expansion of Muslim, Russian, and Chinese empires also expanded global interaction.

These expanding contacts brought significant change. New agriculture transformed the diets of the Old World and the Americas, particularly with domesticated animals from Europe and such Amerindian crops as the potato. European diseases devastated the Amerindian population, facilitating the establishment of large Spanish, Portuguese, French, and British empires. Europe introduced enslaved Africans to relieve the labor shortage. With colonial empires Europe's cities grew richer, and its economies gained strength. But Spain, France, and England faced stiff competition from the Dutch, who introduced innovative economic institutions.

In Asia and Africa, unlike the Americas, the most important changes owed more to internal forces than to European actions. The Portuguese seized control of some important trading ports and networks in the Indian Ocean and pioneered new contacts with China and Japan, and in time the Dutch, French, and English expanded these profitable connections; but in 1750 Europeans were still primarily a maritime force. Asians and Africans generally retained control of their lands and participated freely in overseas trade.

The Islamic world saw the dramatic expansion of the Ottoman Empire in the Middle East and the establishment of the Safavid Empire in Iran and the Mughal Empire in South Asia. In East Asia, China acquired vast new territories and populations, while a new national government in Japan promoted economic development and resisted foreign influence.

Timeline

**1700 — 1750 — 1800**

- **1660** English take Jamaica
- **1700** West Indies are world's main source of sugar
- **1718** French found New Orleans
- **1754–1763** French and Indian War; British take Canada
- **1780–1782** Revolt of Tupac Armaru in Peru

- **1667–1697** Wars of Louis XIV
- England's Glorious Revolution **1688**
- **1712** Peter the Great founds St. Petersburg
- **1700–1800** The Enlightenment
- **1701–1714** War of the Spanish Succession
- **1772–1795** Poland partitioned

- **1680s** Rise of Asante kingdom
- **1720s** Rise of kingdom of Dahomey
- **1750–1800** Growing slave trade reduces population

- **1683** Last Ottoman siege of Vienna
- **1718–1730** Tulip Period of Ottoman Empire; Ottoman military decline
- Fall of Safavid Empire **1722**
- **1736–1747** Nadir Shah reunites Iran

- **1689** Treaty of Nerchinsk
- **1691** British found trading post at Calcutta
- **1736–1799** Reign of Qing emperor Qianlong

# Transformations in Europe

© Cengage Learning

## CHAPTER PREVIEW

### CULTURE AND IDEAS

■ *How did the interplay of traditional beliefs and revolutionary ideas influence the cultural history of early modern Europe?*

### SOCIAL AND ECONOMIC LIFE

■ *What factors contributed to the wealth of some Europeans and the great poverty of others in this period?*

### POLITICAL INNOVATIONS

■ *How did differing policies in the areas of religion, foreign relations, and economics determine the very different experiences of early modern European states?*

**Conclusion**

**ENVIRONMENT + TECHNOLOGY:**
Mapping the World

In the late sixteenth century Dutch cities grew rich from long-distance trade in the Baltic and Mediterranean and in the newly opened markets of South Asia, Africa, and the Americas. Prosperity allowed merchants, ship owners, and even artisans to consume extravagant luxuries previously limited to nobles. They built substantial houses, wore rich clothing, and developed a taste for exotic goods.

The new prosperity also brought the risk of speculation. By the 1570s tulips, introduced by the Ottomans, were avidly collected by Dutch enthusiasts. Scarce and expensive, they became a sign of sophistication and wealth. The collectors and botanists who originally purchased tulips were joined by thousands of eager consumers who recognized potential profit in a rare commodity. As prices surged in the 1620s and 1630s, a speculative market developed and the ownership of tulip bulbs became a form of investment. Confident that prices would continue upward, individuals and partnerships paid extravagant amounts for bulbs. Between December 1636 and February 1637, for example, one of the most popular tulip varieties increased twelve times in value. At the peak of this frenzy the rarest bulbs sold for three times the annual income of a skilled carpenter. Then, in February 1637, the tulip market crashed as panicked investors rushed to unload their bulbs. If some had been made rich in this extraordinary trade, many of those who entered the market at the height of Tulipmania were financially ruined. Such speculative bubbles roiled European economies throughout the early modern period.

The introduction of commercial and financial innovations, such as stock markets, commercial insurance, and expanded property right protections, was part of a dramatic commercial and manufacturing expansion spurred by European exploration and conquest and dynamic social change. By 1750 Europe had brought much of the world under its control. At the same time, wealthy merchants, investors, and manufacturers grew in power relative to Europe's hereditary nobility, cities grew in population relative to the countryside, and secular political and economic institutions grew relative to a church challenged by the Protestant Reformation, religious wars, and the Scientific Revolution.

# CULTURE AND IDEAS

■ How did the interplay of traditional beliefs and revolutionary ideas influence the cultural history of early modern Europe?

During the Reformation, theological controversies broke the religious unity of the Latin Church and contributed to long and violent wars. While the influence of classical ideas from Greco-Roman antiquity increased among better-educated Europeans, some bold thinkers challenged the authority of the ancients. They introduced new ideas about the motion of the planets and the natural world, encouraging others to challenge traditional social and political systems. Once in place, these new ideas would influence revolutionary political and social movements in the period after 1750. Each of these events had its own causes, but the impact of all of them was broadened by the technology of the printing press.

## Early Reformation

In 1500 the **papacy**, the central government of Latin Christianity, held an unrivaled position as Europe's preeminent religious and intellectual authority, although lax clerical standards and corruption were endemic. Recovered from a period when competing popes supported by rival secular rulers disputed control of the church, the papacy now exercised greater power that was funded by larger donations and by income from its enormous real estate holdings. The construction of fifty-four new churches and other buildings in Rome demonstrated the church's power and showcased the artistic Renaissance then under way. The unprecedented size and splendor of the magnificent new Saint Peter's Basilica in Rome was intended to glorify God and enhance the standing of the papacy, but the vast expense of its construction and rich decoration also caused scandal.

The skillful overseer of the design and financing of the Saint Peter's Basilica was Pope Leo X

**papacy** The central administration of the Roman Catholic Church, of which the pope is the head.

(r. 1513–1521), a member of the wealthy Medici (MED-ih-chee) family of Florence, famous for its patronage of the arts. Pope Leo's artistic taste was superb and his personal life free from scandal, but he was more a man of action than a spiritual leader. During his papacy the church aggressively raised funds through the sale of **indulgences**—absolutions for past sins.

A young professor of sacred scripture, Martin Luther (1483–1546), saw this practice and other excesses as intolerably corrupt. Having forsaken money and marriage for a monastic life of prayer, self-denial, and study, Luther found personal consolation in a passage in Saint Paul's Epistle to the Romans stating that salvation resulted from religious faith, not from "doing certain things." That passage led Luther to object to the way preachers emphasized giving money to the church more than they emphasized faith. He complained to Pope Leo and challenged preachers to debate the theology of indulgences.

Theology aside, Pope Leo regarded Luther's letter as a challenge to papal power and moved to silence him. During a debate in 1519, a papal representative led Luther into open disagreement with church doctrines, for which the papacy condemned him. Unable to reform the church from within, Luther burned the papal bull (document) of condemnation, rejected the pope's authority, and began the movement known as the **Protestant Reformation**.

Accusing those whom he called "Romanists" (Roman Catholics) of relying on "good works," Luther insisted that the only way to salvation was through faith in Jesus Christ. He further declared that Christian belief should be based on the word of God in the Bible and on Christian tradition, not on the authority of the pope. Luther's use of the printing press to spread his ideas won him the support of powerful Germans, who responded to his nationalist portrayal

Private Collection/The Bridgeman Art Library

**Luther and the Reformation**  This sixteenth-century woodcut of Martin Luther shows him writing his demands for religious reform with a symbolically oversized quill pen on the door of All Saints Church in Wittenberg, Germany.

of an Italian pope seeking to beautify Rome with German funds.

Luther's denunciation of the ostentation and corruption of the church led others to call for a return to what they saw as authentic Christian practices and beliefs. John Calvin (1509–1564), a Frenchman who abandoned law for theology, became an influential Protestant leader. Calvin also exalted faith over works, but unlike Luther he denied that human faith alone could merit salvation. Salvation, Calvin believed, was a gift God gave to those he "predestined." Calvin also went beyond Luther in curtailing the power of the clergy and simplifying religious rituals. Calvinist congregations elected their governing

**indulgence**  The forgiveness of the punishment due for past sins, granted by the Catholic Church authorities as a reward for a pious act. Martin Luther's protest against the sale of indulgences is often seen as touching off the Protestant Reformation.

**Protestant Reformation**  Religious reform movement within the Latin Christian Church beginning in 1519. It resulted in the "protesters" forming several new Christian denominations, including the Lutheran and Reformed Churches and the Church of England.

# Chronology

| | Politics, Economy, and Culture | Environment and Technology | Warfare |
|---|---|---|---|
| **1500** | **1500s** Spain's golden century<br>**1519** Protestant Reformation begins<br>**1545** Catholic Reformation begins | | **1529** Ottoman siege of Vienna fails<br>**1546–1555** German Wars of Religion<br>**1566–1648** Netherlands Revolt |
| | **Late 1500s** Witch-hunts increase | **1590s** Dutch develop flyboats; Little Ice Age begins | |
| **1600** | **1600s** Holland's golden century<br>**1602** East India Company stocks exchanged in Amsterdam | **1600s** Depletion of forests growing | |
| | **1620s–1637** Tulip bubble in Netherlands | **1609** Galileo's astronomical telescope | **1618–1648** Thirty Years' War<br><br>**1642–1649** English Civil War<br>**1652–1678** Anglo-Dutch Wars |
| | | **1682** Canal du Midi completed | |
| **1700** | **1700s** The Enlightenment begins<br>**1720** Mississippi Company bubble bursts in France | **1720** South Sea Company bubble peaks in England<br>**1750** English mine nearly 5 million tons of coal a year | **1701–1714** War of the Spanish Succession |

committees and in time created regional and national synods (councils) to regulate doctrinal issues. Calvinists also wore simple black clothes and avoided ostentation, stripping churches of statues, most musical instruments, stained-glass windows, incense, and vestments.

The reformers appealed to genuine religious sentiments, but their successes and failures were also due to political conditions. It was no coincidence that German-born Luther had his greatest success among German speakers and linguistically related Scandinavians. Nor was it surprising that peasants and urban laborers sometimes defied their masters by adopting a different faith. Protestants were no more inclined than Roman Catholics to question male dominance in the church and the family, but most Protestants rejected the medieval tradition of celibate priests and nuns and advocated Christian marriage for all adults.

Shaken by the Protestant attack, the Catholic Church initiated internal reforms. A church council meeting in Trent in northern Italy between 1545 and 1563 sought to distinguish Catholic doctrines from Protestant "errors." Bishops allied with the pope dominated the council and reaffirmed the supremacy of the pope and the ecclesiastical authorities in interpreting scriptures, as well as the importance of confession and salvation through both faith and good works. But the council did call for some reform: bishops were to reside in their dioceses, for example, and maintain a theological seminary to train priests.

The creation in 1540 of a new religious order, the Society of Jesus, or "Jesuits," by a Spanish nobleman, Ignatius of Loyola (1491–1556), was among the most important events of the **Catholic Reformation**. Well-educated Jesuits helped stem the Protestant tide by their teaching and preaching (see Map 16.1) and became missionaries overseas (see Chapters 15 and 19).

**Catholic Reformation** Religious reform movement within the Latin Christian Church, begun in response to the Protestant Reformation. It clarified Catholic theology and reformed clerical training and discipline.

**Predominant religion in 1555**

- Lutheran
- Calvinist (Reformed)
- Church of England
- Roman Catholic
- Orthodox
- Muslim
- → Spread of Calvinism
- ▴ Huguenot center
- ◯ Ottoman Empire, 1566

400 Mi.

400 Km.

200

200

0

0

N

**Map 16.1 Religious Reformation in Europe** The Reformation brought greater religious freedom but also led to religious conflict and persecution. In many places the Reformation accelerated the trend toward state control of religion and added religious differences to the motives for wars among Europeans. © Cengage Learning

**Death to Witches** This woodcut from 1574 depicts three women convicted of witchcraft being burned alive in Baden, Switzerland. The scene on the left illustrates the purported witchcraft practiced by the three condemned women.

Art Resource, NY

While traditional folk beliefs were more common in small towns and villages, these beliefs and fears would not have had such deadly consequences if many educated and powerful city dwellers did not believe in the Devil's power to affect society broadly.

It was widely assumed that special powers could be derived from occult knowledge or, in some cases, from a compact with the Devil. In its benign version, practitioners could heal the sick, cause love to flourish, or guarantee good fortune. They could also solve disputes with masters or employers or punish enemies. The malevolent version could cause infertility, illness, or death of loved ones and neighbors, cause crops or businesses to fail, or even provoke epidemics or droughts. The vigor of these local religious traditions ebbed and flowed, and some theologians and jurists questioned the intellectual and religious underpinnings of these assumptions before the mid-sixteenth century. Nevertheless, the fear of witches that swept across Europe in the late sixteenth and seventeenth centuries was testimony to the endurance of these beliefs.

Before this hysteria ended, secular and church authorities had tried approximately 100,000 people and executed 60,000—some three-fourths of them women—for practicing witchcraft. Trial records make it clear that both the accusers and the accused believed that it was possible for individuals to use black magic in concert with the Devil to cause injury to others. Apparently many admitted to having occult powers, though the common use of torture explains most of the confessions of accused witches.

The trials and executions transcended national and religious boundaries, but there were significant

Given the intense emotions stirred by the Protestant Reformation, it is not surprising that both sides persecuted and sometimes executed those of differing views. Bitter "wars of religion" would continue in parts of western Europe until 1648.

## Traditional Thinking and Witch-Hunts

Religious differences continued to generate animosity long after the first generation of reformers, but for both the Protestant north and the Catholic south the widespread **witch-hunts** that Protestants and Catholics undertook in early modern Europe were less about religious doctrine than they were about prevailing European ideas about the natural world. These views blended two distinct traditions. One was an enduring belief in magic and spirits passed down orally from pre-Christian times. The second was the biblical teachings about miracles, saints, and devils heard in church and read by growing numbers in vernacular translations. These Christian teachings coincided easily with beliefs about magic, sorcery, and witchcraft rooted in the distant past.

**witch-hunt** The pursuit of people suspected of witchcraft, especially in northern Europe in the late sixteenth and seventeenth centuries.

differences in regional and national practice. The death toll was highest in German states like Wurzburg and Bamberg, which executed 900 and 600, respectively, between 1626 and 1631, including scores of children. Protestant Scotland also convicted 120 witches who were burned at the stake in 1661 and 1662 alone. But Protestant England and more egalitarian Holland were reluctant to prosecute witches. The relatively strong Catholic states of France and Spain also had low numbers of executions. In Spain the Inquisition limited arrests as early as 1526.

No single reason can explain the witchcraft hysteria in early modern Europe, but these events coincided with rising social tensions, growing rural poverty, and environmental strains. They also coincided with the violent wars of the Reformation period. Far from being an aberration, witch-hunts reflected the tension between popular beliefs and the ambitions of aggressive new religious and political institutions. The Reformation's focus on the Devil—the enemy of God—as the source of evil and the Catholic Counter-Reformation's effort to enforce orthodoxy both helped to propel the brutal persecutions of this period.

## The Scientific Revolution

Beginning in the sixteenth century, European understanding of the natural world shifted away from the physics of the classical Aristotle, who taught that everything on earth was reducible to four elements: earth and water on the surface and air and fire floating above the ground. Experimentation, careful observation, and mathematical calculations challenged the thinking of classical antiquity, newly discovered by Renaissance scholars. Most intellectuals of the **Scientific Revolution** were committed Christians (both Catholic and Protestant) who sought to use science to reinforce religious beliefs. Nevertheless, as this movement gained momentum, European intellectual life became more secular and independent.

Nicholas Copernicus (1473–1543), a Polish monk and mathematician, helped initiate the new era when he proposed that the sun, not the earth, was the center of the universe (see Chapter 12). To escape controversy, Copernicus delayed the publication of his heliocentric (sun-centered) theory until the end of his life. Once disseminated, his research began a

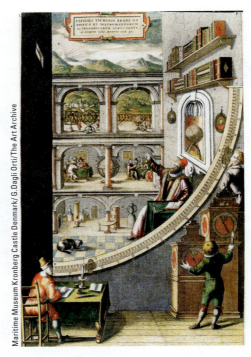

**Tycho Brahe at Work**  Between 1576 and 1597, on the island of Ven between Denmark and Sweden, Tycho built the best observatory in Europe and set a new standard for accurate celestial observations before the invention of the telescope. This contemporary hand-colored engraving shows the Danish astronomer at work.

revolution in the way human beings understood the structure of the heavens.

Other astronomers, including the Danish Tycho Brahe (1546–1601) and his German assistant Johannes Kepler (1571–1630), improved on Copernicus's model, showing that planets actually move in elliptical, not circular, orbits. The most brilliant of the Copernicans was the Italian Galileo Galilei (gal-uh-LAY-oh gal-uh-LAY-ee) (1564–1642). In 1609 Galileo built a telescope through which he took a closer look at the heavens, thus confirming the speculations of other astronomers.

At first, the Copernicans faced formidable resistance because they directly challenged classical and biblical authorities. Many intellectual and religious

**Scientific Revolution**  The intellectual movement in Europe, initially associated with planetary motion and other aspects of physics, that by the seventeenth century had laid the groundwork for modern science.

leaders sought to suppress the new ideas. Following the lead of Martin Luther, most Protestant leaders condemned the heliocentric universe as contrary to the Bible. Catholic authorities did not react immediately, but, when they did act, they more effectively suppressed the new science.

Copernicus died before his book was deemed heretical by Catholic authorities in 1616 and placed on the index of prohibited books. Yet his discoveries helped lead to a more accurate calendar issued in 1582 by Pope Gregory XIII and still used today. Galileo's defense of the heliocentric theory led to a confrontation with the Inquisition. Galileo argued that the Bible was an inspired text, but, when science had established a demonstrable fact, the Bible should be interpreted to coincide with the evidence, since it could not be God's intention to mislead. Despite the controversial nature of his opinions, he continued to publish, pressing for a reliance on physical evidence and accurate measurement. Ordered before the Inquisition in 1633, Galileo was forced to sign a formal renunciation of his research. An apparent victory for tradition, this action put the Catholic Church in untenable opposition to a key early achievement of the new science.

Despite opposition, printed books spread the new scientific ideas across Europe, influencing, among others, the French philosopher and mathematician René Descartes (1595–1650). Descartes played a key role in the development of physics and calculus when he demonstrated the usefulness of algebra to geometry, but the Inquisition's condemnation of Galileo influenced Descartes to delay publication of a potentially controversial work on optics and astronomy in 1633.

In England, Robert Boyle (1627–1691) advocated tirelessly for the use of experimental methods. One of the founders of modern chemistry, he was among the first to publish the details of experiments, including his failures, and demonstrate that air was necessary for the transmission of sound. In 1662 he was also instrumental in founding the Royal Society, whose motto "Nullius in Verba" (nothing in words) was a rallying cry demanding that science be based on experiments alone.

Another Englishman, the mathematician Isaac Newton (1642–1727), began his work in optics and mathematics by building on the work of Boyle and Descartes. Carrying Galileo's demonstration that the heavens and earth share a common physics to its logical conclusion, he formulated mathematical laws that all physical objects obeyed. His Law of Gravity and his role in developing the calculus made him the most famous and influential man of his era, serving as president of the Royal Society from 1703 until his death.

Although Galileo and Descartes, both Catholics, as well as the Protestant Boyle, were convinced that scientific discoveries and revealed religion could be reconciled, most religious and intellectual leaders viewed the new science with suspicion or hostility because it challenged long-established ways of thought. These principal pioneers of the Scientific Revolution showed that the ideas of the Aristotelians and biblical writers were unsupportable in the face of scientific discovery. Using reason to challenge a broader range of unquestioned traditions and superstitions, they changed the world of ideas forever.

## The Early Enlightenment

Advances in scientific thought inspired some to question the reasonableness of everything from agricultural methods to laws, religion, and social hierarchies. Their belief that they could apply the scientific method to economics, politics, and social organization to devise the best policies energized a movement known as the **Enlightenment**. Like the Scientific Revolution, this movement was the work of a few "enlightened" individuals, who often faced bitter opposition. Leading Enlightenment thinkers became accustomed to having their books banned and spending long periods in exile to escape persecution.

Influences besides the Scientific Revolution affected the Enlightenment. The religious warfare and intolerance associated with the struggle between Catholicism and Protestantism undermined the authority of religion for many, as did the killing of suspected witches. Church efforts to impugn the breakthroughs of science also pushed European intellectuals in a secular direction. The leading French thinker Voltaire (1694–1778) declared: "No opinion is worth burning your neighbor for."

**Enlightenment** A philosophical movement in eighteenth-century Europe that fostered the belief that one could reform society by discovering rational laws that governed social behavior and were just as scientific as the laws of physics.

Although many circumstances shaped "enlightened" thinking, new scientific methods and discoveries provided the clearest model for changing European society. Voltaire linked the prestige of the newly ascendant scientific method with his generation's mounting political and social concerns in these terms: "It would be very peculiar that all nature, all the planets, should obey eternal laws" but a human being, "in contempt of these laws, could act as he pleased solely according to his caprice." The English poet Alexander Pope (1688–1774) made a similar point in verse: "Nature and Nature's laws lay hidden in night; / God said, 'Let Newton be' and all was light."

The Enlightenment was more a frame of mind than a coherent movement. Its proponents were clearer about what they disliked than about what changes were necessary. Nearly all were optimistic that—at least in the long run—human beliefs and institutions could be improved. This faith in progress would help foster political and social revolutions after 1750, as Chapter 21 recounts.

While the Catholic Church and many Protestant clergymen opposed the Enlightenment, European monarchs, ambitious to increase power, found anticlerical intellectuals useful allies against church power and wealth. Monarchs and their reforming advisers discovered justification for the expansion of royal authority and modern tax systems. Europe in 1750 was a place where political and religious divisions, growing literacy, and the printing press made it possible for these controversial and exciting new ideas to thrive in the face of opposition from ancient and powerful institutions.

### SECTION REVIEW

- Outraged by corrupt church practices, reformers like Luther and Calvin challenged papal authority and traditional Catholic theology.
- In response to the Protestant reformers, the Catholic Church launched a Counter-Reformation.
- Both Protestants and Catholics, seeking to enforce orthodoxy, sanctioned widespread witch-hunts.
- The thinkers of the Scientific Revolution challenged traditional biblical and classical Greco-Roman conceptions of the cosmos.
- The advances in science prompted Enlightenment thinkers to question many conventional ideas and practices.

## SOCIAL AND ECONOMIC LIFE

■ *What factors contributed to the wealth of some Europeans and the great poverty of others in this period?*

There were large and important differences in the social structures of the major European nations, but there were many shared characteristics as well. European society was dominated by a small number of noble families who monopolized church, government, and military offices and enjoyed many privileges, often including exemption from taxation. Below them was a much larger class of prosperous commoners that included many clergy, bureaucrats, professionals, and military officers as well as merchants, some artisans, and rural landowners. The vast majority of men and women were very poor. Laborers, journeymen, apprentices, and rural laborers struggled to earn their daily bread and often faced unemployment and privation. The poorest members of society lived truly desperate lives, surviving only through guile, begging, or crime. Women remained subordinated to men.

Some social mobility did occur, however. The principal engine of social change was an economy stimulated by long-distance trade and by access to the gold and silver of the Americas. Because cities enjoyed most of this new wealth, they became the centers of opportunity and upward mobility.

**The Bourgeoisie**   Europe's cities grew in response to expanding trade and rising commercial profits. In 1500 Paris was the only northern European city with over 100,000 inhabitants. By 1700 both Paris and London had populations over 500,000, and eleven other European cities contained over 100,000 people.

Urban wealth came from manufacturing and finance, but especially from trade, both within Europe and overseas. The French called the urban class that dominated these activities the **bourgeoisie** (boor-zhwah-ZEE) (burghers, town dwellers). Members of the bourgeoisie poured much of their profits back into their businesses or into new ventures. Even so, most had enough money to live comfortably in

**bourgeoisie**  In early modern Europe, the class of well-off town dwellers whose wealth came from manufacturing, finance, commerce, and allied professions.

**Port of Amsterdam** Ships, barges, and boats of all types are visible in this busy seventeenth-century scene. The large building in the center is the Admiralty House, the headquarters of the Dutch East India Company.  Mansell/TimeLife Pictures/Getty Images

large houses, and some had servants. In the seventeenth and eighteenth centuries wealthier consumers could buy exotic luxuries imported from the far corners of the earth—Caribbean and Brazilian sugar and rum, Mexican chocolate, Virginia tobacco, North American furs, East Indian cotton textiles and spices, and Chinese tea.

The Netherlands provides one of the best examples of this new bourgeois reality. The Dutch Republic was the most egalitarian European country in the early modern period. While it retained an aristocracy, wealthy commoners dominated its economy and politics. Manufacturers and craftsmen turned out a great variety of goods in their factories and workshops. The highly successful textile industry concentrated on the profitable weaving, finishing, and printing of cloth, leaving the spinning to low-paid workers elsewhere. Along with fine woolens and linens, the Dutch made cheaper textiles for mass markets. Other factories in Holland refined West Indian sugar, brewed beer from Baltic grain, cut Virginia tobacco, and made imitations of Chinese ceramics. Free from the censorship and religious persecution imposed in neighboring countries, Holland's intellectuals were active in the Scientific Revolution and early Enlightenment. Its

printers published books in many languages, including manuals with the latest advances in machinery, metallurgy, and agriculture. For a small nation that lacked timber and other natural resources, this was a remarkable achievement.

With a population of 200,000 in 1700, Amsterdam was Holland's largest city and Europe's major port. Huge commercial fleets supported this growth and dominated sea trade in Europe and overseas using ship designs like the *fluit*, or "flyboat," a large-capacity cargo ship developed in the 1590s that was inexpensive to build and required only a small crew, and the heavily armed "East Indiaman" that helped the Dutch establish their supremacy in the Indian Ocean. By one estimate, more than half of all the oceangoing commercial shipping occurred on Dutch ships. Dutch mapmaking supported these distant commercial connections (see Environment and Technology: Mapping the World).

Amsterdam also served as Europe's financial center. Seventeenth-century Dutch banks had such a reputation for security that wealthy individuals and governments from all over western Europe entrusted them with their money. The banks in turn invested these funds in real estate, loaned money to factory

# environment & technology

## Mapping the World

In 1602 Matteo Ricci, a Jesuit missionary in China, printed an elaborate map of the world (see Chapter 19). Working from maps produced in Europe and incorporating the latest knowledge gathered by European maritime explorers, Ricci introduced two changes to make the map more appealing to his Chinese hosts. He labeled it in Chinese characters, and he split his map down the middle of the Atlantic so that China lay in the center. This version pleased the Chinese elite, who considered China the "Middle Kingdom" surrounded by lesser states. A copy of Ricci's map in six large panels adorned the emperor's Beijing palace.

The stunningly beautiful maps and globes of sixteenth-century Europe were the most complete, detailed, and useful representations of the earth that any society had ever produced. The best mapmaker of the century was Gerhard Kremer, who is remembered as Mercator (the merchant) because his maps were so useful to European ocean traders. By incorporating the latest discoveries and scientific measurements, Mercator could depict the outlines of the major continents in painstaking detail, even if their interiors were still largely unknown to outsiders.

To represent the spherical globe on a flat map, Mercator drew the lines of longitude as parallel lines. Because such lines actually meet at the poles, Mercator's projection greatly exaggerated the size of every landmass and body of water distant from the equator. However, Mercator's rendering offered a very practical advantage: sailors could plot their course by drawing a straight line between their point of departure and their destination. Because of this useful feature, the Mercator projection of the world remained in common use until quite recently. To some extent, its popularity came from the exaggerated size this projection gave to Europe. Like the Chinese, Europeans liked to think of themselves as being at the center of things. Yet Europeans also understood their true geographical position better than people in any other part of the world.

**Dutch World Map, 1641**

*It is easy to see why the Chinese would not have liked to see their empire at the far right edge of this widely printed map. Besides the distortions caused by the Mercator projection, geographical ignorance exaggerates the size of North America and Antarctica.*

World Map, from 'Le Theatre du Monde' or 'Nouvel Atlas', 1645 (coloured engraving), Blaeu, Willem (1571-1638)/Bibliotheque des Arts Decoratifs, Paris, France/Archives Charmet/The Bridgeman Art Library owners and governments, and provided capital for big business operations overseas. Individuals seeking higher returns than those provided by banks could purchase shares in a **joint-stock company**, a sixteenth-century forerunner of the modern corporation. Individuals bought and sold shares in specialized financial markets called **stock exchanges**, an Italian innovation transferred to the cities of northwestern Europe in the sixteenth century. The Amsterdam Exchange, founded in 1602, became the greatest stock market in the seventeenth and eighteenth centuries.

The Dutch government played a direct role in this process by pioneering the creation of commercial enterprises like the Dutch East and West India Companies, which were granted trade monopolies with the East and West Indies. France and England soon chartered monopoly trading companies of their own. These companies then sold shares to individuals to raise large sums for overseas enterprises while spreading the risks (and profits) among many investors (see Chapter 17). In this same era large insurance companies were developed to insure long-distance voyages against loss, and by 1700 purchasing insurance had become standard commercial practice. Governments also sought to promote trade by investing in canals to speed transport, lower costs, and drain the lowlands for agriculture. Other governments financed canals as well, including systems of locks to raise barges up over hills. One of the most important was the 150-mile (240-kilometer) Canal du Midi built by the French government between 1661 and 1682 to link the Atlantic and the Mediterranean.

Successful bourgeois merchants in England and France traded wealth for social status. By retiring from their businesses and buying country estates, they could become members of the **gentry**. They loaned money to impoverished peasants and to members of the nobility and in time increased their land ownership. Some sought aristocratic husbands for their daughters. The old nobility found such alliances attractive because of the large dowries that the bourgeoisie provided. Even in colonial settings, some families purchased titles of nobility. While satisfying the desire for status, this move out of the bourgeoisie also removed capital from commerce and production.

## Peasants and Laborers

At the other end of society, serfdom, which bound men and women to land owned by a local lord, declined in western Europe after the great plague of the mid-fourteenth century. As the population recovered, competition for work exerted a downward pressure on wages, reducing the usefulness of serfdom to landowners. In eastern Europe, however, large-scale landowners required serfs to make grain production profitable. Slavery expanded briefly around 1500 in southern Europe, but after 1600 Europeans shipped nearly all African slaves to the Americas. Thus western Europe's dependence on unfree labor was kept at a distance rather than at home (see Chapters 15 and 17).

Legal freedom did not make a peasant's life more secure. Agricultural efficiency had improved little since 1300. As a result, bad years brought famine; good ones provided only small surpluses. The material conditions experienced by the poor in western Europe may have worsened between 1500 and 1750 as the result of warfare, environmental degradation, and economic contractions. Europeans also felt the effects of a century of relatively cool climate that began in the 1590s. During this **Little Ice Age** average temperatures fell only a few degrees, but the effects were startling (see Issues in World History: The Little Ice Age on page 466).

By 1700 high-yielding new crops from the Americas were helping the rural poor avoid starvation. Potatoes sustained life in northeastern and central Europe and in Ireland, while poor peasants in Italy subsisted on maize. Ironically, all of these lands were major exporters of wheat, but agricultural workers could not afford to eat it.

Other rural residents made their living as miners, lumberacks, and charcoal makers. The expanding

**joint-stock company** A business, often backed by a government charter, that sold shares to individuals to raise money for its trading enterprises and to spread the risks (and profits) among many investors.

**stock exchange** A place where shares in a company or business enterprise are bought and sold.

**gentry** In England, the class of landholding families below the aristocracy.

**Little Ice Age** A century-long period of cool climate that began in the 1590s. Its ill effects on agriculture in northern Europe were notable.

iron industry in England provided work for all three, but the high consumption of wood fuel caused serious **deforestation**. One early-seventeenth-century observer lamented: "Within man's memory, it was held impossible to have any want of wood in England. But . . . at present, through the great consuming of wood . . . and the neglect of planting of woods, there is a great scarcity of wood throughout the whole kingdom."[1] Eventually, the high price of wood and charcoal encouraged smelters to use coal as an alternative fuel. England's coal mining increased twelvefold, from 210,000 tons in 1550 to 2,500,000 tons in 1700 and nearly 5 million tons by 1750.

France was more forested than England, but deforestation there prompted Jean Baptiste Colbert, France's minister of finance, to predict that "France will perish for lack of wood." By the late eighteenth century deforestation had become an issue even in Sweden and Russia, where iron production had become a major industry.

Even in the prosperous Dutch towns, half of the population lived in acute poverty. Authorities estimated that permanent city residents who were too poor to tax, the "deserving poor," made up 10 to 20 percent of the population. This left out the large numbers of "unworthy poor"—recent migrants, peddlers traveling from place to place, and beggars (many with horrible deformities and sores) who tried to survive on charity. The pervasive poverty of rural and urban Europe shocked those who were not hardened to it. Around 1580 the mayor of the French city of Bordeaux (bor-DOH) asked a group of visiting Amerindian chiefs what impressed them most about European cities. The chiefs are said to have expressed astonishment at the disparity between the fat, well-fed people and the poor, half-starved men and women in rags. Why, the visitors wondered, did the poor not grab the rich by the throat or set fire to their homes?[2]

In fact, misery provoked many rebellions in early modern Europe. For example, in 1525 peasant rebels in the Alps attacked both nobles and the clergy as representatives of the privileged and landowning classes. They had no love for merchants either, whom they denounced for lending at interest and charging high prices. Rebellions multiplied as rural conditions worsened. In southwestern France alone, some 450 uprisings occurred between 1590 and 1715, many set off by food shortages and tax increases. A rebellion in southern France in 1670 began when a mob of townswomen attacked the tax collector. It quickly spread to the country, where peasant leaders cried, "Death to the people's oppressors!" Authorities dealt severely with such revolts and executed or maimed their leaders.

## Women and the Family

A woman's status was closely tied to her husband's. In some nations a woman could inherit a throne (see Table 16.1 for examples)—in the absence of a male heir. These rare exceptions do not negate the rule that women everywhere ranked below men. Nevertheless, class and wealth defined a woman's position in life more than her sex. The wife or daughter of a rich man, for example, had a materially better life than any poor man. Sometimes a single woman might secure a position of responsibility, as in the case of women from good families who headed convents in Catholic countries. But unmarried women were routinely controlled by fathers and married women by husbands. Some widows controlled property and other assets.

Men and women often chose their own spouses. Privileged families were more likely to arrange marriages than poor ones. Royal and noble families carefully plotted their children's marriages to further family interests. Bourgeois parents were less likely to force their children into arranged marriages, but nearly all found spouses within their own social class, suggesting that the bourgeoisie promoted marriages that buttressed business alliances.

Europeans also married later than people in the rest of the world. While people in other regions usually married in their teens, the sons of Europeans often put off marriage until they could live on their own. Young women worked helping their parents, as domestic

[1]Quoted by Carlo M. Cipolla, "Introduction," *The Fontana Economic History of Europe*, vol. 2, *The Sixteenth and Seventeenth Centuries* (Glasgow: Collins/Fontana Books, 1976), 11–12.

[2]Michel de Montaigne, *Essais* (1588), ch. 31, "Des Cannibales."

**deforestation** The removal of trees faster than forests can replace themselves.

**The Fishwife, 1572**
Women were essential partners in most Dutch family businesses. This scene by the Dutch artist Adriaen van Ostade shows a woman preparing fish for retail sale.

Iberfoto/The Image Works

servants, or in some other capacity to save money for their dowry: the money and household goods—the amount varied by social class—that enabled a young couple to begin marriage independent of their parents. The typical groom in western and central Europe could not hope to marry before his late twenties, and his bride would be a few years younger.

The late age of marriage held down the birthrate and thus limited family size. Even so, about one-tenth of urban births were to unmarried women, often servants. Such newborns were generally left on the doorsteps of churches, convents, or rich households. Many perished. Delayed marriage and poverty helped force unfortunate young women newly arrived from the countryside into brothels.

## SECTION REVIEW

- Early modern European society was more fluid than it appeared, with an expanding economy and improved education promoting some mobility.

- The urban bourgeoisie created much of Europe's wealth through trade, manufacture, finance, and technological innovation.

- Governments sought lucrative alliances with the bourgeoisie, whose wealth afforded them political and social advancement as well as revenue.

- Oppressed by economic and environmental trends, peasants and laborers generally lived in poverty, and their misery often provoked rebellion.

- Although women remained subordinate to men, class and wealth were the main determinants of their positions in life.

## POLITICAL INNOVATIONS

■ *How did differing policies in the areas of religion, foreign relations, and economics determine the very different experiences of early modern European states?*

The monarchs of early modern Europe occupied the apex of the social order, arbitrated intellectual and religious conflicts, and influenced economic life. In addition, royal political agendas introduced new elements of conflict and change.

Though no unified European empire emerged, political centralization increased in separate kingdoms. Frequent civil and international conflicts sometimes promoted cooperation and often encouraged innovation. Leadership in Europe passed from Spain to the Netherlands and then to England and France.

## State Development

Political diversity abounded. City-states, principalities, and a small number of republics existed either independently or bound together in federations, of which the **Holy Roman Empire** of the German heartland was the foremost example. In western Europe strong monarchies emerged and developed national identities.

Dynastic ambitions and historical circumstances combined to favor and then block the creation of an integrated European empire in the early sixteenth century. In 1519, electors of the Holy Roman Empire chose Charles V, the King of Spain, to be emperor. Like his predecessors for three generations, Charles belonged to the powerful **Habsburg** (HABZ-berg) family of Austria, but he had recently inherited the Spanish kingdoms of Castile and Aragon. With these vast resources, Charles hoped to centralize his imperial power and turn back the advance of the Ottoman Empire on Europe's Mediterranean flank while contending with France for dominance of Italy.

Charles and his allies did stop the Ottomans at the gates of Vienna in 1529, but Ottoman attacks continued on and off until 1697. King Francis I of France, who had lost to Charles in the imperial election, worked tirelessly to defeat Charles's ambitions, openly supporting the Ottomans (whom the Europeans called Turks). In addition, German princes swayed by Luther's appeals to German nationalism and the Reformation opposed Charles's defense of Catholic doctrine. These disputes led to open warfare in 1546 (the German Wars of Religion), which drained Charles's treasury and forced him to accept a stalemate in the Mediterranean with the Ottomans.

In the end the ambitions of Charles V were overwhelmed by the scale of his challenges, despite his enormous resources. In the Peace of Augsburg (1555) he recognized the German princes' right to choose either Catholicism or Lutheranism as their state religion and allowed them to keep any church lands

they had seized. This triumph of religious diversity put off German political unification for three centuries. Charles abdicated the Holy Roman and Spanish thrones and retired to a monastery in 1556.

Charles V's son, Philip II, inherited his father's European territories in the low countries and Italy, where quelling unrest would drain his resources for decades, but he also inherited the Spanish throne with its rich American empire. In 1580 Philip inherited the throne of Portugal as well, adding Brazil and Portuguese colonies in Africa and Asia to his Spanish possessions. With this great wealth, he aggressively pursued the geopolitical policies that had thwarted his father.

But the American bullion that enriched Europe brought inflation (rising prices) to Spain, and Philip's effort to seal Spain off from the Protestant Reformation and the Scientific Revolution also imposed economic costs. Spanish guilds and merchants lost ground at a time when technological innovation and commercial expansion grew across northern Europe. Manufactured goods in France, Italy, or other European countries were now cheaper than goods made in Spain, and most goods imported to Spanish colonies were of foreign origin.

Though Philip was ruler of the sixteenth century's mightiest state, his wars against the Ottomans, northern European Protestants, and rebellious Dutch subjects squandered his Iberian wealth, leading to four bankruptcies during his reign and a Spain unprepared to maintain its early domination of the Atlantic when faced by sustained challenges from the English, Dutch, and French.

## The Monarchies of England and France

Although the rulers of Spain, France, and England all enjoyed some success in promoting national political unification and religious unity, the stormy process led to diverse outcomes. Over the course of the seventeenth century, the

---

**Holy Roman Empire** Loose federation of mostly German states and principalities, headed by an emperor elected by the princes. It lasted from 962 to 1806.

**Habsburg** A powerful European family that provided many Holy Roman Emperors, founded the Austrian (later Austro-Hungarian) Empire, and ruled sixteenth- and seventeenth-century Spain.

| TABLE 16.1 | Rulers in Early Modern Western Europe | |
| --- | --- | --- |
| **Spain** | **France** | **England/Great Britain** |
| **Habsburg Dynasty** | **Valois Dynasty** | **Tudor Dynasty** |
| Charles 1 (1516–1556) (Holy Roman Emperor Charles V) Philip II (1556–1598) | Francis I (1515–1547) Henry II (1547–1559) Francis II (1559–1560) Charles IX (1560–1574) Henry III (1574–1589) | Henry VIII (1509–1547) Edward VI (1547–1553) Mary I (1553–1558) Elizabeth I (1558–1603) |
| | **Bourbon Dynasty** | **Stuart Dynasty** |
| Philip III (1598–1621) Philip IV (1621–1665) Charles II (1665–1700) | Henry IV (1589–1610)[a] Louis XIII (1610–1643) Louis XIV (1643–1715) | James I (1603–1625) Charles I (1625–1649)[a,b] (Puritan Republic, 1649–1660) Charles II (1660–1685) James II (1685–1688)[b] William III (1689–1702) and Mary II (1689–1694) Anne (1702–1714) |
| **Bourbon Dynasty** | | **Hanoverian Dynasty** |
| Philip V (1700–1746) Ferdinand VI (1746–1759) | Louis XV (1715–1774) | George I (1714–1727) George II (1727–1760) |

[a] Died a violent death. [b] Was overthrown.
© Cengage Learning

monarchs of England and France faced intense conflict with powerful rivals. Religion was never absent as an issue in these struggles, but the very different constitutional outcomes they produced in these two countries were of more significance in the long run.

To evade any check on his power, King Charles I of England (see Table 16.1) ruled for eleven years without summoning Parliament, his kingdom's representative body. Lacking Parliament's consent to new taxes, he raised funds by coercing "loans" from wealthy subjects and applying existing tax laws more broadly. But in 1640 a rebellion in Scotland forced him to summon Parliament to approve new taxes to pay for an army. Noblemen and churchmen sat in the House of Lords while representatives from towns and counties sat in the House of Commons. Before it would authorize new taxes, Parliament insisted on strict guarantees that the king would never again ignore the body's traditional rights. Charles refused and in 1642 attempted to arrest his critics in the House of Commons, plunging the kingdom into the **English Civil War**.

Militarily defeated in 1648, Charles still refused to compromise. A year later a "Rump" Parliament purged of his supporters ordered his execution. Parliament replaced the monarchy with a republic under Oliver Cromwell, a Puritan general who ruled until his death in 1658. Cromwell expanded England's presence overseas and imposed firm control over Ireland and Scotland, but he was also unwilling to share power with Parliament. Two years after his death, Parliament restored the Stuart line, making it unclear, for a time, which side had won the war.

King James II clarified matters when he refused to respect Parliament's rights by baptizing his heir as a Roman Catholic. Parliament responded by forcing James into exile in the bloodless Glorious Revolution

**English Civil War** (1642–1649) A conflict over royal versus parliamentary rights, caused by King Charles I's arrest of his parliamentary critics and ending with his execution. Its outcome checked the growth of royal absolutism and, with the Glorious Revolution of 1688 and the English Bill of Rights of 1689, ensured that England would be a constitutional monarchy.

**Versailles** Constructed during the reign of Louis XIV of France, the palace of Versailles could house ten thousand people. Surrounded by elaborately landscaped grounds and parks, it became an effective symbol of royal absolutism.

Erich Lessing/Art Resource, NY

of 1688. The Bill of Rights of 1689 formalized this new constitutional order by requiring the king to call Parliament frequently to consent to changes in laws or to raise an army in peacetime. Another law reaffirmed the official status of the Church of England but extended religious toleration to dissenting Puritans.

In France the Estates General, like the English Parliament, represented the traditional rights of the clergy, the nobility, and the towns (that is, the bourgeoisie). The Estates General had asserted its rights during the sixteenth-century French Wars of Religion, when the monarchy was weak. Thereafter France's Bourbon monarchs generally ruled without calling it into session. They put off financial crises by more efficient tax collection and by selling appointments to high government offices, but by 1700 French debt levels challenged traditional fiscal practice. While some historians have used the term *absolutism* to describe the power of French monarchs in this era, even the most powerful, Louis XIV, carefully negotiated his policies with both the nobility and city authorities. While the king's power grew, long-established ways of governing, such as the sale of offices and reliance on patronage networks and personal relationships, continued to frame decision making.

Louis XIV moved his court to a gigantic new palace at **Versailles** (vuhr-SIGH) in 1682. Capable of housing ten thousand people and surrounded by elaborately landscaped grounds and parks, the palace became an effective symbol of growing royal grandeur and power and an arena where the high nobility and ecclesiastical hierarchy interacted with the monarch in a dense cycle of rituals and ceremonies that emphasized royal power.

Most European rulers admired and imitated the centralized powers and apparent absolutist authority of the French monarch until well after 1750. The English model of balanced powers would be widely admired in later times, gaining a favorable press with the beginnings of the Enlightenment. In his influential *Second Treatise of Civil Government* (1690), the English political philosopher John Locke (1632–1704) disputed monarchial claims to absolute authority by divine right. He argued that rulers derived their authority from the consent of the governed and were

**Versailles** The huge palace built for French king Louis XIV south of Paris. The palace symbolized both French power and the triumph of royal authority over the French nobility.

subject to the law. If monarchs overstepped the law, citizens had the right and the duty to rebel.

## Warfare and Diplomacy

In addition to their bitter civil wars, European monarchies engaged in numerous international conflicts provoked in part by efforts to protect or extend colonial empires. Warfare was almost constant (see the Chronology at the beginning of the chapter). As the geographic scope of warfare and the size of armies and navies grew, monarchs expended ever-larger sums of money and caused widespread devastation and death. The worst of the international conflicts, the Thirty Years' War (1618–1648), caused long-lasting depopulation and economic decline in much of the Holy Roman Empire.

Not surprisingly, war-making skills and weaponry improved dramatically, making European armed forces the most powerful in the world. The numbers of men in arms increased steadily. French forces, for example, grew from 88 regiments of infantry and 72 of cavalry in 1691 to 238 regiments of infantry and 94 of cavalry in 1714. Even smaller European states built up impressive armies. Sweden, with under a million people, had one of the finest and best-armed military forces in the seventeenth century. Prussia, a country with fewer than 2 million inhabitants in 1700, had a large, well-disciplined army that made it a major power.

Larger armies required better command structures. The officer corps of the major powers was largely drawn from the nobility, and patronage, not skill, guided promotion and advancement. Training and battlefield control were marginally improved through more frequent drilling for professional troops and the introduction of new signaling techniques, but battlefields remained chaotic. Fortifications were expanded and improved in Europe and in colonial possessions, and even Spain, facing a deep fiscal crisis, borrowed to fortify Cartagena on its Mediterranean coast and Havana. Paying for larger and better-armed fleets proved similarly expensive, but in the face of an intensifying competition for colonial wealth that stretched from the East Indies to the Caribbean and South Atlantic, no great power could afford to cut back.

Safe from the threat of direct invasion, England alone did not maintain a standing army. Its power depended on the navy begun under King Henry VIII, who had spent heavily on ships and promoted a domestic iron industry to supply cannon. The Royal Navy also copied innovative ship designs from the Dutch. The crushing defeat of the Spanish Armada in 1588 by Henry's daughter, Elizabeth I, demonstrated the usefulness of these decisions and accelerated Spain's decline under Philip II. By the early eighteenth century, the Royal Navy surpassed the rival French fleet in numbers. By then, England had merged with Scotland to become Great Britain, annexed Ireland, and built a North American empire.

Although France was Europe's most powerful state, Louis XIV's efforts to expand were increasingly frustrated by a coalition of other powers. In a series of costly eighteenth-century wars beginning with the War of the Spanish Succession (1701–1714), the combination of Britain's naval strength and the land armies of Austria and Prussia blocked French expansionist efforts and prevented the Bourbons from uniting the thrones of France and Spain. France's defeat illustrates the principle of **balance of power** in international relations: the major European states formed temporary alliances to prevent any one state from becoming too powerful (see Map 16.2). These pragmatic alliances were the first successful efforts at international peacekeeping.

## Paying the Piper

European nations struggled to pay for their wars. But the obstacles were formidable, particularly the tax exemptions enjoyed by the nobility and clergy, since they controlled most of Europe's wealth. In Spain, for example, 97 percent of the land was owned by the 3 percent of the population that constituted the nobility. To raise revenue, regressive new taxes were imposed on the peasants and commerce. To collect them governments turned to **tax farmers**, private individuals who advanced the government a fixed sum of money, typically less than 50 percent of the estimated tax

**balance of power** The policy in international relations by which, beginning in the eighteenth century, the major European states acted together to prevent any one of them from becoming too powerful.

**tax farmers** Private individuals or small partnerships who were given contracts to collect taxes for the government. In return tax farmers could keep whatever money they were able to collect above their tax obligation to the government.

**Map 16.2 Europe in 1740** By the middle of the eighteenth century, the great powers of Europe adhering to four different branches of Christianity—Catholic France and Austria, Anglican Britain, Lutheran Prussia, and Orthodox Russia—maintained an effective balance of power by shifting their alliances for geopolitical rather than religious reasons. Spain, the Holy Roman Empire, and the Ottoman Empire were far weaker in 1740 than they had been two centuries earlier. © Cengage Learning

obligation, for the right to collect the tax. In return they could keep whatever money they were able to collect from taxpayers. This allowed governments to avoid creating expensive new bureaucracies, but the system guaranteed corruption and limited revenue growth.

Desperate governments began to find dangerous short-term fiscal expedients attractive, including currency debasement and cynical defaults on debts like Philip II's four bankruptcies. It was inevitable that early capitalism's innovations, such as joint-stock companies and stock markets, would draw governments thwarted by the tax intransigence of the elite to look to these highly speculative novelties to solve fiscal problems. Eventually, markets would grow stronger, but two nearly simultaneous speculative bubbles attached to the French Mississippi Company and the English South Sea Company resulted in spectacularly visible flaws that would force governments to turn to the taxation of reluctant citizens to pay their debts (see Chapter 21).

In 1716 the French government granted John Law, a fugitive Scottish nobleman, a license to create a bank and issue paper money based on the promise to exchange for coins at par. To everyone's surprise, the notes issued by Law's bank not only maintained their value but also were preferred to coins. The value of shares in the bank increased dramatically. Then in 1717 the French government allowed Law to create a monopoly company for development along the Mississippi, a region erroneously believed to have rich mines. The value of the initial shares soared, with prices rising 10 or 20 percent in the course of a few hours. Stories of once-poor servants buying mansions and marrying their children into noble families abounded. As the frenzy mounted, the French government used Law's bank to print more paper money rather than collect taxes. Law then satisfied the public clamor for Mississippi Company shares by imitating this irresponsible behavior. When a nervous French public began to hoard coins and avoid paper currency, Law got the government to discount gold and silver coins against the paper currency and then to restrict individual possession of coins. The subsequent panicked selling of shares in both the bank and the Mississippi Company in 1720 forced Law to run for his life. Paper wealth disappeared in a matter of days, leaving the French government to face its fiscal crisis.

In a similar scheme, the English lord treasurer in 1711 granted exclusive rights to the South Sea Company to trade with the Spanish colonies in the Americas to reduce the British government's huge wartime debt. Holders of war debts were forced to accept shares in the company as payment. Once in possession of the government bonds, the company borrowed new funds based on the supposed security of government debt. At first, the large annual interest payments from the government and a monopoly right to trade slaves to the Spanish colonies made the South Sea Company seem like a profitable investment. With news of the Mississippi Company's success, the government used the South Sea Company to transform another £30,000,000 in debt into shares. When South Sea shares issued at £300 rose to £325, the company issued more stock, even though it had almost no income from its commercial ventures. In January 1720 share prices reached £1,050. With the inevitable crash, thousands of investors were ruined. Among the investors was the scientist Isaac Newton, who said, "I can calculate the motions of the heavenly bodies but not the madness of people."

The rise of the Netherlands as an economic power stemmed from very different policies. The Spanish crown had acquired these resource-poor but commercially successful provinces as part of Charles V's inheritance. But King Philip II's decision to impose Spain's ruinously heavy sales tax and to enforce Catholic orthodoxy drove the Dutch to revolt in 1566 and again in 1572. If successful, those measures would have discouraged business and driven away the Calvinists, Jews, and other key contributors to Dutch prosperity. The Dutch fought with skill and ingenuity, raising and training an army and a navy that were among the most effective in Europe. Unable to bear the military costs any longer, Spain accepted a truce that recognized autonomy in the northern Netherlands in 1609. Finally, in 1648, the independence of the seven United Provinces of the Free Netherlands (their full name) became final.

Rather than being ruined by the long war, the Netherlands emerged as the world's greatest trading nation. This economic success owed much to a decentralized government. During the struggle against Spain, the provinces united around the Prince of Orange, their sovereign and commander-in-chief. But in economic matters each province was free to pursue its own interests. The maritime province of Holland grew rich by favoring commercial interests.

After 1650 the Dutch faced growing competition from England, where business was also allied with government. In a series of wars (1652–1678) England naval might broke Dutch dominance in overseas trade. With government support, the English merchant fleet doubled between 1660 and 1700, and foreign trade rose by 50 percent. State revenue from customs duties tripled. During the eighteenth century Britain's trading position strengthened still more.

The debts run up by the Anglo-Dutch Wars persuaded the English monarchy to enlarge the government's role in managing the economy. The outcome has been called a "financial revolution." The government increased revenues by taxing the formerly exempt landed estates of the aristocrats and by collecting taxes directly instead of relying on tax farmers. To secure cash quickly for warfare and other emergencies and to reduce the burden of debts from earlier wars, England imitated the Dutch by creating a central bank that could issue long-term loans at low rates.

## SECTION REVIEW

- Greater political centralization enabled early modern monarchs to exert increased influence on economic, religious, and social life.

- While the Holy Roman Empire fragmented along religious and political lines, Spain, France, and England achieved greater centralization and religious unity.

- In both England and France, monarchs struggled with rivals over the limits of royal authority.

- Armies grew larger and more sophisticated while European powers strove to maintain a balance of power.

- High military costs drove the European powers to attempt a variety of tax and financial policies, the most successful being those of England and the Netherlands.

The French government also developed its national economy, especially under the royal adviser Jean Baptiste Colbert. Colbert streamlined tax collection, promoted French manufacturing and shipping by imposing taxes on foreign goods, and improved transportation. Yet the power of the wealthy aristocrats kept the French government from following England's lead in taxing wealthy landowners, collecting taxes directly, and securing low-cost loans. Nor did France succeed in managing its debt as efficiently as England.

## CONCLUSION

European historians have used the word *revolution* to describe many different changes taking place in Europe between 1500 and 1750. The expansion of trade has been called a *commercial revolution*, the reform of state spending a *financial revolution*, and the changes in weapons and warfare a *military revolution*. We have also encountered a scientific revolution and the religious revolution of the Reformation.

Yet the years from 1500 to 1750 were not simply—perhaps not even primarily—an age of progress for Europe. For many, the ferocious competition of European armies, merchants, and ideas was a wrenching experience. The growth of powerful states exacted a terrible price in death, destruction, and misery. While the Reformation brought greater individual choice in religion, it also brought widespread persecution. And while the expanding economy benefited the emerging merchant elite and their political allies, most Europeans became worse off as prices rose faster than wages. Finally, new scientific and enlightened ideas ignited controversies long before yielding any tangible results.

The historical significance of this period of European history is clearer when viewed in a global context. What stands out are the powerful and efficient European armies, economies, and governments. From a global perspective, the balance of political and economic power was shifting slowly, but inexorably, in the Europeans' favor. In 1500 the Ottomans threatened Europe. By 1750, Europeans had brought the world's seas and a growing portion of its lands and peoples under their control.

# CHAPTER REVIEW

## CULTURE AND IDEAS

■ *How did the interplay of traditional beliefs and revolutionary ideas influence the cultural history of early modern Europe?* (page 381)

Early modern Europe underwent the Scientific Revolution as well as the fragmentation of the Catholic Church. Traditional antifeminist beliefs and pagan folklore about witchcraft fed a witch-hunting craze that took thousands of lives. Supporting the belief in witchcraft was a more fundamental idea that human misfortune could be blamed on supernatural forces, but this idea was powerfully challenged by pioneers of the Scientific Revolution such as Copernicus and Newton, who showed that the workings of the physical universe could be explained in natural terms. These scientists did not see any conflict between science and religion, and they paved the way for influential figures of the Enlightenment, who believed that human reason was capable of discovering laws that govern social behavior.

## SOCIAL AND ECONOMIC LIFE

■ *What factors contributed to the wealth of some Europeans and the great poverty of others in this period?* (page 388)

Thanks to foreign and domestic trade, European cities in this period experienced rapid growth and the rise of a wealthy commercial class. It was also an era of growing speculative risk and market bubbles like Tulipmania and the South Sea bubble. The Netherlands in particular prospered from expanded manufacturing and trade: with the formation of joint-stock companies and a powerful stock market, Amsterdam became Europe's major port and financial center. For peasants and laborers, however, life did not improve much, although serfdom had all but ended in western Europe. Rural poverty, coupled with the exemption from taxation enjoyed by wealthy landowners, sparked numerous armed rebellions.

## POLITICAL INNOVATIONS

■ *How did differing policies in the areas of religion, foreign relations, and economics determine the very different experiences of early modern European states?* (page 393)

Differing policies in the areas of religion, foreign relations, and economics explain the different histories of Europe's early modern states. Charles V, unable to reconcile the diverse interests of his Catholic and Protestant territories and their powerful local rulers, failed to create a unified Holy Roman Empire. Power struggles in England during this period led to a stronger Parliament, while in France a stronger monarchy emerged, symbolized by Louis XIV's construction of the palace at Versailles. Spain dominated Europe in the sixteenth century, but its failure to suppress revolts in the Netherlands and the costs of other wars led to bankruptcy and decline. In the seventeenth century the Netherlands became the dominant commercial power on the continent. However, the growth of English naval power led to the defeat of the Dutch in the Anglo-Dutch Wars and of France in the early eighteenth century when it attempted to expand its own empire through a union with Spain. Unlike Spain and France, which maintained aristocrats' traditional exemption from taxation, England began to tax their estates, and this policy—together with the establishment of direct taxation and the creation of a central bank from which it could secure low-cost loans—gave England a stronger financial foundation than its rivals enjoyed.

## Key Terms

papacy (p. 381)

indulgence (p. 382)

Protestant Reformation (p. 382)

Catholic Reformation (p. 383)

witch-hunt (p. 385)

Scientific Revolution (p. 386)

Enlightenment (p. 387)

bourgeoisie (p. 388)

joint-stock company (p. 391)

stock exchange (p. 391)

gentry (p. 391)

Little Ice Age (p. 391)

deforestation (p. 392)

Holy Roman Empire (p. 394)

Habsburg (p. 394)

English Civil War (p. 395)

Versailles (p. 396)

balance of power (p. 397)

tax farmers (p. 397)

# The Americas, the Atlantic, and Africa

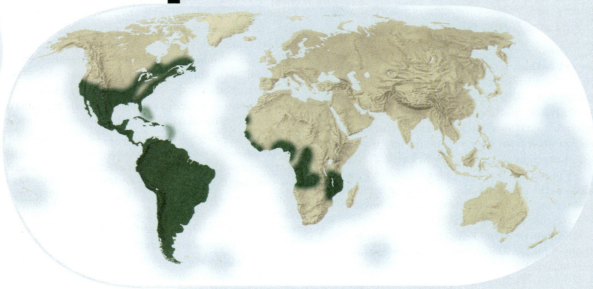

© Cengage Learning

After 1600, Spain became increasingly impoverished and had difficulty protecting its American empire from pirates, privateers, and the rising powers of Europe: the Netherlands, France, and Britain. These nations, like Spain before them, benefited from the advantage that diseases gave to their people in their encounters with Native Americans. As with Spanish colonies before them, the development of English and French colonies in North America in the seventeenth century led to similar patterns of contagion and mortality. In 1616 and 1617 epidemics nearly exterminated New England's indigenous groups, while French fur traders transmitted measles, smallpox, and other diseases as far as Hudson Bay and the Great Lakes.

Although there is very little evidence that Europeans consciously used disease as a tool of empire, they inadvertently increased the rate of contagion by making Native Americans live in denser concentrations. The deadly results of contact with Europeans undermined the ability of native peoples to resist European settlement, and Europeans and their African slaves occupied these depopulated lands. Transformed biologically and culturally, the Americas were subjected to Europeans' political and economic demands.

The colonies of the Americas were crucial pieces of a booming new **Atlantic system**, a network of trading links that moved goods and wealth, as well as peoples and cultures, around the Atlantic. The Atlantic system also affected Africa but less severely than the Americas. Despite the loss of millions to the slave trade, Africa did not suffer population loss due to epidemics as in the Americas. On the contrary, the diseases prevalent in Africa—especially malaria and yellow fever—killed most of the Europeans who visited that continent. As a result, Africans remained in control of their land, except for small enclaves on the coast.

Amerindians, Europeans, and Africans all contributed to the creation of new cultures in the Americas. The societies that arose reflected each colony's mix of native peoples, its connections to the slave trade, and the policies of its European rulers.

# SPANISH AMERICA AND BRAZIL

■ *What role did forced labor play in the main industries of Spanish America and Brazil?*

Within one hundred years of Columbus's first voyage to the Western Hemisphere, the Spanish Empire in America included most of the islands of the Caribbean and a vast area that stretched from northern Mexico to the plains of the Rio de la Plata region (a region that includes the modern nations of Argentina, Uruguay, and Paraguay). Portuguese settlement developed more slowly, but before the end of the sixteenth century, Portugal had occupied most of the Brazilian coast.

Early settlers from Spain and Portugal sought to create colonial societies based on the institutions and customs of their homelands. They viewed society as a vertical hierarchy of estates (classes of society), as uniformly Catholic, and as an arrangement of patriarchal extended-family networks. But despite the imposition of European religious, social, and administrative institutions and the massive loss of life caused by epidemics, indigenous peoples exercised a powerful influence on the development of colonial societies. Aztec and Inka elite families sought to protect their traditional privileges and rights through marriage or less formal alliances with Spanish settlers. They also used colonial courts to defend their claims to land. Nearly everywhere, Amerindian religious beliefs and practices survived beneath the surface of an imposed Christianity. Amerindian languages, cuisines, medical practices, and agricultural techniques also survived the conquest and influenced the development of Latin American culture.

The African slave trade added a third cultural stream to colonial Latin American society. At first, African slaves were concentrated in plantation regions of Brazil and the Caribbean, but by the end of the colonial era, Africans and their descendants were living throughout Latin America, enriching the agricultural practices, music, religious beliefs, cuisine, and social customs of colonial societies.

**Atlantic system** The network of trading links after 1500 that moved goods, wealth, people, and cultures around the Atlantic Basin.

## State and Church

The Spanish crown moved quickly to curb the independent power of the conquistadors and to establish royal authority over both defeated native populations and European settlers. As a result, the highest-ranking Spanish officials in the colonies, the viceroys of New Spain and Peru, enjoyed broad power, but they also faced obstacles to their authority in the vast territories they sought to control. Created in 1535, the Viceroyalty of New Spain, with its capital in Mexico City, included Mexico, the southwest of what is now the United States, Central America, and the islands of the Caribbean. Created five years later, the Viceroyalty of Peru, with its capital in Lima, governed Spanish South America (see Map 17.1). Until the seventeenth century, most colonial officials were born in Spain, but fiscal mismanagement eventually forced the Crown to sell appointments, and later, local-born members of the colonial elite gained many offices.

In the sixteenth century Portugal concentrated its resources and energies on Asia and Africa, because early settlers found neither mineral wealth nor rich native empires in Brazil. Finally, the king appointed a governor-general in 1549 and made Salvador Brazil's capital. In 1720 the king named the first viceroy of Brazil.

The colonial bureaucracies imposed Spanish and Portuguese oversight (and heavy tax burdens) on the silver and gold mines in Spanish America and the sugar plantations in Brazil, justifying their American conquests by assuming an obligation to convert native populations to Christianity. This effort to convert America's native peoples expanded Christianity on a scale similar to its earlier expansion in Europe at the time of Constantine in the fourth century. The Catholic Church undertook the conversion of Amerindians, ministered to the spiritual needs of European settlers, and promoted intellectual life through the introduction of the printing press and the founding of schools and universities. Together, the Spanish and Portuguese colonial governments and the efforts of the Catholic Church brought European language and a more unified culture to the Iberian Americas than would be found in North American settlements.

Although European clergy had arrived in the Americas with the intention of transmitting Catholic Christian belief and ritual without alteration, the linguistic diversity of Amerindian populations and their geographic dispersal over a vast landscape defeated this ambition. Initially, Franciscan missionaries in Mexico tried to extend their reach by creating a seminary to train members of the indigenous elite to become priests. These efforts were abandoned when church authorities discovered that many converts were secretly observing old beliefs and rituals. Although priests at times resorted to forced conversion and the violent repression of native religions, including torture among the Maya in the 1560s, these practices repelled the church hierarchy and were outlawed. Despite European disapproval, Amerindians blended Catholic Christian belief with important elements of traditional native cosmology and ritual that are now embedded in such celebration as saints' days or Catholic rituals associated with the Virgin Mary.

Despite its failures, the Catholic clergy did provide native peoples with some protections against the abuse and exploitation of Spanish settlers. **Bartolomé de Las Casas** (1474–1566), who had arrived in Hispaniola in 1502 and initially lived from the forced labor of Amerindians, was deeply moved by the deaths of so many Amerindians and by the misdeeds of the Spanish. He entered the Dominican Order, becoming the first bishop of Chiapas, in southern Mexico, and spent the remainder of his long life as an advocate for native peoples. His most important achievement was the enactment of the New Laws of 1542, which outlawed the enslavement of Amerindians and limited other forms of forced labor.

After 1600 the terrible loss of Amerindian populations caused by epidemics and resistance to conversion led the Catholic Church to redirect its resources from native regions in the countryside to growing colonial cities and towns with large European populations. This altered mission included the founding of universities and secondary schools, which stimulated urban intellectual life. Over time, the church became the richest institution in the Spanish colonies, controlling ranches, plantations, and vineyards as well as serving as the society's banker.

**Bartolomé de Las Casas** First bishop of Chiapas, in southern Mexico. He devoted most of his life to protecting Amerindian peoples from exploitation. His major achievement was the New Laws of 1542, which limited the ability of Spanish settlers to compel Amerindians to labor for them.

# Chronology

| | Spanish America | Brazil | British America | French America |
|---|---|---|---|---|
| **1500** | **1518** Smallpox arrives in Caribbean<br>**1535** Creation of Viceroyalty of New Spain<br>**1540** Creation of Viceroyalty of Peru<br>**1542** New Laws attempt to outlaw Amerindian enslavement<br>**1545** Silver discovered at Potosí, Bolivia | **1549** Appointment of first Portuguese governor-general of Brazil<br>**1540–1600** Era of Amerindian slavery<br>**After 1540** Sugar begins to dominate the economy | | |
| **1600** | | **By 1620** African slave trade provides majority of plantation workers<br>**1630s** Quilombo of Palmares founded | **1607** Jamestown founded<br>**1620** Plymouth founded<br>**1660–1756** Rapid growth of slavery in Virginia<br>**1664** English take New York from Dutch | **1608** Quebec founded<br><br>**1699** Louisiana founded |
| **1700** | **1713** Beginning of Bourbon dynasty in Spain | **1750–1777** Reforms in Brazil and Spanish America | **1754–1763** French and Indian War | **1760** English take Canada |

## Colonial Economies

The silver mines of Peru and Mexico and the sugar plantations of Brazil dominated the colonial economy and fueled the early development of European capitalism. Profits also promoted the growth of colonial cities, concentrated scarce investment capital and labor resources, and stimulated the livestock industry. Mineral and agricultural exports remain an enduring legacy in Latin America. Silver generated the most wealth and exercised the greatest economic influence in the Spanish colonies, though gold mines were also productive. In 1545, the single richest silver deposit in the Americas was discovered at **Potosí** (poh-toh-SEE) in what is now Bolivia.

Silver mining also altered the environment. Within a short time, wasteful use of forest resources to fuel furnaces for smelting ore led to deforestation near the mining centers. Faced with rising fuel costs, Mexican miners developed an efficient method of chemical extraction that relied on mixing mercury with the silver ore. Silver yields and profits increased, but since mercury is a poison, its use contaminated the environment and sickened the Amerindian workforce.

Indigenous populations had been compelled to provide labor for European settlers in the Americas since Columbus. Until the 1540s Amerindians were divided among settlers in the Spanish colonies and forced to provide labor or goods. This form of forced labor was called **encomienda** (in-co-mee-EN-dah). The discovery of silver in Peru led to use of the *mita*

**Potosí** Located in Bolivia, one of the richest silver mining centers and most populous cities in colonial Spanish America.

**encomienda** A grant of authority over a population of Amerindians in the Spanish colonies. It provided the grant holder with a supply of cheap labor and periodic payments of goods by the Amerindians. It obliged the grant holder to Christianize the Amerindians.

**NEW FRANCE**
(Conquered by England, 1760)

*Mississippi R.*

**ENGLISH COLONIES**
(Independence declared, 1776)

ATLANTIC OCEAN

40°W

40°N

*Colorado R.*

Effective frontier of Spanish settlement

Silver
Silver
**COAHUILA**

*Rio Grande*

**FLORIDA**
(Ceded to England, 1763–1783)

*Gulf of Mexico*

**VICEROYALTY OF NEW SPAIN**

**BAJIO LEÓN** (1535)

Guadalajara ● ✕ Zacatecas
✕ Guanajuato
Mexico City ●
Silver
● Veracruz

Havana ●

Sugar cane
Beef
Tobacco

**HAITI [SAINT-DOMINGUE]**
(Ceded to France, 1697)

Sugar cane
Indigo

Sugar cane

Beef

Sugar cane
**PUERTO RICO**

20°N

Cacao

**BRITISH HONDURAS**

● Guatemala
Silver

**JAMAICA**
(Conquered by England, 1655)

*Caribbean Sea*

**SANTO DOMINGO**

Sugar cane

Sugar cane
Cochineal

Cochineal
Cacao
Indigo

Sugar cane

Pearls

Caracas ●
Cacao

Gold

*Orinoco R.*

*Magdalena R.*

● Bogotá

**GUIANA**

**VICEROYALTY OF NEW GRANADA**
(Separated from Viceroyalty of Peru, 1717, 1739)

Quito ●

Equator 0°

*Amazon R.*

Forest products

**VICEROYALTY OF PERU**
(1590s)

Sugar cane

Lima ●

● Cuzco

**VICEROYALTY OF BRAZIL**
(1720)

Sugar cane ● Pernambuco

Sugar cane
● Salvador

Cacao

PACIFIC OCEAN

Sugar cane

● La Paz

Chuquisaca
(La Plata; Sucre)

✕ Potosí

Diamonds
Gold

Rio de Janeiro
(Capital, 1763)

20°S

*Parana R.*

Yerba
Tobacco

● São Paulo

*ANDES*

**VICEROYALTY OF LA PLATA**
(Separated from Viceroyalty of Peru, 1776)

Wheat

Santiago ●

**AUDIENCIA OF CHILE**
(Retained by Viceroyalty of Peru, 1776)

Buenos Aires ●
Beef and hides

Beef and hides
● Montevideo

0     500    1,000 Km.
0     500    1,000 Mi.

Claimed but not settled by Spain

*Islas Malvinas
(Falkland Islands)*

Cape Horn

80°W     60°W

**Territories claimed by Spain**

▭ Viceroyalty of New Spain
▭ Viceroyalty of New Granada
▭ Viceroyalty of Peru and Audiencia of Chile
▭ Viceroyalty of Rio de la Plata

**Territories claimed by Portugal**

▭ Viceroyalty of Brazil

✕ Silver mine

N

**Map 17.1 Colonial Latin America in the Eighteenth Century** Spain and Portugal controlled most of the Western Hemisphere in the eighteenth century. In the sixteenth century they had created new administrative jurisdictions—viceroyalties—to defend their respective colonies against European rivals. Taxes assessed on colonial products helped pay for this extension of governmental authority. © Cengage Learning

**Legend**

(A) Storage sheds for ore
(B) Two water-driven stamping mills to crush ore
(C) Additional stamping mill
(D) Screen to sort ore
(E) Ore packed in mixing box

(F) Mercury and catalysts added to ore
(G) Amalgamation occurs
(H) Ore dried in furnace
(I) Mercury removed
(J) Refined ore washed
(K) Ore assayed

(L) Poor quality ore remixed with catalysts
(M) Housing
(N) Offices and sheds
(O) Aquaduct
(P) Chapel
(Q) Mill owner's house

© Cengage Learning

**A Bolivian Silver Refinery, 1700** The silver refineries of Spanish America were among the largest industrial establishments in the Western Hemisphere.

(MEE-tah) system of compulsory labor (see Chapters 7 and 14). Under this system, one-seventh of adult male Amerindians were compelled to work for two to four months each year in mines, farms, or textile factories. As the Amerindian population declined with new epidemics, villages began to shorten the period between mita obligations. Instead of serving every seven years, many men returned to the mines after only a year or two, and thousands abandoned traditional agriculture and moved permanently to Spanish mines and farms as paid laborers to avoid mita service and other taxes, weakening Amerindian village life and promoting Amerindian assimilation into Spanish-speaking Catholic colonial society.

The Portuguese had developed sugar plantations using African slave labor on the Atlantic islands of Madeira, the Azores, the Cape Verdes, and São Tomé,

and they quickly transferred this system to Brazil. From roughly 1540 onward sugar dominated the Brazilian economy. Between then and 1600, the Portuguese sugar planters enslaved Amerindians, but as epidemics decimated the Amerindian workforce, planters eventually came to rely more on African slaves. Imports of African slaves rose from an average of two thousand per year in the late sixteenth century to approximately seven thousand per year a century later, outstripping the immigration of free Portuguese settlers.

The mining centers of Latin America exercised global economic influence. American silver increased the European money supply, promoting commercial expansion. Large amounts of silver also flowed to Asia, exchanged for spices, silk, and porcelain. As a result, both Europe and Latin America ran chronic trade deficits with Asia. The sugar plantations of Brazil played a similar role in integrating the economy of the South Atlantic region. Both Spain and Portugal attempted to control the trade of their American colonies, but monopoly commerce and convoy shipping slowed the flow of Europeans goods to the colonies and kept prices high. Frustrated, colonial populations established illegal trade with the English, French, and Dutch. By the middle of the seventeenth century, a majority of European imports were arriving in Latin America illegally.

## Society in Colonial Latin America

With the exception of some early viceroys, few members of Spain's nobility came to the New World. *Hidalgos* (ee-DAHL-goes)—lesser nobles—were well represented, as were Spanish merchants, artisans, miners, priests, and lawyers. Small numbers of criminals, beggars, and prostitutes also found their way to the colonies. Spanish settlers, however, were always a tiny minority in a colonial society numerically dominated by Amerindians and rapidly growing populations of Africans, **creoles** (whites born in America to European parents), and people of mixed ancestry.

Conquistadors and early settlers who received from the Crown grants of labor and tribute goods (*encomienda*) from Amerindian communities as rewards for service to Spain sought to create a hereditary social and political class comparable to the European nobility. But their position was undermined by their abuse of Amerindian communities, the catastrophic effects of the epidemics of the sixteenth century, and the growing power of colonial officials, the clergy, and the richest merchants. The elite of Spanish America included both European immigrants and creoles. Europeans controlled the highest levels of the church and government as well as commerce, while wealthy creoles commonly controlled colonial agriculture and mining. Although tensions between Spaniards and creoles were inevitable, most elite families included both groups.

Before the Europeans arrived in the Americas, the native peoples were members of a large number of distinct cultural and linguistic groups. Cultural diversity and class distinctions were present even in the highly centralized Aztec and Inka Empires. This rich social and cultural complexity was undermined by the effects of conquest and epidemics, and the imposition of Catholic Christianity. The broad application of the racial label *Indian* to all Amerindians helped organize the tribute and labor demands imposed on native peoples while erasing long-standing class and ethnic differences.

Indigenous Amerindian elites struggled to survive. Hereditary native elites established political alliances with colonial administrations and gained some security by becoming their intermediaries with the indigenous masses, collecting Spanish taxes and organizing the labor of their dependents. Some elite Amerindian women married colonists, but over time, these family ties diminished. Indigenous commoners suffered the heaviest burdens of tribute, forced labor, and the loss of native lands. Survivors adapted by embracing elements of colonial culture or entering the market economies of the cities.

Thousands of blacks participated in the conquest and settlement of Spanish America, and the opening of a direct slave trade with Africa added millions more. African slaves arrived in the colonies with different languages, religious beliefs, and cultural practices. European settlers viewed these differences as signs of inferiority that served as a justification for slavery. However, slaves still had an impact on Spanish America beyond serving as a source of labor. Exposure to Iberian culture in West-Central Africa, where many slaves originated, facilitated African influence on the emerging colonial cultures of Latin America. Over time, elements from many African traditions blended and mixed with European (and in some cases Amerindian) languages and beliefs to forge distinct local cultures.

African slaves became skilled artisans, musicians, servants, artists, cowboys, and even soldiers. However, the vast majority worked in agriculture. To escape harsh discipline and backbreaking labor, many slaves rebelled or ran away. Communities of runaways, called *quilombos* (key-LOM-bos) in Brazil and *palenques* (pah-LEN-kays) in Spanish colonies, were common. The largest quilombo was Palmares,

**creoles** In colonial Spanish America, the term used to describe someone of European descent born in the New World. Elsewhere in the Americas, the term is used to describe all nonnative peoples.

where thousands of slaves defended themselves against Brazilian authorities for sixty years until they were finally overthrown in 1694.

Brazil attracted smaller numbers of European immigrants than did Spanish America, and its native populations were smaller and less urbanized than the Aztecs or Inka. Brazil also came to depend on African slave labor earlier than any other American colony, and by the early seventeenth century, Africans and their American-born descendants were by far the largest racial group in that country. As a result, Brazilian colonial society (unlike Spanish Mexico and Peru) was more influenced by African culture than by Amerindian culture.

## Imperial Reform and Resistance

Spain's Habsburg dynasty ended when Charles II died without an heir in 1700, and Philip of Bourbon, grandson of Louis XIV of France, secured the throne after thirteen years of costly war involving the major European powers and factions within Spain. To replenish revenue, Philip V looked to the remarkable economic expansion and population growth of Spanish America in the eighteenth century. Silver production in Mexico and Peru rose steadily, and agricultural exports also

### SECTION REVIEW

- Colonial governments were created to rule distant colonies.
- The Catholic Church led conversion of Amerindian peoples and spread European cultures and languages.
- Silver mining and sugar production dominated colonial Latin American economies.
- Spanish and Portuguese colonies relied on forced labor of Amerindians and African slaves.
- New peoples and new cultures resulted from colonial contacts among Amerindians, Europeans, and Africans.
- Colonial reforms disrupted colonial economic and political accommodations and led to rebellion and resistance.

expanded: tobacco, dyes, hides, chocolate, cotton, and sugar joined the flow of goods to Europe. Spain instituted reforms during this period, reorganizing colonial administration and tax collection to force colonial populations to pay a larger share of the costs of administration and defense. Portugal followed suit, as gold was discovered in Brazil in the 1690s and diamonds after 1720.

Both Spain and Portugal also sought to reduce the power of the Catholic Church in their colonies and to transfer some church wealth to their treasuries. These

Sir Henry Chamberlain, *Views and Costumes of the City and Neighborhoods of Rio de Janeiro,* London, 1822

**Market in Rio de Janeiro** In many of the cities of colonial Latin America, female slaves and black free women dominated retail markets. In this scene from late colonial Brazil, Afro-Brazilian women sell a variety of foods and crafts.

efforts led to a succession of confrontations between colonial officials and the church hierarchy. In the eighteenth century, the clergy could no longer be relied on to support the colonial state, and many colonists saw the reforms as an abuse of power. In the 1770s tax rebellions, urban riots, and Amerindian uprisings tied to these reforms began in Spanish America, and open warfare occurred between "sons of the soil" and "outsiders" in Sáo Paolo, Brazil. A more unified colonial culture had begun to assert itself against the will of distant monarchs.

# ENGLISH AND FRENCH COLONIES IN NORTH AMERICA

■ *What were the differences between the English and the French colonies of North America?*

The North American empires of England and France had much in common with those of Spain and Portugal. They hoped to find precious metals or great indigenous empires like those of the Aztecs and Inka, and their settlers responded to native peoples with a mixture of diplomacy and violence. They also imported large numbers of African slaves.

There were also important differences. The English and French colonies were founded nearly a century after Cortés's conquest of Mexico and the initial Portuguese settlement of Brazil. By the time England and France secured a foothold, trade had increased the integration of world cultural regions. Distracted by ventures elsewhere, neither England nor France imitated the large and expensive colonial bureaucracies that Spain and Portugal established. Instead, private companies and individual proprietors pioneered development. The Protestant Reformation had also helped frame the character of English and French settlement in the Americas. Greater variety in economic activity, political institutions and culture, and social structure was evident here compared with Latin American colonies.

### The South

London investors organized as the Virginia Company took up the challenge of colonizing Virginia in 1607 and 1608. However, 80 percent of the settlers at Jamestown died of disease or Amerindian attack. After the English crown dissolved the Virginia Company because of its mismanagement in 1624, colonists were free to move from the swampy unhealthy Jamestown deeper into the interior, developing a sustainable economy based on furs, timber, and, increasingly, tobacco. The profits from tobacco soon attracted new immigrants and new capital. Along the shoreline of Chesapeake Bay and the rivers that fed it, settlers spread out, developing plantations and farms.

**Indentured servants** eventually accounted for approximately 80 percent of all English immigration to the Chesapeake Bay region. Young European men and women racially and religiously indistinguishable from free settlers paid for their transportation to America by accepting indentures (contracts) that bound them to a term ranging from four to seven years of labor and that provided, at the end of the contract, a small parcel of land, some tools, and clothes. During the seventeenth century, approximately 1,500 indentured servants—mostly male—arrived each year. Initially, high mortality rates among slaves made indentured servants more economical than slaves. But as life expectancy improved, planters calculated that the higher initial cost of buying a slave, who would be owned for life, would contribute to greater profits. As a result, Virginia's slave population grew from 950 in 1660 to 120,000 by 1756.

Ironically, increased dependence on slavery occurred along with the expansion in colonial liberties and political rights. At first, colonial government had been administered by a Crown-appointed governor and by representatives of towns meeting together as the **House of Burgesses**. When elected representatives began to meet alone as a deliberative body, they initiated a form of democratic representation that distinguished the English colonies of North America from the colonies of other European powers. The intertwined evolution of American freedom and slavery gave England's southern colonies a unique and conflicted political character.

**indentured servant**  A migrant to British colonies in the Americas who paid for passage by agreeing to work for a set term ranging from four to seven years.

**House of Burgesses**  Elected assembly in colonial Virginia, created in 1618.

Colonial South Carolina was the most hierarchical society in British North America. Settled first by planters from Barbados in 1670, this colony developed an economy based on plantations and slavery in imitation of the colonies of the Caribbean and Brazil. The richest maintained households in both the countryside and Charleston, the largest city in the southern colonies. Small farmers, cattlemen, artisans, merchants, and fur traders held an intermediate but clearly subordinate social position. At the bottom were the slaves on whom South Carolina depended. African slaves had been present from the founding of Charleston and were instrumental in introducing irrigated rice agriculture and in developing plantations of indigo (a plant that produced a blue dye). Although native peoples remained influential participants in colonial society through commercial contracts and alliances, they were increasingly marginalized.

### New England

New England was colonized by two separate groups of Protestant dissenters. The **Pilgrims** established the coastal colony of Plymouth in present-day Massachusetts in 1620. Although nearly half of the settlers died during the first winter, the colony survived. In 1691, Plymouth was absorbed into the larger Massachusetts Bay Colony of the **Puritans**. By 1643 more than twenty thousand Puritans had settled in the Bay Colony.

Unlike in the southern colonies, most newcomers to Massachusetts arrived with their families. A normal gender balance and a healthy climate resulted in a rapid increase in population. Massachusetts also was more homogeneous and less hierarchical than the southern colonies.

Political institutions evolved from the terms of the Puritans' royal charter. A governor was elected, along with a council of magistrates drawn from the board of directors of the Massachusetts Bay Company. Disagreements between this council and elected representatives of the towns led, by 1650, to the creation of a lower legislative house that selected its own speaker and developed procedures and rules similar to those of the House of Commons in England.

Economically, agriculture met basic needs, but the poor soils and harsh climate did not favor cash crops like tobacco or rice. To pay for imported tools, textiles, and other essentials, the colonists provided commercial and shipping services to the southern colonies, the Caribbean islands, Africa, and Europe. In contrast to Latin America's heavily capitalized monopolies, New England merchants depended on market intelligence, flexibility, and streamlined organization. By 1740, Boston, with 16,000 inhabitants, was the largest city in British North America.

### The Middle Atlantic Region

The rapid economic development and cultural diversity of the Middle Atlantic colonies added to the success of English-speaking North America. The **Iroquois Confederacy**—an alliance among the Mohawk, Oneida, Onondaga, Cayuga, and Seneca peoples—established treaties and trading relationships with the Dutch. When confronted by an English military expedition in 1664, the Dutch surrendered without a fight. James, duke of York and later King James II of England, renamed the colony *New York*. Located at the mouth of the Hudson River, New York City developed as a commercial and shipping center, playing an essential role in connecting the region's grain farmers to the booming markets of the Caribbean and southern Europe. By the early eighteenth century, this colony had a diverse population that included English, Dutch, German, and Swedish settlers as well as a large slave community.

Pennsylvania began as a proprietary colony in 1682 and as a refuge for Quakers, a persecuted religious minority. The founder, William Penn, quickly lost control of the colony's political life, but the colony enjoyed remarkable success. By 1700, Pennsylvania had a population of more than 21,000, and Philadelphia, its capital, soon overtook Boston to become the largest city in the British colonies. Healthy climate,

**Pilgrims** Group of English Protestant dissenters who established Plymouth Colony in Massachusetts in 1620 to seek religious freedom after having lived briefly in the Netherlands.

**Puritans** English Protestant dissenters who believed that God predestined souls to Heaven or Hell before birth. They founded Massachusetts Bay Colony in 1629.

**Iroquois Confederacy** An alliance of five northeastern Amerindian peoples (six after 1722) that made decisions on military and diplomatic issues through a council of representatives. Allied first with the Dutch and later with the English, the Confederacy dominated the area from western New England to the Great Lakes.

"Johnson Hall," by E. L. Henry. Courtesy, Albany Institute of History and Art

**The Home of Sir William Johnson, British Superintendent for Indian Affairs, Northern District**  As the colonial era drew to a close, the British attempted to limit the cost of colonial defense by negotiating land settlements with native peoples, but the growing tide of western migration doomed these agreements. William Johnson (1715–1774) maintained a fragile peace along the northern frontier by building strong personal relations with influential leaders of the Mohawk and other members of the Iroquois Confederacy. His home in present-day Johnstown, New York, shows the mixed nature of the frontier—the relative opulence of the main house offset by the two defensive blockhouses built for protection.

excellent land, and relatively peaceful relations with native peoples attracted free workers without reproducing South Carolina's hierarchical and repressive social order based on slavery. By the early eighteenth century, however, a rich merchant elite was in place and the prosperous city of Philadelphia had a large population of black slaves, servants, and skilled tradesmen.

## Reform and Reorganization in British America

After the period of Cromwell's Puritan Republic (see Chapter 16), the restored Stuart king, Charles II, undertook an ambitious campaign to establish greater control over the colonies. Between 1651 and 1673 a series of Navigation Acts sought to severely limit colonial trade and production that competed directly with English manufacturers. Because the king viewed the New England colonies as centers of smuggling, he temporarily suspended their elected assemblies while appointing colonial governors and granting them new fiscal and legislative powers.

During the eighteenth century the English colonies experienced renewed economic growth and

attracted a new wave of European immigration, but social divisions were increasingly evident. The colonial population in 1770 was more urban, more clearly divided by class and race, and more vulnerable to economic downturns. Crises were provoked when imperial wars with France and Spain disrupted trade in the Atlantic, increased tax burdens, forced military mobilizations, and incited frontier conflicts with Amerindians.

## French America

French settlement patterns more closely resembled those of Spain and Portugal than of England. The French were committed to missionary activity among Amerindian peoples and emphasized the extraction of natural resources—in this case furs.

Coming to Canada after spending years in the West Indies, Samuel de Champlain founded the colony of **New France** at Quebec (kwuh-BEC), on the banks of the St. Lawrence River, in 1608. The European market

**New France**  French colony in North America, with a capital in Quebec, founded in 1608. New France fell to the British in 1763.

for fur, especially beaver, fueled French settlement. Young Frenchmen were sent to live among native peoples to master their languages and customs, and these men and their children by native women organized the fur trade and led French expansion to the west and south. Amerindians actively participated in the trade because they came to depend on the goods they received in exchange for furs—firearms, metal tools, textiles, and alcohol.

The Iroquois Confederacy responded to the increased military strength of France's Algonquin allies by forging commercial and military links with Dutch and later English settlements along the Hudson River. Now well armed, the Iroquois Confederacy nearly eradicated the Huron in 1649 and inflicted a series of humiliating defeats on the French. At the high point of their power in the early 1680s, Iroquois hunters and military forces gained control of much of the Great Lakes region and the Ohio River Valley. A large French military expedition and a relentless attack focused on Iroquois villages and agriculture finally checked Iroquois power in 1701.

In French Canada, the Jesuits led the effort to convert native peoples to Christianity. Building on evangelical efforts in Brazil and Paraguay, French Catholic missionaries mastered native languages,

## SECTION REVIEW

- In contrast to Spanish colonies, the development of British and French colonies was shaped by private companies and individuals.

- North American colonies developed strong regional characters and strong local political traditions. British colonies attracted large numbers of free immigrants, but indentured servitude and slavery were crucial to economic development.

- The southern colonies' dependence on forced labor and plantation agriculture led to a society that was more hierarchical and less democratic that those found in the colonies of New England and the Middle Atlantic region.

- The development of French America was shaped by missionary activity and the fur trade, which was dependent on Amerindian participation.

- Eventually England defeated France and gained control of North America east of the Mississippi.

created boarding schools for young boys and girls, and set up model agricultural communities for converts. Their greatest successes coincided with a destructive wave of epidemics and renewed warfare among native peoples in the 1630s. Nevertheless, native culture persisted.

Although the fur trade flourished, population growth was slow. Founded at about the same time,

**Canadian Fur Traders** The fur trade provided the economic foundation of early Canadian settlement. Fur traders were cultural intermediaries. They brought European technologies and products like firearms and machine-made textiles to native peoples and native technologies and products like canoes and furs to European settlers. This canoe with sixteen paddlers was adapted from the native craft by fur traders to transport large cargoes.
Frances Anne Hopkins, "Shooting the Rapids," Library and Archives Canada, Ref. # C-2774

**Choctaw Village in Louisiana at Time of French Colonial Rule** This scene of village life illustrates the integration of the Choctaw in the colonial economy. The painting places a young African slave and European trade goods in a scene where the Choctaw pursue traditional tasks.
© President and Fellows of Harvard College, Peabody Museum of Archaeology and Ethnology, 41–72–10/20

Virginia had twenty times more European residents by 1627. Canada's small settler population and the fur trade's dependence on Amerindians allowed indigenous peoples to retain greater independence and more control over their encounters with new religious, technological, and market realities. Nevertheless, the French aggressively expanded and in 1699 founded Louisiana, which was also dependent on the fur trade with Amerindians.

France's North American colonies were ultimately threatened by a series of wars with England and the neighboring English colonies. The "French and Indian War" (also known as the Seven Years' War, 1756–1763) proved to be the final contest for the North American empire. England committed a larger military force to the struggle and, despite early defeats, took the French capital of Quebec in 1759. The peace agreement signed the next year forced France to yield Canada to the English and cede Louisiana to Spain.

## PLANTATIONS IN THE WEST INDIES

■ *What factors contributed to the development of plantations in the West Indies?*

The West Indies was the first place in the Americas reached by Columbus and the first region where native populations collapsed, smallpox arriving in 1518. It took a long time to repopulate these islands

and forge economic links with other parts of the Atlantic. But after 1650 sugar plantations, African slaves, and European capital made these islands a major center of the Atlantic economy.

Spanish settlers introduced sugar-cane cultivation into the West Indies shortly after 1500, but these colonies soon fell into neglect as attention shifted to colonizing the American mainland. After 1600 the West Indies revived as a focus of colonization, this time by northern Europeans interested in growing tobacco and other crops. The islands' value mushroomed after the Dutch reintroduced sugar cultivation from Brazil in the 1640s and supplied the African slaves and European capital necessary to create a new economy.

### Sugar and Slaves

The English colony of Barbados illustrates the dramatic transformation that sugar brought to the seventeenth-century Caribbean. In 1640, Barbados's economy depended largely on tobacco, mostly grown by European settlers, both free and indentured. By the 1680s, sugar had become the colony's principal crop, and enslaved Africans were three times as numerous as Europeans. Exporting up to 15,000 tons of sugar a year, Barbados had become the wealthiest and most populous of England's American colonies. By 1700, the West Indian colonies had collectively surpassed Brazil as the world's principal source of sugar.

**Plantation Scene, Antigua, British West Indies** The sugar made at the mill in the background was sealed in barrels and loaded on carts that oxen and horses drew to the beach. By means of a succession of vessels the barrels were taken to the ship that hauled the cargo to Europe. The importance of African labor is evident from the fact that only one white person appears in the painting.

British Library Board

The expansion of sugar plantations in the West Indies required a sharp increase in the volume of the slave trade from Africa. During the first half of the seventeenth century about ten thousand slaves a year had arrived from Africa, most destined for Brazil and the mainland Spanish colonies. In the second half of the century, the trade averaged twenty thousand slaves annually. More than half were intended for the English, French, and Dutch West Indies and most of the rest for Brazil. A century later, the volume of the Atlantic slave trade was three times larger.

What produced this shift in favor of African slaves? Recent scholarship has cast doubts on the once common assertion that Africans were more suited than Europeans to field labor; in fact, both died in large numbers in the American tropics. The West Indian historian Eric Williams has also refuted the idea that the rise of African slave labor was primarily motivated by prejudice. Citing the West Indian colonies' prior use of enslaved Amerindians and indentured Europeans, along with European convicts and prisoners of war, he argued, "Slavery was not born out of racism: rather, racism was the consequence of slavery."[1] Williams suggested that the shift was due to the lower cost of African labor.

Cash-short tobacco planters in the seventeenth century preferred indentured Europeans to African slaves because they cost half as much. However, as the cultivation of sugar spread after 1750, speculators drove land prices in the West Indies so high that the parcel of land promised as part of the payment for indentured servants became expensive. Without the promise of land, wages would have to be raised to attract European laborers. Caribbean sugar planters switched to slaves, and indentured servitude moved to Britain's North American colonies instead, where there was still cheap land.

Rising sugar prices helped West Indian sugar planters afford the higher cost of African slaves. The fact that slaves lived seven years on average after their arrival, while the typical indentured labor contract was for only three or four years, also made slaves a better investment. Dutch and other traders could be relied upon to supply new slaves to meet the demands of expanding plantations. Responding to rising demand, slave prices rose throughout the eighteenth century. These high labor costs were one more factor favoring large plantations over smaller operations.

To find more land for sugar plantations, France and England founded new Caribbean colonies. In 1655 the English wrested the island of Jamaica from the Spanish (see Map 17.1), and in the 1670s the French seized the western half of the large Spanish island of

---

[1]Eric Williams, *Capitalism and Slavery* (Charlotte: University of North Carolina Press, 1944), 7.

Hispaniola. During the eighteenth century this new French colony of Saint Domingue (san doh-MANGH) (present-day Haiti) became the greatest producer of sugar in the Atlantic world, while Jamaica surpassed Barbados as England's most important sugar colony. Later, Spanish Cuba became a major sugar producer.

## Technology and Environment

What made the sugar plantation a complex investment was that it had to be a factory as well as a farm. Fresh-cut cane needed to be crushed within a few hours to extract the sugary sap. Thus for maximum efficiency, each plantation needed its own expensive crushing and processing equipment.

At the heart of the sugar works was the mill where canes were crushed between heavy rollers. From the mill, lead-lined wooden troughs carried cane juice to a series of large copper kettles in the boiling shed, where excess water was boiled off, leaving thick syrup. Workers poured the syrup into conical molds in the drying shed. The sugar crystals that formed in the molds were packed in wooden barrels for shipment to Europe.

To make the operation more efficient and profitable, investors gradually increased the size of the typical West Indian plantation from around 100 acres (40 hectares) in the seventeenth century to at least twice that size in the eighteenth century. A plantation became a huge investment. One source estimated that a planter had to invest nearly £20,000 ($100,000) to acquire a Jamaican plantation of 600 acres (250 hectares) in 1774: a third for the land, a quarter for equipment, and £8,000 for 200 slaves. Jamaica specialized so heavily in sugar production that the island had to import most of its food. Saint Domingue was more diverse in its economy.

In some ways, the mature plantation was environmentally responsible. The crushing mill was powered by water, wind, or animals, not fossil fuels. The boilers were largely fueled by burning crushed cane, and the fields were fertilized by cattle manure. In two respects, however, the plantation was very damaging to the environment: soil exhaustion and deforestation. Instead of rotating sugar with other crops to restore the nutrients naturally, planters found it more profitable to clear new lands when yields declined in the old fields. When land close to the sea was exhausted, planters moved on to new islands. Many of the English who first settled Jamaica were from Barbados, and the pioneer planters on Saint Domingue came from older French sugar colonies. Everywhere in the Caribbean, forests were cleared. By the end of the eighteenth century, deforestation was so complete that only land in the interior of the islands retained dense forests.

The most tragic and dramatic transformation of the West Indies was demographic. During the eighteenth century West Indian plantation colonies

**Caribbean Sugar Mill** The windmill crushes sugar cane, whose juice is boiled down in the smoking building next door. The Crusher Squeezes Juice from the Cane, Antigua, 1823 (print), Clark, William (fl.1823)/British Library, London, UK/© British Library Board. All Rights Reserved/The Bridgeman Art Library were the world's most polarized societies. On most islands, 90 percent or more of the inhabitants were slaves. A small number of very rich men owned most of the slaves and most of the land as well. A few estate managers and government officials existed between master and slave, but it is only a slight simplification to describe eighteenth-century Caribbean society as being made up of a large, abject class of slaves and a small, powerful class of masters.

The profitability of a Caribbean plantation depended on extracting as much work as possible from the slaves through the threat and use of force. On a typical Jamaican plantation, about 80 percent of the slaves actively engaged in productive tasks; the only exceptions were infants, the seriously ill, and the very old. Slave labor was organized by age, sex, and ability. Only 2 or 3 percent of the slaves were house servants. About 70 percent of the able-bodied slaves worked in the fields, generally in one of three labor gangs. Women formed the majority of the field laborers, even in the "great gang" made up of the strongest slaves. A second gang of youths, elders, and less fit slaves did somewhat lighter work. A "grass gang," composed of children under the supervision of an elderly slave, did simple work, such as weeding or collecting grass for the animals. A little over half of adult males did nongang work, tending livestock or serving as blacksmiths and carpenters. The most important artisan slave was the head boiler, who oversaw the delicate process of reducing the cane sap to crystallized sugar and molasses.

Planters often rewarded skilled slaves with food and clothing or time off, but most slaves were compelled to work hard to avoid the lash. Slave gangs were led by a privileged male slave, appropriately called the **driver**, whose job was to ensure that the gang completed its work. Production quotas were high, and slaves toiled in the fields from sunup to sunset, except for meal breaks. Those who fell behind due to fatigue or illness soon felt the sting of the whip. Openly rebellious slaves who refused to work, disobeyed orders, or tried to escape were punished with floggings, confinement in irons, or mutilation.

The harsh conditions of plantation life played a major role in shortening slaves' lives, but the greatest killer was disease. The very young were carried off by dysentery caused by contaminated food and water.

Slaves newly arrived from Africa went through a period of adjustment to a new environment known as **seasoning**, during which one-third, on average, died of unfamiliar diseases. Slaves also suffered from diseases brought with them, including malaria. On one plantation, for example, more than half of the slaves incapacitated by illness had yaws, a painful and debilitating skin disease common in Africa.

Such high mortality greatly added to the volume of the Atlantic slave trade, since plantations had to purchase new slaves every year or two to replace those who died. The additional imports of slaves to permit expansion of the sugar plantations meant that the majority of slaves on most West Indian plantations were African-born. As a result, African religious beliefs, patterns of speech, styles of dress and adornment, and music were prominent parts of West Indian life.

Given the harsh conditions of their lives, it is not surprising that slaves in the West Indies often sought to gain their freedom. Individual slaves often ran away, hoping to elude the men and dogs that would track them. Sometimes large groups of plantation slaves rose in rebellion against their bondage and abuse. For example, a large rebellion in Jamaica in 1760 was led by a slave named Tacky, who had been a chief on the Gold Coast of Africa. One night, his followers broke into a fort and armed themselves. Joined by slaves from nearby plantations, they stormed several plantations, setting them on fire and killing the planter families. Tacky died in the fighting, and three of his lieutenants stoically endured cruel deaths by torture meant to deter others from rebellion.

Because European planters believed that slaves with the strongest African heritage led rebellions, they tried to curtail African cultural traditions. They required slaves to learn the colonial language and discouraged the use of African languages by deliberately mixing slaves from different parts of Africa. In French and Portuguese colonies, slaves were encouraged to adopt Catholic religious practices, though

**driver** A privileged male slave whose job was to ensure that a slave gang did its work on a plantation.

**seasoning** An often difficult period of adjustment to new climates, disease environments, and work routines, such as that experienced by slaves newly arrived in the Americas.

- During the seventeenth and eighteenth centuries, sugar production and slavery expanded rapidly in the West Indies.
- The preference for African slaves grew from the effects of rising sugar prices and land speculation.
- As demand grew, England and France established more island colonies.
- Sugar plantations required larger investments in land, slaves, and machinery than other forms of colonial agriculture.
- The need for efficiency made plantations into large, self-sufficient, and expensive units.
- Sugar plantations had huge human and environmental costs.
- Harsh conditions provoked flight and rebellion; some groups of runaways, maroons, forced authorities to recognize their freedom.

African deities, beliefs, and practices survived. In the British West Indies, where only Quaker slave owners encouraged Christianity among their slaves before 1800, African herbal medicine remained strong, as did African beliefs concerning nature spirits and witchcraft.

As in Latin America, slavery provoked flight. In the Caribbean, runaways were known as **maroons**. Maroon communities were especially numerous in the mountainous interiors of Jamaica and Hispaniola, as well as in the inland parts of the Guianas (guy-AHN-uhs). The Jamaican maroons, after withstanding several attacks by the colony's militia, signed a treaty in 1738 that recognized their independence in return for their cooperation in stopping new runaways and suppressing slave revolts. Unable to win decisive victories, colonial authorities in Spanish, Dutch, and Portuguese colonies signed similar treaties with runaway leaders.

## CREATING THE ATLANTIC ECONOMY

■ *What was the relationship between private investors and European governments in the development of the Atlantic economy?*

The West Indian plantation colonies played a crucial role in the emerging Atlantic economy. At once archaic in its cruel system of slavery and oddly modern in its specialization in a single product, the plantation system profitably dominated a broad region from the Chesapeake to the Caribbean and then to South America and Brazil. African slaves made the plantation economies possible, and profits from the exports of plantation products helped finance commercial and manufacturing expansion. Three other elements went into the creation of a new Atlantic economy: new economic institutions, new partnerships between private investors and governments in Europe, and new working relationships between European and African merchants. This new trading system is a prime example of how European capitalist relationships were reshaping the world.

The Spanish and Portuguese voyages of exploration in the fifteenth and sixteenth centuries were government ventures, and both countries tried to keep their overseas trade with colonies royal monopolies (see Chapters 15). Monopoly control, however, proved both expensive and inefficient. The success of the Atlantic economy in the seventeenth and eighteenth centuries owed much to private enterprise, which made trade more efficient and profitable.

Two European innovations, capitalism and mercantilism, enabled private investors to fund the rapid growth of the Atlantic economy. **Capitalism** was a system of large financial institutions—banks, stock exchanges, and chartered trading companies—that enabled wealthy investors to reduce risks and increase profits (see Chapter 16). Early capitalism was buttressed by **mercantilism**, policies adopted by European states to promote their citizens' overseas trade and defend it, by armed force when necessary.

**maroon** A slave who ran away from his or her master. Often a member of a community of runaway slaves in the West Indies and South America.

**capitalism** The economic system of large financial institutions—banks, stock exchanges, investment companies—that first developed in early modern Europe. *Commercial capitalism*, the trading system of the early modern economy, is often distinguished from *industrial capitalism*, the system based on machine production.

**mercantilism** European government policies of the sixteenth, seventeenth, and eighteenth centuries designed to promote overseas trade between a country and its colonies and accumulate precious metals by requiring colonies to trade only with their motherland country. The British system was defined by the Navigation Acts, the French system by laws known as the *Exclusif*.

**Chartered companies** were one of the first examples of mercantilist capitalism. A charter issued by the government of the Netherlands In 1602 gave the Dutch East India Company a legal monopoly over all Dutch trade in the Indian Ocean. This privilege encouraged private investors to buy shares in the company. They were amply rewarded when the Dutch East India Company captured control of long-distance trade in the Indian Ocean from the Portuguese (see Chapter 16). A sister firm, the **Dutch West India Company**, was chartered in 1621 to engage in the Atlantic trade by seizing sugar-producing areas in Brazil and African slaving ports from the Portuguese.

Such successes inspired other governments to set up their own chartered companies. In 1672, a royal charter placed all English trade with West Africa in the hands of the new **Royal African Company** (RAC), which established its headquarters at Cape Coast Castle, just east of Elmina on the Gold Coast. The French government also chartered East India and West India companies to reduce French dependence on Dutch and English traders. The Spanish and Portuguese governments imitated this model.

French and English governments used military force in pursuit of commercial dominance, especially to break the trading advantages of the Dutch in the Americas. Restrictions on Dutch access to French and English colonies provoked a series of wars with the Netherlands between 1652 and 1678, during which the larger English and French navies defeated the Dutch and drove the Dutch West India Company into bankruptcy.

With Dutch competition in the Atlantic reduced, the French and English limited the privileges of their chartered companies. England opened trade in Africa to any English subject in 1698 on the grounds that ending monopolies would be "highly beneficial and advantageous to this kingdom." It was hoped that such competition would also cut the cost of slaves to West Indian planters, though the demand for slaves soon drove the prices up again.

Such new mercantilist policies fostered competition among the nation's own citizens while using high tariffs and restrictions to exclude foreigners. In the 1660s, England had passes a series of Navigation Acts that confined trade with its colonies to English ships and cargoes. The French called their mercantil-

ist legislation, first codified in 1698, the *Exclusif* (ek-skloo-SEEF), highlighting its exclusionary intentions. Other mercantilist laws defended manufacturing and processing interests in Europe against competition from the colonies, imposing prohibitively high taxes on their manufactured goods and products like refined sugar.

As a result of these mercantilist measures, the Atlantic became Britain, France, and Portugal's most important overseas trading area. The value of imports from West Indian colonies alone accounted for over one-fifth the value of total British imports. The French West Indian colonies played an even larger role in France's overseas trade. Only the Dutch, closed out of much of the American trade, depended more heavily on Asian trade. Profits from the Atlantic economy, in turn, promoted further economic expansion and increased the revenues of European governments.

## AFRICA AND THE ATLANTIC

■ *How was the effect of slavery on Africa different under the Atlantic system?*

The Atlantic system took a terrible toll in African lives. Many died while being marched to African ports for sale. The overall effects on Africa of these losses and of other aspects of the slave trade have been the subject of considerable historical debate. It is clear

**chartered companies** Groups of private investors who paid an annual fee to France and England in exchange for a monopoly over trade to the West Indies colonies.

**Dutch West India Company** Trading company chartered by the Dutch government to conduct its merchants' trade in the Americas and Africa.

**Royal African Company** A trading company chartered by the English government in 1672 to conduct its merchants' trade on the Atlantic coast of Africa.

that the trade's impact depended on the intensity and terms of involvement in different African regions.

Any assessment of the Atlantic system's effects in Africa must also take into consideration the fact that slavery had existed in Africa long before the Atlantic system. Some Africans profited from the trade, marching slaves to the coast chained together or bound to forked sticks, then bartering them to the European slavers for trade goods.

## The Gold Coast and the Slave Coast

The transition to slave trading was not sudden. Even as slaves were becoming Atlantic Africa's most valuable export, goods such as gold, ivory, and timber remained important. For example, during its eight decades of operation from 1672 to 1752, the Royal African Company made 40 percent of its profits from gold, ivory, and forest products. In some parts of West Africa, such non-slave exports remained predominant even at the peak of the Atlantic trade.

African merchants were very discriminating about merchandise they took in exchange for slaves or goods. A ship that arrived with goods of low quality or not suited to local tastes found it hard to purchase a cargo at a profitable price. Textiles, hardware, and guns were in high demand. Of the goods the Royal African Company traded in West Africa in the 1680s, over 60 percent were Indian and European textiles and 30 percent were hardware and weaponry. In the eighteenth century, tobacco and rum from the Americas became welcome imports.

Both Europeans and Africans attempted to drive the best bargain for themselves and sometimes engaged in deceitful practices. The strength of the African bargaining position, however, may be inferred from the fact that as the demand for slaves rose, so too did their price in Africa. In the course of the eighteenth century the value of goods needed to purchase a slave on the Gold Coast doubled and in some places tripled or quadrupled.

African governments on the Gold and Slave Coasts forced Europeans to observe African trading customs and prevented them from taking control of African territory. Rivalry among European nations, each of which established its own trading "castles" along the Gold Coast, also reduced bargaining strength.

How did African kings and merchants obtain slaves for sale? Most accounts agree that prisoners of war were the greatest source of slaves. It is harder to prove that capturing slaves for export was a main cause of wars. An early-nineteenth-century king of Asante stated, "I cannot make war to catch slaves in the bush, like a thief. My ancestors never did so. But if I fight a king, and kill him when he is insolent, then certainly I must have his gold, and his slaves, and his people are mine too. Do not the white kings act like this?"[2] English rulers had indeed sentenced seventeenth-century Scottish and Irish prisoners to forced labor in the West Indies.

## The Bight of Biafra and Angola

In the eighteenth century the slave trade expanded eastward to the Bight (bite) of Biafra. In contrast to the Gold and Slave Coasts, where strong kingdoms predominated, the densely populated interior of the Bight of Biafra contained no large states. Even so, powerful merchant princes of the coastal ports made European traders give them rich presents.

As the volume of the Atlantic trade along the Bight of Biafra expanded in the late eighteenth century, some inland markets evolved into giant fairs, with different sections specializing in slaves and imported goods. In the 1780s an English ship's doctor reported that slaves were "bought by the black traders at fairs, which are held for that purpose, at a distance of upwards of two hundred miles from the sea coast." He reported seeing from twelve hundred to fifteen hundred enslaved men and women arriving at the coast from a single fair.[3]

Angola, south of the Congo estuary, was the greatest source of slaves for the Atlantic trade. This was also the one place along the Atlantic coast where a single European nation, Portugal, controlled a significant amount of territory. Portuguese residents of the main ports served as middlemen between the caravans that arrived from the interior and the ships from Brazil. Many of the slaves sold at Angolan markets were prisoners of war captured by expanding

[2]King Osei Bonsu, quoted in David Northrup, ed., *The Atlantic Slave Trade* (Boston: Houghton Mifflin, 2001), 93.

[3]Alexander Falconbridge, *Account of the Slave Trade on the Coast of Africa* (London: J. Phillips, 1788), 12.

African states. As elsewhere in Africa, such prisoners seem to have been a byproduct of African wars, rather than the objective of the warring parties.

Research has linked other enslavement with environmental crisis in the hinterlands of Angola. During the eighteenth century, these southern grasslands periodically suffered severe droughts, which drove famished refugees to better-watered areas. Powerful African leaders gained control of many refugees and sold the adult males because they were more likely than women and children to escape or challenge the ruler's authority. The most successful of these inland Angolan leaders became heads of powerful new states, stabilizing areas devastated by war and drought and repopulating them with the refugees and prisoners they retained. The slave frontier then moved farther inland. This cruel system worked to the benefit of a few African rulers and merchants at the expense of the many thousands of Africans who were sent to death or perpetual bondage in the Americas.

## European and Islamic Slavery

The ways in which sub-Saharan Africans established new contacts with Europe paralleled their much older pattern of relations with the Islamic world. Africans ceded very little territory to Europeans, and local African rulers kept close tabs on the European trading posts and collected lucrative rents and fees. The size of Africa's slave trade to the Islamic north also seems to have been substantial, if smaller than the transatlantic trade at its peak. Between 1600 and 1800 slave traders sent about 850,000 slaves to Muslim North Africa, and a nearly equal number of slaves from sub-Saharan Africa entered the Islamic Middle East and India by way of the Red Sea and the Indian Ocean.

In contrast to the plantation slavery of the Americas, most African slaves in the Islamic world were soldiers and servants. In the late seventeenth and eighteenth centuries Morocco's rulers employed an army of 150,000 African slaves, trusting their loyalty more than that of recruits from their own lands. Moroccans also used slaves on sugar plantations, as servants, and as artisans. Unlike in the Americas, the majority of African slaves in the Islamic world were women who served wealthy households as concubines, servants, and entertainers. The trans-Saharan slave trade also included a much higher proportion of children than the Atlantic trade.

Like Christians of this period, Muslims saw no moral impediment to owning or trading in slaves. Indeed, Islam considered enslaving "pagans" to be a meritorious act because it brought them into the faith, and it encouraged manumission Although Islam forbade the enslavement of Muslims, Muslim rulers were not strict observers of that rule (see Diversity and Dominance: Slavery in West Africa and the Americas).

While Muslims and Europeans obtained slaves from sub-Saharan Africa, the European trade was larger. The Atlantic trade carried about 8 million Africans to the Americas between 1550 and 1800. During this period the Islamic trade to North Africa and the Middle East transported perhaps 2 million African captives. Scholars generally agree on three points: (1) even at the peak of the trade in the 1700s, sub-Saharan Africa's overall population remained very large; (2) localities that contributed heavily to the slave trade, such as lands near the Slave Coast, suffered acute losses; (3) the ability of a population to recover from losses was related to the proportion of fertile women who were shipped away. The fact that Africans sold fewer women than men into the larger Atlantic trade somewhat reduced the long-term effects of this larger trade.

The slave trade had a mixed impact on sub-Saharan economies. Africans were very particular about what they received in exchange for slaves, and the limited volume of manufactured imports could not overwhelm established African weavers, metalworkers, and other producers. Some imported products like textiles and metal bars stimulated the local production of tools and clothing. While both African and European states benefited by taxing this trade, most of the economic benefits went to European nations and their American colonies, just as the profits from transporting and selling slaves mostly went to European merchants and ship owners. The American colonies were the major beneficiaries of the African slave trade. With the Amerindian population diminished by epidemics and European immigration inadequate to develop American resources, it was the forced labor of African slaves that made possible the enormous wealth produced in a vast region that spread from the

## Slavery in West Africa and the Americas

Social diversity was common in Africa, and the domination of masters over slaves was a feature of many societies. Ahmad Baba (1556–1627) was an outstanding Islamic scholar in the city of Timbuktu. In about 1615 he replied to some questions that had been sent to him. His answers reveal a great deal about the official and unofficial condition of slavery in the Sudan of West Africa, especially in the Hausa states of Kano and Katsina.

You asked: What have you to say concerning the slaves imported from the lands of the Sudan whose people are acknowledged to be Muslims, such as Bornu, . . . Kano, Goa, Songhay, Katsina and others among whom Islam is widespread? Is it permissible to possess them [as slaves] or not?

Know—may God grant us and you success—that these lands, as you have stated are Muslim. . . . But close to each of them are lands in which are unbelievers whom the Muslim inhabitants of these lands raid. Some of these unbelievers are under the Muslims' protection and pay them [taxes]. . . . Sometimes there is war between the Muslim sultans of some of these lands and one attacks the other, taking as many prisoners as he can and selling the captive though he is a free-born Muslim. . . . This is a common practice among them in Hausaland; Katsina raids Kano, as do others, though their language is one and their situations parallel; the only difference they recognize among themselves is that so-and-so is a born Muslim and so-and-so is a born unbeliever. . . .

Whoever is taken prisoner in a state of unbelief may become someone's property, whoever he is, as opposed to those who have become Muslims of their own free will . . . and may not be possessed at all.

A little over a century later another African provided information about enslavement practices in the Western Sudan. Ayuba Suleiman Diallo (ah-YOO-bah SOO-lay-mahn JAH-loh) (1701–?), of the state of Bondu some 200 miles from the Gambia River, was enslaved and transported to Maryland, where he was a slave from 1731 to 1733. When an Englishman learned of Ayuba's literacy in Arabic, he recorded his life story, anglicizing his name to Job Solomon. According to the account, slaves in Bondu did much of the hard work, while men of Ayuba's class were free to devote themselves to the study of Islamic texts.

In February, 1730, Job's father hearing of an English ship at Gambia River, sent him, with two servants to attend him, to sell two Negroes, and to buy paper, and some other necessaries; but desired him not to venture over the river, because the country of the Mandingoes, who are enemies to the people of Futa, lies on the other side. Job not agreeing with Captain Pike (who commanded the ship, lying then at Gambia, in the service of Captain Henry Hunt, brother to Mr. William Hunt, merchant, in Little Tower-street, London) sent back the two servants to acquaint his father with it, and to let him know that he intended to go no farther. Accordingly . . . he crossed the River Gambia, and disposed of his Negroes for some cows. As he was returning home, he stopped for some refreshment at the house of an old acquaintance; and the weather being hot, he hung up his arms in the house, while he refreshed himself. . . . It happened that a company of the Mandingoes, . . . passing by at that time, and observing him unarmed, rushed in, to the number of seven or eight at once, at a back door, and pinioned Job, before he could get his arms, together with his interpreter, who is a slave in Maryland still. They then shaved their heads and beards, which Job and his man resented as the highest indignity; tho' the Mandingoes meant no more by it, than to make them appear like slaves taken in war. On the 27th of February, 1730, they carried them to Captain Pike at Gambia, who purchased them; and on the first of March they were put on board. Soon after Job found means to acquaint Captain Pike that he was the same person that came to trade with him a few days before, and after what manner he had been taken. Upon this Captain Pike gave him free leave to redeem himself and his man; and Job sent to an acquaintance of his father's, near Gambia, who promised to send to Job's father, to inform him of what had happened, that he might take some course to have him set at liberty. But it being a fortnight's [two weeks'] journey between that friend's house and his father's, and the ship sailing in about a week after, Job was brought with the rest of the slaves to Annapolis in Maryland, and delivered to Mr. Vachell Denton. . . .

➤

Mr. Vachell Denton sold Job to one Mr. Tolsey in Kent Island in Maryland, who put him to work in making tobacco; but he was soon convinced that Job had never been used to such labour. He every day showed more and more uneasiness under this exercise, and at last grew sick, being no way able to bear it; so his master was obliged to find easier work for him, and therefore put him to tend the cattle. Job would often leave the cattle, and withdraw into the woods to pray; but a white boy frequently watched him, and whilst he was at his devotion would mock him and throw dirt in his face. This very much disturbed Job, and added considerably to his other misfortunes; all which were increased by his ignorance of the English language, which prevented his complaining, or telling his case to any person about him. Grown in some measure desperate, by reason of his present hardships, he resolved to travel at a venture; thinking he might possibly be taken up by some master, who would use him better, or otherwise meet with some lucky accident, to divert or abate his grief. Accordingly, he travelled thro' the woods, till he came to the County of Kent, upon Delaware Bay. . . . There is a law in force, throughout the [mid-Atlantic] colonies . . . as far as Boston in New England, viz. that any Negroe, or white servant who is not known in the county, or has no pass, may be secured by any person, and kept in the common [jail], till the master of such servant shall fetch him. Therefore Job being able to give no account of himself, was put in prison there.

This happened about the beginning of June 1731, when I, who was attending the courts there, and heard of Job, went with several gentlemen to the [jailer's] house, being a tavern, and desired to see him. He was brought into the tavern to us, but could not speak one word of English. Upon our talking and making signs to him, he wrote a line to two before us, and when he read it, pronounced the words Allah and Mahommed; by which, and his refusing a glass of wine we offered him, we perceived he was a Mahometan [Muslim], but could not imagine of what country he was, or how he got thither; for by his affable carriage, and the easy composure of his countenance, we could perceive he was no common slave.

When Job had been some time confined, an old Negroe man, who lived in that neighborhood, and could speak the Jalloff [Wolof] language, which Job also understood, went to him, and conversed with him. By this Negroe the keeper was informed to whom Job belonged, and what was the cause of his leaving his master. The keeper thereupon wrote to his master, who soon after fetched him home, and was much kinder to him than before; allowing him place to pray in, and in some other conveniences, in order to make his slavery as easy as possible. Yet slavery and confinement was by no means agreeable to Job, who had never been used to it; he therefore wrote a letter in Arabick to his father, acquainting him with his misfortunes,

**Ayuba Suleiman Diallo (1701–?)** Portrait of Ayuba Suleiman Diallo, 1733 (oil on canvas), Hoare, William, of Bath (1707-92)/Private Collection/Photo © Christie's Images/The Bridgeman Art Library

hoping he might yet find means to redeem him. . . . It happened that this letter was seen by James Oglethorpe, Esq. [founder of the colony of Georgia and director of the Royal African Company]; who, according to his usual goodness and generosity, took compassion on Job, and [bought him from his master]; his master being very willing to part with him, as finding him no ways fit for his business.

In spring 1733 Job's benefactors took him to England, teaching him passable English during the voyage, and introduced him to the English gentry. Job attracted such attention that local men took up a collection to buy his freedom and pay his debts, and they also introduced him at the royal court. In 1735 Job returned to Gambia in a Royal African Company ship, richly clothed and accompanied by many gifts.

## QUESTIONS FOR ANALYSIS

1. Since Ahmad Baba points out that Islamic law permitted a Muslim to raid and enslave non-Muslims, do you think that the non-Muslim Mandinka (Mandingoes) would have considered it justifiable to enslave Ayuba, since he was a Muslim?

2. Which aspects of Ayuba Suleiman's experiences of enslavement were normal, and which unusual?

3. How different might Ayuba's experiences of slavery have been had he been sold in Jamaica rather than Maryland?

4. How strictly was the ban against enslaving Muslims observed in Hausaland?

*Source*: Thomas Hodgkin, ed., *Nigerian Perspectives: An Historical Anthology*, 2d ed. (London: Oxford University Press, 1975), 154–156; Thomas Bluett, *Some Memoirs of the Life of Job, the Son of Solomon the High Priest of Boonda in Africa* (London: Richard Ford, 1734), 16–24.

- African trade and cultural relations with European nations paralleled already established relations with Muslim regions.
- Most slaves exported to the Western Hemisphere were prisoners of war.
- In contrast to the plantation slavery of the Americas, most African slaves sent to the Islamic world served as soldiers or servants.
- The wealth created by the labor of African slaves in the Americas significantly expanded capitalism in the seventeenth and eighteenth centuries.

Chesapeake to the Río de la Plata. This wealth accelerated the rapid expansion of Western capitalism in the seventeenth and eighteenth centuries.

## CONCLUSION

The colonial empires of Spain, Portugal, France, and England had many characteristics in common. All subjugated Amerindian peoples, introduced large numbers of enslaved Africans, and transformed the natural environment. Each of the New World empires also reflected the distinctive cultural and institutional heritages of its colonizing power.

Spain's discovery of mineral wealth allowed it to develop the largest and most centralized colonial government. Portugal and France pursued similar objectives, but neither Brazil's agricultural economy, based on sugar, nor France's Canadian fur trade produced the level of centralized control achieved by Spain. There was greater cultural and religious diversity in British North America, and the British colonial government was less centralized and in some cases more responsive to local interests.

From the seventeenth century onward, European powers expanded and created new colonies in the Caribbean. Spain's early control of the region was lost as settlers moved to the mainland once gold and silver were discovered. The British, French, and Dutch also established colonies. While tobacco initially dominated these economies, sugar eventually made these once-isolated islands part of a dynamic trading system controlled from Europe and dependent on slave labor.

European merchants and investors played a central role in the creation of the Atlantic system. By the seventeenth century an adventurous European investor class aggressively promoted colonial production and long-distance trade. The development of banks, stock exchanges, maritime insurance, and chartered companies supported these new ambitions, and the development of the Atlantic system showed their ability to move beyond capturing the benefits of existing trading systems to creating a major new trading network.

The new Atlantic system, a milestone in trade, had great importance in world history as a model of the kind of highly interactive economy that became global in later centuries. However, its transformations were destructive as well as creative, victimizing Amerindians and African slaves while benefiting European commercial and manufacturing interests. Africa played an essential role in the Atlantic system, importing trade goods and exporting slaves to the Americas. However, it was less dominated by the Atlantic system than were Europe's American colonies. Africans remained in control of their continent and interacted culturally and politically more with the Islamic world than with the Atlantic.

## CHAPTER REVIEW

### SPANISH AMERICA AND BRAZIL
■ *What role did forced labor play in the main industries of Spanish America and Brazil?* (page 403)

The development of the Spanish colonies was promoted by the discovery of rich gold and silver mines and by the *encomienda* and *mita*, which forced tens of thousands of indigenous laborers to work in mines, farms, and factories. The sugar industry was crucial to Brazil. At first the enslavement of Amerindians provided labor for the sugar plantations, but eventually Brazil depended on the African slave trade, importing nearly 2 million slaves in the eighteenth century.

## ENGLISH AND FRENCH COLONIES IN NORTH AMERICA

■ *What were the differences between the English and the French colonies of North America?* (page 410)

While French Canada was founded with the hope of mineral wealth, it survived on the modest profits of the fur trade. Like the Spanish and Portuguese, the French also tried to convert the Amerindian peoples. Population grew slowly, and France relied on alliances with native peoples to exploit the fur trade and protect its North American colony. First created by groups of private investors or by religious minorities, the English colonies of North America followed a different path. Because England never established centralized political control over its colonies, settlers exercised more political power. In the northern colonies, a greater gender balance led to a larger population increase than in either the French colonies or the southern colonies. Britain's North American colonies were also economically more diverse than those of France, which relied solely on the fur trade. The northern colonies attracted large numbers of free immigrants, while southern colonies relied on plantation slavery to generate wealth.

## PLANTATIONS IN THE WEST INDIES

■ *What factors contributed to the development of plantations in the West Indies?* (page 414)

The islands of the West Indies were divided among a number of European powers. After devastating epidemics eliminated the indigenous populations, settlers relied heavily on slavery to produce a range of export crops. When settlers and European investors realized sugar's profitability, they were willing to finance the forced transfer of hundreds of thousands of Africans to work the Caribbean plantations. Since Africans and their American-born descendants outnumbered the Europeans across the area, African culture took root and served as an important basis for these new American societies.

## CREATING THE ATLANTIC ECONOMY

■ *What was the relationship between private investors and European governments in the development of the Atlantic economy?* (page 418)

European merchants and investors played a central role in the creation of the Atlantic system. In the century before Columbus they traded over longer distances and introduced new credit mechanisms. By the seventeenth century a more confident and adventurous European investor class was ready to promote colonial production and long-distance trade in a much more aggressive way. The development of banks, stock exchanges, and chartered companies supported these new ambitions.

## AFRICA AND THE ATLANTIC

■ *How was the effect of slavery on Africa different under the Atlantic system?* (page 419)

The Atlantic slave trade that began in the late fifteenth century grew spectacularly after the introduction of sugar to the Caribbean islands. The slave trade provided kingdoms on the coast of West and equatorial Africa with weapons for waging war against the peoples of the interior. These kingdoms then sold their captives to European traders as they had to Islamic traders, but the plantation slavery of the Americas was more brutal and mortality was high. The Atlantic system also had a greater effect on Africa because it enslaved many more Africans than did the Islamic trade. Ultimately, the biggest economic benefit went to European slave merchants and colonies in the Americas, where forced labor created wealth that promoted a capitalist economic system.

## Key Terms

Atlantic system (p. 403)

Bartolomé de Las Casas (p. 404)

Potosí (p. 405)

encomienda (p. 405)

creoles (p. 408)

indentured servant (p. 410)

House of Burgesses (p. 410)

Pilgrims (p. 411)

Puritans (p. 411)

Iroquois Confederacy (p. 411)

New France (p. 412)

driver (p. 417)

seasoning (p. 417)

maroon (p. 418)

capitalism (p. 418)

mercantilism (p. 418)

chartered companies (p. 419)

Dutch West India Company (p. 419)

Royal African Company (p. 419)

# Territorial Empires Between Europe and China

© Cengage Learning

In 1667, Stenka Razin, the leader of a robber band camped on a tributary of the Don River in southern Russia, pillaged a rich convoy of government and merchant barges on the Volga River and sailed southward toward the trading city of Astrakhan. The city's governor was unable to stop his progress, and his band established a new camp by the Caspian Sea at the mouth of the Ural River. From there Razin raided across the sea and down into Iran, defeating both Iranian and Russian armies. In 1670, his forces swollen to 20,000, Razin moved up the Volga, threatening to take Moscow and overthrow the tsar. There a tsarist army finally stopped him, and he was executed in the following year.

Razin's followers were Cossacks, people of various ethnic origins who made their way to southern Russia, many of them escaping serfdom in the north, to live as social equals in societies with minimal government and the power to maintain their independence. Modern Russian culture has glorified Razin in music and poetry as a defender of the poor and foe of noble privilege. A famous folksong portrays him sacrificing his bride for the sake of leading his warriors.

> So that peace may reign forever
> In this band so free and brave
> Volga, Volga, Mother Volga
> Make this lovely girl a grave.

A less lurid historical understanding of his revolt focuses on the unsettled state of the lands north of the Caspian Sea that had once been the center of the Mongol Golden Horde (see Chapter 12). Muslim Tatars, Buddhist Kalmyks from western Mongolia, and Orthodox Christian Ukrainians and Russians mingled in the sparsely populated frontier between the tsars, the Ottoman sultans, and the Iranian shahs.

A new trading axis was in the process of opening, one that built on the old Silk Road and linked the Ottoman, Safavid, and Mughal Empires to the south with a growing Russian Empire to the north. Russia imported cotton and silk textiles from Iran and India and exported furs, leather goods, walrus tusks, and some woolens. While few Russian merchants traveled beyond the tsarist frontiers, Indian and Armenian traders abounded, and Indian family firms resembled the Italian merchant enterprises of the Renaissance era. Twenty-seven Indians resided on the outskirts of Moscow in 1684, along with various Armenian, Iranian, and Bukharan merchants. Ten times that number lived in Astrakhan, which Ivan "the Terrible" had added to his domains in 1556 and defended against Ottoman attack in 1569.

Thus a pattern was set that would last into the twentieth century: while western Europe maintained rigid religious boundaries with very few Muslims living under Christian monarchs, Russia more closely resembled the Muslim empires to its south in tolerating the ethnic and religious diversity that had been a hallmark of Mongol rule.

In the domain of maritime trade, the European powers held a dominant position, but this did not prevent various muslim rulers from carving out their own domains.

## THE OTTOMAN EMPIRE, TO 1750

■ *How did the Ottoman Empire rise to power, and what factors contributed to its transformation?*

The most durable of the post-Mongol Muslim realms was the **Ottoman Empire** (see Map 18.1), founded around 1300. By extending Islamic conquests into eastern Europe starting in the late fourteenth century, and by taking Syria and Egypt from the Mamluk rulers in the early sixteenth century, the Ottomans seemed to re-create the might of the medieval Islamic caliphate. However, the empire actually resembled the new centralized monarchies of Europe (see Chapter 16) more than any medieval model.

Enduring until 1922, the Ottoman Empire survived several periods of wrenching change, some caused by economic and political problems and others by military innovations. These periods of change reveal the problems faced by the land-based empires situated between Europe and China.

**Ottoman Empire** Islamic state founded by Osman in northwestern Anatolia around 1300. After the fall of the Byzantine Empire, the Ottoman Empire was based at Istanbul (formerly Constantinople) from 1453 to 1922. It encompassed lands in the Middle East, North Africa, the Caucasus, and eastern Europe.

**Aya Sofya Mosque in Istanbul**
Originally a Byzantine cathedral, Aya Sofya (in Greek, Hagia Sophia) was transformed into a mosque after 1453, and four minarets were added. It then became a model for subsequent Ottoman mosques. To the right behind it is the Bosporus strait dividing Europe and Asia, to the left the Golden Horn inlet separating the old city of Istanbul from the newer parts. The gate to the Ottoman sultan's palace is to the right of the mosque. The pointed tower to the left of the dome is part of the palace.

mozcann/iStockphoto.com

## Expansion and Frontiers

The Ottoman Empire grew from a tiny state in northwestern Anatolia because of three factors: (1) the shrewdness of its founder, Osman (from which the name *Ottoman* comes), and his descendants, (2) control of a strategic link between Europe and Asia on the Dardanelles strait, and (3) the creation of an army that took advantage of the traditional skills of the Turkish cavalryman and the new military possibilities presented by gunpowder.

Ottoman armies attacked Christian enemies in Greece and the Balkans before conquering neighboring Muslim principalities. In 1389 a strong Serbian kingdom was defeated at the Battle of Kosovo (KO-so-vo), and by 1402 the sultans ruled much of southeastern Europe and Anatolia. In 1453, Sultan Mehmed II, "the Conqueror," laid siege to Constantinople. His forces used enormous cannon to crush the city's walls, dragged warships over a high hill from the Bosporus strait to the city's inner harbor to get around its sea defenses, and finally overcame the city's land walls with direct infantry assaults. The fall of Constantinople—henceforward commonly known as Istanbul—brought to an end over eleven hundred years of Byzantine rule and made the Ottomans seem invincible.

Selim (seh-LEEM) I, "the Grim," conquered Egypt and Syria in 1516 and 1517, making the Red Sea the Ottomans' southern frontier. His son, **Suleiman (SOO-lay-man) the Magnificent** (r. 1520–1566), presided over the greatest Ottoman assault on Christian Europe. Seemingly unstoppable, he conquered Belgrade in 1521, expelled the Knights of the Hospital of St. John

from the island of Rhodes the following year, and laid siege to Vienna in 1529. Vienna was saved by the need to retreat before the onset of winter more than by military action. Later Ottoman historians looked back on the reign of Suleiman as the period when the imperial system worked to perfection, and they spoke of it as the golden age of Ottoman greatness.

While Ottoman armies pressed deeper and deeper into eastern Europe, the sultans also sought to control the Mediterranean. Between 1453 and 1502, the Ottomans fought the opening rounds of a two-century war with Venice, the most powerful of Italy's commercial city-states. The initial fighting left Venice in control of its lucrative islands like Crete and Cyprus for another century. But it also left Venice a reduced military power compelled to pay tribute to the Ottomans.

In the early sixteenth century, merchants from southern India and Sumatra sent emissaries to Istanbul requesting naval support against the Portuguese. The Ottomans responded to Portuguese threats close to their territories, such as at Aden at the southern entrance to the Red Sea, but the flow of eastern luxury products to Ottoman markets was not threatened by Portuguese coastal strongholds, and by century's end the Ottomans had pulled back from maritime commitments outside the Mediterranean Sea to concentrate on defending territory in Europe.

**Suleiman the Magnificent** The most illustrious sultan of the Ottoman Empire (r. 1520–1566); also known as Suleiman Kanuni, "The Lawgiver." He significantly expanded the empire in the Balkans and eastern Mediterranean.

# Chronology

| | Ottoman Empire | Safavid Empire | Mughal Empire | Russian Empire |
|---|---|---|---|---|
| **1500** | **1516–1517** Selim I conquers Egypt and Syria<br>**1520–1566** Reign of Suleiman the Magnificent; peak of Ottoman Empire<br>**1529** First Ottoman siege of Vienna<br><br>**1571** Ottoman naval defeat at Lepanto | **1502–1524** Shah Ismail establishes Safavid rule in Iran<br><br><br><br>**1587–1629** Reign of Shah Abbas the Great; peak of Safavid Empire | **1526** Babur defeats last sultan of Delhi<br><br>**1556–1605** Akbar rules in Agra; peak of Mughal Empire | **1547** Ivan IV adopts title of *tsar*<br><br><br>**1582** Russians conquer Khanate of Sibir |
| **1600** | **1610** End of Anatolian revolts | | **1658–1707** Aurangzeb imposes conservative Islamic regime | **1613–1645** Rule of Mikhail, the first Romanov tsar<br>**1649** Subordination of serfs complete |
| **1700** | **1730** Janissary revolt begins period of Ottoman conservatism | **1722** Afghan invaders topple last Safavid shah<br>**1736–1747** Nadir Shah temporarily reunites Iran; invades India (1739) | **1739** Iranians under Nadir Shah sack Delhi | **1689–1725** Rule of Peter the Great<br>**1712** St. Petersburg becomes Russian capital |

## Central Institutions

By the 1520s, the Ottoman Empire was the most powerful and best-organized state in either Europe or the Islamic world. Its military was balanced between cavalry archers, primarily Turks, and military slaves known as **Janissaries** (JAN-nih-say-rees) [*yeni cheri* in Turkish], who had originated as Christian prisoners of war and been converted to Islam. These new troops gave the Ottomans unusual military flexibility. Since horseback riding and bowmanship were not part of their cultural backgrounds, they readily accepted the idea of fighting on foot and learning to use guns, which at that time were still too heavy and awkward for a horseman to load and fire. The Janissaries lived in barracks and trained all year round.

The recruitment of Janissaries from prisoners changed early in the fifteenth century, when a new system imposed a levy of male children on Christian villages in the Balkans and occasionally elsewhere. Selected children were placed with Turkish families for language learning and then sent to Istanbul for an education that included instruction in Islam, military training, and, for the top 10 percent, skills that could be used in government administration. Senior military commanders and heads of government departments up to the rank of grand vizier were commonly drawn from among the chosen few who received special training.

The cavalrymen were supported by land grants and administered most rural areas in Anatolia and the Balkans. They maintained order, collected taxes, and reported for each summer's campaign with their horses, retainers, and supplies, all paid for from the

**Janissaries** Infantry, originally of slave origin, armed with firearms and constituting the elite of the Ottoman army from the fifteenth century until the corps was abolished in 1826.

**Map 18.1 Muslim Empires in the Sixteenth and Seventeenth Centuries** Iran, a Shi'ite state flanked by Sunni Ottomans on the west and Sunni Mughals on the east, had the least exposure to European influences. Ottoman expansion across the southern Mediterranean Sea intensified European fears of Islam. The areas of strongest Mughal control dictated that Islam's spread into Southeast Asia would be heavily influenced by merchants and religious figures from Gujarat instead of from eastern India. © Cengage Learning

taxes they collected. When not campaigning, they stayed at home.

A galley-equipped navy was manned by Greek, Turkish, Algerian, and Tunisian sailors, usually under the command of an admiral from one of the North African ports. The balance of the Ottoman land forces brought success to Ottoman arms in recurrent wars with the Safavids of Iran, who were slower to adopt firearms, and in the inexorable conquest of

the Balkans. Expansion by sea was less dramatic. A major expedition against Malta in the western Mediterranean failed in 1565. Combined Christian forces also achieved a massive naval victory at the Battle of Lepanto, off Greece, in 1571. But the Ottomans' resources were so extensive that in a year's time they had replaced all of the galleys sunk in that battle.

The Ottoman Empire became cosmopolitan in character. The sophisticated court language,

Osmanli (os-MAHN-lih) (the Turkish form of *Ottoman*), shared basic grammar and vocabulary with Turkish, but Arabic and Persian elements made it distinct from the Turkish spoken by Anatolia's nomads and villagers. Everyone who served in the military or the bureaucracy and conversed in Osmanli was considered to belong to the *askeri* (AS-keh-ree), or "military," class. Members of this class were exempt from taxes and owed their positions to the sultan.

The Ottomans saw the sultan as providing justice for his "flock of sheep" (*raya* [RAH-yah]) and military forces to protect them. In return, the raya paid the taxes that supported both the sultan and the military. In reality, the sultan's government remained comparatively isolated from the lives of most subjects. As Islam gradually became the majority religion in some Balkan regions, Islamic law (the Shari'a [sha-REE-ah]) conditioned urban institutions and social life. Local customs prevailed among non-Muslims and in many rural areas, while non-Muslims looked to their own religious leaders for guidance in family and spiritual matters.

### Crisis of the Military State, 1585–1650

As military technology evolved, cannon and lighter-weight firearms played an ever-larger role on the battlefield. Accordingly, the size of the Janissary corps—and its cost to the government—grew steadily, and the role of the Turkish cavalry diminished. To pay the Janissaries, the sultan started reducing the number of landholding cavalrymen and diverting revenues previously spent on their living expenses and military equipment to the imperial treasury. As inflation caused by a flood of cheap silver from the New World bankrupted many of the remaining landholders, who were restricted by law to collecting a fixed amount of taxes, their land returned to the state. Displaced cavalrymen, armed and unhappy, became a restive element in rural Anatolia.

This complicated situation, exacerbated after 1600 by the climatic deterioration known as the Little Ice Age (see Issues in World History: The Little Ice Age on page 466), resulted in revolts that devastated Anatolia between 1590 and 1610. Former landholding cavalrymen, short-term soldiers released at the end of the campaign season, peasants overburdened by emergency taxes, and even impoverished students of religion formed bands of marauders. Anatolia experienced the worst of the rebellions and suffered greatly from emigration and the loss of agricultural production. But an increase in banditry, made worse by the government's inability to stem the spread of muskets among the general public, beset other parts of the empire as well.

In the meantime, the Janissaries took advantage of their growing influence to gain relief from prohibitions on their marrying and engaging in business. Janissaries who involved themselves in commerce lessened the burden on the state budget, and married Janissaries who enrolled sons or relatives in the corps made it possible in the seventeenth century for the government to save state funds by abolishing forced recruitment. These savings, however, were more than offset by the increase in the total number of Janissaries and in their steady deterioration as a military force, which necessitated the hiring of more and more supplemental troops.

### Economic Change and Growing Weakness

A very different Ottoman Empire emerged from this crisis. Sultans once had led armies. Now they mostly resided in palaces, and the affairs of government were overseen more and more by the chief administrators—the grand viziers. Janissaries, now a hereditary class, became a powerful faction in urban politics, sometimes controlling the tax farms that had replaced land grants as payment for military service (see Chapters 12 and 16). Tax farmers paid specific taxes, such as customs duties, in advance in return for the privilege of collecting a greater amount from the actual taxpayers.

Rural administration, already disrupted by the rebellions, suffered from the transition to tax farms. The former military landholders had kept order on their lands in order to maintain their incomes. Tax farmers were less likely to live on the land. The imperial government therefore faced greater administrative burdens and came to rely heavily on powerful provincial governors or on wealthy men who purchased lifelong tax collection rights and behaved more or less like private landowners.

Military power slowly ebbed. The ill-trained Janissaries sometimes resorted to hiring substitutes to go on campaign, and the sultans relied on partially trained seasonal recruits and on armies raised by the governors of frontier provinces. A second mighty siege of Vienna failed in 1683, and by the middle of the eighteenth century it was obvious to the Austrians and Russians that the Ottoman Empire was weakening. On the eastern front, however, Ottoman exhaustion after many wars was matched by the demise in 1722 of their perennial adversary, the Safavid state of Iran.

Although the Ottoman Empire lacked the wealth of western Europe, it remained much more prosperous than the Russian Empire. As political disorder in Safavid Iran cut deeply into Iranian silk production, overland trade from the East dwindled, but new products also came into vogue. Farmers in Greece, Macedonia, Bulgaria, and Anatolia grew mild-flavored, low-nicotine tobacco (see Environment and Technology: Tobacco and Waterpipes); and coffee, a Yemeni product, rose from obscurity in the fifteenth century to become the rage first in the Ottoman Empire and then in Europe. By 1770, however, Muslim merchants trading in the Yemeni port of Mocha (MOH-kuh) (literally "the coffee place") were charged 15 percent in duties and fees, while European traders, benefiting from long-standing trade agreements with the Ottoman Empire, paid little more than 3 percent.

Such trade agreements, called capitulations (from Latin *capitula*, or "chapter"), were first granted as favors by powerful sultans, but they eventually led to European domination of Ottoman seaborne trade. Nevertheless, the Europeans did not control strategic ports in the eastern and southern Mediterranean comparable to Malacca in the Indian Ocean and Hormuz on the Persian Gulf, so their economic power stopped short of colonial settlement or direct control in Ottoman territories.

A few astute Ottoman statesmen observed the growing disarray of the empire and advised the sultans to reestablish the land grant system and the recruitment of the Janissary corps. Most people, however, did not feel the threat or see Europe as the enemy that would eventually dismantle the empire. The Istanbul elite experimented with European clothing and furniture styles and purchased printed books from the empire's first (and short-lived) press. Ottoman historians named the period between 1718 and 1730 when European fashions were in favor the **Tulip Period** because of the craze for high-priced tulip bulbs that swept Ottoman ruling circles. The craze echoed a Dutch tulip mania that had begun in the mid-sixteenth century, when the flower was intro-

duced into Holland from Istanbul (see Chapter 16), and peaked in 1636 with particularly rare bulbs going for 2,500 florins apiece—the value of twenty-two oxen.

In 1730, however, gala soirees at which guests watched turtles with candles on their backs wander in the dark through massive tulip beds gave way to a conservative Janissary revolt with strong religious overtones. Sultan Ahmed III abdicated, and the leader of the revolt, Patrona Halil (pa-TROH-nuh ha-LEEL), an Albanian former seaman and stoker of the public baths, swaggered around the capital for several months dictating government policies before he was seized and executed.

The Patrona Halil rebellion confirmed the perceptions of a few that the Ottoman Empire was facing severe difficulties. Yet decay at the center spelled benefit elsewhere. In the provinces, ambitious and competent governors, wealthy landholders, urban notables, and nomad chieftains took advantage, and by the middle of the eighteenth century Mamluks had regained a dominant position in Egypt. Though Selim I had defeated the Mamluk sultanate in the early sixteenth century, the practice of buying slaves in the Caucasus and training them as soldiers reappeared by the end of the century in several Arab cities. In Baghdad, Janissary commanders and Georgian Mamluks competed for power, with the

**Tulip Period**  Last years of the reign of Ottoman sultan Ahmed III (1718–1730), during which European styles and attitudes became briefly popular in Istanbul.

## SECTION REVIEW

- The Ottoman Empire grew through the skill of its founding rulers, control of strategic territory, and military power.

- The empire expanded into southern and eastern Europe, the Middle East, and Africa, reaching its height under Suleiman the Magnificent.

- Unwilling to build a strong navy, the Ottomans never adapted to developments in the Indian Ocean.

- The empire rested on the military led by the sultan, and changes in military structure ultimately weakened the state.

- As the imperial economy reoriented toward Europe, the central government weakened, permitting the rise of local powers.

# environment & technology

## Tobacco and Waterpipes

Tobacco, a plant native to the Western Hemisphere, may have been introduced into Ottoman Syria as early as 1570 and was certainly known in Istanbul by 1600. In Iran, one historian noted that when an Uzbek ruler entered the northeast province of Khurasan in 1612 and called for tobacco, it was quickly provided for him, while a Spanish diplomat remarked just a few years later that Shah Abbas, who had banned smoking as a sinful practice, nevertheless permitted an envoy from the Mughal sultan to indulge. European traders initially brought tobacco by sea, but it quickly became a cultivated crop in Mughal India, whence it was exported to Iran. By the middle of the seventeenth century, however, it had also become a significant crop in Ottoman and Safavid territories.

The waterpipe became a distinctive means of smoking in the Islamic world, but when the device came into use is disputed. Iranian historians assert that it was invented in Iran, where one reference in poetry goes back to before 1550. This early date suggests that waterpipes may have been used for smoking some other substance before tobacco became known. Straight pipes of clay or wood were also used, especially in Turkish areas and among poorer people.

The Persian word for a waterpipe, *qalyan*, comes from an Arabic verb meaning "to boil, or bubble." Arabic has two common words: *nargila*, which derives ultimately from the Sanskrit word for "coconut," and *shisha*, which means "glass" in Persian. In India, where coconuts were often used to contain the water, the usual term was *hookah*, meaning "jar." The absence of a clear linguistic indication of the country of origin enhances the possibility that waterpipes evolved and spread before the introduction of tobacco.

All levels of society took to smoking, with women enjoying it as much as men. The leisurely ceremony of preparing and lighting the waterpipe made it an ideal pastime in coffeehouses, which became popular in both the Ottoman and Safavid Empires. In other settings, the size and fragility of

From Rudi Matthee, *The Pursuit of Pleasure: Drugs and Stimulants in Iranian History, 1500–1900* (Princeton: Princeton University Press) p. 125

**Iranian Waterpipe** *Moistened tobacco is placed in cup A, and a glowing coal is put on top of it to make it smolder. When the smoker draws on the stem sticking out to the side, the smoke bubbles up from beneath the water, which cools and filters it. The sophisticated manufacture shown in this drawing, which was rendered in 1622, supports the theory that the waterpipe went through a lengthy period of development before the seventeenth century.*

the waterpipe could cause inconvenience. When traveling, wealthy Iranian men sometimes had a pipe carrier in their entourage who carried the *qalyan* in his hand and had a small pot containing hot coals dangling from his saddle in case his master should wish to light up on the road.

latter emerging triumphant by the mid-eighteenth century. In Aleppo and Damascus, however, the Janissaries came out on top. Meanwhile, in central Arabia, a puritanical Sunni movement inspired by Muhammad ibn Abd al-Wahhab began a remarkable rise beyond the reach of Ottoman power. Although no region declared full independence, the sultan's power was slipping away in all parts of the empire while the Ottoman economy was reorienting itself toward Europe.

# THE SAFAVID EMPIRE, 1502–1722

■ *How did the Safavid Empire both resemble and differ from its neighbors?*

The **Safavid Empire** of Iran (see Map 18.1) resembled its long-time Ottoman foe in many ways: it initially relied militarily on cavalry paid through land grants, and its population spoke several languages and included many non-Muslims. It also had distinct qualities that to this day set Iran off from its neighbors: it derived part of its legitimacy from the pre-Islamic dynasties of ancient Iran, and it adopted the Shi'ite form of Islam.

## Safavid Society and Religion

The ultimate victor in a complicated struggle for power among Turkish chieftains east of the Ottoman lands was Ismail (IS-ma-eel), a boy of Kurdish, Iranian, and Greek ancestry. In 1502, at age sixteen, Ismail proclaimed himself shah of Iran and declared that from that time forward his realm would be devoted to **Shi'ite** Islam, which revered the family of Muhammad's cousin and son-in-law Ali (see Chapter 9). Although Ismail's reasons for compelling Iran's conversion to Shi'ism are unknown, the effect of this radical act was to create a deep chasm between Iran and its Sunni Muslim neighbors. Iran became a truly separate country for the first time since its incorporation into the Islamic caliphate in the seventh century.

The imposition of Shi'ite belief confirmed differences between Iran and its neighbors that had been long in the making. Persian, written in the Arabic script from the tenth century onward, had emerged as the second language of Islam. Iranian scholars and writers normally read Arabic as well as Persian and sprinkled their writings with Arabic phrases, but their Arab counterparts were much less inclined to learn Persian. After the Mongols destroyed Baghdad, the capital of the Islamic caliphate, in 1258, Iran developed largely on its own, having more extensive contacts with India—where Muslim rulers favored the Persian language—than with the Arabs.

In the post-Mongol period, artistic styles in Iran, Afghanistan, and Central Asia also went their own way. Painted and molded tiles and tile mosaics, often in vivid turquoise blue, became the standard exterior decoration of mosques in Iran but were never used in Syria and Egypt. Persian poets raised verse to peaks of perfection that had no counterpart in Arabic poetry, generally considered to be in a state of decline.

To be sure, Islam itself provided a tradition of belief, learning, and law that crossed ethnic and linguistic borders, but Shah Ismail's imposition of Shi'ism set Iran significantly apart. Shi'ite doctrine says that all temporal rulers, regardless of title, are temporary stand-ins for the **Hidden Imam**, the twelfth descendant of Ali, the Prophet Mohammad's cousin and son-in-law who disappeared as a child in the ninth century. Some Shi'ite scholars taught the faithful to calmly accept the world as it was and wait quietly for the Hidden Imam's return. Others maintained that they themselves should play a stronger role in political affairs because they were best qualified to know the Hidden Imam's wishes. These two positions, which still play a role in Iranian Shi'ism, enhanced the self-image of religious scholars as independent of imperial authority and stood in the way of their becoming subordinate government functionaries, as happened in the Ottoman Empire.

Shi'ism also affected popular psychology. Annual commemoration of the martyrdom of Imam Husayn (d. 680), Ali's son and third Imam, regularized an emotional outpouring with no parallel in Sunni lands. Day after day for two weeks, preachers recited the woeful tale to crowds of weeping believers, and elaborate street processions, often organized by craft guilds, paraded chanting and self-flagellating men past crowds of reverent onlookers. Of course, Shi'ites elsewhere observed rites of mourning for Imam Husayn, but the impact of these rites was especially great in Iran, where 90 percent of the population was

**Safavid Empire** Iranian kingdom (1502–1722) established by Ismail Safavi, who declared Iran a Shi'ite state.

**Shi'ites** Muslims belonging to the branch of Islam believing that God vests leadership of the community in a descendant of Muhammad's son-in-law Ali. Shi'ism is the state religion of Iran.

**Hidden Imam** Last in a series of twelve descendants of Muhammad's son-in-law Ali, whom Shi'ites consider divinely appointed leaders of the Muslim community. In occlusion since around 873, he is expected to return as a messiah at the end of time.

Shi'ite. Over time, the subjects of the Safavid shahs came to feel more than ever a people apart.

## A Tale of Two Cities: Isfahan and Istanbul

Outwardly, Ottoman Istanbul looked quite different from Isfahan (is-fah-HAHN), which became Iran's capital in 1598 by decree of **Shah Abbas I** (r. 1587–1629). Built on seven hills beside the narrow Golden Horn inlet, Istanbul boasted a skyline punctuated by the gray stone domes and thin, pointed minarets of the great imperial mosques. The mosques surrounding the royal plaza in Isfahan, in contrast, had unobtrusive minarets and brightly tiled domes. High walls surrounded the sultan's palace in Istanbul. Shah Abbas in Isfahan focused his capital on the giant royal plaza, which was large enough for his army to play polo, and he used an airy palace overlooking the plaza to receive dignitaries and review his troops.

Istanbul's harbor teemed with sailing ships and smaller craft, many of them belonging to a colony of European merchants perched on a hilltop on the other side of the Golden Horn. Isfahan, far from the sea, was only occasionally visited by Europeans. Trade was mostly in the hands of Jews, Hindus, and Jains from India, and especially a colony of Armenian Christians brought in by Shah Abbas.

Beneath these superficial differences, the two capitals had much in common. Wheeled vehicles were scarce in Istanbul and nonexistent in Isfahan. Both cities were built for walking and, aside from the royal plaza in Isfahan, lacked the open spaces common in contemporary European cities. Streets were narrow and irregular. Houses crowded against each other in dead-end lanes. Residents enjoyed their privacy in interior courtyards. Artisans and merchants organized themselves into guilds that had strong social and religious bonds. Shops adjoined one another in the markets.

Women seldom appeared in public, even in Istanbul's mazelike covered market or in Isfahan's long, serpentine bazaar. At home, the women's quarters— called *anderun* (an-deh-ROON), or "interior," in Iran and *harem*, or "forbidden area," in Istanbul—were separate from the public rooms where the men of the family received visitors. In both areas, low cushions, charcoal braziers for warmth, carpets, and small tables constituted most of the furnishings.

SuperStock/Glow Images, Inc.

**Mughal Emperor Jahangir Embracing the Safavid Shah Abbas** Painted by the Mughal artist Abu al-Hasan around 1620, this miniature shows the artist's patron, Jahangir, on the right standing on a lion, dominating the diminutive Shah Abbas, standing on a sheep. Though this may accurately reflect Jahangir's view of their relationship, in fact Shah Abbas was a powerful rival for control of Afghanistan, the gateway to India and the meeting point of the lion and the sheep. The globe the monarchs stand on reflects the spread of accurate geographical ideas into the Muslim world.

The private side of family life has left few traces, but women's society—consisting of wives, children, female servants, and sometimes one or more eunuchs—was not entirely cut off from the outside world. Ottoman court records reveal that women, using male agents, were very active in the urban real estate market. Often they were selling inherited shares of their father's estate, but some both bought and sold real estate on a regular basis and even established

**Shah Abbas I** The fifth and most renowned ruler of the Safavid dynasty in Iran (r. 1587–1629). Abbas moved the royal capital to Isfahan in 1598.

religious endowments for pious purposes. The fact that Islamic law, unlike European codes, permitted a wife to retain her property after marriage gave some women a stake in the general economy and a degree of independence from their spouses. Women also appeared in other types of court cases, where they often testified for themselves, for Islamic courts did not recognize the role of attorney. Although comparable Safavid court records do not survive, historians assume that a parallel situation prevailed in Iran.

European travelers commented on the veiling of women outside the home, but the norm for both sexes was complete coverage of arms, legs, and hair. Miniature paintings indicate that ordinary female garb consisted of a long, ample dress with a scarf or shawl pulled tight over the forehead to conceal the hair. Lightweight baggy trousers were worn under the dress. This mode of dress differed little from that of men. Poor men wore light trousers, a long shirt, a jacket, and a hat or turban. Wealthier men wore over their trousers ankle-length caftans, often closely fitted around the chest.

Public life was a male domain. Poetry and art, both more elegantly developed in Isfahan than in Istanbul, were as likely to extol the charms of beardless boys as pretty women. Despite religious disapproval of homosexuality, attachments to adolescent boys were neither unusual nor hidden. Women who appeared in public—aside from non-Muslims, the aged, and the very poor—were usually slaves. Miniature paintings frequently depict female dancers,

Austrian National Library, picture archive

**Istanbul Family on the Way to a Bath House**   Public baths, an important feature of Islamic cities, set different hours for men and women. Young boys, such as the lad in the turban shown here, went with their mothers and sisters. Notice that the children wear the same styles as the adults.

musicians, and even acrobats in attitudes and costumes that range from decorous to decidedly erotic.

Despite social similarities, the overall flavors of Isfahan and Istanbul were not the same. Isfahan had its prosperous Armenian quarter across the river from the city's center, but it was not as cosmopolitan as Istanbul. Shah Abbas located his capital toward the center of his domain away from any unstable frontier. Istanbul, in contrast, was a great seaport and a crossroads located on the straits separating the sultan's European and Asian possessions. People of all sorts

**Royal Square in Isfahan**   Built by the order of Shah Abbas over a period of twenty years starting in 1598, the open space is as long as five football fields (555 by 172 yards). At the right end, not shown in this photograph, is the entrance to the covered bazaar. The dominating structure is the immense Royal Mosque at the left-hand end. The seven-story "High Porte" pavilion overlooking the far side of the reflecting pool was the entrance to an extensive palace complex, now mostly gone. Its richly painted rooms were used for entertaining guests. Opposite it is a smaller mosque without minarets used only by the ruler and his household.   Georg Gerster/Photo Researchers, Inc.

lived or spent time in Istanbul: Venetians, Genoese, Arabs, Turks, Greeks, Armenians, Albanians, Serbs, Jews, Bulgarians, and more. In this respect, Istanbul conveyed the cosmopolitan character of major seaports from Venice to Canton (Guangzhou), though its prosperity rested on the vast reach of the sultan's territories rather than on the voyages of merchants.

### Economic Crisis and Political Collapse

The silk fabrics of northern Iran were the mainstay of the Safavid Empire's foreign trade. However, the product that eventually became associated with Iran was the deep-pile carpet made by knotting colored yarns around stretched warp threads, work often done by women and girls. Different cities produced distinctive carpet designs.

Overall, Iran's manufacturing sector was neither large nor notably productive. Most of the shah's subjects, whether Iranians, Turks, Kurds, or Arabs, lived by subsistence farming or herding. Neither area of activity recorded significant technological advances during the Safavid period.

The Safavids, like the Ottomans, had difficulty finding the money to pay troops armed with firearms. The crisis occurred somewhat later in Iran because of its geographic distance from Europe. By the end of the sixteenth century, it was evident that a more systematic adoption of cannon and firearms in the Safavid Empire would be needed to hold off the Ottomans and the Uzbeks (UHZ-bex), Turkish rulers who had succeeded the Timurids on Iran's Central Asian frontier (see Map 18.1). Like the Ottoman cavalry a century earlier, warriors from nomadic groups were not inclined to trade their bows for firearms. Shah Abbas responded by establishing a slave corps of year-round soldiers and arming them with guns. The Christian converts to Islam who initially provided the manpower for the new corps were mostly captives taken in raids on Georgia in the Caucasus (CAW-kuh-suhs).

In the late sixteenth century, the inflation caused by cheap silver spread into Iran; then overland trade through Safavid territory declined because of mismanagement of the silk monopoly after Shah Abbas's death in 1629. As a result, the later shahs could not afford to pay their army and bureaucracy. Trying to unseat the nomads from their lands to regain control of taxes was

more difficult and more disruptive militarily than the piecemeal dismantlement of the land-grant system in the Ottoman Empire. The nomads remained cohesive military forces, and pressure from the center simply caused them to withdraw to their mountain pastures. By 1722, the government had become so weak and commanded so little support from the nomadic groups that an army of marauding Afghans was able to capture Isfahan and effectively end Safavid rule.

# THE MUGHAL EMPIRE, 1526–1761

■ *How did the Mughal Empire combine Muslim and Hindu elements into an effective state?*

What distinguished the Indian empire of the Mughal (MOH-guhl) sultans from the empires of the Ottomans and Safavids was the fact that India was a land of Hindus ruled by a Muslim minority. Muslim domain was established by repeated military campaigns from the early eleventh century onward, and even five centuries later Hindus still resented the Muslims. Thus, the challenge facing the Mughals was not just conquering and organizing a large territorial state but also finding a formula for Hindu-Muslim coexistence.

### Political Foundations

Babur (BAH-bur) (1483–1530), the founder of the **Mughal Empire**, was a Muslim descendant of both Timur and Chinggis Khan (*Mughal* is

**Mughal Empire** Muslim state (1526–1857) exercising dominion over most of India in the sixteenth and seventeenth centuries. Fragmentation of power and growth of English imperial strength marked the subsequent period.

Persian for "Mongol"). Invading from Central Asia, Babur defeated the last Muslim sultan of Delhi (DEL-ee) in 1526. Babur's grandson **Akbar** (r. 1556–1605) established the central administration of the expanding state. Under him and his three successors—the last of whom died in 1707—all but the southern tip of India fell under Mughal rule, administered first from Agra and then from Delhi.

Akbar, a brilliant but mercurial man, granted land revenues to military officers and government officials in return for their service. Assignments of land revenue, called *mansabs* (MAN-sab), some large and some small, determined their holders ranks. As in the other Islamic empires, revenue grants were not considered hereditary, and the central government kept careful track of them.

With a population of 100 million, a thriving trade in cotton cloth, and a generally efficient administration, India under Akbar was the most prosperous empire of the sixteenth century. He and his successors faced few external threats and experienced generally peaceful conditions in their northern Indian heartland.

European trade boomed at the port of Surat in the northwest, but merchants from Multan, today on the Indus River in Pakistan, did more business overland with Iran and Russia. Lacking a regular navy, the rulers saw the Europeans—after Akbar's time, primarily Dutch and English, the Portuguese having lost most of their Indian ports—less as enemies than as shipmasters whose support could be procured as needed in return for trading privileges.

## Hindus and Muslims

The Mughal state inherited traditions of religious tolerance from both the Islamic caliphate and the Mongols. Seventy percent of the *mansabdars* (man-sab-DAHRZ) (officials holding land revenues) appointed under Akbar were Muslim soldiers born outside India, but 15 percent were Hindus. Most of the Hindu appointees were warriors from the north called **Rajputs** (RAHJ-putz), one of whom rose to be a powerful revenue minister.

Akbar, the most Illustrious ruler of his dynasty, differed from his Ottoman and Safavid counterparts—Suleiman the Magnificent and Shah Abbas the Great—in his striving for social harmony and not just for

territory and revenue. His marriage to a Rajput princess encouraged reconciliation and even intermarriage between Muslims and Hindus. The birth of a son in 1569 ensured that future rulers would have both Muslim and Hindu ancestry.

Akbar ruled that in legal disputes between two Hindus, decisions would be made according to village custom or Hindu law as interpreted by local Hindu scholars. Shari'a law was for Muslims. Akbar made himself the legal court of last resort.

Akbar also made himself the center of a new "Divine Faith" incorporating Muslim, Hindu, Zoroastrian, Sikh (sick), and Christian beliefs. He liked Sufi ideas, which permeated the religious rituals he instituted at court. To promote serious consideration of his religious doctrines, he personally oversaw, from an elevated catwalk, debates among scholars of all religions assembled in his octagonal audience chamber. When courtiers uttered the Muslim exclamation "Allahu Akbar"—"God is great"—they also understood it in its second grammatical meaning: "God is Akbar."

Akbar's religious views did not survive him, but the court culture he fostered, reflecting a mixture of Muslim and Hindu traditions, flourished until his zealous great-grandson Aurangzeb (ow-rang-ZEB) (r. 1658–1707) reinstituted many restrictions on Hindus. Mughal and Rajput miniature paintings reveled in realistic portraits of political figures and depictions of scantily clad women, even though they brought frowns to the faces of pious Muslims, who deplored the representation of human beings. Most of the leading painters were Hindus. In addition to the florid style of Persian verse favored at court, a new taste developed for poetry and prose in the popular language of the Delhi region. The modern descendant of this language is called *Urdu* in Pakistan and *Hindi* in India.

> **Akbar** Most illustrious sultan of the Mughal Empire in India (r. 1556–1605). He expanded the empire and pursued a policy of conciliation with Hindus.
>
> *mansabs* In India, grants of land given in return for service by rulers of the Mughal Empire.
>
> **Rajputs** Members of a mainly Hindu warrior caste from northwest India. The Mughal emperors drew most of their Hindu officials from this caste, and Akbar married a Rajput princess.

Akbar Tames the Savage Elephant, Hawa'i, Outside the Red Fort at Agra, miniature from the Akbarnama of Abul Fazl, c. 1590 (left-hand side of double page miniature, see 4042) (gouache on paper), Basawan and Chatai (fl.1590)/British Museum, London, UK/The Bridgeman Art Library

**Elephants Breaking Bridge of Boats**  This illustration of an incident in the life of Akbar illustrates the ability of Mughal miniature painters to depict unconventional action scenes. Because the flow of rivers in India and the Middle East varied greatly from dry season to wet season, boat bridges were much more common than permanent constructions.

## Central Decay and Regional Challenges

Mughal power did not long survive Aurangzeb's death in 1707. Some historians consider the land-grant system a central element in the rapid decline of imperial authority, but other factors were at play as well. Aurangzeb's additions to Mughal territory in southern India were not all well integrated into the imperial structure, and strong regional powers arose to challenge Mughal military supremacy. A climax came in 1739 when Nadir Shah, a warlord who had seized power in Iran after the fall of the Safavids, invaded the Mughal capital and carried off to Iran the "peacock throne," the priceless jewel-encrusted symbol of Mughal grandeur. Another throne was found for the later Mughals to sit on; but their empire, which survived in name to 1857, was finished.

In 1723, Nizam al-Mulk (nee-ZAHM al-MULK), the sultan's powerful vizier, gave up on the central government and established his own nearly independent state at Hyderabad in the eastern Deccan. Other officials bearing the title *nawab* (nah-WAHB) became similarly independent in Bengal and Oudh (OW-ad) in the northeast, as did the militant Marathas in the center. In the northwest, simultaneous Iranian and Mughal weakness allowed the Afghans to establish an independent kingdom.

Some of the new regional powers were prosperous and benefited from the removal of the sultan's heavy hand. Linguistic and religious communities, freed from Aurangzeb's religious intolerance, similarly enjoyed greater opportunity for political expression. However, this disintegration of central power favored the intrusion of European adventurers.

In 1741 Joseph François Dupleix (doo-PLAY) took over the presidency of the French stronghold of Pondicherry (pon-dih-CHER-ree), thus beginning a new phase of European involvement in India. He captured the English trading center of Madras and used his small contingent of European and European-trained Indian troops to become a power broker in southern India. Though offered the title *nawab*, Dupleix preferred to operate behind the scenes, using Indian princes as puppets. His career ended in 1754 when he was called home. Deeply involved in European wars, the French government declined further adventures in India. Dupleix's departure opened the way for the British, whose exploits in India are described in Chapter 23.

### SECTION REVIEW

- Founded by Babur, the Mughal Empire grew under Akbar and his successors to encompass most of India.
- The empire prospered through trade and granted trade privileges to Europeans in exchange for naval support.
- Akbar included both Muslims and Hindus in his government, respected Hindu customs, and strove for religious harmony.
- A hybrid culture flourished, but Aurangzeb practiced Muslim intolerance.
- After Aurangzeb's death, the empire declined through foreign invasion, the rise of regional powers, and European encroachment.

# THE RUSSIAN EMPIRE, 1500–1762

■ *What were the similarities between the Christian Russian Empire and the Muslim Ottoman, Safavid, and Mughal Empires to the south?*

Before 1500, the Russian principalities had been dominated by steppe nomads (see Chapter 12). During the next three centuries, however, the rulers of **Muscovy (MUSS-koe-vee)**, the principality based on Moscow (a forest zone north of the steppe), forged an empire that stretched from eastern Europe across northern Asia and into North America. Moving against the Mongol Golden Horde (also known as *Tatars*), the princes of Muscovy ruthlessly annexed the territories of the neighboring Russian state of Novgorod, which lay on the Volga River, in 1478. Prince Ivan IV (r. 1533–1584), known as "the Terrible" (meaning the fearsome), pushed Muscovy's conquests further along the Volga River east and south at the expense of the Tatar khanates of Kazan and Astrakhan.

The Russian church called Moscow the "third Rome" and the successor to Constantinople, which the Ottomans took in 1453, and in 1547 the Russian ruler formally took the title **tsar** (zahr), a title based on the Roman imperial title *caesar* that had been previously reserved for such foreign rulers as the Mongols. Despite these grand titles, in 1600 the empire was poor, backward, and landlocked. Only one seaport—Arkhangelsk near the Arctic circle—connected Russia to the world's oceans. The Crimean Tatars to the south were powerful enough to sack Moscow in 1571, just as Stenka Razin's Cossacks from a nearby region threatened to do a century later. Beyond them, the Ottoman Empire controlled access to the Black Sea, while trade with India had to go through Iran. The kingdoms of Sweden and Poland-Lithuania to the west similarly blocked Russian access to the Baltic Sea.

The one route open to expansion, **Siberia**, turned out to be Russia's version of the New World, an immense northern region of little-known peoples and untapped resources. Particularly prized was the soft, dense fur of sables and other forest animals who were able to survive the long winters. Foragers, reindeer herders, and the Khanate of Sibir were no match for the rifles of Russian troops hired to protect explorers and fur trappers who moved through the frozen forests by river. After reaching the Pacific Ocean during the seventeenth century, the Russians crossed over into Alaska. The Khanate of Sibir fell in 1582, but Russian political control followed more slowly. Beginning in the early seventeenth century, the tsars used Siberia as a penal colony. In the 1640s Russian settlers began to grow grain in the Amur River Valley east of Mongolia, where they came into contact with Chinese authorities (see Chapter 19).

## Russian Society and Politics to 1725

As the empire expanded, it incorporated people with different languages, religious beliefs, and ethnic identities. Orthodox missionaries strove to Christianize the peoples of Siberia, but among the relatively more populous steppe peoples, Islam prevailed as the dominant religion. Differences in how people outside of cities made their living were equally fundamental. Russians tended to live as farmers and hunters, while the peoples newly incorporated into the empire were either herders and caravan workers or hunters and fishers living along the Siberian rivers.

Diversity prevailed even among Russian speakers of Orthodox faith. The name *Cossack*, referring to bands of people living on the steppes between Moscovy and the Caspian and Black Seas, probably comes from a Turkish word for a warrior or mercenary soldier. Actually, Cossacks had diverse origins and beliefs, but they all belonged to close-knit bands, fought superbly from the saddle, and terrified both villagers and legal authorities. Cossack allegiances with rulers were temporary; loyalty to the chiefs of their bands was paramount.

---

**Muscovy**  The Russian principality that emerged gradually during the era of Mongol domination. The muscovite dynasty ruled without interruption from 1276 to 1598.

**tsar (czar)**  From Latin *caesar*, this Russian title for a monarch was first used in reference to a Russian ruler by Ivan III (r. 1462–1505).

**Siberia**  The extreme northeastern sector of Asia, including the Kamchatka Peninsula and the present Russian coast of the Arctic Ocean, the Bering Strait, and the Sea of Okhotsk.

**Cossacks**  Peoples of the Russian Empire who lived outside the farming villages, often as herders, mercenaries, or outlaws. Cossacks led the expansion into Siberia in the sixteenth and seventeenth centuries.

Cossacks provided most of the soldiers employed by the early fur traders, and they founded every major town in Russian Siberia. They also manned the Russian camps on the Amur River and protected settlers. West of the Urals the Cossacks defended Russia against Swedish and Ottoman incursions, but they also preserved their political autonomy (as discussed at the beginning of this chapter).

In the early seventeenth century, a "Time of Troubles" that coincided with the beginning of the Little Ice Age (see Issues in World History, page 466) and that was marked by famine and warfare ended the old line of Muscovite rulers. On separate occasions, Swedish and Polish forces occupied Moscow. Russian aristocrats (boyars [BOY-ars]) responded to this period of internal disorder by electing a new tsar, Mikhail Romanov (ROH-man-off or roh-MAN-off) (r. 1613–1645). Mikhail defended Russia from neighboring powers and inaugurated a new Romanov dynasty, characterizing the Turkish steppe peoples as "infidels" and "barbarians" and Russians as "civilized "and "Christian." Despite this rhetoric, there were many similarities between the Russian Empire and its Muslim neighbors to the south.

Like the sultans and shahs, Moscovy rulers rewarded the military service of nobles with land grants. Peasants were obliged to work for the lord, and the rising commercialization of agriculture raised the value of these labor obligations. Law and custom permitted peasants to change masters during a two-week period each year, which encouraged lords to treat their peasants well, but warfare in the late sixteenth and early seventeenth centuries disrupted peasant life, and many fled to the Cossacks or into Siberia. Those who stayed sold themselves into slavery to keep from starving.

When peace returned, landlords sought to recover the runaways and bind them more tightly to their land. A law change in 1649 eliminated the period when peasants could change masters and ordered runaways to return to their masters, transforming peasants into **serfs**. Like slavery, serfdom was hereditary. In theory the serf was tied to a piece of land, not owned by a master. In practice, strict laws narrowed the difference between serf and slave. In the Russian census of 1795, serfs made up over half the population; landowners made up only 2 percent.

## Peter the Great

The greatest of the Romanov tsars, **Peter the Great** (r. 1689–1725), came to the throne a century or so later than the eminent Muslim potentates Suleiman the Magnificent, the Safavid shah Abbas, and the Mughal sultan Akbar. Whereas Suleiman fought wars with Europeans, and Abbas and Akbar knew Europeans as merchant adventurers, Peter was aware that Europe's wealth and military power had increased enormously. The "Tulip Period" that coincided with Peter's reign reveals Ottoman awareness of Europe, but no Muslim notable could safely sojourn in Christian Europe long enough to master the new techniques of ruling and acquiring power.

When Peter ascended the throne, there were already hundreds of foreign merchants in Moscow, as there were in Istanbul. Military officers from western Europe introduced new weapons and techniques, and Italian builders influenced church and palace architecture. Peter accelerated these tendencies in unprecedented fashion. While his half-sister Sophia governed as regent for him and her sickly brother Ivan, he lived on an estate near the foreigners' quarter outside Moscow, gaining practical skills in blacksmithing, carpentry, shipbuilding, and the arts of war. When Princess Sophia tried to take complete control of the government in 1689, Peter rallied enough support to send her to a monastery, secure the abdication of Ivan, and take charge of Russia. He was still in his teens.

To secure a port on the Black Sea, Peter constructed a small but formidable navy. Describing his wars with the Ottoman Empire as a new crusade to liberate Constantinople from the Muslim sultans, Peter fancied himself the legal protector of Orthodox Christians living under Ottoman rule. His forces seized the port of Azov in 1696 but lost it again in 1713, thus calling a halt to southward expansion.

In the winter of 1697–1698, after his Black Sea campaign, Peter traveled in disguise across Europe

**serf** In medieval Europe, an agricultural laborer legally bound to a lord's property and obligated to perform set services for the lord. In Russia some serfs worked as artisans and in factories; serfdom was not abolished there until 1861.

**Peter the Great** Russian tsar (r. 1689–1725). He enthusiastically introduced Western languages and technologies to the Russian elite and moved the capital from Moscow to the new city of St. Petersburg.

to discover how western European societies were becoming so powerful and wealthy. He paid special attention to ships and weapons, even working for a time as a ship's carpenter in the Netherlands. Upon his return to Russia, Peter resolved to expand and reform his vast but backward empire.

In the long and costly Great Northern War (1700–1721), Peter's modernized armies broke Swedish control of the Baltic Sea, making possible more direct contacts between Russia and Europe. This victory forced the European powers for the first time to recognize Russia as a major power. Then, Peter captured from Sweden the eastern end of the Baltic and built St. Petersburg, his window on the West. In 1712 the city became Russia's capital. To demonstrate Russia's new sophistication, Peter ordered architects to build St. Petersburg's houses and public buildings in the baroque style then fashionable in France.

Peter also pushed the Russian elite to imitate European fashions. He personally shaved off some of his noblemen's long beards to conform to Western styles. To end the traditional seclusion of upper-class Russian women, Peter required officials, military officers, and merchants to bring their wives to the social gatherings he organized in the capital. He also directed the nobles to educate their children.

A decree of 1716 proclaimed that the tsar "is not obliged to answer to anyone in the world for his doings, but possesses power and authority over his kingdom and land, to rule them at his will and pleasure as a Christian ruler." Under this expansive definition of his role, Peter sharply reduced the traditional roles of the boyars in government and the army, brought the Russian Orthodox Church more firmly under state control, built factories and foundries to provide supplies for the military, increased taxes, and imposed more forced labor on the serfs. Peter was an absolutist ruler of the sort then common in western Europe (see Chapter 16), but he is equally comparable to the most authoritarian rulers in the contemporary Muslim empires.

**SECTION REVIEW**

- Russia grew vastly by colonizing Siberia.
- Lacking seaports, Russia relied on overland trade with European and Muslim neighbors.
- Peter the Great copied western European military and economic techniques and imposed a complete autocracy on his subjects.

# THE MARITIME WORLDS OF ISLAM, 1500–1750

■ *What role does maritime history play in the political and economic life of this period?*

As land powers, the Mughal, Safavid, Ottoman, and Russian Empires faced similar problems in the seventeenth and eighteenth centuries. Complex changes in military technology and in the world economy, along with the increasing difficulty of basing an extensive land empire on military forces paid through land grants, affected them all adversely.

The new pressures faced by land powers were less important to seafaring countries intent on turning trade networks into maritime empires. Improvements in ship design, navigation accuracy, and the use of

**The Fontanka Canal in St. Petersburg in 1753**  The Russian capital continued to grow as a commercial and administrative center. As in Amsterdam, canals were the city's major arteries. On the right is a new summer palace built by Peter's successor.

View of the Fontanka River from the grotto and the Guest Palace, etched by Grigory Anikievich Kachalov (1711/12-1759), 1753 (etching with engraving), Makhaev, Mikhail Ivanovich (c.1718-1770) (after) / Hermitage, St. Petersburg, Russia/The Bridgeman Art Library cannon gave an ever-increasing edge to European powers competing with local seafaring peoples. Moreover, the development of joint-stock companies, in which many merchants pooled their capital, provided a flexible and efficient financial instrument for exploiting new possibilities. The English East India Company was founded in 1600, the Dutch East India Company in 1602.

The Ottomans, Safavids, and Mughals did not effectively contest the growth of Portuguese and then Dutch, English, and French maritime power. Muslim shipbuilders, captains, sailors, and traders—and sizable groups of Armenian, Jewish, and Hindu traders—remained aloof from the Europeans. The presence in every port of Muslims following the same legal traditions and practicing their faith in similar ways cemented the Muslims' trading network. Conversion to Islam encouraged the growth of coastal Muslim communities.

Although European missionaries, particularly the Jesuits, tried to extend Christianity into Asia and Africa (see Chapters 15 and 19), most Europeans, the Portuguese excepted, did not treat local converts or the offspring of mixed marriages as full members of their communities. Islam was generally more welcoming. As a consequence, Islam spread extensively into East Africa and Southeast Asia during precisely the same time as rapid European commercial expansion.

## Muslims in Southeast Asia

Historians disagree about the chronology and manner of Islam's spread in Southeast Asia. Arab traders appeared in southern China as early as the eighth century, so Muslims probably reached the East Indies (the island portions of Southeast Asia) at a similarly early date. Nevertheless, the continuing dominance of Indian cultural influences in the area indicates that early Muslim visitors had little impact on local beliefs. Clearer indications of the formation of Muslim communities date from roughly the fourteenth century, with the strongest overseas linkage being to the port of Cambay in India (see Map 18.2) rather than to the Arab world. Islam first took root in port cities and in some royal courts and spread inland only slowly, possibly transmitted by itinerant Sufis.

Although appeals to the Ottoman sultan for support against the Europeans ultimately proved futile, Islam strengthened resistance to Portuguese, Spanish, and Dutch intruders. When the Spaniards conquered the Philippines during the decades following the establishment of their first fort in 1565, they encountered Muslims on the southern island of Mindanao (min-duh-NOW) and the nearby Sulu archipelago. They called them "Moros," the Spanish term for their old enemies, the Muslims of North Africa. In the ensuing Moro wars, the Spaniards portrayed the Moros as greedy pirates who raided non-Muslim territories for slaves. In fact, they were political, religious, and commercial competitors whose perseverance enabled them to establish the Sulu Empire based in the southern Philippines, one of the strongest states in Southeast Asia from 1768 to 1848.

Other local kingdoms that looked on Islam as a force to counter the aggressive Christianity of the Europeans included the actively proselytizing Brunei (BROO-neye) Sultanate in northern Borneo and the **Acheh** (AH-cheh) **Sultanate** in northern Sumatra. At its peak in the early seventeenth century, Acheh succeeded Malacca as the main center of Islamic expansion in Southeast Asia. It prospered by trading pepper for cotton cloth from Gujarat in India. Acheh declined after the Dutch seized Malacca from Portugal in 1641.

How well Islam was understood in these Muslim kingdoms is open to question. In Acheh, for example, a series of women ruled between 1641 and 1699. This practice ended when local Muslim scholars obtained a ruling from scholars in Mecca and Medina that Islam did not approve of female rulers. After this ruling, scholarly understandings of Islam gained greater prominence in the East Indies.

Historians have looked at merchants, Sufi preachers, or both as the first propagators of Islam in Southeast Asia. The scholarly vision of Islam, however, took root in the sixteenth century by way of pilgrims returning from years of study in Mecca and Medina. Islam promoted the dissemination of writing in the region. Some of the returning pilgrims wrote in Arabic, others in Malay or Javanese using Arabic script. As Islam continued to spread, *adat* ("custom"),

**Acheh Sultanate** Muslim kingdom in northern Sumatra. Main center of Islamic expansion in Southeast Asia in the early seventeenth century, it declined after the Dutch seized Malacca from Portugal in 1641.

**Map 18.2 European Colonization in the Indian Ocean, to 1750** Since Portuguese explorers were the first Europeans to reach India by rounding Africa, Portugal gained a strong foothold in both areas. Rival Spain was barred from colonizing the region by the Treaty of Tordesillas in 1494, which limited Spanish efforts to lands west of a line drawn through the mid-Atlantic Ocean. The line carried around the globe provided justification of Spanish colonization in the Philippines. French, British, and Dutch colonies date from after 1600, when joint-stock companies provided a new stimulus for overseas commerce. © Cengage Learning

a form of Islam rooted in pre-Muslim religious and social practices, retained its preeminence in rural areas over practices centered on the Shari'a, the religious law. But the royal courts in the port cities began to heed the views of the pilgrim teachers.

## Muslims in Coastal Africa

Muslim rulers also governed the East African ports that the Portuguese began to visit in

the fifteenth century (see Map 18.2). People living in the millet and rice lands of the Swahili Coast—from the Arabic *sawahil* (suh-WAH-hil) meaning "coasts"—had little contact with those in the dry hinterlands. Throughout this period, the East African lakes region and the highlands of Kenya witnessed unprecedented migration and relocation of peoples because of drought conditions that persisted from the late sixteenth through most of the seventeenth century.

Cooperation among the trading ports of Kilwa, Mombasa, and Malindi was hindered by the thick bush country that separated the cultivated tracts of coastal land and by the fact that the ports competed with one another in the export of ivory; ambergris (AM-ber-grees) (a whale byproduct used in perfumes); and forest products such as beeswax, copal tree resin, and wood. Kilwa also exported gold. In the eighteenth century slave trading, primarily to Arabian ports but also to India, increased in importance. Because Europeans—the only peoples who kept consistent records of slave-trading activities— played a minor role in this slave trade, few records have survived to indicate its extent. Perhaps the best estimate is that 2.1 million slaves were exported between 1500 and 1890, a little over 12.5 percent of the total traffic in African slaves during that period (see Chapter 17).

Initially, the Portuguese favored the port of Malindi, which caused the decline of Kilwa and Mombasa. Repeatedly plagued by local rebellion, Portuguese power suffered severe blows when the Arabs of **Oman** in southeastern Arabia captured their south Arabian stronghold at Musqat (1650) and then went on to seize Mombasa (1698), which had become the Portuguese capital in East Africa. The Portuguese briefly retook Mombasa but lost control permanently in 1729. From then on, the Portuguese had to content themselves with Mozambique in East Africa and a few remaining ports in India (Goa) and farther east (Macao and Timor).

The Omanis created a maritime empire of their own, one that worked in greater cooperation with the African populations. The Bantu language of the coast, broadened by the absorption of Arabic, Persian, and Portuguese loanwords, developed into **Swahili** (swah-HEE-lee), which was spoken throughout the region. Arabs and other Muslims who settled in the area intermarried with local families, giving rise to a mixed population that played an important role in developing a distinctive Swahili culture.

In Northwest Africa the seizure by Portugal and Spain of coastal strongholds in Morocco provoked a militant response. The Sa'adi family, which claimed descent from the Prophet Muhammad, led a resistance to Portuguese aggression that climaxed in victory at the battle of al-Qasr al-Kabir (Ksar el Kebir)

in 1578. The triumphant Moroccan sultan, Ahmad al-Mansur, restored his country's strength and independence. By the early seventeenth century naval expeditions from the port of Salé, referred to in British records as "the Sally Rovers," raided European shipping as far as Britain itself.

Corsairs, or sea raiders, working out of Algerian, Tunisian, and Libyan ports brought the same sort of warfare to the Mediterranean. European governments called these Muslim raiders pirates and slave-takers, and they leveled the same charges against other Muslim mariners in the Persian Gulf and the Sulu Sea. But there was little distinction between the actions of the Muslims and of their European adversaries.

## European Powers in Southern Seas

Through their well-organized Dutch East India Company, the Dutch played a major role in driving the Portuguese from their possessions in the East Indies. Just as the Portuguese had tried to dominate the trade in spices, so the Dutch concentrated at first on the spice-producing islands of Southeast Asia. The Portuguese had seized Malacca, a strategic town on the narrow strait at the end of the Malay Peninsula, from a local Malay ruler in 1511 (see Chapter 15). The Dutch took it away from them in 1641, leaving Portugal little foothold in the East Indies except the islands of Ambon (am-BOHN) and Timor (see Map 18.2).

Although the United Netherlands was one of the least autocratic countries of Europe, the governors-general appointed by the Dutch East India Company deployed almost unlimited powers in their efforts to maintain their trade monopoly. They could even order the execution of their own employees for "smuggling"—that is, trading on their own. Under strong governors-general, the Dutch fought a series of wars against Acheh and other local kingdoms on Sumatra and Java. In 1628 and

**Oman** Arab state based in Musqat, the main port in the southeast region of the Arabian peninsula. Oman succeeded Portugal as a power in the western Indian Ocean in the eighteenth century.

**Swahili** Bantu language with Arabic loanwords spoken in coastal regions of East Africa.

1629 their new capital at **Batavia**, now the city of Jakarta on Java, was besieged by a fleet of fifty ships belonging to the sultan of Mataram (MAH-tah-ram), a Javanese kingdom. The Dutch held out with difficulty and eventually prevailed when the sultan was unable to get effective help from the English.

In the course of the eighteenth century, the Dutch gradually turned from being middlemen between Southeast Asian producers and European buyers to producing crops in areas they controlled, notably in Java. Javanese teak forests yielded high-quality lumber, and coffee, transplanted from Yemen, grew well in the western hilly regions. In this new phase of colonial export production, Batavia developed from being the headquarters town of a far-flung enterprise to being the administrative capital of a conquered land.

## CONCLUSION

The complex changes in military technology and economic organization that were under way in smaller European countries in the seventeenth and eighteenth centuries affected the Ottoman, Safavid, and Mughal Empires adversely. Only Russia, by virtue of a single ruler who was able to learn western European techniques at first hand, found success in adopting some of the changes. By western European standards, however, Russia was still poor and backward when Peter's reign ended in 1762, while the Muslims ruled rich lands that were ripe for European exploitation.

Improvements in ship design, navigation accuracy, and the use of cannon gave an ever-increasing edge to European powers competing with local seafaring peoples. In contrast to the age-old Eurasian belief that imperial wealth came from controlling broad expanses of land, western European rulers promoted joint-stock companies and luxuriated in the prosperity gained from their ever-increasing control of Indian Ocean commerce. Eighteenth-century European observers marveled no less at the riches and industry of these eastern lands than at the fundamental weakness of their political and military systems.

**Batavia** Fort established around 1619 as headquarters of Dutch East India Company operations in Indonesia; today the city of Jakarta.

# CHAPTER REVIEW

## THE OTTOMAN EMPIRE, TO 1750
■ *How did the Ottoman Empire rise to power, and what factors contributed to its transformation?* (page 427)

Strategic location and a centralized army well balanced between mounted bowmen and an infantry armed with gunpowder weapons were key to Ottoman success during the empire's first two centuries. With territorial growth, however, the borders became too distant from the capital for the efficient deployment of a centralized army, and economic pressures, notably those associated with a flood of cheap silver from the New World, forced modifications in the ruling system. Military, and increasingly political, power devolved to commanders and governors in provincial capitals and border districts, while new fiscal arrangements captured more tax revenue for the central government and the Istanbul elite.

## THE SAFAVID EMPIRE, 1502–1722
■ *How did the Safavid Empire both resemble and differ from its neighbors?* (page 434)

The Safavid Empire embodied some of the same Turkish tribal traditions and Islamic governing institutions that were found among the Ottomans, but the formal adoption of Shi'ism as the state religion at the beginning of the sixteenth century created such a gulf between them that these similarities were seldom recognized. In some respects, such as their practice of using Christian prisoners of war as infantry, the Safavids followed the Ottoman lead. By contrast, the Mughals drew military forces from Central Asia and Afghanistan and adopted Persian as the language of government but never enjoyed the religious and cultural homogeneity that was a hallmark of Safavid Iran.

## THE MUGHAL EMPIRE, 1526–1761
■ *How did the Mughal Empire combine Muslim and Hindu elements into an effective state?* (page 437)

Dealing with the Hindu majority in their domain was a continuing problem for the Mughal rulers. Akbar took the path of accommodation by appointing Hindu officials and trying to harmonize religious differences. Aurangzeb, his great-grandson, took the opposite path of persecuting Hindus and exalting Islam. Both rulers enjoyed military success against various Indian adversaries, but neither hit on a formula that would permanently bridge the gap between the Muslim ruling minority and the non-Muslim majority. Nevertheless, by comparison with earlier Indian states, and measured by the problems and successes of the contemporary Ottoman and Safavid realms, Mughal rule must be deemed effective.

## THE RUSSIAN EMPIRE, 1500–1762
■ *What were the similarities between the Christian Russian Empire and the Muslim Ottoman, Safavid, and Mughal Empires to the south?* (page 440)

Like the Ottoman, Safavid, and Mughal Empires, Russia gave land grants for military service. This practice reinforced a system of serfdom, akin to slavery, whereby peasants tilled the land for distant landlords. The absolutist rule of Peter the Great was influenced by absolutist philosophies in western Europe but also resembled the form of rule practiced by the shahs and sultans of the Ottoman, Safavid, and Mughal Empires. Despite fiery rhetoric about "Christians" and "infidels," the Russian Empire closely resembled the Muslim empires to its south in tolerating the ethnic and religious diversity that had also been a hallmark of Mongol rule.

## THE MARITIME WORLDS OF ISLAM, 1500–1750
■ *What role does maritime history play in the political and economic life of this period?* (page 442)

Muslim rulers who saw greater opportunities and dangers along imperial land frontiers than at sea saw nothing threatening in the vigorous commercial activity of the non-Muslim merchants in their realms—Jews, Christians, and Hindus—or even European trading companies. To be sure, the Ottoman navy was a formidable military force in the Mediterranean, and Muslim rulers in Morocco, Oman, and Southeast Asia sometimes reacted effectively to European maritime pressure. But the greatest battles were fought on land, and acquisition or loss of territory was taken by Muslims and non-Muslims alike as a more important sign of an empire's strength than its command of maritime trade routes. European domination of maritime trade, however, eventually outpaced the power of the land-based empires even as it incorporated locals in the maritime trade and in the manufacture of goods like Indian cotton for export.

## Key Terms

Ottoman Empire (p. 427)

Suleiman the Magnificent (p. 428)

Janissaries (p. 429)

Tulip Period (p. 432)

Safavid Empire (p. 434)

Shi'ites (p. 434)

Hidden Imam (p. 434)

Shah Abbas I (p. 435)

Mughal Empire (p. 437)

Akbar (p. 438)

*mansabs* (p. 438)

Rajputs (p. 438)

Muscovy (p. 440)

tsar (p. 440)

Siberia (p. 440)

Cossacks (p. 440)

serf (p. 441)

Peter the Great (p. 441)

Acheh Sultanate (p. 443)

Oman (p. 445)

Swahili (p. 445)

Batavia (p. 446)

# East Asia in Global Perspective

© Cengage Learning

In the sixteenth century Ming China became a driving force in the first truly global economy, one that joined together Asia, Europe, the Americas, and, to a lesser extent, Africa. To meet China's skyrocketing demand for silver, European traders imported American silver and in return shipped silk, spices, tea, and other precious goods back to Europe. Christian missionaries joined European merchants as intellectual middlemen in this global interaction.

At century's end, however, from 1592 to 1598, the Imjin War, a conflict surpassed in violence only by the wars of the nineteenth and twentieth century, embroiled Korea, Japan, and China. After attempting to conquer China, the Japanese finally returned to their islands, leaving the weakened Ming to face other foes. Korea, the devastated battleground, did not recover for centuries.

In the seventeenth century, **Manchu** armies from Manchuria on China's northeast frontier succeeded where Japan had failed. The Ming emperor had slashed the government payroll to pay the army defending Beijing (bay-JING). Among those losing his job was an apprentice ironworker named Li Zicheng (lee ZUH-cheng). By 1630 Li Zicheng had found work as a soldier, but he and his fellow soldiers mutinied when the government failed to provide needed supplies. A natural leader, Li soon headed several thousand Chinese rebels, and in 1635 he and other rebel leaders gained control over much of north-central China.

Wedged between the rebels and the Manchu armies to the north, the Ming government tottered. Li Zicheng's forces moved on Beijing, promising an end to Ming abuses and a restoration of peace and prosperity. In April 1644 Li's forces took the city without a fight. The last Ming emperor hanged himself in the palace garden, bringing to an end the dynasty that had ruled China since 1368.

Li's victory was short-lived, however. Preferring the Manchus to an uneducated warlord, the Ming general Wu Sangui and his new northern allies retook Beijing in June. Li's forces scattered, and a year later he was dead, either a suicide or beaten to death by peasants whose food he tried to steal.[1] Now the new masters of China, the Manchus installed their young sovereign as emperor, declared the beginning of a new dynasty called "Qing" (ching), and over the next two decades hunted down the last of the Ming loyalists and heirs to the throne.

The causes of the changes in governance that affected East Asia in this period differed from those that disrupted the empires discussed in the previous chapter, but the impacts were similarly far-reaching. By the late eighteenth century, China, Korea, and Japan were very different than they had been in 1500.

## EAST ASIA AND EUROPE

■ *How did the West and East Asia affect each other commercially and intellectually?*

European merchants who made their way from Southeast Asia to East Asia in the sixteenth century helped build thriving trade networks. Because of changes in the Ming fiscal system that required taxes to be paid in cash, China had developed an urgent need for silver, consuming as much as 30 percent of the world's total silver output. After 1500, the Americas replaced Japan as China's silver supplier (see Chapter 17), and European ships transported the bullion along Asian trade routes, sometimes operating as middlemen and sometimes as privateers and even pirates.

**Trading Companies and Missionaries**

For European merchants, the China trade was second in importance only to the spice trade of Southeast Asia. China's vast population and manufacturing skills drew a steady stream of ships from western Europe, but enthusiasm for trade developed only slowly at the Ming court (see Chapter 12).

[1]Adapted from Jonathan D. Spence, *The Search for Modern China* (New York: W. W. Norton, 1990), 21–25.

**Manchu** Federation of Northeast Asian peoples who founded the Qing Empire.

In late 1513 a Portuguese ship reached China but was not permitted to trade. Four years later a formal Portuguese embassy got bogged down in Chinese protocol and procrastination, and in 1522 China expelled the Portuguese. The Portuguese finally gained permission to trade from a base in Macao (muh-KOW) on the southern coast in 1557. Spain's China trade was conducted from Manila in the Philippines, where silver-laden galleons arrived from South America. For a time, the Spanish and the Dutch both maintained trading outposts on the island of Taiwan, but in 1662 they were forced to concede control to the Qing, who for the first time incorporated Taiwan into China.

By then, the Dutch East India Company (VOC for Vereenigde Oost-Indische Compagnie) (see Chapter 17) had displaced the Portuguese as the paramount European traders in the Indian Ocean and was establishing itself as the main European trader in East Asia. VOC representatives courted official favor in China by acknowledging the moral superiority of the emperor. This meant performing the ritual kowtow (in which the visitor knocked his head on the floor while crawling toward the throne) to the Ming emperor.

Catholic missionaries accompanied the Portuguese and Spanish merchants to East Asia. The Franciscans and Dominicans pioneered a missionary approach that focused on the poor and low-born. The Jesuits' appeal to the intellectual and political elite was more successful in gaining converts. The outstanding Jesuit of late Ming China, Matteo Ricci (mah-TAY-oh REE-chee) (1552–1610), who resided in Beijing from 1601, became expert in the Chinese language and a scholar of the Confucian classics, and under Ricci's leadership, the Jesuits adapted Catholicism to Chinese cultural traditions. Most importantly, they tolerated Confucian ancestor worship—a move that created a fevered controversy with not only Franciscan and Dominican rivals but also the pope. In 1690 the Chinese emperor wrote to Rome supporting the Jesuit position. When the dispute continued, the Chinese emperor ordered the expulsion of all missionaries who refused to sign a certificate accepting his position. The Jesuit presence in China declined in the eighteenth century. Later Chinese emperors would persecute Christians rather than naming them to high office.

## Chinese Influences on Europe

The exchange of information between Chinese and Europeans went both ways. The Jesuits had introduced the Chinese to the latest European science and technology. Jesuits had also helped create maps in the European style as practical guides to newly conquered regions and as symbols of Qing dominance. One Chinese emperor, Kangxi (KAHNG-shee) (r. 1662–1722) (discussed later in this chapter), considered introducing the European calendar, but protests from the Confucian elite caused him to drop the plan. When Kangxi fell ill with malaria in the 1690s, Jesuit medical treatment (in this case, South American quinine) aided his recovery, and Kangxi ordered the creation of illustrated books in Manchu detailing European anatomical and pharmaceutical knowledge. While the Jesuits brought forward new knowledge of anatomy, the Chinese demonstrated an early form of inoculation, called "variolation," that had helped curtail smallpox after the conquest of Beijing. The technique inspired Europeans to develop other vaccines.

Having learned about China from Jesuit writings, European admiration for China created a demand for Chinese things among the wealthy and aspiring middle classes, including cloisonné jewelry, jade, lacquered and jeweled room dividers, painted fans, and carved ivory (which originated in Africa and was finished in China). Silk, porcelain, and tea were avidly sought. Wallpaper, which began as an adaptation of the Chinese practice of covering walls with enormous loose-hanging watercolors or calligraphy scrolls, was by the mid-1700s exported from special workshops throughout China.

Chinese political philosophy impressed Europeans, too. In the late 1770s poems supposedly written by Emperor Qianlong (chee-YEN-loong) (r. 1736–1796) (discussed later in this chapter) were translated into French and disseminated in intellectual circles. In them the Chinese emperors rule as benevolent despots campaigning against superstition and ignorance, curbing aristocratic excesses, and patronizing science and the arts. This image of a practical, secular, compassionate ruler impressed the French thinker Voltaire, who proclaimed that Chinese emperors were model philosopher-kings and advocated such rulership as a protection against the growth of aristocratic privilege.

# Chronology

| | Korea and Japan | China and Central Asia |
|---|---|---|
| **1500** | **1543** First Portuguese contacts<br><br>**1592** Japanese invasion of Korea | **1517** Portuguese embassy to China |
| **1600** | **1603** Tokugawa Shogunate formed<br><br>**1633–1639** Edicts close down trade with Europe | **1601** Matteo Ricci allowed to reside in Beijing<br><br>**1644** Qing conquest of Beijing<br>**1662–1722** Rule of Emperor Kangxi<br>**1689** Treaty of Nerchinsk with Russia<br>**1691** Qing control of Inner Mongolia |
| **1700** | **1702** Trial of the Forty-Seven Ronin<br><br>**1792** Macartney Mission dispatched from Britain | **1736–1796** Rule of Emperor Qianlong |

## Japan and the Europeans

Europeans also traveled to Japan. Within thirty years of the arrival of the first Portuguese in 1543, warlords known as *daimyo* (DIE-mee-oh) were fighting with Western-style firearms, copied and improved upon by Japanese armorers.

The Japanese welcomed but closely regulated traders from Portugal, Spain, the Netherlands, and England. Aside from a brief boom in porcelain exports in the seventeenth century, few Japanese goods went to Europe, and not much from Europe found a market in Japan. The Japanese sold the Dutch copper and silver, which the Dutch exchanged in China for silks that they then resold in Japan. The Japanese, of course, had their own trade with China.

Portuguese and Spanish merchant ships also brought Catholic missionaries. One of the first, Francis Xavier, went to India in the mid-sixteenth century looking for converts and later traveled throughout Southeast and East Asia. He spent two years in Japan, where he died in 1552, hoping to gain entry to China. Japanese responses to Xavier and other Jesuits were mixed. Many ordinary Japanese found the new faith deeply meaningful, but the Japanese elite more often opposed it as disruptive and foreign. By 1580 more than 100,000 Japanese had become Christians, and one daimyo gave Jesuit missionaries the port city of Nagasaki (NAH-guh-SAHK-kee). In 1613 Date Masamune (DAH-tay mah-suh-MOO-nay), the fierce and independent daimyo of northern Honshu (HOHN-shoo), sent his own embassy to the Vatican by way of the Philippines (where there were significant communities of Japanese merchants and pirates) and Mexico City. Some daimyo converts ordered their subjects to become Christians as well.

By the early seventeenth century there were some 300,000 Japanese Christians and even some Japanese priests. However, suspicions about the intentions of the Europeans turned the samurai regime against Christianity. A decree issued in 1614 banned Christianity and charged its adherents with seeking to overthrow true doctrine, change the government, and seize the country. Some missionaries left Japan; others worked underground. The government began persecutions in earnest in 1617, and the beheadings, crucifixions, and forced recantations over the next several decades destroyed almost the entire Christian community.

To keep Christianity from resurfacing, a series of decrees issued between 1633 and 1639 sharply curtailed trade with Europe. Europeans who entered the

> *daimyo* Literally, "great name(s)." Japanese warlords and great landowners, whose armed samurai gave them control of the Japanese islands from the eighth to the later nineteenth century. Under the Tokugawa Shogunate they were subordinated to the imperial government.

Map of the World, 1671 (woodblock print), Japanese School, (17th century)/Private Collection/The Bridgeman Art Library

**Comprehensive Map of the Myriad Nations**  Thanks to the "Dutch studies" scholars and to overseas contacts, many Japanese were well informed about the cultures, technologies, and political systems of various parts of the world. This combination map and ethnographic text of 1671 enthusiastically explores the differences among the many peoples living or traveling in Asia. The map of the Pacific hemisphere has the north pole on the left and the south pole on the extreme right of the drawing.

country illegally faced the death penalty, and Japanese subjects were required to produce certificates from Buddhist temples attesting to their religious

### SECTION REVIEW

- European merchants pursued trade contacts with China despite official resistance, and missionaries worked successfully until the eighteenth century.

- The Qing and Europeans engaged in productive exchanges of ideas, and Chinese producers supplied growing European consumer markets.

- The Japanese engaged in regulated trade with Europeans, but rising suspicions caused the Japanese to restrict foreign contacts.

orthodoxy and loyalty to the regime. However, the exclusion of Europe was not total. A few Dutch were permitted to reside on a small artificial island in Nagasaki's harbor, and a few Japanese were licensed to supply their needs. What these intermediaries learned about European weapons technology, shipbuilding, mathematics and astronomy, anatomy and medicine, and geography was termed "Dutch studies."

Japanese restrictions on the number of Chinese ships that could trade in Japan were harder to enforce. Regional lords in northern and southern Japan not only pursued overseas trade and piracy but also claimed dominion over islands between Japan and Korea and southward toward Taiwan, including present-day Okinawa.

# JAPANESE UNIFICATION AND THE IMJIN WAR

■ *What was the effect of Japanese unification on Korea and China?*

The Imjin War, the largest pre-twentieth-century conflict in East Asian history, had no European involvement. *Imjin* is the Korean term for the year of the water dragon, but Chinese sources refer to this war by many names, including "the Korean campaign." In Japan today, it is called "Hideyoshi's invasions." Seven years long (1592–1598), the war had lasting effects in Korea, facilitated the demise of the Ming dynasty in China, and produced bad feelings between Japan and Korea that have lasted down to the present.

## Japanese Unification

Japan changed in three different dimensions between 1500 and 1800: internal and external military conflicts, political growth and strengthening, and expanded commercial and cultural contacts. Along with its relatively homogeneous population and natural boundaries, Japan's smaller size made political unification more achievable than in the great empire of China.

The Ashikaga Shogunate had weakened after the Onin War (see Chapter 12), opening opportunities for daimyo across Japan to fight for land and influence. The daimyo pledged a loose allegiance to the Japanese emperor residing in the capital city of Kyoto (KYOH-toh) and to the shogun, the hereditary chief of the imperial government and armies. But neither wielded significant political power. Each daimyo had a castle town, a small bureaucracy, and a band of warriors, his *samurai*. Warfare among the different daimyo was common, and in the late 1500s it culminated in a prolonged civil war. The warlord to emerge victorious was Hideyoshi (HEE-duh-YOH-shi), a lowly peasant who had risen through military ranks.

## The Invasion of Korea

In 1592, buoyed with his success in unifying Japan, the supremely confident Hideyoshi sent a 160,000-man force to the Asian mainland. Various reasons are given for his decision to invade: to impress domestic rivals, to keep major daimyo busy fighting outside of Japan so they could not rebel, to push out Christian daimyo (who made up a sizable force in Korea), to dominate East Asian trade networks. However, even as he was consolidating his control over Japan, Hideyoshi was planning to invade Korea in order to conquer China.

Several centuries of peace and court factionalism had left the Koreans ill prepared to handle the battle-tested samurai-led armies. At the beginning of the war, the Koreans did not have large-scale muskets, though they did possess some cannon, and they suffered disastrous defeats. But although daimyo armies were skilled at land-based fighting, the Japanese navy was unprepared for serious combat. The Koreans deployed ingenious covered warships, or "turtle ships," to intercept a portion of the Japanese fleet and won some twenty-three consecutive naval battles. On land, the Koreans called upon China for help.

Regarding Korea as one of its client states, China obliged, eventually sending 100,000 Chinese troops. After Hideyoshi revoked the short peace China had negotiated, Japanese forces invaded again in 1597, employing brutal punitive measures as they advanced through the Korean peninsula. However, many daimyo were now more interested in securing a few provinces in southern Korea than in supporting Hideyoshi's dream of defeating China. Hideyoshi, in poor health, gave an order to withdraw all troops from Korea, which occurred after his death in 1598. It still took many years for Japan to conclude peace with Korea. Formal relations did not resume until 1617.

The invasion devastated Korea. In the turmoil after the Japanese withdrawal, the Korean *yangban* (ruling class of nobles) laid claim to so much taxpaying land that royal revenues plunged. China also suffered dire consequences. Fighting in Korea depleted the Ming coffers at a time when the empire was also battling peoples to the north. The emperor established a new tax to recover revenue, but this led to protests in the provinces. The battles in Manchuria weakened the Chinese garrisons there, permitting Manchu opposition to consolidate. Manchu forces invaded Korea in the 1620s and eventually compelled Korea to become a tributary state. The Manchus would be in possession of Beijing, China's capital, by 1644.

*samurai* Literally "those who serve," the hereditary military elite of the Tokugawa Shogunate.

**Korean Turtle Boats**  This painting shows a fleet of Korean warships under the command of Admiral Yi SunShin, who repelled numerous attacks by the Japanese in the last decade of the sixteenth century. Admiral Yi is celebrated for his use of the "turtle boats," vessels whose covered decks, possibly made of iron plate, are shown in gray.

## SECTION REVIEW

- A weakened Ashikaga Shogunate led to civil war among the daimyo, from which emerged Hideyoshi, who, as supreme warlord, invaded Korea as a step toward conquering China.

- Although Korean naval victories and the dispatch of Chinese armies to Korea blunted the Japanese invasion, Korea suffered long-lasting devastation.

- The war also weakened the Ming, leading to the dynasty's fall.

## TOKUGAWA JAPAN AND CHOSON KOREA, TO 1800

■ *How did Japan respond to unification and domestic peace, and Korea to the ravages of the Imjin War?*

**Japanese Reunification and Economic Growth**

Despite wartime losses, Japan flourished after Hideyoshi's death. Tokugawa Ieyasu (TOH-koo-GAH-wah ee-ay-YAH-soo) (1543–1616) asserted his domination over other daimyo and in 1603 established a new military regime known as the **Tokugawa Shogunate**. More inward-looking, this shogunal family

concentrated on economic revitalization. Trade from the new administrative capital at Edo (EH-doh) (now Tokyo) along the well-maintained road to the imperial capital of Kyoto promoted the development of the Japanese economy and the formation of other trading centers.

Although the Tokugawa Shogunate gave Japan more political unity than the islands had seen in centuries, the regionally based daimyo retained a great deal of power and autonomy. Economic integration proved to be a more important feature of Tokugawa Japan than political centralization. Because the shoguns required the daimyo to visit Edo frequently, good pedestrian roads and maritime transport linked the city to the castle towns on three of Japan's four main islands. Commercial traffic developed along these routes. Lords received their incomes locally in rice, and they paid their followers in rice. Recipients converted much of this rice into cash, a practice that led to the development of rice exchanges at Edo and at Osaka (OH-sah-kah), where merchants speculated in rice prices. By the late seventeenth century Edo was one of the largest cities in the world, with nearly a million inhabitants.

**Tokugawa Shogunate**  The last of the three shogunates of Japan.

The domestic peace of the Tokugawa era forced the warrior class to adapt to the growing bureaucratic needs of the state. As the samurai became better educated and more attuned to the tastes of the civil elite, they became important customers for merchants dealing in silks, *sake* (SAH-kay) (rice wine), fans, porcelain, lacquer ware, books, and moneylending. The state attempted—unsuccessfully—to curb the independence of the merchants when the economic well-being of the samurai was threatened by low rice prices or high interest rates.

The 1600s and 1700s were centuries of high achievement in artisanship. Japanese skills in steel making, lacquer ware, and pottery were joined by excellence in the production of porcelain, thanks in no small part to Korean experts brought back to Japan after Hideyoshi's invasions, whose advanced skills transformed the Japanese pottery industry. In the early 1600s manufacturers and merchants amassed enormous family fortunes. Several of the most important industrial and financial enterprises—for instance, the Mitsui (MIT-sue-ee) companies—had their origins in sake breweries of the early Tokugawa period and then branched out into manufacturing, finance, and transport.

Wealthy merchants weakened the Tokugawa policy of controlling commerce by cultivating close alliances with their regional daimyo and, when possible, with the shogun himself. By the end of the 1700s the merchant families of Tokugawa Japan held the key to future modernization and the development of heavy industry.

## Japanese Elite Decline and Social Crisis

During the 1700s population growth put a great strain on the well-developed lands of central Japan. In more remote provinces, where the lords promoted new settlements and agricultural expansion, the rate of economic growth was significantly greater.

Also troubling the Tokugawa government in the 1700s was the shogunate's inability to stabilize rice prices and halt the economic decline of the samurai. The Tokugawa government realized that the rice brokers could manipulate prices and interest rates to enrich themselves at the expense of the samurai, who had to convert their rice allotments into cash.

Early Tokugawa laws designed to regulate interest and prices were later supplemented by laws requiring moneylenders to forgive samurai debts. But these laws were not always enforced. By the early 1700s many lords and samurai were dependent on the willingness of merchants to provide credit.

The legitimacy of the Tokugawa shoguns rested on their ability to reward and protect the interests of the lords and samurai who had supported their rise to power. Moreover, the Tokugawa government, like the governments of China, Korea, and Vietnam, accepted the Confucian idea that agriculture should be the basis of state wealth and that merchants, who were considered morally weak, should occupy lowly positions in society. Tokugawa decentralization, however, not only failed to hinder but actually stimulated the growth of commercial activities. From the founding of the Tokugawa Shogunate in 1603 until 1800, the economy grew faster than the population. Household amenities and cultural resources that in China appeared only in the cities were common in the Japanese countryside. Despite official disapproval, merchants enjoyed relative freedom and influence in eighteenth-century Japan. They produced a vivid culture of their own, fostering the development of *kabuki* theater, colorful woodblock prints and silk-screened fabrics, and restaurants.

The "Forty-Seven Ronin" (ROH-neen) incident of 1701–1703 exemplified the ideological and social crisis of Japan's transformation from a military to a civil society. A senior minister provoked a young daimyo into drawing his sword at the shogun's court. For this offense the young lord was sentenced to commit *seppuku* (SEP-poo-koo), the ritual suicide of the samurai. His own followers then became *ronin*, "masterless samurai," obliged by the traditional code of the warrior to avenge their deceased master. They broke into the house of the senior minister and killed him and others in his household. Then they withdrew to a temple in Edo and notified the shogun of what they had done out of loyalty to their lord and to avenge his death.

A legal debate ensued. To deny the righteousness of the ronin would be to deny samurai values. But to approve their actions would create social chaos, undermine laws against murder, and deny the shogunal government the right to try cases of samurai violence. The shogun ruled that the ronin had to die but would be permitted to die honorably by committing seppuku. Traditional samurai values had to surrender to the supremacy of law. The purity of purpose of the ronin is still celebrated in Japan, but since then Japanese writers, historians, and teachers have recognized that the self-sacrifice of the ronin for the sake of upholding civil law was necessary.

## Choson Korea

Despite the Imjin War, the Choson dynasty (1392–1910), established after Mongol rule (see Chapter 12), proved to be the longest-lasting state in East Asian history. The dominant influence on Korean culture had long been China, to which Korean rulers generally paid tribute, and the Choson dynasty aligned itself with the Ming. Even though the Korean and Japanese languages are closely related, Korean printing continued to use Chinese characters for its writing system into the fifteenth century.

In many ways the Choson dynasty was a model Confucian state. The government was staffed by men who passed the civil examination system, modeled on the Chinese institution of the same name. But there was one important difference. In theory, if not in practice, anyone could sit for the civil examinations in China, but by the sixteenth century in Choson Korea, one had to be born into the *yangban* (YAHNG-bahn) class to take an examination and work in any position of real influence in government. Only occasionally was social mobility possible for commoners who tested into the military yangban group, a status typically disdained by the civil yangban.

The yangban, literally "two orders," were a hereditary status group who dominated the civil and military examinations, filling nearly all of the official positions in the national and local governments. Unlike the majority, commoner population, they did not have to pay a household tax, nor did they have to serve in the military (unless they were military yangban). As mentioned in the previous section, the yangban increased their landholdings after the Imjin War, making more land tax-exempt. Revenues fell by two-thirds, preventing Choson Korea from recovering quickly from the war.

The yangban also owned most of Korea's slaves, which at one point made up nearly 30 percent of the population. In addition to privately owned slaves,

**SECTION REVIEW**

- After Hideyoshi's death, the Tokugawa Shogunate unified Japan and moved the capital to Edo (Tokyo).
- Economic growth nourished a new merchant-class culture in Japan.
- Under economic and social pressures, the position of the samurai deteriorated.
- Choson Korea survived Hideyoshi's invasion and modeled itself on the Confucian government of Ming China.
- However, the Korean noble class paid no taxes and laid claim to more land, stifling recovery from wartime devastation.

local governments maintained slaves for a variety of clerical and labor jobs. Even Buddhist temples owned slaves. The slave population dropped to about 10 percent in the eighteenth century, when runaway slaves increased and the poor economy meant that most yangban simply hired poor commoners to work in agriculture.

# FROM MING TO QING

■ *How did China deal with military and political challenges both inside and outside its borders?*

The internal and external forces at work in China were different from those in Japan and operated on a much larger scale, but they led in similar directions. By 1800 China had a greatly enhanced empire, an expanding economy, and growing doubts about the importance of European trade and Christianity.

## Ming Economic Growth, 1500–1644

The economic and cultural achievements of the early Ming Empire (see Chapter 12) continued during the 1500s. But this productive period was followed by many decades of political weakness, warfare, and rural woes until a new dynasty, the Qing from Manchuria, guided China back to peace and prosperity.

European accounts from the early sixteenth century express astonishment at the power, exquisite manufactures, and vast population of the Ming. Ming cities had long been culturally and commercially vibrant (see Material Culture: Four-Wheeled

Vehicles). Many large landowners and absentee landlords lived in town, as did officials, artists, and rich merchants who had purchased ranks or prepared their sons for the examinations. The elite classes had created a brilliant culture in which novels, operas, poetry, porcelain, and painting were closely interwoven. Catering to these urban elites were small businesses that prospered through printing, tailoring, running restaurants, or selling paper, ink, ink-stones, and writing brushes. The imperial government operated factories for the production of ceramics and silks, and enormous government complexes at Jingdezhen and elsewhere invented assembly-line techniques and produced large quantities of high-quality ceramics for sale in China and abroad.

Despite these achievements, serious problems developed that left the Ming Empire economically and politically exhausted. There is evidence that the climate changes known as the Little Ice Age in seventeenth-century Europe affected the climate in China as well (see Issues in World History: The Little Ice Age on page 466). Annual temperatures dropped, reached a low point about 1645, and remained low until the early 1700s. The resulting agricultural distress and famine fueled large uprisings that sped the end of the Ming Empire.

The rapid urban growth and business speculation that were part of the burgeoning trading economy also produced problems. Some provinces suffered from price inflation caused by the flood of silver. In contrast to the growing involvement of European governments in promoting economic growth, the Ming government pursued some policies that hindered growth. Ming governments persisted, despite earlier failed experiments, in issuing new paper money and copper coinage, even after silver had won the approval of the markets. Corruption compounded government problems. Disorder and inefficiency came to plague the imperial factories, touching off strikes in the late sixteenth and seventeenth centuries. During a labor protest at Jingdezhen in 1601, workers threw themselves into the kilns to protest working conditions.

Yet the urban and industrial sectors of later Ming society fared much better than the agricultural sector. Despite knowledge of new African and American crops gained from European traders, farmers were slow to change their ways. Neither the rice-growing regions in southern China nor the wheat-growing regions in northern China experienced a meaningful increase in productivity under the later Ming. After 1500 economic depression in the countryside, combined with recurring epidemics in central and southern China, kept rural population growth in check.

## Ming Collapse and the Rise of the Qing

Environmental, economic, and administrative problems aside, the primary reasons for the fall of the Ming Empire were internal rebellion and threats on the borders. Ming frontiers had long been under pressure from the powerful Mongol federations of the north and west. In the late 1500s large numbers of Mongols were unified by their devotion to the Dalai Lama (DAH-lie LAH-mah), or universal teacher of Tibetan Buddhism. Building on this spiritual unity, a brilliant leader named Galdan restored Mongolia as a regional military power around 1600. At the same time, the Manchus, an agricultural people who controlled the region north of Korea, grew stronger in the northeast.

In the southwest, native peoples repeatedly resisted the immigration of Chinese farmers. Pirates based in Okinawa and Taiwan, many of them Japanese, frequently looted the southeast coast. Ming military resources, concentrated against the Mongols and the Manchus in the north, could not be deployed to defend the coasts. As a result, many southern Chinese migrated to Southeast Asia to profit from the sea-trading networks of the Indian Ocean.

The Imjin War had prompted the Ming to seek the assistance of Manchu troops that they were then unable to restrain. With the rebel leader Li Zicheng in possession of Beijing (see the beginning of this chapter) and the emperor dead by his own hand, a Ming general joined forces with the Manchu leaders in the summer of 1644. Instead of restoring the Ming, however, the Manchus claimed China for their own and began a forty-year conquest of the remaining Ming territories, as well as Taiwan and parts of Mongolia and Central Asia (see Map 19.1).

**Qing Empire** Empire established in China by Manchus who overthrew the Ming Empire in 1644. At various times the Qing also controlled Manchuria, Mongolia, Turkestan, and Tibet. The last Qing emperor was overthrown in 1911.

A Manchu family headed the new **Qing Empire**, and Manchu generals commanded the military forces. But Manchus made up a very small portion of the population. Most Qing officials, soldiers, merchants, and farmers were ethnic Chinese. Like other successful invaders of China, the Qing soon adopted Chinese institutions and policies.

**Emperor Kangxi**   The seventeenth and eighteenth centuries—particularly the reigns of the **Kangxi** (KAHNG-shee) (r. 1662–1722) and Qianlong (chee-YEN-loong) (r. 1736–1796) emperors—saw renewed economic, military, and cultural achievement in China. Roads and waterworks were repaired, transit taxes lowered, rents and interest rates cut, and incentives established for resettling areas devastated by peasant rebellions. Foreign trade was encouraged. Vietnam, Burma, and Nepal sent embassies to the Qing tribute court and carried the latest Chinese fashions back home. Overland routes from Korea to Central Asia revived.

> **Kangxi**  Qing emperor (r. 1662–1722). He oversaw the greatest expansion of the Qing Empire.

**Map 19.1   The Qing Empire, 1644–1783**   The Qing Empire began in Manchuria and captured north China in 1644. Between 1644 and 1783 the Qing conquered all the former Ming territories and added Taiwan, the lower Amur River basin, Inner Mongolia, eastern Turkestan, and Tibet. The resulting state was more than twice the size of the Ming Empire.
© Cengage Learning

The Manchu aristocrats who led the conquest of Beijing and north China dominated the first Qing emperor and served as regents for his young son, who was declared emperor in 1662. This child-emperor, Kangxi, sparred politically with the regents until 1669, when at age sixteen he executed the chief regent and thereby gained real control of the government. An intellectual prodigy who had mastered classical Chinese, Manchu, and Mongolian and memorized the Chinese classics, Kangxi guided imperial expansion and maintained stability until his death in 1722.

### Contact with Russia

In the north, the Qing rulers feared an alliance between Galdan's Mongol state and the expanding Russian presence along the **Amur** (AH-moor) **River**. In the 1680s Qing forces attacked the wooden forts built by hardy Russian scouts on the river's northern bank. Neither empire sent large forces into the Amur territories, so the contest was partly a struggle for the goodwill of the local peoples. The Qing emperor emphasized the importance of treading lightly in the struggle:

> Upon reaching the lands of the Evenks and the Dagurs you will send to announce that you have come to hunt deer. Meanwhile, keep a careful record of the distance and go, while hunting, along the northern bank of the Amur until you come by the shortest route to the town of Russian settlement at Albazin. Thoroughly reconnoiter its location and situation. I don't think the Russians will take a chance on attacking you. If they offer you food, accept it and show your gratitude. If they do attack you, don't fight back. In that case, lead your people and withdraw into our own territories.[2]

Qing forces twice attacked Albazin. The Qing were worried about Russian alliances with other frontier peoples, while Russia wished to protect its access to the furs, timber, and metals concentrated in Siberia and Manchuria (see Chapter 18). The Qing and Russians were also rivals for control of northern Asia's Pacific coast. Seeing little benefit in continued conflict, in 1689 the two empires negotiated the Treaty of Nerchinsk, using Jesuit missionaries as interpreters. The treaty fixed the border along the Amur River and regulated trade across it. Although this was a thinly settled area, the treaty proved important, and the frontier it demarcated has long endured.

Wu Chingteng/Xinhua/Photoshot/Newscom

**Emperor Kangxi**  In a portrait from about 1690, the young Manchu ruler is portrayed as a refined scholar in the Confucian tradition. He was a scholar and had great intellectual curiosity, but this portrait would not suggest that he was also capable of leading troops in battle.

---

[2]Adapted from G. V. Melikhov, "Manzhou Penetration into the Basin of the Upper Amur in the 1680s," in *Manzhou Rule in China*, ed. S. L. Tikhvinshii (Moscow: Progress Publishers, 1983).

**Amur River**  This river valley was a contested frontier between northern China and eastern Russia until the settlement arranged in the Treaty of Nerchinsk (1689).

# Material Culture

## Four-Wheeled Vehicles

**M**ost modern motor transport is based on the principle of the four-wheeled vehicle. Yet prior to the spread of European technologies and tastes in the age of imperialism, four-wheeled vehicles were rarely seen outside of Europe. The wheeled transport of India, East Asia, and Southeast Asia was almost exclusively of the two-wheeled cart variety, though even carts were rare in Japan.

Economically, the two-wheeled cart was generally superior to the four-wheeled wagon throughout the era of animal-drawn transport. The power a team of oxen or horses could exert did not change with the number of wheels. But each added axle, that is, each additional pair of wheels, increased the friction the animals had to overcome in pulling and also added weight to the vehicle. So even though a wagon might have more space than a cart, the weight that could be loaded was invariably smaller.

Four-wheeled vehicles had the additional disadvantage of being difficult to steer. Paved roads were rare, and rutted dirt tracks made for a bumpy ride unless the wheels were of great diameter. Three feet (1 meter) was a common size. However, such large wheels could not turn very far when the front axle pivoted because they hit the frame of the wagon, and raising the wagon-bed more than 3 feet above the ground made the vehicle unstable. Limited to a turning radius of only a few degrees, or more often being constrained by a nonpivoting axle, four-wheeled vehicles could not readily operate in towns and other places where sharp turns were required. Yet making the front wheels smaller so they could turn underneath the wagon-bed made the vehicle difficult to use on rough roads.

Despite these limitations, archaeological evidence shows that both four-wheeled and two-wheeled vehicles were used in Europe, Central Asia, and the Middle East from the fourth millennium B.C.E. onward. By the later days of the Roman Empire, the two-wheeled chariot, formerly the vehicle of warriors, had disappeared, and noblemen had taken to riding horseback. Eventually wagons disappeared in North Africa and the Middle East, but they continued to be used in Europe.

The reasons for European persistence in an inefficient mode of transport are not clear. However, ancient and medieval images suggest that four-wheeled wagons were used primarily for passengers from the upper classes. More specifically, many images show groups of female passengers. Wagons had advantages as conveyances for elite

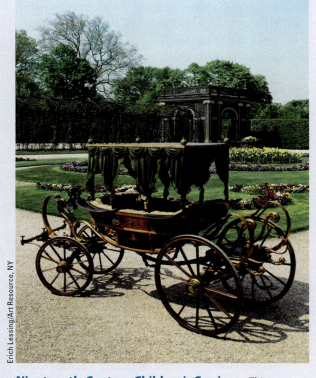

Erich Lessing/Art Resource, NY

**Nineteenth-Century Children's Carriage** *This nineteenth-century children's carriage shows the essential changes that defined the coach. The small front wheels turn under the body of the carriage when the front axle pivots in the center. The back wheels are much larger. And the passenger compartment is suspended on springs that run from the front to the back of the vehicle.*

women. They could easily be enclosed for privacy, and they could hold a noblewoman and her female attendants, thus eliminating the dangers of traveling with only a male driver.

Increased comfort probably played a role in a series of technological improvements that began around the thirteenth century. The word *coach*, of Hungarian origin, signaled the new designs. Pivoting front axles became common, while better paving, particularly in towns, accommodated the required smaller wheels. To reduce jolting, the passenger cabin was first suspended on chains or leather straps and later on springs. Efficient harnessing techniques that had first appeared centuries earlier made possible larger teams of animals, heavier vehicles, and faster speeds. And brakes were developed to help manage the heavier loads.

Coach and carriage designs, particularly associated with the upper classes, became more sophisticated over the following centuries. Charles Darwin's grandfather, Erasmus Darwin, was the first to design a steering system of the type used today on automobiles in which each front wheel turns separately while the axle remains fixed. The four-wheeled coach became the basis for steam locomotives and railway carriages, and eventually for the automobile. Other parts of the world adopted European transport designs as symbols of modernity.

However, the question remains: Why did the Europeans stick with inefficient four-wheeled wagons for over four thousand years when other parts of the world opted exclusively for the two-wheeled alternative? It is unlikely that providing a private traveling compartment for groups of elite women was the sole reason. But the fact that such traveling accommodations became available may offer a technological clue as to why upper-class women in the Middle East, China, India, and other non-European lands were so often prohibited from leaving the house whereas European women enjoyed relatively greater freedom of movement.

## QUESTIONS FOR ANALYSIS

1. Why did most societies prefer two-wheeled transportation?
2. How do different societies solve the problem of providing privacy and safety to women who are traveling?
3. Which is more important in the technological development of transport vehicles, social status or gender?

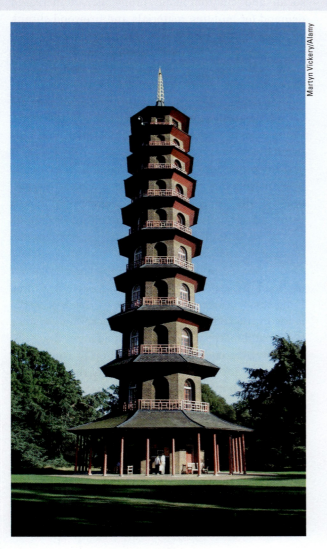

Martyn Vickery/Alamy

**Great Pagoda at Kew Gardens** A testament to Europeans' fascination with Chinese culture is the towering Pagoda at the Royal Botanic Gardens in London. Completed in 1762, it was designed by Sir William Chambers as the principal ornament in the pleasure grounds of the White House at Kew, residence of Augusta, the mother of King George III.

The next step was to settle the Mongolian frontier. Kangxi personally led troops in the great campaigns that defeated Galdan and brought Inner Mongolia under Qing control by 1691.

### Tea and Diplomacy

To maintain control over trade, facilitate tax collection, and suppress piracy, the Qing permitted only one market point for each foreign sector. Thus Europeans could trade only at Canton.

This system worked well enough until the late 1700s, when Britain became worried about its massive trade deficit with China. From bases in India and Singapore, British traders moved eastward and by the early 1700s dominated European trading in Canton, displacing the Dutch. The directors of the East India Company (EIC) anticipated limitless profits from China's gigantic markets and advanced technologies.

In medieval times, tea from China, carried overland to Russia, Central Asia, and the Middle East, had become a prized import. Consumers knew it by its northern Chinese name, *cha*—as did the Portuguese.

Other western Europeans acquired tea from the sea routes and with it the name used in the Fujian province of coastal China and Taiwan: *te*. In much of Europe, tea competed with chocolate and coffee as a fashionable drink by the mid-1600s.

British tea importers accumulated great fortunes. However, the Qing Empire took payment in silver and rarely bought anything from Britain. With domestic revenues declining in the later 1700s, the Qing government needed the silver and was disinclined to loosen import restrictions. To make matters worse, the East India Company had managed its worldwide holdings badly. As it teetered on bankruptcy, its attempts to manipulate Parliament became increasingly intrusive. In 1792 the British government dispatched Lord George Macartney, a well-connected peer with practical experience in Russia and India, to China. Staffed by scientists, artists, and translators as well as guards and diplomats, the **Macartney mission** showed Britain's great interest in the Qing Empire as well as the EIC's desire to revise the trade system.

To fit Chinese traditions, Macartney portrayed himself as a "tribute emissary" come to salute the Qianlong emperor's eightieth birthday. However, he refused to perform the kowtow, though he did agree to bow on one knee as he would to King George III. The Qianlong emperor received Macartney courteously in September 1793 but refused to alter the Canton trading system, open new ports of trade, or allow the British to establish a permanent mission in Beijing. The emperor sent a letter to King George explaining that China had no need to increase its foreign trade, had no use for Britain's ingenious devices and manufactures, and set no value on closer diplomatic ties.

Dutch, French, and Russian missions also failed. European frustration mounted and admiration for China faded. The Qing court would not communicate with foreign envoys or observe the simplest rules of the European diplomatic system. In Macartney's view, China was like a venerable old warship, well maintained and splendid to look at, but obsolete and no longer up to the task.

## Population Growth and Environmental Stress

The Chinese who escorted Macartney and his entourage in 1792–1793 took them through China's prosperous cities and productive farmland. They did not see the economic and environmental decline that had set in during the last decades of the 1700s.

Population growth—a tripling in size since 1500—had intensified demand for food and for more intensive agriculture. With an estimated 350 million people in the late 1700s, China had twice the population of all of Europe. Despite efficient farming and the gradual adoption of New World crops like corn and sweet potatoes, population pressure touched off social and environmental problems. As increased demand for building materials and firewood shrank woodlands, the deforestation, in turn, accelerated wind and water erosion and increased flooding. Dams and dikes were not maintained, and silted-up river channels were not dredged. By the end of the eighteenth century parts of the thousand-year-old Grand Canal linking the rivers of north and south China were nearly unusable, and the towns that bordered it were starved for commerce.

Some interior districts responded to this misery by increasing their output of export goods like tea, cotton, and silk. Some peasants sought seasonal jobs in better-off agricultural areas or worked in low-status jobs as barge pullers, charcoal burners, or night soil (human waste) carriers. Begging, prostitution, and theft increased in the cities, and rebellions broke out in flood-ravaged central and southwestern China. Indigenous peoples concentrated in the less fertile lands in the south and in the northern and western borderlands of the empire often joined in revolts.

The Qing government was not up to controlling its vast empire. It was twice the size of the Ming geographically, but it employed about the same number of officials. The government's dependence on working

**Macartney mission** The unsuccessful attempt by the British Empire to establish diplomatic relations with the Qing Empire.

alliances with local elites had led to widespread corruption and shrinking government revenues. The Qing's spectacular rise had ended, and decline had set in.

## CONCLUSION

It would be a mistake to think of early modern East Asia as three strictly defined countries filled with people who invariably acted on behalf of their homelands in trade or warfare. During the Imjin War, some Japanese, tired of fighting in Korea, decided to join the Ming military and were promoted to high posts by the Chinese. Similarly, some Chinese troops remained in Korea, married local women, and became part of local Korean communities.

Trade and warfare also presented opportunities for groups of people who did not identify with any one country. As a case in point, the Ming-Qing transition and growth in sea trade spurred an increase in piracy during the seventeenth century. The Zheng family dominated piracy in East Asia, defeated the Dutch bases in Taiwan, and eventually worked for the Ming regime to battle the Manchus. The founder of this pirate family, Zheng Zhilong, worked alongside the Dutch and the Portuguese. He was baptized a Catholic and given the name Nicholas Iquan. He married a Japanese woman, and their son, Zheng Chenggong, continued to expand the Zheng enterprise. He is better known as Koxinga, the Portuguese pronunciation for an official title given to him by the Ming. Zheng even pursued state-building activities

such as establishing an office to collect tax and regulating trade in the South China Sea.

Already a vast empire under the Ming, China doubled in size under the Qing, mostly through westward expansion into less densely populated areas. China was land based, just like the Russian, Safavid, Ottoman, and Mughal Empires, with the strengths and problems of administrative control and tax collection that size entailed. The expansion of China incorporated not just new lands but also new peoples. Chinese society had long been diverse, and its geographical, occupational, linguistic, and religious differences grew as the Qing expanded. China had also long used Confucian models, imperial customs, and a common system of writing to transcend such differences and to assimilate elites.

Japan was different. Though nominally headed by an emperor, real power lay with the successive shoguns. However, Japan lacked a centralizing, common political philosophy like China's Confucianism, vast conquered territories, and ethnic diversity. Tokugawa Japan was similar in size and population to France, the most powerful state of western Europe, but its political system was much more decentralized. Japan's efforts to add colonies on the East Asian mainland had failed.

By the late eighteenth century, the weaknesses in China and Japan were becoming more evident and would ultimately make these countries vulnerable to Western aggression. China had once led the world in military innovation, including the first uses of gunpowder, but Chinese armies continued to depend on superior numbers and tactics for their success, rather than on new technology. Infantrymen armed with guns served alongside others armed with bows and arrows, swords, and spears.

The military forces of Japan underwent more innovative changes than those of China and Korea, in part through Western contacts. In the course of its sixteenth-century wars of unification, Japan produced its own gunpowder revolution but thereafter lacked the motivation and the means to stay abreast of the world's most advanced military technology. The samurai preferred swords.

Finally, neither China nor Japan developed navies commensurate with their size and coastlines. Korea had a small but effective navy during the Imjin War, but it could not match China's in strength or size. China's defenses against pirates and other sea invaders were left to the small war junks of its maritime provinces. Japan's naval capacity was similarly decentralized.

# CHAPTER REVIEW

## EAST ASIA AND EUROPE
■ *How did the West and East Asia affect each other commercially and intellectually?* (page 449)

Missionaries and merchants brought European culture to East Asia, and information about Asia traveled back to an interested Europe. Europeans demanded Chinese silk, porcelain, and tea, as well as jewelry, jade, lacquered screens, painted fans, and wallpaper. European political philosophy was influenced by the idea of the Confucian emperor as a philosopher-king. Ideas about weaponry, medicine and anatomy, mapmaking, and astronomy attracted Asian elites. Silver flowed from the new world via European merchant ships in exchange for Chinese consumer goods, but suspicions arose on both sides. European merchants were tightly regulated, and European adaptations to Asian culture erupted in controversy when the Franciscans and Dominicans opposed Jesuit acceptance of ancestor worship. Ultimately Christians were expelled from China and Japan and were later persecuted.

## JAPANESE UNIFICATION AND THE IMJIN WAR
■ *What was the effect of Japanese unification on Korea and China?* (page 453)

After a period of daimyo rivalry and civil war, Hideyoshi emerged victorious. The unification of Japan had seasoned his war forces and inflated his ambitions, and he set his sights on China. Korea became the battleground for the bloody Imjin War. A superior naval strategy helped Korea defend itself against the Japanese, but the experienced Japanese land forces devastated the population. China, which regarded Korea as a tribute state, responded to appeals for help. Hideyoshi never reached China, and the military stalemate eventually caused Japan to withdraw, but only after the Japanese had laid waste to Korea's infrastructure and agriculture. The war also depleted Ming resources, and new taxes for recovery

created internal unrest. A depleted military left vulnerable borders elsewhere. After setting out to conquer the Ming, Hideyoshi facilitated its fall, and other foes would emerge as China's next rulers.

## TOKUGAWA JAPAN AND CHOSON KOREA, TO 1800
■ *How did Japan respond to unification and domestic peace, and Korea to the ravages of the Imjin War?* (page 454)

The unification of Japan under the Tokugawa Shogunate ushered in a long period of relative peace. Commerce and craft industries flourished with sake brewing becoming a particularly profitable business. Merchants as a class commanded little respect, but their ability to manipulate interest rates and rice prices worsened the economic status of the samurai, the military elite.

In the aftermath of the Imjin War, Korean nobles strengthened their position at the expense of the country's recovery. Although aligned with Chinese Confucian culture, Korea's civil service examinations were open only to a hereditary noble class. Nobles filled all government posts and were exempt from taxes and military service. In addition, they were able to expand their landholdings after the war, making more land tax-exempt. At one point, 30 percent of the population were slaves. Royal revenues needed to rebuild fell by an estimated two-thirds.

## FROM MING TO QING
■ *How did China deal with military and political challenges both inside and outside its borders?* (page 456)

China's history illustrates a complex interplay of internal and external forces. During the final days of the Ming dynasty, China suffered from internal rebellions caused by deteriorating economic conditions, to which the Ming responded ineffectively. When Japan invaded, the Ming sought help from the Manchus, who then turned on them and established the Qing Empire. The Qing's settlement of the Amur frontier with Russia illustrates how diplomacy and compromise could serve mutual interests. Finally, the Chinese added new European customers to already extensive internal and external markets and developed both positive and problematic cultural relations with the Jesuits and some other Europeans. From a Chinese perspective, European contacts could be useful but were neither essential nor of great importance.

## Key Terms

Manchu (p. 449)

*daimyo* (p. 451)

*samurai* (p. 453)

Tokugawa Shogunate (p. 454)

Qing Empire (p. 457)

Kangxi (p. 458)

Amur River (p. 459)

Macartney mission (p. 462)

# The Little Ice Age

A giant volcanic eruption in the Peruvian Andes in 1600 affected the weather in many parts of the world for several years. When volcanic ash from the eruption of Mount Huanyaputina (hoo-AHN-yah-poo-TEE-nuh) shot into the upper atmosphere and spread around the world, it screened out sunlight. As a result, the summer of 1601 was the coldest in two hundred years in the Northern Hemisphere.

Archaeologist Brian Fagan has pointed out that Mount Huanyaputina's chilling effects were a spectacular event in a much longer pattern of climate change that has been called the Little Ice Age.[1] Although global climate had been cooling since the late 1200s, in the northern temperate regions the 1590s had been exceptionally cold. Temperatures remained cooler than normal throughout the seventeenth century.

The most detailed information on the Little Ice Age comes from Europe. Glaciers in the Alps grew much larger. Trade became difficult when rivers and canals that had once been navigable in winter froze solid from bank to bank. In the coldest years, the growing season in some places was as much as two months shorter than normal. Unexpectedly late frosts withered the tender shoots of newly planted crops in spring. Wheat and barley ripened more slowly during cooler summers and were often damaged by early fall frosts.

People could survive a smaller-than-average harvest in one year by drawing on food reserves, but when cold weather damaged crops in two or more successive years, the consequences were devastating. Deaths due to malnutrition and cold increased sharply when summer temperatures in northern Europe registered 2.7°F (1.5°C) lower than average in 1674 and 1675 and again in 1694 and 1695. The cold spell of 1694 and 1695 caused a famine in Finland that carried off a quarter to a third of the population.

At the time people had no idea what was causing the unusual cold of the Little Ice Age. Advances in climate history make it clear that the cause was not a single terrestrial event such as the eruption of Mount Huanyaputina. Nor was the Little Ice Age the product of human actions, unlike some climate changes such as today's global warming.

Ultimately, the earth's weather is governed by the sun. In the seventeenth century astronomers in Europe reported seeing fewer sunspots, dark spots on the sun's surface that are indicative of solar activity and thus the sun's warming power. Diminished activity in the sun was primarily responsible for the Little Ice Age.

If the sun was the root cause, the effects of global cooling should not have been confined to northern Europe. Although contemporary accounts are much scarcer in other parts of the world, there is evidence of climate changes around the world in this period. Observations of sunspots in China, Korea, and Japan drop to zero between 1639 and 1700. China experienced unusually cool weather in the seventeenth century, but the warfare and disruption accompanying the fall of the Ming and the rise of the Qing probably were much more to blame for the famines and rural distress of that period.

By itself, a relatively slight decrease in average annual temperature would not have a significant effect on human life outside the northern temperate areas. However, evidence suggests that there was also a significant rise in humidity in this period in other parts of the world. Ice cores drilled into ancient glaciers in the Arctic and Antarctic show increased snowfall. Information compiled by historian James L. A. Webb, Jr., shows that lands south of the Sahara received more rainfall between 1550 and 1750 than they had during the previous era.[2] Increased rainfall would have been favorable for pastoral people, whose herds found new pasture in what had once been desert, and for the farmers farther south whose crops got more rain.

In the eighteenth century the sun's activity began to return to normal. Rising temperatures led to milder winters and better harvests in northern Eurasia. Falling rainfall allowed the Sahara to advance southward, forcing the agricultural frontier to retreat.

---

[1] Brian Fagan, *The Littlest Ice Age: How Climate Made History, 1300–1850* (New York: Basic Books, 2000).

[2] James L. A. Webb, Jr., *Desert Frontier: Ecological Change Along the Western Sahel, 1600–1850* (Madison: University of Wisconsin Press, 1995).

# Part Six

# Revolutions Reshape the World, 1750–1870

ARCTIC OCEAN

Canada
**NORTH AMERICA**
United States
Mexico

Britain
**EUROPE**
France
Spain
Russian Empire
**ASIA**
Ottoman Empire
Algeria
Egypt
**MIDDLE EAST**
China
Japan
India
Burma

NORTH ATLANTIC OCEAN

**AFRICA**
Sokoto Caliphate
Liberia
Ceylon

PACIFIC OCEAN

PACIFIC OCEAN

Colombia
Brazil
**SOUTH AMERICA**
Chile

SOUTH ATLANTIC OCEAN

Cape Colony
Zulu Kingdom

INDIAN OCEAN

**AUSTRALIA**

New Zealand

0  1000 2000 3000 Km.
0  1000  2000  3000 Mi.

© Cengage Learning

| | 1750 | 1775 | 1800 | |
|---|---|---|---|---|
| **AMERICAS** | **1754–1763** French and Indian War | • **1776** U.S. Declaration of Independence • **1789** U.S. Constitution ratified | • **1791** Slaves revolt in Haiti | • **1803** Louisiana Purchase • **1809–1825** Wars for independence in Spanish America |
| **EUROPE** | • **ca. 1750** Industrial Revolution begins in Britain • **1756–1763** Seven Years War | **1789–1799** French Revolution | **1814–1815** Congress of Vienna • **1799–1815** Rule of Napoleon in France | |
| **AFRICA** | **1750–1800** Growing slave trade reduces population | • **1795** Britain takes Cape Colony | • **1809** Sokoto Caliphate founded Shaka founds Zulu kingdom **1818** • | |
| **MIDDLE EAST** | **1769–1772** High point of restored Mamluk influence in Egypt | **1789–1807** Reign of Ottoman sultan Selim III • **1798** Napoleon invades Egypt Muhammad Ali founds dynasty in Egypt **1805** • | | |
| **ASIA AND OCEANIA** | • **1755** Qing conquest of Turkestan **1769–1778** Captain Cook's exploration of Australia, New Zealand • **1765** East India Company rule of Bengal begins | **1796–1804** White Lotus Rebellion in China | East India Company creates Bombay presidency **1818** | |

Between 1750 and 1870, nearly every part of the world experienced dramatic political, economic, and social change. The beginnings of industrialization, the American, French, and Haitian Revolutions, as well as the struggles for independence in Latin America, transformed political and economic life. European nations expanded into Africa, Asia, and the Middle East while Russia and the United States acquired vast new territories.

The Industrial Revolution introduced new technologies and patterns of work that made these societies wealthier and militarily more powerful. Western intellectual life became more secular. The Atlantic slave trade and later slavery itself were abolished, and the first efforts to improve the status of women were made.

The Industrial Revolution led to a new wave of imperialism. France conquered Algeria, and Great Britain expanded its colonial rule in India and established colonies in Australia and New Zealand. European political and economic influence also expanded in Africa and Asia. The Ottoman Empire and the Qing Empire met this challenge by implementing reform programs that preserved traditional structures while adopting elements of Western technology and organization. Though lagging behind western Europe in transforming its economy and political institutions, Russia attempted modernization efforts, including the abolition of serfdom.

The economic, political, and social revolutions that began in the mid-eighteenth century shook the foundations of European culture and led to the expansion of Western power around the globe. Some of the nations of Asia, Africa, and Latin America reformed and strengthened their own institutions and economies, while others pushed for more radical change. After 1870 Western imperialism became more aggressive, and few parts of the world were able to resist it.

| 1825 | 1850 | 1875 |
|---|---|---|
| • **1822** Independence of Brazil | • **1848** Women's Rights Convention in Seneca Falls, New York | **1862–1867** French invasion of Mexico<br>**1861–1865** U.S. Civil War<br>• **1867** Creation of Dominion of Canada |
| • **1830** Revolutions of 1830<br>• **1834** Abolition of slavery in British Empire | **1852–1870** Rule of Napoleon III in France<br>• **1848** Revolutions of 1848 • **1861** Russia abolishes serfdom<br>**1853–1856** Crimean War | |
| • **1821** Republic of Liberia founded | **1836–1839** Afrikaners' Great Trek | • **1869** Jaja founds Opobo |
| • **1826** Ottoman ruler Mahmud II dissolves Janissary corps<br>• **1839** Ottoman ruler Abdul Mejid launches Tanzimat reforms | | • **1860s** Beginning of Young Turk movement<br>• **1869** Suez Canal opens |
| • **1826** East India Company annexes Assam, northern Burma **1839–1842** Opium War<br>**1829–1864** Russia completes conquest of Central Asia | **1850–1864** Taiping Rebellion in China<br>**1857–1858** Sepoy Rebellion in India | |

# Industrial Revolution and Global Impact

© Cengage Learning

Manchester was just a small town in northern England in the early eighteenth century. A hundred years later, it had turned into the fastest-growing city in history. To contemporaries, it was both a marvel and a horror. Prosperous cotton mills were interspersed with workers' housing, built as cheaply as possible. The economist Nassau Senior described these workers' quarters:

> But when I went through their habitations . . . my only wonder was that tolerable health could be maintained by the inmates of such houses. These towns . . . have been erected by small speculators with an utter disregard to everything except immediate profit. . . . Not a house in this street escaped cholera. . . . the streets are unpaved, with a dunghill or a pond in the middle; the houses built back to back, without ventilation or drainage, and whole families occupy each a corner of a cellar or of a garret.[1]

Not everyone deplored the living conditions in the new industrial city. Friedrich Engels, both a factory owner and critic of capitalism, recounted a meeting with a well-to-do citizen:

> One day I walked with one of these middle-class gentlemen into Manchester. I spoke to him about the disgraceful unhealthy slums and drew his attention to the disgusting condition of that part of the town in which the factory workers lived. I declared that I had never seen so badly built a town in my life. He listened patiently and at the corner of the street at which we parted company, he remarked: "And yet there is a great deal of money made here. Good morning, Sir!"[2]

[1]Nassau W. Senior, *Letters on the Factory Act, as it affects the cotton manufacture, addressed to the Right Honourable, the President of the Board of Trade*, 2d ed. (London: Fellows, 1844), 20.

[2]Friedrich Engels, *Condition of the Working Class in England*, trans. and ed. by W. O. Henderson and W. H. Chaloner (Oxford: Blackwell, 1958), 312.

Manchester's rise as a large, industrial city was a result of what historians call the **Industrial Revolution**, the most profound transformation in human life since the beginnings of agriculture. This revolution involved dramatic innovations in manufacturing, mining, transportation, and communications and equally rapid changes in society and commerce. New relationships between social groups created an environment that was conducive to technical innovation and economic growth. The introduction of new technologies and new social and economic arrangements allowed the industrializing countries—first Britain, then western Europe and the United States—to unleash massive increases in production and productivity, exploit the world's natural resources as never before, and transform the environment and human life in unprecedented ways.

Industrialization widened the gap between rich and poor. Those who owned and controlled the innovations amassed wealth and power and lived in spectacular luxury. The middle class of industrializing nations grew rapidly, exercising increased influence in politics and culture. But workers, including children, worked long hours in dangerous factories and lived crowded together in unsanitary tenements.

The effect of the Industrial Revolution around the world was also very uneven. The first countries to industrialize grew rich and powerful, facilitating a second great wave of European imperialism in the nineteenth century. In Egypt and India, the economic and military power of Europe stifled the tentative beginnings of industrialization. The disparity between the industrial and the developing countries that exists today has its origins in the early nineteenth century.

**Industrial Revolution** The transformation of the economy, the environment, and living conditions, occurring first in England in the eighteenth century, that resulted from the use of steam engines, the mechanization of manufacturing in factories, and innovations in transportation and communication.

Manchester from Kersal Moor, 1852 (w/c with bodycolour and gum arabic on paper), Wyld, William (1806–89)/The Royal Collection © 2011 Her Majesty Queen Elizabeth II/The Bridgeman Art Library

**Manchester, the First Industrial City**  The first cotton mills, built on the banks of the River Irwell in northern England, transformed Manchester from a country town into a booming industrial city. The use of chemicals to bleach and dye the cloth and the introduction of steam engines in the early nineteenth century to power the spinning and weaving machines made Manchester, for a time, the most polluted city on earth.

# CAUSES OF THE INDUSTRIAL REVOLUTION

■ *What caused the Industrial Revolution?*

What caused the Industrial Revolution, and why did it develop so rapidly in England in the eighteenth century? The basic preconditions of this momentous event seem to have been population growth, an agricultural revolution, the expansion of trade, and an openness to innovation.

## Preconditions for Industrialization

Population growth fueled the Industrial Revolution by increasing consumer demand and lowering labor costs. Between 1650 and 1850 Europe's population grew from 100 million to 266 million, and the number of city dwellers more than doubled. In England and Wales, for example, the population increased from about 6 million in 1700 to 9 million in 1800 and 18 million by 1850—increases never before experienced in European history. As the pace of manufacturing mounted in the eighteenth century, rural laborers and their families moved to cities in hope of higher earnings and better lives.

The population explosion and urbanization resulted from more widespread resistance to disease and an **agricultural revolution** that provided food for city dwellers and forced poorer peasants off the land. Long before the eighteenth century, the acceptance of the potato and maize from the Americas had increased food supplies in Europe. In the cool and humid regions of Europe, potatoes yielded two or three times more calories per acre than grain. Maize (American corn) was also grown across Europe from northern Iberia to the Balkans.

Prosperous landowners tried new methods and new crops, draining marshes to improve the soil, breeding better livestock whose manure was used to improve fertilizer, and introducing crop rotation. Some "enclosed" their land—that is, consolidated their holdings, including commons that in the past had been open to all. The "enclosure movement" turned the rural poor into tenants and sharecroppers into landless farm laborers. Many moved to the cities to seek work; others became vagrants; still others emigrated to Canada, Australia, and the United States.

Expanding domestic and foreign demand for textiles also led to innovation in Europe. Traditionally, European textiles were produced by skilled artisans organized in guilds using centuries-old technologies, an expensive process that took years. But a system called *proto-industrialization* replaced expensive

**agricultural revolution**  The transformation of farming that resulted in the eighteenth century from the spread of new crops, improvements in cultivation techniques and livestock breeding, and the consolidation of small holdings into large farms from which tenants and sharecroppers were forcibly expelled.

# Chronology

| | Technology | Economy, Society, and Politics |
|---|---|---|
| **1750** | **1702–1712** Thomas Newcomen builds first steam engine<br>**1759** Josiah Wedgwood opens pottery factory<br>**1764** Spinning jenny<br>**1769** Water frame introduced; James Watt patents steam engine<br>**1779** First iron bridge<br>**1785** Samuel Crompton's mule<br>**1794** Eli Whitney's cotton gin | **1 776** Adam Smith's *Wealth of Nations*<br>**1776–1783** American Revolution<br>**1789–1799** French Revolution |
| **1800** | **1800** Alessandro Volta's battery<br>**1807** Robert Fulton's *North River*<br><br>**1837** Wheatstone and Cooke's telegraph; Morse's code<br>**1838** First ships steam across the Atlantic<br>**1840** *Nemesis* sails to China<br>**1840s** Telegraphs cross eastern U.S., western Europe | **1804–1815** Napoleonic Wars<br>**1820s** U.S. cotton industry begins<br>**1833** Factory Act in Britain<br>**1834** Robert Owen's Grand National Consolidated Trade Union<br><br><br>**1847–1848** Irish famine<br>**1848** Collapse of Chartist movement; revolutions in Europe; publication of *Communist Manifesto* |
| **1850** | **1851** Crystal Palace opens in London | **1854** First cotton mill in India |

artisans who typically earned daily wages with proto-industrial workers who were only paid for what they produced. Raw materials and simple machinery, like looms and spinning wheels, were delivered to the homes of farm families and rural jobbers who organized groups of laborers. Complex tasks were subdivided into simple procedures easily mastered by rural workers. Chronic problems with quality control and inefficiencies that resulted from the dispersal of production were offset by increased cloth production and lowered labor costs. (See Diversity and Dominance: Adam Smith and the Division of Labor).

Trade also stimulated a growing interest in technology and innovation among educated people throughout Europe and the America, as well as a much deeper engagement of colonial possessions with foreign markets. Nearly all the European powers profited from plantation colonies in the Americas. But there was also a dramatic expansion of European commerce with markets in Africa and Asia. Europeans of even modest means consumed ever-growing quantities of sugar to sweeten their tea, cof-fee, cocoa, pastries, and candies, and the demand for manufactures like porcelain cups and dinnerware increased as well. At the same time Caribbean planters imported a steeply rising volume of cotton textiles to clothe themselves and their slaves. Initially, these cotton textiles were imported from Asia, but increasing demand led to the creation of domestic cotton textile industries, the first truly modern mechanized industry.

European governments played a key role in this economic expansion. During the eighteenth century the French, Spanish, and British governments sent expeditions around the world to collect plants that could profitably be grown domestically or in their colonies. They offered prizes for scientific discoveries, like determining the longitude of a ship at sea and the accurate measurement of the earth's circumference, and created royal manufacturers that produced fine china, silks, and carpets. As the volume of commerce increased, canal building boomed. Governments also sponsored improvements in road networks, but maintenance was often inadequate. In Britain this neglect

# Diversity & Dominance

## Adam Smith and the Division of Labor

**A**dam Smith (1723–1790), a Scottish philosopher, is famous for his book An Inquiry into the Nature and Causes of the Wealth of Nations, first published in 1776. It was the first work to explain the economy of a nation as a system. Smith criticized the notion, common in the eighteenth century, that a nation's wealth was synonymous with the amount of gold and silver in the government's coffers. Instead, he defined wealth as the amount of goods and services produced by a nation's people. By this definition, labor and its products are an essential element in a nation's prosperity.

In the passage that follows, Smith contrasts two methods of making pins. In one a team of workers divided up the job of making pins and produced a great many every day; in the other pin workers "wrought separately and independently" and produced very few pins per day. It is clear that the division of labor produces more pins per worker per day. But who benefits? Left unsaid is that a pin factory had to be owned and operated by a manufacturer who hired workers and assigned a task to each one.

The illustration shows a pin-maker's workshop in late-eighteenth-century France. Each worker is performing a specific task on a few pins at once, and all the energy comes from human muscles. These are the characteristics of a proto-industrial workshop.

**T**o take an example, therefore, from a very trifling manufacture—but one in which the division of labour has been very often taken notice of—the trade of the pin-maker: a workman not educated to this business (which the division of labour has rendered a distinct trade), nor acquainted with the use of machinery employed in it (to the invention of which the same division of labour has probably given occasion), could scarce, perhaps, with his utmost industry, make one pin in a day, and certainly could not make twenty. But in the way in which this business is now carried on, not only the whole work is a peculiar trade, but it is divided into a number of branches, of which the greater part are likewise peculiar trades. One man draws out the wire, another straights it, a third cuts it, a fourth points it, a fifth grinds it at the top for receiving the head; to make the head requires two or three distinct operations, to put it on, is a peculiar business, to whiten the pins is another; it is even a trade by itself to put them into the paper; and the important business of making a pin is, in this manner, divided into about eighteen distinct operations, which, in some manufactories, are all performed ➤

**A Pin-Maker's Workshop** *The man in the middle (Fig. 2) is pulling wire off a spindle (G) and through a series of posts. This ensures that the wire will be perfectly straight. The worker seated on the lower right (Fig. 3) takes the long pieces of straightened wire and cuts them into shorter lengths. The man in the lower left-hand corner (Fig. 5) sharpens twelve to fifteen wires at a time by holding them against a grindstone turned by the worker in Fig. 6. The men in Figs. 4 and 7 put the finishing touches on the points. Other operations—such as forming the wire to the proper thickness, cleaning and coating it with tin, and attaching the heads—are depicted in other engravings in the same encyclopedia.*

The Pin Factory, plate 2 from Volume IV of the Encyclopedia of Denis Diderot (1713–84) and Jean le Rond d'Alembert (1717–83), 1751–52 (engraving), French School, (18th century)/ Private Collection/The Bridgeman Art Library by distinct hands, though in others the same man will sometimes perform two or three of them. I have seen a small manufactory of this kind where ten men only were employed, and where some of them, consequently, performed two or three distinct operations. But though they were very poor, and therefore but indifferently accommodated with the necessary machinery, they could, when they exerted themselves, make among them about twelve pounds of pins in a day.

There are in a pound upwards of four thousand pins of a middling size. Those ten persons, therefore, could make among them upwards of forty-eight thousand pins in a day. Each person, therefore, making a tenth part of forty-eight thousand pins, might be considered as making four thousand eight hundred pins a day. But if they had all wrought separately and independently, and without any of them having been educated to this peculiar business, they certainly could not each of them have made twenty, perhaps not one pin in a day; that is, certainly, not the two hundred and fortieth, perhaps not the four thousand eight hundredth part of what they are at present capable of performing, in consequence of a proper division and combination of their different operations.

## QUESTIONS FOR ANALYSIS

1. Why does dividing the job of pin-making into ten or more operations result in the production of more pins per worker? How much more productive are these workers than if each one made complete pins from start to finish?

2. How closely does the picture of a pin-maker's workshop illustrate Smith's verbal description?

3. What disadvantage would there be to working in a pin factory where the job was divided as in Smith's example, compared to making entire pins from start to finish?

4. What other examples can you think of, from Adam Smith's day or from more recent times, of the advantages of the division of labor?

*Source*: Adam Smith, *An Inquiry into the Nature and Causes of the Wealth of Nations*, ed. Edward Gibbon Wakefield (London: Charles Knight and Co., 1843), 7–9.

---

led to the formation of private "turnpike trusts" that built numerous toll roads. Authorities in England, France, Prussia, and Spain, among other European nations, recruited skilled artisans from rival nations, subsidized periodicals that disseminated new technologies, and expanded their navies to better protect foreign trade.

## Britain's Advantages

These changes were widespread, but Britain in the eighteenth century had the fastest-growing population, food supply, and overseas trade. Already the world's leading exporter of tools, guns, hardware, clocks, and other manufactured goods (see Map 20.1), Britain took the lead in introducing new technologies and maintained its place as Europe's foremost industrial power to the end of the nineteenth century. After developing machines that multiplied the productive capacities of individual workers in the eighteenth century, British inventors developed efficient steam engines in the nineteenth century that replaced wind, water, and animal power as the source of energy for industrial machinery. Prosperity from good harvests and a booming overseas trade fueled a rising standard of living that stimulated consumption and led to innovation in manufacturing. More important still, Britain had abundant supplies of coal and iron ore, two key ingredients in the Industrial Revolution. Britain's mining and metal industries employed engineers with a tradition of experimentation and innovation, its strong craft tradition trained a large number of skilled mechanics, and its patent system offered inventors the hope of rich rewards by protecting their intellectual property rights. Examples of men who became wealthy and respected for their inventions stimulated others to experiment.

Britain had other advantages as well. At the dawn of the industrial age, it had one of the most fluid societies in Europe. With the exception of the Netherlands, British political power was not as centralized as elsewhere in Europe; its court was less ostentatious, its aristocracy was less powerful, there were fewer obstacles to commerce and manufacturing, and the lines separating the social classes were not as sharply drawn. British commercial culture had long enjoyed the benefits of strong banks, joint-stock companies, a stock market, and commercial insurance. At a time when overland transportation was costly, Britain also had good water transportation thanks to its long coastline, navigable rivers, and a growing network of canals, with none of the duties and tolls that goods had to pay every few miles in France or Spain.

In contrast to Britain, the economies of continental Europe were hampered by high transportation costs, misguided government regulations, and rigid social structures. Once revolutions had swept away Europe's old regimes (see Chapter 21), both private investors and European governments—acutely aware of Britain's head start—recruited British engineers and artisans, created technical schools, eliminated internal tariff barriers, tolls, and other hindrances to trade, and encouraged the formation of joint-stock companies and banks to channel private savings into industrial investments. Rich in coal and iron-ore deposits, first Belgium, and then Germany after 1850, enjoyed industrial booms based on iron, cotton, steam engines, and railroads. The United States was well established as a major industrial power by 1860, having quickly adopted textile and metallurgical technologies developed first in Great Britain. Without abundant coal, France retained a more traditional manufacturing economy until the introduction of electricity late in the nineteenth century.

# THE TECHNOLOGICAL REVOLUTION

■ *What were the key innovations that increased productivity and drove industrialization?*

Five innovations spurred industrialization: (1) mass production through the division of labor, (2) new machines and mechanization, (3) a great increase in the manufacture of iron, (4) the steam engine, and (5) the electric telegraph. While the full realization of these innovations occurred first in Great Britain and then spread to the United States and continental Europe in the nineteenth century, China had achieved the first three during the Song dynasty (960–1279) (see Chapter 11). But China did not develop the steam engine or electricity, innovations that dramatically increased human productivity. The transformation of Western economies through industrialization depended on the application of these new forms of energy to the process of mechanical innovation.

## Mass Production and Mechanization

Before the mid-eighteenth century, only the wealthy could afford fine china, but in 1759, **Josiah Wedgwood**, the son of a potter, started his own pottery business to satisfy the demand from more and more Europeans who wanted to drink their tea, cocoa, and coffee from porcelain because it would not spoil their flavor. He subdivided the work into simple repetitive tasks, such as unloading the clay, mixing it, pressing flat pieces, dipping the pieces in glaze, putting handles on cups, packing kilns, and carrying things from one part of his plant to another. He also used molds instead of the potter's wheel wherever possible, a change that saved labor and created uniform plates and bowls that could be stacked. Wedgwood's china production is a case in point for how **mass production** and the **division of labor** affected traditional industries: workers became more productive and, requiring fewer skills, were paid less. Wedgwood was able to lower the cost of his products while improving their quality, and to offer his wares for sale at lower prices.

**Josiah Wedgwood** English industrialist whose pottery works were the first to produce fine-quality pottery by industrial methods.

**mass production** The manufacture of many identical products by the division of labor into many small repetitive tasks. This method was introduced into the manufacture of pottery and into the spinning of cotton thread.

**division of labor** A manufacturing technique that breaks down a craft into many simple and repetitive tasks that can be performed by unskilled workers. Pioneered in the manufacture of pottery and in other eighteenth-century factories, it greatly increased the productivity of labor and lowered the cost of manufactured goods.

**Map 20.1  The Industrial Revolution in Britain, ca. 1850** The first industries arose in northern and western England. These regions had abundant coal and iron-ore deposits for the iron industry, as well as moist climate and fast-flowing rivers, factors important for the cotton textile industry.
© Cengage Learning

Map labels: Towns with over 20,000 people are shown. 50 400 Thousand, 2.4 Million. Cities with over 100,000 people are labeled. Exposed coalfields. Industrial areas. Centers of woolen cloth production, 18th century. Principal railroads. 0 50 Km. 0 50 Mi.

SCOTLAND; Durham; Cotton and woolen textiles Machinery, Iron; Bradford; Manchester; Leeds; Liverpool; Sheffield; Iron Hardware; Irish Sea; North Sea; WALES; Norwich; Birmingham; Iron Machinery Pottery; Iron; Bristol; Bath; London; Machinery Consumer goods 2°E; Exeter; Tin and copper mining; English Channel

The cotton industry, the largest in this period, illustrates the role of **mechanization**, the use of machines to do work previously done by hand. The cotton plant did not grow in England, but the cloth was so much cooler, softer, and cleaner than wool that wealthy Europeans developed a liking for the costly import. When the powerful English woolen industry persuaded Parliament to forbid the import of cotton cloth, it stimulated attempts to import cotton fiber and make the cloth domestically. Here was an opportunity for enterprising inventors to reduce costs with laborsaving machinery.

Beginning in the 1760s a series of inventions—the spinning jenny, the water frame, and the mule—

**mechanization** The application of machinery to manufacturing and other activities. Among the first processes to be mechanized were the spinning of cotton thread and the weaving of cloth in late-eighteenth- and early-nineteenth-century England.

managers often hired children to tend the spinning machines. Mechanization and cheap labor allowed the price of cloth to fall by 90 percent between 1782 and 1812, and it kept on dropping. Machinery adapted from cotton production quickly transformed the spinning of wool as well. In Belgium in 1810, only 5 of 144 woolen factories were mechanized, but they produced more than 50 percent of total production.

Britain's industrialization made cotton America's most valuable crop. In 1794 the American Eli Whitney patented his mechanical cotton gin, a simple device that separated the seeds from the fiber and made cotton growing economical. This invention permitted the spread of cotton farming into Georgia, then into Alabama, Mississippi, and Louisiana, and finally as far west as Texas. By the late 1850s the southern states were producing a million tons of cotton a year, five-sixths of the world's total. With the help of British immigrants who introduced jennies, mules, and power looms (and Americans willing to ignore the British patent rights), Americans also developed their own cotton industry in the 1820s. By 1840 the United States had twelve hundred cotton mills that served the booming domestic market, two-thirds of them in New England.

**Wedgwood's Potteries**  In Staffordshire, England, Josiah Wedgwood established a factory to mass-produce beautiful and inexpensive china. The bottle-shaped buildings are kilns in which thousands of pieces of china could be fired at one time. Kilns, factories, and housing were all mixed together in pottery towns, and smoke from burning coal filled the air.

*(left margin, rotated)* Mary Evans Picture Library/Alamy

revolutionized the spinning of cotton thread and allowed British industry to undersell high-quality handmade cotton cloth from India. British cotton output increased tenfold between 1770 and 1790, despite the fact that these large-scale producers still depended on water power.

When the boom in thread production and the soaring demand for cloth created bottlenecks in weaving, inventors rose to the challenge with power looms, carding machines, chlorine bleach, and cylindrical printing presses. By the 1830s, large English textile mills powered by steam engines were turning raw cotton into printed cloth. This was a far cry from the cottage industries of the previous century.

Mechanization offered two advantages: increased productivity for the manufacturer and lower prices for the consumer. Whereas in India it took five hundred hours to spin a pound of cotton, the improved, self-regulating mule of 1830 required only eighty minutes. Cotton mills needed few skilled workers, and

### The Iron Industry

For over two thousand years iron had been used throughout Eurasia, Africa, and China for tools, weapons, and household items. Wherever it was produced, however, deforestation eventually drove up the cost of charcoal (used for smelting) and restricted output. Furthermore, iron had to be repeatedly heated and hammered to drive out impurities, a difficult and costly process. Then in 1709 Abraham Darby discovered that coke (coal that has had the impurities removed) could be used in place of charcoal. The resulting metal was of lower quality than charcoal iron but much cheaper to produce, for coal was plentiful. In 1784 British inventor Henry Cort found a way to remove some of the impurities in coke-iron by puddling—stirring the molten iron with long rods—prior to rolling the iron into bars. Cort's process made it possible to produce wrought iron (a soft and malleable form of iron) very cheaply.

By 1790 four-fifths of Britain's iron was made with coke, while other countries still used charcoal. Coke-iron allowed a great expansion in the size of

**Pit Head of a Coal Mine** This is a small coal mine. In the center of this picture stands a Newcomen engine used to pump water. The work of hauling coal out of the mine was still done by horses and mules. The smoke coming out of the smokestack is a trademark of the early industrial era.

Walker Art Gallery, National Museums Liverpool/The Bridgeman Art Library

individual blast furnaces, substantially reducing the cost of iron production. There seemed almost no limit to the quantity of iron that could be produced with coke. Britain's iron production rose fast, from 17,000 tons in 1740 to 3 million tons in 1844, as much as in the rest of the world put together.

In turn, there seemed no limit to the amount of iron that an industrializing society would purchase or the novel applications for this cheap and useful material. In 1779 Abraham Darby III (grandson of the first Abraham Darby) built a bridge of iron across the Severn River. In 1851 Londoners marveled at the **Crystal Palace**, a huge exhibition hall made entirely of iron and glass that showcased British industry but also included exhibits from the colonies and other nations.

The availability of cheap iron made the mass production of objects such as guns, hardware, and tools appealing. However, fitting together the parts of these products required a great deal of labor. To reduce labor costs, manufacturers like the Americans Eli Whitney (firearms) and Eli Terry (clocks) contributed to the development of standardized interchangeable parts that did not require high levels of crasftsmanship. By the mid-nineteenth century, interchangeable parts had been widely adopted in the manufacture of firearms, farm equipment, and sewing machines, and Europeans, who still relied on skilled artisans, had begun to call this the "American system of manufactures" because it was a distinctively American response to a shortage of skilled craftsmen in its immigrant population.

## The Steam Engine

The first machine to transform fossil fuel into mechanical energy was the **steam engine**, a device that set the Industrial Revolution apart from all previous periods of growth and innovation.

Before the eighteenth century, deep mines filled with water faster than horses could pump it out. Scientists understood the concept of atmospheric pressure and had created experimental devices to turn heat into motion, but they had not found a way to put the principles involved to practical use. Then, between 1702 and 1712, Thomas Newcomen developed the first practical steam engine, a huge but

**Crystal Palace** Building erected in Hyde Park, London, for the Great Exhibition of 1851. Made of iron and glass, like a gigantic greenhouse, it was a symbol of the industrial age.

**steam engine** A machine that turns the energy released by burning fuel into motion. Thomas Newcomen built the first crude but workable steam engine in 1712. James Watt vastly improved his device in the 1760s and 1770s. Steam power was later applied to operating machinery in factories and to propelling ships and locomotives.

**The *De Witt Clinton* Locomotive, 1835–1840** The *De Witt Clinton* was the first steam locomotive built in the United States. The high smokestack let the hot cinders cool so they would not set fire to nearby trees, an important consideration at a time when eastern North America was still covered with forest. The three passenger cars are clearly horse carriages fitted with railroad wheels.

Bettmann/Corbis

effective device that could clear water from mines much faster than earlier pumps.

The Newcomen engine's voracious appetite for fuel mattered little in coal mines, where fuel was cheap, but it made the engine too costly for other uses. In 1764 **James Watt**, an instrument maker at Glasgow University in Scotland, was asked to repair the university's model Newcomen engine. Watt realized that the engine wasted fuel because the cylinder had to be alternately heated and cooled. He developed a separate condenser—a vessel into which the steam was allowed to escape, leaving the cylinder always hot and the condenser always cold. Watt patented his idea in 1769 and enlisted the help of the iron manufacturer Matthew Boulton to turn his invention into a commercial product. Their first engines were used to pump water out of copper and tin mines, where fuel was too costly for Newcomen engines. In 1781 Watt invented the sun-and-planet gear, which turned the back-and-forth action of the piston into rotary motion. This allowed steam engines to power machinery in flour and cotton mills, pottery manufactures, and other industries.

Watt's steam engine was the most celebrated invention of the eighteenth century. Because coal supplies seemed unlimited, steam-generated energy appeared to be an inexhaustible source of power that could be used where animal, wind, and water power were lacking. Inspired by the success of Watt's

engine, several inventors put steam engines on boats. The first commercially successful steamboat was Robert Fulton's *North River*, which sailed the Hudson River between New York City and Albany, New York, in 1807. Soon steamboats were launched on the Ohio and the Mississippi, gateways to the Midwest. By 1830 some three hundred steamboats plied the Mississippi and its tributaries. The United States was fast becoming a nation that moved by water.

Oceangoing steam-powered ships were much more difficult to build than river boats, for the first steam engines used so much coal that no ship could carry more than a few days' supply. The *Savannah*, which crossed the Atlantic in 1819, was a sailing ship with an auxiliary steam engine that was used for only ninety hours of its twenty-nine-day trip. Engineers soon developed more efficient engines, and in 1838 two steamers, the *Great Western* and the *Sirius*, crossed the Atlantic on steam power alone.

## Railroads

Steam engines were initially too heavy and weak to pull any weight. After Watt's patent expired in 1800, however, inventors experimented with lighter, more powerful

**James Watt** Scot who invented the condenser and other improvements that made the steam engine a practical source of power for industry and transportation. The watt, an electrical measurement, is named after him.

high-pressure engines. In the early 1800s they built several steam-powered vehicles able to travel on roads or rails. Between 1830 and 1850, a railroad-building mania swept Britain. The first lines linked towns and mines with the nearest harbor or waterway. As passenger traffic soared, entrepreneurs built lines between the major cities and even to small towns. Railroads were far cheaper, faster, and more comfortable than stagecoaches.

Railroads had their most transformative effects in the United States. By the 1840s, 6,000 miles (10,000 kilometers) of track radiated from Boston, New York, Philadelphia, and Baltimore. In the 1850s, 21,000 miles (34,000 kilometers) of additional track were laid, much of it westward across the Appalachians to Memphis, St. Louis, and Chicago. The trip from New York to Chicago, which once took three weeks by boat and on horseback, could be made in forty-eight hours. The railroads opened up the Midwest, dispersing the waves of immigrants, turning the vast prairie into farms to feed the industrial cities of the eastern United States, and creating a prodigious internal market for manufactures.

Railways also accelerated the industrialization of Europe. Belgium, independent since 1830, quickly copied the British. In France and Prussia, construction in the mid-1840s not only satisfied the long-standing need for transportation but also stimulated the iron, machinery, and construction industries. By 1850 Germany had built 3,639 miles (5,856 kilometers) of railroad line and France 1,811 miles (2,915 kilometers).

### Communication over Wires

After the Italian scientist Alessandro Volta invented the battery in 1800, making it possible to produce an electric current, many inventors tried to apply electricity to communication. The first practical **electric telegraph** systems were developed almost simultaneously in England and America. In 1837 in England, Charles Wheatstone and William Cooke introduced a five-wire telegraph, while the American Samuel Morse introduced a code of dots and dashes that could be transmitted with a single wire.

By the late 1840s telegraph wires crisscrossed the eastern United States and western Europe. In 1851 the first submarine telegraph cable was laid across

### SECTION REVIEW

- The technological revolution involved the development of cost-saving machines and processes, such as mass production through the division of labor.
- Beginning in the 1760s a series of inventions mechanized the British cotton industry and stimulated cotton farming in the United States, while American manufacturers pioneered processes involving interchangeable parts.
- Innovations in processing transformed the British iron industry, making cheap iron widely available for various applications.
- With the perfection of the steam engine, steamboats and railroads proliferated, the latter spurring the industrialization of Europe.
- Practical electric telegraphs appeared in England and America and quickly spread.

the English Channel from England to France (cutting the transmission of news from up to four days to minutes). Thus began a network that eventually connected the entire globe. The world was rapidly shrinking, to the applause of Europeans and Americans, for whom speed was a clear measure of progress. No longer was the movement of information limited to the speed of a sailing ship, a galloping horse, or a fast-moving train.

## THE IMPACT OF THE EARLY INDUSTRIAL REVOLUTION

■ *What was the impact of these changes on the society and environment of the industrializing countries?*

The Industrial Revolution led to profound changes in society, politics, and the economy. Early changes—smoky cities, slum neighborhoods, polluted water, child labor in mines and textile mills—were being alleviated by the mid-nineteenth century. But by then national or even international problems were replacing those local ones: business cycles, labor conflicts, and the degradation of entire regions into industrial landscapes.

**electric telegraph** A device for rapid, long-distance transmission of information over an electric wire. It was introduced in England and North America in the 1830s and 1840s and replaced telegraph systems that utilized visual signals such as semaphores.

## The New Industrial Cities

The most dramatic environmental changes occurred in the towns. Never before had towns grown so fast. London, one of the largest cities in Europe in 1700 with 500,000 inhabitants, grew to 1,117,000 by 1800 and to 2,685,000 by 1850, making it the largest city in the world. New York City, already 100,000 strong in 1815, reached 600,000 (including Brooklyn) in 1850. In some areas, towns merged and formed megalopolises, such as Greater London, the English Midlands, central Belgium, and the Ruhr district of Germany.

A great deal of money went into the building of fine homes, churches, museums, and theaters. Yet, by all accounts, the industrial cities grew much too fast. As poor migrants streamed in from the countryside, developers built cheap, shoddy row houses for them to rent. These tenements were dangerously overcrowded, with several families often living in one room. Moreover, town dwellers recently arrived from the country brought country ways with them. People threw their sewage and trash out the windows to be washed down the gutters in the streets. The poor kept pigs and chickens; the rich kept horses; and pedestrians stepped into the street at their own risk. Air pollution from burning coal got steadily worse, and people drank water drawn from wells and rivers contaminated by sewage and industrial runoff. The River Irwell, which ran through Manchester, was, in the words of one visitor, "considerably less a river than a flood of liquid manure."[3]

To the long list of preindustrial diseases (such as smallpox, dysentery, and tuberculosis), industrialization added new ailments. Rickets, a bone disease caused by lack of sunshine, became endemic in dark and smoky industrial cities. Steamships brought cholera from India, causing great epidemics that struck poor neighborhoods especially hard. In the 1850s, the average life expectancy in England was forty years. In Manchester's poorest neighborhoods, it was around seventeen. Shocking reports of slum life eventually led to municipal reforms, such as garbage removal, water and sewage systems, and parks and schools. These measures began to alleviate the ills of urban life after the mid-nineteenth century.

[3]Quoted in Lewis Mumford, *The City in History* (New York: Harcourt Brace, 1961), 460.

## Rural Environments

Long before the Industrial Revolution, wilderness areas had largely disappeared in Britain and much of western Europe. Almost every piece of land was covered with fields, pastures, or towns. The most serious problem was deforestation. People cut timber to build ships and houses, to heat homes, and to manufacture bricks, iron, glass, beer, bread, and many other items.

Americans transformed their environment on a vast scale. Settlers viewed forests not as a valuable resource but as a hindrance to development. In their haste to "open up the wilderness," pioneers felled trees and burned them, built houses and abandoned them when they moved on. The cultivation of cotton was especially harmful. Planters cut down forests, grew cotton for a few years until the soil was depleted, and then moved west, abandoning the land to scrub pines.

In industrializing Europe, raw materials once grown on the land—such as wood, hay, and wool—were replaced by materials found underground, like iron ore and coal, or obtained overseas, like cotton. Across Europe the expansion of coal and iron mining had dramatic effects on the environment. As the population increased and land grew scarcer, the cost of growing feed for horses rose, creating incentives to find new, less land-hungry means of transportation. Likewise, iron became cheaper and wood more expensive. Canal building boomed in Britain, France, and the low countries. The marvels of canal construction—deep-cut tunnels and even aqueducts—were then applied to the railroads. Soon, rattling trains pulled by puffing, smoke-belching locomotives invaded long-isolated districts.

## Working Conditions

Most industrial jobs were unskilled, repetitive, and boring. Factory work did not vary with the seasons or the time of day but began and ended by the clock. Factories used the invention of gas lighting to expand the working day past sunset. Workdays were long, there were few breaks, and foremen watched constantly. Workers who performed one simple task over and over had little sense of achievement or connection to the final product. Industrial accidents were common and could ruin a family. Unlike even the poorest

**An Industrial Canal** In the late eighteenth and early nineteenth centuries, before railroads were introduced, many canals were constructed in England so that barges could transport heavy materials cheaply, such as coal for industrial works and steam engines, stone and bricks for buildings, clay for pottery works, and ores for metal foundries. Canals such as this one, which ran alongside a copper foundry, contributed greatly to Britain's industrial development.

preindustrial farmer or artisan, factory workers had no control over their tools, jobs, or working hours.

Industrial work also had a major impact on women and family life. Women who could not afford servants had always worked, but mostly within the family: spinning and weaving, sewing hats and clothes, preparing food, washing, and doing a myriad other household chores. In rural areas, women also did farm work, especially caring for gardens and small animals. However, factory work was never the main occupation of working women. Most young women who sought paid employment became domestic servants in spite of the low pay, drudgery, and risk of sexual abuse. Other women with small children tried hard to find work they could do at home, such as laundry, sewing, embroidery, millinery, or taking in lodgers.

Those who worked in factories were concentrated in textile mills, because textile work required less strength than metalworking, construction, or hauling. On average, women earned one-third to one-half as much as men. Young unmarried women worked to support themselves or to save for marriage, while married women took factory jobs when their husbands were unable to support the family. Mothers of infants faced a hard choice: whether to leave their babies with wet nurses at great expense or bring them to the factory and keep them quiet with opiates. Rather than working together as a family, husbands and wives increasingly worked in different places.

Even with both parents working, poor families found it hard to make ends meet. As in preindustrial societies, parents thought children should contribute to their upkeep as soon as they were able to. The first generation of industrial workers brought children as young as five or six with them to the factories and mines, since there were no public schools or day-care centers. Employers preferred child workers because they were cheaper and more docile than adults and because they were better able to tie broken threads or crawl under machines to sweep the dust. Mine operators used children to pull coal carts along the low passageways from the coal face to the mine shaft.

Some manufacturers tried to provide more humane environments. When Francis Cabot Lowell built a cotton mill in Massachusetts, he hired the unmarried daughters of New England farmers, promising them decent wages and housing in dormitories under careful moral supervision. Other manufacturers eager to combine profits with morality followed his example. But soon the profit motive won out, and manufacturers imposed longer hours, harsher working conditions, and lower wages. When young women in New England factories went on strike, the mill owners replaced them with Irish immigrants willing to accept lower pay and worse conditions.

Rising demand for cotton also reinforced and expanded the institution of slavery in the Americas. In the 1790s, there were 700,000 slaves of African descent in the United States. As the "Cotton Kingdom" expanded, the number of slaves increased to 3.2 million by 1850, 60 percent located in the cotton region. Similarly, European demand for sugar prolonged plantation slavery in the West Indies and spread it to the coffee-growing regions of southern Brazil. Slavery was an integral part of both commercial capitalism and the Industrial Revolution, not, as some maintained at the time, a consequence of biological differences or biblical injunctions.

## Changes in Society

Industrialization accentuated the polarization of society and disparities of income. In Britain the worst-off were those who clung to an obsolete skill or craft. Even by working more hours, handloom weavers could not compete with power looms and were reduced to destitution. The standard of living of factory workers did not decline steadily like those of handloom weavers but fluctuated wildly with the cycles of economic growth and contraction. During the war years 1792 to 1815, the poor suffered widespread hardship when the price of food rose faster than wages. Then, in the 1820s, real wages and public health began to improve, as industrial production grew at over 3 percent a year, pulling the rest of the economy along. Prices for food, housing, and clothing fell so that even the poor could afford comfortable, washable cotton clothes. Hard times returned in the "hungry forties" when, in 1847–1848, the potato crop failed in Ireland and one-quarter of the Irish population died.

Overall, the benefits of industrialization— cheaper food, clothing, and utensils—did not improve workers' standard of living until the 1850s.

### SECTION REVIEW

- The Industrial Revolution spurred rapid urbanization, causing severe pollution, overcrowding, and myriad health and hygiene problems.

- Industrialization hastened deforestation and brought pollution to rural environments.

- Industrial working conditions were harsh and dangerous, especially for children, until Britain passed child-labor laws.

- Working-class women faced difficult choices between factory work and family obligations, and slavery persisted because of industrialization.

- Industrialization benefited owners more quickly than workers, the former often being able to rise in society, while the cult of domesticity shaped middle class women's lives.

The real beneficiaries of the early Industrial Revolution were the middle class. Most were the sons of middling shopkeepers, craftsmen, or farmers who had a little capital to start a cotton-spinning or machine-building business. Many tried and some succeeded, largely plowing their profits back into the business. A generation later, in the nineteenth century, some newly rich industrialists bought their way into high society. With industrialization came a "cult of domesticity" that removed middle-class women from contact with the business world and left them responsible for the home, the servants, the education of children, and the family's social life.

## NEW ECONOMIC AND POLITICAL IDEAS

■ *How did the Industrial Revolution influence the rise of new economic and political ideas?*

Changes as profound as the Industrial Revolution triggered political ferment and ideological conflict. So many wars and revolutions took place during those years that we cannot neatly separate out the consequences of industrialization from the rest (see Chapter 21). But it is clear that the Industrial Revolution strengthened the ideas of laissez faire (LAY-say fair) and socialism and sparked workers' protests.

### Laissez Faire

The most celebrated exponent of **laissez faire** ("let them do [as they will]") was Adam Smith (1723–1790), a Scottish economist. In *The Wealth of Nations* (1776) Smith argued that if individuals were allowed to seek personal gain, the effect, as though guided by an "invisible hand," would be to increase the general welfare (see Diversity and Dominance: Adam Smith and the Division of Labor). Except to protect private property, the government should refrain from interfering in business; it should even allow duty-free trade with foreign countries.

Although it was true that governments at the time were incompetent at regulating their national economies, it was becoming obvious that industrialization was not improving the general welfare but was causing great misery for some segments of society. Some thinkers blamed the workers' plight on the population boom, which outstripped the food supply and led to falling wages. The workers' poverty, they claimed, was as much a result of "natural law" as was the wealth of successful businessmen, and the only way for the working class to avoid mass famine was to delay marriage and practice self-restraint and sexual abstinence.

Laissez faire provided an ideological justification for a special kind of capitalism: banks, stock markets, and chartered companies allowed investors to obtain profits with reasonable risks but with much less government control and interference than in the past. But not everyone accepted the grim conclusions of the "dismal science," as economics was then termed. Jeremy Bentham (1748–1832) believed that it was possible to maximize "the greatest happiness of the greatest number," if only a Parliament of enlightened reformers would study the social problems of the day and pass appropriate legislation. His philosophy became known as utilitarianism.

### Positivism and Marxism

Some French social thinkers, moved by sincere concern for the poor, offered a more radically new vision of a just civilization. Espousing a philosophy called **positivism**, the Count of Saint-Simon (1760–1825) argued that the scientific method could solve social as well as technical problems. He recommended that the poor, guided by scientists and artists, form workers' communities under the protection of benevolent business leaders. Instead of attracting workers, these ideas found enthusiastic support from bankers and entrepreneurs, who were inspired by them to invest in railroads, canals, and other symbols of modernity. Positivism also influenced the political elites of Brazil and Mexico, who pursued a top-down program of economic development reinforced by harsh police controls and the manipulation of political institutions. Its chief tenets are emblazoned on the Brazilian flag: Order and Progress.

Numerous protest organizations formed across Europe, the most prominent of which—calling themselves *communists*—were led by two German-born intellectuals, Karl Marx (1818–1883) and his long-time collaborator and benefactor Friedrich Engels (1820–1895). They argued that the concentration of wealth and power associated with industrialization had led to the unbearable oppression of industrial workers (whom they called the **proletariat**), that history was dominated by class struggle, and that proletarians would inevitably come together to overthrow the bourgeoisie, the modern class that controlled industry. The final words of *The Communist Manifesto*, published in 1848 with Engels, urged revolutionary action with the challenge "Proletarians of all countries unite!"

### Protests and Reforms

Workers benefited little from the ideas of these middle-class philosophers. Instead, they resisted harsh working conditions in their own ways. They changed jobs frequently and were often absent, especially on Mondays. Periodically, workers rioted, went

**laissez faire** The idea that government should refrain from interfering in economic affairs. The classic exposition of laissez-faire principles is Adam Smith's *Wealth of Nations* (1776).

**positivism** A philosophy developed by the French Count of Saint-Simon. Positivists believed that social and economic problems could be solved by application of the scientific method, leading to continuous progress. Their ideas became popular in France and Latin America in the nineteenth century.

**proletariat** Industrial workers whose oppression was an example of how, according to *The Communist Manifesto*, history was dominated by class struggle between the workers who sold their labor for survival and those who owned the mills, factories, mines, or other means of industrial production and wealth (the bourgeoisie).

on strike, or violently resisted the introduction of new technologies, believing that mechanized production would diminish the value of their skills and force them into poverty. As early as 1767, disgruntled textile workers mobilized to destroy the spinning jenny. In 1779 workers destroyed the machines driven by water power in Blackburn, England, and in 1811 angry lace and stocking workers calling themselves *Luddites* attacked more than one hundred businesses and destroyed nearly every machine in the district.

In the late 1770s, French workers organized protests against "foreign" innovations, attacking British craftsmen and destroying the new machines. In the early stages of the French Revolution (see Chapter 21), popular revolutionary sentiment reinforced the resistance of workers to new machinery and undermined the ability of the government to protect factories. The result was that French artisans retained traditional control of production and France fell decades behind Britain in industrializing.

When wealthy farmers began to introduce reapers and other machines, the rural poor set fires, threatened landlords, demanded higher wages, and broke the machines. This popular movement culminated after 1830 when widespread rural riots forced the British government to mobilize troops and militia in defense of property. In the end, thousands of protestors were arrested and either imprisoned in Britain or transported to Australia as convict laborers.

These violent efforts to block innovation and protect long-established customs in manufacturing and agriculture were superseded by laboring-class organizations focused on workplace reform, higher wages, and expanded political rights. Gradually, workers formed benevolent societies and organized to demand universal male suffrage and shorter workdays. In 1834 Robert Owen founded the Grand National Consolidated Trade Union to lobby for an eight-hour workday; it quickly gained half a million members but collapsed a few months later in the face of government prosecution of trade union activities. The Chartist movement had more success, gathering petitions by the thousands to present to Parliament. Although Chartism collapsed in 1848, it left a legacy of labor organizing.

## SECTION REVIEW

- Industrialization reinforced Adam Smith's laissez-faire, free-market theories even in the face of conditions that prompted competing ideas such as utilitarianism. Many people sought explanations and proposed solutions for the changes in society and the economy.

- Positivists deplored the hardships caused by industrialization but asserted that they could be ameliorated by technological advances and wise policies, while communists advocated revolutionary action.

- Agitation by workers led politicians to investigate the working conditions in mines and factories, especially the work of women and children.

Eventually, mass movements persuaded the British Parliament to investigate conditions in factories and mines and initiate some reforms. The Factory Act of 1833 prohibited the employment of children younger than nine in textile mills and limited the working hours of children between the ages of nine and thirteen to eight hours a day and of fourteen- to eighteen-year-olds to twelve hours. The Mines Act of 1842 prohibited the employment of women and boys under age ten underground. On the European continent, in contrast, the revolutions of 1848 revealed widespread discontent with repressive governments but failed to soften the hardships of industrialization (see Chapter 21).

## THE LIMITS OF INDUSTRIALIZATION OUTSIDE THE WEST

■ How did the Industrial Revolution affect the relations between the industrialized and the nonindustrialized parts of the world?

The spread of the Industrial Revolution in the early nineteenth century transformed the relations of western Europe and North America with the rest of the world. In Egypt and India, cheap industrial imports, backed by the power of Great Britain, delayed industrialization for a century or more, and China was defeated by the products of industrial manufacture. In these three cases, we can discern outlines of the Western domination that has characterized the history of the world since the late nineteenth century.

**A Railroad Bridge Across the Nile** In the second half of the nineteenth century, industrialized nations, especially Great Britain, sent engineers and equipment to build railroads in less industrialized parts of the world, such as India, South Africa, Latin America, and the Middle East. One such railway connected Cairo and Alexandria in Egypt. Here a railroad bridge crosses the Nile at Benha near the pyramids. Corbis

Egypt, strongly influenced by European ideas since the French invasion of 1798, began to industrialize in the early nineteenth century. The driving force was its ruler, Muhammad Ali (1769–1849), a man who was to play a major role in the history of the Middle East and East Africa (see Chapter 22). Wanting to build up the Egyptian economy and military in order to become less dependent on the Ottoman sultan, his nominal overlord, Muhammad Ali imported advisers and technicians from Europe and built cotton mills, foundries, shipyards, weapons factories, and other industrial enterprises. To pay for all this, he made the peasants grow wheat and cotton, which the government bought at a low price and exported at a profit. He also imposed high tariffs on imported goods to force the pace of industrialization.

Muhammad Ali's efforts fell afoul of the British, who did not want a powerful country threatening to interrupt the flow of travelers and mail across Egypt, the shortest route between Europe and India. When Egypt went to war against the Ottoman Empire in 1839, Britain intervened and forced Muhammad Ali

to eliminate all import duties in the name of free trade. Unprotected, Egypt's fledgling industries could not compete with the flood of cheap British products. Thereafter, Egypt exported raw cotton, imported manufactured goods, and became an economic dependency of Britain.

Until the late eighteenth century, India had been the world's largest producer and exporter of cotton textiles, handmade by skilled spinners and weavers. The British East India Company took over large parts of India just as the Industrial Revolution was beginning in Britain. It allowed cheap British factory-made yarn and cloth to flood the Indian market duty-free, putting spinners and handloom weavers out of work. Unlike Britain, India had no factories where displaced handicraft workers could work. Most of them became landless peasants, eking out a precarious living.

Like other tropical regions, India became an exporter of raw materials and an importer of British industrial goods. To hasten the process, British entrepreneurs and colonial officials introduced railroads into the subcontinent. The construction of India's railroad network began in the mid-1850s, along with coal mining to fuel the locomotives and the installation of telegraph lines to connect the major cities.

Some Indian entrepreneurs saw opportunities in the atmosphere of change that the British created. In 1854 the Bombay merchant Cowasjee Nanabhoy Davar imported an engineer, four skilled workers, and several textile machines from Britain and started India's first textile mill. This was the beginning of India's mechanized cotton industry. Despite many gifted entrepreneurs, however, India's industrialization proceeded at a snail's pace, for the government was in British hands and the British did nothing to encourage Indian industry.

Having benefited from a long period of relative political stability, population growth, and commercial expansion, the Qing dynasty saw little reason to focus on foreign trade or promote the new machine technologies that had rapidly transformed the European economy in the first half of the nineteenth century. China continued to play a major role in the major markets of Asia even as European power grew, maintaining a favorable balance of trade that Europe paid for in silver (see Chapter 19). Moreover, China remained an agrarian empire with a conservative elite and a growing peasant population. As such, China focused on the production and distribution of food, rather than on trade, as an effective guarantee of social peace.

This situation was about to change. In January 1840 a shipyard in Britain launched a radically new ship whose iron hull and flat bottom allowed it to navigate in shallow waters, with a steam engine to power it upriver and against the wind. In November the *Nemesis* arrived off the coast of China, heavily armed and ready to reverse the steep trade imbalance long enjoyed by China. Though ships from Europe had been sailing to China for three hundred years, the *Nemesis* was the first steam-powered iron gunboat in Asian waters. It was soon joined by other steam-powered warships that collectively established European control of Chinese rivers, bombarding forts and cities and transporting troops and supplies from place to place along the coast and up the rivers far

more quickly than Chinese soldiers could move on foot. With this new weapon, Britain, a small island nation half a world away, compelled China to recognize the economic and military transformations wrought by industrial innovation in Europe and defeated the largest and most populated country in the world (see Chapter 22).

## CONCLUSION

The Industrial Revolution was the most momentous transformation in history since the beginning of agriculture. The steam engine and other new machines greatly lowered the cost and increased the production of goods like cotton and iron and the speed of transportation and communication.

However, the process caused social upheavals and environmental problems. Many entrepreneurs and businesspeople became very wealthy, while industrial workers—many of them children—worked under appalling conditions and lived in overcrowded tenements in badly polluted cities. Economists and philosophers proposed many theories and offered many solutions to the radical problems of industrial societies.

Industrialization had political consequences on a global scale. A small number of industrializing nations—first Great Britain, then those of western Europe and North America—grew more powerful. Other parts of the world were left behind to become political or economic dependencies of these powerful nations.

Eventually the industrial nations learned to alleviate their social problems, but the disparity between the rich and poor nations persisted for two centuries or more, and the environmental effects of industrialization have changed from local to global.

### SECTION REVIEW

- Industrialization contributed to Europe's and North America's domination of large parts of the world.
- Britain snuffed out the incipient industrialization in Egypt and India and turned these countries intro producers of raw materials.
- Steam-powered iron warships enabled Britain to defeat China.

# CHAPTER REVIEW

## CAUSES OF THE INDUSTRIAL REVOLUTION
■ *What caused the Industrial Revolution?* (page 472)

The Industrial Revolution arose from a combination of factors in European society in the eighteenth and early nineteenth centuries. The population grew, but so did the food supply, thanks to improvements in agriculture. Among upper- and middle-class Europeans, practical subjects like business, science, and technology became fashionable. Great Britain had a particularly fluid society open to talents and enterprise.

## THE TECHNOLOGICAL REVOLUTION
■ *What were the key innovations that increased productivity and drove industrialization?* (page 476)

A series of technological and organizational innovations transformed the manufacture of many products, reducing their costs and increasing their productivity. New machines, assembled in mills, mass-produced cotton thread and cloth. Work formerly done by skilled craftsmen was divided into many simple tasks assigned to workers in factories. New techniques also made iron cheap and abundant. Steam engines provided power to factories, ships, and railroads, while electricity found its first practical application in telegraphy.

## THE IMPACT OF THE EARLY INDUSTRIAL REVOLUTION
■ *What was the impact of these changes on the society and environment of the industrializing countries?* (page 481)

The Industrial Revolution changed people's lives and the environments in which they lived. Cities grew huge, and for most of their inhabitants, unsightly and unhealthy. While middle-class women were consigned to caring for the home and children, working-class women and children as well as men were obliged to earn their living in mines and factories. Rural environments were also transformed as roads, canals, and railroads crisscrossed open land.

## NEW ECONOMIC AND POLITICAL IDEAS
■ *How did the Industrial Revolution influence the rise of new economic and political ideas?* (page 484)

Some thinkers defended the growing disparities between rich and poor in the name of laissez faire. Government and businesspeople eagerly adopted many of the free-market capitalist views of Adam Smith. Others, such as positivists and utopian socialists, criticized the injustices caused by industrialization and offered a new vision of just communities. Still others, like communists, called for revolution. Workers created labor unions, leading political leaders to reexamine the working conditions of factories and mines, especially as they concerned women and children. However, not until the mid-nineteenth century did industrialization begin to raise living standards in the industrialized countries.

## THE LIMITS OF INDUSTRIALIZATION OUTSIDE THE WEST
■ *How did the Industrial Revolution affect the relations between the industrialized and the nonindustrialized parts of the world?* (page 486)

The Industrial Revolution changed life around the world because it gave the newly industrial nations of the West new powers to coerce non-Western societies. In particular, incipient industrialization in Egypt and India was actively thwarted or intentionally ignored, and those countries turned into producers of raw materials and consumers of British goods. British steam-powered gunboats forced China to open its doors to unequal trade.

## Key Terms

Industrial Revolution (p. 471)

agricultural revolution (p. 472)

Josiah Wedgwood (p. 476)

mass production (p. 476)

division of labor (p. 476)

mechanization (p. 477)

Crystal Palace (p. 479)

steam engine (p. 479)

James Watt (p. 480)

electric telegraph (p. 481)

laissez faire (p. 485)

positivism (p. 485)

proletariat (p. 485)

# Revolutionary Changes in the Atlantic World

© Cengage Learning

In August 1791 slaves and free blacks began an insurrection in the plantation district of northern Saint Domingue (san doe-MANG) (present-day Haiti). During the following decade and a half, Haitian revolutionaries abolished slavery; defeated military forces from Britain and France; and achieved independence.

News and rumors about revolutionary events in France had helped move the island's slave community to rebel. These same events had divided the island's white population into royalists (supporters of France's King Louis XVI) and republicans (who sought an end to monarchy). The large free mixed-race population secured some political rights from the French Assembly but were forced into rebellion by the violent resistance of the slave-owning elite.

Among those planning the insurrection was Toussaint L'Ouverture (too-SAN loo-ver-CHORE), a black freedman. This remarkable revolutionary organized the rebels militarily, negotiated with the island's competing factions and with representatives of Britain and France, and wrote his nation's first constitution. Commonly portrayed as a fiend by slave owners, Toussaint became a towering symbol of resistance to oppression to slaves everywhere.

The Haitian slave rebellion was an important event in the political and cultural transformation of the Western world. Profound changes to the economy, politics, and intellectual life occurred as well. The Industrial Revolution (see Chapter 20) increased manufacturing productivity and led to greater global interdependence, new patterns of consumerism, and altered social structures. At the same time, intellectuals questioned the traditional place of monarchy and religion in society. Merchants, professionals, and manufacturers provided an audience for the new intellectual currents and pressed for a larger political role.

This revolutionary era turned the Western world "upside down." The *ancien régime* (ahn-see-EN ray-ZHEEM), the French term for Europe's old order, rested on medieval principles: politics dominated by powerful monarchs, intellectual and cultural life dominated by religion, and economics dominated by hereditary agricultural elites. In the West's new order, commoners entered political life; science took the place of religion in intellectual life; and economies opened to competition.

Revolutionary steps forward were often matched by reactionary steps backward. Imperial powers resisted the loss of colonies; monarchs and nobles struggled to retain their ancient privileges; and church authorities fought against the claims of science. While the liberal and nationalist ideals of the eighteenth-century revolutionary movements were sometimes thwarted in Europe and the Americas, belief in national self-determination and universal suffrage and a passion for social justice continued to animate reformers into the twentieth century.

## PRELUDE TO REVOLUTION: THE EIGHTEENTH-CENTURY CRISIS

■ *How did the costs of imperial wars and the Enlightenment challenge the established authority of monarchs in Europe and the American colonies?*

The cost of wars fought among Europe's major powers over colonies and trade helped precipitate the revolutionary era that began in 1775 with the American Revolution. The struggles of Britain, France, and Spain for political preeminence in western Europe and overseas produced violent conflicts in the eighteenth century. In the Seven Years' War (1756–1763)—known as the French and Indian War in America—Britain gained dominance in North America and India. The enormous cost of these conflicts distinguished them from earlier wars.

However, the intellectual environment transformed by the **Enlightenment** made people much more critical of any effort to extend the power of a monarch or impose new taxes, and it also raised questions about the rights of individuals, applying the methods and questions of the Scientific Revolution to the study of human society (see Chapter 16). Some thinkers challenged long-established religious and political institutions. They argued that if scientists

**Enlightenment** A philosophical movement in eighteenth-century Europe that fostered the belief that one could reform society by discovering rational laws that governed social behavior and were just as scientific as the laws of physics.

could understand the laws of nature, then surely similar forms of disciplined investigation might reveal laws of human nature. The most radical wondered whether society and government could be better regulated and more productive if guided by reason rather than by hereditary rulers and the church.

These new perspectives and the intellectual optimism that fed them helped guide the English political philosopher John Locke (1632–1704). Locke argued in 1690 that governments were created to protect life, liberty, and property and that the people had a right to rebel when a monarch violated these natural rights. In *The Social Contract*, published in 1762, the French-Swiss intellectual Jean-Jacques Rousseau (zhan-zhock roo-SOE) (1712–1778) asserted that the will of the people was sacred and that the legitimacy of monarchs depended on the consent of the people. Although both men believed that government rested on the will of the people, Locke emphasized the importance of the individual, while Rousseau envisioned the people acting collectively because of their shared historical experience.

The Enlightenment is commonly associated with hostility toward religion and monarchy, but Voltaire (1694–1778), one of the Enlightenment's most critical intellects, believed that Europe's monarchs were likely agents of political and economic reform, and he wrote favorably of China's Qing emperors (see Chapter 19). Indeed, sympathetic members of the nobility and reforming European monarchs in Spain, Russia, and Prussia actively sponsored and promoted the dissemination of new ideas, providing patronage for many intellectuals. They recognized that elements of the Enlightenment buttressed their own efforts to expand royal authority at the expense of religious institutions, the nobility, and regional autonomy. Monarchs also understood that the era's passion for science and technology held the potential of fattening national treasuries and improving economic performance.

Women were instrumental in the dissemination of these new ideas. In England large numbers of educated middle-class women purchased and discussed books and pamphlets. Some were important contributors to intellectual life, raising arguments for the rights of women. In Paris wealthy women made their homes centers of debate, intellectual speculation, and free inquiry. Their salons brought together

**Beer Street (1751)** William Hogarth's engraving shows an idealized London street scene where beer drinking is associated with manly strength, good humor, and prosperity. The self-satisfied corpulent figure in the left foreground reads a copy of the king's speech to Parliament. We can imagine him offering a running commentary to his drinking companions as he reads.

philosophers, social critics, artists, members of the aristocracy, and the commercial elite.

The intellectual ferment of the era deeply influenced the expanding middle class, who were eager consumers of the widely available books and inexpensive newspapers and journals. This broadening of the intellectual audience overwhelmed traditional institutions of censorship. New public venues like the thousands of coffeehouses and teashops of cities and market towns also became locations to discuss scientific discoveries, new technologies, and controversial works on human nature and politics, expanding the Enlightenment's influence beyond the literate minority.

The Western Hemisphere shared in Europe's intellectual ferment. Among peoples compelled to accept the dependence and inferiority explicit in colonial rule, the idea that government authority rested on the consent of the governed proved explosive. The efforts of ordinary men and women to resist the growth of government power and the imposition

# Chronology

| | The Americas | Europe |
|---|---|---|
| 1750 | **1756–1763** French and Indian War<br>**1770** Boston Massacre<br>**1776** American Declaration of Independence<br>**1778** U.S. alliance with France<br>**1781** British surrender at Yorktown<br>**1783** Treaty of Paris ends American Revolution<br><br>**1791** Slaves revolt in Saint Domingue (Haiti)<br><br>**1798** Toussaint L'Ouverture defeats British in Haiti | **1756–1763** Seven Years' War<br><br>**1778** Death of Voltaire and Rousseau<br><br>**1789** Storming of Bastille begins French Revolution; Declaration of Rights of Man and of the Citizen in France<br>**1793–1794** Reign of Terror in France<br>**1795–1799** The Directory rules France<br>**1799** Napoleon overthrows the Directory |
| 1800 | **1804** Haitians defeat French invasion and declare independence<br>**1808–1809** Revolutions for independence begin in Spanish South America<br>**1810–1821** Mexican movement for independence<br>**1822** Brazil gains independence<br>**1838** Slavery abolished in British colonies<br>**1848** Women's Rights Convention in Seneca Falls, New York; slavery abolished in French colonies | **1804** Napoleon crowns himself emperor<br>**1804–1814** Napoleon occupies most of Europe<br>**1812** Napoleon fails to conquer Russia<br>**1814** Napoleon abdicates; Congress of Vienna opens<br>**1830** Greece gains independence; revolution in France<br>**1848** Revolutions in France, Austria, Germany, Hungary, and Italy |
| 1850 | **1861–1865** U.S. Civil War; 1863 Emancipation Proclamation; 1865 Thirteenth Amendment abolishes slavery in United States<br>**1873** Puerto Rico abolishes slavery<br>**1886** Cuba abolishes slavery<br>**1888** Brazil abolishes slavery | |

of new cultural forms provided an important political undercurrent to much of the revolutionary agitation and conflict between 1750 and 1850. But spontaneous popular uprisings gained revolutionary potential only when they coincided with ideological division and conflict within the governing class.

## SECTION REVIEW

- Wars fought to protect colonies and trade routes overwhelmed the fiscal resources of European powers.
- Also important were the ideas and critical spirit of the Enlightenment, particularly the political ideas of Locke and Rousseau.
- These new ideas received the support of reformist nobles and monarchs.
- Progressive intellectual debate spread to the colonial societies of the Western Hemisphere.

## THE AMERICAN REVOLUTION, 1775–1800

■ *What were the direct causes of the American Revolution?*

After defeating the French in 1763, the British government faced two related problems in its North American colonies. One was the likelihood of armed conflict with Amerindian peoples as settlers quickly pushed west of the Appalachian Mountains across the Ohio River. Already burdened with war debts, Britain desperately wanted to avoid additional expenditures for frontier defense. The other problem was how to get colonists to shoulder more of the costs of colonial defense and administration. Every effort to impose new taxes or prevent new settlements sparked bitter resentment and protest and ultimately led to violent rebellion.

**Frontiers and Taxes**    The British government's Proclamation of 1763, which sought to establish an effective western limit for settlement, threw into question the claims of thousands of established farmers without effectively protecting Amerindian land. The Quebec Act of 1774 annexed disputed lands to the province of Quebec, thus denying eastern colonies the authority to distribute lands claimed on the basis of original charters. Colonists saw the Quebec Act as tyrannical, and the Amerindian peoples received no relief from the continuous assault on their lands.

In comparison with the French, Spanish, and Portuguese colonies of the Americas, the settlers of the British colonies enjoyed substantial political autonomy. Metropolitan producers and merchants grew rich on colonial consumption of British cloth, porcelains, tea, and other imports, and these goods played a key role in forging a unified colonial culture. When new commercial regulations threatened New England's profitable trade with Spanish and French Caribbean sugar colonies, women from prominent colonial families organized boycotts of British goods. The Stamp Act of 1765, a tax on all legal documents, newspapers, pamphlets, and nearly all printed material, led to angry protests and more boycotts. Although this combination of protest and boycott forced the repeal of the Stamp Act, Britain imposed new taxes and duties in 1767. Parliament also sent British troops to quell colonial riots. Unable to control the streets of Boston, British authorities reacted by threatening colonial liberties, dissolving the colonial legislature of Massachusetts, and dispatching a warship and two regiments of soldiers. Support for a complete break with Britain grew in 1770 when British soldiers fired at an angry Boston crowd, killing five civilians. The "Boston Massacre," which seemed to expose the naked force on which colonial rule rested, radicalized public opinion throughout the colonies.

Parliament attempted to calm colonial opinion by repealing some taxes and duties, then stumbled into another crisis when it granted the East India Company a monopoly for importing tea to the colonies, raising anew the constitutional issue of Parliament's right to tax the colonies. The monopoly also offended wealthy colonial merchants, who were excluded from this profitable commerce. The crisis

Fotosearch/Archive Photos/Getty Images

**The Tarring and Feathering of a British Official, 1774**   British periodicals responded to the rising tide of colonial protest by focusing on mob violence and the breakdown of public order. This illustration portrayed the brutal treatment given John Malcomb, commissioner of customs at Boston. For many in Britain, colonial demands for liberty were little more than an excuse for mob violence.

came to a head in the already politically tense port of Boston when protesters dumped tea worth £10,000 into Boston harbor.

**The Course of Revolution**   As the crisis mounted, patriots created new governing bodies, effectively deposed many British governors and other officials, passed laws, appointed judges, and even took control of colonial militias. Simultaneously, radical leaders organized crowds to intimidate loyalists—people who were pro-British—and to enforce the boycott of British goods. Few thought compromise possible. Elected representatives, meeting in Philadelphia as the Continental

Congress of 1775, now assumed the powers of government, creating a currency and organizing an army. **George Washington** (1732–1799), a Virginia planter who had served in the French and Indian War, was named commander. On July 4, 1776, Congress approved the Declaration of Independence, the document that proved to be the most enduring statement of the revolutionary era's ideology:

> We hold these truths to be self evident: That all men are created equal; that they are endowed by their creator with certain unalienable rights; that among these are life, liberty and the pursuit of happiness; that, to secure these rights, governments are instituted among men, deriving their just powers from the consent of the governed.

This affirmation of popular sovereignty and individual rights influenced the language of revolution and popular protest around the world.

To shore up British authority, Great Britain sent more than 400 ships, 50,000 soldiers, and 30,000 German mercenaries. But this military commitment proved futile. Although British forces won most of the battles, Washington slowly built a competent Continental army and civilian support networks that provided supplies and financial resources. In the final decisive battle, fought at Yorktown, Virginia, an American army, supported by French soldiers, who had allied with the Continentals in 1778, besieged a British army led by General Charles Cornwallis. With escape cut off by a French fleet, Cornwallis surrendered to Washington as the British military band played "The World Turned Upside-Down."

## New Republican Institutions

Ignoring the British example of an unwritten constitution, representatives in each of the newly independent states drafted formal charters and submitted the results to voters for ratification. Europeans were fascinated by these written constitutions and by their formal ratification by the people. Here was the social contract of Locke and Rousseau made manifest. The state constitutions also placed severe limits on executive authority and granted broad powers to legislatures. Many state constitutions included bills of rights to provide further protection against tyranny.

### SECTION REVIEW

- The American Revolution grew from British settlement and tax policies after the French and Indian War.
- New taxes and commercial policies provoked colonial protest and riots in the colonies.
- Armed conflict between British troops and colonists led to the calling of the Continental Congress and the Declaration of Independence.
- French support for the American Revolution proved crucial.
- The American states developed republican institutions and procedures on the state and national levels.
- Although the new government was quite democratic, only a minority of adults gained full rights.

It proved more difficult to frame a national constitution. The Articles of Confederation—the first constitution of the United States—were not accepted until 1781. With the coming of peace in 1783, there was an effort to fashion a new convention. Debate at the **Constitutional Convention**, which began meeting in May 1787, focused on several issues: representation, electoral procedures, executive powers, and the relationship between the federal government and the states. The final compromise provided for a two-house legislature: the lower house (the House of Representatives) to be elected directly by voters and the upper house (the Senate) to be elected by state legislatures. The chief executive—the president—was to be elected indirectly by "electors" selected by ballot in the states (each state had a number of electors equal to the number of its representatives and senators).

Although the U.S. Constitution created the most democratic government of the era, only a minority of the adult population had full political rights. Southern leaders were able to protect the institution of slavery by counting three-fifths of the slave population to allocate the number of congressional representatives. Although women had led prewar boycotts and organized charitable relief during the war, they also were denied political rights in the new republic.

**George Washington**  Military commander of the American Revolution. He was the first elected president of the United States (1789–1797).

**Constitutional Convention**  Meeting in 1787 of the elected representatives of the thirteen original states to write the Constitution of the United States.

# THE FRENCH REVOLUTION, 1789–1815

■ *What were the origins and accomplishments of the French Revolution?*

The French Revolution confronted the entrenched privileges of an established church, monarchy, and aristocracy more directly than the American Revolution did. It also expanded mass participation in political life and radicalized the democratic tradition. But in the end, the passions unleashed in France by revolutionary events could not be sustained.

## French Society and Fiscal Crisis

French society was divided into three estates. The clergy, called the First Estate, numbered about 130,000 in a nation of 28 million. The Catholic Church owned about 10 percent of the nation's land and extracted substantial amounts of wealth from the economy in the form of tithes and ecclesiastical fees. Despite its substantial wealth, the church was exempted from nearly all taxes.

The 300,000 members of the nobility, the Second Estate, controlled about 30 percent of the land and retained ancient rights on much of the rest. Nobles held the vast majority of high administrative, judicial, military, and church positions. Though traditionally barred from some types of commercial activity, nobles were also important participants in wholesale trade, banking, manufacturing, and mining.

The Third Estate included everyone else. There were three times as many members of the bourgeoisie (boor-zhwah-ZEE) in 1774, when Louis XVI took the throne, as there had been in 1715, at the end of Louis XIV's reign. Peasants accounted for 80 percent of the French population. They owned some property and lived decently when crops were good and prices stable. By 1780, however, poor harvests had decreased their incomes.

The nation's poor were a large, growing, and troubling sector. Urban streets swarmed with beggars and prostitutes. Unable to afford decent housing, obtain steady employment, or protect their children, the poor periodically erupted in violent protest and rage. In the countryside, violence was often the reaction to increased dues and fees. In towns and cities, an increase in the price of bread often provided the spark.

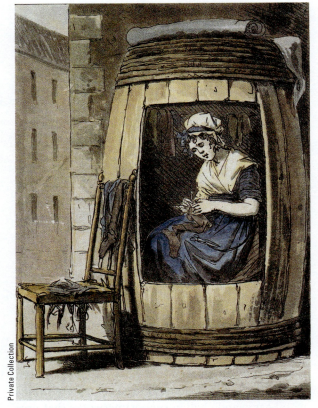

Private Collection

**Parisian Stocking Mender** The poor lived very difficult lives. This woman uses a discarded wine barrel as a shop where she mends socks.

These explosive episodes, however, were not revolutionary in character. The remedies sought were conventional and immediate rather than structural and long term. That was to change when the Crown tried to solve its fiscal crisis by imposing new taxes on the nobility and other groups that in the past had enjoyed exemptions. The effort failed in the face of widespread protests and the refusal of the Parlement of Paris, an appeals court, to register the new tax. Frustrated by these actions, French authorities exiled the members of the Parlement and pushed through a series of unpopular fiscal measures.

Despite the worsening fiscal crisis, the French government took on the heavy burden of supporting the American Revolution, delaying financial collapse by borrowing enormous sums. By the end of the war with Britain, more than half of France's national budget was required to service the debt alone. In 1787, the desperate king called an Assembly of Notables to approve a radical and comprehensive reform of economic and fiscal policy. Despite the fact that the king's advisers selected this assembly from the high nobility, the judiciary, and the clergy, these representatives of France's most privileged classes proved unwilling to support the proposed reforms and new taxes. Instead, they sought to protect their interests by questioning the competence of the king and his ministers to supervise the nation's affairs, thus creating the conditions for political revolution.

## Protest Turns to Revolution

The refusal of the elite to grant needed tax concessions forced the king to call the **Estates General**, a customary consultative body representing the three estates that had not met since 1614. Traditionally, the three estates met separately, and a positive vote by two of the three was required for action. Tradition, however, was quickly overturned when the Third Estate—mostly men of substantial property, including some who were inclined toward constitutional monarchy—refused to conduct business until the king ordered the other two estates to sit with it in a single body. During a six-week period of stalemate, sympathetic clergy, and eventually nobles, joined the debates of the Third Estate, beginning a transition toward an assembly that could claim to represent the nation.

When this expanded Third Estate declared itself the **National Assembly**, the king realized the reformers intended to force him to accept a constitutional monarchy. Louis's agenda for fiscal reform was being displaced by the central ideas of the era: that the people are sovereign and the legitimacy of rulers depends on their fulfilling the people's will. Louis prepared for a confrontation with the National Assembly by moving military forces to Versailles.

A succession of bad harvests beginning in 1785 had propelled bread prices upward throughout France and provoked an economic depression. By the time the Estates General met, nearly a third of the Parisian workforce was unemployed. Hunger and anger marched hand in hand through working-class neighborhoods. When the people of Paris heard that the king was massing troops to arrest the representatives, crowds of common people began to seize arms and mobilize. On July 14, 1789, a crowd attacked the Bastille (bass-TEEL), a medieval fortress used as a prison. The futile defense of the Bastille cost ninety-eight lives before its garrison surrendered. Enraged, the attackers hacked the commander to death and then paraded through the city with his head and that of Paris's chief magistrate stuck on pikes.

These events coincided with uprisings by peasants in the country. Peasants sacked manor houses, destroyed documents that recorded their traditional obligations, refused to pay taxes and dues to landowners, and seized common lands. Forced to recognize the fury raging through rural areas, the National

The Siege of the Bastille, 1789 (gouache on card), Cholat, Claude (18th-19th century) / Musée de la Ville de Paris, Musée Carnavalet, Paris, France / Giraudon / The Bridgeman Art Library

**Parisians Storm the Bastille**  An eyewitness to the storming of the Bastille on July 14, 1789, painted this representation of this epochal event, still celebrated by the French as a national holiday.

**Estates General**  France's traditional national assembly with representatives of the three estates, or classes, in French society: the clergy, nobility, and commoners. The calling of the Estates General in 1789 led to the French Revolution.

**National Assembly**  French Revolutionary assembly (1789–1791). The Estates General gave itself this title when it came together and demanded radical change. In 1789 it passed the Declaration of the Rights of Man and of the Citizen.

New Playing card designs dating from the French Revolution, 1793 (coloured engraving), French School, (18th century)/Private Collection/Archives Charmet/The Bridgeman Art Library

**Playing Cards from the French Revolution**  Even playing cards could be used to attack the aristocracy and Catholic Church. In this pack of cards, "Equality" and "Liberty" replaced kings and queens.

Assembly voted to end traditional obligations and the privileges of the nobility and church, essentially ending the feudal system. Having won this victory, peasants ceased their revolt.

These popular uprisings strengthened the hand of the National Assembly in its dealings with the king and led to passage of the **Declaration of the Rights of Man and of the Citizen**, which was more sweeping in its language than the American Declaration of Independence. Among the enumerated natural rights were "liberty, property, security, and resistance to oppression." The Declaration of the Rights of Man and of the Citizen also guaranteed free expression of ideas, equality before the law, and representative government.

While delegates debated political issues in Versailles, the economic crisis worsened in Paris. The anger of the working women of Paris, struggling to feed their families in the face of high food prices, had a hard edge. On October 5, thousands of women marched the 12 miles (19 kilometers) to Versailles and forced their way into the National Assembly to demand action: "the point is that we want bread," they shouted. The crowd then entered the royal apartments, killed some of the king's guards, and searched for Queen Marie Antoinette (ann-twah-NET), whom they hated as a symbol of extravagance. They then forced the royal family to relocate to Paris.

In the next two years, the National Assembly achieved a radically restructured French society. It passed a new constitution that dramatically lim-

ited monarchial power and abolished the nobility as a hereditary class. Economic reforms swept away monopolies and trade barriers within France. This body was eventually renamed the Legislative Assembly. Its legislators seized church lands to use as collateral for a new paper currency and mandated that priests, who were to be elected, be placed on the public payroll. When the Assembly forced priests to take a loyalty oath, however, many Catholics joined a growing counter-revolutionary movement.

At first, many European monarchs welcomed the weakening of the French king, but by 1791 Austria and Prussia were threatening to intervene in support of the monarchy. The Legislative Assembly responded by declaring war. Although the war went badly at first for French forces, people across France responded patriotically to foreign invasions, forming huge new volunteer armies and mobilizing national resources to meet the challenge. By the end of 1792, French armies had gained the upper hand everywhere.

In this period of national crisis and foreign threat, the French Revolution entered its most radical phase. A failed effort by the king and queen to escape from Paris cost the king his remaining popular support. As foreign armies crossed into France, his behavior was seen as treasonous. In August 1792, the Legislative Assembly suspended his authority and ordered his imprisonment, calling for the formation of a new National Convention to be elected by all men. Swept along by popular passion, the newly elected National Convention convicted Louis XVI of treason, sentenced him to death, and proclaimed France a republic.

**Declaration of the Rights of Man and of the Citizen**  Statement of fundamental political rights adopted by the French National Assembly at the beginning of the French Revolution.

# environment & technology

## The Guillotine

**N**o machine more powerfully symbolizes the revolutionary era than the guillotine. The machine immortalizes Joseph Ignace Guillotin (1738–1814), a physician and member of the French Constituent Assembly. In 1789 Guillotin recommended that executions be made more humane by use of a beheading device. He sought to replace hangings, used for commoners, and beheadings by axe, used for the nobility. Both forms of execution were often conducted with little skill, leading to gruesome and painful deaths. Guillotin believed that a properly designed machine would produce predictable, nearly painless deaths and remove the social distinction between commoners and nobles, embarrassing in a more egalitarian age.

After 1791 execution by beheading became the common sentence for all capital crimes. Another physician, Antoine Louis, secretary of the College of Surgeons, designed the actual machine. Once directed to produce a suitable device, Louis, in many ways a typical technician of his time, systematically examined devices used elsewhere and experimented until satisfied with his results. Praised by contemporaries because it seemed to remove human agency, and therefore revenge, from the death penalty, the guillotine became the physical symbol of the Terror.

**The Guillotine** *The guillotine, introduced as a more humane and democratic alternative to traditional executions, came to symbolize the arbitrary violence of the French Revolution. In this contemporary cartoon Robespierre, the architect of the Terror, serves as executioner while surrounded by guillotines.*

The Art Archive

The guillotine ended the king's life in January 1793. Invented in the spirit of the era as a more humane way to execute the condemned, this machine was to become the bloody symbol of the Revolution (see Environment and Technology: The Guillotine). During this period of repression, called the Reign of Terror (1793–1794), competing factions used rumors of counter-revolutionary plots to justify the use of violence. Approximately 40,000 people were executed or died in prison. This radical phase ended in July 1794 when the Terror's leaders were themselves executed by guillotine.

### Reaction and Dictatorship

Purged of the radicals, the National Convention began to undo the radical reforms. It removed emergency economic controls that held down prices and protected the working class. Gone also was toleration

499

for violent popular demonstrations. When the Paris working class rose in protest in 1795, the Convention reacted with overwhelming military force. It allowed the Catholic Church to regain much of its former influence, but it did not return the church's confiscated wealth. Finally, it ratified a more conservative constitution that protected property, established a voting process that reduced the power of the masses, and created a new executive authority, the Directory.

After losing the election of 1797, the Directory refused to give up power, effectively ending the republican phase of the Revolution. Political authority now depended on coercive force rather than elections. Two years later, a brilliant young general in the French army, **Napoleon Bonaparte** (1769–1821), seized power. Just as the American and French Revolutions had been the start of the modern democratic tradition, the military intervention that brought Napoleon to power in 1799 marked the advent of another modern form of government: popular authoritarianism.

In contrast to the National Convention, Napoleon proved capable of realizing France's dream of dominating Europe and providing effective protection for persons and property at home. Negotiations with the Catholic Church led to the Concordat of 1801, which gave French Catholics the right to practice their religion freely. Napoleon's Civil Code of 1804 asserted two basic principles inherited from the moderate first stage of the French Revolution: equality in law and protection of property. Even some members of the nobility were won over when Napoleon declared himself emperor and France an empire in 1804.

While it reestablished order, the Napoleonic system denied or restricted many individual rights. The Civil Code denied women basic political rights (a process that had begun under the Terror) and only allowed them to participate in the economy with the guidance and supervision of fathers and husbands. Free speech was limited. Criticism of the government, viewed as subversive, was proscribed, and most opposition newspapers disappeared.

Ultimately, the Napoleonic system depended on the success of French arms (see Map 21.1). From Napoleon's assumption of power until his fall, no single European state could defeat the French military. Austria and Prussia were forced to become allies of France. Only Britain, protected by its powerful navy,

remained able to thwart Napoleon's plans to dominate Europe. In June 1812, Napoleon made the fateful decision to invade Russia with 600,000 men, the largest army ever assembled in Europe. Five weeks after occupying Moscow, he was forced to retreat, his army destroyed by the brutal Russian winter and attacks by Russian forces. A broken and battered remnant of 30,000 men made it back to France.

After the debacle in Russia, Austria and Prussia deserted Napoleon and entered an alliance with England and Russia. Unable to defend Paris, Napoleon abdicated the throne in April 1814 and was exiled to the island of Elba off the coast of Italy.

## Retrenchment, Reform, and Revolution

The French Revolution and Napoleon's imperial ambitions had threatened the survival of the old European order by overturning ancient monarchies and tossing aside long-established political institutions. The very existence of the nobility and church had seemed at risk. Under the leadership of the Austrian foreign minister, Prince Klemens von Metternich (MET-uhr-nik) (1773–1859), Britain, Russia, Austria, and Prussia, along with representatives from other countries, worked together in Vienna to create a comprehensive peace settlement that would safeguard the conservative order. Because the participants in the **Congress of Vienna** believed that a strong and stable France was the best guarantee of future peace, the French monarchy was reestablished, and Metternich sought to offset French strength with a balance of power.

Despite the power of the conservative monarchs, popular support for national self-determination and democratic reform grew throughout Europe. In 1821 Greek patriots launched a movement for independence from Ottoman control, and in 1830 Russia, France, and Great Britain forced the Ottoman Empire to recognize Greek independence. That same year,

**Napoleon Bonaparte** General who overthrew the French Directory in 1799 and became emperor of the French in 1804. Failed to defeat Great Britain and abdicated in 1814. Returned to power briefly in 1815 but was defeated and died in exile.

**Congress of Vienna** Meeting of representatives of European monarchs called to reestablish the old order after the defeat of Napoleon I.

**Map 21.1 Napoleon's Europe, 1810** By 1810 Great Britain was the only remaining European power at war with Napoleon. Because of the loss of the French fleet at the Battle of Trafalgar in 1805, Napoleon was unable to threaten Britain with invasion, and Britain was able to assist the resistance movements in Spain and Portugal, thereby helping weaken French power. © Cengage Learning

**Legend:**
- French empire
- Dependent states
- Allied with Napoleon
- At war with Napoleon
- ★ Major battle

**Scale:**
400 Mi.
400 Km.
200
200
0
0

ATLANTIC OCEAN

North Sea

Baltic Sea

Black Sea

Mediterranean Sea

GREAT BRITAIN
- London

KINGDOM OF NORWAY AND DENMARK
- Stockholm
- Copenhagen

KINGDOM OF SWEDEN

RUSSIAN EMPIRE
- St. Petersburg
- Moscow
- Smolensk
- Kiev
- ★ Borodino 1812

SWEDISH POMERANIA

PRUSSIA
- Lübeck
- Hamburg
- Bremen
- Berlin
- Königsberg
- Danzig
- Tilsit
- ★ Friedland 1807

WESTPHALIA
- ★ Auerstädt 1806
- ★ Jena 1806

SAXONY

GRAND DUCHY OF WARSAW

CONFEDERATION OF THE RHINE

BADEN
- Zurich

WÜRTTEMBERG

BAVARIA

SWITZERLAND

AUSTRIAN EMPIRE
- Vienna
- Pressburg
- Buda
- Pest
- ★ Austerlitz 1805
- ★ Wagram 1804

ILLYRIAN PROVINCES

KINGDOM OF ITALY
- Milan
- Genoa
- ★ Marengo 1800

FRANCE
- Paris
- Amiens
- Lunéville
- Marseilles
- Brussels
- ★ Waterloo 1815

KINGDOM OF NAPLES
- Rome
- Naples

KINGDOM OF SICILY
- Palermo
- Malta (Gr. Br.)

Corsica
Elba
Sardinia

SPAIN
- Madrid

PORTUGAL
- Lisbon
- ★ Trafalgar 1805

GIBRALTAR (Gr. Br.)

OTTOMAN EMPIRE
- Constantinople
- Athens

Ionian Is. (Gr. Br.)

Rhine R.
Elbe R.
Neman R.
Danube R.

- The French Revolution grew from mounting social and financial crises after 1763.

- The crisis within the Estates General sparked the Revolution when the Third Estate declared itself the National Assembly.

- Economic crisis and foreign intervention radicalized the Revolution, resulting in the execution of Louis XVI and the Reign of Terror.

- Reacting against the violence of the Terror and exhausted by foreign enemies, France turned to Napoleon Bonaparte, who dominated Europe until he was defeated in 1814.

- Despite conservative retrenchment after Napoleon's fall, liberal reform and revolution continued through the failed 1848 revolutions.

the people of Paris rose up and forced King Charles X to abdicate. His successor, Louis Philippe (loo-EE fee-LEEP) (r. 1830–1848), reestablished the constitution and extended voting privileges.

Despite limited political reform, conservatives continued to hold the upper hand in Europe. Finally, in 1848, the desire for democratic reform and national self-determination and the frustrations of urban workers led to upheavals across Europe. The **Revolutions of 1848** began in Paris, where members of the middle class and workers united to overthrow the regime of Louis Philippe and create the Second French Republic. Adult men were given voting rights, slavery was abolished in French colonies, the death penalty was ended, and a ten-hour workday was legislated for Paris. But Parisian workers' demands for programs to reduce unemployment and lower prices provoked conflicts with the middle class, which wanted to protect property rights. Desiring the reestablishment of order, the French elected Louis Napoleon, a nephew of the former emperor, president in December 1848. Three years later, he overturned the constitution and, after ruling briefly as dictator, proclaimed himself Emperor Napoleon III. He remained in power until 1871. Despite the heroism of the 1848 revolutionaries in Vienna, Rome, and Berlin, they failed to gain either their nationalist or republican objectives. Metternich, the symbol of reaction, fled Vienna in disguise, but little lasting change occurred. Monarchs retained the support not only of aristocrats

but also of professional militaries, largely recruited from among peasants who had little sympathy for urban workers.

## REVOLUTION SPREADS

■ *How did revolution in one country help incite revolutions elsewhere?*

In the Americas the legacies of the American and French Revolutions led to a new round of struggles for independence. News of revolutionary events in France destabilized the colonial regime in Saint Domingue (present-day Haiti) and helped initiate the first successful slave rebellion. The same economic and political forces that had undermined British rule in the colonies that became the United States were present in Spanish America and Brazil.

### The Haitian Revolution

The French colony of Saint Domingue produced two-thirds of France's tropical imports and generated nearly one-third of all French foreign trade. This impressive wealth depended on a brutal slave regime. The harsh punishments and high mortality rate inflicted on the slaves of Saint Domingue were notorious throughout the Caribbean.

In 1789, when news of the meeting of the Estates General arrived on the island, wealthy white planters sent a delegation to Paris to seek more home rule and greater economic freedom. The *gens de couleur* (zhahn deh koo-LUHR), the large mixed-race population of free black planters and urban merchants who owned slaves, also sent representatives. They sought political rights and a limit to racial discrimination, not an end to slavery.

The political turmoil in France weakened the colonial authority, permitting rich planters, poor whites, *gens de couleur*, and slaves to pursue their narrow interests in an increasingly bitter and

**Revolutions of 1848** Democratic and nationalist revolutions that swept across Europe. The monarchy in France was briefly overthrown. In Germany, Austria, Italy, and Hungary the revolutions failed.

***gens de couleur*** Free men and women of color in Haiti. They sought greater political rights and later supported the Haitian Revolution.

Burning of the town of Cap-Francais, Saint-Domingue (Haiti), 1795 (colour engraving), French School, (18th century)/Private Collection/Archives Charmet/The Bridgeman Art Library

**Burning of Cap Français, Saint Domingue, in 1793** In 1791, the slaves of Saint Domingue, France's richest colony, began a rebellion that, after years of struggle, ended slavery and created the Western Hemisphere's second independent nation, Haiti.

confrontational struggle. By 1791 whites and the *gens de couleur* were engaged in open warfare. This breach between the two groups of slave owners gave slaves an opening. Their rebellion began on the plantations of the north and spread through the colony. Rebelling slaves destroyed plantations, killed masters and overseers, and burned crops.

A leadership emerged that relied on elements of African political practice and revolutionary ideology from France to mobilize and direct the rebelling slaves. **Toussaint L'Ouverture** (discussed at the beginning of this chapter), a former domestic slave, swept aside his local rivals, defeated the British expeditionary force in 1798, and then led an invasion of the neighboring Spanish colony of Santo Domingo, freeing slaves there. While Toussaint asserted his loyalty to France, he gave the French government no effective role in local affairs.

In 1802, Napoleon sent a large military force to Saint Domingue as well as Guadeloupe to reestablish both French colonial authority and slavery. At first, French forces were successful, capturing Toussaint and sending him to France, where he died in prison. Eventually, however, the loss of thousands of lives to yellow fever and the resistance of the revolutionaries turned the tide. In 1804 Toussaint's successors declared independence, and the free republic of Haiti

joined the United States as the second independent nation in the Western Hemisphere, but the economy was now in ruins.

## Latin American Revolutions

Revolutionary documents like the American Declaration of Independence and the French Declaration of the Rights of Man and of the Citizen circulated widely in Latin America as well. But it was Napoleon's decision to invade Portugal (1807) and Spain (1808), not revolutionary ideas, that ignited Latin America's struggle for independence.

As a French army neared Lisbon in 1808, the Portuguese royal family fled to Brazil. Once arrived, King John VI maintained his court there for over a decade. In Spain, by contrast, Napoleon forced King Ferdinand VII to abdicate and placed his own brother, Joseph Bonaparte, on the throne. When Spanish patriots fighting against the French created a new political body, the Junta (HUN-tah) Central, they claimed authority over Spain's colonies. A vocal minority of powerful colonists objected.

**Toussaint L'Ouverture** Leader of the Haitian Revolution. He freed the slaves and gained effective independence for Haiti despite military interventions by the British and French.

In 1808 and 1809, popular movements overthrew Spanish colonial officials in Venezuela, Mexico, and Bolivia and created local juntas. In each case, Spanish repression strengthened the resolve for independence. By 1810 Spanish colonial authorities were facing a new round of revolutions.

In Caracas (the capital city of modern Venezuela), a revolutionary junta led by creoles (colonial-born whites) declared independence in 1811. Its leaders were landowners whose aim was to expand their own privileges by eliminating Spaniards from the upper levels of government and the church. They defended slavery and opposed full citizenship for the black and mixed-race majority. The junta's narrow agenda spurred Spanish loyalists to rally thousands of free blacks and slaves to defend the Spanish Empire.

In response, the revolutionary movement placed total political authority in the hands of its military leader **Simón Bolívar** (see-MOAN bow-LEE-varh) (1783–1830), the son of wealthy Venezuelan planters. Bolívar had traveled in Europe and studied the works of the Enlightenment. He was charismatic and effective in mobilizing support, successfully adapting his objectives and policies to attract new allies and build coalitions. He agreed to support emancipation in order to draw slaves and freemen to his cause and to gain military supplies from Haiti.

Military advantage shifted back and forth, but in 1820 a revolt in Spain distracted Spanish forces and swung momentum to Bolivar. After liberating present-day Venezuela, he also liberated Colombia, Ecuador, Bolivia, and finally Peru in 1824. But Bolívar's attempts to draw the former Spanish colonies into a formal confederation failed (see Map 21.2).

Buenos Aires (the capital city of modern Argentina and after Caracas the second important center of revolutionary activity in Spanish South America) declared independence as the United Provinces of the Río de la Plata in 1816. In the south, this coalition of militia commanders, merchants, and ranchers sought to retain control over the territory of the Viceroyalty of Río de la Plata, but a separatist movement defeated these ambitions and Argentina descended into chaos. However, a mixed force of Chileans and Argentines, led by José de San Martín (hoe-SAY deh san mar-TEEN) (1778–1850), liberated Chile in 1820.

The arrival of the Portuguese royal family in Brazil in 1808 had helped to maintain the loyalty of the colonial elite, but with Napoleon's defeat, King John VI returned to Portugal in 1821, leaving his son Pedro in Brazil as regent. By then, some of the Spanish colonies along Brazil's borders had gained independence, and Brazilians began to talk openly of independence. To hold on to Brazil, Pedro aligned himself with rising separatist sentiment, and in 1822 he declared Brazilian independence. Unlike its neighbors, which became constitutional republics, Brazil thus gained independence as a constitutional monarchy with Pedro I, son of the king of Portugal, as emperor. However, Pedro I ran afoul of the dominant slave-owning class because he opposed slavery, and he became unpopular when he used military force to control neighboring Uruguay. The constitutional monarchy was overthrown by republicans in 1889.

**Mexico**    In 1810 Mexico was Spain's wealthiest and most populous colony. The first stage of the revolution against Spain occurred in central Mexico, where ranchers and farmers had aggressively forced Amerindian communities from their traditional agricultural lands. Crop failures and epidemics further afflicted the region's rural poor.

On September 16, 1810, the parish priest of the small town of Dolores, **Miguel Hidalgo y Costilla** (mee-GEHL ee-DAHL-go ee cos-TEE-ah), rang the church bells and attracted thousands. In a fiery speech he urged the crowd to rise up against the oppression of Spanish officials. Tens of thousands of the rural and urban poor soon joined his movement. The Spanish as well as the wealthy Mexicans who owned the ranches and mines recognized the threat posed by the angry masses following Hidalgo, and Spanish forces captured and executed him in 1811.

Although insurgents continued to wage war, colonial rule seemed secure, but in 1821 Colonel Agustín de Iturbide (ah-goos-TEEN deh ee-tur-BEE-deh) and

**Simón Bolívar**    The most important military leader in the struggle for independence in South America. Born in Venezuela, he led military forces there and in Colombia, Ecuador, Peru, and Bolivia.

**Miguel Hidalgo y Costilla**    Mexican priest who led the first stage of the Mexican independence war in 1810. He was captured and executed in 1811.

**Map 21.2 Latin America by 1830** By 1830 patriot forces had overturned the Spanish and Portuguese Empires of the Western Hemisphere. Regional conflicts, local wars, and foreign interventions challenged the survival of many of these new nations following independence. © Cengage Learning

ATLANTIC OCEAN

PACIFIC OCEAN

OREGON COUNTRY (Joint U.S.-British occupation)

BRITISH NORTH AMERICA (CANADA) (Gr. Br.)

UNITED STATES

MEXICO 1821

New York
Philadelphia
Washington, D.C.
Charleston
San Antonio
New Orleans

Mississippi R.
Colorado R.
Rio Grande

Gulf of Mexico

BAHAMA IS. (Gr. Br.)

Havana

CUBA (Spain)

HAITI 1804

PUERTO RICO (Spain)

Mexico City
Veracruz

BRITISH HONDURAS (Gr. Br.)
GUATEMALA
Guatemala City

JAMAICA (Gr. Br.)

Caribbean Sea

TRINIDAD (Gr. Br.)

UNITED PROVINCES OF CENTRAL AMERICA 1823–1839

Panama

Caracas
VENEZUELA
Socorro
Bogotá

BR. GUIANA (Gr. Br.)
DUTCH GUIANA (Neth.)
FRENCH GUIANA (France)

Magdalena R.
Orinoco R.

GRAN COLOMBIA 1819–1830

Quito
ECUADOR

Galápagos Islands

Equator 0°

Amazon R.

EMPIRE OF BRAZIL 1822

Lima

PERU 1824

BOLIVIA 1825
La Paz
Sucre

Salvador

Paraná R.

PARAGUAY 1811

São Paulo
Rio de Janeiro

20°S

CHILE 1817

UNITED PROVINCES OF THE RIO DE LA PLATA 1816

URUGUAY 1828
Montevideo

Valparaíso
Santiago

ARGENTINA
Buenos Aires
Bahía Blanca

PATAGONIA (Disputed between Argentina and Chile)

Islas Malvinas (Falkland Islands)

0    500    1000 Km.
0    500    1000 Mi.

**1811** Year independence gained
  Colony

40°W
40°N
20°N
20°S
80°W
60°W

505

## SECTION REVIEW

- Revolutionary events in France prompted Saint Domingue's whites and *gens de couleur* to demand reforms.

- The French invasion of Portugal and Spain created a political crisis in their American colonies that in turn led to independence movements.

- Under the leadership of Simón Bolívar, several South American countries gained independence.

- Led by the son of the Portuguese king, Brazil gained independence as a monarchy.

- Mexico gained independence after a long and destructive war.

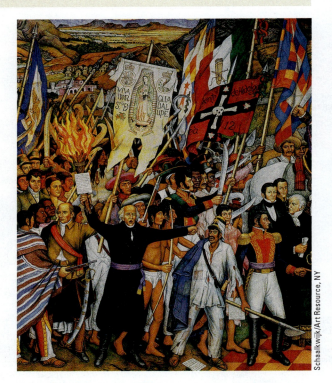

Schaalkwijk/Art Resource, NY

**Miguel Hidalgo y Costilla**  Padre Miguel Hidalgo y Costilla led the first stage of Mexico's revolution for independence by rallying the rural masses. His defeat, trial, and execution made him one of Mexico's most important political martyrs.

other loyalist commanders forged an alliance with insurgents to declare Mexico's independence. The conservative origins of Mexico's independence were made clear by the decision to create a monarchial government and crown Iturbide emperor. In early 1823, however, the army overthrew Iturbide and Mexico became a republic.

# ECONOMIC AND SOCIAL LIBERATION MOVEMENTS

■ *What economic and social liberation movements rose during the nineteenth century?*

The newly independent nations of the Western Hemisphere struggled to realize the Enlightenment ideals of freedom and individual liberty that had helped ignite the revolutions for independence. In both the United States and Latin America, strong antislavery sentiments were expressed during the struggles for independence. But in nearly all the new nations of the Western Hemisphere, revolutionary leaders asserted universal ideals of freedom and citizenship that contrasted sharply with the reality of slavery. Two groups denied full rights under the Constitution, women and free African Americans, played important roles in the abolition of slavery. By century's end, reform movements had made significant progress, but much remained to be done.

**The Abolition of Slavery**  In regions where the export of plantation products was most important—such as the United States, Brazil, and Cuba—the abolition of slavery was achieved with great difficulty. Those who sought to end slavery as an institution were called **abolitionists**. Despite their efforts, slavery survived in most of the hemisphere until the 1850s.

In the United States, some northern states had abolished slavery after the Revolution, and Congress banned the importation of new slaves in 1808. But the expansion of cotton agriculture stalled further progress. In Spanish America tens of thousands of slaves gained freedom by joining revolutionary armies during the wars for independence. After independence,

**abolitionists**  Men and women who agitated for a complete end to slavery. Abolitionist pressure ended the British transatlantic slave trade in 1808 and slavery in British colonies in 1834. In the United States the activities of abolitionists were one factor leading to the Civil War (1861–1865).

most Spanish American republics prohibited the slave trade, but growing international demand for sugar and coffee slowed the achievement of abolition. As prices rose for plantation products, Brazil and Cuba increased their imports of slaves.

After Britain ended its participation in the slave trade in 1807, it negotiated treaties with Spain, Brazil, and other importers of slaves to eliminate the slave trade to the Americas. But enforcement proved difficult. In the Caribbean, where almost 40 percent of all African slaves were shipped, the slave rebellion in Saint Domingue struck terror in the hearts of slave owners and convinced many that any effort to overthrow colonial rule would unleash new insurrections. As a result, there was little local support for abolition in the Caribbean. In these colonies abolition would result from decisions made in Europe by imperial governments.

Abolition in British colonies occurred in 1834, but "freed" slaves were compelled to remain with former masters as "apprentices." Abuses by planters and resistance to apprenticeship by former slaves led to complete abolition in 1838. France abolished slavery in its colonies a decade later. The decision to abolish slavery in the Dutch Empire in 1863 freed 33,000 slaves in Surinam and 12,000 in the Antilles.

During the long struggle to end slavery in the United States, American abolitionists argued that slavery offended both morality and the universal rights asserted in the Declaration of Independence. Southern leaders sought to protect slavery, however, by expanding into new territories in Louisiana and the West. While territorial expansion redrew the map of the United States, it also forced a national debate about slavery that contributed to the election of Abraham Lincoln as president in 1860.

After the election of Lincoln, who was committed to checking the spread of slavery, the southern states where slavery was legal seceded from the United States to form a new nation, the Confederate States of America. During the Civil War (1861–1865) that broke out between the northern states of the Union and the Confederacy, pressure for emancipation rose. Tens of thousands of black freemen and escaped slaves joined the Union army, while hundreds of thousands of slaves fled their masters' plantations and farms for the protection of advancing northern armies. President Lincoln began the abolition of slavery in 1863 by issuing the Emancipation Proclamation, which ended slavery in rebel states not occupied by the Union army. Up to 750,000 lives were lost before the Confederacy surrendered in 1865, making the U.S. Civil War the most destructive conflict in the history of the Western Hemisphere. Also in 1865 the Thirteenth Amendment to the Constitution abolished slavery completely.

After abolition in the United States, slavery continued to survive in Brazil, Puerto Rico, and Cuba. Reformers secured abolition in Puerto Rico in 1873, but in sugar-rich Cuba, abolition was more gradual, with Spain finally abolishing slavery in 1886. In Brazil, however, it was patriotism that won slaves their emancipation. Large numbers of slaves joined the Brazilian army in exchange for freedom during a war with Paraguay (1865–1870), and Brazil abolished slavery in 1888.

## Equal Rights for Women and Blacks

Two groups denied full rights under the Constitution, women and free African Americans, played important roles in the abolition of slavery. Women were among the leaders of the American Anti-Slavery Society and produced effective propaganda against slavery. Eventually, thousands of women joined the abolitionist cause. When social conservatives attacked their highly visible public role, many women became public advocates of female suffrage as well.

In 1848 a group of women angered by their exclusion from an international antislavery meeting issued a call for a conference to discuss women's rights. The resulting **Women's Rights Convention** at Seneca Falls, New York, issued a statement that said, in part, "We hold these truths to be self-evident: that all men and women are equal." While moderates focused on the issues of economic independence and legal rights, increasing numbers of women demanded the right to vote. Others lobbied to gain better conditions for women working outside the home, especially in textile factories.

**Women's Rights Convention** An 1848 gathering of women angered by their exclusion from an international antislavery meeting. They met at Seneca Falls, New York, to discuss women's rights.

Progress toward equality between men and women was equally slow in Canada and in Latin America. Canada's first women doctors received their training in the United States because women could not receive medical degrees until 1895. Argentina and Uruguay were among the first Latin American nations to provide public education for women, and both nations introduced coeducation in the 1870s. Chilean women gained access to some careers in medicine and law in the 1870s. In Brazil, where many women were in the abolitionist movement, four women graduated in medicine by 1882. Throughout the hemisphere more rapid progress occurred in lower-status careers that threatened male economic power less directly, and, by the end of the century, women dominated elementary school teaching.

From Canada to Argentina and Chile, the majority of working-class women, although having no direct involvement in reform movements, succeeded in transforming gender relations in their daily lives. By the end of the nineteenth century, large numbers of poor women worked outside the home on farms, in markets, and, increasingly, in factories.

Throughout the hemisphere, there was little progress toward eliminating racial discrimination. Blacks were denied the vote throughout the southern United States and were subjected to the indignity of segregation—consigned to separate schools, hotels, restaurants, seats in public transportation, and even water fountains. Racial discrimination against men and women of African descent was also common in Latin America, though seldom spelled out in legal codes. Latin Americans tended to view racial identity across a continuum of physical characteristics rather than in the narrow terms of black and white that defined race relations in the United States.

## SECTION REVIEW

- Following independence, American nations eventually abolished the slave trade and slavery.
- The long struggle to achieve women's rights and end racial and ethnic discrimination altered the Western Hemisphere's political culture.

# CONCLUSION

The last decades of the eighteenth century began a long period of revolutionary upheaval in the Atlantic world. Costly wars in Europe and along Europe's colonial frontiers in the Americas and Asia helped to provoke change, forcing European monarchs to impose new and unpopular taxes. The American Revolution initiated these transformations. Having defeated Britain, the citizens of this new American republic created the most democratic government of the time. While full rights were limited and slavery persisted, many Europeans saw this experiment as demonstrating the efficacy of the Enlightenment's most revolutionary political ideas. In the end, however, the compromises over slavery that had made a new Constitution possible in 1787 failed, and the new nation nearly disintegrated after 1860.

The French Revolution led temporarily to a more radical formulation of representative democracy, but it also led to the Terror, which cost tens of thousands of lives, the militarization of western Europe, and a destructive cycle of wars. Yet, despite these terrible costs, the French Revolution propelled the idea of democracy and the ideal of equality far beyond the boundaries established by the American Revolution. The Haitian Revolution, set in motion by events in France, not only created the second independent nation of the Western Hemisphere but also delivered a powerful blow to the institution of slavery. In Europe the excesses of the French Revolution and the wars that followed in its wake promoted the political ascent of Napoleon Bonaparte and democracy's modern nemesis, popular authoritarianism.

Each revolution had its own character. The revolutions in France and Haiti proved to be more violent and destructive than the American Revolution. American revolutionaries defeated Great Britain and established independence without overturning a colonial social and political order that depended on slavery in most of the southern colonies. Revolutionaries in France and Haiti faced more strongly entrenched and more powerful oppositions as well as greater social inequalities than American revolutionaries, and the resistance of privileged elites led inexorably to greater violence. Both French and Haitian revolutionaries also faced powerful foreign interventions that intensified the bloodshed and destructiveness of these revolutions.

The conservative retrenchment that followed the defeat of Napoleon succeeded in the short term. Monarchy, multinational empires, and the established church retained the loyalty of millions of Europeans and could count on the support of many of Europe's wealthiest and most powerful individuals. But liberalism and nationalism continued to stir revolutionary sentiment. The contest between adherents of the old order and partisans of change was to continue well into the nineteenth century. In the end, the nation-state, the Enlightenment legacy of rational inquiry, broadened political participation, and secular intellectual culture prevailed. This outcome was determined in large measure by the old order's inability to satisfy the demands of new social classes tied to an emerging industrial economy. The narrow confines of a hereditary social system could not contain the material transformations generated by industrial capitalism, and the doctrines of traditional religion could not contain the rapid expansion of scientific learning.

These revolutions began the transformation of Western society, but they did not complete it. Only a minority gained full political rights. Women did not achieve full political rights until the twentieth century. Democratic institutions, as in revolutionary France, often failed. Moreover, slavery endured in the Americas past the mid-1800s despite the revolutionary era's enthusiasm for individual liberty, leaving a legacy of racism and discrimination across the Americas.

# CHAPTER REVIEW

## PRELUDE TO REVOLUTION: THE EIGHTEENTH-CENTURY CRISIS

■ *How did the costs of imperial wars and the Enlightenment challenge the established authority of monarchs in Europe and the American colonies?* (page 491)

This era of revolution was, in large measure, the product of a long period of costly warfare among the imperial nations of Europe. Britain and France in particular faced fiscal crises as a result of colonial wars. Using taxes and institutions inherited from the past, they found it increasingly difficult to fund distant wars in the Americas or in Asia. In the British case, the costs of the French and Indian War led the government to attempt to impose unpopular taxes on its colonies. France faced an even more dire fiscal emergency as a result of its aid to the American revolutionaries. The refusal of powerful French interests to accept new taxes forced the king to call the Estates General and ultimately led to the French Revolution.

Meanwhile, the spread of literacy and the greater availability of books helped create an Enlightenment culture more open to reform and to the revolutionary change of existing institutions in Europe and in the Americas. But there were many distinct, even contradictory, currents in the Enlightenment. Nevertheless, the intellectual ferment of the era gave educated men and women the tools to criticize existing political institutions and the confidence to design new ones. The language of liberty and equality, even if poorly realized in the actions of revolutionary governments, proved a powerful solvent when applied to hierarchy and privilege.

## THE AMERICAN REVOLUTION, 1775–1800

■ *What were the direct causes of the American Revolution?* (page 493)

The American Revolution grew from British colonial policy after the French and Indian War. To avoid new military costs, Britain tried unsuccessfully through the Quebec Act to restrict western settlement and thus reduce conflict with the Amerindians. To pay its war debt, Britain imposed new taxes, duties, and commercial regulations on the colonies, including the Stamp Act. These acts led to violent unrest that culminated with the "Boston Massacre." Parliament repealed some of these acts but then gave the British East India Company a tea monopoly, thus provoking more violence. Colonial patriots met in the Continental Congress, assumed government powers, raised an army, and issued the Declaration of Independence.

## THE FRENCH REVOLUTION, 1789–1815

■ *What were the origins and accomplishments of the French Revolution?* (page 496)

The French Revolution erupted from the crises provoked by France's archaic social and tax system, financial collapse, urban unrest, and division between the monarchy and aristocracy. The immediate cause was the crisis within the Estates General, during which the Third Estate broke away and declared itself the National Assembly. Uprisings in Paris and the countryside strengthened the Assembly position, enabling it to press reforms embodied in the Declaration of the Rights of Man and of the Citizen. Further reforms restructured France's society and economy. However, foreign intervention pushed the Legislative Assembly to radical extremes that culminated with the execution of Louis XVI and the Reign of Terror.

Reaction against the Terror resulted in the conservative Directory and in the even more repressive dictatorship of Napoleon Bonaparte. Napoleon's military adventures ultimately led to his fall, and the Congress of Vienna sought to reestablish a conservative balance of power. Despite this retrenchment, revolutionary struggles continued, especially in France, where the 1830 uprising replaced Charles X with Louis-Philippe. In 1848 nationalist and republican revolutions flared throughout Europe. These won few lasting gains, however, and in France they resulted in the imperial rule of Napoleon III.

## REVOLUTION SPREADS

■ *How did revolution in one country help incite revolutions elsewhere?* (page 502)

Though very different in its root causes, the French Revolution was affected by the political ideas of the American Revolution. Those ideas expressed in Paris in turn encouraged Haitians to seek independence. Though the French Republic descended into dictatorship, Napoleon's occupation of Portugal and Spain had repercussions in the Western Hemisphere. The Portuguese king took refuge in Brazil, and after his return to Portugal the Brazilians supported a constitutional monarchy under his son. Different Spanish colonies saw the rise of revolutionary movements, some of which resulted in new independent countries. Each of these movements reflected some of the same rivalries among economic interests and between religious conservatives and champions of Enlightenment ideas.

## ECONOMIC AND SOCIAL LIBERATION MOVEMENTS

■ *What economic and social liberation movements rose during the nineteenth century?* (page 506)

In the newly independent nations of the Americas, the persistence of slavery and gender inequality clashed with the Enlightenment ideals that had fostered their revolutions. Rising demand for export crops after 1800 strengthened slavery in the southern United States and part of Latin America. Although Lincoln issued the Emancipation Proclamation during the Civil War, final abolition did not come until the Thirteenth Amendment passed in 1865. Britain ceased to participate in the slave trade in 1807 and worked to end the Atlantic trade through treaties with slave importers. Although Britain's navy forced compliance on Latin American importers, slavery continued in Brazil, Cuba, and Puerto Rico until late in the nineteenth century. Many women and free blacks were important abolitionists, and a movement for equal rights for these groups emerged. In the United States, women declared equal rights at the Seneca Falls Women's Rights Convention, but progress on gender equality and the elimination of racial discrimination was slow throughout the Western Hemisphere. Racial discrimination was legalized in the southern United States. It also persisted in Latin America without formal codification.

### Key Terms

Enlightenment (p. 491)

George Washington (p. 495)

Constitutional Convention (p. 495)

Estates General (p. 497)

National Assembly (p. 497)

Declaration of the Rights of Man and of the Citizen (p. 498)

Napoleon Bonaparte (p. 500)

Congress of Vienna (p. 500)

Revolutions of 1848 (p. 502)

*gens de couleur* (p. 502)

Toussaint L'Ouverture (p. 503)

Simón Bolívar (p. 504)

Miguel Hidalgo y Costilla (p. 504)

abolitionists (p. 506)

Women's Rights Convention (p. 507)

# CHAPTER 22

## 1800–1870

# Land Empires in the Age of Imperialism

© Cengage Learning

## CHAPTER PREVIEW

### THE OTTOMAN EMPIRE

■ What were the benefits and the drawbacks to the Ottoman Empire of the reforms adopted during the Tanzimat period?

### THE RUSSIAN EMPIRE

■ How did the Russian Empire maintain its status as both a European power and a great Asian land empire?

### THE QING EMPIRE

■ How did the impact of European imperialism on China differ from its impact on Russia and the Ottoman Empire?

### Conclusion

**ENVIRONMENT & TECHNOLOGY:** The Web of War

511

During the late 1860s, a little-known warlord named Yaqub Beg (ya-KOOB Bek) unified several Muslim uprisings in Inner Asia against a foreign Qing occupier. Only a hundred years earlier, in 1759, Qing armies successfully conquered a vast region of Inner Asia and called it Xinjiang (shin-JYAHNG), meaning "new territory" (see Chapter 19). Despite attempts to work with local leaders, tensions between locals and Chinese never eased, and the natives rebelled.

Yaqub took full diplomatic advantage of the empires surrounding him. To his south lay India, controlled by an expanding British Empire. To his north was the Russian Empire, Britain's rival in the quest to gain territory in Inner Asia. Yaqub sent emissaries to both empires in 1868 and signed commercial treaties in 1872 in exchange for their recognition of his rule over Xinjiang. He even received military support from the distant Ottoman Empire, whose ruler bestowed upon him the title "commander of the faithful." For a time it seemed that the Qing might not try to retake Xinjiang. It would be an expensive venture for a government that preferred to spend its money modernizing its army and navy. But fears that Russia might take over neighboring Mongolia drove the Chinese back into Xinjiang, and Yaqub's regime collapsed in 1877.

Yaqub's story illustrates the challenges facing Eurasian empires: old and inefficient ways of governing and an international climate dominated by European dependence on colonial wealth. During the early 1800s rapid population growth and slow agricultural growth affected much of Eurasia. In addition, earlier military expansion had left the land-based empires vulnerable to European military pressure (see Chapter 19). Responses to this pressure varied, with reform gaining headway in some lands, while tradition was reasserted in others. In the long run, attempts to meet western Europe's economic and political demands resulted in an increased foreign debt that further stressed the economies of Eurasian empires.

This chapter contrasts the experiences of the Qing Empire with those of the Russian and Ottoman Empires. Whereas the Qing opted for resistance, the others made varying attempts to adapt and reform. Russia eventually became part of Europe, while the Ottomans and the Qing became subject to ever-greater imperialist pressure. These different responses raise the question of the role of culture in shaping western Europe's relations with the rest of the world in the nineteenth century.

## THE OTTOMAN EMPIRE

■ *What were the benefits and the drawbacks to the Ottoman Empire of the reforms adopted during the Tanzimat period?*

During the eighteenth century the central government of the Ottoman Empire lost much of its power to provincial governors, military commanders, ethnic leaders, and bandit chiefs. In several parts of the empire local officials and large landholders tried to increase their independence and divert imperial funds into their own coffers.

This Ottoman weakness allowed Muhammad ibn Abd al-Wahhab (moo-HAH-muhd ib-uhn ab-dahl-wa-HAHB), a puritanical fundamentalist from Arabia, to take control of the holy cities of Mecca and Medina and deprive the sultan of organizing the annual pilgrimage. Mamluk slave-soldiers, who as a military class that ruled Egypt between 1260 and 1517, reemerged as a military force; and the Ottoman Janissaries, who had evolved into a hereditary military class of that in some provincial areas came into conflict with the mamluks (see Chapter 18), used their Istanbul power base to force Sultan Selim III to abandon efforts to train a modern, European-style army. For the sultans, the outlook was bleak, but the situation unexpectedly changed when France invaded Egypt.

### Egypt and the Napoleonic Example

Napoleon Bonaparte and an invasion force of 36,000 men and four hundred ships invaded Egypt in May 1798. The French quickly defeated the mamluk army. Fifteen months later, after being stopped by Ottoman land and British naval forces in an attempted invasion of Syria, Napoleon secretly left Cairo and returned to France. Three months later he seized power and made himself emperor.

# Chronology

| | Ottoman Empire | Russian Empire | Qing Empire |
|---|---|---|---|
| 1800 | | | 1794–1804  White Lotus Rebellion |
| | | 1801–1825  Reign of Alexander I | |
| | 1805–1849  Muhammad Ali governs Egypt | | |
| | 1808–1839  Rule of Mahmud II | 1812  Napoleon's retreat from Moscow | |
| | 1826  Janissary corps dissolved | 1825  Decembrist revolt | |
| | 1830  Greek independence | 1825–1855  Reign of Nicholas I | |
| | 1839  Abdul Mejid begins Tanzimat reforms | | 1839–1842  Opium War |
| 1850 | 1853–1856  Crimean War | 1853–1856  Crimean War | 1850–1864  Taiping Rebellion |
| | | 1855–1881  Reign of Alexander II | 1856–1860  Arrow War |
| | | 1861  Emancipation of the serfs | |
| | 1876  First constitution by an Islamic governmen | | |

Back in Egypt, his generals were cut off from France by British ships in the Mediterranean and had little hope of remaining in power. They agreed to withdraw in 1801. For the second time in three years, a collapse of military power produced a power vacuum in Egypt. The winner of the ensuing contest was **Muhammad Ali** (moo-HAM-mad AH-lee), whom the sultan had sent with a contingent of Albanian soldiers to restore imperial control. By 1805 he had taken the place of the official Ottoman governor, and by 1811 he had dispossessed the mamluks of their lands and privileges.

Muhammad Ali's rise to power coincided with the meteoric career of Emperor Napoleon I. It is not surprising, therefore, that he adopted many French practices in rebuilding the Egyptian state. Militarily, he established special schools for training artillery and cavalry officers, army surgeons, military band-masters, and others. The curricula of these schools featured European skills and sciences, and Muhammad Ali began to send promising officer trainees to France for education. In 1824 he started a gazette devoted to official affairs, the first newspaper in the Islamic world. As discussed in Chapter 20, Muhammad Ali built various sorts of factories to outfit his new army. These did not prove efficient enough to survive, but they showed a determination to achieve independence and parity with the European powers.

In the 1830s Muhammad Ali's son Ibrahim invaded Syria and instituted some of the changes already under way in Egypt. The improved quality of the new Egyptian army had been proven during the Greek war of independence (discussed later in this chapter), when Ibrahim had commanded an expeditionary force to help the sultan. In response, the sultan embarked on building his own new army in 1826. The two modernized forces met when Ibrahim invaded Anatolia in 1839 and defeated the Ottoman sultan's army. The road to Istanbul seemed open until the European powers intervened and forced a withdrawal to Egypt. Muhammad Ali remained Egypt's ruler, under the suzerainty of the sultan, until his death in 1849, and his family continued to rule the country until 1952. But his dream of making Egypt a mighty country capable of standing up to Europe faded. What survived was the example he had set for the sultans in Istanbul.

**Muhammad Ali**  Leader of Egyptian modernization in the early nineteenth century. He ruled Egypt as an Ottoman governor but had imperial ambitions. His descendants ruled Egypt until overthrown in 1952.

From Ignatius Mouradgea d'Ohsson, *Tableau General de l'Empire Ottoman,* large folio edition, Paris, 1787–1820, pl. 178, following p. 340

**Interior of the Ottoman Financial Bureau** This engraving from the eighteenth century depicts the governing style of the Ottoman Empire before the era of westernizing reforms. By the end of the Tanzimat period in 1876, government offices and the costumes of officials looked much more like those in contemporary European capitals.

## Ottoman Reform and the European Model, 1807–1853

At the end of the eighteenth century, Sultan Selim (seh-LEEM) III (r. 1789–1807), a forward-looking ruler who stayed abreast of events in Europe, introduced reforms to create European-style military units, bring provincial governors under central government control, and standardize taxation. The rise in government expenditures to implement the reforms was supposed to be offset by taxes on selected items, primarily tobacco and coffee. The Janissary military corps preserved their own economic privileges and power by violently resisting the creation of new military units, and the reforms ultimately failed on political rather than economic grounds.

At times, Janissary power produced military uprisings. In the Ottoman territory of **Serbia**, local residents intensely resented the control exercised by Janissary governors. The Orthodox Christians claimed that the Janissaries abused them. In response, Selim threatened to reassign the Janissaries to Istanbul. Suspecting that the sultan wanted to curb their political power, in 1805 the Janissaries revolted and massacred Christians in Serbia. Unable to reestablish central Ottoman rule over Serbia, the sultan had to rely on the ruler of Bosnia, another Balkan province, who joined his troops with the peasants of Serbia to suppress the Janissary uprising. When the threat of Russian intervention prevented the Ottomans from disarming the victorious Serbians, Serbia became effectively independent.

Other opponents of reform included ulama, or Muslim religious scholars, who distrusted the

**Serbia** The Ottoman province in the Balkans that rose up against Janissary control in the early 1800s. After World War II the central province of Yugoslavia.

From Edward William Lane, *The Manners and Customs of the Modern Egyptians* (London: J. M. D & Co. 1860)

**Street Scene in Cairo** This engraving from Edward William Lane's influential travel book, *Account of the Manners and Customs of the Modern Egyptians Written in Egypt During the Years 1833–1835*, conveys the image of narrow lanes and small stores that became stock features of European thinking about Middle Eastern cities.

secularization of law and taxation that Selim proposed. In the face of widespread rejection of his reforms, Selim suspended his program in 1806. Nevertheless, a massive military uprising occurred at Istanbul, and the sultan was deposed and imprisoned. Reform forces recaptured the capital, but not before Selim had been executed. Selim's cousin, Sultan Mahmud (mah-MOOD) II (r. 1808–1839), cautiously revived Selim's program, but he realized that reforms needed to be more systematic and imposed more forcefully. The effectiveness of radical reform in Muhammad Ali's Egypt drove this lesson home,

as did the insurrection in Greece, during which the Egyptian military outperformed the main Ottoman army.

Greek independence in 1830 had dramatic international significance. A combination of Greek nationalist organizations and interlopers from Albania powered the independence movement. Europe's interest in the classical age of Greece and Rome led many Europeans to consider the Greeks' struggle for independence a campaign to recapture their classical glory from Muslim oppression. Some—including English poet Lord Byron, who lost his life in the war—went to Greece to fight as volunteers. When the combined squadrons of the British, French, and Russian fleets, under orders to observe but not intervene in the war, made an unauthorized attack that sank the Ottoman fleet at the Battle of Navarino, Greek victory was assured (see Map 22.1).

Mahmud II concurred with the pro-Greek Europeans in viewing Ottoman military reversals in Greece as a sign of profound weakness. The sultan capitalized on popular outrage over the military setbacks by announcing the creation of a new artillery unit—one he had secretly been training. When the Janissaries revolted in 1826, he bombarded their barracks. The Janissary corps was officially dissolved.

Like Muhammad Ali, Mahmud felt he could not implement major changes without reducing the political power of the religious elite. But Ibrahim attacked from Syria in 1839 before he could restructure the bureaucracy and the educational and legal systems, where ulama power was strongest. Battlefield defeat, the decision of the rebuilt Ottoman navy to switch sides and support Egypt, and the death of Mahmud, all in the same year, left the empire completely dependent on the European powers for survival.

Mahmud's reforming ideas received their widest expression in the **Tanzimat** (TAHNZ-ee-maht) ("reorganization"), a series of reforms begun under his sixteen-year-old son and successor, Abdul Mejid (abdul meh-JEED), in 1839 and strongly endorsed by the European ambassadors. One proclamation called for

**Tanzimat** Restructuring reforms by the nineteenth-century Ottoman rulers, intended to move civil law away from the control of religious elites and make the military and the bureaucracy more efficient.

**Map 22.1  The Ottoman and Russian Empires, 1829–1914** At its height the Ottoman Empire controlled most of the perimeter of the Mediterranean Sea. But in the 1800s Ottoman territory shrank as many countries gained their independence. The Black Sea, where the Turkish coast was vulnerable to assault, became a weak spot as Russian naval power grew. Russian challenges to the Ottomans at the eastern end of the Black Sea and to the Persians east and west of the Caspian aroused fears in Europe that Russia was trying to reach the Indian Ocean. © Cengage Learning

The Ottoman Empire
- Territory lost, 1829–1877
- Territory lost, 1878–1913
- Ottoman Empire in 1914

The Russian Empire
- Russia in 1802
- Territory gained, by 1914

- Persia

public trials and equal protection under the law for all, whether Muslim, Christian, or Jew. It also guaranteed some rights of privacy, equalized the eligibility of men for conscription into the army (a practice copied from Egypt), and provided for a new, formalized method of tax collection that legally ended tax farming in the Ottoman Empire. It took many years and strenuous efforts by reforming bureaucrats, known as the "men of the Tanzimat," to give substance to these reforms.

Over time, one legal code after another—commercial, criminal, civil procedure—was introduced to take the place of the corresponding areas of religious legal jurisdiction. All the codes were modeled closely on those of Europe. The Shari'a, or Islamic law,

gradually became restricted to matters of family law such as marriage and inheritance. As the Shari'a was displaced, job opportunities for the ulama shrank.

European observers praised the reforms for their noble principles and rejection of religious influence. Ottoman citizens were more divided; the Christians and Jews, for whom the Europeans showed the greatest concern, were generally more enthusiastic than the Muslims. Many historians see the Tanzimat as the dawn of modern thought and enlightened government in the Middle East. Others point out that removing the religious elite from influence in government also removed the one remaining check on authoritarian rule.

**Modernized Ottoman Troops** This photograph of a contingent of Imperial Guards in the late nineteenth century shows them equipped and uniformed much like any other European army of the time. The only distinctive feature is the fez, a brimless hat adopted earlier in the century as a symbol of reform.

From one of the original photographic albums of Sultan Abdul Hamid II, 1842–1918/Library of Congress

Like Muhammad Ali, Sultan Mahmud sent military cadets to France and the German states for training. In the 1830s an Ottoman imperial school of military sciences, later to become Istanbul University, was established. Instructors from western Europe taught chemistry, engineering, mathematics, and physics in addition to military history. Military education became the model for more general educational reforms. In 1838 the first medical school was established to train army doctors and surgeons. Later, a national system of preparatory schools was created to feed graduates into the military schools. The subjects that were taught and many of the teachers were foreign, raising the issue of whether Turkish should be a language of instruction. Because it was easier to import and use foreign textbooks than to write new ones in Turkish, French became the preferred language in all advanced professional and scientific training. However, the great majority of students still learned to read and write in Quran schools down to the twentieth century.

In the capital city of Istanbul, the reforms stimulated the growth of a small but cosmopolitan milieu embracing European language and culture. The first Turkish newspaper, a government gazette modeled on that of Muhammad Ali, appeared in 1831. Other newspapers followed, many written in French. Travel to Europe—particularly to England and France—became popular among wealthy Turks. Interest in importing European military, industrial, and communications technology remained strong through the 1800s.

Changes in military practice had unforeseen cultural and social effects. Accepting the European notion that modern weapons and drill required modern military dress, beards were deemed unhygienic and, in artillery units, a fire hazard. Military headgear also became controversial. European military caps, which had leather bills on the front to protect against the glare of the sun, were not acceptable because they interfered with Muslim soldiers' touching their foreheads to the ground in prayer. The compromise was the brimless cap now called the *fez*, which was adopted by the military and then by Ottoman civil officials in the early years of Mahmud II's reign.

The empire's new orientation spread beyond the military. Government ministries that normally recruited from traditional bureaucratic families and relied on on-the-job training were gradually transformed into formal civil services hiring men educated in the new schools. Among self-consciously progressive men, particularly those in government service, European dress became the fashion in the Ottoman cities of the later 1800s, while traditional dress became a symbol of the religious, the rural, and the parochial.

Secularization of the legal code particularly affected non-Muslim Ottoman subjects. Islamic law had required non-Muslims to pay a special head tax that was sometimes explained as a substitute for military service. Under the Tanzimat, the tax was abolished and non-Muslims became liable for military service—unless they bought their way out by paying a new military exemption tax. The new law codes gave all subjects equal access to the civil courts, while the operations of the Islamic law courts shrank. What enhanced the status of non-Muslims most, however, was the strong concern for their welfare consistently expressed by the European powers. The Ottoman Empire became a rich field of operation for Christian missionaries and European supporters of Jewish community life in the Muslim world.

The public rights and political participation granted during the Tanzimat applied specifically to men. Private life, including everything connected to marriage and divorce, remained within the sphere of religious law, and at no time was there a question of political participation or reformed education for women. Indeed, the reforms may have decreased the influence of women. The political changes ran parallel to economic changes that also narrowed women's opportunities.

After silver from the Americas began to flood the empire in the 1600s, workers were increasingly paid in cash rather than in goods, and businesses associated with banking and finance developed. But women were barred from the early industrial jobs and the professions, and traditional "woman's work" such as weaving was increasingly mechanized and done by men.

Nevertheless, in the early 1800s women retained considerable power in the management and disposal of their own property, gained mostly through fixed shares of inheritance. After marriage a woman was often pressured to convert her landholdings to cash in order to transfer her personal wealth to her husband's family, with whom she and her husband would reside. However, this was not a requirement, since men were legally obligated to support their families single-handedly. Until the 1820s many wealthy women retained their say in the distribution of property through the creation of charitable trusts for their offspring. Because these trusts were set up in the religious courts, they could be designed to conform to the wishes of family members. Then, in the 1820s and 1830s the secularizing reforms of Mahmud II transferred jurisdiction over the charitable trusts from religious courts to the state and ended women's control over this form of property.

## The Crimean War and Its Aftermath

Since the reign of Peter the Great (r. 1689–1725), the Russian Empire had been attempting to expand southward at the Ottomans' expense (also discussed later in this chapter in the section on Russia and Asia). His successor, Catherine the Great (r. 1762–1796), had captured control of the north shore of the Black Sea by 1783; by 1815 Russia had pried the Georgian region of the Caucasus away from the Ottomans, and the threat of Russian intervention had prevented the Ottomans from crushing Serbian independence. When Muhammad Ali's Egyptian army invaded Syria in 1833, Russia signed a treaty in support of the Ottomans. In return, the sultan recognized Russia's claim to being the protector of all of the empire's Orthodox subjects. This set the stage for an obscure dispute that resulted in war.

Bowing to British and French pressure, in 1852 the sultan named France Protector of the Holy Sepulchre in Jerusalem. Russia protested, but the sultan held firm. So Russia invaded Ottoman territories in what is today Romania, and Britain and France went to war as allies of the sultan. The real causes of the war went beyond church quarrels in Jerusalem and involved diplomatic maneuvering among European powers over whether the Ottoman Empire should continue to exist and, if not, who should take over its territory. The *Eastern Question* was the simple name given to this complex issue. Though the powers, including Russia, had agreed to save the empire in 1839, Britain subsequently became suspicious of Russian ambitions. Prominent anti-Russian politicians in Britain feared that Russia would threaten the British hold on India.

Between 1853 and 1856 the **Crimean** (cry-ME-uhn) **War** raged in Romania, on the Black Sea, and on the Crimean peninsula. Britain, France, and the Italian kingdom of Sardinia-Piedmont sided with the Ottomans. Britain and France trapped the Russian fleet in the Black Sea, where its commanders decided to sink the ships to protect the approaches to Sevastopol, their main base in Crimea. An army largely made up of British and French troops landed and laid siege to the city. Official corruption and lack of railways hampered the Russians' attempts to supply their forces. On the Romanian front, the Ottomans resisted effectively. At Sevastopol, the Russians were outmatched militarily and suffered badly from disease. Tsar Nicholas died as defeat loomed, leaving his successor, Alexander II (r. 1855–1881), to sue for peace when Sevastopol finally fell three months later.

The Crimean War brought significant changes to all the combatants. The tsar and his government, already beset by demands for the reform of serfdom, education, and the military, were further discredited. In Britain and France, the conflict was accompanied by massive propaganda campaigns. For the first time newspapers effectively mobilized public support for a war. British press accounts so glamorized British participation that the false impression has lingered that Ottoman troops played a negligible role in the conflict. At the time, however, British and French commanders noted the massive losses among Turkish troops in particular. The French press, dominant in Istanbul, promoted a sense of unity between Turkish and French society that continued to influence many aspects of Turkish urban culture.

The larger significance of the Crimean War was that it marked the transition from traditional to modern warfare (see Environment and Technology: The Web of War). All the combatants had previously prided themselves on the use of highly trained cavalry to smash through the front lines of infantry. Cavalry coexisted with firearms until the early 1800s, primarily because early rifles were awkward to load and not very accurate. Cavalry could attack during the intervals between volleys. Then in the 1830s and 1840s percussion caps that did away with pouring gunpowder into the barrel of a musket came into use. In Crimean War battles many cavalry units were destroyed by the rapid fire of rifles that loaded at the breech rather than down the barrel. That was the fate of the famed British Light Brigade, which was sent to relieve an Ottoman unit surrounded by Russian troops.

After the Crimean War, the Ottoman Empire increased its involvement with European commerce. The Ottoman imperial bank was founded in 1840, and a few years later currency reform pegged the value of Ottoman gold coins to the British pound. Sweeping changes in the 1850s expedited the creation of banks, insurance companies, and legal firms throughout the empire. Bustling trade also encouraged a migration from country to city between about 1850 and 1880. Many of the major cities of the empire—Istanbul, Damascus, Beirut, Alexandria, Cairo—expanded. A small but influential urban professional class emerged, as did a considerable class of wage laborers.

However, commercial vigor and urbanization could not make up for declining revenues and the chronic insolvency and corruption of the imperial government. From the conclusion of the Crimean War in 1856 on, the Ottoman government became heavily dependent on foreign loans. In return it lowered tariffs to favor European imports and allowed European banks to open in Ottoman cities. Europeans living in Istanbul and other commercial centers enjoyed **extraterritoriality**, the right to be subject to their own laws and exempt from Ottoman jurisdiction.

As the result of these measures, imported goods multiplied, but—apart from tobacco and the Turkish opium that American traders took to China to compete against British opium from India—Anatolia produced few exports. As foreign debt grew, so did inflationary trends that left urban populations in a precarious position. By contrast, Egyptian cotton exports soared during the American Civil War, when American cotton exports plummeted; but the profits benefited Muhammad Ali's descendants, who had become the hereditary governors of Egypt, rather

**Crimean War** Conflict between the Russian and Ottoman Empires fought primarily in the Crimean peninsula. To prevent Russian expansion, Britain and France sent troops to support the Ottomans.

**extraterritoriality** The right of foreign residents in a country to live under the laws of their native country and disregard the laws of the host country. In the nineteenth and early twentieth centuries, European and American nationals living in certain areas of Chinese and Ottoman cities were granted this right.

# environment & technology

## The Web of War

The lethal military technologies of the mid-nineteenth century that were used on battlefields in the United States, Russia, India, and China were rapidly transmitted from one conflict to the next. This dissemination was due not only to the rapid development of communications but also to the existence of a new international network of soldiers who moved from one trouble spot to another, bringing expertise in the use of new techniques.

General Charles Gordon (1833–1885), for instance, was commissioned in the British army in 1852 and then served in the Crimean War after Britain entered on the side of the Ottomans. In 1860 he was dispatched to China, where he served with British forces during the Arrow War and took part in the sack of Beijing. Afterward, he stayed in China and was assigned to the Qing imperial government until the suppression of the Taipings in 1864, earning himself the nickname "Chinese" Gordon. Gordon later served the Ottoman rulers of Egypt as governor of territory along the Nile. He was killed in Egyptian-ruled Sudan in 1885 while leading his Egyptian troops in defense of the city of Khartoum against an uprising by the Sudanese religious leader, the Mahdi.

Journalism played an important part in the developing web of telegraph communications that sped orders to and from the battlefields. Readers in London could learn details of the drama occurring in the Crimea or in China within a week—or in some cases days—after they occurred. Print and, later, photographic journalism created new "stars" from these war experiences. Charles Gordon was one. Florence Nightingale was another.

In the great wars of the 1800s, the vast majority of deaths resulted from infection or excessive bleeding, not from the wounds themselves. Florence Nightingale (1820–1910), while still a young woman, became interested in hospital management and nursing and went to Prussia and France to study advanced techniques. Before the outbreak of the Crimean War she was credited with bringing about marked improvement in British health care. When the public reacted to news reports of the suffering in the Crimea, the British government sent Nightingale to the region. Within a year of her arrival the death rate in the military hospitals there dropped from 45 percent to under

5 percent. Her techniques for preventing septicemia and dysentery, essentially sanitary measures like washing bed linens after a death and emptying toilet buckets outside, were quickly adopted by those working for and with her. On her return to London, Nightingale established institutes for nursing that soon were recognized as leaders around the world. She herself was lionized by the British public and received the Order of Merit in 1907, three years before her death.

The importance of Nightingale's innovations in public hygiene is underscored by the life of her contemporary, Mary Seacole (1805–1881). A Jamaican woman who volunteered to nurse British troops in the Crimean War, Seacole was repeatedly excluded from nursing service by British authorities. She eventually went to Crimea and used her own funds to run a hospital there, bankrupting herself in the process. The drama of the Crimean War moved the British public to support Seacole after her sacrifices were publicized. She was awarded medals by the British, French, and Turkish governments and today is recognized with her contemporary Florence Nightingale as an innovative field nurse and a champion of public hygiene in peacetime.

Private Collection/The Stapleton Collection/The Bridgeman Art Library

**Florence Nightingale During Crimean War** *This 1856 lithograph shows Florence Nightingale supervising nursing care in a hospital in Scutari (Üsküdar) across the Bosphorus strait from Istanbul. Though the artist may have exaggerated the neatness and cleanliness of the ward, sanitary measures proved the key to Nightingale's raising of the survival rate of sick and wounded soldiers.*

than the Ottoman government. The Suez Canal, which was partly financed by cotton profits, opened in 1869, and Cairo was redesigned and beautified. Eventually overexpenditure on such projects plunged Egypt into the same debt crisis that plagued the empire as a whole.

The decline of Ottoman power and prosperity had a strong impact on a group of well-educated young urban men who aspired to wealth and influence. They doubted that the empire's rulers and the Tanzimat officials who worked for them would ever stand up to European domination. Though lacking a sophisticated organization, these **Young Ottomans** (sometimes called Young Turks, though that term properly applies to a later movement) promoted a mixture of liberal ideas derived from Europe, national pride in Ottoman independence, and modernist views of Islam. Prominent Young Ottomans helped draft a constitution that was promulgated in 1876 by a new and as yet untried sultan, Abdul Hamid II. This apparent triumph of liberal reform was short-lived. With war against Russia again threatening in the Balkans in 1877, Abdul Hamid suspended the constitution and the parliament that had been elected that year. Though he ruthlessly opposed further political reforms, the Tanzimat programs of extending modern schooling, utilizing European military practices and advisers, and making the government bureaucracy more orderly continued during his reign.

## SECTION REVIEW

- After French withdrawal from Egypt, Muhammad Ali seized control and began a French-influenced modernization program.

- His successors continued the program and attacked the Ottoman Empire, but they were thwarted by the European powers.

- The Greek insurrection, European intervention, and Egyptian attack drove the westernizing reform efforts of Mahmud II and his successors.

- The most comprehensive reform initiative was Abdul Mejid's Tanzimat program.

- The Crimean War marked the transition from traditional to modern warfare and drew the Ottoman Empire into greater involvement with European commerce.

- Declining power and prosperity led to the rise of the Young Ottomans.

## THE RUSSIAN EMPIRE

■ *How did the Russian Empire maintain its status as both a European power and a great Asian land empire?*

In 1812, when Napoleon's march on Moscow ended in a disastrous retreat, the European image of Russia changed. Just as Napoleon's withdrawal from Egypt led to Muhammad Ali briefly becoming a political power, so his withdrawal from Russia conferred status on Tsar Alexander I (r. 1801–1825). Conservative Europeans still saw Russia as alien, backward, and oppressive, but they acknowledged its immensity and potential and included the tsar in efforts to suppress revolutionary tendencies throughout Europe.

In several important respects Russia resembled the Ottoman Empire more than the conservative kingdoms of Europe whose autocratic practices it so staunchly supported. Socially dominated by nobles whose country estates were worked by unfree serfs, Russia had almost no middle class. Industry was still at the threshold of development by the standards of the rapidly industrializing European powers, though it was somewhat more dynamic than Ottoman industry. Like Egypt and the Ottoman Empire, Russia engaged in reforms from the top down under Alexander I, but when his conservative brother Nicholas I (r. 1825–1855) succeeded to the throne, iron discipline and suspicion of modern ideas took priority over reform.

**Russia and Europe**    In 1700 only three Russians out of a hundred lived in cities, two-thirds of them in Moscow alone. By the mid-1800s the town population had grown tenfold, though it still accounted for only 6 percent of the total because the territories of the tsars had grown greatly through wars and colonization (see Chapter 18). These figures demonstrate that, like the Ottoman Empire, Russia was an overwhelmingly agricultural land. However, it had poorer transportation than the Ottoman Empire, since many Ottoman cities were

**Young Ottomans** Movement of young intellectuals to institute liberal reforms and build a feeling of national identity in the Ottoman Empire in the second half of the nineteenth century.

seaports. Both empires encompassed peoples speaking many different languages.

Well-engineered roads did not begin to appear until 1817, and steam navigation commenced on the Volga in 1843. Tsar Nicholas I built the first railroad from St. Petersburg, the Russian capital, to his summer palace in 1837. A few years later his commitment to strict discipline led him to insist that the trunk line from St. Petersburg to Moscow run in a perfectly straight line. Industrialization projects depended heavily on foreign expertise. While American engineers oversaw the laying of track and built locomotive workshops, British engineers set up the textile mills that gave woolens and cottons a prominent place among Russia's industries.

Until the late nineteenth century the Russian government's interest in industry was limited. An industrial revolution required educated and independent-minded artisans and entrepreneurs, but Nicholas feared the spread of literacy and modern education—especially anything smacking of liberalism, socialism, or revolution—beyond the minimum needed to train the officer corps and the bureaucracy. He preferred serfs to factory workers, and he paid for imported industrial goods with exports of grain and timber.

Like Egypt and the Ottoman Empire, Russia aspired to Western-style economic development. But when France and Britain entered the Crimean War, they faced a Russian army equipped with obsolete weapons and bogged down by lack of transportation. At a time when European engineers were making major breakthroughs in loading cannon through an opening at the breech end, muzzle-loading artillery remained the Russian standard.

Yet in some ways Russia bore a closer resemblance to other European countries than the Ottoman Empire did. From the point of view of the French and the British, the Cyrillic alphabet and the Russian Orthodox form of Christianity seemed foreign, but they were not nearly as foreign as the Arabic alphabet and the Muslim faith. Britain and France feared Russia as a rival for power in the east, but they increasingly accepted Tsar Nicholas's view of the Ottoman Empire as "the sick man of Europe," capable of surviving only so long as the European powers permitted.

From the Russian point of view, kinship with western Europe was of questionable value. Western-

izers, like the men of the Tanzimat in the Ottoman Empire, put their trust in technical advances and governmental reform. Opposing them were intellectuals known as **Slavophiles**, who considered the Orthodox faith, the solidity of peasant life, and the tsar's absolute rule to be the proper bases of Russian civilization. After Russia's humiliation in the Crimea, the Slavophile tendency gave rise to **Pan-Slavism**, a militant political doctrine advocating unity of all the Slavic peoples, including those living under Austrian and Ottoman rule.

On the diplomatic front, the tsar's inclusion as a major European ruler contrasted sharply with the sultan's exclusion. However, this did not prevent a powerful sense of Russophobia from developing in the West. Britain in particular saw Russia as a threat to India and despised the subjection of the serfs, who gained their freedom from Tsar Alexander II only in 1861, twenty-seven years after the British had abolished slavery. The passions generated by the Crimean War and its outcome affected the relations of Russia, Europe, and the Ottoman Empire for the remainder of the nineteenth century.

### Russia and Asia

The Russian drive to the east in the eighteenth century brought the tsar's empire to the Pacific Ocean and the frontiers of China (see Map 19.1) by century's end. In the nineteenth century Russian expansionism focused on the south. There the backwardness of the Russian military did not matter since the peoples they faced were even less industrialized and technologically advanced. In 1860 Russia established a military outpost on the Pacific coast that would eventually grow into the great naval port of Vladivostok. In Central Asia the steppelands of the Kazakh nomads came under Russian control early in the century, setting the stage for a confrontation with three Uzbek states farther south. They succumbed one by one, beginning

**Slavophiles** Russian intellectuals in the early nineteenth century who favored resisting western European influences and taking pride in the traditional peasant values and institutions of the Slavic peoples.

**Pan-Slavism** Movement among Russian intellectuals in the second half of the nineteenth century to identify culturally and politically with the Slavic peoples of eastern Europe.

in 1865, giving rise to the new province of Turkestan, with its capital at Tashkent in present-day Uzbekistan. In the region of the Caucasus Mountains, the third area of southward expansion, Russia first took over Christian Georgia (1786), Muslim Azerbaijan (ah-zer-by-JAHN) (1801), and Christian Armenia (1813) before gobbling up the many small principalities in the heart of the mountains. Between 1829 and 1864 Dagestan, Chechnya (CHECH-nee-yah), and Abkhazia (ab-KAH-zee-yah) became parts of the Russian Empire.

The drive to the south intensified political friction with Russia's new neighbors: Qing China and Japan in the east, Iran on the Central Asian and Caucasus frontiers, and the Ottoman Empire at the eastern end of the Black Sea. In the latter two instances, Muslim refugees from the territories newly absorbed by Russia spread anti-Russian feelings, though some brought with them modern skills and ideas gained from exposure to Russian administration and education.

The Russian drive to the south added a new element to the Eastern Question. Many British statesmen and strategists reckoned that a warlike Russia would press on until it had conquered all the lands separating it from British India, a prospect that made them shudder, given India's enormous contribution to Britain's prosperity. The competition that ensued over which power would control southern Central Asia resulted in a standoff in Afghanistan, which became a buffer zone under the control of neither. In Iran, the standoff between the powers helped preserve the weak Qajar dynasty of shahs.

### Cultural Trends

Unlike Egypt and the Ottoman Empire, which began to send students to Europe for training only in the nineteenth century, Russia had been in cultural contact with western Europe since the time of Peter the Great (r. 1689–1725). Members of the Russian court knew Western languages, and the tsars employed officials and advisers from Western countries. Peter had also enlisted the well-educated Ukrainian clerics who headed the Russian Orthodox Church to help spread a Western spirit of education. As a result, Alexander I's reforms met a more positive reception than those of Muhammad Ali and Mahmud II. However, his reforms promised more on paper than they brought about in practice. It took many years to develop a sufficient pool of trained bureaucrats to make the reforms effective.

Ironically, much of the opposition to Alexander's reforms came from well-established families that were not at all unfriendly to Western ideas. Their fear was that the new government bureaucrats, who often came from humbler social origins, would act as agents of imperial tyranny. Individuals favoring more liberal reforms, including military officers who had served in western Europe, intellectuals who read Western political tracts, and members of Masonic lodges who exchanged views with Freemasons in the West, formed secret societies of opposition. Some placed their highest priority on freeing the serfs; others advocated a constitution and a republican form of government. When Alexander I died in December 1825, confusion over who was to succeed him encouraged a group of reform-minded army officers to try to take over the government and provoke an uprising. This so-called **Decembrist revolt** failed, and many of the participants were severely punished. These events ensured that the new tsar, Nicholas I, would pay little heed to calls for reform over the next thirty years. His conservative reign realized the liberals' worst fears in the same way that the Tanzimat-inspired bureaucracy of the Ottoman Empire served the despotic purposes of Sultan Abdul Hamid II after 1877.

The great powers meeting in Paris to settle the Crimean War in 1856 forced Russia to return land to the Ottomans in both Europe and Asia. This humiliation spurred Nicholas's son and successor, Alexander II (r. 1855–1881), to institute major new reforms to reinvigorate the country. The greatest of his reforms was the emancipation of the serfs in 1861. He also authorized new joint-stock companies, projected a railroad network to tie the country together, and modernized the legal and administrative arms of government.

Earlier intellectual and cultural trends flourished under Alexander II. More and more people became involved in intellectual, artistic, and professional life. Most prominent intellectuals received some amount of instruction at Moscow University or some German university. Universities also appeared

**Decembrist revolt** Abortive attempt by army officers to take control of the Russian government upon the death of Tsar Alexander I in 1825.

**Raising of the Alexander Monument in St. Petersburg** The death of Alexander I in 1825 brought to power his conservative brother Nicholas I. Yet Alexander remained a heroic figure for his resistance to Napoleon. This monument in Winter Palace Square was erected in 1829.

Visual Connection Archive

in provincial cities like Kharkov in Ukraine and Kazan on the Volga River. Student clubs, along with Masonic lodges, became places for discussing new ideas. As Russian scholars and scientists began to achieve recognition for their contributions to European thought, scholarly careers attracted young men from clerical families, who in turn helped stimulate reforms in religious education.

Just as the Tanzimat reforms of the Ottoman Empire preceded the emergence of the Young Ottomans as a new and assertive political and intellectual force in the second half of the nineteenth century,

so the initially ineffective reforms of Alexander I set in motion cultural currents that would make Russia a dynamic center of intellectual, artistic, and political life under his nephew Alexander II. Thus Russia belonged to two different spheres of development. It entered the nineteenth century a recognized force in European politics, but in other ways it resembled the Ottoman Empire. Rulers in both empires instituted reforms, overcame opposition, and increased the power of their governments. These activities stimulated intellectual and political trends that would ultimately work against the absolute rule of tsar and sultan. Yet Russia would eventually develop much closer relations with western Europe and become an arena for every sort of European intellectual, artistic, and political tendency, while the Ottoman Empire would ultimately succumb to European imperialism.

## THE QING EMPIRE

■ *How did the impact of European imperialism on China differ from its impact on Russia and the Ottoman Empire?*

In 1800 the Qing Empire faced many problems, but no reform movement of the kind initiated by Sultan Selim III emerged in China. Unlike the Ottomans, the Qing did not know that Europeans were making enormous fortunes in the early 1800s or that illegal Chinese trade in opium was helping finance the

### SECTION REVIEW

- Russian society resembled Ottoman society, but Alexander I undertook top-down westernizing reforms.

- Nicholas I's suspicion of Western ideas stalled reform and slowed industrial development.

- Slavophiles opposed westernizers and, after the Crimean War, embraced Pan-Slavism, contributing to Russophobia in the West.

- Russian expansion southward and eastward added vast territories to the empire and caused friction with China, Japan, Iran, and the Ottoman Empire.

- Resistance to Alexander I's bureaucratic reforms sparked the Decembrist revolt, which stiffened Nicholas I's hostility to Western ideas.

- The humiliation of the Crimean War drove Alexander II's reforms, including emancipation of the serfs.

**Trade Warehouse in Guangzhou**  A European merchant enters in the background while Chinese workers pack tea and porcelain.

industrial transformation of England and the United States. China viewed its most serious crises as domestic, not foreign. The Qing emperors had skillfully countered Russian expansion in the 1600s, and instead of facing a Napoleonic threat, they enjoyed the admiration of Jesuit priests, who likened them to enlightened philosopher-kings. So they brushed aside European complaints about the restrictions of the "Canton system" by which the Qing limited and controlled foreign trade, and they rebuffed the British Macartney mission sent to improve trade relations in 1792 (see Chapter 19). Instead, China focused on quelling rebellions and protests, little realizing the significance of European opinion turning against it.

## Economic and Social Disorder

Early Qing successes and territorial expansion sowed the seeds of the domestic and political chaos of the later period. The early emperors encouraged the recovery of farmland, the opening of previously uncultivated areas, and the restoration and expansion of the road and canal systems. These measures expanded the agricultural base and supported a doubling of the population between about 1650 and 1800. Enormous numbers of farmers, merchants, and day laborers migrated in search of less crowded conditions, and a permanent floating population of the unemployed and homeless emerged. By 1800 population strain had caused serious environmental damage in some parts of central and western China.

While farmers tried to cope with agricultural deterioration, other groups vented grievances against the government: minority peoples in central and southwestern China complained about being driven off their lands during the boom of the 1700s, and Mongols resented appropriation of their grazing lands and the displacement of their traditional elites. In some regions, village vigilante organizations took over policing and governing functions from Qing officials who had lost control. Growing numbers of people mistrusted the government, suspecting that all officials were corrupt. The increasing presence of foreign merchants and missionaries in Canton and in the Portuguese colony of Macao aggravated discontent in neighboring districts.

In some parts of China the Qing were hated as foreign conquerors and were suspected of sympathy with the Europeans. In 1794 the White Lotus Rebellion—partly inspired by a messianic ideology that predicted the restoration of the Chinese Ming dynasty and the coming of the Buddha—raged across central China and was not suppressed until 1804. It initiated a series of internal conflicts that continued through the 1800s. Ignited by deepening social instabilities, these movements were sometimes intensified by local ethnic conflicts and by unapproved religions. The ability of some village militias to defend themselves and attack others intensified the conflicts, though the same techniques proved useful to southern coastal populations attempting to fend off British invasion.

## The Opium War and Its Aftermath, 1839–1850

Only slowly did Qing officials become aware of British colonies in India that grew and exported opium and of the major naval base at Singapore through which British opium reached East Asia. The first Qing law banning opium imports had been promulgated in 1729. By 1800, however, opium smuggling had swelled to as many as four thousand chests per year. Though British merchants had pioneered this profitable trade, Chinese merchants likewise profited from distributing the drugs. A price war in the early 1820s stemming from competition between British and American importers raised demand so sharply that as many as thirty thousand chests were being imported by the

1830s. Addiction spread to all levels of Qing society, including high-ranking officials. The Qing emperor and his officials debated whether to legalize and tax opium or to enforce the existing ban more strictly. Having decided to root out the use and importation of opium, in 1839 they sent a high official to Canton to deal with the matter.

Britain considered the ban on opium importation an intolerable limitation on trade, a direct threat to Britain's economic health, and a cause for war. British naval and marine forces arrived on the south China coast in late 1839. The **Opium War** (1839–1842) broke out when negotiations between the Qing official and British representatives reached a stalemate. The war exposed the fact that the traditional, hereditary soldiers of the Qing Empire—the **Bannermen**—were, like the Janissaries of the Ottoman Empire, hopelessly obsolete. As in the Crimean War, the British excelled at sea, where they deployed superior technology. British ships landed marines who pillaged coastal cities and then sailed to new destinations (see Map 22.2). Qing sea forces were no match for Britain's powerful navy. Even in land engagements, Qing resources proved woefully inadequate. The British could quickly transport their troops by sea along the coast, whereas Qing soldiers moved primarily on foot. Moving Qing reinforcements from central to eastern China took more than three months; and when the defense forces arrived, they were exhausted and basically without weapons.

The Bannermen used the few muskets the Qing had imported during the 1700s. The weapons were matchlocks, which required the soldiers to ignite the load of gunpowder in them by hand. Firing the weapons was dangerous, and the canisters of gunpowder that each musketeer carried on his belt were likely to explode if a fire broke out nearby—a frequent occurrence in encounters with British artillery. Most of the

**Opium War**  War between Britain and the Qing Empire that was, in the British view, occasioned by the Qing government's refusal to permit the importation of opium into its territories. The victorious British imposed the one-sided Treaty of Nanking on China.

**Bannermen**  Hereditary military servants of the Qing Empire, in large part descendants of peoples of various origins who had fought for the founders of the empire.

Bannermen, however, had no guns at all and fought with swords, knives, spears, and clubs. Soldiers under British command—many of them Indians—carried percussion-cap rifles, which were far quicker, safer, and more accurate than the matchlocks. In addition, the long-range British artillery could be moved from place to place and proved deadly in the cities and villages of eastern China.

Assuming that British gunboats rode so low in the water that they could not sail up the Chinese rivers, Qing commanders evacuated the coastal areas to counter the British threat. But the British deployed new gunboats for shallow waters and moved without difficulty up the Yangzi River (see Chapter 20).

When the invaders approached Nanjing, the former Ming capital, the Qing decided to negotiate. The

**Map 22.2  Conflicts in the Qing Empire, 1839–1870** In both the Opium War of 1839–1842 and the Arrow War of 1856–1860, the seacoasts saw most of the action. Since the Qing had a weak navy, the well-armed British ships encountered little resistance as they shelled the southern coasts. In inland conflicts, such as the Taiping Rebellion, the opposing armies were massive and slow moving. Battles on land were often prolonged attempts by one side to starve out the other side before making a major assault. © Cengage Learning

**Treaty of Nanking** (the British name for Nanjing) dismantled the old Canton system. The number of **treaty ports**—cities opened to foreign residents—increased from one (Canton) to five (Canton, Xiamen, Fuzhou, Ningbo, and Shanghai [shahng-high]). The island of Hong Kong became a British colony, and British residents in China gained extraterritorial rights. The Qing government agreed to set a low tariff of 5 percent on imports and to pay Britain an indemnity of 21 million ounces of silver as a penalty for having started the war. A supplementary treaty the following year guaranteed Britain **most-favored-nation status**: any privileges that China granted to another country would be automatically extended to Britain as well. This provision effectively prevented the colonization of China, because giving land to one country would have necessitated giving it to all.

With each round of treaties came a new round of privileges for foreigners. In 1860 a new treaty legalized their right to import opium. Later, French treaties established the rights of foreign missionaries to travel in the Chinese countryside and preach their religion. The number of treaty ports grew, too; by 1900 they numbered more than ninety. The treaty system and the principle of extraterritoriality resulted in the colonization of small pockets of Qing territory, where foreign merchants lived at ease.

Greater territorial losses resulted when outlying regions gained independence or were ceded to neighboring countries. Districts north and south of the Amur River in the northeast fell to Russia by treaty in 1858 and 1860; parts of modern Kazakhstan and Kyrgyzstan in the northwest met the same fate in 1864. From 1865 onward the British gradually gained control of territories on China's Indian frontier. In the late 1800s France forced the court of Vietnam to end its tribute relationship to the Qing, while Britain encouraged Tibetan independence.

In Canton, Shanghai, and other coastal cities, Europeans and Americans maintained offices and factories that employed local Chinese as menial laborers. The foreigners built comfortable housing in zones where Chinese were not permitted to live, and they entertained themselves in exclusive restaurants and bars. Around the foreign establishments, gambling and prostitution offered employment to part of the local urban population.

Whether in town or in the countryside, Christian missionaries whose congregations sponsored hospitals, shelters, and soup kitchens or gave stipends to Chinese who attended church enjoyed a good reputation. But just as often the missionaries themselves were regarded as another evil. They seemed to subvert Confucian beliefs by condemning ancestor worship, pressured poor families to put their children into orphanages, and fulminated against footbinding. The growing numbers of foreigners, and their growing privileges, became targets of resentment for a deeply dissatisfied, daily more impoverished, and increasingly militarized society.

### The Taiping Rebellion, 1850–1864

The inflammatory mixture of social unhappiness and foreign intrusion exploded in the great civil war usually called the **Taiping** (tie-PING) **Rebellion**. In Guangxi, where the Taiping movement originated, entrenched social problems had been generating disorders for half a century. Agriculture in the region was unstable, and many people made their living from arduous and despised trades such as disposing of human waste, making charcoal, and mining. Ethnic divisions complicated economic distress. The lowliest trades frequently involved a minority group, the Hakkas, and tensions between them and the majority were rising. Problems may have been intensified by sharp fluctuations in the opium trade and reactions to the cultural and economic impact of the Europeans and Americans in Canton.

Hong Xiuquan (hoong shee-OH-chew-an), the founder of the Taiping movement, experienced all of these influences. Hong came from a humble Hakka

**Treaty of Nanking** The treaty that concluded the Opium War. It awarded Britain a large indemnity from the Qing Empire, denied the Qing government tariff control over some of its own borders, opened additional ports of residence to Britons, and ceded the island of Hong Kong to Britain.

**treaty ports** Cities opened to foreign residents as a result of the forced treaties between the Qing Empire and foreign signatories. In the treaty ports, foreigners enjoyed extraterritoriality.

**most-favored-nation status** A clause in a commercial treaty that awards to any later signatories all the privileges previously granted to the original signatories.

**Taiping Rebellion** A Christian-inspired rural rebellion that threatened to topple the Qing Empire.

background. After years of study, he competed in the provincial Confucian examinations, hoping for a post in government. He failed the examinations repeatedly, and it appears that he suffered a nervous breakdown in his late thirties. Afterward he spent some time in Canton, where he met both Chinese and American Protestant missionaries, who inspired him with their teachings. Hong had his own interpretation of the Christian message. He saw himself as the younger brother of Jesus, commissioned by God to found a new kingdom on earth and drive the Manchu conquerors, the Qing, out of China. The result would be universal peace. Hong called his new religious movement the "Heavenly Kingdom of Great Peace."

Hong quickly attracted a community of believers, primarily Hakkas like himself. They believed in the prophecy of dreams and claimed they could walk on air. Hong and his rivals for leadership in the movement went in and out of ecstatic trances and denounced the Manchus as creatures of Satan. After news of the sect reached the government, Qing troops arrived to arrest the Taiping leaders but were soundly repelled. Local loyalty to the Taipings spread quickly; their numbers multiplied; and they began to enlarge their domain.

The Taipings relied at first on Hakka sympathy and the charismatic appeal of their religious doctrine to attract followers. But as their numbers and power grew, they altered their methods of preaching and governing, replacing the anti-Chinese appeals used to enlist Hakkas with anti-Manchu rhetoric designed to enlist Chinese. They also forced captured villages to join their movement. Once people were absorbed, the Taipings strictly monitored their activities, segregating men and women and organizing them into work and military teams. Women were forbidden to bind their feet (the Hakkas had never practiced footbinding) and participated fully in farming and labor. Brigades of women soldiers took to the field against Qing forces.

As the movement grew, it began to move toward eastern and northern China (see Map 22.2). Panic preceded the Taipings. Villagers feared being forced into Taiping units, and Confucian elites recoiled in horror from the bizarre ideology of foreign gods, totalitarian rule, and walking, working, warring women. But the huge numbers the Taipings were able to muster over-whelmed attempts at local defense. The tremendous growth in the number of Taiping followers required the movement to establish a permanent base. When the rebel army conquered Nanjing in 1853, the Taiping leaders decided to settle there and make it the capital of the new "Heavenly Kingdom of Great Peace."

Qing forces attempting to defend north China became more successful as problems of organization and growing numbers slowed Taiping momentum. Increasing Qing military successes resulted mainly from the flexibility of the imperial military commanders in the face of an unprecedented challenge. In addition, the military commanders received strong backing from a group of civilian provincial governors who had studied the techniques developed by local militias for self-defense. Certain provincial governors combined their knowledge of civilian self-defense and local terrain with more efficient organization and the use of modern weaponry. The result was the formation of new military units in which many of the Bannermen voluntarily served under civilian governors. The Qing court agreed to special taxes to fund the new armies and acknowledged the new combined leadership.

When the Taipings settled into Nanjing, the new Qing armies surrounded the city, hoping to starve out the rebels. The Taipings, however, had provisioned themselves well. They also had the services of several brilliant young military commanders, who mobilized enormous campaigns in nearby parts of eastern China, scavenging supplies and attempting to break the encirclement of Nanjing. For more than a decade the Taiping leadership remained ensconced at Nanjing, and the "Heavenly Kingdom" endured.

In 1856 Britain and France, freed from their preoccupation with the Crimean War, turned their attention to China. European and American missionaries had visited Nanjing, but their reports were discouraging. Hong Xiuquan and the other leaders appeared to lead lives of indulgence and abandon, and more than one missionary accused them of homosexuality. The British and French surveyed the situation without fear of quashing a pious Christian movement. Though the Taipings were not going to topple the Qing, rebellious Nian ("Bands") in northern China added a new threat in the 1850s. A series of simultaneous large insurrections might indeed

**Nanjing Encircled**  For a decade the Taipings held the city of Nanjing as their capital. For years Qing and international troops attempted to break the Taiping hold. By the summer of 1864, Qing forces had built tunnels leading to the foundations of Nanjing's city walls and had planted explosives. The detonation of the explosives signaled the final Qing assault on the rebel capital. As shown here, the common people of the city, along with their starving livestock, were caught in the crossfire. Many of the Taiping leaders escaped the debacle at Nanjing, but nearly all were hunted down and executed.

destroy the empire. Moreover, since the Qing had not observed all the provisions of the treaties signed after the Opium War, Britain and France were now considering renewing war on the Qing themselves.

In 1856 the British and French launched a series of swift, brutal coastal attacks—a second opium war, called the Arrow War (1856–1860)—which culminated in the sacking of the Beijing Summer Palace in 1860. A new round of treaties punished the Qing for not enacting all the provisions of the Treaty of Nanking. Having secured their principal objective, the British and French forces then joined the Qing campaign against the Taipings. Attempts to coordinate the international forces were sometimes riotous and sometimes tragic, but the injection of European weaponry and money helped quell both the Taiping and the Nian rebellions during the 1860s.

The Taiping Rebellion ranks as the world's bloodiest civil war and the greatest armed conflict before the twentieth century. Estimates of deaths range from 20 million to 30 million, caused primarily by starvation and disease. Military engagement consisted of surrounding fortified cities and waiting until the enemy forces died, surrendered, or became too weak to defend themselves. Many sieges continued for months. Reports of people eating grass, leather, hemp, and human flesh were widespread. The dead were rarely buried properly, and epidemic disease was common.

The area of early Taiping fighting was close to the regions of southwest China in which bubonic plague had been lingering for centuries. When the rebellion was suppressed, many Taiping followers sought safety in the highlands of Laos and Vietnam, which soon showed infestation by plague. Within a few years the disease reached Hong Kong. From there it spread to Singapore, San Francisco, Calcutta, and London. In the late 1800s Chinese immigrants were regarded as likely carriers, and apprehension over the possibility of a worldwide outbreak contributed to the passage of discriminatory immigration bans on Chinese in the United States in 1882.

The Taiping Rebellion devastated the agricultural centers of China. Many of the most intensely cultivated regions of central and eastern China were depopulated. Some were still uninhabited decades later, and major portions of the country did not recover until the twentieth century.

Cities, too, were hard hit. Shanghai, a treaty port of modest size before the rebellion, saw its population multiplied many times by the arrival of refugees from war-blasted neighboring provinces. The city then endured months of siege by the Taipings. Major cultural centers in eastern China lost masterpieces of art and architecture; imperial libraries were burned or their collections exposed to the weather; and the printing blocks used to make books were destroyed. While the empire faced the mountainous challenge of dealing with the material and cultural destruction of the war, it also was burdened by a major ecological disaster in the north. The Yellow River changed course in 1855, flooding the southern part of impoverished Shandong province and initiating decades of water shortage along the former riverbed in northern Shandong.

## Decentralization at the End of the Qing Empire, 1864–1875

The Qing government emerged from the 1850s with no hope of achieving solvency. The corruption of the 1700s, attempts in the very early 1800s to restore waterworks and roads, and declining yields from land taxes had bankrupted the treasury. By 1850, before the Taiping Rebellion, Qing government expenditures were ten times revenues. The indemnities demanded by Europeans after the Opium and Arrow Wars compounded the problem. Vast stretches of formerly productive rice land were devastated, and the population was dispersed. Refugees pleaded for relief, and the imperial, volunteer, foreign, and mercenary troops that had suppressed the Taipings demanded unpaid wages.

Britain and France became active participants in the period of recovery that followed the rebellion. To ensure repayment of the debt to Britain, Robert Hart was installed as inspector-general of a newly created Imperial Maritime Customs Service. Britain and the Qing split the revenues he collected. Britons and Americans worked with the Qing government as advisers and ambassadors, attempting to smooth communications between the Qing, Europe, and the United States.

The real work of the recovery, however, was managed by provincial governors who had come to the forefront in the struggle against the Taipings. To prosecute the war, they had won the right to levy their own taxes, raise their own troops, and run their own bureaucracies. These special powers were not entirely canceled when the war ended. Chief among these governors was Zeng Guofan (zung gwoh-FAHN), who—looking to the United States rather than Britain for models and aid—oversaw programs to restore agriculture, communications, education, and publishing, as well as efforts to reform the military and industrialize armaments manufacture. He hired American advisers and sponsored a daring program in which promising Chinese boys were sent to Hartford, Connecticut, a center of missionary activity, to learn English, science, mathematics, engineering, and history. They returned to China to assume positions previously held by foreign advisers. Though he did not advocate for a public role for women, Zeng was convinced by Confucian principles that educated mothers were needed more than ever and provided an advanced classical education for his own daughters. With Zeng's death in 1872, China lost a major force for reform.

A coalition of aristocrats supported the reform and recovery programs after 1850, marking a fundamental structural change in the Qing Empire. Without provincial governors like Zeng Guofan, the empire might have evaporated within a generation. A crucial member of this alliance was Cixi (TSUH-shee), who was known as the "Empress Dowager" after the 1880s. Later observers, both Chinese and foreign, reviled her as a monster of corruption and arrogance. But in the 1860s and 1870s Cixi supported the provincial governors, some of whom became so powerful that they were managing Qing foreign policy as well as domestic affairs.

Tz'u His (1835–1908) Empress Dowager of China 1903 (b/w photo), French Photographer, (20th century)/Private Collection/The Bridgeman Art Library

**Cixi's Allies** In the 1860s and 1870s, Cixi was a supporter of reform. In later years she was widely regarded as corrupt and self-centered and as an obstacle to reform. Her greatest allies were the court eunuchs. Introduced to palace life in early China as managers of the imperial harems, eunuchs became powerful political parties at court. The first Qing emperors refused to allow the eunuchs any political influence, but by Cixi's time the eunuchs once again were a political factor.

No longer a conquest regime dominated by a Manchu military caste and its Chinese civilian appointees, the empire now came under the control of a group of reformist aristocrats and military men, independently powerful civilian governors, and a small number of foreign advisers. Without a strong, central, unified leadership, the Qing could not recover their powers of taxation, legislation, and military command. From the 1860s forward, China disintegrated into a number of large power zones. The Qing court's role now was to ritually legitimate the control of provincial governors.

## CONCLUSION

The Ottoman, Qing, and Russian Empires shared several characteristics both in their early successes and late-stage challenges. All three maintained a flexible approach when incorporating a diverse group of peoples and cultures into their growing empires. Around the mid-eighteenth century, however, the need to maintain order and increase tax revenues pushed rulers to differentiate groups of people, creating stricter hierarchies within each empire and leading to conflict between the rulers and the ruled. The population growth that began in the sixteenth century throughout Eurasia, and that had been sustainable, and beneficial, in the expanding territories of Russia and the Qing, eventually became unsupportable. By the nineteenth century, even the Qing Empire, the largest and most advanced Eurasian empire in terms of commercial economy and efficient bureaucratic structures, could no longer effectively deal with the increasing demographic pressures, regional conflict, and political dysfunctions.

Most of the subjects of the Ottoman, Russian, and Qing rulers did not think of European pressure or competition as determining factors in their lives during the

**SECTION REVIEW**

- Social unrest grew in Qing China through a combination of discontent among the poor and displaced indigenous peoples and resentment of growing European influence.

- Qing attempts to ban opium imports provoked the Opium War with Britain, which exposed Qing military inferiority.

- The Treaty of Nanking gave extraterritoriality and other privileges to Britain and led to further losses to other Western powers.

- Social resentment and foreign intrusion ignited the Taiping Rebellion, which, after the Arrow War, the Qing quelled with British and French aid.

- The rebellion encouraged epidemics, devastated agriculture, produced overcrowded cities filled with refugees, and coincided with environmental disasters.

- The rebellion and China's recovery afterward resulted in a process of decentralization led by reformist aristocrats.

first half of the nineteenth century. They continued to live according to the social and economic institutions they inherited from previous generations. By the 1870s, however, the challenge of Europe had become widely realized. The Crimean War, where European allies achieved a hollow victory for the Ottomans and then pressured the sultan for more reforms, confirmed both Ottoman and Russian military weakness. The Opium War did the same for China. But China, unlike the other empires, was also stricken by rampaging civil war and regional uprisings.

In analyzing the crises of the three empires, historians today stress European economic pressures and observe that all three empires ultimately became insolvent and saw the overthrow of their ruling dynasties. However, at the time what most impressed the Ottomans, Russians, and Chinese was European military superiority, as demonstrated in the Greek war of independence, the Crimean War, and the Opium War. Thus for all three empires, dealing with military emergency took priority over deeper reforms throughout most of the time period of this chapter.

# CHAPTER REVIEW

## THE OTTOMAN EMPIRE

■ *What were the benefits and the drawbacks to the Ottoman Empire of the reforms adopted during the Tanzimat period?* (page 512)

Although the Tanzimat period began with the sultan declaring in 1839 a measure of equality for all Ottoman citizens, improving military performance was the center of the reforming effort. This reform enhanced the role of the military while other administrative changes reduced the social role and governmental influence of the religious elite. The result was an unbalanced reform effort that eventually led to a military takeover of the country.

## THE RUSSIAN EMPIRE

■ *How did the Russian Empire maintain its status as both a European power and a great Asian land empire?* (page 521)

For Russians, defeat in the Crimean War and the revelation that Russian arms were no match for modern European weaponry were counterbalanced by the comparative weakness of the peoples in the east and south into whose territories they aggressively expanded. Thus, while lagging far behind in industrialization and having an inefficient government, Russia, like the other European states, engaged in imperialist expansion.

## THE QING EMPIRE

■ *How did the impact of European imperialism on China differ from its impact on Russia and the Ottoman Empire?* (page 524)

The course of Russian expansion into Asia made it a neighbor of Qing China, but other European powers were seen as greater threats. Britain, France, and the United States used every means available to gain the freedom to exploit China economically. With respect to the Russian and Ottoman empires nearer to home, however, European imperialists—the United States had minimal involvement—considered financial investment to be somewhat less important than limiting Russian expansion or weakening the Ottoman state and improving the lives of its Christian and Jewish populations.

## Key Terms

Muhammad Ali (p. 513)

Serbia (p. 514)

Tanzimat (p. 515)

Crimean War (p. 519)

extraterritoriality (p. 519)

Young Ottomans (p. 521)

Slavophiles (p. 522)

Pan-Slavism (p. 522)

Decembrist revolt (p. 523)

Opium War (p. 526)

Bannermen (p. 526)

Treaty of Nanking (p. 528)

treaty ports (p. 528)

most-favored-nation status (p. 528)

Taiping Rebellion (p. 528)

# State Power, the Census, and the Question of Identity

**B**etween the American Revolution and the last decades of the nineteenth century, new ways of organizing political, economic, and intellectual life transformed Europe and the Americas. One of the less heralded but enduringly significant changes was the expansion of government statistical services.

Bureaucratic departments that depended on reliable statistics to measure the nation's achievements and discover its failures accompanied the rise of the nation-state. Mobilizing resources on a previously unimaginable scale, as exemplified by the modernization of militaries, the internal improvements such as railroads, and the growth in state revenues, became a hallmark of the nation-state. Historians have recently begun examining a less visible but equally important manifestation of growing state power: census taking.

Counting people or estimating their numbers was nothing new. Our best assessments of the Amerindian population of the Western Hemisphere in 1500 rest almost entirely on what were little more than missionary guesses about the numbers they baptized. Spanish and Portuguese kings were eager to count native populations, since "indios" (adult male Amerindians) were subject to labor obligations and tribute payments. So, from the mid-sixteenth century onward, imperial officials conducted regular censuses of Amerindians, adapting practices already in place in Europe.

In the last decades of the eighteenth century, however, the Enlightenment belief that scientific method could be applied to human society attracted both political radicals, like the French Revolutionaries, and reforming monarchs like Maria Theresa of Austria. A science of government, they maintained, could remove the inefficiencies and irrationalities that stood in the way of prosperity and happiness. The French intellectual Condorcet wrote in 1782:

Those sciences, created almost in our own days, the object of which is man himself, the direct goal of which is the happiness of man, will enjoy a progress no less sure than that of the physical sciences. . . . In meditating on the nature of the moral sciences [what we now call the social sciences], one cannot help seeing that, as they are based like the physical sciences on the observation of fact, they must follow the method, acquire a language equally exact and precise, attaining the same degree of certainty.[1]

As confidence in this new "science" grew, governments and practitioners abandoned the term previously used to describe the collection of numbers about society, political arithmetic, in favor of statistics, a term that suggests its close ties to the "state." The new objectives set out by Condorcet and others led to both the formal university training of statisticians and the creation of government statistical services.

The new nation-states self-consciously sought to transform society, sponsoring economic development, education, and improvements in health and welfare. Statistics allowed them to measure the effectiveness of their policies so they counted practically everything: taverns, urban buildings, births and deaths, and arrests and convictions. They also counted their populations with unprecedented thoroughness. Improved statistical reporting allowed governments to measure not only their own progress but also that of their neighbors and rivals.

The revolutionary governments of France modernized the census practices of the overthrown monarchy by spending more money, hiring more census takers, and improving the training of the staff that designed censuses and analyzed results. Great Britain had an official census in 1801, but established a special administrative structure only in the 1830s. In the Western Hemisphere most independent nations provided for "scientific" censuses. The United States Constitution stipulated a census every ten years. Latin American nations, often torn by civil war, took censuses less regularly; but even the poorest nations took censuses when they could. The census itself seemingly confirmed the existence of the government, demonstrating its modernity and seriousness.

Until recently, historians asked few questions about the politics of census design. What could be more objective than rows of numbers? But census managers were uninhibited in proclaiming the usefulness of reliable numbers to the governments that employed them. At the 1860 International Statistical Congress held in London one speaker said, "I think the true meaning to be attached to 'statistics' is not every collection of figures, but figures collected with the sole purpose of applying the principles deduced from them to questions of importance to the state."[2] The desire to be useful meant that statistics might not be fully objective.

Subjectivity was an unavoidable problem. Censuses that identified citizens and foreign residents by place of residence, sex, age, and family relationships within households, as well as specifying profession and literacy, often undercounted the poor and those living in rural areas.

Moreover, because census takers were determined to be politically useful, they were necessarily concerned with issues of nationality and, in the Americas, with race because these characteristics commonly determined political rights and citizenship. The assessment of nationality and race would prove to be among the most politically dubious objectives of the new social sciences.

Though traditional monarchies commonly disregarded nationality, nation-states could not. A country's strength was assumed to depend in large measure on the growth of its national population, a standard that suggested that the growth of minority populations was dangerous. Who was French? Who was Austrian or Hungarian? European statisticians relied on language of use and mother tongue as proxies for nationality, the first term being flexible enough to recognize the assimilation of minorities, the second suggesting a permanent identity based on a person's birth language. Both terms forced bilingual populations to simplify complex identities. Ethnic minorities were sometimes excluded from military careers,

university admission, or other benefits of citizenship. In parts of Spanish America language was a proxy for race. Spanish speakers were citizens in the full sense, even if they were indistinguishable from Amerindians in appearance. Those who spoke indigenous languages were "indios" and therefore subject to special taxes and labor obligations and effectively denied the right to vote.

Beyond justifying discrimination, census categories compressed and distorted the complexity and variety of human society to fit political preconceptions. Large percentages of the residents of Mexico, Peru, and Bolivia, among other parts of the Americas, were descended from both Europeans and Amerindians and, in the Caribbean region, from Europeans and Africans. Census categories could not capture the complexities of these biological and cultural mixtures. We now know that the poor were often identified as "indios" or "blacks" and the better-off were often called something else, "Americanos," "criollos" (creoles), or even whites. Since this process flattened and streamlined the complexities of identity, censuses on their own could not truly reflect the distribution of ethnicity and race in a population.

In Europe the issue of nationality similarly perplexed the census takers and endangered minorities. Politically dominant national majorities usually lived alongside ethnic minorities: Jewish and Polish minorities in areas controlled by German speakers, German speakers among the French, and Serbo-Croatian speakers among Hungarians, for example. The frontiers between these minority populations and their neighbors were always porous. Sexual unions and marriages were common, and two or more generations of a family often lived together in the same household, with the elder members speaking one language and the younger members another. Who was what? In a very real sense, nationality, like race in the Americas, was ultimately fixed by the census process, where the nation-state forced a limited array of politically utilitarian categories onto the rich diversity of ethnicity and culture.

---

**1.** Quoted in James C. Scott, *Seeing like a State. How Certain Schemes to Improve the Human Condition Have Failed* (New Haven: Yale University Press, 1998), 91.

**2.** This discussion relies heavily on Eliza Johnson (now Ablovatski), "Counting and Categorizing: The Hungarian Gypsy Census of 1893" (M.A. Thesis, Columbia University, 1996), especially Chapter III. She quotes from the *Proceedings of the Sixth International Statistical Congress Held in London, 1860,* 379.

# Part Seven

# Global Diversity and Dominance, 1850–1945

© Cengage Learning

| | 1850 | 1870 | 1890 |
|---|---|---|---|
| **AMERICAS** | | **1861–1865** U.S. Civil War    • **1867** Creation of Dominion of Canada | • **1880s** British build railroads in Brazil and Argentina <br> **1880–1914** Immigration from southern and eastern Europe surges | • **1898** Spanish-American War |
| **EUROPE** | • **1851** Majority of British population living in cities <br> • **1856** Transformation of steel and chemical industries begins | **1870–1914** Era of the New Imperialism <br> • **1871** Unification of Germany, Italy | **1894–1906** Dreyfus affair in France |
| **AFRICA** | End of transatlantic slave trade **1867** • | West Africa conquered by France and Britain **1880s** •    **1884–1885** Berlin Africa Conference <br> Nigeria becomes British protectorate **1899** • | • **1896** Ethiopians defeat Italian army at Adowa |
| **MIDDLE EAST** | **1863–1879** Ismail westernizes Egypt <br> • **1869** Suez Canal opens | • **1882** British occupy Egypt <br> • **1878** Ottoman Empire loses most of its European territories | |
| **ASIA AND OCEANIA** | • **1858** Direct British rule in India <br> • **1862** French conquer Indochina | • **1868** Meiji Restoration in Japan <br> First Indian National Congress **1885** • <br> **1884–1887** Russia conquers Central Asia | • **1894** Sino-Japanese War <br> Boxer Rebellion in China **1900** • |

In 1850, the world embraced a huge diversity of societies and cultures, but a preceding century of European imperialist adventures had imposed a common theme on many parts of the globe. During the century that followed, Europe, the United States, and Japan dominated much of the world and tried to convert other peoples to their own cultures and ways of life.

In Europe, mounting tensions led to the Great War of 1914–1918. Russia and China erupted in revolution. Soon after, the heartland of the Ottoman Empire became modern Turkey, while its Arab provinces were taken over by France and Britain.

In the 1930s, amidst a worldwide transformation of lifestyles brought on by new technologies, the political and economic system the European powers crafted after the war fell apart. While the capitalist nations fell into a depression, the Soviet Union industrialized at breakneck speed. In Germany and Japan, extremists sought to solve their countries' grievances by military conquest.

Nationalists in India yearning for independence, as well as nationalists in Latin America seeking an end to foreign military interventions, increased global economic and political tensions as World War II loomed.

The war caused the death of millions of people and the destruction of countless cities. It also weakened Europe's overseas empires. India gained its independence in 1947. Two years later, Mao Zedong led the Chinese communists to victory. Of all the once great powers, only the United States and the Soviet Union remained to compete for global dominance.

---

**1910**      **1930**      **1950**

- **1906–1914** U.S. builds Panama Canal
  - **1917** U.S. enters World War I
- **1911–1920** Mexican Revolution
- **1929** U.S. stock market crash leads to Great Depression
- **1938** Mexico nationalizes oil industry
- **1946** Juan Perón becomes president of Argentina

- **1905** Revolution of 1905 in Russia
- **1922–1945** Fascism in Italy
  - **1917** Russian Revolutions
  - **1933** Hitler takes power in Germany
- **1914–1918** World War I
- **1939–1945** World War II

- **1908** Congo annexed by Belgium
- **1909** African National Congress founded
- **1939–1945** A million Africans serve in World War II

- Balfour Declaration **1917**
- **1922–1938** Atatürk secularizes Turkey
- **1948** State of Israel founded
- **1904** Young Turk reforms in Ottoman Empire
- **1918** Breakup of Ottoman Empire
- **1915–1918** Arab Revolt against Ottomans

- **1904–1905** Russo-Japanese War
- **1910** Korea annexed by Japan
- **1911** Overthrow of Qing dynasty in China
- **1931** Japanese invasion of Manchuria
- **1941** Japan attacks U.S.
- **1945** U.S. atomic bombs force Japanese surrender
- **1947** India and Pakistan win independence
- **1949** Communists take power in China

# Varieties of Imperialism in Africa, India, Southeast Asia, and Latin America

© Cengage Learning

## CHAPTER PREVIEW

### CHANGES AND EXCHANGES IN AFRICA

- Why were imperialists interested in conquering Africa, and how did their presence on that continent change the environment?

### INDIA UNDER BRITISH RULE

- How did Britain secure its hold on India, and what colonial policies led to the beginnings of Indian nationalism?

### SOUTHEAST ASIA AND THE PACIFIC

- What were the social and cultural effects of imperialism in Southeast Asia and the Pacific?

### IMPERIALISM IN LATIN AMERICA

- What were the economic motives behind imperialism in Latin America?

### THE WORLD ECONOMY AND THE GLOBAL ENVIRONMENT

- How did imperialism contribute to the growth and globalization of the world economy?

### Conclusion

**DIVERSITY & DOMINANCE:** Two Africans Recall the Arrival of the Europeans

Like many regions that looked to be coherent countries on the maps drawn by imperialism, Algeria was not a unified realm in 1830 when France landed 35,000 troops outside of Algiers. Five days later, at a cost of 6,000 dead and wounded Frenchmen, the dey of Algiers, an autonomous governor ruling under Ottoman suzerainty, surrendered the city. French nationalists called the invasion a defense of French honor because three years earlier the dey had struck a French diplomat with a fly whisk during an argument over debts lingering from the Napoleonic wars, which had ended more than a decade earlier. Actually the invasion plan had been drawn up by Napoleon himself in 1808 in response to commercial interests in southern France that sought to acquire new land in North Africa.

Control of Algiers, however, did not prevent the king of Morocco from pressing a claim to rule Algeria's western region, nor did it fit the political interests of the country's five major Sufi brotherhoods, which had earlier staged revolts against Ottoman imperialism. The brotherhood that would prove the hardest for the French to defeat was the Qadiriya, which waged a fifteen-year *jihad* (holy war) that only ended in 1847 with the surrender of its leader Abd al-Qadir.

Abd al-Qadir (AHB-dahl-KAH-deer) was only twenty-five when he took over from his father as head of the brotherhood in 1832. The key to Abd al-Qadir's success was a network of religious centers (*zawiyas*) that trained judges and administrators and disseminated his vision of an egalitarian society that would observe Islamic law and be dominated by neither Ottoman officials nor French generals. Other Sufi brotherhoods fought separately against the French, but not as successfully.

Though Abd al-Qadir was allowed to settle in Damascus after his defeat and there pursued an eminent career as a leader of the Muslim community, his historical image is primarily one of resistance to imperialism. Like most movements elsewhere opposing imperialist aggression, Abd al-Qadir's Sufi followers could not prevail against European firepower but laid the groundwork for anticolonial movements that would gain momentum after World War II.

Defenders of imperialism often cite the benefits of European rule in terms of railroad construction, orderly governance, integration of local production with currents of international trade, and similar economic and administrative factors. But the reputations or legends of leaders like Abd al-Qadir would eventually eclipse the memory of some of the generals and administrators who oversaw a massive increase in European imperialism starting in the late eighteenth century.

## CHANGES AND EXCHANGES IN AFRICA

■ *Why were imperialists interested in conquering Africa, and how did their presence on that continent change the environment?*

In the century before 1870 Africa underwent dynamic political changes and a great expansion of foreign trade. While a few indigenous African leaders held out against European imperialism, maps of Africa became tinted with pink and green, the conventional colors of British and French colonies, respectively. The slave trade died under British pressure, and trade in other goods grew sharply. Africans consumed large quantities of imported machine-made textiles, and those rulers who retained a measure of independence purchased European firearms.

### Southern Africa

For many centuries the Nguni (ng-GOO-nee) peoples had farmed and raised cattle in the fertile coast-lands of southeastern Africa (see Map 23.1). When drought hit the region at the beginning of the nineteenth century, an upstart military leader named Shaka (r. 1818–1828) created the **Zulu** kingdom in 1818. Strict military discipline and courage soon made the Zulu the most powerful and most feared fighters in southern Africa. Shaka expanded his kingdom by raiding his African neighbors, seizing their cattle, and capturing their women and children. Although Shaka ruled for little more than a decade, he left behind a

**Zulu** A people of modern South Africa whom King Shaka united in 1818.

Africa and were beginning to refer to themselves as **Afrikaners** (af-rih-KAHN-uhr). Firearms enabled the Afrikaners to win some important battles against the Zulu and other Africans, but they were still a tiny minority surrounded by the populous and powerful independent African kingdoms. The British prohibited further expansion because it invariably led to wars with indigenous Africans; this decision alienated many Afrikaners who had left the British-ruled Cape Colony between 1836 and 1839 to go north in what is called the "Great Trek."

After diamonds were discovered in 1868, Great Britain annexed the diamond area in 1871, further angering Afrikaners. Once in the interior, the British came into conflict first with the Xhosa (KOH-sah) people in 1877 and 1878, and then in 1879 they confronted the Zulu, militarily the most powerful of the African peoples in the region.

The Zulu, led by their king Cetshwayo (set-SHWAH-yo), resented their encirclement by Afrikaners and British. A growing sense of nationalism and their proud military tradition led them into a war with the British in 1879. They defeated the British at Isandlwana (ee-sawn-dull-WAH-nuh), but a few months later they were in turn defeated. Cetshwayo was captured and sent into exile, and the Zulu lands were given to white ranchers.

Relations between the British and the Afrikaners, already tense as a result of British encroachment, took a turn for the worse when gold was discovered in the Afrikaner republic of Transvaal (trans-VAHL) in 1886. In the gold rush that ensued, the British soon outnumbered the Afrikaners.

**Zulu in Battle Dress, 1834** Elaborate costumes helped impress opponents with the Zulus' strength. Shown here are long-handled spears and thick leather shields.

Eileen Tweedy/The At Archive/Art Resource, NY

new national identity destined to clash with European colonial designs.

Southern Africa attracted European settlers first because of its good pastures and farmlands and later because of the discovery of phenomenal deposits of diamonds, gold, and copper, as well as coal and iron ore. The Cape Colony, a Dutch possession that came definitively under British rule after 1806, flourished because of Cape Town's strategic importance as a supply station for ships making the long voyages between Europe and India. With the port city came some twenty thousand descendants of Dutch and French settlers who occupied farms and ranches in the fertile high *veld* (plateau) in the north that two decades of Zulu wars had depopulated.

Despite their European origins, these people thought of themselves as permanent residents of

**Afrikaners**  South Africans descended from Dutch and French settlers of the seventeenth century. Their Great Trek founded new settler colonies in the nineteenth century. Though a minority among South Africans, they held political power after 1910, imposing a system of racial segregation called apartheid after 1949.

# Chronology

| | Slavery | Africa | India and Southeast Asia | Latin America |
|---|---|---|---|---|
| 1750 | | **1795–1802** Britain takes control of Dutch Cape Colony; **1806** British possession becomes permanent | **1756** Black Hole of Calcutta<br>**1765** East India Company (EIC) rule of Bengal begins | |
| 1800 | **1807** Britain outlaws slave trade<br><br><br><br><br><br><br>**1834** Britain frees slaves in its colonies. Indentured labor migrations begin<br><br>**1848** France abolishes slaves in its colonies | **1808** Britain takes over Sierra Leone<br>**1809** Sokoto Caliphate founded<br><br>**1818** Shaka founds Zulu kingdom<br>**1821** Foundation of Liberia<br><br>**1831–1847** Algerians resist French takeover<br>**1836–1839** Afrikaners' Great Trek<br>**1840** Omani sultan moves capital to Zanzibar | **1818** EIC creates Bombay Presidency<br><br>**1826** EIC conquers Assam and northern Burmaco<br>**1828** Brahmo Samaj founded | |
| 1850 | **1867** End of Atlantic slave trade | | **1857–1858** Sepoy Rebellion leads to end of EIC rule<br>**1877** Queen Victoria becomes Empress of India<br>**1885** Indian National Congress formed<br>**1898** Spanish-American War. U.S. takes over Philippines | **1876–1910** Porfirio Díaz, dictator of Mexico<br><br><br>**1898** Spanish-American War. U.S. takes over Cuba |
| 1900 | | **1899–1902** South African (Boer) War<br>**1900s** Railroads connect ports to the interior | | **1910** Mexican Revolution begins<br>**1917** New constitution proclaimed in Mexico |

Britain's invasion of southern Africa was driven in part by the ambition of **Cecil Rhodes** (1853–1902), who once declared that he would "annex the stars" if he could. Rhodes made his fortune in the diamond fields, founding De Beers Consolidated, a company

**Cecil Rhodes (1853–1902)** British entrepreneur and politician involved in the expansion of the British Empire from South Africa into Central Africa. The colonies of Southern Rhodesia (now Zimbabwe) and Northern Rhodesia (now Zambia) were named after him.

**Map 23.1** **Africa in the Nineteenth Century** Expanding trade drew much of Africa into global networks, but foreign colonies in 1870 were largely confined to Algeria and southern Africa. Growing trade, Islamic reform movements, and other internal forces created important new states throughout the continent. © Cengage Learning

that has dominated the world's diamond trade ever since. He then turned to politics. He encouraged a concession company, the British South Africa Company, to push north into Central Africa, where he named two new colonies after himself: Southern Rhodesia (now Zimbabwe) and Northern Rhodesia (now Zam-

bia). The Ndebele (en-duh-BELL-ay) and Shona peoples, who inhabited the region, resisted this invasion, but the machine guns of the British finally defeated them.

The inflow of English-speaking whites into the gold- and diamond-mining areas and British attempts to annex the two Afrikaner republics, Transvaal and

**Map legend:**
- Zanzibari trading post
- Nguni/Ngoni states
- Reformist Muslim states
- Nyamwezi states
- Ethiopia, 1880
- Ethiopia, 1900
- Other states
- European colonies
- → Migrations of the Nguni/Ngoni
- → The Great Trek
- → Trade routes
- External slave trade and date of suppression

Gardiner F. Williams/NGS Image Collection

**South African Diamond Mine**  When diamonds were found in Kimberley, South Africa, in 1868, the discovery precipitated a rush of prospectors from Europe and America. As soon as surface deposits were exhausted, their claims were bought by large companies that could afford the heavy equipment needed to mine deep underground. By the early twentieth century, diamonds came from major industrial mines like the Premier Mine shown here.

ish government expected European settlers in Africa to manage their own affairs, as they were doing in Canada, Australia, and New Zealand. Thus, in 1910 the European settlers created the Union of South Africa, in which the Afrikaners eventually emerged as the ruling element.

Unlike Canada, Australia, and New Zealand, South Africa had a majority of indigenous inhabitants and substantial numbers of Indians and "Cape Coloureds" (people of mixed ancestry). Yet the Europeans were both numerous enough to demand self-rule and powerful enough to deny the vote and other civil rights to the majority. In 1913 the South African parliament passed the Natives Land Act, assigning Africans to reservations and forbidding them to own land elsewhere. This and other racial policies turned South Africa into a land of segregation and oppression.

Simultaneous with the formation of Shaka's Zulu kingdom, Islamic reform movements were creating another cluster of powerful states in the savannas of West Africa. The reformers followed a classic Muslim pattern: a *jihad* (holy war) added new lands, spreading Islamic beliefs and laws among conquered peoples. The largest reform movement was led by Usuman dan Fodio (OO-soo-mahn dahn FOH-dee-oh) (1745–1817), whose armed supporters conquered and combined the older Hausa (HOW-suh) states into a new empire ruled by a caliph in the city of Sokoto. The **Sokoto Caliphate** (1809–1906) was the largest state in West Africa since the sixteenth century (see Map 23.1).

In coastal West Africa, however, the French, who had maintained a foothold in Senegal for centuries,

Orange Free State, led to the South African or Boer War, which lasted from 1899 to 1902. At first the Afrikaners had the upper hand, for they were highly motivated, possessed modern rifles, and knew the land. In 1901, however, Great Britain brought in 450,000 troops and crushed the Afrikaner armies. Ironically, the Afrikaners' defeat in 1902 led to their ultimate victory. Wary of costly commitments overseas, the Brit-

**Sokoto Caliphate**  A large Muslim state founded in 1809 in what is now northern Nigeria.

envisioned building a railroad from the upper Sen-egal River to the upper Niger to open the interior to French merchants. This in turn led the French military to undertake the conquest of the interior. Sokoto remained independent, but after 1890 it was embattled both by neighboring rulers and European encroach-ment. In 1906 the empire came to an end, with France, Britain, and Germany gobbling up various portions.

Farther south, **King Leopold II** of Belgium, fol-lowing the advice of an American journalist and explorer, Henry Morton Stanley, invested his personal fortune in "opening up"—that is, occupying—the Congo Basin, an enormous forested region in the heart of equatorial Africa. With Leopold's money, Stanley returned to Africa from 1879 to 1884 to establish trad-ing posts along the southern bank of the Congo River. At the same time Savorgnan de Brazza, an Italian officer serving in the French army, obtained from an African ruler living on the opposite bank a treaty that placed that area under the "protection" of France.

These events sparked a flurry of diplomatic activ-ity. German chancellor Bismarck called the **Berlin Conference** on Africa of 1884 and 1885. There the major powers agreed that henceforth "effective occu-pation" would replace the former trading relations between Africans and Europeans. Every country with colonial ambitions had to send troops into Africa and participate in the division of the spoils. As a reward for triggering the "scramble" for Africa, Leopold II acquired a personal domain under the name *Congo Free State*, while France and Portugal took most of the rest of equatorial Africa. In this manner, the Euro-pean powers and King Leopold managed to divide Africa among themselves, at least on paper.

Except in Kenya, Northern Rhodesia, and South Africa, where Europeans found the land and climate to their liking and forced Africans to become squat-ters, sharecroppers, or ranch hands on land they had farmed for generations, the colonial rulers declared any land that was not farmed to be "vacant" and gave it to private concession companies. In the Gold Coast (now Ghana), British trading companies bought the cocoa grown by African farmers at low prices and resold it for large profits. The interior of French West Africa lagged behind. Although the region could pro-duce cotton, peanuts, and other crops, the difficulties of transportation limited its development before 1914.

Compared to West Africa, equatorial Africa had few inhabitants and little trade. Rather than try to govern these vast territories directly, authorities in the Congo Free State, the French Congo, and the Por-tuguese colonies of Angola and Mozambique granted huge pieces of land to private concession companies, offering them monopolies on the natural resources and trade of their territories and the right to employ soldiers and impose taxes.

Freed from outside supervision, the companies forced the African inhabitants at gunpoint to pro-duce cash crops and carry them, on their heads or backs, to the nearest railroad or navigable river. The worst abuses took place in the Congo Free State, where a rubber boom made it profitable for private companies to brutalize Africans collecting latex from vines that grew in the forests. After 1906 the British press began publicizing the horrors. The public out-cry that followed, coinciding with the end of the rub-ber boom, convinced the Belgian government to take over Leopold's private empire in 1908. (See Diversity and Dominance: Two Africans Recall the Arrival of the Europeans.)

## Modernization in Egypt and Ethiopia

While colonial states were aris-ing elsewhere, in northeast-ern Africa Egypt and Ethiopia retained their independence and experimented with **modernization**. Muhammad Ali, who ruled Egypt from 1805 to 1849, began a series of reforms aimed at creating a modern Egypt (see Chapter 22). European pressure sharply curtailed these efforts after 1839, but by the end of his reign Egypt's population had nearly doubled; trade with Europe had expanded

**King Leopold II (1835–1909)**  King of Belgium (r. 1865–1909). He was active in encouraging the exploration of Central Africa and became the ruler of the Congo Free State (to 1908).

**Berlin Conference (1884–1885)**  Conference that German chancellor Otto von Bismarck called to set rules for the partition of Africa. It led to the creation of the Congo Free State under King Leopold II of Belgium.

**modernization**  The process of reforming political, military, economic, social, and cultural traditions in imitation of the early success of Western societies, often with little regard for accommodating local traditions in non-Western societies.

by almost 600 percent; and a new class of educated Egyptians was beginning to wield some influence.

Muhammad Ali's grandson Ismail (is-mah-EEL) (r. 1863–1879) placed emphasis on westernizing Egypt. "My country is no longer in Africa," Ismail declared, "it is in Europe."[1] Massive cotton exports during the American Civil War helped finance a network of new irrigation canals, 800 miles (1,300 kilometers) of railroads, a postal service, and dazzling changes in the capital city of Cairo. Once cotton prices returned to normal after 1865, other sources of revenue were needed to finance such projects as the **Suez Canal**, which opened in 1869 and was the greatest construction project of the century. The canal allowed ships to travel between Europe and India in less than two weeks—much less than the month or longer consumed by sailing around Africa and across the Indian Ocean. Ismail even tried to make Egypt the center of an empire reaching into Sudan and Ethiopia.

Instead of making Egypt powerful and independent, ambitious projects like the Suez Canal forced Egypt to borrow from European creditors at high interest rates. Half the Suez Canal was financed by the French; the other half by Egypt. By 1876 foreign debt had risen to £100 million sterling, and the interest payments alone consumed one-third of Egypt's foreign export earnings. To avoid bankruptcy, the Egyptian government sold its shares in the Suez Canal to Great Britain and accepted foreign oversight. When high taxes caused hardship and popular discontent, the French and British persuaded the Ottoman sultan to depose Ismail. This foreign intervention provoked a military uprising under the Egyptian army colonel Arabi Pasha, which threatened the Suez Canal.

Fearing for their investments, the British sent an army into Egypt in 1882. So important was the Suez Canal to Britain's maritime supremacy that they stayed for seventy years. During those years the British ruled Egypt "indirectly"—that is, they maintained the Egyptian government and the fiction of Egyptian sovereignty but retained real power in their own hands.

Eager to develop Egyptian cotton production, the British brought in engineers and contractors to build the first dam across the Nile, at Aswan in Upper Egypt. When completed in 1902, it captured the annual Nile flood and released its waters throughout the year, allowing farmers to grow two, sometimes three, crops a year. The economic development of Egypt by the British enriched a small elite of landowners and merchants, many of them foreigners. Egyptian peasants got little relief from the heavy taxes collected to pay for their country's crushing foreign debt and the expenses of the British army of occupation. Most Egyptians found British rule more onerous than that of the Ottomans. By the 1890s Egyptian politicians and intellectuals were demanding that the British leave.

Beginning in the 1840s, Christian Ethiopia was also modernizing its state, purchasing weapons from European sources and creating strong armies loyal to the ruler. Emperor Téwodros (tay-WOH-druhs) II (r. 1833–1868) and his successor, Yohannes (yoh-HAHN-nehs) IV (r. 1872–1889), brought back under imperial rule large areas of ancient Ethiopia. When King Menelik II (MEN-uh-lik) of Shoa succeeded Yohannes as emperor in 1889, the merger of their separate realms created the modern boundaries of Ethiopia.

## Transition from the Slave Trade

Trade between Africa and the other Atlantic continents more than doubled between the 1730s and the 1780s, then doubled again by 1870.[2] Before about 1825, the slave trade accounted for most of that increase. Western criticism of slavery was rising, however. Once the world's greatest slave traders, the British became the most aggressive abolitionists. During the half century after 1815, Britain spent some $60 million (£12 million) in its efforts to end the slave

> **Suez Canal** Ship canal dug across the Isthmus of Suez in Egypt, designed by Ferdinand de Lesseps. It opened to shipping in 1869 and shortened the sea voyage between Europe and Asia. Its strategic importance led to the British occupation of Egypt in 1882.

---

[1]Quoted in P. J. Vatikiotis, *The History of Modern Egypt: From Muhammad Ali to Mubarak*, 4th ed. (Baltimore: Johns Hopkins University Press, 1991), 74.

[2]David Eltis, "Precolonial Western Africa and the Atlantic Economy," in *Slavery and the Rise of the Atlantic Economy*, ed. Barbara Solow (New York: Cambridge University Press, 1991), table 1.

# Diversity & Dominance

## Two Africans Recall the Arrival of the Europeans

*We know a great deal about the arrival of the Europeans into the interior of Africa from the perspective of the conquerors, but very little about how the events were experienced by Africans. Here are two accounts by African women, one from northern Nigeria whose land was occupied by the British, the other from the Congo Free State, a colony of King Leopold II of Belgium. They show not only how Africans experienced European colonial dominance but also how diverse these African experiences were.*

### Baba of Karo, a Nigerian Woman, Remembers Her Childhood

**W**hen I was a maiden the Europeans first arrived. Ever since we were quite small the *malams* had been saying that the Europeans would come with a thing called a train, they would come with a thing called a motor-car, in them you would go and come back in a trice. They would stop wars, they would repair the world, they would stop oppression and lawlessness, we should live at peace with them. We used to go and sit quietly and listen to the prophecies.

I remember when a European came to Karo on a horse, and some of his foot soldiers went into the town. Everyone came out to look at them, but in Zerewa they didn't see the European. Everyone at Karo ran away—"There's a European, there's a European!"

At that time Yusufu was the king of Karo. He did not like the Europeans, he did not wish them, he would not sign their treaty. Then he say that perforce he would have to agree, so he did. We Habe wanted them to come, it was the Fulani who did not like it. When the Europeans came the Habe saw that if you worked for them they paid you for it, they didn't say, like the Fulani, "Commoner, give me this!

Commoner, bring me that!" Yes, the Habe wanted them; they saw no harm in them.

The Europeans said that there were to be no more slaves; if someone said "Slave!" you could complain to the *alkali* who would punish the master who said it, the judge said, "That is what the Europeans have decreed." The first order said that any slave, if he was younger than you, was your younger brother, if he was older than you was your elder brother—they were all brothers of their master's family. No one used the word "slave" any more. When slavery was stopped, nothing much happened at our *rinji* except that some slaves whom we had bought in the market ran away. Our own father went to his farm and worked, he and his son took up their large hoes; they loaned out their spare farms. Tsoho our father and Kadiri my brother with whom I live now and Babambo worked, they farmed guineacorn and millet and groundnuts and everything; before this they had supervised the slaves' work—now they did their own.

In the old days if the chief liked the look of your daughter he would take her and put her in his house; you could do nothing about it. Now they don't do that.

### Ilanga, a Congolese Woman, Recounts Her Capture by Agents of the Congo Free State

. . . we were all busy in the fields hoeing our plantations, for it was the rainy season, and the weeds sprang quickly up, when a runner came to the village saying that a large band of men was coming, that they all wore red caps and blue cloth, and carried guns and long knives, and that many white men were with them, the chief of whom was Kibalanga (Michaux). Niendo at once called all the chief men to his house, while the drums were beaten to summon the people to the village. A long consultation was held, and finally we were all told to go quietly to the fields and bring in ground-nuts, plantains, and cassava for the warriors who were coming, and goats and fowl for the white men. ➤

The women all went with baskets and filled them, and put them in the road, which was blocked up, so many were there. Niendo then commanded everyone to go and sit quietly in the houses until he gave other orders. This we did, everyone remaining quietly seated while Niendo went up the road with the head men to meet the white chief. We did not know what to think, for most of us feared that so many armed men coming boded evil; but Niendo thought that, by giving presents of much food, he would induce the strangers to pass on without harming us. And so it proved, for the soldiers took the baskets, and were then ordered by the white men to move off through the village. Many of the soldiers looked into the houses and shouted at us words we did not understand. We were glad when they were all gone, for we were much in fear of the white men and the strange warriors, who are known to all the people as being great fighters, bringing war wherever they go. . . .

When the white men and their warriors had gone, we went again to our work, and were hoping that they would not return; but this they did in a very short time. As before, we brought in great heaps of food; but this time *Kibalanga* did not move away directly, but camped near our village, and his soldiers came and stole all our fowl and goats and tore up our cassava; but we did not mind as long as they did not harm us. The next morning it was reported that the white men were going away; but soon after the sun rose over the hill, a large band of soldiers came into the village, and we all went into the houses and sat down. We were not long seated when the soldiers came rushing in shouting, and threatening Niendo with their guns. They rushed into the houses and dragged the people out. Three or four came to our house and caught hold of me, also my husband Oleka and my sister Katinga. We were dragged into the road, and were tied together with cords about our necks, so that we could not escape. We were all crying, for now we knew that we were to be taken away to be slaves. The soldiers beat us with the iron sticks from their guns, and compelled us to march to the camp of *Kibalanga*, who ordered the women to be tied up separately, ten to each cord, and the men in the same way. When we were all collected—and there were many from other villages whom we now saw, and many from Waniendo—the soldiers brought baskets of food for us to carry, in some of which was smoked human flesh (*niama na nitu*).

We then set off marching very quickly. My sister Katinga had her baby in her arms, and was not compelled to carry a basket; but my husband Oleka was made to carry a goat. We marched until the afternoon, when we camped near a stream, where we were glad to drink, for we were much athirst. We had nothing to eat, for the soldiers would give us nothing, so we lay upon the ground, and at night went to sleep. The next day we continued the march, and when we camped at noon were given some maize and plantains, which were gathered near a village from which the people had run away. So it continued each day until the fifth day, when the soldiers took my sister's baby and threw it in the grass, leaving it to die, and made her carry some cooking pots which they found in the deserted village. On the sixth day we became very weak from lack of food and from constant marching and sleeping in the damp grass, and my husband, who marched behind us with the goat, could not stand up longer, and so he sat down beside the path and refused to walk more. The soldiers beat him, but still he refused to move. Then one of them struck him on the head with the end of his gun, and he fell upon the ground. One of the soldiers caught the goat, while two or three others stuck the long knives they put on the ends of their guns into my husband. I saw the blood spurt out, and then saw him no more, for we passed over the brow of a hill and he was out of sight. Many of the young men were killed the same way, and many babies thrown into the grass to die. A few escaped; but we were so well guarded that it was almost impossible.

## QUESTIONS FOR ANALYSIS

1. How do Baba and Ilanga recall their existence before the Europeans came?
2. What did they expect when they first heard of the arrival of Europeans? Instead, what happened to them, their relatives, and their towns?
3. How do you explain the difference between these two accounts?

*Sources*: From M. F. Smith, ed., *Baba of Karo: A Woman of the Muslim Hausa* (New York: Philosophical Library, 1955), 66–68. Edgar Canisius, *A Campaign Amongst Cannibals* (London: R. A. Everett & Co., 1903), 250–256.

trade through naval patrols. This equaled the profits British slave traders had made in the fifty years before the trade was banned in 1807. Although British patrols captured 1,635 slave ships and liberated over 160,000 enslaved Africans, continued demand for slaves in Cuba and Brazil kept the trade going until 1867.

To satisfy their desire for cloth, metals, and other goods after slavery was outlawed, Africans expanded their **"legitimate" trade** (exports other than slaves). The most successful of the new exports from West Africa was palm oil, used by British manufacturers for soap, candles, and lubricants. Though still a major source of slaves until the mid-1830s, the trading states of the Niger Delta emerged as the premier exporters of palm oil. Coastal Africans grew rich and purchased large numbers of male slaves to paddle the giant dugout canoes that transported palm oil from inland markets along the narrow delta creeks to the trading ports.

Suppressing the slave trade helped spread Western cultural influences in West Africa. In 1808, the British had taken over the small colony of Sierra Leone (see-AIR-uh lee-OWN) as a base for their anti-slave trade naval squadron. In the following years, 130,000 men, women, and children taken from "captured" vessels were liberated in Sierra Leone. Christian missionaries helped settle these impoverished and dispirited **recaptives** in and around Freetown, the capital. In time, the mission churches and schools made many converts among such unfortunates.

Sierra Leone's schools also produced a number of distinguished graduates. Samuel Adjai Crowther (1808–1891), freed from a slave ship in 1821, became the first Anglican bishop in West Africa in 1864, administering a pioneering diocese along the lower Niger River. James Africanus Horton (1835–1882), the son of slaves liberated in Sierra Leone, became a doctor and the author of many studies of West Africa.

Other Western cultural influences came from people of African birth or descent returning to their ancestral homeland. In 1821, to the south of Sierra Leone, free black Americans founded a settlement that grew into the Republic of Liberia, a place of liberty at a time when slavery was legal and flourishing in the United States.

With the British patrolling West Africa, slavers moved southward and then around the tip of the continent to eastern Africa, where an existing trade

**SECTION REVIEW**

- In the south, Shaka established a Zulu kingdom that came in conflict with European settlers.
- Differences between the British and Dutch-descended Afrikaners led to the Boer War.
- In the west, Usuman dan Fodio conquered the former Hausa states and formed the Sokoto Caliphate.
- The Suez Canal conferred new economic and political importance on Egypt.
- The abolition of slavery had economic and political consequences.

in slaves to the Islamic world was expanding. Two-thirds of the 1.2 million slaves exported from eastern Africa in the nineteenth century went to markets in North Africa and the Middle East; the other third went to plantations in the Americas and the Indian Ocean.

Between 1800 and 1873 local Arab and Swahili (swah-HEE-lee) owners purchased some 700,000 slaves from inland eastern Africa to do the hard work of harvesting cloves on plantations on Zanzibar Island and the neighboring coast. These territories belonged to the sultanate of Oman, a realm in southeastern Arabia. The sultan had even moved his court to Zanzibar in 1840 to take advantage of the burgeoning trade in cloves. Zanzibar also exported ivory and slaves until British pressure induced the sultan to ban the export of slaves in 1857 and their import in 1873.

# INDIA UNDER BRITISH RULE

■ *How did Britain secure its hold on India, and what colonial policies led to the beginnings of Indian nationalism?*

The people of South Asia felt the impact of European commercial, cultural, and colonial expansion more immediately and profoundly than did the Africans. Europeans laid claim to only small parts of Africa

**"legitimate" trade** Exports from Africa in the nineteenth century that did not include the newly outlawed slave trade.

**recaptives** Africans rescued by Britain's Royal Navy from the illegal slave trade of the nineteenth century and restored to free status.

between 1750 and 1870, but nearly all of India (with three times the population of Africa) came under Britain's direct or indirect rule. After the founding of the East India Company in 1600, it took British interests 250 years to commandeer the colonies and trade of the Dutch, fight off French and Indian challenges, and pick up the pieces of the decaying Mughal (MOO-guhl) Empire.

The might of the Mughal Empire had not lasted long after the reign of Aurangzeb, who died in 1707 (see Chapter 18). In 1739 Iranian invaders sacked Delhi and carried off vast amounts of booty. Indian states also took advantage of Mughal weakness to assert their independence. By midcentury, the Maratha (muh-RAH-tuh) Confederation, a coalition of states in central India, controlled more land than the Mughals did. Several **nawabs** (NAH-wab), a term used for Muslim princes who were nominally deputies of the Mughal emperor, carved out powerful states of their own. Ambitious young "company men" employed by British, French, and Dutch trading companies used hard bargaining, and hard fighting when necessary, to persuade these Indian rulers to allow them to establish coastal trading posts. To protect their fortified warehouses, the companies hired trained Indian troops known as **sepoys** (SEE-poy). In fragmented India, these private armies came to hold the balance of power.

In 1691, the East India Company (EIC) had persuaded the nawab of Bengal in northeast India to allow a company trading post at the fishing port of Calcutta. In 1756 a new nawab overran the post and imprisoned a group of EIC men in a cell so small that many died of suffocation. To avenge their deaths in this "Black Hole of Calcutta," a large EIC force from Madras overthrew the nawab. The weak Mughal emperor was persuaded to acknowledge the EIC's right to rule Bengal in 1765. By 1788 Calcutta had grown into a city of 250,000.

Along with Calcutta and Madras, the third major center of British power was Bombay, on the western coast. There, in 1818, the EIC annexed large territories to form the core of what was called the "Bombay Presidency." This gave the EIC an empire with fifty times the population of the colonies the British had lost in North America.

One goal of the **British raj** (reign) was to remake India on a British model through administrative measures, economic development, and modern technology. But the company men—like the Mughals before them—had to temper their interference with Indian social and religious customs lest they provoke rebellion or lose the support of their Indian princely allies.

The main policy was to create a powerful and efficient system of government. Another British policy was to substitute private property for India's complex and overlapping patterns of landholding. In Bengal this reform worked to the advantage of large landowners, but in Mysore the peasantry gained. Private ownership made it easier for the state to collect the taxes that were needed to pay for administration, the army, and economic reform.

Such policies of "westernization, Anglicization, and modernization," as they have been called, were only one side of British rule. The other side was the bolstering of "traditions"—both real and newly invented. In the name of tradition the Indian princes who ruled nearly half of British India were permitted to expand their power and splendor. The British rulers themselves invented many "traditions"—including elaborate parades and displays, called **durbars**, that were half borrowed from European royal pomp, half from Mughal ceremonies.

The British and Indian elites danced sometimes in close partnership, sometimes in apparent opposition. But the ordinary people of India—women of every status, members of subordinate Hindu castes, the "untouchables" and "tribals" outside the caste system, and the poor generally—found less benefit from the British reforms and much new oppression from the taxes and "traditions."

The transformation of British India's economy was also double-edged. On the one hand, the growth in internal and external trade created many new jobs, as did the expansion of farming: opium in Bengal,

**nawab** Technically, a semi-autonomous deputy of the Mughal emperor but often a Muslim prince allied to British India.

**sepoy** A soldier in colonial India, especially in the service of the British.

**British raj** The rule over much of South Asia between 1765 and 1947 by the East India Company and then by a British government.

**durbar** An elaborate display of political power and wealth in British India in the nineteenth century, ostensibly in imitation of the pageantry of the Mughal Empire.

**Delhi Durbar, January 1, 1903**  The parade of Indian princes on ornately decorated elephants and accompanied by retainers fostered their sense of belonging to the vast empire of India that British rule had created.

largely for export to China (see Chapter 22); coffee in Ceylon; and tea in Assam in northeastern India (ruled by Burma prior to EIC conquest in 1826). On the other hand, competition from cheap cotton goods produced in Britain's industrial mills drove many Indians out of the handicraft textile industry. In the eighteenth century India had been the world's greatest exporter of cotton textiles; in the nineteenth century India increasingly shipped raw cotton fiber to Britain.

Economic changes, including beneficial ones, caused disruption. Thus, local rebellions by displaced ruling elites, disgruntled religious traditionalists, and the economically dispossessed were almost constant during the first half of the nineteenth century. The greatest concern was over the loyalty of Indian sepoys in the EIC's army.

In the early decades of EIC rule, most sepoys came from Bengal. The Bengali sepoys resented the recruitment of other ethnic groups into the army after 1848, such as Sikhs (sicks) from Punjab and Gurkhas from Nepal. Many high-caste Hindus objected to a new law in 1856 requiring new recruits to be available for service overseas, for their religion prohibited ocean travel. Then in 1857 the replacement of the standard muskets by the more accurate Enfield rifles sparked outrage because they required soldiers to use their teeth to tear open the ammunition cartridges, which were greased with animal fat. Fat from cattle offended Hindus; fat from pigs offended Muslims.

A quick change in the cartridge-opening procedure could not forestall a rebellion by Hindu sepoys in May 1857. Muslim sepoys, peasants, and discontented elites joined in. The rebellion was put down ten months later, but it shook this empire to its core.

Historians have attached different names and meanings to the events of 1857 and 1858. Nineteenth-century British historians labeled it the **"Sepoy Rebellion"** or "Mutiny." Seeing in these events the beginnings of the later movement for independence, some modern Indian historians have termed it the "Revolution of 1857."

## Political Reform and Industrial Impact

Regardless of label, the events of 1857–1858 marked a turning point in the history of modern India. In their wake Indians gained a new centralized government, entered a period of rapid economic growth, and began to develop a new national consciousness.

In 1858 Britain eliminated the last traces of Mughal and EIC rule. In their place, a new secretary of state for India in London oversaw Indian policy, and a new governor-general in Delhi acted as the British monarch's viceroy. In November 1858 Queen Victoria, who would assume the title Empress of India in 1877, guaranteed all Indians equal protection of the law and the freedom to practice their religions and social customs, but she also assured Indian princes that so long as they were loyal to the queen British India would respect their control of territories and "their rights, dignity and honour."[3]

Meanwhile, a powerful and efficient bureaucracy controlled India. Members of the elite **Indian Civil Service** (ICS), mostly graduates of Oxford and Cambridge University, held the senior administrative and judicial posts. Numbering only a thousand at the end of the nineteenth century, they visited the villages in their districts, heard lawsuits and complaints, and passed judgments. A far greater number of Indian officials and employees served beneath them. Recruitment into the ICS was by open examination given only in England and thus inaccessible to most Indians. In 1870 only one Indian was a member of the ICS. Subsequent reforms led to fifty-seven Indian appointments by 1887, but there the process stalled.

Beginning in the 1840s a railroad boom gave India its first national transportation network, followed by telegraph lines, and by 1870 India had the fifth largest rail network in the world. The government invested

millions of pounds sterling in other public works as well. Forests were felled to make way for tea plantations. Indian farmers were persuaded to grow cotton and jute for export. Engineers built great irrigation systems to alleviate the famines that periodically decimated whole provinces. As a result, India's trade expanded rapidly.

Most of the exports were agricultural commodities: cotton fiber, opium, tea, silk, and sugar. In return India imported manufactured goods from Britain, including machine-made cotton textiles that undercut Indian hand-loom weavers. Some women found jobs at very low pay on plantations or in the growing cities, where prostitution flourished. Everywhere in India poverty remained the norm.

Easier movement and urbanization promoted the spread of cholera (KAHL-uhr-uh), a disease transmitted through water contaminated by human feces. In 1867, officials demonstrated the close connection between cholera and pilgrims who bathed in and drank from sacred pools and rivers. The installation of a new sewerage system and a filtered water supply (1869) in Calcutta dramatically reduced cholera deaths there. Similar measures in Bombay and Madras also led to great reductions, but most Indians lived in small villages where famine and lack of sanitation kept cholera deaths high.

## Indian Nationalism

Both the successes and failures of British rule stimulated Indian nationalism. The failure of the rebellion of 1857 led some thoughtful Indians to argue that the only way to regain control of their destiny was to reduce their country's social and ethnic divisions.

Individuals such as Rammohun Roy (1772–1833) had promoted development along these lines a generation earlier. A Western-educated Bengali from a Brahmin family, Roy was a successful administrator for the EIC and a student of comparative religion. His

---

[3]Quoted by Bernard S. Cohn, "Representing Authority in Victorian India," in *The Invention of Tradition*, ed. Eric Hobsbawm and Terence Ranger (Cambridge, England: Cambridge University Press, 1983), 165.

**Sepoy Rebellion** The revolt of Indian soldiers in 1857 against certain practices that violated religious customs; also known as the Sepoy Mutiny.

**Indian Civil Service** The elite professional class of officials who administered the government of British India. Originally composed exclusively of well-educated British men, it gradually added qualified Indians.

An Indian Railway Station, 1854 (engraving) (b/w photo), English School, (19th century)/The Illustrated London News Picture Library, London, UK/The Bridgeman Art Library

**Indian Railroad Station, 1866**  British India built the largest network of railroads in Asia. People of every social class traveled by train.

Brahmo Samaj (BRAH-moh suh-MAHJ) (Divine Society), founded in 1828, attracted Indians who sought to reconcile the values of the West with the religious traditions of India. They backed the British outlawing of *sati* (suh-TEE) (widow burning) in 1829 and of slavery in 1834 and sought to correct other abuses of women and female infanticide. Roy and his followers advocated reforming the caste system and urged a

return to the founding principles of the *Upanishads*, ancient sacred writings of Hinduism.

Although Brahmo Samaj remained influential after the rebellion of 1857, many Indian intellectuals turned to Western secular values and nationalism as the way to reclaim India, often aided by European and American missionaries. In 1870 there were 790,000 Indians in over 24,000 elementary and secondary schools, and India's three universities (established in 1857) awarded 345 degrees. Many new nationalists arose from the Indian middle class, and in 1885 nationalists convened the first **Indian National Congress**, which called for a larger Indian role in the civil service and for greater efforts to

## SECTION REVIEW

- Between 1757 and 1857, Britain gained nearly complete control of India.

- The British exploited local traditions and rulers and instituted a colonial government that conferred benefits on those Indians who governed on its behalf, while most of the population lived in worsening conditions.

- The Sepoy Rebellion of 1857–1858 prompted reforms and substantial investments in railroads and other public works.

- In response to modernization, Indian nationalism arose in the educated middle class.

**Indian National Congress**  A movement and political party founded in 1885 to demand greater Indian participation in government. Its membership was middle class, and its demands were modest until World War I. Led after 1920 by Mohandas K. Gandhi, it appealed increasingly to the poor, and it organized mass protests demanding self-government and independence.

reduce poverty. But although the Indian National Congress promoted unity among the country's many religions and social groups, most early members were upper-caste Western-educated Hindus and Parsis. Until it attracted the support of the masses, it could not hope to challenge British rule.

# SOUTHEAST ASIA AND THE PACIFIC

■ *What were the social and cultural effects of imperialism in Southeast Asia and the Pacific?*

The underlying goal of imperialism in the nineteenth century was not territory but trade. Southeast Asia and the Pacific have differing histories, yet all came under intense imperialist pressure. From the far corners of the world came coffee, cocoa, tea, and sugar for the tables of Western consumers, as well as indigo dyes and cotton fibers for the expanding textile factories. In return for the foodstuffs and industrial raw materials that flowed toward Europe and the United States, the factories of the industrialized nations supplied manufactured goods at very attractive prices. In most cases such trade benefited both sides, but there is no question that the industrial nations were the dominant partners.

## Southeast Asia and Indonesia

Until the mid-nineteenth century, independent kingdoms had ruled most of the Southeast Asian peninsula and the Indonesian archipelago. Only Siam (now Thailand) would remain independent. Burma (now Myanmar), which had already lost several provinces to British India, went fully to Britain in a war ending in 1885. Malaya (now Malaysia)—with its Singapore port—also came under British rule. Indochina fell under French control. By the early 1900s, the Dutch has subdued northern Sumatra. (See Map 23.2.)

What all these regions had in common was fertile soil, constant warmth, and heavy rains, along with a long tradition of intensive gardening, irrigation, and terracing. The climate favored the transfer of commercially valuable plants from other parts of the world. Tobacco, cinchona (sin-CHO-nah) (an antimalarial drug), manioc (an edible root crop), maize (corn), and natural rubber came from the Americas; sugar from India; tea from China; and coffee and oil

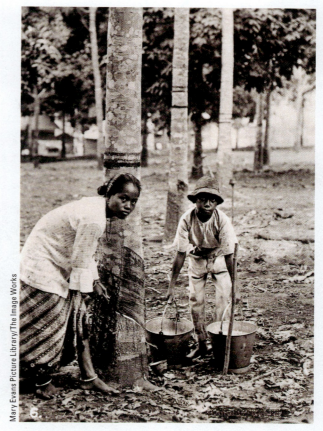

Mary Evans Picture Library/The Image Works

**A Rubber Plantation**  As bicycles and automobiles proliferated in the early twentieth century, the demand for rubber outstripped the supply available from wild rubber trees in the Amazon forest. Rubber grown on plantations in Southeast Asia came on the market from 1910 on. The rubber trees had to be tapped very carefully and on a regular schedule to obtain the latex or sap from which rubber was extracted. In this picture a woman and a boy perform this operation on a plantation in British Malaya.

palms from Africa. By 1914 much of the world's supply of these valuable products—in the case of rubber, almost all—came from Southeast Asia and Indonesia.

Colonialism and population growth spurred many social changes. Agricultural and commercial peoples gradually moved into mountainous and forested areas, displacing groups that practiced hunting and gathering or shifting agriculture and had not experienced as much population growth. Javanese migrating to Borneo and Sumatra are but one example. Immigrants from China and India changed the ethnic composition and culture of every country in

**Map 23.2 Asia in 1914** By 1914, much of Asia was claimed by colonial powers. The southern rim, from the Persian Gulf to the Pacific, was occupied by Great Britain, France, the Netherlands, and the United States. © Cengage Learning

**Territories held by Western powers**

- Great Britain
- France
- Netherlands
- United States
- Russian Empire

- Japan and its territories
- Independent Asian states
- Ottoman Empire
- Major railroads

AFRICA

PACIFIC OCEAN

INDIAN OCEAN

RUSSIAN EMPIRE

JAPANESE EMPIRE

SIBERIA

CHINA

OTTOMAN EMPIRE

ARABIA

INDIA

*Sea of Okhotsk*

*Sea of Japan*

*East China Sea*

*South China Sea*

*Bay of Bengal*

*Arabian Sea*

*Caspian Sea*

*Black Sea*

*Mediterranean Sea*

*Red Sea*

*Aral Sea*

*Lake Balkash*

*Lake Baikal*

Helsinki
St. Petersburg
Riga
Warsaw
Brest-Litovsk
Kiev
Moscow
Omsk
Orenburg
Samara
Kazalinsk
Irkutsk
Chita
Khabarovsk (1858)
Vladivostok (1860)
Harbin

*Trans-Siberian Railway*

AMUR DISTRICT (1858)

MANCHURIA

OUTER MONGOLIA (Russian Influence, 1912)

INNER MONGOLIA

SINKIANG

TIBET

JEHOL

Shenyang (Mukden)
Beijing
Tianjin
Lüshun (Port Arthur) (Japan 1905)
Weihai (Gr. Br. 1898)
Jiaozhou (Ger. 1898)
KOREA (1905, 1910)
Ryuku Is. (Jap.)
Formosa (1895)
Karafuto (1905)
Sakhalin

Nanjing
Shanghai (Gr. Br. 1842)
Wuhan
Fuzhou
Xiamen (Gr. Br. 1842)
Guangzhou (Gr. Br. 1842)
Hong Kong (France 1898)
Zhanjiang (France 1898)
Macao (Port. 1557)
Hainan
Haiphong
Hanoi
Kunming
Chongqing

Philippine Is. (U.S. 1898)
Manila

BRITISH NORTH BORNEO (1888)
SARAWAK (1888)
Borneo
Celebes
New Guinea (Portugal 1859)
Timor (Neth.)
DUTCH EAST INDIES
Java (1619)
Batavia
Sumatra

MALAY STATES (1874, 1909)
Singapore (Gr. Br. 1819)
SIAM
Bangkok
FRENCH INDOCHINA (1859, 1907)
Saigon
BURMA (1852, 1885)
Rangoon
Andaman Is. (Gr. Br.)
Ceylon

BHUTAN
NEPAL
HIMALAYA MTS.
KASHMIR (1846)
PUNJAB
Delhi
Calcutta
Yanaon (Fr.)
Madras
Pondicherry (Fr.)
Karikal (Fr.)
Goa (Port.)
Diu (Port.)
Bombay
Karachi
BALUCHISTAN (1883)
BRITISH SPHERE (1907)
AFGHANISTAN
Kushka
Merv (1884)
Ashkhabad (1881)
Bukhara
Samarkand (1868)
Tashkent (1864)
Andizhan (1871)
Krasnovodsk

IRAN
RUSSIAN SPHERE (1907)
Tehran
Baku
Baghdad
Damascus
Beirut
Constantinople
Ankara
Kars (1878)
Batum (1878)
Suez Canal 1869
KUWAIT (1899)
OMAN (1891)
HADRAMAUT (1888)
WEST ADEN (1903)
Medina
Persian Gulf

*Nile R.*
*Danube R.*
*Dnieper R.*
*Volga R.*
*Amu R.*
*Indus R.*
*Ganges R.*
*Huang He R.*
*Yangzi*
*Mekong R.*

40°N
20°N
Tropic of Cancer
Equator 0°
60°E
80°E
100°E
120°E

0    500    1,000 Mi.
0    500    1,000 Km.

N

the region. Thus the population of the Malay Peninsula became one-third Malay, one-third Chinese, and one-third Indian.

## Australia and New Zealand

Rather than rule indigenous populations, as they had done in India, or set up commercial outposts, as they did in Singapore and Cape Town, British settlers displaced indigenous populations in the new colonies of Australia and New Zealand, just as they had done in North America.

Portuguese mariners had sighted Australia in the early seventeenth century, but it was too remote to be of interest. However, after the English captain James Cook explored New Zealand and the eastern coast of Australia between 1769 and 1778, expanding shipping networks brought in growing numbers of visitors and settlers.

The Australia Cook visited was the home of about 650,000 hunting-and-gathering people whose Melanesian (mel-uh-NEE-zhuhn) ancestors had arrived some forty thousand years earlier. About 250,000 Maori (MOW-ree [ow as in cow]) inhabited the two Islands of New Zealand, lying 1,000 miles (1,600 kilometers) southeast of Australia. They practiced hunting, fishing, and cultivation of root crops that their Polynesian ancestors had introduced around 1200. These two populations were as vulnerable as the Amerindians had been to unfamiliar diseases introduced by new overseas contacts. By the 1890s, only 93,000 aboriginal Australians and 42,000 Maori survived, and British settler populations both outnumbered and dominated them.

The first permanent British settlers in Australia were 736 convicts, of whom 188 were women, sent into exile in 1788. Australian penal colonies grew slowly and had only slight contact with the indigenous population, whom the British called "Aborigines." However, the discovery of gold in 1851 brought a flood of free European settlers (and some Chinese) and hastened the end of the penal colonies. When the gold rush subsided, government subsidies enabled tens of thousands of British settlers to settle "down under." Though it still took more than three months to reach Australia from Britain, by 1860 Australia had a million immigrants, and the settler population doubled during the next fifteen years.

British settlements in New Zealand proceeded more slowly. Initially a few temporary residents along the coast slaughtered seals and exported pelts to Western countries to be made into men's felt hats. A single ship in 1806 took away sixty thousand sealskins, and by the early 1820s overhunting had nearly exterminated the seal population. Sperm whales were also targeted; whalers hunted them near New Zealand for their oil, used for lubrication, soap, and lamps; ambergris (AM-ber-grees), an ingredient in perfume; and whalebone or baleen, a flexible substance used in women's corsets. Military suppression of Maori resistance, a brief gold rush, faster ships, and subsidized passages attracted more British immigrants after 1860. The colony especially courted women immigrants to offset the preponderance of single men. By the early 1880s the fertile agricultural lands of this most distant frontier of the British Empire had a settler population of 500,000.

Britain encouraged the settlers in Australia and New Zealand to become self-governing, following the 1867 model that had formed the Dominion of Canada out of the diverse and thinly settled colonies of British North America. In 1901, a unified Australia emerged from the federation of six separate colonies. New Zealand became a self-governing dominion in 1907.

By gradually turning over governing power to the colonies' inhabitants, Britain accomplished three things. It satisfied the settlers' desire for greater control; it muted demands for independence; and it made the colonial governments responsible for most of their own expenses. Indigenous peoples were outvoted by the settlers or even excluded from voting.

North American patterns also shaped the indigenous peoples' fate. An 1897 Australian law segregated the remaining Aborigines onto reservations, where they lacked the rights of Australian citizens. The requirement that voters had to be able to read and write English kept Maori from voting in early New Zealand elections, but four seats in the lower house of the legislature were reserved for Maori from 1867 on.

## Hawaii and the Philippines, 1878–1902

By the 1890s the United States had a fast-growing population and industries that produced more manufactured goods than they could sell at home. Merchants and bankers began

Bettmann/CORBIS

**Emilio Aguinaldo**  In 1896, a revolt led by Emilio Aguinaldo attempted to expel Spaniards from the Philippines. When the United States purchased the Philippines from Spain two years later, the Filipino people were not consulted. Aguinaldo continued his campaign, this time against the American occupation forces, until his capture in 1901. In this picture, he appears on horseback, surrounded by some of his troops.

to look for export markets. Guam, Hawaii, and the Philippines being naval stations on the route to China, the new expansionists looked in that direction. China was also in the sights of those who agreed with the naval strategist Alfred T. Mahan (mah-HAHN): "Whether they will or no, Americans must now begin to look outward. The growing production of the country requires it."

Some Americans had been looking outward for quite some time. In 1878 the United States obtained the harbor of Pago Pago in Samoa as a coaling and naval station, and in 1887 it secured the use of Pearl Harbor in Hawaii for the same purpose. By 1898 the United States under President William McKinley (1897–1901) had become openly imperialistic and annexed Hawaii as a steppingstone to Asia. As the United States became ever more involved in Asian affairs, Hawaii's strategic location brought an inflow of U.S. military personnel, and its fertile land caused planters to import laborers from Japan, China, and the Philippines. These immigrants soon outnumbered the native Hawaiians.

While large parts of Asia were falling under colonial domination, the people of the Philippines were chafing under Spanish rule. Emilio Aguinaldo, leader of a secret society, rose in revolt. The revolutionaries had a good chance of winning independence, for Spain had its hands full with a revolution in Cuba. Unfortunately for Aguinaldo and his followers, the United States declared war against Spain in April 1898 and quickly overcame Spanish forces in the Philippines and Cuba. After the Spanish defeat, President McKinley realized that a weakened Spain might lose the islands to another imperialist power. Japan, having recently defeated China in the Sino-Japanese War (1894–1895) and annexed Taiwan (see Chapter 24), was eager to expand. So was Germany, which had taken over parts of New Guinea and Samoa and several Pacific archipelagoes during the 1880s. To forestall them, McKinley purchased the Philippines from Spain for $20 million.

The Filipinos were not eager to trade one master for another. For a while, Aguinaldo cooperated with the Americans in the hope of achieving full independence. When his plan was rejected, he rose up again in 1899 and proclaimed the independence of his country. In spite of protests by anti-imperialists in the United States, the U.S. government decided that its global interests outweighed the interests of the Filipino people. In rebel areas, a U.S. army of occupation tortured prisoners, burned villages and crops, and forced the inhabitants into "reconcentration camps." By the end of the insurrection in 1902, the war had cost the lives of 5,000 Americans and 200,000 Filipinos.

After the insurrection ended, the United States attempted to soften its rule with public works and economic development projects. New buildings went up in the city of Manila; roads, harbors, and railroads were built; and the Philippine economy was tied ever more closely to that of the United States. In 1907 Filipinos were allowed to elect representatives to a legislative assembly, but ultimate authority remained in the hands of a governor appointed by the president of the United States. In 1916 the Philippines were the first U.S. colony to be promised independence, a promise that remained unfulfilled for thirty years.

# IMPERIALISM IN LATIN AMERICA

■ *Where were the economic motives behind imperialism in Latin America?*

The United States played a lesser role than Britain and other European countries in the economic dominance that characterized imperialism in Latin America, and business played a more important role than military intervention. But America's clash with Spain over control of the Philippines carried over into Spanish possessions closer to home.

## American Expansionism and the Spanish-American War, 1898

The United States had long had interests in Cuba, the closest and richest of the Caribbean islands and a Spanish colony. American businesses had invested great sums of money in Cuba's sugar and tobacco industries, and thousands of Cubans had migrated to the United States. In 1895 the Cuban nationalist José Martí started a revolution against Spanish rule. American newspapers thrilled readers with lurid stories of Spanish atrocities; businessmen worried about their investments; and politicians demanded that the U.S. government help liberate Cuba.

On February 15, 1898, the U.S. battleship *Maine* accidentally blew up in Havana harbor, killing 266 American sailors. The U.S. government immediately blamed Spain and issued an ultimatum that the Spanish evacuate Cuba. Spain agreed to the ultimatum, but the American press and Congress were eager for war, and President McKinley did not restrain them.

The **Spanish-American War** was over quickly. On May 1, 1898, U.S. warships destroyed the Spanish fleet at Manila in the Philippines. Two months later the U.S. Navy sank the Spanish Atlantic fleet off Santiago, Cuba, and by mid-August Spain was suing for peace. Secretary of State John Hay called it "a splendid little war." The United States purchased the Philippines from Spain but took over Puerto Rico and Guam as war booty. The two islands remain American possessions to this day. Cuba became an independent republic, subject to interference by the United States.

## Economic Imperialism

Latin America achieved independence from Spain and Portugal in the nineteenth century (see Chapter 21), but it suffered from ideological divisions, unstable governments, and violent upheavals, and its societies remained deeply split between wealthy landowners and desperately poor peasants. But Latin America's economic potential was huge, for the region could produce many agricultural and mineral products that were needed by the industrial countries. Foreign merchants, bankers, and Latin American landowners embraced railroads as a means of opening the interior to development. Starting in the 1870s, almost every country in Latin America acquired railroads, usually connecting mines or agricultural regions

**Spanish-American War** U.S. war fought with Spanish in 1898 over control of Cuba, ostensibly because of the sinking of a U.S. ship and also after reports of Spanish atrocities had fanned flames of American popular opinion. Won handily in three months, the war unofficially made Cuba a protectorate of the United States.

with the nearest port rather than linking up the different parts of the interior. All the equipment and building material came from Britain or the United States. So did the money to build the networks, the engineers who designed and maintained them, and the managers who ran them. Latin American political elites encouraged foreign companies with generous concessions as the most rapid way to modernize their countries.

## Mexico

At the beginning of the twentieth century Mexican society was divided into rich and poor and into persons of Spanish, Indian, and mixed ancestry. A few very wealthy families of Spanish origin, less than 1 percent of the population, owned 85 percent of Mexico's land, mostly in huge *haciendas* (estates). A handful of American and British companies controlled most of Mexico's railroads, silver mines, plantations, and other productive enterprises. At the other end of the social scale were Indians, many of whom did not speak Spanish. *Mestizos* (mess-TEE-so), people of mixed Indian and European ancestry, were only slightly better off; most of them were peasants who worked on the haciendas or farmed small communal plots near their ancestral villages.

After independence in 1821, wealthy Mexican families and American companies used bribery and force to acquire millions of acres of good agricultural land from villages in southern Mexico. Peasants lost not only their fields but also their access to firewood and pasture for their animals and had little choice but to work on haciendas. To survive, they had to buy food and other necessities on credit from the landowner's store; eventually, they fell permanently into debt.

Despite many upheavals, in 1910 the government seemed in control. For thirty-four years General Porfirio Díaz (DEE-as) (1830–1915) had ruled Mexico under the motto "Liberty, Order, Progress." To Díaz "liberty" meant freedom for rich hacienda owners and foreign investors to acquire more land. The government imposed "order" through rigged elections, bribes to Díaz's supporters, and summary justice for those who opposed him. "Progress" meant mainly the importing of foreign capital, machinery, and technicians to take advantage of Mexico's labor, soil, and natural resources.

During the Díaz years (1876–1910) Mexico City became a showplace with paved streets, streetcar lines,

electric street lighting, and public parks. New telegraph and railroad lines connected cities and towns throughout Mexico. But this material progress benefited only a handful of well-connected businessmen and lowered the average Mexican's standard of living.

Though a mestizo himself, Díaz discriminated against the nonwhite majority of Mexicans. He and his supporters tried to eradicate what they saw as Mexico's rustic traditions. On many middle- and upper-class tables French cuisine replaced traditional Mexican dishes, and the wealthy traded sombreros and ponchos for European garments. To the educated middle class—the only group with a strong sense of Mexican nationhood—this devaluation of Mexican culture became a symbol of the Díaz regime's failure to defend national interests against foreign influences.

## Revolution and Civil War in Mexico

The **Mexican Revolution** was a social revolution that developed haphazardly under ambitious but limited leaders, each representing a different segment of Mexican society. The first was American-educated Francisco I. Madero (1873–1913), the son of a wealthy landowning and mining family. Strongly opposed to Díaz, he called on his fellow citizens to oppose electing him for a sixth term. This sparked a revolution in 1910 and the election of Madero as Díaz's successor. But although the Madero presidency was welcomed in some quarters, it aroused opposition in others. He was assassinated two years into his presidency by a former supporter, General Victoriano Huerto, who had been encouraged by the American ambassador. U.S. president Woodrow Wilson (1856–1924) disavowed American support, recalled the ambassador, and, concerned about Mexican unrest, sent U.S. Marines to occupy Veracruz.

Angered by the inequities of Mexican society and foreign intervention in Mexico's affairs, Mexico's middle class and industrial workers found new leaders. Calling themselves *Constitutionalists*, Venustiano

**Mexican Revolution** A social revolution that developed haphazardly under ambitious but limited leaders, each representing a different segment of Mexican society. The revolution evolved into civil war for over ten years of armed struggle, but it established a constitution for Mexico.

Topical Press Agency/Getty Images

**Francisco "Pancho" Villa** Francisco "Pancho" Villa led an army of cowboys and ranch hands in northern Mexico during the revolution. He became very popular by confiscating large haciendas and dividing them among the poor. In March 1916 he entered the United States with 500 soldiers and attacked the town of Columbus, New Mexico, provoking an American invasion of Mexico. He was assassinated in 1923.

Carranza, a landowner, and Alvaro Obregón (oh-bray-GAWN), a schoolteacher, overthrew Huerta in 1914. By then, the revolution had spread to the countryside.

**Emiliano Zapata** (sah-PAH-tah) (1879–1919), himself an Indian farmer, led a revolt against the haciendas in the mountains of Morelos, south of Mexico City. For several years Zapata's supporters would periodically come down from the mountains, burn hacienda buildings, and return land to the Indian villages to which it had once belonged.

Another leader appeared in Chihuahua, a northern state where seventeen individuals owned two-fifths of the land and 95 percent of the people had no land at all. Starting in 1913, **Francisco "Pancho" Villa** (1877–1923), a former ranch hand, mule driver, and bandit, organized an army of three thousand men, most of them cowboys. They also seized land from the large haciendas, not to rebuild traditional communities as in southern Mexico but to create family ranches.

After Villa led a failed and unexplained attack on the town of Columbus, New Mexico, the U.S. Army sent General John Pershing on a nine-month mission to hunt him down. The mission was cut short by American entry into World War I, but, like the occupation of Veracruz, it demonstrated increasing American concern for protecting land and business interests in Mexico.

Zapata and Villa enjoyed tremendous popular support but could never rise above their regional and peasant origins to lead a national revolution. The Constitutionalists had fewer soldiers than Zapata and Villa, but they held the major cities, controlled the country's oil exports, and used the proceeds to buy modern weapons. Gradually the Constitutionalists took over most of Mexico. In 1919 they defeated and killed Zapata; Villa was assassinated four years later. An estimated 2 million people lost their lives in the civil war, and much of Mexico lay in ruins.

The Constitutionalists adopted many of their rivals' agrarian reforms, such as restoring communal lands to the Indians of Morelos. They also proposed social programs aimed at workers and the middle class. The Constitution of 1917 promised universal

**Emiliano Zapata (1879–1919)** Revolutionary and leader of peasants in the Mexican Revolution. He mobilized landless peasants in south-central Mexico in an attempt to seize and divide the lands of the wealthy landowners. Though successful for a time, he was ultimately defeated and assassinated.

**Francisco "Pancho" Villa (1877–1923)** A popular leader during the Mexican Revolution. An outlaw in his youth, when the revolution started he formed a cavalry army in the north of Mexico and fought for the rights of the landless in collaboration with Emiliano Zapata. He was assassinated in 1923.

suffrage and a one-term presidency, state-run education, the end of debt peonage, restrictions on foreign ownership of property, and laws specifying minimum wages and maximum hours to protect laborers. However, powerful Mexican forces and the United States sought to prevent full implementation.

In the early 1920s, after years of violence, the Mexican Revolution lost momentum. Only in Morelos did peasants receive land. Carranza, elected in 1917, was killed in an anti-Carranza plot organized by Obregón. In 1928, Obregón was assassinated.

## The Caribbean and Central America, 1901–1914

American intervention in the Western Hemisphere was not limited to Mexico. The nations of the Caribbean and Central America were small and poor, and their governments were corrupt, unstable, and often bankrupt. They seemed to offer an open invitation to foreign interference. A government would borrow money to pay for railroads, harbors, electric power, and other symbols of modernity. When it could not repay the loan, the lending banks in Europe or the United States would ask for assistance from their home governments, which sometimes threatened to intervene. To ward off European intervention, the United States sent in the marines on more than one occasion.

Presidents Theodore Roosevelt (1901–1909), William Taft (1909–1913), and Woodrow Wilson (1913–1921) felt impelled to intervene in the region, though they differed sharply on the proper policy the United States should follow toward the small nations to the south. Roosevelt encouraged regimes friendly to the United States; Taft sought to influence them through loans from American banks; and the moralist Wilson tried to impose clean governments by military means.

Having "liberated" Cuba from Spain, in 1901 the United States forced the Cuban government to accept the Platt Amendment, which gave the United States the "right to intervene" to maintain order on the island. The United States used this excuse to occupy Cuba militarily from 1906 to 1909, in 1912, and again from 1917 to 1922. In all but name Cuba became an American protectorate. U.S. troops also occupied the Dominican Republic from 1904 to 1907 and again in 1916, Nicaragua and Honduras in 1912, and Haiti in

**SECTION REVIEW**

- After the Spanish-American War, Cuba nominally became an independent republic but was subject to constant interference by the United States, which had strong economic stakes in the country.
- U.S. and European countries invested in railroads and other industrial enterprises throughout Latin America.
- Strong economic and social divisions in Mexico contributed to a confused revolution led by various players.
- After a decade of violence Mexico gained a new constitution, but the revolution lost momentum after the 1920s.
- Repeated American interventions in the region peaked with the building of the Panama Canal.

1915. They brought sanitation and material progress but no political improvements.

The United States was especially forceful in Panama, which was a province of Colombia. Here the issue was not corruption or debts but a more vital interest. When the United States acquired Hawaii and the Philippines, it recognized the need for a canal that would allow warships to move quickly between the Atlantic and Pacific Oceans. The main obstacle was Colombia, which refused to give the United States a piece of its territory. In 1903 the U.S. government supported a Panamanian rebellion against Colombia and quickly recognized the independence of Panama. In exchange, it obtained the right to build a canal and to occupy a zone 5 miles (8 kilometers) wide on either side of it. Work began in 1904, and the **Panama Canal** opened on August 15, 1914.

## THE WORLD ECONOMY AND THE GLOBAL ENVIRONMENT

◼ How did imperialism contribute to the growth and globalization of the world economy?

The nineteenth-century imperialists were not traditional conquerors or empire builders like the Spanish conquistadors. They expressed their belief in

**Panama Canal** Ship canal cut across the Isthmus of Panama by U.S. Army engineers; it opened in 1914. It greatly shortened the sea voyage between the east and west coasts of North America. The United States turned the canal over to Panama on January 1, 2000.

progress and their good intentions in the clichés of the time: "the conquest of nature," "the annihilation of time and space," "the taming of the wilderness," and "our civilizing mission."

## Expansion of the World Economy

For centuries Europe had been a ready market for spices, sugar, silk, and other imported products. The Industrial Revolution expanded this demand, especially for stimulants such as tea, coffee, and chocolate. Demand grew even faster for industrial raw materials: agricultural products like cotton, jute for bags, and palm oil for soap and lubricants, and minerals like diamonds, gold, and copper. Some wild forest products eventually came to be cultivated: timber for buildings and railroad ties, cinchona bark, rubber for rainwear and tires, and gutta-percha (gut-tah-PER-cha) (the sap of a Southeast Asian tree) to insulate electric cables.

Economic botany and agricultural science were applied to every promising plant species. European botanists had long collected and classified exotic plants from around the world. In the nineteenth century they founded botanical gardens in Java, India, Mauritius (maw-REE-shuss), Ceylon, Jamaica, and other tropical colonies. These gardens not only collected local plants but also transferred commercially valuable plant species from one tropical region to another. Tobacco, sugar, coffee, tea, and other crops were introduced, improved, and vastly expanded in the colonies of Southeast Asia and Indonesia, and oil-palm plantations were established in Nigeria and the Congo Basin.

Throughout the tropics, land once covered with forests or devoted to shifting slash-and-burn agriculture was transformed into permanent farms and plantations. Even in areas not developed to export crops, growing populations put pressure on the land. In Java and India farmers felled trees to obtain arable land and firewood, terraced hillsides, drained swamps, and dug wells.

## New Labor Migrations

Between 1834 and 1870 many thousands of Indians, Chinese, and Africans went overseas to work, especially on sugar plantations. In the half century after 1870, tens of thousands of Asians and Pacific islanders made similar voyages.

In part these migrations were linked to the end of slavery. After their emancipation in British colonies in 1834, many slaves left the plantations. To compete with sugar plantations in Cuba, Brazil, and the French Caribbean that were still using slave labor, British colonies had to recruit new laborers.

India's impoverished people seemed one obvious alternative. After planters on Mauritius successfully introduced Indian laborers, the Indian labor trade moved to the British Caribbean in 1838. In 1841 the British government also allowed Caribbean planters to recruit Africans whom British patrols had rescued from slave ships and liberated in Sierra Leone and elsewhere. By 1870 nearly 40,000 Africans had settled in British colonies, along with over half a million Indians and over 18,000 Chinese. After the French and Dutch abolished slavery in 1848, their colonies also recruited new laborers from Asia and Africa.

Slavery continued in Cuba until 1886, but the rising cost of slaves led the sugar planters to recruit 138,000 new laborers from China between 1847 and 1873. Indentured labor recruits also became the mainstay of new sugar plantations in places that had never known slave labor. After 1850 American planters in Hawaii recruited labor from China and Japan; British planters in Natal (in South Africa) recruited from India; and those in Queensland (in northeastern Australia) relied on laborers from neighboring South Pacific islands.

Larger, faster ships made transporting laborers halfway around the world affordable. Nevertheless, crowded accommodations encouraged the spread of cholera and other contagious diseases. All of these laborers served under **contracts of indenture**, which bound them to work for a specified period (usually from five to seven years) in return for free passage to their overseas destination. They were paid a small salary and were provided with housing, clothing, and medical care. Indian indentured laborers also received the right to free passage home if they worked a second five-year contract. British Caribbean colonies required forty women to be recruited for every hundred men as

---

**contract of indenture**  A voluntary agreement binding a person to work for a specified period of years in return for free passage to an overseas destination. Before 1800 most indentured servants were Europeans; after 1800 most indentured laborers were Asians.

- Industrialization increased demand for food imports and raw materials in Europe.
- To meet this demand, Europeans studied botany and transformed Southeast Asian forests into commercial plantations.
- As slavery ended, laborers were sent from heavily populated countries like India and China to work in European colonies under contracts of indenture.

a way to promote family life. So many Indians chose to stay in Mauritius, Trinidad, British Guiana, and Fiji that they constituted a third or more of the total population of these colonies by the early twentieth century.

The indentured labor trade reflected the unequal commercial and industrial power of the West, but it was not an entirely one-sided creation. The men and women who signed indentured contracts were trying to improve their lives by emigrating, and many succeeded. Whether for good or ill, more and more of the world's peoples saw their lives being influenced by the existence of Western colonies, Western ships, and Western markets.

## CONCLUSION

What is the global significance of these complex political and economic changes in southern Asia, Africa, the South Pacific, and Latin America? One perspective stresses the continuing and growing imperialist exploitation of non-Europeans. From another perspective what was most important about this period was not the political and military strength of the Europeans but their growing domination of the world's commerce, especially their investment in plantations, railroads, mines, and long-distance ocean shipping. Motives differed somewhat from region to region. Imperialists were drawn to Africa and Southeast Asia by a desire for tropical foodstuffs and industrial raw materials. Land for settlement was the attraction in Australia, New Zealand, and South Africa, as it earlier had been for European settlers in the New World. India and Latin America, having more prosperous middle classes, provided markets for European and American manufactures.

The growing exchanges could be mutually beneficial. As in Europe itself, overseas consumers found industrially produced goods far cheaper and sometimes better than the handicrafts they replaced. Industrialization also created new markets for African and Asian goods, such as vegetable oil from West Africa or rubber from Malaya. There were also negative impacts, as in the case of weavers thrown out of work in India and the beginnings of deforestation in Southeast Asia.

Imperialist military and commercial strength did not reduce Africa, Asia, Latin America, and the Pacific to mere appendages of Europe. While the balance of power shifted in the Europeans' favor between 1750 and 1914, other cultures were still vibrant and local initiatives often dominant. Islamic reform movements, the rise of the Zulu nation, and the Mexican Revolution had as great significance for their respective regions as Western forces.

## CHAPTER REVIEW

### CHANGES AND EXCHANGES IN AFRICA

■ *Why were imperialists interested in conquering Africa, and how did their presence on that continent change the environment?* (page 539)

Imperialists were interested in conquering Africa because they wanted to extract its resources to further their own military and economic power. After the slave trade was abolished, vegetable oils, gold, ivory, diamonds, and rubber were major exports. Their production, such as deep mining for diamonds, transformed the environment, as did the railroads that were constructed to reach the interior. European companies invested in rubber and palm-oil plantations, gold and diamond mines, and other resources. Traditional land-use patterns were disrupted, and all Africans were affected by changes in social and cultural customs. The Suez Canal, a major alteration to the environment, supported much of this activity, and the British also constructed a dam across the Nile to help develop agriculture.

## INDIA UNDER BRITISH RULE

■ *How did Britain secure its hold on India, and what colonial policies led to the beginnings of Indian nationalism?* (page 548)

The British East India Company, using negotiation and force in dealing with local princes, was able to secure control of the cities of Calcutta, Madras, and Bombay. The British instituted a powerful colonial government and skillfully exploited native traditions and local rulers. In 1857–1858 the Sepoy Rebellion prompted a wave of reforms: Queen Victoria promised all Indians freedom of religion and equal protection under the law, and great sums of money were invested in harbors, canals, railroads, and telegraph lines. The rebellion also began to stir feelings of nationalism in thoughtful Indians. In addition, the higher standard of living, missionary influences, and the Indian Civil Service helped form a more educated middle class that became interested in nationalist ideas.

## SOUTHEAST ASIA AND THE PACIFIC

■ *What were the social and cultural effects of imperialism in Southeast Asia and the Pacific?* (page 553)

The effects of colonialism varied throughout Asia, although in all regions the economic profits benefited the Europeans rather than the indigenous peoples. Southeast Asia's fertile soil and heavy rains made farming of various crops, most importantly rubber, quite profitable. As laborers were brought in from overseas, they gradually displaced the earlier inhabitants. A similar situation occurred in Hawaii, where U.S. military personnel and foreign farm laborers eventually outnumbered native Hawaiians. After James Cook had explored New Zealand and eastern Australia, expanded shipping networks brought growing numbers of white settlers there, displacing the native Maori and Australian peoples. Europeans also brought new and devastating diseases, as they had to Amerindian peoples two centuries before: over 80 percent of native New Zealanders and Australians perished in just over a century.

## IMPERIALISM IN LATIN AMERICA

■ *What were the economic motives behind imperialism in Latin America?* (page 557)

Latin America had great economic potential because of its wealth of agricultural and mineral products. The construction of railroads, using equipment, engineers, and funding from Britain and the United States, helped to connect the interior regions with the coastal ports. Americans also saw economic potential in Cuba and invested heavily in the sugar and tobacco industries there. After the Spanish-American War, they issued the Platt Amendment to maintain their influence in Cuba. The United States also supported the Panamanian secession from Colombia in 1903 in order to build the Panama Canal.

## THE WORLD ECONOMY AND THE GLOBAL ENVIRONMENT

■ *How did imperialism contribute to the growth and globalization of the world economy?* (page 560)

Imperialism opened up the world to increased trade and communication. Shipping, canals, and railroads were the most visible means of globalization. Economically valuable plant species were transferred from region to region while the transformation of forests into working plantations and the end of slavery led to the migration of thousands of Indians, Chinese, Africans, and Pacific Islanders to British colonies, above all to the Caribbean, under contracts of indenture.

## Key Terms

Zulu (p. 539)

Afrikaners (p. 540)

Cecil Rhodes (p. 541)

Sokoto Caliphate (p. 543)

King Leopold II (p. 544)

Berlin Conference (p. 544)

modernization (p. 544)

Suez Canal (p. 545)

"legitimate" trade (p. 548)

recaptives (p. 548)

nawab (p. 549)

sepoy (p. 549)

British raj (p. 549)

durbar (p. 549)

Sepoy Rebellion (p. 551)

Indian Civil Service (p. 551)

Indian National Congress (p. 552)

Spanish-American War (p. 557)

Mexican Revolution (p. 558)

Emiliano Zapata (p. 559)

Francisco "Pancho" Villa (p. 559)

Panama Canal (p. 560)

contract of indenture (p. 561)

# The New Power Balance

© Cengage Learning

On July 8, 1853, four American warships, two of them steam-powered, appeared in Edo Bay, close to the capital of Japan. The commander of the fleet, **Commodore Matthew Perry**, delivered a letter from the president of the United States, demanding that Japan open its ports to foreign trade. Japan had had contact with Europe since the sixteenth century, when Portuguese mariners and Jesuit missionaries arrived. The Dutch followed in the seventeenth century. Worried by this Western presence, Japan suppressed Christianity and "excluded" European merchants in 1639, although limited contact was permitted at the port of Nagasaki (see Chapter 19).

While Japan had rejected a similar request delivered by a smaller U.S. naval force in 1845, the sight of Perry's modern, well-armed fleet made clear the dangers associated with refusing his demand. When he returned the following year, the Japanese agreed to end the exclusion policies. Perry's visit also introduced to Japan a compelling array of the Industrial Revolution's technological and scientific triumphs, including a miniature railroad, a short telegraph line, and other marvels. For the next twenty years, Japanese society was torn between those who wanted to retreat into isolation and those who wished to embrace Western ways. For it was now clear that only by industrializing could Japan escape the fate of weaker nations then being taken over by Europe and the United States.

In the late nineteenth century Japan joined the ranks of "great powers" that dominated the world. Great Britain and France had been recognized as great powers long before the industrial age. Russia achieved that status as an ally against Napoleon and began industrializing in the late nineteenth century, as did Germany, the United States, and now Japan. This handful of wealthy industrialized nations imposed on the other peoples of the world a domination more powerful than any experienced before or since.

## TECHNOLOGY ALTERS THE WORLD ECONOMY

■ *What new technologies and industries appeared between 1850 and 1900, and how did they alter the world economy?*

The Industrial Revolution marked the beginning of a massive transformation of the world. Textile mills, railroads, steamships, the telegraph—all spread from Britain to other parts of the world in the nineteenth century (see Chapter 20). By 1890 Germany and the United States had surpassed Great Britain as the world's leading industrial powers. Industrialization also introduced entirely new technologies that revolutionized everyday life and transformed the world economy. Potent combinations of business, engineering, and science led to the institutionalization of engineering schools and research laboratories, which resulted in the discovery of electricity and new steel and chemical industries.

While industrialization brought vast amounts of wealth, it also caused considerable damage to nature and human health. Rapidly growing urban populations in industrializing Europe and America overwhelmed primitive sanitation systems until the last decades of the nineteenth century. In 1858, Londoners experienced *The Big Stink* due to vast quantities of untreated human and industrial waste dumped into the Thames. While coal-burning steam engines powered the new machine age, they also filled the skies of Manchester, England, and other manufacturing centers with dense smog. The coal smoke of railroad locomotives and other steam engines contributed to air pollution as well. More threatening still were pollution-related diseases like typhoid and cholera.

**Railroads**    By the mid-nineteenth century, steam engines had become the prime mover of industry and commerce. Nowhere was this more evident than in the spread of **railroads**. By 1850 the first railroads had proved so successful that every industrializing country, and many that aspired to become industrial, began to build lines. The next fifty years saw a tremendous expansion of the world's rail networks. After a rapid spurt of building new lines,

> **Commodore Matthew Perry** A navy commander who, on July 8, 1853, became the first foreigner to break through the barriers that had kept Japan isolated from the rest of the world for 250 years.
>
> **railroads** Networks of iron (later steel) rails on which steam (later electric or diesel) locomotives pulled long trains at high speeds. The first railroads were built in England in the 1830s. Their success caused a railroad-building boom throughout the world that lasted well into the twentieth century.

## Arrivals from the East

In 1853, Commodore Matthew Perry's fleet sailed into Edo (now Tokyo) Bay. The first steam-powered warships to appear in Japanese waters caused a sensation among the Japanese. In this print done after the Meiji Restoration, the traditionally dressed local samurai go out to confront the mysterious "black ships."

Courtesy of the Trustees of the British Museum/The Art Archive

British railroad mileage leveled off in the 1870s at around 20,000 miles (over 32,000 kilometers). France and Germany built networks longer than Britain's, as did Canada and Russia. Already the nation with the largest railroad network in 1865, the United States increased its mileage eleven times by 1917.

Railroads benefited not only industrialized nations but also regions with abundant raw materials or agricultural products, like South Africa, Mexico, and Argentina, or densely populated countries like Egypt. The British built the fourth largest rail network in the world in their largest colony, India, to reinforce their presence and develop trade.

With one exception, European or American engineers built these railroads with equipment imported from the West. In 1855, barely a year after Commodore Perry's visit, the Japanese instrument maker Tanaka Hisashige built a model steam train that he demonstrated to an admiring audience. In the 1870s the Japanese government hired British engineers to build the first line from Tokyo to Yokohama and sent them home in the 1880s once they had trained Japanese engineers. Within a few years, Japan began manufacturing its own railroad equipment.

Railroads consumed huge amounts of land. Many old cities doubled in size to accommodate railroad stations, sidings, tracks, warehouses, and repair shops. In the countryside, railroads required bridges, tunnels, and embankments. Railroads also consumed vast quantities of timber, initially for fuel and then for ties to support the rails and for bridges. As railroads pushed across the landscape, they often left miles of deforested land on either side of their tracks. At the same time, railroads opened new land to agriculture, mining, and other exploitation of natural resources wherever they were built, becoming major engines of global economic development.

## Steamships and Telegraph Cables

In the mid-nineteenth century, a series of developments radically transformed ocean shipping. First iron, then steel, replaced the wood that had been used for hulls since shipbuilding began. Paddle wheels replaced sails and then were replaced by propellers as engineers built more powerful and fuel-efficient engines. The average size of freighters increased from 200 tons in 1850 to 7,500 tons in 1900. Coaling stations and ports able to handle large ships were built around the world. The Suez Canal, which opened in 1869, shortened the distance between Europe and Asia and triggered a massive switch from sail power to steam (see Chapter 23).

Shipping lines offered fast, punctual, and reliable service for passengers, mail, and perishable freight as the world's merchant ships grew from 9 million tons in 1850 to 35 million tons in 1910. The result was

# Chronology

| | Political Events | Social, Cultural, and Technological Events |
|---|---|---|
| **1850** | 1853–1854 Commodore Matthew Perry visits Japan | **1850s** Laws abolished in Britain that prohibited worker strikes, workers form "friendly societies" **1851** Majority of British population living in cities **1856** First synthetic dye **1859** Charles Darwin, *On the Origin of Species* |
| **1860** | 1860–1870 Unification of Italy 1861–1865 American Civil War 1862–1908 Rule of Empress Dowager Cixi (China) 1868 Meiji Restoration begins modernization drive in Japan | **1861** Emancipation of serfs (Russia) **1866** Alfred Nobel develops dynamite **1866** First successful Transatlantic cable **1867** Karl Marx, *Das Kapital* **1868–1894** Japan undergoes Western-style industrialization and societal changes |
| **1870** | 1870–1871 Franco-Prussian War 1871 Unification of Germany | **1872** Anarchist Mikhail Bakunin expelled from the International Workingman's Association **1879** Thomas Edison develops incandescent lamp |
| **1890** | 1894 Sino-Japanese War | |
| **1900** | 1900 Boxer Uprising (China) 1904–1905 Russo-Japanese War 1905 Revolution in Russia 1910 Japan annexes Korea | **1914** Women win right to vote in 12 U.S. states; British women follow in 1918 |

falling freight costs and greater commercial integration, changes that benefited not only the exporters of industrial products in Europe and North America but also the Asian, African, and Latin American exporters of agricultural and mining products.

At the same time, shipping companies and commercial firms were able to use the new **submarine telegraph cables**—laid across the Atlantic in 1866—to communicate with distant colonies and markets. By the turn of the century, cables connected every country and almost every inhabited island. As they became the indispensable tools of modern shipping and business, the public and the press extolled the "annihilation of time and space."

## The Steel and Chemical Industries

**Steel**, a special form of iron, was reserved for swords, knives, axes, and watch springs until a series of inventions made it the cheapest and most versatile metal ever known. As a result, world steel production rose from a half-million tons in 1870 to 28 million in 1900—10 million produced by the United States, 8 by Germany, and 4.9 by England. Steel became affordable and abundant enough to make rails, bridges, ships, and even "tin" cans meant to be used once and thrown away. But steel mills took as much space as whole towns, belched smoke, and left behind huge hills of waste, degrading the environment.

The chemical industry followed suit. The development of synthetic dyes starting in 1856 delighted consumers with their bright, long-lasting colors and were cheap to produce, but in the process the indigo

**submarine telegraph cables** Insulated copper cables laid along the bottom of a sea or ocean for telegraphic communication. The first short cable was laid under the Hooghly River in Calcutta in 1839; the first successful transatlantic cable was laid in 1866.

**steel** A form of iron that is both durable and flexible. It was first mass-produced in the 1860s and quickly became the most widely used metal in construction, machinery, and railroad equipment.

plantations of India and Latin America were ruined. Chemistry also advanced the manufacture of explosives. In 1866 the Swedish scientist Alfred Nobel found a way to turn nitroglycerin into a stable solid—dynamite. This and other new explosives were useful in mining and the construction of railroads and canals. They also enabled the armies and navies to arm themselves with increasingly accurate and powerful rifles and cannon.

The growing complexity of industrial chemistry made it one of the first fields where science and technology interacted on a daily basis. By the end of the nineteenth century, Germany had the most advanced engineering schools and scientific institutes and the government funded research that helped make it the world's leading producer of dyes, drugs, synthetic fertilizers, ammonia, and nitrates used in making explosives. However, chemical industries also produced tons of toxic effluents that were dumped into rivers.

## Electricity

No innovation of the late nineteenth century changed people's lives as radically as **electricity**. At first, producing electric current was so costly that it was used only for electroplating and telegraphy. Then in 1831 the Englishman Michael Faraday showed that the motion of a copper wire through a magnetic field induced an electric current in the wire. Based on his discovery, inventors in the 1870s devised generators that turned mechanical energy into electric current. Electricity was more flexible and much easier to use than waterpower or the stationary steam engine, which had powered industrialization until then.

Electricity now had a host of new applications. Initially, arc lamps lit up public squares, theaters, and stores. For a while homes continued to rely on gas lamps, which produced a softer light, but in 1879 **Thomas Edison** developed an incandescent lamp well suited to lighting small rooms. In 1882 Edison created the world's first electrical distribution network in New York City. By the turn of the century electric lighting was rapidly replacing gas lamps in the cities of Europe and North America.

Other uses of electricity quickly appeared. Electric streetcars and subways transported people throughout the cities of Europe and North America. Electric motors replaced steam engines and power belts, increasing productivity and improving workers' safety. Commonly dependent on coal-fired generators, electric energy production contributed to air pollution as well. As demand for electricity grew, engineers built hydroelectric plants. The plant at Niagara Falls, on the border between Ontario, Canada, and New York State, produced an incredible 11,000 horsepower when it opened in 1895. At the newly created Imperial College of Engineering in Japan, an Englishman, William Ayrton, became the first professor of electrical engineering anywhere in the world; his students later went on to found major corporations and government research institutes.

## World Trade and Finance

World trade expanded tenfold between 1850 and 1913, transforming varied economies in different parts of the world. The capitalist economies of western Europe and North America, the prime beneficiaries, grew more diversified and prosperous. Industries mass-produced consumer goods for a growing number of middle-class and even working-class customers: soap, canned and packaged foods, ready-made clothes, household items, and small luxuries like cosmetics and engravings. Nonindustrial areas were more vulnerable, for many of them produced raw materials that could be replaced by synthetic substitutes. Nevertheless, the value of exports from tropical nations remained generally high until World War I.

German and American industries surpassed the British, but Great Britain continued to dominate the flow of trade, finance, and information. In 1900 two-thirds of the world's submarine cables were British or passed through Britain, and over half of the world's shipping was British owned. Britain invested one-fourth of its national wealth overseas, much of it in India, the United States, and Argentina, financing railroads, harbors, mines, and other big projects.

**electricity**  A form of energy used in telegraphy from the 1840s on and for lighting, industrial motors, and railroads beginning in the 1880s.

**Thomas Edison**  American inventor best known for inventing the electric light bulb, acoustic recording on wax cylinders, and motion pictures.

- Industrialization spread throughout the world through trade and new technologies.
- Railroads, almost always financed by Western nations, spread to all continents, changing and enlarging cities and facilitating economic growth.
- Steamships and telegraph cables connected continents and encouraged trade.
- In three new industries—steel, chemicals, and electricity—the United States and Germany surpassed Great Britain.
- World trade boomed in an age of globalization.

Despite global expansion, capitalist economies were prey to periodic depressions in which workers lost their jobs and investors their fortunes. Because of the close connection among the industrial economies, the collapse of a bank in Austria in 1873 triggered a depression that spread to the United States, causing mass unemployment. Worldwide recessions also occurred in the mid-1880s and mid-1890s. Fears that recession would result from industrial production growing faster than the capacity of traditional markets to consume goods helped justify new imperialist adventures by the United States and the European powers to expand markets and gain protected access to raw materials in Asia, Africa, and Latin America (see Chapter 23).

## SOCIAL CHANGES

■ *How did the societies of the industrial countries change during this period?*

As industry and technology ensured steady food supplies, fast-growing populations swelled cities to unprecedented size. Millions of Europeans emigrated to the Americas, Australia, and New Zealand, and nonindustrial workers from Africa, China, India, the Pacific, and elsewhere were recruited to work on distant plantations, in mines, and on railroads (see Chapter 23). The roles of women and men also became more isolated, and women found their lives dramatically altered by economic and technological change, both in the home and in the public sphere.

**Population Growth and Urbanization**

The population of Europe grew faster from 1850 to 1914 than ever before or since, almost doubling from 265 million to 468 million. Much of the increase came from a drop in mortality, as epidemics and starvation became less common. The Irish famine of the 1840s was the last peacetime famine in European history. North American wheat supplemented Europe's food supplies, and new technologies like canning and refrigeration made food abundant year-round, permitting the export of Argentine beef and mutton to Europe. Meat, fruit, vegetables, and oils became part of the daily fare of city dwellers.

In 1851, Britain became the first nation with a majority of its population living in towns and cities. By 1914, 80 percent of Britain's population was urban, as was 60 percent of Germany's population and 45 percent of France's. London grew from 2.7 million in 1850 to 6.6 million in 1900. New York, expanded to include five boroughs, reached 3.4 million by 1900. In the English Midlands, in the German Ruhr, and around Tokyo Bay, fast-growing towns fused into one another, filling in the fields and woods that had once separated them.

In early industrial cities, the poor crowded together in unsanitary tenements. However, new urban technologies transformed city life for most residents. Pipes brought in clean water and carried away sewage. At the same time, gas and then electric lighting made cities safer at night. By the end of the century, municipal governments in Europe and North America provided police and fire protection, schools, parks, and other amenities unheard of a century earlier.

As sanitation improved, urban death rates fell below birthrates for the first time. Confident that their children would survive infancy, couples began to limit the number of children they had. To accommodate the growing population, urban planners laid out new cities on rectangular grids, and middle-class families moved to suburban developments on the edges of cities. In Paris older neighborhoods with narrow crooked streets and rickety tenements were replaced with broad boulevards and modern apartment buildings. Paris became the "city of lights," a model for city planners from New Delhi to Buenos

**Paris Lit Up by Electricity, 1900**  The electric light bulb was invented in the United States and Britain, but Paris made such extensive use of the new technology that it was nicknamed "city of lights." To mark the Paris Exposition of 1900, the Eiffel Tower and all the surrounding buildings were illuminated with strings of light bulbs while powerful spotlights swept the sky.

Aires. By 1900, electric streetcars and subways allowed working-class people to live miles from their workplaces.

In fast-growing cities such as London, New York, and Chicago, newcomers arrived so quickly that housing construction and municipal services could not keep up. Immigrants who saved money to reunite their families could not afford costly municipal services. As a result, the poorest neighborhoods remained as overcrowded, unhealthy, and dangerous as they had been since the early decades of industrialization.

While urban environments improved in many ways, air quality worsened. Coal, burned to power steam engines and heat buildings, polluted the air, coating everything with a film of grimy dust. And the thousands of horses that pulled carts and carriages covered the streets with their waste, causing a terrible stench.

## Middle-Class Women's "Separate Sphere"

In English-speaking countries the period from about 1850 to 1901 is known as the **Victorian Age**. The expression refers not only to the reign of Queen Victoria of England (r. 1837–1901) but also to rules of behavior and to an ideology surrounding the family and the relations between men and women. The Victorians contrasted the masculine ideals of strength and courage with the feminine virtues of beauty and kindness, and they idealized the home as a peaceful and loving refuge from the dog-eat-dog world of competitive capitalism.

**Victorian Age**  The reign of Queen Victoria of Great Britain (r. 1837–1901). The term is also used to describe late-nineteenth-century society, with its rigid moral standards and sharply differentiated roles for men and women and for middle-class and working-class people.

**Separate Spheres in Great Britain**  In the Victorian Age, men and women of the middle and upper classes led largely separate lives. In *Aunt Emily's Visit* (1845), we see women and children at home, tended by a servant. *The Royal Exchange*, meanwhile, was a place for men to transact business.

Victorian morality claimed to be universal, yet it best fit upper- and middle-class European families. Men and women were thought to belong in **"separate spheres."** While successful businessmen worked or relaxed in men's clubs, their wives spent their time rearing children, running the household, and enhancing the family's social status. However, constant financial pressure caused many less privileged women to work outside the home for wages or take in laundry or low-wage piecework, like sewing for garment companies, to supplement household income.

Before electric appliances, maintaining a middle-class home involved enormous amounts of work. Families were larger, and middle-class couples entertained often and lavishly. Carrying out these tasks required servants. A family's status and the activities and lifestyle of the "mistress of the house" depended on the availability of servants to help with household tasks. Only families that employed at least one full-time servant were considered middle class.

Toward the turn of the century modern technology began to transform middle-class homes. Plumbing eliminated the pump and the outhouse. Central heating replaced fireplaces, stoves, and endless dusting. Gas and electricity lit houses and cooked food without soot, smoke, and ashes. But the vacuum cleaners and washing machines of the twentieth century did not mean less housework for women. As families acquired new household technologies, they raised their standards of cleanliness. Meanwhile, young working-class women increasingly preferred factory or office work to domestic service, and the burden of housework more often fell on the mistress of the house.

Unlike the rich of previous eras, who handed their children over to wet nurses and tutors, Victorian women nursed their own babies and supervised the education of their children, even if they employed governesses. Girls' education was very different from that of boys. While boys were being prepared for business or professional life, girls learned embroidery, drawing, and music—social graces that enhanced their marriage prospects.

Victorian morality frowned on middle-class women working. Young women could work until they got married, but only in genteel places like stores and offices, never in factories. When the typewriter and telephone entered the business world in the 1880s, businessmen turned to educated young women who worked for lower wages than men. Operating these machines was stereotyped as women's work.

**"separate spheres"**  Nineteenth-century idea in Western societies that men and women, especially of the middle class, should have clearly differentiated roles in society: women as wives, mothers, and homemakers; men as breadwinners and participants in business and politics.

Jimmy Sime/Hulton Archive/Getty Images

**Emmeline Pankhurst Under Arrest** The leader of the British women's suffrage movement frequently called attention to her cause by breaking the law to protest discrimination against women. Here she is being arrested and carried off to jail by the police.

Most professional careers were closed to women. Until late in the century, few universities granted women degrees. In the United States higher education was available to women only at elite colleges in the East and teachers' colleges in the Midwest. European women had fewer opportunities. Before 1914 very few women became doctors, lawyers, or professional musicians.

The first profession open to women was teaching, due to laws calling for universal compulsory education. By 1911, for instance, 73 percent of all teachers in England were women. They were considered well suited to teaching young children and girls—an extension of the duties of Victorian mothers—but only until marriage. When a woman married, she was expected to become pregnant right away and stay home to take care of her own children.

A home life, no matter how busy, did not satisfy all middle-class women. Some became volunteer nurses or social workers, receiving little or no pay. Others organized to fight prostitution, alcohol, and child labor. By the turn of the century a few chal-

lenged male domination of politics and the law. Suffragists, led in Britain by Emmeline Pankhurst and in the United States by Elizabeth Cady Stanton and Susan B. Anthony, demanded the right to vote. By 1914 U.S. women had won the vote in twelve states. British women won the vote in 1918.

**Working-Class Women** In the new industrial cities, men and women no longer worked together at home or in the fields. The separation of work and home affected women even more than men. Women formed a majority of the workers in the textile industries and in domestic service. Yet working-class women needed to keep homes and raise children as well as earn their living. As a result, they led lives of toil and pain, considerably harder than the lives of their menfolk. In Japan, as in Ireland and New England, tenant farmers, squeezed by rising taxes and rents, were forced to send their daughters to work in textile mills. Others became domestic servants, commonly working sixteen or more hours a day, six and a half days a week, for little more than room and board, usually in attics or basements. Without appliances, much of their work was physically hard: hauling coal and water up stairs, washing laundry by hand. Female servants were also vulnerable to sexual abuse by their masters or their masters' sons, and the majority of families fired servants who got pregnant rather than embarrass the master of the house.

Young women often preferred factory work to domestic service. Here, too, Victorian society practiced a strict division of labor by gender. Men worked in construction, iron and steel, heavy machinery, or on railroads; women worked in textiles and the clothing trades, extensions of traditional women's household work (see Material Culture: Cotton Clothing). Appalled by the abuses of women and children in the early years of industrialization, most industrial countries passed protective legislation limiting the hours or forbidding the employment of women in the hardest and most dangerous occupations, such as mining and foundry work. Such legislation reinforced gender divisions in industry, keeping women in low-paid, subordinate positions. Female factory workers earned between one-third and two-thirds of men's wages.

Married women with children were expected to stay home, even if their husbands did not make enough to support the family. Yet they had to contribute to the family's income. Families who had room to spare, even a bed or a corner in the kitchen, took in boarders. Many women did piecework such as sewing dresses, making hats or gloves, or weaving baskets at home. The hardest and worst-paid work was washing other people's clothes. Overall, many poor women worked at home ten to twelve hours a day and

enlisted the help of their small children, perpetuating practices long outlawed in factories.

## THE STRUGGLE BETWEEN CAPITAL AND LABOR

■ How did industrialism contribute to the socialist and labor movements?

Strained relations between industrial employers and workers spawned labor movements and new forms of radical politics. **Socialism** was an ideology developed by radical thinkers who questioned the sanctity of private property and argued in support of industrial workers against their employers. **Labor unions** were organizations formed by industrial workers to defend their interests in negotiations with employers. The socialist and labor movements were never identical. Most of the time they were allies; occasionally they competed for the support of workers.

The growing wealth and power of new industrial elites and the harsh living and working conditions experienced by industrial workers led to the formation of labor unions, the creation of the first social welfare policies, demands for voting rights, and, for some, the dream of revolutionary transformation. Those seeking a revolution were divided among numerous parties and factions. **Karl Marx** was a formidable theorist of revolution as well as a major contestant for power within the diverse and contentious world of left-leaning politics (see Chapter 20). Heir to the Enlightenment's enthusiasm for reason and logic, he identified his revolutionary ideal as "scientific socialism," although his adherents commonly called themselves communists. Marx believed that industrial capitalism would ultimately lead to a social order

### SECTION REVIEW

- As European population grew, millions migrated to other continents.
- Cities grew to enormous size, changing in character and posing difficult housing, sanitation, and environmental problems.
- Middle-class women inhabited a "separate sphere" from men and devoted their lives to their homes and families, but a few fought for equal rights.
- Gender divisions widened between working-class men and women. Working-class women, who had to keep a home while earning a living, led hard lives.

**socialism** A political ideology that originated in Europe in the 1830s. Socialists advocated government protection of workers from exploitation by property owners and government ownership of industries. This ideology led to the founding of socialist or labor parties throughout Europe in the second half of the nineteenth century.

**labor union** An organization of workers in a particular industry or trade, created to defend the interests of members through strikes or negotiations with employers.

**Karl Marx** German journalist and philosopher, founder of the Marxist branch of socialism. He is known for two books: *Manifesto of the Communist Party* (1848) and *Das Kapital* (Vols. I–III, 1867–1894).

# Material Culture

## Cotton Clothing

Of all the things that bring us comfort, nothing compares to cotton. For clothes, sheets, and towels, it is the world's favorite textile. And no wonder: cotton is cool next to the skin, can be dyed in bright colors, absorbs moisture, and, unlike other fabrics such as wool, can be washed easily.

The use of cotton for clothing has a long history dating back to 3000 B.C.E., when it was grown in the Indus River Valley. Originally, the cotton plant was grown and the cloth woven only in India, Mexico, Peru, and a few other places in the tropics. The Maya wove fine textiles from cotton and traded them with other parts of Mesoamerica. Indian cottons were particularly fine and exported as luxury items to China and Rome. Cotton replaced hemp clothing in China in the time of the Mongols and was used extensively for turbans, pants, and other items of clothing. The Arabs spread cotton growing and weaving to the Middle East and Spain. By the tenth century, it was a major crop in Iran and elsewhere in the region. Many of our names for particular kinds of cotton fabric come from cities in India, like *calico* (from Calicut) or *madras*, or in the Middle East, like *damask* (from Damascus) or *muslin* (from Mosul in Iraq).

Around 800 C.E., Arab merchants brought cotton cloth to Europe, where it became as precious as silk. Five centuries later Italy borrowed Arab techniques to develop its own cotton industry. With the invention of machines like the spinning jenny and the water frame in the eighteenth century (see Chapter 20), cotton became less precious and more available. Cotton thread and cloth were the first items to be mass-produced in the Industrial Revolution, with important consequences for India, the American South, and other countries.

Mass production means mass consumption. In the nineteenth century, for the first time, the poor could afford to wear bright, colorful clothes and—even more important—to wash them. Wealthy European families hired seamstresses and tailors who came to the house, took measurements, and returned a few days later with finished clothes. Other women sewed clothes for themselves and their families.

Sewing by hand was time-consuming and increasingly costly compared to the declining price of cloth. By

**The Sewing Machine**  *The Japanese imported many innovations from the West after the Meiji Restoration of 1868. Among the most popular were Western-style clothing and sewing machines.*
Image copyright © The Metropolitan Museum of Art. Image source: Art Resource, NY

the mid-nineteenth century, prosperity and a faster pace of life in Europe and America provided an incentive for inventors to devise a machine that could sew. In 1850, Isaac Singer manufactured the first practical machine for commercial use. A few years later, he designed the "Singer Family Sewing Machine" with an iron stand and a foot-treadle for home use. By 1891 Singer alone had manufactured 10 million machines in the United States and Europe. Some were industrial machines sold to makers of ready-to-wear clothes in the new garment districts. Others were home models, some inexpensive enough for the working class. There were even portable models that seamstresses could take with them to their clients' homes.

The combination of cotton cloth and sewing machines revolutionized clothing. A shirt that took fourteen and a half hours to sew by hand could be made in an hour and a quarter on a machine; an apron could be made in nine minutes instead of an hour and a half. Now the poor could afford to own several shirts, skirts, or pants, even underwear. Better-off homemakers subscribed to fashion magazines, bought patterns, and made blouses and dresses, even complicated items like crinolines and hoopskirts, which would once have been too tedious to sew by hand.

Today, the world uses more cotton than any other fiber. China is the largest producer (and consumer) of cotton, followed by the United States, India, and Pakistan. Almost all of the cotton clothing sold is produced on powerful computerized machines in the developing countries of Asia and Latin America.

divided between a wealthy powerful few and a mass of exploited and impoverished workers. This division, once in place, would lead to revolution. A dictatorship of the proletariat would then abolish private property, distribute the material benefits and scientific progress achieved by the Industrial Revolution to society in general, and end poverty and injustice.

Many of those committed to revolutionary change rejected Marx's insistence that revolution depended on the proletariat taking up arms. Others doubted that his imagined dictatorship of the proletariat, or, indeed, any government, could avoid recreating the inequality and injustice that already oppressed the poor. The Russian intellectual, Mikhail Bakunin (1814–1876), argued forcibly that peasants, displaced and unemployed artisans, and other exploited groups also had revolutionary potential and, consequently, that many parts of Europe were ready for revolution. He also dismissed as naive Marx's faith in a future workers' government.

Bakunin exercised a powerful influence over the development of **anarchism**, the chief revolutionary alternative to communism. Anarchists believed that revolution could be achieved through direct action by individuals and small groups, what they called *propaganda of the deed*. The result of this movement's development was a series of assassinations and bombings that shook the political structures of Europe and America. These attacks included the bombings of the opera (1893) and Corpus Christi celebration (1896) in Spain and the Haymarket bombing in Chicago (1896). They also included the assassinations of President Carnot of France (1894), Prime Minister Cánovas del Castillo of Spain (1897), Empress Elizabeth of Austria (1898), King Umberto of Italy (1900), and President McKinley of the United States (1901).

The conflict between Marx and Bakunin culminated in 1872 when Bakunin and his adherents were expelled from the revolutionary umbrella organization, the International Workingman's Association. While the followers of Marx forced Bakunin from the center of revolutionary activity, his followers remained a potent source of political violence and working-class mobilization in Italy, Spain, and Argentina well into the twentieth century.

Since the beginning of the nineteenth century, workers had united to create "friendly societies" for

## SECTION REVIEW

- The plight of workers led Karl Marx to predict a future workers' revolution, while Mikhail Bakunin's anarchist ideas spawned acts of violence and rebellion in many countries.
- Labor movements and unions worked to improve workers' pay and working conditions.

mutual assistance in times of illness, unemployment, or disability. Laws that forbade workers to strike were abolished in Britain in the 1850s and in the rest of Europe soon thereafter. Labor unions sought not only better wages but also improved working conditions and insurance against illness, accidents, disability, and old age. They grew slowly because they required a permanent staff and a great deal of money to sustain their members during strikes. Still, by the end of the century British labor unions counted 2 million members, and German and American unions had 1 million members each. They also became a political force in democratic countries, advocating improved wages and working conditions.

# NATIONALISM AND THE RISE OF ITALY, GERMANY, AND JAPAN

■ *How was nationalism transformed from a revolutionary to a conservative ideology?*

The most influential idea of the nineteenth century was **nationalism**. French revolutionaries defined people, previously considered the subjects of a sovereign, as the citizens of a *nation*—a concept identified with a territory, the state that ruled it, and the culture of its people.

**anarchism** Movement of revolutionaries who wanted to abolish all private property and governments, usually by violence, and replace them with free associations of groups.

**nationalism** A political ideology that stresses people's membership in a nation—a community defined by a common culture and history as well as by territory. In the late eighteenth and early nineteenth centuries, nationalism was a force for unity in western Europe. In the late nineteenth century it hastened the disintegration of the Austro-Hungarian and Ottoman Empires. In the twentieth century it provided the ideological foundation for scores of independent countries emerging from colonialism.

## Language and National Identity in Europe Before 1871

Language was usually the crucial element in creating a feeling of national unity. It was important both as a way to unite the people of a nation and as the means of persuasion by which political leaders could inspire their followers. Yet language and citizenship seldom coincided.

The fit between France and the French language was closer than in most large countries, though some French-speakers lived outside of France and some French people spoke other languages. Italian- and German-speaking people, however, were divided among many small states. Living in the Austrian Empire were peoples who spoke German, Czech, Slovak, Hungarian, Polish, and other languages. Even where people spoke a common language, they could be divided by religion or institutions. The Irish, though English-speaking, were mostly Catholic, whereas the English were primarily Protestant.

The idea of redrawing the boundaries of states to accommodate linguistic, religious, or cultural differences was revolutionary. In Italy and Germany it led to the forging of large new states out of many small ones in 1871. In central and eastern Europe, nationalism threatened to break up large states into smaller ones.

Until the 1860s nationalism was associated with **liberalism**, the revolutionary middle-class ideology that emerged from the French Revolution; it asserted the sovereignty of the people and demanded constitutional government, a national parliament, and freedom of expression (see Chapter 21). The most famous nationalist of the early nineteenth century was the Italian liberal Giuseppe Mazzini (jew-SEP-pay mots-EE-nee) (1805–1872), who led a failed revolution in 1848 in Italy. Russia, Prussia, and Austria tried but could not quash Mazzini's idea of nationhood and liberty for peoples oppressed by tyrants and foreigners. The revolutions of 1848 convinced conservatives that governments could not keep citizens out of politics and that, if properly managed, they could strengthen rather than weaken the state (see Chapter 21). A new generation of conservative political leaders learned how to preserve the status quo through public education, universal military service, and colonial conquests, all of which built a sense of national unity.

## The Unification of Italy, 1860–1870

By midcentury, popular sentiment was building throughout Italy for unification. Opposing it were Pope Pius IX, who abhorred everything modern, and Austria, which controlled two Italian provinces, Lombardy and Venetia. The prime minister of Piedmont-Sardinia, Count Camillo Benso di Cavour, saw the rivalry between France and Austria as an opportunity to unify Italy. He secretly formed an alliance with France, then instigated a war with Austria in 1858. The war triggered uprisings throughout northern and central Italy in favor of joining Piedmont-Sardinia, a moderate constitutional monarchy under King Victor Emmanuel.

If the conservative, top-down approach to unification prevailed in the north, a more radical approach was still possible in the south. In 1860 the fiery revolutionary **Giuseppe Garibaldi** (jew-SEP-pay gary-BAHL-dee) and a small band of followers landed in Sicily and then in southern Italy, overthrew the Kingdom of the Two Sicilies, and prepared to found a democratic republic. The royalist Cavour, however, took advantage of the unsettled situation to sideline Garibaldi and expand Piedmont-Sardinia into a new Kingdom of Italy. Unification was completed with the addition of Venetia in 1866 and the Papal States in 1870.

The process of Italian unification illustrates the shift of nationalism from a radical democratic idea to a conservative method of building popular support for a strong centralized government, even an aristocratic and monarchical one.

## The Unification of Germany, 1866–1871

Some German nationalists wanted to unite all Germans under the Catholic Austrian throne. Others wanted to exclude Austria with its many non-Germanic peoples and unite all other German-speaking areas under Lutheran Prussia. The Prussian state had two

**liberalism** A political ideology that emphasizes the civil rights of citizens, representative government, and the protection of private property. This ideology, derived from the Enlightenment, was especially popular among the property-owning middle classes of Europe and North America.

**Giuseppe Garibaldi** Italian nationalist and revolutionary who conquered Sicily and Naples and added them to a unified Italy in 1860.

advantages: (1) the newly developed industries of the Rhineland, and (2) the first European army to make use of railroads, telegraphs, breech-loading rifles, steel artillery, and other products of modern industry.

The king of Prussia, Wilhelm I (r. 1861–1888), had entrusted the running of his government to his chancellor, the brilliant and authoritarian aristocrat **Otto von Bismarck** (UTT-oh von BIS-mark) (1815–1898), who was determined to use the Prussian military and German nationalism to advance the interests of the Prussian state. In 1866 Prussia attacked and defeated Austria. To everyone's surprise, Prussia took no Austrian territory. Instead, Prussia and some smaller states formed the North German Confederation, the nucleus of a future Germany. Then in 1870, Bismarck attacked France. In this "Franco-Prussian War," German armies used their superior firepower and tactics to achieve a quick victory.

The spoils of victory included a large indemnity and the two provinces of Alsace and Lorraine (see Map 24.1). To the Germans, this region was German because a majority of its inhabitants spoke German. To the French, it was French because most of its inhabitants considered themselves French. These two conflicting definitions of nationalism kept enmity between France and Germany smoldering for decades.

## The West Challenges Japan

In Japan a completely different political organization was in place. The emperor was revered but had no power. Instead, Japan was governed by the Tokugawa Shogunate—a secular government under a military leader, or *shogun*, that had come to power in 1600 (see Chapter 19). Local lords, called *daimyo*, were permitted to control their lands and populations with very little interference from the shogunate.

Because this system did not permit the coordination of resources necessary to resist a major invasion, the shoguns attempted to minimize exposure to foreigners. In the early 1600s they prohibited foreigners from entering Japan and Japanese from going abroad. The most flagrant violators of these rules were powerful lords in southern Japan who ran large pirate or black-market operations. These lords benefited from the decentralization of the shogunal political system. But when a genuine foreign threat was suggested—as when, in 1792, Russian and British ships were spotted

off the Japanese coast—the local lords realized that a decentralized Japan was perilously weak.

Some regional lords began to develop their own reformed armies, arsenals, and shipyards. By the 1800s Satsuma (SAT-soo-mah) and Choshu (CHOE-shoo), two large domains in southern Japan, had become wealthy and ambitious, enjoying high rates of revenue and population growth. Their remoteness from the capital Edo (now Tokyo) and their economic vigor also fostered a strong sense of local self-reliance.

This situation changed with the 1853 arrival of Commodore Matthew C. Perry's fleet (discussed at the beginning of this chapter). Perry demanded that Japan open its ports to trade and allow American ships to refuel and take on supplies during their voyages between China and California. His demands sparked a crisis in the shogunate. After consultation with the provincial daimyo, the shogun's advisers advocated capitulation to Perry, pointing to China's humiliating defeats in the Opium and Arrow Wars (see Chapter 22). In 1854, when Perry returned, representatives of the shogun indicated their willingness to sign the Treaty of Kanagawa (KAH-nah-GAH-wah), modeled on the unequal treaties between China and the Western powers. Angry and disappointed, some provincial governors began to encourage an underground movement calling for the destruction of the Tokugawa regime and the banning of foreigners from Japan.

Tensions between the shogunate and some provincial leaders, particularly in Choshu and Satsuma, increased in the early 1860s. When British and French ships shelled the southwestern coasts in 1864 to protest the treatment of foreigners, the action enraged the provincial samurai, who rejected the Treaty of Kanagawa. Young, ambitious, educated men who faced mediocre prospects under the rigid Tokugawa class system emerged as provincial leaders. In 1867 the Choshu leaders Yamagata Aritomo and Ito Hirobumi finally realized that they should stop warring with their rival province, Satsuma, and join forces to rebel against the shogunate.

**Otto von Bismarck** Chancellor (prime minister) of Prussia from 1862 until 1871, when he became chancellor of Germany. A conservative nationalist, he led Prussia to victory against Austria (1866) and France (1870) and was responsible for the creation of the German Empire in 1871.

**Map 24.1 Unification of Germany, 1866–1871** Germany was united after a series of short, successful wars by the kingdom of Prussia against Austria in 1866 and against France in 1871. © Cengage Learning

## The Meiji Restoration and the Modernization of Japan, 1868–1894

The civil war was intense but brief. In 1868 provincial rebels overthrew the Tokugawa Shogunate and declared young emperor Mutsuhito (moo-tsoo-HEE-toe) (r. 1868–1912) "restored." The new leaders called their regime the **Meiji (MAY-gee) Restoration** after Mutsuhito's reign name (*Meiji* means "enlightened rule"). The "Meiji oligarchs," as the new rulers were known, were extraordinarily talented and far-sighted. Though imposed from above, the Meiji Restoration marked as profound a change as the French Revolution (see Map 24.2).

The oligarchs knew they would have to transform their institutions and their society. In the Char-

> **Meiji Restoration** The political program that followed the destruction of the Tokugawa Shogunate in 1868, in which a collection of young leaders set Japan on the path of centralization, industrialization, and imperialism.

Map 24.2 **Expansion and Modernization of Japan, 1868–1918** As Japan acquired modern industry, it followed the example of the European powers in seeking overseas colonies. Its colonial empire grew at the expense of its neighbors: Taiwan was taken from China in 1895; Karafutu (Sakhalin) from Russia in 1905; and all of Korea became a colony in 1910. © Cengage Learning

**Legend:**
- Japan in 1875
- Territory gained by Japan from 1894 to 1910
- **1905** Year Japan gained control
- Major Japanese manufacturing area
- Japanese railroads in 1889
- Japanese railroads in 1918

ter Oath issued in 1868, the young emperor included a prophetic phrase: "Knowledge shall be sought throughout the world and thus shall be strengthened the foundation of the imperial polity." It was to be the motto of a new Japan, which embraced all foreign ideas, institutions, and techniques that could strengthen the nation. The literacy rate in Japan was the highest in Asia at the time, and the oligarchs shrewdly exploited it in their introduction of new educational systems, a conscript army, and new communications. The government was able to establish heavy industry, without extensive foreign debt, thanks to decades of industrial development and financing in the provinces in the earlier 1800s.

The Meiji leaders copied the government structure of imperial Germany. They modeled the new Japanese navy on the British and the army on the Prussian. They introduced Western-style postal and telegraph services, railroads and harbors, banking, clocks, and calendars. To learn the secrets of Western strength, they sent hundreds of students to Britain, Germany, and the United States. Western-style clothing and hairstyles and garden parties and formal dances became popular.

The Granger Collection, NYC

**Japan's New Army**  After the Meiji Restoration in 1868, the leaders of the new government set out to make Japan "a rich country with a strong army." They modeled the new army on the European armies of the time, with Western-style uniforms, rifles, cannon, and musical instruments.

Especially interested in Western technology, the government opened vocational, technical, and agricultural schools, founded four imperial universities, and brought in foreign experts to advise on medicine, science, and engineering. To encourage industrialization, the government set up state-owned enterprises to manufacture cloth and inexpensive consumer goods for sale abroad. The first Japanese industries exploited their workers ruthlessly, just as the first industries in Europe and America had done. In 1881 the government sold these enterprises to private investors, mainly large *zaibatsu* (zye-BOT-soo), or conglomerates, encouraging individual technological innovation. Thus the carpenter Toyoda Sakichi

founded the Toyoda Loom Works (now Toyota Motor Company) in 1906; ten years later he patented the world's most advanced automatic loom.

## Nationalism and Social Darwinism

In many countries, the dominant group used nationalism to impose its language, religion, or customs on minority populations. The Russian Empire attempted to "Russify" its diverse ethnic populations. The Spanish government made Spanish compulsory in the schools, newspapers, and courts of its Basque- and Catalan-speaking provinces. Immigrants to the United States were expected to learn English.

Some people attempted to use science to support the harsh inequalities of gender, ethnicity, and class common across Europe and the Americas. One of the most influential scientists of the century, and the one whose ideas were most widely appropriated and misinterpreted, was the English biologist **Charles Darwin** (1809–1882), who based his theory of evolution on the observations he made during a research voyage in South America and while observing English livestock breeders. His famous book, *On the Origin of Species* (1859), argued that, over the course of hundreds of thousands of years, living beings had either evolved in the struggle for survival or become extinct. The philosopher Herbert Spencer (1820–1903) and others took up Darwin's idea of "natural selection" and coin-

**Charles Darwin (1809–1882)**  Author of *On the Origin of Species* (1859), which developed the theory of evolution through natural selection.

**SECTION REVIEW**

- Nationalism, the most powerful new ideology of the nineteenth century, defined nations primarily on the basis of language.
- Cavour and Garibaldi helped unify Italy between 1860 and 1870, and Bismarck unified Germany from 1866 to 1871.
- In response to Western intrusion, provincial Japanese lords launched the Meiji Restoration and quickly transformed Japan into a modern industrial nation.
- During this era, Charles Darwin's theory of evolution was often misinterpreted to justify the power of the privileged few.

ing the phrase "survival of the fittest" applied it to human society. Extreme Social Darwinists developed elaborate pseudo-scientific theories of racial and ethnic differences, claiming that they were the result not of history but of biology. Although not based on any research, these ideas gave a scientific-sounding justification for the power of the privileged.

# THE GREAT POWERS OF EUROPE, 1871–1900

■ *How did the forces of nationalism affect the major powers of Europe?*

After the middle of the century, politicians and journalists discovered how easily they could whip up popular frenzy against neighboring countries. Rivalries over colonial territories, ideological differences between liberal and conservative governments, and even minor border incidents or trade disagreements contributed to a growing international tension.

## Germany at the Center of Europe

International relations revolved around Germany, because Germany was located in the center of Europe and had the most powerful army on the European continent. After creating a unified Germany in 1871, Bismarck worked to maintain the peace in Europe. To isolate France, he forged a loose coalition with Austria-Hungary and Russia that held for twenty years.

Bismarck proved equally adept at manipulating mass politics at home. To weaken the influence of middle-class liberals, he extended the vote to all adult men. By imposing high tariffs on manufactured goods and wheat, he gained the support of both the wealthy industrialists of the Rhineland and the great landowners of eastern Germany. He stole the thunder of the socialists by introducing social legislation—medical, unemployment, and disability insurance and old-age pensions—long before other industrial countries. Under his leadership, the German people developed a strong sense of national unity and pride in their industrial and military power.

In 1888 Wilhelm I was succeeded by his grandson Wilhelm II (r. 1888–1918), who dismissed Chancellor Bismarck. Wilhelm II talked about his "global policy" and demanded that Germany, with the mightiest army and the largest industrial economy in Europe, deserved a colonial empire, "a place in the sun."

France had difficulty reconciling itself to being second to Germany. Its population and its army lagged far behind Germany's, and its industry was growing more slowly, because it had lost the iron and coal mines of Lorraine in 1871. The French people were also deeply divided politically: some were monarchists and Catholics, but a growing number held republican and anticlerical views. Despite these problems, a long tradition of popular participation in politics and a strong sense of nationhood, reinforced by a fine system of public education, gave the French people a deeper cohesion than appeared on the surface.

Great Britain was the only other country in Europe with a democratic tradition. The British government alternated smoothly between the Liberal and Conservative Parties, and the income gap between rich and poor gradually narrowed. Nevertheless, Britain had problems. One was Irish resentment of English occupation and rule. Another was the British economy. Great Britain lagged behind the United States and Germany in such important industries as steel, chemicals, electricity, and textiles. Germany was even catching up in shipbuilding. Finally, Britain's far-flung empire was a constant drain on Britain's finances.

## The Conservative Powers: Russia and Austria-Hungary

The forces of nationalism weakened rather than strengthened Russia and Austria-Hungary. Their populations were far more divided, socially and ethnically, than were the German, French, or British peoples.

Nationalism was most divisive in the Austrian Empire. The decision to rename itself the Austro-Hungarian Empire in 1867 appeased its Hungarian critics but alienated its Slavic-speaking minorities. The Austro-Hungarian Empire still considered itself a great power and attempted to dominate the Balkans. This strategy irritated Russia, which thought of itself as the protector of Slavic peoples everywhere, and it eventually led to war (see Chapter 25).

**The Doss House**  Late-nineteenth-century cities showed more physical than social improvements. This painting by Makovsky of a street in St. Petersburg contrasts the broad avenue and impressive new buildings with the poverty of the crowd.

Russia was the most misunderstood country in Europe. Its enormous size and population led many Europeans to exaggerate its military potential, but it was weakened by national and social divisions. All in all, only 45 percent of the peoples of the tsarist empire spoke Russian. To strengthen the bonds between the monarchy and the Russian people and promote industrialization by enlarging the labor

### SECTION REVIEW

- A united Germany, the most powerful state in Europe, became a threat to peace under Wilhelm II.

- France and Great Britain, though liberal democracies, faced difficulties at home and overseas.

- Russia and Austria-Hungary, two conservative empires, failed to adapt their politics to the modernization of their societies.

pool, the moderate conservative Tsar Alexander II (r. 1855–1881) emancipated the peasants from serfdom in 1861. That measure, however, did not create a modern society but only turned serfs into farm workers with few skills and little capital. Though "emancipated," the great majority of Russians had little education, few legal rights, and no say in the government.

After Alexander's assassination in 1881, his successors Alexander III (r. 1881–1894) and Nicholas II (r. 1894–1917) reluctantly permitted half-hearted attempts at social change. Industrialization consisted largely of state-sponsored projects, such as railroads, iron foundries, and armament factories, and led to social unrest among urban workers. Wealthy landowning aristocrats dominated the Russian court and administration and blocked most reforms.

The weaknesses in Russia's society and government became glaringly obvious after Russia's defeat in the Russo-Japanese War of 1904–1905 (discussed later in this chapter). The shock of defeat caused a revolution in 1905, forcing Tsar Nicholas II to grant a constitution and permit an elected Duma (parliament). But as soon as he was able to rebuild the army and the police, he reverted to the traditional despotism of his forefathers. Small groups of radical intellectuals, angered by the contrast between the wealth of the elite and the poverty of the common people, began plotting the violent overthrow of the tsarist autocracy.

## CHINA, JAPAN, AND THE WESTERN POWERS

■ *How did Western pressure affect East Asia?*

After 1850 China and Japan—the two largest countries in East Asia—felt the influence of the Western powers as never before, but their responses were completely opposite. China resisted Western influence and became weaker, while Japan transformed itself into a major industrial and military power. One reason for this difference was the Western powers' heavy involvement in China. More important was the difference between the Chinese and Japanese elites' attitudes toward foreign cultures.

### China in Turmoil

China had been devastated by the Taiping (tie-PING) Rebellion that raged from 1850 to 1864 (see Chapter 22). The French and British took advantage of China's weakness to demand treaty ports where they could trade at will and freely import opium.

China's attempts to resist these changes were ultimately self-defeating. A Chinese "self-strengthening movement" tried in vain to bring about reform by reducing government expenditures and eliminating corruption. The **Empress Dowager Cixi** (TSUH-shee) (r. 1862–1908), who had once encouraged the construction of shipyards, arsenals, and telegraph lines, opposed railways and other foreign technologies that could carry foreign influences to the interior. Government officials, who did not dare resist the Westerners outright, secretly encouraged crowds to attack and destroy the intrusive devices. They were able to slow the foreign intrusion, but in doing so, they denied themselves the best means of defense against foreign pressure.

### Japan Confronts China

The motive for the transformation of Japan was defensive—to protect the nation from the Western powers—but the methods that protected Japan could also be used for Japanese conquest. Japan's path to imperialism was laid out by **Yamagata Aritomo**, a leader of the Meiji oligarchs. He believed that an independent Japan required a "sphere of influence" that included Korea, Manchuria, and part of China (see Map 24.2). If other countries controlled this sphere, Japan would be at risk. To protect this sphere of influence, Yamagata insisted, Japan must accelerate its military industrialization, culminating in the building of battleships.

As Japan grew stronger, China was growing weaker. In 1894 the two nations went to war over Korea. The Sino-Japanese War lasted less than six months, and it forced China to evacuate Korea, cede Taiwan and the Liaodong (li-AH-oh-dong) Peninsula, and pay a heavy indemnity. France, Germany, Britain, Russia, and the United States, upset at seeing a newcomer join the ranks of the imperialists, made Japan give up Liaodong in the name of the "territorial integrity" of China. In exchange for their "protection," the Western powers then made China grant them territorial and trade concessions, including ninety treaty ports.

In 1900 Chinese officials around the Empress Dowager Cixi encouraged a series of antiforeign riots known as the Boxer Uprising. Military forces from the European powers, Japan, and the United States put down the riots and occupied Beijing. Emboldened by China's obvious weakness, Japan and Russia competed for possession of the mineral-rich Chinese province of Manchuria.

Japan's participation in the suppression of the Boxer Uprising demonstrated its military power in

**Empress Dowager Cixi** Empress of China and mother of Emperor Guangxi. She put her son under house arrest, supported antiforeign movements, and resisted reforms of the Chinese government and armed forces.

**Yamagata Aritomo** One of the leaders of the Meiji Restoration.

## SECTION REVIEW

- China was weakened by the Taiping Rebellion, a reactionary government under Empress Dowager Cixi, and the demands of the West.
- Japan, in contrast, built up its military and industrial strength and became another imperial power, taking advantage of China's weakness to seize Korea, Taiwan, and southern Manchuria.

East Asia. Then in 1905, Japan surprised the world by defeating Russia in the Russo-Japanese War. By the Treaty of Portsmouth that ended the war, Japan established a protectorate over Korea. In spite of Western attempts to restrict it to the role of junior partner, Japan continued to increase its influence. It gained control of southern Manchuria, with its industries and railroads, and in 1910 it finally annexed Korea, joining the ranks of the world's colonial powers.

## CONCLUSION

The late nineteenth century witnessed the most rapid changes in technology, society, and politics that had ever taken place until that time. The changes were concentrated in a few regions of the world—Europe, the United States, and Japan—but would have repercussions everywhere.

Two primary causes—industrialization and nationalism—were responsible for the changes. Industrialization provided an abundance of goods as well as new and much better means of transportation and communication. After 1850, some of the worst abuses of industrialization that had characterized the previous age were attenuated, and new technologies promised to improve the lives of workers, city dwellers, and women.

Industrialization and the new politics of national identity increased the power of certain states but threatened others. States founded on a strong sense of national identity, such as France and Japan, found that the politics of nationalism benefited them and their citizens. But nationalism could also threaten the cohesion of multinational states like Russia and Austria-Hungary or weaken traditional states like China. The two great revolutions of the eighteenth and early nineteenth centuries—the industrial and the political—were about to destabilize the world, first in the nonindustrial regions, and then in the very heartland of the industrial world (see Chapter 25).

# CHAPTER REVIEW

## TECHNOLOGY ALTERS THE WORLD ECONOMY

■ *What new technologies and industries appeared between 1850 and 1900, and how did they alter the world economy?* (page 565)

After World War I broke out in 1914, many people, especially in Europe, looked back on the period from 1850 to 1914 as a golden age. For some, and in certain ways, it was. Industrialization was a powerful torrent changing Europe, North America, and East Asia. While shipping and railroads increased their global reach, new technologies—electricity, the steel and chemical industries, and the global telegraph network—contributed to the enrichment and empowerment of the industrial nations. World trade increased tenfold during this period, and many countries' economies were transformed.

## SOCIAL CHANGES

■ *How did the societies of the industrial countries change during this period?* (page 569)

With these new technologies, memories of the great scourges—famines, wars, and epidemics—faded. Clean water, electric lights, and railways began to improve the lives of city dwellers, even the poor. Municipal services made city life less dangerous and chaotic. Goods from distant lands, even travel to other continents, came within the reach of millions. Middle-class women continued to focus on domestic pursuits and lived in a "separate sphere" from men. Many working-class women took jobs in the textile industry, yet their work outside the home did not lessen their domestic and child-rearing responsibilities. At the same time women mobilized in large numbers to demand political rights.

## THE STRUGGLE BETWEEN CAPITAL AND LABOR
■ *How did industrialization contribute to socialist and labor movements?* (page 573)

Industrialization created a large class of factory and railroad workers, and Karl Marx predicted that a class struggle between industrial workers and employers would lead to revolution. Anarchism, a rival revolutionary philosophy, included all who were oppressed as potential revolutionary agents. Anarchism shook the political structures of Europe and America with terrorist attacks and remained a potent source of political violence and working-class mobilization in Italy, Spain, and Argentina well into the twentieth century. Socialism became more an intellectual current than a revolutionary movement. By the turn of the century, liberal political reforms had taken hold in western Europe. Through labor unions, workers did achieve some measure of recognition and security.

## NATIONALISM AND THE RISE OF ITALY, GERMANY, AND JAPAN
■ *How was nationalism transformed from a revolutionary to a conservative ideology?* (page 575)

The framework for all these changes was the nation-state. Until the 1860s nationalism was associated with liberalism, but later generations of conservatives used public education, military service, and colonial conquests to build a sense of national unity. By 1871 both Italy and Germany had become unified states. In Japan, the Meiji Restoration restored power to the emperor and ushered in a period of Western influences.

## THE GREAT POWERS OF EUROPE, 1871–1900
■ *How did the forces of nationalism affect the major powers of Europe?* (page 581)

The world economy, international politics, and even cultural and social issues revolved around a handful of countries—the great powers—that believed they controlled the destiny of the world. These included the most powerful European nations of the previous century, as well as three newcomers—Germany, the United States, and Japan—that were to play important roles in the future. Under the leadership of Bismarck, the German people developed a strong sense of national pride. Religious differences proved to be a hindrance to nationalism in France. Great Britain's problems were due to economic issues and Irish resentment of English rule.

## CHINA, JAPAN, AND THE WESTERN POWERS
■ *How did Western pressure affect East Asia?* (page 583)

Japan responded to western pressure by imitating the industrialized countries and adopting many of their institutions and attitudes. Japan's efforts to acquire a European-style colonial empire led to successful wars with China and Russia. China's response to the west was much less successful, partly because of western intrusions into the chinese economy in the name of free trade and partly because of internal divisions.

## Key Terms

Commodore Matthew Perry (p. 565)
railroads (p. 565)
submarine telegraph cables (p. 567)
steel (p. 567)
electricity (p. 568)
Thomas Edison (p. 568)
Victorian Age (p. 570)
"separate spheres" (p. 571)
socialism (p. 573)
labor union (p. 573)
Karl Marx (p. 573)
anarchism (p. 575)
nationalism (p. 575)
liberalism (p. 576)
Giuseppe Garibaldi (p. 576)
Otto von Bismarck (p. 577)
Meiji Restoration (p. 578)
Charles Darwin (p. 580)
Empress Dowager Cixi (p. 583)
Yamagata Aritomo (p. 583)

# The Crisis of the Imperial Order

© Cengage Learning

On June 28, 1914, Archduke Franz Ferdinand, heir to the throne of Austria-Hungary, was riding in an open carriage through Sarajevo, a city Austria had annexed six years earlier. When the carriage stopped momentarily, Gavrilo Princip, a member of a pro-Serbian conspiracy, fired his pistol twice, killing the archduke and his wife.

Those shots ignited a global conflict. All previous wars had caused death and destruction, but they were also marked by heroism and glory. In this new war, four years of bitter fighting produced no victories, no gains, and no glory, only death for millions of soldiers. The war became global as the Ottoman Empire fought against Britain and Japan attacked German positions in China. France and Britain involved their empires in the war and brought Africans, Indians, Australians, and Canadians to Europe to fight and labor on the front lines. Finally, in 1917, the United States entered the fray.

In this chapter, we will look at the causes of war between the great powers, the consequences of that conflict in Europe, the Middle East, and Russia, and the upheavals in China and Japan.

## ORIGINS OF THE CRISIS IN EUROPE AND THE MIDDLE EAST

■ *What led to the outbreak of the First World War?*

When the twentieth century opened, the world seemed firmly under the control of the great powers. Its first decade saw peace, economic growth, and the spread of new technologies: airplanes, automobiles, radio, and cinema. The only international war of the period, the Russo-Japanese War (1904–1905), ended quickly with a decisive Japanese victory.

However, two major changes undermined the apparent stability of the world. In Europe, Germany challenged Britain at sea and France in Morocco. The Ottoman Empire grew weaker, leaving a dangerous power vacuum. The resulting chaos in the Balkans gradually drew the European powers into a web of hostilities.

### The Ottoman Empire and Balkans

By 1900, the once-great Ottoman Empire had become the "sick man of Europe" and began losing its outlying provinces. Between 1902 and 1913, Macedonia rebelled, Austro-Hungary annexed Bosnia, Crete merged with Greece, and Albania became independent. In 1912–1913 Serbia, Bulgaria, Romania, and Greece chased the Turks out of the Balkans. France and Britain controlled Ottoman finances, taxes, railroads, mines, and public utilities.

In reaction, the Turks began to assert themselves against rebellious minorities and meddling foreigners. Many officers in the army, the most Europeanized segment of Turkish society, blamed Sultan Abdul Hamid II (r. 1876–1909) for the decline of the empire. In 1908–1909, a revolutionary group known as "Young Turks" plotted to overthrow the sultan and reinstate a stillborn constitution that he had suspended in 1876. The new regime reinvigorated the Tanzimat reform movement (see Chapter 22) that had begun in the early nineteenth century. At the same time, it cracked down on Greek and Armenian minorities. Galvanized by their defeat in the Balkan Wars, the Turks hired a German general to modernize their armed forces. The dangerous mixture of modern armies and nationalism was not limited to the Ottoman Empire, however.

### Nationalism, Alliances, and Military Strategy

Nationalism united the citizens of France, Britain, Italy, and Germany behind their respective governments and gave them tremendous cohesion and strength of purpose. But nationalism could divide as well as unify. In the large but fragile multinational empires—Russia, Austria-Hungary, and the Ottoman Empire—ethnic and religious minorities were stirring. The easy victories in the colonial wars (see Chapter 23) had led some in power to believe that only war could heal the divisions in their societies.

What turned the assassination of Franz Ferdinand into a conflict involving all the great powers was the system of alliances that had accumulated over the previous decades. Germany stood at Europe's center as the most heavily industrialized country in Europe. Its army was the best trained and equipped, and its battleships were challenging Great Britain's naval supremacy. Germany joined Austria-Hungary and Italy in the Triple Alliance in 1882. When in 1907 Britain, France, and Russia formed an Entente (on-TONT) ("understanding"), Europe was divided into two blocs of roughly equal power (see Map 25.1).

The alliance system was cursed by inflexible military planning. Anticipating war, military planners in France and Germany had worked out elaborate railroad timetables to mobilize their respective armies in a few days. Other countries were less well prepared. Russia with its underdeveloped rail system needed several weeks. Britain, with a tiny volunteer army, had no mobilization plans. German generals, believing that the British would stay out of a European war, made plans to defeat France in a matter of days and then transport the entire army by train across Germany to the Russian border before Russia could fully mobilize.

On July 28, 1914, emboldened by the backing of Germany, Austria-Hungary declared war on Serbia, triggering mobilization plans in other countries. The next day, Russia ordered general mobilization to force Austria to back down. On August 1, France honored its treaty obligation to Russia and ordered general mobilization. Minutes later Germany did the same. War was now unavoidable.

The German General Staff expected France to capitulate before the British could get involved. But on August 3, when German troops entered Belgium, Britain demanded their withdrawal. When Germany refused, Britain declared war on Germany.

# THE "GREAT WAR" AND THE RUSSIAN REVOLUTIONS, 1914–1918

■ *How did war lead to revolution in Russia?*

Throughout Europe, people greeted the outbreak of war with parades and flags, expecting a quick victory.

The German sociologist Max Weber wrote: "This war, with all its ghastliness, is nevertheless grand and wonderful. It is worth experiencing."[1] Very few imagined that their side might not win. No one foresaw that everyone would lose.

**Stalemate, 1914–1917** The generals' carefully drawn plans went awry from the start. Believing that a spirited attack would always prevail, French generals hurled their troops against the well-defended German border and suffered a crushing defeat. By early September, the Germans held Belgium and northern France and were fast approaching Paris. German victory seemed assured. But when Russia attacked, German troops needed for the final push into France were shifted to the eastern front. A gap opened between two German armies along the Marne River, into which moved France's last reserves. At the Battle of the Marne, the Germans were thrown back several miles.

During the next month, both sides spread out until they formed an unbroken battlefront extending over 300 miles (some 500 kilometers) from the North Sea to the border of Switzerland. All along this **western front**, machine guns provided an almost impenetrable defense against advancing infantry but were useless for the offensive because they were too heavy for one man to carry and took too much time to set up. To escape the deadly streams of bullets, soldiers dug holes in the ground, connected the holes to form shallow trenches, and then dug communications trenches to the rear. Within weeks, the battlefields were scarred by lines of trenches several feet deep, their tops protected by sandbags and their floors covered with planks.

For four years, generals on each side again and again ordered their thousands of young men to climb out of their trenches, race across the open fields, and be mowed down by enemy machine-gun fire. Poison gas added to the horror of battle.

---

[1]Frank B. Tipton, *A History of Modern Germany since 1815* (Berkeley: University of California Press, 2003), 295.

**western front** A line of trenches and fortifications in World War I that stretched without a break from Switzerland to the North Sea. Scene of most of the fighting between Germany, on the one hand, and France and Britain, on the other.

# Chronology

| | Europe and North America | Middle East | East Asia |
|---|---|---|---|
| **1900** | **1907** British-Russian Entente | **1909** Young Turks overthrow Sultan Abdul Hamid | **1900** Boxer Uprising in China<br>**1904–1905** Russo-Japanese War |
| **1910** | **1912–1913** Balkan Wars<br>**1914** Assassination of Archduke Franz Ferdinand sparks World War I<br>**1916** Battles of Verdun and the Somme<br>**1917** Russian Revolutions; United States enters the war<br>**1918** Armistice ends World War I<br>**1918–1921** Civil war in Russia<br>**1919** Treaty of Versailles | **1915** British defeat at Gallipoli<br>**1916** Arab Revolt in Arabia<br>**1917** Balfour Declaration<br>**1919–1922** War between Turkey and Greece | **1911** Chinese revolutionaries led by Sun Yat-sen overthrow Qing dynasty<br>**1915** Japan presents Twenty-One Demands to China<br>**1919** May Fourth Movement in China |
| **1920** | **1923–1928** New Economic Policy in Russia | **1922** Egypt nominally independent<br>**1923** Mustafa Kemal proclaims Turkey a republic<br>**1932** Britain grants Iraq official independence | **1927** Guomindang forces occupy Shanghai and expel communists |

The year 1916 saw the bloodiest and most futile battles of the war. The Germans attacked French forts at Verdun, losing 281,000 men and causing 315,000 French casualties. In retaliation, the British attacked the Germans at the Somme River and suffered 420,000 casualties—60,000 on the first day alone—while the Germans lost 450,000 and the French 200,000.

This was not warfare as it had ever been waged before; it was mass slaughter. Neither side could win, for the armies were stalemated by trenches and machine guns. During four years of the bloodiest fighting the world had ever seen, the western front moved no more than a few miles one way or another.

At sea, the war was just as inconclusive. As soon as war broke out, the British cut the German overseas telegraph cables, blockaded the coasts of Germany and Austria-Hungary, and set out to capture or sink all enemy ships still at sea. The German High Seas Fleet, built at enormous cost, seldom left port. Only once, in May 1916, did it confront the British Grand Fleet. At the Battle of Jutland, off the coast of Denmark, the two fleets lost roughly equal numbers of ships, and the Germans escaped back to their harbors.

In early 1915, in retaliation for the British naval blockade, Germany announced a blockade of Britain by submarines. German submarines attacked every vessel they could. One attack sank the British ocean liner *Lusitania*, killing 198 people, 139 of them Americans. When the United States protested, Germany ceased its submarine campaign, hoping to keep America neutral.

## The Home Front and the War Economy

The war economy transformed civilian life. In France and Britain, food rations were allocated according to need, improving nutrition among the poor. Unemployment vanished, and thousands of Africans, Indians, and Chinese were recruited for heavy labor in Europe. Employers also hired women to fill jobs in steel mills, mines, and munitions plants. Women became streetcar drivers, mail carriers, and police officers or found work in the burgeoning government bureaucracies. Many

**Map 25.1 The First World War in Europe** After an initial surge through Belgium into northern France, the German offensive bogged down for four years along the western front. To the east, the German armies conquered a large part of Russia during 1917 and early 1918. Despite spectacular victories in the east, Germany lost the war because its armies collapsed along the strategically important western front. © Cengage Learning

**Main map labels:**

ATLANTIC OCEAN

North Sea

Baltic Sea

Black Sea

Mediterranean Sea

Adriatic Sea

NORWAY
SWEDEN
FINLAND
Helsinki
Petrograd (St. Petersburg)
Moscow
RUSSIA
Don R.
Dnieper R.
Kiev
UKRAINE

Treaty of Brest-Litovsk, March 1918
Armistice line, December 1917
Farthest Russian advance, 1914

ESTONIA
LATVIA
Riga
LITHUANIA
Wilno (Vilnius)
COURLAND
BELARUS
Masurian Lakes 1914
E. PRUSSIA 1914
Tannenberg 1914
Brest-Litovsk
Warsaw
KINGDOM OF POLAND (Russia)
Vistula R.
MAY 1915
GALICIA
Dniester R.
TRANSYLVANIA

British blockade line
Jutland 1916
DENMARK
Kiel
Berlin
Elbe R.
GERMANY
Rhine R.
LUXEMBOURG
ALSACE-LORRAINE
NETHERLANDS
Louvain
BELGIUM
Western front
Paris
Seine R.
Loire R.
Bordeaux
Garonne R.
FRANCE
Rhône R.

GREAT BRITAIN
London
IRELAND

SPAIN
Ebro R.

AUSTRIA-HUNGARY
Vienna
Budapest
Danube R.
AUG. 1917
Caporetto 1917
MAR. 1918
Italian front
SWITZERLAND
ITALY
Po R.
Rome
Elba
Corsica
Sardinia
Balearic Is.

ROMANIA
Bucharest
BULGARIA
SERBIA
Sarajevo
MONTENEGRO
ALBANIA
1917-1918
GREECE
1915
Balkan front

Constantinople
OTTOMAN EMPIRE
Dardanelles
Gallipoli 1915
Cyprus
Crete
Malta
Sicily
Tunis
TUNISIA (France)

**Main map legend:**
- Triple Entente and its Allies
- Central Powers
- Neutral nations
- Greatest extent of territory gained by Germany-Austria
- Battle line

Scale: 0 200 400 Mi. / 0 200 400 Km.

**Inset map labels:**

English Channel
Dover
Calais
Ostend
FLANDERS
Ghent
Antwerp
Brussels
BELGIUM
Liège
NETHERLANDS
Scheldt R.
Meuse R.
ARDENNES
LUXEMBOURG
Coblenz
Cologne
Ruhr R.
Rhine R.
Moselle R.
GERMANY
Saar R.
LORRAINE
St. Mihiel
Strasbourg
ALSACE
Mulhouse
Basel
Épinal
Nancy
Verdun
Châlons-sur-Marne
ARGONNE FOREST
Sedan
Reims
St. Quentin
Somme
Somme R.
Amiens
Arras
Compiègne
Belleau Wood
Chateau-Thierry
Marne II
Marne R.
Marne I
Aisne R.
Paris
Seine R.
FRANCE

**Inset map legend:**
- Germany, 1914
- German offensive, 1915
- Greatest extent of territory gained by Germany, Sept. 1914
- Front at beginning of 1915
- German offensive, Summer 1918
- Armistice line, November 1918
- Major battle

Scale: 0 25 50 Mi. / 0 25 50 Km.

joined auxiliary military services as doctors, nurses, mechanics, and ambulance drivers. These positions gave thousands of women a sense of participation in the war effort and a taste of personal and financial independence.

The British naval blockade punished Germany's civilians. German chemists developed synthetic explosives and fuel, but not synthetic food. Wheat flour disappeared, replaced first by rye, then by potatoes and turnips, then by acorns and chestnuts, and finally by sawdust. After the failure of the potato crop in 1916 came the "turnip winter," when people had to survive on 1,000 calories per day, half the normal amount that an active adult needs. Women, children, and the elderly were especially hard hit. Even soldiers went hungry.

Abroad the British and French overran all of Germany's African colonies except German East Africa, which remained undefeated until the end of the war (see Map 25.1). In many African colonies, war policies imposed heavy taxes, low prices for requisitioned supplies, and military recruitment. Many Europeans stationed in Africa left to join the war, leaving areas with little or no European presence. Over a million Africans served in the various armies, and perhaps three times that number were drafted as porters to carry army equipment. In some places these impositions provoked African uprisings that lasted for years.

One country grew rich during the war: the United States, which for two and a half years stayed technically neutral while its companies did a roaring business supplying France and Britain with food and war materiel. After the United States entered the war in 1917, civilians were exhorted to help the war effort by investing their savings in war bonds and growing food in backyard "victory gardens." Employment created by the war opened up jobs for women and African Americans.

## The Ottoman Empire at War

On August 2, 1914, the Turks signed a secret alliance with Germany. In November they joined the fighting, hoping to gain land at Russia's expense. But the campaign in the Caucasus proved disastrous for both sides. Suspecting the local Armenians of being pro-Russian, the Turks forced them to march from their homelands across the mountains in the winter, a trek during which hundreds of thousands

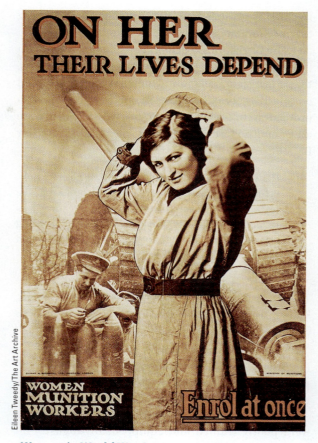

**Women in World War I** Women played a more important role in World War I than in previous wars. As the armies drafted millions of men, employers hired women for essential war work. This poster extols the importance of women workers in supplying munitions.

died of hunger, exposure, and outright slaughter. Famine stalked the empire.

The Turks also closed the Dardanelles, the strait between the Mediterranean and Black Seas (see Map 25.1). When a British attack on the Dardanelles failed disastrously at the Battle of Gallipoli, they tried to subvert the Ottoman Empire from within by promising the emir (governor) of Mecca, Hussein ibn Ali, a kingdom of his own. In 1916 Hussein started an Arab revolt against the Turks. His son **Faisal I** (FIE-sahl) led an Arab army into Palestine and Syria in support of

**Faisal I (1885–1933)** Arab prince, leader of the Arab Revolt in World War I. The British made him king of Iraq in 1921, and he reigned under British protection until 1933.

the British advance from Egypt, thereby contributing to the Ottoman defeat.

The British made promises to Chaim Weizmann (hi-um VITES-mun), leader of the British Zionists, that a Jewish homeland in Palestine could be carved out of the Ottoman Empire and placed under British protection. In November 1917, as British armies were advancing on Jerusalem, Foreign Secretary Sir Arthur Balfour wrote:

> His Majesty's Government view with favor the establishment in Palestine of a national home for the Jewish people and will use their best endeavours to facilitate the achievement of that object, it being clearly understood that nothing shall be done which may prejudice the civil and religious rights of existing non-Jewish communities in Palestine.[2]

The British did not foresee that this statement, known as the **Balfour Declaration**, would lead to conflicts between Palestinians and Jewish settlers.

## Double Revolution in Russia, 1917

Russia began the war with the largest army in the world, but its generals were incompetent, supplies were lacking, and soldiers were poorly trained and equipped. In August 1914 two Russian armies were thrown back in eastern Germany. Russia did better against the Austro-Hungarian army but again was defeated by the Germans. In 1916, after a string of defeats, the Russian army ran out of ammunition and other essential supplies. Soldiers were ordered into battle unarmed and told to pick up the rifles of fallen comrades.

With so many men in the army, railroads broke down for lack of fuel and parts, and crops rotted in the fields. Civilians faced shortages and widespread hunger. In the cities food and fuel became scarce. During the bitterly cold winter of 1916–1917, factory workers and housewives had to line up in front of grocery stores before dawn to get food. The court of Tsar Nicholas II, however, remained as extravagant and corrupt as ever.

When food ran out in Petrograd (St. Petersburg), the capital, in early March 1917, housewives and women factory workers staged mass demonstrations. Soldiers mutinied and joined striking workers to form *soviets* (councils) to take over factories and barracks. A few days later, the tsar abdicated, and leaders of the parliamentary parties, led by Alexander Kerensky, formed a Provisional Government. Thus began what Russians called the "February Revolution" because their calendar was two weeks behind the one in use elsewhere.

Revolutionary groups came out of hiding. Most numerous were the Social Revolutionaries, who advocated redistributing land to the peasants. The Social Democrats, a Marxist party, were divided. The Mensheviks, who advocated electoral politics and reform in the tradition of European socialists, had a large following among intellectuals and factory workers. The **Bolsheviks** were a small but tightly disciplined group dedicated to revolution. **Vladimir Lenin** (1870–1924), the Bolshevik leader, became a revolutionary in his teens when his older brother was executed for plotting to kill the tsar. His goal was to create a party that would lead the revolution rather than wait for it.

In early April 1917, the German government, hoping to destabilize Russia, allowed Lenin to travel from Switzerland to Russia in a sealed railway car. As soon as he arrived in Petrograd, he announced his program: immediate peace, all power to the soviets, and transfers of land to the peasants and factories to the workers. This plan proved immensely popular among soldiers and workers exhausted by the war.

When the Provisional Government ordered another offensive against the Germans, Russian soldiers deserted by the hundreds of thousands, throwing away their rifles and walking back to their villages. The Bolsheviks, meanwhile, were gaining support among the workers of Petrograd and the soldiers and sailors stationed there. On November 6,

**Balfour Declaration**  Statement issued by Britain's foreign secretary Arthur Balfour in 1917 favoring the establishment of a Jewish national homeland in Palestine.

**Bolsheviks**  Radical Marxist political party founded by Vladimir Lenin in 1903. Under Lenin's leadership, the Bolsheviks seized power in November 1917 during the Russian Revolution.

**Vladimir Lenin (1870–1924)**  Leader of the Bolshevik (later Communist) Party. He lived in exile in Switzerland until 1917, then returned to Russia to lead the Bolsheviks to victory during the Russian Revolution and the civil war that followed.

---

[2]Walter Z. Laqueur and Barry Rubin, eds., *The Arab-Israeli Reader: A Documentary History of the Middle East Conflict*, 4th ed. (New York: Penguin Books, 1984), 18.

akg-images/Newscom

**Lenin the Orator**   The leader of the Bolshevik revolutionaries was a spellbinding orator. Here Lenin is addressing Red Army soldiers in Sverdlov Square, Moscow, in 1920.

1917 (October 24 in the Russian calendar), they rose up and took over the city. This "October Revolution" overthrew the Provisional Government and the Bolsheviks arrested Mensheviks, Social Revolutionaries, and other rivals.

The Bolsheviks nationalized all private land and ordered the peasants to hand over their crops without compensation. The peasants, having seized their landlords' estates, resisted. In the cities the Bolsheviks took over the factories and drafted the workers into compulsory labor brigades. To enforce his rule, Lenin created the Cheka, a secret police force with powers to arrest and execute opponents. The Bolsheviks also sued for peace with Germany and Austria-Hungary. By the Treaty of Brest-Litovsk, signed on March 3, 1918, Russia lost territories containing a third of its population and wealth.

## The End of the War in Western Europe, 1917–1918

Like many Americans, President **Woodrow Wilson** wanted to stay out of the European conflict. For nearly three years he kept the United States neutral and tried to persuade the belligerents to compromise. But in late 1916, Germany's decision to starve the British by using submarines to sink food ships risked bringing the United States into the war. Germany was willing to gamble that Britain and France would collapse before the United States could send a decisive number of troops.

The German gamble failed. The British organized their merchant ships into convoys protected by destroyers, and on April 6 President Wilson asked the United States Congress to declare war on Germany.

On the western front, the two sides were so evenly matched in 1917 that the war seemed unlikely to end until one side or the other ran out of young men. Losing hope of winning, soldiers began to mutiny. In May 1917, before the arrival of U.S. forces, fifty-four of one hundred French divisions along the western front refused to attack. At Caporetto, Italian troops were so demoralized that 275,000 were taken prisoner.

Between March and August 1918, German general Erich von Ludendorff launched a series of surprise attacks that pushed to within 40 miles

**Woodrow Wilson (1856–1924)**  President of the United States (1913–1921) and a leading figure at the Paris Peace Conference of 1919. He was unable to persuade the U.S. Congress to ratify the Treaty of Versailles or join the League of Nations.

(64 kilometers) of Paris, but victory eluded him. Meanwhile, every month brought another 250,000 American troops to the front. In August the Allies counterattacked, and the Germans began a retreat that could not be halted, for German soldiers, many of them sick with the flu, had lost the will to fight.

In late October Ludendorff resigned, and sailors in the German fleet mutinied. Two weeks later, Kaiser Wilhelm fled to Holland as a new German government signed an armistice. At 11 A.M. on November 11, the guns on the western front went silent.

# PEACE AND DISLOCATION IN EUROPE, 1919–1929

■ *What role did the war play in eroding European dominance in the world?*

The Great War lasted four years. It took almost twice as long for Europe to recover. Millions of people had died or been disabled; political tensions lingered; and national economies remained depressed until the mid-1920s. The return of peace and prosperity in the late 1920s soon proved illusory.

## The Impact of the War

It is estimated that between 9 million and 10 million soldiers died, almost all of them young men. Perhaps twice that many returned home wounded, gassed, or shell-shocked, many of them disabled for life. In addition, the war created millions of refugees.

France welcomed 1.5 million refugees, but the preferred destination was the United States. About 800,000 immigrants succeeded in reaching it before immigration laws passed in 1921 and 1924 closed the door to eastern and southern Europeans. Canada, Australia, and New Zealand adopted similar restrictions on immigration. The Latin American republics welcomed European refugees, but their poverty discouraged potential immigrants.

One unexpected disaster was the great influenza epidemic of 1918–1919, which started among soldiers heading for the western front. This was no ordinary flu but a virulent strain that infected almost everyone on earth and killed one person in every forty. Half a million Americans perished in the epidemic—five times as many as died in the war. Worldwide, some 20 million people died.

The war also caused serious damage to the environment. No place on earth was ever so completely devastated as the scar across France and Belgium known as the western front. The fighting ravaged forests and demolished towns. The earth was gouged by trenches, pitted with craters, and littered with ammunition, broken weapons, chunks of concrete, and the bones of countless soldiers. After the war, it took a decade to clear away the debris, rebuild the towns, and create dozens of military cemeteries with neat rows of crosses stretching for miles.

## The Peace Treaties

In early 1919 delegates of the victorious Allies met in Paris. The defeated powers were kept out until the treaties were ready for signing. Russia, in the throes of civil war, was not invited.

From the start, three men dominated the Paris Peace Conference: U.S. president Wilson, British prime minister David Lloyd George, and French premier Georges Clemenceau (zhorzh cluh-mon-SO). They ignored the Italians, who had joined the Allies in 1915, and paid even less attention to the smaller European nations. They rejected the Japanese proposal that all races be treated equally and ignored the call of the Pan-African Congress for attention to the concerns of Africans. They also ignored delegates who did not represent sovereign states—the Arab revolt leader Faisal, the Zionist Chaim Weizmann, and several Armenian delegations.

Each man had his agenda. Wilson wanted to apply the principle of self-determination, by which he meant creating nations that reflected ethnic or linguistic divisions. He proposed a **League of Nations**, a world organization to safeguard the peace and foster international cooperation. His idealism clashed with the more hardheaded and self-serving nationalism of the Europeans. Lloyd George insisted that Germany pay a heavy indemnity. Clemenceau wanted Germany to return Alsace and Lorraine, cede the industrial Saar region to France, and make the Rhineland a buffer state.

The result was a series of compromises that satisfied no one. The European powers formed a League of Nations, but the U.S. Congress refused to let the United States join. France recovered Alsace and Lorraine but was unable to detach the Rhineland and had to content itself with vague promises of British and American protection if Germany ever rebuilt its army. Britain acquired new territories in Africa and the Middle East but was greatly weakened by human losses and the disruption of its trade.

On June 28, 1919, the German delegates reluctantly signed the **Treaty of Versailles** (vuhr-SIGH). Germany was forbidden to have an air force and was permitted only a token army and navy. It also gave up large parts of its eastern territory to a newly reconstituted Poland. The Allies made Germany promise to pay reparations, but they did not set a figure or a period of time for payment. A "guilt clause," which was to rankle for years to come, obliged the Germans to accept "responsibility for causing all the loss and damage" of the war. The treaty left Germany humiliated but largely intact and potentially the most powerful nation in Europe. Establishing a peace neither of punishment nor of reconciliation, it was one of the great failures in history.

In eastern Europe, the Allies created new national states in the lands lost by the old Russian, German, and Austro-Hungarian Empires. Austria and Hungary became separate states; Poland was resurrected after over a century; Czechoslovakia and Yugoslavia were created from parts of Austria-Hungary. These small nations all contained disaffected minorities

and were safe only as long as Germany and Russia remained weak.

## Russian Civil War and the New Economic Policy

Fighting continued in Russia for another three years after the end of the Great War. The Bolshevik Revolution had provoked Allied intervention, and, in December 1918, civil war broke out in Russia. The communists—as the Bolsheviks now called themselves—held central Russia, but all the surrounding provinces rose up against them. Counter-revolutionary armies led by former tsarist officers obtained weapons and supplies from the Allies. However, by 1921 the superior discipline of the Red Army, led by Leon Trotsky, gave the communists victory.

Gradually, the communists reunited the old Russian Empire. In 1920 Ukrainian communists declared the independence of a Soviet republic in the Ukraine; then in 1922, this merged with Russia to create the Union of Soviet Socialist Republics (USSR), or Soviet Union. In 1920–1921 the Red Army reconquered the oil-rich Caucasus and established Soviet control over Central Asia. In 1922 the new Soviet republics of Georgia, Armenia, and Azerbaijan joined the USSR.

By then, the Russian economy was in a state of ruin. Factories and railroads had shut down, and farmland had been devastated and livestock killed. Lenin decided to release the economy from party and government control. In 1923, he announced the **New Economic Policy** (NEP), which allowed peasants to own land and sell their crops, private merchants to trade, and private workshops to produce goods

**League of Nations** International organization founded in 1919 to promote world peace and cooperation but greatly weakened by the refusal of the United States to join. It proved ineffectual in stopping aggression by Italy, Japan, and Germany in the 1930s, and it was superseded by the United Nations in 1945.

**Treaty of Versailles (1919)** The treaty imposed on Germany by France, Great Britain, the United States, and other Allied powers after World War I. It demanded that Germany dismantle its military and give up some lands to Poland. It humiliated but did not weaken Germany.

**New Economic Policy** Policy proclaimed by Vladimir Lenin in 1923 to encourage the revival of the Soviet economy by allowing small private enterprises. Joseph Stalin ended the NEP in 1928 and replaced it with a series of Five-Year Plans.

and sell them on the free market. Only the biggest businesses, such as banks, railroads, and factories, remained under government ownership.

The relaxation of controls had an immediate effect. Production began to climb, and food and other goods became available. In the cities, food remained scarce because farmers used their crops to feed their livestock rather than sell them. But the NEP reflected no change in the communist goal of creating a modern industrial economy without private property. It merely provided breathing space—what Lenin called "one step back to advance two steps forward." This meant investing in heavy industry and electrification, moving farmers to the new industries, and providing food for the urban workers. In other words, it meant making the peasants, the great majority of the Soviet people, pay for the industrialization of Russia.

When Lenin died in January 1924, his associates jockeyed for power. Leon Trotsky, commander of the Red Army, had the support of many "Old Bolsheviks" who had joined the party before the Revolution, but Joseph Stalin, general secretary of the Communist Party, got the support of the majority and filled the party bureaucracy with individuals loyal to himself. In January 1929, he forced Trotsky to flee the country. Then, as absolute master of the party, he prepared to industrialize the Soviet Union at breakneck speed.

### An Ephemeral Peace

After the war came five years of painful recovery and readjustment (1919–1923), followed by six years of growing peace and prosperity (1924–1929). In the first period, the German government had printed money recklessly to fund reparations payments, causing a devastating inflation. As Germany teetered on the brink of civil war, radical nationalists tried to overthrow the government. Finally, the German government issued a new currency and promised to resume reparations payments, and the French, who had occupied the Ruhr when reparation payments ceased, agreed to withdraw their troops.

Then in 1924 the vexed issue of reparations vanished as Germany borrowed money from New York banks to make its payments to France and Britain, which used the money to repay their wartime loans from the United States. This triangular flow of money stimulated the rapid recovery of the European econo-

**SECTION REVIEW**

- The Great War left millions dead or disabled and caused environmental devastation. The influenza epidemic of 1918–1919 killed millions more.
- France, Britain, and the United States dominated the Paris Peace Conference, refusing to listen to other voices, and humiliating but not weakening Germany with the Treaty of Versailles.
- When Austria-Hungary and Russia fell apart, several smaller nations arose in Europe, creating another source of potential conflict.
- After the Bolshevik victory in the Russian civil war, the Russian economy was in ruins, and Stalin took power.
- Prosperity returned in 1924–1929 when Germany resolved its reparations issues, primarily through U.S. bank loans that flowed from Germany through France and Britain and back to the United States.

mies. France began rebuilding its war-torn northern zone; Germany recovered from its hyperinflation and joined the League of Nations; and in the United States a boom began that was to last for over five years.

While their economies flourished, governments grew more cautious and businesslike. Yet Germany and the Soviet Union did not accept their borders with the small nations that had arisen between them. In 1922 they signed a secret pact allowing the German army to conduct maneuvers in Russia (in violation of the Versailles treaty) in exchange for German help in building up Russian industry.

For a time, the League of Nations proved adept at resolving issues pertaining to health, labor relations, and postal and telegraph communications. But without U.S. participation, sanctions against states that violated League rules carried little weight.

## CHINA AND JAPAN: CONTRASTING DESTINIES

■ *Why did China and Japan follow such divergent paths in this period?*

China and Japan took different directions in the early twentieth century. Still in need of deep internal reform, giant China went through a revolution but soon collapsed into chaos. Japan's reforms before 1900 had gained it industry and a powerful military, which it used to take advantage of China's weakness.

**The Bund in Shanghai** On the Bund, the most important street in Shanghai, banks, corporate headquarters, and luxury hotels faced the waterfront where ships from around the world docked. Although Shanghai was China's industrial and commercial center, many of its workers loaded and unloaded ships by hand or pulled wealthy customers in rickshaws.

Bettmann/Corbis

## Revolution in China

China's population—about 400 million in 1900—was the largest of any country in the world and growing fast. Most Chinese worked incessantly, survived on a diet of grain and vegetables, and spent their lives in fear of floods, bandits, and tax collectors. Peasant plots averaged half what they had been two generations earlier. Meanwhile, landowners lived off the rents of their tenants. Officials, chosen through an elaborate examination system, enriched themselves from taxes and the government's monopolies on salt, iron, and other products. Wealthy merchants handled China's growing import-export trade in collaboration with foreign companies. The contrast between the squalor in which most urban residents lived and the luxury of the foreigners' enclaves in the treaty ports sharpened the resentment of educated Chinese.

When China's Empress Dowager Cixi (TSUH-shee) died in 1908, eight years after the Boxer Uprising that she had encouraged (see Chapter 24), the Revolutionary Alliance led by **Sun Yat-sen** (soon yot-SEN) (Sun Zhongshan, 1867–1925) prepared to take over. Sun had spent much of his life in Japan, Eng-

land, and the United States, plotting the overthrow of the Qing dynasty. His tenacious spirit and his ideas, a mixture of nationalism, socialism, and Confucian philosophy, attracted a large following. A revolutionary assembly elected Sun president of China in December 1911, and the last Qing ruler, the boy-emperor Puyi, abdicated the throne. But Sun had no military forces at his command. To avoid a clash with the army, he resigned after a few weeks, and a new national assembly elected **Yuan Shikai** (you-AHN she-KIE), the most powerful of the regional generals, president of the new Chinese republic.

Yuan was an able military leader, but he had no political program. When Sun reorganized his followers into a political party called the **Guomindang**

**Sun Yat-sen (1867–1925)** Chinese nationalist revolutionary, founder and leader of the Guomindang until his death. He attempted to create a liberal democratic political movement in China but was thwarted by military leaders.

**Yuan Shikai (1859–1916)** Chinese general and first president of the Chinese Republic (1912–1916). He stood in the way of the democratic movement led by Sun Yat-sen.

(gwo-min-dong) (National People's Party), Yuan quashed every attempt at creating a Western-style government and harassed Sun's followers.

## Japan and World War I

Japan's population reached 60 million in 1925 and was increasing by a million a year. The crash program of industrialization begun in 1868 by the Meiji oligarchs (see Chapter 24) accelerated during the First World War when the Japanese suddenly found their textiles, consumer goods, and munitions in great demand.

The Japanese economy grew four times faster than western Europe's and eight times faster than China's. Blessed with a rainy climate and many fast-flowing rivers, Japan expanded its hydroelectric capacity. By the mid-1930s, 89 percent of Japanese households had electric lights, compared with 44 percent of British households.

The *zaibatsu* (zie-BOT-soo), four giant corporations—Mitsubishi, Sumitomo, Yasuda, and Mitsui—that controlled most of Japan's industry and commerce profited the most. Farmers, who constituted half of the population, remained poor; some, in desperation, sold their daughters to textile mills or into domestic service, where young women formed the bulk of the labor force. Labor unions were weak and repressed by the police.

Japan was quick to join the Allied side in World War I. Japanese forces soon conquered the German colonies in the northern Pacific and on the coast of China, and then turned their attention to the rest of China. In 1915, Japan presented China with Twenty-One Demands, which would have turned it into a virtual protectorate. Britain and the United States persuaded Japan to soften the demands but could not prevent it from keeping the German coastal enclaves and extracting railroad and mining concessions at China's expense. Thus began a bitter struggle between the two countries that was to last for thirty years.

## China in the 1920s

To many educated Chinese, the Western powers' decision at the Paris Peace Conference to agree to Japan's seizure of the German enclaves in China was a cruel insult. On May 4, 1919, students demonstrated

in front of the Forbidden City of Beijing. Despite a government ban, the May Fourth Movement spread to other parts of China.

China's regional generals—the warlords—still supported their armies through plunder and arbitrary taxation, frightening off trade and investment. While neglecting the dikes and canals on which Chinese farmers depended, they fought one another and protected the gangsters who ran the opium trade. During the warlord era, China grew poorer. Only the treaty ports prospered.

Sun Yat-sen tried to make a comeback in Guangzhou (Canton) in the early 1920s. Though not a communist, he was impressed with the efficiency of Lenin's revolutionary tactics and let a Soviet adviser reorganize the Guomindang along Leninist lines. He also welcomed members of the newly created Chinese Communist Party into the Guomindang.

When Sun died in 1925, the leadership of his party passed to Chiang Kai-shek (chang kie-shek) (1887–1975). An officer and director of the military academy, Chiang trained several hundred young officers who remained loyal to him thereafter. In 1927 he determined to defeat the regional warlords. Moving north from his base in Canton, he briefly formed an alliance with the communists. Once Shanghai was occupied, however, he allied himself with local gangsters to crush the labor unions and decimate the communists, whom he considered a threat. He then defeated or co-opted most of the other warlords and established a dictatorship.

Chiang's government issued ambitious plans to revitalize the economy, but his administrators were neither competent like the Japanese officials of the Meiji Restoration nor ruthless like the Russian Bolshevik modernizers. Instead, the government attracted thousands of opportunists whose goals were to "become officials and get rich" by taxing and plundering businesses. In the countryside tax collectors and landowners squeezed the peasants ever harder.

> **Guomindang** Nationalist political party founded on democratic principles by Sun Yat-sen in 1912. After 1925, the party was headed by Chiang Kai-shek, who turned it into an increasingly authoritarian movement.

# THE NEW MIDDLE EAST

■ *How did the Middle East change as a result of the war?*

At the Paris Peace Conference, France, Britain, and Italy proposed to divide the territories of the Ottoman Empire among themselves, but their ambitions clashed with President Wilson's ideal of national self-determination. While Turkish nationalists fought for and achieved independence, the Arab-speaking territories of the old Ottoman Empire became part of the League of Nations' new **mandate system**, run by French and British administrations charged with promoting "the material and moral well-being and the social progress of the inhabitants." In Palestine, Zionists accelerated Jewish immigration (see Map 25.2).

## The Rise of Modern Turkey

At the end of the war, Allied forces occupied the Ottoman Empire and made the sultan give up most of his lands. But they had to reckon with Mustafa Kemal, a war hero who formed a nationalist government in central Anatolia with the backing of fellow army officers. His armies defeated a Greek army of occupation in western Anatolia in 1922. An ensuing population exchange moved hundreds of thousands of Greeks to Greece and brought Muslims from that country to Turkey.

As a war hero and proclaimed savior of his country, Mustafa Kemal was able to impose wrenching changes on his people. An outspoken modernizer, he was eager to bring Turkey closer to Europe as quickly as possible. He abolished the sultanate, declared Turkey a secular republic in 1923, and introduced European laws. In a radical break with Islamic tradition, he suppressed Muslim courts, schools, and religious orders and replaced the Arabic alphabet with the Latin alphabet.

Women received civil equality, including the right to vote and to be elected to the national assembly. Kemal forbade polygamy and instituted civil marriage and divorce. He even changed people's clothing, strongly discouraging women from veiling their faces, and ordering Turkish men to wear European brimmed hats instead of the fez. He ordered everyone to take a family name, choosing the name **Atatürk** ("father of the Turks") for himself.

## Arab Lands and the Question of Palestine

Among the Arab people, the thinly disguised colonialism of the mandate system set off protests and rebellions. Arabs viewed the European presence not as liberation from Ottoman oppression, but as foreign occupation.

The British attempted to control the Middle East with a mixture of bribery and intimidation. They made Faisal, leader of the Arab Revolt, the first king of Iraq and used aerial bombing of rebellious nomads to quell opposition. In 1931 they reached an agreement with King Faisal's government. A year later Britain granted Iraq official independence in exchange for a military alliance, the right to keep two air bases, and an assured flow of petroleum. France, meanwhile, sent thousands of troops to Syria and Lebanon to crush nationalist uprisings.

In Egypt, as in Iraq, the British substituted a phony independence for official colonialism. They declared Egypt independent in 1922 but reserved the right to station troops in the Suez Canal zone to secure their link with India. Despite nationalist opposition, Britain was successful in keeping Egypt in limbo—neither independent nor a colony—thanks to an alliance with King Fuad (sultan, 1917–1922; king 1922–1936) and conservative Egyptian politicians who feared both secular and religious radicalism.

**mandate system** Allocation of former German colonies and Ottoman possessions to the victorious powers after World War I, to be administered under League of Nations supervision.

**Atatürk (1881–1938)** The founder of modern Turkey. He distinguished himself as a war hero in World War I and expelled a Greek expeditionary army from Anatolia in 1921–1922. He replaced the Ottoman Empire with the Turkish Republic in 1923. As president, he pushed through a radical westernization and reform of Turkish society.

# Diversity & Dominance

## The Middle East After World War I

During the First World War, Entente forces invaded and occupied Palestine, Mesopotamia, and Syria. This raised the question of what to do with these territories after the war. Would they be returned to the Ottoman Empire? Would they simply be added to the colonial empires of Britain and France? Or would they become independent Arab states?

The following documents illustrate the diversity of opinions among various groups planning the postwar settlement: Great Britain, concerned with defeating Germany and maintaining its empire; the United States, basing its policies on lofty principles; and Arab delegates from the Middle East, seeking self-determination.

In the early twentieth century, in response to the rise of anti-Semitism in Europe, a movement called Zionism had arisen among European Jews. Zionists, led by Theodore Herzl, hoped for a return to Israel, the ancestral homeland of the Jewish people. For two thousand years this land had been a province of various empires—Roman, Byzantine, Arab, and Ottoman—and was inhabited by Arabic-speaking people, most of whom practiced the Islamic religion.

During the war the British government was receptive to the idea of establishing a Jewish homeland in Palestine. It was motivated by the need to win the war, but it also considered the more distant future. The result was a policy statement, sent by Foreign Secretary Arthur James Balfour to Baron Rothschild, a prominent supporter of the Zionist movement in England. This statement, called the "Balfour Declaration," has haunted the Middle East ever since.

### The Balfour Declaration of 1917

Foreign Office
November 2nd, 1917

Dear Lord Rothschild:

I have much pleasure in conveying to you, on behalf of His Majesty's Government, the following declaration of sympathy with Jewish Zionist aspirations which have been submitted to, and approved by, the Cabinet:

His Majesty's Government view with favor the establishment in Palestine of a national home for the Jewish people, and will use their best endeavors to facilitate the achievement of this object, it being clearly understood that nothing shall be done which may prejudice the civil and religious rights of existing non-Jewish communities in Palestine, or the rights and political status enjoyed by Jews in any other country.

I should be grateful if you would bring this declaration to the knowledge of the Zionist Federation.

Yours,
Arthur James Balfour

On January 8, 1918, the American president Woodrow Wilson issued his famous Fourteen Points proposal to end the war. Much of his speech was devoted to European affairs or to international relations in general, but one of his fourteen points referred to the Arab world.

### Woodrow Wilson's Fourteen Points

What we demand in this war . . . is that the world be made fit and safe to live in; and particularly that it be made safe for every peace-loving nation which, like our own, wishes to live its own life, determine its own institutions, be assured of justice and fair dealing by the other peoples of the world as against force and selfish aggression. All the peoples of the world are in effect partners in this interest, and for our own part we see very clearly that unless justice be done to others it will not be done to us. The programme of the world's peace, therefore, is our programme; and that programme, the only possible programme, as we see it, is this:

XII. The Turkish portions of the present Ottoman Empire should be assured a secure sovereignty, but the other nationalities which are now under Turkish rule should be assured an undoubted security ➤

➤ of life and an absolutely unmolested opportunity of autonomous development. . . .

*When the war ended, the victorious Allies assembled in Paris to determine, among other things, the fate of the former Arab provinces of the Ottoman Empire. Arab leaders had reason to doubt the intentions of the great powers, especially Britain and France. When the Allies decided to create mandates in the Arab territories on the grounds that the Arab peoples were not ready for independence, Arab leaders expressed their misgivings, as in the following statement:*

## Memorandum of the General Syrian Congress, July 2, 1919

We the undersigned members of the General Syrian Congress, meeting in Damascus on Wednesday, July 2nd, 1919, made up of representatives from the three Zones, viz., The Southern, Eastern, and Western, provided with credentials and authorizations by the inhabitants of our various districts, Moslems, Christians, and Jews, have agreed upon the following statement of the desires of the people of the country who have elected us. . . .

1. We ask absolutely complete political independence for Syria. . . .

3. Considering the fact that the Arabs inhabiting the Syrian area are not naturally less gifted than other more advanced races and that they are by no means less developed than the Bulgarians, Serbians, Greeks, and Roumanians at the beginning of their independence, we protest against Article 22 of the Covenant of the League of Nations, placing us among the nations in their middle stage of development which stand in need of a mandatory power.

4. . . . . relying on the declarations of President Wilson that his object in waging war was to put an end to the ambition of conquest and colonization, . . . and believing that the American Nation is furthest from any thought of colonization and has no political ambition in our country, we will seek the technical and economic assistance from the United States of America, provided that such assistance does not exceed 20 years.

5. In the event of America not finding herself in a position to accept our desire for assistance, we will seek this assistance from Great Britain, also provided that such does not prejudice our complete independence and unity of our country and that the duration of such assistance does not exceed that mentioned in the previous article.

6. We do not acknowledge any right claimed by the French Government in any part whatever of our Syrian country and refuse that she should assist us or have a hand in our country under any circumstances and in any place.

7. We opposed the pretensions of the Zionists to create a Jewish commonwealth in the southern part of Syria, known as Palestine, and oppose Zionist migration to any part of our country; for we do not acknowledge their title but consider them a grave peril to our people from the national, economical, and political points of view. Our Jewish compatriots shall enjoy our common rights and assume our common responsibilities.

## QUESTIONS FOR ANALYSIS

1. Was there a contradiction between Balfour's proposal to establish "a national home for the Jewish people" and the promise "that nothing shall be done which may prejudice the civil and religious rights of existing non-Jewish communities in Palestine"? If so, why did he make two contradictory promises?

2. How would Woodrow Wilson's statements about "an absolutely unmolested opportunity of autonomous development" apply to Palestine?

3. Why did the delegates to the General Syrian Congress object to the plan to create mandates in the former Ottoman provinces? What alternatives did they offer?

4. Why did the delegates object to the creation of a Jewish commonwealth?

---

*Sources*: The Balfour Declaration, *The Times* (London), November 9, 1917. Memorandum of the General Syrian Congress, *Foreign Relations of the United States: Paris Peace Conference*, vol. 12 (Washington, DC: Government Printing Office, 1919), 780–781.

**Map 25.2 Territorial Changes in the Middle East After World War I** The defeat and dismemberment of the Ottoman Empire at the end of World War I resulted in an entirely new political map of the region. The Turkish Republic inherited Anatolia and a small piece of Europe, while the Ottoman Empire's Arab provinces were divided between France and Great Britain. Only Iran and Egypt did not change. © Cengage Learning

**Legend (map key):**
- Ottoman Empire in 1914
- British protectorate in 1914
- Area controlled under mandates from the League of Nations, 1920
- British Mandate
- French Mandate
- International boundaries, 1923

**Map labels:**
BULGARIA · GREECE · Istanbul (Constantinople) · Black Sea · Ankara · Izmir (Smyrna) · TURKEY · SOVIET UNION · Batum · Ceded by Soviet Union in 1921 · Kars · ARMENIANS · Baku · Caspian Sea · AZERBAIJANIS · Tabriz · Dodecanese (It.) · Crete · Cyprus (Gr. Br.) · Aleppo · Euphrates R. · KURDS · Mosul · SYRIA · IRAQ · Tigris R. · Tehran · PERSIA (IRAN) · LEBANON · Beirut · Damascus · Baghdad · Mediterranean Sea · PALESTINE · Jerusalem · Amman · Karbala · Najaf · Kut el Amara · Cairo · Suez Canal · TRANSJORDAN · Basra · KUWAIT · NEUTRAL ZONE · NEUTRAL ZONE · Persian Gulf · BAHRAIN · QATAR · Gulf of Oman · EGYPT · HEJAZ (Independent 1916; to Nejd 1925) · Boundary undefined · Red Sea · Medina · Riyadh · NEJD (SAUDI ARABIA) · TRUCIAL OMAN · OMAN · Boundary undefined · Nile R. · Jiddah · Mecca · ASIR (Independent 1917; to Nejd 1920) · 20°N · ANGLO-EGYPTIAN SUDAN · ERITREA · YEMEN (Independent 1918) · HADHRAMAUT · Boundary undefined · Arabian Sea · Socotra (Gr. Br.) · ADEN · Blue Nile R. · ABYSSINIA · FRENCH SOMALILAND · Gulf of Aden · 10°N · BRITISH SOMALILAND · ITALIAN SOMALILAND

Scale: 0 150 300 Km. · 0 150 300 Mi.

Hulton Archive/Getty Images

**The Jewish Settlement of Palestine** Thousands of Jews fleeing persecution and discrimination in Europe settled on the land and founded *kibbutzim,* or collective farms. In this picture taken in 1912, an eighty-four-year-old immigrant from Russia plows the land.

As soon as Palestine became a British mandate in 1920, Jewish immigrants, encouraged by the Balfour Declaration of 1917, arrived to join the small community that had immigrated in the nineteenth century. Most settled in the cities, but those supporting a socialist version of Zionism established *kibbutzim,* or communal farms. The purchases of land by Jewish agencies angered the indigenous Arabs, especially tenant farmers who were evicted to make room for settlers. In 1920–1921 riots erupted between Jews and Arabs. When far more Jewish immigrants arrived than they had anticipated, the British tried to limit immigration, thereby alienating the Jews without mollifying the Arabs. Increasingly, Jews arrived without papers, smuggled in by militant Zionist organizations. In the 1930s the country was torn by

strikes and guerrilla warfare that the British could not control. In the process, Britain earned the hatred of both sides.

**SECTION REVIEW**

- Former Arab provinces of the Ottoman Empire became "mandates" under French or British control.
- Mustafa Kemal (Atatürk) expelled the Greek minority from Anatolia and founded the Turkish Republic, then pushed it toward secular reform.
- As Middle Eastern society modernized, the Arabs became more politically active but had to endure the mandate system.
- Jewish immigration to Palestine caused growing tensions between Jews, Arabs, and the British.

# CONCLUSION

In the late 1920s it seemed that the victors in the Great War might reestablish the prewar prosperity and European dominance of the globe. But the spirit of the 1920s was not real peace; instead it was the eye of a hurricane. The Great Depression and World War II were in the offing.

The Great War caused a major realignment among the nations of the world. France and Britain, the two leading colonial powers, emerged economically weakened despite their victory. The war brought defeat and humiliation to Germany but did not reduce its military or industrial potential. It destroyed the old regime of Russia, leading to civil war and revolution from which the victorious powers sought to isolate themselves.

Two other old empires—the Austro-Hungarian and the Ottoman—were divided into many smaller and weaker nations.

Japan took advantage of the European conflict to develop its industries and press its demands on a China weakened by domestic turmoil and social unrest. The United States emerged as the most prosperous and potentially most powerful nation, restrained only by the isolationist sentiments of many Americans.

In the Middle East, the fall of the Ottoman Empire awakened aspirations of nationhood among the Turkish and Arab inhabitants and Jewish immigrants. These aspirations were thwarted when france and Great Britain tried to impose their rule upon the former Ottoman lands, causing conflicts and bitter enmities.

# CHAPTER REVIEW

## ORIGINS OF THE CRISIS IN EUROPE AND THE MIDDLE EAST

■ *What led to the outbreak of the First World War?* (page 587)

In 1914 the great powers of Europe had not had a major conflict in decades and believed a war would be quick and victorious. The two alliances they formed—the Central Powers and the Entente—were locked into a rigid timetable of mobilizations and railroad schedules. When competing nationalist movements in the Balkans triggered a conflict between Serbia and Austria-Hungary, the alliances quickly drew Russia, Germany, France, and Britain into this conflict.

## THE "GREAT WAR" AND THE RUSSIAN REVOLUTIONS, 1914–1918

■ *How did war lead to revolution in Russia?* (page 588)

Russia was the least prepared for war. Chaotic mobilization and a string of defeats disrupted the economy, causing severe shortages. As the war progressed,

soldiers began to desert, and the government lost control of the army and the population. The moderate government that replaced the tsar in March 1917 could neither satisfy the people nor pursue the war. Its failure allowed the Bolsheviks to overthrow it in a second revolution.

## PEACE AND DISLOCATION IN EUROPE, 1919–1929

■ *What role did the war play in eroding European dominance in the world?* (page 594)

France, Great Britain, and Italy expected to reap the benefits of victory and expand their empires at the expense of the defeated powers. However, with the exception of the United States, which withdrew to the Western Hemisphere, the victors were exhausted and impoverished and had lost the will to fight in colonial wars. Meanwhile, the idea of self-determination had spread to the Middle East and Asia, where nationalist politicians and their followers were determined to resist European dominance.

## CHINA AND JAPAN: CONTRASTING DESTINIES

■ *Why did China and Japan follow such divergent paths in this period?* (page 596)

After 1868, Japan established a strong government and built an industrial economy comparable to those of Europe. Meanwhile, China, long ruled by the Qing dynasty, erupted after 1911 in civil wars in which warlords and political factions vied for power. The Japanese military and major industries seized the opportunity of Europe's involvement in the Great War to build up Japan's economy at China's expense.

## THE NEW MIDDLE EAST

■ *How did the Middle East change as a result of the war?* (page 599)

In Anatolia, the heartland of the Ottoman Empire, a movement for national unity led by Kemal Atatürk fought for and achieved Turkish independence. In the predominantly Arab lands, nationalist leaders decried European domination. Jewish immigration into Palestine provoked a violent reaction from the Arabs, which their British overlords found hard to control.

### Key Terms

western front (p. 588)

Faisal I (p. 591)

Balfour Declaration (p. 592)

Bolsheviks (p. 592)

Vladimir Lenin (p. 592)

Woodrow Wilson (p. 593)

League of Nations (p. 595)

Treaty of Versailles (p. 595)

New Economic Policy (p. 595)

Sun Yat-sen (p. 597)

Yuan Shikai (p. 597)

Guomindang (p. 598)

mandate system (p. 599)

Atatürk (p. 599)

# Revolutions in Living

© Cengage Learning

In 1869 three Japanese businessmen, an entrepreneurial former cook, a green grocer, and a wagon builder, responded to government concerns about urban congestion and applied for a license to build a *jinriksha* ("man-power-vehicle"). They described it as "a little seat in the Western style, mounted on wheels so that it can be pulled about. It does not shake as much as the usual cart, and it is easy to turn round. It will not hinder other traffic, and since it can be pulled by one person, it is very cheap."[1] Their first vehicles, which quickly came to be called rickshaws, appeared a year later. A year after that, in 1871, Japan enacted its first patent law, and the three applied for exclusive manufacturing rights. However, so many workshops were by then turning out rickshaws that their application was denied.

An alternative claim of invention arose when an irascible American Baptist missionary named Jonathan Goble petitioned the Tokyo Metropolitan Government to grant him a share of the tax levied on the thirty thousand rickshaws then officially registered. He claimed to be the inventor, and a number of Westerners living in Japan supported him, some stating that Goble had built the first rickshaw for his ailing wife, and others that he had designed it at the request of a Japanese officer for use in the "imperial pleasure gardens."

The Japanese version of the story, which was reinforced in 1900 by government cash awards to the three businessmen, is highly credible since two-wheeled carts with a similar arrangement of shafts for pulling were in use on Japanese farms and for transporting loads well before European carriages came to be known through the "opening of Japan" in the 1850s (see Chapter 24). Moreover, Japan became the export source for rickshaws throughout Asia and the Indian Ocean region. The Goble story, however, made better sense to Westerners, who had a hard time crediting non-Europeans with inventiveness.

---

[1]F. Calvin Parker, *Jonathan Goble of Japan: Marine, Missionary, Maverick* (Lanham, MD: University Press of America, 1990), 222.

People today often look back and marvel at the changes their parents and grandparents lived through in the twentieth century. Movies, radio, television, telephones, automobiles, and airplanes all developed during the first half of the century. Familiar patterns of daily life gave way to new assumptions about many aspects of human life, with important differences according to what part of the world a person lived in.

## NEW TECHNOLOGY OUTSIDE THE INDUSTRIALIZED WORLD

■ *How were Asians and Africans impacted by technology and innovation differently from Europeans and Americans?*

Before we discuss changes in the way people lived in the West between 1900 and 1950, we will consider how other parts of the world adapted local cultural traditions to the changing times and thereby took their societies in distinctive directions. A new technology could originate in the West or the East, but the point of origin did not determine its impact.

The rickshaw discussed at the beginning of this chapter provides a rare example of an Asian invention transforming urban life in ways unfamiliar to Europeans and Americans. The rickshaw stimulated the growth of Asian cities like Shanghai, Beijing, Singapore, Calcutta, and Bombay and reached across the Indian Ocean to Madagascar and South Africa. Much like European villagers entered the urban economy by way of unskilled manufacturing jobs, tens of thousands of unskilled Asian workers flocked to these cities to become rickshaw pullers, and eventually to stimulate a labor movement. Since a rickshaw puller usually ran rather than walked, the rickshaw cut the expense of personal transport in half while doubling its speed—and did not bury the streets under horse manure, the plague of Western cities. In Asia the rickshaw effectively enlarged the area of cities that had previously been scaled for pedestrians, transforming urban life in the Eastern Hemisphere just as streetcars had earlier done in Europe and America.

Some Western technologies were influentially adapted in the non-Western world. Photography and film contributed to feelings of national identity and common experience even in lands that were internally divided by language and ethnicity. In India, the first full-length feature screening occurred in 1912 two years after **Auguste and Louis Lumière**, who had premiered the first motion pictures in Paris in 1895, held motion picture demonstrations all over the world. Movies also caught on quickly in Japan. Not just for entertainment, newsreels and documentaries became major sources of information throughout the world, especially after the advent of sound in the late 1920s.

Practical photography began in Europe in 1839, and forty years later an efficient way was developed for printing photographs in newspapers. Photographic images soon became common throughout the world, often as picture postcards. European photographers, however, tended to look upon Asians and Africans, particularly seminude women, as exotic subjects and thereby catered to common European assumptions about racial superiority.

Non-European photographers rarely became known outside their home countries. Chinese newspapers and magazines usually published images without naming the photographers. A dozen early photographers became famous in Japan, however, possibly because popular woodblock prints had created an audience. In Iran, despite Muslim clerical disapproval of making images of human beings, the ruler Naser al-Din Shah (r. 1848–1896) shot some forty-eight thousand pictures, including members of his own family and even nudes and prisoners.

Photography enabled newspapers, magazines, and advertisements to inform even illiterate people about what their country and their fellow citizens

Hung Chung Chih/Shutterstock.com

**Rickshaw Traffic**  Invented in 1869, the rickshaw transformed urban life in East Asia and the lands bordering on the Indian Ocean.

looked like, who was ruling them, and how traditional elites and prosperous Europeanized families lived. Thus photography contributed to feelings of national identity and common experience even in lands that were internally divided by language and ethnicity.

From the 1890s onward, electricity transformed home life in Europe and North America by attracting private customers. Outside Europe and North America, however, the small size of the middle class limited private subscription. Electricity might be supplied to streetlights, tramways, and factories, but an appliance-oriented lifestyle was slow to develop. By contrast, the foot-operated sewing machine and manually wound phonograph found wider global acceptance than any other appliances before World War II.

Radio development was uneven. Outside of North America, where 600 stations were broadcasting by 1924, the new medium was often limited by governments. Radio developed vigorously in Japan, Shanghai, and most Latin American countries and became an outlet for local cultural and political programming. In India and Africa, on the other hand, British and French colonial authorities imposed strict controls on radio transmissions and programming.

## SECTION REVIEW

- Rickshaws contributed to urbanization, making transport in cities easier and faster and bringing rickshaw pullers to the city for employment.

- Technologies such as movies and photography were embraced and adapted in non-Western countries creating cultural cohesion and informing illiterate populations.

- The electrical appliance culture of the West spread slowly in parts of the world with small middle class populations.

**Auguste (1862–1954) and Louis (1864–1948) Lumière**  French inventors of motion pictures whose equipment demonstrations abroad stimulated the growth of cinema around the world.

# Chronology

| | Technology | India | Africa | Latin America |
|---|---|---|---|---|
| **1900** | **1903** Wright brothers fly first airplane | **1905** Viceroy Curzon splits Bengal; mass demonstrations | **1900s** Railroads connect ports to the interior | **1876–1910** Porfirio Diaz, dictator of Mexico |
| | | **1906** Muslims found All-India Muslim League | | |
| | | **1911** British transfer capital from Calcutta to Delhi | | **1911–1919** Mexican Revolution |
| | **1912** First feature-length movie in India | | **1912** African National Congress founded | |
| | **1913** Henry Ford introduces assembly-line production | | | |
| | **1915–1920** Women gain vote in Norway, Russia, Canada, Germany, Britain, and United States | | | **1917** New constitution proclaimed in Mexico |
| **1920** | **1920** Commercial radio begins in United States | **1919** Amritsar Massacre | **1920s** J. E. Casely Hayford organizes political movement in British West Africa | |
| | **1923** Magaret Sanger opens first birth control clinic | | | |
| | **1925** Commercial radio begins in Japan | **1929** Gandhi leads Walk to the Sea | | **1928** Plutarco Elías Calles founds Mexico's National Revolutionary Party |
| **1930** | | **1930s** Gandhi calls for independence; he is repeatedly arrested | | **1930–1945** Getulio Vargas, dictator of Brazil |
| | **1932** Empire State Building opens | | | **1934–1940** Lázaro Cárdenas, president of Mexico |
| | | | | **1938** Cárdenas nationalizes Mexican oil industry; Vargas proclaims Estado Novo in Brazil |
| | | **1939** British bring India into World War II | **1939–1945** A million Africans serve in World War II | |
| **1940** | | **1940** Muhammad Ali Jinnah demands a separate nation for Muslims | | **1943** Juan Perón leads military coup in Argentina |
| | | **1947** Partition and independence of India and Pakistan | | **1946** Perón elected president of Argentina |

# NEW WAYS OF LIVING IN THE INDUSTRIALIZED WORLD

■ *How did daily life and thought change in early-twentieth-century industrialized countries?*

World War I left a deep imprint on European society and culture. The centuries-old European distinction between aristocrats and commoners faded. Advances in science offered astonishing new insights into the mysteries of nature and the universe. New technologies, many of them pioneered in the United States, promised to change the daily lives of millions of people (see Environment and Technology: New Materials). At the same time, new cultural trends developed that had profound effects.

## Class and Gender

So many European aristocrats died on the battlefields that with them went their class's long domination of the army, the diplomatic corps, and other elite sectors of society. On both sides of the Atlantic, engineers, businessmen, lawyers, and other professionals rose to prominence, increasing the relative importance of the middle class.

At the same time, governments had expanded during the war and continued to grow, providing housing, highways, schools, public health, broadcasting, and other services. The ambitions and tastes of the rapidly expanding middle class became increasingly evident in the postwar period, while the role of the working class remained about the same.

Women's lives changed more rapidly in the 1920s than ever before. Although the end of the war marked a retreat from wartime job opportunities, some women remained in the workforce. The young and wealthy enjoyed more personal freedoms; they drove cars, played sports, traveled alone, and smoked in public. For others, the upheavals of war brought more suffering than liberation. Millions of women had lost their male kin in the war or in the great influenza epidemic. After the war many single women led lives of loneliness and destitution.

In Europe and North America, advocates of women's rights had been demanding the vote for women since the 1890s. New Zealand was the only nation to grant women the vote before the twentieth century. Norway followed in 1915, Russia in 1917, and Canadians and Germans in 1918. Britain gave women over thirty the vote in 1918 and later extended it to younger women. The Nineteenth Amendment to the U.S. Constitution granted suffrage to American women in 1920. Women in Turkey began voting in 1934. Everywhere, their influence on politics was less radical than feminists had hoped and conservatives had feared. Even when it did not transform politics and government, however, the right to vote was a potent symbol.

On both sides of the Atlantic, women participated in social reform movements to prevent mistreatment of women and children and industrial workers. In the United States such reforms were championed by progressives like Jane Addams (1860–1935), who founded a settlement house in a poor neighborhood and received the Nobel Peace Prize in 1931. In Europe reformers were generally aligned with Socialist or Labor Parties.

Among the most controversial, and eventually most effective, of the reformers were those who advocated contraception, such as the American **Margaret Sanger** (1883–1966). Her campaign brought her into conflict with many authorities, who equated birth control with pornography. Finally, in 1923 she was able to found a birth control clinic in New York. In France, the government prohibited contraception and abortion in 1920 in an effort to increase the birthrate and make up for the loss of so many young men in the war.

## Revolution in the Sciences

At the end of the nineteenth century, a revolution in physics undermined the old certainties about nature. Physicists discovered that atoms, the building blocks of matter, are not indivisible, but consisted of far smaller subatomic particles. In 1900 the German physicist **Max Planck** (1858–1947) found that atoms emit or absorb energy in discrete amounts called *quanta*. Few people understood these findings at the time, much less **Albert Einstein**'s (1879–1955) pronouncement in 1916 that time, space, energy, and mass are not fixed but are relative to one another. But the new physics promised to unlock the secrets of matter and provide humans with plentiful—and potentially dangerous—new sources of energy.

The new social sciences were more understandable, and thus more unsettling, for they challenged Victorian morality and middle-class values. **Sigmund Freud** (1856–1939), a Viennese physician, developed the technique of psychoanalysis to probe the minds of his patients. His technique uncovered hidden layers of emotion and desire repressed by social restraints.

**Margaret Sanger (1883–1966)**  American nurse and author; pioneer in the movement for family planning; organized conferences and established birth control clinics.

**Max Planck (1858–1947)**  German physicist who developed quantum theory and was awarded the Nobel Prize for physics in 1918.

**Albert Einstein (1879–1955)**  German physicist who developed the theory of relativity, which states that time, space, and mass are relative to each other and not fixed.

**Sigmund Freud (1856–1939)**  Austrian psychiatrist, founder of psychoanalysis. He argued that psychological problems were caused by traumas, especially sexual experiences in early childhood, that were repressed in later life. His ideas caused considerable controversy among psychologists and in the general public. Although his views on repressed sexuality are no longer widely accepted, his psychoanalytic methods are still very influential.

**Rural Japan Before World War I** This village scene from Japan reflects the taste for landscapes and ordinary life typical of the earliest photographers in Japan, both European and Japanese. The popularity of such scenes in earlier colored woodcuts may have influenced the choice of such subjects.

"The primitive, savage and evil impulses have not vanished from any individual, but continue their existence, although in a repressed state,"[2] he warned. Meanwhile, sociologists and anthropologists had begun the empirical study of societies, both Western and non-Western. Before the war the French sociologist Emile Durkheim (1858–1917) had come to the then shocking conclusion that "there are no religions that are false. All are true after their own fashion."[3]

If the words *primitive* and *savage* applied to Europeans as well as to other peoples, and if religions were all equally "true," then what remained of the superiority of Western civilization? Cultural relativism, as the new approach to human societies was called, could be as unnerving as relativity in physics.

## The New Technologies of Modernity

In North America, even working-class people could afford some of the new products of inventors' ingenuity. Mass consumption lagged in Europe, but science and technology were just as advanced, and public fascination with the latest inventions—the cult of the modern—was just as strong.

No innovation attracted more public interest more than airplanes. In 1903, two young American mechanics, **Wilbur and Orville Wright**, built the first aircraft that was heavier than air and could be maneuvered in flight. From that moment on airplanes fascinated people. During the Great War, the exploits of air aces relieved the tedium of news from the front.

The first flight of **KLM Royal Dutch Airlines**, the oldest continuously operating airline, took off in 1920. That year it carried 440 passengers and 22 tons of cargo. Its most important service as an air link to the Dutch East Indies (now Indonesia) began in 1929. Every country with imperial possessions saw international air service as a political necessity.

Electricity's impact on home life was more sweeping. The first home use of electricity was for lighting, thanks to the economical and long-lasting incandescent bulb (see Chapter 24). Then electrical utilities joined manufacturers in advertising electric irons, fans, washing machines, hot plates, radios, and other electrical appliances. After the war, radio moved from the battlefield into the home. The first commercial station began broadcasting in Pittsburgh in 1920. By 1930, hundreds of stations were broadcasting news, sports, soap operas, and advertisements to 12 million homes in North America. Another medium that spread explosively in the 1920s was film. Motion pictures had begun in France in 1895 and flourished in Europe. In the United States, filmmaking started at almost the same time, but American filmmakers saw the medium's potential to entertain audiences rather than preserve outstanding theatrical performances. After World War I, filmmaking took root and flourished in

[2]Ragnhild Fiebig von Hase and Ursula Lehmkuhl, *Enemy Images in American History* (Oxford: Berghahn Books, 1997), 5.

[3]Sigmund Freud, *Three Contributions to the Theory of Sex*, tran. A. A. Brill, 2 ed. (Washington: Nervous and Mental Health Disease Publishing Company, 1920), 40.

**Wilbur (1867–1912) and Orville (1871–1948) Wright** American bicycle mechanics; the first to build and fly an airplane, at Kitty Hawk, North Carolina, December 7, 1903.

**KLM Royal Dutch Airlines** Oldest major airline, operating since 1920 in Europe and connecting to the Dutch East Indies in 1929.

## New Materials

Nineteenth-century commerce brought many raw materials from European colonies and other far-away places into industrial use. Examples include rubber, a Southeast Asian tree sap called gutta-percha used for electrical insulation, Central Asian camel's hair used for transmission belts, and whale oil for lighting. These exotic materials were valuable, but they did not change the age-old pattern of almost every useful item being manufactured from natural substances.

The first half of the twentieth century saw a revolutionary change in this pattern. Metallurgists and chemists led the way in creating new materials that wrought permanent changes in the look and feel of everyday life. Materials science would go on to become one of the most important areas of technical innovation in later decades.

Though aluminum follows oxygen and silicon as the third most abundant element, it combines so readily with other elements that it was not discovered until 1827. Initially as precious as silver, a 2.4-kilogram piece was installed as the capstone of the Washington Monument in 1884. Four years later, however, almost simultaneously in the United States and France, an inexpensive electrolytic method of extracting the metal from bauxite ore was discovered. The lightweight, noncorrosive metal now became available for all manner of uses, from airplanes, beginning with a design by the German Hugo Junkers in 1917, to aluminum foil, which was invented in 1910.

Stainless steel, made by combining noncorrosive chromium with steel, was invented in 1912, and its many uses accustomed people to thinking of metal products as shiny. Electroplating with chromium came into use in 1924 in Germany and two years later in the United States. The shiny, rust-free metal, which could be deposited as a thin film on either a metallic or plastic base, found numerous uses from musical instruments to automobiles.

Plastics were invented at about the same time. Alexander Parkes invented celluloid, a stable form of explosive guncotton—itself made by soaking fine cotton in sulfuric and nitric acids—and exhibited it at London's Great Exhibition in 1862. The first thermoplastic, it could be molded above a certain temperature but became solid when it cooled. It was used for detachable men's shirt collars,

imagebroker/Alamy

**Bakelite Jewelry**  *This pioneering plastic was so attractive that it was made into jewelry. However, its ease of manufacture, hardness, and resistance to electricity, heat, and chemicals suited it to thousands of other uses from clarinets to wire insulation to kitchenware. During World War II it was even considered as a replacement for the copper penny.*

ping-pong balls, and photographic film, but it was both fragile and flammable.

Belgian-born Leo Hendrik Baekeland invented Bakelite, a more durable plastic that was also attractive enough to be used for jewelry in 1907. Five years later the Swiss chemist Jacques E. Brandenberger, trying to discover a way of waterproofing cloth, experimented with a cellulose-based coating that failed to stick to the cloth and instead peeled off in a clear sheet. Thus was cellophane invented. In the 1930s an American, Richard Drew, coated cellophane with adhesive and Scotch tape was born.

And there were others. Silklike rayon, 1904; isoprene synthetic rubber, 1909; vinyl, 1926; neoprene synthetic rubber, 1931; plexiglass, 1933; nylon, 1935; Lucite, 1936; fiberglass, 1938—the list goes on, with even more new materials being developed in the later decades of the century.

### QUESTIONS FOR ANALYSIS

1. Why do we take for granted a material environment constructed from manufactured substances that did not even exist before 1900?
2. What are the objects we use every day made of?
3. Why did new materials find such broad acceptance?

Japan, India, Turkey, Egypt, and a suburb of Los Angeles, California, called Hollywood. American and European movie studios were both successful in exporting films, since silent movies presented no language problems. Then in 1927 the United States introduced the first "talking" motion picture, *The Jazz Singer*, which changed all the rules. Hollywood studios began the diffusion of American culture that has continued to this day.

Advances in medicine—some achieved in the war—saved many lives. Wounds were regularly disinfected, and **Marie Curie** (1867–1934), the French discoverer of x-rays, organized radiology vans to help army doctors diagnose fractures during the Great War. Cities built costly water supply and sewage treatment systems. By the 1920s indoor plumbing and flush toilets were becoming common even in working-class neighborhoods. Interest in cleanliness entered private life. Doctors and home economists bombarded women with warnings and advice on how to banish germs. Soap and appliance manufacturers filled women's magazines with advertisements for products to help keep homes and clothing spotless and meals fresh and wholesome. The decline in infant mortality and improvements in general health and life expectancy in this period owe as much to the cult of cleanliness as to advances in medicine.

**First Aluminum Airplane** From the Wright Brothers' first aircraft in 1903 down to the air battles of World War I, wood, cloth, and wire made up the wings and bodies of airplanes. Metals were too heavy for anything but engines and weapons until the German manufacturer Hugo Junkers designed the first aluminum flying machine, shown here, in 1917.

## Technology and the Environment

Two new technologies—the skyscraper and the automobile—transformed the urban environment even more radically than the railroad had done. At the end of the nineteenth century architects had begun to design ever-higher buildings using load-bearing steel frames and elevators. Major corporations in Chicago and New York competed to build the most daring buildings in the world, such as New York's fifty-five-story Woolworth Building (1912). A building boom in the late 1920s produced dozens of skyscrapers, culminating with the eighty-six-story Empire State Building in New York in 1932. In the 1920s the Swiss **Le Corbusier** (luh cor-booz-YEH) (1887–1965) outlined a new approach to architecture that featured simplicity of form, absence of surface ornamentation, easy manufacture, and inexpensive materials such as concrete and glass in what came to be known as the International Style.

Meanwhile, instead of being blamed for their exhaust emissions, automobiles were praised as the solution to urban pollution: as they replaced horse-drawn carts and carriages, tons of manure disappeared from city streets. The assembly line pioneered by Henry Ford in 1913 mass-produced vehicles in ever-greater volume and at falling prices. By 1929 the

**Marie Curie (1867–1934)** Twice winner of the Nobel Prize, the Polish Maria (Marie, in French) Sklodowska worked in Paris and, with her husband Pierre Curie, discovered the element radium and radioactivity, changing the knowledge of matter and the treatment of many diseases. In World War I, she convinced wealthy patrons to donate vehicles for use as X-Ray centers and traveled to aid doctors in detecting fractures and shrapnel in wounded soldiers.

**Le Corbusier (1887–1965)** Professional name of architect Charles-Éduard Jenneret who led a modernist movement away from surface decoration and toward form following function.

United States had one car for every five people. The most important environmental effect of automobiles was suburban sprawl. Middle-class families could now live in single-family homes too far apart to be served by public transportation, and cities acquired rings of automobile suburbs. It was less common for Europeans to own automobiles; their premodern narrow streets adapted less easily to passenger automobiles. In the countryside outside European cities, however, high-speed expressways—*autostrada* in Italy and *autobahn* in Germany—became sources of national pride.

Technological advances also transformed rural economies. In 1915 Ford introduced a gasoline-powered tractor, and by the mid-1920s these versatile machines began replacing horses. Larger farms profited most from this innovation, while small farmers sold their land and moved to the cities. Tractors and other expensive equipment hastened the transformation of agriculture from family enterprises to larger businesses, or in the USSR to collective farms with state-owned tractor stations (see Chapter 27).

In India, Australia, Latin America, and the western United States, engineers built dams and canals to generate electricity, control floods, and irrigate dry lands. The immediate benefits of dams and irrigation far outweighed such distant consequences as salt deposits on irrigated lands and harm to fishing industries.

## SECTION REVIEW

- Government bureaucracies and the middle class grew after the war, but not the working class.
- In many countries, women gained the right to vote and led reform movements.
- Max Planck and Albert Einstein led a revolution in physics.
- Social scientists like Sigmund Freud undermined the old certainties of European culture by revealing a dark side to human nature.
- After the Wright brothers' first flight, other aviation pioneers set flying records.
- Electricity, radio, and cinema changed lifestyles and cultures, and the cult of cleanliness improved health.
- American cities were transformed by skyscrapers, and the automobile led to the creation of suburbs.

# A NEW INDIA, 1905–1947

■ *Why did the educated elites of India want independence? What were ordinary Indians hoping for?*

Some parts of the world, such as India, became much more involved in the emerging technologically oriented culture than others, such as sub-Saharan Africa (discussed later in this chapter). The consequences of this inequality of access to "modern" developments are still felt today.

Under British rule India acquired railroads, harbors, modern cities, and cotton and steel mills, as well as an active and worldly middle class. The economic transformation of the region awakened in this educated middle class a sense of national dignity that demanded political fulfillment. In response, the British gradually granted India limited political autonomy while maintaining overall control. Religious and communal tensions among the Indian peoples were carefully papered over, and when the British, exhausted by World War II (see Chapter 27), withdrew in 1947, violent conflicts tore India apart (see Map 26.1).

### The Land and the People

Despite periodic famines, notably between 1896 to 1900, when 2 million people died of starvation, the Indian population grew from 250 million in 1900 to 319 million in 1921 and 389 million in 1941. This growth caused landless young men to converge on the cities, exceeding the number of jobs available in the slowly expanding industries. Many of them entered the urban economy as rickshaw pullers. To produce timber for construction and railroad ties and to clear land for tea and rubber plantations, foresters cut down most of the tropical hardwood forests that had covered the subcontinent in the nineteenth century. In spite of deforestation and extensive irrigation, the amount of land available to peasant families shrank with each successive generation.

Economic development hardly benefited the average Indian. After paying rent to landowners, interest to village moneylenders, and taxes to the government, peasants—always the great majority—had little left to improve their land or raise their standard of living. The government protected property owners, from village moneylenders all the way up to the maharajahs (mah-huh-RAH-juh) or ruling princes, who

**Map 26.1  The Partition of India, 1947**  Before the British, India was divided among many states, ethnic groups, and religions. When the British left in 1947, the subcontinent split along religious lines. The predominantly Muslim regions in the northwest and East Bengal in the east formed the new nation of Pakistan. The predominantly Hindu center became the Republic of India. Jammu and Kashmir remained disputed territories and poisoned relations between the two new countries. © Cengage Learning

owned huge tracts of land. The cities were crowded with craftsmen, traders, and workers of all sorts, most very poor. Although the British had banned the burning of widows on their husbands' funeral pyres, in other respects women's lives changed little under British rule.

Indians also spoke many different languages. As a result of British rule, increasing trade and travel, and newspapers like *The Times of India*, established under that name in 1861, English became the common medium of communication for the Western-educated middle class. This new class of English-speaking bureaucrats, professionals, and

merchants was to play a leading role in the independence movement.

The majority of Indians practiced Hinduism and were subdivided into hundreds of castes (*jati*), each affiliated with a particular occupation. Hinduism discouraged intermarriage and other social interactions among the castes and with non-Hindus. Until displaced by the British in the eighteenth century, Muslim rulers had dominated northern and central India, and Muslims now constituted one-quarter of the Indian population but formed a majority in the northwest and in eastern Bengal. They felt discriminated against by both British and Hindus.

## British Rule and Indian Nationalism

Colonial India was ruled by a viceroy appointed by the British government and administered by a few thousand members of the Indian Civil Service. Drawn mostly from the English gentry, they liked to think of India as a land of lords and peasants. They believed it was their duty to protect the Indian people from the dangers of industrialization, while defending their own positions from Indian nationalists.

As Europeans they admired modern technology but tried to control its introduction into India so as to maximize the benefits to Britain and to themselves. For example, they encouraged railroads, harbors, telegraphs, and other communications technologies, as well as irrigation and plantations, because these increased India's foreign trade and strengthened British control. Yet, they discouraged the cotton and steel industries and limited the training of Indian engineers, ostensibly to spare India the social upheavals that had accompanied the Industrial Revolution in Europe, while actually protecting British industry from Indian competition.

At the turn of the century most Indians—especially peasants, landowners, and princes—accepted British rule. But the Europeans' racist attitude toward dark-skinned people increasingly offended Indians who had learned English and absorbed English ideas of freedom and representative government, only to discover that racial quotas excluded them from the Indian Civil Service, the officer corps, and prestigious country clubs.

In 1885 a small group of English-speaking Hindu professionals founded a political organization called the **Indian National Congress**. For twenty years its members respectfully petitioned the government for access to higher administrative positions and for a voice in official decisions, but they had little influence. Then, in 1905, Viceroy Lord Curzon divided the province of **Bengal** in two to improve the efficiency of its administration. This decision, made without consulting anyone, angered not only educated Indians, who saw it as a way to lessen their influence, but also millions of uneducated Hindu Bengalis, who found themselves outnumbered by Muslims in East Bengal. Soon Bengal was the scene of demonstrations, boycotts of British goods, and even incidents of anti-British violence.

Muslims, fearful of Hindu dominance elsewhere in India, founded the **All-India Muslim League** in 1906. The government responded by granting Indians a limited franchise based on wealth. Muslims, however, were on average poorer than Hindus, possibly because many poor and low-caste Hindus had converted to Islam to escape caste discrimination. Accordingly, the British instituted separate representation and different voting qualifications. Then, in 1911, the British transferred the capital of India from Calcutta to Delhi (DEL-ee), the former capital of the Mughal (MOO-guhl) emperors. These changes raised the political consciousness of all Indian classes and religions, giving rise to two mass movements: one by Hindus and one by Muslims.

Fearful of social upheavals, the British resisted the idea that India could, or should, industrialize. Their geologists looked for minerals like coal and manganese that British industry required. However, when the only Indian member of the Indian Geological Service, Pramatha Nath Bose, wanted to prospect for iron ore, he had to resign because the government wanted no part of an Indian steel industry that might compete with that of Britain. Bose joined forces with Jamsetji Tata, a Bombay textile magnate who decided to produce steel anyway. With the help of German and American engineers and equipment, Tata's son Dorabji opened the first steel mill in India in 1911, in a town called Jamshedpur in honor of his father. Although it produced only a fraction of the steel that India required, Jamshedpur became a powerful symbol of Indian national pride.

**Indian National Congress**  A movement and political party founded in 1885 to demand greater Indian participation in government. Its membership was middle class, and its demands were modest until World War I. Led after 1920 by Mohandas K. Gandhi, it appealed increasingly to the poor and organized mass protests demanding self-government and independence.

**Bengal**  Region of northeastern India. It was the first part of India to be conquered by the British in the eighteenth century and remained the political and economic center of British India throughout the nineteenth century. The 1905 split of the province into predominantly Hindu West Bengal and predominantly Muslim East Bengal (now Bangladesh) sparked anti-British riots.

**All-India Muslim League**  Political organization founded in India in 1906 to defend the interests of India's Muslim minority. Led by Muhammad Ali Jinnah, it attempted to negotiate with the Indian National Congress. In 1940, the League began demanding a separate state for Muslims, to be called Pakistan.

During World War I Indians supported Britain enthusiastically; 1.2 million men volunteered for the army, and millions more voluntarily contributed money to the government. Many expected the British to reward their loyalty with political concessions. Others organized to demand a voice in the government. Responding to the agitation, the British government announced in 1917 "the gradual development of self-governing institutions with a view to the progressive realization of responsible government in India as an integral part of the British Empire." This sounded like a promise of self-government, but the timetable was so vague that nationalists denounced it as a devious maneuver to postpone India's independence.

On April 13, 1919, in the city of Amritsar, General Reginald Dyer ordered his troops to fire into a peaceful crowd of some 10,000 demonstrators, killing at least 379 and wounding 1,200. While waves of angry demonstrations swept over India, the British House of Lords voted to approve Dyer's actions, and a fund was raised in appreciation of his services. Indians interpreted these gestures as showing British contempt for their colonial subjects, effectively bringing to a close the period of gradual accommodation.

## Mahatma Gandhi and Militant Nonviolence

For the next twenty years, violent uprisings and harsh repression, possibly even war, seemed imminent. That the worst did not come to pass was due to **Mohandas K. Gandhi** (GAHN-dee) (1869–1948), a man known to his followers as "Mahatma," the "great soul."

Gandhi began life with every advantage. His wealthy family sent him to England for his education. After his studies he lived in South Africa and practiced law for the small Indian community there. During World War I he returned to India and was one of many Western-educated Hindu intellectuals who joined the Indian National Congress.

Unlike many radical political thinkers of his time, Gandhi denounced the popular ideals of power, struggle, and combat. Instead, inspired by both Hindu and Christian ideals, he preached the saintly virtues of *ahimsa* (uh-HIM-sah) (nonviolence) and *satyagraha* (suh-TYAH-gruh-huh) (the search for truth). He refused to countenance violence among his followers and called off several demonstrations when they turned violent.

In 1921 Gandhi gave up the Western-style suits worn by lawyers and the fine raiment of wealthy Indians and henceforth wore simple peasant garb: a length of homespun cloth below his waist (*dhoti*) and a shawl to cover his torso. He spoke for the farmers and the outcasts, whom he called *harijan* (HAH-ree-jahn), "children of God." He attracted ever-larger numbers of followers among the poor and the illiterate, who soon began to revere him; and he transformed the cause of Indian independence from an elite movement of the educated into a mass movement with a quasi-religious aura.

Gandhi was a brilliant political tactician and a master of public relations gestures; he also knew how to use the new media. In 1929, for instance, he led a few followers on an 80-mile (129-kilometer) walk, camped on a beach, and gathered salt from the sea in a blatant and well-publicized act of civil disregard for the government's monopoly on salt. But he discovered that unleashing the power of popular participation was one thing and controlling its direction was quite another. Within days of his "Walk to the Sea," demonstrations of support broke out all over India, in which the police killed a hundred demonstrators and arrested over sixty thousand.

Many times during the 1930s Gandhi threatened to fast "unto death," and several times he came close to death, to protest the violence of both the police and his followers and to demand independence. He was repeatedly arrested and spent a total of six years in jail. But every arrest made him more popular. He became an iconic figure not only in his own country but also in the Western media. In the words of historian Percival Spear, he made the British "uncomfortable in their cherished field of moral rectitude," and he gave Indians the feeling that theirs was the ethically superior cause.

**Mohandas K. Gandhi (1869–1948)** Leader of the Indian independence movement and advocate of nonviolent resistance. After being educated as a lawyer in England, he returned to India and became leader of the Indian National Congress in 1920. He appealed to the poor, led nonviolent demonstrations against British colonial rule, and was jailed many times. Soon after independence he was assassinated for attempting to stop Hindu-Muslim rioting.

**Gandhi's Salt March to the Sea**  Mohandas Gandhi, bareheaded and more simply dressed than his followers, led a march of 80 miles to collect sea salt in an act of civil disobedience. News photographs like this played a key role in popularizing his cause and displaying his saintly habits. To his left one man carries a sitar and another has a drum hanging from his shoulder.

## India Moves Toward Independence

In the 1920s, slowly and reluctantly, the British handed over control of "national" areas such as education, the economy, and public works to Indians. They also gradually admitted more Indians into the Civil Service and the officer corps. Economically, Indian politicians obtained the right to erect high tariff barriers against imports to protect India's infant industries. Behind these barriers, Indian entrepreneurs built plants to manufacture iron and steel, cement, paper, textiles, sugar, and other products. While early industrialization did not improve the lives of the Indian peasants or urban poor, it created a class of wealthy Indian businessmen who supported the Indian National Congress and its demands for independence. Though paying homage to Gandhi, they preferred his designated successor as leader of the Indian National Congress, **Jawaharlal Nehru** (NAY-roo) (1889–1964).

Unlike Gandhi, Nehru looked forward to creating a modern industrial India.

Congress politicians won regional elections but continued to be excluded from the viceroy's cabinet, the true center of power. When World War II began (see Chapter 27), Viceroy Lord Linlithgow declared war without consulting a single Indian. The Congress-dominated provincial governments resigned in protest and found that boycotting government offices increased their popular support. When the British offered to give India its independence once the war ended, Gandhi demanded full independence immediately. His "Quit India" campaign aroused popular

**Jawaharlal Nehru (1889–1964)**  Indian statesman who succeeded Mohandas K. Gandhi as leader of the Indian National Congress. He negotiated the end of British colonial rule in India and became India's first prime minister (1947–1964).

demonstrations against the British and provoked a wave of arrests, including his own.

Most Indian soldiers felt they were fighting to defend their country rather than to support the British Empire. As in World War I, Indians contributed heavily to the Allied war effort, supplying 2 million soldiers and enormous amounts of resources, especially the timber needed for emergency construction. A small number of Indians were so anti-British that they joined the Japanese side.

## Partition and Independence

When the war ended, Britain's new Labor Party government prepared for Indian independence, but deep suspicions between Hindus and Muslims complicated the process. The break between the two communities had started in 1937, when the Indian National Congress won provincial elections and refused to share power with the Muslim League. In 1940 the leader of the League, **Muhammad Ali Jinnah** (JIH-nah) (1876–1948), demanded what many Muslims had been dreaming of for years: a country of their own, to be called Pakistan.

As independence approached, talks between Jinnah and Nehru broke down and violent rioting between Hindus and Muslims broke out. Gandhi's appeals for tolerance and cooperation fell on deaf ears. The British made frantic proposals to keep India united, but their authority was waning fast.

In early 1947 the Indian National Congress accepted the partition of India into two states, one secular but dominated by Hindus, the other Muslim. On August 15 British India gave way to a new India and Pakistan. The Indian National Congress, led by Nehru, formed the first government of India; Jinnah and the Muslim League established a government for the provinces that made up Pakistan.

Violent clashes between Muslims and Hindus marred any celebration of independence. Throughout the land, Muslim and Hindu neighbors turned on one another, and armed members of one faith hunted down people of the other faith. For centuries Hindus and Muslims had intermingled throughout most of India. Now, leaving most of their possessions behind, Hindus fled from predominantly Muslim areas, and Muslims fled from Hindu areas. Trainloads of desperate refugees

were attacked and massacred by members of the opposite faith. Within a few months some 12 million people had abandoned their ancestral homes and a half-million lay dead. In January 1948 Gandhi died too, gunned down by an angry Hindu refugee.

When the dust cleared, few Hindus remained in Pakistan, and Muslims were a minority in all but one state of India. That state was Kashmir, a strategically important region in the foothills of the Himalayas. India annexed Kashmir because the local maharajah was Hindu and because the state held the headwaters of the rivers that irrigated millions of acres of Indian farmland. The majority of the inhabitants of Kashmir were Muslims, however, and would have joined Pakistan if they had been allowed to choose. The annexation of Kashmir turned India and Pakistan into bitter enemies that fought several wars over the next half century.

**SECTION REVIEW**

- The inequities of British rule caused the rising class of English-speaking Indian professionals to create an independence movement.
- Changes in colonial administration and voting rights played upon religious divisions and created parallel Hindu and Muslim political movements.
- World War I and its aftermath stimulated nationalist agitation, which turned violent after the Amritsar Massacre.
- Employing militant nonviolence, Gandhi built a morally charged mass independence movement.
- Under Nehru's leadership, Indians pushed for greater independence, but World War II subordinated India to British interests.
- After gaining independence, India split into two states, and violence erupted between Hindus and Muslims.

**Muhammad Ali Jinnah (1876–1948)** Indian Muslim politician who founded the state of Pakistan. A lawyer by training, he joined the All-India Muslim League in 1913. As leader of the League from the 1920s on, he negotiated with the British and the Indian National Congress for Muslim participation in Indian politics. From 1940 on, he led the movement for the independence of India's Muslims in a separate state of Pakistan, founded in 1947.

# MEXICO, ARGENTINA, AND BRAZIL, 1917–1949

■ *How did the most powerful Latin American economies and political cultures change in the aftermath of World War I?*

Though some parts of the world, notably Latin America, were untouched by the fighting, they were still struck by the disruptions of the postwar period. After a decade of violence that saw revolutionaries turn into political leaders only to be assassinated in the new Republic of Mexico (see Chapter 23), former general and interior minister Plutarco Elías Calles (KAH-yace) was elected president and served from 1924 to 1928. Calles reinvigorated the revolutionary principles of an exhausted country. He founded the National Revolutionary Party, or PNR (the abbreviation of its name in Spanish), which governed the country from 1929 to 2000, becoming a symbol for populist reform and a forum where all the pressure groups and vested interests—labor, peasants, businessmen, landowners, the military, and others—worked out compromises.

**Lázaro Cárdenas** (LAH-sah-roe KAHR-dih-nahs), chosen by Calles to be president in 1934, brought peasants' and workers' organizations into the party, removed generals from government positions, and implemented the reforms promised in the constitution. Cárdenas redistributed 44 million acres (17.6 million hectares) to peasant communes, replaced church-run schools with government schools, and nationalized the railroads and other businesses.

Most dramatic was the expropriation of foreign-owned oil companies. In the early 1920s Mexico was the world's leading producer of oil, but a handful of American and British companies exported almost all of it. In 1938 Cárdenas seized the foreign-owned oil industry, which had gained importance with the wartime recognition that modern armies ran on gasoline. The American and British oil companies expected their governments to come to their rescue, perhaps with military force. But Mexico and the United States chose to resolve the issue through negotiation, and Mexico retained control of its oil.

The Royal Navy was now set to continue its rule of the seas undaunted by supply problems, but Britain's strategic security had become dependent on control of Iran, a nominally independent country, and of Iraq, a part of the Ottoman Empire. Oil supplies had become an essential feature of world military calculations, and with the accelerating spread of motorized land transport after World War I, the civilian economies of the industrialized world became equally dependent.

This dependency lies behind a myriad of military and political decisions made over the subsequent decades, making the division between producing countries with surplus oil to sell and consuming countries reliant on a steady supply of imported fuel a crucial factor in world affairs.

When Cárdenas's term ended in 1940, Mexico was still a land of poor farmers with a small industrial base, but the political system was free of both chaos and dictatorships. The wealthy few no longer monopolized land and resources; the military was tamed; the Catholic Church no longer controlled education; and the nationalization of oil had demonstrated Mexico's independence.

## The Transformation of Argentina

Most of Argentina consists of *pampas* (POM-pus), flat, fertile land that is easy to till, much like the prairies of the midwestern United States and Canada. Throughout the nineteenth century, Argentina's economy was based on two exports, the hides of longhorn creole cattle and the wool of merino sheep, which roamed the pampas in huge herds. At the end of the nineteenth century railroads and refrigerator ships that transported meat safely changed not only the composition of Argentina's exports but also the way they were produced. European consumers preferred the soft flesh of Lincoln sheep and Hereford cattle to the tough, sinewy meat of creole cattle and marino sheep. The valuable Lincolns and Herefords, however, had to be carefully bred and receive a diet of alfalfa and oats. To safeguard them, the pampas had to be divided, cultivated, and fenced with barbed wire. Once fenced, the

**Lázaro Cárdenas (1895–1970)** President of Mexico (1934–1940). He brought major changes to Mexican life by distributing millions of acres of land to the peasants, bringing representatives of workers and farmers into the inner circles of politics, and nationalizing the oil industry.

land could be used to produce wheat as well as beef and mutton. Within a few years grasslands that had stretched to the horizon were transformed into farmland. Like the North American Midwest, the pampas became one of the world's great producers of wheat and meat.

Argentina's government represented the interests of the *oligarquía* (oh-lee-gar-KEE-ah), a very small group of wealthy landowners. They also owned fine homes in Buenos Aires (BWAY-nos EYE-res), a city that was built to resemble Paris, traveled frequently to Europe, and spent so lavishly the French coined the superlative "rich as an Argentine." Focused on producing wheat and meat, they were content to let British companies build Argentina's railroads, processing plants, and public utilities. In exchange for its agricultural exports, Argentina imported almost all its manufactured goods from Europe and the United States. So important were British interests in the Argentinean economy that English, not Spanish, was used on the railroads.

## Brazil and Argentina, to 1929

Before the First World War, Brazil produced most of the world's coffee and cacao, grown on vast estates, and natural rubber, gathered by Indians from rubber trees growing wild in the Amazon rain forest. Planters and rubber exporters made up Brazil's elite. Like their Argentinean counterparts, they spent extravagantly, building palaces in Rio de Janeiro (REE-oh day zhuh-NAIR-oh) and one of the world's most beautiful opera houses in Manaus (meh-NOWSE), deep in the Amazon. As in Argentina, British companies built railroads, harbors, and other infrastructure and imported most manufactured goods.

Both Argentina and Brazil had small but outspoken middle classes that demanded a share in government and looked to European models. The poor, at the bottom of the social pyramid, were mainly Spanish and Italian immigrants turned landless laborers and meat processors in Argentina and sharecroppers and plantation workers in Brazil, many descended from slaves.

Rubber exports collapsed after 1912, replaced by cheaper plantation rubber from Southeast Asia. The outbreak of war put an end to imports from Europe

as Britain and France focused all their industries on war production and Germany was cut off entirely. These disruptions weakened the landowning class. In Argentina the urban middle class obtained the secret ballot and universal male suffrage in 1916 and elected a liberal politician, **Hipólito Irigoyen** (ee-POH-lee-toe ee-ree-GO-yen), as president. To a certain extent, the United States replaced the European countries as suppliers of machinery and consumers of coffee. European immigrants built factories to manufacture textiles and household goods. Desperate for money to pay for the war, Great Britain sold many of its railroad, streetcar, and other companies to the governments of Argentina and Brazil.

South America prospered during the postwar years. Trade with Europe resumed; export prices for agricultural exports remained high; and both Argentina and Brazil used accumulated profits to industrialize and improve their transportation systems and public utilities. Nevertheless, workers and middle-class professionals demanded social reforms and a larger voice in politics. In Argentina, students' and workers' demonstrations were brutally crushed. In Brazil junior officers rebelled several times, calling for universal suffrage, social reforms, and freedom for labor unions. Though they accomplished little, these demonstrations laid the groundwork for later reformist movements. In neither country did the urban middle class take power away from the wealthy landowners. Instead, the two shared power at the expense of both landless peasants and urban workers.

Though Argentina and Brazil moved forward, new technologies again left them dependent on the advanced industrial countries. Brazilians are justly proud that the first person to fly an airplane outside the United States was Alberto Santos-Dumont, a Brazilian. But he did so in 1906 in France, where he lived most of his life and had access to engine manufacturers and technical assistance. Aviation reached Latin America after World War I, when European and American companies such as Aéropostale and

**Hipólito Irigoyen (1850–1933)** Argentine politician, president of Argentina from 1916 to 1922 and 1928 to 1930. The first president elected by universal male suffrage, he began his presidency as a reformer but later became conservative.

Pan American Airways introduced airmail service between cities and linked Latin America with the United States and Europe.

Before and during World War I, radio was used only for point-to-point communications. Transmitters powerful enough to send messages across oceans or continents were complex and expensive with antennas covering many acres. They used as much electricity as a small town.

Right after the war, the major powers scrambled to build powerful transmitters on every continent to take advantage of the boom in international business and news reporting. However, no Latin American country possessed the knowledge or funds to build its own transmitters. Four powerful radio companies—one British, one French, one German, and one American—formed a cartel to control all radio communications in Latin America. Thus, even as Brazil and Argentina were asserting state control over their railroads and older industries, as Mexico had done with its oil industry, the major industrial countries controlled the diffusion of the newer aviation and radio technologies.

## The Depression and the Vargas Regime in Brazil

The Depression hit Latin America as hard as Europe and the United States and was in many ways a more important turning point for the region than either world war. As long-term customers cut back their orders, the value of agricultural and mineral exports fell by two-thirds between 1929 and 1932. Argentina and Brazil could no longer afford imported manufactured goods. An imploding economy also undermined their shaky political systems. Like European countries, Argentina and Brazil veered toward authoritarianism.

In 1930 **Getulio Vargas** (jay-TOO-lee-oh VAR-gus) (1883–1954), a state governor, staged a coup and proclaimed himself president of Brazil. He proved to be a masterful politician. He wrote a new constitution that broadened the franchise and limited the president to one term. He also raised import duties and promoted national firms and state-owned enterprises, culminating in the construction of the Volta Redonda steel mill in the 1930s. By 1936 industrial

production had doubled, especially in textiles and small manufactures. Brazil was on its way to becoming an industrial country. Vargas's policy, called **import-substitution industrialization**, became a model for other Latin American countries attempting to break away from neocolonial dependency.

The industrialization of Brazil brought all the familiar environmental consequences. Powerful new machines allowed the reopening of old mines and the digging of new ones. Cities grew as poor peasants looking for work arrived from the countryside. In Rio de Janeiro and São Paulo (sow PAL-oh), the poor turned steep hillsides and vacant lands into immense *favelas* (feh-VEL-luhs) (slums) of makeshift shacks.

The countryside also was transformed. Scrubland was turned into pasture or planted in wheat, corn, and sugar cane. Even the Amazon rain forest—half of the land area of Brazil—was affected. In 1930 American industrialist Henry Ford invested $8 million to clear land along the Tapajós River and prepare it to become the site of the world's largest rubber plantation. Ford encountered opposition from Brazilian workers and politicians; the rubber trees proved vulnerable to diseases; and he had to abandon the project—but not before leaving 3 million acres (1.2 million hectares) denuded of trees.

Although Vargas instituted many reforms favorable to urban workers, he refused to take measures to help the millions of landless peasants or challenge the great landowners. Prohibited by his own constitution from being reelected in 1938, Vargas staged another coup, abolished the constitution, and instituted the

**Getulio Vargas (1883–1954)**  Dictator of Brazil from 1930 to 1945 and from 1951 to 1954. Constitutionally barred from another term in 1938 and fearful of a military takeover, he suspended elections and created Estado Novo ("New State"), a dictatorship that emphasized industrialization and helped the urban poor but did little to alleviate the problems of the peasants.

**import-substitution industrialization**  An economic system aimed at building a country's industry by restricting foreign trade. It was especially popular in Latin American countries such as Mexico, Argentina, and Brazil in the mid-twentieth century. It proved successful for a time but could not keep up with technological advances in Europe and North America.

Estado Novo (esh-TAH-doe NO-vo), or "New State," with himself as supreme leader. He abolished political parties, jailed opposition leaders, and turned Brazil into a fascist state, though one that contributed troops and ships to the Allied war effort once the Second World War broke out.

### Argentina After 1930

Economically, the Depression hurt Argentina badly. Politically, however, the consequences were delayed. In 1930 General José Uriburu (hoe-SAY oo-ree-BOO-roo) overthrew the popularly elected President Irigoyen. For thirteen years the generals and the oligarchy ruled, doing nothing to lessen the poverty of the workers or the frustrations of the middle class. When World War II broke out, Argentina remained officially neutral.

In 1943 another military revolt flared, this one among junior officers led by Colonel **Juan Perón** (hoo-AHN pair-OWN) (1895–1974). The intentions of the rebels were clear:

> Civilians will never understand the greatness of our ideal; we shall therefore have to eliminate them from the government and give them the only mission which corresponds to them: work and obedience.[4]

Once in power the officers took over the highest positions in government and business and began to lavish money on military equipment and their own salaries. Their goal, inspired by Nazi victories, was nothing less than the conquest of South America.

As the war turned against the Nazis, the officers saw their popularity collapse. Perón, however, had other plans. Inspired by his charismatic wife **Eva Duarte Perón** (AY-vuy doo-AR-tay pair-OWN) (1919–1952), he appealed to the urban workers. Eva became the champion of the *descamisados* (des-cah-mee-SAH-dohs), or "shirtless ones," and campaigned tirelessly for social

Bettmann/Corbis

**Juan and Eva Perón**  Juan Perón's presidency of Argentina (1946–1955) relied on his, and especially on his wife Eva's, popularity with the working class. To sustain their popularity, they often organized parades and demonstrations in imitation of the fascist dictators of Europe. This picture shows them riding in a procession in Buenos Aires in 1952.

**Juan Perón (1895–1974)**  President of Argentina (1946–1955, 1973–1974). As a military officer, he championed the rights of labor. Aided by his wife Eva Duarte Perón, he was elected president in 1946. He built up Argentinean industry, became very popular among the urban poor, but harmed the economy.

**Eva Duarte Perón (1919–1952)**  Wife of Juan Perón and champion of the poor in Argentina. She was a gifted speaker and popular political leader who campaigned to improve the life of the urban poor by founding schools and hospitals and providing other social benefits.

---

[4]George Blankenstein, *Perón's Argentina* (Chicago: Unversity of Chicago Press, 1953), 37.

benefits and for the cause of women and children. With his wife's help, Perón won the presidency in 1946 and created a populist dictatorship in imitation of the Vargas regime in Brazil.

Like Brazil and Mexico, Argentina industrialized rapidly under state sponsorship. Perón spent lavishly on social welfare projects as well as on the military, depleting the capital that Argentina had earned during the war. Though a skillful demagogue who played off the army against the navy and both against the labor unions, Perón could not create a stable government. When Eva died in 1952, he lost his political skills (or perhaps they were hers) and soon thereafter was overthrown in yet another military coup.

# SUB-SAHARAN AFRICA, 1900–1945

■ *Why was Africa so little involved in the transformations of that era?*

When nationalist movements threatened European rule in Asia in the early twentieth century, Africa was still being subjected to the economic and political forces of imperialism, but it would be a mistake to conclude that developments in Africa would have resembled those in India or China if imperialism had started sooner. Affected by a long history of racism, Europeans maintained that people who were accustomed to bare subsistence would work fewer hours if their pay was raised rather than strive to better their standard of living (the way European workers theoretically would). This theory stigmatized African labor and justified paying subsistence wages.

### Colonial Africa: Economic and Social Changes

Outside of Algeria, Kenya, and South Africa, few Europeans lived in Africa. In 1930 Nigeria, with a population of 20 million, was ruled by 386 British officials and by 8,000 policemen and military personnel, of whom 150 were European. Yet even such a small presence stimulated deep social and economic changes.

Since the turn of the century, the colonial powers had built railroads from coastal cities to mines and plantations in the interior to transport raw materials. But few Africans benefited from these changes. Colonial governments took lands from Africans and sold or leased them to European companies or to white settlers. Large European companies dominated wholesale commerce, while Indians, Greeks, and Syrians handled much of the retail trade.

Where land was divided into small farms, some Africans benefited from the boom. Farmers in the Gold Coast (now Ghana [GAH-nuh]) profited from the high price of cacao, as did palm-oil producers in Nigeria and coffee growers in East Africa. In most of Africa women played a major role in the retail trades, selling cloth, food, pots and pans, and other items in the markets. Many maintained their economic independence and kept their household finances separate from those of their husbands, following a custom that predated the colonial period.

For many Africans, however, economic development meant working in European-owned mines and plantations, often under compulsion. Colonial governments were eager to develop the resources of their territories but would not pay wages high enough to attract workers. Instead, they used their police powers to force Africans to work under harsh conditions for little or no pay. In the 1920s, when the government of French Equatorial Africa decided to build a railroad from Brazzaville to the Atlantic coast, a distance of 312 miles (502 kilometers), it drafted 127,000 men to carve a roadbed across mountains and through rain forests. Lacking adequate food, clothing, and medical care, 20,000 of them died, an average of 64 deaths per mile of track.

Eye Ubiquitous/SuperStock

**Making Palm Oil** Oil palms produce two products, a red palm oil squeezed from the pulpy fruit and a yellow palm kernel oil extracted from the fruit's seeds with a simple press. Because it stands up well to heat, it is widely used as a cooking oil and is a major export crop in West Africa and other tropical regions.

Europeans prided themselves on bringing modern health care to Africa; yet before the 1930s there was too little of it to help the majority of Africans, and other aspects of colonialism actually worsened public health. Migrants and soldiers spread syphilis, gonorrhea, tuberculosis, and malaria. Sleeping sickness and smallpox epidemics raged throughout Central Africa. In recruiting men to work, colonial governments also depleted rural areas of farmers needed to plant and harvest crops. Forced requisitions of food to feed the workers left the remaining populations undernourished and vulnerable to diseases. Not until the 1930s did colonial governments realize the negative consequences of their labor policies and begin to invest in agricultural development and health care for Africans.

In 1900 Ibadan (ee-BAH-dahn) in Nigeria was the only city in sub-Saharan Africa with more than 100,000 inhabitants; fifty years later, dozens of cities had reached that size. Africans migrated to cities because they offered hope of jobs and excitement and, for a few, the chance to become wealthy.

However, migrations damaged family life, for almost all the migrants were men leaving women in the countryside to farm and raise children. Cities built during the colonial period had racially segregated housing, clubs, restaurants, hospitals, and other institutions. Racial discrimination was most rigid in the white-settler colonies of eastern and southern Africa.

**Religious and Political Changes**

Traditional religious belief could not explain the dislocations that foreign rule, migrations, and sudden economic changes brought to the lives of Africans. Many therefore turned to Christianity or Islam for guidance.

Christianity, introduced into Africa by Western missionaries (except in Ethiopia, where it was indigenous), was most successful in West and South Africa, where the European influence was strongest. Mission schools, which taught both craft skills and basic literacy, provided access to employment as minor functionaries, teachers, and shopkeepers. These schools

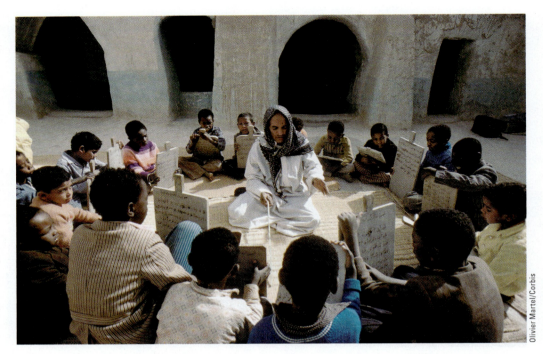

**A Quranic School**  In Muslim countries, religious education is centered on learning to read, write, and recite the Quran, the sacred book of the Islamic religion, in the original Arabic. This picture shows boys in a Libyan madrasa (Quranic school) studying writing and religion.

also imparted Western political ideas to a new educated elite. Many Africans read the suffering of their own peoples into the biblical stories of Moses and the parables of Jesus. The churches trained some pupils to become catechists, teachers, and clergymen. Independent Christian churches associated Christian beliefs with radical ideas of racial equality and political participation.

Islam spread inland from the East African coast and southward from the Sahel (SAH-hel) through the influence and example of Arab and African merchants. Islam also emphasized literacy—in Arabic rather than a European language—and was less disruptive of traditional African customs such as polygamy.

In a few places, such as Dakar in Senegal and Cape Town in South Africa, small numbers of Africans could obtain secondary education. Even smaller numbers went on to college in Europe or America. Though few in number, they became the leaders of political movements. The contrast between the liberal ideas imparted by Western education and the

realities of racial discrimination under colonial rule contributed to the rise of nationalism among educated Africans. In Senegal **Blaise Diagne** (dee-AHN-yuh) agitated for African participation in politics and fair treatment in the French army. In the 1920s J. E. Casely Hayford began organizing a movement for greater autonomy in British West Africa. In South Africa, Western-educated lawyers and journalists founded the **African National Congress** in 1912 to

**Blaise Diagne (1872–1934)**  Senegalese political leader. He was the first African elected to the French National Assembly. During World War I, in exchange for promises to give French citizenship to Senegalese, he helped recruit Africans to serve in the French army. After the war, he led a movement to abolish forced labor in Africa.

**African National Congress**  An organization dedicated to obtaining equal voting and civil rights for black inhabitants of South Africa. Founded in 1912 as the South African Native National Congress, it changed its name in 1923. Though it was banned and its leaders were jailed for many years, it eventually helped bring majority rule to South Africa.

## SECTION REVIEW

- Colonial rule developed Africa's economies at the expense of its peoples' livelihoods and health.

- Many Africans turned to Christianity or Islam; some, especially those who participated in World War II, began to demand independence.

- New media had little influence in Africa.

defend the interests of Africans. These nationalist movements were partly inspired by the ideas of Pan-Africanists from America such as W. E. B. Du Bois and Marcus Garvey, who advocated the unity of African peoples around the world. Before World War II, however, they were small and had little influence.

The new media of cinema and radio had little impact on Africa. The first attempts at radio broadcasting occurred in South Africa in 1924, and down to World War II, the South African Broadcasting Corporation established a monopoly over the medium and broadcast only in English and Afrikaans. Efforts in other colonies likewise targeted European listeners, with the exception of British West Africa—Sierra Leone, Ghana, and Nigeria—where African languages were utilized. After 1936 the British authorities began to see radio as a medium for reaching Africans who did not understand English. Africa also had almost no cinematic presence prior to World War II, apart from fourteen Tarzan films made in Hollywood between 1918 and 1949. A few films were made for British and Afrikaner audiences in South Africa, but the French issued a decree in 1934 prohibiting the shooting of movies.

During the Second World War (see Chapter 27) increased forced labor, inflation, and requisitions of raw materials had a profound effect even on Africans who were far removed from the theaters of war. Yet the war also brought hope. During the campaign to oust the Italians from Ethiopia, Emperor **Haile Selassie** (HI-lee seh-LASS-ee) (r. 1930–1974) led his own troops into Addis Ababa, his capital, and reclaimed his title. A million Africans served as soldiers and carriers in Burma, North Africa, and Europe. They listened to Allied propaganda in favor of European liberation movements and against Nazi racism and returned to their countries with new and radical ideas.

## CONCLUSION

The narratives of world war, global depression, and varying regional development do not incorporate the profound change in ways of living that affected most parts of the world, to a greater or lesser degree, between 1900 and 1950. Europe's colonies, and the nonindustrialized world in general, witnessed increases in political awareness and contact with the world at large that stemmed in large part from the adoption of new technologies like electricity and airplanes, but also from media technologies. The latter incorporated themes and images from local cultural sources and helped mold national consciousness.

The industrialized world experienced the same flood of new inventions but was more strongly affected at a popular level. Respect for science grew along with an expectation that science would continue indefinitely to improve human lives. This was the cult of the modern. Social science and a concern for social welfare, health, and the rights of women were part of this trend.

Imperialism being focused as always on benefits for the home country, colonial administrators in different parts of the world tried to control the flow of global technological and ideological changes. Having a larger and better-educated middle class than many other non-European lands, India entered more fully into the new ways of living than did sub-Saharan Africa. Political and cultural independence became a realizable goal in the former, where Mahatma Gandhi's nonviolent movement pioneered an entirely new form of political activism. In the latter region, however, European racism and the unwavering favoritism shown to European settlers stifled almost all attempts at change. In Latin America, economic imperialism similarly guaranteed that most benefits of the new revolutions in living would go to the wealthiest people.

**Haile Selassie (1892–1975)** Emperor of Ethiopia (r. 1930–1974) and symbol of African independence. He fought the Italian invasion of his country in 1935 and regained his throne during World War II, when British forces expelled the Italians. He ruled Ethiopia as a traditional autocracy until he was overthrown in 1974.

## CHAPTER REVIEW

### NEW TECHNOLOGY OUTSIDE THE INDUSTRIALIZED WORLD

■ *How were Asians and Africans impacted by technology and innovation differently from Europeans and Americans?* (page 607)

Outside the United States and Europe, innovations were adapted to local cultural conditions. India and Japan, for example, spawned their own film industries that reflected their own aesthetic traditions, while newsreels and photography were used to inform illiterate populations. These new media helped create a culturally cohesive identity. The rickshaw contributed to urbanization from Asia to Africa. These technologies were able to thrive locally because they were less expensive than technologies like railroads and steelmills.

### NEW WAYS OF LIVING IN THE INDUSTRIALIZED WORLD

■ *How did daily life and thought change in early-twentieth-century industrialized countries?* (page 609)

Many women who had participated in the war effort remained in the workforce and demanded voting and other rights. Governments took on new responsibilities for education, public health, and social welfare. Automobiles, movies, and radio broadcasts were eagerly adopted. Advances in the sciences, especially in physics and psychology, undermined the old cultural certainties, while birth control and family planning provoked considerable opposition from traditionalists.

### A NEW INDIA, 1905–1947

■ *Why did the educated elites of India want independence? What were ordinary Indians hoping for?* (page 614)

In the late nineteenth century, educated Indians began to resent the racist condescension with which they were treated by their colonial overlords. They believed that they could govern India and develop its economy better than the British could. Mahatma Gandhi's leadership of a powerful but non-violent independence movement galvanized both Hindus and Muslims. However, as British withdrawal neared, other political leaders played on religious identity and brought about a partition of the country.

### MEXICO, ARGENTINA, AND BRAZIL, 1917–1949

■ *How did the most powerful Latin American economies and political cultures change in the aftermath of World War I?* (page 620)

Three countries, Mexico, Brazil, and Argentina, contained well over half of Latin America's land, population, and wealth. Their societies remained deeply split between wealthy landowners and desperately poor peasants even after independence, and their economies remained dependent on foreign investment and the exchange of raw materials and agricultural products for foreign manufactured goods. World War I disrupted this trade, weakening the landowning classes, and workers and the middle class demanded reforms. However, the Depression, more than the war, brought about the most dramatic changes in Latin America. Dependence on foreign investment had made economic growth difficult to achieve, and democracy was fragile. Authoritarian leaders emerged who attempted to make Latin American countries more independent and to industrialize Latin American economies.

## SUB-SAHARAN AFRICA, 1900–1945
■ *Why was Africa so little involved in the transformations of that era?* (page 624)

Sub-Saharan Africa was still under colonial rule when the Northern Hemisphere was engulfed in the First and Second World Wars. Colonial powers built cities, railroads, harbors, mines, and plantations. But the new media was monopolized by Europeans or white settlers or prohibited altogether, while Africans were forced to provide labor at subsistence wages that kept workers from accruing the benefits of industrialization. Many turned to Christianity or Islam for spiritual guidance during these upheavals.

## Key Terms

Auguste (1862–1954) and Louis (1864–1948) Lumière (p. 608)

Margaret Sanger (p. 610)

Max Plank (p. 610)

Albert Einstein (p. 610)

Sigmund Freud (p. 610)

Wilbur and Orville Wright (p. 611)

KLM Royal Dutch Airlines (p. 611)

Marie Curie (p. 613)

Le Corbusier (p. 613)

Indian National Conference (p. 616)

Bengal (p. 616)

All-India Muslim League (p. 616)

Mohandas K. Gandhi (p. 617)

Jawaharlal Nehru (p. 618)

Muhammad Ali Jinnah (p. 619)

Lázaro Cárdenas (p. 620)

Hipólito Irigoyen (p. 621)

Getulio Vargas (p. 622)

import-substitution industrialization (p. 622)

Juan Perón (p. 623)

Eva Duarte Perón (p. 623)

Blaise Diagne (p. 626)

African National Congress (p. 626)

Haile Selassie (p. 627)

# CHAPTER 27

## 1929–1949

# The Collapse of the Old Order

© Cengage Learning

**CHAPTER PREVIEW**

### THE STALIN REVOLUTION
- *How did the Soviet Union change under Stalin?*

### THE DEPRESSION
- *What caused the Depression, and what effects did it have on the world?*

### THE RISE OF FASCISM
- *How did fascism in Italy and Germany lead to the Second World War?*

### EAST ASIA, 1931–1945
- *Why did Japan invade Manchuria?*

### THE SECOND WORLD WAR
- *How was the war fought, and why did Japan and Germany lose?*

### THE CHARACTER OF WARFARE
- *How did science and technology change the nature of warfare?*

### Conclusion

**DIVERSITY & DOMINANCE:** Women, Family Values, and the Russian Revolution

630

Before the First World War the Italian poet Filippo Marinetti exalted violence as noble and manly: "We want to glorify war, the world's only hygiene—militarism, deed, destroyer of anarchisms, the beautiful ideas that are death-bringing, and the subordination of women."[1] His friend Gabriele d'Annunzio added: "If it is a crime to incite citizens to violence, I shall boast of this crime."[2] Poets are sometimes more prescient than they imagine.

Most survivors of World War I had learned to abhor violence, and after the trauma of World War I, the world seemed to return to what U.S. president Warren Harding called "normalcy": prosperity in Europe and America, European colonialism in Asia and Africa, U.S. domination of Latin America, and peace almost everywhere. But in 1929 normalcy vanished. The Great Depression spread around the world, and for a few, war and domination became a creed, a goal, and a solution to their problems. Governments turned against one another in desperate attempts to protect their people's livelihood.

The Japanese military tried to save their country from the Depression by conquering China, which erupted in revolution. In Germany many blamed their troubles on communists and Jews and turned to the Nazis, who promised to save German society by crushing others. In the Soviet Union, Stalin used energetic and murderous means to force his country into a communist version of the Industrial Revolution.

As the old order collapsed, the world was engulfed by a second Great War, one far more global and destructive than World War I. In World War II, entire countries were conquered in a matter of weeks, fighter planes and bombers targeted civilians, and, finally, atomic bombs obliterated entire cities.

At the end of World War II much of Europe and East Asia lay in ruins, and millions of destitute refugees sought safety in other lands. The European colonial powers were either defeated or so weakened that

they could no longer prevent their Asian and African subjects from demanding independence.

## THE STALIN REVOLUTION

■ *How did the Soviet Union change under Stalin?*

After **Joseph Stalin** (1879–1953) achieved total mastery over the USSR in 1929 (see Chapter 25), he led it through an economic and social transformation that turned it into a great industrial and military power and intensified both admiration for and fear of communism throughout the world.

### Five-Year Plans

Stalin's ambition to turn the USSR into an industrial nation was not intended initially to produce consumer goods for a mass market or enrich individuals. Instead, his aim was to increase the power of the Communist Party domestically and that of the Soviet Union in relation to other countries. By building up Russia's industry, Stalin was determined to prevent a repetition of the humiliating defeat Russia had suffered at the hands of Germany in 1917.

Stalin encouraged rapid industrialization through a series of **Five-Year Plans**, a system of centralized control copied from the German experience or World War 1. The goal of the first Five-Year Plan was to quintuple the output of electricity and double that of heavy industry: iron, steel, coal, and machinery. Beginning in October 1928, the Communist government created whole industries and cities from scratch, then trained millions of peasants to work in the new factories, mines, and offices. In every way except actual fighting, Stalin's Russia resembled a nation at war.

Rapid industrialization hastened environmental changes. Hydroelectric dams turned rivers into

---

[1]Apollonio Umbro, ed., *Documents of Twentieth Century Art: Futurist Manifestos* (New York: Viking Press, 1973), 23.
[2]Richard F. Hamilton and Holger H. Herwig, *Decisions for War, 1914–1917* (Cambridge: Cambridge University Press, 2004), 199.

**Joseph Stalin (1879–1953)** Bolshevik revolutionary, head of the Soviet Communist Party after 1924, and dictator of the Soviet Union from 1928 to 1953. He led the Soviet Union with an iron fist, using Five-Year Plans to increase industrial production and terror to crush all opposition.

**Five-Year Plans** Plans that Joseph Stalin introduced to industrialize the Soviet Union rapidly, beginning in 1928. They set goals for the output of steel, electricity, machinery, and most other products and were enforced by the police powers of the state. They succeeded in making the Soviet Union a major industrial power before World War II.

strings of reservoirs. Roads, canals, and railroad tracks cut the landscape. Forests and grassland were turned into farmland. From an environmental perspective, the Five-Year Plans resembled the transformation that had occurred in the United States and Canada a few decades earlier.

## Collectivization of Agriculture

Since the Soviet Union was still a predominantly agrarian country, the only way to pay for these massive investments, provide the labor, and feed the millions of new industrial workers was to squeeze the peasantry. Stalin therefore proceeded with the most radical social experiment conceived up to that time: the collectivization of agriculture.

Collectivization meant consolidating small private farms into vast collectives and making the farmers work together in commonly owned fields. Each collective was expected to supply the government with a fixed amount of food and distribute what was left among its members. Collectives were to become outdoor factories through the techniques of mass production and the use of machinery. Collectivization was expected to bring the peasants once and for all under government control so they never again could withhold food supplies, as they had done during the period of Lenin's New Economic Policy (see Chapter 25).

The government mounted a massive propaganda campaign to enlist the farmers' support. At first all seemed to go well, but soon *kulaks* (COO-lock) ("fists"), the better-off peasants, began to resist giving up all their property. When soldiers came to force them into collectives at gunpoint, they burned their crops, smashed their equipment, and slaughtered their livestock. Within a few months they slaughtered half of the Soviet Union's horses and cattle and two-thirds of the sheep and goats. In retaliation, Stalin ruthlessly ordered the "liquidation of kulaks as a class" and incited the poor peasants to attack their wealthier neighbors. Over 8 million kulaks were arrested. Many were executed, and the rest were sent to slave labor camps, where most starved to death.

The peasants who were left had been the least successful before collectivization and proved to be the least competent after. Many were sent to work in factories. The rest were forbidden to leave their

Poster concerning the 1st 5 Year Plan with a photograph of Joseph Stalin 1879-1953), 'At the end of the Plan, the basis of collectivization must be completed', 1932 (colour litho), Klutchis (fl.1932)/Deutsches Plakat Museum, Essen, Germany/Archives Charmet/The Bridgeman Art Library

**The Collectivization of Soviet Agriculture**  One of the goals of collectivization was to introduce modern farm machinery. This poster highlights Josef Stalin's personal connection with mechanization. The tractors and operators were assigned to tractor stations, which then supplied them to individual collective farms.

farms. With half of their draft animals gone, they could not plant or harvest enough to meet the swelling demands of the cities. Yet government agents took whatever they could find, leaving little or nothing for the farmers themselves. After bad harvests in 1933 and 1934, a famine swept through the countryside, killing some 5 million people, about one in every twenty farmers.

Stalin's second Five-Year Plan, designed to run from 1933 to 1937, was originally intended to produce consumer goods. But when the Nazis took over Germany in 1933 (discussed later in this chapter), Stalin changed the plan to emphasize heavy industries that could produce armaments. Between 1927 and 1937, the Soviet output of metals and machines increased fourteen-fold while consumer goods became scarce and food was rationed. After a decade of Stalinism, the Soviet people were more poorly clothed, fed, and

# Chronology

| | United States, Europe, and North Africa | Asia and the Pacific |
|---|---|---|
| 1920 | **1928** Stalin introduces Five-Year Plans and the collectivization of agriculture<br>**1929** Great Depression begins in United States | |
| 1930 | **1931** Great Depression reaches Europe<br>**1933** Hitler comes to power in Germany | **1931** Japanese forces occupy Manchuria<br>**1934–1935** Mao leads communists on Long March |
| 1935 | | **1937** Japanese troops invade China, conquer coastal provinces; Chiang Kai-shek flees to Sichuan<br>**1937–1938** Japanese troops take Nanjing |
| | **1939** (Sept. 1) German forces invade Poland | |
| 1940 | **1940** (March–April) German forces conquer Denmark, Norway, the Netherlands, and Belgium<br>**1940** (May–June) German forces conquer France<br>**1940** (June–Sept.) Battle of Britain<br>**1941** (June 21) German forces invade USSR | **1941** (Dec. 7) Japanese aircraft bomb Pearl Harbor<br>**1942** (Jan.–March) Japanese conquer Thailand, Philippines, Malaya<br>**1942** (June) U.S. Navy defeats Japan at Battle of Midway |
| | **1942–1943** Allies and Germany battle for control of North Africa<br>**1943** Soviet victory in Battle of Stalingrad<br>**1943–1944** Red Army slowly pushes Wehrmacht back to Germany<br>**1944** (June 6) D-day: U.S., British, and Canadian troops land in Normandy | |
| 1945 | **1945** (May 7) Germany surrenders | **1945** (Aug. 6) United States drops atomic bomb on Hiroshima<br>**1945** (Aug. 14) Japan surrenders<br>**1945–1949** Civil war in China<br>**1949** (Oct. 1) Communists defeat Guomindang; Mao proclaims People's Republic of China |

housed than they had been before Lenin's New Economic Policy.

## Terror and Opportunities

The 1930s brought both terror and opportunities to the Soviet people. The forced pace of industrialization, the collectivization of agriculture, and the uprooting of millions of people could be accomplished only under duress. To prevent any possible resistance or rebellion, Stalin's secret police force created a climate of suspicion and fear.

First "Old Bolsheviks" and high officials were put on trial; then the terror spread steadily downward. The government regularly made demands that people could not meet, so everyone was guilty of breaking some regulation. People from all walks of life were arrested, some on mere suspicion or because of a false accusation by a jealous coworker or neighbor, some for expressing a doubt or working too hard or not hard enough, some for being related to someone previously arrested, some for no reason at all. Millions of people were sentenced without trials. At the height of the terror, some 8 million were sent to *gulags* (GOO-log) (labor camps), where perhaps a million died each year of exposure or malnutrition. To its victims the terror seemed capricious and random.

Yet Stalin's regime received the support of many Soviet citizens. Suddenly, with so many people gone and new industries and cities being built everywhere, there were opportunities for those who remained, especially the poor and the young. Women entered careers and jobs previously closed to them, becoming steelworkers, physicians, and office managers; but they retained their household and child-rearing duties, receiving little help from men (see Diversity and Dominance: Women, Family Values, and the Russian Revolution). People who moved to the cities, worked enthusiastically, and asked no questions could hope to rise into the upper ranks of the Communist Party, the military, the government, or the professions—where the privileges and rewards were many.

Stalin's brutal methods helped the Soviet Union industrialize faster than any country had ever done. By the late 1930s the USSR was the world's third largest industrial power, after the United States and Germany. To foreign observers it seemed to be booming with construction projects and labor shortages. Even anti-Communist observers admitted that government planning worked. To millions of Soviet citizens who took pride in the new strength of their country, and to many foreigners who contrasted conditions in the Soviet Union with the unemployment and despair in the West, Stalin's achievement seemed worth any price.

# THE DEPRESSION

■ *What caused the Depression, and what effects did it have on the world?*

On October 24, 1929—"Black Thursday"—the New York stock market went into a dive. Within days stocks had lost half their value. Their value continued to fall for three years. Thousands of banks and businesses collapsed. Millions of workers lost their jobs. The stock market crash started the deepest and most widespread depression in history.

**Economic Crisis** As consumers reduced their purchases, businesses cut production, laying off thousands of workers. Female employees were the first laid off on the grounds that men had to support families while women worked only for "pin money." Jobless men deserted their families. Small farmers went bankrupt and lost their land. By mid-1932 the American economy had shrunk by half, and 25 percent of the workforce was unemployed. Many observers thought that free-enterprise capitalism was doomed.

In 1930 the U.S. government, hoping to protect American industries from foreign competition, imposed the highest import duty in American history. In retaliation, other countries also raised their tariffs. As a result, global industrial production declined by 36 percent between 1929 and 1932, while world trade dropped by a breathtaking 62 percent.

**Depression in Industrial Nations** This massive economic upheaval had profound political repercussions. In the United States, Franklin D. Roosevelt was elected president in 1932 on a "New Deal" platform of government programs to stimulate and revitalize the economy. British and French governments also intervened in their economies, and they remained democratic. In Germany and Japan, as economic grievances worsened long-festering political resentments, radical leaders came to power and turned their nations into military machines, hoping to acquire, by war if necessary, empires large enough to support self-sufficient economies.

**Depression in Nonindustrial Regions** The Depression affected Asia, Africa, and Latin America, but very unevenly. Because a wall of new import duties protected India's infant industries from foreign competition, living standards stagnated but did not drop. The Depression added little to China's problems, which were more political than economic.

However, countries that depended on exports were hard hit by the Depression. When automobile production dropped by half in the United States and Europe, so did imports of rubber, devastating the economies of Southeast Asia. Egypt, dependent on cotton exports, was also affected, and in the resulting political strife, the government became autocratic and unpopular. The industrialization of Argentina and Brazil was set back a decade or more by the loss of export markets, and in response, military officers seized power in several Latin American countries, consciously imitating dictatorships emerging in Europe (see Chapter 26).

Southern and Central Africa recovered from the Depression quickly because falling prices made their gold and other minerals more valuable. But this mining boom benefited only a small number of mine owners and investors. For Africans, it was a mixed blessing, for mining provided men with jobs and cash wages, while women stayed behind in the villages to manage without their husbands' help.

**SECTION REVIEW**

- The New York stock market crash of 1929 caused business and bank failures and massive unemployment.

- The Depression soon spread to all industrial nations, especially Germany and Japan.

- Nonindustrial countries, especially those that depended on exports to industrial countries, were also hard hit; only southern and central Africa were spared.

- In the face of this threat, some countries turned to dictatorship to save their economies.

## THE RISE OF FASCISM

■ *How did fascism in Italy and Germany lead to the Second World War?*

The Russian Revolution and its Stalinist aftermath frightened property owners in Europe and North America. In western Europe and North America, middle- and upper-income voters took refuge in conservative politics. In southern and central Europe,

**Two Views of the American Way**  In this classic photograph, *Life* magazine photographer Margaret Bourke-White captured the contrast between advertisers' view of the ideal American family and the reality of bread lines for the poor.

Time Life Pictures/Getty Images

## Women, Family Values, and the Russian Revolution

The Bolsheviks were of two minds on the subject of women. They were opposed to bourgeois morality and to the oppression of women, especially working-class women, under capitalism. But what to put in its place?

Alexandra Kollontai was the most outspoken of the Bolsheviks on the subject of women's rights. She advocated the liberation of women, the replacement of housework by communal kitchens and laundries, and divorce on demand. Under socialism, love, sex, and marriage would be entirely equal, reciprocal, and free of economic obligations. Childbearing would be encouraged, but children would be raised communally: "The worker mother . . . must remember that there are henceforth only our children, those of the communist state, the common possession of all workers."

In a lecture she gave at Sverdlov University in 1921, Kollontai declared:

. . . it is important to preserve not only the interests of the woman but also the life of the child, and this is to be done by giving the woman the opportunity to combine labour and maternity. Soviet power tries to create a situation where a woman does not have to cling to a man she has learned to loathe only because she has nowhere else to go with her children, and where a woman alone does not have to fear for her life and the life of her child. In the labour republic it is not the philanthropists with their humiliating charity but the workers and peasants, fellow-creators of the new society, who hasten to help the working woman and strive to lighten the burden of motherhood. . . . I would like to say a few words about a question which is closely connected with the problem of maternity—the question of abortion, and Soviet Russia's

attitude toward it. On 20 November 1920 the labour republic issued a law abolishing the penalties that had been attached to abortion. What is the reason behind this new attitude? Russia after all suffers not from an overproduction of living labour but rather from a lack of it. Russia is thinly, not densely populated. Every unit of labour power is precious. Why then have we declared abortion to be no longer a criminal offence? . . .

Abortion exists and flourishes everywhere, and no laws or punitive measures have succeeded in rooting it out. A way round the law is always found. But "secret help" only cripples women; they become a burden on the labour government, and the size of the labour force is reduced. Abortion, when carried out under proper medical conditions, is less harmful and dangerous, and the woman can get back to work quicker. Soviet power realizes that the need for abortion will only disappear on the one hand when Russia has a broad and developed network of institutions protecting motherhood and providing social education, and on the other hand when women understand that *childbirth is a social obligation*; Soviet power has therefore allowed abortion to be performed openly and in clinical conditions.

Besides the large-scale development of motherhood protection, the task of labour Russia is to strengthen in women the healthy instinct of motherhood, to make motherhood and labour for the collective compatible and thus do away with the need for abortion. This is the approach of the labour republic to the question of abortion, which still faces women in the bourgeois countries in all its magnitude. In these countries women are exhausted by the dual burden of hired labour for capital and motherhood. In Soviet Russia the working woman and peasant woman are helping the Communist Party to build a new society and to undermine the old way of life that has enslaved women. As soon as woman is viewed as being essentially a labour unit, the key to the solution of the complex question ➤

of maternity can be found. . . . The emancipation of women can only be completed when a fundamental transformation of living is effected; and life-styles will change only with the fundamental transformation of all production and the establishment of a communist economy. The revolution in everyday life is unfolding before our very eyes, and in this process the liberation of women is being introduced in practice.

*Fifteen years later Joseph Stalin reversed the Soviet policy on abortion.*

The published draft of the law prohibiting abortion and providing material assistance to mothers has provoked a lively reaction throughout the country. It is being heatedly discussed by tens of millions of people and there is no doubt that it will serve as a further strengthening of the Soviet family. . . .

When we speak of strengthening the Soviet family, we are speaking precisely of the struggle against the survivals of a bourgeois attitude towards marriage, women, and children. So-called "free love" and all disorderly sex life are bourgeois through and through, and have nothing to do with either socialist principles or the ethics and standards of conduct of the Soviet citizens. Socialist doctrine shows this, and it is proved by life itself.

The elite of our country, the best of the Soviet youth, are as a rule also excellent family men who dearly love their children. And vice versa: the man who does not take marriage seriously, and abandons his children to the whims of fate, is usually also a bad worker and a poor member of society. . . .

It is impossible even to compare the present state of the family with that which obtained before the Soviet regime—so great has been the improvement towards greater stability and, above all, greater humanity and goodness. The single fact that millions of women have become economically independent and are no longer at the mercy of men's whims, speaks volumes. Compare, for instance, the modern woman collective farmer who sometimes earns more than her husband, with the pre-revolutionary peasant woman who completely depended on her husband

and was a slave in the household. Has not this fundamentally changed family relations, has it not rationalized and strengthened the family? The very motives for setting up a family, for getting married, have changed for the better, have been cleansed of atavistic and barbaric elements. Marriage has ceased to be a matter of sell-and-buy. Nowadays a girl from a collective farm is not given away (or should we say "sold away"?) by her father, for now she is her own mistress, and no one can give her away. She will marry the man she loves. . . .

We alone have all the conditions under which a working woman can fulfill her duties as a citizen and as a mother responsible for the birth and early upbringing of her children.

A woman without children merits our pity, for she does not know the full joy of life. Our Soviet women, full-blooded citizens of the freest country in the world, have been given the bliss of motherhood. We must safeguard the family and raise and rear healthy Soviet heroes!

## QUESTIONS FOR ANALYSIS

1. How does Kollontai expect women to be both workers and mothers without depending on a man? How would Soviet society make this possible?
2. Why does Alexandra Kollontai advocate the legalization of abortion in Soviet Russia? Does she view abortion as a permanent right or as a temporary necessity?
3. Why does Stalin characterize a "lighthearted, negligent attitude toward marriage" and "all disorderly sex life" as "bourgeois through and through"?
4. How does Stalin's image of the Soviet family differ from Kollontai's? Are his views a variation of her views, or the opposite?

*Sources*: First selection from Alexandra Kollontai, "The Labour of Women in the Revolution of the Economy," in *Selected Writings of Alexandra Kollontai*, translated by Alix Holt (Lawrence Hill & Company, 1978), pp. 148–149. Second selection from *Discussion of the Law on Abolition of Legal Abortion*, Pravda, Editorials of May 28 and June 9, 1936. English translation in Rudolf Schlesinger, ed., *Changing Attitudes in Soviet Russia: The Family in the USSR*, London, Routledge & Kegan Paul, 1949, pp. 251–54, 268–69.

the war had turned people's hopes of victory to bitter disappointment. Radical politicians quickly became adept at appealing to people's fears. They promised to bring back full employment, stop the spread of communism, and achieve the territorial conquests that World War I had denied them.

## Mussolini's Italy

The first country to seek radical answers was Italy. World War I, which had never been popular, left thousands of veterans who found neither pride in their victory nor jobs in the postwar economy. Unemployed veterans and violent youths banded together into *fasci di combattimento* (fighting units) to demand action and intimidate politicians. When workers threatened to strike, factory and property owners hired gangs of these *fascisti* to defend them.

**Benito Mussolini** (1883–1945), a spellbinding orator, quickly became the leader of the **Fascist Party**, which glorified warfare and the Italian nation. By 1921 the party had 300,000 members, many of whom used violent methods to repress strikes, intimidate voters, and seize municipal governments. A year later Mussolini threatened to march on Rome if he was not appointed prime minister. The government gave in.

Mussolini then proceeded to install Fascist Party members in all government jobs, crush all opposition parties, and jail anyone who criticized him. The party took over the press, public education, and youth activities and gave employers control over their workers. The Fascists lowered living standards but reduced unemployment and provided social security and public services. They proved to be neither ruthless radicals nor competent administrators.

What Mussolini and the Fascist movement really excelled at was bombastic speeches, spectacular parades, and signs everywhere proclaiming "Il Duce (eel DOO-chay) [the Leader] is always right!" Mussolini's genius was to apply the techniques of modern mass communications and advertisement to political life. Billboards, movie footage, and radio news bulletins galvanized the masses in ways never before done in peacetime. His techniques of whipping up public enthusiasm were not lost on other radicals. By the 1930s fascist movements had appeared in most European countries, as well as in Latin America, China, and Japan.

## Hitler's Germany

Like Mussolini, **Adolf Hitler** (1889–1945) had served in World War I and looked back fondly on the clear lines of authority and the camaraderie he had experienced in battle. After the war, he used his gifts as orator to appeal to Germans disappointed at their country's humiliation and formed the National Socialist German Workers' Party—**Nazis** for short. While serving a brief jail sentence he wrote *Mein Kampf* (mine kompf) (*My Struggle*), in which he outlined his goals and beliefs, but when it was published in 1925, almost no one took seriously its intense hatred for Jews, on whom he blamed every disaster that had befallen Germany, or its ideas of a "master race" of Aryans (he meant Germans, Scandinavians, and Britons), a degenerate "Alpine" race of French and Italians, and an inferior race of Russian and eastern European Slavs, fit only to be slaves of the master race. He glorified violence, which would enable the "master race" to defeat and subjugate all others.

But when the Depression hit, the Nazis gained supporters among the unemployed, who believed Nazi promises of jobs for all, and among property owners frightened by the growing popularity of communists. In March 1933, as leader of the largest party in Germany, Hitler became chancellor.

Once in office, he quickly assumed dictatorial power, just as Mussolini had done. He put Nazis in charge of all government agencies, educational

**Benito Mussolini (1883–1945)**   Fascist dictator of Italy (1922–1943). He led Italy to conquer Ethiopia (1935), joined Germany in the Axis pact (1936), and allied Italy with Germany in World War II. He was overthrown in 1943 when the Allies invaded Italy.

**Fascist Party**   Italian political party created by Benito Mussolini during World War I. It emphasized aggressive nationalism and was Mussolini's instrument for the creation of a dictatorship in Italy from 1922 to 1943.

**Adolf Hitler (1889–1945)**   Born in Austria, Hitler became a radical German nationalist during World War I. He led the National Socialist German Workers' Party—the Nazis—in the 1920s and became dictator of Germany in 1933. He led Europe into World War II.

**Nazis**   German political party led by Adolf Hitler, emphasizing nationalism, racism, and war. When Hitler became chancellor of Germany in 1933, the Nazis became the only legal party and an instrument of Hitler's absolute rule. The party's formal name was National Socialist German Workers' Party.

**A Nazi Rally** Hitler organized mass rallies at Nuremberg to whip up popular support for his regime and to indoctrinate young Germans with a martial spirit. Thousands of men in uniform marched in torch-lit parades before Hitler and his top officials.

institutions, and professional organizations; banned all other political parties; and threw their leaders into concentration camps. The Nazis deprived Jews of their citizenship and civil rights, prohibited them from marrying "Aryans," ousted them from the professions, and confiscated their property. In August 1934 Hitler proclaimed himself *Führer* (FEW-rer) ("leader") and called Germany the "Third Reich," the third German empire after the Holy Roman Empire of medieval times and the German Empire of 1871 to 1918.

The Nazis' economic and social policies were spectacularly effective. The government undertook massive public works projects and gave contracts to businesses to manufacture weapons. Women who had entered the workforce during and after World War I were urged to concentrate on "*Kinder, Kirche, Kuche*" (children, church, kitchen), releasing jobs for men. By 1936, business was booming, unemployment was at its lowest level since the 1920s, and living standards were rising. Hitler's popularity soared because most Germans believed their economic well-being outweighed the loss of liberty.

## The Road to War, 1933–1939

What Hitler really wanted was not prosperity or popularity, but conquest. As soon as he came to office, he began to build up the armed forces. Meanwhile, he tested the reactions of the other powers through a series of surprise moves followed by protestations of peaceful intent.

In 1933, when Hitler withdrew Germany from the League of Nations, France and Britain hesitated to retaliate by blockading or invading Germany. Two years later, he announced that Germany was going to introduce conscription, build up its army, and create an air force—in violation of the Versailles treaty. Instead of protesting, Britain signed a naval agreement with Germany. The message was clear: neither

Britain nor France was willing to risk war by standing up to Germany. The United States, absorbed in its own domestic economic problems, had reverted to isolationism.

By 1938 Hitler decided that his rearmament plans were far enough advanced that he could afford to escalate his demands. In March, Germany invaded Austria, without protest from its German-speaking citizens. Then came Czechoslovakia. Hitler first demanded autonomy for its German-speaking borderlands, then their annexation to Germany. At the Munich Conference of September 1938, the leaders of France, Britain, and Italy gave him everything he wanted to keep him from starting a war. Hitler learned that aggression paid off.

The democracies' policy of "appeasement" ran counter to the European balance-of-power tradition for three reasons. The first was the deep-seated fear of war among people who had lived through World War I. The second was fear of communism. The conservative politicians who ruled France and Britain were more afraid of Stalin than of Hitler, for Hitler claimed to respect Christianity and private property. The third cause was the very novelty of fascist tactics. Britain's prime minister, Neville Chamberlain, assumed that political leaders (other than the Bolsheviks) were honorable men and that an agreement was as valid as a business contract. Thus, when Hitler promised "no further territorial demands," Chamberlain believed him.

After Munich, it was too late to stop Hitler, short of war. Germany and Italy were now united in an alliance called the Axis. In March 1939, Germany invaded what was left of Czechoslovakia. Belatedly realizing that Hitler could not be trusted, France and Britain sought Soviet help. Stalin, however, distrusted the "capitalists" as much as they distrusted him. When Hitler offered to divide Poland between Germany and the Soviet Union, Stalin accepted. The Nazi-Soviet Pact of August 23, 1939, freed Hitler from the fear of a two-front war and gave Stalin time to build up his armies. One week later, on September 1, German forces swept into Poland, and the war was on.

# EAST ASIA, 1931–1945

■ *Why did Japan invade Manchuria?*

When the Depression ruined Japan's export trade, especially in silk and rice, ultranationalists, including young army officers, resented their country's dependence on foreign trade and what they believed was unnecessary party politics that sullied the righteousness of the divine imperial will. If only Japan had a colonial empire, they thought, it would not be beholden to the rest of the world. But Europeans and Americans had already taken most potential colonies in Asia. Japanese nationalists saw the conquest of China, with its vast population and resources, as the solution to their country's problems.

Meanwhile, in China the Guomindang (see Chapter 25) was becoming stronger and preparing to challenge the Japanese presence in Manchuria, a province rich in coal and iron ore. Junior officers in the Japanese army, frustrated by the caution of their superiors, took action. In September 1931 they blew apart railroad track as a pretext for invading Manchuria (*Manchukuo*) (man-CHEW-coo-oh) and recognizing its "independence," while in reality putting Manchukuo under Japanese control. Those in Tokyo who disapproved of the attack were persuaded by the overwhelmingly positive reaction expressed by the public, press, and even leftist critics.

The U.S. government condemned the Japanese conquest, and the League of Nations refused to recognize Manchukuo and urged the Japanese to remove their troops from China. Persuaded that the Western powers would not fight, Japan resigned from the League.

During the next few years, the Japanese built railways and heavy industries in Manchuria and northeastern China and sped up their rearmament. The government grew more authoritarian, jailing thousands of dissidents. On several occasions, ultranationalists, many of them junior officers, mutinied or assassinated leading political figures, receiving only mild punishments, and generals and admirals sympathetic to their views replaced more moderate civilian politicians.

### The Long March

Until the Japanese seized Manchuria, the Chinese government seemed to be creating conditions for a national recovery. The main challenge to the government of **Chiang Kai-shek** (chang kie-shek) came from the Chinese communists, who were industrial workers and who worked in alliance with the nationalists until 1927, when Chiang Kai-shek arrested and executed communists and labor leaders alike (see Chapter 25).

The few communists who escaped the mass arrests fled to the remote mountains of Jiangxi (jang-she), in southeastern China. Among them was **Mao Zedong** (ma-oh zay-dong) (1893–1976), a farmer's son who had left home to study philosophy.

In the early 1920s Mao discovered the works of Karl Marx, joined the Communist Party, and soon became one of its leaders. In Jiangxi, Mao began studying conditions among the peasants, in whom communists had previously shown no interest. He planned to redistribute land from the wealthier to the poorer peasants, thereby gaining adherents for the coming struggle with the Guomindang army.

Mao's reliance on the peasantry was a radical departure from Marxist-Leninist ideology, which stressed the backwardness of the peasants and pinned its hopes on industrial workers. Mao was also an advocate of women's equality. Before 1927 the communists had organized the women who worked in Shanghai's textile mills, the most exploited of all Chinese workers. Later, in their mountain stronghold in Jiangxi, they organized women farmers, allowed divorce, and banned arranged marriages and footbinding.

The Guomindang army pursued the communists into the mountains, building small forts throughout the countryside. Rather than risk direct confrontations, Mao responded with guerrilla warfare. Whereas government troops often mistreated civilians, Mao insisted that his soldiers help the peasants, pay a fair price for food and supplies, and treat women with respect. In spite of their good relations with the peasants of Jiangxi, the communists decided to break out of the southern mountains and trek to Shaanxi (SHAWN-she), an even more remote province in northwestern China. The so-called **Long March** took them 6,000 miles (nearly 9,700 kilometers) in one year, 17 miles a day over desolate mountains and through swamps and deserts, pursued by the army and bombed by Chiang's aircraft. Of the 100,000 communists who left Jiangxi in October 1934, only 4,000 reached Shaanxi a year later.

### The Sino-Japanese War, 1937–1945

On July 7, 1937, Japanese troops attacked Chinese forces near Beijing. As in 1931, the junior officers who ordered the attack quickly obtained the support of their commanders and then, reluctantly, of the government. By November, Japanese troops had seized Beijing, Tianjin, Shanghai, and other coastal cities, and the Japanese navy blockaded the entire coast of China.

Once again, the United States and the League of Nations denounced the Japanese atrocities. Yet the Western powers were too preoccupied with events in Europe and with their own economic problems to risk a military confrontation in Asia. When the Japanese sank a U.S. gunboat and shelled a British ship on the Yangzi River, the U.S. and British governments

**Chiang Kai-shek (1886–1975)** Chinese military and political leader. Succeeded Sun Yat-sen as head of the Guomindang in 1925; headed the Chinese government from 1928 to 1948; fought against the Chinese communists and Japanese invaders. After 1949 he headed the Chinese nationalist government in Taiwan.

**Mao Zedong (1893–1976)** Leader of the Chinese Communist Party (1927–1976). He led the communists on the Long March (1934–1935) and rebuilt the Communist Party and Red Army during the Japanese occupation of China (1937–1945). After World War II, he led the communists to victory over the Guomindang.

**Long March (1934–1935)** The 6,000-mile flight of Chinese communists from southeastern to northwestern China. The communists, led by Mao Zedong, were pursued by the Chinese army under orders from Chiang Kai-shek. The four thousand survivors of the march formed the nucleus of a revived communist movement that defeated the Guomindang after World War II.

responded only with righteous indignation and pious resolutions.

The large Chinese armies were poorly led and armed and lost every battle. Within a year Japan controlled the coastal provinces of China and the lower Yangzi and Yellow River Valleys, China's richest and most populated regions, but the Chinese people continued to resist, either in the army or with the communist guerrilla forces. Japan's periodic attempts to turn the tide by conquering one more piece of China only pushed it deeper into the quagmire.

Warfare between the Chinese and Japanese was incredibly violent. In the winter of 1937–1938 Japanese troops took Nanjing, raped 20,000 women, killed roughly 200,000 prisoners and civilians, and looted and burned the city. To slow them down, Chiang ordered the Yellow River dikes blasted open, causing a flood that destroyed four thousand villages, killed 890,000 people, and made millions homeless. Two years later, when the communists ordered a massive offensive, the Japanese retaliated with a "kill all, burn all, loot all" campaign, destroying hundreds of villages down to the last person, building, and farm animal.

The Chinese government, led by Chiang Kai-shek, escaped to the mountains of Sichuan in the center of the country. There Chiang built up a huge army, not to fight Japan but to prepare for a future confrontation with the communists. The army drafted over 3 million men, even though it had only a million rifles and could not provide food or clothing for all its soldiers. The Guomindang raised farmers' taxes, even when famine forced farmers to eat the bark of trees. Such taxes were not enough to support both a large army and the thousands of government officials and hangers-on who had fled to Sichuan. To avoid taxing its wealthy supporters the government printed money, causing inflation, hoarding, and corruption.

From his capital of Yan'an in Shaanxi province, Mao also built up his army and formed a government. Unlike the Guomindang, the communists listened to the grievances of the peasants, especially the poor, to whom they distributed land confiscated from wealthy landowners. Because they presented themselves as the only group in China that was serious about fighting the Japanese, they obtained support and intelligence from farmers in Japanese-occupied territory, turning military reversals into propaganda victories.

## SECTION REVIEW

- Seeing conquest as a solution to its economic problems, in 1931 Japan conquered Manchuria.
- The Chinese government under Chiang Kai-shek fought both the Japanese and the communists led by Mao Zedong, who fled into the mountains of northern China.
- The communists supported both peasants and women, while Chiang Kai-shek taxed farmers, printed money, and diverted war efforts to prepare to fight the communists.
- In 1937, Japanese forces conquered the coastal provinces of China; in the ensuing violent war, the Chinese communists offered the most effective resistance and Japan gained few real advantages.

# THE SECOND WORLD WAR
■ *How was the war fought, and why did Japan and Germany lose?*

The Second World War was much bigger and deadlier than the first in every way. It was fought around the world, from Norway to New Guinea and from Hawaii to Egypt, and on every ocean. It was a total war that showed how effectively industry, science, and nationalism could be channeled into mass destruction.

**The War of Movement**   In World War II motorized weapons gave back the advantage to the offensive. Opposing forces moved fast, their victories hinging as much on the aggressive spirit of their commanders and the military intelligence they obtained as on numbers of troops and firepower.

The Wehrmacht (VAIR-mokt), or German army, was the first to learn this lesson. It not only had tanks, trucks, and fighter planes, but also had perfected their combined use in a tactic called *Blitzkrieg* (BLITS-creeg) (lightning war): fighter planes scattered enemy troops and disrupted communications, tanks punctured the enemy's defenses, and then, with the help of the infantry, they encircled and captured enemy troops. At sea, both Japan and the United States had developed aircraft carriers that could launch planes against targets hundreds of miles away.

Armies ranged over vast theaters of operation, and countries were conquered in days or weeks. The

**Soviet Tanks at Stalingrad** In the winter of 1942–1943, the Red Army encircled a German army at Stalingrad, a strategic city in southern Russia that marked the furthest eastward advance of the Wehrmacht. The Soviets deployed their new T-34s, the best tanks in the world at the time. Unlike the Germans, Soviet soldiers were equipped with warm winter uniforms with a white outer layer for camouflage in the snow.

belligerents mobilized the economies of entire continents, squeezing them for every possible resource. They tried not only to defeat their enemies' armed forces but—by blockades, submarine attacks, and bombing raids—to damage the economies that supported those armed forces. They thought of civilians as legitimate targets and, later, as vermin to be exterminated.

## War in Europe and North Africa

It took less than a month for the Wehrmacht to conquer Poland. Britain and France declared war on Germany but took no military action. Meanwhile, the Soviet Union invaded eastern Poland and the Baltic republics. Although the Poles fought bravely, their infantry and cavalry were no match for German and Russian tanks. During the winter of 1939–1940, Germany and the Western democracies faced each other in what soldiers called a "phony war."

In March 1940 Hitler went on the offensive again, conquering Denmark, Norway, the Netherlands, and Belgium in less than two months. In May he attacked France. Although the French army had as many soldiers, tanks, and aircraft as the Wehrmacht, its morale was low and it quickly collapsed. By the end of June Hitler was master of all of Europe between Russia and Spain.

Germany still had to face Britain. The British had no army to speak of, but they had other assets: the English Channel, the Royal Navy and Air Force, and a tough new prime minister, Winston Churchill. The Germans knew they could invade Britain only by gaining control of the airspace over the Channel, so they launched a massive air attack—the Battle of Britain—lasting from June through September. The attack failed because the Royal Air Force used radar and code-breaking to detect approaching German planes.

Frustrated in the west, Hitler turned his attention eastward. In June 1941, the Wehrmacht invaded the Soviet Union. In five months it conquered the Baltic states, Ukraine, and half of European Russia, captured a million prisoners of war, and stood at the very gates of Moscow and Leningrad (now St. Petersburg). The USSR seemed on the verge of collapse when suddenly the weather turned cold, machines froze, and the fighting came to a halt. Like Napoleon, Hitler had ignored the climate of Russia at his peril.

The next spring the Wehrmacht renewed its offensive and surrounded Leningrad in a siege that was to cost a million lives. Leaving Moscow aside, it turned toward the Caucasus and its oil wells. In August the Germans attacked **Stalingrad** (now Volgograd), the key to the Volga River and the supply of oil. For months, German and Soviet soldiers fought over every street and every house. When winter came, the Red Army counterattacked and encircled the city, and in February 1943, the remnants of the German army in Stalingrad surrendered. Hitler had lost his greatest gamble (see Map 27.1).

From Europe the war spread to Africa. During 1941 British forces conquered Italian East Africa and invaded Libya as well. The Italian rout in North Africa brought the Germans to the rescue. During 1942, the German army and the forces of the British Commonwealth seesawed back and forth across the deserts of Libya and Egypt. Because the British could decode German messages and had more weapons and supplies, they were finally able to expel the Germans from Africa in May 1943.

### War in Asia and the Pacific

The war presented Japan with the opportunity to take over European colonies in Southeast Asia, with their abundant oil, rubber, and other strategic materials. After Japanese forces occupied Indochina in September 1940, the United States stopped shipments of steel, scrap iron, oil, and other products that Japan desperately needed. This left Japan with three alternatives: give up its conquests, as the Americans insisted; face economic ruin; or widen the war. Japan chose war. On December 7, 1941, Japanese planes bombed the U.S. naval base at **Pearl Harbor**, sinking or damaging scores of warships but missing the aircraft carriers, which were at sea. Then, in early 1942, the Japanese conquered all of Southeast Asia and the Dutch East Indies. They soon began to confiscate food and raw materials and demand heavy labor from the inhabitants.

Japan's dream of an East Asian empire seemed within reach, but the Pearl Harbor attack had finally mobilized the United States. In April 1942 American planes bombed Tokyo. In May the U.S. Navy defeated a Japanese fleet in the Coral Sea, ending Japanese plans to conquer Australia. A month later, at the **Battle of Midway**, Japan lost four of its six largest aircraft carriers. Without them, Japan faced a long and hopeless war (see Map 27.2).

### The End of War

America's entry into the war also helped the Soviet Union capitalize on the advantage it had won in the Battle of Stalingrad. Aided by a growing stream of supplies from the United States, the Red Army began pushing the Wehrmacht back toward Germany. The Western powers, meanwhile, staged two invasions of Europe. Beginning in July 1943, they captured Sicily and invaded Italy. Italy signed an armistice, but German troops held off the Allied advance for two years. Then on D-day (June 6, 1944), 156,000 British, American, and Canadian troops landed on the coast of Normandy in western France. Within a week, the Allies had more troops in France than Germany did. To meet this growing force, Hitler had to transfer part of the Wehrmacht from the eastern front. Despite advancing armies on three sides, Germany held out for almost a year. On May 7, 1945, a week after Hitler committed suicide, German military leaders surrendered.

By June 1944, U.S. bombers were also attacking Japan from newly captured island bases in the Pacific, and U.S. submarines were sinking large numbers of Japanese merchant ships, cutting Japan off from its sources of oil and other raw materials. After May 1945, with Japanese fighters grounded for lack of fuel, U.S. planes began destroying Japanese shipping, industries, and cities at will.

**Stalingrad** City in Russia, site of a Red Army victory over the German army in 1942–1943. The Battle of Stalingrad was the turning point in the war between Germany and the Soviet Union. Today Volgograd.

**Pearl Harbor** Naval base in Hawaii attacked by Japanese aircraft on December 7, 1941. The sinking of much of the U.S. Pacific Fleet brought the United States into World War II.

**Battle of Midway** U.S. naval victory over the Japanese fleet in June 1942, in which the Japanese lost four of their best aircraft carriers. It marked a turning point in World War II.

**Hiroshima** City in Japan, the first to be destroyed by an atomic bomb, on August 6, 1945. The bombing hastened the end of World War II.

On August 6, 1945, the United States dropped an atomic bomb on **Hiroshima**, killing some 80,000 people in a flash and leaving about 120,000 more to die from burns and radiation. Three days later another atomic bomb destroyed Nagasaki. On August 14 Emperor Hirohito gave the order to lay down arms. Two weeks later Japanese leaders signed the terms of surrender. The war was officially over.

## Collapse of the Guomindang and Communist Victory

The Japanese surrender meant the end of Japanese occupation for much of China. The United States gave millions of dollars in aid and weapons to the Guomindang, all the while urging "national unity" and a "coalition government" with the communists. But Chiang used all means available to prepare for a

**Map 27.1  World War II in Europe and North Africa**  In a series of quick and decisive campaigns from September 1939 to December 1941, German forces overran much of Europe and North Africa. There followed three years of bitter fighting as the Allies slowly pushed the Germans back. © Cengage Learning

**Legend:**
- Hitler's Greater Germany
- Allied with Germany
- Occupied by Germany and its allies
- Grand Alliance
- Neutral nations
- ★ Major battle

Siege of Leningrad, Sept. 1941–Jan. 1944

Siege of Stalingrad, Aug. 21, 1942–Jan. 31, 1943

German surrender: Reims, May 7, 1945 Berlin, May 8, 1945

Battle of Britain, fall 1940

Rhine Crossing, March 7, 1945

Battle of the Bulge, Dec. 1944

Invasion of Normandy, June 6, 1944

Axis troops occupy Vichy France, Nov. 10 and 11, 1942

VICHY FRANCE (Occupied Nov. 1942)

Allies land in Provence, Aug. 15, 1944

Monte Cassino, May 1944

Salerno, Sept. 1943

Rome (Liberated June 1944)

Allies invade Sicily and Italy, July–Sept. 1943

Sicily, July 1943

Casablanca, Nov. 1942

Rommel defeated in Tunisia; Axis troops evacuated, May 1943

El Alamein, summer 1942

**Map 27.2 World War II in Asia and the Pacific** Having conquered much of China between 1937 and 1941, Japanese forces launched a sudden attack on Southeast Asia and the Pacific in late 1941 and early 1942. American forces slowly reconquered the Pacific islands and the Philippines. In August 1945, the atomic bombing of Hiroshima and Nagasaki forced Japan's surrender. © Cengage Learning

civil war. The Guomindang started with many advantages, more troops and weapons, U.S. support, and control of China's cities. But their behavior eroded whatever popular support they had. As they moved into formerly Japanese-held territory, they acted like an occupation force, taxing the people they "liberated" more heavily than the Japanese had, looting businesses, and enriching themselves at the expense of the population. Chiang's government had printed money so fast that it lost all value. In the countryside the Guomindang's brutality alienated the peasants.

In contrast, the communists' land reform programs had won them popular support, which was even more important than the weapons brought over by Guomindang soldiers, who began deserting by the thousands, and the Japanese equipment seized

Bettmann/CORBIS

**Hiroshima After the Atomic Bomb**  On August 6, 1945, an atomic bomb destroyed the city, killing some eighty thousand people. This fire truck, stationed at the Hiroshima Fire Department, is one of the few identifiable objects in the photo. It was located 4,000 feet from ground zero.

by the Soviets in the last weeks of the war. By 1949, the Guomindang armies were collapsing everywhere, defeated more by their own greed and ineptness than by the communists. As the communists advanced, high-ranking members of the Guomindang fled to Taiwan, protected from the mainland by the U.S. Navy. On October 1, 1949, Mao Zedong announced the founding of the People's Republic of China.

## SECTION REVIEW

- World War II was a war of machines and movement covering entire continents and oceans.
- Germany quickly conquered most of continental Europe but failed to subdue Britain.
- Soviet troops halted Germany's invasion at Stalingrad, and Britain drove German forces from North Africa.
- Despite initial successes, Japan lost critical battles, particularly Midway, and never could match U.S. war production.
- With the help of vital U.S. resources, the Western powers defeated Germany, while the United States pressed Japan, dropping two atomic bombs to force its surrender.
- In China, Mao's communists won the civil war with the Guomindang by gaining support from the people.

## THE CHARACTER OF WARFARE

■ *How did science and technology change the nature of warfare?*

The war left an enormous death toll. Recent estimates place the figure at close to 60 million deaths, six to eight times more than in World War I. Over half of the dead were civilian victims of massacres, famines, and bombs. The Soviet Union lost between 20 and 25 million people, more than any other country. China suffered 15 million deaths; Poland lost some 6 million, of whom half were Jewish; the Jewish people lost another 3 million outside Poland. Over 4 million Germans and over 2 million Japanese died. Great Britain lost 400,000 people, and the United States 300,000.

One reason for the terrible toll in human lives and suffering was a change in moral values, as belligerents identified not just soldiers but entire peoples as enemies. Some even labeled their own ethnic minorities as "enemies." Another reason for the devastation was the appearance of new technologies that carried destruction deep into enemy territory, far beyond the traditional battlefields.

## The Science and Technology of War

Scientists made many contributions to the technology of warfare. Chemists found ways to make synthetic rubber from coal or oil. Physicists perfected radar, which warned of approaching enemy aircraft and submarines. Others broke enemy codes and developed antibiotics that saved the lives of countless wounded soldiers.

Aircraft development was especially striking. As war approached, German, British, and Japanese aircraft manufacturers developed fast, maneuverable fighter planes. U.S. industry produced aircraft of every sort but was especially noted for heavy bombers designed to fly in huge formations and drop tons of bombs on enemy cities. Germany responded with radically new designs, including the first jet fighters, low-flying pilotless buzz bombs, and long-range V-2 missiles.

In October 1939, President Roosevelt received a letter from physicist Albert Einstein, a Jewish refugee from Nazism, warning of the dangers of nuclear power. Fearing that Germany might develop a nuclear bomb first, Roosevelt placed the vast resources of the U.S. government at the disposal of physicists and engineers. By 1945 they had built two atomic bombs, each one powerful enough to annihilate an entire city.

## Bombing Raids

The Germans began the war from the air, but it was the British and Americans who excelled at large-scale urban bombardment. Since it was very hard to pinpoint individual buildings, especially at night, air raids were aimed at weakening the morale of civilian populations.

In May 1942, 1,000 British planes dropped incendiary bombs on Cologne, setting fire to the old city. Between July 24 and August 2, 1943, 3,330 British and American bombers set fire to Hamburg, killing 50,000 people. Later raids destroyed Berlin, Dresden, and other German cities. The bombing raids against Germany killed 600,000 people—more than half of them women and children—and injured 800,000, but they failed to break the morale of the German people. The only effective bombing raids were those directed against oil depots and synthetic fuel plants; by early 1945, they had almost brought the German war effort to a standstill.

American bombing raids on Japanese cities were even more devastating that the fire-bombing of German cities, for Japanese cities were built of wood. In March 1945, a large raid set Tokyo ablaze, killing 80,000 people and leaving a million homeless. Five months later, each atomic bomb did as much damage as a thousand-plane raid.

## The Holocaust

The Nazis killed defenseless civilians on an even larger scale. Their murders were not the byproducts of some military goal but a calculated policy of extermination.

Their first targets were Jews. Soon after Hitler came to power, he deprived German Jews of their citizenship and legal rights. When eastern Europe fell under Nazi rule, the Nazis herded its large Jewish population into ghettos in the major cities, where many died of starvation and disease. Then, in early 1942, the Nazis decided to carry out Hitler's "final solution to the Jewish problem" by applying modern industrial methods to the slaughter of human beings. German companies built huge extermination camps in eastern Europe. Every day, trainloads of cattle cars arrived at the camps and disgorged thousands of captives and the corpses of those who had died of starvation or asphyxiation along the way. The strongest survivors were put to work and fed almost nothing until they died. Women, children, the elderly, and the sick were shoved into gas chambers and asphyxiated with poison gas. **Auschwitz**, the biggest camp, was a giant industrial complex designed to kill up to twelve thousand people a day. This mass extermination, now called the **Holocaust** ("burning"), claimed some 6 million Jewish lives.

**Auschwitz** Nazi extermination camp in Poland, the largest center of mass murder during the Holocaust. Close to a million Jews, Gypsies, communists, and others were killed there.

**Holocaust** Nazis' program during World War II to kill people they considered undesirable. Some 6 million Jews perished during the Holocaust, along with millions of Poles, Gypsies, communists, socialists, and others.

## The Home Front

Rapid military movements and air power carried the war into people's homes in China, Japan, Southeast Asia, and Europe. Armies swept through the land, confiscating food, fuel, and anything else of value. Bombers and heavy artillery pounded cities into rubble, leaving only the skeletons of buildings, while survivors cowered in cellars. Air-raid sirens awakened people throughout the night. Millions fled their homes in terror. Of all the major belligerents, only Americans escaped such nightmares, and war production ended the joblessness of the Depression years.

The war demanded an enormous production effort from civilians. In the face of advancing Germans in 1941, the Soviets dismantled over fifteen hundred factories and rebuilt them in the Ural Mountains and Siberia, where workers soon turned out more tanks and artillery than the Axis. American factories produced an unending supply of ships, aircraft, trucks, tanks, and other materiel for the Allied effort. The Axis powers could not compete with the vast outpouring.

Hulton Deutsch Collection/Corbis

**U.S. Army Medics and Holocaust Victims**  When Allied troops entered the Nazi concentration camps, they found the bodies of thousands of victims of the Holocaust. In Dachau in southern Germany, two U.S. Army medics are overseeing a truckload of corpses to be taken to a burial site.

With so many men mobilized for war, women were responsible for much of this production. Six million American women entered the labor force, 2.5 million of them in manufacturing jobs previously considered "men's work." Soviet women took over half of all industrial and three-quarters of all agricultural jobs. In other belligerent countries, women also played major roles in the war effort, replacing men in fields, factories, and offices. The Nazis, in contrast, believed that German women should stay home and bear children, and they imported 7 million "guest workers"—a euphemism for captured foreigners.

Besides the Jews, the Nazis killed 3 million Polish Catholics—especially professionals, army officers, and the educated—in an effort to reduce the Polish people to slavery. They also exterminated homosexuals, Jehovah's Witnesses, Gypsies, the disabled, and the mentally ill—all in the interests of "racial purity." Whenever a German was killed in an occupied country, the Nazis retaliated by burning a village and all its inhabitants. After the invasion of Russia the Wehrmacht was given orders to execute all captured communists, government employees, and officers. They also worked millions of prisoners of war to death or let them die of starvation.

## War and the Environment

As in World War I, battles scarred the landscape, leaving behind spent ammunition and damaged equipment. Retreating armies flooded large areas of China and the Netherlands. The bombing of cities left ruins that remained visible for a generation or more. The main cause of environmental stress, however, was not the fighting but the economic development that sustained it.

As war industries boomed—the United States increased its industrial production fourfold during the war—so did the demand for raw materials. Mining companies opened new mines and towns in Central Africa to supply strategic minerals. Latin American countries deprived of manufactured imports began building their own steel mills, factories, and shipyards. In India, China, and Europe, timber felling accelerated far beyond forest regrowth. Yet, the environmental impact of the war was quite modest compared to the damage inflicted on the earth by the long consumer boom that began after World War II.

## CONCLUSION

During the two decades from 1929 to 1949, industrialization and nationalism led to Depression, political violence, and war. In the Soviet Union, Joseph Stalin used terror to turn his country into a modern industrial state prepared for war. In the United States and western Europe, a shaky economy based on credit and speculation collapsed, throwing millions out of work and causing worldwide misery. France and Britain survived by making their colonial empires purchase their products. In Italy, Germany, and Japan the economic turmoil, the disillusionment with liberal parliamentary politics, and nationalist resentments played into the hands of extremists who believed that war offered solutions to their nations' problems.

The Second World War was not just another war between states and armed forces, but a war against peoples. Of the roughly 60 million people who died in the war, most were civilians. Modern industrial technologies like aviation that had been developed for peaceful purposes, as well as new scientific breakthroughs like nuclear physics, were turned into engines of destruction. The war that resulted was by far the most violent and deadly in the history of humanity.

# CHAPTER REVIEW

## THE STALIN REVOLUTION

■ *How did the Soviet Union change under Stalin?* (page 631)

After the Great War ended, the world seemed to return to its prewar state, but it was an illusion. In the Soviet Union, Joseph Stalin was determined to turn his country into a modern industrial sate at breakneck speed, regardless of the human cost. Several million people— most of them peasants—died, and millions more were enslaved during the Five-Year Plans and the collectivization of agriculture. By 1914 Soviet industry was much better prepared for a war with Germany than it had been in 1914–1917.

## THE DEPRESSION

■ *What caused the Depression, and what effects did it have on the world?* (page 634)

In 1929, after a few years of prosperity, excessive speculation based on shaky loans caused the New York stock market to collapse. Within a few months, the world economy fell into the Great Depression, which threw millions out of work, not only in the industrial nations but also throughout the world. Countries such as France and Britain survived the Depression by making their colonial empires purchase their products. Countries that were dependent on exports, such as Germany and Japan, suffered more. Only the USSR and southern

Africa, where gold became more valuable, boomed during the 1930s.

## THE RISE OF FASCISM

■ *How did fascism in Italy and Germany lead to the Second World War?* (page 635)

In Italy, the government that was already fascist became more tyrannical. Mussolini installed Fascist Party members in all government jobs and jailed anyone who criticized him. In Germany, economic collapse led people to entrust their government to Adolf Hitler and his Nazi followers, who quickly set to work establishing a totalitarian government. Nazi Germany's rebuilding of its military and its invasion of Austria and Czechoslovakia were greeted with a policy of appeasement by Western democracies, until finally they could no longer overlook Germany's intentions.

## EAST ASIA, 1931–1945

■ *Why did Japan invade Manchuria?* (page 640)

The Depression hit Japan hard because the worldwide demand for silk and rice collapsed. Japan saw China as a potential new colony with a vast population and resources to help solve its economic problems. In 1931, Japan conquered Manchuria and proceeded to build railways and heavy industries there. The United States and the League of Nations protested but did little else. The Sino-Japanese War, which began with the Japanese invasion of Beijing in 1937, was a long and brutal war that became a drain on the Japanese economy and resources. Meanwhile, the communists, led by Mao Zedong, were slowly gaining support in the Chinese countryside.

## THE SECOND WORLD WAR

■ *How was the war fought, and why did Japan and Germany lose?* (page 642)

Italy conquered Ethiopia in 1935, and Japan attacked China in 1937, while the Western democracies disapproved but took no action. War began in Europe in 1939 when Germany conquered Poland and thenk, in the following Spring, Denmark, Norway, the low countries and France. The war turned global when Germany invaded the Soviet Union and Japan attacked the United States in 1941. The Allies won because of Russia's hard fighting and victory at Stalingrad; the Allies' overwhelming materiel resources, especially those of the United States; the invasion of D-day, which put enough men on the European continent to finally drive Germany back; and U.S. naval victories in the Pacific and the use of atomic weapons against Japan.

## THE CHARACTER OF WARFARE

■ *How did science and technology change the nature of warfare?* (page 647)

The Second World War was by far the deadliest and most horrific in history. Modern mechanized forces swept across entire nations and oceans. Their targets were not only each other's armed forces, but their civilian populations as well. Though Germany had considerable scientific and technical talent, the war favored the nations with the most heavy industries, namely, the United States and the Soviet Union. The Allies destroyed German and Japanese cities with fire-bombs, and the United States dropped atomic bombs on Hiroshima and Nagasaki. Of the roughly 60 million people who died in the war, most were civilians.

## Key Terms

| | |
|---|---|
| Joseph Stalin (p. 631) | Long March (p. 641) |
| Five-Year Plans (p. 631) | Stalingrad (p. 644) |
| Benito Mussolini (p. 638) | Pearl Harbor (p. 644) |
| Fascist Party (p. 638) | Battle of Midway (p. 644) |
| Adolf Hitler (p. 638) | Hiroshima (p. 644) |
| Nazis (p. 638) | Auschwitz (p. 648) |
| Chiang Kai-shek (p. 641) | Holocaust (p. 648) |
| Mao Zedong (p. 641) | |

# Famines and Politics

Human history is filled with tales of famines—times when crops failed, food supplies ran out, and people starved.

## Natural Famines

India, dependent on the monsoon rains, has been particularly prone to such calamities, with famines striking two to four times a century, whenever the rains fail for several years in succession. Three times in the eighteenth century famines killed several million people. The nineteenth century was worse, with famines in 1803–1804, 1837–1838, 1868–1870, and 1876–1878. The famine of 1876–1878 also afflicted northern China, causing between 9 and 13 million deaths from hunger and from the diseases of malnutrition. There were even incidents of cannibalism, as starving adults ate starving children.

When drought hit a region, it decimated not only the human population but also the animals they relied on to transport crops or plow the land. When water levels dropped in rivers and canals, food could not be transported by boat to areas where people were starving.

## Commercial Famines

That all changed in the nineteenth century. Railroads and steamships could transport foodstuffs quickly across great distances, regardless of the weather. Great Britain became dependent on imports of wheat and beef. Yet the global death toll from starvation has been far higher since the mid-nineteenth century than ever before. Why?

Consider Ireland. By the early nineteenth century the potato had become the main source of nutrition for the Irish people. Potatoes grew abundantly and produced more calories per acre than any other crop, allowing the population to increase dramatically.

In 1845 a blight turned the potatoes in the fields black, mushy, and inedible. The harvest was ruined the following year as well. It recovered slightly in 1847 but was bad again in 1848. Tens of thousands died of starvation, while hundreds of thousands died from the diseases that strike malnourished people, especially dysentery, typhus, or cholera. Travelers saw corpses rotting in their hovels or on the sides of roads. Altogether, a million or more people died, while another million emigrated, reducing the population of Ireland by half.

Throughout those years, Ireland exported wheat to England, where people had money to pay for it. Food cost money, and the Irish, poor even before the famines, could not afford to buy the wheat. The British government was convinced that interfering with the free market would only make things worse. Relief efforts were half-hearted at best; the official responsible for Irish affairs preferred to leave the situation to "the operation of natural causes."

The same held true in India, like Ireland a colony of Great Britain. The drought of 1876–1878 killed over 5 million Indians in the Deccan region, while British officials were helpless or indifferent. Part of the problem was transportation. In the 1870s most goods were still transported in bullock carts, but the bullocks also starved during the drought. Another obstacle was political. The idea that governments should be responsible for feeding the population was unthinkable at the time. So millions starved in the Deccan, while the Punjab exported wheat to Britain.

Over the next twenty years, so-called famine railways were built in the regions historically most affected by the failures of the monsoon. When drought struck again at the end of the century, the railways were ready to transport food to areas that had previously been accessible only by bullock carts. However, the inhabitants of the affected regions were too poor to buy what little food there was, so grain merchants bought all the stocks, hoarded them until the price rose, and then used the railways to transport them to regions where people had more money. The government was still reluctant to interfere with free enterprise.

In the twentieth century, governments do take responsibility for their own people as well as for people in other countries, but commercial famines still exist. When a catastrophic flood covered half of Bangladesh in 1974, its disorganized government sold its stocks of rice to merchants (who exported it to India) rather than distributing it. Thousands died. Survival depended on food shipped from donor countries.

## Political Famines

In the twentieth century global food supplies were always adequate for the population of the world, and transportation was seldom a problem. Yet the century witnessed the most murderous famines ever recorded.

In 1942 the Japanese army had conquered Burma, a rich rice-producing colony. Food supplies in Bengal, which imported rice from Burma, dropped by 5 percent. As prices began to rise, merchants bought stocks of rice and held them, hoping that prices would continue to increase. Sharecroppers sold their stocks to pay off their debts. Meanwhile, the railroads that in peacetime would have carried food from other parts of India were fully occupied with military traffic. By the time Viceroy Lord Wavell ordered the army to transport food to Bengal in October 1943, between 1.5 and 2 million Bengalis had died.

Worst of all were the famines caused by deliberate government policies. The most famous was the famine of 1932–1933 caused by Stalin's collectivization of agriculture. The Communists tried to force the peasants to give up their land and

livestock and join collectives, where they could be made to work harder and provide food for the growing cities and industries. When the peasants resisted, their crops were seized. Millions were sent to prison camps, and millions of others died of starvation.

An even worse famine took place in China from 1958 to 1961 during the "Great Leap Forward" (see Chapter 28). Communist Party chairman Mao Zedong decided to hasten the transformation of China into a communist state by relying not on the expertise of economists and technocrats but on the enthusiasm of the masses. Farms were consolidated into huge communes. Peasants were told to make steel out of household utensils in backyard furnaces. The harvest of 1959 was poor, and later ones were even worse. The amount of grain per person declined from 452 pounds (205 kilograms) in 1957 to 340 pounds (154 kilograms) in 1961. Since the Central Statistical Bureau had been shut down, the central government was unaware of the shortages and demanded ever higher requisitions of food to feed the army and urban and industrial workers and to export to the Soviet Union to pay off China's debts. The amount of food left to the farmers was between one-fifth and one-half of their usual subsistence diet. From 1958 to 1961 between 20 and 30 million Chinese are estimated to have starved or died of the diseases of malnutrition. It was the worst famine in the history of the world. Mao denied its existence.

The destruction or requisitioning of crops also caused famines in the Russian civil war of 1921–1922, the Japanese occupation of Indochina in 1942–1945, and the Great Leap Forward. In the 1970s and 1980s, droughts in Africa were used to crush rebellions: the governments of Ethiopia and Sudan denied that their people were hungry and prevented food shipments from reaching drought victims.

In the world today, natural disasters are as frequent as ever, and many countries are vulnerable to food shortages. No one now claims that governments have no business providing food to the starving. However, humanitarian feelings compete with other political agendas, and the specter of politically motivated famines still stalks the world.

# Part Eight

# Perils and Promises of a Global Community, 1945 to the Present

© Cengage Learning

|  | **1950** | **1960** | **1970** |
|---|---|---|---|
| **AMERICAS** | • **1945** United Nations charter signed in San Francisco<br>• **1946** International Monetary Fund and World Bank founded<br>• **1952** U.S. tests first hydrogen bomb | Military takes power in Brazil **1964** •<br>Cuban Revolution **1959** •<br>• **1962** Cuban missile crisis<br>Neil Armstrong walks on moon **1969** • | Military coup overthrows Allende in Chile **1973** • |
| **EUROPE** | **1948–1952** Marshall Plan helps rebuild western Europe<br>• **1949** NATO founded • **1955** Warsaw Pact formed<br>Soviet troops crush revolt in Hungary **1956** • • **1957** Common Market founded | • **1961** Berlin Wall built | • **1968** Student uprising in France |
| **AFRICA** | Apartheid becomes official in South Africa **1948** •<br>Guinea wins independence from France **1958** •<br>Ghana first British colony in West Africa to win independence **1957** • | • **1960** Nigeria, Congo, Somalia, Togo win independence<br>• **1963** Kenya independent | **1970–1980** White domination of Rhodesia yields to international pressure |
| **MIDDLE EAST** | • **1948** State of Israel founded; first Arab-Israeli War<br>**1954–1962** Algerian war for Independence | • **1956** Suez crisis<br>• **1960** Organization of Petroleum Exporting Countries founded | • **1967** Six Day Arab- Israeli War<br>October Arab-Israeli War leads to oil embargo, price hikes **1973** • |
| **ASIA AND OCEANIA** | • **1949** Indonesia wins independence from Netherlands<br>Communist Revolution in China **1949** •<br>**1951–1953** Korean War<br>**1954–1975** Vietnam War | | **1966–1969** Cultural Revolution in China<br>Japan becomes world economic power **1970s** • **1971** Independence of Bangladesh |

654

**CHAPTER 28**
The Cold War and Decolonization,
1945–1999

**CHAPTER 29**
New Challenges in a New Millennium

After World War II an increasingly interconnected world faced new hopes and fears. The United Nations promoted peace, international cooperation, and human rights. Colonized peoples gained independence, and global trade expanded. At the same time the United States and the Soviet Union, victorious former allies in the war against the Axis, mobilized every resource in a global contest for economic and political influence. This "Cold War" led to nuclear stalemate as well as a new round of warfare, dispelling dreams of world peace. Wars in Korea and Vietnam, as well as proxy conflicts—local or regional wars in which the superpowers armed, trained, and financed the combatants—pitted the United States against communist regimes.

Following the Cold War nuclear proliferation and terrorism became top concerns. The 9/11 attacks by Muslim extremists on the World Trade Center and the Pentagon triggered an American-led "global war on terrorism." The ensuing invasions of Afghanistan and Iraq made the Middle East a top danger spot.

The industrialized nations, including Germany and Japan, recovered quickly from World War II.

Elsewhere economic development came slowly, except in a handful of countries: South Korea, Taiwan, Brazil, Argentina, and, after 2000, China and India. In Africa and other poor regions, population growth usually offset economic gains.

Although the Green Revolution of the 1960s and the fruits of genetic engineering thirty years later alleviated much world hunger, industrial growth and automobile use increased pollution and competition for petroleum supplies. Global warming became an international concern, along with overfishing, deforestation, and endangerment of wild species.

Globalization affected culture as well. Transnational corporations selling uniform products threatened localized economic enterprises, and Western popular culture aroused fears of cultural imperialism, fear offset in part by the rise of Asian economic powers. The Internet and the emergence of English as the global language improved international communication but also stimulated fears that cultural diversity would be lost.

| 1980 | 1990 | 2000 |
|---|---|---|
| • **1976** Military takes power in Argentina | **1983–1989** Democracy restored in Brazil, Argentina, Chile | • **1994** NAFTA agreement among Canada, U.S., Mexico • **1994** Maya uprising in southern Mexico | • **2001** Terrorists attack New York, Washington, D.C. |
| • **1975** Helsinki Accords | **1980** Solidarity union founded in Poland   Fall of communist regimes in eastern Europe **1989** •   End of USSR **1991** • | • **1990** Reunification of Germany   Introduction of euro **1999** •   **1992–2000** Disintegration of Yugoslavia | European Union admits ten new members **2004** •   • **2005** Terrorists bomb London buses |
| • **1975** Angola and Mozambique win independence from Portugal | • **1985** Africa equals Europe in population | **1994–1999** Nelson Mandela president of South Africa   • **1999** Democracy restored in Nigeria | |
| • **1979** Islamic Revolution overthrows shah of Iran   **1980–1988** Iran-Iraq War | • **1991** Persian Gulf War | • **2003** U.S., Britain invade, occupy Iraq | • **2006** Israel and Hezbollah war in Lebanon |
| • **1979** USSR enters war in Afghanistan   • **1980s** Taiwan, South Korea, Singapore industrialize | • **1989** Chinese troops suppress Tiananmen Square protest | • **1997** Asian financial crisis starts in Thailand   • **1999** East Timor wins independence from Indonesia | |

# The Cold War and Decolonization

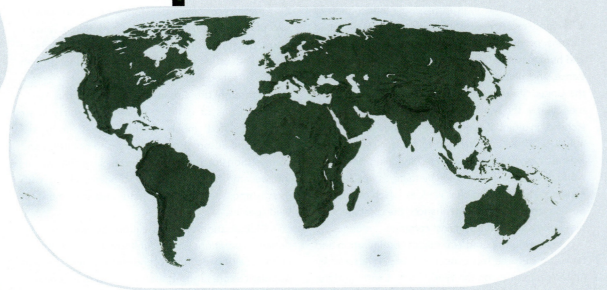

© Cengage Learning

On January 1, 1959, the thirty-two-year-old Fidel Castro entered Havana, Cuba, after having successfully defeated the dictatorship of Fulgencio Batista (ful-HEHN-see-oh bah-TEES-tah). Castro had initiated his revolution in 1953 with an attack on a military barracks, but the attack failed. At his trial, Castro proclaimed that his objectives were the restoration of Cuban democracy and the institution of reforms designed to ameliorate the effects of underdevelopment.

In his September 26, 1960, United Nations address, Castro offered a broad internationalist and anti-imperialist criticism of the world's developed nations and of the United Nations. Claiming that the United States had supported the Batista dictatorship to protect American investors, he outlined an ambitious program of new revolutionary reforms in Cuba, which included concentrating power in the hands of its closest allies and nationalizing most American investments.

The Cuban government and the United States were already heading for confrontation because of Castro's policies when Cuba became a flash point in the Cold War. In 1961 the United States tried and failed to overthrow Castro. Castro retaliated by declaring himself a socialist and forging an economic and military alliance with the Soviet Union that led in 1962 to the Cuban Missile Crisis.

The intensity of the Cold War, with its accompanying threat of nuclear destruction, obscured a postwar phenomenon of more enduring importance: the colonial empires were overthrown, and Western influence declined in Asia, Africa, and Latin America. The leaders who headed these new nations were sometimes able to use Cold War antagonism to their own advantage when they sought economic or military assistance. Some, like Castro, became frontline participants in this struggle.

## THE COLD WAR

■ *What were the major threats to world peace during the Cold War?*

The wartime alliance between the United States, Great Britain, and the Soviet Union had been an uneasy one. Political and economic leaders in the industrialized West had viewed socialism as a threat to free markets and private property. With the defeat of Germany, growing Soviet assertiveness in Europe and communist insurgencies in China and elsewhere seemed to confirm the threat of worldwide revolution.

Each side viewed every action by its rival as a direct threat. Fearful of growing Soviet power, the United States and the nations of western Europe established a military alliance in 1949, the **North Atlantic Treaty Organization (NATO)**. Soviet leaders, struggling to recover from their terrible war losses and feeling themselves surrounded by hostile nations, responded by creating their own military alliance, the **Warsaw Pact**, in 1955. The **Cold War** of suspicion and distrust between these two alliances would now play out on a worldwide stage.

### The United Nations

Founded on October 1945, the **United Nations** had two main bodies: the General Assembly, with representatives from all fifty-one member states; and the Security Council, with five permanent members—China (until 1971 the anticommunist Chinese government based in Taiwan), France, Great Britain, the United States, and the Soviet Union—and seven rotating members. The United Nations operated by majority vote, except that the five permanent members of the Security Council had veto power in that chamber. All signatories to the United Nations Charter renounced war and territorial conquest. Yet the permanent members often exercised their vetoes to protect their allies and interests. From time to time the United Nations

**North Atlantic Treaty Organization (NATO)** Organization formed in 1949 as a military alliance of western European and North American states against the Soviet Union and its east European allies.

**Warsaw Pact** The 1955 treaty binding the Soviet Union and countries of eastern Europe in an alliance against the North Atlantic Treaty Organization.

**Cold War** The ideological struggle between communism (Soviet Union) and capitalism (United States) for world influence. The Cold War came to an end when the Soviet Union dissolved in 1991.

**United Nations** International organization founded in 1945 to promote world peace and cooperation. It replaced the League of Nations.

sent observers or peacekeeping forces to monitor truces or other international agreements.

The decolonization of Africa and Asia greatly swelled the size of the General Assembly. As many newly independent countries looked to the United Nations for material assistance and access to a wider political world, the General Assembly became an arena for debates over issues like decolonization and development.

In the early years of the United Nations, General Assembly resolutions carried great weight. An example is a 1947 resolution that sought to divide Palestine into sovereign Jewish and Arab states. Gradually, though, the flood of new members produced a voting majority concerned more with poverty, racial discrimination, and the struggle against imperialism than with the Cold War. As a result, Western powers increasingly disregarded the General Assembly, allowing new countries to have their say but not to act collectively.

May Day Parade in Red Square, 9th May 1967 (colour photo)/Moscow, Russia/© Mirrorpix/The Bridgeman Art Library

**May Day Parade 1967**  At the height of the Cold War the annual May Day celebration in Moscow became a demonstration of Soviet military might.

## Capitalism and Communism

In July 1944, economic specialists representing over forty countries met at Bretton Woods, a New Hampshire resort, to devise a new international monetary system. The signatories eventually agreed to fix exchange rates. They also created the International Monetary Fund (IMF) and **World Bank** to provide funds for reconstructing Europe and helping needy countries.

The Soviet Union attended the Bretton Woods Conference and signed the agreements, but by 1946 suspicion between the Soviet Union and the West undermined cooperation. While the United States held reserves of gold and the rest of the world held reserves of dollars to maintain the stability of the monetary system, the Soviet Union established a closed monetary system for itself and for allied communist regimes in eastern Europe. In Western countries, supply and demand determined prices; in the Soviet command economy, government agencies allocated resources, labor, and goods and set prices, irrespective of market forces.

Many leaders of newly independent states preferred the Soviet Union's socialist example to the capitalism of their former colonizers. Thus, the relative success of economies patterned on Eastern or Western models became an element in the Cold War. Each side trumpeted economic successes measured by industrial output, changes in per capita income, and productivity gains.

After World War II, the United States enjoyed prosperity and an international competitive advantage, while European economies were still heavily damaged from the war. To support European reconstruction, the American **Marshall Plan** provided more than $20 billion to Europe by 1961. In 1948, European nations also promoted economic cooperation and

**World Bank**  A specialized agency of the United Nations that makes loans to countries for economic development, trade promotion, and debt consolidation. Its formal name is the International Bank for Reconstruction and Development.

**Marshall Plan**  U.S. program to support the reconstruction of western Europe after World War II. By 1961 more than $20 billion in economic aid had been dispersed.

# Chronology

| | International Crises | Decolonization |
|---|---|---|
| **1945** | **1947–1948** Soviet blockade of Berlin<br>**1949** NATO formed | **1947** Partition of India<br>**1949** Dutch withdraw from Indonesia |
| **1950** | **1950–1953** Korean War<br>**1952** United States detonates first hydrogen bomb<br>**1954** Jacobo Arbenz overthrown in Guatemala, supported by CIA | **1954** CIA intervention in Guatemala; defeat at Dienbienphu ends French hold on Vietnam |
| **1955** | **1955** Warsaw Pact created<br>**1956** Soviet Union suppresses Hungarian revolt; Suez War pits Israel, England, and France against Egypt<br>**1957** Soviet Union launches first artificial satellite into earth orbit | **1955** Bandung Conference<br><br>**1957** Ghana becomes first British colony in Africa to gain independence<br>**1959** Triumph of Fidel Castro's revolution in Cuba |
| **1960** | **1961** East Germany builds Berlin Wall<br>**1961** Bay of Pigs (Cuba)<br>**1962** Cuban Missile Crisis<br>**1967** Six-Day War between Israel and Arab neighbors<br>**1968** Nuclear Non-Proliferation Treaty | **1960** Shootings in Sharpeville intensify South African struggle against apartheid; Nigeria becomes independent<br>**1962** Algeria wins independence |
| **1970** | **1973** Yom Kippur War between Israel and Egypt<br>**1974** OPEC raises world oil prices<br>**1975** End of Vietnam War<br>**1979** Shah of Iran overthrown in Islamic Revolution | **1971** Bangladesh secedes from Pakistan |
| **1980** | **1980–88** Iran-Iraq War<br><br>**1989** Berlin Wall falls | **1983** United States invades Grenada<br><br>**1989** United States arrests president of Panama |
| **1990** | **1991** Disintegration of Soviet Union | **1990** Nelson Mandela released from prison in South Africa<br>**1994** Nelson Mandela elected president of South Africa<br>**1997** Hong Kong passes from British control to become part of the People's Republic of China<br>**1999** United States cedes Panama Canal to Panama |

integration with the creation of the Organization of European Economic Cooperation (OEEC). After cooperative policies on coal and steel proved successful, some OEEC countries lowered tariffs to encourage trade. In 1957 France, West Germany, Italy, the Netherlands, Belgium, and Luxembourg signed a treaty creating the **European Economic Community (EC)**, also known as the **Common Market**. By 1963, a resurgent European economy had doubled 1940 output, and by the 1970s the EC nations had nearly overtaken the United States in industrial production. The economic alliance expanded after 1970 as Great Britain, Denmark, Greece, Ireland, Spain, Portugal, Finland, Sweden, and Austria joined.

**European Economic Community (Common Market)** An organization promoting economic unity in Europe, formed in 1957 by consolidation of earlier, more limited agreements. With the addition of many new nations it became the European Union (EU) in 1993.

Prosperity brought dramatic changes to western Europe. Wages increased and social welfare benefits expanded. Governments increased spending on health care, unemployment benefits, old-age pensions, public housing, and grants to poor families. Richer nations subsidized poorer nations, and the combination of economic growth and income redistribution raised living standards and fueled demand for consumer goods.

The Soviet experience was dramatically different. Even though the Soviet Union was more devastated than western Europe at the end of the Second World War, it also had enormous natural resources, a large population, and abundant energy—all of which initially contributed to its recovery. Moreover, Soviet planners had made large investments in technical and scientific education, and the Soviet state had developed heavy industry in the 1930s and war years. But as the postwar period progressed, the inefficiencies of bureaucratic control became obvious. By the 1970s the economic gap with the West had widened. Soviet industry failed to meet domestic demand for clothing, housing, food, automobiles, and consumer electronics. In addition, agricultural production failed to meet even domestic needs. More significant still, the Soviet Union fell behind the West in civilian-sector technological innovation.

## West Versus East

For Germany, Austria, and Japan, peace brought foreign military occupation and governments controlled by the victors. The Soviet Union initially seemed willing to accept governments in neighboring states that included a mix of parties as long as they were not hostile to local communist groups or to the Soviets. Many were willing to embrace the communists as a hedge against those who had supported fascism or cooperated with the Germans. As relations between the Soviets and the West worsened in the late 1940s, communists gained a series of political victories across eastern Europe. Western leaders saw the emergence of communist regimes in Poland, Czechoslovakia, Hungary, Bulgaria, Romania, Yugoslavia, and Albania as a threat.

In 1946 Great Britain's wartime leader, Winston Churchill, said in a speech in Missouri, "From Stettin in the Baltic to Trieste in the Adriatic, an iron curtain has descended across the Continent. . . . I am convinced there is nothing they [the communists] so much admire as strength, and there is nothing for which they have less respect than weakness, especially military weakness." The phrase **iron curtain** became a watchword of the Cold War.

Increased hostility did not lead to a direct military confrontation between the two powerful alliances, however. In the waning days of World War II, the United States had seemed amenable to the Soviet desire for access to the Mediterranean through the Turkish straits. But in July 1947, the U.S. **Truman Doctrine** offered military aid to strengthen Turkish and Greek resistance to Soviet military pressure and subversion. In 1951, Turkey and Greece were admitted to NATO.

The West tested Eastern resolve by encouraging divisions within the Warsaw Pact, contributing to armed uprisings in Hungary and peaceful reform efforts in Czechoslovakia. Both were crushed by Soviet troops—Hungary in 1956 and Czechoslovakia in 1968—while the West stood by.

The East tested Western resolve as well. In 1947–1948, the Soviet Union blockaded the British, French, and American zones of Berlin (located in Soviet-controlled East Germany) and in 1961 built the Berlin Wall to prevent East Germans from fleeing to West Berlin. The political and ideological boundaries of the Cold War were established by these events.

A more explosive crisis erupted in Korea. At the end of World War II, Soviet troops were left in control north of the thirty-eighth parallel, while American troops controlled the south. When no agreement could be reached on holding countrywide elections, communist North Korea and a noncommunist South Korea became independent states in 1948. Two years later, North Korea invaded South Korea. In the absence of the Soviet delegation, the UN Security Council condemned the invasion and called on its members to come to the defense of South Korea.

**iron curtain** Winston Churchill's term for the Cold War division between the Soviet-dominated East and the U.S.-dominated West.

**Truman Doctrine** Foreign policy initiated by U.S. president Harry Truman in 1947. It offered military aid to help Turkey and Greece resist Soviet military pressure and subversion.

In the ensuing **Korean War**, which lasted until 1953, the United States was the primary military ally of South Korea. Military progress by American and South Korean forces stalled when the People's Republic of China entered the war in support of North Korea's communist regime. The United States feared that launching attacks into China might prompt China's ally, the Soviet Union, to retaliate. The contending armies eventually reached a stalemate along the thirty-eighth parallel. The two sides agreed to a truce but not a formal peace treaty. As a result, fear of renewed warfare has lingered until the present.

## The United States and Vietnam

The most important postwar communist movement arose in French Indochina in Southeast Asia. The Vietnamese leader Ho Chi Minh (hoe chee min) (1890–1969) had spent several years in France during World War I and helped form the French Communist Party. After training in Moscow, he returned to Vietnam to found the Indochina Communist Party in 1930. Ho Chi Minh's nationalist coalition, called the Viet Minh, fought the French with help from the People's Republic of China. Under President Dwight D. Eisenhower (1953–1961), the United States provided limited support to the French but ultimately decided not to prop up French colonial rule in Vietnam, perceiving that the European colonial empires were doomed. After a brutal struggle, the French stronghold of Dienbienphu (dee-yen-bee-yen-FOO) fell in 1954, marking the end of France's colonial enterprise. Ho's Viet Minh government took over in the north, and a noncommunist nationalist government ruled in the south.

After winning independence, communist North Vietnam supported a communist guerrilla movement—the Viet Cong—against the noncommunist government of South Vietnam. When President John F. Kennedy (served 1961–1963) changed American policy to support the South Vietnamese government of President Ngo Dinh Diem (dee-YEM), North Vietnam committed its military forces more directly to the war with support from the Soviet Union and the Republic of China. Although Kennedy knew that the Diem government was corrupt and unpopular, he feared that a communist victory would encourage communist movements throughout Southeast Asia

and alter the Cold War balance of power. Kennedy increased the number of American military advisers while hoping that a more popular and honest government would come to power. But Diem's overthrow and execution only brought new rulers just as corrupt and unpopular, resulting in some popular South Vietnamese support for the Viet Cong and Hanoi's drive for national reunification.

Lyndon Johnson (served 1963–1969), who became president after Kennedy was assassinated, gained congressional support for an unlimited U.S. military deployment that eventually reached 500,000 troops. Despite battlefield success in the **Vietnam War**, the United States failed to achieve a comprehensive victory. In the massive 1968 Tet Offensive, the Viet Cong guerrillas and their North Vietnamese allies suffered significant losses but gained military credibility.

With a clear victory now unlikely, the antiwar movement in the United States grew in strength. President Johnson, having begun his administration committed to a broad program of social reforms and civil rights initiatives called the Great Society, was instrumental in passing major civil rights legislation that responded to the heroic campaign for voting rights and integration led by Martin Luther King, Jr. As the commitment of U.S. troops in Vietnam grew, a massive antiwar movement applied the tactics of the civil rights movement to end the war. Growing economic problems and a rising tide of antiwar rallies, soon acquiring an international character, undermined support for Johnson, who declined to seek reelection.

In 1973 a treaty between North Vietnam and the United States ended U.S. involvement in the war and promised future elections. Two years later, in violation of the treaty, Viet Cong and North Vietnamese troops overran the South Vietnamese army and captured the southern capital of Saigon, renaming it Ho

**Korean War (1950–1953)** Conflict that began with North Korea's invasion of South Korea and that came to involve the United Nations (primarily the United States) allying with South Korea and the People's Republic of China allying with North Korea.

**Vietnam War (1954–1975)** Conflict pitting North Vietnam and South Vietnamese communist guerrillas against the South Vietnamese government, aided after 1961 by the United States.

Dana Stone/Black Star

**The Vietnamese People at War** American and South Vietnamese troops burned many villages to deprive the enemy of civilian refuges. This policy undermined support for the South Vietnamese government in the countryside.

Chi Minh City. They then united the two Vietnams in a single state ruled from the north. Over a million Vietnamese and 58,000 Americans had died during the war. As the victors imposed a new economic and political order, hundreds of thousands of refugees from South Vietnam left for the United States and other Western nations.

While the United States had justified its military involvement in South Vietnam as an effort to defend against the spread of communism in the region, the communist-led government of a newly reunited Vietnam soon found itself at war with its communist neighbors. In 1975 communist revolutionaries (the Khmer Rouge) gained power in Cambodia, Vietnam's western neighbor. Not only did this brutal regime led by Pol Pot execute more than 1 million of their fellow

citizens, but they also provoked a war with the communist government of Vietnam in 1978. A Vietnamese force of more than 150,000 defeated the Khmer Rouge and set up an occupation government, but a resilient guerrilla force drove the Vietnamese out after a decade of war. The Vietnamese invasion of Cambodia also led to a two-month-long war with the Republic of China, which favored the Cambodians.

## The Race for Nuclear Supremacy

The terrible devastation of Hiroshima and Nagasaki by atomic weapons (see Chapter 27) framed the strategic decisions in the Korean and Vietnamese wars. The Soviet Union had exploded its first nuclear device in 1949. The United States exploded a far more powerful hydrogen bomb in 1952, but the Soviet Union followed suit less than a year later. As a result, the United States took care not to directly challenge the Soviet Union or China (a nuclear power from 1964) during the Korean or Vietnamese conflicts. But the threat of superpowers willing to use nuclear weapons to protect their vital interests spread fear around the world.

Everyone's worst fears seemed about to be realized in the **Cuban Missile Crisis** of 1962. When the Soviet Union deployed nuclear-tipped missiles in Cuba in response to the U.S. missiles in Turkey, the world held its breath. Confronted by unyielding, diplomatic pressure and military threats from President Kennedy, the Soviet Union backed down and pulled the missiles from Cuba. Subsequently, the United States removed its missiles from Turkey.

Arms limitations also saw progress. In 1963 Great Britain, the United States, and the Soviet Union agreed to ban the testing of nuclear weapons in the atmosphere, in space, and under water, thus reducing the danger of radioactive fallout. In 1968 the United States and the Soviet Union together proposed the Nuclear Non-Proliferation Treaty (NPT) signed by 137 countries.

Space exploration was another offshoot of the nuclear arms race. The contest to build larger and more accurate missiles prompted the superpowers

**Cuban Missile Crisis (1962)** Brink-of-war confrontation between the United States and the Soviet Union over the latter's placement of nuclear-armed missiles in Cuba.

## SECTION REVIEW

- The United Nations was created to manage international disputes and facilitate decolonization and development.
- The United States developed the Marshall Plan to aid European recovery from the devastation of World War II.
- The Cold War was a confrontation between two military alliances, NATO and the Warsaw Pact, and two distinct economic systems, capitalism and communism.
- The United States and the Soviet Union avoid a direct conflict, but the Cold War led to wars in Korea and Vietnam.
- The development of nuclear weapons made the Cold War a threat to the survival of the human race and led to nonproliferation treaties.

to prove their skills in rocketry by launching space satellites. The Soviet Union placed a small *Sputnik* satellite into orbit around the earth in October 1957, thereby administering a deep shock to American pride and confidence. The United States responded with its own satellite three months later. In 1969, two Americans, Neil A. Armstrong and Edwin E. ("Buzz") Aldrin, became the first humans to walk on the moon.

# DECOLONIZATION AND NATION BUILDING

■ *What problems did less developed nations face?*

Whereas the losing countries in World War I were stripped of colonies, it was primarily countries on the winning side in World War II that ended up losing their colonies (see Map 28.1). Circumstances differed profoundly from place to place. In some Asian countries, where colonial rule was of long standing, new states possessed viable industries, communications networks, and education systems. In other countries, notably in Africa, decolonized nations faced dire economic problems and internal disunity.

Despite their differences, a sense of kinship arose among the nations of Latin America, Africa, and Asia. All shared feelings of excitement and rebirth. As North Americans, Europeans, and the Chinese settled into the exhausting deadlock of the Cold War, visions of independence and national development captivated the rest of the world.

## Challenges of Nation Building

Each former colony had its own history and followed its own route to independence. Fifty-one nations signed the United Nations Charter in the closing months of 1948. During the United Nations' first decade, twenty-five new members joined, a third of them upon gaining independence. During the next decade, forty-six more new members were admitted, nearly all of them former colonial territories.

All spoke with one voice about their need for economic and technical assistance and the obligation of the wealthy nations to satisfy those needs. However, these new nations had difficulty finding a collective voice in a world increasingly oriented toward two superpowers. Antagonistic ethnic, religious, and linguistic groups strained the stability of fledgling governments trying to build an infrastructure.

Though some developing nations—particularly in Asia—attained substantial benefits from rapid technological change and world economic integration, many new nations faced basic problems of educating their citizens, nurturing industry, and escaping the economic constraints imposed by former imperialist masters that often maintained ownership of key resources. Wrenching social change accompanied the opening of markets to foreign investment and competition. The environment suffered severe pressures from oil exploration and transport to support the growing economies of the wealthy nations and from deforestation and urbanization in poor regions. Increased globalization coincided with increased inequality in many nations.

## The Superpowers and the Nonaligned Movement

Although the East-West superpower rivalry dominated world affairs, newly independent nations had concerns that were primarily domestic and regional. Their challenge was to pursue their ends within the bipolar structure of the Cold War—and when possible to take advantage of the East-West rivalry. In short, the superpowers dominated the world but did not control it. As time progressed, they dominated it less and less.

As one of the most successful leaders of the decolonization movement, Indonesia's President Sukarno

**Map 28.1 Decolonization, 1947–1990** Independence was achieved a decade or so earlier in South and Southeast Asia than in Africa. © Cengage Learning

**1960 Year independence achieved**

**Former ruler**

Great Britain
France
Netherlands
Italy
Belgium
Portugal
United States
Other

**ATLANTIC OCEAN**

GREAT BRITAIN
NETHERLANDS
BELGIUM
FRANCE
SPAIN
PORTUGAL
ITALY

**PACIFIC OCEAN**

JAPAN

NORTH KOREA 1948
SOUTH KOREA 1948 (From Japan)

PHILIPPINES 1946

NORTH VIETNAM 1954 (Unified 1975)
SOUTH VIETNAM 1954
CAMBODIA 1953
LAOS 1949
MYANMAR (BURMA) 1947

BRUNEI 1984 (From Gr. Br.)
MALAYSIA 1963
SINGAPORE 1965 (From Malaysia)
INDONESIA 1949
TIMOR-LESTE 1999 (From Indonesia)

PAPUA NEW GUINEA 1975 (From Australia)

PAKISTAN 1947
BANGLADESH 1973
INDIA 1947
SRI LANKA (CEYLON) 1948
MALDIVES 1975 (From Gr. Br.)

**INDIAN OCEAN**

OMAN 1971
P.D.R. OF YEMEN 1967
YEMEN (Unified 1990)
BAHRAIN 1971
QATAR 1971
UNITED ARAB EMIRATES 1971
KUWAIT 1961
IRAQ 1932
JORDAN 1946
SYRIA 1944
LEBANON 1944
ISRAEL 1948
CYPRUS 1960
MALTA 1964 (From Gr. Br.)

SEYCHELLES 1976 (From Gr. Br.)
COMOROS 1975 (From France)
MAURITIUS 1968 (From Gr. Br.)

MADAGASCAR 1960

SOMALIA 1960
DJIBOUTI 1977
ETHIOPIA
ERITREA 1993 (From Ethiopia)
SUDAN 1956
EGYPT 1922
LIBYA 1951
CHAD 1960

KENYA 1963
UGANDA 1962
DEM. REP. OF CONGO 1960
RWANDA 1962
BURUNDI 1962
TANZANIA 1964
MALAWI 1964
ZAMBIA 1964
ZIMBABWE 1980
MOZAMBIQUE 1975
SWAZILAND 1968
LESOTHO 1966
BOTSWANA 1966
SOUTH AFRICA (Republic 1961)
NAMIBIA 1990 (From South Africa)
ANGOLA 1975

CENTRAL AFRICAN REPUBLIC 1960
CAMEROON 1960
GABON 1960
REPUBLIC OF CONGO 1960
EQUATORIAL GUINEA 1968 (From Spain)
SÃO TOMÉ AND PRINCIPE 1975 (From Port.)
NIGERIA 1960
TOGO 1960
BENIN 1960
GHANA 1957
CÔTE D'IVOIRE 1960
NIGER 1960
BURKINA FASO 1960
MALI 1960
ALGERIA 1962
TUNISIA 1957

GUINEA 1958
LIBERIA 1820s
SIERRA LEONE 1961
GUINEA-BISSAU 1974
GAMBIA 1965
SENEGAL 1960
CAPE VERDE 1975 (From Port.)
MAURITANIA 1960
WESTERN SAHARA 1975 (From Spain) (Morocco)
MOROCCO 1956

Caspian Sea
Black Sea
Mediterranean Sea
Arabian Sea
Bay of Bengal

Tropic of Cancer
Tropic of Capricorn
Equator 0°

N

0   1,000   2,000 Mi.
0   1,000   2,000 Km.

© Cengage Learning

AP Photo/George Sweers

**Bandung Conference, 1955** India's Jawaharlal Nehru (in white hat) was a central figure at the conference held in Indonesia to promote solidarity among nonaligned developing nations.

was an appropriate figure to host a 1955 meeting of twenty-nine African and Asian countries at Bandung, Indonesia, that proclaimed solidarity among those fighting against colonial rule. This conference marked the beginning of an effort by the many new, poor, mostly non-European nations emerging from colonialism to gain more influence in world affairs. The terms **nonaligned nations** and **Third World**, which became commonplace in the following years, signaled these countries' collective stance toward the rival sides in the Cold War. If the West, led by the United States, and the East, led by the Soviet Union, represented two worlds locked in mortal struggle, the Third World consisted of everyone else.

Leaders of so-called Third World countries preferred the label *nonaligned*, which signaled their independence from Soviet or U.S. control. However, because the Soviet Union supported national liberation movements and the nonaligned movement

included communist countries such as China, Western leaders did not take the term *nonaligned* seriously. They saw Sukarno, Nehru, Nkrumah, and Egypt's Gamal Abd al-Nasser (gah-MAHL AHB-d al–NAH-suhr) as stalking horses for a global campaign to extend Soviet influence. This may have also been the hope of some Soviet leaders, who were quick to offer military and financial aid to many nonaligned countries.

For the movement's leaders, however, nonalignment was primarily a way to extract money and support from one or both superpowers. By flirting with the Soviet Union or its ally, the People's Republic of China, some skilled nonaligned leaders were able to

**nonaligned nations** Developing countries that announced their neutrality in the Cold War.

**Third World** Term applied to a group of developing countries who professed nonalignment during the Cold War.

gain from both sides. Nasser, who had led a military coup against the Egyptian monarchy in 1952, and his successor Anwar al-Sadat (al-seh-DAT) played this game well. The United States offered to build a dam at Aswan (AS-wahn), on the Nile River, to increase Egypt's electrical generating and irrigation capacity, but it withdrew the offer when Egypt turned to the Soviet Union for armaments in 1956. The Soviet Union then committed to building the dam.

Later that same year Israel, Great Britain, and France conspired to invade Egypt, aiming to overthrow Nasser, regain the Suez Canal that had recently been nationalized, and secure Israel from any Egyptian threat. The invasion succeeded militarily, but both the United States and the Soviet Union pressured the invaders to withdraw, thus saving Nasser's government. In 1972 Sadat evicted Soviet military advisers, but a year later he used his Soviet weapons to attack Israel. After he lost that war, he disengaged from the Soviets and sought increased aid from the United States.

Numerous other countries adopted similar balancing strategies. In each case, local leaders sought to develop their nations' economies and assert or preserve their nations' interests. Manipulating the superpowers was a means toward those ends and implied very little about true ideological orientation.

## New Nations in South and Southeast Asia

After partition in 1947 the independent states of India and Pakistan were strikingly dissimilar (see Chapter 26). Muslim Pakistan defined itself according to religion and quickly fell under the control of military leaders. Though 90 percent of India's population was Hindu, this much larger republic was secular. It inherited most of the considerable industrial and educational resources the British had developed, along with the larger share of trained civil servants and military officers.

The decision of the Hindu ruler of the northwestern state Jammu and Kashmir to join India without consulting his overwhelmingly Muslim subjects led to a war between India and Pakistan in 1947 that ended with an uneasy truce. Pakistan and India have since fought two wars: a brief one in 1965 over Kashmir, and another in 1971 when East Bengal, with

India's help, seceded from Pakistan to form the new nation of Bangladesh. Despite the truce between the two nations, Kashmir remained a flash point, with new clashes in 1999 and 2000. India, Pakistan, and Bangladesh have found cooperation difficult and have pursued markedly different economic, political, religious, and social paths.

Elsewhere in the region, nationalist movements won independence as well. Britain granted independence to Burma (now Myanmar [my-ahn-MAHR]) in 1948 and established the Malay Federation that year. Singapore, once a member of the federation, became an independent city-state itself in 1965. In 1946, the United States kept its promise of postwar independence for the Philippine Islands but retained close economic ties and leases on military bases. In the Dutch East Indies, a military confrontation resulted in Dutch withdrawal in 1949, and an architect and nationalist named Sukarno (1901–1970) became dictator of the resource-rich but underdeveloped nation of Indonesia. He ruled until 1965, when a military coup ousted him, eliminated the powerful Communist Party, and targeted the large Chinese ethnic community in an attempt to force assimilation.

## The Struggle for Independence in Africa

In the quarter-century between 1955 and 1980, African nationalists succeeded in ending European colonial rule. Mostly they gained independence peacefully, but where European settlers were numerous, violence became the norm.

In 1954, the Muslim people of Algeria rebelled against France. Having lost Indochina, France was determined to hold on to Algeria because 10 percent of the Algerian population was European and Algeria's economy was strongly oriented toward France. Both sides fought with great brutality. When Algeria finally won independence in 1962, the departure of the colonists undermined Algeria's economy, since few Arabs had received technical training or had management experience. None of the other African independence movements matched the Algerian struggle in scale or brutality.

Many African leaders dedicated their lives to winning independence. Kwame Nkrumah (KWAH-mee nn-KROO-muh) (1909–1972), for example, spent

**Jomo Kenyatta**  Kenya's newly elected premier, Jomo Kenyatta, cheered by crowds in Nairobi in 1963. Kenyatta (waving ceremonial "whisk") had led the struggle to end British colonial rule in Kenya.

a decade studying philosophy and theology in the United States, where he absorbed ideas about black pride and independence propounded by W. E. B. Du Bois and Marcus Garvey. When he returned to the Gold Coast in 1947 to work for independence, Great Britain had already freed its Asian colonies. Nkrumah quickly united the people of Ghana behind him and won independence without bloodshed. He became prime minister of Ghana (formerly the Gold Coast) in 1957, the first British colony in West Africa to achieve independence. However, Nkrumah proved more effective as an international spokesman than as an administrator, and he was overthrown in 1966 by a disaffected group of army officers.

Jomo Kenyatta (ca. 1894–1978) traveled a more difficult road in Kenya, where a substantial number of European coffee planters strengthened British desire to retain control. A protest movement among the Kikuyu (kih-KOO-you) people, which settlers called the "Mau Mau," became violent. After 1952, British troops hunted down movement leaders and resettled the Kikuyu. The British charged Kenyatta with being a Mau Mau leader, imprisoned him, and then put him in internal exile for eight years during a declared state of emergency. Released in 1961, Kenyatta negotiated with the British to write a constitution for an independent Kenya, and in 1964 he was elected the nation's first president. Kenyatta proved to be an effective, though autocratic, ruler.

In contrast, African leaders in the French colonies of sub-Saharan Africa were slow to call for full independence. They believed in the promises of political and civil rights made in 1944 by General Charles de Gaulle at a conference in Brazzaville. This Brazzaville conference also promised to expand French education at the village level, to improve health services, and to open more lower-level administrative positions to Africans, but the word *independence* was never mentioned.

African leaders also realized that some French colonies—such as Ivory Coast, with coffee and cacao exports, fishing, and hardwood forests—had good economic prospects, while others, such as landlocked, desert Niger, did not. Furthermore, they recognized the importance of French investment. Ultimately, however, African patriotism prevailed everywhere. Guinea, under the dynamic leadership of Sékou Touré (SAY-koo too-RAY), gained full independence in 1958, and the others did the same in 1960.

In southern Africa, European settlers fought hard to hold on. The African struggle against Portuguese rule in Angola and Mozambique dragged on until the overthrow of the antidemocratic government of Portugal in 1974; independence was granted the following year. After a ten-year fight, European settlers in the British colony of Southern Rhodesia accepted African majority rule in 1980. The new government renamed the country Zimbabwe, the name of a great city built long before the arrival of Europeans.

Only South Africa and neighboring Namibia remained in the hands of European minorities much longer. After World War II, the white minority government of South Africa achieved effective independence in 1961 but imposed a system of extreme racial segregation called *apartheid* (a-PART-hite) in which the cities, best jobs, and most of the land were reserved for Europeans. Africans and others classified as "non-whites" were subjected to strict limitations on place of residence, right to travel, and access to jobs and public facilities.

The African National Congress (ANC), formed in 1912, led opposition to apartheid (see Diversity and Dominance: Race and the Struggle for Justice in South Africa). After police fired on demonstrators in the African town of Sharpeville in 1960 and banned all peaceful political protest by Africans, a lawyer named Nelson Mandela (b. 1918) organized guerrilla resistance by the ANC. Mandela was sentenced to life in prison in 1964 and the government persecuted the ANC, but it was unable to defeat the movement. Facing growing opposition internationally, South Africa freed Mandela from prison in 1990 and began the transition to majority rule.

## SECTION REVIEW

- Newly independent nations faced the challenge of developing their economies and educating their peoples.
- Some new nations aligned themselves with the United States or with the Soviet Union, but many referred to themselves as nonaligned.
- Independence in India and Pakistan led to war over Kashmir, which has continued to cause conflict.
- Algeria gained independence from France after a long and violent revolution.
- West African colonies eventually gained independence from Great Britain and France through negotiation.
- In southern African colonies, large white populations resisted independence, and whites in South Africa instituted the system of segregation called apartheid.

# REVOLUTIONS, REFORM, AND REPRESSION IN LATIN AMERICA

■ *How did U.S. policies during the Cold War affect Latin America?*

Although Latin America had achieved independence from colonial rule more than a hundred years earlier, it struggled in the postwar decades over foreign ownership and social inequality. European and American companies dominated the economies of the region, creating a semicolonial order (see Chapters 21 and 23). Foreigners controlled Chile's copper, Cuba's sugar, Colombia's coffee, Guatemala's bananas, and the communication networks of several countries. Even in a country like Mexico, where the ruling Institutional Revolutionary Party, or PRI, was committed to revolutionary independence and economic development, a yawning gulf between rich and poor persisted. According to one estimate from the mid-1960s, some three hundred foreign and eight hundred Mexican companies dominated the country, and some two thousand families controlled much of the nation's wealth. At the other end of the economic scale were the millions of poor Mexicans struggling to survive. Thwarted by limited opportunities at home, millions of Mexicans migrated to the United States.

**Guatemala and the CIA**  Jacobo Arbenz Guzmán, elected president of Guatemala in 1951, was typical of Latin American leaders like Perón of Argentina and Vargas of Brazil (see Chapter 25), who confronted powerful foreign interests. His expropriation of large estates angered the United Fruit Company, a U.S. corporation that dominated banana exports and held vast tracts of land in reserve. Reacting to reports that Arbenz was becoming friendly toward communism, the U.S. Central Intelligence Agency (CIA) sponsored a takeover by the Guatemalan military in 1954. CIA intervention removed Arbenz, but it also condemned Guatemala to decades of governmental instability and violence.

## The Cuban Revolution

In Cuba, U.S. companies owned 40 percent of raw sugar production, 23 percent of nonsugar industry, 90 percent of telephone and electrical services, and 50 percent of public service railways. The needs of the U.S. economy largely determined Cuban foreign trade and held back development. Profits went north to the United States or to a small class of wealthy Cubans, many of foreign origin. Cuba's ruler during that period, Fulgencio Batista, became a symbol of corruption, repression, and foreign economic domination.

In 1959, a popular rebellion forced Batista to flee the country (see the discussion at the beginning of this chapter). Fidel Castro, the leader of the rebels, his brother Raul Castro, and Ernesto ("Che") Guevara (CHAY guh-VAHR-uh), the main theorist of communist revolution in Latin America, created a new regime. Within a year, Castro's government had redistributed land, lowered urban rents, and raised wages, effectively transferring 15 percent of the national income from the rich to the poor. Within two years the Castro government had nationalized the property of almost all U.S. corporations in Cuba as well as the wealth of Cuba's elite. This action resulted in a blockade by the United States, the flight of middle-class and technically trained Cubans, a drop in foreign investment, and the beginning of chronic food shortages.

Little evidence supports the view that Castro was committed to communism before the revolution, but his commitment to break the economic and political power of the United States in Cuba led him to turn

**Fidel Castro Arrives in Havana** Castro and his supporters overthrew a brutal dictatorship and began the revolutionary transformation of Cuba that led to a confrontation with the United States.

to the Soviet Union for economic aid. In doing so, he unwittingly committed his nation to economic stagnation and dependence on a foreign power as damaging as the previous relationship with the United States had been.

In April 1961, some fifteen hundred Cuban exiles trained and armed by the CIA landed at the Bay of Pigs in an effort to overthrow Castro. The Cuban army defeated the attempted invasion in a matter of days, partly because the new U.S. president, John F. Kennedy, decided not to provide all the air support that the plan (drawn up by the previous Eisenhower administration) originally called for. The failure of the Bay of Pigs invasion tarnished the reputation of the United States and the CIA and helped precipitate the Cuban Missile Crisis. Fearful of a new invasion, Castro placed Soviet nuclear weapons as well as missiles and bombers in Cuba.

Armed revolutionary movements that imitated the tactics and objectives of Cuba's bearded revolutionaries experienced little success. Among the thousands to lose their lives was Che Guevara, captured and executed in 1967 by Bolivian troops trained by the United States. Nevertheless, Castro had demonstrated that revolutionaries could successfully challenge American

# Diversity & Dominance

## Race and the Struggle for Justice in South Africa

One of South Africa's martyrs in the struggle against apartheid was the thinker and activist Steve Biko (1946–1977). Biko was one of the founders of the Black Consciousness Movement, which focused on the ways in which white settlers had stripped Africans of their freedom. Between 1975 and 1977 police arrested and interrogated him four times. After his arrest in August 1977, the police severely beat him and denied him medical care. His death in police custody caused worldwide outrage.

[T]hese are not the people we are concerned with [those who support apartheid]. We are concerned with that curious bunch of nonconformists who explain their participation in negative terms: that bunch of do-gooders that goes under all sorts of names—liberals, leftists etc. These are the people who argue that they are not responsible for white racism and the country's "inhumanity to the black man." These are the people who claim that they too feel the oppression just as acutely as the blacks and therefore should be jointly involved in the black man's struggle for a place under the sun. In short, these are the people who say that they have black souls wrapped up in white skins.

The role of the white liberal in the black man's history in South Africa is a curious one. Very few black organisations were not under white direction. True to their image, the white liberals always knew what was good for the blacks and told them so. The wonder of it all is that the black people have believed in them for so long. It was only at the end of the 50s that the blacks started demanding to be their own guardians.

Nowhere is the arrogance of the liberal ideology demonstrated so well as in their insistence that the problems of the country can only be solved by a bilateral approach involving both black and white. . . . Hence the multiracial political organisations and parties and the "nonracial" student organisations, all of which insist on integration not only as an end goal but also as a means.

The integration they talk about is first of all artificial in that it is a response to conscious manoeuvre rather than to the dictates of the inner soul. In other words the people forming the integrated complex have been extracted from various segregated societies with their in built [sic] complexes of superiority and inferiority and these continue to manifest themselves even in the "nonracial" setup of the integrated complex. As a result the integration so achieved is a one-way course, with the whites doing all the talking and the blacks the listening. . . .

. . .

It will not sound anachronistic to anybody genuinely interested in real integration to learn that blacks are asserting themselves in a society where they are being treated as perpetual under-16s. One does not need to plan for or actively encourage real integration. Once the various groups within a given community have asserted themselves to the point that mutual respect has to be shown then you have the ingredients for a true and meaningful integration. At the heart of true integration is the provision for each man, each group to rise and attain the envisioned self. Each group must be able to attain its style of existence without encroaching on or being thwarted by another. Out of this mutual respect for each other and complete freedom of self-determination there will obviously arise a genuine fusion of the life-styles of the various groups. This is true integration.

From this it becomes clear that as long as blacks are suffering from [an] inferiority complex—a result of 300 years of deliberate oppression, denigration and derision—they will be useless as co-architects of a normal society where man is nothing else but man for his own sake. Hence what is necessary as a prelude to anything else that may come is a very strong grassroots build-up of black consciousness such that blacks can learn to assert themselves and stake their rightful claim.

Thus in adopting the line of a nonracial approach, the liberals are playing their old game. They are claiming a "monopoly on intelligence and moral judgement" and setting the pattern and pace for the realisation of the black man's aspirations. They want to remain in good books ➤

with both the black and white worlds. They want to shy away from all forms of "extremisms," condemning "white supremacy" as being just as bad as "Black Power!" They vacillate between the two worlds, verbalising all the complaints of the blacks beautifully while skillfully extracting what suits them from the exclusive pool of white privileges. But ask them for a moment to give a concrete meaningful programme that they intend adopting, then you will see on whose side they really are. Their protests are directed at and appeal to white conscience, everything they do is directed at finally convincing the white electorate that the black man is also a man and that at some future date he should be given a place at the white man's table.

*In the following selection Anglican bishop Desmond Tutu (b. 1931) expressed his personal anguish at the death of Steve Biko, summarizing Biko's contributions to the struggle for justice in South Africa. Tutu won the Noble Peace Prize in 1984 and was named archbishop in 1988. From 1995 to 1998 he chaired the Truth and Reconciliation Commission, which investigated atrocities in South Africa during the years of apartheid. He stated that his objective was to create "a democratic and just society without racial divisions."*

When we heard the news "Steve Biko is dead" we were struck numb with disbelief. . . . But no, dear friends, he is dead and we are still numb with grief, and groan with anguish. . . .

It all seems such a senseless waste of a wonderfully gifted person, struck down in the bloom of youth, a youthful bloom that some wanted to see blighted. What can be the purpose of such wanton destruction? . . . How long can we go on appealing for a more just ordering of society where we all, black and white together, count not because of some accident of birth or a biological irrelevance—where all of us black and white count because we are human persons, human persons created in your own image.

God called Steve Biko to be his servant in South Africa—to speak up on behalf of God, declaring what the will of this God must be in a situation such as ours, a situation of evil, injustice, oppression and exploitation. God called him to be the founder father of the Black Consciousness Movement against which we have had tirades and fulminations. It is a movement by which God, through Steve, sought to awaken in the Black person a sense of

his intrinsic value and worth as a child of God, not needing to apologise for his existential condition as a black person, calling on blacks to glorify and praise God that he had created them black. Steve, with his brilliant mind that always saw to the heart of things, realised that until blacks asserted their humanity and their personhood, there was not the remotest chance for reconciliation in South Africa. For true reconciliation is a deeply personal matter. It can happen only between persons who assert their own personhood, and who acknowledge and respect that of others. You don't get reconciled to your dog, do you? Steve knew and believed fervently that being pro-black was not the same thing as being anti-white. The Black Consciousness Movement is not a "hate white movement," despite all you may have heard to the contrary. He had a far too profound respect for persons as persons, to want to deal with them under readymade, shopsoiled [sic] categories.

All who met him had this tremendous sense of a warm-hearted man, and as a notable acquaintance of his told me, a man who was utterly indestructible, of massive intellect and yet reticent; quite unshakeable in his commitment to principle and to radical change in South Africa by peaceful means; a man of real reconciliation, truly an instrument of God's peace, unshakeable in his commitment to the liberation of all South Africans, black and white, striving for a more just and more open South Africa.

## QUESTIONS FOR ANALYSIS

1. What are Steve Biko's charges against white liberals in South Africa?
2. What was the proper role for whites in the anti-apartheid movement according to Biko?
3. How does Bishop Tutu's eulogy differ from the political spirit and point of view expressed in Biko's 1970 essay?
4. According to Bishop Tutu, what were Biko's strongest characteristics? Were these characteristics demonstrated in Biko's essay?

*Sources*: First selection from Steve Biko, *I Write What I Like*, ed. by Aelred Stubbs C.R., Bowerdean Publishing Co., Ltd.; second selection from Bishop Desmond Tutu, *Crying in the Wilderness: The Struggle for Justice in South Africa*, ed. John Webster (William B. Eerdmans Publishing Co., 1982), pp. 61–63.

power and put in place a radical program of economic and social reform in the Western Hemisphere.

## The Era of Violence and Repression

In the 1970s Latin America entered a dark era of political violence. Revolutionary movements challenged the established order, and democratic governments were overturned by military revolts. A region of weak democracies in 1960 became a region of military dictatorships with little patience for civil liberties and human rights fifteen years later.

The ongoing confrontation between Fidel Castro and the United States contributed to regional crisis. The fact that the Cuban communist government survived opposition from the United States energized the revolutionary left throughout Latin America. In response, the United States increased support for its political and military allies, training many of the military leaders who led coups during this period.

Brazil was the first nation to experience the conservative reaction to the Cuban Revolution. Claiming that Brazil's civilian political leaders could not protect the nation from communist subversion, the army overthrew the government of President João Goulart (ju-wow go-LARHT) in 1964. Once in power, the military suspended the constitution, outlawed political parties, and exiled former presidents and opposition leaders. Death squads—illegal paramilitary organizations sanctioned by the government—detained, tortured, and executed thousands of citizens. The dictatorship also undertook an ambitious economic program that promoted industrialization through import substitution (see Chapter 25). Using tax and tariff policies, the Brazilian dictatorship successfully compelled foreign-owned companies to increase investment in manufacturing, especially the auto industry.

This combination of dictatorship, violent repression, and government promotion of industrialization came to be called the "Brazilian Solution." Elements of this "solution" spread across much of the region. In 1970 Chile's newly elected president, **Salvador Allende** (sal-VAH-dor ah-YEHN-day), undertook an ambitious program of socialist reforms and nationalized Chile's heavy industry and mines, including the American-owned copper companies that domi-

nated the economy. From the beginning of Allende's presidency, the administration of President Richard Nixon (served 1969–1973) opposed the Allende reforms. Supported by the United States, General Augusto Pinochet (ah-GOOS-toh pin-oh-CHET) led a military uprising that overthrew Allende in 1973. President Allende and thousands of Chileans died in the uprising, and thousands more were jailed, tortured, and imprisoned without trial. Pinochet rolled back Allende's socialist innovations, reduced state participation in the economy, and encouraged foreign investment.

In 1976 Argentina followed Brazil and Chile into dictatorship. Juan Perón (see Chapter 26) had been exiled in 1955 after a military uprising, but with Argentina torn by political violence he was allowed to return and was then elected president in 1973. Perón insisted that his third wife, Isabel Martínez de Perón (EES-ah-bell mar-TEEN-ehz deh pair-OWN), be his vice president, and she inherited the presidency after his death in 1974, but Argentina suffered during her weak administration, wracked by inflation, terrorism, and labor protests. Impatient with her policies, the military seized power and suspended the constitution in 1976. During the next seven years it fought what it called the **Dirty War** against terrorism. More than nine thousand Argentines lost their lives; thousands of others endured arrest and torture before democracy was restored.

Yet some revolutionary movements persisted, reaching a peak in 1979 in Nicaragua with the overthrow of the corrupt dictatorship of Anastasio Somoza. This broad alliance of revolutionaries and reformers called themselves **Sandinistas** (sahn-din-EES-tahs), from Augusto César Sandino, who had led Nicaraguan opposition to U.S. military intervention

**Salvador Allende (1908–1973)** Socialist president of Chile who was elected in 1970 and overthrown and killed by the military in 1973.

**Dirty War** Suppression of leftist groups by the Argentine military (1976–1983) characterized by the use of illegal imprisonment, torture, and executions.

**Sandinistas** Members of a leftist coalition that overthrew the Nicaraguan dictator Anastosio Somoza in 1979 and attempted to install a socialist economy. The United States financed an armed uprising against the Sandinista government. In 1990 the Sandinistas lost power after a national election.

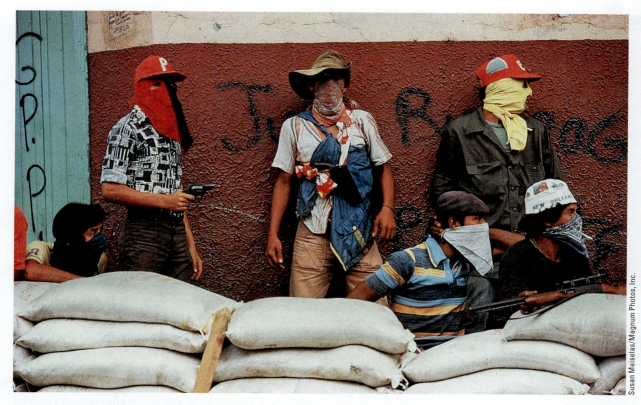

**The Nicaraguan Revolution Overturns Somoza**  A revolutionary coalition that included Marxists drove the dictator Anastasio Somoza from power in 1979. The Somoza family had ruled Nicaragua since the 1930s and maintained a close relationship with the United States.

between 1927 and 1932. The Sandinistas sought to imitate the Soviet-style economy of Cuba, nationalizing the properties of the Nicaraguan elite and U.S. companies.

U.S. president Jimmy Carter (served 1977–1980) stopped the flow of U.S. arms to regimes with the worst records of human rights violations and reestablished Panamanian sovereignty of the Panama Canal in 1999, but he failed to find common ground with the intransigent Sandinistas. Ronald Reagan (served 1981–1989), who succeeded Carter as president, vigorously opposed both the Nicaraguan Revolution and a revolutionary movement in neighboring El Salvador. When the U.S. Congress would not support U.S. military intervention, Reagan turned to a proxy force of anti-Sandinista Nicaraguans, called *Contras* (counter-revolutionaries). Overconfident Sandinistas responded by calling for free elections in 1990, but they badly miscalculated. Exhausted

by more than a decade of violence, Nicaraguans rejected the Sandinistas and elected a middle-of-the-road coalition led by Violeta Chamorro (vee-oh-LET-ah cha-MOR-roe).

The Reagan administration also thwarted the FMLN (Farabundo Martí [fah-rah-BOON-doh mar-TEE] National Liberation Front) guerrilla movement in El Salvador by training the Salvadoran army and providing hundreds of millions of dollars in military assistance. Chastened by the Sandinista defeat, the FMLN negotiated for peace with the brutal dictatorship that had been responsible for the deaths of critics, even those in the Catholic clergy, and transformed themselves into a civilian political party.

Violence also abated when right-wing military dictatorships in Brazil, Chile, and Argentina came to an end between 1983 and 1990, brought down by their own excesses and by popular desires for a return to constitutional democratic government. But the U.S.

invasion of the tiny Caribbean nation of Grenada in 1983 and the arrest of Panamanian dictator General Manuel Noriega (MAN-wel no-ree-EGG-ah) in 1989 were powerful reminders of American power in the region, and the United States pushed Latin American nations to remove limitations on foreign investment, eliminate many social welfare programs, and reduce public-sector employment.

# JAPAN, CHINA, AND THE FOUR TIGERS

■ *Why were developments in China so different from those in other parts of East Asia?*

East Asia had suffered as much as Europe from the Second World War. Eastern China had been invaded and occupied by Japanese forces from 1937 to 1945, and the rest of China had been the scene of a long and bitter civil war (1934–1949) between the nationalist (or Guomindang) army supported by the United States and the communist People's Liberation Army (see Chapter 27). War continued on the Korean peninsula until 1953. After that, it took several decades before prosperity came to East Asia.

## The Japanese Economic Miracle

Japan signed a peace treaty with most of its former enemies in 1951 and regained independence from American occupation the following year. Renouncing militarism and its imperialist past, Japan remained on the sidelines throughout the Korean War. Its new constitution, written under American supervision in 1946, allowed only a limited self-defense force, banned the deployment of Japanese troops abroad, and gave the vote to women.

With peace restored, the Japanese focused their resources on rebuilding industries and expanding trade. During the U.S. occupation, Japan became closely tied to the West by trade and soon benefited from the postwar recovery. At the same time, controls placed on Japan by peace conditions kept its military expenditures low during the Cold War, providing an exceptional environment to invest in economic development and infrastructure.

Three industries that took advantage of government aid and new technologies were key to Japan's emergence as an economic superpower after 1975. Electricity was in short supply in 1950, and Tokyo suffered from chronic power outages. Japan responded by constructing a power grid between 1951 and 1970 that produced 60 million kilowatts of electricity. Most of this new capacity came from hydroelectric sources. At the same time steel production and shipbuilding developed rapidly, placing Japan among world leaders in both industries.

The Japanese industrial model differed from the American and European models. During the American occupation, Japanese industrial conglomerates known as *zaibatsu* were broken up. Although ownership of major industries became less concentrated, new industrial alliances appeared. These formed six major *keiretsu* (kay-REHT-soo), each of which included a major bank as well as firms in industry, commerce, and construction tied together in an interlocking ownership structure. Minor keiretsu could also form around a corporation, like Toyota, and its major suppliers. These industrial combinations developed close relationships with the government, which imposed tariffs and import regulations to inhibit foreign competition. Such support was crucial in fostering the development of Japan's major industries.

Through the 1970s and 1980s, the Japanese superiority in manufactured goods produced huge trade surpluses. Attempts by the United States and the

*keiretsu* Alliances of corporations and banks that dominate the Japanese economy.

European Community to pry open the Japanese market through negotiation had only limited success. In 1990, Japan's trade surplus with the rest of the world was double that of 1985. Many experts assumed that Japan's competitive advantages would propel it past the United States as the world's preeminent industrial economy. But its economy began to stall at the end of the decade when Japanese real estate and stock markets became overvalued and prices collapsed. By the end of the 1990s Japan's GDP had suffered a loss greater than that suffered by the United States in the Great Depression.

## Mao's Zedong's Many Revolutions

While Japan benefited from being outside the Cold War, China was deeply involved in Cold War politics. When Mao Zedong (maow dzuh-dong) and the communists defeated the nationalists in 1949 and established the People's Republic of China (PRC) (see Chapter 27), their main ally and arms supplier was the Soviet Union, although by 1956 the PRC and the Soviet Union had diverged politically. Mao had his own notions of communism that focused strongly on the peasantry, which the Soviets had ignored in favor of the industrial working class.

Mao's Great Leap Forward in 1958 was intended to propel China into the ranks of world industrial powers. His plan relied on maximizing the output of small-scale, village-level industries and instituting mass collectivization in agriculture. It took over a decade for this small-scale industrialization to result in record levels of agricultural and industrial production, but these policies demonstrated Mao's willingness to carry out massive economic and social experiments of his own devising.

In 1966, in another nationwide radical program called the **Cultural Revolution**, Mao ordered the mass mobilization of Chinese youth into Red Guard units to ward off the stagnation and bureaucratization he saw in the Soviet Union. To this end, Red Guard units criticized and purged teachers, party officials, and intellectuals for "bourgeois values." Internal party conflict continued until 1971, when Mao admitted that attacks on individuals had gotten out of hand. The last years of the Cultural Revolution were dominated by radicals led by Mao's wife, Jiang Qing (jyahn ching), who restricted artistic and intellectual activity.

The rift between the PRC and the Soviet Union allowed U.S. president Richard Nixon (served 1969–1974) to revive relations with China. In 1971 the United States agreed to allow the PRC to join the United Nations and occupy China's permanent seat on the Security Council, displacing the Chinese nationalist government on Taiwan. The following year, Nixon visited Beijing, initiating a new era of cooperation between the People's Republic of China and the United States.

## The Four Tigers

A few other Asian states imitated the Japanese model of close cooperation between government and industry. South Korea overcame the devastation of the Korean War in little more than a decade through a combination of inexpensive labor, strong technical education, and sustained domestic capital reserves. It developed heavy industries like steel and shipbuilding, as well as consumer industries like automobiles and consumer electronics. Japanese investment and technology transfers accelerated this process.

Taiwan, Hong Kong, and Singapore moved so rapidly in the same direction that these three nations and South Korea were called the **Asian Tigers**. Taiwan suffered a number of political reverses, including the loss of its United Nations seat to the People's Republic of China in 1971 and the withdrawal of diplomatic recognition by the United States. Nevertheless, it achieved remarkable economic progress, based on smaller, more specialized companies and investment in the People's Republic of China.

Hong Kong and Singapore were former British colonies with limited resources. Singapore's economy rested on its busy port and on banking and commercial services. After separating from Malaysia in 1965, this society of around 4 million people diversified by building textile and electronics industries. Hong Kong's economic prosperity, based on its ports as well as its banking and commercial services, was increasingly

**Cultural Revolution (China)** Campaign in China ordered by Mao Zedong to purge the Communist Party of his opponents and instill revolutionary values in the younger generation.

**Asian Tigers** South Korea, Taiwan, Hong Kong, and Singapore, so called because their economies expanded so fast.

tied to China's growing economy. Worried about Hong Kong's reintegration into the People's Republic of China in 1997, local capitalists moved significant amounts of capital to safe havens like the United States and Canada, but in recent years Hong Kong has regained its dynamism and is now even more closely tied to the rapidly developing Chinese economy.

These **newly industrialized economies (NIEs)** all had disciplined and hardworking labor forces, and all invested heavily in education. As early as 1980 Korea had as many engineering graduates as Germany, Britain, and Sweden combined. These countries also emphasized outward-looking export strategies and had high rates of personal saving—about 35 percent of GDP—that allowed them to fund investment in new technology. Like Japan, they practiced government sponsorship and protection. Despite this momentum, the region was deeply shaken by a financial crisis that began in 1997. Like the recession that afflicted Japan in 1990, a combination of bad loans, weak banks, and the international effects of currency speculation led to a deep regional crisis that was stabilized only by the efforts of the United States, Japan, and international institutions like the International Monetary Fund.

## NATIONAL AND RELIGIOUS CONFLICTS IN THE MIDDLE EAST

■ *What roles did nationalism and religious identity play in Middle Eastern politics?*

Independence came gradually to the Arab countries of the Middle East. Syria and Lebanon gained independence when the League of Nations mandate system ended after World War II. Iraq, Egypt, and Jordan enjoyed nominal independence between the two world wars but remained under indirect British control until the 1950s.

## The Arab-Israeli Conflict

Overshadowing all Arab politics, however, was the struggle with Israel. British policy on Palestine between the wars oscillated between favoring Zionist Jewish immigrants and the indigenous Palestinian Arabs. After the war, under intense pressure to resettle European Jewish refugees, Britain turned the Palestine problem over to the United Nations. In November 1947 the General Assembly voted in favor of partitioning Palestine into two states, one Jewish and one Arab. The Jewish community made plans to declare independence, while the Palestinians, who felt the proposed land division was unfair, reacted in horror and took up arms. When Israel declared its independence in May 1948, neighboring Arab countries sent armies to help the Palestinians crush the newborn state.

Israel prevailed and some 700,000 Palestinians became refugees, finding shelter in United Nations refugee camps in Jordan, Syria, Lebanon, and the Gaza Strip (a bit of coastal land on the Egyptian-Israeli border). The right of these refugees to return home remains a focal point of Arab politics today. In 1967, Israel responded to threatening military moves by Egypt's Nasser by preemptively attacking Egyptian and Syrian air bases. In six days, Israel won a smashing victory. It also won control of Jerusalem (previously split with Jordan), the West Bank, the Gaza Strip, the strategic Golan Heights in southern Syria, and the entire Sinai Peninsula (see Map 28.2). Acquiring all of Jerusalem satisfied Jews' deep longing to return to their holiest city, but Palestinians continued to regard Jerusalem as their destined capital, and Muslims in many countries protested Israeli control of the Dome of the Rock, a revered Islamic shrine located in the city. These acquisitions resulted in a new wave of Palestinian refugees.

The rival claims to Palestine continued to plague Middle Eastern politics. The Palestine Liberation Organization (PLO), headed by Yasir Arafat (AR-uh-fat),

**newly industrialized economies (NIEs)** Rapidly growing new industrializing nations of the late twentieth century, including the Asian Tigers.

**Map 28.2** **Middle East Oil and the Arab-Israeli Conflict, 1947–1973** Private European and American companies had long controlled oil resources. In the 1960s OPEC negotiated agreements for sharing control and eventually establishing national ownership. This set the stage for the use of oil as a weapon in the 1973 Arab-Israeli war as well as for subsequent price increases. © Cengage Learning

Soviet occupation, 1979–1989
U.S. aid to rebels, 1980s
International and Northern Alliance
forces defeat Taliban, 2001

U.S. troops, 1958, 1983–1984

U.S. arms sales, 1955–1978:
$20.8 billion
Shah overthrown, 1979
American hostages taken,
1979–1981

Principal center of al-Qaeda
activity, 2004–

U.S. and allies launch
First U.S.-Iraq War, 1991

U.S. arms sales, 1980s,
during Iran-Iraq War
Iraq invades Kuwait, 1990
Second U.S.-Iraq War, 2003

Al-Qaeda headquarters,
1992–1996

Oil embargo, 1973
Source of 17% of U.S. oil imports
in 1975
Largest buyer of U.S. arms, 1978

Bombing of USS *Cole*
by al-Qaeda, 2000

U.S. troops assist in relief of
famine, 1992–1993.
U.S. troops withdrawn, 1994.
U.S.-backed Ethiopian invasion
removes Islamist government,
2006

Members of the Organization of
Petroleum Exporting Countries
(OPEC)

Oil fields

**ARAB-ISRAELI
CONFLICT**

Jewish state after UN partition
of Palestine, 1947

Israel after War of 1948–1949

Area controlled by Israel after
Six-Day War, 1967

Israeli-occupied area after
Yom Kippur War, 1973

By Egyptian-Israeli agreements of 1975 and
1979, Israel withdrew from the Sinai in 1982.
In 1981 Israel annexed the Golan Heights.
Through negotiations between Israel and
the PLO, Jericho and the Gaza Strip were
placed under Palestinian self-rule, and Israeli
troops were withdrawn in 1994. In 1994
Israel and Jordan signed an agreement
opening their borders and normalizing their
relations.

waged guerrilla war against Israel, frequently engaging in acts of terrorism. The militarized Israelis were able to blunt or absorb these attacks and launch counter-strikes that involved assassinations and bombings. Though the United States proved a firm friend to Israel and the Soviet Union armed the Arab states, neither superpower saw the struggle between Zionism and Palestinian nationalism as a vital concern—until oil became a political issue.

## The Oil Crisis of 1973

The phenomenal concentration of oil wealth in the Middle East—Saudi Arabia, Iran, Iraq, Kuwait, Libya, Qatar, Bahrain, and the United Arab Emirates—was not fully realized until after World War II, when demand for oil rose sharply as civilian economies recovered. In 1960, as world demand rose, oil-producing states formed the **Organization of Petroleum Exporting Countries (OPEC)** to promote their collective interest in higher revenues.

Oil politics and the Arab-Israeli conflict intersected in October 1973 during the Yom Kippur War. Surprise attacks by Syria and Egypt threw the Israelis into temporary disarray, but Israel won a clear military victory in the end. Supported by military supplies from the United States, it drove back Syrian forces and trapped an Egyptian army at the Suez Canal's southern end. The United States then arranged a cease-fire and the disengagement of forces. But before that could happen, the Arab oil-producing countries voted to embargo oil shipments to the United States and the Netherlands as punishment for their support of Israel.

The implications of using oil as an economic weapon profoundly disturbed the worldwide oil industry. Prices rose—along with feelings of insecurity. In 1974 OPEC responded to the turmoil in the oil market by quadrupling prices, setting the stage for massive transfers of wealth to the producing countries and provoking a feeling of crisis throughout the consuming countries.

## Islamic Revolutions in Iran and Afghanistan

Although the Arab-Israel conflict and the oil crisis concerned both superpowers, the prospect of direct military involvement remained remote. When unexpected crises developed in Iran and Afghanistan, however, significant strategic issues came to the foreground. Both countries adjoined Soviet territory. Exercising post–Vietnam War caution, the United States reacted with restraint. The Soviet Union chose a bolder and ultimately disastrous course.

Muhammad Reza Pahlavi (REH-zah PAH-lah-vee) succeeded his father as shah of Iran in 1941. In 1953, covert intervention by the U.S. Central Intelligence Agency (CIA) helped the shah retain his throne in the face of a movement to overturn royal power. Even after nationalizing the foreign-owned oil industry, the shah continued to enjoy American support. When oil income mushroomed following the price increases of the 1970s, the United States encouraged the shah to spend his nation's growing wealth on advanced American weaponry. By the 1970s popular resentment against the shah's dependence on the United States, the ballooning wealth of the elite families that supported him, and the brutality, inefficiency, malfeasance, and corruption of his government led to mass opposition.

**Ayatollah Ruhollah Khomeini** (A-yat-ol-LAH ROOH-ol-LAH ko-MAY-nee), a Shi'ite (SHE-ite) philosopher-cleric who had spent most of his eighty-plus years in religious and academic pursuits, became the voice and symbolic leader of the opposition. Massive protests forced the shah to flee Iran and ended the monarchy in 1979. In the Islamic Republic of Iran, which replaced the monarchy, Ayatollah Khomeini was supreme arbiter of disputes and guarantor of the religious legitimacy. Elections were held, but monarchists, communists, and other groups opposed to the idea of an Islamic Republic were barred from office. Shi'ite clerics with little training for government service emerged in many of the highest posts, and stringent measures were taken to replace Western styles and culture with Islamic norms. Universities temporarily closed as their faculties were purged of secularists and monarchists.

**Organization of Petroleum Exporting Countries (OPEC)** Organization formed in 1960 by oil-producing states to promote their collective interest in generating revenue from oil.

**Ayatollah Ruhollah Khomeini (1902–1989)** Shi'ite philosopher and cleric who led the overthrow of the shah of Iran in 1979 and created an Islamic republic.

James Pozarik/Getty Images

**Shortage at the Pumps** As prices rose in the late 1970s, consumers tried to hoard supplies by filling gas cans at neighborhood stations. For the first time gas prices exceeded $1 a gallon.

Women were compelled to wear modest Islamic garments outside the house, while semi-official vigilante committees policed public morals and cast a pall over entertainment and social life.

The United States under President Carter had criticized the shah's repression, but the overthrow of a long-standing ally and the creation of the Islamic Republic were blows to American prestige. Khomeini saw the United States as a "Great Satan" and encouraged Islamic revolutionary movements elsewhere, to the distress of both the United States and Israel. In November 1979, Iranian radicals seized the U.S. embassy in Tehran and then held fifty-two diplomats hostage for 444 days. Americans felt humiliated by their inability to rescue the hostages or negotiate their release.

In the fall of 1980, shortly after negotiations for the release of the hostages began, **Saddam Husain (sah-DAHM hoo-SANE)**, the ruler of neighboring Iraq, invaded Iran to topple the Islamic Republic. His own dictatorial rule rested on a secular Arab-nationalist philosophy and long-standing friendship with the Soviet Union, which supplied his army. He feared that

Iran's revolutionary fervor would infect his own country's Shi'ite majority and threaten his power. While the war pitted American weapons in Iranian hands against Soviet weapons in Iraqi hands, the superpowers avoided overt involvement. Covertly, however, the Reagan administration sent arms via Israel to Iran, hoping to gain the release of other American hostages held by Muslim radicals in Lebanon and to secretly finance the Contra war against the Sandinista government of Nicaragua. When this deal came to light in 1986, the resulting political scandal intensified American hostility toward Iran. Openly tilting toward Iraq, President Reagan sent the U.S. Navy to the Persian Gulf, ostensibly to protect nonbelligerent shipping. This threatening move helped persuade Iran to accept a cease-fire in 1988.

While the United States experienced anguish and frustration in Iran, the Soviet Union found itself

**Saddam Husain (1937–2006)** President of Iraq from 1979 until overthrown by the American invasion in 2003. Waged war on Iran from 1980 to 1988. His invasion of Kuwait was repulsed in the Persian Gulf War of 1991.

**SECTION REVIEW**

- The politics of the postwar Middle East came to be dominated by the Arab-Israeli conflict.

- In response to an Arab-Israeli war, the Arab nations cut off oil exports, causing a severe economic crisis.

- In Iran, a radical anti-American Islamic revolution led by Ayatollah Khomeini overthrew the shah and established an anti-Western Shi'ite republic in 1979, after which Sunni Iraq attacked Iran.

- The Soviets intervened in Afghanistan in 1979 but failed to defeat religiously inspired Afghan guerrilla forces backed by the United States and Pakistan.

facing even more serious problems in neighboring Afghanistan. In 1978 a Marxist party with a secular reform agenda seized power in Afghanistan. Offended by these efforts to reform education and grant rights to women, traditional ethnic and religious leaders led a successful rebellion. In 1979, the Soviet Union responded by sending its army to Afghanistan to bolster communist rule.

With the United States, Saudi Arabia, and Pakistan paying, equipping, and training Afghan rebels, the Soviet Union found itself in the same kind of unwinnable war the United States had stumbled into in Vietnam. Unable to justify the continuing drain on manpower, morale, and economic resources and facing widespread domestic discontent, Soviet leaders finally withdrew their troops in 1989. The Afghan communists held on for another three years, and then rebel groups took control of the entire country and began to fight among themselves over who should rule.

In this chaotic situation a radical Islamic party with close ties to Pakistan, the Taliban, took power in 1996. They installed a harsh religious regime and soon faced armed opposition. The Taliban had received financial support from the Saudi Arabian Osama bin Laden during their rise to power and later provided him with protection as he organized al-Qaeda (discussed in Chapter 29).

# THE END OF THE BIPOLAR WORLD

■ *What led to the collapse of the Soviet bloc?*

Few in 1980 predicted the startling collapse of the Soviet Union and the socialist nations of the Warsaw Pact. The once-independent nations and ethnic groups brought within the Soviet Union and the eastern European nations seemed securely transformed by the experiences and institutions of communism. But this arrangement was nearly finished.

## Crisis in the Soviet Union

Under U.S. president Ronald Reagan and the Soviet Union's general secretary Leonid Brezhnev (leh-oh-NEED BREZ-nef), the rhetoric of the Cold War remained intense. Massive new U.S. investments in armaments placed heavy burdens on a Soviet economy already suffering from shortages and mismanagement. Obsolete industrial plants and centralized planning stifled initiative and led to a declining standard of living relative to the West, while the arbitrariness of the bureaucracy, the manipulation of information, and deprivations created a crisis in morale.

Despite the growing discontent, Brezhnev refused to modify his unsuccessful policies. But he could not escape criticism. In a series of powerful books, the writer Alexander Solzhenitsyn (sol-zhuh-NEET-sin) castigated the Soviet system and particularly the Soviet prison camps. He won a Nobel Prize in literature but was charged him with treason and expelled from the country in 1974. *Samizdat* (sah-meez-DAHT), self-published underground writings by critics of the regime, circulated widely despite government efforts to suppress them.

By the time **Mikhail Gorbachev** (GORE-beh-CHOF) took up the reins of the Soviet government in 1985, war weariness, economic decay, and vocal protest had reached critical levels. Casting aside Brezhnev's hard line, Gorbachev authorized major reforms in an attempt to stave off total collapse. His policy of political openness (*glasnost*) permitted criticism of the government and the Communist Party. His policy of *perestroika* (per-ih-STROY-kuh) ("restructuring") was an attempt to address long-suppressed economic problems by moving away from central state

**Mikhail Gorbachev (b. 1931)** Head of the Soviet Union from 1985 to 1991. His liberalization effort improved relations with the West, but he lost power after his reforms led to the collapse of the communist governments in eastern Europe.

***perestroika*** Policy of "restructuring" that was the centerpiece of Mikhail Gorbachev's efforts to liberalize communism in the Soviet Union.

planning and toward a more open economic system. In 1989 he ended the unpopular war in Afghanistan.

## The Collapse of the Socialist Bloc

Events in eastern Europe were very important in forcing change on the Soviet Union. In 1980 protests by Polish shipyard workers in the city of Gdansk led to the formation of **Solidarity**, a labor union that grew to 9 million members. The Roman Catholic Church in Poland, strengthened by the elevation of a Pole, Karol Wojtyla (KAH-rol voy-TIL-ah), to the papacy as John Paul II in 1978, gave strong moral support to the protest movement. As Gorbachev loosened political controls in the Soviet Union after 1985, communist leaders elsewhere lost confidence in Soviet resolve, and critics and reformers in Poland and throughout eastern Europe were emboldened.

Beleaguered Warsaw Pact governments vacillated between relaxation of control and suppression of dissent. As the Catholic clergy in Poland had supported Solidarity, Protestant and Orthodox religious leaders aided the rise of opposition groups elsewhere. This combination of nationalism and religion provided a powerful base for opponents of the communist regimes. Threatened by these forces, communist governments sought to quiet the opposition by seeking solutions to their severe economic problems. They turned to the West for trade and financial assistance and opened their nations to travelers, ideas, styles, and money from Western countries, all of which accelerated the demand for change.

By the end of 1989, communist governments across eastern Europe had fallen. The dismantling of the Berlin Wall, the symbol of a divided Europe and the bipolar world, vividly represented this transformation. In Poland, Hungary, Czechoslovakia, and Bulgaria, communist leaders decided that change was inevitable and initiated political reforms. When Romanian dictator Nicolae Ceausescu (nehk-oh-LIE chow-SHES-koo) refused to surrender power, he provoked a rebellion that ended with his arrest and execution. The comprehensiveness of these changes became clear in 1990, when Solidarity leader Lech Walesa (leck wah-LEN-sah) was elected president of Poland and dissident playwright Vaclav Havel (vah-SLAV hah-VEL) was elected president of Czechoslovakia. That same year, East and West Germany were reunited, and the

**The Fall of the Berlin Wall**  The Berlin Wall was the most important symbol of the Cold War. Constructed to keep residents of East Germany from fleeing to the West and defended by armed guards and barbed wire, it was the public face of communism. As the Soviet system fell apart, the residents of East and West Berlin broke down sections of the wall.

_Bossu Regis/Corbis Sygma_

eastern Baltic states of Lithuania, Estonia, and Latvia declared independence from the Soviet Union.

The end of the Soviet Union then came suddenly in 1991. Gorbachev's efforts to transform the Soviet system could not keep up with the tide of change sweeping through the region. After communist hardliners botched a poorly conceived coup against Gorbachev, disgust with communism boiled over. Boris Yeltsin, the president of the Russian Republic and a long-time member of the Communist Party, led popular resistance to the coup in Moscow and emerged as the most powerful leader in the country. Russia, the largest republic in the Soviet Union, was effectively

**Solidarity**  Polish trade union created in 1980 to protest working conditions and political repression. It began the nationalist opposition in eastern Europe.

taking the place of the disintegrating USSR. In September 1991, as the sixteen smaller republics of the Soviet Union declared their independence, the Congress of People's Deputies voted to dissolve the union. Mikhail Gorbachev went into retirement.

## CONCLUSION

Shortly after World War II, the Soviet Union and the Western democracies led by the United States began to prepare for a new round of hostilities, establishing competing military alliances and attempting to influence the new governments of nations formerly occupied by the Axis. Each side portrayed this tension as a struggle between irreconcilably different social and economic systems. The boundary that separated the United States and its allies and the Soviet Union and its allies, and that Churchill called an "iron curtain," was soon defended by massive armies and powerful nuclear weapons.

This Cold War quickly became global in character as distant civil wars, regional conflicts, and nationalist revolutions were transformed by support provided by these rivals for global ascendancy. Many of the flash points in this war were provided by the desire of colonized peoples to establish independent nations. The most powerful force in the postwar era was nationalism, the desire of peoples to control their own destinies. This reality was obscured by the global contest of the Cold War.

In Africa, the Middle East, South Asia, and Latin America, this desire to throw off foreign controls led to the creation of scores of new nations by the 1970s. Each nation's struggle had its own character. While in India these passions led to a partition into two states, similar sentiments led in China to the overthrow of a weak pro-Western government and the creation of a communist dictatorship. In much of Africa, the Middle East, and the Caribbean, nationalism overturned colonial rule. In the Middle East the desire for self-government was complicated by the creation of the state of Israel. In Latin America, where most nations had been independent for well over a century, nationalist passions focused on a desire for economic independence and an end to foreign military interventions. For this reason Castro found it easy to connect his revolutionary ambitions to anticolonial movements elsewhere.

The end of Japanese control in Korea and Vietnam led to territorial partitions that separated Soviet-leaning and Western-allied polities. Civil war and foreign interventions soon followed. In both cases the Soviet Union and China supported communist forces. The United States committed large military forces to protect the anticommunist governments, gaining a stalemate in Korea and eventually losing in Vietnam. While these outcomes were mixed for the superpowers, the wars were contained and managed so as to prevent direct engagement and nuclear conflict.

# CHAPTER REVIEW

## THE COLD WAR

■ *What were the major threats to world peace during the Cold War?* (page 657)

The arms race associated with the rivalry between the West and the Soviets produced the largest peacetime militaries in world history. The reliance of both sides on nuclear weapons meant that any direct conflict had the potential to escalate into a global holocaust. For more than fifty years massed armies faced each other across Europe. This confrontation was projected into space, as each side sought to advertise its technological capacity through satellite launches and finally a moon landing. During the Cold War, leaders of the opposing alliances viewed their struggle as a global conflict between irreconcilable systems. This meant that every popular movement, revolution, or civil war was strategically important and could involve the superpowers or their allies. Because fighting each other directly would have risked escalation to the level of nuclear exchange, they carefully avoided crises that might provoke such confrontations. Nevertheless, the antagonism led to protracted and costly wars in Korea and especially Vietnam.

## DECOLONIZATION AND NATION BUILDING
■ *What problems did less developed nations face?* (page 663)

Decolonization occurred on a vast scale. Each nation had to organize and institute some form of government, but few were able to do so without experiencing coups, rewritten constitutions, or regional rebellions. Most of the new nations, while trying to establish political stability, also faced severe economic challenges. Some new governments openly sided with one superpower of the other, and skilled leaders in the nonaligned countries could play the powers off each other and extract money and support from both.

## REVOLUTIONS, REFORM, AND REPRESSION IN LATIN AMERICA
■ *How did U.S. policies during the Cold War affect Latin America?* (page 668)

Latin American nationalists aimed for economic independence and an end to foreign intervention. Fidel Castro identified these goals with those of countries struggling for independence in Asia and Africa. However, fear of communist revolution led the United States to support counter-revolutionary uprisings, coups, and military dictatorships in several Latin American countries, often causing disruption and hardship.

## JAPAN, CHINA, AND THE FOUR TIGERS
■ *Why were developments in China so different from those in other parts of East Asia?* (page 674)

Protected by the American strategic umbrella, Japan turned its energies to building the world's second largest capitalist economy, and it was quickly followed by the four Asian Tigers. In China, in contrast, the victory of the communists over the nationalists and Cold War hostility toward the United States and its allies allowed Mae Zedong to instigate social revolutions along communist lines.

## NATIONAL AND RELIGIOUS CONFLICTS IN THE MIDDLE EAST
■ *What roles did nationalism and religious identity play in Middle Eastern politics?* (page 676)

In the Middle East, nationalist movements were directed not just at former colonial powers but also at Israel and its allies in the West. The nationalist desire of Israelis to have their own country was partly inspired by religious feelings and came in direct conflict with the identical desire of Palestinians. In Iran, nationalists rejected Western and communist dominance, while in Afghanistan, a communist coup aroused opposition. In both areas nationalism found expression in a revival of Islamic identity.

## THE END OF THE BIPOLAR WORLD
■ *What led to the collapse of the Soviet bloc?* (page 680)

Economic decline caused by inefficiencies in the communist system, as well as defeat in Afghanistan, weakened the hold of the Communist Party on the Soviet people and of the USSR on the nations of eastern Europe. As communists lost control, first the eastern European nations and then the smaller republics of the Soviet Union declared their independence.

## Key Terms

North Atlantic Treaty Organization (NATO) (p. 657)
Warsaw Pact (p. 657)
Cold War (p. 657)
United Nations (p. 657)
World Bank (p. 658)
Marshall Plan (p. 658)
European Economic Community (Common Market) (p. 659)
iron curtain (p. 660)
Truman Doctrine (p. 660)
Korean War (p. 661)
Vietnam War (p. 661)
Cuban Missile Crisis (p. 662)
nonaligned nations (p. 665)
Third World (p. 665)
Salvador Allende (p. 672)
Dirty War (p. 672)
Sandinistas (p. 672)
*keiretsu* (p. 674)
Cultural Revolution (China) (p. 675)
Asian Tigers (p. 675)
newly industrialized economies (NIEs) (p. 676)
Organization of Petroleum Exporting Countries (OPEC) (p. 678)
Ayatollah Ruhollah Khomeini (p. 678)
Saddam Husain (p. 679)
Mikhail Gorbachev (p. 680)
*perestroika* (p. 680)
Solidarity (p. 681)

© Cengage Learning

The workday began normally at the World Trade Center in lower Manhattan on the morning of September 11, 2001. The fifty thousand people who worked there were making their way to the two 110-story towers. Suddenly, at 8:46 A.M., an American Airlines Boeing 767 with 92 people on board, traveling at a speed of 470 miles per hour (756 kilometers per hour), crashed into floors 94 to 98 of the north tower, igniting the 10,000 gallons (38,000 liters) of fuel in its tanks. Just before 9:03 A.M. a United Airlines flight with 65 people on board and a similar fuel load hit floors 78 to 84 of the south tower.

As the burning jet fuel engulfed the collision areas, the buildings' occupants struggled through smoke-filled corridors and down dozens of flights of stairs. Many of those trapped above the crash sites used cell phones to say good-bye to loved ones. Rather than endure the flames and fumes, a few jumped to their deaths.

Just before 10 o'clock, temperatures had risen to the point that the steel girders in the impacted area of the south tower suddenly gave way. The collapsing upper floors crushed the floors underneath one by one, engulfing lower Manhattan in a dense cloud of dust. Twenty-eight minutes later the north tower pancaked in a similar manner. Miraculously, most of the buildings' occupants had escaped before the towers collapsed. Besides the people on the planes, nearly 2,600 lost their lives, including some 400 police officers and firefighters helping in the evacuation.

That same morning another American Airlines jet crashed into the Pentagon, killing all 64 people on board and 125 others inside the military complex near Washington, D.C. Passengers on a fourth plane managed to overpower their hijackers, and the plane crashed in rural Pennsylvania, killing all 45 on board.

The four planes had been hijacked by teams of Middle Eastern men who slit the throats of service and flight personnel and seized control. Of the nineteen hijackers, fifteen were from Saudi Arabia. All had links to an extremist Islamic organization, al-Qaeda (ahl–KAW-eh-duh) (the base or foundation), commanded by a rich Saudi named Usama bin Laden (oo-SAH-mah bin LAH-din) who was incensed with American political, military, and cultural influence in the Middle East. The men were educated and well traveled, had lived in the United States, and spoke English. Some had trained as pilots so that they could fly the hijacked aircraft.

The hijackers left few records of their motives, but the acts spoke for themselves. The World Trade Center was a focal point of international business, the Pentagon the headquarters of the American military. The fourth plane was probably meant to hit the Capitol or the White House, the legislative and executive centers of the world's only superpower.

The events of September 11, which became commonly referred to as 9/11, can be understood on many levels. The hijackers and those who sympathized with them saw themselves as engaged in a holy struggle against economic, political, and military institutions they believed to be evil. People directly affected, political leaders around the world, and most television watchers described the attacks as evil deeds against innocent victims.

To understand why the nineteen attackers were heroes to some and terrorists to others, one needs to explore the historical context of global changes at the turn of the millennium and the ideological tensions they have generated. The unique prominence of the United States in every major aspect of global integration, as well as its support for pro-American governments overseas, also elicits sharply divergent views.

## GLOBALIZATION AND THE WORLD ECONOMY

■ *What are the main benefits and dangers of growing political, economic, and cultural integration?*

The turn of the millennium saw the intensification of **globalization** trends that had been building since the 1970s. Growing trade and travel and new technologies were bringing all parts of the world into closer economic, political, and cultural interdependence. The collapse of the Soviet Union had completed the dissolution of territorial empires that had been under

**globalization** The economic, political, and cultural integration and interaction of all parts of the world brought about by increasing trade, travel, and technology.

way throughout the twentieth century. In their place were some two hundred independent nations, a growing number of which embraced democratic institutions. However, increasing interdependency also facilitated a global economic crisis that exploded in 2008 when the massive accumulation of debt at the financial institutions in the gigantic U.S. economy (larger than the economies of the next five countries combined—Japan, Germany, Great Britain, China (including Hong Kong), and France—became unsustainable.

## New Technologies and the World Economy

Since 1945 the global economy has expanded more rapidly than at any time in the past. Wave after wave of technological innovations have led to faster, cheaper communications and transportation as well as improvements in industrial and agricultural technologies. The material abundance would have amazed those who experienced the first Industrial Revolution (see Chapter 20). Improvements in existing technologies accounted for much of the developed world's productivity during the 1950s and 1960s, with both capitalist and socialist governments expanding highway systems, improving railroads, and constructing airports and nuclear plants. But new technologies played a role, too—none more so than the computer.

Few had anticipated that a silicon chip containing the computer's brains would lead to smaller, faster computers and now tablets and smart phones that when combined with the Internet would create a communication revolution. Access to a vast international database of research, opinion, entertainment, and commerce brought peoples and markets closer, and computer innovation also improved efficiency and product quality by allowing most modern industries to rely on small dedicated computers to control and monitor machines or, following Japan's early lead, incorporate robots into manufacturing and mining.

In the post–World War II years, many companies with multinational ownership and management invested in and marketed products throughout the world. These transnational corporations became the primary agents for technological change. By the end of the twentieth century the growing economic power of corporations in industrialized nations

allowed them to invest directly in the mines, plantations, and public utilities of less developed regions. International trade agreements and open markets furthered the process. Not only did Ford, Nissan, BMW, and other car companies produce and sell cars internationally, but their shareholders, workers, and managers also came from numerous nations.

The location of manufacturing plants overseas and the acquisition of corporate operations by foreign buyers rendered such global firms as transnational as the products they sold. In the 1970s and 1980s American brand names like Levi's, Coca-Cola, Marlboro, Gillette, McDonald's, and Kentucky Fried Chicken were global phenomena. But in time Asian names— Honda, Hitachi, Sony, Sanyo, and Mitsubishi—were blazoned in neon and on giant video screens on the sides of skyscrapers, along with European brands such as Nestlé, Mercedes, Pirelli, and Benetton. Since 1979, China's emergence as a global industrial power has accelerated this process of integration and diffusion.

As transnational manufacturers, agricultural conglomerates, and financial giants became wealthier and more powerful, they increasingly escaped the controls imposed by national governments. If labor costs were too high in Japan, antipollution measures too intrusive in the United States, or taxes too high in Great Britain, transnational companies relocated— or threatened to do so. In 1945, for example, the U.S. textile industry was located in low-wage southern states, dominating the American market and exporting to the world. As wages in the American South rose and global competition increased, producers began relocating plants to Puerto Rico in the 1980s and to Mexico after NAFTA went into effect in 1994 (discussed later in this chapter). Now China is the primary manufacturer of textiles.

## Globalization and Economic Crisis

The expansion of global trade and communications and the privatization of government enterprises fueled an economic boom in the 1990s that cooled abruptly in the wake of 9/11. The rate of growth in world trade fell from 13 percent in 2000 to only 1 percent in 2001.

However, growth in China and India resumed quickly, and the very large populations of these two

# Chronology

| | Politics | Economics and Society |
|---|---|---|
| **2000** | **2000** Al-Qaeda attacks American destroyer USS *Cole* in Yemen | |
| **2001** | **2001** Terrorists destroy the World Trade Center and damage the Pentagon on September 11<br>**2001** United States armed forces overthrow Taliban regime in Afghanistan | **2001–2003** Terrorist attacks trigger global recession<br>**2001** Shanghai Cooperation Organization formed<br>**2001** United Statess withdraws from Kyoto Protocol on global warming |
| **2002** | | **2002** Euro currency adopted in twenty-seven European countries |
| **2003** | **2003** United States and allies invade Iraq | |
| **2004** | **2004** Terrorists bomb Spanish trains<br>**2004–2009** Genocidal conflict ongoing in Darfur region of Sudan | **2004** Ten new members admitted to European Union |
| **2005** | **2005** Terrorists bomb London transit system | |
| **2006** | **2006** Israel attacks Hezbollah in Lebanon in response to its seizure of Israeli soldiers | |
| **2007** | **2007** Assassination of Benazir Bhutto deepens political crisis in Pakistan | |
| **2008** | | **2008** Collapse of mortgage debt bubble in United States triggers global recession |
| **2010** | | **2010** China becomes world's second largest economy |
| **2011** | **2011** Usama bin Laden killed by American raiders in Pakistan<br>**2011** Arab Spring uprisings force government change in Egypt, Tunisia, Libya, and Yemen | |

countries marked them as future world economic powers. Their growth increased pressure on world energy supplies; however, the United States continued to consume a quarter of the world's petroleum production and by 2013 had resumed its position as the world's largest producer through the production of oil derived from shale deposits. OPEC's manipulation of world oil prices, combined with political instability in the Middle East, had caused crude oil prices to soar between 1973 and 1985. But aside from those years, the average price of oil remained consistently below $20 per barrel (adjusted for inflation) throughout the second half of the twentieth century. In the year 2000, however, oil prices began to rise again because of confidence in world economic expansion. By 2008 a barrel of crude had spiked to $145, fueling ambitious economic programs in major oil producers

like Russia, Venezuela, Iran, Saudi Arabia, and the small sheikhdoms of the Persian Gulf, as well as in the newer OPEC states Ecuador, Nigeria, and Angola. With the economic crisis of 2008, prices fell abruptly, but by 2013 the price per barrel was back in the $90–$100 range.

Regional trade associations came into being to promote growth, reduce the economic vulnerability of member states, and, less explicitly, balance American economic dominance. The twenty-seven-member European Union (EU) was the most successful (see Map 29.1), adopting in 2002 a new common currency, the euro, that competed with the U.S. dollar for investment and banking. However, unequal levels of development among members became a source of crisis in 2009 when an economic downturn devastated European stock markets, increasing unemployment.

**Map 29.1 Regional Trade Associations, 2004** International trade and development are major concerns of governments in developed and developing countries. NAFTA, Mercosur, and the EU are free-trade areas. The other associations promote trade and development. © Cengage Learning

**NAFTA** (North American Free Trade Agreement)

Canada
Mexico
United States

**MERCOSUR** (Mercado Comun del Cono Sur)

Argentina
Brazil
Paraguay (suspended, 2012)
Uruguay
Venezuela

**EU** (European Union)

Austria
Belgium
Bulgaria
Cyprus
Czech Republic
Denmark
Estonia
Finland
France
Germany
Greece
Hungary
Ireland
Italy
Latvia
Lithuania
Luxembourg
Malta
Netherlands
Poland
Portugal
Romania
Slovakia
Slovenia
Spain
Sweden
United Kingdom

**ECOWAS** (Economic Community of West African States)

Benin
Burkina Faso
Cape Verde
Côte d'Ivoire
The Gambia
Ghana
Guinea
Guinea-Bissau
Liberia
Mali
Niger
Nigeria
Senegal
Sierra Leone
Togo

**PAFTA** (Pan-Arab Free Trade Area):

Algeria
Bahrain
Egypt
Iraq
Jordan
Kuwait
Lebanon
Libya
Morocco
Oman
Palestinian Authority
Qatar
Saudi Arabia
Sudan
Syria
Tunisia
United Arab Emirates
Yemen

**SADC** (Southern African Development Community)

Angola
Botswana
Democratic Republic of the Congo
Lesotho
Madagascar
Malawi
Mauritius
Mozambique
Namibia
Seychelles
South Africa
Swaziland
Tanzania
Zambia
Zimbabwe

**SAFTA** (South Asian Free Trade Agreement)

Afghanistan
Bangladesh
Bhutan
India
Maldives
Nepal
Pakistan
Sri Lanka

**APEC** (Asia-Pacific Economic Cooperation Forum)

Australia
Brunei
Canada
Chile
China
Hong Kong
Indonesia
Japan
Malaysia
Mexico
New Zealand
Papua New Guinea
Peru
Philippines
Russia
Singapore
South Korea
Taiwan
Thailand
United States
Vietnam

With this crisis, the idea of the euro, a common currency that symbolized Europe's progress toward unity, came into question because some member states like Greece were not at liberty to devalue their currency to reduce the debt they could no longer cover with their shrunken economies. Wealthier countries, led by Germany, urged austerity over investment and thereby further increased unemployment and discontent. In an increasingly globalized network of financial markets and institutions, Europe's debt crisis generated economic anxiety from Japan to New York City.

Despite the EU's expansion, the North American Free Trade Agreement (NAFTA), which eliminated tariffs among the United States, Canada, and Mexico in 1994, governed the world's largest free-trade zone. Yet heated debate in the United States over illegal immigration across the Mexican border limited popular enthusiasm for the agreement. The third largest free-trade zone, Mercosur, created by Argentina, Brazil, Paraguay (now suspended), and Uruguay in 1991 and subsequently expanded to include five associate members, visualized a parliament consisting of eighteen representatives from each member state. Other free-trade associations operated in West Africa, southern Africa, Southeast Asia, Central America, the Pacific Basin, and the Caribbean.

The Shanghai Cooperation Organization (SCO), formed in 2001 with China, Russia, and four former Soviet Central Asian republics (Kazakhstan, Kyrgystan, Tajikistan, and Uzbekistan), originally pursued common security interests, such as combating separatist movements and terrorism. But the organization's five observer members—Iran, India, Pakistan, Afghanistan, and Mongolia—the first a major oil exporter and the latter two possessing rich unexploited mineral deposits, lent credence to its twenty-year plan for reducing barriers to trade and population movement. Iran, which formally applied for full membership in 2008, posed a special problem insofar as U.S.-led international pressures to curb its nuclear program encountered resistance from both Russia and China.

Because of the inequalities and downturns that are intrinsic to free economic markets, the global bodies that tried to manage world trade and finance found it hard to convince poorer nations that they were not concerned only with the welfare of richer countries. In 1995 the world's major traders established the **World Trade Organization (WTO)** to encourage reduced barriers and enforce international agreements. When Russia became the 157th member in 2012, the largest economy not to be included was Iran. The WTO has had many critics and has regularly encountered street protests during its ministerial meetings. Some protesters have claimed that the organization's idea of free trade enables low-cost foreign manufacturers to attract business and shrink the job opportunities in richer states; others have demanded continuing tariff protection for local farmers.

The International Monetary Fund (IMF) and the World Bank (see Chapter 28), established to help economically troubled nations, have also been criticized for giving conditional assistance and mandating such unpopular economic reforms as terminating government subsidies for basic foodstuffs, cutting social programs, and liberalizing investment. A 2002 United Nations meeting in Monterrey, Mexico, pledged increased attention to the problem of economic despair, especially in Africa, though these commitments have seldom resulted in increased support.

The global financial crisis that began in 2008 had complicated roots. In 1997 the investment boom in Asian markets burst and investment shifted to the United States, where now massive growth in imported goods and unprecedented increases in housing prices spurred a rapid increase in the U.S. stock market. At the same time, money from overseas was invested in the U.S. treasury, which helped fund the wars in Afghanistan and Iraq while lowering taxes. The American national debt climbed dramatically.

When housing prices collapsed in 2008, many homeowners who had borrowed money using their homes as collateral (at these higher values) found themselves so deeply in debt on their mortgages that they lost their homes. New and risky lending techniques spread these bad debts throughout the banking system. Stock prices fell, banks teetered on the brink of collapse, and employers laid off workers they could no longer afford or did not need as consumer demand plummeted. The effects spread worldwide.

**World Trade Organization (WTO)** An international body established in 1995 to foster and bring order to international trade.

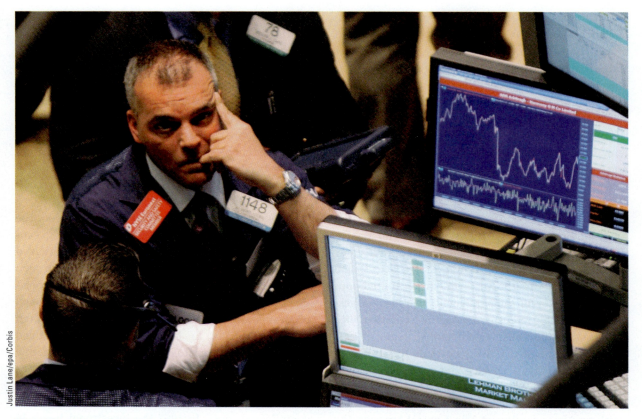

Justin Lane/epa/Corbis

**Watching Financial Markets Fall**  After years of economic boom, much of it fueled by inflated housing prices in the United States and ingenious new financial instruments that concealed risk, the world's stock markets fell drastically in 2008–2009. American stocks lost approximately one-third of their value. The banking crisis and resulting unemployment reminded economists of the Great Depression of the 1930s. People in all walks of life—from heads of state, to retirees, to ordinary workers—were forced to reappraise their financial situations.

Economists proclaimed it the worst economic crisis since the Great Depression of the 1930s.

In President Barack Obama's first weeks in office in January 2009, he proposed a series of steps, including massive increases in government spending, to jolt the economy back to health. Some of the plans yielded fruit, such as a rescue of the American automobile industry. Others were stymied after 2010 by partisan debate in the House of Representatives about whether the national debt or unemployment took precedence. Economic recovery remained slow and fragile in both the United States and the European Union. The trade expansion that had signaled the promise of globalization at the beginning of the century faded from memory, and the interdependence that had bound the world's economies in a cycle of growth became a dead weight that dragged many countries down.

## China Rejoins the World Economy

After Mao Zedong's death in 1976, the Chinese communist leadership began economic reforms that relaxed state control, allowing more initiative and permitting individuals to accumulate wealth. Under China's leader **Deng Xiaoping** (dung shee-yao-ping), China permitted foreign investment for the first time since the communists came to power in 1949. Between 1979 and 2005 foreign direct investment in China grew to more than $600 billion as McDonald's, General Motors, Coca-Cola, Airbus, Toyota, and many other foreign companies began doing business. As a result,

**Deng Xiaoping (1904–1997)**  Communist Party leader who forced Chinese economic reforms after the death of Mao Zedong.

Robert Van Der Hilst/Getty Images

**Shanghai—Old Meets New** The city of Shanghai is one of the great success stories in a rapidly growing Chinese economy, but its prosperity has left many behind. In this photo a poor man crosses a street in Shanghai's rich, modern commercial district carrying goods in hand-woven baskets balanced on a neck yoke, a technology thousands of years old.

by 2010 China had become a major industrial power and the world's most important exporting nation. But state-owned enterprises still employed more than 100 million workers, and most foreign-owned companies were limited to special economic zones. The result was a dual industrial sector—one modern, efficient, and connected to international markets, the other directed by political decisions. In 2010 China became the world's second largest economy, surpassing Japan.

Despite this enormous achievement, the Chinese people remain substantially poorer than people in mature industrial economies. Per capita GDP (GDP divided by population) has reached only $5,413.57, whereas advanced industrial economies have a per capita GDP of $42,063. However, China is now richer than much of the developing world. Latin America has a per capita GDP of $4,299, the Middle East $2,329, and sub-Saharan Africa $940.

**SECTION REVIEW**

- Improvements in existing technology and new technologies such as the computer have improved manufacturing efficiency and connections among producers and consumers from different regions and nations.

- Globalization has created a more integrated world economy, reducing the ability of a single nation to escape the effects of distant events.

- Global interdependence and rapid economic expansion and speculation led to a global financial crisis in 2008 that plunged the world into the worst economic slowdown since the Great Depression of the 1930s.

- China experienced three decades of rapid growth after Deng Xiaoping reformed and modernized its economy, and thus far it has weathered the worldwide financial crisis.

China's expansion has depended heavily on exports. While the Chinese economy continued to grow during the worldwide 2008 recession, some economists wonder if a deep contraction will hit the Chinese economy as it has others after a period of speculation-fueled investment.

## THE QUESTION OF VALUES

■ *What roles do religious beliefs and secular ideologies play in the contemporary world?*

As people around the world first faced the opportunities of globalization and then the fear of global recession, they tried to make sense of these changes in terms of their own value systems. With 6 billion people, the world was big enough to include many different approaches, whether religious or secular, local or international, traditional or visionary. In some cases, however, conflicting visions fed violence.

**Faith and Politics** Religious beliefs increasingly inspired political actions during the second half of the twentieth century, and the trend intensified in the new century. Though for Americans this change reversed two centuries of growing secularism, Western analysts did not agree on the cause of the religious revival.

Evangelical Protestants became a powerful conservative political force in the United States, and

Catholic opposition to abortion, homosexuality, marriage of priests, and admission of women to the priesthood characterized conservative belief worldwide. In Israel, ultra-orthodox Jews played a leading role in settling the West Bank and Gaza, the Palestinian territories captured by Israel in 1967, and vehemently resisted both Israel's unilateral withdrawal from Gaza in 2005 and subsequent plans for withdrawal from the West Bank. And in India, Hindu zealots made the BJP party a powerful political force.

Yet Islam became the focus of most discussions of faith and politics (see Diversity and Dominance: Conflict and Civilization). The birth of the Islamic Republic of Iran in the revolution of 1979 made visible a current of Muslim political assertiveness that had been building in several Muslim countries for twenty years. But by the year 2000 acts of **terrorism** perpetrated by non-Iranian Muslim groups claiming to be acting for religious reasons were capturing the headlines.

Terrorism is a political tactic by which comparatively weak militants use violent acts against civilians to convince a frightened public that danger is everywhere and the government is incapable of protecting them. Though terrorism has a long history, the instantaneous communications and the tradition in the news business of publicizing violence increased its effectiveness from the 1980s onward.

Bombings, kidnappings, and assassinations made political sense to all sorts of political groups: Palestinians confronting Israel; national separatists like the Tamils in Sri Lanka, Basques in Spain; Chechens in Russia; Catholic and Protestant extremists in Northern Ireland; and racial militias in Rwanda and Darfur, to name a few. But al-Qaeda gained the lion's share of attention because it targeted the United States and Europe, concentrated on spectacular attacks, drew from Muslims all over the world, and made effective use of news coverage and audiovisual communications.

Their media star and ideological spokesman, **Usama bin Laden**, was born into a wealthy Saudi family and educated as an engineer. He fought against the Soviet Union in Afghanistan and trained a core group of fighters called al-Qaeda. Though his family disowned him and Saudi Arabia stripped him of his citizenship, his calls for holy war (*jihad*) and his

portrayal of the United States as a puppet-master collaborating with Israel to murder innocent Muslims and supporting the suppression of Muslim political movements by authoritarian Muslim governments made sense to millions of Muslims, even if only a very few committed themselves to follow him into battle.

Al-Qaeda blew up American embassies in Kenya and Tanzania in 1998, crippled the U.S. Navy destroyer *Cole* during a port call in Yemen in 2000, and then capped everything by attacking the World Trade Center and the Pentagon on 9/11. When the "global war on terrorism" declared by President George Bush (served 2001–2008) failed to eliminate bin Laden, his mystique grew; and the American toppling in 2001 of the Taliban regime in Afghanistan, which had sheltered Bin Laden, and invasion of Iraq in 2003 convinced many Muslims that Bin Laden was right. Further terrorist attacks—by Indonesians on tourists on the island of Bali in 2002, by North Africans on commuter trains servicing Madrid in 2004, by English-born Muslims on the London transit system in 2005, and by Pakistanis on luxury hotels in Mumbai, India, in 2008—made it clear that the violence unleashed by al-Qaeda had become decentralized and that recruits and cells might no longer be taking orders from bin Laden. Even after an American commando operation killed bin Laden in his hideout in Pakistan in 2011, groups affiliated with al-Qaeda continued to operate in Yemen, Libya, and Mali.

In trying to explain a current of violence that seemed to be centered on Muslims, some analysts argued that Islam itself encouraged violence against non-Muslims and that conservative Muslims like Usama bin Laden were opposed to freedom and modernity. The counterargument pointed out that the vast majority of Muslims saw their religion as one of peace, that al-Qaeda used modern military and

**terrorism**   Political belief that extreme and seemingly random violence will destabilize a government and permit the terrorists to gain political advantage. Though an old technique, terrorism gained prominence in the late twentieth century with the growth of worldwide mass media that, through their news coverage, amplified public fears of terrorist acts.

**Usama bin Laden (1957–2011)**   Saudi-born Muslim extremist who funded the al-Qaeda organization that was responsible for several terrorist attacks, including those on the World Trade Center and the Pentagon in 2001.

propaganda techniques, and that many of its operatives, like bin Laden himself, graduated from modern technical programs. To those who argued that the United States instigated al-Qaeda's wrath by supporting Israel and stationing troops in Saudi Arabia, others pointed out that the United States had championed the Muslim cause in Bosnia in 1992–1995, driven the secular dictator Saddam Husain out of Kuwait in 1991, and supported the popular uprisings of the Arab Spring in 2011.

## Universal Rights and Values

Alongside the growing influence of religion on politics, efforts to promote adherence to universal human rights also expanded. The modern human rights movement grew out of the French Declaration of the Rights of Man (1789) and the U.S. Constitution (1787) and Bill of Rights (1791). Over the next century, the logic of universal rights moved Westerners to undertake international campaigns to end slave trading and slavery throughout the world and to secure equal rights for women.

International organizations in the twentieth century secured agreement on labor standards, the rules of war, and the rights of refugees. The pinnacle of those efforts was the **Universal Declaration of Human Rights**, passed by the United Nations General Assembly in 1948, which proclaimed itself "a common standard of achievement for all peoples and nations." Its thirty articles condemned slavery, torture, cruel and inhuman punishment, and arbitrary arrest, detention, and exile. The Declaration called for freedom of movement, assembly, and thought. It asserted rights to life, liberty, and security of person; to impartial public trials; and to education, employment, and leisure. The principle of equality was most fully articulated in Article 2:

> Everyone is entitled to all the rights and freedoms set forth in this Declaration, without distinction of any kind, such as race, color, sex, language, religion, or political or other opinion, national or social origin, property, birth or other status.[1]

This passage reflected an international consensus against racism and imperialism and a growing acceptance of the importance of social and economic equality. Most newly independent countries joining the United Nations willingly signed the Declaration because it implicitly condemned European colonial regimes.

Besides the official actions of the United Nations and various national governments, **nongovernmental organizations (NGOs)** have been important forces promoting human rights. Amnesty International, founded in 1961, concentrates on gaining the freedom of people who have been tortured or imprisoned without trial and campaigns against summary execution by government death squads or other gross violations of rights. Other NGOs have devoted themselves to famine relief, refugee assistance, and health care around the world. Médecins Sans Frontières (Doctors Without Borders), founded in 1971, was awarded the Nobel Peace Prize in 1999 for offering medical assistance in scores of crises.

While NGOs often worked on individual situations in specific countries, other universal goals became enshrined in international agreements. Such agreements made genocide a crime and promoted environmental protection of the seas, of Antarctica, and of the atmosphere. However, the United States and a few other nations were greatly concerned that such treaties would unduly limit their sovereignty or threaten their national interests. For this reason the U.S. Congress delayed ratifying the 1949 convention on genocide until 1986. More recently the United States demanded exemption for Americans from the jurisdiction of the International Criminal Court, created in 2002 to try international criminals, declaring that "enemy combatants" taken prisoner during the "global war on terrorism" should not be treated in accordance with the Third Geneva

---

[1]"Universal Declaration of Human Rights," in *Twenty-five Human Rights Documents* (New York: Center for the Study of Human Rights, Columbia University, 1994), 6.

**Universal Declaration of Human Rights** A 1948 United Nations covenant binding signatory nations to the observance of specified rights.

**nongovernmental organizations (NGOs)** Nonprofit international organizations devoted to investigating human rights abuses and providing humanitarian relief. Two NGOs won the Nobel Peace Prize in the 1990s: International Campaign to Ban Landmines (1997) and Doctors Without Borders (1999).

# Diversity & Dominance

## Conflict and Civilization

In 1993 Samuel P. Huntington, a professor of government at Harvard University, published "The Clash of Civilizations?" in the journal Foreign Affairs. *This article provoked extraordinary debate, particularly after the 9/11 attacks on the World Trade Center and the Pentagon. Some readers deemed it an accurate description of a post–Cold War world in which Islamic countries were destined to conflict violently with the countries of Europe and North America. Others saw it as imprecise in its failure to clarify what a "civilization" is, imperialistic in its unquestioning assumption of Western superiority, and encouraging of anti-Muslim prejudice.*

The interactions between civilizations vary greatly in the extent to which they are likely to be characterized by violence. Economic competition clearly predominates between the American and European subcivilizations of the West and between both of them and Japan. On the Eurasian continent, however, the proliferation of ethnic conflict, epitomized at the extreme in "ethnic cleansing," has not been totally random. It has been most frequent and most violent between groups belonging to different civilizations. In Eurasia the great historic fault lines between civilizations are once more aflame. This is particularly true along the boundaries of the crescent-shaped Islamic bloc of nations from the bulge of Africa to central Asia. Violence also occurs between Muslims, on the one hand, and Orthodox Serbs in the Balkans, Jews in Israel, Hindus in India, Buddhists in Burma and Catholics in the Philippines. Islam has bloody borders.

*Rejoinders to Huntington's thesis saw it as a cornerstone of the aggressive policies adopted by the Bush administration after 9/11. As an alternative, they stressed the common values held by peaceful societies and the need for intercultural understanding. Mohammed Khatami, the president of the Islamic Republic of Iran, found support for a more positive framing of the matter when the United Nations, following his proposal, declared 2001 the year of "Dialogue Among Civilizations." Almost simultaneously, the Organization of the Islamic Conference (now called the Organization of Islamic Cooperation), a fifty-seven-member international body headquartered in Saudi Arabia and composed of states with large Muslim populations, elaborated upon this concept in the "Tehran Declaration on Dialogue Among Civilizations."*

## Tehran Declaration on Dialogue Among Civilizations

Praise be to Allah and peace and blessing be upon His prophet and kin and companion.

The representatives of Heads of State and Government of OIC member states . . . [recognizing] the United Nations General Assembly resolution 53/22, designating the year 2001 as the United Nations year of Dialogue among Civilizations;

Guided by the noble Islamic teachings and values [*each of the following principles is accompanied by reference to a verse in the Quran*] on human dignity and equality, tolerance, peace and justice for humankind, and promotion of virtues and proscription of vice and evil;

Drawing upon the Islamic principles of celebration of human diversity, recognition of diversified sources of knowledge, promotion of dialogue and mutual understanding, genuine mutual respect in human interchanges, and encouragement of courteous and civilized discourse based on reason and logic;

Reaffirming the commitment of their Governments to promote dialogue and understanding among various cultures and civilizations, aimed at reaching a global consensus to build a new order for the next millennium founded in faith as well as common moral and ethical values of contemporary civilizations;

Requests the Secretary-General of the OIC to submit this declaration for endorsement to the Chairman of the Eighth Islamic Summit and the 26th Islamic Conference of Foreign Ministers for appropriate action:

A) General principles of dialogue among civilizations

1. Respect for the dignity and equality of all human beings without distinctions of any kind and of nations large and small;

2. Genuine acceptance of cultural diversity as a permanent [quality] of human society and a cherished asset for the advancement and welfare of humanity at large;

3. Mutual respect and tolerance for the views and values of various cultures and civilizations, as well as the right of members of all civilizations to preserve their cultural heritage and values, and rejection of desecration of moral, religious or cultural values, sanctities and sanctuaries;

➤

4. Recognition of diversified sources of knowledge throughout time and space, and the imperative of drawing upon the areas of strengths, richness and wisdom of each civilization in a genuine process of mutual enrichment;

5. Rejection of attempts for cultural domination and imposition as well as doctrines and practices promoting confrontation and clash between civilizations;

6. Search for common grounds between and within various civilizations in order to face common global challenges;

Acceptance of cooperation and search for understanding as the appropriate mechanism for the promotion of common universal values as well as for the suppression of global threats;

7. Commitment to participation of all peoples and nations, without any discrimination, in their own domestic as well as global decision-making and value distribution processes;

8. Compliance with principles of justice, equity, peace and solidarity as well as fundamental principles of international law and the United Nations Charter. . . .

A few years later, a joint proposal by the governments of Spain and Turkey received a similar endorsement by the United Nations. This led to the creation of the Alliance of Civilizations. The underlying principles of this organization were expressed in the 2006 report of its "High-Level Group," a body of eminent political, intellectual, and spiritual figures from around the world.

## Alliance of Civilizations Report of the High-Level Group

I. Bridging the World's Divides

1.1 Our world is alarmingly out of balance. For many, the last century brought unprecedented progress, prosperity, and freedom. For others, it marked an era of subjugation, humiliation and dispossession. Ours is a world of great inequalities and paradoxes: a world where the income of the planet's three richest people is greater than the combined income of the world's least developed countries; where modern medicine performs daily miracles and yet 3 million people die every year of preventable diseases; where we know more about distant universes than ever before, yet 130 million children have no access to education; where despite the existence of multilateral covenants and institutions, the international community often seems helpless in the face of conflict and genocide. For most of humanity, freedom from want and freedom from fear appear as elusive as ever.

1.2 We also live in an increasingly complex world, where polarized perceptions, fueled by injustice and inequality, often lead to violence and conflict, threatening international stability. Over the past few years, wars, occupation and acts of terror have exacerbated mutual suspicion and fear within and among societies. Some political leaders and sectors of the media, as well as radical groups have exploited this environment, painting mirror images of a world made up of mutually exclusive cultures, religions, or civilizations, historically distinct and destined for confrontation.

1.3 The anxiety and confusion caused by the "clash of civilizations" theory regrettably has distorted the terms of the discourse on the real nature of the predicament the world is facing. The history of relations between cultures is not only one of wars and confrontation. It is also based on centuries of constructive exchanges, cross-fertilization, and peaceful co-existence. Moreover, classifying internally fluid and diverse societies along hard-and-fast lines of civilizations interferes with more illuminating ways of understanding questions of identity, motivation and behavior. Rifts between the powerful and the powerless or the rich and the poor or between different political groups, classes, occupations and nationalities have greater explanatory power than such cultural categories. Indeed, the latter stereotypes only serve to entrench already polarized opinions. Worse, by promoting the misguided view that cultures are set on an unavoidable collision course, they help turn negotiable disputes into seemingly intractable identity-based conflicts that take hold of the popular imagination. It is essential, therefore, to counter the stereotypes and misconceptions that deepen patterns of hostility and mistrust among societies.

## QUESTIONS FOR ANALYSIS

1. How important are culture and religion, as opposed to governing ideology or economic inequality, in explaining current world conflicts?

2. Can idealistic statements by governments be effective in curbing acts of violence carried out by individual zealots or terrorist groups?

3. Should general statements about culture play a role at the level of personal relations in the neighborhood, the workplace, or the classroom?

Sources: Samuel P. Huntington, "The Clash of Civilizations?," Foreign Affairs 72, no. 3 (Summer 1993). "The Tehran Declaration on Dialogue Among Civilizations," Organization of the Islamic Conference, www.isesco.org.ma/english/publications/dig/CH11.php; "High-Level Group Report," Alliance of Civilizations, available online at www.unaoc.org/content/view/64/94/lang,english/.

Convention (1950) on humane treatment of prisoners of war.

## Women's Rights

The women's rights movement, which began on both sides of the North Atlantic in the nineteenth century, became an important human rights issue in the twentieth century. Rights for women became accepted in Western countries and were enshrined in the constitutions of many nations newly freed from colonial rule. In 1979 the United Nations General Assembly adopted the Convention on the Elimination of All Forms of Discrimination Against Women, and in 1985 the first international conference on the status of women, sponsored by the United Nations Division for the Advancement of Women, was held in Nairobi, Kenya. A second conference in Beijing ten years later added momentum to the movement. By 2012, all but seven UN member countries—Iran, Palau, Somalia, Sudan, South Sudan, Tonga, and the United States—had ratified the convention, though the United States and Palau had signed it without ratification.

Besides highlighting the similarity of the problems women face around the world, international conferences have also revealed great variety in the views and concerns of women. Feminists from the West, who had been accustomed to dictating the agenda and who had pushed for the liberation of women in other parts of the world, sometimes found themselves accused of having narrow concerns and condescending attitudes. Some non-Western women complained about Western feminists' endorsement of sexual liberation and about the deterioration of family life in the West. While agreeing with Western feminists' concerns about female circumcision, a form of genital mutilation that can cause chronic infections or permanently impair sexual enjoyment, some non-Western feminists found the issue less important than poverty, rape, and AIDS.

The conferences were more important for the attention they focused on women's issues than for the solutions they generated. The search for a universally accepted women's rights agenda proved elusive because of local concerns and strong disagreement on abortion and other issues. Nevertheless, increases in women's education, access to employment, political participation, and control of

**SECTION REVIEW**

- The second half of the twentieth century has seen an increase in political action inspired by religious belief.
- Militant Islam has risen in response to the claim that the United States supports such authoritarianism in many Muslim countries.
- Universal standards of human rights have gained wider acceptance and underlie the work of the United Nations, individual states, and NGOs.
- Concepts of human rights have expanded to address genocide and environmental protection.
- Global debates on women's rights have addressed a variety of economic, political, and social problems but have also involved clashes over cultural values.

fertility augured well for the eventual achievement of gender equality.

Such efforts raised the prominence of human rights as a global concern and put pressure on governments to consider human rights when making foreign policy decisions. Skeptics observed, however, that a Western country might successfully prod a non-Western country to improve its human rights performance—for example, by granting women better access to education and careers—but that reverse criticism of a Western country often fell on deaf ears—for example, condemnation of the death penalty in the United States. For such critics the human rights movement was seen not as an effort to make the world more humane but as another form of Western cultural imperialism. Still, support for universal rights has grown, especially because increasing globalization has made common standards of behavior more important.

## THE CHALLENGE OF POPULATION GROWTH

■ *What explains differences in the rate of population growth among the world's regions?*

The empowerment of women and deep ideological divisions concerning abortion contributed to a wide-ranging debate over population growth. For most of human history, population growth was viewed as beneficial, and human beings were seen as a source of wealth. Since the late eighteenth century, however, population growth has been viewed with increasing alarm. Some feared that food supplies could not keep up with population growth. Others foresaw class and ethnic struggle as numbers overwhelmed resources. By the second half of the twentieth century, population growth was increasingly seen as a threat to the environment.

## The Industrialized Nations

From the late eighteenth to the early twentieth centuries, educated Europeans were ambivalent about the rapid increase in human population. Some saw it as a blessing that would promote economic well-being. Others warned that the seemingly relentless increase would bring disaster. The best-known pessimist was the English cleric **Thomas Malthus**, who in 1798 argued that unchecked population growth would outstrip food production. To terrify his European readers, he claimed that a visitor to China "will not be surprised that mothers destroy or expose many of their children; that parents sell their daughters for a trifle; . . . and that there should be such a number of robbers. The surprise is that nothing still more dreadful should happen."[2]

The population of Europe almost doubled between 1850 and 1914, putting enormous pressure on rural land and urban housing and overwhelming fragile public institutions. This dramatic growth forced a large wave of immigration across the Atlantic, helping to develop the Western Hemisphere and invigorating the Atlantic economy. Population growth also contributed to Europe's Industrial Revolution by lowering labor costs and increasing consumer demand.

In the generation that came of age after World War II, the views of Malthus were casually dismissed as industrial and agricultural productivity multiplied supplies of food and other necessities while expanded female employment, older age at marriage, and more effective family planning slowed the birthrate. By the 1960s Europe and other industrial societies had made the **demographic transition** to lower fertility rates (average number of births per woman) and reduced mortality. This meant that the median age in the world's most developed nations rose from twenty-nine years in 1950 to thirty-seven years by 2000.

In much of Europe and Japan, fertility levels are so low that population would fall without immigration. Japanese women have an average of 1.4 children, while Italian women have 1.2. Although Sweden tries to promote fertility with cash payments, tax incentives, and job leaves to families with children, the average number of births per woman is 1.4. By comparison, the average African woman now has 4.6 children. Higher levels of female education and employment, the material values of consumer culture, and access to contraception and abortion explain the low fertility of mature industrial nations.

As fertility has declined in the industrialized nations of western Europe, the combination of abundant food, improved hygiene, and more effective medicines and medical care has lengthened human lives. In 2000 about 20 percent of the population in Europe was sixty-five or over. By 2050 this proportion will rise to over one-third. Italy soon will have more than twenty adults fifty years old or over for each five-year-old child. Because of higher fertility and greater levels of immigration, the United States is moving in this direction more slowly than western Europe; by 2050 the median age in Europe will be fifty-two, while it will be thirty-nine in the United States. The combination of falling fertility and rising life expectancy in the industrialized nations presents a challenge very different from the one foreseen by Malthus. As the

---

[2]Quoted in Antony Flew, "Introduction," in Thomas Robert Malthus, *An Essay on the Principle of Population and a Summary View of the Principle of Population* (New York: Penguin Books, 1970), 30.

**Thomas Malthus (1766–1834)** Eighteenth-century English intellectual who warned that population growth threatened the future generations because, in his view, it would always outstrip increases in agricultural production.

**demographic transition** A change in the rates of population growth. Before the transition, both birthrates and death rates are high, resulting in a slowly growing population; then the death rate drops but the birthrate remains high, causing a population explosion; finally the birthrate drops and the population growth slows down. This transition took place in Europe in the late nineteenth and early twentieth centuries, in North America and East Asia in the mid-twentieth century, and, most recently, in Latin America and South Asia.

| TABLE 29.1 | Population for World and Major Areas, 1750–2050 |

**Population Size (Millions)**

| Major Area | 1750 | 1800 | 1850 | 1900 | 1950 | 2000 | 2050* |
|---|---|---|---|---|---|---|---|
| World | 791 | 978 | 1,262 | 1,650 | 2,521 | 6,122 | 8,909 |
| Africa | 106 | 107 | 111 | 133 | 221 | 796 | 1,803 |
| Asia | 502 | 635 | 809 | 947 | 1,399 | 3,680 | 5,222 |
| Europe | 163 | 203 | 276 | 408 | 547 | 728 | 632 |
| Latin America and the Caribbean | 16 | 24 | 38 | 74 | 167 | 520 | 768 |
| North America | 2 | 7 | 26 | 82 | 172 | 316 | 448 |
| Oceania | 2 | 2 | 2 | 6 | 13 | 31 | 46 |

**Percentage Distribution**

| Major Area | 1750 | 1800 | 1850 | 1900 | 1950 | 2000 | 2050* |
|---|---|---|---|---|---|---|---|
| World | 100 | 100 | 100 | 100 | 100 | 100 | 100 |
| Africa | 13.4 | 10.9 | 8.8 | 8.1 | 8.8 | 13.1 | 20.2 |
| Asia | 63.5 | 64.9 | 64.1 | 57.4 | 55.5 | 60.6 | 58.6 |
| Europe | 20.6 | 20.8 | 21.9 | 24.7 | 21.7 | 12.0 | 7.1 |
| Latin America and the Caribbean | 2.0 | 2.5 | 3.0 | 4.5 | 6.6 | 8.6 | 8.6 |
| North America | 0.3 | 0.7 | 2.1 | 5.0 | 6.8 | 5.2 | 5.0 |
| Oceania | 0.3 | 0.2 | 0.2 | 0.4 | 0.5 | 0.5 | 0.5 |

* Estimated.

*Source*: J. D. Durand, "Historical Estimates of World Population: An Evaluation" (Philadelphia: University of Pennsylvania, Population Studies Center, 1974, mimeographed); United Nations, *The Determinants and Consequences of Population Trends*, vol. 1 (New York: United Nations, 1973); United Nations, *World Population Prospects as Assessed in 1963* (New York: United Nations, 1966); United Nations, *World Population Prospects: The 1998 Revision* (New York: United Nations, forthcoming); United Nations Population Division, Department of Economic and Social Affairs, *World Population to 2300*. 2004. http://www.un.org/esa/population/publications/longrange2/WorldPop2300final.pdf.
© Cengage Learning

number of retirees increases relative to the number of employed people, the cost of a broad array of social services, including retirement income, medical services, and housing supplements for the elderly, may become unsustainable.

## The Developing Nations

At current rates, 95 percent of all future population growth will be in developing nations (see Table 29.1). A comparison between Europe and Africa illustrates these changes. In 1950 Europe had more than twice the population of Africa. By 1985 Africa's population had drawn even. According to projections, its population will be three times larger than Europe's by 2050.

By the late 1970s, the demographic transition had not occurred in the poorer countries, and the issue of population growth became politicized. Leaders in some developing nations argued that larger populations would increase national power. Industrialized, mostly white, nations raised concerns about rapid population growth in Asia, Africa, and Latin America. Populist political leaders in these regions asked whether these concerns were racist. The question temporarily disarmed Western advocates of birth control.

However, once the economic shocks of the 1970s and 1980s revealed the vulnerability of poor nations, governments in the developing world jettisoned policies that promoted population growth. In the 1970s the government of Mexico had encouraged high fertility, and population rose to 3 percent per year. In the 1980s Mexico rejected these policies and began to promote birth control, leading by the 1990s to an annual population growth of 1.7.

Mortality rates have also increased in some areas as improved transportation facilitates the transmission of disease. The rapid spread of HIV/AIDS is an

**Chinese Family-Planning Campaign**  To slow population growth, the Chinese government has sought to limit parents to a single child. Billboards and other forms of mass advertising have been an essential part of the campaign.

example of this phenomenon. Less developed regions with poorly funded public health institutions and with few resources to invest in prevention and treatment experience the highest rates of infection and the greatest mortality. Of the countries with the highest HIV/AIDS rates in 2010, thirty-seven are in Africa, three in Asia, and six in Latin America and the Caribbean. These countries are home to 87 percent of all HIV/AIDS infections. By 2007 approximately 25 million people had died of AIDS and another 33 million were infected worldwide. Prevention programs and improved drug therapies have slowed both mortality and infection rates, with the greatest successes registered in rich countries with the greatest medical resources.

After 2000, rapid population growth continued in the developing world even as birthrates fell. Birthrates fell most steeply in countries experiencing the most rapid economic development. In China the birthrate fell from 42 births per thousand in 1950 to a First World level of 13 today. In this same period birthrates declined from 43 per thousand to 23 in India, another fast-growing economy. Latin America's birthrate declined from 43 per thousand in 1950 to 19 in 2010. Birthrates fell more slowly in sub-Saharan Africa and in Muslim countries like Pakistan and Afghanistan. Regardless of these changes, birthrates remain more than twice as high in the developing world as in the mature industrial nations, with the highest levels in the poorest countries.

## Old and Young Populations

Population pyramids generated by demographers clearly illustrate the profound transformation in human reproductive patterns and life expectancy since World War II. Figure 29.1 shows the 2001 age distributions in Pakistan, South Korea, and Sweden—nations at three different stages of economic development. Sweden is a mature industrial nation. South Korea is rapidly industrializing and has surpassed many European nations in both industrial output and per capita wealth. Pakistan is a poor, traditional Muslim nation with rudimentary industrialization, low educational levels, and little effective family planning.

**Figure 29.1  Age Structure Comparison**  Islamic Nation (Pakistan), Non-Islamic Developing Nation (South Korea), and Developed Nation (Sweden), 2001.

*Source*: U.S. Bureau of the Census, *International Database*, 2001.

In 2001 nearly 50 percent of Pakistan's population was under age sixteen. The resulting pressures on the economy have been extraordinary. Every year approximately 150,000 men reach age sixty-five—and another 1.2 million turn sixteen. Pakistan, therefore, has to create more than a million new jobs a year or face growing unemployment and declining wages. Sweden confronts a different problem. Sweden's aging population, growing demand for social welfare benefits, and declining labor pool mean that its industries may become less competitive and living standards may decline. In South Korea, a decline in fertility dramatically altered the ratio of children to adults, creating an age distribution similar to that of western Europe.

## SECTION REVIEW

- In the twentieth century the developed nations made the demographic transition to low birthrates, while the developing nations began by stressing higher birthrates.

- World population more than doubled between 1950 and 2000.

- In developed nations, falling birthrates and longer life expectancy will strain the ability of governments to care for an older population.

- Developing nations will contribute most of the world's future population growth, despite changing economies and population-planning efforts.

# UNEQUAL DEVELOPMENT AND THE MOVEMENT OF PEOPLES

■ *How have differences in wealth between nations influenced global migration patterns?*

Two characteristics of the postwar world should now be clear. First, world population has increased to startlingly high levels, and much of the increase has been, and will continue to be, in the poorest nations. Second, despite decades of experimentation with state-directed economic development, most nations that were poor in 1960 are still poor today. There are notable exceptions. In Asia, first Japan, then the Asian Tigers (Taiwan, Singapore, South Korea, and Hong Kong), and more recently China have generated high rates of growth and are now among the world's most competitive industrial powers. In recent years Brazil, Mexico, India, and Turkey have also experienced significant growth. This industrial transformation has increased a world demand for raw materials that has enriched a small number of oil-exporting nations.

## The Problem of Inequality

The persistence of poverty despite the global economic expansion has led to deepening inequality. The industrialized nations of the Northern Hemisphere now enjoy a larger share of the world's wealth than they did a century ago. As a result, the gap between rich and poor nations has grown

**Garbage Dump in Manila, Philippines** In Third World nations thousands of poor families live by sorting and selling bottles, aluminum cans, plastic, and newspapers in urban landfills.

wider. China's spectacular rise as an industrial power since 1980 is a strong indicator that some once-poor countries can become competitive. Nevertheless, the vast majority of the world's population continues to live in poverty.

There are many measures of the comparative relative wealth of nations; GDP (gross domestic product) per capita measured in U.S. dollars is among the most common. In 2010 the per capita GDP of Luxembourg was the highest in the world, $104,512; the U.S. figure was $46,702 and the Japanese figure $43,063. The countries of the European Union were generally rich, but some of the former Soviet satellites admitted to the EU recently have the GDP per capita of developing nations. France and Germany have per capita GDPs of $39,170 and $39,852, respectively. The poorest countries in the European Union, Bulgaria and Romania, have per capita GDPs similar to Russia's: $6,335, $7,539, and $10,481, respectively.

Many countries in the developing world now approach the poorest tier of European countries in per capita GDP: Mexico, $9,133; Brazil, $10,993; Chile, $12,640; South Africa, $7,272; and Gabon, $8,768. But many more countries, especially in Asia and Africa, remain very poor: the Philippines, $2,140; India, $1,375; Pakistan, $1,019; Nigeria, $1,242; and Sudan, $1,538. The poorest, like Haiti, Kenya, and Bangladesh, have per capita GDP levels under $1,000.

## International and Internal Migration

The combination of intractable poverty and growing population has generated a surge in international immigration. With the exception of Japan, large numbers of legal and illegal immigrants from poor nations with growing populations are entering the developed industrial nations. Few issues have stirred more controversy. Even moderate voices sometimes frame this discussion as a competition among peoples.

When an expanding European economy first confronted labor shortages in the 1960s, nations promoted guest worker programs and other inducements

| TABLE 29.2 | | The World's Metropolitan Areas (population of 10 million or more) | | | | | | |
|---|---|---|---|---|---|---|---|
| City | 1970 | City | 1990 | City | 2011 | City | 2025 |
| 1 Tokyo | 23.3 | 1 Tokyo | 32.5 | 1 Tokyo | 37.2 | 1 Tokyo | 38.7 |
| 2 New York | 16.2 | 2 New York | 16.1 | 2 Delhi | 22.7 | 2 Delhi | 32.9 |
| | | 3 Mexico City | 15.3 | 3 Mexico City | 20.4 | 3 Shanghai | 28.4 |
| | | 4 São Paulo | 14.8 | 4 New York | 20.4 | 4 Mumbai | 26.6 |
| | | 5 Mumbai | 12.4 | 5 Shanghai | 20.2 | 5 Mexico City | 24.6 |
| | | 6 Osaka-Kobe | 11.0 | 6 São Paulo | 19.9 | 6 New York | 23.6 |
| | | 7 Calcutta | 10.9 | 7 Mumbai | 19.7 | 7 São Paulo | 23.2 |
| | | 8 Los Angeles | 10.9 | 8 Beijing | 15.6 | 8 Dhaka | 22.9 |
| | | 9 Seoul | 10.5 | 9 Dhaka | 15.4 | 9 Beijing | 22.6 |
| | | 10 Buenos Aires | 10.5 | 10 Calcutta | 14.4 | 10 Karachi | 20.2 |
| | | | | 11 Karachi | 13.9 | 11 Lagos | 18.9 |
| | | | | 12 Buenos Aires | 13.5 | 12 Calcutta | 18.7 |
| | | | | 13 Los Angeles | 13.4 | 13 Manila | 16.3 |
| | | | | | | 14 Los Angeles | 15.7 |
| | | | | | | 15 Shenzhen | 15.5 |
| | | | | | | 16 Buenos Aires | 15.5 |
| | | | | | | 17 Guangzhou | 15.5 |
| | | | | | | 18 Istanbul | 14.9 |
| | | | | | | 19 Cairo | 14.7 |
| | | | | | | 20 Kinshasa | 14.5 |
| | | | | | | 21 Chongqing | 13.6 |
| | | | | | | 22 Rio de Janeiro | 13.6 |
| | | | | | | 23 Bangalore | 13.2 |

*Source*: International Migration Report 2002, United Nations, Department of Economic and Social Affairs, Population Division, "World Urbanization Prospects: The 1999 Revision," p. 6. The United Nations is the author of the original material. Reprinted by permission of United Nations Publications.
© Cengage Learning

to immigration. However, attitudes toward immigrants changed as the size of immigrant populations grew, particularly during periods of economic contraction like the 2008 recession. Facing higher levels of unemployment, native-born workers see immigrants as competitors willing to work for lower wages and less likely to support labor unions.

Immigrants' native cultures in Latin America, Africa, and the Middle East also encourage early marriage and large families, and these high fertility rates among immigrants contribute to tensions. For example, Spain briefly became the major immigrant-receiving nation in the EU, and the immigrant component of Spain's population rose from 2.1 to 14.1 percent between 1990 and 2010, with foreign-born mothers accounting for 10 percent of all births. Since

the beginning of the recession in 2008, immigration to Spain has slowed and birthrates of both native-born and foreign-born have fallen. But even in this altered context, immigrant populations have increased in Europe and the United States, and the resulting cultural conflicts have tested definitions of citizenship and nationality.

Large-scale migrations within developing countries are a related phenomenon. Migration from rural areas to urban centers increased threefold between 1925 and 1950; the pace of migration then accelerated (see Table 29.2). While slums around the major cities of developing nations are seen as signs of social breakdown and economic failure, life in these urban slums was generally better than life in the countryside. A World Bank study estimated that three out of four rural-to-urban migrants made economic gains. Residents of cities in sub-Saharan Africa, for example, were six times more likely than rural residents to have safe water. An unskilled migrant from the depressed northeast of Brazil could triple his or her income by moving to Rio de Janeiro.

As the scale of rural-to-urban migration grew, these benefits became more elusive. In the cities of the developing world, basic services have been crumbling under the pressure of rapid population growth. In Mexico City and Manila, among the world's largest cities, tens of thousands live in garbage dumps, scavenging for food. In Rio de Janeiro alone an estimated 350,000 abandoned children live in the streets and parks, begging, selling drugs, stealing, and engaging in prostitution to survive. Some nations have tried to relocate migrants back to the countryside. Indonesia, for example, has relocated more than a half-million urban residents since 1969.

# TECHNOLOGICAL AND ENVIRONMENTAL CHANGE

■ *How has technological change affected the global environment in the recent past?*

Technological innovation powered the economic expansion that began after World War II. New technologies increased productivity and disseminated human creativity. They also altered the way people lived, worked, and played. Because most of the economic benefits were initially concentrated in the advanced industrialized nations, technology

increased the power of those nations relative to the developing world. This has changed in the last decade with globalization and the rising industrial role of China. Even within developed nations, postwar technological innovations did not benefit all classes, industries, and regions equally. There were losers as well as winners. Governments in the developing world were often hard-pressed to control the actions of powerful transnational corporations, for example. As a result, the worst abuses of labor or the environment usually occurred in poor nations.

Population growth and increased levels of migration and urbanization multiplied the numbers of acres farmed and the number of factories, intensifying environmental threats. In the early twenty-first century, loss of rain forest, soil erosion, global warming, air and water pollution, and extinction of species threatened the quality of life and the survival of human societies. Environmental protection, like the acquisition of new technology, has progressed most in societies with the greatest economic resources.

## Conserving and Sharing Resources

In the 1960s environmental activists and political leaders began warning about the devastating environmental consequences of population growth, industrialization, and the expansion of agriculture onto marginal lands. Assaults on rain forests, the disappearance of species, and the poisoning of streams and rivers raised public consciousness. Environmental damage occurred in the advanced industrial economies and in the poorest of the developing nations. Perhaps the worst environmental record was achieved in the former Soviet Union, where industrial and nuclear wastes were routinely dumped with little concern for environmental consequences.

The expanding global population required increasing quantities of food, housing, energy, and other resources as the twentieth century ended (see Map 29.2). In the developed world, the consumer-driven economic expansion of the post–World War II years became an obstacle to addressing environmental problems, since modern economies depend on a profligate consumption of goods and resources. When consumption slows, industrial nations enter a recession, as recently demonstrated in 2008. How

Stephanie Maze/CORBIS

**Loss of Brazilian Rain Forest**   The destruction of large portions of Brazil's virgin rain forest has come to symbolize the growing threat to the environment caused by population growth and economic development. In this photograph we see the scale of environmental destruction.

could the United States, Germany, Japan, or China change consumption patterns to protect the environment without endangering corporate profits, wages, and employment levels?

Environmental pressures have also been extreme in the developing countries where population growth has been most dramatic. In Brazil, India, and China, for example, the need to expand food production led to rapid deforestation and the extension of farming and grazing onto marginal lands. The results were predictable—erosion and pollution—but many developing countries saw exploitation of their environmental resources and industrialization as the solution to their rapidly growing populations. Their argument was compelling: Why should Indians or Brazilians remain poor while Americans, Europeans, and Japanese grew rich?

## Responding to Environmental Threats

Despite the gravity of environmental threats, there were many successful efforts to preserve and protect the environment. The Clean Air Act, the Clean Water Act, and the Endangered Species Act were passed in the United States in the 1970s as part of an environmental effort that included the nations of the European Community and Japan. Environmental awareness spread by means of the media and grassroots political movements, and most nations in the developed world enforced strict antipollution laws and sponsored massive recycling efforts. Many also encouraged resource conservation by rewarding energy-efficient factories and manufacturers of fuel-efficient cars and by promoting the use of alternative energy sources such as solar and wind power.

Environmental efforts produced significant results. In western Europe and the United States, air quality improved dramatically. In the United States, smog levels fell nearly a third from 1970 to 2000, even though the number of automobiles increased more than 80 percent. Emissions of lead and sulfur dioxide were down as well. The Great Lakes, Long Island Sound, and Chesapeake Bay were all much cleaner at the end of the century than they had been in 1970. The rivers of North American and Europe also improved.

New technologies made much of the improvement possible. Pollution controls on automobiles, planes, and factory smokestacks reduced harmful emissions. Similar progress was made in the chemical industry. Scientists identified the chemicals that threaten the ozone layer, and the phase-out of their use in new appliances and cars began.

Clearly the desire to preserve the natural environment was growing around the world. In the developed nations, continued political organization and enhanced awareness of environmental issues seemed likely to lead to step-by-step improvements in environmental policy. In the developing world and most of the former Soviet bloc, however, population pressures and weak governments were major obstacles to effective environmental policies. Since the 1990s the rapid expansion of China's industrial sector has put additional pressure on the environment. In China, for example, respiratory disease caused by pollution is the leading cause of death. It now seems likely that industrialized nations will have to fund global improvements and that the cost will be high.

## Global Warming

Until the 1980s environmental alarms focused mainly on localized episodes of air and water pollution, exposure to toxic substances, waste management, and the disappearance of wilderness. The development of increasingly powerful computers and complex models of ecological interactions in the 1990s, however, made people aware of the global scope of certain environmental problems.

Many scientists and policymakers came to perceive global warming, the slow increase of the temperature of the earth's lower atmosphere, as an environmental threat requiring preventive action on an international scale. The warming is caused by a layer of atmospheric gases (carbon dioxide, methane, nitrous oxide, and ozone) that allow solar radiation to reach earth and warm it but that keep infrared energy (heat) from radiating from earth's surface back into space. Called the *greenhouse effect*, this process normally keeps the earth's temperature at a level suitable for life. However, increases in greenhouse-gas emissions—particularly from the burning of fossil fuels in industry and transportation—have added to this insulating atmospheric layer.

**Flooding in Bangladesh**
Typhoon-driven floods submerge the low-lying farmlands of Bangladesh with tragic regularity. Any significant rise in the sea level will make parts of the country nearly uninhabitable.

David Greedy/Getty Images

## Population Density and Water Stress

**Water stress**

Low–
medium High

| | High | Medium | Low | Extremely low | No data |

Population density

**Map 29.2  Fresh Water Resources**  This map links population density and the availability of water. Red areas are highly stressed environments where populations use at least 40 percent or more of available water. Less stressed environments are blue. The deeper the shade of red or blue, the greater the environmental stress.?  *Source:* From "Global Water Stress," *National Geographic, September 2002,* pp. 14–16. Reprinted by permission of the National Geographic Society. © Cengage Learning

Map labels: PACIFIC OCEAN, AUSTRALIA, ANTARCTICA, North China Plain, Yangzi R., Ganges R., Bay of Bengal, INDIAN OCEAN, SIBERIA, Huang He, ASIA, Persian Gulf, Aral Sea, EUROPE, Nile, AFRICA, SAHARA, Mediterranean Sea, Victoria Falls, ARCTIC OCEAN, Arctic Circle, GREENLAND, NORTH AMERICA, GREAT PLAINS, Colorado R., Grande R., Mississippi R., The Everglades, Gulf of Mexico, ATLANTIC OCEAN, Tropic of Cancer, Equator, Tropic of Capricorn, Antarctic Circle, Orinoco R., Amazon R., SOUTH AMERICA, Río de la Plata, PACIFIC OCEAN

Recent events have confirmed predictions of global temperature increases and melting glaciers and icecaps. Record heat hit northern Europe in the summer of 2003. Greenland glaciers and Arctic Ocean sea ice are melting at record rates, and a huge section of the Antarctic ice shelf broke up and floated away. Andean glaciers are shrinking so fast they could disappear in a decade, imperiling water supplies for drinking, irrigation, and hydroelectric production. Drought has affected much of the United States in recent years, and in 2002 Australia experienced the "Big Dry," its worst drought in a century.

Despite this evidence, governments of the industrialized countries that produce the most greenhouse gases have been slow to adopt measures stringent enough to reduce emissions because of the negative effects they believe this could have on their economies. Fearing limits on gas emissions could cripple their plans for industrial and economic expansion, many nations hesitated to sign the 1997 Kyoto Protocol, the first international agreement to impose penalties on countries that failed to cut greenhouse-gas emissions. It was a major environmental victory when Japan added its signature in March 2001, but to the consternation of many world leaders, President George W. Bush rejected the agreement, reluctant to burden American business. Shortly after being elected in 2008, President Barack Obama declared that "the United States will once again . . . lead the world toward a new era of global cooperation on climate change"; however, the issue of global warming played no role during the presidential election of 2012 until the tropical superstorm Sandy dealt a devastating blow to New York and New Jersey, vindicating

the prediction that the increased energy in the atmosphere caused by global warming would produce severe weather anomalies around the world.

## GLOBAL CULTURE
■ *How has technology contributed to the process of global interaction?*

Because of changes in electronic technology, today political and economic events have almost instantaneous impact in all parts of the world. A global language, a global educational system, and global forms of artistic expression have all come into being. Trade, travel, and migration have made a common popular culture unavoidable. These changes have delighted and enriched some but angered others.

### The Media and the Message

The fact that the most pervasive elements of global culture have their origins in the West has raised concerns in many quarters about **cultural imperialism**. Critics complain that entertainment conglomerates are flooding the world's movie theaters and television screens with Western images and that goods catering to Western tastes but manufactured in countries with low labor costs, like China and Indonesia, are flooding world markets. In this view, global marketing is especially insidious in trying to shape a world with a Western outlook based on capitalist ideology, while suppressing or devaluing traditional cultures and alternative ideologies. As the leader of the capitalist world, the United States is seen as the primary culprit.

But in truth, technology plays a more central role than ideology in spreading Western culture. Even though imperialist forces old and new shape choices, democratic forces are also at work as people around the world make their selections in the cultural marketplace. Thus a diversity of voices is more characteristic of cultural globalization than the cultural imperialism thesis maintains.

**SECTION REVIEW**

- Population growth and urbanization have led to deforestation and water and air pollution.
- Poorer countries feel their resources are being exploited by richer countries.
- Government measures and new technologies are reducing air and water pollution.
- Global warming caused by the accumulation of greenhouse gases will continue to affect the planet in coming decades.

**cultural imperialism** Domination of one culture over another by a deliberate policy or by economic or technological superiority.

## Technological Innovations

The pace of cultural globalization began to quicken during the economic recovery after World War II. The Hollywood films and American jazz recordings that had become popular in Europe and parts of Asia continued to spread. The birth of electronic technology opened contacts with large numbers of people who could never have afforded to go to a movie or buy a record.

The first step was the development of cheap transistor radios that could run on a couple of small batteries. Perfected by American scientists in 1948, transistors replaced power-hungry tubes in radios and other devices. Small portable transistor radios, most made in Asia, spread rapidly in parts of the world where homes lacked electricity.

Television, which became widely available to Western consumers in the 1950s, spread to poorer parts of the world in the 1980s and 1990s after mass production and cheap transistors made sets more affordable. Outside the United States, television broadcasting was usually a government monopoly at first, following the pattern of telegraph and postal service and radio broadcasting. Governments expected news reports and other programming to disseminate a unified national viewpoint.

Government monopolies eroded as the high cost of television production opened up global markets for American soap operas, adventure series, and situation comedies. By the 1990s a global network of satellites brought privately owned television broadcasting to even remote areas of the world, and first the VCR (videocassette recorder), followed by DVD players, provided an even greater variety of programs to people everywhere.

As a result of wider circulation of programming, people often became familiar with different dialects and languages. People in Portugal have become avid fans of Brazilian soap operas, and immigrants from Albania and North Africa often arrive in Italy with a command of Italian learned from Italian stations whose signals they could pick up at home. CNN (Cable News Network) expanded its international market after becoming the most-viewed and informative news source during the 1991 Persian Gulf War, when it broadcast live from Baghdad. CNN's fundamentally American viewpoints stimulated broadcasters in other countries to develop their own round-the-clock coverage. Al-Jazeera, based in the Persian Gulf emirate of Qatar, offered video footage and interpretation that differed greatly from American coverage of the war in Iraq in 2003.

The Internet's linkage of academic, government, and business networks began to transform world culture in the early twenty-first century. With the easy-to-use graphic interface of the World Wide Web in 1994, the number of users skyrocketed, with myriad users of "e-commerce" sites and blogs (Web logs), easy access to entertainment as well as information, and social media sites, including Facebook (2004) and Twitter (2006). Smart phones, connected to the Web, were initially used to transmit pictures and keep in touch with friends, but the Arab Spring of 2011 saw them develop as tools for communication among antiregime protesters as well.

As had happened so often throughout history, technological developments had unanticipated consequences. Although the new telecommunications and entertainment technologies derived disproportionately from American inventions, Japan and other East Asian nations came to dominate the manufacture and refinement of electronic devices. Non-Western countries that had adopted telephones late and had limited networks of copper wire benefited most from the improved communication. In 2012 the United States ranked 114th in per capita cellular phone use, sandwiched between the Congo Republic and the Dominican Republic. Qatar topped the list as the country with the highest per capita use.

Lawren Lu/Photodisc/Getty Images

**Always Connected** Two students simultaneously apply the power of smartphone, tablet, and laptop to a project.

**Japanese Comic Books**
After World War II comic magazines emerged as a major form of publication and a distinctive product of culture in Japan. Different series are directed to different age and gender groups. Issued weekly and running to some three hundred pages in black and white, the most popular magazines sell as many copies as do major newsmagazines in the United States.

Eye Ubiquitous/Photoshot

## The Spread of Pop Culture

For most of history, popular culture consisted of folk tales and highly localized styles of dress, cooking, music, and visual expression. Only the literate few had full access to the riches of a broader "great tradition," such as Confucianism, Islam, or Buddhism. In modern times, government school systems increased literacy rates but also promoted specifically national values and cultural tastes. Prescribed languages of instruction eroded the use and memory of local languages and traditions. In their place there arose **global pop culture**.

Initially, the content was heavily American. Singer Michael Jackson was almost as well known to the youth of Tanzania and Thailand as to American fans. Businesses sought out basketball star Michael Jordan and championship golfer Tiger Woods to endorse their products. American television programs, following in the path of American movies, acquired immense followings and inspired local imitations.

But the United States had no monopoly on global pop culture. Latin American soap operas, *telenovelas*, had a vast following in the Americas, eastern Europe, and elsewhere. Mumbai, India, long the world's largest producer of films, made or inspired more films for international audiences, like the 2009 Academy Award–winning *Slumdog Millionaire*. And the martial arts filmmakers of Hong Kong saw their style flourish in high-budget international spectaculars like director Ang Lee's *Crouching Tiger, Hidden Dragon* (2000) and the *Matrix* trilogy (1999–2003), which relied heavily on Hong Kong fight choreographers.

## Emerging Global Culture

While the globalization of popular culture has been criticized, cultural links across national and ethnic boundaries at a more elite level have generated little controversy. The end of the Cold War reopened intellectual and cultural contacts between former adversaries, making possible such things as Russian-American collaboration on space missions and extensive business contacts among former rivals. The English language, modern science, and higher education became the key elements of this **global elite culture**.

The emergence of English as the first global language began with the British Empire's introduction of the language to far-flung colonies. After achieving

**global pop culture**　Popular cultural practices and institutions that have been adopted internationally, such as music, the Internet, television, food, and fashion.

**global elite culture**　At the beginning of the twenty-first century, the attitudes and outlook of well-educated, prosperous, Western-oriented people around the world, largely expressed in European languages, especially English.

independence in the wake of World War II, most former colonies continued using English as an official language because it provided national unity and a link to the outside world that local languages could not. Countries that chose instead to make a local language official often found the decision counterproductive. Indian nationalists who had pushed Hindi to be India's official language found that students taught in Hindi were unable to compete internationally because of poor knowledge of English. Sri Lanka, which had made Sinhala its official language in 1956, reversed itself in 1989 after reports that prominent officials were sending their children to private English-language schools.

The use of English as a second language was greatly stimulated by the importance of the United States in postwar world affairs. Individuals recognized the importance of mastering English for successful business, diplomatic, and military careers. After the collapse of Soviet domination, students in eastern Europe flocked to study English instead of Russian. Ninety percent of students in Cambodia (a former French colony) chose to study English, even though a Canadian agency offered a sizable cash bonus if they would study French. In the 1990s China made the study of English as a second language nearly universal from junior high school onwards.

English has become the language of choice for most international academic conferences, business meetings, and diplomatic gatherings. International organizations that provide equal status to many languages, such as the United Nations and the European Union, often conduct informal committee meetings in English. In cities throughout the world, signs and notices are commonly posted in the local language and English. Writers from Africa and India have received high honors for novels written in English, as have Arab and Caribbean authors for works written in French. Nevertheless, world literature remains highly diverse in form and language.

By contrast, science and technology have become standardized components of global culture. Though imperialism helped spread the Western disciplines of biology, chemistry, and physics around the world, their importance expanded even further after decolonization as students from newly independent nations sought to compete at an international level. Standardization of scientific terms, weights and measures, and computer codes underlay the worldwide expansion of commerce.

The third pillar of global elite culture is the university. The structure and curricula of modern universities are nearly indistinguishable around the world, permitting students today to cross national boundaries as freely as medieval students in the European mainland (see Chapter 13) or the Muslim world (see Chapter 9). Instruction in the pure sciences varies little from place to place, and standardization is nearly as common in applied sciences such as engineering and medicine and only slightly less so in the social sciences.

While university subjects are taught in many languages, instruction in English is spreading rapidly. Because discoveries are often first published in English, advanced students in science, business, and international relations need to know that language to keep up with the latest developments. Many courses in northern European countries have long been offered in English, and elsewhere in Europe courses taught in English have facilitated the EU's efforts to encourage students to study outside their home countries.

## Enduring Cultural Diversity

Although protesters regularly denounce the "Americanization" of the world, a closer look suggests that cultural globalization is more complex. Although English has spread widely as a second language, global culture is primarily a second culture that dominates some contexts but does not displace other traditions. From this perspective, American music, fast food, and fashions are more likely to add to a society's options than to displace local culture.

Japan first demonstrated that a country with a non-Western culture could industrialize effectively. Individuality was less valued in Japan than the ability of each person to fit into a group, whether as an employee, a member of an athletic team, or a student in a class. Moreover, the Japanese considered it unmannerly to directly contradict, correct, or refuse the request of another person. From a Western point of view, these Japanese customs seemed to discourage individual initiative and personality development and to preserve traditional hierarchies. Even though Japanese women often worked outside the home, they responded only slowly to the American and European feminist advocacy of gender equality. However, the Japanese approach to social relations was well suited to an industrial economy. The efficiency, pride in workmanship, and group solidarity of Japanese workers played a major role in transforming Japan into an economic power by the 1980s, although it proved less well adapted to the severe economic slowdown that began in the 1990s.

As awareness of the economic impact of Japanese culture and society began to spread, it became apparent that Taiwan and South Korea, along with Singapore and Hong Kong (a British colony before being reunited with China in 1997), were developing dynamic industrial economies of their own. Today India and the People's Republic of China are following the same path without forsaking their national tastes and heritages.

This does not mean that the world's cultural diversity is secure. Every decade a number of minority languages cease to be spoken. Televised national ceremonies or performances for tourists may prevent folk customs and costumes from dying out, but they also tend to devitalize rituals that once had many local variations. While a century ago it was possible to recognize the nationality of people from their clothing and grooming, today most urban men dress the same the world over, although women's clothing shows greater variety. As much as one may regret the disappearance or commercialization of some folkways, most anthropologists would agree that change is characteristic of all healthy cultures. What doesn't change risks extinction.

## SECTION REVIEW

- The global pervasiveness of Western culture has provoked charges of U.S. cultural imperialism.
- Technology such as radio, television, and the Internet has played a major role in the spread of Western culture since World War II.
- Technology has also contributed to the emergence of a global pop culture that blends a variety of cultural elements from different countries.
- A global elite culture has also developed combining the English language, science, and higher education.
- Despite globalizing forces, cultural diversity remains strong, if not completely secure.

# CHAPTER REVIEW

## GLOBALIZATION AND THE WORLD ECONOMY
■ *What are the main benefits and dangers of growing political, economic, and cultural integration?*
(page 685)

Dramatic changes in technology—especially in computers, communication networks, and the media—have helped integrate national and regional economies into a global economy that has benefited from improved efficiencies and a growing demand. The expansion of global trade and communications and the privatization of government enterprises fueled an economic boom in the 1990s that cooled abruptly in the wake of 9/11. Many nations joined a variety of trade organizations to promote growth and reduce the vulnerability created by American economic dominance. Global interdependence and rapid economic expansion and speculation led to a global financial crisis in 2008 that plunged the world into the worst economic slowdown since the Great Depression of the 1930s. The spectacular growth in the economy of China, fueled by the world's insatiable demand for its products, has been the most impressive change in the global economy.

## THE QUESTION OF VALUES

◼ *What roles do religious beliefs and secular ideologies play in the contemporary world?* (page 691)

In much of the world, religious movements are gaining adherents. The growing influence of Islam has been particularly important, in part as a reaction to Western values and Western imperialism. Extremists have used religion as an excuse to commit acts of terrorism. Meanwhile, certain universal values are also gaining ground. Among the most important are human rights and the rights of women.

## THE CHALLENGE OF POPULATION GROWTH

◼ *What explains differences in the rate of population growth among the world's regions?* (page 696)

Population changes mean that the richer nations have an aging population and growth has slowed. The populations of Latin America and Asia have also slowed, but not as fast as they did in the mid-twentieth century. Per capita income and industrialization play key roles in differences between countries. Countries with higher wages and educational levels generally have smaller families. Meanwhile, despite severe health problems such as HIV/AIDS, especially in the poorest regions, such as sub-Saharan Africa, the population is still growing fast and therefore consists predominantly of young people.

## UNEQUAL DEVELOPMENT AND THE MOVEMENT OF PEOPLES

◼ *How have differences in wealth between nations influenced global migration patterns?* (page 700)

The poor, particularly those living in rural areas, are leaving their homes in search of better opportunities. Most migrate to cities in their home countries, in numbers that far outstrip the ability of cities to provide jobs, housing, education, water, and sanitation. Many others cross continents and seas at great expense and risk to reach the richer countries of Europe and North America. Though they are willing to work hard for little pay, their presence is often resented by the native inhabitants, who fear the changes in culture and customs that immigrants bring.

## TECHNOLOGICAL AND ENVIRONMENTAL CHANGE

◼ *How has technological change affected the global environment in the recent past?* (page 703)

A growing economy has had profound effects on the global environment. The burning of fossil fuels and the release of other chemical emissions have caused the earth's climate to warm considerably since the mid-twentieth century. Technology has reduced polluting emissions, and advances in chemistry have helped protect the ozone layer as well. More warming is yet to come, however, which will cause changes in the weather and a rise in sea levels. International efforts to alleviate these problems have begun, but so far they have been insufficient to curb pollution and to slow down global warming.

## GLOBAL CULTURE

◼ *How has technology contributed to the process of global interaction?* (page 707)

Global communications have encouraged the rise of two common global cultures. Popular culture, especially in dress, food, and entertainment, initially reflected Western tastes and commercial interests but now includes many elements from other cultures. The parallel growth of a global elite culture has resulted from the spread of the English language, modern science, and increasingly uniform university curricula.

## Key Terms

globalization (p. 685)

World Trade Organization (WTO) (p. 689)

Deng Xiaoping (p. 690)

terrorism (p. 692)

Usama bin Laden (p. 692)

Universal Declaration of Human Rights (p. 693)

nongovernmental organizations (NGOs) (p. 693)

Thomas Malthus (p. 697)

demographic transition (p. 697)

cultural imperialism (p. 707)

global pop culture (p. 709)

global elite culture (p. 709)

# GLOSSARY

**Abbasid Caliphate** Descendants of the Prophet Muhammad's uncle, al-Abbas, the Abbasids overthrew the Umayyad Caliphate and ruled an Islamic empire from their capital in Baghdad (founded 762) from 750 to 1258. (p. 215)

**abolitionists** Men and women who agitated for a complete end to slavery. Abolitionist pressure ended the British transatlantic slave trade in 1808 and slavery in British colonies in 1834. In the United States the activities of abolitionists were one factor leading to the Civil War (1861–1865). (p. 506)

**Acheh Sultanate** Muslim kingdom in northern Sumatra. Main center of Islamic expansion in Southeast Asia in the early seventeenth century, it declined after the Dutch seized Malacca from Portugal in 1641. (p. 443)

**Aden** Port city in the modern south Arabian country of Yemen. It has been a major trading center in the Indian Ocean since ancient times. (p. 340)

**Adolf Hitler (1889–1945)** Born in Austria, Hitler became a radical German nationalist during World War I. He led the National Socialist German Workers' Party—the Nazis—in the 1920s and became dictator of Germany in 1933. He led Europe into World War II. (p. 638)

**African National Congress** An organization dedicated to obtaining equal voting and civil rights for black inhabitants of South Africa. Founded in 1912 as the South African Native National Congress, it changed its name in 1923. Though it was banned and its leaders were jailed for many years, it eventually helped bring majority rule to South Africa. (p. 626)

**Afrikaners** South Africans descended from Dutch and French settlers of the seventeenth century. Their Great Trek founded new settler colonies in the nineteenth century. Though a minority among South Africans, they held political power after 1910, imposing a system of racial segregation called apartheid after 1949. (p. 540)

**Agricultural Revolutions** The change from food gathering to food production that occurred between ca. 8000 and 2000 B.C.E. Also known as the Neolithic Revolution. (p. 10)

**agricultural revolution** The transformation of farming that resulted in the eighteenth century from the spread of new crops, improvements in cultivation techniques and livestock breeding, and the consolidation of small holdings into large farms from which tenants and sharecroppers were forcibly expelled. (p. 472)

**Akbar** Most illustrious sultan of the Mughal Empire in India (r. 1556–1605). He expanded the empire and pursued a policy of conciliation with Hindus. (p. 438)

**Akhenaten** Egyptian pharaoh (r. 1353–1335 B.C.E.). He built a new capital at Amarna, fostered a new style of naturalistic art, and created a religious revolution by imposing worship of the sun-disk. (p. 34)

**Albert Einstein (1879–1955)** German physicist who developed the theory of relativity, which states that time, space, and mass are relative to each other and not fixed. (p. 610)

**Alexander** King of Macedonia in northern Greece. Between 334 and 323 B.C.E. he conquered the Persian Empire, reached the Indus Valley, founded many Greek-style cities, and spread Greek culture across the Middle East. Later known as Alexander the Great. (p. 100)

**Alexander Nevskii** Prince of Novgorod (r. 1236–1263). He submitted to the invading Mongols in 1240 and received recognition as the leader of the Russian princes under the Golden Horde. (p. 291)

**Alexandria** City on the Mediterranean coast of Egypt founded by Alexander. It became the capital of the Hellenistic kingdom of the Ptolemies. It contained the famous Library and the Museum, a center for leading scientific and literary figures. Its merchants engaged in trade with areas bordering the Mediterranean and the Indian Ocean. (p. 102)

**All-India Muslim League** Political organization founded in India in 1906 to defend the interests of India's Muslim minority. Led by Muhammad Ali Jinnah, it attempted to negotiate with the Indian National Congress. In 1940, the League began demanding a separate state for Muslims, to be called Pakistan. (p. 616)

**altepetl** An ethnic state in ancient Mesoamerica, the common political building block of that region. (p. 346)

**amulet** Small charm meant to protect the bearer from evil. Found frequently in archaeological excavations in Mesopotamia and Egypt, amulets reflect the religious practices of the common people. (p. 16)

**Amur River** This river valley was a contested frontier between northern China and eastern Russia until the settlement arranged in the Treaty of Nerchinsk (1689). (p. 459)

**anarchism** Movement of revolutionaries who wanted to abolish all private property and governments, usually by violence, and replace them with free associations of groups. (p. 575)

**Anasazi** Important culture of what is now the southwest United States (700–1300 C.E.). Centered on Chaco Canyon in New Mexico and Mesa Verde in Colorado, the Anasazi culture built multistory residences and worshiped in subterranean buildings called kivas. (p. 170)

**aqueduct** A conduit, either elevated or underground, that used gravity to carry water from a source to a location—usually a city—that needed it. The Romans built many aqueducts in a period of substantial urbanization. (p. 119)

**Arawak** Amerindian peoples who inhabited the Greater Antilles of the Caribbean at the time of Columbus. (p. 359)

**Armenia** One of the earliest Christian kingdoms, situated in eastern Anatolia and the western Caucasus and occupied by speakers of the Armenian language. (p. 204)

**Ashikaga Shogunate** The second of Japan's military governments headed by a shogun (a military ruler). Sometimes called the Muromachi Shogunate. (p. 302)

**Ashoka** Third ruler of the Mauryan Empire in India (r. 273–232 B.C.E.). He converted to Buddhism and broadcast his precepts on inscribed stones and pillars, the earliest surviving Indian writing. (p. 145)

**Asian Tigers** South Korea, Taiwan, Hong Kong, and Singapore, so called because their economies expanded so fast. (p. 675)

**Atahuallpa** Last ruling Inka emperor of Peru. He was executed by the Spanish. (p. 372)

**Atatürk (1881–1938)** The founder of modern Turkey. He distinguished himself as a war hero in World War I and expelled a Greek expeditionary army from Anatolia in 1921–1922. He replaced the Ottoman Empire with the Turkish Republic in 1923. As president, he pushed through a radical westernization and reform of Turkish society. (p. 599)

**Atlantic system** The network of trading links after 1500 that moved goods, wealth, people, and cultures around the Atlantic Basin. (p. 403)

**Auguste (1862–1954) and Louis (1864–1948) Lumière** French inventors of motion pictures whose equipment demonstrations abroad stimulated the growth of cinema around the world. (p. 608)

**Augustus** Honorific name of Octavian, founder of the Roman Principate, the military dictatorship that replaced the failing rule of the Roman Senate. After defeating all rivals, between 31 B.C.E. and 14 C.E. he laid the groundwork for several centuries of stability and prosperity in the Roman Empire. (p. 112)

**Auschwitz** Nazi extermination camp in Poland, the largest center of mass murder during the Holocaust. Close to a million Jews, Gypsies, communists, and others were killed there. (p. 648)

**australopithecines** The several extinct species of humanlike primates that existed from about 4.5 million years ago to 1.4 million years ago (genus *Australopithecus*). (p. 6)

**Ayatollah Ruhollah Khomeini (1902–1989)** Shi'ite philosopher and cleric who led the overthrow of the shah of Iran in 1979 and created an Islamic republic. (p. 678)

**ayllu** Andean lineage group or kin-based community. (p. 173)

**Aztec** The Mexica-dominated alliance that created a powerful empire in central Mexico (1325–1521). (p. 346)

**Babylon** The largest and most important city in Mesopotamia. It achieved particular eminence as the capital of the Amorite king Hammurabi in the eighteenth century B.C.E. (p. 13)

**balance of power** The policy in international relations by which, beginning in the eighteenth century, the major European states acted together to prevent any one of them from becoming too powerful. (p. 397)

**Balfour Declaration** Statement issued by Britain's foreign secretary Arthur Balfour in 1917 favoring the establishment of a Jewish national homeland in Palestine. (p. 592)

**Bannermen** Hereditary military servants of the Qing Empire, in large part descendants of peoples of various origins who had fought for the founders of the empire. (p. 526)

**Bantu** Collective name of a large group of sub-Saharan African languages and the peoples speaking these languages. (p. 201)

**Bartolomé de Las Casas** First bishop of Chiapas, in southern Mexico. He devoted most of his life to protecting Amerindian peoples from exploitation. His major achievement was the New Laws of 1542, which limited the ability of Spanish settlers to compel Amerindians to labor for them. (p. 404)

**Bartolomeu Dias** Portuguese explorer who in 1488 led the first expedition to sail around the southern tip of Africa from the Atlantic and sight the Indian Ocean. (p. 363)

**Batavia** Fort established around 1619 as headquarters of Dutch East India Company operations in Indonesia; today the city of Jakarta. (p. 446)

**Battle of Midway** U.S. naval victory over the Japanese fleet in June 1942, in which the Japanese lost four of their best aircraft carriers. It marked a turning point in World War II. (p. 644)

**Beijing** China's northern capital, first used as an imperial capital in 906 and now the capital of the People's Republic of China. (p. 294)

**Bengal** Region of northeastern India. It was the first part of India to be conquered by the British in the eighteenth century and remained the political and economic center of British India throughout the nineteenth century. The 1905 split of the province into predominantly Hindu West Bengal and predominantly Muslim East Bengal (now Bangladesh) sparked anti-British riots. (p. 616)

**Benito Mussolini (1883–1945)** Fascist dictator of Italy (1922–1943). He led Italy to conquer Ethiopia (1935), joined Germany in the Axis pact (1936), and allied Italy with Germany in World War II. He was overthrown in 1943 when the Allies invaded Italy. (p. 638)

**Berlin Conference (1884–1885)** Conference that German chancellor Otto von Bismarck called to set rules for the partition of Africa. It led to the creation of the Congo Free State under King Leopold II of Belgium. (p. 544)

**Bhagavad-Gita** The most important work of Indian sacred literature, a dialogue between the great warrior Arjuna and the god Krishna on duty and the fate of the spirit. (p. 146)

**bipedalism** The ability to walk upright on two legs, characteristic of hominids. (p. 6)

**Black Death** An outbreak of bubonic plague that spread across Asia, North Africa, and Europe in the mid-fourteenth century, carrying off vast numbers of persons. (p. 309)

**Blaise Diagne (1872–1934)** Senegalese political leader. He was the first African elected to the French National Assembly. During World War I, in exchange for promises to give French citizenship to Senegalese, he helped recruit Africans to serve in the French army. After the war, he led a movement to abolish forced labor in Africa. (p. 626)

**Bolsheviks** Radical Marxist political party founded by Vladimir Lenin in 1903. Under Lenin's leadership, the Bolsheviks seized power in November 1917 during the Russian Revolution. (p. 592)

**Borobodur** A massive stone monument on the Indonesian island of Java, erected by the Sailendra kings around 800 C.E. The winding ascent through ten levels, decorated with rich relief carving, is a Buddhist allegory for the progressive stages of enlightenment. (p. 152)

**bourgeoisie** In early modern Europe, the class of well-off town dwellers whose wealth came from manufacturing, finance, commerce, and allied professions. (p. 388)

**British raj** The rule over much of South Asia between 1765 and 1947 by the East India Company and then by a British government. (p. 549)

**bronze** An alloy of copper with a small amount of tin (or sometimes arsenic), which is harder and more durable than copper alone. The term *Bronze Age* is applied to the era—the dates of which vary in different parts of the world—when bronze was the primary metal for tools and weapons. (p. 19)

**bubonic plague** A bacterial disease of fleas that can be transmitted by flea bites to rodents and humans; humans in late stages of the illness can spread the bacteria by coughing. Because of its very high mortality rate and the difficulty of preventing its spread, major outbreaks have created crises in many parts of the world. (p. 285)

**Buddha** An Indian prince named Siddhartha Gautama, who renounced his wealth and social position. After becoming "enlightened" (the meaning of *Buddha*), he enunciated the principles of Buddhism. This doctrine evolved and spread throughout India and to Southeast, East, and Central Asia. (p. 140)

**Byzantine Empire** Historians' name for the eastern portion of the Roman Empire from the fourth century onward, taken from *Byzantion*, an early name for Constantinople, the Byzantine capital city. The empire fell to the Ottomans in 1453. (p. 229)

**caliphate** Office established in succession to the Prophet Muhammad, to rule the Islamic empire; also the name of that empire. (p. 213)

**calpolli** A group of up to a hundred families that served as a social building block of an altepetl in ancient Mesoamerica. (p. 346)

**capitalism** The economic system of large financial institutions—banks, stock exchanges, investment companies—that first developed in early modern Europe. *Commercial capitalism,* the trading system of the early modern economy, is often distinguished from *industrial capitalism*, the system based on machine production.    (p. 418)

**caravel**  A small, highly maneuverable three-masted ship used by the Portuguese and Spanish in the exploration of the Atlantic.    (p. 361)

**Carthage**  City located in present-day Tunisia, founded by Phoenicians around 800 B.C.E. It became a major commercial center and naval power in the western Mediterranean until defeated by Rome in the third century B.C.E.    (p. 49)

**Catholic Reformation**  Religious reform movement within the Latin Christian Church, begun in response to the Protestant Reformation. It clarified Catholic theology and reformed clerical training and discipline.    (p. 383)

**Cecil Rhodes (1853–1902)**  British entrepreneur and politician involved in the expansion of the British Empire from South Africa into Central Africa. The colonies of Southern Rhodesia (now Zimbabwe) and Northern Rhodesia (now Zambia) were named after him.    (p. 541)

**Celts**  Peoples sharing common linguistic and cultural features that originated in Central Europe in the first half of the first millennium B.C.E.    (p. 73)

**Champa rice**  Quick-maturing rice that can allow two harvests in one growing season. Originally introduced into Champa from India, it was later sent to China as a tribute gift by the Champa state.    (p. 273)

**Chang'an**  City in the Wei River Valley in eastern China. It became the capital of the early Han Empire. Its main features were imitated in the cities and towns that sprang up throughout the Han Empire.    (p. 127)

**Charlemagne**  King of the Franks (r. 768–814); emperor (r. 800–814). Through a series of military conquests he established the Carolingian Empire, which encompassed all of Gaul and parts of Germany and Italy. Though illiterate himself, he sponsored a brief intellectual revival.    (p. 229)

**Charles Darwin (1809–1882)**  Author of *On the Origin of Species* (1859), which developed the theory of evolution through natural selection.    (p. 580)

**chartered companies**  Groups of private investors who paid an annual fee to France and England in exchange for a monopoly over trade to the West Indies colonies.    (p. 419)

**Chavín**  The first major urban civilization in South America (900–200 B.C.E.). Its capital, Chavín de Huántar, was located high in the Andes Mountains of Peru. Chavín became politically and economically dominant in a densely populated region that included two distinct ecological zones, the Peruvian coastal plain and the Andean foothills.    (p. 161)

**Chiang Kai-shek (1886–1975)**  Chinese military and political leader. Succeeded Sun Yat-sen as head of the Guomindang in 1925; headed the Chinese government from 1928 to 1948; fought against the Chinese communists and Japanese invaders. After 1949 he headed the Chinese nationalist government in Taiwan.    (p. 641)

**chiefdom**  Form of political organization with rule by a hereditary leader who held power over a collection of villages and towns. Less powerful than kingdoms and empires, chiefdoms were based on gift giving and commercial links.    (p. 172)

**Chimú**  Powerful Peruvian civilization based on conquest. Located in the region earlier dominated by Moche. Conquered by Inka in 1465.    (p. 178)

**chinampas**  Raised fields constructed along lakeshores in central Mexico to increase agricultural yields.    (p. 164, 347)

**Chinggis Khan**  The title of Temüjin when he ruled the Mongols (1206–1227). It means the "oceanic" or "universal leader." Chinggis Khan was the founder of the Mongol Empire.    (p. 281)

**Choson**  The Choson dynasty ruled Korea from the fall of the Koryo kingdom to the colonization of Korea by Japan.    (p. 300)

**Christopher Columbus**  Genoese mariner who in the service of Spain led expeditions across the Atlantic, reestablishing contact between the peoples of the Americas and the Old World and opening the way to Spanish conquest and colonization.    (p. 363)

**city-state**  A small independent state consisting of an urban center and the surrounding agricultural territory. A characteristic political form in early Mesopotamia, Archaic and Classical Greece, Phoenicia, and early Italy.    (p. 16)

**civilization**  An ambiguous term often used to denote more complex societies but sometimes used by anthropologists to describe any group of people sharing a set of cultural traits.    (p. 15)

**Cold War**  The ideological struggle between communism (Soviet Union) and capitalism (United States) for world influence. The Cold War came to an end when the Soviet Union dissolved in 1991.    (p. 657)

**Commodore Matthew Perry**  A navy commander who, on July 8, 1853, became the first foreigner to break through the barriers that had kept Japan isolated from the rest of the world for 250 years.    (p. 565)

**Confucius**  Western name for the Chinese philosopher Kongzi (551–479 B.C.E.). His doctrine of duty and public service had a great influence on subsequent Chinese thought and served as a code of conduct for government officials.    (p. 63)

**Congress of Vienna**  Meeting of representatives of European monarchs called to reestablish the old order after the defeat of Napoleon I.    (p. 500)

**conquistadors**  Early-sixteenth-century Spanish adventurers who conquered Mexico, Central America, and Peru.    (p. 371)

**Constantine**  Roman emperor (r. 312–337). After reuniting the Roman Empire, he moved the capital to Constantinople and made Christianity a favored religion.    (p. 120)

**Constitutional Convention**  Meeting in 1787 of the elected representatives of the thirteen original states to write the Constitution of the United States.    (p. 495)

**contract of indenture**  A voluntary agreement binding a person to work for a specified period of years in return for free passage to an overseas destination. Before 1800 most indentured servants were Europeans; after 1800 most indentured laborers were Asians.    (p. 561)

**Cossacks**  Peoples of the Russian Empire who lived outside the farming villages, often as herders, mercenaries, or outlaws. Cossacks led the expansion into Siberia in the sixteenth and seventeenth centuries.    (p. 440)

**creoles**  In colonial Spanish America, the term used to describe someone of European descent born in the New World. Elsewhere in the Americas, the term is used to describe all non-native peoples.    (p. 408)

**Crimean War**  Conflict between the Russian and Ottoman Empires fought primarily in the Crimean peninsula. To prevent Russian expansion, Britain and France sent troops to support the Ottomans.    (p. 519)

**Crusades**  (1095–1204) Armed pilgrimages to the Holy Land by Christians determined to recover Jerusalem from Muslim rule. The Crusades brought an end to western Europe's centuries of intellectual and cultural isolation.    (p. 250)

**Crystal Palace**  Building erected in Hyde Park, London, for the Great Exhibition of 1851. Made of iron and glass, like a gigantic greenhouse, it was a symbol of the industrial age.    (p. 479)

**Cuban Missile Crisis (1962)** Brink-of-war confrontation between the United States and the Soviet Union over the latter's placement of nuclear-armed missiles in Cuba.   (p. 662)

**Culhuacán** Multiethnic Mesoamerican state south of and historically connected with Teotihuacan.   (p. 168)

**cultural imperialism** Domination of one culture over another by a deliberate policy or by economic or technological superiority.   (p. 707)

**Cultural Revolution (China)** Campaign in China ordered by Mao Zedong to purge the Communist Party of his opponents and instill revolutionary values in the younger generation.   (p. 675)

**culture** Socially transmitted patterns of action and expression. *Material culture* refers to physical objects such as dwellings, clothing, tools, and crafts. Culture also includes arts, beliefs, knowledge, and technology.   (p. 5)

**cuneiform** A system of writing in which wedge-shaped symbols represented words or syllables. It originated in Mesopotamia and was used initially for Sumerian and Akkadian but later was adapted to represent other languages of western Asia. Literacy was confined to a relatively small group of administrators and scribes.   (p. 15)

**Cyrus** Founder of the Achaemenid Persian Empire. Between 550 and 530 B.C.E. he conquered Media, Lydia, and Babylon. Revered in the traditions of both Iran and the subject peoples, he employed Persians and Medes in his administration and respected the institutions and beliefs of subject peoples.   (p. 84)

*daimyo* Literally, "great name(s)." Japanese warlords and great landowners, whose armed samurai gave them control of the Japanese islands from the eighth to the later nineteenth century. Under the Tokugawa Shogunate they were subordinated to the imperial government.   (p. 451)

**Daoism** Chinese school of thought, originating in the Warring States Period with Laozi. Daoism offered an alternative to the Confucian emphasis on hierarchy and duty, emphasizing instead understanding the "path" of nature.   (p. 63)

**Darius I** Third ruler of the Persian Empire (r. 521–486 B.C.E.). He crushed the widespread initial resistance to his rule and gave major government posts to Persians rather than to Medes. He established a system of provinces and tribute, began construction of Persepolis, and expanded Persian control in the east (Pakistan) and west (northern Greece).   (p. 85)

**Decembrist revolt** Abortive attempt by army officers to take control of the Russian government upon the death of Tsar Alexander I in 1825.   (p. 523)

**Declaration of the Rights of Man and of the Citizen** Statement of fundamental political rights adopted by the French National Assembly at the beginning of the French Revolution.   (p. 498)

**deforestation** The removal of trees faster than forests can replace themselves.   (p. 392)

**Delhi Sultanate** Centralized Indian empire of varying extent, created by Muslim invaders.   (p. 332)

**democracy** System of government in which all "citizens" (however defined) have equal political and legal rights, privileges, and protections, as in the Greek city-state of Athens in the fifth and fourth centuries B.C.E.   (p. 90)

**demographic transition** A change in the rates of population growth. Before the transition, both birthrates and death rates are high, resulting in a slowly growing population; then the death rate drops but the birthrate remains high, causing a population explosion; finally the birthrate drops and the population growth slows down. This transition took place in Europe in the late nineteenth and early twentieth centuries, in North

America and East Asia in the mid-twentieth century, and, most recently, in Latin America and South Asia.   (p. 697)

**Deng Xiaoping (1904–1997)** Communist Party leader who forced Chinese economic reforms after the death of Mao Zedong.   (p. 690)

**dhows** Characteristic cargo and passenger ships of the Arabian Sea.   (p. 338)

**Diaspora** Greek word meaning "dispersal," used to describe the communities of a given ethnic group living outside their homeland. Jews, for example, spread from Israel to western Asia and Mediterranean lands in antiquity and today can be found throughout the world.   (p. 46)

**Dirty War** Suppression of leftist groups by the Argentine military (1976–1983) characterized by the use of illegal imprisonment, torture, and executions.   (p. 672)

**division of labor** A manufacturing technique that breaks down a craft into many simple and repetitive tasks that can be performed by unskilled workers. Pioneered in the manufacture of pottery and in other eighteenth-century factories, it greatly increased the productivity of labor and lowered the cost of manufactured goods.   (p. 476)

**driver** A privileged male slave whose job was to ensure that a slave gang did its work on a plantation.   (p. 417)

**Druids** The class of religious experts who conducted rituals and preserved sacred lore among some ancient Celtic peoples.   (p. 74)

**durbar** An elaborate display of political power and wealth in British India in the nineteenth century, ostensibly in imitation of the pageantry of the Mughal Empire.   (p. 549)

**Dutch West India Company** Trading company chartered by the Dutch government to conduct its merchants' trade in the Americas and Africa.   (p. 419)

**electricity** A form of energy used in telegraphy from the 1840s on and for lighting, industrial motors, and railroads beginning in the 1880s.   (p. 568)

**electric telegraph** A device for rapid, long-distance transmission of information over an electric wire. It was introduced in England and North America in the 1830s and 1840s and replaced telegraph systems that utilized visual signals such as semaphores.   (p. 481)

**Emiliano Zapata (1879–1919)** Revolutionary and leader of peasants in the Mexican Revolution. He mobilized landless peasants in south-central Mexico in an attempt to seize and divide the lands of the wealthy landowners. Though successful for a time, he was ultimately defeated and assassinated.   (p. 559)

**Empress Dowager Cixi** Empress of China and mother of Emperor Guangxi. She put her son under house arrest, supported antiforeign movements, and resisted reforms of the Chinese government and armed forces.   (p. 583)

**encomienda** A grant of authority over a population of Amerindians in the Spanish colonies. It provided the grant holder with a supply of cheap labor and periodic payments of goods by the Amerindians. It obliged the grant holder to Christianize the Amerindians.   (p. 405)

**English Civil War** (1642–1649) A conflict over royal versus parliamentary rights, caused by King Charles I's arrest of his parliamentary critics and ending with his execution. Its outcome checked the growth of royal absolutism and, with the Glorious Revolution of 1688 and the English Bill of Rights of 1689, ensured that England would be a constitutional monarchy.   (p. 395)

**Enlightenment** A philosophical movement in eighteenth-century Europe that fostered the belief that one could reform society by discovering rational laws that governed social behavior and were just as scientific as the laws of physics.   (p. 387, 491) *equites* In ancient Italy, prosperous landowners second in wealth and status to the senatorial aristocracy. The Roman emperors allied with this group to counterbalance the influence of the old aristocracy and used the equites to staff the imperial civil service. (p. 112)

**Estates General** France's traditional national assembly with representatives of the three estates, or classes, in French society: the clergy, nobility, and commoners. The calling of the Estates General in 1789 led to the French Revolution. (p. 497)

**Ethiopia** East African highland nation lying east of the Nile River. (p. 204)

**European Economic Community (Common Market)** An organization promoting economic unity in Europe, formed in 1957 by consolidation of earlier, more limited, agreements. With the addition of many new nations it became the European Union (EU) in 1993. (p. 659)

**Eva Duarte Perón (1919–1952)** Wife of Juan Perón and champion of the poor in Argentina. She was a gifted speaker and popular political leader who campaigned to improve the life of the urban poor by founding schools and hospitals and providing other social benefits. (p. 623)

**evolution** The biological theory that, over time, changes occurring in plants and animals, mainly as a result of natural selection and genetic mutation, result in new species. (p. 5)

**extraterritoriality** The right of foreign residents in a country to live under the laws of their native country and disregard the laws of the host country. In the nineteenth and early twentieth centuries, European and American nationals living in certain areas of Chinese and Ottoman cities were granted this right. (p. 519)

**Faisal I (1885–1933)** Arab prince, leader of the Arab Revolt in World War I. The British made him king of Iraq in 1921, and he reigned under British protection until 1933. (p. 591)

**Fascist Party** Italian political party created by Benito Mussolini during World War I. It emphasized aggressive nationalism and was Mussolini's instrument for the creation of a dictatorship in Italy from 1922 to 1943. (p. 638)

**Ferdinand Magellan** Portuguese navigator who led the Spanish expedition of 1519–1522 that was the first to sail around the world. (p. 364)

**fief** In medieval Europe, land granted in return for a sworn oath to provide specified military service. (p. 238)

**First Temple** A monumental sanctuary built in Jerusalem by King Solomon in the tenth century B.C.E. to be the religious center for the Israelite god Yahweh. The Temple priesthood conducted sacrifices, received a tithe or percentage of agricultural revenues, and became economically and politically powerful. (p. 45)

**Five-Year Plans** Plans that Joseph Stalin introduced to industrialize the Soviet Union rapidly, beginning in 1928. They set goals for the output of steel, electricity, machinery, and most other products and were enforced by the police powers of the state. They succeeded in making the Soviet Union a major industrial power before World War II. (p. 631)

**foragers** People who support themselves by hunting wild animals and gathering wild edible plants and insects. (p. 8)

**Francisco "Pancho" Villa (1877–1923)** A popular leader during the Mexican Revolution. An outlaw in his youth, when the revolution started he formed a cavalry army in the north of Mexico and fought for the rights of the landless in collaboration with Emiliano Zapata. He was assassinated in 1923. (p. 559)

**Francisco Pizarro** Spanish explorer who led the conquest of the Inka Empire of Peru in 1531–1533. (p. 372)

**Fujiwara** Aristocratic family that dominated the Japanese imperial court between the ninth and twelfth centuries. (p. 272)

**Funan** An early complex society in Southeast Asia between the first and sixth centuries C.E. It was centered in the rich rice-growing region of southern Vietnam, and it controlled the passage of trade across the Malaysian isthmus. (p. 151)

*gens de couleur* Free men and women of color in Haiti. They sought greater political rights and later supported the Haitian Revolution. (p. 502)

**gentry** In China, the class of prosperous families, next in wealth below the rural aristocrats, from which the emperors drew their administrative personnel. Respected for their education and expertise, these officials became a privileged group and made the government more efficient and responsive than in the past. (p. 127)

**gentry** In England, the class of landholding families below the aristocracy. (p. 391)

**George Washington** Military commander of the American Revolution. He was the first elected president of the United States (1789–1797). (p. 495)

**Getulio Vargas (1883–1954)** Dictator of Brazil from 1930 to 1945 and from 1951 to 1954. Constitutionally barred from another term in 1938 and fearful of a military takeover, he suspended elections and created Estado Novo ("New State"), a dictatorship that emphasized industrialization and helped the urban poor but did little to alleviate the problems of the peasants. (p. 622)

**Ghana** First known kingdom in sub-Saharan West Africa between the sixth and thirteenth centuries C.E. Also the modern West African country once known as the Gold Coast. (p. 216)

**Giuseppe Garibaldi** Italian nationalist and revolutionary who conquered Sicily and Naples and added them to a unified Italy in 1860. (p. 576)

**global elite culture** At the beginning of the twenty-first century, the attitudes and outlook of well-educated, prosperous, Western-oriented people around the world, largely expressed in European languages, especially English. (p. 709)

**globalization** The economic, political, and cultural integration and interaction of all parts of the world brought about by increasing trade, travel, and technology. (p. 685)

**global pop culture** Popular cultural practices and institutions that have been adopted internationally, such as music, the Internet, television, food, and fashion. (p. 709)

**Gold Coast** Region of the Atlantic coast of West Africa occupied by modern Ghana; named for its gold exports to Europe from the 1470s onward. (p. 363)

**Golden Horde** Mongol khanate founded by Chinggis Khan's grandson Batu. It was based in southern Russia and quickly adopted both the Turkish language and Islam. Also known as the Kipchak Horde. (p. 288)

**Gothic cathedrals** Large churches originating in twelfth-century France; built in an architectural style featuring pointed arches, tall vaults and spires, flying buttresses, and large stained-glass windows. (p. 315)

**Grand Canal** The 1,100-mile (1,771-kilometer) waterway linking the Yellow and the Yangzi Rivers. It was begun in the Han period and completed during the Sui Empire. (p. 255)

**Great Ice Age** Geological era that occurred between ca. 2 million and 11,000 years ago. (p. 6)

**"great traditions"** Historians' term for a literate, well-institutionalized complex of religious and social beliefs and practices adhered to by diverse societies over a broad geographical area. (p. 199)

**Great Western Schism** A division in the Latin (Western) Christian Church between 1378 and 1415, when rival claimants to the papacy existed in Rome and Avignon. (p. 323)

**Great Zimbabwe** City, now in ruins (in the modern African country of Zimbabwe), whose many stone structures were built between about 1250 and 1450, when it was a trading center and the capital of a large state. (p. 340)

**guild** In medieval Europe, an association of men (rarely women), such as merchants, artisans, or professors, who worked in a particular trade and banded together to promote their economic and political interests. Guilds were also important in other societies, such as the Ottoman and Safavid Empires. (p. 314)

**Gujarat** Region of western India famous for trade and manufacturing; the inhabitants are called Gujaratis. (p. 336)

**gunpowder** A mixture of saltpeter, sulfur, and charcoal, in various proportions. The formula, brought to China in the 400s or 500s, was first used to make fumigators to keep away insect pests and evil spirits. In later centuries it was used to make explosives and grenades and to propel cannonballs, shot, and bullets. (p. 265)

**Guomindang** Nationalist political party founded on democratic principles by Sun Yat-sen in 1912. After 1925, the party was headed by Chiang Kai-shek, who turned it into an increasingly authoritarian movement. (p. 598)

**Gupta Empire** A powerful Indian state based, like its Mauryan predecessor, on a capital at Pataliputra in the Ganges Valley. It controlled most of the Indian subcontinent through a combination of military force and its prestige as a center of sophisticated culture. (p. 146)

**Habsburg** A powerful European family that provided many Holy Roman Emperors, founded the Austrian (later Austro-Hungarian) Empire, and ruled sixteenth- and seventeenth-century Spain. (p. 394)

**hadith** A tradition relating the words or deeds of the Prophet Muhammad; next to the Quran, the most important basis for Islamic law. (p. 221)

**Haile Selassie (1892–1975)** Emperor of Ethiopia (r. 1930–1974) and symbol of African independence. He fought the Italian invasion of his country in 1935 and regained his throne during World War II, when British forces expelled the Italians. He ruled Ethiopia as a traditional autocracy until he was overthrown in 1974. (p. 627)

**Hammurabi** Amorite ruler of Babylon (r. 1792–1750 B.C.E.). He conquered many city-states in southern and northern Mesopotamia and is best known for a code of laws, inscribed on a black stone pillar, illustrating the principles to be used in legal cases. (p. 17)

**Han** A term used to designate (1) the ethnic Chinese people who originated in the Yellow River Valley and spread throughout regions of China suitable for agriculture and (2) the dynasty of emperors who ruled from 206 B.C.E. to 220 C.E. (p. 126)

**Hanseatic League** An economic and defensive alliance of the free towns in northern Germany, founded about 1241 and most powerful in the fourteenth century. (p. 313)

**Harappa** Site of one of the great cities of the Indus Valley civilization of the third millennium B.C.E. It was located on the northwest frontier of the zone of cultivation (in modern Pakistan). (p. 134)

**Hatshepsut** Queen of Egypt (r. 1473–1458 B.C.E.). She dispatched a naval expedition to Punt (possibly northeast Sudan or Eritrea), the faraway source of myrrh. There is evidence of opposition to a woman as ruler, and after her death her name and image were frequently defaced. (p. 33)

**Hebrew Bible** A collection of sacred books containing diverse materials concerning the origins, experiences, beliefs, and practices of the Israelites. Most of the extant text was compiled by members of the priestly class in the fifth century B.C.E. and reflects the concerns and views of this group. (p. 43)

**Hellenistic Age** Historians' term for the era, usually dated 323–30 B.C.E., in which Greek culture spread across western Asia and northeastern Africa after the conquests of Alexander the Great. The period ended with the fall of the last major Hellenistic kingdom to Rome, but Greek cultural influence persisted until the spread of Islam in the seventh century C.E. (p. 101)

**Henry the Navigator** Portuguese prince who promoted the study of navigation and directed voyages of exploration down the western coast of Africa in the fifteenth century. (p. 361)

**Hernán Cortés** Spanish explorer and conquistador who led the conquest of Aztec Mexico in 1519–1521 for Spain. (p. 371)

**Herodotus** Heir to the technique of *historia* ("investigation/research") developed by Greeks in the late Archaic period. He came from a Greek community in Anatolia and traveled extensively, collecting information in western Asia and the Mediterranean lands. He traced the antecedents and chronicled the wars between the Greek city-states and the Persian Empire, thus originating the Western tradition of historical writing. (p. 92)

**Hidden Imam** Last in a series of twelve descendants of Muhammad's son-in-law Ali, whom Shi'ites consider divinely appointed leaders of the Muslim community. In occlusion since around 873, he is expected to return as a messiah at the end of time. (p. 434)

**hieroglyphics** A system of writing in which pictorial symbols represented sounds, syllables, or concepts. It was used for official and monumental inscriptions in ancient Egypt. Because of the long period of study required to master this system, literacy in hieroglyphics was confined to a relatively small group of scribes and administrators. (p. 23)

**Hinduism** A general term for a wide variety of beliefs and ritual practices that have developed in the Indian subcontinent since antiquity. Hinduism has roots in ancient Vedic, Buddhist, and south Indian religious concepts and practices. It spread along the trade routes to Southeast Asia. (p. 141)

**Hipólito Irigoyen (1850–1933)** Argentine politician, president of Argentina from 1916 to 1922 and 1928 to 1930. The first president elected by universal male suffrage, he began his presidency as a reformer but later became conservative. (p. 621)

**Hiroshima** City in Japan, the first to be destroyed by an atomic bomb, on August 6, 1945. The bombing hastened the end of World War II. (p. 644)

**history** The study of past events and changes in the development, transmission, and transformation of cultural practices. (p. 5)

**Hittites** A people from central Anatolia who established an empire in Anatolia and Syria in the Late Bronze Age. With wealth from the trade in metals and military power based on chariot forces, the Hittites vied with New Kingdom Egypt for control of Syria-Palestine before falling to unidentified attackers around 1200 B.C.E. (p. 32)

**Holocaust** Nazis' program during World War II to kill people they considered undesirable. Some 6 million Jews perished during the Holocaust, along with millions of Poles, Gypsies, communists, socialists, and others. (p. 648)

**Holy Roman Empire** Loose federation of mostly German states and principalities, headed by an emperor elected by the princes. It lasted from 962 to 1806. (p. 240, 394)

**hominid** The biological family that includes humans and humanlike primates. (p. 6)

***Homo erectus*** An extinct human species. It evolved in Africa about 1.8 million years ago. (p. 7)

*Homo habilis*  The first human species (now extinct). It evolved in Africa about 2.3 million years ago.   (p. 6)

*Homo sapiens*  The current human species. It evolved in Africa sometime between 400,000 and 100,000 years ago.   (p. 8)

**hoplite**  A heavily armored Greek infantryman of the Archaic and Classical periods who fought in the close-packed phalanx formation. Hoplite armies—militias composed of middle- and upper-class citizens supplying their own equipment—were for centuries superior to all other military forces.   (p. 89)

**horse collar**  Harnessing method that increased the efficiency of horses by shifting the point of traction from the animal's throat to the shoulders; its adoption favors the spread of horse-drawn plows and vehicles.   (p. 248)

**House of Burgesses**  Elected assembly in colonial Virginia, created in 1618.   (p. 410)

**humanists (Renaissance)**  European scholars, writers, and teachers associated with the study of the humanities (grammar, rhetoric, poetry, history, languages, and moral philosophy), influential in the fifteenth century and later.   (p. 319)

**Hundred Years' War (1337–1453)**  Series of campaigns over control of the throne of France, involving English and French royal families and French noble families.   (p. 323)

**Ibn Battuta**  Moroccan Muslim scholar, the most widely traveled individual of his time. He wrote a detailed account of his visits to Islamic lands from China to Spain and the western Sudan.   (p. 329)

**Il-khan**  A "secondary" or "peripheral" khan based in Persia. The Il-khans' khanate was founded by Hülegü, a grandson of Chinggis Khan, and was based at Tabriz in the Iranian province of Azerbaijan. It controlled much of Iran and Iraq.   (p. 288)

**import-substitution industrialization**  An economic system aimed at building a country's industry by restricting foreign trade. It was especially popular in Latin American countries such as Mexico, Argentina, and Brazil in the mid-twentieth century. It proved successful for a time but could not keep up with technological advances in Europe and North America.   (p. 622)

**indentured servant**  A migrant to British colonies in the Americas who paid for passage by agreeing to work for a set term ranging from four to seven years.   (p. 410)

**Indian Civil Service**  The elite professional class of officials who administered the government of British India. Originally composed exclusively of well-educated British men, it gradually added qualified Indians.   (p. 551)

**Indian National Congress**  A movement and political party founded in 1885 to demand greater Indian participation in government. Its membership was middle class, and its demands were modest until World War I. Led after 1920 by Mohandas K. Gandhi, it appealed increasingly to the poor, and it organized mass protests demanding self-government and independence.   (p. 552)

**Indian National Congress**  A movement and political party founded in 1885 to demand greater Indian participation in government. Its membership was middle class, and its demands were modest until World War I. Led after 1920 by Mohandas K. Gandhi, it appealed increasingly to the poor and organized mass protests demanding self-government and independence.   (p. 616)

**Indian Ocean Maritime System**  In premodern times, a network of seaports, trade routes, and maritime culture linking countries on the rim of the Indian Ocean from Africa to Indonesia.   (p. 191)

**indulgence**  The forgiveness of the punishment due for past sins, granted by the Catholic Church authorities as a reward for a pious act. Martin Luther's protest against the sale of indulgences is often seen as touching off the Protestant Reformation.   (p. 382)

**Industrial Revolution**  The transformation of the economy, the environment, and living conditions, occurring first in England in the eighteenth century, that resulted from the use of steam engines, the mechanization of manufacturing in factories, and innovations in transportation and communication.   (p. 471)

**Inka**  Largest and most powerful Andean empire. Controlled the Pacific coast of South America from Ecuador to Chile from its capital of Cuzco.   (p. 348)

**investiture controversy**  Dispute between the popes and the Holy Roman Emperors over who held ultimate authority over bishops in imperial lands.   (p. 241)

**Iron Age**  Historians' term for the period during which iron was the primary metal for tools and weapons. The advent of iron technology began at different times in different parts of the world.   (p. 30)

**iron curtain**  Winston Churchill's term for the Cold War division between the Soviet-dominated East and the U.S.-dominated West.   (p. 660)

**Iroquois Confederacy**  An alliance of five northeastern Amerindian peoples (six after 1722) that made decisions on military and diplomatic issues through a council of representatives. Allied first with the Dutch and later with the English, the Confederacy dominated the area from western New England to the Great Lakes.   (p. 411)

**Islam**  Religion expounded by the Prophet Muhammad on the basis of his reception of divine revelations, which were collected after his death into the Quran. In the tradition of Judaism and Christianity, and sharing much of their lore, Islam calls on all people to recognize one creator god—Allah—who rewards or punishes believers after death according to how they led their lives.   (p. 211)

**Israel**  In antiquity, the land between the eastern shore of the Mediterranean and the Jordan River, occupied by the Israelites from the early second millennium B.C.E. The modern state of Israel was founded in 1948.   (p. 43)

**James Watt**  Scot who invented the condenser and other improvements that made the steam engine a practical source of power for industry and transportation. The watt, an electrical measurement, is named after him.   (p. 480)

**Janissaries**  Infantry, originally of slave origin, armed with firearms and constituting the elite of the Ottoman army from the fifteenth century until the corps was abolished in 1826.   (p. 429)

**Jawaharlal Nehru (1889–1964)**  Indian statesman who succeeded Mohandas K. Gandhi as leader of the Indian National Congress. He negotiated the end of British colonial rule in India and became India's first prime minister (1947–1964).   (p. 618)

**Jesus**  A Jew from Galilee in northern Israel who sought to reform Jewish beliefs and practices. He was executed as a revolutionary by the Romans. Hailed as the Messiah and son of God by his followers, he became the central figure in Christianity, a belief system that developed in the centuries after his death.   (p. 118)

**joint-stock company**  A business, often backed by a government charter, that sold shares to individuals to raise money for its trading enterprises and to spread the risks (and profits) among many investors.   (p. 391)

**Joseph Stalin (1879–1953)**  Bolshevik revolutionary, head of the Soviet Communist Party after 1924, and dictator of the Soviet Union from 1928 to 1953. He led the Soviet Union with an iron fist, using Five-Year Plans to increase industrial production and terror to crush all opposition.   (p. 631)

**Josiah Wedgwood** English industrialist whose pottery works were the first to produce fine-quality pottery by industrial methods.   (p. 476)

**Juan Perón (1895–1974)** President of Argentina (1946–1955, 1973–1974). As a military officer, he championed the rights of labor. Aided by his wife Eva Duarte Perón, he was elected president in 1946. He built up Argentinean industry, became very popular among the urban poor, but harmed the economy.   (p. 623)

**junk** A very large flatbottom sailing ship produced in the Tang, Song, and Ming Empires, specially designed for long-distance commercial travel.   (p. 264)

**Kamakura Shogunate** The first of Japan's decentralized military governments (1185–1333).   (p. 273)

*kamikaze* The "divine wind," which the Japanese credited with blowing Mongol invaders away from their shores in 1281.   (p. 302)

**Kangxi** Qing emperor (r. 1662–1722). He oversaw the greatest expansion of the Qing Empire.   (p. 458)

**Karl Marx** German journalist and philosopher, founder of the Marxist branch of socialism. He is known for two books: *Manifesto of the Communist Party* (1848) and *Das Kapital* (Vols. I–III, 1867–1894).   (p. 573)

**karma** In Indian tradition, the residue of deeds performed in past and present lives that adheres to a "spirit" and determines what form it will assume in its next life cycle. The doctrines of karma and reincarnation were used by the elite in ancient India to encourage people to accept their social position and do their duty.   (p. 139)

*keiretsu* Alliances of corporations and banks that dominate the Japanese economy.   (p. 674)

**khipus** System of knotted colored cords used by preliterate Andean peoples to record information.   (p. 173, 349)

**Khubilai Khan** Last of the Mongol Great Khans (r. 1260–1294) and founder of the Yuan Empire.   (p. 294)

**Kievan Russia** State established at Kiev in Ukraine around 880 by Scandinavian adventurers asserting authority over a mostly Slavic farming population.   (p. 229)

**King Leopold II (1835–1909)** King of Belgium (r. 1865–1909). He was active in encouraging the exploration of Central Africa and became the ruler of the Congo Free State (to 1908).   (p. 544)

**KLM Royal Dutch Airlines** Oldest major airline, operating since 1920 in Europe and connecting to the Dutch East Indies in 1929.   (p. 611)

**Korean War (1950–1953)** Conflict that began with North Korea's invasion of South Korea and that came to involve the United Nations (primarily the United States) allying with South Korea and the People's Republic of China allying with North Korea.   (p. 661)

**Koryo** Korean kingdom founded in 918 and destroyed by a Mongol invasion in 1259.   (p. 270)

**Kush** An Egyptian name for Nubia, the region alongside the Nile River south of Egypt, where an indigenous kingdom with its own distinctive institutions and cultural traditions arose beginning in the early second millennium B.C.E.   (p. 68)

**labor union** An organization of workers in a particular industry or trade, created to defend the interests of members through strikes or negotiations with employers.   (p. 573)

**laissez faire** The idea that government should refrain from interfering in economic affairs. The classic exposition of laissez-faire principles is Adam Smith's *Wealth of Nations* (1776).   (p. 485)

**lama** In Tibetan Buddhism, a teacher.   (p. 294)

**Lázaro Cárdenas (1895–1970)** President of Mexico (1934–1940). He brought major changes to Mexican life by distributing millions of acres of land to the peasants, bringing representatives of workers and farmers into the inner circles of politics, and nationalizing the oil industry.   (p. 620)

**League of Nations** International organization founded in 1919 to promote world peace and cooperation but greatly weakened by the refusal of the United States to join. It proved ineffectual in stopping aggression by Italy, Japan, and Germany in the 1930s, and it was superseded by the United Nations in 1945.   (p. 595)

**Le Corbusier (1887–1965)** Professional name of architect Charles-Éduard Jeanneret who led a modernist movement away from surface decoration and toward form following function.   (p. 613)

**Legalism** In China, a political philosophy that emphasized the unruliness of human nature and justified state coercion and control. The ruling class invoked it to validate the authoritarian nature of the regime and its profligate expenditure of subjects' lives and labor. It was later superseded by a more benevolent Confucian doctrine of governmental moderation.   (p. 62)

**"legitimate" trade** Exports from Africa in the nineteenth century that did not include the newly outlawed slave trade.   (p. 548)

**liberalism** A political ideology that emphasizes the civil rights of citizens, representative government, and the protection of private property. This ideology, derived from the Enlightenment, was especially popular among the property-owning middle classes of Europe and North America.   (p. 576)

**Library of Ashurbanipal** A large collection of writings drawn from the ancient literary, religious, and scientific traditions of Mesopotamia. It was assembled by the seventh-century B.C.E. Assyrian ruler Ashurbanipal. The many tablets unearthed by archaeologists constitute one of the most important sources of present-day knowledge of the long literary tradition of Mesopotamia.   (p. 42)

**Linear B** A set of syllabic symbols, derived from the writing system of Minoan Crete, used in the Mycenaean palaces of the Late Bronze Age to write an early form of Greek. It was used primarily for palace records, and the surviving Linear B tablets provide substantial information about the economic organization of Mycenaean society and tantalizing clues about political, social, and religious institutions.   (p. 37)

**Li Shimin** One of the founders of the Tang Empire and its second emperor (r. 626–649). He led the expansion of the empire into Inner Asia.   (p. 256)

**Little Ice Age** A century-long period of cool climate that began in the 1590s. Its ill effects on agriculture in northern Europe were notable.   (p. 391)

**llama** A hoofed animal indigenous to the Andes Mountains. It was the only domesticated beast of burden in the Americas before the arrival of Europeans. The use of llamas to transport goods made possible specialized production and trade among people living in different ecological zones and fostered the integration of these zones by Chavín and later Andean states.   (p. 162)

**loess** A fine, light silt deposited by wind and water. It constitutes the fertile soil of the Yellow River Valley in northern China.   (p. 58)

**Long March (1934–1935)** The 6,000-mile flight of Chinese communists from southeastern China to northwestern China. The communists, led by Mao Zedong, were pursued by the Chinese army under orders from Chiang Kai-shek. The four thousand survivors of the march formed the nucleus of a revived communist movement that defeated the Guomindang after World War II.   (p. 641)

**ma'at** Egyptian term for the concept of divinely created and maintained order in the universe. The divine ruler was the earthly guarantor of this order. (p. 22)

**Macartney mission** The unsuccessful attempt by the British Empire to establish diplomatic relations with the Qing Empire. (p. 462)

*Mahabharata* A vast epic chronicling the events leading up to a cataclysmic battle between related kinship groups in early India. It includes the Bhagavad-Gita. (p. 146)

**Mahayana Buddhism** "Great Vehicle" branch of Buddhism followed in China, Japan, and Central Asia. The focus is on reverence for Buddha and for bodhisattvas, enlightened persons who have postponed nirvana to help others attain enlightenment. (p. 141)

**Malacca** Port city in the modern Southeast Asian country of Malaysia, founded about 1400 as a trading center on the Strait of Malacca. (p. 342)

**Mali** Empire created by indigenous Muslims in western Sudan of West Africa from the thirteenth to fifteenth century. It was famous for its role in the trans-Saharan gold trade. (p. 333)

**mamluks** Under the Islamic system of military slavery, Turkish military slaves formed an important part of the armed forces of the Abbasid Caliphate of the ninth and tenth centuries. Mamluks eventually founded their own state, ruling Egypt and Syria (1250–1517). (p. 216)

**Manchu** Federation of Northeast Asian peoples who founded the Qing Empire. (p. 449)

**Mandate of Heaven** Chinese religious and political ideology developed by the Zhou, according to which it was the prerogative of Heaven, the chief deity, to grant power to the ruler of China and to take away that power if the ruler failed to conduct himself justly and in the best interests of his subjects. (p. 62)

**mandate system** Allocation of former German colonies and Ottoman possessions to the victorious powers after World War I, to be administered under League of Nations supervision. (p. 599)

**manor** In medieval Europe, a large, self-sufficient landholding consisting of the lord's residence (manor house), outbuildings, peasant village, and surrounding land. (p. 237)

*mansabs* In India, grants of land given in return for service by rulers of the Mughal Empire. (p. 438)

**Mansa Kankan Musa** Ruler of Mali (r. 1312–1337). His pilgrimage through Egypt to Mecca in 1324–1325 established the empire's reputation for wealth in the Mediterranean world. (p. 335)

**Mao Zedong (1893–1976)** Leader of the Chinese Communist Party (1927–1976). He led the communists on the Long March (1934–1935) and rebuilt the Communist Party and Red Army during the Japanese occupation of China (1937–1945). After World War II, he led the communists to victory over the Guomindang. (p. 641)

**Margaret Sanger (1883–1966)** American nurse and author; pioneer in the movement for family planning; organized conferences and established birth control clinics. (p. 610)

**Marie Curie (1867–1934)** Twice winner of the Nobel Prize, the Polish Maria (Marie, in French) Sklodowska worked in Paris and, with her husband Pierre Curie, discovered the element radium and radioactivity, changing the knowledge of matter and the treatment of many diseases. In World War I, she convinced wealthy patrons to donate vehicles for use as X-Ray centers and traveled to aid doctors in detecting fractures and shrapnel in wounded soldiers. (p. 613)

**maroon** A slave who ran away from his or her master. Often a member of a community of runaway slaves in the West Indies and South America. (p. 418)

**Marshall Plan** U.S. program to support the reconstruction of western Europe after World War II. By 1961 more than $20 billion in economic aid had been dispersed. (p. 658)

**mass deportation** The forcible removal and relocation of large numbers of people or entire populations. The mass deportations practiced by the Assyrian and Persian Empires were meant as a terrifying warning of the consequences of rebellion. They also brought skilled and unskilled labor to the imperial center. (p. 41)

**mass production** The manufacture of many identical products by the division of labor into many small repetitive tasks. This method was introduced into the manufacture of pottery and into the spinning of cotton thread. (p. 476)

**Mauryan Empire** The first state to unify most of the Indian subcontinent. It was founded by Chandragupta Maurya in 324 B.C.E. and survived until 184 B.C.E. From its capital at Pataliputra in the Ganges Valley it grew wealthy from taxes on agriculture, iron mining, and control of trade routes. (p. 144)

**Max Planck (1858–1947)** German physicist who developed quantum theory and was awarded the Nobel Prize for physics in 1918. (p. 610)

**Maya** Mesoamerican civilization concentrated in Mexico's Yucatán Peninsula and in Guatemala and Honduras but never unified into a single empire. Major contributions were in mathematics, astronomy, and development of the calendar. (p. 165)

**Mecca** City in western Arabia; birthplace of the Prophet Muhammad and ritual center of the Islamic religion. (p. 211)

**mechanization** The application of machinery to manufacturing and other activities. Among the first processes to be mechanized were the spinning of cotton thread and the weaving of cloth in late-eighteenth- and early-nineteenth-century England. (p. 477)

**medieval** Literally "middle age," a term that historians of Europe use for the period from roughly 500 to 1300, signifying its intermediate point between Greco-Roman antiquity and the Renaissance. (p. 229)

**Medina** City in western Arabia to which the Prophet Muhammad and his followers emigrated in 622 to escape persecution in Mecca. (p. 212)

**megaliths** Structures and complexes of very large stones constructed for ceremonial and religious purposes in Neolithic times. (p. 12)

**Meiji Restoration** The political program that followed the destruction of the Tokugawa Shogunate in 1868, in which a collection of young leaders set Japan on the path of centralization, industrialization, and imperialism. (p. 578)

**Memphis** The capital of Old Kingdom Egypt, near the head of the Nile Delta. Early rulers were interred in the nearby pyramids. (p. 23)

**mercantilism** European government policies of the sixteenth, seventeenth, and eighteenth centuries designed to promote overseas trade between a country and its colonies and accumulate precious metals by requiring colonies to trade only with their motherland country. The British system was defined by the Navigation Acts, the French system by laws known as the *Exclusif*. (p. 418)

**Meroë** Capital of a flourishing kingdom in southern Nubia from the fourth century B.C.E. to the fourth century C.E. In this period Nubian culture shows more independence from Egypt and the influence of sub-Saharan Africa. (p. 68)

**Mexican Revolution** A social revolution that developed haphazardly under ambitious but limited leaders, each representing a different segment of Mexican society. The revolution evolved into civil war for over ten years of armed struggle, but it established a constitution for Mexico. (p. 558)

**Miguel Hidalgo y Costilla** Mexican priest who led the first stage of the Mexican independence war in 1810. He was captured and executed in 1811.  (p. 504)

**Mikhail Gorbachev (b. 1931)** Head of the Soviet Union from 1985 to 1991. His liberalization effort improved relations with the West, but he lost power after his reforms led to the collapse of the communist governments in eastern Europe.  (p. 680)

**Ming Empire** Empire based in China that Zhu Yuanzhang established after the overthrow of the Yuan Empire. The Ming emperor Yongle sponsored the building of the Forbidden City and the voyages of Zheng He. The later years of the Ming saw a slowdown in technological development and economic decline.  (p. 296)

**Minoan** Prosperous civilization on the Aegean island of Crete in the second millennium B.C.E. The Minoans engaged in far-flung commerce around the Mediterranean and exerted powerful cultural influences on the early Greeks.  (p. 36)

**mita** Andean labor system based on shared obligations to help kinsmen and work on behalf of the ruler and religious organizations.  (p. 173)

**Moche** Civilization of north coast of Peru (200–700 C.E.). An important Andean civilization that built extensive irrigation networks as well as impressive urban centers dominated by brick temples.  (p. 174)

**Moctezuma II** Aztec emperor who died while in custody of the Spanish conquistador Hernán Cortés.  (p. 371)

**modernization** The process of reforming political, military, economic, social, and cultural traditions in imitation of the early success of Western societies, often with little regard for accommodating local traditions in non-Western societies.  (p. 544)

**Mohandas K. Gandhi (1869–1948)** Leader of the Indian independence movement and advocate of nonviolent resistance. After being educated as a lawyer in England, he returned to India and became leader of the Indian National Congress in 1920. He appealed to the poor, led nonviolent demonstrations against British colonial rule, and was jailed many times. Soon after independence he was assassinated for attempting to stop Hindu-Muslim rioting.  (p. 617)

**Mohenjo-Daro** Largest of the cities of the Indus Valley civilization, centrally located in the extensive floodplain of the Indus River in contemporary Pakistan.  (p. 134)

**moksha** The Hindu concept of the spirit's "liberation" from the endless cycle of rebirths. There are various avenues—such as physical discipline, meditation, and acts of devotion to the gods—by which the spirit can distance itself from desire for the things of this world and be merged with the divine force that animates the universe.  (p. 139)

**monasticism** Living in a religious community apart from secular society and adhering to a rule stipulating chastity, obedience, and poverty. It was a prominent element of medieval Christianity and Buddhism. Monasteries were the primary centers of learning and literacy in medieval Europe.  (p. 241)

**Mongols** A people of this name is mentioned as early as the records of the Tang Empire, living as nomads in northern Eurasia. After 1206 they established an enormous empire under Chinggis Khan, linking western and eastern Eurasia.  (p. 281)

**monotheism** Belief in the existence of a single divine entity. Some scholars cite the devotion of the Egyptian pharaoh Akhenaten to Aten (sun-disk) and his suppression of traditional gods as the earliest instance. The Israelite worship of Yahweh developed into an exclusive belief in one god, and this concept passed into Christianity and Islam.  (p. 46)

**monsoon** Seasonal winds in the Indian Ocean caused by the differences in temperature between the rapidly heating and cooling landmasses of Africa and Asia and the slowly changing ocean waters. These strong and predictable winds have long been ridden across the open sea by sailors, and the large amounts of rainfall that they deposit on parts of India, Southeast Asia, and China allow for the cultivation of several crops a year.  (p. 137)

**monsoon** Seasonal winds in the Indian Ocean caused by the differences in temperature between the rapidly heating and cooling landmasses of Africa and Asia and the slowly changing ocean waters. These strong and predictable winds have long been ridden across the open sea by sailors, and the large amounts of rainfall that they deposit on parts of India, Southeast Asia, and China allow for the cultivation of several crops a year.  (p. 330)

**most-favored-nation status** A clause in a commercial treaty that awards to any later signatories all the privileges previously granted to the original signatories.  (p. 528)

**movable type** Type in which each individual character is cast on a separate piece of metal. It replaced woodblock printing, allowing for the arrangement of individual letters and other characters on a page, rather than requiring the carving of entire pages at a time. It may have been invented in Korea in the thirteenth century.  (p. 266)

**Mughal Empire** Muslim state (1526–1857) exercising dominion over most of India in the sixteenth and seventeenth centuries. Fragmentation of power and growth of English imperial strength marked the subsequent period.  (p. 437)

**Muhammad Ali Jinnah (1876–1948)** Indian Muslim politician who founded the state of Pakistan. A lawyer by training, he joined the All-India Muslim League in 1913. As leader of the League from the 1920s on, he negotiated with the British and the Indian National Congress for Muslim participation in Indian politics. From 1940 on, he led the movement for the independence of India's Muslims in a separate state of Pakistan, founded in 1947.  (p. 619)

**Muhammad Ali** Leader of Egyptian modernization in the early nineteenth century. He ruled Egypt as an Ottoman governor but had imperial ambitions. His descendants ruled Egypt until overthrown in 1952.  (p. 513)

**Muhammad** Arab prophet (570–632 C.E.); founder of religion of Islam.  (p. 211)

**mummy** A body preserved by chemical processes or special natural circumstances, often in the belief that the deceased will need it again in the afterlife.  (p. 26)

**Muscovy** The Russian principality that emerged gradually during the era of Mongol domination. The muscovite dynasty ruled without interruption from 1276 to 1598.  (p. 440)

**Muslim** An adherent of the Islamic religion; a person who "submits" (in Arabic, *Islam* means "submission") to the will of God.  (p. 211)

**Mycenae** Site of a fortified palace complex in southern Greece that controlled a Late Bronze Age kingdom. In ancient epic poems, Mycenae was the base of King Agamemnon, who commanded the Greeks besieging Troy. Contemporary archaeologists call the complex Greek society of the second millennium B.C.E. "Mycenaean."  (p. 37)

**Napoleon Bonaparte** General who overthrew the French Directory in 1799 and became emperor of the French in 1804. Failed to defeat Great Britain and abdicated in 1814. Returned to power briefly in 1815 but was defeated and died in exile.  (p. 500)

**Nasir al-Din Tusi** Persian mathematician and cosmologist whose academy near Tabriz provided a model for heavenly motions that helped to inspire the Copernican model of the solar system.  (p. 290)

**National Assembly** French Revolutionary assembly (1789–1791). The Estates General gave itself this title when it came together and demanded radical change. In 1789 it passed the Declaration of the Rights of Man and of the Citizen. (p. 497)

**nationalism** A political ideology that stresses people's membership in a nation—a community defined by a common culture and history as well as by territory. In the late eighteenth and early nineteenth centuries, nationalism was a force for unity in western Europe. In the late nineteenth century it hastened the disintegration of the Austro-Hungarian and Ottoman Empires. In the twentieth century it provided the ideological foundation for scores of independent countries emerging from colonialism. (p. 575)

**nawab** Technically, a semi-autonomous deputy of the Mughal emperor but often a Muslim prince allied to British India. (p. 549)

**Nazis** German political party led by Adolf Hitler, emphasizing nationalism, racism, and war. When Hitler became chancellor of Germany in 1933, the Nazis became the only legal party and an instrument of Hitler's absolute rule. The party's formal name was National Socialist German Workers' Party. (p. 638)

**Neo-Assyrian Empire** An empire extending from western Iran to Syria-Palestine, conquered by the Assyrians of northern Mesopotamia between the tenth and seventh centuries B.C.E. They used force and terror and exploited the wealth and labor of their subjects. They also preserved and continued the cultural and scientific developments of Mesopotamian civilization. (p. 40)

**Neo-Babylonian kingdom** Under the Chaldaeans (nomadic kinship groups that settled in southern Mesopotamia in the early first millennium B.C.E.), Babylon again became a major political and cultural center in the seventh and sixth centuries B.C.E. After participating in the destruction of Assyrian power, the monarchs Nabopolassar and Nebuchadnezzar took over the southern portion of the Assyrian domains. (p. 53)

**neo-Confucianism** Term used to describe new approaches to understanding classic Confucian texts that became the basic ruling philosophy of China from the Song period to the twentieth century. (p. 265)

**Neolithic** The period of the Stone Age associated with the ancient Agricultural Revolution(s). (p. 10)

**New Economic Policy** Policy proclaimed by Vladimir Lenin in 1923 to encourage the revival of the Soviet economy by allowing small private enterprises. Joseph Stalin ended the NEP in 1928 and replaced it with a series of Five-Year Plans. (p. 595)

**New France** French colony in North America, with a capital in Quebec, founded in 1608. New France fell to the British in 1763. (p. 412)

**newly industrialized economies (NIEs)** Rapidly growing new industrializing nations of the late twentieth century, including the Asian Tigers. (p. 676)

**new monarchies** Historians' term for the monarchies in France, England, and Spain from 1450 to 1600. The centralization of royal power was increasing within more or less fixed territorial limits. (p. 324)

**nomads** People without permanent, fixed places of residence, whose way of life and means of subsistence require them to periodically migrate, often with their herds of domesticated animals, to a familiar series of temporary seasonal encampments. (p. 70)

**nonaligned nations** Developing countries that announced their neutrality in the Cold War. (p. 665)

**nongovernmental organizations (NGOs)** Nonprofit international organizations devoted to investigating human rights abuses and providing humanitarian relief. Two NGOs won the Nobel Peace Prize in the 1990s: International Campaign to Ban Landmines (1997) and Doctors Without Borders (1999). (p. 693)

**North Atlantic Treaty Organization (NATO)** Organization formed in 1949 as a military alliance of western European and North American states against the Soviet Union and its east European allies. (p. 657)

**Olmec** The first Mesoamerican civilization. Between about 1200 and 400 B.C.E., the Olmec people of central Mexico created a vibrant civilization that included intensive agriculture, wide-ranging trade, ceremonial centers, and monumental construction. The Olmec had great cultural influence on later Mesoamerican societies. (p. 158)

**Oman** Arab state based in Musqat, the main port in the southeast region of the Arabian peninsula. Oman succeeded Portugal as a power in the western Indian Ocean in the eighteenth century. (p. 445)

**Opium War** War between Britain and the Qing Empire that was, in the British view, occasioned by the Qing government's refusal to permit the importation of opium into its territories. The victorious British imposed the one-sided Treaty of Nanking on China. (p. 526)

**Organization of Petroleum Exporting Countries (OPEC)** Organization formed in 1960 by oil-producing states to promote their collective interest in generating revenue from oil. (p. 678)

**Ottoman Empire** Islamic state founded by Osman in northwestern Anatolia around 1300. After the fall of the Byzantine Empire, the Ottoman Empire was based at Istanbul (formerly Constantinople) from 1453 to 1922. It encompassed lands in the Middle East, North Africa, the Caucasus, and eastern Europe. (p. 293, 427)

**Otto von Bismarck** Chancellor (prime minister) of Prussia from 1862 until 1871, when he became chancellor of Germany. A conservative nationalist, he led Prussia to victory against Austria (1866) and France (1870) and was responsible for the creation of the German Empire in 1871. (p. 577)

**Paleolithic** The period of the Stone Age associated with the evolution of humans. (p. 7)

**Panama Canal** Ship canal cut across the Isthmus of Panama by U.S. Army engineers; it opened in 1914. It greatly shortened the sea voyage between the east and west coasts of North America. The United States turned the canal over to Panama on January 1, 2000. (p. 560)

**Pan-Slavism** Movement among Russian intellectuals in the second half of the nineteenth century to identify culturally and politically with the Slavic peoples of eastern Europe. (p. 522)

**papacy** The central administration of the Roman Catholic Church, of which the pope is the head. (p. 240, 381)

**papyrus** A reed that grows along the banks of the Nile River in Egypt. From it was produced a coarse, paperlike writing medium used by the Egyptians and many other peoples in the ancient Mediterranean and Middle East. (p. 23)

**Parthians** Iranian ruling dynasty between ca. 250 B.C.E. and 226 C.E. (p. 189)

**pastoralism** A way of life dependent on moving large herds of small and large stock to new pastures and watering places throughout the year. (p. 11)

**patron/client relationship** In ancient Rome, a fundamental social relationship in which the patron—a wealthy and powerful individual—provided legal and economic protection and assistance to clients, men of lesser status and means, and in return the clients supported the political careers and economic interests of their patron. (p. 109)

**Paul** A Jew from the Greek city of Tarsus in Anatolia, he initially persecuted the followers of Jesus but, after receiving a revelation on the road to Syrian Damascus, became a Christian.

Taking advantage of his Hellenized background and Roman citizenship, he traveled throughout Syria-Palestine, Anatolia, and Greece, preaching the new religion and establishing churches. Finding his greatest success among pagans ("gentiles"), he began the process by which Christianity separated from Judaism.   (p. 118)

*pax Romana* Literally, "Roman peace," it connoted the stability and prosperity that Roman rule brought to the lands of the Roman Empire in the first two centuries C.E. The movement of people and trade goods along Roman roads and safe seas allowed for the spread of cultural practices, technologies, and religious ideas.   (p. 117)

**Pearl Harbor** Naval base in Hawaii attacked by Japanese aircraft on December 7, 1941. The sinking of much of the U.S. Pacific Fleet brought the United States into World War II.   (p. 644)

**Peloponnesian War** A protracted (431–404 B.C.E.) and costly conflict between the Athenian and Spartan alliance systems that convulsed most of the Greek world. The war was largely a consequence of Athenian imperialism. Possession of a naval empire allowed Athens to fight a war of attrition. Ultimately, Sparta prevailed because of Athenian errors and Persian financial support.   (p. 100)

*perestroika* Policy of "restructuring" that was the centerpiece of Mikhail Gorbachev's efforts to liberalize communism in the Soviet Union.   (p. 680)

**Pericles** Aristocratic leader who guided the Athenian state through the transformation to full participatory democracy for all male citizens, supervised construction of the Acropolis, and pursued a policy of imperial expansion that led to the Peloponnesian War. He formulated a strategy of attrition but died from the plague early in the war.   (p. 93)

**Persepolis** A complex of palaces, reception halls, and treasury buildings erected by the Persian kings Darius I and Xerxes in the Persian homeland. It is believed that the New Year's festival was celebrated here, as well as the coronations, weddings, and funerals of the Persian kings, who were buried in cliff-tombs nearby.   (p. 86)

**Persian Wars** Conflicts between Greek city-states and the Persian Empire, ranging from the Ionian Revolt (499–494 B.C.E.) through Darius's punitive expedition that failed at Marathon (490 B.C.E.) and the defeat of Xerxes's massive invasion of Greece by the Spartan-led Hellenic League (480–479 B.C.E.). This first major setback for Persian arms launched the Greeks into their period of greatest cultural productivity. Herodotus chronicled these events in the first "history" in the Western tradition.   (p. 94)

**Peter the Great** Russian tsar (r. 1689–1725). He enthusiastically introduced Western languages and technologies to the Russian elite and moved the capital from Moscow to the new city of St. Petersburg.   (p. 441)

**pharaoh** The central figure in the ancient Egyptian state. Believed to be an earthly manifestation of the gods, he used his absolute power to maintain the safety and prosperity of Egypt.   (p. 22)

**Phoenicians** Canaanites living on the coast of modern Lebanon and Syria in the first millennium B.C.E. From major cities such as Tyre and Sidon, Phoenician merchants and sailors explored the Mediterranean, engaged in widespread commerce, and founded Carthage and other colonies in the western Mediterranean.   (p. 47)

**pilgrimage** Journey to a sacred shrine by Christians seeking to show their piety, fulfill vows, or gain absolution for sins. Other religions also have pilgrimage traditions, such as the Muslim pilgrimage to Mecca and the pilgrimages made by early Chinese Buddhists to India in search of sacred Buddhist writings.   (p. 250)

**Pilgrims** Group of English Protestant dissenters who established Plymouth Colony in Massachusetts in 1620 to seek religious freedom after having lived briefly in the Netherlands.   (p. 411)

**polis** The Greek term for a city-state, an urban center and the agricultural territory under its control. It was the characteristic form of political organization in southern and central Greece in the Archaic and Classical periods. Of the hundreds of city-states in the Mediterranean and Black Sea regions settled by Greeks, some were oligarchic, others democratic, depending on the powers delegated to the Council and the Assembly.   (p. 89)

**positivism** A philosophy developed by the French Count of Saint-Simon. Positivists believed that social and economic problems could be solved by application of the scientific method, leading to continuous progress. Their ideas became popular in France and Latin America in the nineteenth century.   (p. 485)

**Potosí** Located in Bolivia, one of the richest silver mining centers and most populous cities in colonial Spanish America.   (p. 405)

**printing press** A mechanical device for transferring text or graphics from a woodblock or type to paper using ink. Presses using movable type first appeared in Europe in about 1450.   (p. 321)

**proletariat** Industrial workers whose oppression was an example of how, according to *The Communist Manifesto*, history was dominated by class struggle between the workers who sold their labor for survival and those who owned the mills, factories, mines, or other means of industrial production and wealth (the bourgeoisie).   (p. 485)

**Protestant Reformation** Religious reform movement within the Latin Christian Church beginning in 1519. It resulted in the "protesters" forming several new Christian denominations, including the Lutheran and Reformed Churches and the Church of England.   (p. 382)

**Ptolemies** The Macedonian dynasty, descended from one of Alexander the Great's officers, that ruled Egypt for three centuries (323–30 B.C.E.). From their magnificent capital at Alexandria on the Mediterranean coast, the Ptolemies largely took over the system created by Egyptian pharaohs to extract the wealth of the land, rewarding Greeks and Hellenized non-Greeks serving in the military and administration.   (p. 102)

**Puritans** English Protestant dissenters who believed that God predestined souls to Heaven or Hell before birth. They founded Massachusetts Bay Colony in 1629.   (p. 411)

**pyramid** A large, triangular stone monument, used in Egypt and Nubia as a burial place for the king. The largest pyramids, erected during the Old Kingdom near Memphis, reflect the Egyptian belief that the proper and spectacular burial of the divine ruler would guarantee the continued prosperity of the land.   (p. 22)

**Qin** A people and state in the Wei River Valley of eastern China that conquered rival states and created the first Chinese empire (221–206 B.C.E.). The Qin ruler, Shi Huangdi, standardized many features of Chinese society and ruthlessly marshaled subjects for military and construction projects, engendering hostility that led to the fall of his dynasty shortly after his death. The Qin framework was largely taken over by the succeeding Han dynasty.   (p. 125)

**Qing Empire** Empire established in China by Manchus who overthrew the Ming Empire in 1644. At various times the Qing also controlled Manchuria, Mongolia, Turkestan, and Tibet. The last Qing emperor was overthrown in 1911.   (p. 457)

**Quran** Book composed of divine revelations made to the Prophet Muhammad between roughly 610 and his death in 632; the sacred text of the religion of Islam.   (p. 213)

**railroads** Networks of iron (later steel) rails on which steam (later electric or diesel) locomotives pulled long trains at high speeds. The first railroads were built in England in the 1830s. Their success caused a railroad-building boom throughout the world that lasted well into the twentieth century.   (p. 565)

**Rajputs** Members of a mainly Hindu warrior caste from northwest India. The Mughal emperors drew most of their Hindu officials from this caste, and Akbar married a Rajput princess.   (p. 438)

**Ramesses II** A long-lived ruler of New Kingdom Egypt (r. 1290–1224 B.C.E.). He reached an accommodation with the Hittites of Anatolia after a standoff in battle at Kadesh in Syria. He built on a grand scale throughout Egypt.   (p. 35)

**Rashid al-Din** Adviser to the Il-khan ruler Ghazan, who converted to Islam on Rashid's advice.   (p. 289)

**recaptives** Africans rescued by Britain's Royal Navy from the illegal slave trade of the nineteenth century and restored to free status.   (p. 548)

**reconquest of Iberia** Beginning in the eleventh century, military campaigns by various Iberian Christian states to recapture territory taken by Muslims. In 1492 the last Muslim ruler was defeated, and Spain and Portugal emerged as united kingdoms.   (p. 324)

**Renaissance (European)** A period of intense artistic and intellectual activity, said to be a "rebirth" of Greco-Roman culture. Usually divided into an Italian Renaissance, from roughly the mid-fourteenth to mid-fifteenth century, and a Northern (trans-Alpine) Renaissance, from roughly the early fifteenth to early seventeenth century.   (p. 318)

**Revolutions of 1848** Democratic and nationalist revolutions that swept across Europe. The monarchy in France was briefly overthrown. In Germany, Austria, Italy, and Hungary the revolutions failed.   (p. 502)

**Romanization** The process by which the Latin language and Roman culture became dominant in the western provinces. Indigenous peoples in the provinces often chose to Romanize because of the political and economic advantages that it brought, as well as the allure of Roman success.   (p. 117)

**Roman Principate** A term used to characterize Roman government in the first three centuries C.E., based on the ambiguous title *princeps* ("first citizen") adopted by Augustus to conceal his military dictatorship.   (p. 112)

**Roman Republic** The period from 507 to 31 B.C.E., during which Rome was largely governed by the aristocratic Roman Senate.   (p. 109)

**Roman Senate** A council whose members were the heads of wealthy, landowning families. Originally an advisory body to the early kings, in the era of the Roman Republic the Senate effectively governed the Roman state and the growing empire. Under Senate leadership an empire of unprecedented extent in the lands surrounding the Mediterranean Sea.   (p. 109)

**Royal African Company** A trading company chartered by the English government in 1672 to conduct its merchants' trade on the Atlantic coast of Africa.   (p. 419)

**sacrifice** A gift given to a deity, often with the aim of creating a relationship, gaining favor, and obligating the god to provide some benefit to the sacrificer, sometimes in order to sustain the deity and thereby guarantee the continuing vitality of the natural world.   (p. 91)

**Saddam Husain (1937–2006)** President of Iraq from 1979 until overthrown by the American invasion in 2003. Waged war on Iran from 1980 to 1988. His invasion of Kuwait was repulsed in the Persian Gulf War of 1991.   (p. 679)

**Safavid Empire** Iranian kingdom (1502–1722) established by Ismail Safavi, who declared Iran a Shi'ite state.   (p. 434)

**Sahel** Belt south of the Sahara; literally "coastland" in Arabic.   (p. 198)

**Salvador Allende (1908–1973)** Socialist president of Chile who was elected in 1970 and overthrown and killed by the military in 1973.   (p. 672)

*samurai* Literally "those who serve," the hereditary military elite of the Tokugawa Shogunate.   (p. 453)

**Sandinistas** Members of a leftist coalition that overthrew the Nicaraguan dictator Anastosio Somoza in 1979 and attempted to install a socialist economy. The United States financed an armed uprising against the Sandinista government. In 1990 the Sandinistas lost power after a national election.   (p. 672)

**Sasanid Empire** Iranian empire, established around 224, with a capital in Ctesiphon, Mesopotamia. The Sasanid emperors established Zoroastrianism as the state religion. Islamic Arab armies overthrew the empire around 651.   (p. 208)

**satrap** The governor of a province in the Achaemenid Persian Empire, often a relative of the king. He was responsible for protection of the province and for forwarding tribute to the central administration. Satraps in outlying provinces enjoyed considerable autonomy.   (p. 85)

**savanna** Tropical or subtropical grassland, either treeless or with occasional clumps of trees. Most extensive in sub-Saharan Africa but also present in South America.   (p. 199)

**schism** A formal split within a religious community.   (p. 232)

**scholasticism** A philosophical and theological system, associated with Thomas Aquinas, devised to reconcile Aristotelian philosophy and Roman Catholic theology in the thirteenth century.   (p. 319)

**Scientific Revolution** The intellectual movement in Europe, initially associated with planetary motion and other aspects of physics, that by the seventeenth century had laid the groundwork for modern science.   (p. 386)

**scribe** In the governments of many ancient societies, a professional position reserved for men who had undergone the lengthy training required to be able to read and write using cuneiform, hieroglyphics, or other early, cumbersome writing systems.   (p. 18)

**Scythians** Term used by the ancient Greeks for the nomadic peoples living on the steppe north of the Black and Caspian Seas.   (p. 71)

**seasoning** An often difficult period of adjustment to new climates, disease environments, and work routines, such as that experienced by slaves newly arrived in the Americas.   (p. 417)

**"separate spheres"** Nineteenth-century idea in Western societies that men and women, especially of the middle class, should have clearly differentiated roles in society: women as wives, mothers, and homemakers; men as breadwinners and participants in business and politics.   (p. 571)

**sepoy** A soldier in colonial India, especially in the service of the British.   (p. 549)

**Sepoy Rebellion** The revolt of Indian soldiers in 1857 against certain practices that violated religious customs; also known as the Sepoy Mutiny.   (p. 551)

**Serbia** The Ottoman province in the Balkans that rose up against Janissary control in the early 1800s. After World War II the central province of Yugoslavia.   (p. 514)

**serf** In medieval Europe, an agricultural laborer legally bound to a lord's property and obligated to perform set services for the lord. In Russia, later, some serfs worked as artisans and in factories; serfdom was not abolished there until 1861.   (p. 237, 441)

**shaft graves** A term used for the burial sites of elite members of Mycenaean Greek society in the mid-second millennium B.C.E. At the bottom of deep shafts lined with stone slabs, the bodies were laid out along with gold and bronze jewelry, implements, weapons, and masks.   (p. 37)

**Shah Abbas I** The fifth and most renowned ruler of the Safavid dynasty in Iran (r. 1587–1629). Abbas moved the royal capital to Isfahan in 1598.   (p. 435)

**shamanism** The practice of identifying special individuals (shamans) who will interact with spirits for the benefit of the community. Characteristic of the Korean kingdoms of the early medieval period and of early societies of Central Asia.   (p. 270)

**Shang** The dominant people in the earliest Chinese dynasty for which we have written records (ca. 1750–1045 B.C.E.).   (p. 60)

**Shi Huangdi** Founder of the short-lived Qin dynasty and creator of the Chinese Empire (r. 221–210 B.C.E.). He is remembered for his ruthless conquests of rival states, standardization of practices, and forcible organization of labor for military and engineering tasks. His tomb, with its army of life-size terracotta soldiers, has been partially excavated.   (p. 125)

**Shi'ites** Muslims belonging to the branch of Islam believing that God vests leadership of the community in a descendant of Muhammad's son-in-law Ali. Shi'ism is the state religion of Iran.   (p. 213)

**Shi'ites** Muslims belonging to the branch of Islam believing that God vests leadership of the community in a descendant of Muhammad's son-in-law Ali. Shi'ism is the state religion of Iran.   (p. 434)

**Siberia** The extreme northeastern sector of Asia, including the Kamchatka Peninsula and the present Russian coast of the Arctic Ocean, the Bering Strait, and the Sea of Okhotsk.   (p. 440)

**Sigmund Freud (1856–1939)** Austrian psychiatrist, founder of psychoanalysis. He argued that psychological problems were caused by traumas, especially sexual experiences in early childhood, that were repressed in later life. His ideas caused considerable controversy among psychologists and in the general public. Although his views on repressed sexuality are no longer widely accepted, his psychoanalytic methods are still very influential.   (p. 610)

**Silk Road** Caravan routes connecting China and the Middle East across Central Asia and Iran.   (p. 187)

**Simón Bolívar** The most important military leader in the struggle for independence in South America. Born in Venezuela, he led military forces there and in Colombia, Ecuador, Peru, and Bolivia.   (p. 504)

**Slavophiles** Russian intellectuals in the early nineteenth century who favored resisting western European influences and taking pride in the traditional peasant values and institutions of the Slavic peoples.   (p. 522)

**"small traditions"** Historians' term for a localized, usually nonliterate, set of customs and beliefs adhered to by a single society, often in conjunction with a "great tradition."   (p. 199)

**socialism** A political ideology that originated in Europe in the 1830s. Socialists advocated government protection of workers from exploitation by property owners and government ownership of industries. This ideology led to the founding of socialist or labor parties throughout Europe in the second half of the nineteenth century.   (p. 573)

**Socrates** Athenian philosopher (ca. 470–399 B.C.E.) who shifted the emphasis of philosophical investigation from questions of natural science to ethics and human behavior.

He attracted young disciples from elite families but made enemies by revealing the ignorance and pretensions of others, culminating in his trial and execution by the Athenian state.   (p. 96)

**Sokoto Caliphate** A large Muslim state founded in 1809 in what is now northern Nigeria.   (p. 543)

**Solidarity** Polish trade union created in 1980 to protest working conditions and political repression. It began the nationalist opposition in eastern Europe.   (p. 681)

**Song Empire** Empire in central and southern China (960–1126) while the Liao people controlled the north. Empire in southern China (1127–1279; the "Southern Song") while the Jin people controlled the north. Distinguished for its advances in technology, medicine, astronomy, and mathematics.   (p. 263)

**Spanish-American War** U.S. war fought with Spanish in 1898 over control of Cuba, ostensibly because of the sinking of a U.S. ship and also after reports of Spanish atrocities had fanned flames of American popular opinion. Won handily in three months, the war unofficially made Cuba a protectorate of the United States.   (p. 557)

**Srivijaya** A state based on the Indonesian island of Sumatra between the seventh and eleventh centuries C.E. It amassed wealth and power by a combination of selective adaptation of Indian technologies and concepts, control of the lucrative trade routes between India and China, and skillful showmanship and diplomacy in holding together a disparate realm of inland and coastal territories.   (p. 151)

**Stalingrad** City in Russia, site of a Red Army victory over the German army in 1942–1943. The Battle of Stalingrad was the turning point in the war between Germany and the Soviet Union. Today Volgograd.   (p. 644)

**steam engine** A machine that turns the energy released by burning fuel into motion. Thomas Newcomen built the first crude but workable steam engine in 1712. James Watt vastly improved his device in the 1760s and 1770s. Steam power was later applied to operating machinery in factories and to propelling ships and locomotives.   (p. 479)

**steel** A form of iron that is both durable and flexible. It was first mass-produced in the 1860s and quickly became the most widely used metal in construction, machinery, and railroad equipment.   (p. 567)

**steppe** An ecological region of grass- and shrub-covered plains that is treeless and too arid for agriculture.   (p. 70, 199)

**stock exchange** A place where shares in a company or business enterprise are bought and sold.   (p. 391)

**Stone Age** The historical period characterized by the production of tools from stone and other nonmetallic substances.   (p. 7)

**submarine telegraph cables** Insulated copper cables laid along the bottom of a sea or ocean for telegraphic communication. The first short cable was laid under the Hooghly River in Calcutta in 1839; the first successful transatlantic cable was laid in 1866.   (p. 567)

**sub-Saharan Africa** Portion of the African continent lying south of the Sahara.   (p. 195)

**Suez Canal** Ship canal dug across the Isthmus of Suez in Egypt, designed by Ferdinand de Lesseps. It opened to shipping in 1869 and shortened the sea voyage between Europe and Asia. Its strategic importance led to the British occupation of Egypt in 1882.   (p. 545)

**Suleiman the Magnificent** The most illustrious sultan of the Ottoman Empire (r. 1520–1566); also known as Suleiman Kanuni, "The Lawgiver." He significantly expanded the empire in the Balkans and eastern Mediterranean.   (p. 428)

**Sumerians** The people who dominated southern Mesopotamia through the end of the third millennium B.C.E. (p. 15)

**Sunnis** Muslims belonging to branch of Islam believing that the community should select its own leadership. The majority religion in most Islamic countries. (p. 214)

**Sun Yat-sen (1867–1925)** Chinese nationalist revolutionary, founder and leader of the Guomindang until his death. He attempted to create a liberal democratic political movement in China but was thwarted by military leaders. (p. 597)

**Swahili** Bantu language with Arabic loanwords spoken in coastal regions of East Africa. (p. 445)

**Swahili Coast** East African shores of the Indian Ocean between the Horn of Africa and the Zambezi River; from the Arabic *sawahil*, meaning "shores." (p. 339)

**Taiping Rebellion** A Christian-inspired rural rebellion that threatened to topple the Qing Empire. (p. 528)

**Tamil kingdoms** The kingdoms of southern India, inhabited primarily by speakers of Dravidian languages, which developed in partial isolation, and somewhat differently, from the Arya north. They produced epics, poetry, and performance arts. Elements of Tamil religious beliefs were merged into the Hindu synthesis. (p. 146)

**Tang Empire** Empire unifying China and part of Inner Asia (618–907). The Tang emperors presided over a magnificent court at their capital, Chang'an. (p. 256)

**Tanzimat** Restructuring reforms by the nineteenth-century Ottoman rulers, intended to move civil law away from the control of religious elites and make the military and the bureaucracy more efficient. (p. 515)

**tax farmers** Private individuals or small partnerships who were given contracts to collect taxes for the government. In return tax farmers could keep whatever money they were able to collect above their tax obligation to the government. (p. 397)

**Tenochtitlan** Capital of the Aztec Empire, located on an island in Lake Texcoco. Its population was above 150,000 on the eve of the Spanish conquest. Mexico City was constructed on its ruins. (p. 346)

**Teotihuacan** A powerful city-state in central Mexico (100 B.C.E.–750 C.E.). Its population was about 150,000 at its peak in 600. (p. 163)

**terrorism** Political belief that extreme and seemingly random violence will destabilize a government and permit the terrorists to gain political advantage. Though an old technique, terrorism gained prominence in the late twentieth century with the growth of worldwide mass media that, through their news coverage, amplified public fears of terrorist acts. (p. 692)

**theater-state** Historians' term for a state that acquires prestige and power by developing attractive cultural forms and staging elaborate public ceremonies (as well as redistributing valuable resources) to attract and bind subjects to the center. Examples include the Gupta Empire in India and Srivijaya in Southeast Asia. (p. 147)

**Thebes** Capital city of Egypt and home of the ruling dynasties during the Middle and New Kingdoms. Monarchs were buried across the river in the Valley of the Kings. (p. 23)

**Theravada Buddhism** "Way of the Elders" branch of Buddhism followed in Sri Lanka and much of Southeast Asia. Theravada remains close to the original principles set forth by the Buddha; it downplays the importance of gods and emphasizes austerity and the individual's search for enlightenment. (p. 141)

**third-century crisis** Historians' term for the political, military, and economic turmoil that beset the Roman Empire during much of the third century C.E.: frequent changes of ruler, civil wars, barbarian invasions, decline of urban centers, and near-destruction of long-distance commerce and the monetary economy. After 284 C.E. Diocletian restored order by making fundamental changes. (p. 120)

**Third World** Term applied to a group of developing countries who professed nonalignment during the Cold War. (p. 665)

**Thomas Edison** American inventor best known for inventing the electric light bulb, acoustic recording on wax cylinders, and motion pictures. (p. 568)

**Thomas Malthus (1766–1834)** Eighteenth-century English intellectual who warned that population growth threatened the future generations because, in his view, it would always outstrip increases in agricultural production. (p. 697)

**three-field system** A rotational system for agriculture in which two fields grow food crops and one lies fallow. It gradually replaced the two-field system in medieval Europe. (p. 308)

**Tibet** Country centered on the high, mountain-bounded plateau north of India. Tibetan political power occasionally extended farther to the north and west between the seventh and thirteenth centuries. (p. 259)

**Timbuktu** City on the Niger River in the modern country of Mali. It was founded by the Tuareg as a seasonal camp sometime after 1000. As part of the Mali Empire, Timbuktu became a major terminus of the trans-Saharan trade and a center of Islamic learning. (p. 343)

**Timur** Member of a prominent family of the Mongols' Chagatai Khanate, Timur through conquest gained control over much of Central Asia and Iran. He consolidated the status of Sunni Islam as orthodox, and his descendants, the Timurids, maintained his empire for nearly a century and founded the Mughal Empire in India. (p. 289)

**Tiwanaku** Name of capital city and empire centered on the region near Lake Titicaca in modern Bolivia (375–1000 C.E.). (p. 175)

**Tokugawa Shogunate** The last of the three shogunates of Japan. (p. 454)

**Toltecs** Powerful postclassic empire in central Mexico (900–1175 C.E.). It influenced much of Mesoamerica. Aztecs claimed ties to this earlier civilization. (p. 168)

**Toussaint L'Ouverture** Leader of the Haitian Revolution. He freed the slaves and gained effective independence for Haiti despite military interventions by the British and French. (p. 503)

**trans-Saharan caravan routes** Trading network linking North Africa with sub-Saharan Africa across the Sahara. (p. 195)

**Treaty of Nanking** The treaty that concluded the Opium War. It awarded Britain a large indemnity from the Qing Empire, denied the Qing government tariff control over some of its own borders, opened additional ports of residence to Britons, and ceded the island of Hong Kong to Britain. (p. 528)

**Treaty of Versailles (1919)** The treaty imposed on Germany by France, Great Britain, the United States, and other Allied powers after World War I. It demanded that Germany dismantle its military and give up some lands to Poland. It humiliated but did not weaken Germany. (p. 595)

**treaty ports** Cities opened to foreign residents as a result of the forced treaties between the Qing Empire and foreign signatories. In the treaty ports, foreigners enjoyed extraterritoriality. (p. 528)

**tributary system** A system in which, from the time of the Han Empire, countries in East and Southeast Asia not under the direct control of empires based in China nevertheless enrolled as tributary states, acknowledging the superiority of the emperors in China in exchange for trading rights or strategic alliances. (p. 257)

**tribute system** A system in which defeated peoples were forced to pay a tax in the form of goods and labor. The forced transfer of food, cloth, and other goods subsidized the development of large cities. An important component of the Aztec and Inka economies. (p. 347)

**trireme** Greek and Phoenician warship of the fifth and fourth centuries B.C.E. It was sleek and light, powered by 170 oars arranged in three vertical tiers. Manned by skilled sailors, it was capable of short bursts of speed and complex maneuvers. (p. 95)

**tropical rain forest** High-precipitation forest zones of the Americas, Africa, and Asia lying between the Tropic of Cancer and the Tropic of Capricorn. (p. 199)

**tropics** Equatorial region between the Tropic of Cancer and the Tropic of Capricorn. It is characterized by generally warm or hot temperatures year-round, though much variation exists due to altitude and other factors. Temperate zones north and south of the tropics generally have a winter season. (p. 329)

**Truman Doctrine** Foreign policy initiated by U.S. president Harry Truman in 1947. It offered military aid to help Turkey and Greece resist Soviet military pressure and subversion. (p. 660)

**tsar (czar)** From Latin *caesar*, this Russian title for a monarch was first used in reference to a Russian ruler by Ivan III (r. 1462–1505). (p. 292, 440)

**Tulip Period** Last years of the reign of Ottoman sultan Ahmed III (1718–1730), during which European styles and attitudes became briefly popular in Istanbul. (p. 432)

**tyrant** The term the Greeks used to describe someone who seized and held power in violation of the normal procedures and traditions of the community. Tyrants appeared in many Greek city-states in the seventh and sixth centuries B.C.E., often taking advantage of the disaffection of the emerging middle class and, by weakening the old elite, unwittingly contributing to the evolution of democracy. (p. 90)

**tzompantli** Images of impaled skulls in scenes of human sacrifice included in the decoration of a prominent public buildings and temples in Tula. (p. 168)

**Uighurs** A group of Turkish-speakers who controlled their own centralized empire from 744 to 840 in Mongolia and Central Asia. (p. 259)

**ulama** Muslim religious scholars. From the ninth century onward, the primary interpreters of Islamic law and the social core of Muslim urban societies. (p. 219)

**Umayyad Caliphate** First hereditary dynasty of Muslim caliphs (661 to 750). From their capital at Damascus, the Umayyads ruled an empire that extended from Spain to India. Overthrown by the Abbasid Caliphate. (p. 213)

**umma** The community of all Muslims. A major innovation against the background of seventh-century Arabia, where traditionally kinship rather than faith had determined membership in a community. (p. 212)

**United Nations** International organization founded in 1945 to promote world peace and cooperation. It replaced the League of Nations. (p. 657)

**Universal Declaration of Human Rights** A 1948 United Nations covenant binding signatory nations to the observance of specified rights. (p. 693)

**universities** Degree-granting institutions of higher learning. Those that appeared in the countries of western Europe from about 1200 onward became the model of all modern universities. (p. 318)

**Urdu** A Persian-influenced literary form of Hindi written in Arabic characters and used as a literary language since the 1300s. (p. 343)

**Usama bin Laden (1957–2011)** Saudi-born Muslim extremist who funded the al-Qaeda organization that was responsible for several terrorist attacks, including those on the World Trade Center and the Pentagon in 2001. (p. 692)

***varna/jati*** Two categories of social identity of great importance in Indian history. Varnas are the four major social divisions: the Brahmin priest class, the Kshatriya warrior/administrator class, the Vaishya merchant/farmer class, and the Shudra laborer class. Within the system of varnas are many jatis, regional groups of people who have a common occupational sphere and who marry, eat, and generally interact with other members of their group. (p. 138)

**Vasco da Gama** Portuguese explorer. In 1497–1498 he led the first naval expedition from Europe to sail to India, opening an important commercial sea route. (p. 363)

**vassal** In medieval Europe, a sworn supporter of a king or lord committed to rendering specified military service to that king or lord. (p. 238)

**Vedas** Early Indian sacred "knowledge"—the literal meaning of the term—long preserved and communicated orally by Brahmin priests and eventually written down. These religious texts, including the thousand poetic hymns to various deities contained in the *Rig Veda*, are our main source of information about the Vedic period (ca. 1500–500 B.C.E.). (p. 138)

**Versailles** The huge palace built for French king Louis XIV south of Paris. The palace symbolized both French power and the triumph of royal authority over the French nobility. (p. 396)

**Victorian Age** The reign of Queen Victoria of Great Britain (r. 1837–1901). The term is also used to describe late-nineteenth-century society, with its rigid moral standards and sharply differentiated roles for men and women and for middle-class and working-class people. (p. 570)

**Vietnam War (1954–1975)** Conflict pitting North Vietnam and South Vietnamese communist guerrillas against the South Vietnamese government, aided after 1961 by the United States. (p. 661)

**Vladimir Lenin (1870–1924)** Leader of the Bolshevik (later Communist) Party. He lived in exile in Switzerland until 1917, then returned to Russia to lead the Bolsheviks to victory during the Russian Revolution and the civil war that followed. (p. 592)

**Wari** Andean civilization culturally linked to Tiwanaku, perhaps beginning as a colony of Tiwanaku. (p. 175)

**Warsaw Pact** The 1955 treaty binding the Soviet Union and countries of eastern Europe in an alliance against the North Atlantic Treaty Organization. (p. 657)

**western front** A line of trenches and fortifications in World War I that stretched without a break from Switzerland to the North Sea. Scene of most of the fighting between Germany, on the one hand, and France and Britain, on the other. (p. 588)

**Wilbur (1867–1912) and Orville (1871–1948) Wright** American bicycle mechanics; the first to build and fly an airplane, at Kitty Hawk, North Carolina, December 7, 1903. (p. 611)

**witch-hunt** The pursuit of people suspected of witchcraft, especially in northern Europe in the late sixteenth and seventeenth centuries. (p. 385)

**Women's Rights Convention** An 1848 gathering of women angered by their exclusion from an international antislavery meeting. They met at Seneca Falls, New York, to discuss women's rights. (p. 507)

**Woodrow Wilson (1856–1924)** President of the United States (1913–1921) and a leading figure at the Paris Peace Conference of 1919. He was unable to persuade the U.S. Congress to ratify the Treaty of Versailles or join the League of Nations.   (p. 593)

**World Bank**  A specialized agency of the United Nations that makes loans to countries for economic development, trade promotion, and debt consolidation. Its formal name is the International Bank for Reconstruction and Development.   (p. 658)

**World Trade Organization (WTO)**  An international body established in 1995 to foster and bring order to international trade.   (p. 689)

**Xiongnu**  A confederation of nomadic peoples living beyond the northwest frontier of ancient China. Chinese rulers tried a variety of defenses and stratagems to ward off these "barbarians," as they called them, and finally succeeded in dispersing the Xiongnu in the first century C.E.   (p. 129)

**Yamagata Aritomo**  One of the leaders of the Meiji Restoration.   (p. 583)

**yin/yang**  In Chinese belief, complementary factors that help to maintain the equilibrium of the world. Yang is associated with masculine, light, and active qualities; yin with feminine, dark, and passive qualities.   (p. 66)

**Yongle**  The third emperor of the Ming Empire (r. 1403–1424). He sponsored the building of the Forbidden City, a huge encyclopedia project, the expeditions of Zheng He, and the reopening of China's borders to trade and travel.   (p. 296)

**Young Ottomans**  Movement of young intellectuals to institute liberal reforms and build a feeling of national identity in the Ottoman Empire in the second half of the nineteenth century.   (p. 521)

**Yuan Empire**  Empire created in China and Siberia by Khubilai Khan.   (p. 282)

**Yuan Shikai (1859–1916)**  Chinese general and first president of the Chinese Republic (1912–1916). He stood in the way of the democratic movement led by Sun Yat-sen.   (p. 597)

**Zen**  The Japanese word for a branch of Mahayana Buddhism based on highly disciplined meditation. It is known in Sanskrit as *dhyana*, in Chinese as *chan*, and in Korean as *son*.   (p. 265)

**Zheng He**  An imperial eunuch and Muslim, entrusted by the Ming emperor Yongle with a series of state voyages that took his gigantic ships through the Indian Ocean, from Southeast Asia to Africa.   (p. 297)

**Zhou**  The people and dynasty that took over the dominant position in north China from the Shang and created the concept of the Mandate of Heaven to justify their rule. The Zhou era, particularly the vigorous early period (1045–771 B.C.E.), was remembered in Chinese tradition as a time of prosperity and benevolent rule.   (p. 61)

**ziggurat**  A massive pyramidal stepped tower made of mud bricks. It is associated with religious complexes in ancient Mesopotamian cities, but its function is unknown.   (p. 16)

**Zoroastrianism**  A religion originating in ancient Iran that became the official religion of the Achaemenids. It centered on a single benevolent deity, Ahuramazda, who engaged in a struggle with demonic forces before prevailing and restoring a pristine world. It emphasized truth-telling, purity, and reverence for nature.   (p. 87)

**Zulu**  A people of modern South Africa whom King Shaka united in 1818.   (p. 539)